Probation, Parole, and Community Corrections
in the United States

Sixth Edition

Dean John Champion
Texas A & M International University

PEARSON
Prentice
Hall

Upper Saddle River, New Jersey 07458

Library of Congress Cataloging-in-Publication Data

Champion, Dean John
  Probation, parole, and community corrections in the United States / by Dean J.
Champion.—6th ed.
     p. cm.
  Rev. ed. of: Probation, parole, and community corrections. 5th ed. Upper
Saddle River, N. J. : Pearson/Prentice Hall, c2005.
  ISBN 0-13-613058-5
  1. Probation—United States. 2. Parole—United States. I. Champion, Dean
J. Probation, parole, and community corrections. II. Title.
  HV9304.C463 2008
  364.6'30973—dc22

                                        2007000502

Editor-in-Chief: Vernon R. Anthony
Senior Acquisitions Editor: Tim Peyton
Associate Editor: Sarah Holle
Editorial Assistant: Jillian Allison
Marketing Manager: Adam Kloza
Production Editor: Patty Donovan, Pine Tree Composition
Production Liaison: Barbara Marttine Cappuccio
Managing Editor: Mary Carnis
Manufacturing Manager: Ilene Sanford
Manufacturing Buyer: Cathleen Petersen
Senior Design Coordinator: Miguel Ortiz
Cover Design: Eva Ruutopold
Cover Image: Getty Images/Photodisc
Formatting: Laserwords Pvt. Ltd
Printer/Binder: R.R. Donnelley & Sons

Chapter Opening Photo Credits

p. 1 A. Ramey, PhotoEdit; **p. 31** Al Dodge;
p. 76 Michael Newman, PhotoEdit; **p. 127** Robert
Harbison; **p. 313** Mikael Karlsson, Arresting Images; **p. 382** Mikael Karlsson, Arresting Images; **p.
429** Les Stone, Corbis/Sygma; **p. 471** Andrew Lichtenstein, Aurora & Quanta Product; **p. 503** Gary
Wagner, Gary Wagner Photography; **p. 615** David J.
Sams, Stock Boston.

Pearson Prentice Hall™ is a trademark of Pearson Education, Inc.
Pearson® is a registered trademark of Pearson plc
Prentice Hall® is a registered trademark of Pearson Education, Inc.

Pearson Education LTD., *London*
Pearson Education Australia Pty. Limited, *Sydney*
Pearson Education Singapore, Pte. Ltd
Pearson Education North Asia Ltd., *Hong Kong*
Pearson Education Canada, Ltd., *Toronto*
Pearson Education de Mexico, S.A. de C.V.
Pearson Education—Japan, *Tokyo*
Pearson Education Malaysia, Pte. Ltd.
Pearson Education, Upper Saddle River, *New Jersey*

10 9 8 7 6 5 4 3 2 1
ISBN 0-13-613058-5

Contents

Chapter 3

An Overview of Community Corrections: Types, Goals, and Functions   65

Chapter 4

Sentencing and the Presentence Investigation Report: Background, Preparation, and Functions   113

Chapter 5

Probation and Probationers: History, Philosophy, Goals, and Functions   163

Chapter 6

Programs for Probationers   204

Chapter 7

Jails and Prisons   261

Chapter 8

Parole and Parolees

Chapter 9

Early Release, Parole Programs, and Parole Revocation   366

Chapter 10

Probation/Parole Organization and Operations: Recruitment, Training, and Officer—Client Relations

436

Chapter 11

Probation and Parole Professionals   489

Chapter 12

Offender Supervision: Types of Offenders and Special Supervisory Considerations   534

Chapter 13

Juvenile Probation and Parole

Chapter 14

Evaluating Programs: Balancing Service Delivery and Recidivism Considerations   652

Preface

Probation, Parole, and Community Corrections, Sixth Edition, is about adults and juveniles who have been convicted of criminal offenses or adjudicated as delinquent and are punished. Judges may sentence offenders to incarceration in prison or jail for a definite period or they may suspend the sentence, subject to the offender's compliance with certain conditions. Judges may also sentence offenders to incarceration for a fixed period of years; offenders may serve only a portion of that time. Parole boards, the court, or others may authorize the early release of offenders, again subject to certain conditions.

Some adult and juvenile offenders are permitted by the courts to remain free in their communities, provided that they comply with certain conditions. Other offenders are granted early release from incarceration under similar provisions. These offenders will be supervised by officers and agencies as provided by law. This book is also about the personnel and agencies who monitor these offenders.

The distinction between probation and parole is not clear-cut. Probation applies to a class of programs for those offenders sentenced to incarceration but who have had their incarcerative sentences conditionally suspended. Parole applies to those programs for offenders who have been incarcerated but have been released prior to serving the full term of their incarceration. Therefore, parolees are convicted or adjudicated offenders who have been incarcerated but have been released before their sentences have been fully served. Probationers are convicted or adjudicated offenders who are ordered to serve nonincarcerative conditional sentences in the community in lieu of incarceration.

In both instances, parolees and probationers are supervised by parole and probation officers. But there are other classes of offenders whose activities are monitored by these officers as well. Sometimes, offenders are granted diversion by the court. Diversion is a pretrial alternative whereby offenders may avoid prosecution altogether. If offenders successfully comply with the conditions of their diversion, then criminal charges against them are either dropped or reduced in seriousness when they complete their diversionary period.

Distinguishing clearly between probation and parole is difficult for at least two reasons. First, there are many probation and parole programs, and several of them overlap. Thus, the clients of a specific program may be comprised of both probationers and parolees. Second, there are many different kinds of probationers and parolees to be supervised. There is disagreement among professionals about which programs are most effective. Furthermore, there are disagreements about the philosophical objectives of probation and parole programs. This book describes the objectives of probation and parole and whether these objectives are achieved. Understanding these philosophies will be enhanced through an examination of the history of parole and probation in the United States. Besides describing probation and parole programs, various classes of offenders are portrayed. Additionally, several problems associated with the selection and training of probation and parole officers are highlighted, including their relationships with offender-clients.

Juvenile offenders pose special problems for those assigned to supervise them. A profile of juvenile offenders is also presented, together with a discussion of several controversial issues associated with processing juveniles. The juvenile justice system is gradually acquiring several characteristics that are making its distinctiveness less apparent compared with the criminal justice system. Larger numbers of juveniles are being processed as adult offenders, either through statutes or recommendations from prosecutors and juvenile judges. Since 1966, juveniles have been granted certain constitutional rights equivalent to those of adult offenders. Some of these rights are described, and the influence of these rights upon juvenile probation and parole programs is examined.

One premise of this book is that all components of the criminal and juvenile justice systems are interrelated to varying degrees. While experts contend that these systems are better described as loosely related processes, each component has an impact on each of the other components. Police discretion influences the disposition of adult and juvenile offenders. In turn, the courts influence police discretion and affect prisons and jails through particular sentencing practices. Prison and jail problems such as overcrowding often overburden probation and parole officers with excessive offender caseloads. Varying offender caseloads influence the quality of officer–offender interaction and the ultimate effectiveness of probation and parole programs. Ineffective probation and parole programs may increase the number of repeat offenders who come to the attention of police when they commit new crimes. Thus, probation and parole programs do not exist in a vacuum, unaffected by other agencies and organizations.

Probation and parole policy decisions are sometimes politically motivated. However, economic considerations and limited human resources also play important parts in shaping correctional priorities. The influence of political and economic considerations on probation and parole programs as well as officer effectiveness is described.

The book has the following features, which add to its value as a teaching tool. First, there are questions for review at the end of each chapter to facilitate group discussion and class assignments. Second, a comprehensive glossary is provided in order for students to look up unfamiliar words. All key words that are mentioned in each chapter are boldfaced and included in a glossary in an appendix. At chapter ends, Internet sites are included that may be used for further study. Suggested further readings are also provided. A comprehensive, up-to-date bibliography is included for those students who wish to do additional reading and learn more about the different subjects presented. All chapters are summarized, highlighting the major points. Each chapter opens with interesting vignettes relevant for the material to be covered. Another feature is that persons who work in probation and parole services are profiled as Career Snapshots. Students should find these personality highlights of interest, since these have been written by practitioners in the field in different capacities.

A unique and interesting feature contained in each chapter is a box describing probation and parole in a foreign country. Thus, the probation and parole systems of 14 different countries are featured, giving readers a strong comparative perspective about how probationers and parolees are managed throughout the world. There are many similarities with U.S. practices as well as contrasts and differences. For instructors, an Instructor's Manual is provided, together with a test-generated CD. The Instructor's Manual includes synopses of chapters, key objectives of each chapter, and short-answer essay questions to use for examination preparation. Powerpoint is also available.

While every effort has been made to include the most up-to-date information in various tables throughout the text, there is a continuous updating of information by the U.S. government and other data sources. There is always at least a one-year delay between the time information is compiled and reported by any federal or state agency. Thus, in 2006 the most current information available about probationers and parolees was for 2004, with 2005 estimates. Generally, the trend and descriptive information reported, even the research literature and contemporary findings, remain fairly stable over time. Few surprises are encountered across years about innovative programming and theories. But if students want the most current information available, such as midyear reports, this information may be accessed via the Internet and various web sites. At each chapter end, several Internet addresses are provided that can be accessed and where current information about probationers, parolees, and other populations can be found.

The author wishes to acknowledge the following persons who have reviewed the manuscript in its various editions and have given their comments about how this edition could be improved. I am grateful for their suggestions and note that any possible factual mistakes are my own: Silvina Ituarte, California State University—East Bay; Beth M. Huebner, University of Missouri—St. Louis; and Lior Gideon, John Jay College of Criminal Justice—New York. I encourage anyone using this book to contact me for additional examination information and for other ancillary materials, which I will be pleased to provide in different software formats on diskette. I wish to thank Tim Peyton, my Prentice Hall editor, for his supportive efforts as my book has gone through various developmental stages. I would also like to thank Sarah Holle, my Associate Editor, for her encouragement and efforts in coordinating the review process, assembling and researching photos for inclusion, and many other endless forms of assistance rendered to me as this edition has progressed to completion.

Dean John Champion
Department of Applied, Behavioral Sciences,
and Criminal Justice
Texas A & M International University

CHAPTER 1 | *Criminal Justice System Components: Locating Probation and Parole*

Chapter Outline

Chapter Objectives

As the result of reading this chapter, the following objectives will be realized:

1. Provide a brief overview and description of the components of the criminal justice system.
2. Distinguish between probation and parole and specifying those agencies and organizations within these categories.
3. Describe traditional offender categorizations including property offenders and violent offenders, first-offenders, recidivists, and career criminals.
4. Describe the *Uniform Crime Reports* and the *National Crime Victimization Survey* and their weaknesses and strengths.
5. Describe particular types of specialized offenders, including drug/alcohol-dependent offenders, offenders who are mentally ill, and sex offenders.

• *Ramos was on probation in California for DWI (driving while intoxicated). One probation condition was that Ramos was to submit his person, property, and automobile, or any object under his control, to search and seizure by any probation officer or other peace officer at any time of the day or night, with or without a warrant. While on probation, Ramos was prohibited from possessing or consuming any alcoholic beverages and/or illegal drugs. A subsequent search in the middle of the night by Ramos's probation officer yielded various alcoholic beverages and illegal drugs secreted in various places in Ramos's automobile and house. The probation officer, together with a deputy sheriff, took Ramos into custody and a report was made to court concerning Ramos's probation and his violation of one or more conditions of it. Ramos objected to the search of his premises and automobile, contending that the search was unlawful. Therefore, the seized items should not be used against him in a probation revocation proceeding. An appellate court ruled against Ramos, noting that the purpose of a search condition is to deter the commission of a crime and the protect the public, and the effectiveness of the deterrent is enhanced by the potential for random searches. By accepting probation, Ramos consented to a waiver of his Fourth Amendment right in order to avoid incarceration. Therefore, whenever a probationer agrees to permit a warrantless search of his person, car, and house, he voluntarily waives whatever claim of privacy he might otherwise have had. [People v. Ramos, 101 P.3d 478, 21 Cal.Rptr.3d 575 (Cal.Sup.Nov.2004)].*

• *Carlson had worked as a physician's assistant for several years and was subsequently convicted of defrauding various health care providers and insurance companies by obtaining large quantities of prescription drugs for illicit sale to others and to fuel his own narcotics addiction. The federal district court ordered Carlson to a term of supervised release. One of several conditions of Carlson's supervised release was that he should not perform any work in the medical field. Subsequently Carlson obtained a job working as an orthopedic physician's assistant. This work came to his probation officer's attention and the court was notified. The government moved to revoke Carlson's term of supervised release and Carlson appealed, alleging that the employment prohibition condition was unreasonable. The appeals court disagreed, holding that Carlson's employment as an orthopedic physician's assistant placed him in close proximity to prescription medication, and that he used sample medications obtained through his employment on at least two occasions. The court concluded that a condition of supervised release prohibiting probationers from engaging in a specific occupation is proper if it determines that*

(1) a reasonably direct relationship existed between the defendant's occupation and the conduct relevant to the conviction offense, and (2) imposition of such a restriction is reasonably necessary to protect the public because there is reason to believe, that absent such a restriction, the probationer will continue to engage in unlawful conduct similar to that for which he was convicted. [United States v. Carlson, 406 F.3d 529 (U.S.8thCir.Apr.) (2005)].

• *Sczubelek was convicted on several counts of bank robbery and sentenced to a term of confinement. Subsequently he was placed on supervisory release with various conditions. Shortly after Sczubelek was placed on supervised release, the Congress passed the DNA Act, which made the submission of a DNA sample a mandatory condition of supervised release for certain offenses, including bank robbery. A DNA sample was sought from Sczubelek, who challenged the law on Fourth Amendment grounds and refused to submit a blood sample. He appealed to the Third Circuit who heard his case. The Circuit Court rejected Sczubelek's argument that his Fourth Amendment right against unreasonable searches and seizures would be violated if the government took a sample of his blood. The Court noted that although the collection of DNA samples went well beyond the supervision of an individual on supervised release, the appropriate analysis would be to assess the reasonableness of seizing Sczubelek's blood under a totality of circumstances test. Applying this test, the Court held that taking Sczubelek's blood sample was not unreasonable. Several factors were considered in reaching this conclusion. These were that (1) the intrusion of a blood test is minimal; (2) an individual on supervised release has a reduced expectation of privacy; (3) the government has an interest in accurate criminal investigations and prosecutions that are compelling and DNA sampling could reasonably advance that interest; and (4) the government had an additional interest in protecting society from future criminal violations committed by those under probation supervision. [United States v. Sczubelek, 402 F.3d 175 (U.S.3rd.Cir.March) (2005)].*

• *Chism was an Indiana probationer who had previously been convicted of conspiracy to deliver cocaine and driving while intoxicated. He was ordered to serve time on home detention with electronic monitoring. Chism was required to wear an ankle bracelet that sent a signal to a monitoring box in his home. The box was connected through a telephone line to be monitored by the central community corrections agency. On several occasions during his probation and home confinement, Chism spent several nights away from home without the permission of his probation officer. He was brought back into court later and his probation orders were revoked and modified. Subsequently Chism was placed under supervision and supervised by a global positioning satellite system, which permitted community corrections officials to identify his exact location at any given moment. Furthermore, Chism was ordered to pay a monthly maintenance fee to defray the costs of global position satellite tracking. Chism objected both to being monitored by global position satellite tracking and having to pay for it. He claimed that such supervision was unconstitutional. An Indiana appeals court disagreed. The Court distinguished between global satellite tracking devices that required a client's consent to allow corrections personnel to watch or listen to things happening inside the offender's home and those devices that a court may require without the offender's consent, devices that simply tell whether the offender is there or not, without transmitting images or sound. Chism's monitoring fell in the later category, and thus the fact that global position satellite tracking tells corrections officials where Chism is when he is not at home does not destroy its status as a device that broadcasts only his location. The monitoring requirement imposed on Chism was therefore constitutional and proper. [Chism v. State, 824 N.E.2d 334 (Ind.Sup.March) (2005)].*

These cases indicate that probation and parole are both conditional sentences and releases from incarceration, either immediately following conviction for a crime or after a period of incarceration in a prison or jail. The conditions imposed relate to behavioral requirements and involve agreements between the state and probationers/parolees based on mutual trust. The reward for probationers/parolees is freedom, which is either limited or completely unrestricted. The penalties for violating this trust involve loss of freedom through incarceration or more restrictive forms of probation/parole supervision. This book is about all types of programs involving convicted offenders, and where such programs include diverse conditions of supervised release. These programs are almost always operated in communities and are designed to supervise offender behaviors more or less intensively. These are broadly labeled probation, parole, or community corrections.

INTRODUCTION

This chapter is an overview of the **criminal justice system**. Probation and parole are identified in relation to various criminal justice system components. The first part of this chapter defines crime and distinguishes between several types of crime. Different offense categories are listed by which offenders are classified. Two popular crime information sources are described. These are the *Uniform Crime Reports (UCR)* and the *National Crime Victimization Survey (NCVS)*. Several criticisms of these information sources are listed. Additional descriptions are provided for both traditional offenders and special-needs offenders. These classifications include first-offenders and recidivists, drug/alcohol dependent offenders, offenders who are mentally and/or physically challenged, and those with HIV/AIDS and other communicable diseases. Major components of the criminal justice system are identified and described, including law enforcement, prosecutorial decision making, courts and court processing, and corrections. When a crime is committed and someone is charged with committing it, the criminal justice system processes the offender through a series of established stages. The final part of the chapter looks at probation and parole. Probation and parole are defined as essentially different programs, although there are many similarities among these programs for convicted offenders.

AN OVERVIEW OF THE CRIMINAL JUSTICE SYSTEM

The criminal justice system consists of **law enforcement**, the **courts**, and **corrections**. Law enforcement officers attempt to control crime and apprehend criminals. The courts determine a defendant's guilt or innocence and sentence convicted offenders. Corrections punishes, manages, and rehabilitates those who have been sentenced. Ideally, this is how things are supposed to work. In actual practice, however, the criminal justice system is seriously flawed. Many criminals are never caught. Many of those criminals who are apprehended never go to trial. Many of those whose cases go to trial are acquitted even though they are guilty of the offenses charged. Many convicted offenders are never incarcerated. Many incarcerated offenders are never rehabilitated. They leave prisons and jails only to resume their criminal activity. Considerable responsibility is given to corrections personnel. Much is expected of those working directly with offenders. Not only are they expected to provide inmates with food, shelter, and basic living requirements, but they are also supposed to rehabilitate them and make them suitable for return to society as law-abiding citizens. As we will see in later chapters, corrections falls far short of this goal. But we will also see that it is not necessarily the fault of corrections for the low incidence of **offender rehabilitation**. Besides institutional corrections, such as prisons and jails, personnel who work in **probation, parole,** and **community corrections** are heavily involved with offender supervision and operate programs designed to rehabilitate or reintegrate offender-clients. These personnel are also expected to accomplish the difficult task of supervising and offering different forms of assistance to their clients with the express purpose of making them law-abiding citizens. Again, it will be disclosed that **probation officers (POs)** and **parole officers (POs)** often fail to achieve their personal and departmental objectives. However, the reasons for their client failures are often beyond their direct control.

Entry into the criminal justice system begins with the commission of a crime, followed by the **arrest** of one or more suspected perpetrators of that crime (McKean and Raphael, 2002). Assuming **offenders** have been identified and apprehended, their movement through the criminal justice system is similar for both the state and federal processing. Persons suspected of committing crimes are arrested, booked, and charged with one or more offenses. If there are successful **prosecutions** of **defendants** by **prosecutors,** they are found guilty and sentenced by judges. Probation is one sentencing option imposed by judges in lieu of incarceration. **Probationers** are allowed to remain free in their communities, although they must abide by certain probation conditions for a period of time. Another option is parole. Parole is an **early release** from prison or jail, permitting convicted offenders the opportunity of living in their communities, again with parole program restrictions and conditions. Convicted offenders who have served some time in jail or prison before earning early release are called **parolees**.

This book describes what happens to offenders who are either sentenced to probation or granted parole after serving a portion of their sentence in prison. In both situations, these offenders must obey several program conditions. Otherwise, their probation or parole may be revoked or cancelled. A **parole revocation** means that parolees may be returned to prison for some or all of the remainder of their original sentences. For probationers, a **probation revocation** may mean incarceration, or it may mean a more intensive form of supervision by probation by program officials. Enforcing the conditions of probation and parole are **probation** and **parole officers (POs)**. The designation, PO, is used to refer either to probation or parole officers throughout this text. Offenders are required to report to their POs regularly and to comply with other rules and regulations. Thus, a second major goal of this book is to describe the personnel and programs that manage probationers and parolees.

Figure 1.1 is a diagram of the criminal justice system, showing the commission of a crime that leads to an arrest. Other phases of offender processing are also depicted. Figure 1.1 also shows that if offenders are juveniles, they are sent to the juvenile justice system.

POs often collaborate with community agencies that provide special services for offenders. For example, in the state of Washington, a program has been established to treat **sex offenders**. It is called the Special Sex Offender Sentencing Alternative (SSOSA) (Starzyk and Marshall, 2003). Probation officers assist community **corrections officers** with their supervisory chores in overseeing large numbers of sex offenders. Some of these offenders were **recidivists,** meaning that they had been convicted of one or more previous crimes. Some amount of **recidivism** is a part of all probation and parole programs, regardless of how carefully they are established and how closely offenders are supervised. **Recidivism rates** were lower for those sex offenders who participated in the community treatment and were under the close supervision of both probation

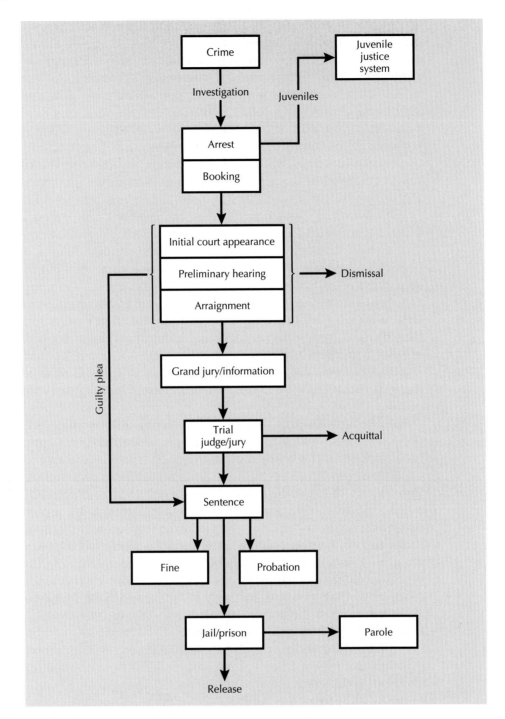

FIGURE 1.1   An overview of the criminal justice system.
From Champion, 5th edition, *Probation, Parole, and Community Corrections.*

and community agency personnel. The SSOSA program has had similar results in other cities throughout the state. Thus, depending on the **jurisdiction,** POs may be assigned to supervise (1) adult probationers and/or parolees; (2) juvenile probationers and/or parolees; and/or (3) offenders with special needs. While POs perform many other duties, their primary responsibility is the management and supervision of nonincarcerated offenders.

All probationers and parolees are a part of corrections. Corrections is the aggregate of programs, services, facilities, and organizations responsible for the management of people who have been accused or convicted of criminal offenses. This book focuses largely on the nonincarcerative dimension of corrections, although some attention will be given to jails or prisons, where offenders may receive treatment or assistance for their needs or problems. More often than not, inmates of prisons or jails are influenced by those they associate with while confined. These associations may not be positive or therapeutic. In fact, the criminogenic environment of prisons and jails and social interactions with other inmates often leads to and explains probation or parole program failures.

TYPES OF OFFENSES

Crimes are violations of the law by people held accountable by the law. Two general categories of crime are **felonies** and **misdemeanors**.

Felonies and Misdemeanors

Felonies.   A **felony** is a major crime that carries potentially severe penalties of one or more years in prison or jail and **fines.** Fines are monetary assessments that accompany a conviction for one or more crimes. Fines are prescribed by statute. Usually, statutory penalties are associated with all felonies and include both fines and/or incarceration in a state or federal prison for one or more years. Felonies include arson, murder, rape, burglary, robbery, vehicular theft, and aggravated assault. In recent years, stalking behavior, where persons follow others with the intent of harming or annoying them, has been promoted to a serious felony (Maxey, 2002). In about two-thirds of all states, the death penalty may be imposed as the maximum punishment, primarily in cases involving premeditated murder of another. Both misdemeanor and felony convictions mean that offenders acquire criminal records. Some jurisdictions have a third class of crimes. A certain type of minor offense may be known as a **summary offense** or an infraction or simply a violation. These are petty crimes and ordinarily carry penalties of fines only. Also, convictions for these petty offenses will not result in a criminal record. Examples of summary offenses are speeding or dumping litter from an automobile on a public highway.

Misdemeanors.   A **misdemeanor** is a minor or petty offense. Misdemeanor offenses carry less severe penalties compared with major crimes or felonies. Misdemeanor offenses may result in fines and/or incarceration for less than one year. A **misdemeanant** is someone who commits a misdemeanor and may be incarcerated in a local jail. Examples of misdemeanors include making a false financial statement to obtain credit, prostitution, shoplifting, and criminal trespass.

Violent and Property Crimes

Violent crimes are characterized by extreme physical force, including murder or homicide, forcible rape, child sexual abuse, assault and battery by means of a dangerous weapon, robbery, and arson (Black, 1990:371). Sometimes these offenses are referred to as **crimes of violence**, **crimes against the person**, because persons are directly involved as victims and affected emotionally and physically as a result of the crime's commission. Nonviolent offenses include crimes such as burglary, vehicular theft, embezzlement, fraud, forgery, and larceny. These are often referred to as **crimes against property**, and although persons are indirectly victimized or affected by such offenses, their lives and physical well-being are not directly jeopardized by such acts. Two sources that report crime in the United States are the *Uniform Crime Reports* and the *National Crime Victimization Survey*.

Apart from the types of crimes against the person listed above, there are several other crime categorizations that have been increasingly visible in recent years. For instance, crimes committed against persons of particular races, ethnicities, or religions have increased the concern of law enforcement. Some of the first hate crimes in the United States were directed against blacks by the Ku Klux Klan. Burning crosses would be placed in the yards in front of homes of blacks, or their churches and homes would be torched. Lynchings of blacks were a fairly common occurrence, especially in some of the Southern states. These crimes are called **hate crimes** and are indicative of intolerance of others' different views or beliefs.

Hate crimes are evident in such actions as church arsons and destruction of religious symbols in cemeteries and other places. They involve many different kinds of persons. Gay persons may be targeted, because certain people may be repulsed by the gay lifestyle. In some instances, deaths have resulted. Special legislation has been passed to create specific penalties for hate crimes, and harsh punishments are administered to violators upon conviction. Other types of crime include campus crime. These crimes occurring on school premises may be simple thefts, or they may involve the destruction of school property or its defacement.

The *Uniform Crime Reports* and the *National Crime Victimization Survey*

The Uniform Crime Reports (UCR).   *The Uniform Crime Reports (UCR)* is published annually by the **Federal Bureau of Investigation (FBI)**. This publication includes statistics about the number and kinds of crimes reported in the United States annually by over 15,000 law enforcement agencies. The *UCR* is the official compendium of crime statistics for the United States. The *UCR* is compiled by gathering information about twenty-nine types of crime from reporting law enforcement agencies. Crime information is requested from all rural and urban law enforcement agencies and is subsequently reported to the **FBI**. The FBI has established a **crime classification index**. **Index offenses** include eight serious types of crime used by the FBI to measure crime trends. These are arson, murder and nonnegligent manslaughter, aggravated assault, robbery, motor vehicle theft, forcible rape, larceny-theft, and burglary. Information is also compiled about twenty-one less serious offenses ranging from forgery and counterfeiting to curfew violations and runaways. Index offense information is presented in the *UCR* for each state, city, county, and township that has submitted crime information during the most recent year. The *UCR* is published annually by the U.S. Government Printing Office.

Criticisms of the UCR.   Although the *UCR* publishes the most current crime figures available from reporting law enforcement agencies, this information is inaccurate in several respects. First, when criminals are questioned about other crimes they have committed, there are discrepancies between *UCR* figures and **self-reported information**. Many criminals are not caught for many of the crimes they have committed. Therefore, there is considerably more crime committed annually than is disclosed by official estimates published in the *UCR*. Second, not all law enforcement agencies report crimes in uniform ways. For instance, North Dakota has no forcible rape category for this type of sex crime. This doesn't mean that rape doesn't occur in that state. Rather, North Dakota classifies forcible rape as "gross sexual imposition." Third, more aggressive enforcement of certain laws in different jurisdictions may lead to more arrests, although there are few convictions. Furthermore, not all law enforcement agencies report their crime figures consistently. Also, many crimes are never reported to the police. Finally, when a crime report is submitted to the *UCR,* only the most serious offense is often reported. Thus, if someone robs a convenience store, shoots and kills the clerk, injures customers, and steals a car before being captured by police, the police department will report only the most serious offense, or "murder or nonnegligent manslaughter," rather than all of the other offenses the perpetrator committed. Thus, there is good reason for experts to believe that the *UCR* greatly underestimates the amount of crime committed in the United States.

The National Crime Victimization Survey (NCVS). The limitations of the *UCR* and other official documents measuring the amount of crime in the United States have caused some persons to draw comparisons between the *UCR* and the ***National Crime Victimization Survey (NCVS),*** which is conducted annually by the United States Bureau of the Census. The *NCVS* is a random survey of approximately 60,000 dwellings, about 127,000 persons age 12 and over, and approximately 50,000 businesses. Smaller samples of persons from these original figures form the database from which annual crime estimates are compiled. Carefully worded questions lead people to report incidents that can be classified as crimes. This material is statistically manipulated in such a way as to make it comparable with *UCR* statistics. This material is usually referred to as **victimization data**.

The *NVCS* distinguishes between **victimizations** and **incidents**. A victimization is the basic measure of the occurrence of a crime and is a specific criminal act that affects a single victim. An incident is a specific criminal act involving one or more victims. However, the *NCVS* has certain persistent problems similar to the *UCR*. Some crime victims cannot remember when or where the offense against them occurred. Other victims are reluctant to report a rape, particularly if the rapist is known to them, such as a family member or close friend. Often, crimes are committed in the workplace, where employees steal goods from their employers. Much **white-collar crime**, or crime conducted in the course of one's occupation, is handled internally and not reported, sometimes because those involved don't believe the crimes are serious enough to warrant police intrusion. Nonreporting is also related to victim fear, feelings of helplessness or apathy, the perceived powerlessness of police, and fear of the authorities themselves. The poor are especially reluctant to report crime because they fear reprisals from the criminals who are often known to them. Also, police may detect evidence of other crimes or statutory violations such as health code infractions, illegal aliens, and overcrowded apartment dwellings. Regardless of these shortcomings, the *UCR* and *NCVS* are better than no information. Researchers find many uses for the information from both sources.

In recent years, summary statistical information in the *Uniform Crime Reports* and other official sources has gradually been replaced by the **National Incident-Based Reporting System (NIBRS)**. This system involves the collection of incident-level data for a broad range of offenses. Thus, a more accurate picture of the amount of crime committed in the United States can be gleaned from an examination of NIBRS figures.

CLASSIFYING OFFENDERS

Distinguishing between different types of offenders is fairly easy, particularly if we classify them strictly on the basis of the crimes they have committed. However, some burglars are more violent or dangerous than others. Some rapists are more aggressive than other rapists. Some murderers are more dangerous than other murderers. Prisons and jails must place their inmates according to the most appropriate form of supervision. Various classification schemes have been devised and are used by prison and jail officials to determine which **level of custody** is most appropriate for each inmate. Corrections officials want to know which inmates should be isolated from other inmates and which ones should be permitted to associate with other inmates under more general supervision. Some inmates may pose physical threats either to themselves or to other inmates. Aggressive and violent prisoners can exploit, injure, or kill weaker inmates. Some inmates are suicide risks. Yet other inmates have mental illnesses or suffer from poor social adjustment (Povner, 2002). Classification schemes used by prison officials are also measures of the varying risks posed by inmates to others.

Probation and parole agencies also have a vested interest in classifying offenders accurately. Different probation programs target particular types of offenders, although the effectiveness of classification is sometimes questionable (Brown, 2000). Some offenders may be impaired mentally or physically. Some may have personality disorders or poor self-concepts. Yet other offenders may have serious alcohol or drug dependencies. Thus, various treatment programs are designed to meet specific offender needs, such as narcotics addiction (Weedon, 2002). These classification problems are pervasive for both adult and juvenile offenders (Underwood and Falwell, 2002). Several additional offender classifications have been developed for probation and parole programs. These traditional offender classifications include first-offenders and recidivists or career criminals.

Traditional Offender Categorizations

Besides violent and property offenders, two additional classifications include (1) first-offenders and (2) recidivists and career criminals.

First-Offenders. **First-offenders** are those who commit one or more crimes but have no previous history of criminal behavior. There is nothing especially unique about first-offenders. They may commit violent crimes or **property crimes**. First-offenders may be male or female. They may be old or young. They may or may not have records as juvenile **delinquents**. No useful blanket generalizations can be made about first-offenders other than the fact they have no previous criminal history. First-offenders who commit only the offense for which they were apprehended and prosecuted and are unlikely to commit future crimes are called **situational offenders**. Situational offenders may commit serious crimes or petty offenses. The situation itself creates the unique conditions leading to the criminal act. An argument between husband and wife over something trivial may lead to the death of one of the spouses. An argument between a convenience store clerk and a customer may lead to a serious altercation, even death. Serious financial pressures or setbacks may prompt situational offenders to commit embezzlement.

BOX 1.1

FIRST-OFFENDERS AND REPEAT-OFFENDERS: PROBATION OR INCARCERATION?

Should the Following Persons Receive Prison or Probation for Their Crimes?

- Roger G. is a 23-year-old first-offender. He was arrested by undercover officer for soliciting for prostitution with a young-looking male in a California park. Roger G. is a middle-level executive with an advertising firm in Los Angeles. He has never been arrested for any crime. He was booked at the Los Angeles County Jail and released on his own recognizance. When the prosecutor reviewed Roger G.'s case, he recommended diversion. Roger G. was placed on a one-year diversion program, without conditions. Two months later, Roger G. was arrested again, this time for soliciting a young man for prostitution in a Southern California bar. Roger G. was convicted of soliciting for prostitution. The charge carries up to one year in jail and a fine. What should the judge do?

- Gerald M., age 26, was convicted of aggravated assault and carjacking in Florida. He and two friends stopped an elderly couple at a traffic light in Miami and, at gunpoint, made them exit their car. Gerald M. hit the man with his pistol when the man resisted exiting the vehicle. Later, Gerald M. and his friends were caught in the stolen car. They were arrested and charged with aggravated assault in the incident. Aggravated assault carries a maximum prison term of

20 years. A presentence investigation report of Gerald M. shows that he has multiple arrests for petty larceny, theft, vehicular theft, and one assault charge arising from a disagreement with a bar patron. He has been on probation for various offenses twice. Gerald M.'s lawyer requested probation for Gerald M., noting that he had been crime-free for three years. What should the judge do?

- Juanita C., age 22, lives in San Francisco. She has been using drugs for four years. She dropped out of high school in the 10th grade and has worked at a fast-food restaurant off and on for two years. Presently she is unemployed. She was arrested while attempting to deliver 1 kilo of cocaine for her boyfriend, a man who is on probation himself for drug trafficking and use. The punishment for such an offense carries a life term. Juanita C. is from a broken home and grew up in an abusive household. She was sexually assaulted by her father and uncle since she was 9 years of age. The family has received little or no counseling or guidance from family protective services. Juanita C.'s attorney is asking the judge for probation. What should the judge do?

- Adam Z. is a teller at a small bank in Iowa. Recently, Adam Z. was arrested and convicted for forging names of

(*continued*)

BOX 1.1 (*Continued*)

bank customers and making unauthorized withdrawals from their accounts. The maximum penalty for such an offense is up to 5 years in prison and a $50,000 fine. Adam Z. claims that he wanted to pay off some of his student loan debt and only targeted accounts of wealthier bank customers. He acknowledged the wrongfulness of his actions and accepted responsibility for them. He has no prior criminal record. The amounts taken from customer accounts total $12,275, and Adam Z. has agreed to make financial restitution to the bank. What should the judge do?

- Michella D. is a 19-year-old gang member. She was recently involved in a drive-by shooting of a rival female gang member in Detroit. She shot at and seriously wounded two innocent bystanders in her attempt to gun down the rival gang member, who escaped without injury. Michella D. has confessed to the crime, and through a plea agreement, she has agreed to compensate the victims for their lost wages and perform 400 hours of community service. Her crime carries a penalty of up to 10 years in prison and a mandatory 2-year term for the use of a firearm during the commission of a felony. She is a first-offender, although her probation officer has noted in a presentence investigation report that she has serious alcohol and drug problems. She is a high school dropout and has a history of self-mutilation. What should the judge do?

What Happened?

- Roger G. received a 90-day suspended sentence and a one-year probationary term. The judge ordered Roger G. to attend sex therapy counseling for six months.

- Gerald M. received a six-year prison sentence for aggravated assault. His request for probation was denied.

- Juanita C. received three years' probation, with special conditions. The conditions included that she enroll and successfully complete a drug treatment program and that she receive regular counseling and medical therapy for her cocaine and methamphetamine addictions.

- Adam Z. was sentenced to two years' probation, with restitution orders to repay the bank in full for the embezzled money. Adam Z. is also required to obtain and maintain a job unaffiliated with handling money and to report monthly to the probation office during his probationary term. If he successfully completes the terms of his probation, his record will be ordered expunged by the court.

- Michella D. was sentenced to 2 years to be served in a state mental hospital where she can receive treatment for her addictions and because of the mandatory term to be served as the result of using a firearm during the commission of a felony. Her record will be reviewed when she completes her hospitalization and a probation recommendation may be made.

Often, first-offenders are given special treatment by different components of the criminal justice system. Prosecutors are inclined to give first-offenders another chance by either diverting them from the criminal justice system entirely or downgrading the seriousness of their instant offense. These persons are frequently good candidates for community treatment programs. If they have not become deeply entrenched in criminal activity, there is a good chance that one or more programs can reach them and help them to become more law-abiding. Probation departments also target first-offenders as most eligible for their programs. Knowing one's criminal history can indicate much about whether their participation in these community programs will be worthwhile and/or successful.

Recidivists.   Besides first-offenders and situational criminals, some offenders are **recidivists** who continue to commit new offenses. Even after they have been apprehended, prosecuted, and incarcerated, many offenders continue their criminal activity when released. Sometimes these persons are called **persistent offenders**, **persistent felony offenders**, or **habitual offenders**, **repeat offenders**, or **chronic offenders**. These appellations underscore the frequency and persistence of one's offending. Many programs devised by probation and parole departments are not particularly effective for helping hardcore recidivists. Some offenders will continue to reoffend no matter how carefully certain community programs are designed (Zhang & Jung, 2006).

Career Criminals.   **Career criminals** are offenders who earn their living from the crimes they commit. Their criminal activity is a craft, involving expertise and special training. Career criminals are those who have reached a stage of criminality where they view crime as an occupation or profession. Many of these offenders are more bothersome than dangerous. They frequently commit petty offenses involving theft, burglary, and vandalism. When they are punished, they are often overpenalized. This is the result of legislation where repeat offenders are subject to harsher penalties, even life imprisonment without the possibility of parole, if they are convicted of numerous petty crimes and are nonviolent toward others. Understandably, it is difficult for probation and parole officials to tailor programs that will rehabilitate or cure career criminals from their patterns of criminal activity.

CRIMINAL JUSTICE SYSTEM COMPONENTS

The primary components of the criminal justice system include **(1) law enforcement; (2) prosecutorial decision making; (3) courts and judges; and (4) corrections.**

Law Enforcement

All law enforcement agencies vest their officers with **arrest** powers. Police officers have the authority to make arrests whenever law violations occur within their jurisdictions. These arrest powers include apprehending anyone suspected of committing crimes. Offenses justifying arrests may range from traffic violations to first-degree murder, forcible rape, or kidnapping. Law enforcement officers are empowered to enforce the laws and statutes of their jurisdictions. Primarily an investigative body, the FBI has arrest powers involving violations of over 200 federal laws. FBI agents observe all appropriate jurisdictional boundaries associated with their position. These agents do not issue traffic citations or monitor speeders on interstate highways. Accordingly, state troopers seldom investigate and arrest counterfeiters or conspirators in interstate gambling or drug trafficking.

Arrest and Booking.   An arrest means taking a crime suspect into custody. Ordinarily, police officers make arrests of those suspected of committing crimes. Once defendants have been taken into custody, they are booked. **Booking** is an administrative procedure that furnishes personal background

 **BOX 1.2**

Daniel P. Hoffman
Chief of Police, Fairbanks Police Department, Fairbanks, Alaska

Statistics:

B.S. (wildlife biology), University of Alaska–Fairbanks; M.S. (justice administration), University of Alaska–Fairbanks.

Background and Work History:

If you are entering the workforce in the criminal justice system, you will undoubtedly interact with countless police officers, many of whom will profess that "this was the only job they ever wanted to do." While I have worked at the Fairbanks Police Department for nearly 18 years and have risen to the rank of Chief, I am not one of those people.

I graduated high school in Anchorage, Alaska, in 1983 and began my undergraduate work in wildlife biology at the University of Alaska–Fairbanks (UAF) on an academic scholarship. If you had told me at the time that I would end up working as a career police officer, I would have thought you were nuts! I spent four wonderful years at UAF, punctuated by great summers of field work in Alaska, including moose studies in the Interior, geese studies on the Yukon-Kuskokwim Delta, and guiding fly fisherman in Katmai National Park and Preserve.

A funny thing happened during my senior year, as I started taking a more realistic assessment of my chosen field. I realized that most of the fun and enjoyable field work that I had done was, and would continue to be, performed by seasoned technicians, as the true wildlife biologists spent a great deal of their time doing statistical data analysis and generating academic papers. This was not an appealing long-term prospect. As luck would have it, my older brother had graduated a few years ahead of me from the University of Alaska–Anchorage with a criminal justice degree and was working as a police officer in Kenai. Having spent some time

with him and doing some ride-alongs on patrol, I began to wonder if I could integrate the excitement I found in police work into my career. Natural Resource law enforcement seemed to be the obvious choice. I immediately added a criminal justice minor to my degree program, and I went through the selection and screening process to attend the Alaska Department of Public Safety Training Academy in Sitka as a self-sponsored candidate.

Working alongside municipal officer-recruits from around the state, many of whom were already employed by their sponsoring agencies, I surprisingly graduated as the class valedictorian and class honor-graduate in 1987. I returned to UAF for the Spring Semester, completing my degree and graduating. Then I began my first season as a Fish and Wildlife Enforcement Officer with the Alaska State Troopers on the Kenai Peninsula, a seasonal position that normally ran May through September.

Once again, reality collided with expectations. While I looked forward to spending a significant amount of time enforcing trapping, hunting, and sport-fishing regulations, I quickly learned that the big bucks (and hence, big violations) in Alaska are found in the commercial fisheries, and thus the majority of enforcement efforts are geared toward this area. After spending the majority of this season working the drift-fleet and set-netters of the Cook Inlet salmon fisheries, I was looking to regain my land-lubber status. I had greatly enjoyed living in Fairbanks during my college years; when I saw a recruitment/advertisement for the

Fairbanks Police Department, I decided on a whim to travel up and test. I competed with over 300 applicants for one of three positions, and I was fortunate enough to be hired. I suppose the rest, they say, is history.

Beginning in 1989 I spent the next 6 years working as a patrol officer on the streets of Fairbanks. This was definitely a learning experience for me, as I had come from a relatively sheltered, two-parent home, where I was afforded an ideal, Norman Rockwell–like upbringing. Dealing with thieves, drug users, sexual deviants, and other offenders—all set against a backdrop of pervasive family dysfunction—certainly broadened my horizons. I spent the next 3 years working as a patrol sergeant, where I first began to develop my supervisory and administrative skills.

The following four years were spent as the sergeant in charge of our Detective Division, where I managed all of our department's significant felony case investigations. After investigating scores of robberies, sexual assaults, and other serious crimes, and after closing 13 of the 14 homicides that we investigated, I was promoted to Lieutenant and came back to patrol. A short time later, I was assigned to the Deputy Chief's position, and now I serve as our department's Chief of Police.

Looking back on my career to this point, there are still times that I wonder, "How the heck did I end up as a cop, much less our Chief?" I believe the answer lies in the fact that I've always had a strong work ethic, and that I would always strive to do the best job that I could, no matter what the nature of my position/assignment was. I believe the other factor that has contributed most to my professional development and success is the fact that I truly care about both the personnel in my agency and about our community as a whole. When you have a strong work ethic, and when you care about what you are doing, most choices regarding work habits, time/resource allocation, and other factors tend to resolve themselves pretty easily.

Advice to Students:

Based on my own experiences, my first piece of advice is that you shouldn't feel compelled to follow the traditional career track. The value and applicability of a college education is often debated among practicing law enforcement officers. While I have met many superb and accomplished officers who did not have the benefit of a college education, I believe that the overall experience of completing a coordinated curriculum is a highly valuable one. Interaction with faculty and students of differing backgrounds and beliefs will help instill an openmindedness that is critical for police officers, both in approaching criminal investigation, as well as in dealing with the diverse populations that we serve. Completion of a 4-year curriculum requires forethought, planning, and disciplined follow-through, which would translate well toward any career. As you might surmise from my own background, I believe that a 4-year degree in nearly any discipline carries a strong value; I would not give hiring preference to a potential police applicant for his/her criminal justice degree, as compared to an applicant who had a 4-year degree in any of the hard sciences, such as business or engineering. My only other piece of advice is to care about what you are doing, no matter where your career evolution takes you. If you truly care, and work hard to do the best job you can possibly do, you just never know where you might end up!

information of offenders for law enforcement officials. Booking includes compiling a file for defendants, including their name, address, telephone number, age, place of employment, relatives, and other personal data. The extensiveness of the booking procedure varies among jurisdictions. In some jurisdictions, the suspect may be photographed and fingerprinted, while in others, defendants may answer a few personal, descriptive questions.

 **BOX 1.3**

INTERNATIONAL SNAPSHOT: PROBATION AND PAROLE IN SOUTH AFRICA

The criminal justice system of South Africa applies to a culturally diverse population of Africans. Approximately 76 percent of the population is black, 13 percent white, 8.5 percent coloreds, and the remainder Indians. The racial segregationist policy of Apartheid established a racial pecking order and distributed varying privileges according to three racial/ethnic subdivisions: white, colored, and black. Apartheid was subsequently rejected, and following the seating of a new South African government in 1994, free enterprise and integration were implemented. Several problems relating to housing, land, unemployment, and crime were produced and exacerbated as the result of these changes. However, the South African government had in place a preexisting criminal justice system to deal with criminal offenders. As governmental changes occurred, so did changes in the criminal justice system.

Between 1995 and 2005, numerous changes in the criminal laws and procedures of South Africa have been made. Prior to 1995, one of the most important developments leading to South Africa's contemporary criminal justice system was the Criminal Procedure Act of 1977, which has been amended several times subsequently. Among the original provisions of this act was the empowerment of magistrates to impose a minimum of 1 year and a maximum of 3 years of correctional supervision upon offenders after receiving a favorable report from a correctional official or probation officer. Another provision authorized the court to impose sentences of imprisonment not exceeding 5 years on accused persons where after serving one-sixth of the sentence offenders could be placed under correctional supervision in their communities. In 1991 on a provincial basis, different provinces were authorized to impose a community sentencing option for offenders deemed not to pose community risks. As specified under the Criminal Procedure Act of 1977, the requirements for correctional supervision included the following for any eligible offender in lieu of incarceration in prison:

1. Not pose a threat to the community.
2. Have a fixed, verifiable address.
3. Have a means of support to be financially independent.

South Africa has evolved a clear pattern of Pre-Trial Services (PTS). The major aim of PTS is to enable courts to make more informed bail decisions. Information about alleged offenders is collected by probation officers, similar to presentence investigation reports. However, the discretionary power to make bail decisions rests exclusively with magistrates. PTS thus provides the courts with much greater and detailed information about suspects. The implications of such PTS actions are to help ensure that (1) dangerous suspects are less likely to be released on bail; (2) petty offenders are released on bail with warnings or granted affordable bail; (3) all accused persons are closely supervised while on bail, thus reducing the likelihood of witness intimidation or court delays due to failure to appear; and (4) a decrease in the sheer number of prisoners awaiting trial occurs. Estimates are that without PTS, the number of prisoners held in South African prisons and jails would double.

South Africa also has implemented a diversion program to divert certain types of low-risk offenders from the criminal justice system. The aims of diversion are to prevent first-offenders from prolonged or frequent encounters with the criminal justice system; to promote conformity to the laws; and prevent persons from being imprisoned. Diversion is believed therapeutic as a rehabilitative action. Diversion is restricted largely to persons ages 14–18, although under special circumstances, diversion may be granted to older or younger offenders. South Africa now includes victim–offender mediation, family group conferencing associated with restorative justice programming; and outdoor experience programs for youths.

One program used by different South African provinces is the One Stop Youth Justice Center, or Stepping Stones. Stepping Stones consists of a police charge officer, a youth court and welfare component staffed by a probation officer, and children and youth care workers placed in local communities. Their aims are to divert youths away from the justice system or prevent them from advancing deeper into the system; to provide them with necessary services to meet their needs; to work with them and their families in a holistic way to enable them to acquire coping skills and vocational/educational training; to focus on the least restrictive sentencing options; and to give young people the opportunity to correct the wrongs committed through their actions. Thus, restitution and community service are stressed as sanctions, especially for more youthful offenders.

Pursuant to an investigation of various parole systems in other countries by a South African delegation in 1992–1993, the Department of Correctional Services was charged with the supervision of parolees, to be placed under community corrections. An autonomous Correctional Supervision and Parole Board was established to determine (1) definite dates of parole release of convicted offenders, (2) the communities where offenders should be placed, and (3) the parole conditions to be followed during the parole term. These requirements pertain to any person sentenced to:

1. Imprisonment for corrective training, where they may be detained in prison for a period of 2 years and may not be placed on parole until he or she has served at least 12 months.

2. Imprisonment for the prevention of a crime, where they may be detained in a prison for a period of 5 years and may not be placed on parole until he or she has served at least 2 years and 6 months of the sentence.

3. Life imprisonment, and such persons may not be placed on parole until they have served at least 25 years of the sentence; although a person who is age 65 may be placed on parole if he or she has served at least 15 years of their original sentence.

The Correctional Supervision and Parole Board makes both parole and parole revocation decisions.

General conditions for persons serving terms on either probation or parole include the following:

1. Refraining from committing criminal offenses.

2. Complying with any reasonable instructions by the court.

3. Refraining from making any contact with particular persons.

4. Refraining from threatening any persons by word or action.

Differing levels of supervision for offenders are determined by their level of seriousness. The most serious offenders are supervised more intensively than the least serious offenders. A classification system for all offenders is in the process of being devised. The classification system is oriented toward assessing not only risks posed by offenders but their needs. Thus, community officials charged with their eventual supervision can anticipate necessary rehabilitative and reintegrative services. The following supervision categories guide the nature of correctional supervision:

Maximum supervision cases: visited four times per month

Medium supervision cases: visited twice per month

Minimum supervision cases: visited once per month

Both parole and probation in South Africa may include house arrest; victim compensation; community service; correctional programming for treatment of drug/alcohol abuse and other problems; restrictions to one's community; fixed addresses; alcohol/drug monitoring; searches; obligations to seek and maintain employment.

It should not be inferred from these community-based initiatives that South Africa has abandoned incarceration as a punishment option. Indeed, South Africa endorses incarceration as the most appropriate punishment for those who pose the most serious community threats. In 2005 there were 239 correctional centers throughout

(continued)

BOX 1.3 (Continued)

South Africa in the different provinces. Eight women's centers and 131 men-only centers existed, with the remainder comprising institutions housing both male and female inmates. The total inmate population in 2005 was estimated at 155,800, with 3,200 of these inmates being female. There were 33,000 correctional officers and 5,000 correctional staff. Thus, there is an approximate 1 to 5 staff–inmate ratio. Inmates were serving terms of varying lengths, with 19,000 serving 7- to 10-year terms; 23,500 serving 10- to 15-year terms; 11,000 servicing 15- to 20-year terms; and 6,300 serving life terms. Fewer than 10,000 inmates were serving terms of less than 2 years. The death penalty was abolished in 1995. Inmates under age 18 numbered approximately 2,200. The number of parolees in 2005 was 31,300, while the number of probationers was 20,500. It is unknown how many persons are on bail at any given time, or who are on diversionary programs, since records of such actions are difficult to obtain from courts.

The prison system has been inspected frequently, both by government officials and world rights organizations. Generally, South African prisons are clean, decent, and humane institutions. A heavy emphasis is placed on vocational training. Most prisons have brick-laying schools and stress work related to construction and furniture production. In fact, the South African prison system has been modeled after various U.S. prisons, including several prison systems in Ohio and other states. Like many U.S. prisons, South African prisons have experienced chronic overcrowding in past years. For instance, in 2001 there was sufficient space in South African prisons to accommodate 102,048 prisoners, although at that time, 170,959 prisoners were being warehoused in these facilities, causing overcrowded conditions. Thus, more emphasis on nonincarcerative sanctions has promoted a broader variety of community corrections sanctions that are now in place. A general reduction in the prison population has occurred, and various community corrections programs are increasingly used in the different South African provinces.

Adapted from Mark Shaw, *Reforming South Africa's Criminal Justice System*, Crime and Policing Policy Project, 1996; Ronald Mpuru Ntuli and Sonwabo Victor Dlula, "Enhancement of Community-Based Alternatives to Incarceration at All Stages of the Criminal Justice Process in South Africa," Department of Correctional Services, 2004; *Correctional Statistics,* Department of Correctional Services, South Africa, 2005; Reginald A. Wilkinson, "Republic of South Africa: Department of Correctional Services," *Association of State Correctional Administrators Newsletter,* June 1998; M.S. Moatshe, "Budget Vote: Correctional Services," Republic of South Africa, June 2004.

Bail.   When defendants are arrested, a decision is made by prosecutors whether these persons will be brought to trial at some future date. If there is a trial, most defendants can obtain temporary release from detention. Criminal defendants may be **released on their own recognizance (ROR)**. **Bail** is only available to those entitled to bail. Those not entitled to bail include suspects likely to flee the jurisdiction if released temporarily, as well as those who pose a danger to others or themselves. Bail is a surety to procure the release of those under arrest and to ensure that they will appear later to face criminal charges in court.

While bail has been a part of the American landscape since its inception as a nation, research about bail and who should receive it has been sporadic. In 1961 the Vera Institute of Justice, a research organization, undertook the task of examining the bail issue. A large part of Vera's interest in bail was that large numbers of offenders were overcrowding jails and prisons. Many persons were spending long periods of time in jail awaiting their trials, and/or bail amounts were set so high that most persons entitled to bail could not afford to post it.

The Vera Institute studied bail in a landmark investigation, which came to be known as the Manhattan Bail Project (Currie, 2001:2). Subsequently, Vera staff presented a sample of New York judges with a list of persons they believed should be granted bail, based on their family roots, ties with the city, employment record, and other factors. They made release recommendations to these judges. These release recommendations were that judges should release these persons on their own recognizance. Interestingly, it was discovered as a result of this project that those released on their own recognizance by these criminal court judges had twice the appearance rate later at their trials compared with offenders who were released on traditional posting of different bail amounts. This study had a profound effect on bail reform, and the Bail Reform Act of 1966 was passed, in part based on Vera's investigations and positive findings. Large numbers of persons were subsequently released in most jurisdictions on their own recognizance with positive reappearance results.

However, nearly 20 years later, the Bail Reform Act of 1984 was passed. This Act was a part of the Comprehensive Crime Control Act of 1984, which was sweeping legislation designed to address numerous issues related to criminal prosecutions (Tarlow, 2005:1). The essence of the Bail Reform Act of 1984 was to make it more difficult for persons to obtain bail by shifting the burden to defendants to show why they would not pose a danger to others or be flight risks if released pending their subsequent trials. Today, judges still release defendants on their own recognizance, primarily because of the substantial overcrowding problems faced by jails, but also because not all persons charged with crimes pose a danger to others.

Bail is ordinarily specified at the time criminal suspects are brought before a judge or magistrate in an **initial appearance**. An initial appearance involves a preliminary specification of criminal charges against the defendant. Presiding judges may specify bail or they require defendants to be held until a **preliminary hearing** or **preliminary examination** can be convened for the purpose of establishing **probable cause**. At the conclusion of preliminary hearings, bail may be ordered or suspects may be released on their own recognizance.

In the federal system, U.S. Probation Officers perform various **pretrial services**. These services include conducting investigations of certain persons who have been charged with federal crimes. Recommendations are often made by these federal officers to U.S. Magistrates regarding an offender's bail eligibility. U.S. Magistrates want to know whether a defendant poses a flight risk or poses a danger to others if freed on bail. Federal probation officers furnish the court with important information about the nature of the charges against defendants. These officers work closely with the U.S. Attorney's Office and determine whether to recommend bail. Thus, probation officers (POs) have considerable discretionary powers in their decision making. Often judges are persuaded by POs to follow their recommendations with positive consequences. As we will see in this and future chapters, POs have even more far-reaching discretionary powers that influence the life chances of offenders throughout the criminal justice system.

Prosecutorial Decision Making

Prosecutions. After suspects have been arrested and booked for alleged violations of the law, a prosecutor examines their cases and the evidence against them and determines whether these suspects should be prosecuted. Not all arrests for serious crimes result in **prosecutions.** Furthermore, not all prosecutions result in convictions. A prosecution is the carrying forth of criminal proceedings against a person culminating in a trial or other final disposition, such as a guilty plea in lieu of trial. Prosecutors make these decisions and they are influenced by a consideration of factors such as the adequacy of evidence, whether there are eyewitnesses, and the seriousness of the crime.

Screening and Prioritizing Cases.   The prosecuting attorney screens cases and determines which ones have the highest probability for conviction. **Screening cases** involves determining the priority to be given particular kinds of cases such as murder or vehicular theft. Some cases lack merit or have insufficient evidence to sustain a criminal conviction. In other instances, there may be so many criminal cases to prosecute that not all of them can be prosecuted. Thus, prosecutors must prioritize their cases and prosecute only the most serious ones. Prosecutors also decide whether certain cases should be dropped.

Prosecutors act as negotiators between defendants, their attorneys, and judges. Prosecutors attempt to work out mutually advantageous arrangements between the state and defendants. The role of a **defense counsel** is to secure for clients the best possible outcome, preferably an acquittal. The stage is set for negotiations. Prosecutors want guilty pleas from defendants. Defendants, who may or may not be guilty of the offenses alleged, weigh the alternatives. Considering the strength of the evidence and other factors, defendants, after consulting with their attorneys, may decide to plead guilty, provided the government makes adequate concessions. Sentences resulting from trial convictions are often more severe than those imposed as the result of plea-bargained convictions for the same offenses.

Plea Bargaining.   Over 90 percent of all felony convictions in the United States are obtained prior to trial through **plea bargaining**. Plea bargaining is a preconviction agreement between the defendant and the state whereby the defendant pleads guilty with the expectation of either a reduction in the charges, a promise of sentencing leniency, or some other governmental concession short of the maximum penalties that could be imposed under the law. Plea bargaining is not exclusively an American phenomenon.

Plea bargaining is largely discretionary with prosecutors who use this tool as a means of regulating case flow, managing case backlogs, and facilitating case completion. Without plea bargaining occurring in most jurisdictions, the criminal justice system would probably be seriously impaired and grind to a halt. This is because almost every case would be subject to more lengthy trials and the costs and personpower involved would be prohibitive.

Four types of plea bargaining are described as follows. The first type is **implicit plea bargaining,** where defendants plead guilty with the expectation that they will receive more lenient sentences than if they were to go to trial and be found guilty by a jury. Generally, plea bargaining results in greater leniency in sentencing compared with a sentence derived from a jury finding of guilty at the conclusion of a **criminal trial**. A second type is **sentencing recommendation bargaining**, where the prosecutor proposes a sentence in exchange for a guilty plea. A third type is **charge reduction bargaining**, where the prosecutor downgrades charges in exchange for a guilty plea. This is sometimes called **overcharging**. A fourth type of plea bargaining is **judicial plea bargaining,** where the judge makes a plea offer to a defendant, such that if the defendant pleads guilty, the judge will impose a specific lenient sentence. Sentence recommendation bargaining and charge reduction bargaining are probably the most frequently used in plea negotiating.

Prosecutors do not have the authority to grant probation to any criminal defendant in exchange for a guilty plea. Prosecutors can only recommend probation to judges. Judges are the ultimate arbiters, and they decide whether to approve or disapprove any plea agreement. The plea bargaining process is important to any criminal defendant entering into negotiations with government prosecutors. Several constitutional rights are waived by defendants, and they acquire a criminal record. In the present context, plea bargaining is any offer or recommendation of sentencing leniency in exchange for a guilty plea from a defendant.

Informations, Indictments, and Presentments. If prosecutors persist in a prosecution against certain defendants, they have several options for commencing criminal proceedings. Prosecutors may file an **information**, or a formal criminal charge against a defendant. In about half of all states, a **grand jury** convenes and may issue an **indictment** or **presentment** against criminal suspects. Indictments and presentments are also charges stemming from grand jury consideration of evidence against the accused. Indictments are charges against criminal suspects brought by the grand jury at the request of prosecutors. Presentments are criminal charges against the accused where the grand jury has acted on its own authority. These actions simply specify that sufficient evidence exists to establish probable cause that a crime has been committed and the accused committed it. A **true bill** indicates that the grand jury has found sufficient evidence to establish probable cause that the accused committed a crime. No true bills issue from grand jury action and indicate that insufficient evidence exists to establish probable cause. If a **no true bill** or **no bill** is issued, suspects are most often freed from further criminal prosecutions.

Arraignments. Trials are preceded by an **arraignment**. An arraignment is a formal proceeding where the finalized list of charges is furnished to criminal defendants. Arraignments also are held for the purposes of entering a plea (e.g., guilty, not guilty, guilty but mentally ill) and determining a trial date. In a worst-case scenario, suppose a criminal defendant pleads not guilty to a criminal charge. When this happens, a trial date is established and a trial is scheduled where one's guilt or innocence can be determined by a judge or jury.

Courts and Judges

Court Dockets and Judicial Workloads. In many federal district courts as well as state criminal courts, court calendars are glutted with cases. About 85 percent of these cases are civil, and they consume considerable court time. The remainder of the cases are criminal. The courtroom is the place where a defendant's guilt is ultimately determined. It functions as a public forum for the airing of all relevant information and evidence in the case. The government presents its evidence against the accused, and the defense counters with its own evidence. Witnesses are called to testify both for and against the accused, and defendants have the right to cross-examine their accusers and to offer testimony and evidence in their own behalf. The courtroom is also the place where the sufficiency of evidence against the accused is tested. The prosecution carries the burden of proof against the accused and must establish one's guilt **beyond a reasonable doubt**.

Speedy Trials and Case Processing.   All defendants are entitled to a **jury trial** in any criminal proceeding as a matter of right, if the charges are serious and could result in incarceration for a period of six months or more. This applies to either misdemeanors or felonies. A jury is an objective, impartial body of persons who convene to hear the case against the accused and make a determination of guilt or innocence on the basis of the factual evidence presented. Despite speedy trial measures, streamlined case processing, and other court reforms, most state and federal judges are overworked and their dockets are glutted with case backlogs. Therefore, judges encourage prosecutors to work out arrangements with defendants, if possible, so that the number of trials can be at least minimized. About 10 percent of all criminal cases eventually proceed to trial. When defendants are convicted, most jurisdictions require probation officers at judicial direction to prepare reports about the convicted offender's background. These reports are time-consuming and take up a great deal of a PO's daily work routine. One result of the Speedy Trial Act of 1974, which prompted more rapid case processing, is that POs now must respond to judicial orders and prepare more of these reports more frequently. Thus, the time that POs can allocate to offenders and offender rehabilitation is diminished somewhat as they are faced with more paperwork from the courts.

Sentencing and Implications for Convicted Offenders.   Defendants who are found not guilty are acquitted and freed from the criminal justice system. When defendants are found guilty, an appeals process exists at both the state and local levels whereby these defendants may appeal the verdict and request a new trial. In the meantime, convicted offenders are sentenced.

Several options are available to judges in sentencing criminal defendants. For example, first-offenders may receive light sentences and not be incarcerated. However, convicted offenders with prior records will probably receive harsher sentences. Judges may sentence offenders to incarceration in a local jail or regional prison for a specified period of time. If the judge sentences convicted offenders to some nonincarcerative punishment, defendants may be placed on probation for a prescribed period.

Probation is a sentence involving a conditional suspension of incarceration, usually with several behavioral provisions or conditions. These conditions are often prescribed by law. Although this is not an exhaustive list, these conditions include (1) not associating with other known criminals, (2) refraining from committing future criminal acts, (3) obtaining and maintaining employment, and/or (4) participating in appropriate medical or counseling programs and therapy. Also, in many cases, judges must sentence convicted offenders to prison according to prescribed statutes. These are mandatory statutory provisions that bind judges and restrict their discretionary powers. Generally, however, convicted offenders collectively fall under the supervision of corrections.

Corrections

The last component of the criminal justice system is corrections. Corrections includes all of the agencies, organizations, and personnel who deal with convicted offenders after court processing and convictions. Typically, corrections are associated with **jails** and **prisons**. Jails are typically short-term confinement facilities operated by cities and county governments. They are usually used for persons enduring short-term confinement for misdemeanor offenses or for persons charged with more serious offenses who are awaiting trial. Prisons are long-term facilities that are more self-contained and house inmates serving sentences of one or more years. While prisons and jails are important features of the corrections system, they are hardly the dominant components of it. By 2003, approximately 7 million adults were under some form of correctional supervision in the United States. There were over 1 million prison inmates and about 750,000 jail inmates (Glaze, 2003).

Jail and Prison Overcrowding. Frequently, there is little room in many prisons and jails to house new convicted offenders. This is **overcrowding**. By 2006, 33 states were under court order to decrease their prison inmate populations to comply with health and safety standards as well as other factors (U.S. Department of Justice, 2006). Among other states, Texas, Tennessee, and Louisiana have been targeted for rehabilitative reforms by the courts. **Prison overcrowding** and **jail overcrowding** are primarily responsible for the large increase in the number of nonincarcerated offenders currently under some form of correctional supervision. Overcrowding in jails or prisons occurs whenever the operating capacity of any jail or prison is exceeded by the number of inmates it is intended to accommodate. Many judges have reported that prison overcrowding is a significant factor in their sentencing decisions whether to incarcerate convicted offenders. One increasingly important factor affecting prison populations in both state and federal facilities is the growing population of noncitizen felony offenders (Cohn et al., 2002).

Judicial Discretion in Sentencing Offenders. Judges frequently have considerable latitude in sentencing criminal offenders. Besides sentencing offenders to incarceration, judges may impose other sentences, including **community service,** restitution, and even probation (Nellis, 2002). There are at least two other sentencing options. Judges may issue what is called a **suspended imposition of a sentence** or a **suspended execution of a sentence**. A suspended imposition of a sentence means that the judge or jury has found the defendant guilty of the offense. However, the judge suspends imposing the sentence or temporarily delays imposing the sentence. The sentence may actually involve a 3-year prison term. But the judge doesn't impose this sentence immediately. Rather, the judge temporarily suspends the sentence so that the offender can satisfy certain conditions. These conditions may require the offender to make restitution, pay a monthly maintenance fee to the probation department, remain law-abiding, submit monthly reports to show regular employment, and submit to drug or alcohol tests. The period of time covered by this suspended imposition of a sentence may be up to one year. Once the offender has completed this period prescribed by the judge and has satisfied all of these imposed conditions, the judge will suspend the 3-year prison term. Actually, the judge usually orders the guilty verdict set aside and dismisses the charges against the offender. Thus, the suspended imposition of a sentence is a constitutional, statutorily authorized form of judicial clemency, similar to a pardon. The net result is that there is no conviction, despite a prior verdict of guilty.

In a suspended execution of a sentence, imagine the same scenario as above. A judge or jury has found the defendant guilty of a crime and a 3-year prison term may be imposed upon that conviction. However, in this case, the judge enters a judgment of conviction but postpones executing the sentence. Again, the judge sets forth various conditions the offender must satisfy, including restitution to victims, payment of fines, maintenance fees to a probation department, community service, and remaining employed and law-abiding. Again, the period of sentence suspension may be up to a year. Once the time interval is completed and the offender has complied with all of the judge's behavioral requirements, then the judge suspends the 3-year prison term and the offender is freed. However, the conviction remains on the person's record. Depending on the seriousness of the charges against defendants, and depending on the particular jurisdiction, judges may or may not have the power to suspend sentences, either their imposition or execution.

Assisting judges in their sentencing decisions are probation officers who often prepare reports on convicted offenders. These reports contain sentencing recommendations that many judges are inclined to follow. Subsequently, parole-eligible offenders will face parole boards and these reports prepared by POs will be consulted as a part of their decision making.

In 2006, the probation and parolee population exceeded 7 million. Among the factors considered by trial judge when sentencing offenders are (1) the nature and circumstances of the offense and the history and characteristics of the defendant; (2) the need for the sentence imposed to reflect the seriousness of the offense, to promote respect for the law, to afford adequate **deterrence** to criminal conduct, and to protect the public from further crimes of the defendant; (3) the kinds of educational or training services, medical care, or other correctional treatment that might be appropriate for any particular defendant; (4) the kinds of sentences available; and (5) the need to avoid unwarranted sentence disparities among defendants with similar records who have been found guilty of similar conduct. Judges may have too much unregulated power, and that may result in questionable decision making such as excessive leniency for violent offenders and sending nonserious juveniles to criminal courts for processing. Numerous sentencing reforms have been dedicated to controlling judicial discretion at all levels, although no sentencing scheme seems to work perfectly.

The Availability of Community Services and Facilities.   Many citizens equate corrections with punishment involving incarceration. In reality, a majority of convicted offenders are never incarcerated. Rather, they are permitted the freedom of living in their communities under some form of **alternative sentencing** or **creative sentencing**. Alternative sentencing involves some form of community service, some degree of restitution to victims of crimes, becoming actively involved in educational or vocational training programs, or becoming affiliated with some other productive activity (Holcomb and Glenn, 2006). Two goals of alternative sentencing are enabling offenders to avoid the criminal label of imprisonment and allowing convicts to participate in rehabilitative and reintegrative community programs. Community programs are designed to provide convicted offenders with needed services and therapy while they remain free in their communities. Alternative sentencing is also intended to reduce jail and prison overcrowding and reduce correctional operating costs.

PROBATION AND PAROLE DISTINGUISHED

Probation is considered a front-end sentence, whereby judges impose conditional sentences in lieu of incarceration. In most cases, probationers do not serve time in either jail or prison. Rather, they must comply with an extensive list of probation program conditions as specified by the court. Probationers remain free within the jurisdiction of sentencing judges while on probation. If probationers violate one or more conditions of their probation orders while on probation, judges decide whether to revoke or terminate their probation programs.

In contrast, parole is early release from prison or jail by a **parole board**. Most states have parole boards that convene to determine whether inmates should be released short of serving their full sentences. Since almost all jails and prisons in the United States are overcrowded, any mechanism that might reduce such overcrowding is viewed favorably, particularly by state legislatures. Parole is one such mechanism. Parole differs from probation in that parolees have spent a period of time in a jail or prison. All parolees have in common the fact that they have previously been inmates of some state or federal facility. Another feature of parole is that parole boards have jurisdiction over parolees and decide whether they should be released short of serving their full incarcerative terms.

SUMMARY

The major components of the criminal justice system include law enforcement, prosecution and the courts, and corrections. Probation and parole are integral features of corrections, which includes all organizations and personnel who manage offenders who have been convicted of crimes. Probation is a conditional sentence imposed by a judge in lieu of incarceration, while parole is conditional early release from prison granted by a parole board.

The entire criminal justice process starts whenever a crime is committed. Crimes are violations of the law by persons held accountable under the law. They may be distinguished as either misdemeanors or felonies, and they may involve property or **violence**. Official sources of crime in the United States are the *Uniform Crime Reports (UCS)* and the *National Crime Victimization Survey (NCVS)*. Both of these sources are flawed in various respects. Both official sources are considered underestimates of the actual amount of crime committed in the United States annually. When persons are arrested for a crime, they are booked. Prosecutors decide whether to prosecute defendants. Prosecutors prioritize cases if their caseloads are particularly large. Over 90 percent of all criminal defendants enter guilty pleas to criminal charges in exchange for sentencing leniency. This process is known as plea bargaining. For other defendants, trials are held where juries or judges determine their guilt or innocence. If defendants are convicted through trial, judges must sentence offenders to some type of punishment. All sentences are a type of punishment, although the punishment does not always involve incarceration. Probation is a punishment, although it is a nonincarcerative alternative. Probationers must comply with numerous probation program conditions and behavioral restrictions.

Judges decide whether to place offenders on probation or send them to jails or prisons. Sentencing offenders depends on the seriousness of their offenses and their prior records. Jails are short-term facilities intended to house minor offenders and pretrial detainees. Prisons are long-term and self-contained facilities designed to accommodate more serious offenders for longer time periods. Depending on the type of crime they have committed, offenders are classified in different ways to determine their level of custody and/or the nature of their treatment or assistance. Some offenders are first-offenders, while others may be recidivists or career criminals. Those offenders with prior criminal records usually receive harsher treatment from judges when sentenced. Some offenders are designated as special-needs criminals. They may have AIDS or some other communicable illness. They may be handicapped in some respect, or psychologically or mentally impaired. Some offenders may have drug or alcohol dependencies and require special treatment or counseling. Other offenders may be sex offenders and **child sexual abusers** requiring extraordinary therapy.

Corrections is expected to accommodate all types of offenders. Depending on how offenders are sentenced, different corrections agencies or institutions will be responsible for offender supervision. Those sentenced by judges to probation are supervised by probation agencies and probation officers, while parole officers and agencies supervise those who have been paroled from either state or federal penitentiaries by parole boards. **Community-based corrections** are intended to assist both probationers and parolees in various ways in order to enhance the likelihood that they will complete their respective probation or parole programs successfully. The long-term goal of these agencies and organizations is to cause their clients to become law-abiding so that they will refrain from future criminal activity.

QUESTIONS FOR REVIEW

1. What is the *Uniform Crime Reports (UCR)?* What kinds of information does it report? What can you say about its accuracy relative to general crime and crime trends in the United States?

2. What is the *National Crime Victimization Survey (NCVS)?* How does it differ from the *UCR?* Explain. Do you believe it is more accurate as a reflection of the amount of crime in the United States? Why or why not?

3. What are the major components of the criminal justice system? Which part of the system deals with convicted offenders? Explain briefly the functions of this component relative to convicted offenders.

4. What is a crime? Distinguish between two general categories of crime. Explain how each is treated in terms of punishment. You answer can include both the location where offenders might be housed as well as the sentence lengths judges might commonly impose.

5. What are index offenses? What is their usefulness regarding crime in the United States and crime trends?

6. Differentiate between a victimization and an incident.

7. Who are situational offenders? What can you speculate about their amount of expected recidivism in the future? Explain.

8. What is recidivism and what are some of the ways it is measured? Why is recidivism used as a measure of a program's success or failure?

9. What are four different types of plea bargaining? Give an example of each from any hypothetical information you may have.

10. What is meant by alternative or creative sentencing? Give some examples of it.

SUGGESTED READINGS

Carmichael, S.E. and A.R. Piquero (2006). "Deterrence and Arrest Ratios." *International Journal of Offender Therapy and Comparative Criminology* **50**:71–87.

Chappell, A.T., J.M. MacDonald, and P.W. Manz (2006). "The Organizational Determinants of Police Arrest Decisions." *Crime and Delinquency* **42**:287–306.

Dembo, R., et al. (2005). "Evaluation of the Impact of a Policy Change on Diversion Program Recidivism and Justice System Costs." *Journal of Offender Rehabilitation* **41**:93–122.

Merritt, Nancy, Terry Fain, and Susan Turner (2006). "Oregon's Get Tough Sentencing Reform: A Lesson in Justice System Adaptation." *Criminology and Public Policy* **5**:5–36.

Muller, Nicholas and Karen Dunlap (2006). "Effective Supervision and Gun Violence Reductions." *APPA Perspectives* **30**:34–37.

Orth, U., L. Montada, and A. Maercker (2006). "Feelings of Revenge, Retaliation Motive, and Posttraumatic Stress Reactions in Crime Victims." *Journal of Interpersonal Violence* **21**:229–243.

INTERNET CONNECTIONS

American Bar Association
http://www.abanet.org/crimjust/links.html

Criminal justice links
http://www.lawguru.com/ilawlib/96.htm

Federal Judicial Center
http://www.fjc.gov

History of Federal Bureau of Prisons
http://www.bop.gov/lpapg/pahist.html

Legal Resource Center
http://www.crimelynx.com/research.html

National Institute of Justice
http://www.ojp.usdoj.gov/nij

State court links
http://www.doc.state.co.us/links

State criminal justice links
http://www.statesnews.org/other_resources/law_and_justice.htm

U.S. Department of Justice
http://www.usdoj.gov/02organizations/02_1.html

Vera Institute of Justice
http://www.vera.org

CHAPTER 2 | *Theories of Offender Treatment*

Chapter Outline

As the result of reading this chapter, the following objectives will be realized:

1. Describing biological theories of criminal conduct, including abnormal physical structure, heredity, and biochemical disturbances.
2. Describing psychological theories, including psychoanalytic theory, cognitive development theory, and social learning theory.
3. Understanding sociological and/or sociocultural theories, including differential association, anomie theory, the subculture theory of delinquency, and social control theory.
4. Understanding conflict/Marxist theory.
5. Understanding reality therapy and social casework.
6. Understanding the differences between various theories and how they relate to different offender programs.
7. Determining which theories are best for explaining offender behaviors and program development.

• *It happened in Indiana in 1992. A youth, Joseph Corcoran, age 17, was accused of murdering his parents. At the time, insufficient evidence linked the youth with the crimes. His parents had been shot to death, and the police could not discover a murder weapon or determine a motive for why Corcoran would kill his parents. No other suspects were arrested at that time for the murders of Joseph's parents, Jack and Kathryn Corcoran. Subsequently, Joseph Corcoran was released. However, five years later, Joseph Corcoran, now age 22, walked downstairs in the home where he was living and shot to death his older brother, James Corcoran, age 30; his sister's fiance, Robert Scott Turner, age 32; Douglas A. Stillwell, age 30; and Timothy G. Bricker, age 30. The others were friends of the family. Joseph Corcoran went across the street to the home of a neighbor and asked him to call the police. When the police arrived, Joseph said, "You might as well just arrest me." He told an investigating officer that he killed everyone because he thought they were talking about him and became angry. All four persons had been sitting in the living room eating pizza and watching television. Joseph Corcoran's sister, Kelly Nieto, said, "I knew right then and there that he had killed my parents. Everything's gone. He's ruined my life." Police say that Joseph Corcoran opened fire on everyone with a semiautomatic rifle. A defense counsel for Corcoran argued in court later that Corcoran was "delusional" and seemed "paranoid." Joseph Corcoran was later convicted and sentenced to death.*

• *It happened in Arkansas in 2001. Rickey Dale Newman, age 35, was a homeless person living near some railroad tracks. One evening he spotted Marie Cholette, age 46, who was also living near the railroad tracks. Cholette, who was from Ft. Worth, Texas, had been staying in the train yard for several weeks. She had told others that she was a member of the Freight Train Riders of America, a gang of homeless persons who frequently hitched rides on freight trains to travel from one location to another. Newman lured Cholette into a wooded area one evening, telling her that he had something to drink. Suddenly, he turned on her and overwhelmed her. He tied her to a tree and began cutting her with a knife. He cut off portions of her breasts and slit her from her sternum to her pelvic area. After cutting other parts of her body, he poured gasoline over her and set her on fire. He then took portions of her body and put them in a pot, cooking them. Later, he put her remains under a makeshift tent composed of tarps and lumber. Newman was apprehended later, since other homeless persons recalled seeing him with Cholette earlier.*

Newman confessed, giving as the reason that Cholette lied about being in the Freight Train Riders of America gang. He said, "I was gonna punish her good. She represented herself as a member of our gang and she was murdered for it. I tortured her, murdered her, and set her on fire. I think if you're man enough to do the crime, you should be man enough to take the punishment." Later following his conviction, several civil rights groups filed petitions and appeals on his behalf, citing mental disease or defect. Newman was outraged. Newman said, "I feel like people need to stay out of my business and let me get on with dying. There's nothing wrong with me."

• *It happened in Texas in October 1998. A woman, Kiersa Alexandra Paul, age 24, was jogging in a remote area of a park. She was assaulted and then killed by David Martinez, a 20-something local with the nickname "Wolfman." The woman was later discovered by other joggers. She was covered by a pair of unbuttoned shorts and her legs were spread open. She had marks on her body consistent with strangulation, blunt force trauma, bruising of both nipples, cuts on her neck and stomach, and forceful sexual intercourse. Martinez came to the attention of police because he was riding Paul's bicycle and carrying her bicycle bag. They arrested Martinez and seized a Swiss army pocket knife. Forensic tests determined that hairs found on Paul matched Martinez as well as semen taken from the dead woman's vagina and panties. Blood on the pocket knife matched Paul's. Martinez was subsequently convicted of Paul's murder and sentenced to death. He did not express or show remorse for the murder.*

• *Terry Neal, an 18-year-old man from Oklahoma, was found dead in his apartment. Investigation revealed that Neal was a homosexual who frequented a section of Oklahoma City known as a district for homosexual prostitution. Witnesses recall Neal in the company of a teenage boy. His description was distributed to area police and residents, and the name of James Fisher, Jr., was mentioned by an acquaintance, who said Fisher had bragged about killing a fag. Fisher was picked up by police in Buffalo, New York, where he was extradited back to Oklahoma. Following a lengthy interrogation, Fisher confessed. He related that Neal met him downtown and took him to Neal's apartment where they had sex. After sex, Fisher hit Neal with a wine bottle, which broke, and stabbed him in the neck several times with the broken end of the bottle. Fisher then took Neal's television set and sold it to a friend. Fisher drove Neal's car to New York where he was subsequently apprehended. Fisher said, "I was in Oklahoma doing anything to try and make some money. Later, after I hit him with the bottle, I took his TV and sold it." Police recovered Fisher's prints from Neal's apartment and automobile. Fisher, age 18, was convicted of first-degree murder and sentenced to death. [Source: Adapted from ProDeathPenalty.com, "July 2005 Executions," October 1, 2005].*

INTRODUCTION

Why do people rob? Why do people murder others? Why are there child sexual abusers? Why do people assault others? Why are there rapists? For several centuries, scientists have attempted to explain crime, its causes, and how it can most effectively be treated. This chapter describes several theories or explanations for committing crimes. Theories are explanatory schemes that attempt to link events with presumed causes of those events. Subsequent research attempts to show the predictive utility of theories and the events that they are designed to explain.

Because probationers and parolees have been convicted of crimes, they have often been studied by researchers who delve into their motives and intent. This inquiry has led to the formulation of various treatments designed to rehabilitate offenders or cause them to change their criminal ways. These treatments are also known as interventions. Interventions are experiences interjected into the lives of persons at different ages in order to cause changes in their future circumstances. For instance, in elementary schools, some students have been identified as being at risk of becoming delinquent. They may be socially isolated or exhibit psychological problems. They may be indifferent to authority or simply refuse to obey a teacher's instructions. Psychologists and others have devised terms to account for some of this behavior. Attention-deficit disorder, or ADD, is used to explain why some students have difficulty staying "on task" in classroom situations. Some students are hyperactive, and they have medications prescribed for them to control their hyperactivity.

In short, interventions with at-risk youths or with adult probationers and parolees are intended to correct their current behaviors and cause them to become law-abiding. If we look hard enough at any particular intervention, we will usually find some criminological theory lurking in the background. There are those, for example, who believe that youthful offenders should not be exposed to the trappings of juvenile courts, which are increasingly like criminal courts in their appearance. Thus, it has been advocated that for many of these youths, they should be sheltered from these formal proceedings and diverted from the juvenile justice system if possible. In the interest of protecting or insulating certain youths from criminal court–like proceedings, therefore, it is believed that they will not define themselves as criminals or delinquents. And as a result, they may be saved from a life of crime by being treated in some way rather than punished through incarceration or probation. Labeling theory is the explanatory scheme behind this type of diversionary action. Youths can avoid the criminal taint or label of being criminal or delinquent. Thus, if they don't define themselves that way, they will have a better chance of becoming rehabilitated.

Interventions in preschool or in one's early school years, which target at-risk youths, are designed to provide them with opportunities they might not otherwise have because of their socioeconomic circumstances. Being at risk doesn't always mean being socioeconomically deprived, however. There are risk factors such as family violence or instability, drug use, alcohol consumption, social isolation, bullying, and other circumstances that cause some youths to be identified by authorities as being at risk (Klein, Bartholomew, and Hibbert, 2002). What should be done to rescue these youths from the circumstances that are believed to contribute to their future potential criminal conduct? Various types of counseling and therapeutic interventions are attempted that target some of these at-risk youths. The idea is to help them understand themselves and acquire better self-concepts and self-esteem. Social isolates are drawn out and put into school groups and activities. They are provided with social opportunities and learning experiences that they otherwise might not have. Behind these types of interventions are theories known as differential or limited opportunity.

For other youthful offenders in their teens, boot camps are used to instill discipline within them. We have examined boot camps earlier, and they are military-like interventions where self-esteem, self-respect, acceptance of responsibility, and respect for authority are heightened. Many juveniles are attracted to gangs and engage in delinquent or criminal conduct because they lack the resistance to avoid delinquent groups or criminal organizations. Boot camps are designed, in part, to assist participants in acting independently without having to rely on delinquent gangs for esteem and recognition. A theory of delinquent subcultures underlies many boot camp programs that are operating in the United States today.

This chapter describes different theories of criminal and delinquent behavior. Explored are biological theories, psychological theories, and sociological theories that have been used to explain deviant and criminal conduct. These theories are important to understand, since they are linked closely with the interventions used by POs in relation with their clients. Furthermore, these theories are the basis for many of the experiences and programs to which probationer/parolee/clients are exposed. The chapter concludes by evaluating these theories in terms of their predictive utility. Which theory is best? No single theory is universally accepted by all criminologists. No single theory dominates PO policy and practice. Nevertheless, PO work is often couched in one type of theory or another. Thus, we can more effectively understand why POs orient themselves to clients in particular ways through a knowledge of the theories that drive their behaviors and the interventions they utilize.

THEORIES OF CRIMINAL BEHAVIOR

A **theory** is a set of assumptions that attempts to explain and predict relationships between phenomena. The primary functions of theories are to explain and predict. Regarding probationer recidivism, we are interested in explaining why certain probationers commit new offenses while on probation. We are also interested in predicting the occurrence of these crimes. Criminologists conduct statistical studies to identify circumstances of probationers who cannot remain law-abiding. They might suggest that such probationers were unemployed or underemployed, or that they were on drugs or under the influence of alcohol, or had associated with other known criminals prior to committing these new offenses. If adolescents join a delinquent gang and commit burglaries or engage in gang fights, the criminologist might say that these adolescents had unstable home environments, were not doing well in school, or needed peer companionship and esteem. Thus, several theories may be needed to account for one's criminal conduct.

Observers disagree about the objectives of probation and parole. Some see probation and parole as rehabilitative, while others see it as a deterrent to crime. Yet others see the objective of probation and parole as purely punitive. There are those who believe that probation and parole embraces all of these objectives. Understanding the causes of crime and criminal behavior is useful in designing effective treatment strategies that can be useful in the rehabilitative and reintegrative process. The criminal justice system, including the statutes applicable to sanctioning criminal offenders, has evolved over several centuries. The influence of various theories of criminal behavior on probationer and parolee conduct and the development of subsequent interventions used in their treatment are apparent. Many theories of criminal behavior can be grouped into three general categories that stress different causal factors: (1) biological theories; (2) psychological theories; and (3) sociological or sociocultural theories.

Between 1890 and 2000, there has been a major theoretical shift in the thinking of criminologists about why people commit crimes. Early theories of crime emphasized factors inside persons or internal to them. Bad blood, malfunctioning glands, physical deformities, having a criminal personality, having criminal drives or tendencies, possession by evil spirits, heredity, and mental illness are some of the many internal concepts advanced to explain deviant behavior generally and criminal behavior specifically (Hooton, 1939; Yochelson and Samenow, 1976).

During the 1940s and 1950s, some criminologists changed their thinking about criminal behavior to those phenomena occurring external to the individual such as the person's social status or sociocultural position, group pressures and gang conformity, antisocial criminal patterns, associating with criminals, labeling one's self as a criminal, or learning to be a criminal. While this shift has not been overtly acknowledged, it is apparent that the emergence of violent delinquent gangs and social circumstances of adult offenders have undermined existing internal explanations of criminal behavior. Another indication of this shift is the subtle change in research literature that explains crime and describes criminality. Although interpretations of trends in the criminological research literature are largely impressionistic, explanations of crime today emphasize causal factors that differ from those emphasized in the 1920s and 1930s.

This shift does not mean that professionals have abandoned internal explanations for external ones. Rather, external theories are currently more popular than internal theories. This popularity may be seen in the treatment and rehabilitation of criminal offenders. Manipulating the external environment of criminals, their home life, or associates seems easier to accomplish than modifying their genetic structure, driving out evil spirits, or erasing criminal propensities, whatever they might be. Of course, there are other explanations for this shift. Recent theoretical developments in sociology and psychology have emphasized the importance of social or external factors in predicting criminal behavior. Also, criminologists have learned more about genetic makeup, the role of diet in altering personality characteristics, and the medical control of various psychological disorders. Interestingly, these and similar developments have recently renewed interest in some of the more popular internal explanations for criminal behavior.

For example, sociobiologists believe that body chemistry and genetic makeup are crucial in determining all human behavior, including deviance and criminal conduct (Wilson and Herrnstein, 1985). **Sociobiology** is the scientific study of the causal relation between genetic structure and social behavior. Some of the treatment programs currently used for offenders are based, in part, on this biological explanation for criminal behavior.

One important issue shared by all of these theories, regardless of their intuitive value, innovativeness, or general interest, is whether they can be used to explain and predict criminal behavior. How can each theory be applied? Can effective rehabilitative programs be developed for probationers and parolees? Can any of these theories be used to control criminal behavior or prevent crime? These practical questions are often used to assess the adequacy of any of the theories described here.

Some of these theories of criminal behavior may seem archaic in view of our current state of scientific knowledge. But their impact may be measured or evaluated according to their influence on correctional policies and other criminal justice issues. Thus, while a theory of criminal behavior may be refuted and found to be false, it nevertheless may have important implications for the policies of various agencies within the criminal justice system. For instance, one theory of criminal behavior shown to be false was that heredity transmitted criminal characteristics genetically from one generation to the next. During the 1930s and 1940s, thousands of state and federal prisoners were sterilized, because it was believed that their sterilization would prevent the birth of new generations of criminal offspring.

But evaluations of these theories are not limited to strictly pragmatic criteria. Sometimes, explanations of criminal behavior are abstract and provide contextual backgrounds for other, more practical theories. For instance, sociologists say that the social class structure of the United States explains certain kinds of crimes. Crime fluctuates among neighborhoods as well as among social classes. Evidently, there is some connection between the social class structure and crime. But it is unlikely that major changes will soon occur in the social class structure of the United States that affect crime or crime rates. But this fact doesn't preclude criminologists from using social class as an explanation for crime and crime trends. And it probably encourages POs to orient themselves in particular ways toward probationers or parolees according to the nature of the neighborhoods where they live as well as their ethnic or racial backgrounds and general socioeconomic information.

BIOLOGICAL THEORIES

Biological theories of criminal behavior include (1) abnormal physical structure, (2) hereditary criminal behaviors, and (3) biochemical disturbances.

Abnormal Physical Structure

One biologically based set of theories has attempted to link **abnormal physical structures** with criminal behaviors. A pioneer of the school of thought that criminals may be identified by their abnormal or unusual physical characteristics was the Italian physician Cesare Lombroso (1835–1909). He coined the expression, "born criminals." In fairness to Lombroso, his beliefs about the relation between physique and criminal propensities were developed during the period when Charles Darwin's theory of evolution was deemed quite credible in science. Darwin argued that humans evolved from lower life forms, and that some humans were more advanced in their biological development than others. Less advanced humans had visible physical characteristics closely associated with the physical features of criminals. Thus, Lombroso's explanation of crime made much more sense than it does today.

Lombroso said that (1) criminals are, by birth, a distinct type; (2) this type can be recognized by asymmetrical craniums, long lower jaws, flattened noses, scanty beards, and low sensitivity to pain; (3) these characteristics do not themselves cause crime but assist in our identification of personalities disposed toward criminal behavior; (4) such persons cannot refrain from criminal behavior except under unusual social circumstances; and (5) different physical features are associated with different kinds of crime.

Originally, Lombroso argued that 100 percent of the prison population was comprised of born criminals, but in subsequent years, he modified this figure to about 40 percent. His treatise on the subject was published in 1876 and was expanded into three volumes (Lombroso, 1918). His views later were known as the "Italian school" or the "positive school," because direct empirical indicators of criminal tendencies could be identified (i.e., cranium shape, jaw angles, body hair, etc.) compared with other speculation about criminal conduct.

Lombroso's studies of Italian prison inmates led him to observe that many had long, sloping foreheads, pointed ears, narrow or shifty eyes, receding chins, and overly long arms. Subsequent comparisons of other prisoners with the nonincarcerated population-at-large have revealed no significant differences in physical characteristics between criminals and noncriminals, however. One explanation for Lombroso's views about physique and criminal behavior is that often, persons with odd appearances are rejected by others. This rejection might lead them to follow deviant or criminal paths. The labeling theory of deviant behavior described later in this chapter examines this phenomenon more fully.

Lombroso's views still enjoy popularity in the media whenever particularly bizarre events occur. For instance, the late Truman Capote wrote a nonfictional work titled *In Cold Blood.* This book detailed the murder of an entire Kansas family by two drifters. These men were apprehended, tried and convicted of murder, and executed. At or about the time of their execution, their photographs appeared in *The Saturday Evening Post.* The writer of the article suggested that readers observe that one of the murderers had a face made up from two parts where the two parts did not quite match up with one another. Attention was drawn to portions of the murderer's photograph showing that one eye was not level or even with the other, the mouth curved down on one side and up on the other side, and that the ears were unevenly matched. This physical description was provided in a popular national magazine in the late 1960s.

A popular outgrowth of Lombroso's positivist thinking was the concept of various body types by Sheldon (1949). Sheldon classified persons into three distinct categories: (1) **endomorphs** (fat, soft, plump, jolly); (2) **ectomorphs** (thin, sensitive, delicate), and (3) **mesomorphs** (strong, muscular, aggressive, tough). Sheldon wrote extensively about the behavioral characteristics of each body type. He devised a complex numerical system where persons possessed features of one body type to a greater degree than the other two types. He eventually developed crude indices from which generalizations about criminal behavior could be made. He said that ectomorphs tend to commit forgery, fraud, or burglary (passive, nonviolent crimes), whereas mesomorphs tend to commit robbery, rape, murder, assault, and other physically demanding crimes. Sheldon believed that body type was a cause of particular types of criminal conduct. Subsequent studies and extensive research by criminologists and others have failed to support Sheldon's theory.

Hereditary Criminal Behaviors

Heredity as a cause of criminal conduct suggested the inheritance of certain physical and behavioral characteristics from parents or ancestors. Whether people became criminals depended on their lineage or hereditary background. If one's ancestors were cattle rustlers, thieves, or rapists, then the offspring would also tend to be cattle rustlers, thieves, or rapists. Little scientific evidence exists supporting this theory.

A more recent heredity-based theory of criminal behavior is the **XYY syndrome.** "X" and "Y" are labels assigned to the human sex chromosomes. Males are *XY,* while females are *XX.* These sex chromosomes, *X* and *Y,* are inherited from the mother and father. The father transmits the *Y* or aggressive chromosome, while the *X* or "passive" chromosome comes from the mother. Occasionally, infants are born with an *XYY* (doubly aggressive?) chromosomatic pattern.

In the 1960s, researchers were intrigued by the discovery that Richard Speck had an *XYY* chromosomatic pattern. At the time, Speck was in prison for the brutal murder of eight student nurses in Chicago. Could this extra *Y* chromosome have caused his violent behavior? Geneticists have investigated the

XYY syndrome in selected, captive-audience situations: prisons. Their data show that (1) there appears to be more *XYY* people in the criminal population compared with the general population, and (2) less than 5 percent of the prison population has the *XYY* syndrome. Thus, the *XYY* syndrome is not a consistent cause of criminal behavior.

Biochemical Disturbances

A third group of biologically based theories of criminal behavior focuses on biochemical disturbances and glandular malfunctions as inducing criminal acts. The thyroid, adrenal, pituitary, and hypothalamus glands have been linked with different kinds of aggressive and antisocial behavior. Glands have been shown to control metabolism, growth, and activity levels. Hyperactivity, or abnormally active behavior, is often associated with oversecretions or undersecretions of various hormones. However, recent medical developments have led to a greater understanding of our biochemical functions and to the development of drugs and synthetic chemicals that can control abnormal behavior. Thorazine is administered to mental patients to control various psychotic disorders. Diazepam, an antidepressant, is used to treat severe alcohol withdrawal or to help patients manage severe anxiety or stress. These products alter hormonal states and permit some regulation of deviant and criminal behavior.

For more than a few probationers and parolees who are sex offenders, various drugs have been utilized to contain their sexual urges (Mears et al., 2003). Together with counseling and medicine, many sex offenders are leading normal lives today as probationers and parolees. This is because their problems are believed to be hormone related to a degree. And chemical imbalances can be regulated with proper drug therapies.

PSYCHOLOGICAL THEORIES

Another set of theories about criminal conduct is based in psychology, the study of individual behavior. By studying individual behavior, psychologists try to explain the inner workings of the mind. Since various components of the criminal justice system must determine criminal intent and the defendant's mental competence to stand trial, prosecutors and defense attorneys often turn to psychologists for help. Psychologists and psychiatrists, physicians who specialize in treating mental disorders, are often asked to examine defendants and give their expert testimony in court. Psychological theories of criminal behavior have also influenced correctional and rehabilitative programs. Psychological counselors and psychiatrists play key roles in contemporary criminal rehabilitative therapy. Three psychological theories are presented here. They include (1) psychoanalytic theory; (2) cognitive development theory; and (3) social learning theory.

Psychoanalytic Theory

Psychoanalytic theory was created by the Austrian neurologist Sigmund Freud (1856–1939). Frustrated by the primitive technology of his day, Freud tried to explain the human personality and mental disorders through the interaction of the concepts of the **id**, the **ego**, the **superego**, and the **libido**. The id is the "I want" associated with the behavior of infants. Getting a two-year-old to share his or her jellybeans or ice cream is near impossible. As children grow, they learn that the id cannot always be satisfied. The child cannot have everything he or she wants. Therefore, the id is eventually controlled by the ego, which embodies society's standards and conventional rules. As the child matures into adolescence, moral values are incorporated into the personality. Moral values are the domain of the superego. The libido is the sex urge or drive, which Freud believed was inborn. Freud explained criminal behavior as a function of an inadequately developed ego, the controlling mechanism for the id. When persons fail to control their impulses and disregard the rights and feelings of others, their aggressive behaviors often follow deviant paths and criminal acts occur (Johansson-Love and Geer, 2003). Rape may be the result of an uncontrollable libido, and theft may be the result of a poorly developed ego, according to Freud.

Some counseling centers and rehabilitative agencies work with offenders to assist them in improving their self-concept as well as their ability to function normally around others. Encouraging people to talk out their problems and exchange personal information with others through group therapy and encounter sessions are ways for offenders to gain greater control over their behaviors. The halfway house concept is one intervention designed to gradually assist offenders in integrating back into society once they have left prison or jail. The transition experience may be abrupt. However, halfway house personnel, together with other offenders, provide a social support system for newly released inmates who can learn to cope with societal demands for law-abiding behavior. Furthermore, these houses provide some amount of counseling assistance. If they can't, then there is a community network of services available to halfway house clients. All probationers and parolees have access to necessary community services, if needed. Many of these services are oriented toward improving one's self-concept and feelings of self-worth.

More than a few POs have bought into the idea that some of their clients have underdeveloped egos and psychological problems that must be resolved through some form of counseling or therapy. This type of approach is used by enablers, brokers, and educators, and it reflects a social work orientation toward the PO role. POs using this approach in dealing with their clients would be more inclined to recommend some form of counseling, individually or in a group, for offenders who violate one or more program conditions. They would be less likely to report program infractions compared with enforcers.

Cognitive Development Theory

Cognitive development theory stresses **cognitive development** through a learning process involving various stages. Jean Piaget (1896–1980) was one of the first to stress the importance of the cognitive stages of development and the idea that all normal individuals pass through the same sequential periods in the growth or maturing of their ability to think or to gain knowledge and awareness of themselves and their environment. As a child moves through various stages of development, he or she acquires an awareness of people, objects, and, especially, standards of behavior or judgments of right and wrong (Piaget, 1948).

Piaget's notions about cognitive development have been modified and expanded by Kohlberg (1963). Kohlberg has described six stages in the development of a person's moral judgment. These levels or stages, according to Kohlberg, reflect a different type of relationship between the individual and his or her society. Kohlberg divides the six stages into three categories: (1) the preconventional level, (2) the conventional level, and (3) the postconventional level. Kohlberg says that very young children, some adolescents, and many criminals are in the preconventional stage of development. Thus, psychologists supporting this theory associate criminal behavior with inadequate moral development during childhood. Some gender bias is inherent in Kohlberg's scheme, because conventional role conformity traditionally encourages males in our culture to acquire protective/aggressive behaviors, while females are socialized to be more submissive and nurturing.

A contrary perspective has been devised by Yochelson and Samenow (1976). These researchers reject the notion that criminal behavior is the direct result of one's environment. Rather, they believe that those who become criminals do so because they want to. At a very early age, youths seek associations with others who may be delinquent. The excitement of committing delinquent acts becomes a self-perpetuating influence in their lives. As these youths graduate to more serious offenses as adults, the same excitement urges them to carry out criminal acts. Yochelson and Samenow believe that free will rather than one's environment determines whether a criminal career pattern will be pursued. Thus, if criminal behavior is to be decreased or eliminated by any conventional treatment program, it is imperative that psychologists and others try to dissuade these people from thinking about committing crimes. Changing their thoughts about crime will lead to a cessation of their criminal behaviors. But Yochelson and Samenow do not answer the question of why these people "think" about engaging in criminal acts. In short, little support exists for their position. However, their theorizing is an interesting contrast with the work of Kohlberg and others who stress environmental experiences as primary ingredients for stimulating criminal behavior.

Social Learning Theory

Applied to criminology, **social learning theory** is that criminal behavior is learned by modeling the behaviors of others who are criminals. It does not propose that criminal conduct is copied or imitated. Rather, those who use others as models for their criminal behavior do so as the result of strong incentives to do so (Bandura, 1977). Deviant and criminal conduct as well as conventional conduct stems from the process of reinforcement, whereby people perceive others who are rewarded (by goods, money, or social status) for conforming to conventional rules or are punished for deviating from those same rules. This type of reinforcement, called external reinforcement, is seen as a crucial social reinforcement mechanism that propels people toward conventional behavior. People also derive reinforcement from internal sources. Some people may engage in self-punishment when they perceive themselves behaving badly, or they may reward themselves for self-perceptions of conformity and appropriate behavior. Most important, reinforcement arises from observing others being rewarded for their conduct. Depending on the environment in which people are socialized, reinforcement may stem from conventional sources or from unconventional ones. Those who observe a criminal being rewarded with goods, money, social status, or acclaim may be motivated to model or emulate this deviant or criminal behavior.

In those instances where people do not fit in with certain social groups, or if they are unsuccessful in adapting to social situations and perceive little or no reward for their conventional behavior, they may learn other behaviors for which rewards of various kinds are forthcoming. Such conduct may be criminal conduct, and it can yield rewards from others who are criminal. This type of situation reinforces deviant conduct and dissuades people from adopting conventional modes of behavior.

Social learning theory fails to explain the roles played by close friends, family, and other agencies of socialization in modifying one's conventional or unconventional conduct (Rebellon, 2002). It stresses psychological factors and alludes to certain stimulus–response behavior patterns reflected by behaviorism. Its main value is that it focuses our attention on the social contexts in which conventional or unconventional conduct is acquired. However, it does not adequately explain the process of acquiring these behaviors.

SOCIOLOGICAL AND/OR SOCIOCULTURAL THEORIES

Sociological and sociocultural theories are as equally diverse as psychological theories. There is considerable interplay between psychological and sociological perspectives. However, sociologists focus more closely on the social processes involved in criminal conduct, as well as the importance of social structure. They believe that forces or processes in the external social environment lead people to commit criminal acts. **Social process theories** stress external forces as causes of criminal conduct, in contrast to the internal forces emphasized by biological and psychological theories. Several popular sociological theories of criminal behavior are (1) differential association, (2) anomie theory, (3) strain theory, (4) labeling theory, (5) social control theory, and (6) conflict/Marxist theory.

FIGURE 2.1   Boys being questioned by the police.

Differential Association Theory

The sociologist Edwin Sutherland (1893–1950) is credited with formulating perhaps the best-known sociological theory of crime. Sutherland's theory, known as **differential association theory,** was formally presented in the 1920s, and a few researchers still use it to explain some forms of adult crime. Sutherland used the differential association concept to explain the process by which persons became criminals. As the name implies, association with criminals is an important part of this process. However, it is an oversimplification of Sutherland's theory to state that simple association with criminals causes a person to become a criminal. The theory is more complex than that. In some respects, Sutherland's theory is an outgrowth of **cultural transmission theory,** developed by Shaw and McKay (1929). These sociologists believed that criminal behavior patterns are transmitted in much the same manner as culture is transmitted through **socialization**. Socialization is learning through contact with others, or social learning.

 **BOX 2.1**

 **CAREER SNAPSHOT**

Veronica Perry
Chief Probation Officer, Medina County, Ohio

Statistics:

B.S. (criminal justice), Kent State University; Masters of Justice Administration, Tiffin University.

Background:

Deviant criminal behavior has always been an area of human behavior that has fascinated me, and I decided early on that I'd like to further my study of this topic even though I was unsure of what future career opportunities existed in the field. I received my bachelor's degree in criminal justice from Kent State University in 1986 and my master's of justice administration from Tiffin University in 2004. During my undergraduate studies, I took a class in probation and decided that this was a field I could work in that would help me better understand the criminal population. As a result of taking this probation class, I realized that I would like a job that afforded me more direct contact with the courts and the opportunity to manage a criminal caseload.

Well, I'd like to tell you that although I do consider myself very lucky because ultimately I did get my dream job, it didn't happen quite as quickly as a young college graduate might presume it would. After waitressing for several months, working as a legal assistant (aka "glorified secretary") for approximately one year, working as an officer administrator for a small law firm for approximately two years, and ultimately taking a $5,000 pay cut, I got hired by the Cuyahoga County Adult Probation Department, located in Cleveland, Ohio, and I couldn't have been happier to accept the job (albeit I could have done without the pay reduction!).

Experiences:

After working in the trenches as an adult felony probation officer for eight years wherein we were required to manage very large caseloads (ranging from 150–450 felony offenders) comprised mostly of inner-city, drug-addicted, and usually poverty-stricken probationers, the challenges of *successfully* managing your caseload became greater and greater. Often we were required to collect monies from individuals who could barely feed themselves, but yet somehow they managed to find the funds to sustain their drug habits. A good percentage of these clients were either unwilling or incapable of following the court's orders and therefore they entered the vicious cycle of positive drug tests, lapses in payments, failures to report, and new arrests.

The beauty of working with an inner-city population in a large urban town was that there was no time to be bored. The challenges were frequent and steady; training was ample; and there were many community resources to draw from. The shortcomings of such a large caseload were the constant time constraints that resulted in limited contact with each client, ultimately making most of a probation officer's efforts seem futile, consequently resulting in serious burnout.

At about the same time that I could take no more caseload mania, I was promoted to a management position and became a supervisor in 1997. The old adage, "Watch what you wish for," was quickly ringing home. My new job duties removed me entirely from line staff duties and I no longer dealt directly with the population I was so curious about. I learned quickly that I missed the direct probationer contact and have on many occasions reflected back on those times with somewhat of a longing for my old duties.

My problems no longer revolved around my caseload of strangers and telling funny stories, such as my favorite one about the probationer who submitted his pregnant girlfriend's urine sample for a drug test, not knowing that I had recent knowledge of this plot, and upon his next report to my office I gave him the good news and the bad news: "The good news is that your urine is clean; the bad news is that you are pregnant and under arrest!"

My new duties as a supervisor now revolved around eight former colleagues and all of their personal issues as well as their professional issues—a dynamic I never considered until I got the job, and truth be told, it was the hardest job I ever had to perform. It is much easier to be responsible for felony convicts with whom you have no personal relationship than for individuals you know personally. It was quite a challenge transitioning from being their peer for eight years to now becoming their boss. It took some time for me to acclimate to my new role and to the way some people tended to distance themselves because I was now a manager.

However, three years after being promoted to supervisor and accepting the reality that my day-to-day duties revolved around staff administration and management rather than probationer caseloads, I was ready for a greater challenge, a change of environment, and more autonomy, which I believed a smaller department would provide me.

In 2000 I was hired as Chief Probation Officer for the Medina County Adult Probation Department. The transition from working in a large urban population for 12 years to working in a much smaller suburban population was a welcome change. I presently supervise a staff of 12 employees who embrace the meaning of team work and who were hired on merit rather than political affiliations, as was at times the case at my previous job. I am extremely fortunate to work with judges who afford me much autonomy and trust me to run the department as I see fit while sincerely supporting me and my administrative decisions.

Advice to Students:

My advice to students who want to become probation officers is to be passionate about their career choice, to work very hard, and to find a role model who will help them develop a strong set of professional ethics, who will guide them throughout their career. I believe that it is crucial to take courses that not only interest you, but ones that also inspire you, and I highly recommend internships for all students so that they can get a practical idea of what the field realistically entails. Finally, having a positive "can-do" attitude is fundamental for any challenge you face, either personally, professionally, or academically. Good luck!

Expanding on the work of Shaw and McKay, Sutherland outlined a fairly elaborate multidimensional social interaction process that would induce a person to adopt criminal behaviors. The dimensions of differential association theory include (1) frequency, (2) duration, (3) priority, and (4) intensity. The transmission of deviant (and criminal) cultural values and behaviors occurs in a social learning context. In this context, the potential criminal has frequent contact with criminals. These frequent contacts are of some lasting duration. Priority and intensity are more elusive concepts in Sutherland's scheme. Priority refers to either the lawful or criminal behavior learned in early childhood. This persists throughout a person's life to reinforce criminal behaviors whenever associations with criminals occur. Intensity is the degree of emotional attachment to either conventional or criminal groups and the prestige allocated to each. Thus, criminal behaviors acquired at an early age and reinforced through frequent and lengthy emotional attachments with one or more criminals are seen as the primary contributing factors explaining why people become criminals.

Professionals involved in corrections programs have shown some respect for Sutherland's differential association ideas over the years. In some jurisdictions, first-offenders are not placed in the same cells with more seasoned repeat-offenders. But this policy is a luxury. It is relinquished when incarceration rates are high and prison funding is low. Thus, because of overcrowding, penal authorities sometimes mix all inmates, regardless of the nature or seriousness of the crimes they have committed. This overcrowding situation has caused some observers to label prisons and jails as institutions of higher criminal learning, where more seasoned criminals teach first-offenders how to avoid being apprehended the next time.

Critics of differential association theory have said that Sutherland's terms are difficult to define and understand. What is meant by an intense relation? How frequent is frequent? Also, Sutherland's theory does not explain all types of criminal conduct. Although Sutherland intended his theory to account for most criminal behavior, numerous exceptions to his scheme over the years caused him to believe that additional factors such as opportunity and individual needs were equally important and ought to be considered. Therefore, he eventually adopted multiple-factor theoretical explanations for criminal conduct in later years and gave less attention to differential association (Short, 2002).

Closely related to differential association theory and applied to juveniles is **neutralization theory**. POs who work with juveniles frequently encounter youths who deny responsibility for what they have done. They deny that they caused anyone injury or they claim that the victim deserved whatever injuries were received. These youths are living examples of what Gresham Sykes and David Matza (1957) called neutralization theory. Neutralization theory is the explanation of delinquency that holds that delinquents experience guilt whenever they commit crimes, although simultaneous, they respect the legitimacy of the social order of their community. Their delinquency is episodic rather than chronic. They are said to drift into delinquent conduct. Drifting means that they must first neutralize their legal and moral values with rationalizations of various kinds (Boehnke and Winkels, 2002).

Most juveniles spend their early years on a behavioral continuum ranging between unlimited freedom and total control or restraint. These persons drift toward one end of the continuum or the other, depending on their social and psychological circumstances. If youths have strong attachments with those who are delinquent, then they "drift" toward the unlimited freedom end of the continuum and perhaps engage accordingly in delinquent activities. However, the behavioral issue is not clear-cut. Juveniles most likely have associations with normative culture as well as the delinquent subculture. Therefore, at least some delinquency results from rationalizations created by youths that render delinquent acts acceptable under the circumstances. Appropriate preventative therapy for such delinquents might be to undermine their rationales for delinquent behaviors through empathic means.

Rationalizations used by juveniles to account for their misconduct include that there is no real victim; that they believe their victim deserved to be injured; that they committed their crimes for family members or friends; that the police and others are out to get them; that no one actually was hurt by whatever they did; and that the delinquency was not really their fault. PO dealings with juveniles frequently disclose such rationalizations. Thus, they are able to understand why some delinquents do not accept any responsibility or exhibit remorse when they have done something wrong. But neutralization theory posits that delinquents do, indeed, feel guilt at some level. POs can use this guilt to their advantage when prescribing appropriate community therapies for juvenile offenders.

Anomie Theory or Innovative Adaptation

The use of anomie in **anomie theory** is a misnomer. Anomie literally means normlessness, or a condition when the norms or behavioral expectations are unknown, undefined, or in conflict. People seldom experience true normlessness. Robert King Merton (1938, 1957) is credited with developing anomie theory, which was originally proposed by the French sociologist Emile Durkheim (1858–1917). Anomie theory states that all people in society are taught to pursue certain culturally approved goals. These people are also taught socially acceptable or approved institutionalized means by which these goals may be achieved. Merton's theory of anomie emphasized the ways that persons adapt to goal attainment and the means they use to achieve these goals. He referred to these as the **modes of adaptation**. Merton said that persons either accept or reject the goals of their society. Also, they either accept or reject the approved means to achieve those goals (Merton, 1938).

According to Merton, conformity is the most common adaptation. People accept the culturally approved goals and the socially approved means to achieve them. People might want a new car or a new home, and they will work patiently at socially acceptable jobs so that they may eventually acquire these possessions. However, some people accept the culturally approved goals, but they reject the means to achieve those goals. For instance, a trustee at a state prison once confided that he had been an "A" student at a large California university. He was majoring in business administration and planned a business career. At the end of his third year, however, he decided the educational process was too slow, and that his calculations of future earnings were too low for his particular desires. He said, "I decided that to get what I want fast, I've got to have a lot of money. The best place to get a lot of money fast is a bank. So I started robbing banks." His adaptation to the goals/means relation was innovation. His criminal behaviors were the innovative means he substituted to achieve certain desired, culturally approved goals.

Much criminal behavior, according to Merton, is innovative behavior. And this mode of adaptation was the focus of his theory of anomie. Merton's theory also tried to explain drug abusers and alcohol users. These people have been labeled as retreatists because they withdraw from others and reject culturally approved goals as well as the means to achieve them. Such people may be unemployed, vagrant, or otherwise indifferent about achieving the culturally approved goals sought by others. Other adaptation forms included in Merton's scheme are ritualism (rejecting the goals, accepting the means) and rebellion (accepting and rejecting some of the goals and means and substituting new goals and means). Ritualists might be people who conclude that they will never have the nice home and new car, but they will nevertheless work at their socially approved jobs until retirement. In contrast, rebels reject the goals and the means and are interested in creating new societal goals through revolution or rebellion.

Merton's theory of anomie is particularly relevant for explaining property crimes such as burglary and larceny. The people who commit these crimes may want material wealth or expensive possessions, but they are unwilling or unable to earn money through socially acceptable occupations. Thus, they will likely seek goal attainment through innovative means. Merton's theory is economically based and concerned with gaining access to certain success goals. It may be that Merton made an erroneous assumption that poor persons are more prone toward criminal behavior than rich persons. Furthermore, Merton has not explained the embezzlement or tax fraud of successful business executives. It might be, however, that such criminals are simply seeking a culturally approved goal through innovative means. Another criticism is that the theory does not explain noneconomic crimes such as aggravated assault or rape. However, anomie is not intended to explain these kinds of offenses. Finally, Merton's scheme does not seem to deal well with criminal behavior as a process.

Merton's scheme presents several adaptations persons can make in attaining goals and choosing the means to achieve those goals. It is a static theory rather than a dynamic one. Merton's innovative mode is more or less an automatic response that is almost always regarded as deviant and/or criminal. By comparison, differential association theory analyzes such dynamic processes as the duration and intensity of social associations that encourage and condone criminal acts. Sutherland's differential association theory about white-collar criminals and Merton's innovative modes of adaptation may be linked theoretically to the **theory of opportunity**. According to this theory, middle- and upper-class persons have more opportunities to gain access to and achieve success goals, whereas lower-class persons lack these opportunities. Therefore, lower-class persons tend to achieve success by achieving certain deviant and/or criminal objectives that are respected by other criminals.

The Subculture Theory of Delinquency

During the 1950s, sociologist Albert Cohen (1955) focused on and described **delinquent subcultures**. Delinquent subcultures exist, according to Cohen, within the greater societal culture. But these **subcultures** contain value systems and modes of achievement and gaining status and recognition apart from the mainstream culture. Thus, if we are to understand why many juveniles behave as they do, we must pay attention to the patterns of their particular subculture.

The notion of a delinquent subculture is fairly easy to understand, especially in view of the earlier work of Shaw and McKay (1929). While middle- and upper-class children learn and aspire to achieve lofty ambitions and educational goals and receive support for these aspirations from their parents as well as predominantly middle-class teachers, lower-class youths are at a distinct disadvantage at the outset. They are born into families where these aspirations and attainments may be alien and rejected. Their primary familial role models have not attained these high aims themselves. At school, these youths are often isolated socially from upper- and middle-class juveniles, and therefore, social attachments are formed with others similar to themselves. Perhaps these youths dress differently from other students, wear their hair in a certain style, or use coded language when talking to peers in front of other students. They acquire a culture unto themselves, one that is largely unknown to other students. In a sense, much of this cultural isolation is self-imposed. But it functions to give them a sense of fulfillment, of reward, of self-esteem and recognition apart from other reward systems. If these students cannot achieve one or more of the various standards set by middle-class society, then they create their own standards and prescribe the means to achieve those standards.

Cohen is quick to point out that delinquency is not a product of lower socioeconomic status per se. Rather, children from lower socioeconomic statuses are at greater risk than others of being susceptible to the rewards and opportunities a subculture of delinquency might offer in contrast with the system's middle-class reward structure. Several experiments have subsequently been implemented with delinquents, where these subcultures have been targeted and described, and where the norms of these subcultures have been used as intervening mechanisms to modify delinquent behaviors toward nondelinquent modes of action. The Provo Experiment was influenced, to a degree, by the work of Cohen (Empey and Rabow, 1961). Samples of delinquent youths in Provo, Utah, were identified in the late 1950s and given an opportunity to participate in group therapy sessions at Pine Hills, a large home in Provo that had been converted to an experimental laboratory.

In cooperation with juvenile court judges and other authorities, Pine Hills investigators commenced their intervention strategies assuming that juvenile participants (1) had limited access to success goals, (2) performed many of their delinquent activities in groups rather than alone, and (3) committed their delinquent acts for nonutilitarian objectives rather than for money (Empey and Rabow, 1961). These investigators believed that since the delinquents had acquired their delinquent values and conduct through their subculture of delinquency, they could "unlearn" these values and learn new values by the same means. Thus, groups of delinquents participated extensively in therapy directed at changing their behaviors through group processes. The investigators believed that their intervention efforts were largely successful and that the subcultural approach to delinquency prevention and behavioral change was fruitful.

An interesting variation on the subcultural theme is the work of Wolfgang and Ferracuti (1967). It will be recalled that Wolfgang and other associates investigated large numbers of Philadelphia boys in a study of birth cohorts. In that study, he found that approximately 6 percent of all boys accounted for over 50 percent of all delinquent conduct from the entire cohort of over 9,000 boys (Wolfgang, Figlio, and Sellin, 1972). These were chronic recidivists who were also violent offenders. Wolfgang has theorized that in many communities, there are subcultural norms of violence that attract youthful males. They regard violence as a normal part of their environment; they use violence, and respect the use of violence by others. On the basis of evidence amassed by Wolfgang and Ferracuti, it appeared that predominantly lower-class and less-educated males formed a disproportionately large part of this **subculture of violence**. Where violence is accepted and respected, its use is considered normal and normative for the users. Remorse is an alien emotion to those using violence and who live with it constantly. Thus, it is socially ingrained as a subcultural value.

The subcultural perspective toward delinquent conduct is indicative of a strain between the values of society and the values of a subgroup of delinquent youths (Grietens, Rink, and Hellinckx, 2003). Therefore, some researchers have labeled the subcultural perspective a **strain theory**. The strain component is apparent since although many lower SES youths have adopted middle-class goals and aspirations, they may be unable to attain these goals because of their individual economic and cultural circumstances. This is a frustrating experience for many of these youths, and such frustration is manifested by the strain to achieve difficult goals or objectives (Agnew et al., 2002). While middle-class youths also experience strain in their attempts to achieve middle-class goals, it is particularly aggravating for many lower-class youths, since they sometimes do not receive the necessary support from their families. Merton's anomie theory greatly influenced the development of strain theory.

Obviously, a myriad of other explanations for delinquent conduct have been advanced by various theorists. Those selected for more in-depth coverage above are by no means the best theories to account for delinquency. Their inclusion here is merely to describe some of the thinking about why juveniles might be attracted toward delinquent conduct. Some of the other approaches that have been advocated include **containment theory** and **differential reinforcement theory**.

Containment theory is closely associated with the work of sociologist Walter Reckless (1967). Reckless outlined a theoretical model consisting of "pushes" and "pulls" in relation to delinquency. By pushes he referred to internal personal factors, including hostility, anxiety, and discontent. By pulls he meant external social forces, including delinquent subcultures and significant others. The containment dimension of his theoretical scheme consisted of both outer and inner containments. Outer containments, according to Reckless, are social norms, folkways, mores, laws, and institutional arrangements that induce societal conformity. By inner containments, Reckless referred to individual or personal coping strategies to deal with stressful situations and conflict. These strategies might be a high tolerance for conflict or frustration and considerable ego strength. Thus, Reckless combined both psychological and social elements in referring to weak attachments of some youths to cultural norms, high anxiety levels, and low tolerance for personal stress. These persons are most inclined to delinquent conduct. A key factor in whether juveniles adopt delinquent behaviors is their level of self-esteem. Those with high levels of self-esteem seem most resistant to delinquent behaviors if they are exposed to such conduct while around their friends.

In 1966, Robert Burgess and Ronald Akers attempted to revise Sutherland's differential association theory and derived what they termed differential reinforcement theory. Differential reinforcement theory actually combines elements from labeling theory and a psychological phenomenon known as conditioning. Conditioning functions in the social learning process as persons are rewarded for engaging in certain desirable behaviors and refraining from certain undesirable behaviors. Juveniles perceive how others respond to their behaviors (negative reactions) and may be disposed to behave in ways that will maximize their rewards from others. Also, in some respects, Burgess and Akers have incorporated certain aspects of the "looking-glass self" concept originally devised by the theorist Charles Horton Cooley. Cooley theorized that people learned ways of conforming by paying attention to the reactions of others in response to their own behavior. Therefore, Cooley would argue that we imagine how others see us. We look for others' reactions to our behavior and make interpretations of these reactions as either good or bad reactions. If we define others' reactions as good, we will feel a degree of pride and likely persist in the behaviors. But, as Cooley indicated, if we interpret their reactions to our behaviors as bad, we might experience mortification. Given this latter reaction or at least our interpretation of it, we might change our behaviors to conform to what others might want and thereby elicit approval from them. While these ideas continue to interest us, they are difficult to conceptualize and investigate empirically. Akers and others have acknowledged such difficulties, although their work is insightful and underscores the reality of a multidimensional view of delinquent conduct.

Labeling Theory

Another theory of criminal behavior is **labeling theory**. Labeling theory is linked closely with the work of Edwin Lemert (1951), although Howard S. Becker (1963) and John Kitsuse (1962) were among its early advocates. Labeling theory pertains to the social definitions of criminal acts rather than the criminal acts themselves. Labeling theory attempts to answer at least two questions: (1) What is the process whereby persons become labeled as criminals or deviants? and (2) How does such labeling influence the persons labeled as deviant?

The basic assumptions of labeling theory are: (1) no act is inherently criminal; (2) persons become criminals by social labeling or definition; (3) all persons at one time or another conform to and deviate from laws; (4) getting caught begins the labeling process; (5) the person defined as criminal will develop a criminal self-definition; and (6) the person will seek others similarly defined and develop a criminal subculture (Bernburg and Krohn, 2003).

There are two types of deviation: primary and secondary. Primary deviations involve violations of law that often can be and frequently are overlooked. College students who pull pranks such as disassembling the university president's car and reassembling it on the roof of the women's dormitory are mildly chided by police rather than arrested for criminal vehicular theft. Secondary deviations occur when violations of the law have become incorporated into a person's lifestyle or behavior pattern. Usually, by the time secondary deviations have occurred, the offender has accepted the label of deviant or criminal and is on the road toward joining a criminal subculture (Lemert, 1951).

Many labeling theorists say they are not interested in explaining criminal acts. Instead, they want to explain the social process of labeling and one's personal reaction to being labeled. Nevertheless, a strong explanatory element is prevalent. In effect, the labeling theorist is saying that persons who react to social labeling by defining themselves as deviant or criminal will not only engage in further criminal activity, they will also seek out others like themselves and form criminal subcultures. This subcultural development is the equivalent of rejecting the rejectors. Some evidence of the influence of labeling may be found by examining arrest rates by race and social class. Labeling theorists argue that the most likely targets of labeling are persons who are young, nonwhite, and of lower socioeconomic statuses. These persons are most likely to be labeled by police and others as deviant or inclined to be criminal.

More arrests tend to be made in high-crime areas. Coincidentally, high-crime areas tend to be low-rent districts that attract a disproportionately large number of the poor and ethnic and racial minorities. These are the same areas that tend to attract larger numbers of police such that arrest rates will be increased. Also, law enforcement officers may be more inclined to take advantage of persons of lower socioeconomic statuses. When compared with middle- or upper-class citizens, lower-class persons have fewer resources and lack the legal sophistication to resist or retaliate within the legal system. Again, deviance or criminal conduct is like a social status that, once assigned, changes the relationship the person has with others (Bernburg and Krohn, 2003).

Labeling theory is an external explanation for criminal behavior. Criminal behavior is whatever lawmakers—an external source—say it is. A criminal is whomever a society labels as criminal. The offender's acceptance of the label criminal merely completes the process, and leads the offender to seek the companionship of others labeled as deviants. In some respects, labeling theory involves some interplay between the social and psychological realms. The offender reacts to social definitions, the offender interprets or defines him- or herself as deviant or criminal, and the offender forms subcultures with others in an effort to win acceptance and preserve self-worth.

However, labeling theory fails to account for the people who either reject deviant labels or successfully unlabel themselves as criminals or deviants. It also inadequately explains occasional offenders or weekend deviants, persons leading two morally different lives by associating with diverse community elements. Finally, persons who engage in victimless crimes or crimes where the victim is a willing participant (e.g., gambling and prostitution) seem to escape the psychological effects of being labeled a deviant. The theory does not explain the mental compartmentalization these people seem to use in refusing to define themselves as deviants.

It is interesting to note that most probation and parole program agreements reflect critical elements of labeling theory. Among most provisions are that probationers and parolees are not to associate or have contact with any known criminals. Furthermore, visits to prisons or jails to visit incarcerated friends or relatives is strictly prohibited. PO approval is required for any contact to be made among offenders. What other reason would there be to deny one a chance to visit his or her friends acquired while incarcerated or to associate with friends in the community who also happen to have criminal records?

Social Control Theory

Sometimes referred to as **bonding theory, social control theory** focuses on the processual aspects of becoming bonded or attached to the norms and values of society (Hirschi, 1969). As the bonds between society and people become stronger, the possibility that people will engage in deviant or criminal behaviors becomes weaker. Bonding consists of several dimensions. These include (1) attachment, the emotional or affective dimension linking us with significant others whose opinions we respect and whose admonitions we follow; (2) commitment, the energy expended by an individual in particular activities, either conventional or unconventional; (3) belief, a person's moral definition of the propriety of particular conduct, that the laws and rules should be obeyed; and (4) involvement, the degree of intensity with which one is involved in conventional conduct or with which one espouses conventional values.

BOX 2.2

INTERNATIONAL SNAPSHOT: PROBATION AND PAROLE IN SOUTH KOREA

South Korea is a centralized nation-state with a government consisting of administration, legislation, and judicature. The criminal justice system is highly centralized, although there are correctional centers and other services operating in various Korean communities. Much of the contemporary criminal justice system is influenced by the enactment of the Criminal Law of 1953, although this law has been extensively revised and supplemented through 2005.

The legal classification system of South Korea distinguishes between three types of offenses, including crimes breaching a national interest, such as rebellion; crimes breaching a social interest, such as arson; and crimes breaching personal interests, such as larceny, robbery, murder, and drug offenses. Regarding the third category of personal-interest offenses, South Korean officials distinguish between serious offenses and less serious offenses, much as the United States differentiates between felonies and misdemeanors. Punishments are proportional to the type of crime committed. Crimes are further distinguished according to whether they are violent crimes or property crimes. Violent crimes include any crime causing physical injury, such as assault, rape, murder, and robbery. Property crimes are largely nonviolent and include embezzlement, breach of trust, theft, fraud, and damage or vandalism.

South Korea has stringent drug laws. These laws were implemented in 1992–1993 and include several categories of drug offenses. The Narcotics Act of 1992 distinguishes between more addictive drugs and transactions involving heroin and cocaine; marijuana (the Cannabis Control Act); and methamphetamine (the Psychotropic Substances Control Act). It is a crime to sell, produce, cultivate, manufacture, smuggle, possess, or use any substances or materials listed under the Narcotics Act, and serious penalties are imposed when persons are convicted for different types of drug offenses.

In 2005 and for the past several decades, there has been a very low murder rate in South Korea. Fewer than 2 murders per 100,000 persons have been committed in any given year. Rapes have occurred at the rate of about 15 per 100,000 persons, while theft and property crimes occur at the greatest rate, at about 200 per 100,000 per year. The Supreme Public Prosecutor's Office is charged with the prosecution of all criminal offenses. The age of criminal responsibility in South Korea is 14. However, persons ranging in age from 14 to 20 are specially treated under juvenile laws. Any youth under age 18 who is convicted of a criminal offense cannot be sentenced to capital punishment or life imprisonment.

There are approximately 3,400 police branch offices located in various communities throughout South Korea. Police officers investigate crimes and arrest offenders, who are transferred to local holding areas for trial. Since the early 1990s South Korea has established an active victims' rights agenda, with greater citizen input in criminal matters, including sentencing and other activities. Victims are actively involved in the sentencing process and have the right to speak and give their punishment recommendations to judges, although judges have the final word on one's punishment upon conviction.

When criminal suspects are arrested, most are entitled to bail. Suspects also have the right to examine evidence against them; the right to avoid particular judges; the right to appeal; the right to trial by a judicial panel; the right to confess or avoid confession; and the right to either a private attorney or public defender. South Korea has no preliminary hearing phase. Juries are not used in criminal proceedings. Judicially appointed prosecutors, working on behalf of the Ministry of Justice, bring cases against criminal suspects and have a broad range of discretionary powers. Thus, prosecutors may indict, refuse to indict, or suspend indictments against suspects at their discretion. For juveniles, most of the time prosecutors seek protective and rehabilitative

(continued)

BOX 2.2 (Continued)

dispositions instead of incarceration in juvenile facilities. If there is a need to confine juvenile offenders, South Korea operates several up-to-date vocational/technical schools where juvenile offenders are housed. They are permitted weekly visits with their families in cottages provided on the premises. They receive excellent vocational and educational instruction to prepare them for law-abiding lives.

For adult offenders and depending on the seriousness of their offenses, prosecutors may recommend bail or they may require defendants held without bail for trial. About 10 percent of all offenders have criminal trials annually. Most other offenders are subject to a broad range of community sanctions. Judges have broad sentencing powers and exclusively determine one's punishment. They can require confinement in prison, jail, fines, forfeiture, and other penalties, including probation. Those imprisoned may be paroled at a later date. Fines are the most frequently used penalties, especially for property offenders.

Numbers of prisoners, probationers, and parolees suggest that probation is most often used as a criminal sanction. There are about 90,000 prisoners in South Korean prisons. Only about 4 percent of all prisoners are female. All South Korean prisons are designed to provide useful labor for inmates that is significant in their eventual rehabilitation and reintegration. South Korea rewards good institutional conduct with parole, especially for vocational trainees who have performed well at their assigned prison tasks while confined. While not all inmates are required to do so, most participate in classes and/or vocational/educational training while imprisoned. Inmates accumulate points for good conduct, and they may become eligible for furloughs, more progressive institutional treatment, and special privileges. Some inmates participate in work/study release programs.

Although probation in Korea was unofficially used for various offenders in 1982, the probation system was not officially established until 1989. At that time, 12 probation offices and 6 branch offices were opened in various cities. Subsequently, special offices have been created for the supervision of sex offenders and domestic violence offenders, among others. The probation system of South Korea today is one of the most advanced probation systems compared with other industrialized countries. The emphasis of South Korean probation is on education, counseling, and guidance leading to rehabilitation and societal reintegration. In 2005 there were approximately 200,000 probationers and 70,000 parolees of different designations. Supervising these offenders were 495 probation officers in approximately 30 probation and parole offices in various cities.

Probationers are subject to various probation conditions, including community service orders and attendance center orders. Community service orders are intended to make criminals serve society in various ways by providing useful unpaid labor services for a period of time while remaining free within their communities. Thus, this system is similar to that used in the United States. The intent of community service orders in South Korea includes also the opportunity for offenders to repent, to recover their self-esteem, to inspire their labor spirits, and to help them become reintegrated into society as law-abiding members. Attendance center orders are designed especially for those with various drug and alcohol addictions or dependencies. Typically these addicted offenders, and also certain mentally ill offenders, attend lectures and receive other services through their local probation and parole offices for a period of time, again while remaining free within their communities. Thus, the intent of attendance center activities is to enhance a law-compliance spirit, understand the damages of the crimes they have committed, and to build up and foster their mental health and adaptability in society generally. Thus, this is closely connected with rehabilitation and societal reintegration.

Probation and parole guidelines provide for the following:

1. Legal matters of observation (allowing probation officers access to a client's premises for the purpose of monitoring their behavior while on probation or parole).
2. An obligation to reside in one's residence and remain employed.
3. An obligation to maintain a good family relationship.

4. An obligation to obey all probation officer directives.

5. An obligation to make advance reports if traveling for more than one month.

Special conditions of probation and parole also include abstinence from alcohol or drugs, avoiding certain areas, and other behavioral requirements. In 2005 caseloads for probation officers were about 380 offenders per year. Between 1989 and 2005, over 150,000 persons have been assisted while on probation or parole with a high degree of successfulness.

Prospective parolees are subject to the orders of a Parole Examination Committee. This committee is charged with investigating all matters of adult inmates in determining their eligibility for early release. They may examine pre-sentence investigation reports prepared by probation officers much like those consulted and prepared for offenders by probation officers in the United States. Details of one's offense are examined in-depth by this committee, including their living conditions, family relations, friendships and acquaintances, and potential societal adaptability. Interviews with prospective parolees are conducted, and these

interviews may include victim participation, family members, and other interested parties, including probation officers.

Time guidelines exist for different categories of offenders. These guidelines are specified below.

South Korean officials suggest that their version of probation and parole is most similar to those of England and the United States. Dispositions of suspensions of executions of sentences or suspensions of indictments, protective dispositions, release on probation or parole, and other conditions are intended to reintegrate offenders into their communities and prevent further criminality.

One innovation introduced by South Korean probation officials is the creation of volunteer probation officers, which aggressively involves citizens in one's rehabilitation. Volunteer probation officers are called members of the Crime Prevention Volunteer Committee. Originally, there were three committees: the Rehabilitation Aid Committee, created in 1961; the Juvenile Guidance Committee, established in 1981; and the Protection Committee, created in 1989. In 1996, the Crime Prevention Volunteer Committee was created through the Supreme Public Prosecutor's

Criminal Offenders	Length and Nature of Punishment/Parole/Probation
1. Those receiving suspended sentences or probation	Probation of one year or less
2. Those under suspended execution of sentence	Probation of one year or less
3. Parolees	Remaining period of one's original sentence
4. Juveniles on probation	Up to 2 years
5. Juveniles released from Juvenile Training School	6 months–2 years
6. Parolees whose prison terms have provisionally expired	3 years
7. Domestic violence offenders	6 months
8. Those under suspension of indictment	6 months–1 year
9. Those subject to suspended execution of sentence on probation	Community service: 500 hours or less
10. Community service orders or attendance center orders	Community service: 200 hours or less
11. Juveniles over age 16 subject to community service orders	200 hours or fewer community service
12. Community service orders for domestic violence offenders	100 hours or fewer community service

(continued)

BOX 2.2 (*Continued*)

Office. The functions of this committee are to conduct crime prevention activities and support the activities of the probation and parole offices. Committee members (1) deploy crime prevention activities in their communities; (2) provide offenders with counseling; (3) assist in job searches and financial aid; and (4) comply with other related concerns regulated by the Minister of Justice. More specifically, committee members work to minimize school violence by monitoring and relating with juveniles more closely; by providing counseling and special instruction to those under suspension of indictment; by assisting probation officers in the guidance and supervision of their clients; and by supporting job searches, vocational training, care, and financial aid.

It is believed that offender reintegration and rehabilitation are facilitated with greater community participation through the volunteer probation officer program. Qualities for the selection of volunteers include those considered socially desirable in their character and conduct; those who possess a passionate attitude for social services; and those who are healthy and active. Appointments of volunteers are for three-year terms. Assignments of probationers to volunteers are made on the basis of community and offender needs. Their involvement is highly individualized.

Sources: Adapted from World Book of Criminal Justice Facts, New York, January 2006; Graeme R. Newman, "South Korea," World Factbook of Criminal Justice Systems, 2002; Probation and Parole in South Korea, Seoul, Korea: Korean Institute of Criminology, 2005; Woo Sik Chung, "The Volunteer Probation Officer System in Korea," Probation and Parole System, Seoul, Korea: Korean Probation and Parole Office, 2006.

Persons who have strong attachments with conventional groups and their opinions, who manifest beliefs in the values of the group, who are intensely involved in these groups' activities, and who expend considerable energy in these activities will probably not become deviant or exhibit criminal conduct. But if one or more of these bonding dimensions are weakened, people stand a better chance of deviating from the expectations of conventional society. For instance, when people cease to believe that the group they associate with is important and/or exhibits the right values or standards, a weakening of the bond occurs (Le, 2002). It may be that a delinquent gang can lure youths away from conventional groups by permitting them to develop close attachments and involvements in delinquent gang activity. A type of rivalry occurs between one's conventional bonds and the developing bonds of less conventional social groups.

Hirschi's social control theory builds on the differential association theory developed by Sutherland. Sutherland's dimensions of intensity and priority appear closely related to Hirschi's notions of attachment, commitment, and involvement. While Sutherland attempted to account for white-collar crime, Hirschi has used his bonding theory to explain juvenile delinquency. In Hirschi's investigation of a sample of junior and senior high school youth in California, he found that those students who exhibited strong attitudes and attachments to teachers and school officials were less inclined to engage in delinquent activity. These were also those earning higher grades and making a more successful adjustment to the rigors of schoolwork than students with weaker bonds. As for youths engaged in delinquent activity, Hirschi found that they were frequently the poor performers academically, disliked school, and had few positive experiences with school faculty and officials.

Hirschi's theory has been criticized for several reasons. First, it fails to specify the precise relation between these bonding dimensions and conventional and nonconventional conduct. Many youths have attachments to both conventional and nonconventional groups, and yet no clear pattern of delinquency or nondelinquency emerges as a result. Which dimensions have the greatest weight in predicting deviant conduct? What are the roles of parents and church officials in the lives of these youths? How does social class function as an explanatory variable?

Social control theory is strongly psychological, since it holds that one's mental attachments and beliefs are critical in linking the individual to society's conventional norms. This theory may explain why certain individuals reject conventional behavior for deviant conduct, but it cannot be used to predict which youths among large groups will turn to crime. Hirschi's emphasis on school experiences is an inherent weakness, because it does not account for bonding processes that take place outside of school settings. Its application is restricted to explaining deviance among adolescents who are in school (Bowers, Langhinrichsen-Rohling, and Arata, 2006).

Conflict/Marxist Theory

Sometimes called **Marxist criminology, conflict criminology, critical criminology,** or **radical criminology, conflict/Marxist theory** explains criminal conduct by focusing our attention on the people who have the political power to define crime for the rest of society. According to this theory, the masses can be divided into the have-nots, the poor people who are manipulated and controlled by the haves, the rich and powerful people who have vested interests in capital, industry, and business.

Statistically, persons in the lower socioeconomic strata are arrested more frequently than those in the upper socioeconomic strata. These facts do not mean that those in the lower socioeconomic categories commit more crime. Instead, these statistics show that the ruling elite has targeted these poor people for harassment. This harassment is a strategy for maintaining the status quo and preserving existing societal arrangements that perpetuate and legitimize the power of the "haves." This theory also asserts that one reason for the formal creation of the police in 1829 was to protect the interests of those in power. These interests exert considerable influence on how crime is defined. Vagrancy and loitering laws were created, in part, as a means for keeping people from wandering about, looking for better jobs and work.

Conflict/Marxist theory is a general scheme to account for societal characteristics. It does not explain individual behaviors or the behavior of small groups. It is not linked with any particular social process of acquiring criminal behaviors, and it defines criminal behavior as the result of legislative definitions created by the rich and powerful. To use this theory for creating a specific plan to deal with crime and influence the lives of probationers and parolees, we would have to change our basic social and economic structure.

REALITY THERAPY

Reality therapy was created by William Glasser (1976). Glasser was a psychiatrist by training and accepted developmental theory as an explanation of deviant conduct up to a point. Glasser rejected the developmental theoretical explanation that once a cause is known for a particular criminal behavior, the problem can be dealt with by having the probationer/parolee/client understand the problem's origins. Reality therapy is a confrontational method of behavior modification where one's criminality is simply unacceptable to a PO. Glasser contends that all persons are born with two primary psychological needs. There is a need for love and a need for acceptance, self-worth, or recognition. Those POs who practice reality therapy must acquire the trust of their clients and get close to them emotionally. POs must therefore cultivate a tentative friendship between themselves and their clients, so that their clients can feel free to disclose things about themselves.

POs using reality therapy must get emotionally involved with their clients. The PO is not interested in trying to understand one's prior circumstances and what led to their present circumstances. The focus is on the present, and the intent of the PO is to assist clients in evaluating their behavior and why it is unacceptable. Thus, it is unimportant to know the etiology of one's criminality. All too often, this is used as a crutch by the client. Many clients love to rationalize their conduct as being the product of a miserable childhood or poor upbringing or bad social circumstances in their school years.

Reality therapy works best if the PO is able to establish a support group of several clients. Sympathy and excuses are rejected. The PO does not label the client as sick or disturbed. Rather, there are problems that are unacceptable and they need to be dealt with and resolved. The PO is an enabler in this regard. Glasser says the POs can assist their clients by helping them devise better plans for the future. Where appropriate, the PO should lavish the client with praise for acceptable, law-abiding conduct as a reinforcement.

Reality therapy has been criticized because some clients feel uncomfortable disclosing things about themselves on an intimate level. For some clients, they prefer rejecting a PO's help rather than risk accepting it, because they expect to be disappointed when the therapy doesn't work. POs who work hard to cultivate close relationships with clients may actually drive them away emotionally. Therefore, reality therapy is an intervention that should be used only by selected POs who are qualified and disposed to working with hard-to-manage offenders.

SOCIAL CASEWORK

Social casework is an intervention technique that is service-oriented. It is the development of a relation between the PO and his or her clients with a problem-solving context, and coordinated with the appropriate use of community resources. Social casework rests on three basic tenets: (1) assessment, or gathering and analyzing relevant information on which to base a plan for one's client; (2) planning, or thinking about and organizing facts into a meaningful, goal-oriented explanation; and (3) intervention, or implementation of the plan.

Social casework is a product of social work, which emerged as an intervention strategy during the 1920s. Important to social workers are human relations skills and the capacity to mobilize community resources to assist clients. POs who use the social casework method for assisting their clients attempt to find solutions for their problems that interfere with or minimize their effectiveness as persons. If parolees or probationers have difficulty seeking and maintaining continuous employment, social caseworker–POs can assist them in resolving problems that may be inhibiting them from being successful in this regard.

Good social caseworkers acquire understandings of their clients and attempt to assist them in developing constructive solutions to their problems. They are concerned with client self-esteem and feelings of self-worth. They want clients to be able to function apart from the caseworker. Thus, they provide clients with encouragement and moral support, together with necessary training from community resources. They are reassuring and believe strongly in counseling and guidance as strategies for coping and behavioral changes.

WHICH THEORY IS BEST?: AN EVALUATION

Theories about Adult Offenders

There is no single theory to explain crime or criminal conduct that is universally accepted by all researchers as the best one. Each theory has strengths and weaknesses and has exerted varying degrees of influence on the criminal justice system in processing offenders. Two important criteria for evaluating theories of criminal behavior are the extent to which they enable us to explain and predict that behavior. An evaluation of these theories suggests that creating a satisfactory theory stringently meeting these criteria is quite difficult.

 **BOX 2.3**    **CAREER SNAPSHOT**

Stephen Walters
University of Houston–Clear Lake

Statistics:

B.S. (sociology), Southwest Missouri State University; M.A. (sociology), Central Missouri State University; M.S. (criminal justice administration), Central Missouri State University; Ph.D. (sociology), University of Montana.

Background and Experience:

For the last 30 years I have been a university professor, teaching primarily in the field of criminal justice. For a brief period of time, I took a break from teaching and was employed as a correctional officer. My experience working in corrections has motivated a great deal of my research, which has been published in several criminal justice journals, and my forthcoming work, *Correctional Officers in America* (with Tom Caywood). My current research projects include smuggling on the Texas–Mexico border and contemporary maritime piracy.

Theoretical Perspective:

My research in criminology has recently been affected by routine activities theory. This theory takes into account three variables that are necessary for a crime to occur. First, there must be motivated offenders; that is, persons who are willing to commit criminal acts. Most theories in criminology stop here. However, routine activities theory goes further, and it explains that motivated offenders cannot commit crime without two other variables being present. For a crime to occur, there must secondly be suitable targets, targets that are not only profitable, but also accessible to the criminal. Finally, this theory asserts that the presence or absence of capable guardians is also important for understanding crime. For example, if one wants to understand the crime of smuggling, one must first have an individual who is motivated to smuggle contraband. But even having a motivated smuggler

(continued)

BOX 2.3 (*Continued*)

will not ensure that the crime will actually occur. The smuggler must also have a suitable target, in this case, a border that is easy to cross unnoticed. Yet even a motivated smuggler and a suitable target will not guarantee that a criminal act will occur. If the border were patrolled by a large number of competent defenders (e.g., law enforcement, border patrol, immigration and naturalization officers), it would be impossible for the smuggler to get his product to market. Only when you have a motivated offender, an accessible target, and a lack of competent defenders will a crime occur. Thus it is important for the criminologist to not only understand why people commit crimes, but also to understand the nature of the environment and the efficiency of the defenders, if present.

Advice to Students:

I would advise students of criminal justice to get as broad an education as possible.

Criminal justice is an interdisciplinary activity, drawing knowledge from a variety of academic disciplines. Supporting one's criminal justice education with coursework from psychology, sociology, biology, social work, or business, to name a few, will help students not only to better understand crime, but also to increase their number of career choices within the field of criminal justice.

I also encourage students to become familiar with research methods and statistical analysis. These skills are not only important for those students who plan on attending graduate school, but they are also quite useful to students planning on directly entering criminal justice employment upon graduation. Many criminal justice agencies now do evaluative research "in-house," and students who are able to conduct this type of research are desirable to many criminal justice employers.

Most of the theories presented, regardless of whether they were biological, psychological, or sociological, emphasized single-factor causation. One factor (e.g., glands, genes, improper or inadequate ego development, or anomie) was usually featured as the chief cause of criminal behavior, and all other factors were either subordinated or ignored.

One problem with evaluating these theories is that often the historical context in which they were generated is overlooked. As we have already seen, Cesare Lombroso's work on the relation between physique and criminal behavior was devised during the time when Charles Darwin's *Origin of the Species* was popular. Biological evolution was considered to be an important explanation for certain kinds of social behaviors in the 1870s as well as for the next several decades. Assessing Lombroso's work in view of our current knowledge makes his theorizing seem comical. In contrast, psychologists investigated the influence of an air pollutant, ozone, on criminal behavior in 1987. James Rotton, a psychologist at Florida International University, has estimated that every year, ozone provokes hundreds of cases of family violence in large cities with bad air. How will this theory be viewed by criminologists and others 100 years from now (Champion, 2005)?

In all likelihood, criminal behavior is the result of a combination of these factors. It is insufficient to rely entirely on a single cause for such a complex phenomenon. There are criminals of every size and shape and variety. The same crimes such as murder or robbery are committed by many different kinds of people for a variety of reasons. It may be that in time of war, murdering the enemy will cause someone to be a hero, whereas murder in other contexts and at other times would be punished severely. However, there is a problem with developing conglomerate or "holistic" theories, because they may not be theories at all in the formal sense.

Obviously, explanations advanced by Lombroso and Sheldon attaching significance to one's body structure have little or no predictive value. We cannot look at someone and determine from their physical features whether they are criminals or will become criminals. Also, genetic structure fails to explain and predict criminal behavior. Theories emphasizing the id, ego, and superego as crucial determinants of social conduct are very difficult to test empirically. Such phenomena cannot be extracted from persons and dissected and examined microscopically. If we rigorously apply the standards of science and empiricism and subject all explanations advanced to the most scrupulous experiments and tests, all theories of criminal behavior presented in this chapter fail such tests.

Theories about Delinquency

Assessing the importance or significance of theories of delinquency is difficult. First, almost all causes of delinquent conduct that have been advocated by experts during the past century continue to interest contemporary investigators (Garbarino et al., 2002). The most frequently discounted and consistently criticized views are the biological ones, although as we have seen, sociobiology and genetic concomitants of delinquent conduct persist to raise unanswered questions about the role of heredity in the delinquency equation. Psychological explanations seem more plausible than biological ones, although the precise relation between the psyche and biological factors remains unknown. If we focus on psychological explanations of delinquency as important in fostering delinquent conduct, almost invariably we involve certain elements of one's social world in such explanations. Thus, one's mental processes are influenced in various ways by one's social experiences. Self-definitions, important to psychologists and learning theorists, are conceived largely in social contexts, in the presence of and through contact with others. It is not surprising, therefore, that the most fruitful explanations for delinquency are those that seek to blend the best parts of different theories that assess different dimensions of youths, their physique and intellectual abilities, personalities, and social experiences. Intellectual isolationism or complete reliance on either biological factors exclusively, psychological factors exclusively, or sociological factors exclusively may simplify theory construction, but in the final analysis, such isolationism is unproductive. Certainly, each field has importance and makes a contribution toward explaining why some youths exhibit delinquent conduct and why others do not. Applying a purely pragmatic approach in assessing the predictive and/or explanatory utility of each of these theories, we may examine contemporary interventionist efforts that seek to curb delinquency or prevent its resurgence.

Program successes are often used as gauges of the successfulness of their underlying theoretical schemes (Stouthamer-Loeber and Loeber, 2002). Since no program is 100 percent effective at preventing delinquency, it follows that no theoretical scheme devised thus far is fully effective. Yet, the wide variety of programs that are applied today to deal with different kinds of juvenile offenders indicates that most psychological and sociological approaches have some merit and contribute differentially to delinquency reduction. As we will see in subsequent chapters, policy decisions are made throughout the juvenile justice system and are often contingent upon the theoretical views adopted by politicians, law enforcement personnel, prosecutors and judges, and correctional officials at every stage of the justice process. For the present, we may appreciate most views because of their varying intuitive value and selectively apply particular approaches to accommodate different types of juvenile offenders.

FIGURE 2.2   Teen boys shoplifting.
Courtesy of Jim Smith, Photo Researchers, Inc.

A bottom line concerning theories of delinquency generally is that their impact has been felt most strongly in the area of policymaking rather than in behavioral change or modification. Virtually every theory is connected in some respect to various types of experimental programs in different jurisdictions. The intent of most programs has been to change behaviors of participants. However, high rates of recidivism characterize all delinquency prevention innovations, regardless of their intensity or ingenuity. Policy decisions implemented at earlier points have long-range implications for present policies in correctional work. Probationers and parolees as well as inmates and divertees, adults and juveniles alike, are recipients or inheritors of previous policies laid in place by theorists who have attempted to convert their theories into practical experiences and action.

Current policy in juvenile justice favors the "get-tough" orientation, and programs are increasingly sponsored that heavily incorporate accountability and individual responsibility elements. At an earlier point in time, projects emphasizing rehabilitation and reintegration were rewarded more heavily through private grants and various types of government funding. No particular prevention, intervention, or supervision program works best. Numerous contrasting perspectives about how policy should be shaped continue to vie for recognition among professionals and politicians. The theories that have been described here are indicative of the many factors that have shaped our present policies and practices.

TREATMENT PROGRAMS AND THEORIES

One way of evaluating these theories is to examine the successes that have resulted when these theories have been applied at various stages of the criminal justice process. Which theories seem to be most influential in formulating policies in our various correctional institutions? Which theories receive the most consistent emphasis and support from foundations that underwrite research projects examining the causes of criminal behavior? To identify which theories seem most popular, it might be helpful to study parole board hearings. Parole boards determine whether incarcerated prisoners should be released before serving their full sentences. Parole boards consider many factors in deciding whether an offender should be released. Did the inmate behave properly in prison? Did they exhibit any unusual behavioral disorders? What is the likelihood that these offenders will be able to cope effectively with life on the "outside"? Halfway houses, places where parolees can stay temporarily in the community until they can find appropriate employment and housing, were created to help offenders adjust to life outside prison.

Have inmates had vocational training, group therapy, or rehabilitative counseling? What are the reports of the counselors who interacted with these inmates and listened to their problems? All answers to these questions combine to form a release quotient or salient factor score. This is a numerical value that predicts inmates' chances of living on the outside in the community with others and not committing new crimes (Wolf, 2002).

Differential association theory seems influential in parole decisions and the conditions prescribed for parolees. For instance, persons who are paroled are required not to associate with other known criminals as one of several parole conditions. But many parolees violate this condition because the community has labeled them as ex-convicts. This community rejection makes it difficult for these former criminals to obtain employment. Thus, in a sense, society compels these persons to seek social attachments with other criminals. This frustrates their efforts to go straight and refrain from further criminal activity.

One way of determining which delinquency theories are most popular and/or influence policy and administrative decision making relative to juveniles is to catalog the ways offenders are treated by the juvenile justice system after their apprehension by police or others. A preliminary screening of juvenile offenders may result in some being diverted from the juvenile justice system. One manifest purpose of such diversionary action is to reduce the potentially adverse influence of labeling on these youths. A long-term objective of diversion is to minimize recidivism among divertees. While some experts contend that the intended effects of diversion, such as a reduction in the degree of social stigmatization toward status offenders, are presently unclear, inconsistent, and insufficiently documented, other professionals endorse diversion programs and regard them as effective in preventing further delinquent conduct among first-offenders. In fact, the preponderance of evidence from a survey of available literature is that diversion, while not fully effective at preventing delinquent recidivism, nevertheless tends to reduce it substantially.

Implicit in most studies of recidivism among youth has been the idea that minimizing formal involvement with the juvenile justice system has been favorable for reducing participants' self-definitions as delinquent and avoiding the delinquent label. Thus, labeling theory seems to have been prominent in the promotion of diversionary programs. Furthermore, many divertees have been exposed to experiences that enhance or improve their self-reliance and independence. Many youths have learned to think out their problems rather than act them out unproductively or antisocially. When we examine the contents of these programs closely, it is fairly easy to detect aspects of bonding theory, containment theory, and differential reinforcement theory at work in the delinquency prevention process (Antonopoulos, 2002).

Besides using diversion per se with or without various programs, there are elements or overtones of other theoretical schemes that may be present in the particular treatments or experiences juveniles receive as they continue to be processed throughout the juvenile justice system. At the time of adjudication, for example, juvenile judges may or may not impose special conditions to accompany a sentence of probation. Special conditions may refer to obligating juveniles to make restitution to victims, to perform public services, to participate in group or individual therapy, or to undergo medical treatment in cases of drug addiction or alcohol abuse. It may be that those youths who receive probation accompanied by special conditions are less likely to recidivate compared with those youths who receive probation unconditionally.

Learning to accept responsibility for one's actions, acquiring new coping skills to face crises and personal tragedy, improving one's educational attainment, and improving one's ego strength to resist the influence of one's delinquent peers are individually or collectively integral parts of various delinquency treatment programs, particularly where the psychological approach is strong. For example, a juvenile education program was implemented at the East Lansing (Kansas) Penitentiary in the late 1970s. Delinquent youths currently on probation and residing in three Kansas counties near the penitentiary were obligated to participate in the program, which stressed introducing the juveniles to the realities of prison life. These juveniles participated from June to October 1980. In a follow-up investigation of their recidivism rates compared with a sample of other delinquents not exposed to the program, self-reported delinquency was considerably lower among previous program participants than among those who did not participate in the program. Researchers concluded that the experience of life in prison was to a degree therapeutic, and it appeared to change the perceived status of most participants.

Several programs in various jurisdictions may function as alternatives to state training schools. These programs include outdoor educational activities and wilderness challenges that encourage youths to learn useful skills and confront their fears. For those designated as "children at risk," preschool programs such as Headstart, parent training programs such as the Oregon Learning Center, selected school programs intended to increase the achievement of lower income children, and voluntary youth service programs such as California's Conservation Corps provide many participating youths with opportunities to avoid delinquent behavioral patterns. Together with psychodrama, cognitive-behavioral techniques were used by the Clinic of the Wayne County, Michigan, Juvenile Court and were intended to reduce participants' aggressive, acting-out tendencies and build their ego strength. A High School Personality Questionnaire was administered to all adolescents participating in the program to chart before–after program changes. Researchers reported positive results, where juveniles tended to exhibit higher ego strength, less introversive tendencies, and less antisocial behavior after program participation. Intervention techniques included behavioral contracting, monetary reinforcement, and alternative behavior rehearsals, together with psychodrama, as methods for reducing these delinquents' acting-out tendencies.

Group therapy is an option applied to the treatment of juvenile delinquents. Group therapy seems particularly effective for more aggressive adolescents. Much of this group therapy research is conducted in residential settings, such as group homes. In these less traditional, nonthreatening circumstances, juveniles seem to be more amenable to behavioral change and improved conduct.

During the late 1970s, a program known as "Getting It Together" was established in a large-city juvenile court jurisdiction. The program emphasized a combination of affective (emotional) and social skills training designed to assist those with immature personalities and who exhibited neurotic behaviors. Over the next several years, many delinquent youths participated in this program. A majority reported improved self-esteem and socially mature behavior, better communication skills with authorities and parents, greater self-control, more positive values, and more adequate job skills. Ego strength levels for most participating youths improved, as did the quality of peer relationships and a reduction of various sexual problems. This program, in addition to other similar enterprises, has been guided to a great degree by social learning theory.

SUMMARY

Theories explain and predict relationships between various phenomena. Criminologists theorize about criminal behavior and describe the characteristics of persons convicted of crimes as well as their motives. Efforts are made to determine whether or not criminals have the necessary *mens rea* or guilty mind or criminal disposition in the crimes they commit. Nineteenth-century biological theories of criminal behavior stressed the importance of physical characteristics as indicators of criminal propensities. One biological theory determined that criminal behavior was hereditary. Other biological explanations focused on body type as a predictor. These theories have been discounted. Biochemical imbalance or glandular problems were also believed linked with criminal conduct, although no consistent evidence exists to support such beliefs.

Psychoanalytic theory developed by Freud emphasizes early selfish behaviors of infants that sometimes remain uncontrolled as children grow older. The id, or "I want," part of the personality remains unchecked by the ego, or that part of the personality that includes the standards and conventional rules of society. Again, criminal behavior is one predictable result. The psychological theory of moral development emphasizes developmental stages in the lives of children. As they grow and mature, they incorporate into their personality systems certain socially acceptable behavior patterns. Sometimes, disruptions occur in these stages, and criminal conduct results.

Sociological or sociocultural theories of criminal behavior stress social and environmental factors as influential in promoting criminal conduct. One sociological theory, anomie, is that people experience a conflict between aspiring to achieve socially acceptable goals and the culturally approved means to achieve those goals. People adapt to this conflict in different ways. Some persons engage in innovative or unconventional behavior to achieve desired objectives. A third sociological theory is labeling. According to this theory, deviance is whatever a group says it is. Labeling theory involves no moral judgments of criminal actions. Rather, attention is directed at social definitions of criminal behavior and a person's responses to being labeled as criminal.

An evaluation of these theories may be made according to several criteria. Can we predict criminal behavior by using them? Which are most useful for helping us to understand why people commit crimes? In addition to evaluating their usefulness in predicting crime, these theories can be evaluated by considering the importance each is given in various sectors of the criminal justice system. Counseling programs, group therapy, and rehabilitative practices in prison settings are strongly influenced by psychological theories. Correctional institutional policies and guidelines are influenced strongly by differential association theory and the labeling perspective. Finally, single-factor explanations of criminal behavior have inherent weaknesses, because they highlight one variable or circumstance and ignore others. The best explanations are those that combine the best elements of several theoretical schemes.

There are several theories of delinquency. Similar to theories about adult criminality, theories of delinquency may be grouped into biological, psychological, and sociological explanations. Biological theories strongly imply a causal relation between physique and other genetic phenomena and delinquent behaviors. Psychological theories include psychoanalytic theory devised by Sigmund Freud and promoted by others. Social learning theory is similar to psychoanalytic theory, although it stresses imitation of significant others. Concentric zone theory postulates that ecological factors such as the nature of urban growth create living situations conducive to delinquent conduct.

A popular sociological view of delinquency is labeling theory. Those who engage in wrongdoing may come to adopt self-definitions as delinquents, particularly if significant others and the police define them as delinquents. Having frequent contact with the juvenile justice system enhances such labeling for many youths. Labeling theorists often argue that delinquents are acting out the behaviors others expect from them. Closely related to labeling theory is bonding theory, where juveniles develop either close or distant attachments to schools, teachers, and peers. Delinquency is regarded as a function of inadequate bonding or a weakening of social attachments. Other theories include containment theory, neutralization or drift theory, and differential association. Each of these views suggests the power or attraction of group processes in the onset of delinquent conduct.

Theories of delinquency are often evaluated according to how they influence public policy relating to juvenile conduct and its prevention or treatment. Diversionary programs that prevent further juvenile contact with the juvenile justice system are influenced largely by labeling theory, since it is believed that youths will become more deeply entrenched in juvenile conduct to the extent that they are exposed to the formal system and juvenile courts. Individual and group therapy, often a part of treatment programs for errant juveniles, seek to use ego development strategies coupled with various learning methods to improve self-definitions, reduce antisocial behaviors, and promote more healthy attitudes toward others. Programs that emphasize personal responsibility for one's actions or encourage youths to become more active in decision making seem to make a difference in reducing recidivism among program participants. No theory is universally accepted, however.

QUESTIONS FOR REVIEW

1. Why is it important to study biological explanations of criminal behavior to understand probationers and parolees? How valid are sociobiological explanations of one's unlawful conduct while on probation or parole?

2. Compare and contrast labeling theory with differential association theory. Which theory directs attention to the nature of the crime committed? Which theory directs attention to the societal reaction toward the offender? Which theory do you feel is the most "sociological" of the two?

3. What evidence exists to support the idea that body type has something to do with the causes of criminal behavior? Give some of the supporting information, regardless of its scientific benefits or lack of them.

4. What is a theory of criminal behavior? What are some important objectives of such theories? Can these objectives be used to evaluate whether certain criminal theories are good or bad? Why or why not? Give an example.

5. Of the three different categories of criminal behavior theories, which one do you prefer and why? Name your favorite theory discussed in the category you have chosen, and explain why it is your favorite.

6. What is meant by the shift from internal to external explanations of criminal behavior? What emphasis is placed on each perspective? Which perspective is popular currently? Why do you think this is so?

7. How do psychoanalytic theory and developmental theory differ?

8. Some people read about "differential association" theory and decide that Edwin Sutherland meant that associating with criminals would make someone turn out to be a criminal. Is this what Sutherland was really saying? What are the characteristics of differential association theory? Why are they important in explaining criminal conduct?

9. Discuss the "labeling" process of becoming a deviant. What factors seem to be most important in this theoretical explanation of criminal behavior? What are the assumptions or principles of labeling theory?

10. Differentiate between primary and secondary deviation. Give two examples of situations where two different persons would commit the same criminal acts, but one person gets arrested and convicted and the other is only scolded. Why do you think situations like this occur?

SUGGESTED READINGS

Bernsburg, J.G., M.D. Krohn, and C.J. Rivera (2006). "Official Labeling: Criminal Embeddedness, and Subsequent Delinquency: A Longitudinal Test of Labeling Theory." *Journal of Research in Crime and Delinquency* **43**:67–88.

Gomez-Smith, Z. and A.R. Piquero (2005). "An Examination of Adult-Onset Offending." *Journal of Criminal Justice* **33**:515–525.

Ozbay, O. and Ozcan, Y.Z. (2006). "Classic Strain Theory and Gender." *International Journal of Offender Therapy and Comparative Criminology* **50**:21–38.

Ryan, Timothy P. (2006). "Incarceration Therapy: Local Approaches." *Corrections Today* **68**:18–20.

Walters, G.D. (2006). "Use of the Psychological Inventory of Criminal Thinking Styles to Predict Disciplinary Adjustment in Male Inmate Program Participants." *International Journal of Offender Therapy and Comparative Criminology* **50:**166–173.

INTERNET CONNECTIONS

Advances in Criminological Theory
http://www.newark.rutgers.edu/rscj/ journals/advances.htm

Criminological Theory on the Web
http://www.home.attbi.com/~ddemelo/ crime/crimetheory.html

Criminology theory
http://www.roxbury.net/crimtheorypast2 .html

North Carolina Department of Corrections Offender Treatment Programs
http://www.doc.state.nc.us/Substance/ Treatment.htm

Offender treatment programs
http://www.house.state.mo.us/bills/HB407 .htm

Sex Offenders Treatment Program
http://www.auditor.leg.state.mn.us/sexoff .htm

Understanding criminological theory
http://www.faculty.ncwc.edu/toconnor/ 301/crimtheo.htm

<table>
<tr><td>CHAPTER 3</td><td>An Overview of Community Corrections: Types, Goals, and Functions</td></tr>
</table>

Chapter Outline

Chapter Objectives

As the result of reading this chapter, the following objectives will be realized:

1. Examining the meaning of community corrections.
2. Discussing the origination of community corrections acts as well as the general nature of community corrections programs today.
3. Defining the characteristics and history of community corrections programs.
4. Highlighting the goals and functions of community corrections programs.
5. Discussing selected issues in community corrections, including public resistance to them.
6. Describing the NIMBY syndrome.
7. Describing offender needs and community safety.
8. Explaining the general nature of services delivery and rehabilitation.
9. Defining intermediate punishments and discussing their variation throughout the United States.
10. Defining home confinement and its goals, functions, and effectiveness.
11. Profiling home confinement clients and their potential for program success.
12. Discussing selected issues related to home confinement.
13. Identifying and describing electronic monitoring systems.
14. Comparing and contrasting the relative effectiveness of home confinement and electronic monitoring as viable alternatives to incarceration or more intensive supervised probation programs.
15. Discussing the future of electronic monitoring and home confinement as offender management tools in future decades.

• *Jungers was convicted in a California criminal court of assaulting his girlfriend who was also the mother of his child and placed on probation. One probation condition was that Jungers was prohibited from having contact with the woman. However, the woman was entitled to initiate contact with Jungers, if the woman chose to do so. Subsequently, Jungers violated a probation condition by failing to notify his probation officer of a change of his address. His probation was revoked but was reinstated, with the same conditions. Jungers was also placed in a special program, Teen Challenge, a residential treatment program, for one year. In the meantime, he married the woman he had previously been convicted of assaulting. He moved to change his probation conditions to permit him unlimited contact with her. The court upheld the original probation conditions, noting that domestic violence was the conviction offense, that Jungers had a problem with anger, and that he had previously used threats and intimidation to control the woman he eventually married. As before, the court ordered Jungers not to initiate contact with the woman, but it permitted her to initiate contact with him on occasion if she wanted to do so. Contending that forbidding him from associating with his wife violated his associational rights as well as his right to privacy, Jungers appealed. The court upheld Jungers's probation conditions, holding that the probation conditions had to be carefully tailored and reasonably related to the compelling state interest in reforming and rehabilitating Jungers. The elimination of domestic violence was a compelling state interest. Noting that some victims of domestic violence often remained in abusive relationships, the court went on to hold that the restriction on Jungers's ability to contact his wife was appropriate under the circumstances. [People v. Jungers, 25 Cal.Rptr.3d 873 (Cal.App.March) (2005)].*

• *Saulsby was convicted in Louisiana of a property crime. Saulsby was placed on probation. While Saulsby was on probation, sheriff's deputies were advised by an unknown informant that Saulsby was involved in illegal narcotics activity and surveillance of Saulsby and his residence was set up by the Sheriff's Office. While the surveillance did not disclose any evidence of illegal narcotics trafficking, the Sheriff's Office notified Saulsby's probation officer, Berger. Berger went to Saulsby's residence and determined that he wasn't at home. Berger and some sheriff's deputies waited for Saulsby to return and when he did, he was searched as he exited his vehicle. He was carrying $1,000 in cash, and Berger said that to his knowledge, Saulsby was unemployed. Berger and sheriff's deputies proceeded to search Saulsby's residence where a large amount of cocaine was discovered in Saulsby's closet. Saulsby was subsequently convicted of possessing cocaine and appealed, contending that his Fourth Amendment right against unreasonable search and seizure had been violated. An appeals court heard the case and sided with Saulsby. The court noted that in determining whether a warrantless search by a probation officer is reasonable, the court must consider (1) the scope of the particular intrusion; (2) the manner in which it was conducted; (3) the justification for initiating it; and (4) the place in which it was conducted. The court said that Berger had testified that he had received information that Saulsby was involved in illegal narcotics activity, but it is unclear who actually provided this information. It is also unclear what the sheriff's department advised Berger about Saulsby's alleged drug activities. Berger also did not specify how extensive a search was conducted, only that cocaine was discovered in Saulsby's closet. Berger did not see any evidence of illegal drug activity before he searched Saulsby or his residence. Furthermore, no evidence existed to indicate that Saulsby's original offense was related to narcotics. The court held, therefore, that the search of Saulsby and his residence was unreasonable and in violation of his Fourth Amendment rights. The narcotics were excluded as evidence against him. Thus, while persons on probation have a reduced expectation of privacy, they are not totally bereft of privacy rights.* [State v. Saulsby, *892 So.2d 655 (La.App.Dec.) (2004)*].

• *Williams is a Florida probationer. Williams's probation officer noted that on one particular occasion, Williams had failed to file his required monthly report. Furthermore, it was discovered by his probation officer that Williams was living on the street. This behavior was defined as "changing one's residence without notifying one's probation officer." The probation officer reported these apparent probation violations to the court, where Williams's case was reviewed for possible revocation action. The judge revoked Williams's probation and Williams appealed, arguing that he had recently been forced to leave his residence by his landlord and without prior notice. Also, Williams claimed that because of his homeless circumstances, he was unable to file a timely report during that particular interval of time. An appellate court reversed the revocation action, noting that Williams had faithfully complied with all probation conditions, had filed timely reports both before and after the month where a report was not filed, and that he had no control over being forced to leave his residence without prior notice. Williams had also attempted to contact his probation officer during the time interval while he was living on the street, but he was unable to locate the officer. In view of the evidence, Williams did not willfully fail to obtain his probation officer's consent before changing his residence, and his contact with the probation officer and regular report filing, both before and after being forcibly removed from his residence, show a reasonable effort by Williams to comply with his probation conditions.* [Williams v. State, *896 So.2d 805 (Fla.Dist.App.Feb.) (2005)*].

• *Rand was convicted in federal court of identity theft, where he had fraudulently obtained credit cards and money through an identity theft scheme. He was sentenced to 21 months in prison and ordered to pay $57,000 in restitution to victims during his supervised release following his imprisonment. Rand appealed the restitution order, contending that some of the restitution applied to victims who were originally unnamed or identified in the indictment against him or acknowledged as victims in his guilty plea. The government responded that the restitution order was related to all included losses* *related to street addresses Rand and his co-conspirators specifically admitted to using in the course of their conspiracy. All of the losses included in the restitution orders stemmed from fraudulent acts taken pursuant to a single identity theft conspiracy, the specific conduct to which Rand pleaded guilty, and were related to individuals who were directly harmed by Rand's criminal conduct in the course of his scheme. The appellate court upheld the restitution order as valid. [United States v. Rand, 403 F.3d 489 (U.S.7thCir.April) (2005)].*

• *Parrish was a Florida probationer who had been convicted of drug crimes. When Parrish was sentenced, the judge sentenced Parrish to standard probation without conditions. Later, the probation office subjected Parrish to numerous drug tests and urinalyses and blood and breath tests, requiring Parrish to pay for them. Furthermore, the probation office directed Parrish to undergo drug abuse evaluation and attend a drug treatment program, again at his own expense. Parrish appealed, arguing that these drug tests, drug evaluation, and drug treatment program were not valid requirements of his probation program since the court had failed to list them as special conditions in his original probation orders. An appellate court held for Parrish, noting that the condition of Parrish's probation, which required him to pay costs of urinalysis and various blood and breath tests, were special conditions of probation that had to be pronounced at sentencing. Moreover, the condition requiring Parrish to undergo drug abuse evaluation and drug treatment were also special conditions of probation that had to be pronounced at sentencing. Because the trial court failed to comply with Florida's statutory requirements in this regard, these conditions had to be set aside. [Parrish v. State, 898 So.2d 1074 (Fla.Dist.App.April) (2005)].*

INTRODUCTION

These scenarios involve probationers and parolees under different types of supervision within their own communities in various jurisdictions. These probationers and parolees or clients are supervised within their own communities. The broad categorical term for such supervision is community corrections. Since the mid-1970s, increasing numbers of jurisdictions have relied on community corrections as an alternative to incarceration, believing that many offenders can be effectively monitored and supervised within their own communities. The successfulness of community corrections has been firmly established. Most jurisdictions have discovered that community corrections not only eases prison and jail overcrowding, but the cost of supervising offenders in their own communities is but a fraction of the cost of imprisonment.

This chapter is organized as follows. First, community corrections is defined and contrasted with intermediate punishments. A historical context of the development and philosophy of community corrections is provided. Several characteristics of community-based corrections programs are described. Various goals and functions of community corrections programs are presented. Community corrections clients are also profiled. Next, an overview of different types of community corrections programs is presented. Three kinds of community-based correctional programs include home confinement, electronic monitoring, and day reporting. Each of these types of programs is described, including their functions and goals, advantages and disadvantages, and primary features.

The chapter concludes with a discussion of selected community-based correctional issues. These issues relate to public opposition toward community-based corrections programs; the privatization of community-based correctional programs; and whether community-based corrections are true punishments. Some persons have been critical of community-based corrections because they have involved net-widening, or drawing in certain clients who would not be subject to any type of supervision if these programs did not exist. Other issues pertain to the management and operations of community-based corrections, the quality of services delivery, and staff training and education.

COMMUNITY CORRECTIONS AND INTERMEDIATE PUNISHMENTS

Community-based corrections is the broad array of correctional programs established at the community level that provide alternatives to incarceration (Marion, 2002). These community-based programs are intended to continue one's punishment, but in the context of the community rather than in a prison or jail. Another term that is often used synonymously with community corrections is **intermediate punishments.** Intermediate punishments include any community-based programs that are somewhere between standard probation and incarceration. The conceptual confusion between community corrections and intermediate punishments is easily explained. This author conducted a content analysis of over 600 articles and books extracted from the *Criminal Justice Abstracts* in 2001. These articles and books were selected according to the key words "community corrections" and "intermediate punishments." An inspection of the abstracts of these articles and books disclosed a remarkably high number of similarities.

Let's examine a few articles that focused on "intermediate punishments" or "intermediate sanctions." For instance, Karol Lucken (1997a) examined intermediate punishments as including home confinement and day reporting programs. Henry Sontheimer and Traci Duncan (1996) investigated intermediate sanctions in Pennsylvania, and these included community service, restitution, house arrest/electronic monitoring, residential work release, intensive supervision, and other programs. David Rasmussen and Bruce Benson (1994) examined various intermediate punishment programs in Florida, including day fines, shock incarceration, intensive probation supervision, electronic monitoring, house arrest, and day reporting. A fourth source, an article by Kevin Courtright, Bruce Berg, and Robert Mutchnick (1997:19), indicated among other things that "if offenders who would have been sentenced to standard probation are now being sentenced to an intermediate punishment program, e.g., house arrest, intensive supervision, or electronic monitoring . . . then net-widening would have occurred."

Next, let's examine several articles that focused on "community corrections," "community-based corrections," or "community-based sanctions." Research reported by Jody Sundt and her associates (1998:25) investigated public opinions about different types of sanctions to be imposed on fictitious criminals with specific types of criminal histories. Sundt et al. reported that "given the community-based options, respondents preferred sentencing offenders to halfway houses or house arrest . . . rather than strict probation." In an essay describing Michigan's Community Corrections Act (CCA), Patricia Clark (1995:68) has noted that "since the implementation of Michigan's CCA, community service work, electronic monitoring, day reporting, employment, and drug testing and treatment programs have been initiated and expanded in most communities in the state." And in a definitive study of community corrections conducted by

Robert Sigler and David Lamb (1995:7), types of community corrections included the following: regular probation; intensive probation; shock probation; work release; electronic monitoring; house arrest; halfway house; victim restitution and fines; and community service.

What is clear is that the differences between community-based corrections and intermediate punishments are unclear. The primary reason for this lack of clarity is that virtually all intermediate punishments are community-based sanctions. All intermediate punishment programs are located in communities, where offenders are permitted various freedoms to work at jobs, attend school, and/or participate in different forms of individual or group therapy. All intermediate punishment programs have behavioral conditions. Virtually every intermediate punishment program is administered by a probation or parole agency or by a private organization. All intermediate punishment clients are under some form of supervision by these agencies or organizations. The intensity of such supervision varies according to the agency and program requirements.

Some states, such as Florida, have a program known as **community control.** According to Florida officials, community control is not intensive supervised probation or parole. Rather, it is home confinement, often coupled with **electronic monitoring.** However, Florida clouds the picture by describing how community control involves frequent face-to-face contacts between probationers and parolees and their supervisors; that curfews are strictly enforced; and that probation and parole officers have deliberately low caseloads of 20 or fewer clients so as to allow officers to supervise offenders closely or intensively. This description of community control sounds a lot like intensive supervised probation/parole, and it has all of the identifying characteristics of community corrections.

A fine line is sometimes drawn between programs that offer offenders community freedoms but require them to be monitored frequently and intensively (e.g., repeated drug and alcohol testing through urinalysis, curfew checks, unannounced but frequent inspections of one's residence), and programs that place offenders in designated locations, such as their homes or halfway houses. But the simple fact is that **professionals** themselves obscure the differences between community-based programs by lumping together any and all programs that involve client freedom but some form of community supervision, regardless of its nature or intensity (Hobbs, Jablonski, and Ahern, 2006). In this text, we will define community corrections as any community-based program designed to supervise convicted offenders in lieu of incarceration, either at the city, county, state, or federal level; that provides various services to client/offenders; that monitors and furthers client/offender behaviors related to sentencing conditions; that heightens client/offender responsibility and accountability regarding the payment of fines, victim compensation, community service, and restitution orders; and that provides for a continuation of punishment through more controlled supervision and greater accountability.

Various community-based correctional alternatives include programs, such as intensive probation or parole supervision, home confinement, electronic surveillance or monitoring, narcotics and drug deterrence, work furlough programs or work release, study release, day reporting centers, and probationer violation and restitution residential centers (Israel and Dawes, 2002). Also included under the community corrections umbrella are programs such as diversion, **pretrial release,** and pre-parole. Community corrections programs can also be distinguished according to the controlling authority. Community-based correctional programs may be community-run (locally operated, but lacking state funding and other external support); community-placed (programs that are located in communities but do not network with any community agency); and community-based (programs that are locally operated but are also financially supplemented from outside sources; programs that network with other community agencies and the criminal justice system). There is considerable interstate variation in community-based correctional programs. However, there have been efforts in recent years among different jurisdictions to network with one another as a means of information dissemination and sharing regarding particular community corrections programs.

The term may also refer to any of several different programs designed to closely control or monitor offender behaviors. Since there are several possible meanings of intermediate punishments, the term is widely applied, correctly or incorrectly, to a variety of community-based offender programs involving nonincarcerative sanctions. Major distinguishing features of intermediate punishments are the high degree of offender monitoring and control of offender behaviors by program staff. Other characteristics of intermediate punishments include curfews, where offenders must observe time guidelines and be at particular places at particular times; frequent monitoring; and contact with program officials. The amount and type of frequent monitoring or contact varies with the program, although daily visits by probation officers at an offender's workplace or home are not unusual.

One semantic problem is that the intensive supervision refers to different levels of monitoring or officer–offender contact, depending on the jurisdiction. Intermediate punishments are intended for prison- or jail-bound offenders. Therefore, offenders who are probably going to receive probation anyway are considered the least likely candidates for these more intensively supervised programs. However, judges often assign these low-risk probation-bound offenders to intermediate punishment programs anyway. This practice tends to defeat the goals of such programs, because the programs target offenders who would otherwise occupy valuable prison or jail space unnecessarily. Cluttering these intensive supervision programs with offenders who don't need close supervision is a waste of money, time, and personnel. When this occurs, it is referred to as **net-widening.** Offenders are given considerable freedom of movement within their communities, although it is believed that such intensive monitoring and control fosters a high degree of compliance with program requirements. It is also suspected that this intensive supervision deters offenders from committing new crimes.

THE COMMUNITY CORRECTIONS ACT

A **community corrections act** is the enabling medium by which jurisdictions establish local community corrections agencies, facilities, and programs. A generic definition of a community corrections act is a statewide mechanism through which funds are granted to local units of government to plan, develop, and deliver correctional sanctions and services at the local level. The overall purpose of this mechanism is to provide local sentencing options in lieu of imprisonment in state institutions.

The aim of community corrections acts is to make it possible to divert certain prison-bound offenders into local, city-, or county-level programs where they can receive treatment and assistance rather than imprisonment. Usually, those offenders who are eligible or otherwise qualify for community corrections programs are low-risk, nonviolent, nondangerous offenders. Community corrections acts also target those incarcerated offenders who pose little or no risk to the public if released into the community under close parole supervision. Thus, community corrections acts function to alleviate prison and jail overcrowding by diverting certain jail- or prison-bound offenders to community programs.

For instance, Wisconsin implemented a community corrections act in the early 1990s. This act was designed to provide alternatives to both incarceration and new prison construction by encouraging local communities to provide appropriate community sanctions for adult and juvenile offenders. At the time Wisconsin implemented its community-based programs, there were 196,000 crimes committed in the state annually, largely by recidivists. Wisconsin community corrections currently utilizes a variety of programs as a part of its community corrections, including home confinement, day reporting centers, halfway houses, electronic monitoring, and intensive supervised probation and parole to supervise its 68,000 offenders. Under present fiscal allocations, the annual cost of these community-based programs to the state averages $1,500 per offender.

In 2005, there were over 225,000 offenders on probation in Ohio, with about 70,000 of these involved in community corrections programs (U.S. Department of Justice, 2006). Targeted offenders include nonviolent clients who participate in both residential and nonresidential placement options. These placement options include work release and halfway house programs, intensive supervised probation, day reporting centers, home confinement, community service, and standard probation. Personnel conduct urinalyses of clients as well as other forms of behavioral monitoring. Ohio programming staff look for the following resident/client traits:

1. A demonstrated willingness to comply with program rules and regulations.
2. A motivation to work on individual treatment plans as described by program staff.
3. A target population pool that consists primarily of nonviolent offenders, including but not limited to misdemeanants, probation-eligible felony offenders, and parolees who are amenable to community sanctions (Latessa, Travis, and Holsinger, 1997:2–10).

THE PHILOSOPHY AND HISTORY OF COMMUNITY CORRECTIONS

The philosophy of community corrections is to provide certain types of offenders with a rehabilitative and reintegrative milieu, where their personal abilities and skills are improved, and where their chances for recidivism are minimized (Nijboer et al., 2002). The primary purpose of community-based correctional programs is to assist probationers in becoming reintegrated into their communities, although parolees are assisted by such programs as well. It is not so much the case that probationers (in contrast with parolees) have lost touch with their communities through incarceration, but rather they have the opportunity of avoiding confinement and remaining within their communities to perform productive work to support themselves and others and to repay victims for losses suffered.

A secondary purpose of community-based programs is to help alleviate prison and jail overcrowding by accepting those offenders who are not dangerous and pose the least risk to society. Of course, the difficulty here is attempting to sort those most dangerous offenders from those least dangerous. Assessments of offender risk are not infallible, and often, persons predicted to be dangerous may never commit future violent offenses or harm others. At the same time, some risk instruments may suggest that certain offenders will be nonviolent and not dangerous, although the offender will turn out to be dangerous. These two types of offenders are called **false positives** and **false negatives.** False positives are offenders considered dangerous based on independent criteria such as their prior institutional conduct or prior record of offending, although they do not pose a danger to others. False negatives are offenders believed to be nonviolent on the basis of independent criteria, such as **risk assessment instruments** and psychological evaluations, although they turn out to be dangerous by subsequently harming others and committing violent offenses. In order to reduce the risks posed by false negatives and improve the likelihood of releasing false positives, community corrections acts acknowledge that: (1) states should continue to house violent offenders in secure facilities; (2) judges and prosecutors need a variety of punishments; and (3) local communities cannot develop these programs without additional funding from such legislatures.

Several common elements that are believed essential to the success of community-based corrections include (1) prison/jail-bound offenders are targeted, rather than adding additional punishments to those who would have otherwise remained in the community; (2) financial subsidies are provided to local government and community agencies; (3) a performance factor is implemented to ensure funds are used for the act's specific goals; (4) local advisory boards in each local community assess local needs, propose improvements in the local criminal justice system, and educate the general public about the benefits of alternative punishments; (5) advisory boards submit annual criminal justice plans to the local government (Champion, 2005); (6) there is a formula for allocating funds; (7) local communities participate voluntarily and may withdraw at any time; and (8) there are restrictions on funding high-cost capital projects as well as straight probation services.

Community-based corrections appears to be working, because these programs offer mechanisms for ensuring and maintaining public safety and security. These community-based programs have been demonstrated to be safer and less costly than incarceration, especially when the right, eligible nonviolent clients are targeted for inclusion in such programs.

California was one of the first states to implement a community corrections program. California's **Probation Subsidy Program** was implemented in 1965. This program provided local communities with supplemental resources to manage larger numbers of probationers more closely. A part of this subsidization provided for **community residential centers** where probationers could check in and receive counseling, employment assistance, and other forms of guidance or supervision. Soon, other states, such as Colorado and Oregon, established their own community-based programs to assist probationers and others. However, it took at least another decade for large-scale philosophical shifts to occur among different U.S. jurisdictions so that community corrections could be implemented more widely.

Community-based programs are geared to assist offenders by providing nonsecure lodging, vocational/educational training, job assistance, and a limited amount of psychological counseling. Such programs perform rehabilitative and reintegrative functions. One of the first official acknowledgments of the need for community-based programs as a possible front-end solution to prison and jail overcrowding was the 1967 **President's Commission on Law Enforcement and Administration of Justice.** Subsequently, the National Advisory Commission on Criminal Justice Standards and Goals as well as the Law Enforcement Assistance Administration encouraged the establishment of community-based programs as alternatives to incarceration in 1973 and provided extensive financial sponsorship for such programs.

The growing use of community-based programs has occurred for at least three reasons. First, the 1967 President's Commission on Law Enforcement and Administration of Justice indicated that community-based monitoring of offenders is much cheaper than incarceration. The **Law Enforcement Assistance Administration (LEAA)** provided considerable funding for experiments in community-based programming. Second, since incarceration has been unable to offer the public any convincing evidence that large numbers of inmates emerge rehabilitated, community corrections programs will not be any worse. Community-based correctional programs are perhaps the major form of offender management today. Offender management, control, and punishment are key functions of community corrections.

Prisons are increasingly considered destructive for both offenders and society, another important reason for community-based correctional programs. Many inmates who are confined in prisons for several years become accustomed to an alien lifestyle unlike anything occurring within their communities. There is physical separation from an offender's family unit and friends. Inmates are subject to demeaning experiences and treatment not designed to equip offenders with the necessary skills to cope with life on the outside when they are eventually released.

CHARACTERISTICS, GOALS, AND FUNCTIONS OF COMMUNITY CORRECTIONS PROGRAMS

Community-based programs vary in size and scope among communities, although they share certain characteristics such as the following:

1. Community-based program administrators have the authority to oversee offender behaviors and enforce compliance with their probation conditions.
2. These programs have job referral and placement services where paraprofessionals or others act as liaisons with various community agencies and organizations to facilitate offender job placement.
3. Administrators of these programs are available on premises on a 24-hour basis for emergency situations and spontaneous assistance for offenders who may need help.
4. One or more large homes or buildings located within the residential section of the community with space to accommodate between 20 and 30 residents are provided within walking distance of work settings and social services.
5. A professional and paraprofessional staff "on call" for medical, social, or psychological emergencies.
6. A system is in place for heightening staff accountability to the court concerning offender progress.

Community-based corrections is not intended to free thousands of violent felons into communities. Rather, these programs advocate the continued use of incarceration for violent offenders. However, a portion of prison-bound offenders might benefit by becoming involved in community-based correctional programming. Community-based corrections seeks to preserve offender attachments with their communities by diverting them from incarceration and housing them in local neighborhoods. Thus, there is a strong reintegrative objective that drives such community programming. One of the major obstacles for implementing community-based corrections on a large scale is community opposition because of fear and a lack of understanding about how such programming is operated.

Citizens are entitled to believe that freeing dangerous felons into their communities certainly poses some degree of risk to public safety. There is also the view that offenders who remain free also remain unpunished (Sigler and Lamb, 1996). But community-based corrections are replete with the characteristics associated with punishment. All community-based correctional programs are considered to be continuations of punishments for offenders. For instance, offender/clients must pay restitution to victims, perform public service, pay fines and maintenance fees, adhere to stringent rules and curfews, put up with unannounced searches of their premises by POs, and they must comply with other seemingly unreasonable behavioral restrictions and limitations. Indeed, some offenders have opted for imprisonment instead of probation or parole, since they regard probation or parole as a substantial intrusion on their privacy. They would rather serve out their time or "max out" their sentences and be free of the criminal justice system entirely rather than be subjected to all of the rules and regulations associated with community-based corrections programs (Clear and Dammer, 2000).

The Goals of Community-Based Corrections

The goals of community corrections programs include (1) facilitating offender reintegration, (2) fostering offender rehabilitation, (3) providing an alternative range of offender punishments, and (4) heightening offender accountability.

Facilitating Offender Reintegration. It is considered advantageous for both offenders and correctional personnel to supervise as many offenders in their communities as possible. One reason is that continued community involvement means continuous and hopefully positive contact with one's family and close friends. Also, there is a broader range of social and psychological services available to offenders compared with their opportunities for personal growth and development while in prison or jail. Convicted offenders who remain free in their communities can help with community-based correctional programming operating costs, work at jobs to support themselves and their families, and take advantage of vocational/technical and educational programs available through local colleges and universities. Some offenders require closer monitoring than others. Therefore, it is imperative that community-based correctional programs devise effective screening mechanisms for their clients in order to diagnose their needs accurately. Offender reintegration is therefore an important objective of community-based correctional programs in most states.

Fostering Offender Rehabilitation. A major goal of any community-based correctional program is rehabilitation. Rehabilitation occurs when community correctional clients, offenders, participate in vocational, educational, and/or counseling programs that are intended to improve their coping skills. These programs are particularly beneficial for first-time nonviolent offenders. Several jurisdictions disclose that they have much lower rates of recidivism among community-based correctional clientele compared with offenders who have been incarcerated (Herbst, 2006). In Texas, for instance, community corrections clients have exhibited recidivism rates of 31 percent compared with a 50 percent recidivism rate among former inmates of Texas penitentiaries. In another program in a large urban probation department in another state, officials operate a program known as SAFE-T. SAFE-T adopts cognitive-behavioral approaches that target contemporary youth culture. While SAFE-T is oriented toward more youthful offenders, it has promise also for young adults. Clients are exposed to a four-month series of 32 group sessions. These sessions are led by probation officers who have been intensively trained in group work methods and exposed to urban youth culture. Clients are guided in establishing personal responsibility and learning how to cope with others who may be involved in drugs, alcohol, or illicit activities (Fals, 2003).

Providing an Alternative Range of Offender Punishments.   The range of punishments is vast within community-based corrections. Programs are tailored to fit clients from all age groups, including those with diverse needs and special problems, such as addictions to drugs or alcohol, learning disabilities, or vocational/educational deficiencies. Community centers are created under community corrections acts to assist clients in filling out job applications or overcoming illiteracy. Individual and group counseling are offered to different clients in need of such assistance. The private sector has become increasingly involved in the treatment of community-based correctional clients, and program expansion and diversification has occurred in many cities and communities.

Heightening Offender Accountability.   One of the primary reasons that traditional unsupervised probation has been unsuccessful in rehabilitating offenders is that all too often, probationers are completely unsupervised. They may be permitted simply to fill out a one-page report of their work activities and submit these to probation offices by mail. This means absolutely no direct supervision of these offenders occurs. This condition exists whenever there are large numbers of offenders on probation and relatively few probation officers available to supervise them. One aim of community-based corrections, therefore, is to provide substantial supervision and services to those in need. Substance abusers comprise a class of clients requiring special assistance and intervention. Often these offenders have committed crimes in the past to acquire the drugs they need to satisfy their addictions. With appropriate intervention and accountability mechanisms established, many of these offenders can overcome their addictions and accept responsibility for their actions. Over time, they learn to cope and overcome their substance dependencies to the extent that they can perform full-time jobs and support their dependents. Heightening offender accountability is a key goal of community-based correctional programs, both in the United States and elsewhere, such as Australia and Canada.

The Functions of Community-Based Corrections

Community-based corrections perform the following functions: (1) client monitoring and supervision to ensure program compliance, (2) ensuring public safety, (3) employment assistance, (4) individual and group counseling, (5) educational training and literacy services, (6) networking with other community agencies and businesses, and (7) alleviating jail and prison overcrowding.

Client Monitoring and Supervision to Ensure Program Compliance.   When offenders are sentenced to a community corrections program, it is expected that they will comply with all program conditions. The nature of their supervision is more or less intense in order to ensure program compliance. Victim compensation, restitution, and/or community service are often crucial program components. Public safety is enhanced to the extent that program requirements are enforced by community-based correctional personnel. Measures must be established to ensure that offenders comply with court orders and participate in designated programs. This is especially important for those clients designated as having substance abuse problems and dependencies and are in need of receiving special drugs to aid them in their withdrawal process.

 **BOX 3.1**

CAREER SNAPSHOT

Robert D. Newman
Intensive Supervision Probation Officer Community Corrections Act Project Director

Statistics:

B.A. (psychology), University of Akron; B.A. (sociology), University of Akron; M.C.J. (forensic psychology), Tiffin University.

Background:

My path to the field of probation is a little different from most probation officers. After high school, I planned to take some time off from school before I was talked into taking classes at Cuyahoga Community College. I was working full time and going to school full time but I was sick of the dead-end jobs I held. I really enjoyed my psychology classes and decided to transfer to the University of Akron and pursue my B.A. As part of my electives at Akron, I took several criminology and sociology courses. When it came down to my final semester, my counselor noticed that I was one class short of a second B.A. in sociology, and so I postponed graduation for one more semester and completed an internship with the Summit County Medical Examiner. This allowed me to graduate with separate degrees in sociology and psychology. I was ready for a real job. The only problem was that there were no jobs available.

Throughout my years in college, I worked construction as a subcontractor four days per week. In April 2001 I was involved in a severe car accident that injured my neck and back, and suddenly I could no longer work the 16-hour days my construction job required. As fate would have it, I noticed an advertisement in the local paper for an adult probation officer position. I had no real expectations of landing the job, but the pay was equal to or even a little better than what I had been making and I was desperate, and so I applied. I specifically remember the day of my interview and the day I received the call informing me that I had the job. I was interviewed on September 10, 2001, and was given the job on September 11, 2001. My official start date was October 1, 2001. I have now been with the Medina County Adult Probation Department for over five years and was named Community Corrections Act Project Director in 2005.

Work Experiences:

When I started with Medina County, I was hired as an Intensive Supervised Probation (ISP) officer. The ISP program in Ohio is funded through grants awarded by the Department of Rehabilitation and Corrections. These grants are the result of the Community Corrections Act (CCA), passed in 1979 and revised in 1995. The main objective of the CCA

(continued)

BOX 3.1 (Continued)

was to assist local criminal justice systems in providing local sanctions instead of relying on local jails and/or state prisons. The revision in 1995 greatly expanded the powers of the CCA and the ability of communities to develop new programs to reduce recidivism in addition to reducing the prison/jail populations. Medina County won a grant to start an ISP program shortly after this revision.

My first day on the job, things were a little hectic. I was introduced to everyone in the office and sat through the morning's court docket. In the afternoon I was given a brief overview of my new caseload of offenders and was informed that I would be meeting with most of them in two days. I spent the next day observing another officer interview her probationers, and the day after that, I was given a list and informed that I would be interviewing 25–30 probationers that day. Since that first day, I have become much more comfortable working with the offenders, and in 2005, I was named the Project Director for Medina County's ISP program.

When I first started with Medina County, ISP caseloads were between 60 and 70 offenders per officer. At one point, my caseload topped out at 94. By comparison, state guidelines recommended ISP caseloads consist of 30–35 offenders. We only had two ISP officers and so we were very busy. Since then, the state has revised the standards for all CCA grant programs, including ISP, and we have been able to revamp our ISP program. Our caseloads are still above state guidelines but we are down to 45–55 offenders per ISP officer. This smaller caseload allows us to more closely monitor the high-risk offenders typically placed on ISP. While general supervision officers meet with their probationers once per month, ISP officers start out meeting them once per week. This frequent contact is vital to properly supervising the typical ISP offender. Because ISP is more intense, the offenders we receive are usually violent, judicial release, sexually oriented, and/or repeat offenders who may not perform as well under less scrutiny.

Besides meeting with offenders once each week, my job duties include arresting probation violators, testifying in court proceedings, conducting home and employment visits on probationers, and writing presentence investigations (PSIs). The most enjoyable aspects of my job are the variety of tasks I'm required to do and the fact that no two days are ever alike. Boredom is never a problem in probation. In my short time as a probation officer, I have learned many things from the offenders I supervise. Things like: Tylenol can cause a positive test for cocaine, Hydrocodone contains morphine and cocaine, and two glasses of wine at dinner will cause you to blow a .251 blood alcohol content the following day. These are just some of the hundreds of excuses I get to hear every day from probationers who have tested positive for drugs or violated their probation in one way or another. Of course, none of these statements are true, but the entertainment value really keeps the job interesting. I even had one female claim, "I tested positive for cocaine because there is cocaine residue trapped in the mucous membrane of my nose due to a sinus infection I had when I last used cocaine, more than 1 year ago." She won the award for the most amusing and most disgusting excuse ever.

Another of the more entertaining aspects of probation is the random home visits we conduct on offenders. When an offender is placed on probation, he or she signs a list of conditions that he or she agrees to abide by. One of these conditions is a waiver of their Fourth Amendment rights to search and seizure. This allows us to visit them at home at any time, day or night. When we do these home visits, they are unannounced and we are usually accompanied by a police officer. We are generally looking for any weapons or drugs the offender may have in his or her home. Occasionally, we find more than we were looking for. I have found hardcore pornography hidden in a sex offender's bathroom floor. Not all that unusual except he was 18 and living with his very religious mother who nearly fainted when she saw what we were pulling out of her home. She did more to punish him than I ever could have done. Some of the more bizarre items we have found include sex toys (this is why we wear gloves); used

BOX 3.1 (*Continued*)

condoms; nude pictures; and a pair of very dirty women's underwear in a kitchen cabinet. Upon knocking on the door, I have been greeted by a semi-nude female as well as a couple wrapped in a single bed sheet. I've even found a naked man hiding in the shower of a married female probationer, who was not her husband. Most of the home visits are low-key affairs with no problems, but sometimes, things get a little harried.

In my five years with Medina County, I've been involved in one foot chase, two car/foot chases, and I've had one gun pulled on me. Since our department is not armed, we never do home visits alone. When I had the gun pulled on me, I happened to be with another unarmed probation officer conducting a routine house check. The offender's father refused to allow us into the home and pulled a handgun. We calmly backed away and called for police from a safe distance. Since then I have rarely gone on a home visit without an armed police officer. During the foot chase, we arrived at a defendant's house to arrest him on a probation violation. While his father-in-law met us at the door, he jumped out of a window and fled into a field and eventually hid in a nearby woods. After calling in five sheriff's deputies and a K-9 Unit, we managed to track him down about four miles away. This pursuit lasted more than two hours and covered railroad tracks, woods, a field, and a shallow river, and it ultimately ruined a perfectly good pair of shoes and a suit.

The worst pursuit I've ever been involved with also started with me attempting to serve a probation violation on an offender. He was in his late 40s and lived with his parents. When we arrived, his mother told us he was sleeping in the basement. A sheriff's sergeant and I went downstairs but saw no sign of him. We started back up the stairs when I noticed a small crawlspace behind the bed. I called for the defendant to come out and the door started to open. About that time, I noticed a handgun sitting on a dresser near the bed. I tried to stay between the defendant and the gun, but as soon as he was out of the crawlspace, he ran upstairs and outside. I followed him and managed to grab the tailgate of his truck as he started to speed away. After being dragged for 10–15 feet, I realized what I was doing and let go. Unfortunately, this defendant got away. However, he was picked up during a traffic stop several weeks later and eventually went to prison. While the occasional pursuit can be exciting, safety should always be a probation officer's main concern.

Besides the occasional pursuit, working with offenders is often very frustrating. While you or I may look at the offender's situation and think, "I would do anything I had to in order to avoid going to prison," offenders do not see things the same way. They never stop to think about the consequences of using drugs or skipping court-ordered drug treatment. It takes time before you can view the world through the eyes of an offender. Everything seems to boil down to instant gratification with no thought of the future. Some offenders have to violate probation once and spend some time in jail before they realize they are in a serious situation. Other offenders never get the big picture and repeatedly violate, eventually ending up incarcerated. It was probably a year or 18 months of working with offenders before I could understand them. Once that happened, I was able to notice what set an offender off on the road to violation and the times of year probationers all seemed to violate. Anytime there is a life-altering event (death in the family, loss of a job), offenders are more likely to use drugs or alcohol. The holidays and early summer are notorious times for drug usage. Knowing these things doesn't always help me prevent it from happening, but it does give me the understanding of why offenders violate probation. Figuring out why is the key to reducing my frustration when offenders refuse to help themselves by following the rules of their probation.

Advice to Students:

My best advice to students is to believe in yourself. No one can prevent you from succeeding except you. Figure out what you want out of life and your job and go get it. As far as advice specific to a job in criminal justice:

1. Education is key. Learn as much as you can about the job you want before you apply.

(continued)

BOX 3.1 (Continued)

2. Do an internship in a criminal justice field. It is very beneficial on a resume and can lead to full-time employment.

3. Network. Meet as many people in your desired field as possible. These connections can only help you when it comes time to find employment.

4. Work on your writing and public speaking skills. Speaking in front of a full courtroom and the occasional television camera can be nerve-wracking at first. The better you are to begin with, the more comfortable you will feel. This also helps on job interviews.

5. Never trust offenders. This may seem harsh but it is for your own good. Offenders will use every tactic imaginable to manipulate you. It only takes

one time being burned before you learn your lesson.

6. Never take anything an offender says personally. I've been called many names and dealt with many angry probationers, but I never let it get to me. Always remember that you are doing your job and that is all.

7. Do not take the stress of your job home with you. Sometimes the job can really get to you, dealing with offenders, their families, and even the decisions of some judges, but you must leave it all at the office or you'll go crazy.

8. Most importantly, enjoy the work you do. If you're not happy in your job, then you should probably find another line of work.

Between 1994 and 1995, for example, a sample of 109 Washington State offenders participated in a program known as Moral Recognition Therapy (MRT). The MRT program was a community-based correctional program designed to increase moral reasoning and decrease hedonistic and sensation-seeking tendencies among offender/clients. These offenders were compared with 101 offenders in a control group who did not attend the program. Considerably more program violations occurred among offenders in the control group not exposed to the MRT program. When compared with the control group of offenders, MRT clients exhibited significantly less recidivism, much lower drug usage, a higher employment rate, more stable living conditions with their families, lower numbers of program violations, and significantly fewer rearrests. Greater program compliance under **community-based supervision** has been observed elsewhere, such as Idaho, California, Wyoming, Pennsylvania, and other states.

Ensuring Public Safety.   Community-based corrections is greatly concerned with the matter of public safety. Clients selected for inclusion in these community-based programs are carefully screened so that those likely to pose the most risk or danger to others are excluded. The supervisory safeguards, such as curfew and drug/alcohol abuse checks, are intensive (Addy and Parker, 2006). Offender-clients are selected primarily on the basis of their low-risk profile and the prospect that they will complete their programs successfully.

Employment Assistance.   An important objective of community corrections is to provide offender-clients with job assistance. Many of these clients do not know how to fill out job application forms. Other clients do not know how to interview properly with prospective employers. Minimal assistance from staff of community-based corrections agencies can do much to aid offenders in securing employment and avoiding further trouble with the law (Taylor et al., 2006).

Individual and Group Counseling.   Many offender-clients who become involved in community corrections programs have drug or alcohol dependencies. Often, these offenders have difficulty getting along with others and coping with societal expectations. These offenders have certain social, psychological, and physical needs that must be treated, either through individual or group counseling (Lucken, 1997a). Many community corrections agencies have established such counseling programs for these offenders. In Colorado, for instance, a community-based correctional program was established to furnish offender/clients with various services, including employment assistance, counseling, and networking opportunities with various support groups, such as Alcoholics Anonymous. The average daily program cost per offender was only $6.07 compared with the cost of imprisonment ($52.68 per day per inmate). Furthermore, the community correctional clientele had a recidivism rate of only 23 percent compared with a 65 percent rate of recidivism for probationers and parolees not involved in community programs. In fact, most of the recidivism among community corrections clients related to technical program violations rather than new criminal offenses. This much lower recidivism rate was attributable to the greater variety of services made available to clients through these community-based programs.

Educational Training and Literacy Services.   It is surprising for some citizens to learn that many offenders cannot read or write. Thus, whenever they are released, either on probation or parole, they find it difficult to find and retain good jobs in the workplace. Most jobs require minimal reading and writing skills. A significant proportion of offenders lack these basic skills. In Arizona, for instance, a task force investigated the literacy level of Arizonans and found that over 400,000 of them were functionally illiterate. Another 500,000 did not have a high school diploma. About 60 percent of Arizona's prison inmates had a reading level at about the sixth grade. Seeking to remedy this situation, Arizona implemented L.E.A.R.N. labs, or the Literacy, Education, and Reading Network, to remedy learning and educational deficiencies among its probationers and inmates. One purpose of this program is to raise the educational and reading level of offender-clients so that they will be more competitive in the workplace.

Community-based correctional programming is increasingly offering educational experiences to offenders who are illiterate or do not have reading levels commensurate with the jobs they are seeking to provide for themselves and their families. Greater use is being made of needs instrumentation for the purpose of screening program-eligible offenders and determining which needs they have and how best those needs can be met.

Besides working with offenders with educational deficiencies, community-based corrections also targets offenders with particular disabilities under the Americans with Disabilities Act. Community-based correctional personnel are learning to cater to diverse offender needs, including sex offender counseling, gang affiliation and separation, cultural diversity issues, anger management training, and health care.

Networking with Other Community Agencies and Businesses.   An important function of community corrections is to network with various community agencies and businesses to match offender-clients with needed treatments and services. Community corrections agencies may not have a full range of offender services. Cooperative endeavors are necessary if certain offenders are to receive the type of treatment they need most. Sometimes, the networking performed by community corrections enables offender-clients to obtain vocational and educational training, or perhaps group or individual counseling. Networking with businesses enables community corrections personnel to determine job availability. Thus, community corrections offers a valuable job placement service for those offenders who have difficulty finding work.

Alleviating Jail and Prison Overcrowding.   Community-based corrections alleviates some amount of jail and prison overcrowding. In New York, for instance, it costs about $40,000 per prisoner per year for prison housing. In contrast, community-based offender monitoring, which offers more intensive offender supervision but less than full incarceration, costs the state about $4,500 per prisoner (U.S. Department of Justice, 2006).

SELECTED ISSUES IN COMMUNITY CORRECTIONS

Several important issues relating to community-based correctional programs include: (1) public resistance to locating community programs in communities; (2) punishment and public safety versus offender rehabilitation and reintegration; (3) net-widening; (4) the privatization of community-based corrections agencies; and (5) services delivery.

Public Resistance to Locating Community Programs in Communities (the NIMBY Syndrome: "Not In My Backyard")

Community resistance is found whenever a community plans to establish a rehabilitation center for offenders in particular neighborhoods. Community corrections personnel are interested in locating their facilities near city centers and within walking distance of schools, hospitals, counseling centers, and workplaces. These staff believe that neighborhood environments important to offender therapy necessary for offender rehabilitation and reintegration. Locating community-based services within communities is critical, therefore, since offenders can experience the freedoms and responsibilities associated with their probation and parole programs.

However, some citizens, especially those whose homes are located near these community-based centers and services, believe that they are endangered by the presence of convicted felons roaming about freely near them and their children. Some citizens believe that their property values are adversely affected, and that they will have difficulty selling their property if they decide to move. After all, who wants to live near a home that houses numerous convicted felons? This common community reaction often results from the fact that most persons don't understand what community-based corrections is all about and how it is intended to operate. Community corrections staff refer to it as the **NIMBY syndrome.** NIMBY is an acronym meaning "Not In My Backyard." The NIMBY syndrome means that while many neighborhood residents believe in correctional rehabilitation and that community corrections help offenders to readjust their lives to normal community living, these same persons would prefer that corrections agencies should be located in neighborhoods other than their own (Evans, 2005).

Communities manifest the NIMBY syndrome for several reasons. They may fear crime and expect that close contact with offenders may endanger them. They may have attitudes about and views toward offenders that are unrealistic.

They may be afraid facilities that serve the needs of community offenders will adversely affect the neighborhood and lower property values. Educating the public and increasing their awareness of what these programs are all about and how offenders are supervised or monitored can overcome many of the adverse influences of the NIMBY syndrome. But it is difficult to change community thinking in the short term (Evans, 2005).

Punishment and Public Safety versus Offender Rehabilitation and Reintegration

Public safety is a perennial issue raised whenever community corrections seeks to establish agencies within neighborhoods. There is substantial evidence that the general public has an intense fear of crime, and that this fear of crime has led them to oppose the idea of community corrections programming for dangerous felons. Residents are repelled by the idea that they will have convicted felons roaming freely among them. At the same time, corrections officials cite the need to place certain offenders into communities where they can learn to function normally in law-abiding ways. Offenders need community experience, while community residents need to feel safe. Thus, public safety is often at odds with the **rehabilitative ideal** of community corrections programs. The cost of treating and supervising offenders in their communities is considerably less than incarcerating offenders in jails or prisons. This is a largely undisputed fact. However, there is considerable disagreement over whether permitting some offenders to remain in their communities either unsupervised or supervised is the functional equivalent of punishment. The dilemma is deciding whether it is therapeutic for offenders to remain within their communities where their reintegration and rehabilitation may be maximized, or whether their freedom places law-abiding citizens at risk. Both of these views are valid.

Interestingly, if offender/clients presently or formerly under some type of community-based supervision were to be asked whether they view their programs as punishments, they would probably agree. This is because of the extensive behavioral restrictions and program requirements that they are obligated to comply with as clients. These offenders are constantly being tested for various illegal substances. They are subject to unannounced visits from community-based correctional personnel, including probation and parole officers, at any hour of the day or night. They are monitored in diverse ways, through telephonic or face-to-face checks with employers and work associates. They must submit weekly or monthly reports and proof of employment. They must refrain from any criminal activity. They must not associate with certain types of persons. They cannot possess or use firearms for any reason, even hunting. In short, they are subject to many intrusions that ordinary citizens routinely avoid. But because citizens see these criminals free within their communities, they perceive this freedom as some form of leniency and certainly not punishment.

The dilemma over whether community corrections is a punishment may be an issue of dollars and cents. Community corrections programs seek to preserve public safety by screening prospective clients and including only those most likely to succeed. He believes that imprisonment should be reserved only for the most violent offenders who pose the greatest danger to public safety. Furthermore, the bulk of current jail and prison inmates are largely nonviolent offenders who are capable of becoming safely reintegrated into their communities under some form of monitoring of close supervision. Their remediation perhaps ought to be a key correctional priority.

Many offenders derive numerous rehabilitative benefits from community-based programs. Proof of community-based programming effectiveness is manifested by lower recidivism rates among community corrections clientele, which is also a gauge of supervisory effectiveness of correctional staff. It is also manifested by the increasing number of countries throughout the world who are developing community-based correctional programming for a portion of their criminal populations. Researchers in the United States and elsewhere declare that how offenders are supervised makes a significant difference in their potential for recidivism (Oldfield and Oldfield, 2002). For instance, community-based correctional personnel may supervise their clients as enforcers, treating their clients in ways similar to police officer–offender encounters. Such a supervisory style emphasizes rules and punitiveness. Another supervisory style is prosocial, where problem solving and empathy are key supervisory tactics in relation to offender/clients. Studies of this prosocial approach to offender supervision suggest that offender/clients respond more positively and perceive their supervisors as supportive rather than punitive. The result is that recidivism rates among those supervised in prosocial ways are up to 50 percent less than offenders who are supervised punitively.

Net-Widening

Net-widening occurs whenever offender/clients are included in community programs simply because those programs exist. If the programs did not exist, then these offender/clients would probably be placed on probation. Thus, the mere existence of a community-based correctional program raises questions about who should be included in the program. The clear intent of most community-based correctional programs is to encompass jail- or prison-bound offenders who might benefit more from community treatment rather than incarceration. Decisions about which offenders should be placed in community-based programs and which offenders should be incarcerated are most often made by judges. Judges are influenced by probation officers, who often make sentencing recommendations.

Community-based correctional programs often screen prospective clients and determine their eligibility. Some of the criteria used in the screening process include whether the community agency can provide the right type of assistance for particular offenders; whether certain offenders have undesirable behaviors, habits, or prior records; and whether certain offenders are considered amenable to various treatment strategies. If community corrections officers determine that certain offenders are ineligible for their programs, then they can refuse to admit them.

Most community-based corrections agencies have a strong vested interest in including offenders in their programs who are the most likely to be successful in their compliance with program requirements and program completion. Often, the most nonviolent offenders are selected as clients. They have behavioral histories of compliance with authority. They are considered the best risks. When these offenders are included in community programs and more serious offenders are excluded, a self-serving selection process is set in motion where the programming outcomes for certain clients are highly predictable. Some corrections professionals refer to this process as **creaming,** as in skimming the cream from fresh milk. Applied to those considered eligible for community-based programs, creaming means that only those who show the greatest promise of being successful in their programs will be included in those programs. When these offender/clients eventually succeed and complete their program requirements successfully, program supervisors are not especially surprised. In fact, they may be delighted. This usually means that these same successful offender/clients will leave their programs and be the least likely to reoffend compared with more serious offenders who were barred from community corrections programs initially in the screening process. Thus, low recidivism rates among such offender/clients is quite predictable. Since most community corrections agencies depend on state or federal resources to defray their operating costs, a showing of low recidivism rates is the most direct indication of the program's success as a rehabilitative medium. The program will most likely continue to be funded by one or more government sources. This is a somewhat cynical view, although it is based largely on political reality.

Avoiding net-widening is difficult. As long as community-based corrections agencies serve gatekeeping functions and screen prospective jail- or prison-bound clients for inclusion or exclusion, only the least violent and most compliant offenders will be drawn into these programs. Judicial discretion is also important. Judges have the power to order particular jail- or prison-bound offenders to community programs, where such programs exist. All of these decisions require considering the value of particular types of community-based correctional programming and prospective offender/client needs and characteristics.

Privatization of Community-Based Correctional Agencies

Some proportion of the chronic overcrowding problems of jails and prisons has been alleviated through community-based correctional programs. Through community corrections acts, many communities have established programs to accommodate jail- or prison-bound offenders. Thus, some scarce prison and jail space has been made available for more serious offenders through various types of community programming. However, the public sector has been unable to provide necessary rehabilitative services for large numbers of offenders. Increasingly, the private sector has made a concerted effort to establish itself as a legitimate alternative to public community corrections.

The **privatization** of corrections, or the intrusion of private industry into community programs and the administration of jail and prison systems, is succeeding in furthering the public relations image of corrections generally in the community by suggesting greater control of prisons and offender programs by the private sector (Francis, 2006). In 2005, for example, private corporations supervised at least 100,000 inmates in over 250 prisons, while over 400 privately operated jails and detention facilities accommodated over 90,000 prisoners (U.S. Department of Justice, 2006). During the next decade, the proportion of offenders supervised either institutionally or in the community will multiply greatly as the demand for privately operated correctional services increases.

At least five reasons have been given for why privately run community-based treatment programs would be regarded as a progressive solution to present-day jail and prison overcrowding. These reasons include:

1. Privatization would break the traditional treatment–custody link and the resulting corruption from overconcern with custody and control. A greater incentive would exist to make rehabilitation work if the profit motive were present, since profits are ordinarily related to program effectiveness.
2. Privatization would result in more, not less, accountability if program rehabilitation objectives fail. Systems linking payment or contract renewal to the quality and effectiveness of services provided would make private vendors more accountable and responsive.

3. The infusion of private interests into corrections would promote experimentation with new ideas and strategies for offender treatment and rehabilitation. Under existing management schemes, the routinization of policy is commonplace, with little or no innovativeness.

4. The introduction of business into offender rehabilitation may enhance the political acceptability of correctional treatment. In short, the public relations dimension of corrections would be enhanced and greater community acceptance would ensue.

5. Privatization is consistent with capitalist philosophy, and this basic compatibility would make sense since it offers businesses the chance to make money from corrections.

Major criticisms of privatization of both institutional and community corrections are that (1) private enterprise removes control of offenders from professional corrections personnel; (2) it creates accountability issues for the courts; (3) private enterprise would encourage more prisons and community-based facilities to warehouse larger numbers of offenders because of the profit motive; (4) private enterprise would lead to a downgrading of supervisory quality by reducing the standards by which personnel are trained to monitor dangerous offenders; and (5) it is unconstitutional for private enterprise to sanction state and federal offenders.

Pro-privatization arguments are that (1) private agencies can respond more quickly to problems of financing than legislatures and other political organizations; (2) it can make initial capital investments in facility construction, thus saving the states billions of dollars; (3) private enterprise can decrease the amount of government liability arising from lawsuits brought by clients against program administrators and staff; (4) they can operate more efficiently and at less cost than public agencies; and (5) private enterprise staff are usually drawn from public sector correctional positions where they have already been professionally trained.

The fact is that there is no constitutional prohibition against using private enterprise as an option to publicly operated correctional facilities, either institutionally or within the community. Under the theory of **agency,** the government may direct private corporations to establish different types of correctional facilities, as long as these facilities are in compliance with state and federal guidelines. Thus, the government vests private corporations with the authority to supervise offenders, both juvenile and adult, under different conditions and for varying periods. All privately operated correctional programs are subject to the same mechanisms of accountability, control, and regulation as publicly operated facilities (Lucken, 1997b).

A major difference between private and public correctional facilities is their relative cost effectiveness. Private enterprise is able to compete more vigorously with public facilities in providing a broad range of services to offender/clients. A comparative study of privately and publicly operated correctional organizations in Louisiana, for instance, disclosed that compared with state-operated facilities, private correctional agencies were able to operate in more cost-effective ways; reported fewer critical incidents; provided safer work environments for employees and safer living environments for offenders; judiciously and effectively used inmate disciplinary actions to maintain order; deployed fewer security personnel while achieving higher safety levels; had proportionately more offenders complete their basic education, literacy, and vocational training courses; and equaled or surpassed the number of offender screenings for community corrections placements. Similar findings about privatization have been disclosed for other state jurisdictions, such as Florida, Washington, and Wisconsin (Aos, Roman, and Beckman, 2006). The use of privately operated correctional programs in other countries has also resulted in positive outcomes compared with publicly operated agencies and organizations.

Services Delivery

Delivering the appropriate services for offenders is often a difficult task for community corrections agencies. Assessments of offender-clients are frequently superficial, largely because of understaffing or underfunding. Sometimes, offenders have several types of problems that are difficult to diagnose and treat. Historically, services delivery has been deficient in many community corrections programs, where supervisory chores and offender accountability have been regarded as primary goals.

One way to ensure that services delivery is offender-relevant and appropriate is to individualize the needs of specific offenders. For instance, many persons are placed in probation and parole programs who have undiagnosed mental illnesses or suffer from other mental or physical impairments. Appropriate diagnostic procedures must be in place in order for community corrections personnel to determine each offender's needs. If any particular agency is not equipped to deal with certain offender needs, then the agency should be in a position to network with other community agencies to make sure that the necessary services are provided in a timely manner. For instance, Texas has a Special Needs Parole Program that provides for an early parole review for offenders with special health needs who require 24-hour skilled nursing care and supervision. Although inmates considered for Special Needs Parole are at a higher risk of recidivating and have committed more severe offenses than regular parole cases, the parole board approves them at a higher rate for early release to particular community-based programs where they can obtain necessary mental health services. Improved screening, referral, and review processes increase the program's use without increasing public safety risks. An additional feature of this program is that those offenders with significant medical problems and who represent little or no threat to public safety are detected and diverted from prison to more cost-effective community programs for appropriate treatment (Wasserman and Kaplan, 2006).

Many offender/clients released to community-based correctional programs have substance abuse problems and dependencies (Gahl et al., 2006). Often, substance abuse led to their convictions, and when they are released into the community under some form of supervision, they are unable to refrain from substance abuse without strong intervention and assistance from appropriate community agencies. Many of these offenders pose substantial supervision problems for POs and other supervisors, who must monitor their progress. Any effective community-based treatment and rehabilitation program must be prepared to cope directly or indirectly with substance abusers, since they pose more significant problems for supervisory agencies than any other class of offenders. One innovative idea is to create mental health courts for such persons similar to the establishment of drug courts for drug-dependent offenders (Witt, 2006).

HOME CONFINEMENT PROGRAMS

There are many types of community-based correctional programs. One of the most frequently used programs is home confinement, also known as house arrest or **home incarceration.**

Home Confinement Defined

Home confinement or **house arrest** is a community-based program consisting of confining offenders to their residences for mandatory incarceration during evening hours, curfews, and/or on weekends. Home confinement is a sentence imposed by the court. Offenders may leave their residences for medical reasons or employment. Additionally, they may be required to perform community service or pay victim restitution and/or supervisory fees.

Home confinement is not new. St. Paul the Apostle was detained under house arrest in biblical times. In the 1600s, Galileo, the astronomer, was forced to live out the last eight years of his life under house arrest. In 1917, Czar Nicholas II of Russia was detained under house arrest until his death. And during Czar Nicholas II's reign, Lenin was placed under house arrest for a limited period. St. Louis was the first city in the United States to use home confinement in 1971. St. Louis officials originally limited its use to juvenile offenders, although home confinement became more widespread over the next several decades in many other jurisdictions (Courtright et al., 1997).

The Early Uses of Home Confinement

Florida was the first state to officially use home confinement on a statewide basis. As originally conceived by this Act, Florida's community control house arrest is not an intensive supervision program. Offenders are confined to their own homes, instead of prison, where they are allowed to serve their sentences. The cost of home confinement is only about $10 per day compared with about $50 per day in operating costs for imprisonment (U.S. Department of Justice, 2006). Florida statutes regard community control as a form of intensive supervised custody in the community, including surveillance on weekends and holidays, administered by officers with restricted caseloads. It is an individualized program in which the freedom of an offender is restricted within the community, home, or noninstitutional residential placement and specific sanctions imposed and enforced. Community control officers work irregular hours and at night to help ensure that offenders stay in their homes except while working at paid employment to support themselves and dependents.

In Florida, community controllees or offenders eligible for the house arrest program include low-risk, prison-bound criminals. They are expected to comply with the following program requirements:

1. Contribute from 150 to 200 hours of free labor to various public service projects during periods ranging from six months to one year.
2. Pay a monthly maintenance fee of $30–50 to help defray program operating costs and officer salaries.
3. Compile and maintain daily logs accounting for their activities; these logs are reviewed regularly by officers for accuracy and honesty.

4. Pay restitution to crime victims from a portion of salaries earned through employment.

5. Remain gainfully employed to support themselves and their dependents.

6. Participate in vocational/technical or other educational courses or seminars, which are individualized according to each offender's needs.

7. Observe a nightly curfew and remain confined to their premises during late evening hours and on weekends, with the exception of court-approved absences for health-related reasons or other purposes.

8. Submit to monitoring by officials 28 times per month either at home or at work.

9. Maintain court-required contacts with neighbors, friends, landlords, spouses, teachers, police, and/or creditors (Champion, 2005).

The record of successes through home incarceration in Florida has been impressive. By 2005, 11,500 offenders were under house arrest and intensive supervision by probation officers (U.S. Department of Justice, 2006). There have been relatively few program failures. Most of these failures are persons who have committed technical program violations, such violating curfew.

Under Florida's home confinement program, **community control house arrest,** offenders eligible for home confinement fall into three categories: (1) those found guilty of nonforcible felonies; (2) probationers charged with technical or misdemeanor violations; and (3) parolees charged with technical or misdemeanor violations. The basic conditions for home confinement cases include:

1. Report to home confinement officer at least four times a week, or if employed part time, report daily.

2. Perform at least 140 hours of public service work, without pay, as directed by the home confinement officer.

3. Remain confined to residence except for approved employment, public service work, or other special activities approved by the home confinement officer.

4. Make monthly restitution payments for a specified total amount.

5. Submit to and pay for urinalysis, breathalyzer, or blood specimen tests at any time as requested by the home confinement officer or other professional staff to determine possible use of alcohol, drugs, or other controlled substances.

6. Maintain an hourly account of all activities in a daily log to be submitted to the home confinement officer upon request.

7. Participate in self-improvement programs as determined by the court or home confinement officer.

8. Promptly and truthfully answer all inquiries of the court or home confinement officer, and allow the officer to visit the home, employer, or elsewhere.

9. For sex offenders, the court requires, as a special condition of home confinement, the release of treatment information to the home confinement officer or the court (Florida Advisory Council, 2006).

House arrest programs such as Florida's are increasingly common, especially in those states with prison overcrowding problems. Home confinement programs for both juveniles and adults have been established and are proliferating in both federal and state jurisdictions. Additional conditions are usually imposed, including substance abuse counseling and treatment, victim compensation, and community service. Figure 3.1 shows a generic home confinement agreement.

Some Examples of Home Confinement in Action.   Conventional home confinement systems usually require offenders to wear bracelets or anklets that emit electronic signals. This is electronic monitoring and will be discussed in greater detail in the following section. Offenders must remain in their homes during evening hours, and they are permitted leave from their dwellings only for medical or work-related purposes. The electronic bracelets or anklets worn by home confinement clients are capable of detecting whether clients move out of range of their home monitoring stations, which are semi-permanent fixtures in their dwellings. POs may conduct random visits to one's dwelling at times when the offender must be at home. Voice verification may be effected by telephone. Also, POs may conduct drive-bys with electronic receptors to make an unobtrusive check to see if the offender is on his or her premises at particular times. In some instances, video cameras are installed in one's home and are activated from some central location as another means of verifying the offender's whereabouts. In 2005 there were 22 companies manufacturing and distributing wrist/ankle electronic surveillance products. Targeted for inclusion in home confinement programs are carefully selected nonviolent offenders who have either been removed or diverted from high-cost incarcerative facilities (Champion, 2005).

In another instance, the Dane County Sheriff's Office in Wisconsin uses SpeakerID. SpeakerID permits the sheriff's department to confine certain nonviolent offenders to their homes. The SpeakerID program started by supervising 8–12 offenders, and in 1998 it was supervising 30–35 offenders. Two staff members at the jail run the program and monitor offenders. SpeakerID uses voice verification for persons sentenced to home confinement. These persons are telephoned at random times, and their voices are compared with digitalized recordings previously made of offenders' vocal patterns. Such voice verification is about 97 percent accurate. If SpeakerID does not get a successful match or an answer on the first call, then the number is automatically redialed for authentication. After a maximum of four unsuccessful attempts, the sheriff's office is notified of a possible violation, and a deputy goes to the offender's residence for a face-to-face visit. If the offender is not there, this is grounds for terminating one's program and returning the offender to jail. Eligibility requirements for the home confinement program include being nonviolent, employed, and having a relatively stable family environment. If the offender has formerly been in prison or jail, then prior institutional good conduct is considered together with these other qualifying characteristics.

A third type of home confinement program that is also used in tandem with electronic monitoring has been described. It occurred during October 1992 through October 1993 and was referred to as Western County, since it was located in Western Pennsylvania (Courtright et al., 1997:19). The Western County program primarily targeted DUI or DWI offenders, although other low-risk offenders were subsequently included. First-offenders are mandated to spend 48 hours in jail, second-time offenders spend 30 days in jail, and third-time offenders spend 90 days in jail. In Western County, however, these DWI or DUI offenders were permitted to serve their varying times under a home confinement program. The program was overseen by a probation officer. Those typically sentenced to home confinement were convicted of DUI or DWI, bad checks, retail theft (shoplifting), simple assault, and second-degree burglary. Excluded offenders included those

HOME CONFINEMENT PROGRAM PARTICIPANT AGREEMENT

1. I _____ have been placed in the Home Confinement Program. I agree to comply with all program rules set forth in this agreement, and the instructions of my probation officer. Failure to comply with this Agreement or any instructions of my officer will be considered a violation of my supervision and may result in an adverse action. I agree to call my officer immediately if I have any questions about these rules or if I experience any problems with the monitoring equipment.

2. I will remain at my approved residence at all times, except for employment and other activities approved in advance by my probation or pretrial services officer. Regularly occurring activities are provided for in my written weekly schedule which remains in effect until modified by my officer. I must obtain my officer's advance permission for any special activities (such as doctor's appointments) that are not included in my written schedule.

3. I shall not deviate from my approved schedule except in an emergency. I shall first try to get the permission of my officer. If this is not possible, I must call my officer as soon as I am able to do so. If I call during non-business hours, I will leave a message on my officer's answering machine, including my name, the date, the time, a brief description of the emergency, and my location or destination. I agree to provide proof of the emergency as requested by my officer.

4. While under home confinement supervision, I agree to wear a non-removable ankle bracelet which will be attached by my officer.

5. I agree to provide and maintain a telephone, with modular telephone connectors, at my residence and maintain telephone and electrical service there at my own expense.

6. On the line to which the monitoring equipment is connected, I agree to not have party lines, telephone answering machines, cordless telephones, "call forwarding," "Caller ID," "call waiting," and other devices and services that may interfere with the proper functioning of the electronic monitoring equipment.

7. I agree to allow a monitoring device (receiver/dialer) to be connected to the telephone and the telephone outlet at my residence.

8. I acknowledge receipt of receiver/dialer number _____, and transmitter number _____. I understand that I will be held responsible for damage, other than normal wear, to the equipment. I also understand that if I do not return the equipment, or do not return it in good condition, I may be charged for replacement or the repair of the equipment and I agree to pay these costs. I understand that I may be subject to felony prosecution if I fail to return my monitoring equipment.

9. I agree to not move, disconnect, or tamper with the monitoring device (receiver/dialer).

10. I agree to not remove or tamper with the ankle bracelet (transmitter) except in a life-threatening emergency or with the prior permission of my officer.

11. I agree to allow authorized personnel to inspect and maintain the ankle transmitter and receiver/dialer.

12. I agree to return the receiver/dialer and transmitter to my officer upon demand.

13. I agree that I will not make any changes in the telephone equipment or services at any residence without prior approval of my officer.

14. I agree to provide copies of my monthly telephone bill when requested by my officer.

15. I agree to notify my officer immediately if I lose electrical power at my residence, if I have to remove the ankle bracelet because of an emergency, or if I experience any problems with the monitoring equipment. During non-business hours, I agree to call my officer and leave a message on his/her answering machine including my name, the date, the time, and the nature of my problem. If there is a power problem, I agree that I will call and leave another message when the power is restored. I also agree to notify my officer of any problems with my telephone service as soon as I am able to do so.

16. I agree that I will not attempt to use my telephone when the Receiver/Dialer's "Phone Busy" or "Phone Indicator" light is on.

17. I understand that my officer will use telephone calls and personal visits to monitor my compliance with my approved schedule. If I fail to answer the telephone or door when I am supposed to be at home, my officer will conclude that I am absent, and in violation of my curfew restrictions.

18. I understand that my officer must be able to contact me at work at any time. If I do not have a job with a fixed location (as in construction work) my officer must be able to locate me by calling my employer and promptly obtaining my work location. I also understand that jobs that do not meet these requirements are not permitted while I am under home confinement supervision. I understand that all job changes must be approved in advance by my officer.

19. I agree to refrain from the excessive use of alcohol or any use of controlled substances unless the controlled substance is prescribed by a licensed medical practitioner.

20. I understand that I will be required to undergo periodic, unscheduled urine collection and testing.

21. I agree to comply with all other conditions of my release and supervision as imposed by the court or parole board.

22. I understand and agree that all telephone calls from the monitoring connector to my residence will be tape-recorded by the monitoring contractor.

23. I understand that I may be ordered to pay all or part of the daily cost of my electronic monitoring. If so ordered, I agree, as directed by my officer, to pay _____ per day directly to the monitoring service.

24. Additional Rules (As needed)

I acknowledge that I have received a copy of these rules and that they have been explained to me. I understand that I must comply with these rules until _____, or until otherwise notified by my probation/parole officer. I further understand that any violations of these rules will also constitute a violation of supervision and may cause immediate adverse action.

_____   _____

FIGURE 3.1   Home Confinement Agreement.

previously convicted of violent crimes and sex offenses. Additional selection criteria included mandatory drug/alcohol treatment or counseling; payment of monitoring fees; and compliance with all other program rules and regulations, including curfew and periodic substance abuse checks. Home confinement participants paid a monthly maintenance fee of $25. All participants were required to be employed or actively seek employment if unemployed. The program compliance rate was 84 percent, meaning that only 16 percent of all clients recidivated. Most of these were technical program violations, however. Program revocation occurred in less than 2 percent of all cases. Thus, the program was considered successful and did not place the community at risk (Courtright et al. 1997:21–22).

The Goals of Home Confinement Programs

The goals of home confinement programs include the following:

1. To continue the offender's punishment while permitting the offender to live in his or her dwelling under general or close supervision.
2. To enable offenders to perform jobs in their communities to support themselves and their families.
3. To reduce jail and prison overcrowding.
4. To maximize public safety by ensuring that only the most qualified clients enter home confinement programs and are properly supervised.
5. To reduce the costs of offender supervision.
6. To promote rehabilitation and reintegration by permitting offenders to live under appropriate supervision within their communities.

There are several advantages and disadvantages of home confinement or house arrest. Among the advantages she notes are (1) it is cost effective; (2) it has social benefits; (3) it is responsive to local citizen and offender needs; and (4) it is easily implemented and is timely in view of jail and prison overcrowding. Some of the more important disadvantages of home confinement are (1) house arrest may actually widen the net of social control; (2) it may narrow the net of social control by not being a sufficiently severe sentence; (3) it focuses primarily on offender surveillance; (4) it is intrusive and possibly illegal; (5) race and class bias may enter into participant selection; and (6) it may compromise public safety. Some of these advantages and disadvantages will be addressed at length below as issues concerning home confinement where electronic monitoring is also used.

A Profile of Home Confinement Clients

No precise figures exist for describing home confinement clientele. Unofficial estimates for 2006 show that approximately 120,000 offenders were in home confinement programs and supervised generally by probation departments (U.S. Department of Justice, 2006). An examination of the screening procedures and eligibility requirements of different home confinement programs currently operating among the states suggests that most home confinement clients are nonviolent first-offenders. They tend to have close family ties, are married and live with their spouses, and are employed full time. They do not have drug or alcohol dependencies. Compared with clients in other types of probation and parole programs, home confinement clients tend to have higher amounts of education and vocational skills. They also tend to be older, age 30 or above.

Selected Issues in Home Confinement

Because home confinement means permitting some misdemeanants and felons the opportunity of living in personal dwellings within their communities, this type of programming is not seen by the public as particularly punitive. As a result, several issues have been raised about whether home confinement is a viable punishment option and should be used. These issues include but are not limited to the following: (1) home confinement may not be much of a punishment; (2) whether home confinement is constitutional; (3) public safety versus offender needs for community reintegration; and (4) home confinement may not be much of a crime deterrent.

Home Confinement May not be Much of a Punishment.   The public tends to view offenders confined to their homes as more of a luxury than a punishment. It may even lead some persons to contemplate committing crimes, since they might reason that being confined to one's home isn't that bad of a punishment. However, the experiences of clients who have been confined to their homes for a period of weeks or months suggest that home confinement is very much a punishment.

One reason home confinement is perceived as less than true punishment compared with incarceration in a jail or prison is that the courts do not equate time served at home with time served in prison. In 1990 an Illinois defendant, Ramos, was confined to his parent's home for several weeks under house arrest while awaiting trial for a crime. He was not permitted to leave the premises except to work or receive medical treatment. Later, Ramos was convicted of the crime and asked the court to apply the time he spent at home toward the time he would have to serve in prison. The court denied his request, holding that his home confinement did not amount to custody (*People v. Ramos,* 1990). This decision has been made in many other states at the appellate level, as well as in federal cases where home confinement has been imposed as a condition of probation or parole.

Also, when offenders leave their residences without permission while under home confinement, they are not charged with escaping from prison; rather, they are guilty of a technical program violation. Lubus, a convicted Connecticut offender, was sentenced to house arrest. At some point, he failed to report to his supervising probation officer. The officer claimed this was the equivalent of an "escape" and sought to have him prosecuted as an escapee. The Connecticut Supreme Court disagreed, indicating that unauthorized departures from community residences are not the same as unauthorized departures from halfway houses, mental health facilities and hospitals, and failures to return from furloughs or work release (*State v. Lubus,* 1990). Thus, if the courts are unwilling to consider home confinement to be the equivalent of incarceration in a prison or jail, why should the public feel differently?

Whether Home Confinement is Constitutional.   Some scholars have argued that home confinement is unconstitutional because it involves various warrantless intrusions into one's premises by POs at any time for supervisory purposes. But this argument has no legal merit. State legislatures, the U.S. Congress, and the U.S. Supreme Court determine what is or is not unconstitutional. Thus far, home confinement has not been declared unconstitutional by the U.S. Supreme Court. Home confinement is simply one of several approved community corrections alternatives specified under every state community corrections act. The intent of the act is to provide alternative community punishments in lieu of incarceration in jails or prisons. A reduction in jail and prison inmate populations is sought, and more than a few offenders, particularly the least serious ones, have often been diverted to some type of community corrections punishment. Offenders diverted to community corrections programs should be those who are determined to be in need of more restrictive monitoring or supervision compared with standard probationers or standard parolees.

Perhaps the most compelling argument that overcomes the constitutionality issue is that any sentence of home confinement is strictly voluntary (Rhoades and Venegas, 2006). Judges give offenders a choice—they can accept home confinement and its accompanying conditions and restrictions, or they can go to jail or prison. Any criminal court judge contemplating using home confinement as a punishment for any particular offender must determine whether that offender agrees in writing with the program conditions. The Fourth Amendment issue of illegal search and seizure has also been raised. Some offenders believe that one's residence is a sacred place and that random curfew checks and travel restrictions are unreasonable. If offenders do not wish to enter home confinement programs with those restrictions, then they can choose jail or prison. It is up to them, not the courts. Since those offenders who accept the program conditions waive certain constitutional rights, then the Fourth Amendment issue becomes irrelevant.

In virtually every jurisdiction, the appellate courts have held that there is no fundamental right to receive probation or any other community-based sentence (*Speth v. State,* 1999). Granting probation of any kind is within the discretion of the trial court, and offenders who are sentenced to probation must declare their objections to any probation condition when they are sentenced. If any defendant finds any probation condition objectionable, then the court has the discretion to withdraw the probationary sentence and impose an incarcerative one. Convicted offenders who receive sentences of probation are considered to have waived any issues and rights regarding any conditions imposed on appeal later. In the Alabama case of *Ford v. State* (1999), for instance, Ford was a convicted offender who was sentenced to a prison term, but who was subsequently ordered by the court to serve a term of probation, with conditions, in lieu of incarceration. However, Ford objected to the stringent probationary terms and declared that he would rather serve his time in jail. An Alabama appellate court held that because Ford did not accept the judge's offer of probation, the judge cannot order probation unless Ford indicates that he is willing to accept it. In this case, Ford was sentenced to prison for the duration of his original sentence.

Public Safety versus Offender Needs for Community Reintegration.   In any community corrections program, corrections staff consider public safety to be a primary consideration. This is why eligibility requirements are strict and why such careful screening of potential home confinement candidates occurs. If offenders are first-timers without prior records, and if their conviction offenses are nonviolent, they are considered for inclusion. But the absence of a prior record is no guarantee that an offender will automatically qualify. Predictions are made, usually on the basis of sound criteria, about one's success chances.

There are obvious problems with placing convicted felons in home confinement programs. They have the freedom to leave their dwellings and roam about their communities freely. Only detection by a PO can result in terminating one's program. Home confinement does not control offender behaviors. Rather, it is a less expensive alternative to incarceration, and only the most eligible offenders are given an opportunity to participate in such programs. The therapeutic value of home confinement and avoiding the criminal taint of incarceration are believed essential to an offender's rehabilitation and reintegration. Public safety is enhanced through the sound application of strenuous selection criteria. However, no selection criteria are foolproof. House arrest may be worth it, however, despite the occasional home confinement failures.

Home Confinement May not be Much of a Crime Deterrent.   Does home confinement function as a crime deterrent? No, it isn't supposed to function as a crime deterrent. The primary function of home confinement is to enable POs to maintain a high degree of supervisory control over an offender's whereabouts. No home confinement program can claim that house arrest deters crime from occurring. However, there are several controls that deter those on home confinement programs from violating their program requirements, such as treatment for drug or alcohol abuse and imposing curfews.

ELECTRONIC MONITORING PROGRAMS

Frequently accompanying home confinement is **electronic monitoring** (Tumperi, 2006). Primarily designed for low-risk, petty offenders, particularly misdemeanants and first-offender felons, electronic monitoring is a growing alternative to incarceration in prison or jail. Several manufacturers, such as GOSSlink, BI Incorporated, and Controlec, Inc., produce tamper-resistant wrist and ankle bracelets that emit electronic signals that are often connected to telephone devices and are relayed to central computers in police stations or probation departments.

Electronic Monitoring Defined

Electronic monitoring (EM) is the use of telemetry devices to verify that offenders are at specified locations during particular times. Electronic devices such as

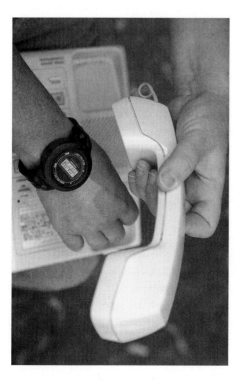

FIGURE 3.2   Electronic wrislet verifies offender location at particular times.
Courtesy of A. Ramey, PhotoEdit

wristlets or anklets are fastened to offenders and must not be removed by them during the course of their sentence. The sanction for tampering with an offender's telemetry device is strong, consisting of a revocation of privileges and return to prison or jail. In 2006 it was reported in a survey of over 90 percent of all U.S. jurisdictions that 135,000 clients were under some form of EM supervision (U.S. Department of Justice, 2006). Government sources confirm that in 2006 there were over 2,500 EM programs operating in the United States, with 145,000 EM units being used. The average cost of EM per offender per day nationally in 2005 was $6.50, with a cost variation ranging from $5 to $18 depending on the jurisdiction. This is a fraction of the expense of maintaining inmates under jail or prison supervision. Incarceration costs averaged between $40–120 per prisoner per day in 2006 as a comparison (U.S. Department of Justice, 2006).

Early Uses of Electronic Monitoring

The first commercial use of EM devices occurred in 1964 as an alternative to incarcerating mental patients and certain parolees. In subsequent years, EM was extended to include monitoring office work, employee testing for security clearances, and many other applications (Tumperi, 2006). The feasibility of using electronic devices to monitor probationers was investigated by various researchers during the 1960s and 1970s, although New Mexico officially sanctioned its use for criminal offenders in 1983.

New Mexico Second Judicial District Judge Jack Love implemented a pilot project in 1983 to electronically monitor persons convicted of drunk driving and various white-collar offenses. The New Mexico Supreme Court examined the program and approved it subject to the voluntary consent and participation of offenders as a condition of their probation and as long as their privacy, dignity, and families were protected. Offenders were required to wear anklets or wristlets that emitted electronic signals that could be intercepted by probation officers conducting surveillance operations.

Following the New Mexico experiment, other jurisdictions commenced using a variety of EM systems for supervising parolees, probationers, inmates of jails and prisons, and pretrial releasees. Both praised and condemned by criminal justice practitioners, EM seems to be the most promising and cost-effective solution to the problems of prison overcrowding and the management of **probation officer caseloads.** Until the advent of EM devices, the idea of confining convicted offenders to their homes as a punishment was simply unworkable, unless a jurisdiction was willing to pay for the continuous monitoring services of a probation officer. In 1983 an electronic device was used to monitor low-risk offenders in New Mexico. In the next few years, experiments with EM devices were tried in Florida, California, and Kentucky.

The use of EM is presently global. Successful EM programs have been reported in England, Canada, and the Netherlands. For instance, a study of EM was conducted in Greater Manchester, Norfolk, and Berkshire, United Kingdom. Approximately 375 offenders were placed on EM with curfew orders in 1996 and investigated for nearly two years. These were compared with 2,400 offenders who were given community service orders and 2,900 offenders who were placed on probation without any type of EM. Recidivism rates were lowest among those who were electronically monitored, with a recidivism rate of only 18 percent (Martinez, 2006). Those most likely to receive EM were convicted of nonviolent offenses, including theft, burglary, and driving without a license.

BOX 3.2

In 2006 Thailand had a population of approximately 65 million. The size of Thailand is comparable to France or Texas. About 90 percent of the nation consists of Thais, with other races/ethnicities making up the remainder. Thailand has a king as well as a legislature and a judicial branch, which consists of the Constitutional Court, the Courts of Justice, and the Administrative Courts. The country is considered a constitutional monarchy and has 76 provinces. Education is compulsory and there is a 98 percent literacy rate, one of the highest literacy rates in the world. With the exception of Bangkok and other major cities, Thailand is mostly rural, noted for its extensive rice production. Although Thailand has a king, this position is largely symbolic, since the Thai legal system is a blend of traditional Thai and Western laws.

Thailand's courts of justice have jurisdiction over all criminal and civil cases. The highest court is the Supreme Court of Justice. There are lesser courts, Courts of Appeals and Courts of the First Instance, which are the equivalent of U.S. state trial courts. The National Assembly of Thailand makes laws, while provincial officials at different levels, including the police and courts, enforce these laws.

In 2005, there were approximately 650,000 crimes reported, with nearly 300,000 defendants. The definition of crime in Thailand is unusual compared with U.S. crime definitions. For instance, Thailand distinguishes between violent crime (e.g., murder, robbery, kidnapping), crimes against the person (e.g., murder, assault, rape), property crimes (e.g., theft, blackmail, possession of stolen goods, vandalism), interesting crimes (e.g., motorcycle theft, car theft, cattle theft, taxi robbery, cheating and fraud), and victimless crimes (e.g., gambling, pornography, prostitution, and narcotics offenses). The largest type of crime committed was victimless crime (over 80 percent of all reported crimes), with narcotics offenses accounting for over 65 percent of all crimes in this category. Gambling was a close second. The most frequent type of "interesting crime" was motorcycle theft, while assaults and murder made up the majority of crimes against the person and violent crimes.

Current laws require Thai police to make arrests with judicial warrants. Arrested persons are entitled to know the charges being filed against them, and a presumption of innocence exists. Detainees have a right to a lawyer present during their questioning. Depending on the offenses alleged, most prisoners are entitled to bail until trial is held. Prosecutors bring cases against criminal defendants. All prosecutors are expected to have law degrees, either from Thailand or another country. They must have passed the exam of the Institute of Legal Education of the Thai Bar Association. They may be no younger than 25 years of age and have good moral conduct. They should be financially secure. They must pass a physical and be mentally stable, to be determined by medical and psychological examinations. Once public prosecutors are in place, they may only be removed from office through death, resignation, retirement, transfer to another governmental appointment, or being expelled or dismissed for cause.

Arrested persons may be held in pretrial detention. Pretrial detention may be permitted for up to 60 days. About 25 percent of those in Thai prisons and jails are pretrial detainees. There is no trial by jury. Judges decide cases based on evidence presented. Two or more judges may sit and decide more complex or serious cases. There is no time limit governing how long trials last. Some trials may last for years. Indigent defendants are entitled to publicly appointed counsel. Maximum penalties include death by lethal injection, as the result of a 2001 law. However, persons under the age of 18 cannot receive the death penalty. All sentences are indeterminate. Furthermore, all death sentences are appealable. The number of executed offenders is not large. Between 1997 and 2004, there

(continued)

BOX 3.2 (Continued)

were 48 executions, with only four executions in 2004. While the death penalty is imposed more frequently than it is applied, this is the result of pardons being granted. These royal pardons permanently set aside death sentences for convicted offenders. In lieu of execution, many offenders will serve their lives in prison.

The prison population grew from 100,900 in 1996 to a high of 245,800 in 2002, and then the prison population systematically declined to 162,000 in 2005. However, correctional officer personpower escalated slightly during this time interval, from 10,113 officers in 1996 to 10,979 officers in 2005. One reason for the substantial decline in the prison population is the passage of the Drug Rehabilitation Act of 1991. This Act involved participating with Thailand's military organization in establishing at least 25 military camps where numerous drug prisoners could be transferred and treated. This program of diverting drug offenders away from prisons to military treatment camps has been slowly implemented, since Thailand has no effective means for identifying those with drug dependencies. Only the most obvious cases have been targeted. The primary objective of these military camps is to provide rehabilitative therapy to those most in need of such drug abuse treatment.

Initially, drug treatment programs were operated by the Department of Corrections in the prisons themselves. But in 1993 the idea of a therapeutic community (TC) was adopted by the prison system, which sought to integrate courts and communities in ways that would further the rehabilitation of drug offenders. TC in prison is a well-patterned treatment program aiming to help drug offenders to quit drug use permanently with the support of peer groups and families. It has been reported that recidivism among drug abusers has significantly declined with the implementation of TC. The Thailand Department of Corrections has established three major treatment programs. These include:

1. Prisoner's Welfare Program. The aims of this program are to (a) treat old-age offenders, (b) treat ill offenders, (c) treat handicapped offenders, and (d) treat foreign prisoners.

2. Rehabilitative Program. The aims of this program are to provide (a) vocational training, (b) formal vocational education, (c) religious services, (d) welfare services, and (3) recreation.

3. Special Rehabilitative Program. The aims of this program are to (a) rehabilitate sex offenders, (b) rehabilitate property offenders, (c) rehabilitate drug dealers, (d) rehabilitate violent offenders, (e) rehabilitate domestic violence offenders, and (f) provide a program for ideals and stability.

Thailand has also established various community corrections programs aimed at offender rehabilitation and reintegration. The aims of these programs, usually operated at the community level, are to provide public protection by keeping offenders in custody or under close supervision and aid in the prevention of recidivism. The responsibilities and mission of community corrections are to:

1. Provide a level of supervision and custody that will offer maximum protection to the community.

2. Rehabilitate convicted offenders in order to achieve a successful adjustment upon their return to the society.

3. Provide various alternative programs for convicted offenders.

4. Provide an institutional environment that is consistent with United Nations standards with minimum rules for the treatment of prisoners and related recommendations to the extent that existing circumstances allow.

5. Reduce overcrowding by encouraging the use of various alternative nonimprisonment programs for offenders who are not suited for institutional confinement.

6. Promote the knowledge of correctional techniques through systematic evaluation and research.

Despite these community correctional goals, a definitive community corrections system has not been fully realized. Much of

BOX 3.2 (Continued)

the rehabilitation and reintegration that occurs takes place within prison systems. In 2004 Thai officials implemented a five-year program to revise and upgrade its Department of Corrections, with the overall goal to become an outstanding agency among Asian countries. The mission of the Department of Corrections is overtly stated as taking offenders into custody and equipping them with professional skills, and rehabilitating them through meaningful and effective activities. Overall goals include helping inmates acquire professional skills, overcome their drug or alcohol addictions, create better citizens among inmates, focus activities in prisons more on learning than on punishment, using better governance or leadership in prison administration and operation, and use innovative treatment philosophies in inmate management and improvement. The 2006 strategic plan involved:

1. Improving management and leadership skills of prison directors.
2. Improving human resource management for the Department of Corrections.
3. Improving the welfare system for officers.
4. Establishing consistent standards for all prisons and correctional institutions.
5. Providing secure custody for high-profile offenders.
6. Renovate prison infrastructure and improve security systems.
7. Seek greater partnerships in corrections and community justice.

Little is known presently about the nature of probation and parole officer jobs. There is a Probation Department funded by the Ministry of Justice. In 2000 a community-based corrections seminar was held in Bangkok as a means of sharing information with probation officers in other cities and countries. Over 97 percent of all offenders who are tried in Thai courts receive suspended sentences. Many of these are placed on probation for various terms. Probation is regarded as an acceptable alternative to incarceration and it reduces significantly the amount of prison overcrowding. Two agencies are responsible for coordinating probationers. One is the Adult Probation Service, which oversees adult probationers. Another responsible for supervising youthful offenders is the Observation and Protection Center. Since 2000 other agencies have been created partly as the result of information-sharing about probation services in other countries. For instance, there is a Rehabilitation Center for Drug Addictions and a Mediation Project in Communities. These particular measures are regarded as preferable to traditional imprisonment.

In order to be eligible for probation, offenders must be facing incarceration of three or fewer years, and the present conviction offense was not committed while the offender was already on probation for another offense. Offenders sentenced to probation will be supervised by probation officers employed by the Thai government as well as volunteer probation officers. Korea has a similar volunteer probation officer program. Volunteer probation officers are recruited from among upstanding Thai community residents and seek to assist offenders in becoming rehabilitated and reintegrated into their communities. A nonprofit Offender's Rehabilitation program was created in 1995 to establish halfway houses for those released on probation or parole. Financial support and other types of assistance are provided.

Regarding the Department of Corrections and prison releases, no precise figures are available about the numbers of inmates who have been released conditionally on parole. Historically inmates have served flat time or whatever prison sentences they have received, although many prisoners have been released short of serving their full sentences through royal pardons and sentence commutations. The discretionary powers of the courts are such that little is known about how many cases are diverted or directed to probation or to any form of community corrections. It is

(continued)

BOX 3.2 (Continued)

clear, however, that one of Thailand's long-term goals is to integrate offender treatment with community stakeholders, including offender families, victims, relatives, the public, private agencies, and correctional institutions.

In 2006, for instance, a celebration was anticipated inasmuch as it was the 60th year of the king's accession to the throne of Thailand. In honor of such a significant event, it was expected that up to 27,700 prisoners who are not anticipated to confront transitional problems back into society would be freed from prisons all over the country. Approximately 300 prisoners would be released who would be expected to have transitional problems. In these latter circumstances, shelter, foster family placement, vocational funding, and other services would be provided these offenders from the government. All released prisoners will receive social service assistance, depending on their needs. The objective of these royal pardons is to enable these released persons to restart their lives as productive citizens of society.

Almost every Thai prison has a pre-release center. These centers offer services for those offenders about to be released back into society. These centers are referred to as temporary prisons and have low security. Most prisoners will receive agricultural training skills and other special services to equip them to become law-abiding. These centers have been operated by Thai prisons for many years.

There have been several clear recommendations concerning the creation of effective community-corrections programming in Thailand in recent years. These recommendations have promoted the idea of greater professionalism among Thai probation officers and volunteer probation officers; an emphasis on caseload reductions among officers to improve their effectiveness in supervising offenders; and making greater use of government resources for mediation programs, offender vocational/educational assistance, and other rehabilitation initiatives.

Sources: Adapted from Thailand Department of Corrections, *Statistics,* February 2006; Bureau of Democracy, Human Rights, and Labor, "Thailand," February 22, 2006; Department of Corrections, "Thailand Department of Corrections," Nonthaburi, Thailand, January 2006; Bureau of East Asian and Public Affairs, "Background Note: Thailand," October 2005; Bureau of Rehabilitation, Department of Corrections, "Death Penalty in Thailand," November 2005.

Similarly successful results have been reported in Canada where numerous offenders have been placed on EM accompanied by various community-based treatments. Offender recidivism was far lower in electronically monitored programs compared with those programs where EM was not used. In the Canadian study, a control sample of inmates receiving treatment without the EM condition was compared with a matched sample of electronically monitored offenders. Rehabilitative services were more effectively delivered under EM conditions.

Types of Electronic Monitoring Systems

There are four general categories of EM equipment. Two of these categories include devices that use telephones at the monitoring location, while the remaining two categories include radio signal-emitting systems where radio signals are received either by portable or stationary units.

Continuous Signaling Devices.   **Continuous signaling devices** use a miniature transmitter strapped to the offender. The transmitter broadcasts an encoded signal that is picked up by a receiver-dialer in the offender's home. The signal is relayed to a central receiver over telephone lines.

Programmed Contact Devices.   **Programmed contact devices** are similar to the continuous signal units, except that a central computer calls at random hours being monitored to verify that offenders are where they are supposed to be. Offenders answer the telephone and their voices are verified by computer.

Cellular Telephone Devices.   Apparatuses are also transmitters worn by offenders. This emits a radio signal, which is received by a local area monitor. Such systems can monitor as many as 25 offenders simultaneously.

Continuous Signaling Transmitters.   **Continuous signaling transmitters** are also worn by the offender and emit a continuous electronic signal. Portable receiver units are used by probation officers so they may drive by an offender's home and verify the offender's presence. Drive-by checks by POs are not only useful for detecting an offender's presence at his or her dwelling, but also whether the offender is attending prescribed counseling sessions or meetings, such as Alcoholics Anonymous or at one's workplace.

EM systems may be either passive or active. In passive systems, offenders have to answer a telephone and speak to a PO or insert the transmitter into the home monitoring device to verify one's presence. Some passive systems emit signals so that if offenders move out of range (150–500 yards away from the home monitoring device), an alarm sounds and the central monitoring center is alerted. Active systems emit electronic signals on a continuous basis, and such signals have their personalized signature and can be tracked by POs or by global positioning system technology. Victims may be protected from offenders as well, since these devices can be programmed to alert POs if offenders enter a specified range around the victim.

Home monitoring systems have the capability of reporting tampering or the loss of electrical power. They have memory retention capability so all saved messages can be restored after power outages. Sufficient battery backup power is provided for up to 48 hours. Mechanisms are waterproofed to protect against pests and infestation. And internal antennae are installed to prevent offender tampering. Electronic transmitters worn on the wrist or ankle are light and manageable, no larger than a pack of cigarettes. They are shockproof and waterproof, thus allowing offenders to bathe or swim without damaging the system's internal components. They are also tamperproof and cannot be removed except by special devices in the possession of POs. Any tampering is easily detected, since these EM devices are often composed of shiny black plastic. POs are equipped with field monitoring devices and can track an offender's whereabouts anywhere in public.

Electronic Monitoring with Home Confinement

In many jurisdictions, EM is used together with home confinement. One of the greatest benefits of using both of these supervisory methods is that client reintegration and rehabilitation are facilitated. A study of 261 probationers and parolees was conducted over several years, and data were compiled from a Family Environment Scale and the Beck Depression Inventory. These are personality assessment devices to measure a client's responsiveness to community-based treatment programming. The most significant factor contributing to an offender's positive reintegration with his or her community was electronically monitored house arrest, which tended to facilitate one's integration and personal improvement. Similar outcomes have been observed in the United States and elsewhere.

Some Examples of Electronic Monitoring in Action.   One particularly good example of the use of electronic monitoring with home confinement occurred in Virginia. In 1989, Chesterfield County received a $34,470 state grant to investigate the feasibility of home confinement as an alternative to imprisonment. The Chesterfield County Jail was suffering from chronic overcrowding with 156 inmates, nearly twice its rated capacity (*Richmond Times-Dispatch,* 1990). The county acquired 30 watch-size monitoring transmitters, activator devices, and computer equipment for a one-year trial period of an EM home incarceration program. In this case, selected inmates were fitted with a black monitoring transmitter, which was attached to their wrists with a black plastic wristband. The wristband is waterproof and the only way it can be removed is by cutting it off. The transmitter fits into a second piece of equipment called the verifier, which also goes home with the inmate. The verifier device plugs into a telephonic device. The verifier is then called at random times during the day by a computer located in the county jail offices. The inmate has 10 seconds to answer the telephone and state his name and time on the receiver. Then he inserts the wrist transmitter into a slot on the verifier. The transmitter sends an electronic tone back to the computer, verifying that the correct monitor has responded to the telephone call. The entire system is fully automated, with the offender's voice recorded and the results of the electronic signal printed out at the jail.

If the wrist monitor fails to activate the verifier or if the inmate doesn't answer the telephone, the computer redials the home in two minutes. If there is no answer, a third call is made. If there is still no answer, a sheriff's deputy visits the offender's home directly to verify his whereabouts. Violating home confinement or removing the electronic device are program violations that can result in probation or parole revocation. Furthermore, offenders pay $5.50 daily to offset the EM costs. Since Chesterfield County uses the devices for jail-bound offenders, there is some relief from jail overcrowding (*Richmond Times-Dispatch,* 1990:100).

In another application of EM, the U.S. Probation Office for the Southern District of Mississippi experimented with EM beginning in 1994 (Champion, 2007). The selection criteria for federal offenders included the following: no history of violence or mental illness and no severe substance abuse history. Subsequently, the federal EM program began to include more serious types of offenders, including substance abusers who tested positive for alcohol or drugs, and irresponsible offenders, who often failed to report, failed to complete community service, or made false statements to their POs. Candidates for EM placement did exhibit good work histories, however, including relatively stable home environments. Increasing numbers of pretrial defendants and post-sentence nonviolent offenders were added to the list of program-eligible clientele. For all clients, an approved daily activity schedule was established, which permitted offenders to be "out of range" for certain periods during the day for work purposes or hospital or counseling visits. Arrangements were made with the EM manufacturer and supplier for daily facsimile reports of offender departures from, and arrivals to, the residence. This high-precision information made it possible to detect minor violations, such as missing one's curfew.

Interestingly, program personnel found that when offender/clients began wearing electronic wristlets or anklets, an "incredible deterrent effect" was observed. The bracelet, which transmitted an electronic signal for reception by a home monitoring unit, served as a constant reminder to offenders to comply with specified program requirements. Face-to-face visits on an irregular basis and at random times further increased offender compliance with program specifications. Some EM clients were also placed in home confinement. The federal EM program exhibited a 92 percent success rate, with only 8 percent of the offenders recidivating (Champion, 2005).

Arguments For and Against Electronic Monitoring

Arguments favoring the use of EM are: (1) EM assists offenders in avoiding criminogenic atmosphere of prisons or jails and helps reintegrate them into their communities; (2) EM permits offenders to retain jobs and support families; (3) EM assists probation officers in their monitoring activities and has potential for easing their caseload responsibilities; (4) EM gives judges and other officials considerable flexibility in sentencing offenders; (5) EM has the potential of reducing recidivism rates more than existing probationary alternatives; (6) EM is potentially useful for decreasing jail and prison populations; (7) EM is more cost effective in relation to incarceration; and (8) EM allows for pretrial release monitoring as well as for special treatment cases such as those who abuse substances, those who are mentally retarded, women who are pregnant, and juveniles.

Arguments against EM include: (1) some potential exists for race, ethnic, or socioeconomic bias by requiring offenders to have telephones or to pay for expensive monitoring equipment and/or fees (ironically, some jurisdictions report that many offenders enjoy better living conditions in jail or prison custody compared with their residences outside of prison); (2) public safety may be compromised through the failure of these programs to guarantee that offenders will go straight and not endanger citizens by committing new offenses while free in the community; (3) EM may be too coercive, and it may be unrealistic for officials to expect full offender compliance with such a stringent system; (4) little consistent information exists about the impact of electronic monitoring on recidivism rates compared with other probationary alternatives; (5) persons frequently selected for participation are persons who probably don't need to be monitored anyway; (6) technological problems exist making electronic monitoring somewhat unreliable; (7) EM may result in widening the net by being prescribed for offenders who otherwise would receive less costly standard probation; (8) EM raises right to privacy, civil liberties, and other constitutional issues such as Fourth Amendment search and seizure concerns; (9) much of the public interprets this option as going easy on offenders and perceives electronic monitoring as a nonpunitive alternative; and (10) the costs of electronic monitoring may be more than published estimates.

A Profile of Electronic Monitoring Clients

It is difficult to articulate specific criteria that are applicable to all electronically monitored clients. Some clients are juveniles, while others are awaiting trial. Many are probationers where electronic monitoring has been specified as a condition of their probation. Others are parolees who are placed under an electronic monitoring program for short periods following their early release.

Some offenders have been convicted of domestic violence–related crime and may require greater supervision than EM provides (Ames and Dunham, 2002). However, electronic monitoring isn't for all offenders. Ordinarily, those considered for electronic monitoring have been charged with or convicted of minor, nonviolent offenses such as property offenders (e.g., burglars, larcenists and thieves, automobile thieves, shoplifters, embezzlers). Prospective clients include those who have no prior records. Some offenders might be nonviolent, but they may be chronic offenders with lengthy criminal histories. Thus, if there is a great likelihood that certain prospective clients might reoffend, then they would be barred from participating in an electronic monitoring program.

Selected Issues in Electronic Monitoring

Invariably, electronic monitoring has generated considerable controversy since its inception in the 1960s. Any attempt to employ electronic means in offender supervision is going to raise one or more issues about the suitability and/or legality of these devices. Electronic monitoring is no exception. Some of the more important issues are described here. The following list is fairly thorough, although not comprehensive: (1) the ethics of electronic monitoring; (2) the constitutionality of electronic monitoring and client rights; (3) punishment versus rehabilitation and reintegration; (4) the public safety issue; (5) deterrence; and (6) privatization and net-widening.

The Ethics of Electronic Monitoring.   One criticism of EM is the potential for the ultimate political control of the public. Is EM ethical? One response is to consider the fundamental purpose or intent of EM. Is EM intentionally designed to snoop on private citizens? No. Is EM intentionally designed to invade one's privacy? No. Is EM intentionally designed to assist POs in verifying an offender's whereabouts? Yes. Is EM capable of detecting program violations in lieu of direct PO supervision? Yes.

Perhaps the ethics of EM becomes more relevant or focused if we theoretically project what the limits of electronic monitoring might be in some future context. Some critics might be justified, therefore, in contending that if we use electronic monitoring for a limited purpose today (e.g., to verify an offender's whereabouts), what other uses might be made of electronic monitoring in future years (e.g., intruding into bedrooms to detect criminal sexual acts or other possible criminal behaviors)? Presently, EM equipment is placed in convenient areas, such as kitchens or living rooms. Video-capable EM equipment is also presently limited to verifying one's identity and whether drug or alcohol program violations have occurred. No one has suggested that cameras be placed in one's bedroom or bathroom to be activated at the whim of an equipment operator. If there is an issue to be raised here, then it would be the reasonableness issue.

One extreme extrapolation of the use of EM has been suggested by Toombs (1995). Given present-day technology and the existence of numerous satellite surveillance systems, it may be possible to surgically implant electronic transponders in offenders. Such transponders could be implanted in ways that would make their removal difficult. Furthermore, any attempt to remove an implanted transponder would trigger an alarm and immediately immobilize the offender. A satellite surveillance system could be significantly less costly than present prison operations. Such a system would permit community-based programs to use EM in the design of individualized treatment programs to maximize various types of assistance for offenders so that they can live acceptably in society. However, there are strong ethical objections to such monitoring methods, that involve physically intrusive procedures such as surgical implants. Less intrusive methods, such as the use of electronic pulse emission by wristlets and anklets worn by offenders and tracked by global positioning satellites, or transmissions of an offender's whereabouts over either telephone lines or wireless networks, even the Internet, are being devised. Preferred EM methods aim toward supervising low-risk offenders who are least likely to reoffend.

The Constitutionality of Electronic Monitoring and Client Rights.   Certain legal issues about EM are presently unresolved, although the constitutionality of EM has never been successfully challenged. Many of the same legal arguments raised regarding the constitutionality of home confinement are also raised about EM. But like home confinement, offenders who are placed in EM programs must agree to abide by all EM program conditions. If any particular offender doesn't want to be placed in an EM program, then the judge can impose incarceration in a jail or prison. The consensual nature of offender participation in such programs undermines virtually all constitutional challenges that might be raised. Perhaps the most compelling constitutional issue relates to whether EM discriminates against particular offenders who do not have permanent dwellings or telephones. However, the range of EM options is such that discrimination is not a factor. Anyone can be outfitted with some type of EM device to suit the circumstance. POs can conduct drive-bys or checks with handheld EM equipment to verify an offender's whereabouts without actually using telephonic equipment.

Punishment versus Rehabilitation and Reintegration.   Another criticism is that home confinement and electronic monitoring are not really punishments at all, because offenders are not assigned to hard time behind jail or prison walls (Batchelder and Pippert, 2002). The average length of time offenders are placed on electronic monitoring is about 80 days. Thus, critics might claim that less than three months is insufficient time to accomplish any significant reintegration or rehabilitation. But the overwhelming evidence supports EM as a rehabilitative and reintegrative tool.

The Public Safety Issue.   Whenever offenders are placed on EM and/or home confinement, they are free to commit new crimes if they wish to do so. They are not incapacitated; therefore, they pose possible risks to public safety. However, the criteria used for selecting offenders as EM clients are very strenuous. For example, the Nevada County Probation Department uses electronic monitoring with home confinement as a means of providing an alternative incarceration site besides jail. Participants are eligible for electronic monitoring if they meet the following criteria:

1. Participants must be assessed as low-risk offenders.
2. Participants must exhibit good conduct while in jail.
3. They must be physically and mentally capable of caring for themselves or be in circumstances where another person can provide their needed care.
4. Participants must have a verifiable local address as well as a telephone and electricity at their home location.
5. They must have no less than 10 days and no more than 90 days to serve in jail.

6. Participants must pay an administrative fee of $10 per day while being monitored.

7. Participants cannot have any holds or warrants from other jurisdictions while on the program.

8. Participants must wear an electronic anklet and have a field monitoring device placed in their home.

9. Participants must have the support and cooperation of family members.

10. Participants must seek and maintain employment while on the program.

11. Participants just participate in any specified rehabilitative programs while on the program.

12. Participants must volunteer to participate in the program.

Although violent felons are generally rejected as potential candidates for community corrections programs such as EM, there are instances where EM has been used to monitor their behaviors. The Georgia Board of Pardons and Paroles used EM on a sample of paroled violent felons, for instance, in 1995. Subsequently, a follow-up assessment of EM was done to determine whether it was an effective deterrent to recidivism. While EM was found to have no direct effect on the likelihood of recommitment to prison or time until failure when relevant demographic and criminal history variables were controlled, it was found that those on EM remained in their communities longer than those not on EM. Specific categories of offenders were also investigated, including sex offenders. Sex offenders on EM were far less likely to return to prison than sex offenders not on EM. While the study results suggested that EM was only incidental to program failure, there was at least some indication that it could be used successfully in future years with additional behavioral controls and supervision (Finn and Muirhead-Steves, 2002).

Deterrence.   Despite the sophistication of our technology, it can be beaten. POs have found that some offenders have installed call forwarding systems so that when the computers dial their telephone numbers automatically, the calls may be forwarded electronically to cell telephones elsewhere. Also, some offenders have devised tape-recorded messages so that electronic voice verifications are deceived about the offender's actual whereabouts. Some offenders may convert their homes into a criminal base of operations, conducting fencing operations, fraud, illegal drug exchanges, and other criminal activity without attracting suspicion from the POs who supervise them. Thus, there is some question as to whether EM deters persons from committing crimes. But we must remember the primary objective of EM: It is not a behavior control mechanism; it is a means of determining an offender's whereabouts at particular times. Thus, although deterrence from criminal activity is desirable, it is not the primary objective of EM.

Privatization and Net-Widening.   EM is susceptible to privatization by outside interests. Companies that manufacture EM equipment and the wristlets and anklets worn by offenders already are involved to a great degree in the implementation and operation of home confinement programs in various jurisdictions. They train probation officers and others in the use of EM equipment, and they offer instruction to police departments and probation agencies on related matters of **offender control**. Thus, it is conceivably a short step to complete involvement by private interests in this growing nonincarcerative alternative.

Another concern is the potential EM has for net-widening. Some officials have said that judges and others may use these options increasingly for larger numbers of offenders who would otherwise be diverted to standard probation involving minimal contact with probation officers. In order for home confinement and EM to be maximally effective at reducing jail and prison overcrowding and not result in the feared net-widening, only jail- or prison-bound offenders should be considered for participation in these programs. EM supervision has interested other countries in recent years, and this supervisory method is growing (Albrecht, 2002).

DAY REPORTING CENTERS

For many furloughees and work/study releasees, community residences or centers are established to facilitate their work or educational placement and assist them in other needs they might have. These are known as **day reporting centers.** Sometimes called invisible jails, day reporting centers are a hybrid of intensive probation supervision, house arrest, and early release. Day reporting is a highly structured, nonresidential program utilizing supervision, sanctions, and services coordinated from a central focus (Champion, 2007). In 2006 there were approximately 350 day reporting centers in the United States. Unofficial estimates from 90 percent of the reporting state and federal jurisdictions surveyed for 2006 indicate that 30,229 offenders were under some form of day reporting center supervision (U.S. Department of Justice, 2006). It is more likely that perhaps as many as 30,000 or more offenders are actually participating in day reporting center programs in the United States presently.

Day reporting centers are conveniently located in the midst of various pre-parole releasees living within the community. These centers handle the daily activities and provide minimum supervision for participating work and study releasees and furloughees. Many of these offender-clients have special conditions associated with their work/study release or furlough programs, such as restitution to victims and payment of program costs and supervisory fees. Also, clients must be checked to determine if they are involved in drug or alcohol abuse. Day reporting centers assist authorities in providing these services and offender monitoring. Another function of day reporting centers is to assist clients in job placement and completing job applications. In some instances, these programs provide some educational and vocational opportunities to prepare them for better-paying jobs.

Several guidelines for operating day reporting centers have been established. These include the following:

1. Sign a contract with participants spelling out expectations about home, work, schooling, financial matters, drug tests, counseling, community service, and restitution.
2. Notify the police department in the offender's hometown.
3. Set a curfew; 9:00 P.M. is frequent.
4. Require an advance copy of the participant's daily itinerary points.
5. Perform spot-checks of the participant's home, job, other itinerary points.
6. Institute proper urinalysis procedures—this is crucial; twice a week is typical.

7. Schedule telephone checks more heavily on Thursday, Friday, and Saturday nights.

8. Establish services—addiction education, parenting, and transition skills are popular topics (Schmitz, Wassenberg, and Patterson, 2000).

Day reporting center clients should have the following characteristics: (1) good candidates for day reporting centers include those convicted of drug offenses, larceny, driving while intoxicated, breaking and entering of commercial buildings, and similar charges (Massachusetts excludes sex offenders and, for the most part, violent offenders); (2) offenders without an identified victim; (3) those with a home to go to (check); and (4) typically, inmates within six months of release (Champion, 2005).

In a study of juveniles assigned to day reporting programs in several Illinois counties, day reporting was supplemented with drug treatment, individual and group counseling, education, life skills courses, and Moral Recognition Therapy. The programs were highly successful in modifying criminal and substance-abusing behaviors of participating juveniles (Schmitz et al., 2000). Reasons given for the positive results were that day reporting maximized family involvement, school enrollment, and employment. Day reporting generally appears to be a successful intervention, particularly where prospective clients are carefully screened, supervised, and given appropriate treatments or therapies.

An Example of a Day Reporting Center in Action

Liz Marie Marciniak (2000) has provided a detailed description of a day reporting center established in southeastern North Carolina as the result of monies supplied through the 1994 North Carolina Structured Sentencing Act. In North Carolina, day reporting center programs are a special condition of probation. That is, judges may sentence offenders to probation with the special condition that they attend day reporting centers and participate in prescribed programming. Marciniak obtained a sample of 1,026 cases where day reporting had been included in probationary sentences as a special condition. The North Carolina Day Reporting Center program was set up as follows:

1. A four-phase program lasting 12 months.

2. Offenders must check in between one to six times per week, depending on the special conditions of their probation programs.

3. Clients must be employed or engaged in a concentrated job search while in the program.

4. Day reporting center clientele assess offenders for substance abuse problems, educational/vocational courses, and mental health needs, and appropriate referrals are made to other community agencies or organizations.

5. The day reporting center offers GED classes, literacy training, adult basic skills, parenting, Alcoholics Anonymous, Narcotics Anonymous, drug education, and individual counseling.

6. All offenders must develop and submit daily itineraries to their case managers.

7. All offenders must submit to random drug tests at the center.

8. The center operates on a three-strikes system, so that once a client accrues three strikes, he or she is terminated from the program (strikes include missed or late appointments, swearing, assaulting a case manager, positive drug screens, and technical or legal violations of one's probation conditions).

9. All clients are under intensive supervised probation.

10. All clients must observe a curfew from 7:00 P.M. to 7:00 A.M.

11. All clients must have contact with their probation officer five times per week.

12. All clients must submit to warrantless searches of their residences.

13. All clients must submit to random drug tests at their residences.

14. All clients must perform community service as specified in their probation orders.

15. All clients must work or attend school.

About half of all offenders supervised by the day reporting program were sentenced to the program by a judge. The other half were sent to the program as a way of intensifying their regular probation programs, usually for committing technical program violations. Marciniak concluded as the result of her study that those who participated in the day reporting program had many rehabilitative advantages compared with other probationers not involved in the program. One interesting result of Marciniak's research about day reporting centers was that the clients did not differ in their recidivism rates compared with other probationers not involved in day reporting. However, she observed that individual clients who did participate in day reporting were able to earn their GED degrees, have substance abuse counseling, take literacy courses, and take anger management classes. Thus, recidivism rate comparisons, at least in Marciniak's view, do not give us a full and accurate portrayal of the benefits of day reporting programs for involved clients.

SUMMARY

Community corrections refers to any community-based correctional program designed to supervise convicted offenders in lieu of incarceration, including payment of fines, victim compensation and restitution, and community service. Community corrections involves any type of intermediate punishment, ranging somewhere between standard probation and incarceration. Such programs involve halfway houses, day reporting centers, work release, study release, furloughs, home confinement, electronic monitoring, and intensive supervised probation. These community-based programs are located in neighborhoods and provide a rehabilitative and reintegrative milieu for offender-clients. These facilities also function as a continuation of punishment.

Community corrections are established largely through community corrections acts. These acts fund service agencies at the local level and are intended to divert jail- or prison-bound offenders. These community-based corrections programs attempt to facilitate offender reintegration into society, offender rehabilitation, heighten offender accountability, and provide a range of nonincarcerative punishments. Functions of community corrections are to monitor and supervise offender-clients to ensure program compliance (e.g., victim compensation, restitution, community service orders); ensure public safety; offer job placement and employment assistance; provide individual and group counseling; provide educational training and literacy services; network with other agencies to maximize services to offender-clients; and to alleviate jail and prison overcrowding.

Major issues of community corrections concern the controversy of locating community corrections programs within communities, thereby posing a potential risk to citizens. Some persons believe that community corrections is not punishment at all. There is a struggle between meeting offender needs with reintegrative programs and ensuring public safety. Possible net-widening may occur, simply because community programs have been established. Growing privatization of community corrections suggests that large-scale use of incarceration as a punishment may occur as privatization of these programs expands. Many community corrections programs are underequipped and understaffed. Many staff of these agencies have not been trained adequately to deal with diverse populations of offenders. Special-needs offenders pose unique problems that are sometimes difficult to resolve. The growth of community corrections as well as the rise of professionalization of staff suggests that these programs are becoming more effective at meeting the needs of growing numbers of offender-clients.

Home confinement is an intermediate punishment consisting of confining offenders to their residences for mandatory incarceration during evening hours, curfews, and/or on weekends. Home confinement as a punishment was first used in St. Louis, Missouri, in 1971. It was adopted statewide in Florida in 1983. Offenders on home confinement may be assigned to community service, may be required to pay maintenance fees of the program, and may be required to pay restitution to victims. Other requirements may include participation in vocational/educational courses, observance of curfews, submit to random drug and alcohol checks, and maintain other court-required contacts. The goals of home confinement programs are to reduce jail and prison overcrowding, reduce offender costs, foster rehabilitation and reintegration among offender-clients, ensure public safety, and to continue one's punishment under nonincarcerative conditions.

Often used in conjunction with home confinement is electronic monitoring. Electronic monitoring is the use of telemetry devices to verify that offenders are at specified locations during particular times. Electronic monitoring was first used in New Mexico to monitor the behaviors of those convicted of drunk driving. Various forms of electronic monitoring include continuous signaling devices, programmed contact devices, cellular telephone devices, and continuous signal transmitters. Most persons on electronic monitoring pose little or no risk to public safety. They are often first-offenders and are nonviolent. Many of the same issues that are associated with home confinement also apply to electronic monitoring. These issues pertain to the ethics of electronic monitoring, certain possible constitutional rights violations, the punishment versus rehabilitation or reintegration issue, the concern for public safety, the crime deterrence issue, and the issue of privatization and possible net-widening.

Day reporting centers are also used as mechanisms for supervising low-risk and nonviolent offenders. Support services are made available through such programs, and most research about the successfulness of day reporting clientele has been favorable. Day reporting is regarded as an important rehabilitative and reintegrative tool when clients are properly screened and supervised, and when they receive appropriate therapies and treatments.

QUESTIONS FOR REVIEW

1. What is meant by community-based corrections?

2. What are the major functions of community corrections programs?

3. In what sense is there a conflict between ensuring public safety and providing a community environment to promote offender therapy and reintegration? Discuss.

4. What is the general philosophy of community corrections? Based on what you have read up to now, is this philosophy consistent with the "get tough" movement? Why or why not? Explain.

5. What are some of the major criticisms of electronic monitoring?

6. How is it possible for net-widening to occur under electronic monitoring? Explain.

7. What are the major constitutional issues raised about the use of electronic monitoring? How does one's voluntariness to become involved in electronic monitoring programs influence the credibility of these constitutional issues?

8. What are some of the pro's and con's associated with electronic monitoring?

9. What are some of the general characteristics of electronic monitoring clients? Why is it difficult to profile these offenders adequately? Explain.

10. Discuss five major issues related to electronic monitoring.

SUGGESTED READINGS

Erez, Edna, Peter R. Ibarra, and Norman A Lurie (2004). "Electronic Monitoring of Domestic Violence Cases: A Study of Two Bilateral Programs." *Federal Probation* **68**:15–20.

Gable, Ralph Kirkland and Robert S. Gable (2005). "Electronic Monitoring: Positive Intervention Strategies." *Federal Probation* **69**:21–25.

Gelb, Adam (2006). "COMPSTAT for Community Corrections." *APPA Perspectives* **30**:30–33.

Moore, S. and P. Scourfield (2005). "Eliminating the Visible: Exploring the Community Response to Anti-Social Behavior." *Crime Prevention and Community Safety: An International Journal* **7**:51–61.

Padgett, Kathy G., William D. Bales, and Thomas G. Blomberg (2006). "Under Surveillance: An Empirical Test of the Effectiveness and Consequences of Electronic Monitoring." *Criminology and Public Policy* **5**:61–92.

Renzema, Marc and Evan Mayo-Wilson (2005). "Can Electronic Monitoring Reduce Crime for Moderate to High-Risk Offenders?" *Journal of Experimental Criminology* **1**:215–237.

INTERNET CONNECTIONS

American Community Corrections Institute
http://www.accilifeskills.com/

American Correctional Association: Past, Present, and Future
http://www.corrections.com/aca/pastpresentfuture/history.htm

American Probation and Parole Association
http://www.appa-net.org

BI Incorporated
http://www.bi.com

Center for Community Corrections
http://www.communitycorrectionsworks.org/

Center for Restorative Justice
http://www.ssw.che/.umn.edu/rjp

Citizen Probation
http://www.citizenprobation.com/

Fairfax County Pre-Release Center
*http://www.g2.to/fairfax/departments/
prc/prc*

Federal Prison Consultants
http://www.federalprisonconsultants.com

Home Confinement Program
*http://thwp.uscourts.gov/
homeconfine-ment.html*

International Community Corrections
Association
http://www.iccaweb.org

National Institute on Drug Abuse
http://www.nida.nih.gov

New York Corrections History Society
http://www.correctionshistory.org

New York State Probation Officer's
Association
http://www.nyspoa.com/

Probation agency links
http://www.cppca.org/link

Probation and parole sites
http://www.angelfire.com/md/ribit/states

<table>
| CHAPTER 4 | *Sentencing and the Presentence Investigation Report: Background, Preparation, and Functions* |
</table>

CHAPTER 4 | *Sentencing and the Presentence Investigation Report: Background, Preparation, and Functions*

Chapter Outline

Chapter Objectives

As the result of reading this chapter, the following objectives will be realized:

1. Describing presentence investigation reports and other relevant documents used by judges in imposing sentences and evaluating offender risk.
2. Examining presentence investigation reports and their contents.
3. Illustrating presentence investigation reports prepared by state and federal agencies.
4. Explaining and describing the purposes of sentencing hearings.
5. Examining the views of judges concerning sentencing felons.
6. Describing attempts to predict dangerousness and public risk of those placed on probation.
7. Describing the decision to place convicted offenders into probation programs and highlighting sentencing trends.
8. Describing aggravating and mitigating circumstances as sentencing considerations.

• *Cox was a parole-eligible New York inmate who was denied parole on various grounds, some of which were contained in a presentence investigation report that had been prepared at the time of his sentencing and incarceration. The conviction offense was aggravated assault, robbery, and murder, and Cox, together with a co-defendant, was identified as a shooter during the crime's perpetration. When the New York parole board rejected Cox's parole bid, he appealed, alleging that the contents of his presentence investigation report were inaccurate and prejudicial. Cox claimed that a surviving victim recanted her testimony that Cox was a shooter, and that a dying victim stated that Cox's co-defendant was the shooter, not Cox. Thus, information contained in the presentence investigation report was allegedly inaccurate, and that it was irrational of the parole board to rely on the presentence investigation report in support of his parole denial. A judge granted Cox an appeal and a New York Appellate Court heard the case. The court rejected Cox's arguments and declared that Cox had been given time to challenge the accuracy of his presentence investigation report at the time of his sentencing but did not do so. The court said that Cox's production of favorable testimony, even though contradicted by other evidence on record, does not provide a basis for departing from the rule that a defendant is not permitted to collaterally attack a presentence report. Having failed to timely challenge the accuracy of the presentence reports' description of the events underlying the crimes of which he was convicted, Cox cannot now argue that the parole board's statutorily mandated consideration of that report was irrational. [Cox v. N.Y. State Division of Parole, 783 N.Y.S.2d 410 9 (N.Y.Sup.App.Div.Oct.) (2004)].*

• *Hannis was convicted of four counts of possession of cocaine. Hannis received an eight-year sentence for Count I, and four two-year sentences for Counts II, III, and IV. Counts II, III, and IV were to run concurrently with each other but consecutively with Count I. After serving less than two years for Counts II, III, and IV, Hannis was paroled but his parole was almost immediately revoked. The Indiana parole board declared that Hannis must serve the unserved portion of his original eight-year sentence for Count I. Hannis appealed, contending that the consecutive nature of the sentences was improper. However, an appeals court disagreed with Hannis. The court declared that whenever a defendant is released either to parole or probation, he is not completely discharged from his sentence. Rather, the term continues to run. In this case, while Hannis was granted parole for Counts II, III, and IV for cocaine possession, he was still expected to serve the remainder of the eight-year sentence for Count I. There is nothing improper or unconstitutional about consecutive sentences imposed by the court [Hannis v. Deuth, 816 N.E.2d*

872 (Ind.App.Oct.) (2004)]. Such consecutive sentences have been imposed and upheld in virtually every other state court, including federal courts. [United States v. Deutsch, *403 F.3d 915 (U.S.7thCir.April) (2005)].*

• *Nathan Washington, age 27, and R.J. Brooks, age 22, robbed several convenience stores in Maryland. Video footage from one of the convenience stores identified Washington and authorities apprehended him shortly thereafter. Washington cooperated with investigators and gave them the name of Brooks, who was subsequently apprehended in Georgia, where he had fled. He was extradited to Maryland where both defendants stood trial for aggravated robbery of six convenience stores. On one occasion, a store clerk was shot in the shoulder by one of the defendants, allegedly Washington. However, Washington claimed that Brooks had been the shooter and confessed to participating in the robberies. Washington and Brooks were tried separately, with Washington testifying against Brooks. Both defendants were found guilty. In a plea bargain agreement, Washington received a five-year term, while Brooks received a 25-year-to-life term for his role in the robberies at the conclusion of his trial. Were these widely disparate sentences fair, since both men had participated equally in the multiple robberies?* [Adapted from the Associated Press, "Robbers Sentenced in Convenience Store Crime Spree," May 15, 2006].

• *Ameline was a convicted federal offender who was sentenced according to the U.S. sentencing guidelines. The guidelines provide punishment ranges expressed in months and are closely associated with one's prior criminal history and the base offense level associated with the conviction offense(s). At the time of Ameline's sentencing, a federal probation officer submitted a pre-sentence investigation report to the court, and the report was used to fix Ameline's base offense level in determining how many months he must serve. In a timely manner, Ameline disputed certain information contained in the report as inaccurate, false, and misleading, and thus the report was unreliable and should not be used in his sentencing. However, the district court judge rejected Ameline's claim, thus treating the factual statements made in the report as presumptively accurate. Furthermore, the court declared that Ameline must bear the burden of proving the inaccuracy of any statement contained in the pre-sentence investigation report. Ameline appealed and the Ninth Circuit Court of Appeals heard his case. The court set Ameline's sentence aside, declaring that although the pre-sentence investigation report is essential to the sentencing process, there is nothing sacrosanct about the information contained in the report. In the present case, Ameline raised specific objections to certain facts stated in the report; he raised these objections in a timely fashion; and the government bore the burden to produce reliable evidence to establish the factual basis for the court's base level offense determination.* [United States v. Ameline, *400 F.3d 646 (U.S.9thCir.Feb.) (2005)].*

INTRODUCTION

Decisions by judges about the types of sentences to be imposed are not always clear-cut. Every trial is different from the next. Sentencing offenders is not as easy as it appears at first glance. This chapter is about the sentencing process. Sentencing is a major concern of those who advocate justice reforms. The federal government and most states have passed new sentencing legislation in response to criticisms that present sentencing practices that are discriminatory according to gender, race or ethnic background, and/or socioeconomic status. Four different types of sentencing schemes are described, including indeterminate, determinate, presumptive or guidelines-based, and mandatory sentencing. Several important sentencing issues are examined.

In most major felony cases and in some minor misdemeanor cases, judges request probation officers to prepare reports about convicted offenders who are about to be sentenced. These reports are called **pre-sentence investigation reports,** or **PSIs.** These PSIs are described, including their functions, contents, and preparation. Probation officers have many duties and responsibilities. Among these responsibilities is a duty to the court to conduct investigations into the backgrounds of convicted offenders and determine relevant information about them. This information is eventually delivered to judges in a report that becomes useful in determining the most appropriate sentence. Besides the probation officer's observations, factual information is acquired about an offender's family, educational background, and family relations. If there are persons who have been victimized by the offender, sometimes PSIs will contain **victim impact statements** to set forth the nature of injuries or damage sustained. These statements are helpful to judges when considering if there are any circumstances that might warrant harsher penalties. Sometimes PSIs are privately prepared. Additionally, they may contain statements from offenders about their version of events. All of this material is described and explained.

The next section of the chapter describes the sentencing hearing. An important part of the sentencing hearing is the opportunity for judges to weigh any aggravating or mitigating circumstances that might heighten or lessen the severity of one's sentence. Both sides speak out on behalf of or against the convicted offender in order to persuade the judge to be lenient or severe in the sentence imposed. Both state and federal jurisdictions have identified specific factors that are considered either aggravating or mitigating. These factors are statutory and must be considered by the sentencing authority. Several of these factors are listed and described. Whenever PSI reports are prepared for the court, it is the probation officer's responsibility to identify both aggravating and mitigating circumstances for judges and include them in their PSI reports. The chapter concludes with a discussion of the changing responsibilities of probation officers resulting from various sentencing reforms.

THE SENTENCING PROCESS: TYPES OF SENTENCING SYSTEMS AND SENTENCING ISSUES

Functions of Sentencing

The **Sentencing Reform Act of 1984** restated a number of sentencing objectives that have guided sentencing judges in their leniency or harshness toward convicted defendants. Some of these objectives have been made explicit by various states and local jurisdictions in past years, while others have been implicitly incorporated into prevailing sentencing guidelines. Some of the more important functions of sentencing are (1) to promote respect for the law; (2) to reflect the seriousness of the offense; (3) to provide just punishment for the offense; (4) to deter the defendant from future criminal conduct; (5) to protect the public from the convicted offender; and (6) to provide the convicted offender with educational and/or vocational training or other rehabilitative assistance. The purposes of sentencing include punishment or retribution, deterrence, custodial monitoring or incapacitation, and rehabilitation.

To Promote Respect for the Law.   When offenders are sentenced, judges send a message to the criminal community. If the sentence is too lenient, then the message is that offending will not be punished harshly. Therefore, many offenders may engage in further criminal conduct believing that even if they are subsequently apprehended, they will not be punished severely. Most judges attempt to impose sentences that are fair or equitable. They may use legislated standards of punishment, such as fines and prescribed terms of incarceration. Or they may impose less stringent sentences than the maximums prescribed by law. Their ultimate aim is to promote respect for the law. Their intended message is that if the law is violated, violators will be sanctioned. Ideally, this view promotes respect for the law and functions as a deterrent to would-be criminals.

To Reflect the Seriousness of the Offense.   One objective of sentencing is to match the sentence with the seriousness of the offense. More serious crimes deserve harsher punishments. Violent criminals are usually punished more severely than property offenders, because violent crimes often result in serious bodily injury or death. Property can be replaced while life cannot. Thus, punishments should be proportional to the seriousness of the crime. Some observers believe, however, that regardless of the punishment, no sanction is a definite deterrent to future offending. Nevertheless, most judges tend to impose sentences that reflect a crime's seriousness. Thus, the more serious the offense, the harsher the penalty.

To Provide Just Punishment for the Offense.   In recent years, sentencing policies in most jurisdictions in the United States have shifted to reflect the **justice model,** which is a legitimization of the power of the state to administer sanctions. The justice model emphasizes punishment as a primary objective of sentencing, an abolition of parole, an abandonment of the rehabilitative ideal, and determinate sentencing.

To Deter Future Criminal Conduct.   Not only is sentencing designed as a punishment to fit the crime, but it is also designed to function as a deterrent to future criminal offending. At least two major actions have been designed to equate offense seriousness with harsher penalties. The most significant legislation has been the establishment of habitual offender or repeat offender laws, whereby those convicted of three or more felonies are sentenced to life imprisonment. California has a "three strikes and you're out" law where repeat offenders are sentenced to life-without-parole terms. This get-tough action was designed to deter violent recidivists, such as robbers and murderers. The thinking is that if repeat violent offenders have not learned their lesson by the time they are convicted of their third violent offense, then they should be locked up permanently.

To Protect the Public from Convicted Offenders.   Incarcerating convicted offenders is the most direct way of protecting the public from them. If they are locked up, they cannot perpetrate crimes against citizens. Longer sentences generally mean longer periods where criminals cannot victimize others. Some persons believe that all criminals should be locked up for some period of time, in order to insulate a vulnerable public from their criminal activities.

To Provide the Convicted Offender with Educational and Vocational Training and/or Other Rehabilitative Assistance.   This is the rehabilitative function of sentencing. Rehabilitation has always been a fundamental goal of sentencing. A prevailing belief is that some attempt should be made to reform criminals while they are incarcerated. We should not merely warehouse offenders. Rather, educational and vocational programs should be offered in order to help those who are interested in helping themselves. It is better to provide some services for those who will use them productively rather than to withhold all rehabilitative services because of those who will never be rehabilitated.

Types of Sentencing

During the last several decades, sentencing practices in most states have undergone transformation. There is disagreement about the number and types of sentencing systems currently used by the states. Furthermore, new sentencing schemes continue to be proposed in contrast to existing ones. The following types of sentencing schemes are used in most jurisdictions: (1) indeterminate sentencing; (2) determinate sentencing; (3) mandatory sentencing; and (4) presumptive sentencing.

Indeterminate Sentencing.   The most frequently used sentencing for many years was **indeterminate sentencing.** Indeterminate sentencing occurs where the court sets either explicit (according to statute) or implicit upper and lower limits on the amount of time to be served by the offender, and where the actual release date from prison is determined by a parole board. The judge may sentence an offender to "one to ten years," or "not more than five years," and a parole board determines when the offender may be released within the limits of those time intervals. In the "one to ten year" scenario, an inmate may be released early by a parole board after serving at least one year of the sentence. The parole board may release the inmate after two or three years. Early release is often based on an inmate's institutional behavior. Good behavior is rewarded by early release, while bad conduct may result in an inmate having to serve the entire 10-year sentence. At the end of the 10-year sentence, however, the jurisdiction must release the inmate since all of the sentence will have been served.

Determinate Sentencing.   **Determinate sentencing** is a fixed term of incarceration that must be served in full, less any good time earned while in prison. **Good time** is the reduction in the amount of time incarcerated amounting to a certain number of days per month for each month served. If inmates obey the rules and stay out of trouble, they accumulate good time credit, which accelerates their release from incarceration. In states using determinate sentencing, parole boards have no discretion in determining an inmate's early release (Florida Department of Corrections, 2006). In 2005 there were 26 states that used determinate sentencing. A total of 35 states used both indeterminate and determinate sentencing in 2005 (U.S. Department of Justice, 2006).

Three types of good time credit can be accumulated by inmates to influence their early release chances. These are (1) **statutory good time,** where inmates acquire good time by serving time without problems or incidents; (2) **earned good time,** where inmates acquire good time by good behavior, participation in education or self-improvement programs and work programs; and (3) **meritorious good time,** where good-time credit is earned by exceptional act or service. Inmates may earn all three types of good time during their imprisonment. For example, Nebraska authorizes statutory good time of 7.5 days per month, up to one-half maximum term reduction; earned days: 7.5 days per month served; total of 15 days per month per 30 days served. In North Dakota, 5 days of statutory good time are allowed per month; up to 2 additional days per month may be granted for extraordinary acts by inmates; 5 days per month of earned good time (given for performance at work, school, or treatment programs; all must comply to earn good time; all inmates are given the highest possible amount of good time to be earned upon entrance; if they become noncompliant with programming, they receive an "incident report" (write-up), and the Adjustment Committee sanctions loss of good time.

Several variations on good-time accumulation are as follows. New Hampshire adds 150 days to one's minimum sentence; these days are reduced by earning 12.5 days per month for exemplary conduct; failure to earn this good time means inmates must serve additional time beyond minimum sentence. In Ohio, one day of statutory good time per month up to a total sentence reduction of 3 percent may be accumulated, while one day per month of earned good time can be accumulated. The Federal Bureau of Prisons permits up to 54 days per year of statutory good time. Actually, 54 days a year is approximately 15 percent of one's sentence. This fits the federal sentencing model where offenders are expected to serve at least 85 percent of their sentences before becoming eligible for parole. The federal government has encouraged individual states to adopt **truth-in-sentencing provisions** whereby incarcerated offenders must serve most of their original sentences before being considered eligible for parole. Various states have adopted these truth-in-sentencing provisions in their sentencing schemes in exchange for federal grant monies for correctional improvements.

Presumptive Sentencing. Presumptive or **guidelines-based sentencing** is a specific sentence, usually expressed as a range of months, for each and every offense or offense class. The sentence must be imposed in all unexceptional cases, but when there are mitigating or aggravating circumstances, judges are permitted some latitude in shortening or lengthening sentences within specific boundaries. An example of the sentencing grid used by the federal government with a guidelines-based or presumptive sentencing scheme is the **U.S. sentencing guidelines grid** shown in Figure 4.1. States, such as Minnesota, have also used these grids with different variations on punishment ranges and crime definitions. Across the top of Figure 4.1 are criminal history categories ranging from I to VI. These are from least to worst in terms of numbers of points associated with one's criminal history. The greater the criminal history, the greater the numbers of points. Someone who is a first-offender would be in category I, for instance. A repeat-offender with multiple convictions and possibly involving violence would fit into category VI.

Down the left-hand side of the grid are offense levels, ranging from 1 to 43. These represent a crime's seriousness. All crimes are scored. The more serious the crime, the larger the score. Notice that the larger the score, the months in the body of the grid increase. Where one's offense level and criminal history intersect defines the range of months judges will use for sentencing purposes. In a 30- to 40-month scenario, for instance, 35 months would be the presumptive sentence, or the middle-range sentence imposed, absent any factors that would tend to increase or decrease one's punishment. Upward departures from 35 to 40 months would occur if someone showed extreme cruelty in the commission of the offense or was a gang leader, for instance. A downward departure from 35 months to 30 months might occur if the offender cooperated with police and helped them capture others who committed the crime as well.

In Figure 4.1, four different zones are shown, from Zone A through Zone D. These zones represent a sentenced offender's eligibility for probation or some other type of punishment. For instance, Zone A sentencing ranges include "0"

SENTENCING TABLE
(in months of imprisonment)

Offense Level	Criminal History Category (Criminal History Points)					
	I (0 or 1)	II (2 or 3)	III (4, 5, 6)	IV (7, 8, 9)	V (10, 11, 12)	VI (13 or more)
1	0-6	0-6	0-6	0-6	0-6	0-6
2	0-6	0-6	0-6	0-6	0-6	1-7
3	0-6	0-6	0-6	0-6	2-8	3-9
4	0-6	0-6	0-6	2-8	4-10	6-12
5	0-6	0-6	1-7	4-10	6-12	9-15
6	0-6	1-7	2-8	6-12	9-15	12-18
7	0-6	2-8	4-10	8-14	12-18	15-21
8	0-6	4-10	6-12	10-16	15-21	18-24
9	4-10	6-12	8-14	12-18	18-24	21-27
10	6-12	8-14	10-16	15-21	21-27	24-30
11	8-14	10-16	12-18	18-24	24-30	27-33
12	10-16	12-18	15-21	21-27	27-33	30-37
13	12-18	15-21	18-24	24-30	30-37	33-41
14	15-21	18-24	21-27	27-33	33-41	37-46
15	18-24	21-27	24-30	30-37	37-46	41-51
16	21-27	24-30	27-33	33-41	41-51	46-57
17	24-30	27-33	30-37	37-46	46-57	51-63
18	27-33	30-37	33-41	41-51	51-63	57-71
19	30-37	33-41	37-46	46-57	57-71	63-78
20	33-41	37-46	41-51	51-63	63-78	70-87
21	37-46	41-51	46-57	57-71	70-87	77-96
22	41-51	46-57	51-63	63-78	77-96	84-105
23	46-57	51-63	57-71	70-87	84-105	92-115
24	51-63	57-71	63-78	77-96	92-115	100-125
25	57-71	63-78	70-87	84-105	100-125	110-137
26	63-78	70-87	78-97	92-115	110-137	120-150
27	70-87	78-97	87-108	100-125	120-150	130-162
28	78-97	87-108	97-121	110-137	130-162	140-175
29	87-108	97-121	108-135	121-151	140-175	151-188
30	97-121	108-135	121-151	135-168	151-188	168-210
31	108-135	121-151	135-168	151-188	168-210	188-235
32	121-151	135-168	151-188	168-210	188-235	210-262
33	135-168	151-188	168-210	188-235	210-262	235-293
34	151-188	168-210	188-235	210-262	235-293	262-327
35	168-210	188-235	210-262	235-293	262-327	292-365
36	188-235	210-262	235-293	262-327	292-365	324-405
37	210-262	235-293	262-327	292-365	324-405	360-life
38	235-293	262-327	292-365	324-405	360-life	360-life
39	262-327	292-365	324-405	360-life	360-life	360-life
40	292-365	324-405	360-life	360-life	360-life	360-life
41	324-405	360-life	360-life	360-life	360-life	360-life
42	360-life	360-life	360-life	360-life	360-life	360-life
43	life	life	life	life	life	life

Zone A: Offense Levels 1–8
Zone B: Offense Levels 9–10
Zone C: Offense Levels 11–12
Zone D: Offense Levels 13–43

FIGURE 4.1   U.S. Sentencing Guidelines Grid.

months, which means that at the judge's discretion, probation might be imposed. Thus, probation-eligible offenders sentenced in U.S. district courts would be eligible for probation if their sentence fell within Zone A. Zones B through D suggest other sentencing options. Zone B, for instance, may include probation also, but with home confinement or electronic monitoring. Persons whose sentences lie in Zone C must serve at least half of their sentence in prison. Those in Zone D must serve their maximum sentences in prison within the guidelines range. Under present federal laws, federal prisoners may accrue 54 days per year against their maximum sentences as good-time credit, which is the equivalent of a 15 percent sentence reduction for every year served.

Presumptive sentencing has the following aims: (1) to establish penalties commensurate with harm caused by the criminal activity; (2) to produce a fairer system of justice; (3) to reduce the typical severity of penalties; (4) to incarcerate only the most serious offenders; (5) to reduce discretionary power of judges and parole authorities; (6) to allow special sentences for offenders where the circumstances are clearly exceptional; (7) to eliminate early release procedures for inmates, and (8) to make participation in treatment or rehabilitative programs completely voluntary by inmates with no effect on their terms of incarceration.

By 2005, 95 percent of the states had reformed their sentencing laws so that an offender's parole eligibility was either eliminated or made more difficult (U.S. Sentencing Commission, 2006). Accompanying these reforms were changes relating to modifying the amount of good time inmates can earn and how good time should be calculated. Therefore, while the certainty of incarceration has increased under determinate sentencing, the sentences served are often shorter compared with what they might have been under indeterminate sentencing. Presumptive sentencing has become increasingly popular in other countries such as England (Roberts, 2002).

Mandatory Sentencing. Mandatory sentencing is the imposition of an incarcerative sentence of a specified length, for certain crimes or certain categories of offenders, and where no option of probation, suspended sentence, or immediate parole eligibility exists. California, Hawaii, Illinois, Kentucky, and Michigan are a few of the many states that have enacted mandatory sentencing provisions for certain offenses. As has been previously stated, Michigan imposes a two-year additional sentence of **flat time** (where offenders must serve the full two years without relief from parole) if they use a dangerous weapon during the commission of a felony. In Kentucky, those convicted of being habitual offenders are sentenced to life without parole in prison for violating Kentucky's Habitual Offender Statute. Usually, mandatory sentences including life imprisonment are prescribed for those who use dangerous weapons during the commission of a crime, habitual offenders with three or more prior felony convictions, and major drug dealers. But some critics question whether any significant deterrent value is obtained from such mandatory sentencing laws, since attorneys and judges find numerous ways to circumvent them to suit their own purposes (Boswell et al., 2002).

Sentencing Issues

This section examines briefly some of the major sentencing issues that continue to plague most jurisdictions. Issues are usually questions that need to be addressed and are not, as yet, resolved. Issues also involve factors that must be considered when sentencing offenders. While a discussion of all sentencing issues that might be included here is beyond the scope of this book, several important issues have been selected here. These are (1) whether convicted offenders should be placed on probation or incarcerated; (2) the fact of jail and prison overcrowding; (3) the ineffectiveness of rehabilitation; and (4) offender needs and public safety.

Probation or Incarceration?   Should offenders be placed on probation or in jail or prison? This is often a difficult judicial decision. Probation officers might recommend probation to judges when filing a PSI report for some convicted offender, although the court may disregard this recommendation. The just-deserts philosophy is a dominant theme in American corrections today, and judges appear to be influenced by this philosophy as reflected in the sentences they impose. Generally, their interest is imposing sentences on offenders that are equated with the seriousness of the conviction offense.

Jail and Prison Overcrowding.   Jail and prison overcrowding conditions influence judicial discretion in sentencing offenders. Judges have many sentencing options, including incarceration or a non-jail/prison penalty such as fines, probation, community service, restitution to victims, halfway houses, treatment, or some combination of these. It is precisely because of this broad range of discretionary options associated with the judicial role as well as the independence of other actors in the criminal justice system that has led to jail and prison overcrowding becoming the most pressing problem facing the criminal justice system today.

As we have seen, there have been drastic changes in the sentencing policies of most states and the federal government. As increasing numbers of jurisdictions adopt tougher sentencing policies and implement sentencing schemes that will keep offenders behind bars for longer periods, present jail and prison overcrowding conditions are only exacerbated by these policies. In many instances, judges have no choice but to impose incarceration for specified durations on convicted offenders. Judges are obligated to impose mandatory terms for offenders convicted of particular offenses. Often, they have little latitude to depart from whatever sentences are required under the law. When the U.S. sentencing guidelines were implemented in 1987, for instance, the discretion of federal court judges to impose probation as an alternative to incarceration was drastically curtailed. The pre-guidelines use of probation applied to over 60 percent of all convicted federal offenders. In the post-guidelines aftermath, less than 15 percent of all convicted federal offenders are granted probation at the discretion of federal judges. This automatically means greater use of existing federal prison space by larger numbers of convicted offenders sentenced to incarcerative terms. An emerging dilemma is that proportionately larger numbers of nonviolent offenders are being incarcerated when it is quite likely that they would do well in community programs instead.

The Ineffectiveness of Rehabilitation.   The failure of incarceration or various nonincarcerative alternatives to rehabilitate large numbers of offenders for long periods may not necessarily be the fault of those particular programs but rather the nature of clients served by those programs. It is generally acknowledged that jail and prison do not rehabilitate. While most prisons and some jails have one or more programs designed to assist inmates to develop new vocational skills and to counsel them, the effectiveness of these programs is questionable. Understaffing is a chronic problem often attributable to the lack of funding for such programs. Also, the equipment used in prison technical education programs is often outdated. If inmates earn an educational certificate, it often bears the name of the prison facility where the degree or accomplishment was acknowledged. Thus, employers are deterred from hiring such persons. Furthermore, many of these institutions are principally concerned with the custody and control of their inmate populations, and rehabilitation is a remote consideration for them.

One important reason that rehabilitation is less effective in prison and jail settings is that they are chronically overcrowded. In some instances, the overcrowding level in certain prisons approaches the cruel and unusual punishment level, where court intervention is required. Thus, there may be an extensive array of vocational and educational programs within different prison settings, but overcrowding means that not all inmates can take advantage of these services. Furthermore, the effectiveness of services delivery is adversely impacted because too many inmates in classes interfere with learning potential and teacher performance.

Offender Needs and Public Safety. As the courts move voluntarily or involuntarily toward the greater use of **felony probation,** judicial concern is increasingly focused on determining which offenders should be incarcerated and which ones should not be imprisoned. Therefore, in recent years several investigators have attempted to devise prediction schemes that would permit judges and other officials to predict a convicted defendant's dangerousness. Obviously, this concern is directed toward the preservation of public safety and minimizing public risks possibly arising from placing violent and dangerous offenders on probation rather than imprisoning them.

 **BOX 4.1**

 **CAREER SNAPSHOT**

Patricia Haas
Senior Probation and Parole Officer
Domestic Violence Unit, Delaware Department of Correction, Probation and Parole

Statistics:

A.A. (criminal justice), Delaware Technical and Community College; B.S. (behavioral sciences), Wilmington College.

Background:

I always had an interest in social work and working with delinquents, and so choosing criminal justice as a major was the obvious choice for me. While in school I chose to complete an internship in order to fulfill my degree requirements. There were several options, but probation and parole seemed like the best fit since it was a combination of both law enforcement and social work. I was assigned to an adult probation and parole office, and during this internship, I got to see all aspects of the job. I knew immediately that this was what I wanted to do for a living. Following my internship I was fortunate enough to be hired as a part-time casual/seasonal employee while I was completing my education. During this employment, I basically filled in

wherever I was needed. For example, if an officer was out sick or on vacation, I would oversee their caseload in their absence. The experience that I gained during that time was invaluable for me as it really gave me a taste of what the job would be like. It gave me experience in casework and interviewing offenders, which gave me a definite advantage over other college graduates applying for the same job. I was eventually hired on full time and completed the Basic Officer's Training Course in 1998.

Work Experiences:

Working in community corrections can be a very challenging and rewarding experience. Every day is something different and new, and so being flexible is a trait that will get you far in

(*continued*)

BOX 4.I (Continued)

this field. One minute you can be sitting behind your desk finishing paperwork, while the next minute you could be out in the field arresting someone or called to court to testify in a case. What makes Delaware different from other states is that probation and parole officers have warrantless arrest and search powers. We also prosecute all of our own Violation of Probation hearings. Officers act as prosecutors and present the evidence to the judge at a formal hearing and make revocation recommendations. Good oral communication and public speaking skills are a must for this aspect of the job.

My work experience with probation and parole has varied over the past 7½ years. For the first year or so, I supervised what Delaware calls a "Level I" caseload. This is essentially an administrative caseload and it consisted of over 1,000 offenders. Those cases were first-time offenders and misdemeanor crimes that required little supervision. For the past six years I have worked in the Domestic Violence Unit supervising intimate violence cases, child abuse, and elder abuse cases. A domestic violence caseload is extremely challenging because of the volatile nature of the cases. The recidivism rate is high and as a result, most of these cases end up in violation status. We treat our cases as "zero tolerance" and if someone is arrested for a new domestic offense against the same or new victim, then they are arrested for violation of probation as well.

In addition to dealing with the offender, you also have a victim to deal with, which is another reason this caseload can be challenging. Most recently our department received a federal grant funded by the Delaware Criminal Justice Council through the U.S. Department of Justice, Violence Against Women Office, for a victim advocate position. The advocate is now responsible for contacting the victims to check on their welfare during the probation term. The advocate also educates the victim regarding probation supervision. This has been an immense help to our unit since it has freed up a lot of our time to complete other important tasks.

Our unit works closely with other state agencies, including child and adult protective services. Supervision of domestic offenders is close and intensive. We not only monitor compliance of the court order, but all "no contact" and "protection from abuse (PFA)" orders. Fieldwork is absolute and necessary in this unit. It's important to get inside of the offender's home to look for signs of continued abuse, as domestic violence frequently goes unreported. Oftentimes you can get a chance to meet the victim at the home and gauge her well-being. You also want to make sure that the offender is complying with any "no contact" orders that may have been imposed, and doing home visits is one way to verify this. Our unit is on call 24 hours a day, 7 days a week, to respond to police if someone who is on probation or parole supervision is arrested for a new domestic violence crime. Most recently I have accepted a position utilizing SCRAM alcohol monitoring technology. This technology is new to our state and I am excited about being a part of this pilot program. I will be assisting management in devising and implementing the policy for this program. Currently they are targeting domestic violence and felony DUI offenders for this program.

Working with the domestic violence unit and with victims of crime has led to other career opportunities for me. I completed a crisis response training offered by the National Organization for Victim's Assistance (NOVA) in 2003. I have been called out to assist FEMA during natural disasters, such as hurricanes in Florida in 2004 and Hurricane Katrina in 2005. I have also spoken about domestic violence at the statewide Delaware Law Enforcement Training conference, and I have taught new cadets in our basic officer's training course. The department has sent me to numerous trainings over the past several years, including the National Domestic Violence conference and the American Probation and Parole Association (APPA) conference.

Advice to Students:

My advice to students considering entering this field is to make sure that this is what you want to do, as the work can be hard and stressful and the pay is less than desirable. Complete an internship, if available at your college or university, and/or volunteer with a particular agency. The "hands-on" experience that you will acquire will be beneficial in determining your career path and could also help lead to full-time employment.

Most states have laws permitting officials to detain criminal defendants on the basis of the defendant's perceived dangerousness. The legal test used is called the dangerous-tendency test, which is the propensity of a person to inflict injury (Black, 1990:394; *Frazier v. Stone,* 1974). Dangerousness is interpreted differently depending on the particular jurisdiction. In 21 states, for example, dangerousness is defined as a history of prior criminal involvement (Champion, 1994). This history may include a prior conviction, probation or parole status at the time of arrest, or a pending charge when the defendant is arrested. In seven states, the type of crime with which the offender is charged defines dangerousness (e.g., a violent crime such as aggravated assault, robbery, or homicide). And in 23 states, judicial discretion determines dangerousness. However, many offenders, even those convicted of numerous offenses, are nonviolent and not dangerous. We may tend to overincarcerate these types of offenders when they can function normally within their own communities under close supervision as an alternative in confinement in a jail or prison.

THE ROLE OF PROBATION OFFICERS IN SENTENCING

Probation officers are closely connected with the sentencing process, regardless of the type of sentencing scheme used by any particular jurisdiction. Different aspects of their roles relative to sentencing are listed and described below.

1. POs prepare pre-sentence investigation reports at the request of judges. Probation officers play a fundamental role in sentencing. At the request of judges, probation officers prepare pre-sentence investigation reports, or PSIs, for various convicted offenders. While a more comprehensive definition will be provided in the following section, it is sufficient for now to know that PSI reports are more or less extensive compilations of situational and personal details about offenders, their crimes, crime victims, and any other relevant information yielded during the investigative process.

2. POs classify and categorize offenders. Before sentences are imposed or sentence lengths are contemplated, probation officers do some preliminary categorizing of their offender-clients. Different classification schemes are used depending on the jurisdiction.

3. POs recommend sentences for convicted offenders. Besides preparing PSI reports, POs also make recommendations to judges about the sentences they believe are warranted under the circumstances associated with given offenses. In several states, POs are guided by presumptive sentencing guidelines or guidelines-based sentencing schemes. Using a numerical system, they can weigh various factors and generate a score. Usually associated with this score are various incarcerative lengths, expressed in either years or months. The

power of PO sentence recommendations should not be underestimated. Many POs either look for information in their investigations of offenders that confirms or justifies their sentence recommendations or for information that might lead to a modification or rejection of their recommendations. Their own work dispositions determine which investigative mode they tend to follow.

4. Probation officers work closely with courts to determine the best supervisory arrangement for probationer-clients. When offenders are sentenced to probation, POs may or may not supervise them closely. Usually, the greater the likelihood that an offender will recidivate, the more supervision will be directed toward that offender.

5. Probation officers are a resource for information about any extralegal factors that might impact either positively or adversely on the sentencing decision. Thus, judges may rely heavily on probation officer reports on whether certain offenders are socially situated so that they can comply with different probation conditions. If judges want to impose restitution in particular cases, will offenders be able to repay the victims for damages inflicted? The PO has a fairly good sense of whether certain offenders will be able to comply with this and other probation conditions. POs also work with atypical offenders, including transgendered and transsexual individuals. Because reintegration into society may be difficult for some of these persons, POs can assist the court in recommending appropriate treatment interventions and other strategies potentially useful in their rehabilitation (Poole, Whittle, and Stephens, 2002).

PRE-SENTENCE INVESTIGATION (PSI) REPORTS: INTERSTATE VARIATIONS

Whether a conviction is obtained through plea bargaining or a trial, a **pre-sentence investigation (PSI)** is often conducted on instructions from the court. The result is a **pre-sentence investigation report.** This investigation is sometimes waived in the case of negotiated guilty pleas, because an agreement has been reached between all parties concerning the case disposition and nature of sentence to be imposed (Walklate, 2002).

When requested by federal district judges, PSIs are usually prepared within a 60-day period from the time judges make their requests. While there is no standard PSI format among states, most PSIs contain similar information. A pre-sentence investigation report is a document prepared, usually by a probation agency or officer, which provides background information on the convicted offender, including name, age, present address, occupation (if any), potential for employment, the crime(s) involved, relevant circumstances associated with the crime, family data, evidence of prior record (if any), marital status, and other relevant data. Although it was much more informally prepared contrasted with contemporary PSIs, **John Augustus** has been credited with drafting the first one in 1841. It has been estimated that there are over 1.5 million PSI reports prepared by probation officers annually in the United States (U.S. Department of Justice, 2005).

PSIs are written summaries of information obtained by the probation officer through interviews with the defendant and an investigation of the defendant's background. An alternative definition is that PSI reports are narrative summaries of an offender's criminal and noncriminal history, used to aid a judge in determining the most appropriate decision as to the offender's sentence for a crime. These documents are often partially structured in that they require probation officers to fill in standard information about defendants. PSIs also contain summaries or accounts in narrative form highlighting certain information about defendants and containing sentencing recommendations from probation officers. In some instances, space is available for the defendant's personal account of the crime and why it was committed.

In most felony convictions in local, state, and federal trial courts, a pre-sentence investigation is conducted. The purpose of this investigation is to assist the judge in determining the most appropriate punishment or sentence for the convicted defendant. This investigation is usually made by a probation officer attached to the court and consists of a check of all relevant background information about a convicted defendant.

A pre-sentence report is prepared from the facts revealed from the investigation. This report varies considerably in focus and scope from jurisdiction to jurisdiction, but it should contain at least the following items:

1. a complete description of the situation surrounding the criminal activity;
2. the offender's educational background;
3. the offender's employment history;
4. the offender's social history;
5. the residence history of the offender;
6. the offender's medical history;
7. information about the environment to which the offender will return;
8. information about any resources available to assist the offender;
9. the probation officer's view of the offenders' motivations and ambitions;
10. a full description of the defendant's criminal record; and
11. a recommendation from the probation officer as to the sentence disposition (Black, 1990:1184).

An informal component of many PSIs is the **narrative** prepared by the probation officer. In many instances, judges are persuaded to deal more leniently or harshly with offenders, depending on how these narratives have been prepared. Probation officers exercise considerable discretion to influence the favorableness or unfavorableness of these reports for offenders. One important factor is the probation officer's judgment of the degree of public risk posed by the offender if placed on probation. Thus, probation officers must attempt to predict an offender's future behavior. This is one of the most difficult tasks associated with probation work. Assessments of offender risk to the public will be examined later in this chapter. A sample PSI report is illustrated in the chapter appendix.

The PSI report is an informational document prepared by a probation officer, which contains the following personal data about convicted offenders, the conviction offense(s), and other relevant data:

1. Name
2. Address
3. Prior record including offenses and dates
4. Date and place of birth
5. Crime(s) or conviction offense and date of offense
6. Offender's version of conviction offense
7. Offender's employment history
8. Offender's known addiction to or dependency on drugs or alcohol or controlled substances of any kind

9. Statutory penalties for the conviction offense
10. Marital status
11. Personal and family data
12. Name of spouse and children, if any
13. Educational history
14. Any special vocational training or specialized work experience
15. Mental and/or emotional stability
16. Military service, if any, and disposition
17. Financial condition including assets and liabilities
18. Probation officer's personal evaluation of offender
19. Sentencing data
20. Alternative plans made by defendant if placed on probation
21. Physical description
22. Prosecution version of conviction offense
23. Victim impact statement prepared by victim, if any
24. Codefendant information, if codefendant is involved
25. Recommendation from probation officer about sentencing
26. Name of prosecutor
27. Name of defense attorney
28. Presiding judge
29. Jurisdiction where offense occurred
30. Case docket number and other identifying numbers (e.g., Social Security, driver's license, etc.)
31. Plea
32. Disposition or sentence
33. Location of probation or custody

The Administrative Office of the United States Courts uses standardized PSIs including five core categories that must be addressed in the body of the report. These are: (1) the offense, including the prosecution version, the defendant's version, statements of witnesses, codefendant information, and a victim impact statement; (2) prior record, including juvenile adjudications and adult offenses; (3) personal and family data, including parents and siblings, marital status, education, health, physical and mental condition, and financial assets and liabilities; (4) evaluation, including the probation officer's assessment, parole guideline data, sentencing data, and any special sentencing provisions; and (5) recommendation, including the rationale for the recommendation and voluntary surrender or whether the offender should be transported to the correctional institution on his own or should be transported by U.S. Marshals. Under existing federal sentencing guidelines implemented in November 1987, PSIs have not been eliminated. Rather, they now include material besides that listed above regarding an offender's **acceptance of responsibility** for the crime. Judges select sentences for offenders from a sentencing table and may lessen or enhance the severity of their sentences, based on probation officer recommendations, offender acknowledgment of wrongdoing or acceptance of responsibility, or other criteria.

BOX 4.2

INTERNATIONAL SNAPSHOT: PROBATION AND PAROLE IN FRANCE

The government of France is highly centralized. There are both criminal and civil justice systems serving 22 regions and 36,000 municipalities. Since 1994 France has established new criteria for different crime categories. The three major crime categories are:

1. Contraventions: petty offenses associated with fines as punishments (e.g., minor traffic offenses, breaches of bylaws, minor assaults, noise offenses)
2. Delits: offenses of greater importance and possibly requiring confinement for periods ranging from 6 months to 10 years and possible fines (e.g., theft, manslaughter, assault, drug offenses, driving while intoxicated)
3. Crimes: the most serious offenses punishable by imprisonment of from 10 years to life and possible fines (there is no death penalty in France) (e.g., murder, rape, robbery, kidnapping or abduction)

The age of accountability is 18, although criminal charges may be brought against persons ages 13 to 17; however, the law recommends the use of educational measures rather than punitive incarcerative sanctions. Juvenile courts operate in the traditional manner on an individualized case-by-case basis similar to the *parens patriae* philosophy in U.S. juvenile courts. Juvenile offenders age 13–17 face possible maximum punishments of one-half of the legal punishments that could be imposed on persons age 18 or older. About a third of all cases involving juveniles between 13–17 usually result in some type of confinement for short periods. About 1 percent of the French prison population consists of juveniles.

Defenses to alleged criminal conduct are similar to those in the United States. Accused defendants may claim insanity, duress or coercion, mistake or ignorance of the law, self-defense, and personal necessity. Statutes of limitations exist and differ according to offense severity. In the case of contraventions, there is a one-year statute of limitations. Delits have a 3-year time limit, while crimes have a 10-year time limit. Certain offenses, known as crimes against humanity, have no statute of limitations.

The French court system is somewhat complex. The lowest court, the Police Court, deals with summary offenses or violations of the law such as reckless driving or public intoxication, and maximum fines of 25,000 francs or punishments of two months or less of confinement in a jail are heard and decided. The next higher-level court is the Correctional Court, which has jurisdiction over all crimes involving a maximum punishment of 10 years in prison. A third court is the Assize Court, which can impose life sentences for the most serious offenses. The Assize Court is comprised of three-judge panels who hear and decide cases. Juries of nine persons are used in the most serious cases, and jurors are drawn from local communities similar to veniremen lists in U.S. cities. The numbers of jurors in different courts may range from 6–12 depending on the jurisdiction. In 2006 there were over 7,000 judges, of which approximately 50 percent are female. All judges are recruited and judicial posts are competitive following a two-year training program at the National School of Magistrature.

Serious criminal investigations are conducted by public prosecutors. These persons and their deputies are under the control of the Public Ministry. The tasks of public prosecutors are to direct the police when they proceed with criminal investigations; receive complaints filed by victims of crimes; assess whether there are sufficient grounds for legal action to be taken; order that inquiries shall be continued by an investigating judge; represent society in court against criminals and make sentence recommendations; and following a verdict, ensure that the verdict is implemented.

(continued)

BOX 4.2 (*Continued*)

Following a crime's commission, the crime is investigated. If a defendant is identified, an accusation is made. Accused persons are considered innocent until proven guilty in court. All defendants are entitled to counsel. If they cannot afford counsel, it will be appointed for them at government expense. Evidence gathering is distributed among the police, the prosecutors, and even the victims, who can present a wide variety of evidence to the court during a trial. Bail is optional according to the seriousness of the offense, and judges decide whether particular defendants are entitled to bail. Depending on the level and quality of evidence against particular suspects, persons may be held without bail until trial. Inquiries against particular defendants can be made for up to six months, although an additional six-month extension for particular inquiries may be granted. Prosecutors may request that certain accused persons be held in custody during the duration of these inquiries. When the evidence compilation is complete and sufficient evidence warrants a prosecution, a trial is conducted. The burden of proof is on the state. If there is insufficient evidence against certain accused persons, then cases may be dropped. If an accused person held in pretrial detention is subsequently found guilty of the charged offense(s), then the time spent in pretrial detention is deducted from the sentence of imprisonment subsequently imposed.

There is no plea bargaining in France. Accused persons are not permitted to plead guilty. They may confess to the crimes they are charged with committing, but these confessions become evidence against them in court and influence the nature of sentences imposed. When defendants are found guilty, judges have the sole responsibility of imposing sentences upon them. Influencing the sentencing process are victims who may testify during a sentencing hearing. The prosecutor and defense counsel may give their opinions and sentencing suggestions. Expert witnesses, such as psychiatrists and counselors, can also testify and give sentencing suggestions. But the rule of judges is

absolute. Judges generally abide by recommendations of experts when imposing sentences on offenders.

Sentencing judges have broad powers of discretion. Capital punishment was abolished in France in 1981, although life sentences may be imposed. Judges do not use sentencing guidelines, and all cases are individualized depending on the evidence presented and offense seriousness, offender attitudes, and other factors. All sentences may be appealed, however. French judges may impose probation if they choose. Actually for custodial sentences of up to five years, sentences of probation are frequently imposed. Supervision of probationers in France is under the judiciary supervision of probation judges (*Juge de l'application des peines*). Sentences are controlled by an agency known as the *service penitentiaire d'insertion et de probation,* which is comprised of social workers. Probationary terms may be imposed for up to three years.

Besides probation orders, community orders may also be imposed. For petty offenders, sentences of community service may be imposed, requiring offenders to perform from 40 to 240 hours of community service. In 2006 there were over 40,000 community service orders issued following convictions for less serious offenses. Particularly for minor offenses, fines are imposed as well as other sanctions. Depending on the offense, fines ranging from 100,000 to 300,000 francs may be imposed. Theft is subject to three years' imprisonment and/or 300,000 francs as a fine, for instance. Persons who are assessed fines but because of personal circumstances cannot pay them cannot be jailed. Alternative punishments or creative sentencing is therefore encouraged in cases involving indigent defendants. The probation system in France supervised over 200,000 probationers in 2006. Probationers in France are expected to seek and maintain employment, support their families, seek counseling and other forms of assistance, depending on the nature of their conviction offense, and engage in productive vocational or educational training, if necessary. Their activities are closely monitored by probation officers who work under the jurisdiction of the judicial probation service. Almost all probation officers are in fact social workers who counsel and work with offenders during their probationary terms. Job assistance and other counseling activities are performed. While the probation service uses some volunteers, professional social workers do not consider volunteers effective in performing quasi-probation officer tasks. Thus, volunteers work with various offenders by teaching them how to read and write. Only trained professionals should oversee offender aftercare, however.

A growing interest in community corrections in France has been observed. One major reason is that the French prison system is notoriously overcrowded. The French prison service is overseen by the Ministry of Justice. In 2005, there were 14 regional prison administration offices managing nearly 200 prisons throughout France and French territories. About 30,000 civil servants worked in the prison department. There were 22,000 prison officers and 2,000 social workers. The central prison department is located in Paris. It includes a special training center.

The French prison system is broken down as follows. There are remand centers, or *Maisons d'arrêt,* in charge of minor offenders serving shorter sentences of 12 months or less. A second type of facility is a *Centres de détention,* which manages offenders who are capable of being rehabilitated. Social rehabilitation is promoted and discipline is minimal. A third type of prison is the *Centres pénitentiarires,* which are similar to remand centers. *Maisons centrales* are a fourth type of facility in charge of accommodating long-term and habitual criminals. Security rather than rehabilitation is emphasized. Finally, there are *Centres de semi-liberté,* which are the equivalent of day reporting centers in the United States. Inmates may work at jobs in their communities during daytime hours but must report back to these centers during evening hours. Most inmates in these centers are serving shorter sentences. The prison population in France in 2005 was in excess of 60,000 inmates, with space available for 58,000. Thus, overcrowding was evident. However, there is high inmate turnover. The average sentence length in France in 2005 was about 10 months. Prison labor is purely voluntary and not compulsory. Vocational and educational activities are provided for interested prisoners. About 20 percent of all prisoners in 2005 could not read or write. But certain prison initiatives have been implemented to assist these prisoners to achieve a minimal level of academic comprehension.

Prison authorities have the discretion to grant particular prisoners *semi-liberté,* where they are permitted to leave their prisons during daytime hours and work or study in their communities. Thus, there is a heavy emphasis on community reintegration. These measures are used to assist prisoners in avoiding job loss and to permit them to receive medical treatment of psychological counseling or other types of assistance. Frequently probation judges make such determinations of which inmates are eligible for *semi-liberté.* Probation judges may also grant furloughs or short-term leaves to particular inmates, particularly those serving sentences of 12 months or less.

The official use of parole in France commenced in 1885, almost contemporaneous with the implementation of parole in the United States. Actually the National Prison Association (later the American Correctional Association) was formed in 1870 and met in the United States for the first time. Prison officials from various countries attended and shared prison and inmate management information. It is likely that this meeting was responsible for experimentation with various types of inmate programs, including parole. Parole is regarded not only as a means of alleviating prison overcrowding in France today, but also as a means of meaningfully reintegrating offenders back into society. In 2005 approximately 7,000 paroles were granted, up from 4,900 paroles granted in 1999. One factor affecting the granting of parole is the difficulty in finding employment for parolees.

(continued)

BOX 4.2 (*Continued*)

Parole and parole orders are granted today by the *juge de l'application des peines,* if the sentence being served is less than 10 years, or if the remaining time to be served in prison is less than 3 years. Full judicial hearings are held and paroles are either granted or denied particular parole-eligible offenders. Paroled offenders are supervised similar to those supervised by probation officers or social workers. Special conditions may accompany both probation and parole programs, including curfews, drug and alcohol monitoring, and searches of one's residence. If parolees or probationers violate one or more conditions of their particular programs, their programs will be terminated and they will be imprisoned to serve their full terms as a punishment. In some special cases, pardons may be granted by the President of France.

Sources: Adapted from Isabelle Miquel, "French Criminal Justice System," London Conference, 2002; Jackques Borricand, "France," *World Factbook of Criminal Justice Systems,* 2006; Sophie M. Clavier, "Perspectives on French Criminal Law," Paris, France, 1997; *Criminal Justice System of France,* Paris, France, 2006.

Judges frequently treat the PSI in a way similar to how they treat plea bargain agreements. They may concur with probation officer sentencing recommendations, or they may ignore the recommendations made in these reports. However, since most convictions occur through plea bargaining, the only connection a judge usually has with the defendant before sentencing is through the PSI report. In federal district courts, judges may decide not to order PSIs if they feel there is sufficient information about the convicted offender to "enable the meaningful exercise of sentencing discretion, and the court explains this finding on the record" (18 U.S.C., Rule 32(c)(1), 2004). If the defendant wishes, the PSI and report may be waived, with court permission.

The Confidentiality of PSI Reports

The general public is usually excluded from seeing the contents of PSI reports. They serve numerous purposes. Their functions and uses will be discussed later in this section. It is imperative that confidentiality be maintained concerning these reports. Often they contain the results of tests or examinations, psychiatric or otherwise. Probation officers contact one's former employers and work associates and include a summary of interview information as a part of the narrative. Ordinarily, only those court officials and others working closely on a particular case have a right to examine the contents of these reports. All types of information are included in these documents. Convicted offenders are entitled to some degree of privacy relative to a PSI report's contents.

The federal government requires the disclosure of the contents of PSIs to convicted offenders, their attorneys, and to attorneys for the government at least 10 days prior to actual sentencing (18 U.S.C., Sec. 3552(d), 2004). At state and local levels, this practice varies, and the PSI report may or may not be disclosed to the offender. Under 18 U.S.C., Fed. R. Cr. Proc. 32(c)(3)(B) (2004), some information in the PSI may be withheld from the defendant. The report may contain confidential information such as a psychiatric evaluation or a sentencing recommendation. The presiding judge determines those portions of the PSI report to be disclosed to offenders and their counsels. Anything disclosed to defendants must also be made available to the prosecutors. Some federal courts have interpreted these provisions to mean that convicted offenders should have greatly restricted access to these PSI reports. Indeed, many federal prisoners have filed petitions under the **Freedom of Information Act (FOIA)** in order to read their own PSI reports in some judicial districts. This Act makes it possible for private citizens to examine certain public documents containing information about them, including IRS information or information compiled by any other government agency, criminal or otherwise. This is a drastic way of gaining access to a document that may or may not contain erroneous information about the offender, the circumstances of the offense, and other relevant information. Some persons believe that the post-sentence disclosure of PSI reports to prisoners ought to be converted into a routine function rather than as a right to be enjoyed only after exhausting the provisions of the FOIA.

At least one state, California, permits an examination by the public of any PSI report filed by any state probation office for up to 10 days following its filing with the court. Under exceptional circumstances, however, even California courts may bar certain information from public scrutiny if a proper argument can be made for its exclusion. Usually, a good argument would be potential danger to one or more persons who have made statements or declarations in the report. Furthermore, some witnesses or information-givers do so only under the condition that they will remain anonymous. This anonymity guarantee must be protected by the court. But as has been previously indicated, most jurisdictions maintain a high level of confidentiality regarding PSI documents and their contents.

The Preparation of PSI Reports

Most PSI reports are prepared by probation officers at the direction of criminal court judges. There are several different approaches to PSI report preparation. In about half of the states, PSI report preparation is mandatory for all felony offense convictions (U.S. Department of Justice, 2005). Other factors may prompt PSI report preparation, such as when incarceration of a year or longer is a possible sentence; when the offender is under 21 or 18 years of age; and when the defendant is a first-offender. In several states, statutes provide for mandatory PSI report preparation in any felony case where probation is a possible consideration. When probation is not a consideration, then the PSI report preparation is sometimes optional or discretionary with particular judges. Finally, PSI reports may be wholly discretionary with the presiding judge. Some variations in state policies regarding the preparation of PSI reports include the following:

New Jersey
PSI report = required in all felony cases; suggested in misdemeanor cases involving one or more years' incarceration

Connecticut
PSI report = mandatory for any case where incarceration is one or more years

Pennsylvania
PSI report = mandatory for any case where incarceration is one or more years

District of Columbia
PSI report = required unless offenders waive their right to one with court permission

California

PSI report = mandatory for all felony convictions; discretionary for misdemeanor cases

Arizona

PSI report = mandatory for anyone where incarceration is a year or more; may be ordered in other cases

Texas

PSI report = totally discretionary with the judge (Administrative Office of U.S. Courts, 2006).

How Long Does It Take to Prepare a PSI Report?   No standard time can be given for PSI report preparation and completion. Some PSI reports are short and can be completed in a few hours, while others are very long and take several days to complete. A large amount of a PO's time is consumed with PSI report preparation. Much investigative time is required for POs to verify an offender's prior employment, compile educational records, conduct interviews with family members, obtain victim and/or witness information, analyze court records, review police reports of the arrest and crime details, and many other types of necessary and relevant information; this activity is only the preliminary step in the process of PSI report preparation. Officers must still sit down at their computers and prepare these reports. Most probation agencies do not have adequate secretarial staff where such information can be dictated and subsequently transcribed and converted into a written report. Therefore, POs must often write their own reports. Computer literacy, therefore, is a good asset if one wants to become a PO.

Functions and Uses of PSI Reports

While no standard format exists for PSI report preparation among the states, many PSIs are patterned after those used by the Administrative Office of the United States Courts in the Appendix of this chapter. The PSI report was adopted formally by the Administrative Office of the United States Courts in 1943, with many subsequent revisions. Prior to 1943, informal reports about offenders were often prepared for judges by court personnel. Probably the earliest informal PSI was prepared in 1841 by John Augustus, the father of probation in the United States (Champion, 2005). PSI reports for the U.S. District Courts and the U.S. Probation Office serves at least five important functions. These include:

1. To aid the court in determining the appropriate sentence for offenders.
2. To aid probation officers in their supervisory efforts during probation or parole.
3. To assist the Federal Bureau of Prisons and any state prison facility in the classification, institutional programming, and release planning for inmates.
4. To furnish the U.S. Parole Commission and other parole agencies with information about the offender pertinent to a parole decision.
5. To serve as a source of information for research (Administrative Office of U.S. Courts, 2006).

Providing information for offender sentencing is the primary function of a PSI. It continues to be an important function, since judges want to be fair and impose sentences fitting the crime. If there are mitigating or aggravating circumstances that should be considered, these factors appear in the report submitted to the judge. Aiding POs in their supervisory efforts is an important report objective because proper rehabilitative programs can be individualized for different offenders. If vocational training or medical help is needed, the report suggests this. If the offender has a history of mental illness, psychological counseling or medical treatment may be appropriate and recommended. This information is also helpful to ancillary personnel who work in community-based probation programs and supervise offenders with special problems such as drug or alcohol dependencies. PSIs assist prisons and other detention facilities in their efforts to classify inmates appropriately. Inmates with special problems or who are handicapped physically or mentally may be diverted to special prison facilities or housing where their needs can be addressed by professionals. Inmates with diseases or viruses such as AIDS can be isolated from others for health purposes.

Another function of federal PSIs is that they are used in early-release decision making by parole boards. In those jurisdictions where parole boards determine an inmate's early release potential, PSIs provide valuable background information about inmates and their past circumstances. Furthermore, criminologists and others are interested in studying those sentenced to various terms of incarceration or probation. Background characteristics, socioeconomic information, and other relevant data assist researchers in developing explanations for criminal conduct. An examination of PSIs may help corrections professionals devise more effective adaptation and reintegration mechanisms, permitting inmates to make a smoother transition back into their respective communities.

A General Summary of PSI Report Functions among the States

A primary function of PSI reports is to provide sentencing judges with an impression of the offender's background and prospects for rehabilitation. Judges can make fairer sentencing decisions if they know more about offenders to be sentenced. If offenders are placed on probation, the PSI permits probation officers to determine offender needs more clearly and to be more helpful in assisting offenders in locating jobs or completing applications for vocational/educational training. Thus, PSI reports help probation officers in their officer/client supervision planning. This planning may include community service, restitution to crime victims, assignment to community-based corrections agencies, house arrest/electronic monitoring, or some other nonincarcerative alternative.

Probation officers are expected to assess the offender's dangerousness and public risk. They classify and categorize offenders into various risk categories. These risk assessments may suggest that some offenders are considered extremely dangerous and should not be granted probation. Judges may accept these recommendations or at least consider them in the sentencing process.

For inmates, PSI reports are of value to parole boards in determining one's early release and the conditions accompanying the granting of parole. This fact underscores both the short-term and the long-term relevance and importance of PSI reports for influencing an offender's chances at securing freedom from the criminal justice system. Offenders may be prison inmates for many years. When they appear before parole boards 15, 20, or even 30 years after they have been incarcerated for their crimes, the parole boards refer to their PSI reports that were originally prepared at the time of their sentencing. These "ancient" documents contain important information about the offender's earlier circumstances. Even though much of this material is badly dated, parole boards consider it in their early-release decision making.

A fourth function of PSIs is to permit probation officers or other supervisory authorities greater monitoring capability over offenders sentenced to some form of probation. The report contains background information, personal habits, and names of acquaintances of the offender. Should it become necessary to apprehend probationers for any probation violation or new crime alleged, the PSI also functions as a locating device. A fifth function of PSIs is to provide research material for scholars to conduct investigations of crime patterns, parole board decision making, judicial sentencing trends, and other related phenomenon. This function is unrelated to offender sentencing decisions, and it is closely tied to academic interests in the criminal justice process.

Criticisms of PSI Report Preparation

PSIs have been criticized in recent years because of the subjectivity inherent in their preparation. Probation officers report both factual background information as well as their personal impressions about offenders. Sometimes POs have overpredicted an offender's antisocial behavior, while at other times POs have made recommendations for leniency for those offenders who may pose substantial risks to public safety. PO supervisors encourage their officers not to oversimplify offender backgrounds when preparing these PSI reports.

Investigations of probation officer behaviors in PSI preparation have disclosed diverse perspectives and levels of experience ranging from rehabilitative to legalistic. One reasonable expectation of POs is that they possess some understanding of human nature in their report preparations. Many officers lack such understanding. They rely on personal feelings and impressions, and thus, it is difficult to avoid bias and subjectivity in PSI report preparation. Despite these shortcomings, most POs do their best to produce objective documents for use by judges and parole boards.

The Defendant's Sentencing Memorandum

The Administrative Office of the United States Courts (Probation Division) has recommended the inclusion of the offender's version of the offense (Administrative Office of U.S. Courts, 2006). These statements are the **defendant's sentencing memorandum.** If such statements are prepared, they should be prepared with the assistance of defense counsel and attached to the PSI report filed by the probation officer. Often, these memorandums contain mitigating information, and the severity of one's sentence might be reduced. While these memorandums are not required by law in many jurisdictions, the offender's acceptance of responsibility weighs heavily in affecting the sentence federal judges impose.

The Inclusion of Victim Impact Statements

In some jurisdictions, victims of crimes are required to submit their own versions of the offense as a **victim impact statement (VIS).** The victim impact statement is a statement made by the victim and addressed to the judge for consideration in sentencing. It includes a description of the harm inflicted on the victim in terms of financial, social, psychological, and physical consequences of the crime. It also includes a statement concerning the victim's feelings about the crime, the offender, and a proposed sentence. Although the federal government and states have no statutes currently requiring victims to file such statements with the court prior to sentencing, proponents of victim compensation regard victim impact statements as an increasingly important part of the sentencing process. This is seen as a form of victim participation in sentencing, and a victim impact statement is given similar weight compared with the offender's version of events. Usually, these victim impact statements are not required. They pertain exclusively to the direct effects of the crime and are regarded as aggravating circumstances just as the offender's sentencing memorandum serves as a basis for mitigating circumstances. While victim participation in sentencing raises certain ethical, moral, and legal questions, indications are that victim impact statements are used with increasing frequency and appended to PSI reports in various jurisdictions.

Victim impact statements may be oral or written or both. A written statement prepared by a victim becomes an attachment to the PSI report. The victim or victims create a written account of how the crime and offender influenced them, usually adversely. The victim or victim's relatives may also make a verbal statement at the offender's sentencing hearing (*Booth v. Maryland,* 1987). Proponents of victim impact statements believe that such statements personalize the sentencing process by showing that actual persons were harmed by certain offender conduct. Also, victims' rights advocates contend that victims have a moral right to influence one's punishment (Walklate, 2002).

Privatizing PSI Report Preparation

The Private Preparation of PSI Reports.   Sometimes PSIs are prepared by private corporations or individuals. Criminological Diagnostic Consultants, Inc., in Riverside, California, founded by brothers William and Robert Bosic, is a corporation that prepares privately commissioned PSIs for defense attorneys and others. William Bosic is a former prison counselor and probation officer, while his brother, Robert, is a retired police officer. Their claim is, "We don't do anything different from the probation department; we just do it better." While the average cost of a government-prepared PSI averages about $250, privately prepared PSIs cost from $200 to $2,000 or more. The cost depends on the PSI contents, such as whether psychiatric evaluations of offenders are conducted. The amount of investigative detail required in particular cases influences preparation costs as well. Increasing numbers of PSIs are being prepared privately, often by ex-POs. The quality of private PSI report preparation varies greatly.

Most jurisdictions accept privately prepared PSI reports to accompany the official PSI report prepared by a PO. These private-sector PSIs are often prepared by former probation officers or criminal justice consultants. A defendant's **sentencing memorandum** contains similar PSI information, especially the defendant's version of what happened, and any mitigating factors that would lessen sentencing severity. This independently prepared report serves to make the official PSI more objective, and to clarify or resolve facts that may be in dispute.

THE SENTENCING HEARING

Under Rule 32 of the Federal **Rules of Criminal Procedure** (18 U.S.C., 2007), the contents of a PSI must be disclosed to defendants and their counsels, although some information is exempt from disclosure. Mental or psychological reports, interviews with family members or a personalized account of the defendant's marital problems, and certain personal observations by the probation officer and court are potentially excludable from PSIs.

A **sentencing hearing** is held where both prosecutors and defense counsel can respond to the contents of the PSI report. Offenders and their attorneys can comment on the PSI report and amend it with additional information. The role of defense attorneys is especially crucial at this stage because they can negotiate with the PO who prepared the report as well as the victims, and they can make timely legal attacks on erroneous information that might be included. In addition to considering the contents of a PSI, the oral and written reports furnished by victims and the offenders themselves, and attorney arguments both from the prosecution and defense, judges use their best judgment in arriving at the most equitable sentence for offenders. Judges consider mitigating and aggravating circumstances surrounding the offense, the age, psychological and physical condition, and social/educational background of the offender, and the minimum and maximum statutory penalties of incarceration and/or fines accompanying the crime in arriving at a decision. Judges also take into account both **aggravating circumstances** and **mitigating circumstances.**

AGGRAVATING AND MITIGATING CIRCUMSTANCES

Aggravating Circumstances

Aggravating circumstances are those factors that intensify the severity of punishment. Some of the factors considered by judges to be aggravating include:

1. whether the crime involved death or serious bodily injury to one or more victims;
2. whether the crime was committed while the offender was out on bail facing other criminal charges;
3. whether the offender was on probation, parole, or work release at the time the crime was committed;
4. whether the offender was a recidivist and had committed several previous offenses for which he or she had been punished;
5. whether the offender was the leader in the commission of the offense involving two or more offenders;
6. whether the offense involved more than one victim and/or was a violent or nonviolent crime;
7. whether the offender treated the victim(s) with extreme cruelty during the commission of the offense; and
8. the offender used a dangerous weapon in the commission of the crime and the risk to human life was high.

If the convicted defendant has one or more aggravating circumstances accompanying the crime committed, the judge is likely to intensify the punishment prescribed. More aggravating circumstances usually means longer sentences, incarceration in lieu of probation, and/or a sentence to be served in a maximum-security prison rather than a minimum- or medium-security prison. Mitigating circumstances may influence judges to be lenient with defendants and impose probation.

Mitigating Circumstances

Mitigating factors are those circumstances that might lessen the crime's severity. Some of these circumstances include:

1. The offender did not cause serious bodily injury by his or her conduct during the commission of the crime.
2. The convicted defendant did not contemplate that his or her criminal conduct would inflict serious bodily injury on anyone.
3. The offender acted under duress or extreme provocation.
4. The offender's conduct was possibly justified under the circumstances.
5. The offender was suffering from a mental incapacitation or physical condition that significantly reduced his or her culpability in the offense;
6. The offender cooperated with authorities in apprehending other participants in the crime or in making restitution to the victims for losses suffered.
7. The offender committed the crime through motivation to provide necessities for him- or herself or his or her family.
8. The offender did not have a previous criminal record.

If the offender has one or more mitigating circumstances associated with the crime, the judge may reduce the severity of the imposed sentence. First-offenders and nonviolent criminals are likely to be considered as prime candidates for alternative sentencing that does not involve incarceration. But chronic recidivists or repeat-offenders, career criminals, or those who have committed violent acts are likely to be punished severely. Both aggravating and mitigating circumstances are contained in PSI reports.

A PRE-SENTENCE INVESTIGATION REPORT FROM WISCONSIN

Several states, such as North Dakota, provide forms for PSI report preparation. Probation officers must fill in the blanks on these forms, with explicit information requested. However, a growing number of states are using a more free-flowing format for their PSI reports. As long as specific information is included, there is great variation in how such PSI reports are formatted.

The following material presents a rather detailed PSI report from the State of Wisconsin. Wisconsin authorizes general PSI preparations without adhering to a fixed PSI format. Thus, there are some components of Wisconsin PSI reports that may not be applicable for particular offenders. The intent of Wisconsin officials is to individualize these reports to fit offender characteristics, needs, and sentence recommendations. The Wisconsin Department of Corrections states that the purpose of any PSI is a careful study of how the individual's personal characteristics, environmental factors, and behavioral patterns have interacted to produce the present situation. The agent must comply with confidentiality laws when securing and disclosing medical, psychiatric, psychological, and educational information. Courts may order PSI reports following conviction and prior to imposition of sentence for felony cases. Investigation due dates are usually set by the court. Below is a real PSI report based on an actual criminal incident and conviction. The names of offenders and other parties as well as geographical locations have been changed for purposes of anonymity.

STATE OF WISCONSIN

Department of Corrections

PRE-SENTENCE INVESTIGATION

Date

August 10, 1996

Name and DOB

John Ming
November 20, 1962

PRESENT OFFENSE

Description of Offense

Attempted Sexual Assault. Offense date is November 3, 1995. This offense involves an incident in which a 29-year-old nude woman's body was discovered on a rural road. The body had been decapitated, and the woman's head and articles of bloody clothing were discovered on another road three miles away. It was discovered that the woman, in an intoxicated condition, had accompanied some men from a tavern who reportedly took the woman to their apartment, forced her to engage in sexual intercourse, then at least one of the men attacked the woman with a kitchen knife, cut her throat, then decapitated her. Four men were eventually charged in the offense, including the defendant, Mu Chou (life sentence), Bok Suk Kim (life sentence), and Raymond Phu (10 years). Mr. Ming admits that he resides at the apartment where the offense occurred, but denies any involvement in or knowledge of the offense until his arrest two weeks later. He was not released on bond. Rationale: "I never see girl, I don't know about it."

Offender's Version

The subject is a 34-year-old Chinese National male, first-offender, who is currently confined in the Briggs Unit facing a 10-year sentence in Madison County for one count of Attempted Sexual Assault. The subject states that on or about November 3, 1995, during an unknown time he allegedly committed the offense of Attempted Sexual Assault on a 29-year-old female, but he denies the Attempted Sexual Assault and any knowledge of the woman's murder or decapitation. He admits to occasional marijuana use at age 27; admits to three prior arrests resulting in a two-year probationary term for DWI. He states that he left the apartment for an unknown period of time, and when he returned, his friends and the woman were gone. He admits that there was blood on the floor and in the bedroom where the woman was allegedly raped by the other men.

Victim's Statement

Not applicable

PRIOR RECORD

Juvenile Record

No record of juvenile arrests

Adult Record

Three prior arrests for DWI; sentenced to two years' probation; claims completed.

Pending Charges

One detainer warrant from U.S. Immigration "Hold"

Correctional Experience

Good jail report from Madison County Jail from jail authorities

Offender's Explanation of Record

Claims no contact with father, mother, or two siblings; claims single; residence unstable; education claims high school completed; employment claims "laborer"; home stability poor due to lack of contact with family; admits to experimental use of marijuana at age 27; current offense of Attempted Sexual Assaulting a 29-year-old female and allegedly cutting her head off, subject denies; speaks little English.

PERSONAL HISTORY

Academic/Vocational Skills

Subject states he completed 12 years of school in China. Subject worked as "laborer" but did not elaborate on what "laborer" did.

Employment

Worked as "laborer" at various jobs in different states; would not disclose which establishments employed him. No information is forthcoming about subject's past educational level or occupations in his native country of China. He has been in English classes in Indiana for about a year prior to coming to Wisconsin. While in Wisconsin the subject worked in a few different jobs. He bussed tables in a restaurant, worked in a furniture factory, and did some janitorial work. He then moved to Madison where he worked for the ABC Packing Company as a meat cutter.

Financial Management

Has given no indication of ability to manage financial affairs.

Marital/Alternate Family Relationships

Has not seen family for many years.

Companions

Has no close associates presently. Admits to knowing other men who were convicted of woman's murder only because they were also Oriental and in the tavern when he was there. He admits to being drunk when he left tavern but denies any involvement in woman's murder.

Emotional Health

See attached Psychiatric Evaluation.

Physical Health

Transferred to mental health unit at Briggs for psychiatric and psychological evaluation. Subject was referred because he was mute, refused to eat, and exhibited unusual behavior. Subject appeared detached, withdrawn, in distress, and depressed. His blood pressure was low, he had lost much weight, and he appeared to be dehydrated. He would give no information to medical staff. He would sit in one place on his bunk for seven or eight hours at a time. At that time he stated that he was very nervous and scared. He had been making statements that he needed to stay in prison because he would not have anything on the outside now. He flooded his cell on one occasion and became quite unresponsive. His physical and mental condition deteriorated further. He lost 26 pounds of weight because he was not eating. He was transferred to the medical unit for acute care. When received, the subject was on Haldol C, 15 mgs., TID and Cogentin, 2 mgs. BID. The subject may have been a suicide risk and was placed on suicide precaution status. The subject began to eat on the second day of his admission. The subject is being treated for a positive TB test with INH. The file reflects no other medical problems at this time.

Mental Ability

The subject is now 34 years old, a frail looking, Chinese male who was dressed in a disheveled Department of Corrections white uniform. He looked undernourished. He was mute and had poor eye contact. He was able to answer one question by head movement at one time. His mood seemed depressed to euthymic. He had an inappropriate smile at some part of his evaluation. There was no indication that subject had delusions or hallucinations, although he reportedly has history of having fairly loose delusions and grandiose delusions in the past. The rest of his mental status examination was not tested because of his uncooperativeness and because he remained mute.

Chemical Usage

Subject admitted to using marijuana and drinking beer. Presently on prescribed medications as indicated.

Sexual Behavior

Convicted of Attempted Sexual Assault, subject denies. Has no close friends or acquaintances.

Military

None

Religion

Born into Buddhist faith; now is nondenominational.

Leisure Activities

None determined.

Residential History

Taipei, Taiwan	1962–1985
Lafayette, Indiana	1985–1986
Madison, Wisconsin	1986–present

SUMMARY AND CONCLUSIONS

Agent's Impressions

Ming is a Line Class I inmate, unassigned due to his mental health status. He needs recreational therapy. He does not attend any educational, vocational, or character development programs due to his mental status. He is not a gang member. Ming is receiving INH for TB prevention. Ming denies any mental health treatment in society and denies suicide attempts. Ming has been diagnosed with Schizoeffective Disorder, Bipolar Type Rule out Bipolar Disorder, Mixed with Psychotic Features, Rule Out Schizophrenia, Chronic, Catatonic Type with Acute Exacerbation. Alcohol use in remission. Addicted to Cannabis, in remission due to incarceration. Interviews with Ming indicate that he is unwilling or unable to relate any new information to this officer about his present offense. Ming maintains he is not guilty and claimed he did not know any details about the present offense until he was arrested. Ming claims he does not know if he was ever physically or sexually assaulted and has never been married and has no children. Ming claims he cannot remember if he engaged in sex with prostitutes. Due to the subject's past probation for DWI, it appears he may need monitoring in the area of alcohol usage. He may also benefit from psychological counseling.

Restitution Information

Not applicable

Recommendation

Recommend that Ming be confined in mental unit at Briggs until such time as his eating behavior is stabilized. Recommend Ming for psychological counseling. Statutory punishment of 10 years should be imposed. Ming must accept responsibility for his actions, since this officer interviewed two other persons convicted of the murder and they give consistent accounts of Ming's involvement in the female victim's murder and decapitation. Both subjects accused Ming of committing the decapitation and joking about it later. Other than mental problems contained in psychiatric evaluation, there are no outstanding mitigating circumstances that would cause this officer to recommend sentencing leniency or a shorter incarcerative term at this time.

1. Confinement is necessary to protect the public from further criminal activity.
2. The subject is in need of correctional treatment that can most effectively be provided through confinement.
3. Nonconfinement would unduly depreciate the seriousness of the instant offense.

Probation is not recommended.

John J. Beecher, Probation Officer, Madison County

PSYCHIATRIC EVALUATION
WISCONSIN DEPARTMENT OF CORRECTIONS

NAME: John Ming
WDOJ#:   47324568
DATE: July 15, 1996
EXAMINER: Dominique Daws, M.D.

SOURCE OF INFORMATION:

Patient and WDOC Records.

PERTINENT MEDICAL HISTORY:

The patient's chart indicates that he has tuberculosis Class II and he is currently taking medication for this. He has no allergies to medications.

PERTINENT PSYCHIATRIC AND LEGAL HISTORY:

Reports in patient's brown chart indicated that he has a history of psychiatric hospitalizations and was given the diagnoses of Psychotic Disorder, NOS, Alcohol Abuse, and Cannabis Abuse. During that hospitalization, he was given Ativan 1 mg po hs prn for his complaint of having difficulty sleeping. He was also treated with other psychotropic medications prior to his discharge. His final diagnosis was Schizophrenia, Chronic, Undifferentiated Type, Alcohol Abuse, and Cannabis Abuse. His previous records also indicated that he had experienced delusional thinking such as thinking that he has special powers and special knowledge of prediction of the future, and he had worldwide powerful activities. His mental status on his psychiatric hospitalization indicated that he made a statement that he went with too many gods in the war, saw them and talked to them, go with them anywhere, and that they told him things about the CIA and the life of Americans and that the American religions were always at odds with his religion. Social History done at Briggs indicated that patient reported being arrested one time in Indianapolis, Indiana, for not having any money for a bus ticket. He reportedly spent a week in jail and a friend paid the fine and got him out. He was also arrested once in Lafayette, Indiana, for driving while intoxicated. He was released and was told to appear in court, which he did not do and which led to his being arrested later for failure to appear. He reportedly paid a fine and as a result was discharged. The patient is reportedly serving a ten-year sentence for murder.

FAMILY HISTORY:

There is no available information about the patient's family or history of medical or psychiatric illness at this time.

SOCIAL HISTORY:

This information is obtained from the social history compiled during the patient's hospitalization at Briggs. The patient was reportedly born in Taipei, Taiwan, and his family all reside in Taipei. He reportedly went to school there. He was not married. He came to the United States in 1985 as a refugee, is staying in Indiana for one year, and worked in a factory in Madison, Wisconsin, for three years prior to his present incarceration. For additional Social History, please read Social History in the brown chart.

MENTAL STATUS EXAMINATION:

The patient is 34 years old, a frail looking, Chinese male who was dressed in a disheveled white WDOC uniform. He looked undernourished. He was mute and he had poor eye contact. He was able to answer one question by head movement at one time. There were no indications that patient had delusions or hallucinations. The rest of his mental status examination was not tested because of his uncooperativeness and for him remaining mute.

SUMMARY OF POSITIVE FINDINGS AND TARGET SYMPTOMS:

This 34-year-old male reportedly came to the United States as a refugee in 1985 and has been living with friends in Madison prior to his incarceration. He reportedly is serving a 10-year sentence for murder. His records indicated that he has a history of delusions and hallucinations and was hospitalized at a mental hospital with a diagnosis of Undifferentiated Schizophrenia, Alcohol Abuse, and Cannabis Abuse. He reportedly was observed to have unusual behavior at Briggs, remaining mute and not making eye contact with anyone and was observed looking at his wall while in his cell. He also started refusing to eat, causing him to lose weight. The patient was transferred to the medical unit at Briggs electively mute and not eating, although he started eating the next day. The patient at this time remains mute, although he started to answer by moving his head. It is possible that this patient has a Schizoaffective Disorder and a possible Bipolar Disorder in addition to his history of Alcohol and Cannabis Abuse.

DIAGNOSIS:

Axis I:	295.70 Schizoaffective Disorder, Bipolar Type
	Rule Out Bipolar Disorder, Mixed with Psychotic Features 296.64
	Rule Out Schizophrenia, Chronic, Catatonic Type with Acute Exacerbation 295.24
	305.00 Alcohol Abuse, in remission due to incarceration
	305.20 Cannabis Abuse, in remission due to incarceration
Axis II:	799.90 Deferred
Axis III:	Tuberculosis Class II
Axis IV:	Severe (incarceration and no family support)
Axis V:	Current GAF: 20 Highest GAF Past Year: 0

PROGNOSIS:

Poor.

_____

Dominique Daws, MD

RECOMMENDATIONS:

It is recommended that Inmate Ming be kept in acute care until he is stabilized. He should do well on a dorm unit once he has achieved some remission.

PROGNOSIS:

Guarded.

_____   _____
Raul Hastings, ACP III   William G. Fraley, Ph.D.
Staff Psychologist   Supervising Psychologist

REASON FOR REFERRAL:

Inmate Ming was informed that the contents of this report would be shared with the appropriate treating personnel and the evaluation was completed following inmate's tacit consent.

This inmate is a thin, frail, 34-year-old Chinese male who understands English better than he can speak it. Records indicate that he has been hospitalized before. His travel card indicates that he is serving time for Rape. He allegedly cut off the victim's head. There is some question as to whether he might have been charged with the crime, and did not actually participate in the decapitation. This was a gang-rape situation. Inmate Ming has been electively mute since his admission to Briggs. He will look at this examiner, however, he makes no verbal response. Records indicate that he has experienced delusional thinking in the past. He has verbalized special powers, special knowledge, and has been able to predict the future. He has been diagnosed at Psychotic Disorder, NOS, Schizoaffective Disorder, Depressed, and Schizoaffective Disorder, Bipolar Type. There has also been some question as to whether or not he may be a catatonic schizophrenic.

MENTAL STATUS:

Inmate Ming cannot be interviewed or tested at this time because of his refusal to talk. He does not appear to be attending to hallucinations. He appears flat, withdrawn, depressed, detached, and medicated.

PSYCHOMETRICS:

Not applicable.

This is a real PSI and psychiatric evaluation of an offender who is currently incarcerated in another state. The names of the offender, accomplices, probation officers, and physicians were changed for reasons of confidentiality.

CHANGING RESPONSIBILITIES OF PROBATION OFFICERS RESULTING FROM SENTENCING REFORMS AND TRENDS

The probation officer role has transformed as different states have changed their sentencing laws. Under indeterminate sentencing formerly used by the federal district courts, for example, the U.S. Probation Office had its POs collect diverse information about prospective probationers and present this information in a subsequent sentencing hearing. POs embellished their reports frequently with personal observations and judgments. They also recommended sentences to federal district court judges, based on their own impressions of each case. However, the implementation of the U.S. sentencing guidelines in 1987 modified the PO's role greatly. Now, POs must learn to add and subtract points from one's **offense seriousness score** according to whether a drug transaction occurred within a specified distance of a school, whether the offender used a dangerous weapon during the commission of the crime, and/or whether offenders accepted responsibility for their actions. In drug cases, amounts of drugs must be factored into an increasingly complex formula to determine where an offender's case might be categorized. Fortunately, much of this calculating has been computerized to make it easier for POs to determine one's offense level and crime seriousness.

Ellen Steury (1989:95–96) illustrates the complexity of score determination under the federal sentencing guidelines with a hypothetical example. She describes the following:

A hypothetical offense situation might be helpful in portraying the mechanics of the guidelines. Consider the case of a defendant convicted of armed robbery, where the facts are as follows: (1) the robbery offense; (2) was carefully planned; (3) $23,000 was stolen; (4) the robber pointed a gun at the teller; (5) no injuries occurred; (6) the offender had three previous felony convictions, of which two carried terms of imprisonment longer than 13 months and one carried a term of probation; (7) the offender had been out of prison six months at the time of committing the instant offense, but was not under legal sentence at the time of the offense; (8) had no other currently pending charges; (9) confessed to the crime, wholly cooperated with law enforcement authorities, and offered restitution. In the ordinary case, this fact situation would require the court to sentence the offender to a term of imprisonment between 57 months (4 years, 9 months) and 71 months (5 years, 11 months). In the hypothetical situation detailed above, each of the items would carry the following values:

1. The robbery itself carries a base level score of 18.
2. The "more than minimal planning" does not affect the sentence in the case of robbery, but it does (inexplicably) in other offenses such as burglary, property damage or destruction, embezzlement, and aggravated assault.
3. The amount of money taken increases the base level by two points.
4. Brandishing a firearm increases the base level by another three points.
5. The fact that no victim injuries occurred avoids other possible level increases, which would otherwise be calculated on the basis of the degree of the injury.
6. The criminal history score totals nine points, comprised of three points for each sentence of imprisonment longer than thirteen months, and one point for the sentence of probation; while the recency of the latest imprisonment incurs two additional points.
7. The absence of other pending charges avoids a possible score increase.
8. The confession, coupled with the cooperation and the volunteered restitution, might persuade the court to conclude that the offender had "accepted responsibility" for the crime, which could result in decreasing the offense level score by two points.

In the above example, the offense points sum to 21, and the criminal history points sum to 9. The sentencing range associated with offense level 21 and the criminal history score of 9 (Category IV) is 57–71 months. Defendants so sentenced, or the government, could appeal by claiming that the guidelines had been incorrectly applied (18 U.S.C., Sec. 3742(a)(2) and Sec. 3742(b)(2), 2007). An appellate court would review the case.

If the sentencing court in its wisdom believed that the offender deserved less than 57 months or more than 71 months, a departure from the guidelines would be allowable, provided a written justification from the judge accompanied the departure. In such cases, defendants (if the sentence were longer than the maximum specified by the guidelines) or the government (if the sentence were shorter than the minimum specified by the guidelines) could appeal for a review of the stated reasons given by the judge for the departure (18 U.S.C., Sec. 3742(a)(3)(A) and Sec. 3742(b)(3)(A), 2007).

Frank Marshall, a federal PO with the U.S. Probation Office in Philadelphia in 1989, has commented about several significant changes in PO work as the result of the federal sentencing guidelines that went into effect in November 1987. He says that the U.S. Parole Commission was scheduled to be abolished in 1992, and that all future parolees would be placed under the supervision of the U.S. Probation Office. A new term, **supervised release,** would replace terms such as parole and special parole in future years. Marshall also says that POs would acquire more sentencing responsibilities with the sentencing change. Federal district court judges increasingly rely on PO work for determining appropriate sentences of offenders. At the same time, fewer convicted offenders are eligible for probation or diversion (Marshall, 1989:153–164). In the years following the sentencing guidelines, for example, federal sentencing patterns shifted dramatically so that probation as a sentence was imposed about 10–12 percent of the time in the post-guidelines period compared with 60–65 percent probation sentences in the pre-guidelines period (Champion, 1994). This pattern continues (Champion, 2005). The federal sentencing guidelines have drastically reduced the number of persons eligible for and receiving probation. The work of federal POs is not substantially reduced, however, since they now supervise parolees under supervised release and their PSI report preparation has become increasingly complex.

SUMMARY

Sentencing is a crucial stage in offender processing. Many factors are considered in determining the appropriateness of the sentences convicted criminals receive. Much depends on the type of sentencing scheme used by any particular jurisdiction. Four major sentencing schemes include indeterminate sentencing, determinate sentencing, presumptive or guidelines-based sentencing, and mandatory sentencing. Indeterminate sentencing involves a judge imposing a term of years and where parole boards determine one's early release from jail or prison. Determinate sentencing also involves a sentence imposed by the judge, but offenders are released according to the amount of good time they accumulate while confined. Good time credit may be statutory, earned, or meritorious. Parole boards are not involved in the early release of inmates sentenced under determinate sentencing. Guidelines-based or presumptive sentencing involves utilizing established sentencing ranges, usually expressed in numbers of months, which fit particular crimes and are associated with offenders with particular criminal histories. Judges are obligated to stay within preapproved guidelines in the sentences they impose, although they may depart from these guidelines provided they furnish a written rationale for doing so. Mandatory sentences must be served despite the judge's beliefs or feelings. One intent of sentencing reform and generating different sentencing schemes is to yield an equitable punishment proportional to the offense committed, and to remove from the sentencing equation all extralegal factors, including one's age, socioeconomic status, gender, race, or ethnicity.

Offenders who are about to be sentenced usually have a sentencing hearing. These hearings are important because they provide an opportunity for both victims and offenders to make statements favoring their respective positions. Victim impact statements reflect how the conduct of the offender influenced the lives of victims. Offenders themselves can furnish the court with positive information in an attempt to persuade sentencing judges to be lenient. Defendants' sentencing memorandums are used to detail the offender's version of the crime and why it was committed. Also considered are reports submitted by probation officers.

The role of probation officers has become increasingly varied and complex. Probation officers must classify and categorize offenders and prepare presentence investigation reports about them at the direction of criminal court judges. These reports contain recommended sentences for offenders. Judges may either consider or disregard such recommendations. However, most judges seem to take such recommendations seriously. Probation officers also work closely with the courts to ensure that the best supervisory arrangement for offenders is provided if probation is used as a sentencing option.

The pre-sentence investigation report, or PSI, is an important document. It contains many bits of information, including a summary of the offense and circumstances about it, the offender's background, and the impact of the offense on victims, if any. PSI reports are confidential court documents, although designated persons are permitted to see them at various times in different jurisdictions. Whether reports are prepared is contingent upon prevailing statutes in given jurisdictions as well as the discretion of sentencing judges. PSI reports perform functions, including assisting judges in imposing the best sentences for offenders, aiding POs during their supervisory efforts with probationer-clients, assisting prison officials in their inmate classification decision making, assisting parole boards in their early-release decision making, and serving as a source for research. Offenders may attach a memorandum of their version of events as well as any exculpatory information that might mitigate their sentences.

QUESTIONS FOR REVIEW

1. How are indeterminate and determinate sentencing distinguished? Under each sentencing scheme, how do offenders gain early release from jail or prison?
2. What is mandatory sentencing? What are some examples of mandatory sentences?
3. What are guidelines-based or presumptive sentences?
4. What are some general purposes of sentencing reform?
5. What are some general functions performed by probation officers? How do their functions relate to offender sentencing?
6. What are some differences between aggravating and mitigating circumstances? What are some examples of each? At what point in offender processing are such circumstances considered important?
7. What is a pre-sentence investigation? Who prepares this report? Are such reports always prepared for all offenders? Under what circumstances would PSIs be prepared?
8. What information is usually provided in a PSI? What functions do PSIs serve?
9. What are false positives and false negatives? How do they relate to risk assessment instruments?
10. What are several criticisms of probation?

SUGGESTED READINGS

Denov, Myriam S. and Kathryn M. Campbell (2005). "Understanding the Causes, Effects and Responses to Wrongful Conviction." *Journal of Contemporary Criminal Justice* **21**:224–249.

Fearn, N.E. (2005). "A Multilevel Analysis of Community Effects on Criminal Sentencing." *Justice Quarterly* **22**:452–487.

Hurst, D.R. and L.A. Foley (2005). "Filicide and Insanity Defense: Legal Authoritarianism and Empathy as Predictors of Guilt." *American Journal of Forensic Psychology* **23**:81–91.

Kurlychek, Megan C. and Brian D. Johnson (2004). "The Juvenile Penalty: A Comparison of Juvenile and Young Adult Sentencing Outcomes in Criminal Court." *Criminology* **42**:485–517.

Mitchell, O. (2005). "A Meta-Analysis of Race and Sentencing Research: Explaining the Inconsistencies." *Journal of Quantitative Criminology* **21**:439–466.

INTERNET CONNECTIONS

Bureau of Justice Statistics
http://www.ojp.usdoj.gov/bjs/correct.htm

Bureau of Justice Statistics Courts and Sentencing Statistics
http://www.ojp.usdoj.gov/bjs/stsent.htm

Coalition for Federal Sentencing Reform
http://www.mn.sentencing.org

National Association of Pretrial Services
http://www.napsa.org

National Criminal Justice Reference Service
http://www.ncjrs.org

Punishment and Sentencing
http://www.uaa.alaska.edu/just/just110/courts4.html

Sentencing Advisory Panel
http://www.sentencing-advisory-panel.gov.uk/

Sentencing Project
http://www.sentencingproject.org/

U.S. Courts
http://www.flmp.uscourts.gov/Presentence/presentence

U.S. Probation Department of Southern District of Ohio
http://www.ohsp.uscourts.gov/pdfs/psi.pdf

U.S. Sentencing Commission
http://www.ussc.gov/

Vera Institute of Justice Projects: State Sentencing and Corrections Program
http://www.vera.org/project/project1_1.asp?section_id=26

APPENDIX

SAMPLE FEDERAL PSI REPORT

IN THE UNITED STATES DISTRICT COURT
FOR THE NORTHERN DISTRICT OF OHIO

UNITED STATES OF AMERICA)
)
)
              v.   )   Docket No. 07-00014-01
)
     Michael Mali   )

PRESENTENCE REPORT

Prepared for:	The Honorable Kelly G. Green United States District Judge
Prepared by:	Craig T. Doe United States Probation Officer (216) 633-6226
Sentencing Date:	September 15, 2007 at 9:00 a.m.
Offense:	Count One: Conspiracy to Violate Federal Narcotics Laws (18 U.S.C. 846) 10 years to life/ $4,000,000 fine
Release Status:	Detained without bail since 6/19/06
Identifying Data:	
Date of Birth:	March 19, 1973
Age:	34
Race:	Black
Sex:	Male
Social Security Number:	881-22-4444
Address:	24 Apple Street Breaker Bay, Maryland 10012
SS#:	333-33-3333

FBI#:	102-631-476
USM#:	07-214670-1
Other ID#:	Not applicable.
Education:	11th grade
Dependents:	Two
Citizenship:	U.S.
Aliases:	None.
Detainers:	None.
Codefendants:	Sammy Maples - CR 07-00015-1
	John Smith - CR 07-00016-1

Assistant U.S. Attorney	Defense Counsel
Mr. Robert Prosecutor	Mr. Arthur Goodfellow
U.S. Courthouse	113 Main Street
Breaker Bay, Maryland	Breaker Bay, Maryland
(216) 333-3333	(216) 444-4444

Date report prepared: August 21, 2007
Revised September 3, 2007

Part A. The Offense

Charge(s) and Conviction(s)

1. Michael Mali, Sammy Maples, and John Smith were named in a two-count indictment returned by the Eastern District of Maryland grand jury on November 1, 2006. Count one charges that from December 1998 until June 19, 2005 the defendants conspired to violate the federal narcotics laws, in violation of 18 U.S.C. 846. Count two charges that on June 19, 2005, the defendants possessed with intent to distribute 500 grams or more of heroin, in violation of 18 U.S.C. §§ 812, 841(a)(1), 841(b)(1)(B) and 18 U.S.C. § 2.

2. On July 20, 2007, Michael Mali, Sammy Maples, and John Smith pled guilty to count one and are scheduled to be sentenced on September 30, 2007. All of the above defendants have pled guilty in accordance with the terms of written plea agreements which require a plea of guilty to count one in return for the dismissal of count two in the original indictment.

3. The assistant U.S. attorney has filed a motion pursuant to 18 U.S.C. § 3553(e) and U.S.S.G. § 5K1.1, advising that the defendants have provided substantial assistance to the Government. Accordingly, the Government will recommend a sentence below the mandatory minimum sentence and applicable guideline range.

The Offense Conduct

4. This case was initiated by the Drug Enforcement Administration in early January 2003 upon the receipt of information from a confidential informant that Michael Mali and Sammy Maples were involved in the distribution of multiple-ounce quantities of heroin from an apartment located in the Breaker Bay, Maryland housing project. Subsequent investigation revealed that Mali and Maples were regularly distributing heroin to John Smith. After several months of investigation and surveillance, drug enforcement agents learned that Smith regularly purchased heroin from Mali and Maples, and sold the heroin

to Leon Williams, who would travel from the Breaker Bay area each month to Bodega Bay, Maryland, a small community approximately 200 miles south of Breaker Bay. Williams gave Smith the money to purchase heroin, but generally waited in a parked car near the housing project while Kent conducted the heroin transaction inside apartment 4J in the housing project. Mali and Maples relied on a number of heroin sources, including two unidentified Asian males, and on at least two occasions, John Smith.

5. According to information provided by a confidential informant and testimony presented at Leon Williams's trial, sometime in September 2006, Mali met Smith in November 2002 while they were being held by local police authorities on unrelated drug charges. While in custody, Mali told Smith that he sold small quantities of heroin in Breaker Bay and relied on various suppliers. Mali complained that his suppliers were unreliable and frequently provided him with heroin of poor quality. Smith, although cautious and somewhat suspicious of Mali, revealed that he might be aware of other suppliers whom Mali might use once he was released from custody and ready to resume his drug distribution operation. The two exchanged telephone numbers and agreed to discuss Smith's suppliers in the future. Several days later, Mali was released from custody and shortly thereafter resumed his heroin distribution operation with his partner Sammy Maples.

6. In early December 2002 Mali contacted Smith by telephone and discussed the possibility of obtaining 10 ounces of heroin. After several weeks of negotiations, Smith agreed to meet with Mali at Mali's apartment, accompanied by an unidentified Hispanic male. Prior to entering the apartment building in late January 1999, Smith was observed handling a package, which investigators later learned contained 300 grams of heroin, to the Hispanic male. Once inside the apartment, Mali tested a small sample of the heroin, and agreed to purchase the package of heroin for $70,000. Mali gave Smith the $70,000 in cash, and in turn, Smith directed the Hispanic male to give Mali the package of heroin. A short time later, Smith and his companion were observed leaving Mali's apartment.

7. Later that afternoon, Federal agents observed Leon Williams driving a 2002 Porsche in the vicinity of the housing project. Williams parked the vehicle nearby and was observed carrying a brown duffle bag as he entered the housing project where he proceeded to Mali's apartment. According to the confidential informant, once inside the apartment, Williams spoke briefly to Mali and Maples, and Mali and Williams proceeded to a back bedroom where Mali was known to weigh and package drugs. A few moments later, Williams and Mali returned to the living room of the apartment and Mali was carrying the brown duffle bag that Williams had brought to the apartment. Mali then emptied the duffle bag that contained a large sum of U.S. currency, bound in $50, $20, and $10 denominations. Mali assured Williams that he would find the heroin to be of high quality and agreed to provide additional quantities of heroin to Williams whenever his out-of-town buyer needed them. A short time later, Williams left the apartment and returned to the vehicle.

8. For over a year, agents maintained surveillance on Mali's apartment, and on many occasions, the agents monitored Smith's arrival at Mali's apartment followed by the arrival of Williams. On each occasion, Williams would remain outside, sitting in the 2002 Porsche, while Smith entered Mali's apartment. Smith would deliver a large duffle bag to the apartment and return a short time later carrying a small package under his arm. On June 14, 2005 an undercover agent of the Drug Enforcement Administration posing as a drug purchaser met with Mali in the vicinity of the housing project to negotiate the purchase of 10 grams of heroin. Mali told the undercover agent that he expected to receive a shipment of heroin the following day and that, while he anticipated transacting a large heroin deal with another out-of-town customer, he would be able to sell the undercover agent 10 grams of heroin from the shipment for $7,000.

9. For the next two days, Federal agents maintained 24-hour surveillance on the housing project and Mali's residence. On June 19, 2005 the agents observed Smith when he arrived at Mali's residence carrying a shopping bag. Smith arrived at the apartment with the shopping bag and had a gun which was visible in his waistband. Smith remained in Mali's apartment and a short time later, Williams arrived. Williams was carrying a blue gym bag. Shortly therafter the agents entered the apartment and the defendants scattered. The agents observed Maples, Williams, and Smith seated in a back bedroom of the apartment, and they were all placed under arrest without incident. Other Federal agents, who

were positioned outside of the apartment building, observed Mali as he jumped out of the apartment's kitchen window had landed in a patch of bushes on the ground below, where he was placed under arrest. At the time of Mali's arrest, a loaded .38 caliber revolver was found in the bushes near the spot where Mali landed. In addition, other agents proceeded to the parked Porsche. Agents recovered a .357 magnum revolver from Williams' waistband. Williams told agents that he had driven to Breaker Bay from Bodega Bay and had visited some friends.

10. The agents searched Mali's apartment and recovered a large quantity of suspected heroin from the toilet that the defendants attempted to destroy. The agents safeguarded the seized narcotics using plastic bags. The following day, the bags were reopened and the water/heroin solution was drained into plastic bottles for laboratory submission. According to the results of a later laboratory report, the agents recovered an additional 725.12 grams of 20 percent pure heroin. In addition, the agents recovered an additional 55.4 grams of 20 percent pure heroin from the top of the refrigerator in the kitchen, and heroin residue from a table in the bedroom, along with an Ohaus triple beam scale, a strainer, and other drug-related paraphernalia. Moreover, the agents seized $1032,160 in cash bundles of U.S. currency from the blue gym bag that the agents had previously observed being carried by Williams, and $16,870 from Williams' jacket pockets.

11. The agents then proceeded to apartment 6J where, according to confidential informant information, Mali was believed to store narcotics proceeds and other property. The apartment was occupied by Michael Mali's mother, Carol Mali, who consented to the search of the apartment. Agents recovered an additional $13,000 in cash and jewelry, later appraised to be valued at $50,000.

12. All of the participants in the offense shared equally important functions in this loosely organized heroin distribution operation. Defendant John Smith was the supplier for the June transactions. Michael Mali and Sammy Maples were the brokers, while Williams was a buyer, who authorities believe operated a street-level heroin distribution operation in Bodega Bay, Maryland, and he frequently traveled to Breaker Bay to purchase heroin. A total of 1090.52 grams (or slightly more than one kilogram) of heroin was distributed during the course of this offense, which has an estimated wholesale value of $350,000.

Victim Impact

13. There were no victims in this offense.

Adjustment for Obstruction of Justice

14. Although Mali attempted to flee prior to his arrest, he was apprehended almost immediately. The probation officer has no other information to suggest that the defendant impeded or obstructed justice.

Adjustment for Acceptance of Responsibility

15. During an interview with drug enforcement officials shortly after his arrest, and later during an interview with the probation officer, Mali readily admitted his involvement in this offense. In substance, Mali acknowledged that he had participated in this conspiracy to distribute heroin and takes full responsibility for his conduct.

Offense Level Computation

16. The 2007 edition of the *Guidelines Manual* has been used in this case.

17. Base Offense Level: The guideline for 18 U.S.C. 846 is found in U.S.S.G. § 2D1.4. That section provides that the base offense level for a narcotics conspiracy shall be the same as if the object of the conspiracy or attempt had been completed. In this case, the defendant conspired to distribute 1,090.52 grams of heroin. In accordance with the provisions found in U.S.S.G. § 2D1.1(a)(3)(c)(6), the base offense level is 32.   32

18. Specific Offense Characteristics: Pursuant to the provision in U.S.S.G. § 2D1.1(b)(1) because the agents retrieved a loaded .38 caliber revolver in the bushes where the defendant was arrested, the offense level is increased by two levels.   +2

19. Victim Related Adjustments: None   0

20. Adjustment for Role in the Offense: None   0

21. Adjustment for Obstruction of Justice: None   0

22. Adjustment for Acceptance of Responsibility: The defendant has shown recognition of responsibility for the offense and a reduction of two levels for Acceptance of Responsibility is applicable under U.S.S.G. § 3E1.1.   −2

23. Total Offense Level: 32

Chapter Four Enhancements

24. Career Criminal Provision: In accordance with the provisions found in U.S.S.G. § 4B1.1, because the defendant was at least 18 years old at the time of the instant offense, and the defendant had at least two prior felony controlled substance convictions as detailed below, Mali is a career criminal and the adjusted offense level is 37.   37

25. Adjustment for Acceptance of Responsibility: The defendant has shown recognition of responsibility for the offense and a reduction of two levels for Acceptance of Responsibility is applicable under U.S.S.G. § 3E1.1.   −2

26. Total Offense Level: 35

Part B. The Defendant's Criminal History

Juvenile Adjudications

27. None

Adult Criminal Convictions

	Date of Arrest	Conviction/ Court	Date Sentence Imposed/Disp.	Guidelines/ Points
28.	3/2/93	Criminal sale of controlled substance, Class D Felony, Breaker Bay Superior Court, Breaker Bay, MD Dkt. #86541	9/23/93, 5 years probation	4A1.1(c) ... 1

The defendant was represented by counsel. Mali was arrested, along with Sidney Reynolds, after Breaker Bay police officers observed them selling a quantity of heroin to a third individual not arrested. At the time of arrest, the police recovered 20 glassine envelopes of heroin which, according to a later laboratory report, had a total net weight of 3 grams. Mali was represented by counsel and subsequently pled guilty as noted above, although during his interview with the Breaker Bay county probation officer, he denied his guilt in the offense, stating that he pled guilty in return for the assurance that he would be placed on probation supervision. According to local county probation records, Mali successfully completed probation supervision and was given an early discharge from that supervision on September 27, 1994.

| 29. | 4/4/95 | Criminal sale of controlled substance, Class C Felony, Breaker Bay Superior Court, Breaker Bay, Dkt. # 869215 | 10/24/95, 2 to 4 years imprisonment, paroled 8/4/96, parole revoked 2/27/97, MD returned to custody. | 4A1.1(a) | 3 |

The defendant was represented by counsel. Police officers observed the defendant passing glassine envelopes to others in exchange for money. At the time of his arrest, police officers recovered 55 glassine envelopes containing 2.5 grams of heroin and 16 glassine envelopes containing 26 grams of cocaine, marked "Freeze," wrapped to Mali's arm. Mali failed to return to court as scheduled on July 26, 1994, and a bench warrant was issued for his arrest. The defendant was subsequently returned to court when he was arrested on a new unrelated charge. During his interview with the probation officer, Mali freely acknowledged possession of the narcotics, although he explained that the drugs were for his own personal use. Mali was arrested on the below-listed charges shortly after his release on parole. According to State parole officials, the defendant's parole was violated and he was returned to state custody. His sentence ran to expiration.

| 30. | 4/14/98 | Criminal possession of marijuana, 5th degree, Class B Misd., Breaker Bay Criminal Court, Breaker Bay, MD Dkt. # 245678 | 9/27/98 7 days imprisonment | 4A1.1(a) | 1 |

The defendant was represented by counsel. Mali was arrested and originally charged with assault, resisting arrest and criminal possession of marijuana, while at liberty on bail in connection with the above-mentioned offense.

| 31. | 8/19/01 | Robbery, 3rd degree, Class E Felony, Breaker Bay Superior Court, Breaker Bay, MD Dkt. # 258769 | 2/27/02 18 months probation | | 3 |

The defendant was represented by counsel. Mali was arrested by Breaker Bay Transit police officers after he snatched a gold chain from a victim's neck. According to the victim, who sustained minor injuries, the defendant approached him at gunpoint and demanded that he remove the gold chain. When the victim resisted, Mali snatched the chain and fled, but was apprehended when he ran into two transit officers who were standing nearby. Officers determined that Mali was intoxicated on the basis of a urinalysis test conducted later. No firearm was recovered from Mali, and Mali said he didn't have a firearm; rather, he pointed a cell phone at the victim pretending that it was a gun. Mali was placed on probation for 18 months.

Criminal History Computation

32. The criminal convictions above result in a subtotal criminal history score of 8.

33. At the time when the instant offense was committed, Mali was on probation supervision. In accordance with the provisions of U.S.S.G. § 4A1.1(d), two points are added.

34. The instant offense was committed less than two years following Mali's previous conviction. As such, pursuant to U.S.S.G. § 4B1.1, one point is added.

35. The total criminal history score is 11, and according to the sentencing table found in chapter 5, part A, 10 to 12 criminal history points establish a criminal history category of V; however, the defendant's criminal history category is enhanced to a VI because he is considered a career criminal.

36. As detailed above, the defendant has three prior felony convictions involving controlled substances and a crime of violence, and as such pursuant to the provisions found in U.S.S.G. § 4B1.1, Mali is a career criminal and his criminal history category must be a VI.

Part C. Offender Characteristics

Personal and Family Data

37. Michael Mali was born on March 19, 1973, in Breaker Bay, Maryland, to the union of Carlos and Carol Mali, nee Hewson. His parents were never married and seldom lived together making it necessary for his mother to obtain public assistance for financial support. According to the defendant, his father died in 1991 following a massive heart attack. Prior to his death, the father collected public assistance for financial support and had difficulty maintaining employment. Michael has one brother, David Mali, age 43, who was reared by his maternal grandmother in Washington, DC. David was previously convicted of narcotics charges in the District of Columbia in May, 1992, and sentenced to 30 months imprisonment. At the present time, David is serving a three-year term of supervised release in this district and is living with their mother, age 67, at the Breaker Bay public housing development in an apartment where the defendant was arrested in the instant offense.

38. The defendant was reared by his paternal grandmother, Claudia Mali, now age 75, who has resided at the Breaker Bay housing project at 1430 Bird Avenue for the past 30 years. According to the defendant, he has a good relationship with his mother and brother, David, although he acknowledged that he has not seen them in several months primarily because his mother abuses alcohol and is difficult to talk to when she is intoxicated.

39. According to the defendant's grandmother, she assumed responsibility for Michael when he was approximately 12 years old because of the frequent fights and discord in the mother's residence which is located in a nearby building within the same housing project. Michael was a quiet child and was frequently neglected by his mother who never provided a positive living environment for Michael and frequently allowed him to miss school. The defendant's mother has a reported history of narcotics abuse and was frequently hospitalized and treated for alcohol and narcotics abuse. The grandmother explained that she was employed as a laundry worker prior to her retirement eight years ago and now collects Social Security insurance and retirement benefits for financial support. She explained that she has always felt that Michael had the potential for positive contributions to the community but was frequently sidetracked by his friends.

40. The defendant has never been married, but from 1996-1998 maintained a long-term relationship with his former girlfriend, Jackie Smith, now age 27. This union produced one child, Chanel Mali, now age 5, who currently resides with Smith's mother in an apartment at the Breaker Bay housing project. Several attempts to contact Ms. Smith have been unsuccessful.

41. Simultaneously from 1994 until the present, Mali has maintained an ongoing relationship with Mary Santeangelo, now age 26. The union has produced one child, Cynthia Mali, who was born on

October 1, 1997. Mali states that for approximately four months prior to his arrest, he was residing in a third-floor apartment in a three-family house in Bodega Bay, Maryland, which he shared with Ms. Santeangelo that rented for $500 a month. Mali states that after his arrest, Ms. Santeangelo lost the apartment because she was unable to pay the rent and now resides with her mother in an apartment on the lower west side of Breaker Bay. Attempts to contact Ms. Santeangelo have proven negative in that she has failed to appear at the probation office for several scheduled interviews. While the defendant describes his relationship with Ms. Dee in positive terms, he has elected to reside with his grandmother upon his release from custody.

Physical Condition

42. Michael Mali is 5' 7" tall and weighs 170 pounds. He has brown eyes and brown hair, and at the time of our interview, he wore a mustache and goatee. The defendant states that he is in good general health, but noted that he was hospitalized in April 1994 and treated for a gunshot wound to the arm, which he states he received from a stray 9mm hollowpoint round fired by his co-defendant, Sammy Maples, at someone else in a dispute. While medical records have been requested and are awaited, the defendant states that the bullet broke his arm and he still has bullet fragments in his arm. In addition, Mali noted that he was hospitalized in 1997 after he received a stab wound on his left arm during an argument with his then girlfriend, Jackie Smith.

Mental and Emotional Health

43. The defendant states that he has never been seen by a psychiatrist and describes his overall mental and emotional health as good. We have no documented evidence to suggest otherwise. During our interview, the defendant communicated effectively, but his demeanor is street-wise and tough.

Substance Abuse

44. The defendant states that prior to his arrest he drank alcohol almost every day; however, he does not believe that he is in need of alcohol treatment. The defendant revealed that he has smoked marijuana regularly since 1988 and from 1990–1993, he inhaled cocaine and smoked crack cocaine. According to Mali, prior to his state incarceration, he spent approximately $200 a day to support his cocaine addiction, but has been relatively drug-free since his release from state custody. While in State custody, Mali completed the Network Substance Abuse Program. He attended an out-patient treatment program for a brief period after he tested positive for cocaine in January 1999. At the time of his arrest in this offense, a urine specimen collected from the defendant by a pretrial services officer tested positive for marijuana and opiates.

Educational and Vocational Skills

45. Mali attended Breaker Bay High School from September 1987 until October 1990, when he was discharged in the first semester of the 12th grade at age 17. According to school officials, the defendant had a poor scholastic record, but had an average attendance record and attitude. According to State corrections records, the defendant was administered the BETA IQ test in November 1988 and scored 93. The defendant enrolled in adult education programming and a pre-GED course in July 1994 until December 1999, but was discharged from the program due to disciplinary action. While in the program he was characterized as an average student, according to available academic reports.

Employment Record

46. Mali states that he was briefly employed by messenger services prior to his state prison terms. While under probation supervision, Mali was gainfully employed for a messenger service, was a waiter, and later a cook, until approximately February 1998. Mali was also employed as a porter and dishwasher, earning $6.00 an hour, with Caroline's at Breaker Bay Sea Port from October 2, 1991 until he resigned in February, 1996. According to a representative from Caroline's, Mali was a reliable and good worker, and he would be considered for rehire.

47. Mali candidly admitted that during significant periods of employment, he sold marijuana, cocaine, and heroin to support himself. Mali asserts that he has earned as much as $18,000 a day from his narcotics activities. While such claims cannot be directly verified, the Government seized approximately $13,000 in cash and $5,500 in jewelry from the apartment of the defendant's mother on the day of the defendant's arrest. Mali states that he used the money to enjoy the "fast life," which included the purchase of a 2005 Audi 5000, also recently seized by the Government.

Financial Condition: Ability to Pay

48. The defendant prepared a signed financial statement, wherein he reported no assets or liabilities. His counsel has been appointed by the court, and a recent credit bureau inquiry reveals that the defendant has never established credit. Mali has no known sources of income and upon his release he will be financially dependent upon others.

Part D: Sentencing Options

Custody

49. Statutory Provisions: The minimum term of imprisonment for this offense, a Class A felony, is ten years and the maximum term of imprisonment is life, pursuant to 18 U.S.C. 846 and 841(b)(1)(A).

50. Guideline Provisions: Based upon a total offense level of 35 and a criminal history category of VI, the guideline imprisonment range is 292 to 365 months.

Impact of Plea Agreement

51. Under the plea agreement, Mali has entered a guilty plea to count one, the conspiracy count, in return for the dismissal of all other counts. Pursuant to U.S.S.G. § 3D1.2(d), counts involving the same transaction are grouped together into a single group. All of the substantive counts in this offense pertain to the same transactions. Accordingly a conviction on the additional counts would not affect the offense level or any other guideline calculation.

Supervised Release

52. Statutory Provisions: If a term of imprisonment is imposed, a term of supervised release of five years must also be imposed, pursuant to 18 U.S.C. 3583(b)(2).

53. Guideline Provisions: The guideline range for a term of supervised release is at least five years, pursuant to U.S.S.G. § 5B1.1(b)(1).

Probation

54. Statutory Provisions: The defendant is ineligible for probation, pursuant to 18 U.S.C. 846 and 841(b)(1)(A).

55. Guideline Provisions: The defendant is ineligible for probation, pursuant to U.S.S.G. § 5B1.1(b)(1).

Fines

56. Statutory Provisions: The maximum fine for this offense is $4,000,000, pursuant to 18 U.S.C. 846 and 841(b)(1)(A).

57. A special assessment of $50 is mandatory, pursuant to 18 U.SC. 3013.

58. Guideline Provisions: Pursuant to .S.S.G. § 5E1.2(c)(3), the minimum fine for this offense is $20,000 and the maximum fine is $4,000,000.

59. Subject to the defendant's ability to pay, the court shall impose an additional fine amount that is at least sufficient to pay the costs to the Government of any imprisonment, probation, or supervised release, pursuant to U.S.S.G. § 5E1.2(i). the most recent advisory from the Administrative Office of the U.S. Court suggests that a monthly cost of $1,210.05 be used for imprisonment, a monthly cost of $91.66 for supervision, and a monthly cost of $938.44 for community confinement.

Restitution

60. Restitution is not an issue in this case.

Denial of Federal Benefits

61. Statutory Provisions: Pursuant to 18 U.S.C. 862, upon a second conviction for possession of a controlled substance a defendant may be declared ineligible for any or all Federal benefits for up to five years as determined by the court.

62. Guideline Provisions: Pursuant to U.S.S.G. § 5F1.6, the court may deny eligibility for certain Federal benefits of any individual convicted of distribution or possession of a controlled substance.

Part E. Factors that May Warrant Departure

63. The assistant U.S. attorney has filed a motion pursuant to 18 U.S.C. § 3553(e) and U.S.S.G. § 5K1.1, advising that the defendant has provided substantial assistance to the Government. Accordingly, the Government will recommend a sentence below the mandatory minimum sentence and applicable guideline range.

Respectfully submitted,

Frank D. Gilbert
Chief Probation Officer

By

_____

John W. Phillips
U.S. Probation Officer

Reviewed and Approved:

_____

William Hackett
Supervising U.S. Probation Officer

SENTENCING RECOMMENDATION

United States v. Michael Mali,
U.S. District Court, Eastern District

Custody

Statutory maximum:	10 years to life
Guideline range:	292 to 365 months
Recommendation:	180 months

Fine

Statutory maximum:	$4,000,000
Guideline range:	$20,000 to $4,000,000
Recommendation:	$0

Supervised Release

Statutory maximum:	5 years
Guideline range:	At least 5 years
Recommended sentence:	5 years

Probation

Statutory term:	Ineligible
Guideline term:	Ineligible
Recommended term:	Not applicable

Restitution

Statutory provisions:	Not applicable
Guideline provisions:	Not applicable
Recommended sentence:	Not applicable

Special Assessment

Statutory provisions:	$50
Guideline provisions:	$50
Recommended sentence:	$50

Justification:

We have been advised by the assistant U.S. attorney, who has filed a motion for downward departure in this case, that Mali entered into a cooperation agreement shortly after his arrest. In addition to his testimony at the trial of another defendant, Mali has reportedly provided substantial and extraordinary cooperation relative to organized crime figures, over and beyond the scope of the instant offense. While the Government has filed a motion for downward departure, the conduct in this offense, coupled with the defendant's prior criminal record, would have otherwise supported a sentence near the higher end of the guideline range. Mali has an extensive criminal record, which includes two prior drug-related convictions. At the age of 34, Mali has a limited employment record and, by his own admission, has primarily supported himself through lucrative narcotics trafficking. He has a history of violence and appears to be extremely street-wise and tough. As such, his overall prognosis for rehabilitation is extremely poor, he poses a risk for recidivism, and a sentence of 15 years imprisonment appears appropriate for the protection of the community.

The mandatory five-year statutory term of supervised release is recommended in this case with a special condition requiring drug testing and treatment in view of the defendant's history of drug and alcohol abuse. While the defendant is subject to the provision of Federal benefit denial, in view of his expected prison sentence, these provisions will expire prior to his release from custody. The defendant does not have the ability to pay a fine at this time. No fine is recommended and therefore, the fine payment should be waived by the court. Although the court may deny Federal benefits to the defendant for up to five years, denial of such benefits is not recommended. Unless the defendant were to receive less than a five-year sentence in this case, the period of ineligibility would expire while he is incarcerated.

Voluntary Surrender

The defendant has been detained without bail since his arrest. In light of his conviction and expected lengthy prison sentence, Mali is not eligible for voluntary surrender in accordance with the provisions found in 18 U.S.C. 3143(a)(2).

Recommendation

It is respectfully recommended that sentence in this case be imposed as follows:

Pursuant to the Sentencing Reform Act of 1984, it is the judgment of the court that the defendant, Michael Mali, is hereby committed to the custody of the Bureau of Prisons to be imprisoned for a term of 180 months.

Upon release from imprisonment, the defendant shall be placed on supervised release for a term of five years. Within 72 hours of release from the custody of the Bureau of Prisons, the defendant shall report in person to the probation office in the district to which the defendant is released.

While on supervised release, the defendant shall not commit another Federal, state, or local crime. The defendant shall be prohibited from possessing a firearm or other dangerous device, and he shall not possess a controlled substance. In addition, the defendant shall comply with the standard conditions of supervised release as recommended by the United States Sentencing Commission. The defendant shall also comply with the following special conditions of supervised release: The defendant shall participate in a program of testing and treatment for drug and alcohol abuse, as directed by the probation officer, until such time as the defendant is released from the program by the probation officer.

THE COURT FINDS that the defendant does not have the ability to pay a fine.

IT IS ORDERED that the defendant pay a special assessment in the amount of $50 for Count one which shall be due immediately.

Respectfully submitted,

Frank D. Gilbert
Chief Probation Officer

By

John W. Phillips
U.S. Probation Officer

Reviewed and Approved:

_____

William Hackett
Supervising U.S. Probation Officer

Date: September 12, 2007

ADDENDUM TO THE PRESENTENCE REPORT

The probation officer certifies that the presentence report, including any revision thereof, has been disclosed to the defendant, his attorney, and counsel for the Government, and that the content of the Addendum has been communicated to counsel. The Addendum fairly states any objections they have made.

OBJECTIONS

By the Government

The Government has no objections.

By the Defendant

The defense attorney has no objections.

CERTIFIED BY

Frank D. Gilbert
Chief Probation Officer

By

_____

John W. Phillips
U.S. Probation Officer

Reviewed and Approved:

_____

William Hackett
Supervising U.S. Probation Officer

Chapter Outline

Chapter Objectives

As the result of reading this chapter, the following objectives will be realized:

1. Defining probation.
2. Distinguishing probation from parole.
3. Describing the historical development of probation and the various persons instrumental in its occurrence and adoption in the United States.
4. Discussing the different functions served by probation.
5. Distinguishing between first-offenders and recidivists.
6. Examining selected probation trends.
7. Describing the early origins of probation and the subsequent development of modern probation programs in the United States.
8. Describing several popular models that have been used as patterns for modern probation programs.
9. Describing the historical bases of diversion and those clients most likely to qualify for it.
10. Highlighting some of the major criticisms and functions of diversion.
11. Examining the process of alternative dispute resolution and its functions.
12. Identifying several models used by probation officers to guide their supervision of offender-clients.
13. Describing victim–offender reconciliation projects and their functions.
14. Describing judicial discretion in the probation process.

DO ANY OF THESE CASES DESERVE PROBATION?

• *Rick M., age 46, is a detective in a large Midwestern city. He has a drinking problem and gambles heavily through online gaming on the Internet. He is divorced with four dependent children and pays substantial child support and alimony. Recently he has been reporting late for work, failing to file timely reports associated with his criminal investigations, and other detectives suspect him of drinking on the job. None of this has been reported to superiors. In January 2006 Rick M. is picked up by police officers in a routine sweep of drug dealers in a high drug-trafficking area of the city. He identifies himself as a detective and professes to be working undercover. The arresting officers turn him over to other detectives, together with eight ounces of cocaine in glassine envelopes Rick M. was carrying. An investigation reveals that Rick M. has over $140,000 in gambling debts and has maxed out his credit cards. The illegal drugs he possessed were taken surreptitiously from the evidence room at the police station. Rick M. was selling drugs for money and using the proceeds to gamble. A subsequent drug test reveals that Rick M. is not using drugs. However, he admits to having serious drinking and gambling problems. An 18-year veteran of the police force, Rick M. has received prior commendations for meritorious police work leading to the arrests and convictions of many serious offenders. Rick M.'s case is turned over to the district attorney. Rick M.'s lawyer advises that Rick M. has declared bankruptcy and has voluntarily entered a rehabilitation clinic to work on his drinking and gambling addictions. What should the district attorney do?*

• *Vincent G., age 29, is a drug user and dealer. He traffics in crack cocaine, methamphetamines, and other illegal narcotics and substances. He is arrested by police officers who charge him with drug trafficking and possession. A preliminary investigation reveals that Vincent G. is a college graduate, earned a master's degree, taught in a high school for five years, and is divorced with two children. He has no prior criminal record.*

He has confessed to dealing drugs for eight months prior to his arrest. He advises that some friends introduced him to cocaine about two years earlier, and that he believes he is addicted to cocaine. He acknowledges that he sells drugs in order to sustain his drug habit. In discussions with the district attorney and his lawyer, Vincent G. agrees to give up his sources for drugs in exchange for sentencing leniency. What sentence should Vincent G. receive?

• Craig R., age 52, is a sex offender. He has been convicted on three prior occasions for various sex offenses, including soliciting a 14-year-old male child for sex, attempted sexual assault of a 15-year-old girl, and sodomy of a 12-year-old male from his church. Recently Craig R. was arrested for attempted sexual assault of a 16-year-old male, also a member of his church, who reported the incident to his mother. Craig R. was arrested on the attempted sexual assault charge and held without bond. Subsequently in a jury trial, a jury found Craig R. guilty of the attempted sexual assault charge, which carries a penalty of 15 years to life. The primary aggravating circumstances are Craig R.'s prior arrests and convictions and the sexual assault of a child. What sentence should the judge impose?

• Lakeesha Blake, age 31, has a prior record of four prostitution convictions, soliciting of prostitution, three convictions for petty theft, and one conviction for petty larceny. She has spent two years in jail and has been on probation numerous times for different offenses. Recently she was apprehended for stealing some lipstick from a K-Mart store. Unable to afford private counsel, Blake was assigned a public defender. Blake admits to having the lipstick in her possession but claims that she was going to pay for it. Her present situation is that she is unemployed, living with her aunt, and does part-time laundry work for neighbors. She has no drug or alcohol problems. The prosecutor scans her record and notes that when she was on probation in the past, her behavior was without incident. But her long record of convictions is working against her. The prosecutor plea bargains the case with the public defender and advises that she will recommend leniency and probation to the judge in exchange for a guilty plea to simple larceny. What sentence should the judge impose?

• Jerry J. is 22 years old, started his career of crime early at the age of 9 stealing automobiles for a car theft ring, and is a gang member. He has been convicted four times for vehicular theft, and in each case, Jerry J. was placed on probation. This time Jerry J. is facing charges of conspiracy to commit vehicular theft, together with several other co-defendants, who are also gang members. Jerry J.'s public defender has argued that Jerry J.'s home life has been problematic, with an alcoholic father and drug-dependent mother. Jerry J. has had several jobs at auto body shops, but these jobs have been short-lived. Jerry J. has never been employed by any single company or establishment for longer than 3 months. Jerry J.'s defense counsel is asking the judge for probation in exchange for Jerry J.'s admission to possession of a stolen car, a lesser-included offense to the conspiracy charge. Given Jerry J.'s prior criminal record and gang affiliation, should the judge accept the plea bargain agreement and place Jerry J. on probation again?

WHAT HAPPENED?

• Rick M. was placed on diversion, allowed to keep his job and retirement benefits, and has agreed to participate in alcohol and gambling addiction treatment programs for a two-year period. The record of his arrest will be expunged following his diversionary period. Rick M. attends Alcoholics Anonymous meetings as well as Gamblers Anonymous meetings. He has been reassigned to a desk job at the police station, where he works in fingerprint identification.

• *Vincent G. was given a five-year suspended sentence. He was placed on probation and ordered to attend addiction classes to deal with his cocaine dependency. He was ordered to obtain work and remain employed during the period of his probation. Presently he is under intensive supervised probation and submits to biweekly drug and alcohol checks.*

• *Craig R. was sentenced to 15 years to life for the attempted sexual assault charge. The judge ordered sex offender therapy and counseling for Craig R. while imprisoned.*

• *Lakeesha Blake was sentenced to 9 months in the county jail and given credit against her sentence for time served. Following her sentence, she was ordered to intensive supervised probation. She was also ordered to perform 100 hours of community service and pay $2,500 in court costs, fines, and restitution.*

• *The judge rejected Jerry J.'s bid and sentenced him to a mandatory five years in prison to be following by a probationary term of five years. Jerry J. will be intensively supervised while on probation, and he must not have any contact with his former gang associates. He must seek employment and perform community service.*

INTRODUCTION

These scenarios are examples of many types of cases judges throughout the United States decide every day. Each case is decided on its own merits. Different jurisdictions are involved and there are numerous variations in sentences imposed for seemingly similar offenses. One thread common to all cases above is that in each situation, the presiding judge had a decision to make. Should the offender receive probation?

This chapter is about probation in the United States. The first section defines probation and places it in a historical context. Probation is unique to the United States and its origins date to the 1830s. Besides describing the historical antecedents of probation and its emergence throughout the nation, the philosophy of probation is presented. Next, various models that practitioners use for dealing with probationers is described. These models are orientations that influence the types of treatments or programs designed for probationers. These models also reflect the nature of political sentiment at particular points in our history, ranging from primarily treatment-centered and rehabilitation-oriented to more justice-oriented, due-process frames of reference for guiding PO and probation agency thinking and practice. Several important functions of probation are also presented. The chapter concludes with a profile of probationers, including first-offenders and recidivists.

The final part of the chapter examines several pretrial options available to prosecutors whenever low-level, nonserious types of offenders have committed crimes. It is not always feasible to pursue criminal charges against certain defendants, especially when such cases can be resolved through less stigmatized civil proceedings. Thus, two options are presented, including pretrial diversion and alternative dispute resolution. Both of these options require court approval, although they often result in satisfactory resolutions of disputes between complainants and offenders. In recent years, restorative justice has been used to describe a slightly different civil dispute resolution option available to prosecutors and the courts. This process is described. The chapter concludes with a brief discussion of judicial discretion in probation decision making.

PROBATION DEFINED

Probation is releasing convicted offenders into the community under a conditional suspended sentence, avoiding imprisonment, showing good behavior, under the supervision of a probation officer (Black, 1990:1202). The word *probation* derives from the Latin usage *probatio. Probatio* means a period of proving or trial and forgiveness. Thus, offenders who prove themselves during the trial period by complying with the conditions of their probation are forgiven and released from further involvement with the criminal justice system. Their criminal records may not be expunged or forgotten, but at the very least, they avoid incarceration.

Probation is applied among the states in many different ways. In some states, probation is granted for particular crimes, whereas in other states, the same type of offense might draw prison or jail time. In order to understand the nature and reasons for this variation when probation is imposed, we must examine interstate variation of criminal statutes as well as federal criminal laws. Every state or federal criminal statute carries statutory sanctions. These sanctions always provide for the *possibility* of incarceration and/or a fine, depending on the seriousness of the offense. In Tennessee, for instance, a convicted shoplifter is punished by a fine of *not more than* three hundred dollars ($300) or imprisonment for *not more than* six (6) months, or both (T.C.A., 39-3-1124, 2007). A conviction for violating a federal criminal law, such as the willful destruction of United States government property not exceeding the sum of $100, is punishable by a fine of *not more than* $1,000 or by imprisonment for *not more than* one year, or both (18 U.S.C. Sec. 1361, 2007). If United States government property damage exceeds $100, the punishment escalates to a fine of *not more than* $10,000 or imprisonment for *not more than* ten years, or both (18 U.S.C., Sec. 1361, 2007).

The important phrase in these statutes is *not more than.* Judges have the discretionary power to sentence offenders to the maximum penalties provided by law (e.g., whatever maximum penalties are provided in each criminal statute). Or judges may decide to impose no penalties. A third option is that they may impose a portion of the maximum sentence prescribed by the particular criminal statute. Sometimes, a judge may declare, "You are hereby sentenced to six months in the county jail and ordered to pay a $500 fine—the six-month sentence is suspended upon the payment of a $500 fine and court costs." Or the judge may say, "You are sentenced to four years in prison, but I suspend the four-year sentence and I order you placed on probation for four years." All judges have diverse sentencing options.

In the federal system, until November 1987, federal judges were encouraged to refrain from incarcerating convicted offenders. In fact, 18 U.S.C., Sec. 3582 (2007) says that "recognizing that imprisonment is not an appropriate means of promoting correction and rehabilitation," the court (judge) should consider any relevant policy statements by the Sentencing Commission and recommend an appropriate sentence for the defendant. Furthermore, 18 U.S.C., Sec. 3651 (2007) provides that judges may grant probation for any offense not punishable by death or life imprisonment, when they are satisfied that the ends of justice and the best interest of the public as well as the defendant will be served. Within this same section, the period of probation is limited to five years, regardless of more excessive penalties associated with the original sentence and fine. Several states have followed these federal guidelines in the writing of their own sentencing provisions and guidelines.

THE HISTORY OF PROBATION IN THE UNITED STATES

Many American laws and judicial procedures in the United States have been influenced by early British common law and judicial customs. Also, evidence shows a distinct British influence on United States prison architecture and design as well as other corrections-related phenomena.

Judicial Reprieves and Releases on an Offender's Recognizance

During the late 1700s and early 1800s, English judges increasingly exercised their discretion in numerous criminal cases by granting convicted offenders **judicial reprieves.** Under English common law, judicial reprieves were suspending the incarcerative sentences of convicted offenders. These were demonstrations of judicial leniency, especially in those cases where offenders had no prior records, had committed minor offenses, and where the punishments were deemed excessive by the courts. Judges believed that in certain cases, incarceration would serve no useful purpose. While no accurate records are available about how many convicted offenders actually received judicial reprieves in English courts during this period, the practice of granting judicial reprieves was adopted by some judges in the United States.

Judges in Massachusetts courts during the early 1800s typically used their discretionary powers to suspend incarcerative sentences of particular offenders. Jail and prison overcrowding no doubt influenced their interest in devising options to incarceration. One of the more innovative judges of that period was Boston Municipal Judge Peter Oxenbridge Thatcher. Judge Thatcher used judicial leniency when sentencing offenders. He also sentenced some offenders to be released on their own recognizance (ROR), either before or after their criminal charges had been adjudicated. Thatcher's decision to release convicted offenders on their own recognizance amounted to an indefinite suspension of their incarcerative sentences. Thatcher believed that such sentences would encourage convicted offenders to practice good behavior and refrain from committing new crimes.

While judicial reprieves and suspensions of incarcerative sentences for indefinite periods continued throughout the nineteenth century, the United States Supreme Court declared this practice unconstitutional in 1916. The Supreme Court believed that such discretion among judges infringed the "separation of powers" principle by contravening the powers of the legislative and executive branches to write laws and ensure their enforcement. However, during the 1830s when releases on an offender's own recognizance and judicial reprieves flourished, the stage was set for the work of another Boston correctional pioneer.

John Augustus, the Father of Probation in the United States

Many court practices in the United States have been inherited from England, but there are many exceptions. In corrections, probation is one of those exceptions. Probation in the United States was conceived in 1841 by the successful cobbler or shoemaker and philanthropist **John Augustus,** although historical references to this phenomenon may be found in writings as early as 422–437 B.C. Of course, the actions of Judge Thatcher have been regarded by some scholars as probation, since he sentenced convicted offenders to release on their own recognizance instead of jail. However, John Augustus is most often credited with pioneering probation in the United States, although statutes existed at the time to label it or how it should be conducted (Champion, 2005).

The Temperance Movement against alcohol provided the right climate for using probation. Augustus attempted to rehabilitate alcoholics and to assist those arrested for alcohol-related offenses. Appearing in a Boston municipal court one morning to observe offenders charged and sentenced for various crimes, Augustus intervened on behalf of a man charged with being a "common drunkard" (Augustus, 1852). Instead of placing the convicted offender in the **Boston House of Corrections,** Augustus volunteered to supervise the man for a three-week period and personally guaranteed his reappearance later. Knowing Augustus's reputation for philanthropy and trusting his motives, the judge agreed with this proposal. When Augustus returned three weeks later with the drunkard, the judge was so impressed with the man's improved behavior that he fined him only one cent and court costs, which were less than $4.00. The judge also suspended the six-month jail term. Between 1841 and 1859, the year Augustus died, nearly 2,000 men and women were spared incarceration because of Augustus's intervention and supervision.

Augustus attracted several other philanthropic volunteers to perform similar probation services. These volunteers worked with juvenile offenders as well as with adults. However, few records were kept about the dispositions of juveniles. Thus, the precise number of those who benefited from the work of Augustus and his volunteers is unknown. In all likelihood, several thousand youths probably were supervised effectively as informal probationers.

The Ideal-Real Dilemma: Philosophies in Conflict

Probation was a true correctional innovation in 1841. Before Augustus's work, offenders convicted of criminal offenses were either fined, imprisoned, or both. Between 1790 and 1817, sentences in United States courts had to be served in their entirety (Champion, 2005). Federal prisoners increased beyond the government's capacity to confine them, and overcrowding became a critical correctional issue. Today, jail and prison overcrowding is the greatest problem confronting corrections. After 1817, prison systems began releasing some prisoners early before serving their full terms. These **early release** decisions were often made informally by prison administrators, with court approval. Thus, the informal use of parole in the United States technically preceded the informal use of probation by several decades.

Presently, the **get-tough movement** is pressing for a return to sentencing policies that were practiced in the early 1800s, where convicted offenders had to serve their full incarcerative terms. The get-tough movement is not a specific association of persons with a defined membership list who band together for the purpose of creating harsher punishments for criminal offenders. Rather, the term is used to characterize a general philosophy meaning tougher criminal laws, longer imprisonment lengths for convicted offenders, greater fines, and closer supervision of those who are placed on either probation or parole.

Prison and jail overcrowding continue to frustrate efforts by judges and others to incarcerate larger numbers of convicted offenders for their full sentences. Court-ordered prison and jail inmate population reductions shorten the actual amount of time served by inmates. Logistical considerations involving where convicted offenders may be housed often conflict with the philosophy of just-deserts and punishment. Furthermore, the constitutional rights of inmates must be preserved. These include the right to prison and jail environments that ensure inmate health and safety. While no constitutional provisions exist that require prison and jail administrators to provide comfortable quarters for inmates, penal authorities are obligated to ensure that their incarcerative environments are not "cruel and unusual" and in violation of the Eighth Amendment (Faulkner, 2002).

Public Reaction to Probation

Many citizens believe that probation actually means coddling offenders and causes them not to take their punishment seriously (Arthur, 2000). In the 1840s, Augustus himself was criticized by the press, politicians, and especially jailers. The livelihood of jailers was based on the cost of care and inmate accommodations, including provisions for food and clothing. Jailer income was based on the numbers of prisoners housed in jails. The greater the occupancy, the greater the jailer's income. Under such a system of jailer rewards, some jailers embezzled funds intended for inmate food and clothing for their own use. While it is unknown how much embezzlement occurred among jailers while this arrangement thrived, it is known that more than a few jailers profited from large inmate populations.

Augustus's philanthropy indirectly decreased profiteering among those jailers embezzling funds allocated for inmate care. The lack of an effective system of accountability for these funds explains why the Boston House of Corrections, as well as other Massachusetts jails of that period, was described as a "rat-infested hellhole to be avoided if at all possible" (Gura, 2002). But Augustus could not save everyone from incarceration. In fact, that was not his intention. He only wanted to rescue those he felt worthy of rehabilitation. Therefore, Augustus screened offenders by asking them questions and engaging in informal background checks of their acquaintances and personal habits. Particularly, he limited his generosity to first-offenders or those never before convicted of a criminal offense. By Augustus's own account, only one offender out of nearly 2,000 ever violated his trust (Gura, 2002). Pre-sentence investigations (PSIs) are now routinely conducted in all United States courts where defendants have been convicted of felonies or less serious crimes where they may be incarcerated.

When Augustus died in 1859, probation did not die with him. Various prisoner's and children's aid societies, many religiously based, continued to volunteer their services to courts in the supervision of convicted offenders on a probationary basis. Another philanthropist, **Rufus R. Cook,** continued Augustus's work as well, particularly assisting juvenile offenders through the Boston Children's Aid Society in 1860 (Timasheff, 1941:10). **Benjamin C. Clark,** a philanthropist and volunteer probation officer, assisted in probation work with court permission throughout the 1860s.

Massachusetts became the first state to pass a probation statute in 1878, since Augustus's probation activity originated in Boston. This statute authorized the mayor of Boston to hire the first probation officer, Captain Savage, a former police officer. He was supervised by the Superintendent of Police. Thus, probation was given official recognition, although it was based on political patronage. Several other states passed similar statutes before 1900. In 1901, New York enacted a statutory probation provision similar to that of Massachusetts. Between 1886 and 1900, a number of "settlements" were established, primarily in impoverished parts of cities, for the purposes of assisting the poor and improving the lot of the disadvantaged. These settlements were experimental efforts to aid in the solution of the social and industrial problems engendered by the modern conditions of life in a great city, and they were to figure prominently in the development and use of probation during that period.

In 1893, **James Bronson Reynolds,** an early prison reformer, was appointed headworker of the **University Settlement,** a private facility in New York operated to provide assistance and job referral services to community residents. When New York passed the probation statute in 1901, Reynolds seized this opportunity to involve the University Settlement in probation work. Interestingly, the statute itself prohibited compensation for persons performing "probation officer" chores. Probation work was to be simply another facet of the full-time work they did.

For example, many early probation officers worked as police officers, deputies, or clerks in district attorney's offices. The statute also provided that private citizens would serve as probation officers without cost to the city or county. Thus, the voluntary and privately operated University Settlement project was ideally suited to experiments with future probationers. Besides, Reynolds was a member of several political committees including the Executive Committee of the Prison Association of New York, and his connections directly benefited the University Settlement as a new probation facility. Despite political opposition to Reynolds and the program he attempted, volunteers are widely used today in various capacities by both publicly and privately operated agencies and programs that serve the needs of probationers. Volunteers work in halfway houses, provide foster care for dependent youths, and perform a large number of services that assist POs in the performance of their jobs. Without volunteers, the work of POs would be considerably more burdensome.

By 1922, 22 states had provided for probation in their corrections systems. During the late 1800s and early 1900s, federal district judges were also releasing certain offenders on their own recognizance following the pattern of Massachusetts and other states, often utilizing the services of various state probation officers to supervise offenders. The federal government implemented probation formally through a bill sponsored by the Judicial Committee of the House of Representatives on March 4, 1925. The United States Attorney General was given control of probation officers through another bill in 1930. The Federal Juvenile Delinquency Act was passed on June 16, 1938, so that probation could apply to juveniles as well as to adults, although "general probation" for both juveniles and adults had already been created technically through the 1925 and 1930 acts (Timasheff, 1941:64–66). Thus, all states had juvenile probation programs by 1927, and by 1957, all states had statutes authorizing the use of probation as a sanction for adults where appropriate. Figure 5.1 summarizes the major developments influencing the evolution of probation in the United States.

Today probation operates very differently from the way it was originally conducted in 1841. Also, dramatic changes have occurred in the forms of probation used and approved by the court. Among other things, technological developments have spawned several different kinds of offender management systems compared with the traditional probation officer/client face-to-face relation.

Year	Event
1791	Passage of Bill of Rights
1817	New York passes first good-time statute
1824	New York House of Refuge is founded
1830	Judge Peter Oxenbridge Thatcher in Boston introduces release on one's own recognizance
1836	Massachusetts passes first recognizance with monetary sureties law
1841	John Augustus introduces probation in the United States in Boston
1863	Gaylord Hubbell, warden of the State Correctional Facility at Ossining, New York (Sing Sing), visits Ireland and is influenced by Walter Crofton's ticket of leave or mark system; later led to good-time credits earned by prisoners for early release
1869	Elmira Reformatory established in New York, with early release dates set by the board of managers
1870	Establishment of the National Prison Association (later the American Correctional Association), emphasizing indeterminate sentencing and early release
1876	Zebulon Brockway releases inmates on parole from Elmira Reformatory
1878	First probation law passed by Massachusetts
1899	Illinois passes first juvenile court act, creating special juvenile courts
1906	Work release originates in Vermont through informal sheriff action
1913	Huber Law or first work release statute originates in Wisconsin
1916	U.S. Supreme Court declares that sentences cannot be indefinitely suspended by courts; rather, this right is a legislative right
1918	Furlough program begun in Mississippi
1932	44 states have parole mechanisms
1954	All states have parole mechanisms
1965	Prisoner Rehabilitation Act passed by Congress applicable to federal prisoners
1967	*Mempa v. Rhay* case decided involving probationer; court-appointed counsel must be appointed for probationers who are in jeopardy of having their probation programs revoked; any indigent must be represented by counsel at any stage where substantial rights of accused may be affected
1972	*Morrissey v. Brewer,* U.S. Supreme Court case involving parolee; declared parolees entitled to minimum due process rights before parole programs are revoked; also required two-stage hearings for parole revocations, to determine if allegations are true and what punishment(s) should be imposed

FIGURE 5.1   Developments Influencing the Growth and Change of Probation in the United States.

Year	Event
1973	*Gagnon v. Scarpelli,* U.S. Supreme Court case involving probationer, equated probation revocation with parole revocation; entitled to a two-stage hearing before probation is revoked
1976	Maine abolishes parole
1983	*Bearden v. Georgia,* U.S. Supreme Court case declaring that probationers who were indigent and could not pay fines could not have their probation programs revoked solely on that basis
1984	Sentencing Reform Act passed; created U.S. Sentencing Guidelines, implemented in 1987; federal probation use reduced from 65 percent to 10 percent as the result of newly implemented presumptive guidelines
1985	*Black v. Romano,* U.S. Supreme Court case declaring that judges are not obligated to consider options other than incarceration for probationers whose programs are revoked
1987	*Board of Pardons v. Allen,* U.S. Supreme Court declared that parolee was entitled to statement of reasons for parole denial from parole board
1998	*Pennsylvania Board of Probation and Parole v. Scott,* U.S. Supreme Court declares Fourth Amendment right not applicable in parole revocation proceedings, where parole officer enters one's premises without a warrant and seizes incriminating evidence which is later used in parole revocation action

FIGURE 5.1   *(CONTINUED)*

THE PHILOSOPHY OF PROBATION

Probation in the 2000s has undergone significant changes in its general conception and implementation. Presently there are diverse opinions among experts about how probation should be reconceptualized and reorganized (Arthur, 2000). One observer suggests that the reason for these disagreements and confusion is a general lack of understanding about what probation does and for whom. Even though probation supervises two-thirds of all convicted felons in the United States, it receives little publicity or financial support. The idea of proving, or trial, or forgiveness implied by probation says much about its underlying philosophy. The primary aim of probation is to give offenders an opportunity to prove themselves by remaining law-abiding. Avoiding jail or prison is a powerful incentive to refrain from committing new crimes. Helping to promote probation as a viable alternative to imprisonment are various societal views about the rehabilitative value of prisons and jails. One belief is that incarceration does not deter crime. In fact, locking up offenders only makes matters worse, according to some observers. Newly confined offenders learn more about crime from more experienced, hardcore prisoners. Also, new prison and jail construction is costly. Higher taxes are required to pay for this construction.

Probation is far less expensive. Some forms of probation, such as electronic monitoring and home confinement, are both effective and cheap client management tools. This thinking minimizes the importance of rehabilitation as an important aim of incarceration. Offender punishment, containment, and control should be the priorities of incarceration. While it may be true that some rehabilitation may occur among some offenders, this is an unintended fringe benefit.

However, more than a few observers question whether incarceration should be applied to all criminals. The state-of-the-art presuming to differentiate those who deserve incarceration from those who don't deserve incarceration is imperfect. Many offenders are imprisoned for minor crimes, and a significant proportion of these persons will never reoffend. Many convicted offenders are placed on probation as well, but we know that a substantial number of these clients continue to commit new crimes. Inmates themselves have appraised incarceration and probation accordingly. Some inmates have reported that they would rather do more time in prison than have to adhere to a probation program with strings attached. At the same time, some inmates believe that probation should not be granted to certain offenders, while incarceration should be rejected as a sanction for other criminals.

For guidance about the general philosophy of probation, we can examine the original intent of its pioneer, John Augustus. Augustus wanted to reform offenders. He wanted to rehabilitate common drunks and petty thieves. Thus, **rehabilitation** was and continues to be a strong philosophical aim of probation. But over time, probation has changed from the way Augustus originally viewed it. Let's look at how Augustus supervised his probationers. First, he stood their bail in the Boston Municipal Court. Second, he took them to his home or other place of shelter, fed them, and generally looked after them. He may have even provided them with job leads and other services through his many friendships as well as his political and philanthropic connections. In short, Augustus provided his probationers with fairly intensive supervision and personalized assistance, financial and otherwise. He supervised approximately 100 probationers a year between 1841 and 1859. We know that he kept detailed records of their progress. In this respect, Augustus compiled what are now called pre-sentence investigations, although he usually made extensive notes about offenders and their progress after they had been convicted. He showed great interest in their progress, and no doubt many of these probationers were emotionally affected by his kindness and generosity. According to Augustus's own assessment of his performance, rehabilitation and reformation were occurring at a significant rate among his clients.

But this oversimplifies the philosophy of probation. It has many overtones. For example, John Augustus's goal was behavioral reform. Much of his philanthropy was directed toward those offenders with drinking problems. He believed that some offenders would change from drunkenness and intemperance to sobriety and honesty, if they could avoid the stigma imprisonment. Several religious principles guided Augustus's belief, as well as the views of the Temperance Society to which he belonged.

The major difficulty with pinning down a specific philosophy of probation is that among the public and professionals, there are diverse impressions of what probation is or should be. But the word that recurs most often is rehabilitation. Regardless of the form of rehabilitation prescribed by the court when offenders are sentenced, probation appears beneficial by diverting offenders from incarceration (Farrall et al., 2002).

Present-day probation has become streamlined and bureaucratic. While there are exceptions among probation officers, relatively few take interest in their clients to the extent that they feed and clothe them and look after their other personal needs. No probation officers sit in municipal courtrooms waiting for the right kinds of offenders who will be responsive to personalized attention and care. No probation officers eagerly approach judges with bail bonds and assume personal responsibility for a probationer's conduct, even if for brief periods.

Today, probation officers define their work in terms of client caseloads and officer/client ratios. Much paperwork is required for each case, and this consumes over half of a probation officer's time on the job. If we have strayed far from Augustus's original meaning of what probation supervision is and how it should be conducted, it is probably because of bureaucratic expediency. There are too many probationers and too few probation officers. It is hardly unexpected that the public has gradually become disenchanted with the rehabilitative ideal probation originally promised.

 **BOX 5.1**

 **CAREER SNAPSHOT**

Sterling Wheeler
Senior Probation Officer, New Hampshire Department of Corrections

Statistics:

B.S., Northeast Louisiana University

Background:

My first significant job after graduating from Northeast Louisiana University was working for the Tallulah Police Department in Tallulah, Louisiana. It was here that I learned how to deal with people firmly, fairly, and consistently. I was lucky, since I had a great mentor at that time, Early Pickney, a captain who is now the chief. He exudes confidence. I quickly learned that in dealing with the public, you have to show confidence; after all, all eyes are on you when you carry a badge and a weapon. Upward mobility is tough when you are working in a small town, and so a friend of mine suggested that I consider corrections. As it turned out, it was the best thing for me.

I began my corrections debut as a correctional officer working for the Mississippi Department of Corrections. Within a short period of time, I was promoted to sergeant and managed a 500-bed male housing unit. At that time, Mississippi was ranked last in the nation in terms of salary. Even more discouraging was the fact that we were only paid once a month. I left Mississippi and worked briefly as a deputy for the El Paso County Sheriff's Office before meeting my fiancé and relocating to New Hampshire. Currently I am a probation/parole officer for New Hampshire and have been for the past 16 years. Within that time, I have worked on the High Intensity Surveillance Unit that was responsible for assisting high-risk or the most dangerous offenders to transition back into their communities.

The Profession:

It never ceases to amaze me the looks on people's faces when I tell them what I do for a living; that is, I supervise adults placed on

(continued)

BOX 5.1 (*Continued*)

probation and parole. They assume I work in the juvenile system. My job involves a lot of paperwork along with visiting offenders' homes, contacting offenders at their places of employment, contacting offenders' therapists or counselors, and at the same time, assessing offender risk of relapsing or reoffending.

When offenders become a high-risk-to-reoffend or are noncompliant, we do have the power to make arrests. For example, I received information that a parolee who went to prison as a habitual drunk driving offender was seen operating a motor vehicle without a driver's license. I found the parolee behind the wheel of a vehicle. He was counseled and strongly discouraged not to drive. A good probation/parole officer has to follow up to make sure that offenders are complying with their probation/parole program conditions. During the course of supervision, we get to know the backgrounds and habits of offenders we oversee. Having that information makes us unique in the criminal justice system. A week later I spotted the offender operating a motor vehicle again and arrested him.

Another example that comes to mind is when we received information from a local police department that a probationer was at a motel, possibly doing drugs. My fellow probation/parole officers and I went to the motel. Although I could have gone directly to the motel door and announced my presence, I realized that would give the offender time to dispose of the drugs. Instead, we devised a plan to get the offender to open the door. One of the officers called the room and invited the motel room occupants to a free turkey dinner. Without hesitation, the offender exited his room only to be greeted by probation/parole officers. Inside the motel room, we discovered a large quantity of cocaine. An inspection of the probationer's vehicle produced an AK-47 assault rifle, two fully loaded banana clip magazines, and a metal container with plenty of ammunition.

My job allows me to interact with judges, prosecutors, and defense attorneys on a regular basis. Our dual roles as social workers/law enforcement officers are unique in that we are the "eyes and ears" of the court and parole board. When offenders are placed on supervision, they lose a big chunk, but not all, of their constitutional rights, such as the diminished right to privacy or going out of the state without probation office permission. We conduct rehabilitative inspections to determine whether offenders have been compliant with their supervision conditions. As a result of these unannounced inspections, various types of weapons and drugs have been discovered, confiscated, and removed from the community, thus making the community safer.

The Best Part of the Job:

I love doing fieldwork. Fieldwork includes visiting offenders in their homes, which are usually their comfort zones. I really get a sense of how well offenders are adjusting to community life. Another thing I enjoy about this job is making the community safer by helping to rehabilitate offenders. You can do that by affording the offender a variety of opportunities for self-improvement and arresting those who are noncompliant. It works to your advantage to encourage offenders to engage in positive activities such as obtaining a part-time job or developing new and law-abiding friends. Being a probation/parole officer allows one to sharpen their investigative skills. This is beneficial whenever you are doing pre-sentence investigation reports for the courts, looking for a fugitive, or just verifying an offender's story. I cannot put enough emphasis on gathering information. Finally, I love the flexibility this job offers. You can tailor your work schedule to suit the amount and nature of supervision required for particular offenders. For instance, if you impose a curfew on a high-risk offender, it is important that you check on that offender after the established curfew. This sends the message to the offender that you are thinking of that person, but more importantly, it lets the offender know that you take curfew violation seriously.

The Worst Part of the Job:

Probably one of the most significant "negatives" of what I do is seeing probationers and parolees who are given ample and frequent opportunities to change their negative behaviors, but who choose not to change. Probation/parole typically does not get much public attention, and that can impact the amount of funding your department receives, although we continue to promote and be involved in public safety.

The rehabilitative aim of probation has not been abandoned. Rather, it has been rearranged in a rapidly growing list of correctional priorities. One dominant, contemporary philosophical aim of probation is offender control. If we can't rehabilitate offenders, at least we can devise more effective ways of managing them while they are on probation. As a result, the development of several alternative punishments, each connected directly with increased offender supervision and control, has occurred. The community is most frequently used for managing growing offender populations. Many community corrections programs have been established to accommodate different types of offenders. Observers generally agree that the future of probation is closely connected with the effectiveness of community corrections. And the key to effective community corrections is effective client management through more intensive supervised release. However, investigators have found that in some jurisdictions, those who are placed under intensive supervision in their communities do not pose any greater risk to the public than those who have served prison terms and are subsequently paroled. According to some authorities, probation serves several purposes.

1. Probation keeps those convicted of petty crimes from the criminogenic environment of jails and prisons. Prisons are viewed as colleges of crime where inmates are not rehabilitated, but rather, learn more effective criminal techniques.

2. Probation helps offenders avoid the stigma of the criminal label. Some authorities believe that once offenders have been labeled as delinquent or criminal, they will act out these roles by committing subsequent offenses.

3. Probation allows offenders to integrate more easily with noncriminals. Offenders may hold jobs, earn a living for their families and themselves, and develop more positive self-concepts and conforming behaviors not likely acquired if incarcerated.

4. Probation is a practical means by which to ease the problems of prison and jail overcrowding. Greater use of probation is a major **front-end solution** to jail and prison overcrowding. Thus, probation serves the purely logistical function of enabling correctional institutions to more effectively manage smaller inmate populations.

MODELS FOR DEALING WITH CRIMINAL OFFENDERS

Those who supervise offenders either on probation or parole operate from a variety of different offender management assumptions. Depending on the assumptions made about offenders and the programs used to manage them, different supervisory styles and approaches may have different client outcomes. For instance, some probation officers are more law enforcement–oriented than others.

Some officers believe that their roles should be as educators or enablers. Assisting clients in finding jobs or locating housing may be more important to some officers than whether a client commits a technical program infraction, such as committing a curfew violation or failing a drug test. Therefore, we should acquire an understanding of probation officer work ideologies in order to determine which ideologies seem most effective at reducing client recidivism rates. Several models are presented below. These represent different ways of approaching the officer/client relation. These models are: (1) the treatment or medical model; (2) the rehabilitation model; (3) the justice/due process model; (4) the just-deserts model; and (5) the community model.

The Treatment or Medical Model

Despite the religious, moral, and philanthropic interests that influenced the early practice of probation, its current rehabilitative nature derives from the **treatment model** of treating criminals. Also known as the **medical model,** the medical model considers criminal behavior as an illness to be remedied. The custodial approach of incarcerating criminals does not treat the illness; rather, it separates the ill from the well. When released from incarceration, the ill continue to be ill and are likely to commit further crimes. The nonincarcerative alternative, probation, permits rehabilitation to occur, through treatment programs and therapeutic services not otherwise available to offenders under conditions of confinement. Additionally, rehabilitative measures within prison and jail settings have been taken through the creation and use of vocational/technical, educational, and counseling programs as parallels to the treatment received by nonincarcerated probationers (Rhoades and Venegas, 2006).

Some observers claim the fundamental flaw of the treatment model is that offenders are treated as objects. But selectively applying probation to some offenders and not to others leads to more fundamental criticisms justifiably associated with inequitable treatment on the basis of gender, race/ethnic status, socioeconomic differences, and other factors.

The Rehabilitation Model

Closely related to the treatment or medical model is the **rehabilitation model.** This model stresses rehabilitation and reform. Although rehabilitation may be traced to William Penn's work in correctional reform, the most significant support for the rehabilitation orientation came from Zebulon Brockway's Elmira Reformatory in 1876. Eventually, federal recognition of rehabilitation as a major correctional objective occurred when the Federal Bureau of Prisons was established on May 14, 1930. Although the first federal penitentiary was built in 1895 in Leavenworth, Kansas, it took thirty-five more years for an official federal prison policy to be devised. The original mandate of the Bureau of Prisons called for rehabilitating federal prisoners through vocational and educational training, as well as the traditional individualized psychological counseling that was associated with the treatment model. In later years, encounter groups, group therapy, and other strategies were incorporated into federal prison operations and policy as alternative rehabilitative methods.

Between 1950 and 1966, over 100 prison riots occurred in federal facilities. These incidents were sufficient for officials to reconsider the rehabilitation model and define it as ineffective for reforming prisoners. There were other weaknesses of this model as well. Similar to the treatment model that preceded it, the rehabilitation model stresses "individual" treatment or reform, and as a result, inmate sanctions have often been individualized. This means that those who have committed similar offenses of equal severity might receive radically different rehabilitation or punishment. The inequity of this individualized system is apparent, and in many jurisdictions, such inequities in the application of sanctions have been associated with race, ethnicity, gender, or socioeconomic status.

The 1960s and 1970s are regarded as the **Progressive Era** where rehabilitation was stressed by liberals for both incarcerated and nonincarcerated offenders. However, rising crime rates and the recidivism of probationers and parolees stimulated a public backlash against social reform programs. Studies conducted in the 1970s disclosed the apparent lack of success of rehabilitation programs, including probation. While some critics contend that these studies are inconclusive and misleading, one result was the general condemnation of rehabilitation and specific probation alternatives. Despite these criticisms, rehabilitation continues to be a strong correctional goal (Treglia, 2006).

The Justice/Due Process Model

While the rehabilitation ideal has not been abandoned, it has been supplemented by an alternative known as the justice or **due process model.** The justice model is not intended to replace the rehabilitative model, but rather to enhance it. Probation practices in the United States have been influenced by the justice model in recent years through the imposition of more equitable sentences and fairness. Sentencing reforms have been undertaken to eliminate sentencing disparities attributable to race/ethnic background, gender, or socioeconomic status. The justice model applied to probation stresses fair and equitable treatment. Probably the most important reason citizens oppose the use of probation is that they do not define probation as punishment. In response to this criticism, several views have been expressed including the following:

1. Probation is a penal sanction whose main characteristic is punitive.
2. Probation should be a sentence, not a substitute for a real sentence threatened after future offenses.
3. Probation should be part of a single, graduated range of penal sanctions available for all levels of crime except for the most serious felonies.
4. The severity of the probation sentence should be determined by the quality and quantity of conditions (e.g., restitution or community service).
5. Neither the length of term nor any condition should be subject to change during the sentence, unless the conditions are violated.
6. Conditions should be justified in terms of seriousness of offense.
7. Where conditions are violated, courts should assess additive penalties through show-cause hearings.

The Just-Deserts Model

The **just-deserts model** or **deserts model** emphasizes equating punishment with the severity of the crime. In this respect, Beccaria's ideas are evident in the development of just-deserts as a punishment orientation. Offenders should get what they deserve. Therefore, retribution is an important component. Just-deserts dismisses rehabilitation as a major correctional aim. It alleges that offenders ought to receive punishments equivalent to the seriousness of their crimes. If rehabilitation occurs during the punishment process, this is not undesirable, but it is also not essential. Applying the just-deserts philosophy, offenders sentenced to prison would be placed in custody levels fitting the seriousness of their crimes. Petty offenders who commit theft or burglary might be sentenced to minimum-security facilities with few guards and fences. Accordingly, robbers, rapists, and murderers would be placed in maximum-security prisons under close supervision. If offenders are sentenced to probation, their level of supervision would be adjusted to fit the seriousness of their offenses. The more serious the offense, the more intensive the supervision.

The just-deserts model has emerged in recent years as a popular alternative to the rehabilitation model, which influenced correctional programs for many decades. Penal and sentencing reforms among jurisdictions are currently consistent with the just-deserts approach. Public pressure for applying the just-deserts orientation in judicial sentencing, including greater severity of penalties imposed, has stimulated the get-tough movement.

The Community Model

The **community model** is a relatively new concept based on the correctional goal of offender reintegration into the community. Sometimes called the reintegration model, the community model stresses offender adaptation to the community by participating in one or more programs that are a part of community-based corrections. More judges are using community-based corrections because they are in place within the community and because they offer a front-end solution to prison and jail overcrowding. Often, offenders are accommodated in large homes where curfews and other rules are imposed. Food, clothing, and employment assistance are provided. Sometimes, counselors and psychiatrists are on call to assist their clients with serious adjustment or coping problems if they occur. Some community interventions are geared to assisting battered women in understanding the abusive behaviors of others and the implications of spousal abuse for their original offending behaviors (Ferraro, 2003; Holt et al., 2003).

The primary strengths of the community model are that offenders are able to reestablish associations with their families and have the opportunity to work at jobs where a portion of their wages earned can be used for victim restitution, payment of fines, and defrayment of program maintenance costs. Furthermore, offenders may participate in psychological therapy or educational and vocational programs designed to improve their work and/or social skills. POs often function as brokers, locating important and necessary community services for their offender/clients. POs also provide a means whereby offenders can obtain employment.

The community model uses citizen involvement in offender reintegration. Often, paraprofessionals may assist probation officers in their paperwork. Community volunteers also assist offenders by performing cleaning and kitchen work. Occasionally, important community officials may be members of boards of directors of these community-based services, further integrating the community with the correctional program. However, the presence of community celebrities is sometimes purely symbolic, where they are figureheads exclusively and seldom become actively involved in these programs. Nevertheless, these healthy liaisons with community residents generally increase community acceptance of offenders and offender programs. With such community support, offenders have a better chance of adapting to community life. In recent years, operators of community-based offender programs have been keenly aware of the importance of cultivating links with the community, especially with community leaders.

FUNCTIONS OF PROBATION

The functions of probation are closely connected with its underlying philosophy. Within the rehabilitation context, the primary functions of probation are: (1) crime control; (2) community reintegration; (3) rehabilitation; (4) punishment; and (5) deterrence.

Crime Control

Crime control as a probation function stems directly from the fact that probationers are often supervised more or less closely by their POs. Jurisdictions with large numbers of probationers have difficulty supervising these offenders closely. This is because there simply aren't enough POs to do the job of supervision properly. In many cases, probationers either mail in a form to the probation office weekly or monthly. This form is usually a checklist where the offenders report any law infractions, their most recent employment record, and other factual information. They may also pay pre-established fees to defray a portion of their probation costs and maintenance. Of course, much of this information is self-reported and subjective. It is difficult, if not impossible, to verify the veracity of these self-report statements without some alternative supervisory scheme. Most of the time, probation agencies simply do not have the resources to conduct checks of this self-reported information. If offenders are rearrested within the jurisdiction supervising them, this is often how they come to the attention of probation offices again (Martinez, 2006).

Precisely how much crime control occurs as the result of probation is unknown. When offenders are outside the immediate presence of probation officers, they may or may not engage in undetected criminal activity. Standard probation offers little by way of true crime control, since there is minimal contact between offenders and their probation officers. However, it is believed that even standard probation offers some measure of crime control by extending to probationers a degree of trust as well as minimal behavioral restrictions. It would be misleading to believe that no monitoring occurs under standard probation supervision. Probation officers are obligated to make periodic checks of workplaces and conversations with an offender's employer disclose much about how offenders are managing their time. But again, limited probation department resources confine these checks to so much cursory and superficial activity. Placing offenders on probation and requiring them to comply with certain conditions succeeds to some extent as a method of crime control.

Community Reintegration

One obvious benefit for offenders receiving probation is that they avoid the criminogenic environment of incarceration. This is because they remain in the communities and benefit from **community reintegration.** Offenders on probation usually maintain jobs, live with and support their families, engage in vocational/technical training or other educational programs, receive counseling, and lead otherwise normal lives. While minimum-security prisons and some jails do afford prisoners opportunities to learn skills and participate in programs designed to rehabilitate them, nothing about prisons and jails comes close to the therapeutic value of remaining free within the community.

Rehabilitation

One benefit of probation is that it permits offenders to remain in their communities, work at jobs, support their families, make restitution to victims, and perform other useful services. In addition, offenders avoid the criminogenic influence of jail or prison environments. It is most difficult to make the transformation from prison life to community living, especially if an inmate has been incarcerated for several years. Prison life is highly regulated, and the nature of confinement bears no relation to life on the outside. The community reintegration function of probation is most closely associated with its rehabilitative aim.

Punishment

Is probation a punishment? Those on probation think it is. There are many behavioral conditions accompanying probation orders. Any violation can lead to having one's probation program revoked and the offender may be incarcerated in a jail or prison as a result. Filing a late monthly report is a technical violation. Being absent from work without a legitimate excuse might also be a violation of an offender's probation terms. Other sanctions may be imposed as a part of standard probation, although they do not involve direct or frequent contact with the probation officer. For example, the judge may order the convicted offender to make restitution to victims, to pay for damages and medical bills sustained through whatever crime was committed. Public service of a particular type may be required, and others may be asked to report on the offender's work quality in the service performed. And, of course, the offender may be fined. A portion of an offender's wages may be garnished by the court regularly during the term of probation as payment toward the fine assessed. The offender must sustain regular employment in order to meet these court-imposed fine obligations and community service. These are punishments and place virtually all probationers at risk of losing their freedom for violating one or more conditions of their probation programs (Rhoades and Venegas, 2006).

Deterrence

Does probation deter criminals from committing new crimes? Not much. Because of the low degree of offender control associated with standard probation supervision, which often means no supervision at all, recidivism rates are higher than those associated with offenders in more intensively supervised intermediate punishment programs. Observers disagree about the deterrent effect probation serves. Although no national standard exists about what is a respectable or successful recidivism level, 30 percent has been defined by various researchers as a cutting point, where more successful probation programs have recidivism rates below 30 percent. Thus, the deterrent value of probation may vary according to the standard by which deterrence is measured. Traditional probation programs have recidivism rates of about 65 percent, meaning that only 35 percent of the probationers do not commit new crimes.

A PROFILE OF PROBATIONERS

The profile of probationers in the United States changes annually. Each year, the probation population includes increasing numbers of felony offenders (Champion, 2005). At the beginning of 2003, there were 3,995,165 adults on probation in the United States. This is a 26.6 percent increase since 1995. The average annual increase in probationers was 3.1 percent. Several states with the largest numbers of probationers include Texas (431,981), Georgia (402,694), California (374,701), and Ohio (218,239). Table 5.1 shows a distribution of the number of adults on probation at yearend 2004.

Some of the characteristics of persons on probation in the United States are illustrated in Table 5.2. Table 5.2 shows a comparison of probationers for the years 1995, 2000, and 2004. Approximately 77 percent of all probationers were male in 2004. Between 1995 and 2004, the proportion of female probationers increased from 21 to 23 percent. The racial distribution of probationers hasn't changed much during this same period. White probationers increased to 56 percent in 2004 from 53 percent in 1995, while black probationers declined slightly to 30 percent from 31 percent for the same time interval. The proportion of Hispanic probationers declined slightly from 14 to 12 percent between 1995–2004.

TABLE 5.1

Adults on Probation, 2004

Region and jurisdiction	Probation population, 1/1/04	2004 Entries	Exits	Probation population, 12/31/04	Percent change, 2004	Number on probation per 100,000 adult residents, 12/31/04
U.S. total	4,144,782	2,217,900	2,210,400	4,151,125	0.2%	1,884
Federal	30,601	12,780	14,895	28,346	−7.4%	13
State (reported)	4,087,012	1,957,306	1,951,231	4,122,779	—	—
State (estimated)	4,114,181	2,205,100	2,195,500	4,122,779	0.2%	1,871
Northeast	689,053	263,100	254,700	697,508	1.2%	1,671
Connecticut	52,192	15,656	15,756	52,092	−0.2	1,955
Maine	9,855	5,676	6,209	9,322	−5.4	901
Massachusetts	166,464	76,800	79,800	163,471	−1.8	3,301
New Hampshire	3,987	1,595	1,297	4,285	7.5	431
New Jersey	130,303	45,166	32,154	143,315	10.0	2,190
New York	126,138	38,647	42,758	122,027	−3.3	833
Pennsylvania	137,206	4,157	3,476	167,180	—	1,747
Rhode Island	25,929	6,279	6,123	26,085	0.6	3,117
Vermont	9,810	4,919	4,998	9,731	−0.8	2,000
Midwest	943,026	593,700	585,200	951,498	0.9%	1,922
Illinois	144,454	62,354	62,937	143,871	−0.4	1,518
Indiana	118,773	93,918	96,260	116,431	−2.0	2,511
Iowa	21,413	15,080	13,679	22,832	6.6	1,004
Kansas	14,740	19,577	20,008	14,309	−2.9	697
Michigan	179,486	124,000	127,400	176,083	−1.9	2,323

(continued)

TABLE 5.1   (CONTINUED)

Region and jurisdiction	Probation population, 1/1/04	2004 Entries	Exits	Probation population, 12/31/04	Percent change, 2004	Number on probation per 100,000 adult residents, 12/31/04
Minnesota	110,046	66,775	62,595	114,226	3.8	2,959
Missouri	54,543	25,105	25,816	53,832	−1.3	1,232
Nebraska	18,412	15,282	15,700	17,994	−2.3	1,371
North Dakota	3,566	2,525	2,404	3,687	3.4	744
Ohio	218,239	140,800	131,100	227,891	4.4	2,626
South Dakota	5,236	3,310	3,243	5,372	2.6	926
Wisconsin	54,118	24,929	24,077	54,970	1.6	1,308
South	1,652,705	932,100	915,300	1,668,111	0.9%	2,196
Alabama	39,660	14,700	17,500	36,795	−7.2	1,071
Arkansas	28,164	8,388	7,424	29,128	3.4	1,403
Delaware	18,921	15,083	15,279	18,725	−1.0	2,940
District of Columbia	7,116	6,944	6,313	7,747	8.9	1,745
Florida	286,769	246,200	251,800	281,170	−2.0	2,099
Georgia	402,694	217,100	200,400	419,350	—	—
Kentucky	28,869	20,200	15,800	33,286	15.3	1,051
Louisiana	36,813	14,350	12,693	38,470	4.5	1,148
Maryland	77,875	40,018	41,217	76,676	−1.5	1,842
Mississippi	19,116	8,483	6,275	21,324	11.6	990
North Carolina	113,161	60,069	61,693	111,537	−1.4	1,737
Oklahoma	28,326	14,044	13,935	28,435	0.4	1,068
South Carolina	40,354	13,972	15,470	38,856	−3.7	1,224
Tennessee	44,359	25,700	21,400	47,392	6.8	1,051
Texas	431,981	198,130	201,338	428,773	−0.7	2,643
Virginia	41,663	25,409	23,602	43,470	4.3	769
West Virginia	6,864	3,300	3,200	6,977	1.6	488
West	829,397	416,200	440,300	805,662	−2.9%	1,620
Alaska	5,406	998	857	5,547	2.6	1,187
Arizona	65,554	43,660	39,871	69,343	5.8	1,652
California	374,701	177,896	167,745	384,852	2.7	1,463
Colorado	55,297	29,400	26,500	58,108	5.1	1,698
Hawaii	20,165	8,541	7,260	21,446	6.4	2,224
Idaho	42,375	36,762	34,930	44,580	—	—
Montana	6,914	4,000	3,700	7,221	4.4	1,005
Nevada	12,159	6,755	6,393	12,521	3.0	723
New Mexico	15,899	8,414	6,588	17,725	11.5	1,256
Oregon	43,415	17,183	16,163	44,435	2.3	1,620
Utah	10,339	5,490	5,585	10,244	−0.9	621
Washington	172,511	75,300	122,600	125,222	−27.4	2,654
Wyoming	4,662	1,846	2,090	4,418	−5.2	1,134

Source: Lauren E. Glaze and Seri Palla (2005). *Probation and Parole in the United States, 2004.* Washington, DC: U.S. Department of Justice. (p. 4)

Table 5.2 also shows that proportionately greater numbers of probationers are entering probation programs without serving any jail time first. In 2004, 76 percent of the probationers entered probation without incarceration, up from 72 percent in 1995. There were proportionately slightly lower successful completions of probation programs in 2004 (60 percent), compared with a successful completion of 62 percent in 1995. About 15 percent of all probationers were returned to incarceration in 2004

TABLE 5.2

Characteristics of Adults on Probation, 1995, 2000, and 2004

Characteristic	1995	2000	2004
Total	100%	100%	100%
Gender			
Male	79%	78%	77%
Female	21	22	23
Race/Hispanic origin			
White[a]	53%	54%	56%
Black[a]	31	31	30
Hispanic	14	13	12
American Indian/Alaska Native[a]	1	1	1
Asian/Native Hawaiian/other Pacific Islander[a]	—	1	1
Status of probation			
Direct imposition	48%	56%	56%
Split sentence	15	11	8
Sentence suspended	26	25	24
Imposition suspended	6	7	10
Other	4	1	1
Status of supervision			
Active	79%	76%	74%
Residential/other treatment program	**	**	1
Inactive	8	9	9
Absconder	9	9	9
Warrant status	**	**	5
Supervised out of State	2	3	2
Other	2	3	—
Type of offense			
Felony	54%	52%	49%
Misdemeanor	44	46	50
Other infractions	2	2	1
Most serious offense			
Sexual assault	**	**	3%
Domestic violence	**	**	6
Other assault	**	**	10
Burglary	**	**	5
Larceny/theft	**	**	12
Fraud	**	**	5
Drug law violations	**	24	26
Driving while intoxicated	16	18	15
Minor traffic offenses	**	6	7
Other	84	52	10
Adults entering probation			
Without incarceration	72%	79%	76%
With incarceration	13	16	14
Other types	15	5	10
Adults leaving probation			
Successful completions	62%	60%	60%

(continued)

TABLE 5.2 (CONTINUED)			
Characteristic	**1995**	**2000**	**2004**
Incarceration	21	15	15
With new sentence	5	3	8
With the same sentence	13	8	6
Unknown	3	4	1
Absconder[b]	**	3	4
Discharge to custody, defainer, or warrant	**	1	1
Other unsuccessful[b]	**	11	10
Death	1	1	1
Other	16	9	9

Note: For every characteristic there were persons of unknown type. Detail may not sum to total because of rounding.
**Not available.
—Less than 0.5%.
[a]Excludes persons of Hispanic origin.
[b]In 1995 "absconder" and "other unsuccessful" statuses were reported among "other."

compared with 21 percent in 1995 for various program violations. About half (49 percent) of all probationers in 2004 were on probation for felony convictions. Less frequent use was made of split sentencing in 2004, where 8 percent of all offenders sentenced to probation were also obligated to do some jail time compared with 15 percent in 1995. There were slightly fewer suspended sentences (24 percent) in 2004 compared with 26 percent suspended sentences in 1995 (Glaze and Palla, 2005:6).

FIRST-OFFENDERS AND RECIDIVISTS

Probation decision making is solely at the discretion of criminal court judges. Judges receive sentencing assistance from probation officers, who are frequently directed to prepare background investigations of PSI reports of convicted offenders. These reports summarize the basic information relating to the offense. To the extent that judges must impose specific sentences in particular cases under mandatory sentencing laws, their hands are tied. For instance, if an offender uses a firearm during the commission of an offense in Michigan, Michigan criminal court judges must impose a two-year additional sentence for using a firearm during the commission of a felony. This mandatory punishment, which must be served after one's original sentence for the conviction offense imposed, is intended as a deterrent against the use of dangerous weapons by criminals. It doesn't always work.

Because of the diversity of offenders, their crimes, their prior records or criminal histories, their ages, family stability, work record, and a host of other factors, judges attempt to develop and apply a consistent set of sentencing standards to cover each convicted offender. Thus, some individuality in sentencing occurs. Where such individualization occurs, extralegal factors often function to influence judicial decision making. These factors include race or ethnicity, gender, age, socioeconomic status, and demeanor/attitude. Many offenders are habitual offenders and chronic recidivists. Judges tend to impose harsher sentences on such persons because of their offending chronicity. Those with extensive prior records of offending, especially those previously convicted of violent offenses, are less likely to be considered for probation.

Other factors are considered as well, and judges are virtually powerless to do anything about them. For example, if a state has a jail or prison overcrowding problem, then this overcrowding might obligate judges to impose nonincarcerative sentences, such as probation, more often than incarcerative sentences. But in many jurisdictions, judges are ignorant of the overcrowding conditions of their jails and prisons, and they may impose jail or prison terms for convicted offenders, only to find out later that the convicted offenders were released because there was no jail or prison accommodations for them.

Most probationers share the following characteristics:

1. Probationers tend to be first-offenders or low-risk offenders.
2. More property offenders than violent offenders are considered for probation.
3. More convicted females are considered for probation than convicted males.
4. Not having a history of drug or alcohol use or abuse is considered as a positive factor in granting probation.
5. If there are no physical injuries resulting from the convicted offender's actions, and/or if no weapons were used to commit the crime, the chances for probation are greater.

CIVIL MECHANISMS IN LIEU OF PROBATION

Increasingly, because of the large volume of offenders being arrested for various crimes, prosecutors are faced with burgeoning numbers of criminal cases. Many of these cases involve petty offenses, although even the least serious crimes consume valuable court time. Thus, not every criminal case can be prosecuted, even if prosecutors had the personpower to initiate such prosecutions. There simply aren't enough courts and judges to handle the great volume of criminal cases. Two alternative solutions chosen by prosecutors in a growing number of jurisdictions is to target certain low-level criminal cases for alternative dispute resolution, where a civil court or other authorized body meets with victims and offenders to work out a civil remedy; and diversion, where a criminal case is temporarily suspended from the criminal justice system while offenders must engage in constructive, remedial work or programs and resolve their disputes with victims. Consider the following scenarios:

- Two men leave a strip club intoxicated and attempt to locate their car. Unable to find it, they see a car with keys left in the ignition. They get in the car and drive home. Police officers investigating a report of a stolen car later that evening spot the car in one of the men's driveway. The man admits to taking the car but says he was drunk at the time. He intended to return the car after he sobered up and retrieve his own car. He and his friend are arrested for vehicular theft.

- A man is staying in an out-of-town motel attending a professional conference. Someone knocks on his door and he answers. It is a young woman dressed in a miniskirt and halter top. She asks if he'd like some company. He allows her into his room and she asks for a drink. The man offers her $50 for some sex. The woman produces a badge and identifies herself as an undercover vice officer. The man is arrested for soliciting. He is a respected professor from an out-of-state university.

- It is Christmas time and a young woman passes an unlocked car in a Toys R Us parking lot. There are wrapped gifts in the backseat of the car. She opens the door and takes some of the gifts. Shortly thereafter she is arrested by police for theft. The woman has no criminal record and is recently divorced. She has little money and two small children at home. Her idea to steal the gifts was an on-the-spot decision, and she had no idea what she had taken. She assumed the gifts might be for children.

- A man is shopping in a K-Mart store. He passes the jewelry section and notices a diamond ring with a price tag, which is lying on the floor. He picks it up and pockets it. He leaves the store subsequently with his other purchases but a store employee and police officer arrest him shortly thereafter for theft. The man is a local radio personality and has no criminal record. He is ashamed for what he did and said that he doesn't know why he pocketed the $700 ring.

- An elderly man is driving on a highway when a teenager cuts him off while changing lanes. Angered by being cut off, the man speeds up and rams the rear of the teenager's vehicle. The teenager's car goes out of control and scrapes the highway guard rail. The elderly man is arrested by the highway patrol down the road for assault with a vehicle and leaving the scene of an accident.

- A bank teller is running short of $5 bills in her cash drawer and goes to the head teller for 100 $5 bills wrapped in cash bands. The head teller mistakenly gives her two packs of $5 bills instead of one pack. The bank teller notices the extra cash but says nothing. Later that day, she pockets the extra pack of bills. When the tellers balance at the end of the day, the bank teller checks in her cash drawer with the vault teller, while the head teller is $500 short. The following day, the bank teller is arrested by police officers because the erroneous cash exchange was videotaped. The tape shows the bank teller slipping the extra bills into her purse. She breaks down and cries, telling authorities that she has been behind in her monthly payments on credit cards and "didn't think the bank would miss the money." It is her first offense.

None of these cases excites prosecutors. Two drunks driving off in a vehicle where the owner left the keys in the ignition, a professor offering an undercover officer money for sex in his hotel room, a woman taking gifts from an unlocked car, a man pocketing a ring off the floor from a department store, an elderly man with a temporary case of road rage, and a bank teller pocketing some $5 bills are bothersome cases for most prosecutors. Sure, they are crimes. Justice says that people should pay for the crimes they commit. But should each and every one of these cases be prosecuted to the fullest extent of the law? Should we hold trials for all of these cases and attempt to imprison these offenders? For many prosecutors, the idea of a civil resolution of some or all of these cases seems like a reasonable alternative, especially under the different circumstances of the individual scenarios above. Thus, prosecutors may opt for diversion or alternative dispute resolution. Both of these procedures effectively removes a case from the criminal justice system, at least temporarily, while one or more civil remedies are sought.

Civil procedure and criminal procedure involve two separate systems. The most common portrayal of civil procedure is *Judge Judy* on television. This popular program resolves disputes between parties within certain monetary limits, with Judge Judy in action as the impartial arbiter. Civil wrongs or **torts** are commonly settled in civil actions. In all civil actions, damages are sought, not criminal convictions. A man in a bar fight would like to have his missing teeth replaced. A man soliciting for prostitution might be obligated to receive some type of counseling instead of jail. A man whose tools were stolen would like them replaced or returned. A man whose garage door was smashed would like it replaced. A married couple who assaults one another outside of a casino could benefit from marital counseling. A woman whose money is stolen by another person would like to have her money back.

Many of these solutions are restorative in nature, where stolen or damaged property is restored. But in the process, the perpetrators should be held accountable for their actions with some type of punishment. They must do something besides pay for damages to show their contrition, and they must accept responsibility for whatever they did. In recent years, this process has become known as **restorative justice,** which is every action that is primarily oriented toward doing justice by repairing the harm that has been caused by a crime (Schaefer, et al., 2006). Restorative justice usually means a face-to-face confrontation between the victim and perpetrator, where a mutually agreeable restorative solution is proposed and agreed upon. A key feature of restorative justice is equity, where all parties not only agree on the proposed solution, but offender accountability is also heightened (Lemley, 2006). The offender needs to know that whatever was done has serious consequences and accept responsibility for those consequences. A victim suffered either through injuries or property loss (Schaefer et al., 2006). Two types of programs similar to restorative justice are presented in the next section. These are alternative dispute resolution and diversion (Goff and Goff, 2006).

Any victim can seek damages in a civil court as a remedy for being victimized. In an increasing number of cases, however, those who allegedly offend against victims may be prosecuted as criminals in the criminal justice system. But in numerous instances, the offenses alleged are petty or minor. Even though the criminal justice system might define certain conduct as criminal, that conduct might be redefined as a civil wrong. If conduct that could be defined as criminal is actually reinterpreted as a civil wrong or a tort, then civil mechanisms can be brought into action to resolve or mediate disputes between victims and offenders. Besides pursuing cases against offenders in civil actions, victims can seek compensation through other means, such as alternative dispute resolution.

Alternative Dispute Resolution

In cases involving minor criminal offenses, one option increasingly used by the prosecution is **alternative dispute resolution (ADR).** ADR is a community-based, informal dispute settlement between offenders and their victims. Most often targeted for participation in these programs are misdemeanants. A growing number of ADR programs are being implemented throughout the nation. With its early roots in the Midwest, **victim–offender reconciliation** or ADR programs now exist in over 100 U.S. jurisdictions, 54 in Norway, 40 in France, 25 in Canada, 25 in Germany, 18 in England, 20 in Finland, and eight in Belgium.

In growing circles, ADR is also known as restorative justice (Schaefer et al., 2006). ADR involves the direct participation of the victim and offender, with the aim of mutual accommodation for both parties. The emphasis of ADR is on restitution rather than punishment. There are small costs associated with it compared with trials, and criminal **stigmatization** is avoided. However, it is sometimes difficult to decide which cases are best arbitrated through ADR and which should be formally resolved through trial. This should not be interpreted as meaning that juveniles are excluded from ADR. There are specific programs in various jurisdictions especially tailored for juvenile offenders (Doelling, Hartmann, and Traulsen, 2002). In a growing number of jurisdictions, many criminal cases are being diverted from the criminal justice system through ADR. ADR is a relatively new phenomenon, but it is recognized increasingly as a means whereby differences between criminals and their victims can be resolved through a conciliation, mediation, or arbitration process. **Restitution** or **victim compensation** also makes such programs easier for victims to accept.

The Dispute Settlement Center, Durham, North Carolina.   A good example of ADR is the Dispute Settlement Center of Durham (DSCD), which was established in North Carolina in 1983. Originally, the DSCD received financial assistance from the Orange County Dispute Settlement Center, the Human Relations Commission of the City of Durham, and Hassle House, a local drop-in center for youths. Michael Wendt was hired as the first DSCD director in March 1983. By 1988, the DSCD was a full-time operation with a board of directors.

Early activities of the DSCD included training staff members in the art of **mediation.** Mediation is the process of working out amicable and mutually satisfactory agreements between offenders and victims in disputes. Training was conducted by attorneys affiliated with the North Carolina division of the American Bar Association. A balanced pool of mediators was selected to represent a cross-section of the gender, racial, and ethnic composition of the community. A total of 38 volunteers were trained in the first mediator pool for the DSCD. In 1990 an office building was constructed to accommodate all DSCD activities.

Presently the DSCD considers numerous minor criminal cases that have been referred by the Durham County District Court. Referrals come from a daily review of new arrest warrants issued at the court clerk's office. Some of the cases heard by the DSCD include bad-check writing, divorce and family mediation, drive-by shooting injuries, landlord–tenant disputes, traffic and parking complaints, workplace mediation, school mediation, shoplifting cases, petty theft, burglary, and criminal trespass. Some of the cases excluded from DSCD action include domestic violence, child abuse, alcohol and drug abuse, and incidents involving serious and untreated mental illness.

Criminal matters are usually referred to the DSCD with a letter from the court, which says "A warrant has been sworn out against you by _____ alleging that you committed the criminal offense of _____. You can avoid having to appear in criminal court by submitting this matter to mediation." Respondents are provided with a specific hearing time and are informed that they may reschedule if necessary, as long as the revised time occurs prior to the court date set for the case. The letter closes by saying, "If you choose not to appear at the Dispute Settlement Center or mediation is not successful, you must be in Criminal Court at a specific time and place."

The process of mediation involves two mediators, the victim, and the perpetrator. Ground rules are established where neither party may interrupt the other while speaking. Complainants are then asked to describe the problem from their perspective. Respondents are asked to respond to complainants' comments and to indicate their views regarding the dispute. Mediators focus on having the parties clearly state their positions and on exploring common perspectives and areas of disagreement.

If the mediation session does not appear to be working out, mediators may meet with each party individually to discuss their particular perceptions and possible solutions. Such private meetings with individual participants may disclose evidence or information that one of the parties feels uncomfortable about sharing among all present. Mediators may also ask each party to consider further steps. If and when disputants reach an agreement, the terms are written down and signed by both parties. The agreement has the legal status of a written contract and is enforceable. About 90 percent of all mediations result in such agreements. If the case was originally referred by the district attorney's office, the parties also sign a letter stating, "As a result of mediation, an agreement has been reached. We, the undersigned, request that all pending criminal charges in the above case be dismissed." The letter is signed by the complainant, the respondent, and the two mediators who handled the case.

BOX 5.2

INTERNATIONAL SNAPSHOT: PROBATION AND PAROLE IN RUSSIA

Russia is considered a federative state with a president. The laws of Russia are contained in the Russian constitution, federal constitutional law, federal laws, and laws of subjects of federation. The Ministry of Internal Affairs oversees the penitentiary system and all law enforcement agencies. The court system of Russia has a Supreme Court and a variety of lower courts. Criminal laws are contained in the Criminal Code, the Criminal Procedure Code, the Criminal Punishment Execution Code, and the Law on the Justice System. Other specialized legal codes and compendiums exist.

The age of criminal responsibility in Russia is 16. Persons over 14 years old bear criminal responsibility only for murder, major bodily injury, rape, kidnapping, and other violent acts. Any act not included in the Criminal Code is not a crime. Crimes are classified according to whether they are major or minor. Major offenses are crimes such as rape, kidnapping, murder, treason, espionage, crimes against the justice system, and all other serious violent crimes. Minor crimes include offenses against property, such as theft or burglary, hooliganism, and offenses against public order. Another class of offenses pertains to drugs. Drug offenses include the unlawful production, distribution, transportation, stealing, or use of illegal drugs. The nature of the alleged offense and subsequent conviction determine the type of correctional institution where offenders will be housed. In 2005 there were over 4 million crimes reported. Accurate and current information about the amount and nature of crime committed in Russia is rare, since there is evidence of significant underreporting. It has been estimated that only 5 percent of all rapes are ever reported, for instance. A majority of offenses reported are property offenses, such as vehicular theft. Murders account for a very small proportion of crimes, while about 80,000 crimes reported were drug offenses. Interestingly, in over 75 percent of all crimes committed, victims were relatives or friends of the perpetrators. Nevertheless, the reliability of crime information is highly questionable.

Overseeing citizen safety in every Russian community is the Militia. The Militia is a public agency charged with protecting life, physical health, rights and freedoms of citizens, and protecting property. The Militia is authorized to use force to effect arrests of suspects. A major task of the Militia is crime prevention. The Militia is under the jurisdiction of the Ministry of Internal Affairs. Each city has a local Militia to perform crime control and investigative functions.

(*continued*)

BOX 5.2 (*Continued*)

Special detachments of Militia or police are called "watching units." Numbers of Militia personnel vary according to the crime rates, with usually one Militia officer per 50 crimes committed. For juveniles, delinquency inspectors are appointed. There is one delinquency inspector for every 4,000–5,000 youths under age 16.

The world community has been critical of Russian criminal justice over the last few decades. Some of the reasons for these criticisms pertain to lengthy pretrial detentions of suspects, which may be of durations in excess of three years. Also, Militia detentions appear to be somewhat arbitrary, despite explicit laws to the contrary. Chronically overcrowded labor colonies exist with deplorable conditions, with high rates of disease and inmate deaths due to illnesses. Beatings, torture, and rape are commonplace in such colonies, some of which are designated as educational labor colonies.

Suspects who are being investigated may be held in Special Isolation Facilities (SIZOs). SIZOs are pretrial detention facilities. Approximately 400,000 persons were held in SIZOs awaiting trial in 2005. Also, about 100,000 persons are held in police detention centers for varying periods, awaiting dispositions of their cases. Health and sanitation standards in these facilities at all levels of government are low due to lack of funding. It is not uncommon to see prisons with inmate populations in excess of 200 percent of their operating capacity.

When accused persons are arrested, they have the right to be advised of the charges against them. They may present evidence in their own behalf and be represented by counsel. If they cannot afford counsel, the government will appoint public counsel for them. Defendants have the right to reject certain judges or trial participants, and at the conclusion of proceedings where a conviction is forthcoming, all prisoners are entitled to appeal their convictions. Court-appointed persons to represent defendants are known as counselors, and they must be a member of the Russian bar. Russian courts utilize juries in various cities. The jury system

was introduced in the early 1990s, and thus, evidence of the successfulness of the jury system in Russia is inconclusive. Juries are used at the discretion of the offender, and juries only decide questions of fact. Only persons between the ages of 25 and 70 may be on juries.

Defendants accused of less serious crimes may deposit money as a form of bail prior to their trial. The amount of bail is determined by the nature of the offense, by a prosecutorial recommendation, and by the judge. About 20 percent of all accused offenders were held in pretrial detention prior to their trials in 2005. Pretrial detention is used only if one's punishment for an offense is one or more years. Alternatives to trial include transferring cases to juvenile jurisdiction, verbal reprimands by judges, and transferring cases to comrades' courts.

Judges decide sentences of offenders who are convicted of crimes, either through a trial by jury or bench trial. Individual judicial decision making regarding sentencing is done for those whose punishments do not exceed five years. For those whose punishments can exceed five years in prison, then one's punishment is assessed and imposed by three-judge panels who sit and decide punishments. Sentences imposed are by majority vote in serious cases. The maximum punishment for the most serious offenses in Russia is the death penalty. Approximately 60–70 executions a year are conducted.

For less serious offenses, great judicial discretion may be exercised. There are many possible punishments, including imprisonment for indeterminate terms, fines, performing work in lieu of prison (community service), adverse publicity, dismissal from one's office or job, deprivation of the right to hold certain positions or perform certain activities, restitution for financial damages, confiscation of property (asset forfeiture), and other sanctions. Imprisonment upon conviction for a criminal offense involves placement in a labor camp. Nearly 2 million persons were in Russian labor camps in 2005. Thus, Russia surpasses the United States regarding the number of imprisoned offenders annually. About 5 percent of all prisoners in Russia are women. The labor camps engage prisoners in various vocational activities, often related to agriculture. All prisoners confined in labor camps must work at one type of job or another. They are paid a minimum wage for the labor they perform. As a reward for good behavior and excellent work, prisoners may be given opportunities for furloughs or temporary leaves from these labor camps, to visit families or obtain jobs. Prisoners may also be permitted to spend additional money for food or goods. They may be permitted to receive mail or parcels from family or friends. A crude version of parole exists, in that through an inmate's good work, one may be released from part of one's punishment and placed in less restrictive punishment in one's community. In 2005 some cities and towns in Russia were experimenting with restorative justice and community corrections programming on a limited basis.

Sources: Adapted from Ilya V. Nikiforov, "Russia," *World Factbook of Criminal Justice Systems,* December 2002; Foreign Broadcast Information Service, "Russia," October 2004; Penal Reform Internationale, "Introduction to Alternatives to Imprisonment," Paris, France, January 2005; Ministry of Internal Affairs, *Offenders and Punishments,* Moscow, Russia, January 2006; Bureau of Democracy, Human Rights, and Labor, "Country Reports on Human Rights Practices," February 23, 2001.

In 2006 there were 28 community dispute settlement centers throughout North Carolina. Over 31,000 disputes have been satisfactorily resolved with further criminal prosecution. About 55 percent of these disputes were originally referred by the criminal court. Presently the DSCD receives its funding from state appropriations and the Administrative Office of the U.S. Courts. The impact of volunteer mediators should not be underestimated. In 2005, for example, the average mediator spent 460 hours performing board service; 450 hours mediating disputes; 132 hours performing clerical and other support functions; 83 hours facilitating groups; 65 hours conducting training sessions; 40 hours of fundraising; and 10 hours engaging in community outreach.

Not all DSCD cases are successfully resolved. In fact, in some isolated instances, there have been lethal consequences. For instance, a name-calling incident involving two students at a local high school escalated to a beating of one of the students by friends of the other student. Subsequently, some of the students in one of the groups engaged in a drive-by shooting of an innocent pedestrian while attempting to kill another student. Warrants were sworn out for attempted murder against several students believed to be involved in the drive-by shooting. However, police were unable to positively ID the gunman. The prosecutor feared that the case might be dropped for lack of evidence, and therefore, he referred the case to the DSCD for mediation between the two student groups. Fifteen students and 30 parents agreed to participate in mediation. Student peer mediators ensured that all involved in the shooting participated in the mediation hearing. After one hour, the two groups apologized to each other. Parents of 11 out of 13 students who had sworn out warrants against other students agreed to have their cases dismissed. The parties signed forms requesting dismissals and the cases were dismissed by the criminal court judge. The parents of two other students persisted in their complaints, however, and took their cases to court. But when the parties reached court, the judge dismissed the two cases since the two larger groups of students had reconciled.

The DSCD conducted a survey of all disputants who had been served by the center several years after it had been operating. About 88 percent of all disputes had resulted in agreements. Between 85 and 95 percent of all disputants indicated that they were satisfied with the results from DSCD mediation. The primary result of the DSCD program was that it illustrated how an energetic and creative mediation program can provide a wide range of rehabilitative services to the community. While the DSCD was not 100 percent successful, it is clear that numerous cases that otherwise would have consumed valuable criminal court time were resolved through civil means, and to most everyone's satisfaction.

Victim–Offender Reconciliation Projects

Another version of alternative dispute resolution is victim–offender reconciliation, a specific form of conflict resolution between the victim and the offender. A face-to-face encounter is the essence of this process. Elkhart County, Indiana, has been the site of the **Victim–Offender Reconciliation Project (VORP)** since 1987. The primary aims of VORPs are to (1) make offenders accountable for their wrongs against victims, (2) reduce recidivism among participating offenders, and (3) heighten responsibility of offenders through victim compensation and repayment for damages inflicted.

VORP was established in Kitchener, Ontario, in 1974 and was subsequently replicated as PACT, or Prisoner and Community Together, in northern Indiana near Elkhart. Subsequent replications in various jurisdictions have created different varieties of ADR, each variety spawning embellishments, additions, or program deletions deemed more or less important by the particular jurisdiction. The Genessee County (Batavia), New York, Sheriff's Department established a VORP in 1983, followed by programs in Valparaiso, Indiana; Quincy, Massachusetts; and Minneapolis, Minnesota in 1985. In Quincy, for instance, the program was named EARN-IT and was operated through the Probation Department. More than 25 different states have one or another version of VORP. One of these sites involved a study of offender recidivism and ADR. Investigations of ADR and its effectiveness have tended to reduce recidivism among affected offenders.

Cross-site analyses of ADR programs in other jurisdictions suggest results comparable to those in Indiana. VORPs have been evaluated in several other jurisdictions, including Orange County, California. Over a thousand interviews were conducted in both pre-mediation and post-mediation periods, as well as with persons in several groups not participating in ADR. Most victims and offenders reported greater satisfaction and perceptions of fairness for victims, as well as a much higher rate of restitution completion by offenders. VORPs have been increasingly established outside of the United States with similarly successful results (Champion, 2005).

Pretrial Diversion

Pretrial diversion is a procedure whereby criminal defendants are diverted to either a community-based agency for treatment or assigned to a counselor for social and/or psychiatric assistance (Johnston, 2006). Pretrial diversion may involve education, job training, counseling, or some type of psychological or physical therapy. Diversion is the official halting or suspension of legal proceedings against a criminal defendant or juvenile after a recorded justice system entry, and possible referral of that person to a treatment or care program administered by a nonjustice agency or private agency. Technically, diversion is not true probation in that the alleged offender has not been convicted of a crime.

The thrust of diversion is toward an informal administrative effort to determine (1) whether nonjudicial processing is warranted; (2) whether treatment is warranted; (3) if treatment is warranted, which one to use; and (4) whether charges against the defendant should be dropped or reinstated (Johnston, 2006).

Diversion is intended for first-offenders who have not committed serious crimes. It is similar to probation because offenders must comply with specific conditions established by the court. Successful completion of those conditions usually leads to a dismissal of charges against the defendant. A **totality of circumstances** assessment of each offender's crime is made by the prosecutor and the court, and a decision about diversion is made. Each case is considered on its own merits. Those charged with driving while intoxicated may be diverted to attend Alcoholics Anonymous meetings or special classes for drunk drivers as a part of their diversion. Often, diverted defendants must pay monthly fees or **user fees** during the diversion period to help defray expenses incurred by the public or private agencies who monitor them.

Unconditional and Conditional Diversion.   Most **diversion programs** in the United States include one or more behavioral conditions and prescribe involvement in treatment programs such as Alcoholics Anonymous, driver's training schools, and/or individual or group psychological counseling. However, a **diversion program** may simply specify that offenders known as **divertees** should be law-abiding and submit monthly reports and user fees for the duration of their diversion terms. When an offender is placed in such a program, it is called a **unconditional diversion program.** Unconditional diversion programs place no restrictions on a divertee's behavior, and there are no formal controls operating through which divertee behaviors can be monitored.

A **conditional diversion program** involves some behavioral monitoring by probation officers or personnel affiliated with local probation departments in cities or counties. The degree of monitoring depends on the conditions of the diversion program and the special needs of divertees. For the least monitored divertees, monthly contact with the probation department by letter or telephone may be all that is required, together with the payment of a monthly maintenance fee, which may range from $10–100 or more. Divertees are often required to submit a statement regularly (usually monthly or weekly) indicating their present successful employment, family support, and other pertinent data.

The History and Philosophy of Diversion.   Diversion originated in the United States through the early juvenile courts in Chicago and New York in the late 1800s. There were concerted efforts by religious groups and reformers to keep children from imprisonment of any kind, since children over eight years of age were considered eligible for adult court processing. Cook County, Illinois, implemented a diversion program for youthful offenders in 1899 (Champion, 2005). The underlying philosophy of diversion is community reintegration and rehabilitation, where offenders avoid the stigma of incarceration and the public notoriety accompanying appearances and trials. In most state courts where diversion is condoned, diversion does not entirely remove offenders from court processing, since the court usually must approve prosecutorial recommendations for diversion in each case. Since these approvals are often conducted in less publicized hearings, a divertee's crimes are less likely to be scrutinized publicly. When an offender completes his or her diversion program successfully, one of two things happens. First, the offender's arrest record pertaining to that offense is erased through an **expungement** and the prosecution is terminated. If this event doesn't occur, then the second optional result is a downgrading of the original criminal charge to a lesser offense and a resulting conviction. For instance, a first-offender charged with felony theft may have his or her offense downgraded to misdemeanor theft following the successful completion of the diversion program. Either way, for offenders who are permitted diversion, their diversion programs are win–win situations.

Functions of Diversion.   Some of the more important functions are:

1. To permit divertees the opportunity of remaining in their communities where they can receive needed assistance or treatment, depending on the nature of the crimes charged.
2. To permit divertees the opportunity to make restitution to their victims where monetary damages were suffered and property destroyed.
3. To permit divertees the opportunity of remaining free in their communities to support themselves and their families, and to avoid the stigma of incarceration.
4. To help divertees avoid the stigma of a criminal conviction.
5. To assist corrections officials in reducing prison and jail overcrowding by diverting less serious cases to nonincarcerative alternatives.
6. To save the courts the time, trouble, and expense of formally processing less serious cases and streamlining case dispositions through informal case handling.
7. To make it possible for divertees to participate in self-help, educational, or vocational programs.
8. To preserve the dignity and integrity of divertees by helping them avoid further contact with the criminal justice system and assisting them to be more responsible adults capable of managing their own lives.
9. To preserve the family unit and enhance family solidarity and continuity.

This list highlights the rehabilitative nature of diversion. Presently, it is unknown about how much diversion affects the court system and court case-loads. Accurate estimates of those placed on diversion are difficult to determine, primarily because of the potential for record expungements. Once these criminal records or arrest warrants for various charges have been expunged, the media and official agencies usually cannot access them. Literally, they cease to exist.

Criteria Influencing Pretrial Diversion.   Who qualifies for pretrial diversion? First, it helps to be a first-offender. First-offenders who are charged with petty crimes are the most likely candidates for diversion programs. Those barred from such programs might include the following:

1. Those with prior drug offense convictions, former drug offense divertees, and/or who traffic in drugs.
2. Those convicted of a felony within the previous five-year period.
3. Those whose current offense involves violence.
4. Those who are past or present probation or parole violators.

Other relevant criteria used by different jurisdictions for deciding which offenders deserve to be included in diversion programs are:

1. The age of the offender
2. The residency, employment, and familial status of the offender
3. The prior record of the offender
4. The seriousness of the offense
5. Aggravating or mitigating circumstances associated with the commission of the offense.

Criticisms of Diversion.   Not everyone favors using diversion as a means of removing those charged with crimes from the criminal justice system, even on a temporary basis. They believe that diversion is too lenient on criminals. Critics of diversion generally focus on the nonpunitive nature of diversion conditions, which are often no conditions.

Other criticisms include that diversion is an inappropriate punishment for criminals and that it does not deal effectively with offenders. Furthermore, some critics allege that diversion leads to net-widening. Another criticism is that diversion excludes female offenders. Some observers think that diversion resolves an offender's case without the benefit of due process. For instance, whenever a prosecutor examines a case, the evidence against the defendant, and other pertinent circumstances, an offer of diversion may be made. If the offer is accepted, this is a tacit admission by the defendant that he or she is guilty of the offense(s) alleged. If the offer of diversion is rejected, then prosecutors can always exercise their option to pursue criminal charges against the defendant later in court. Thus, diversion assumes guilt without a trial (Johnston, 2006).

However, supporters of diversion say that diversion greatly reduces offender recidivism when applied appropriately. For instance, a sample of first-time offenders was placed on diversion in Vanderburgh County, Indiana, during the mid-1990s. A sample of 243 divertees was studied. The recidivism rate for those who successfully completed their diversion programs was only 9 percent, while those who did not successfully complete their programs had 39 percent recidivism. Those favoring diversion also counter by arguing that diversion enables divertees to avoid the stigma and criminogenic atmosphere of prisons and jails. Furthermore, there does not appear to be any gender discrimination that applies to diversion programs in any jurisdiction. Males appear equally likely to receive diversion compared with females. The idea that guilt is assumed without the benefit of a criminal trial is difficult to overcome. This is precisely what prosecutors assume. However, the benefit of freedom to live within the community without restriction, and the fact that participation in diversion is strictly voluntary, outweighs the argument that one's right to due process is somehow jeopardized. If someone charged with a crime really wants to fight it in court, then they can exercise their constitutional rights and have a trial in the matter.

JUDICIAL DISCRETION AND THE PROBATION DECISION

Criminal court judges play a pivotal role in the sentencing process. They decide which sentences to impose, and they determine the severity or leniency of those sentences. Most judges have a variety of sentencing options, ranging from probation to incarceration. They can even impose some incarceration interspersed with some probation.

Judges are guided in their sentencing decisions by the different standards of the jurisdictions of their criminal courts. Probation officers assist them by preparing PSI reports about offenders who are awaiting sentencing for different types of crimes. Probation officers frequently append their own sentencing recommendations to these PSI reports, although judges are only obligated to consider them. No judge is bound by the contents of PSIs. However, if judges are in jurisdictions with sentencing guidelines or presumptive sentencing schemes, these schemes provide for particular sentencing ranges, usually expressed in months, which function as guides for judges to follow. Again, there is no hard-and-fast rule obligating judges to follow these guidelines, no matter how binding they may appear. The only constraints upon judges are mandatory sentencing provisions. If cases come before them where particular sentences are mandated, they must impose these sentences. For instance, if a repeat-offender is convicted of being an habitual offender, many state statutes provide for mandatory terms of life without parole. Therefore, judges have no discretion in these cases and must impose life-without-parole terms.

Judges have considerable latitude in the sentences they impose. Judges may impose probation. They may also impose probation with special conditions. These special conditions are appended to probation orders issued by the sentencing judge. Probationers must comply with all of these conditions or they are subject to having their probation programs revoked. They may be placed in a jail or prison for the duration of their sentences. While most states by law suggest conditions to be imposed on new probationers, judges generally have complete discretion to accept, modify, or reject these conditions. In Texas, for instance, judges may impose some of the following special conditions of probation on offenders:

1. Probationer shall not open a checking account.
2. Probationer must attend basic education or vocational training as directed by the supervising probation officer.
3. Probationer must notify any prospective employer regarding criminal history, if position of financial responsibility is involved.
4. Probationer shall be assigned to the highest level of supervision or supervision caseload until appropriate level of supervision is further established by objective assessment instrument and supervision case classification.
5. Probationer shall comply with any other condition specified herein (e.g., no controlled substances).
6. Probationer shall participate in a mental health/mental retardation treatment or counseling program as directed by the supervising probation officer.
7. Probationer shall make restitution payments as required by supervising probation officer in an amount to be set by the court. By the 10th of each month, payments (cashier's check or money order) shall be paid to the Texas Department of Criminal Justice Probation Division, Capital Station, Texas, 78711.
8. Probationer shall submit to a substance (alcohol/narcotics) treatment program, which may include urinalysis monitoring, attendance at scheduled counseling sessions, driving restrictions, or related requirements as directed by supervising probation officer.

9. Probationer shall not contact victim(s).

10. Probationer shall not enter the specified county without prior written judicial approval.

Judges circle the appropriate special conditions above and attach these to one's probation order. The probationer must agree with these conditions and other program requirements and sign the form. If the prospective probationer refuses to sign the form, then probation will be denied. Judges cannot force offenders into probation programs against their wishes.

Probation conditions are usually classified as general or specific. General conditions are imposed on all probationers, while specific conditions are only applied to certain probationers. Judges usually use a previously adopted set of standard probation conditions, which include the following: (1) make periodic reports to their probation officer; (2) notify the officer about changes in employment or residence; (3) obtain permission for out-of-state travel; (4) refrain from possessing firearms; (5) not associate with known criminals; and (6) obey the law.

Original sentencing judges or their courts maintain jurisdiction over all probationers for the duration of their probationary terms. If any probationer violates one or more program conditions and these violations are detected, the information is transmitted to the court. The judge considers the evidence in a special hearing before the court and decides what to do. The judge may intensify a probationer's supervision or place the offender under home confinement with electronic monitoring. The judge may require probation officers to make frequent checks of the offender's premises and test the offender for drugs, alcohol, or other substances that may be prohibited.

Judges are responsive to what the public wants and they attempt to impose sentences that fit the particular offense. But those most directly involved in the enforcement of conditions of a probationer's program are probation officers. These officers are the primary link between the court and their probationer-clients. As far as the court is concerned, probation officers should stress the following in their supervisory responsibilities:

1. The public wants probation to deliver public safety.
2. Probation can both raise public safety and help probationers become law-abiding citizens.
3. Probation needs to enforce probation orders and help offenders.
4. The idea "get tough on probationers" doesn't need to lead to more imprisonment; in fact, it could lead to an increase in general deterrence (Champion, 2005).

Recommendations from judges to probation officers include the following admonitions:

1. Public safety comes first.
2. Probation officers should spend more time supervising offenders who pose the greatest risk to public safety.
3. Probation officers should be assigned to supervise specific geographical areas rather than being randomly assigned to offenders.

4. Permissive practices should be abandoned, and in their place a response that is certain and incorporates graduated sanctions to deal with technical violations.

5. Probation should encourage involvement of other agencies, organizations, and interest groups in offender treatment.

6. Program performance should be used as the measure for the allocation of resources (Champion, 2005).

Although probation officers are given a great deal of supervisory responsibility over sentenced offenders on probation, their initial input through PSI report preparation in certain jurisdictions is mixed. Probation officers are often excluded entirely from sentencing decisions that are plea bargained. Judicial discretion may operate to the probation officer's disadvantage in some cases. Part of the problem is the growing bureaucratization of probation services and a general breakdown in communication between judges and probation agencies.

Judges have broad discretion, therefore, in heightening offender accountability. Judges may impose restitution orders or community service as a means of maximizing offender responsibilities. Restitution to victims by offenders may be mandated by legislative statute. In Pennsylvania, for instance, judges must impose restitution on probationers whenever damages are easy to quantify. Whenever restitution orders are imposed, they generally work to minimize one's potential for being rearrested. Also, offenders who are married, employed, and older are less likely to be rearrested.

Judicial discretion and the special conditions of probation they impose are valid so long as they (1) do not violate the constitution; (2) are reasonable; (3) are unambiguous; and (4) are intended to promote the rehabilitation of the offender and/or the protection of society. In recent years, the job of sentencing offenders has become less perfunctory. Judges are increasingly exercising what some persons term **therapeutic jurisprudence,** which attempts to combine a "rights" perspective—focusing on justice, rights, and equality issues—with an "ethic of care" perspective—focusing on care, interdependence, and response to need (Steinman, 2006). Thus, judging and sentencing offenders is increasingly becoming a collaborative enterprise between the court and community. Sentencing judges attempt to create appropriate dispositional outcomes, including securing treatment and social services for offenders who are sentenced. This is where the special conditions of probation can come into play and influence the offender's life chances significantly. The public seems to desire a more involved and responsive judiciary. Thus, the judiciary is gradually being transformed into a process removed somewhat from the traditional one followed for so many decades. A comparison of the traditional process with the transformed court process is shown below.

Traditional Process	**Transformed Process**
■ Dispute resolution	■ Problem-solving dispute avoidance
■ Legal outcome	■ Therapeutic outcome
■ Adversarial process	■ Collaborative process
■ Claim-or case-oriented	■ People-oriented
■ Rights-based	■ Interest-or needs-based

- Emphasis placed on adjudication
- Interpretation and application of law
- Judge as arbiter
- Backward looking
- Precedent-based
- Few participants and stakeholders
- Individualistic
- Legalistic
- Formal
- Efficient

- Emphasis placed on post-adjudication and alternative dispute resolution
- Interpretation and application of social science
- Judge as coach
- Forward looking
- Planning-based
- Wide range of participants and stakeholders
- Interdependent
- Common-sensical
- Informal
- Effective

Thus, the orientation underlying therapeutic jurisprudence directs the judge's attention beyond the specific dispute before the court and toward the needs and circumstances of the individuals involved in the dispute. All participants in the process of creating safer communities, including judges and probation officers, must stay focused on their areas of influence, ensure ongoing interagency training needs to become the norm, and continue a focus on policy development built on reliable research. Many criminal justice organizations, including the courts and probation departments, are partnering increasingly with other criminal justice organizations in a greater effort to create safer communities and more law-abiding probationer-clients.

SUMMARY

Probation derives from the word *probatio,* which means a period of proving or trial and forgiveness. It was formally recognized by statute in Massachusetts in 1878, although a Massachusetts reformer, John Augustus, is credited with introducing it in the United States in 1841 as part of his philanthropy and temperance beliefs. Those most likely placed on probation include first-time offenders, particularly those convicted of nonviolent crimes. Currently, probation refers to any conditional nonincarcerative sentence imposed by judges for a criminal conviction. Probation differs from parole in that probationers do not ordinarily serve time in either a prison or jail, whereas parolees are former inmates of such institutions who have been released early by parole boards. Judges control probationers, whereas parolees are dependent upon parole board discretion for their early release from incarceration.

Not everyone agrees that probation is a suitable punishment for criminal offenders. Those most likely to receive sentences of probation are nondangerous first-offenders, whereas recidivists and dangerous offenders are least likely to receive it. Proponents of probation argue that it prevents persons from succumbing to the criminogenic influence of prisons and jails. The stigma of being labeled as a criminal may compel some persons to commit new crimes as one result of being incarcerated. Probation means avoiding to some extent this criminal label. Probation also alleviates prison and jail overcrowding. Also, probation permits offenders to remain in their communities and become reintegrated to do lawful and useful activities. Opponents of probation say that it coddles offenders and creates attitudes among criminals that they will not really be punished if they commit crimes.

Those most likely to receive probation are property offenders or those who have been convicted of less serious offenses. However, virtually *every* crime category has at least some persons who have been granted probation. The average length of probation for most offenders varies between 24 and 36 months, although those convicted of the most serious crimes have the longest probation lengths. The use of probation is also contingent upon the nature of the sentencing scheme in any jurisdiction. Guidelines-based sentencing schemes and mandatory sentencing procedures restrict judicial options in sentencing considerably. Nevertheless, most jurisdictions throughout the United States report greater use of probation annually.

Before criminal cases are prosecuted, prosecutors, judges, and offenders sometimes enter into agreements to have their cases disposed of through civil mechanisms. An umbrella term, restorative justice, has been used to depict any action that is primarily oriented toward doing justice by repairing the harm that has been caused by a crime. One civil mechanism involving offender mediation with one or more victims is alternative dispute resolution (ADR). ADR is a community-based, informal dispute settlement process. Usually targeted for involvement in such programs are misdemeanants, although low-level nonviolent felons may become involved in the ADR process, depending on the circumstances. Another option available to prosecutors is pretrial diversion. Diversion means to temporarily suspend a case from the criminal justice process and divert offenders to community-based agencies for treatment and/or supervision for a period of time. Once this process is completed, one's criminal record may be either downgraded to a lesser offense or completely expunged. Victim–offender reconciliation projects (VORPs) are becoming increasingly common as methods for reducing clogged criminal court dockets and case backlogs in prosecutors' offices.

At the hub of any preconviction action is the criminal court judge. Criminal court judges have broad discretionary powers and can impose any one of several different punishments. Judges may impose probation for offenders who are considered good candidates for such programs. These offenders are usually low-risk, nonviolent offenders with no prior criminal records. Increasing numbers of offenders have substance abuse problems or mental illnesses, and judges can proscribe special conditions of probation in order for these persons to receive appropriate treatment from community-based agencies. Increasingly, the judiciary is moving toward greater collaboration with community agencies and organizations to deliver sentences that not only preserve public safety, but tend to hold offenders accountable to their victims in restorative ways.

QUESTIONS FOR REVIEW

1. What does probation mean? Where and when did it originate in the United States?
2. Describe the early use of probation in the United States.
3. Compare and contrast the rehabilitative, treatment-oriented correctional philosophy with the justice model. Give some arguments favoring either perspective.
4. What do you see as the relative merits of probation as an alternative to incarceration? Do you think everyone is in favor of probation? Why or why not? Explain.

5. Identify three persons associated with the early use of probation in the United States.

6. What is meant by alternative dispute resolution? What are some of its functions?

7. What is pretrial diversion? Who usually qualifies for pretrial diversion?

8. What are two important optional consequences for those who successfully complete their diversionary programs?

9. What is restorative justice and why is it important?

10. What is the nature of judicial discretion in probation decision making?

SUGGESTED READINGS

Burnett, R. and F. McNeill (2005). "The Place of the Officer–Offender Relationship in Assisting Offenders to Desist from Crime." *Probation Journal 52:*221–242.

Elechi, O.O. (2005). "Repairing Harm and Transforming African-American Communities Through Restorative Justice." *Community Safety Journal 4:*29–36.

Johnson, B.D. (2005). "Contextual Disparities in Guidelines Departures: Courtroom Social Contexts, Guidelines Compliance, and Extralegal Disparities in Criminal Sentencing." *Criminology 43:*761–796.

Marinos, V. (2005). "Thinking About Penal Equivalents." *Punishment and Society 7:*441–455.

Schlesinger, T. (2005). "Racial and Ethnic Disparity in Pretrial Criminal Processing." *Justice Quarterly 22:*170–192.

INTERNET CONNECTIONS

Abuse of Judicial Discretion
http://www.constitution.org/abus/discretion/judicial/judicial_discretion.htm

American Arbitration Association
http://www.adr.org/index2.1.jsp

Association of Pretrial Professionals of Florida
http://www.appf.org/

Colorado Council of Mediators
http://www.coloradomediation.org/

CPR Institute for Dispute Resolution
http://www.cpradr.org/home1.htm

Grundy County Probation Department
http://www.grundyco.com/probation.htm

History of American Probation and Parole Associaton
http://www.appa-net.org/about%20appa/history.htm

Massachusetts Council on Family Mediation
http://www.divorcenet.com/ma-mediators.html

Montana Mediation Association
http://www.mtmediation.org/

National Association for Community Mediation
http://www.nafcm.org/

National Association of Pretrial Services Agencies
http://www.napsa.org/

National Association of Probation Executives
http://www.napchome.org/

Pretrial Procedures
http://www.uaa.alaska.edu/just/just110/courts2.html

Pretrial Services Resource Center
http://www.pretrial.org/

Probation philosophy
http://www.appa-net.org/about%20appa/probatio.htm

| *Programs for Probationers*

Chapter Outline

Chapter Objectives

As the result of reading this chapter, the following objectives will be realized:

1. Describing standard probation programs, including their weaknesses and strengths.
2. Understanding several intensive supervised probation programs, including programs from Georgia, Idaho, and South Carolina.
3. Describing shock probation and split sentencing, including the philosophy and objectives of these sentencing alternatives.
4. Assessing the effectiveness of split sentencing and shock probation as related to client successes.
5. Understanding the weaknesses, strengths, functions, and goals of boot camps as youth-oriented measures to improve accountability and discipline.

DO ANY OF THESE PERSONS QUALIFY FOR PROBATION?

• *Wilcox is a convicted sex offender in Massachusetts. As a part of his probation, he was ordered to have no unsupervised contact with anyone under the age of 16. While on probation, Wilcox allegedly followed several young girls in his automobile to their home, and repeatedly drove around the block and past their home, staring at where they lived each time he passed in his car. One of the girls called the police who sent a unit to investigate. Wilcox was stopped by police officers and disclosed that he was a probationer. The probation office was contacted and Wilcox's probation officer sought to have his probation revoked by violating the probation order prohibiting contact with anyone under the age of 16. Wilcox objected, claiming that "driving around a neighborhood where young girls happen to live" does not violate the "forbidden contact" condition of his probation orders. Should Wilcox's probation be continued? [Commonwealth v. Wilcox, 823 N.E.2d 808 (Mass.App.March) (2005)].*

• *Ramirez-Franco was convicted of a property offense in federal court in California. The judge imposed several conditions of probation, including that Ramirez-Franco should abstain from abusing prescription medications during his probation or supervised release; that he shall participate in outpatient substance abuse treatment and submit to drug and alcohol testing; and that he shall abstain from using alcohol. Since Ramirez-Franco's pre-sentence investigation report contained no evidence of his drug or alcohol use or abuse and drugs and alcohol were unrelated to the property offense conviction, Ramirez-Franco objected to these supervised release conditions. The Ninth Circuit Court of Appeals heard his appeal. Should these probation conditions be a part of Ramirez-Franco's probation or supervised release program? Should his supervised release without these conditions be approved? [United States v. Ramirez-Franco, 122 Fed.App. 324 (U.S.9thCir.Jan.) (2005)].*

• *Stott was convicted in an Indiana court of child molestation and placed on a term of probation. One of his probation conditions was that he is prohibited from having any contact from any children under the age of 18 and from being within 1,000 feet of any school or day-care center. Stott opposed these conditions, saying that they were unusually severe, unconstitutionally vague, and improper. An appellate court heard the matter. How should the court decide on the appropriateness and constitutionality of these conditions? [Stott v. State, 822 N.E.2d 176 (Ind.App.Jan.) (2005)].*

• *Hernandez was a Florida offender convicted of a crime and sentenced to probation for a period of years. Hernandez completed his probationary term and was subsequently arrested for driving while intoxicated (DWI) and causing serious bodily injury. The original sentencing judge declared that Hernandez was in violation of his original probation orders and declared that he must serve an extended probationary term following his conviction for the DWI offense. Should Hernandez have to serve an additional probationary term after his original probationary term has expired? [Hernandez v. State, 889 So.2d 913 (Fla.Dist.App.Dec.) (2004)].*

• *McClellan, an Illinois defendant, entered a guilty plea to aggravated criminal sexual abuse. She was placed on a term of probation with conditions including that she must successfully complete a therapy program. Subsequently she enrolled in the therapy program but was discharged from it because she continued to maintain her innocence regarding the underlying crime. It was recommended that she undergo individualized therapy. Thereafter she was readmitted to group therapy and made substantial improvements regarding her adjustment to treatment. Nonetheless, authorities in charge of the program noted that she had made minimal or no progress in her ability to disclose her abusive history. She was ultimately discharged from the program as "unsuccessful." Although it was recommended that she retake individual therapy, she only completed an intake evaluation during the course of three appointments. The trial court revoked her probation and she appealed. How should the Illinois court of appeals decide this case? [People v. McClellan, 820 N.E.2d 578 (Ill.App.Dec.) (2004)].*

WHAT HAPPENED?

• *Wilcox's probation program was revoked. While the Commonwealth was not required to prove that Wilcox intended to violate the probation order, it was only required to show that Wilcox's act constituting the violation was voluntary. In the present case, Wilcox's intent was quite direct. He followed the young girls in his car with a persistence that bordered on stalking, and he came within such close proximity to these girls that he instilled fear. This conduct was sufficient to constitute violation of Wilcox's probation orders.*

• *The Ninth Circuit Court of Appeals decided that certain conditions of Ramirez-Franco's probation orders were improperly imposed, because the need for such conditions was not supported by the record or the pre-sentence investigation report. Ramirez-Franco was placed on supervised release (probation) without these additional conditions and restrictions.*

• *The Indiana appeals court declared that whenever a probationer attacks one or more conditions of his or her supervision, the courts will balance three factors: (1) the purpose to be served by probation; (2) the extent to which constitutional rights enjoyed by law-abiding citizens should be enjoyed by probationers; and (3) the legitimate needs of law enforcement. In Stott's case, the court declared that restricting a sex offender's access to locations where other potential victims are present will not only further the defendant's rehabilitation but will also protect those whom the defendant may harm. In Stott's case, the prohibition was specific and accurately defined. It served the purpose of keeping Stott from being where children, potential victims, might congregate. The condition was also constitutional. Stott was placed on probation with these conditions.*

• *A Florida appeals court declared that in Hernandez's case, the original sentencing judge lacked the jurisdiction to impose an additional probationary term. Once Hernandez had successfully completed the original probationary term, the sentencing judge lost jurisdiction over him. The additional probationary term imposed on Hernandez was set aside.*

• *The court declared that the trial court had the right to impose a sex-offender therapy program and treatment as one of McClellan's probation conditions. But one condition pertaining to counseling said merely that "the defendant shall complete sex-offender counseling." McClellan did, in fact, enroll in and take a sex-offender counseling program and participate in both individual and group therapy. That the therapy was deemed "unsuccessful" by therapists is irrelevant to this specific condition of McClellan's probation. Furthermore, McClellan's failure to take follow-up counseling recommended as the resul.t of her mental health evaluation does not constitute a failure on her part to complete the sex-offender counseling program. The order revoking McClellan's probation program was set aside and her program was continued.*

INTRODUCTION

This chapter begins with an examination of **standard probation** and **intensive supervised probation** as alternatives to incarceration. After a determination of guilt in criminal court, some convicted offenders are sentenced to probation for a period of years. Several probation programs are featured. We have already described the history, philosophy, and functions of probation. In this chapter we explore several popular probation options, including specific programs of intensive supervised probation.

The final part of this chapter examines shock probation, split sentencing and boot camps as increasingly used probation variations and options. The goals and effectiveness of shock probation are presented. Boot camps are described, including some of the more popular models developed in various states. Boot camp participants are profiled. The effectiveness of boot camps are discussed, together with several criticisms of it. The costs of these nonincarcerative options are compared with the costs of incarceration, and several trends in diversion and probation are described. Probation revocation is examined.

STANDARD PROBATION

Standard probation supervision in many jurisdictions is essentially no supervision at all. When offenders are convicted of one or more crimes, judges sentence a portion of these convicted offenders to a probation program in lieu of incarceration. These programs may or may not have conditions. Prospective probationers are required to sign a form outlining the conditions of their probation. Compliance with the probation program conditions is monitored closely by POs. However, these officers are often so overworked and understaffed that they cannot possibly oversee all of the activities of their probationer/clients. The caseloads or numbers of offenders POs are assigned to supervise vary among jurisdictions. Offender caseloads may be as high as 2,000 in some cities or counties, while in others, the caseloads may be 30 or fewer. Caseloads vary according to the type of program, the number of offenders, and the number of probation officers who are available.

Standard probation is considered by many critics to be the most ineffective probationary form. Often, probationers may contact their probation officers by telephone and avoid face-to-face visits. Additionally, the requirements of their probationary programs are often less stringent compared with more intensive probation programs. The caseloads of POs in some jurisdictions are so high that officers cannot devote special attention to those offenders in the greatest need of special attention. This is the great failing of standard probation. There are no easy solutions to this problem. The probation department can only do so much in view of its staffing problems and varying clientele. And there is no relief in sight. The chances are that this probation form is growing rather than declining, despite high recidivism rates among standard probationers.

Another problem with probation is that often, those in administrative positions in probation departments attach greater importance to those things that enhance paper-processing, office efficiency, and career development rather than to those things that directly affect probationers. For instance, a study of the Massachusetts probation system was conducted. It involved a mail survey that yielded 500 responses. These responses were supplemented with interviews and field efforts involving 60 different criminal courts and more than 400 individuals. The resulting report addressed at least 60 different improvements in Massachusetts probation programs. But a more selective list of those improvements receiving the greatest priority and attention is significant, not because of what is included, but rather, what is excluded. The list of 11 priority concerns is as follows:

1. The review and redefinition of the overall mission of probation.
2. Career advancement opportunities for all personnel.
3. Greater emphasis on affirmative action.
4. Adjustments in the staffing level in some courts.
5. Increased training opportunities.
6. Substantially improved physical facilities.
7. Immediate attention to computerizing the central file.
8. Formation of citizen advisory groups.
9. Substantially improved social services for offenders.
10. Specific attention to the unique needs of the various trial court departments.
11. An immediate and forceful public education campaign to enlist support for improved social services from all branches of government and the general public (Spangenberg et al., 1987).

All but one of these improvement recommendations has to do with office policy, office efficiency, office work, office environment, public relations with the community, and office relations with courts. It is unclear about what is meant by "improved social services for offenders." Ideally, probation offices exist to supervise offenders. Many probation departments act as brokers between the agency and various community businesses, to identify potential work places where probationer-clients might find and maintain employment. Probationer assistance has always been a mission of probation departments. However, most of these key priorities are unrelated directly to assisting probationers, except for improving their social activities, whatever they may be. This may be one reason why some observers have declared that probation is in trouble.

Seamless Probation

In recent years, some of the major problems confronting probation and parole agencies have been targeted by researchers and investigated. One problem is the pervasive fragmentation of services that exist for probationers and other clients under some form of PO supervision. This problem of services fragmentation is easy to understand. A probation department exists, in large part, to oversee probationers, supervise their behavior, and monitor their participation in court-ordered treatments and other services. There are vast differences among probation departments concerning how POs perform their jobs (Petersilia, 2005; Taxman, 2004). No clear-cut, consistent probation office objectives are in place to guide individual POs in the performance of their supervisory tasks. Some officers administer urinalyses to selected probationers at random times at offenders' homes. Other POs conduct such tests, or have them conducted by probation office staff, when probationers appear for their monthly visits. Those who test positive for drugs or alcohol may be verbally reprimanded and warned. Others may be targeted for probation revocation, which is a formal process initiated by the probation officer and involves a lot of paperwork. The end result may be an intensification of one's probation program or a short jail sentence. If the problem continues with particular probationers following verbal and/or more formal sanctions, then judges can imprison these offenders for longer terms.

One assumption, and a highly questionable one, is that once an errant probationer is confined in a prison or jail, he or she will automatically receive treatment for their drug or alcohol dependencies or other issues. This is most often not the case. If offenders who commit technical program violations are placed under more intensive supervision, the assumption, and also a highly questionable one, is that they will be monitored more closely to ensure that they are in compliance with the program requirements and that they will receive necessary treatments and services.

Many offenders slip through the proverbial cracks in the system. They skillfully avoid or minimize their participation in treatment, educational programming, vocational services, mental health counseling, anger management courses, drug counseling and therapy, and a host of other court-ordered services. Caseloads of POs are so high in many jurisdictions that it is difficult to monitor all offenders equally and consistently. There is a great deal of individualization in PO supervisory methods as well. Richard Seiter (2002:53) has observed that during the past 15 years or so, the dominant style of casework supervision, which emphasizes assisting offenders with problems, counseling, and working to make sure the offender successfully completes supervision, has shifted to a style of surveillance supervision, which emphasizes the monitoring of offenders to catch them when they fail to meet all of their required probation program conditions. When Seiter asked various POs what they regarded as the most important aspects of their jobs relative to their clients, many said that it was most important for them to monitor offender behavior, refer them to community agencies based on their needs, help them maintain employment, and hold offenders accountable for their behaviors (Seiter, 2002:53).

The major problem with monitoring offender behaviors and making referrals to community agencies where offenders may receive needed services is that (1) monitoring of all offenders equally and consistently is quite difficult if not impossible in view of high PO caseloads, and (2) POs seldom have time to follow up with each offender to determine his or her attendance at referred treatments or services (Pelissier and Cadigan, 2004). There is little coordination of tasks and responsibilities within most probation agencies to ensure PO effectiveness in relation to client care. POs may assume that if they make referrals, there will be automatic compliance from their clients and these referrals will result in successful interventions to cure client problems, whatever they might be. But again, this assumption is flawed because of a variety of factors, not the least of which is higher caseloads and diminished time to spend with individual probationers as paperwork and other tasks escalate for individual POs annually.

One promising solution to the fragmentation-of-services problem, especially for those probationers with drug dependencies or other deficiencies (e.g., little educational or vocational training, lack of job skills, mental health issues), is **seamless probation.** Seamless probation is an integrated model of care where the treatment (social services) and supervision staff (POs) jointly conduct screenings and assessments for treatment and offer cognitive-behavioral therapeutic group sessions. Offenders are transitioned into different levels of care as they progress through their treatment programs, by either increasing or decreasing the level of care (Alemi et al., 2004).

One example of seamless probation in action is a national demonstration project that was conducted by the Office of National Drug Control Policy and involved an integrated model of substance abuse treatment for offenders (Taxman, Simpson, and Piquero, 2002). The seamless system included substance abuse treatment with a duration of at least 9 months with two levels of care, drug testing, and graduated sanctions for drug-involved offenders. Experimental groups (those in the seamless group) were compared with a matched sample of probationers (the control group that was merely referred to treatment services under a traditional model followed by most probation agencies). The probationers with drug dependencies and who were involved in the seamless probation model exhibited substantial reductions in their drug use and dependency as well as less criminal behavior over time compared with the control group. In effect, the seamless probation supervision co-located treatment providers with POs, and their efforts were highly coordinated in their work with offenders with drug dependencies. From a cost–benefit perspective, preliminary results revealed that probation officers spent about 7 percent of their time in seamless probation, while 84 percent of them spent their time in traditional supervision. The relative cost per offender per day was $12 for seamless probation PO involvement compared with $7 per offender per day under traditional supervision. The findings disclosed that there were significantly higher costs associated with asking POs to coordinate their treatment of offenders with conventional treatment providers compared with their traditional supervision of offenders, which involved no coordination with others. However, the substantial reduction in recidivism and greater successfulness of offenders under seamless probation in overcoming their problems and remaining crime-free and less drug dependent may be worth the additional cost (Alemi et al., 2004). As will be seen in subsequent chapters, the seamless supervision initiative has spread to parole departments and to offenders with problems besides drug dependencies, such as mental illness or physical impairments.

Federal and State Probation Orders

Standard probation among the states is quite diverse, although the conditions of probation share many of the same characteristics. The U.S. Probation Department oversees adult probationers as well as certain juveniles who have been sentenced by U.S. Magistrates or federal district court judges for federal crimes. As the result of the U.S. Sentencing Guidelines, the use of probation in the federal system since 1987 has been drastically reduced. In the pre-guideline period prior to 1987, probation was granted by federal district court judges about 65 percent of the time. At the beginning of 2006, the proportion of federal offenders who were granted probation is about 10–15 percent (U.S. Department of Justice, 2006). Below are some examples of standard probation orders. Figure 6.1 shows a U.S. district court probation form indicating specific standard conditions of probation. A reading of these conditions will disclose that federal standard probation and supervised release is geared toward crime control and heightening offender accountability. Besides paying fines and restitution, federal offenders must report

---

Conditions of Probation and Supervised Release

UNITED STATES DISTRICT COURT
FOR THE

_____

Name _____   Docket No. _____

Address _____

Under the terms of your sentence, you have been placed on probation/supervised release (strike one) by the Honorable _____, United States District Judge for the District of _____. Your term of supervision is for a period of _____, commencing _____.

While on probation/supervised release (strike one) you shall not commit another Federal, state, or local crime and shall not illegally possess a controlled substance. Revocation of probation and supervised release is mandatory for possession of a controlled substance.

CHECK IF APPROPRIATE:

☐   As a condition of supervision, you are instructed to pay a fine in the amount of _____ ; it shall be paid in the following manner _____ .

☐   As a condition of supervision, you are instructed to pay restitution in the amount of _____ to _____ ; it shall be paid in the following manner _____ .

☐   The defendant shall not possess a firearm or destructive device. Probation must be revoked for possession of a firearm.

☐   The defendant shall report in person to the probation office in the district to which the defendant is released within 72 hours of release from the custody of the Bureau of Prisons.

☐   The defendant shall report in person to the probation office in the district of release within 72 hours of release from the custody of the Bureau of Prisons.

It is the order of the Court that you shall comply with the following standard conditions:

(1)   You shall not leave the judicial district without permission of the Court or probation officer;

(2)   You shall report to the probation officer as directed by the Court or probation officer, and shall submit a truthful and complete written report within the first five days of each month;

(3)   You shall answer truthfully all inquiries by the probation officer and follow the instructions of the probation officer;

FIGURE 6.1   United States District Court Conditions of Probation and Supervised Release.

(4)   You shall support your dependents and meet other family responsibilities;

(5)   You shall work regularly at a lawful occupation unless excused by the probation officer for schooling, training, or other acceptable reasons;

(6)   You shall notify the probation officer within 72 hours of any change in residence or employment;

(7)   You shall refrain from excessive use of alcohol and shall not purchase, possess, use, distribute, or administer any narcotic or other controlled substance, or any paraphernalia related to such substances, except as prescribed by a physician;

(8)   You shall not frequent places where controlled substances are illegally sold, used, distributed, or administered;

(9)   You shall not associate with any persons engaged in criminal activity, and shall not associate with any person convicted of a felony unless granted permission to do so by the probation officer;

(10)   You shall permit a probation officer to visit you at any time at home or elsewhere, and shall permit confiscation of any contraband observed in plain view by the probation officer;

(11)   You shall notify the probation officer within 72 hours of being arrested or questioned by a law enforcement officer;

(12)   You shall not enter into any agreement to act as an informer or a special agent of a law enforcement agency without the permission of the Court;

(13)   As directed by the probation officer, you shall notify third parties of risks that may be occasioned by your criminal record or personal history or characteristics, and shall permit the probation officer to make such notifications and to confirm your compliance with such notification requirement.

The special conditions ordered by the Court are as follows:

Upon a finding of violation of probation or supervised release, I understand that the Court may (1) revoke supervision or (2) extend the term of supervision and/or modify the conditions of supervision.

These conditions have been read to me. I fully understand the conditions, and have been provided a copy of them.

(Signed) _____   _____

                               Defendant   Date

_____   _____

U.S. Probation Officer/Designated Witness   Date

FIGURE 6.1 (Continued).

periodically to the probation office. Probationers cannot possess firearms. They cannot leave their jurisdictions without permission from the federal court. Probationers must work at jobs unless otherwise involved in educational or vocational programs or are undergoing psychological counseling for mental health or substance abuse problems. They must refrain from excessive use of alcohol, and they are forbidden from taking illegal drugs. Even their associations with others and the places they may visit are restricted. Probationers must make their dwellings available at any time for a PO's inspection and search for contraband. Also note in Figure 6.1 that space has been provided for judges to add special conditions of probation, which may include various community-based sanctions, including home confinement, electronic monitoring, day reporting, and other activities that are deemed necessary for an offender's rehabilitation and reintegration. Figure 6.2 shows a federal monthly service report.

The conditions of standard probation for prospective Florida probationers are fairly standard for most other state standard probation programs. Under Florida probation guidelines supplied to judges, the following conditions do not require oral pronouncement in court by a judge. Rather, they are prepared in

U.S. PROBATION OFFICE
MONTHLY SUPERVISION REPORT FOR THE MONTH OF ______________, 20 _____.

Name	Court Name *(if different)*:

PART A: RESIDENCE *(If new address, attach copy of lease/purchase agreement)*

Street Address, Apt. Number: Own or Rent?	Home Phone: Cellular Phone: Pager:
City, State, Zip Code:	Persons Living With You:
Secondary Residence Own or Rent?	Did you move during the month? □ Yes □ No
Mailing Address *(if different)*: E-Mail Address	If yes, date moved: ______________ Reason for Moving:

PART B: EMPLOYMENT *(If unemployed, list source of support under Part D.)*

Name, Address, Phone No. of Employer:	Name of Immediate Supervisor: / Is your employer aware of your criminal status: □ Yes □ No
	How many days of work did you miss? __________ Why?
	Position Held: / Gross Wages: / Normal Work Hours:
Did you change jobs? □ Yes □ No Were you terminated? □ Yes □ No	If changed jobs or terminated, state when and why:

PART C: VEHICLES *(List all vehicles owned or driven by you)*

1. Year/Make/Model/Color:	Mileage:	Tag Number: Vehicle I.D.#:	Owner:
2. Year/Make/Model/Color:	Mileage:	Tag Number: Vehicle I.D.#:	Owner:

PART D: MONTHLY FINANCIAL STATEMENT

Net Earnings from Employment: *(Attach Proof of Earnings)* ________ Other Cash Inflows: ________ TOTAL MONTHLY CASH INFLOWS: ________ TOTAL MONTHLY CASH OUTFLOWS: ________	Do you rent or have access to: a post office box? □ Yes □ No a safe deposit box? □ Yes □ No a storage space? □ Yes □ No Name and Address of Location: Box No. or Space
Do you have checking account(s)? □ Yes □ No Bank Name: ________ Account No: ________ Balance: ________ Do you have savings account(s)? □ Yes □ No Bank Name: ________ Account No: ________ Balance: ________ Attach a complete listing of all other financial account information, if you have multiple accounts.	Does your spouse, significant other, or dependant have a checking or savings account that you enjoy the benefits of or make occasional contributions toward? □ Yes □ No Bank Name: ________ Account No: ________ Balance: ________

List all expenditures over $500 (including e.g., goods, services, or gambling losses)

Date	Amount	Method of Payment	Description of Item

FIGURE 6.2 Monthly Service Report for U.S. Probation Office.

PROB 8
(09/00)

Page 2

PART E: COMPLIANCE WITH CONDITIONS OF SUPERVISION DURING THE PAST MONTH	
Were you questioned by any law enforcement officers? ☐ Yes ☐ No If yes, date: _____ Agency: _____ Reason: _____	Were you arrested or named as a defendant in any criminal case? ☐ Yes ☐ No If yes, when and where? _____ Charges: _____ Disposition: _____

(Attach copy of citation, receipt, charges, disposition, etc.)

Were any pending charges disposed of during the month? ☐ Yes ☐ No If yes, date: _____ Court: _____ Disposition: _____	Was anyone in your household arrested or questioned by law enforcement? ☐ Yes ☐ No If yes, whom? _____ Reason: _____ Disposition: _____
Do you have any contact with anyone having a criminal record? ☐ Yes ☐ No If yes, whom? _____	Do you possess or have access to a firearm? ☐ Yes ☐ No If yes, why? _____
Did you possess or use any illegal drugs? ☐ Yes ☐ No If yes, type of drug: _____	Did you travel outside the district without permission? ☐ Yes ☐ No If yes, when and where? _____

Do you have a special assessment, restitution, or fine? ☐ Yes ☐ No   If yes, amount paid during the month:

Special Assessment: _____   Restitution: _____   Fine: _____

NOTE: ALL PAYMENTS TO BE MADE BY MONEY ORDER (POSTAL OR BANK) OR CASHIER'S CHECK ONLY.

Do you have community service work to perform? ☐ Yes ☐ No Number of hours completed this month: _____ Number of hours missed: _____ Balance of hours remaining: _____	Do you have drug, alcohol, or mental health aftercare? ☐ Yes ☐ No If yes, did you miss any sessions during this month? ☐ Yes ☐ No Did you fail to respond to phone recorder instructions? ☐ Yes ☐ No If yes, why? _____
WARNING: ANY FALSE STATEMENTS MAY RESULT IN REVOCATION OF PROBATION, SUPERVISED RELEASE, OR PAROLE, IN ADDITION TO 5 YEARS IMPRISONMENT, A $250,000 FINE, OR BOTH. (18 U.S.C. § 1001)	I CERTIFY THAT ALL INFORMATION FURNISHED IS COMPLETE AND CORRECT. _____ _____ SIGNATURE DATE
REMARKS: _____ _____ U.S. Probation Officer Date	RECEIVED _____Mail _____OC _____HC _____CC RETURN TO:

FIGURE 6.2 (Continued).

written form and a copy is submitted to the offender for his or her consent and signature. These conditions are as follows:

1. Probationer must report to the probation supervisor as directed.
2. Probationer must permit supervisors to visit him or her at his or her home or elsewhere.
3. Probationer must work faithfully at suitable employment insofar as may be possible.
4. Probationer must remain within a specified place.
5. Probationer must make reparation or restitution to the aggrieved party for the damage or loss caused by his or her offense in an amount to be determined by the court.

6. Probationer must make payment of the debt due and owing to a county or municipal detention facility for medical care, treatment, hospitalization, or transportation received by the probationer while in that detention facility.

7. Probationer must support his or her legal dependents to the best of his or her ability.

8. Probationer must make payment of debt due and owing to the state subject to modification based on change in circumstances.

9. Probationer must pay any application fee assessed and attorney's fees and costs assessed subject to modification based on change of circumstances.

10. Probationer must not associate with persons engaged in criminal activities.

11. Probationer must submit to random testing as directed by the correctional probation officer or the professional staff of the treatment center where he or she is receiving treatment to determine the presence of alcohol or use of alcohol or controlled substances.

12. Probationer is prohibited from possessing, carrying, or owning any firearm unless authorized by the court and consented to by the probation officer.

13. Probationer is prohibited from using any intoxicants to excess or possessing any drugs or narcotics unless prescribed by a physician. The probationer shall not knowingly visit places where intoxicants, drugs, or other dangerous substances are unlawfully sold, dispensed, or used.

14. Probationer will attend an HIV/AIDS awareness program consisting of a class of not less than two hours or more than four hours in length, the cost of which shall be paid by the offender, if such a program is available in the county of the offender's residence.

15. Probationer shall pay not more than $1 per month during the term of probation to a nonprofit organization established for the sole purpose of supplementing the rehabilitative efforts of the Department of Corrections.

Florida also imposes certain special conditions of probation similar to the federal standard probation conditions. These are as follows:

1. Probationer is required to be intensively supervised and under probation officer surveillance.

2. Probationer is required to maintain specified contact with the probation officer.

3. Probationer shall be confined to an agreed-upon residence during hours away from employment and public service activities.

4. Probationer shall perform mandatory public service.

5. Probationer shall be supervised by means of an electronic monitoring device.

6. Probationer placed on electronic monitoring shall be monitored 24 hours a day.

7. Probationers placed on electronic monitoring will be subject to investigation and supervision by a probation officer 24 hours a day.

8. The court shall receive a diagnosis and evaluation of any probationer for appropriate community treatment (Florida Department of Corrections, 2006).

In the Florida Department of Corrections, for instance, several different types of public service or **community service** are prescribed. These include: (1) maintenance work on any property or building owned or leased by any state, county, or municipality or any nonprofit organization or agency; (2) maintenance work on any state-owned, county-owned, or municipally owned road or highway; (3) landscaping or maintenance work in any state, county, or municipal park or recreational area; (4) work in any state, county, or municipal hospital or any developmental services institution or other nonprofit organization or agency. For Florida offenders convicted of drug crimes, they may be required to pay a fine ranging from $500 to $10,000; perform at least 100 hours of public service; submit to routine and random drug testing; and participate, at their own expense, in some appropriate self-help group, such as Narcotics Anonymous, Alcoholics Anonymous, or Cocaine Anonymous, if available. In 2001, the Florida Department of Corrections reported that 145,098 offenders were on probation, with 107,078, or 81 percent, on standard probation. The remainder of nonincarcerated clients were under other forms of supervision, such as community control, pretrial intervention, or post-prison release (Florida Department of Corrections, 2006).

One of the major problems with standard probation is high offender recidivism. Most jurisdictions throughout the United States report recidivism rates of 60 percent or higher for offenders who are placed on standard probation. Some attempt has been made to reduce these high recidivism rates by establishing programs that involve much more intensive offender monitoring and supervision. These programs are categorically called **intensive supervised probation (ISP) programs.**

INTENSIVE SUPERVISED PROBATION (ISP)

An intensive supervised probation (ISP) program or an **intensive probation supervision (IPS) program** is an increasingly common method of supervising offenders who require closer monitoring. Also known as traditional probation, ISP is a type of intermediate punishment, since it is somewhere between standard probation and incarceration. One short-range goal of intermediate punishments is to reduce prison and jail overcrowding. There is government endorsement of this ISP program goal as well as support within the professional community (Bond-Maupin and Maupin, 2002). Other types of intermediate punishments include electronic monitoring, home incarceration, **community-based supervision,** and **community-based corrections.** These programs will be examined at length in subsequent chapters. Offenders are assigned probation officers who arrange frequent contacts with their clients on a face-to-face basis. These contacts may be weekly, a few times a week, or daily. ISP is a special form of traditional probation where the intensity of offender monitoring is greatly increased and the conditions of probation are considerably more stringent. The logic is that the greater the amount of contact between the probationer and PO will function as an incentive for greater offender compliance with program requirements. Known in some circles as smart sentencing, ISP often involves greater client/officer contact, which may mean that POs are more frequently accessible to clients if they are experiencing personal or financial difficulties, social stresses, or other problems.

There is considerable variation in ISP programs among jurisdictions, since probation officer caseloads vary. These caseloads depend on the financial resources of the jurisdiction and local definitions of the maximum number of clients probation officers must supervise. ISP in many jurisdictions limits the number of offender-clients to 30 per probation officer. In some jurisdictions, the maximum number of offenders supervised may be limited to 15 or 20 (U.S. Department of Justice, 2006). Also influencing one's caseload is the nature of supervisory technology used. In Florida, for example, CrimeTrax is used as an advanced method of tracking offenders through the use of global positioning satellite (GPS) technology. Using this method of tracking offenders, Florida POs can locate particular offenders on particular streets at certain times of the day or night. While GPS isn't yet foolproof, it does provide a futuristic supervisory option, which is likely to be adopted by more jurisdictions in future years. Thousands of staff hours may be saved by GPS tracking (Frost, 2002).

Intensive supervised probation programs have received mixed reactions among the public. One problem is that many of these programs, their objectives, and the ways they are being implemented are misunderstood by community residents and interpreted in the most unfavorable light. Despite the fact that these programs monitor probationers more closely than standard probation supervision and are tougher on offenders by comparison, many citizens believe that offender freedom in the community is not an acceptable punishment.

There is no standard definition for ISP, although all ISP programs feature small offender caseload sizes (Champion, 2007). "Intensive" is a relative term, but the basic idea is to increase the intensity of supervision for designated probationers in order to satisfy public demand for applying a just punishment. Some persons distinguish between standard probation and intensive surveillance coupled with substantial community service and/or restitution. But probably the best way of conceptualizing what ISP means is to identify ISP program components that have been operationalized in several states (Harris and Lo, 2002).

Three Conceptual Models of ISP

Before examining several state ISP programs, three conceptual models of ISP will be described. These models will help to explain not only interstate variations in ISP programs but also their individual rationales. These include (1) the justice model; (2) the limited risk control model; and (3) the traditional, treatment-oriented model. Table 4.1 contrasts these three models and highlights several of their important features.

The Justice Model.   The justice model makes no pretense of being anything other than punishment-centered, but not to the point of being unfair to offenders. The penalty should fit the crime committed, and the offender should receive his just-deserts. This model emphasizes (a) daily contact between offenders and probation officers, (b) community service orders, and/or (c) restitution. No counseling is required, nor is any participation in any specific rehabilitative program.

The Limited Risk Control Model.   The **limited risk control model** is based on anticipated future criminal conduct and uses risk assessment devices to place offenders within an effective control range. This model fits a presumptive sentencing format specifying ranges of penalties or varying control levels depending on risk assessment scores. Thus, judges would rely on predictions of probable future criminal conduct and sentence offenders to one of three degrees of community supervision (e.g., minimum, regular, and intensive). Compared with the justice model, the limited risk control model appears more flexible and provides for

TABLE 6.1

The Justice, Limited Risk Control, and Traditional, Treatment-Oriented Models Compared by Intensive Supervised Probation Factors

Program Elements	JM	LRCM	TTOM
1. Recommended caseload	"low"	10	"low"
2. Daily contact with probation officer. . .	Yes	No	No
3. Weekly contact with probation officer. . .	No	Yes	20 times per month, variable
4. Community service. . .	Yes	Optional	Yes
5. Restitution. . .	Yes	Optional	Yes
6. Field visits. . .	Yes	Yes	Optional
7. Probation fees. . .	Yes	Yes	Optional
8. Curfew. . .	Yes	Optional	Yes
9. Shock probation. . .	Optional	No	Yes
10. Offender volunteers for program. . .	No	No	Yes
11. Periodic committee review of offender progress. . .	No	Yes	Yes
12. Use of risk assessment devices. . .	No	Yes	Optional
13. Minimum time in ISP.	6 mo.	Individual, but 90 days minimum	12 mo.
14. Normal program length. . .	6–36 mo.	Variable	18 mo.
15. House arrest. . .	Optional	No	Optional
16. Fines. . .	Optional	Optional	Yes
17. Counseling. . .	No .	Probably	Probably
18. Voc/Rehab Training..	No	Probably	Probably

JM = Justice Model; LRCM = Limited Risk Control Model; and TTOM = Traditional, Treatment-Oriented Model. *Source:* James M. Byrne. "The Control Controversy: A Preliminary Examination of Intensive Supervision Programs in the United States." *Federal Probation* **50**:4–16, 1986. [public domain]

periodic reassessments of predicted offender behaviors and corresponding adjustments of degrees of communit supervision. Table 6.1 shows a comparison of the justice, limited risk control, and traditional treatment-oriented models.

The Traditional, Treatment-Oriented Model.   The **traditional, treatment-oriented model** stresses traditional rehabilitative measures that seek to reintegrate the offender into the community through extensive assistance. While this model may include elements of the justice and limited risk control models, its primary aim is long-term change in offender behavior. Therefore, this model includes strategies such as (a) developing individual offender plans for life in the community such as work, study, or community service; (b) full-time employment and/or vocational training; and/or (c) using community sponsors or other support personnel to provide assistance and direction for offenders.

No states currently use the justice model exclusively. States using the limited risk control model include Oregon and Massachusetts. Several other states have initiated ISP programs as well. Georgia created an ISP program in 1982. Two other state programs were commenced in 1984. These included ISP programs in Idaho and South Carolina. The Georgia, New Jersey, Idaho, and South Carolina plans are being featured here because (1) they represent four different approaches to the problem of managing probationers, and (2) other states have incorporated many of the elements of these programs into their own ISP programs.

 BOX 6.1

CAREER SNAPSHOT

James Dalton
Probation Agent, Faribault County, Blue Earth, Minnesota

Statistics:

B.S. (corrections), Mankato State College

Background:

I graduated from Minnesota State University–Mankato in 1971. I started my career in corrections working for three months at St. Cloud Reformatory in St. Cloud, Minnesota. St. Cloud Reformatory is a prison for young offenders ages 18 to 25. I absolutely hated this job and wasn't there for more than a few hours before I was thinking about transferring someplace, any place other than in a prison. It has to be the most depressing job you can have. I have had great admiration for those who make it a career. But it's not for me. I transferred to State Training School in Red Wing, Minnesota. This is a correctional facility for serious juvenile offenders. I worked there for two years and then transferred to Field Probation.

I originally worked with both juveniles and adult misdemeanants as a probation agent, but presently, I only work with misdemeanant adults. I think that the variety of jobs in the corrections field was helpful to me, since I now have a better understanding of the difficulties that each field of work involves. It is too bad that there isn't more emphasis on diversified background of experiences for people in the field. It always amused me to hear about the conflicts between institutional personnel and field services. I think that most of these conflicts occur because of the ignorance of the unique problems each field has to deal with. The one thing I like about my present job is the freedom that I have in this position. We are confronted with different problems in the community and are encouraged to look for new and better ways to resolve these issues. We will always complain about paperwork, and I don't think that this type of problem will ever be resolved. If you think there might be a national conspiracy with the paper companies, you might be right. I remember when we got our first computers and were told that we would be creating a paperless environment. They lied to us. We generate more paperwork now than ever before. I used to kid my children when they were young, and I said that if they wanted to know who the SOB was who was responsible for all the trees being cut down to make paper, that it was their dad.

Experiences:

One incident I recall had to do with personal safety. I had a juvenile on my caseload who was convicted of a very serious felony. I had a choice of recommending

(continued)

BOX 6.1 (*Continued*)

that he go to a correctional facility or to a therapeutic program. I went to his home at night (my first mistake) to tell him of my recommendation. I thought his parents would be relieved to learn that I wasn't going to recommend him for placement in a correctional facility (my second mistake). Their home was in the country and surrounded by trees. When I got there I went into the home and sat down at a large oak table. Present were the juvenile and the juvenile's mother, uncle, and grandparents. I told them what I was going to recommend. There was complete silence and then the uncle said there was no way the child was going to leave his home. He got up from the table, went behind me, and said nothing. At the time I thought I was either going to get a knife in my back or bullet in my head or get strangled. I froze and didn't say or do anything. He then went back to his seat at the table. The whole incident was to intimidate me. Which he did. I quickly left the home, never to return there. The juvenile was placed in the therapeutic program and was there for nearly a year. About halfway through the program, he started to tell the staff at the program some of his family's secrets. This eventually brought about felony counts against some of his relatives and investigations of felonious behavior of some of his family's friends. At the time I went to their home, I had no idea of the "family secrets." What I learned from this experience was that if you need to give individuals bad news, you do it on your own turf, not on theirs. Sometimes you don't have a choice, but if you do, then you talk with them in the relative safety of your office or a police station or a court. When police talk about the most dangerous thing about their job, they usually refer to going to someone's home to make an arrest. If it's dangerous for them to go to a home for an arrest, it's very dangerous for you to confront people in their own homes also.

Another incident involved a client on my caseload who was charged with assault. What had happened was that he was getting a tattoo from a friend of his. His payment for the tattoo was a case of beer. The victim (the guy who was giving him the tattoo) was drinking beer while working on his friend's tattoo. Anyway, he started to fall in love with his friend and made an advance on him. The client didn't appreciate the advance and hit him. He didn't get his complete tattoo and was charged with assault. I was looking at the tattoo on his arm and the other guy had misspelled his girlfriend's name. I didn't have the courage to tell him. Anyway, the moral of this story is, do not give any beer to the person who is giving you a tattoo until after the tattoo is completed. This holds true for your surgeon was well.

One time I had a client come into my office with his eyebrows burned off. He had pin hole burns in his jacket. He didn't look so good. I asked him what had happened and he said that he blew himself up. I asked him how he did that and he said that he had a wood-burning stove in his garage and it went out, and so he poured some gasoline on it. I went over to his garage and there was an imprint of his body (the sheet rock was crushed on the side of the garage where he landed after the explosion).

In another case I got a call on Christmas Eve from a family who was having problems with one of their children. When I got there I found out that two of the children had been fighting. What had happened was that one of the children had been misbehaving and so the parent took away his Christmas gift and gave it to the other child. And so now we have one child with two gifts and the other without any gifts. I didn't have any easy answers for that one.

Advice to Students:

One of the difficulties of probation work with juveniles is that if your own children are close in age to the children you work with on your caseload, then your own kids might be threatened or assaulted because the delinquent clients you work with don't like you or the restrictions or sanctions that you have recommended. I was lucky in that matter since neither of my children were ever hurt, but I had heard enough stories from other agents who weren't so lucky. Whenever I asked my children what they did to protect themselves, they said they played dumb about whatever information was presented to them from some of my delinquent clients. They also never talked about my profession. I guess I don't have any advice regarding this other than to talk with other agents to see how they resolve these and similar types of problems.

You don't save all youths you work with. That only happens in the movies. You don't take the blame and you don't take the credit for any changes that happen to the people on your caseload. People have free will and all you can do is help and guide them. You are inundated with negative people doing negative things. I think everyone in this field needs healthy diversions from their work. If you take your work home with you, you won't get the mental rest you need for the next day. You also need to develop a sense of humor. Someone once said that humor is the thing that helps you overcome

the bumps in the road. I think they're right. Take time to smell the roses. Spend a lot of time with your children. It's great for you, and it's great for your children. You will have a better understanding of others in the process. I remember an incident where some group home parents were having trouble with their own children, and several agents were talking about it. We came to the conclusion that the reason the child was misbehaving was that the parents were spending so much time with the delinquents housed in their home that their own children were being ignored. The only way their own children thought they could get their parents' attention was to be delinquents themselves and "act out." If I could do it all over again, I would have two majors in college that were not related. That way you have more choices regarding your life's work. The two most important decisions you make in life are (1) your job and (2) your spouse. These decisions are made when you are relatively young and have little experience.

The Georgia ISP Program

In the 1970s Georgia had the highest per capita incarceration rate in the United States. Because of prison overcrowding and the spillover effect into Georgia's jails to house their prison overflow, Georgia was desperate to devise a workable probation program. After spending much money on feasibility studies and considering alternatives to incarceration, Georgia's ISP was put into effect in 1982 (Bralley and Provost, 2001).

Georgia Program Elements.   The **Georgia Intensive Supervision Probation Program (GISPP)** has established several punitive intensive probation conditions that parallel the justice model. Three phases of the program were outlined according to the level of control, Phase I being the most intensive supervision and Phase III being the least intensive. These standards include:

1. Five face-to-face contacts per week in Phase I (decreasing to two face-to-face contacts per week in Phase III).
2. 132 hours of mandatory community service.
3. Mandatory curfew.
4. Mandatory employment.
5. Weekly check of local arrest records.
6. Automatic notification of arrest elsewhere via State Crime Information Network listings.

7. Routine alcohol and drug screens.

8. Assignment of one probation officer and one surveillance officer to 25 probationers or one probation officer and two surveillance officers to 40 probationers (surveillance officers have corrections backgrounds or law enforcement training and make home visits, check arrest records, and perform drug/alcohol tests, among other duties).

9. Probation officer determines individualized treatment (e.g., counseling, vocational/educational training) for offender.

10. Probation officer is liaison between court and offender and reports to court regularly on offender's progress from personal and surveillance observations and records.

The Successfulness of the Georgia ISP Program.   The successfulness of the GISPP thus far has been demonstrated by low recidivism rates among offenders under ISP (recidivism rates are almost always used as measures of probation program effectiveness). Compared with paroled offenders and others supervised by standard probation practices, the GISPP participants had systematically lower recidivism rates depending on their risk classification. Classifications of risk consisted of low risk, medium risk, high risk, and maximum risk. Reconvictions for these groups were 25 percent, 16 percent, 28 percent, and 26 percent, respectively, compared with parolees who had considerably higher reconviction rates for all risk groupings. Figure 6.3 shows an example of the New Jersey conditions of placement of individuals on intensive supervised probation for comparative purposes.

The Idaho ISP Program

The **Idaho Intensive Supervised Probation Program** was launched as a pilot project in 1982. Initially, a team consisting of one PO and two surveillance officers closely supervised a small group of low-risk offenders who normally would have been sent to prison. The program was quite successful. In October 1984, Idaho established a state-wide ISP program with legislative approval. This step was seen as a major element in the get-tough-on-crime posture taken by the state.

Elements of the Idaho ISP Program.   When implemented in 1984, the ISP program operated in teams, consisting of two POs and a Section Supervisor responsible for supervising a maximum of 25 high-risk clients. This team was required to work evenings and in shifts. POs carried firearms while performing their duties. The court-referred clientele for these POs and supervisors consisted of felony probationers or parolees who were classified at a maximum level of supervision. All clients had lengthy criminal records of violent crimes and were in need of intensive supervision. Clients were obligated to stay in their programs for four to six months and had to complete two major phases of supervision.

The first phase consisted of seven face-to-face visits per week, four of which occurred in the clients' homes. Phase II reduced the number of face-to-face contacts with clients per week to four. Both phases included random day or night checks for possible curfew violations, drug and/or alcohol abuse, and any other possible program violation. Probationers who violated one or more program conditions received either verbal warnings or informal staff hearings, where several additional program conditions might be imposed, including community service. Perhaps those probationers in Phase II would be returned to Phase I.

Idaho ISP Program Effectiveness.   Between 1984 and 1992, the Idaho Department of Corrections has processed 2,487 clients. About 63 percent of these probationers have completed the program successfully. During 1992, 179 clients were under ISP of one form or another. The overall rate of technical violations, such as curfew violations, drinking, and unauthorized travel, was only about 28 percent, while the rate of new felonies charged was only 1.3 percent. The major result of this ISP program has been a drastic reduction in new convictions for felonies among successful program participants.

The South Carolina ISP Program

In order to ease prison overcrowding in South Carolina, a legislative mandate was given in 1984 to establish an ISP program for state-wide use. The South Carolina Department of Probation, Parole, and Pardon Services (DPPPS) was responsible for the **South Carolina Intensive Supervised Probation Program** implementation. The primary aims of the ISP program were to heighten surveillance of participants, increase PO/client contact, and increase offender accountability. Like Idaho, South Carolina started their ISP program as a pilot or experimental project. Their program goal was to involve 336 probationers during the first year of operation. By 2005, 33,356 offenders had been processed through the ISP program (U.S. Department of Justice, 2006).

South Carolina ISP Program Elements.   Offenders placed in South Carolina ISP programs must pay a $10 per week supervision fee. Supervision fees are not particularly unusual in many ISP programs. Clients are supervised by specialized POs known as intensive agents with caseloads of no more than 35 offenders at any given time. Weekly face-to-face contacts with offenders are mandatory, together with visits to neighbors, friends, employers, and service providers of probationers. POs in the South Carolina program act as liaisons between the private sector and their clients, lining up job possibilities. Thus, POs do some employment counseling when necessary.

Offender Classification for Participation.   Each offender is classified according to risk and needs (Tjaden and Layton, 2006). Then POs tailor individual program requirements to fit these offender needs. The level of supervision over particular offenders is influenced by their particular risk level determined through risk assessment. The goal of DPPPS POs is to provide offenders with the proper balance of control and assistance. Thus, the ISP program is also supplemented with curfews, electronic monitoring, and house arrest or home incarceration elements for certain high-risk offenders. Offenders sentenced to home incarceration are in a program known as ISP Home Detention and confined to their homes from 10:00 P.M. to 6:00 A.M., excepting authorized leaves from home by their supervising POs. Offenders are subject to random visits from POs, day or night. Clients must work or seek employment; undergo medical, psychiatric, or mental health counseling or other rehabilitative treatment; attend religious services; or perform community service work.

The length of their stay in this ISP program varies from three to six months. Electronic monitoring is used to supplement this program. Offenders are placed on electronic monitoring and must wear an electronic wristlet or anklet for the first 30 days. After successfully completing the first 30-day period of ISP, they are taken off electronic monitoring and subject to a 60-day period of simple voice verification. Such verification occurs by telephone means, where POs call offenders at particular times to verify their whereabouts. Offenders give requested information over the telephone, and electronic devices verify whether the voice pattern transmitted matches that of the offender being called.

Like POs in the Idaho program, POs in the DPPPS work in shifts, in order that offenders can be checked both day and night. Thus, there are First and Second Shift Surveillance Teams. The DPPPS also uses paraprofessionals in Operation Specialist capacities. These persons assist POs in performing surveillance work, particularly in the larger counties throughout the state.

Effectiveness of the South Carolina ISP Program.   The ISP program in South Carolina appears successful. Less than 10 percent of the probationers who have participated in the South Carolina ISP program have had their programs revoked due to new offenses rather than for technical program violations. Using the arbitrary 30 percent recidivism standard for determining whether a program is or is not successful, the South Carolina ISP program is successful for both its probationers as well as its parolees.

Criticisms of the Georgia, Idaho, and South Carolina ISP Programs

A general criticism leveled at any ISP program is that it does not achieve its stated goals. Some observers say that victims are ignored in probation decision making. Yet others say that ISP programs contribute to net-widening, by bringing certain offenders under the ISP program umbrella who really do not need to be intensively supervised. Simultaneously, an equally vocal aggregate of critics praises ISP for alleviating prison inmate overcrowding and providing a meaningful option to incarceration. Among the ISP program components in certain jurisdictions that have drawn criticism have been supervision fees. These costs are normally incurred by probationer-clients. But even this particular issue is hotly debated. The controversy over ISP programs will likely remain unresolved for many years.

Regardless of their disputed effectiveness, the fact is that different ISP programs have been developed and used in other states. For example, several elements of the Georgia model have been adopted by Colorado, Nevada, Oregon, and Washington. These states have not copied Georgia precisely in their probation guidelines, but their newly developed programs resemble the Georgia program to a high degree.

The Georgia program has been both praised and criticized. First, it has demonstrated low rates of recidivism. Convicted criminals who participate in the program do not commit new offenses with great frequency. The ISP program has alleviated some prison overcrowding by diverting a large number of offenders to probationary status rather than incarceration. The most important criticism of Georgia's program credibility pertains to those selected for inclusion in it. Fewer than 30 percent of the offenders placed on ISP in Georgia consist of maximum-risk cases. Thus, most Georgia ISP probationers are those least likely to recidivate anyway. Also, the division of labor between probation officers and surveillance officers has not been as clear as originally intended. Surveillance officers perform many of the same functions as standard probation officers. Therefore, it is difficult to formulate a clear caseload picture for regular Georgia probation officer functions.

Another criticism is that Georgia handpicks its clients for ISP involvement. The selection process deliberately includes low- to medium-risk offenders with the greatest potential to succeed. Deliberately excluded are the most serious offenders with the least success likelihood. In fact, some researchers have said the current composition of ISP clients consists of persons who would have been diverted from prison anyway. In order for ISP programs to be effective, more high-risk offenders ought to be targeted for inclusion rather than those most likely to succeed.

New Jersey's ISP program has received several criticisms. First, offenders must volunteer. And volunteers are not automatically included in the program. In fact, only 25 percent of all applicants are accepted. The most serious felons are excluded, thus creating a "bias" toward lower recidivism among those served by the program. Furthermore, the fact that participants must be incarcerated for a short time is tantamount to shock probation or shock parole. Therefore, space in prison is consumed at least temporarily by persons eventually selected for ISP.

The Idaho and South Carolina ISP programs exhibit relatively low rates of recidivism for their participating offenders. Compared with the Georgia and New Jersey programs, these programs rely fairly heavily on the use of risk assessment instruments for recruiting clients and determining their level of intensive supervision. The South Carolina program element involving the payment of a $10 per week supervision fee is only a token amount, but it nevertheless is regarded by staff as heightening offender accountability and serves as a reminder that they are paying for their crimes, even if the payment is hardly excessive. POs in both Idaho and South Carolina perform functions as liaisons when they unite their clients with receptive employers. Furthermore, the integrated use of home confinement and electronic monitoring, together with frequent face-to-face visits and checks by supervising POs, means that offender control is heightened.

SHOCK PROBATION AND SPLIT SENTENCING

Shock Probation

Shock probation, also referred to as **split sentencing,** first appeared as a federal split sentencing provision in 1958, although the California legislature had authorized a bill permitting judges to impose a combination of incarceration and probation for the same offender in the early 1920s. The term *shock probation* was later coined by Ohio in 1964. Ohio was the first state to use shock probation. It has been characterized as a brief application of the rigors of imprisonment (in Ohio, 90–130 days served) that will deter criminal behavior and not impede the readjustment of the individual upon release. Shock probation has been used increasingly in other states in recent years. In more than a few jurisdictions,

NEW JERSEY CONDITIONS OF PLACEMENT OF ADULTS ON INTENSIVE SUPERVISION

I have applied for, and been granted, an opportunity to be placed on intensive supervision by the Resentencing Panel for a period of _____. Based on the plan I submitted, the Resentencing Panel believes that I am capable of living a useful and law-abiding life in the community and has suspended my sentence with the condition that I comply with the provisions of the intensive supervision program. My being granted the opportunity of intensive supervision is subject to my compliance with the plan I submitted as part of my application along with the conditions listed below. If there is probable cause to believe that I have committed another offense or if I have been held to answer thereto, the Resentencing Panel will commit me to the institution to which I have been sentenced, without bail, to await trial on the new charges. I am required to notify promptly my ISP officer if I am arrested at any time during my sentence to the intensive supervision program.

1. I will obey the laws of the United States and the laws and ordinances of any jurisdiction to which I may be assigned.
2. I will report as directed by the court or my ISP officer.
3. I will permit the ISP officer to visit my home.
4. I will answer promptly, truthfully, and completely all inquiries made by my ISP officer and report any address or residence change to that officer. If the change of address or residence is outside the region in which I am under supervision, I will request approval of my ISP officer at least thirty days in advance of such change.
5. I will cooperate in any medical and/or psychological examination, tests and/or counseling my ISP officer recommends.
6. I will support my dependents, meet my family responsibilities, continue gainful employment, and/or pursue such alternatives as may be part of the program and promptly notify my ISP officer prior to any change in my place of employment or if I find myself out of work.
7. I will participate in a counseling program as scheduled by my ISP officer.
8. I will not leave the State of New Jersey without permission from my ISP officer.
9. I will not have in my possession any firearm or other dangerous weapon.
10. I will perform community service in accordance with the ISP officer.
11. I will participate in group activities scheduled by my ISP officer.
12. I will maintain a diary of my activities while under supervision.
13. I will maintain weekly contact with my community sponsor and network team.

I will comply with the following conditions of intensive supervision imposed in accordance with N.J.S.A. 2C:45-1 et. seq., as communicated to me by my ISP officer.

_____I will pay a fine of $_____ in strict accord with the terms described.
_____I will make restitution of $_____ in strict accord with the terms described.
_____I will pursue the course of study or vocational training described.
_____I will attend/reside in the facility described for the required period of time.
_____I will refrain from frequenting the unlawful or disreputable places or consorting with the disreputable persons described.

_____
_____
_____

_____
Signature of ISP Client

_____
Date

FIGURE 6.3   New Jersey Conditions of Placement of Adults on Intensive Supervion.

problem drinkers, DWI cases, and drug abusers have been targeted for shock probation programs.

Some persons have wondered whether shock probation is an appropriate term, since offenders sentenced to shock probation are actually incarcerated in a jail or prison for a short period, primarily for shock value. Shock probation stems from the fact that judges initially sentence offenders to lengthy terms of incarceration, usually in a jail. After offenders have been in jail for short intervals (e.g., 30, 60, 90, or 120 days), they are brought before the judge where they are sentenced to probation. This type of sentence shocks and surprises these offenders, since they didn't expect to receive probation. Offenders who have been resentenced under these circumstances are **shock probationers.** The shock of incarceration is supposed to be a deterrent against further offending. It is anticipated that recidivism rates among shock probationers will be low.

Split Sentencing

There is a difference between split sentencing and shock probation. Split sentencing means that the judge imposes a **combination sentence,** a portion of which includes incarceration and a portion of which includes probation. Thus, the judge may sentence the offender up to one year, with a maximum incarceration of six months. The remainder of the sentence is to be served on probation. Violating one or more conditions of probation may result in reincarceration, however.

Most states have authorized the use of one of three general types of either split sentencing or shock probation by judges in the sentencing of low-risk offenders. These types include (1) the California scheme, where jail is attached as a condition of probation; (2) the federal scheme under the 1987 sentencing guidelines, where supervised release of up to five years may follow sentences of imprisonment of more than one year (the length of supervised release varies according to the crime classification and ranges from one year for misdemeanors to five years); and (3) the Ohio scheme, where a judge resentences offenders within a 130-day incarcerative period to a probationary sentence. Other states including Texas have similar systems, although incarcerative periods are often longer than 130 days before resentencing to probation is considered (U.S. Department of Justice, 2006).

Other terms used to describe these phenomena are **mixed sentence, intermittent confinement,** and **jail as a condition of probation.** A mixed sentence is imposed by a judge whenever an offender has committed two or more offenses. The judge imposes a separate sentence for each offense. One sentence may involve probation, while the other may involve incarceration. The judge decides whether the two sentences are to be served concurrently or consecutively. The intermittent sentence is imposed whenever the offender is sentenced to a term requiring partial confinement. Perhaps the offender must serve weekends in jail. A curfew may be imposed. In all other respects, the nature of intermittent sentencing is much like probation. Finally, jail as a condition of probation is an option whereby the judge imposes a fixed jail term to be served prior to the offender's completion of a sentence of probation.

The Philosophy and Objectives of Shock Probation

Shock Probation and Deterrence.   Deterrence is one of shock probation's primary themes. Another prominent philosophical objective is reintegration. Confining offenders to jail for brief periods and obligating them to serve their remaining months on probationary status enables them to be employed, support themselves and their families, and otherwise be productive citizens in their communities. The freedom shock probation allows permits offenders to receive specialized attention and to participate in programs designed to deal with their problems. Ideally, exposure to jail should be sufficiently traumatic to cause offenders to want to refrain from further criminal activity.

Shock Probation and Rehabilitation.   Consistent with the philosophy of shock probation and split sentencing generally are community reintegration and rehabilitation. A brief exposure to incarceration followed by release into the community permits offenders to hold jobs, support themselves and their families, pay restitution to victims, perform various public services, and/or participate in therapeutic or educational programs designed to help them with their special problems.

Shock Probation and Creative Sentencing.   Judges are permitted greater flexibility in the punishments they impose for low-risk offenders. Short-term incarceration is one form of creative sentencing.

Shock Probation as a Punishment.   The confinement phase of shock probation is considered a punishment. Low-risk offenders who have never been incarcerated are able to understand what it is like to be locked up without the freedoms to which they have become accustomed while living in their communities.

Shock Probation and Offender Needs.   Short-term confinement in a jail enables judges to determine appropriate services and therapies needed by offenders. Jail reports often disclose certain offender needs that must be addressed through community agencies. Judges can configure a suitable probationary punishment that includes programs that directly address particular offender needs.

Shock Probation and Offender Accountability.   Shock probation heightens offender awareness of the seriousness of their crimes. For many low-risk offenders, spending three or four months in jail is a sufficiently punishing experience to cause them to reflect on the seriousness of the crimes they committed and to accept responsibility for their actions.

Shock Probation and Community Safety.   There is some question as to whether short-term incarceration ensures community safety. Eventually, shock probationers will be placed on probation within their communities. However, some authorities have acknowledged that short-term incarceration does satisfy the public's demand for punitiveness where the law has been violated.

The Effectiveness of Shock Probation

Is shock probation effective? The answer to this question depends on what is expected from shock probation. If shock probation is expected to deter offenders from future offending, then it appears to be modestly successful in those jurisdictions where it has been used. Recidivism rates among shock probationers tend to be fairly low, averaging under 30 percent. Perhaps this is due primarily to the fact that low-risk, nonviolent offenders are most often selected as targets of shock probation sentences. Thus, those least likely to reoffend are included in the broad class of shock probationers and receive this special sanction.

If shock probation is expected to alleviate prison and jail overcrowding, the results are mixed. Shock probation is one viable alternative to alleviating prison overcrowding. This is because most offenders sentenced to shock probation will serve brief terms of confinement, usually in county jails. Thus, they will not occupy valuable long-term prison space that should be reserved for more serious or dangerous offenders. Nevertheless, shock probationers do occupy some jail space, even if their periods of confinement are relatively short. The high turnover among jail inmates suggests that shock probation has only an imperceptible effect on jail overcrowding.

BOOT CAMPS

Closely related to shock probation is **shock incarceration** or **boot camps.** In the case of shock incarceration or boot camps, convicted offenders are jailed or otherwise confined, but their confinement resembles military boot camp training. Shock probation involved sentencing offenders to a plain jail term, with no participation in any military-like programs. In contrast, shock incarceration or boot camp programs do provide military-like regimentation and regulation of inmate behavior.

FIGURE 6.4   General Patrick H. Brady Boot Camp Correctional Facility.

Boot Camps Defined

Boot camps are highly regimented, military-like, short-term correctional programs (90–180 days) where offenders are provided with strict discipline, physical training, and hard labor resembling some aspects of military basic training; when successfully completed, boot camps provide for transfers of participants to community-based facilities for nonsecure supervision. By 2006, boot camps had been formally established in most of the states (Champion, 2007).

Boot camps were officially established in 1983 by the Georgia Department of Corrections Special Alternative Incarceration (SAI), the general idea for boot camps originated some time earlier in the late 1970s, also in Georgia. The usual length of incarceration in boot camps varies from three to six months. During this period, boot camp participants engage in marching, work, and classes that are believed useful in one's rehabilitation. Usually, youthful offenders are targeted by these programs.

The Rationale for Boot Camps

Boot camps were established as an alternative to long-term, traditional incarceration. An outline for boot camps indicates that:

1. A substantial number of youthful first-time offenders now incarcerated will respond to a short but intensive period of confinement followed by a longer period of intensive community supervision.
2. These youthful offenders will benefit from a military-type atmosphere that instills a sense of self-discipline and physical conditioning that was lacking in their lives.
3. These same youths need exposure to relevant educational, vocational training, drug treatment, and general counseling services to develop more positive and law-abiding values and become better prepared to secure legitimate future employment.
4. The costs involved will be less than a traditional criminal justice sanction that imprisons the offender for a substantially longer period of time.

Goals of Boot Camps

Boot camps have several general goals. These goals include: (1) rehabilitation /reintegration; (2) discipline; (3) deterrence; (4) ease prison/jail overcrowding; and (5) vocational, educational, and rehabilitative services.

To Provide Rehabilitation and Reintegration. Boot camp programs are designed to improve one's sense of purpose, self-discipline, self-control, and self-confidence through physical conditioning, educational programs, and social skills training, all within the framework of strict military discipline. The time youthful offenders spend in boot camps is not especially lengthy. The emphasis upon discipline and educational skills is calculated to provide structure for participants, which was lacking in their previous family and social environment. Thus, there are both rehabilitative and reintegrative objectives sought by most boot camp programs.

To Provide Discipline.   Boot camps are intended to improve one's discipline. Many youthful offenders find it difficult to accept authority and often refuse to learn in traditional classroom or treatment environments. Within the context of a boot camp program, however, there are incentives to become involved in program activities. Most boot camp programs also include educational elements pertaining to literacy, academic and vocational education, intensive value clarification, and resocialization.

To Promote Deterrence.   Being thrust into a military-like atmosphere is a frightening experience for many boot camp clients. It is believed that a highly regimented boot camp experience will cause most participants to lead more law-abiding lives when they successfully complete their programs. However, there have been numerous boot camp failures. These failures have caused some observers to regard boot camp programs with some amount of skepticism. It has been recommended, for instance, that more selective criteria should be used to include those clients most amenable to change under military-like boot camp conditions. Furthermore, post-release follow-ups should be conducted of boot camp clientele to gauge program effectiveness. In some instances, boot camp staff have appeared to be overzealous in exercising their authority over youthful offenders. Thus, several ethical questions have been generated about how much control these authorities should have and how that control should be applied, especially where youthful offenders are involved.

To Ease Prison and Jail Overcrowding.   Boot camps are believed to have a long-term impact on jail and prison overcrowding. One primary purpose of boot camps is to divert prison-bound youthful offenders to a structured environment where they can learn discipline and become rehabilitated. Compared with the population of jail and prison inmates, the total number of boot camp clientele accounts for only a small fraction of these populations, however. Thus, it is doubtful whether boot camps seriously ease prison or jail overcrowding to a significant degree.

To Provide Vocational and Rehabilitative Services.   Most boot camp programs offer educational and/or vocational training to clients. Rehabilitative services might include drug abuse intervention counseling, mental health services, and sex offender therapy (Fabelo, 2002).

A Profile of Boot Camp Clientele

Who can participate in boot camps or shock incarceration programs? Participants may or may not be able to enter or withdraw from boot camps voluntarily. It depends on the particular program. Most boot camp participants are prison-bound youthful offenders convicted of less serious, nonviolent crimes, and who have never been previously incarcerated. Depending on the program, there are some exceptions (Nicol and McCree, 2006). Participants may either be referred to these programs by judges or corrections departments or they may volunteer. They may or may not be accepted, and if they complete their programs successfully, they may or may not be released under supervision into their communities.

 **BOX 6.2**

Michigan Department of Corrections Special Alternative Incarceration (SAI).

The Michigan Department of Corrections has implemented a 90-day boot camp program called Special Alternatives Incarceration (SAI). Program elements include the following:

1. Physical training
2. Work at a trade
3. Life skills course
4. Stress management training
5. Group counseling
6. Job seeking
7. Substance abuse awareness
8. Adult basic education

Education sessions are conducted over 10 weeks, with each weekly session lasting 70 minutes. Clients are assessed for substance abuse problems. Michigan's intensive post-release program may include 120-day residential placement and electronic monitoring. All graduates are required to undergo a minimum of 18 months of community supervision, with the first four months including intensive daily supervision.

The Harris County (Texas) Regimented Intensive Probation Program (CRIPP)

In Harris County, Texas, the CRIPP program has the following features:

1. Military model, militaristic chain of command.
2. Staff consists of volunteers from deputies of Harris County Sheriff's Department.
3. Handles convicted criminal offenders under probation supervision.
4. Probationers supervised for 90-day period by Drill Instructors.
5. Program accommodates 48 probationers as a "group" who begin and end as a group.
6. Regimen: breakfast at 4:00 A.M.; physical training; lunch at 11:00 A.M.; more physical

training, barracks cleanup; general orders; dinner at 3:00 P.M.; more physical training; day ends with lights out at 10:00 P.M.; participants wear uniforms and combat boots, where different types of uniforms distinguish between different levels of probationers.

7. Services provided include medical, vocational, physical, social (drug and alcohol counseling) programs; coping and life skills programs.
8. Participants required to practice good grooming and personal hygiene habits; structured activities designed to prepare them for successful reintegration into society.
9. Program activities are mandatory.

The Mississippi Regimented Inmate Discipline (RID) Program

Established in Mississippi, the RID program has the following program features:

1. 140 inmates in minimum-security camp.
2. Judges control inmate selection process, according to broad statutory criteria.
3. Program features physical training, drill and ceremony, hard labor, and treatment.
4. No vocational or educational program.
5. Released inmates live in halfway houses, perform community service; subsequently released to regular probation supervision.

The Alabama Disciplinary Rehabilitation Unit (DRU)

This program includes the following characteristics:

1. Twelve-step program used by Alcoholics Anonymous
2. Drug and alcohol services
3. Camp psychologist counseling sessions
4. Judges control selection process with DRU as a condition of probation.

5. Program includes physical training, drill, hard work; two exercise and drill periods daily, with eight-hour hard labor periods in between.

6. Participants perform limited community services.

7. Drug abuse education and information about sexually transmitted diseases (Cowles, Castellano, and Gransky, 1995 :14–22).

Boot Camp Programs

While boot camp programs share certain features, there are obviously different program components among these boot camps to make them fairly distinctive from the others. It is interesting to note which features are included or excluded from one program to the next.

Jail Boot Camps

Jail boot camps are short-term programs for jail inmates serving short sentences of less than one year. In 2005 there were 20 jail boot camp programs operating in U.S. jails involving 3,004 inmates (U.S. Department of Justice, 2006). In Washoe County, Nevada, for instance, a jail boot camp was established in May 1995. A wide range of ages was represented, with no explicit minimum or maximum age restrictions. The main goals of the Washoe program were to instill in inmates a positive attitude by stressing academic achievement, coping skills, anger and money management, and good work habits. The intent was to inspire the inmate to succeed in society after he leaves jail. Six basic objectives were sought: (1) inmates will develop good work habits and skills; (2) inmates will no longer sit idle while they are held in jail; (3) members will partially repay the community for the cost of their incarceration; (4) members will become more self-sufficient; (5) members will adjust more smoothly back into society; and (6) the recidivism rate will be reduced.

Known as the Highly Intensive Supervision, Training, and Education Program (HISTEP), the Washoe County program was implemented through the Washoe County Sheriff's Office and involved 452 inmates. Five levels were incorporated in the program. Levels I and II ran for six weeks. During these weeks, inmates were introduced to the military way of life. Physical training, inspections, and educational classes were conducted in somewhat of a shock environment, breaking inmates out of the traditional general inmate population mold. Various tests were administered to determine their educational and personality maturity levels. Skills classes were taught, emphasizing anger management, communication, building self-esteem, decision making, parenting techniques, and financial management. Core values were also taught. These core values were a sense of responsibility, pride, and acceptable behavior in various real-life situations. Level III initiated members to the fundamentals of seeking employment, writing resumes, exploring employment resources, and learning interviewing techniques. This level lasted eight weeks. Levels IV and V included work at the jail at a jail industry job. The inmate received a small hourly wage, part of which was used to support the program. Work furloughs were made available to certain inmates who would reside within the jail during evening hours but would work at a job outside the jail during the day. Again, jail inmate wages would be divided into offsetting program costs, establishing a small inmate savings account, and commissary items. Levels IV and V lasted eight weeks. Thus, the program was designed for inmates to leave the jail with a job skill, a job, and money in the bank.

Washoe County Jail officials have conducted a follow-up of the number of inmates who went through the program during the period May 1995 through August 1996. Of the 452 entering the HISTEP program, 30 percent, or 138, completed it. Of the successful jail boot camp inmates who completed the program, the recidivism rate was only 11 percent. Considering substantially higher rates of recidivism associated with standard probation and parole programs and other community-based or intermediate punishments, the 11 percent recidivism figure was interpreted by Washoe officials as a very positive indicator of their HISTEP program success. It is not possible to generalize Washoe County's HISTEP success rate to other jurisdictions with substantial accuracy, although this program does seem to be typical of other jail boot camp programs presently operating in other jurisdictions.

The Effectiveness of Boot Camps

Are boot camps or shock incarceration programs successful? Programs with recidivism rates of 30 percent or less are considered successful by many criminal justice professionals. If we use this standard as a measure of boot camp effectiveness, there seems to be considerable support in the literature for their effectiveness. For instance, a Louisiana IMPACT (Intensive Motivational Program of Alternative Correctional Treatment) program reported that during the first six months of community supervision following boot camp participation, between 7 and 14 percent of the boot camp clients recidivated compared with from 12 to 23 percent of the boot camp dropouts or those who failed to complete the program. A New York Rikers Boot Camp has reported recidivism rates of 23 percent among its graduates. However, a 38 percent recidivism rate was reported by a Georgia SAI (Special Alternative Incarceration) program. Generally recidivism rates continue to be low among boot camp participants (Benda, Toombs, and Peacock, 2002). The simple fact is that because most of these boot camp programs were established during the late 1980s and 1990s, there hasn't been much evaluation research about boot camp program effectiveness.

It is difficult to draw clear conclusions from these preliminary investigations of boot camp costs. In 2002 there were between 50 and 100 different boot camps operating in the United States. Little evaluation research has been made available about them and whether they are effective. There are major differences among these boot camps in the clientele selected for inclusion, however. Some boot camps are designated for those with substance abuse problems, while other programs are intended for those with disciplinary problems and who are relatively drug-free. Different selection criteria exist, therefore, and all programs are operated in different ways. The general impression we might draw from existing literature about boot camps is that they appear to be reasonably successful for those who complete programming requirements (Benda et al., 2002). This would suggest that more rigorous criteria ought to be used when targeting participants for boot camp involvement.

FEMALE PROBATIONERS AND PAROLEES: A PROFILE

In 2004, females accounted for 23 percent of all probationers and 12 percent of all parolees (Glaze and Palla, 2005:6, 9). Women were most represented proportionately in various property offense categories, such as fraud (40 percent) and larceny (24 percent). Overall, women made up about 25 percent of all probationers convicted of property offenses. On the average, women are sentenced to probation more often than men. But this is likely attributable to the fact that male and female offenders have different offending patterns. Males are involved to a greater degree in violent offending, while females are involved to a greater degree in more passive offending, such as fraud and burglary (Harrison and Beck, 2003:10). Another explanation for these sentencing differences is that judges have tended to be more paternalistic toward female offenders in the past. In recent years, however, presumptive or guidelines-based sentencing schemes used by different states and the federal government have caused male–female sentencing differentials to narrow. Generally, the rate of female offending and incarceration has increased both dramatically and systematically since the early 1980s. This does not necessarily mean that there is a new breed or a more dangerous female offender in society—rather, more women are being subject to less lenient treatment by a more equitable criminal justice system. Some observers have labeled this phenomenon gender parity (Festervan, 2003).

Regarding parole, women tended to be distributed in ways similar to their conviction patterns. This proportion is similar to the proportionate distribution of women incarcerated in federal and state prisons. With a few exceptions, female parolee distributions by conviction offense were similar to their original conviction offense patterns. The female failure rate while on probation or parole is approximately the same as it is for male probationers and parolees, about 65 percent (U.S. Department of Justice, 2006).

Special Programs and Services for Female Offenders

In 1992, the American Correctional Association formulated a National Correctional Policy on Female Offender Services (Festervan, 2003). This policy is as follows.

Introduction: Correctional systems must develop service delivery systems for accused and adjudicated female offenders that are comparable to those provided to males. Additional services must also be provided to meet the unique needs of the female offender population.

Statement: Correctional systems must be guided by the principle of parity. Female offenders must receive the equivalent range of services available to other offenders, including opportunities for individualized programming and services that recognize the unique needs of this population. The services should:

1. Ensure access to a range of alternatives to incarceration, including pretrial and post-trial diversion, probation, restitution, treatment for substance abuse, halfway houses, and parole services.
2. Provide acceptable conditions of confinement, including appropriately trained staff and sound operating procedures that address this population's needs in such areas as clothing, personal property, hygiene, exercise, recreation, and visitation with children and family.

3. Provide access to a full range of work and programs designed to expand economic and social roles of women, with emphasis on education; career counseling and exploration of nontraditional as well as traditional vocational training; relevant life skills, including parenting and social and economic assertiveness; and pre-release and work/education release programs.

4. Facilitate the maintenance and strengthening of family ties, particularly those between parent and child.

5. Deliver appropriate programs and services, including medical, dental, and mental health programs, services to pregnant women, substance abuse programs, child and family services, and provide access to legal services.

6. Provide access to release programs that include aid in establishing homes, economic stability, and sound family relationships.

Criticisms of Women's Prison and Community Programming

Studies of some of the continuing problems associated with women's prisons and community-based treatment services have been conducted. Typical female offenders tend to be young, either single, divorced, or separated; educated at a level approximating the general population; lacking in work skills and dependent upon public assistance; overrepresentative of minority groups; and having a high probability of physical and/or sexual abuse victimization and a history of substance abuse (Sharp and Muraskin, 2003).

It is generally acknowledged that women's prisons and programming for women in community-based correctional programs have not compared favorably with programs and facilities for men (Dalley, 2002). For instance, programs for female offenders have been poorer in quality, quantity, variability, and availability in both the United States and Canada. Despite these inequities, courts generally declare that men and women in prisons do not have to be treated equally, and that separate can be equal when men's and women's prisons are compared. There are exceptions, however. In 1979, the case of *Glover v. Johnson* (1979) involved the Michigan Department of Corrections and the issue of equal programming for female inmates. A class action suit was filed on behalf of all Michigan female prison inmates to the effect that their constitutional rights were violated because they were being denied educational and vocational rehabilitation opportunities that were then being provided to male inmates only. Among other things, the Michigan Department of Corrections was ordered to provide the following to its incarcerated women: (1) two-year college programming; (2) paralegal training and access to attorneys to remedy past inadequacies in law library facilities; (3) redo inmate wage policy to ensure that female inmates were provided equal wages; (4) female inmates were to have access to programming at camps previously available only to male inmates; (5) enhanced vocational offerings; (6) apprenticeship opportunities; and (7) prison industries, which previously existed only at men's facilities. Several similar cases in other jurisdictions have been settled without court action (Connecticut, California, Wisconsin, and Idaho).

The *Glover* case is like the tip of the iceberg when it comes to disclosing various problems associated with women's prisons and other corrections institutions for women. The following are criticisms that have been leveled against women's correctional facilities in the last few decades. Some of these criticisms have been remedied in selected jurisdictions.

1. No adequate classification system exists for female prisoners. Women from widely different backgrounds with diverse criminal histories are celled with one another in most women's prisons. This is conducive to greater criminalization during the incarceration period. Furthermore, most women's prisons have only medium-security custody, rather than a wider variety of custody levels to accommodate female offenders of differing seriousness and dangerousness. Better classification methods should be devised.

2. Most women's prisons are remotely located; thus, many female prisoners are deprived of immediate contact with out-of-prison educational or vocational services that might be available through study or work release.

3. Women who give birth to babies while incarcerated are deprived of valuable parent–child contact. Some observers contend this is a serious deprivation for newborn infants.

4. Women have less extensive vocational and educational programming in the prison setting.

5. Women have less access to legal services; in the past, law libraries in women's facilities were lacking or nonexistent; recent remedies have included provisions for either legal services or more adequate libraries in women's institutions.

6. Women have special medical needs, and women's prisons do not adequately provide for meeting these needs.

7. Mental health treatment services and programs for women are inferior to those provided in men's facilities.

8. Training programs that are provided to women do not permit them to live independently and earn decent livings when released on parole (Champion, 2005).

Because of the rather unique role of women as caregivers for their children, many corrections professionals rule the imprisonment of women differently from the imprisonment of men. For various reasons, female imprisonment is opposed on moral, ethical, and religious grounds. Legally, these arguments are often unconvincing. In an attempt to at least address some of the unique problems confronting female offenders when they are incarcerated or when they participate in community-based programs, some observers have advocated the following as recommendations:

1. Institute training programs that would enable imprisoned women to become literate.

2. Provide female offenders with programs that do not center on traditional gender roles—programs that will lead to more economic independence and self-sufficiency.

3. Establish programs that would engender more positive self-esteem for imprisoned women and enhance their assertiveness and communication and interpersonal skills.

4. Establish more programs that would allow imprisoned mothers to interact more with their children and assist them in overcoming feelings of guilt and shame for having deserted their children. In addition, visitation areas for mothers and children should be altered to minimize the effect of a prison-type environment.

5. An alternative to mother-and-child interaction behind prison bars would be to allow imprisoned mothers to spend more time with their children outside of the prison.

6. Provide imprisoned mothers with training to improve parenting skills.

7. Establish more programs to treat drug-addicted female offenders.

8. Establish a community partnership program to provide imprisoned women with employment opportunities.

9. Establish a better classification system for incarcerated women—one that would not permit the less-hardened offender to be juxtaposed with the hardened female offender.

10. Provide in-service training (sensitivity awareness) to assist staff members (wardens, correctional officers) in understanding the nature and needs of incarcerated women (Champion, 2005).

Other observers have recommended the establishment and provision for an environment that would allow all pregnant inmates the opportunity to rear their newborn infants for a period of one year and provide counseling regarding available parental services, foster care, guardianship, and other relevant activities pending their eventual release. Some women's facilities have cottages on prison grounds where inmates with infants can accomplish some of these objectives. One of these is the **Program for Female Offenders, Inc. (PFO).** The PFO was established in 1974 as the result of jail overcrowding in Allegheny County, Pennsylvania (Festervan, 2003). The PFO is a work-release facility operated as a nonprofit agency by the county. It is designed to accommodate up to 36 women and space for six preschool children. It was originally created to reduce jail overcrowding, but because of escalating rates of female offending and jail incarceration, the overcrowding problem persists.

When the PFO was established, the Allegheny County Jail was small. Only twelve women were housed there. Nevertheless, agency founders worked out an agreement with jail authorities so that female jail prisoners could be transferred to PFO by court order. Inmate-clients would be guilty of prison breach if they left PFO without permission. While at PFO, the women would participate in training, volunteering in the community, and learning how to spend their leisure time with the help of a role modeling and parent education program for mothers and children. The program is based on freedom reached by attaining levels of responsibility. In the mid-1980s, a much larger work-release facility was constructed in Allegheny County. Currently, over 300 women per year are served by PFO. PFO authorities reserve the right to screen potential candidates for work release. In 1992 the following companion projects were implemented in Allegheny County (Champion, 2005):

1. Good-time project at the county jail

2. Male work-release center accommodating 60 beds

3. Development of criminal justice division in county government

4. Drug treatment/work-release facility at St. Francis Health Center's Chemical Dependency Department

5. Development of a male job placement program

6. Expansion of the existing THE PROGRAM Women's Center

7. Expansion of the retail theft project

The successfulness of THE PROGRAM is demonstrated by its low 3.5 percent recidivism rate in the community program and only a 17 percent recidivism rate at the residential facility. Over $88,000 has been collected in rent, $27,000 in fines, and $8,000 in restitution to victims of the female offenders. For the male offenders, $106,500 has been collected in rent and $107,400 in fines and restitution. Long-range plans for THE PROGRAM call for a crime prevention program, including a day care center, intervention therapy for drug-abusing families, intensive work with preschool children who are already showing evidence of impending **delinquency,** and a scholarship program. Plans also include expanding THE PROGRAM's services to more areas throughout Pennsylvania (Champion, 2005).

In the early 1990s, the Kansas Department of Corrections established a program for women with children that has been patterned after PATCH (Parents and Their Children), which was created by the Missouri Department of Corrections and MATCH (Mothers and Their Children) operated by the California Department of Corrections. The Kansas program is known as the **Women's Activities and Learning Center (WALC).** WALC was started with a grant from the U.S. Department of Education under the Women's Educational Opportunity Act and is based in Topeka. The Topeka facility has a primary goal of developing and coordinating a broad range of programs, services, and classes and workshops that will increase women offenders' chances for positive reintegration with their families and society upon release. A visiting area at the center accommodates visitations with female inmates and their children. Thus, women with children are given a chance to take an active part in caring for their children. Mothers acquire some measure of a mother–child relationship during incarceration. They are able to fix meals for their children and have recreation with them in designated areas. Various civic and religious groups contribute their volunteer resources to assist these women. Both time and money are expended by outside agencies and personnel, such as the Kiwanis, the Kansas East Conference of the United Methodist Church, and the Fraternal Order of Police.

One advantage of WALC is that it provides various programs and courses in useful areas such as parenting, child development, prenatal care, self-esteem, anger management, nutrition, support groups, study groups, cardiopulmonary resuscitation, personal development, and crafts. The parenting program, for instance, is a 10-week course where inmate-mothers meet once a week to discuss their various problems. In order to qualify for inclusion in this program, female inmates must be designated as "low risk," "minimum security," and have no disciplinary reports filed against them during the 90 days prior to program involvement. When the 10-week course is completed, the women are entitled to participate in a three-week retreat sponsored by the Methodist Church. The retreat includes transportation for inmates, with fishing, horse-riding, hay rides, and game-playing for mothers and their children. Volunteers and a correctional officer are present during the retreat experience. Since September 1991, more than 300 women and 500 children have participated in the WALC program with a low rate of recidivism (Champion, 2005).

New York's Prison Nursery/Children's Center. At the Bedford Hills, New York, Correctional Facility, a 750-woman maximum-security prison constructed in 1933, a Children's Center was established in 1989–1990. Since 1930, New York legislation provided for women in prison to keep their babies. Authorities at Bedford Hills believe that it is important for women to maintain strong ties with their families during incarceration. Furthermore, they believe that women will have a greater chance at reintegration and lower recidivism as the opportunity for familial interaction increases. As a result, there is a positive impact on babies, since they can remain with and be nurtured by their mothers. Not all women incarcerated at Bedford Hills are eligible to participate in the prison nursery program. A woman's criminal background, past parenting performance, disciplinary record, and educational needs are examined and assessed before they are accepted. Women who are selected are expected to make the best use of their time by developing their mothering skills and caring for their infants. They are also expected to participate in various self-help programs of a vocational and educational nature. The center's main program goal is to help women preserve and strengthen family ties and receive visits from their children as often as possible in a warm, nurturing atmosphere. Through the various classes and programs offered at Bedford Hills, women acquire a better understanding of their roles as parents and are able to reinforce their feelings of self-worth (Roulet, 1993:5).

Roulet (1993:6) says that women whose babies are born while incarcerated may keep them at Bedford for up to one year. Babies are delivered in a hospital outside of prison, and the mother and infant live in the nursery for as long as the child remains. If it is likely that the mother will be paroled by the time the infant is 18 months old, then the infant may remain with the mother with special permission until that date. It is important to keep mothers and children together as much as possible while at Bedford Hills. The child's welfare is of utmost concern to authorities (Roulet, 1993:6). Such bonding is considered significant at reducing rates of recidivism among paroled Bedford Hills women.

More women are being convicted of drug offenses annually. Three-fourths of all women inmates are in need of substance abuse treatment, although only 30 percent of all incarcerated women have conviction offenses involving drugs (Grabarek, Bourke, and Van Hasselt, 2002). Most offenders had dropped out of high school or had not received the GED. Most had been unable to hold a job for longer than six months. Presently, most of the surveyed institutions offer vocational and educational courses for these women. Two-thirds offer college courses and 70 have pre-release programs. Most facilities have institutional work assignments, and about half have parenting prgrams (Festervan, 2003). These policy changes involve increased opportunities for women to work and/or participate in vocational and educational programming originally available only to male inmates. Major changes have occurred in classification, visitation, and housing. Clothing policy changes have also been effected. Many of these changes have been occasioned by the parity issue, where women's facilities are brought more in line with men's facilities. In most instances, this has meant improved services delivery to women's prisons. Most prison and community correctional policy changes have benefited women generally. Each year, the conditions in women's facilities are being improved and services delivery to these institutions and community agencies is being expanded.

CONTINUUMS OF SANCTIONS

For both male and female probationers and depending on the jurisdiction, different probation programs are prescribed by judges. Offenders with drug or alcohol dependencies will likely be referred to or required to meet with social service agencies designed to deal with these dependencies. From descriptions of several probation programs presented earlier, it is apparent that many behavioral requirements are in place to ensure that offenders remain law-abiding throughout the duration of their programming. But not all offenders comply with all of their program requirements all of the time. Their supervising POs detect program violations and must make decisions about consequences to impose. One immediate solution would be to report the offender to the court for whatever violation is detected. Once formal court action is initiated, the process of probation revocation begins. Using a worst-case scenario, the result of such formal revocation proceedings may be a jail or prison term. However, most probation agencies recognize that more than a few offenders are going to need guidance and closer supervision than others. There are various types of violations that are not equally serious. Therefore, in most jurisdictions, a **continuum of sanctions** has been established. This continuum of sanctions extends from verbal reprimands by POs directly to the offender, and ultimately, if the offender persists in committing more program violations, various types of escalating punishments and restrictions may be imposed.

One example of a state using a continuum of sanctions is Iowa. Iowa has instituted a five-level continuum of sanctions that gradually increases the penalties for probation program violations (Iowa Department of Corrections, 2005). These levels are shown as follows:

Level I: Noncommunity-based corrections sanctions, including the following:

1. Self-monitored sanctions. Self-monitored sanctions that are not monitored for compliance, including, but not limited to, fines and community service.

2. Other than self-monitored sanctions. Other than self-monitored sanctions that are monitored for compliance by other than the district department of correctional services, including, but not limited to, mandatory mediation, victim and offender reconciliation, and noncommunity-based corrections supervision.

Level II: Probation and parole options consisting of the following:

1. Monitored sanctions. Monitored sanctions are administrative sanctions that are monitored for compliance by the district department of correctional services and include, but are not limited to, low-risk offender-diversion programs.

2. Supervised sanctions. Supervised sanctions are regular probation or parole supervision and any conditions established by the probation or parole agreement or by court order.

3. Intensive supervision sanctions. Intensive supervision sanctions provide levels of supervision that include electronic monitoring, day reporting, live-out programs for persons on work release or who have violated particular statutes, and institutional work release.

Level III: Quasi-incarceration sanctions. Quasi-incarceration sanctions are those supported by residential facility placement or 24-hour electronic monitoring, including, but not limited to, the following:

1. Residential treatment facilities
2. Operating while intoxicated offender treatment facilities
3. Work release facilities
4. House arrest with electronic monitoring

Level IV: Short-term incarceration designed to be of short duration, including, but not limited to, the following:

1. Twenty-one (21)-day shock incarceration for persons who violate particular statutes
2. Jail for less than 30 days
3. Violators' facilities
4. Prison with sentence consideration

Level V: Incarceration, which consists of the following:

1. Prison
2. Jail for 30 days or longer

Iowa applies these levels by describing them to all offenders initially when they enter their probation programs. Each Iowa judicial district implements an intermediate criminal sanctions program and shall consist of Levels I, II, and III, with sublevels of 1 and 3 under Level IV of the corrections continuum. These shall be operated in accordance with an intermediate criminal sanctions plan adopted by the chief judge of the judicial district and the director of the judicial district department of correctional services. The plan adopted shall be designed to reduce probation revocations to prison through the use of incremental, community-based sanctions for probation violations. The plan shall be subject to rules adopted by the department of corrections, and the plan should include a requirement for transferring individuals between levels in the continuum. The provisions shall include a requirement that the reasons for the transfer be in writing and that an opportunity for the individual to contest the transfer be made available. Nothing shall limit the district department's ability to seek a revocation of the client's probation if such action is deemed necessary (Iowa Department of Corrections, 2005).

In Wichita County, Texas, the Adult Probation Department has set forth a continuum of sanctions of probationers and others under supervision, including parolees (Wichita County Adult Probation, 2006). These sanctions include the following:

1. *Verbal counseling.* The officer explains the violation and details the consequences the offender faces for continued noncompliance. An example is the client failing to report for a scheduled office visit or visits.

2. *Written reprimand.* The behavior, because of its seriousness or repetitiveness, warrants additional action. The officer can put in writing the consequences that will be taken if the behavior continues. An example is the officer putting into writing that the next time the client fails to make a payment, the officer will request an administrative hearing.

3. *Agreed modification of probation.* The officer chooses to impose a sanction on the offender due to noncompliance. The officer may choose one or more of the sanctions listed in the agreed modification to correct the behavior. The sanctions include, but are not limited to, the offender working additional community service hours, attending outpatient substance abuse treatment, attending classes or programs that address anger of cognitive restructuring, and time in jail. The officer will limit the sanction to a period of time sufficient to bring the defendant into compliance. The agreed modification must be signed by the client and filed in the District Court Clerk's Office. The agreed modification becomes a required condition of the defendant's probation. An example is the defendant has a positive drug test. The probation officer uses the agreed modification with the defendant agreeing to attend outpatient substance abuse treatment to Serenity House (a drug treatment facility in Wichita County) or the Helen Farabee Intensive Substance Abuse Program (another treatment facility in Wichita County).

4. *Administrative hearing.* The officer is unable to change the noncompliant behavior of the defendant. The officer requests the supervisor to address the noncompliant behavior in a formal setting that requires the defendant to develop a plan of action to correct the behavior. An example is an offender is several months behind in court-ordered payments. The supervisor, in a formal setting, requires the defendant to provide a detailed budget of income and expenses and a plan to correct the arrearages. The supervisor and defendant sign an agreement and the officer monitors compliance based on the signed plan. If the plan is not met by the defendant, another sanction up to and including a violation report to the District Attorney is imposed.

5. *Violation report.* The officer notifies the District Attorney that the client is not in compliance with one or more terms of the probation and details the action taken by the department to correct the noncompliant behavior. The officer makes a recommendation of an appropriate action to be taken up and including revoking the defendant's probation.

The Wichita County Adult Probation sanctions continuum ranges from verbal reprimands from the supervising PO eventually to a violation report, which will result in a formal judicial hearing. The purpose of the hearing is to determine whether the client's probation program will be revoked. Judges have several options at this point. They can move the offender to an intensive supervised probation program or they can incarcerate the offender, similar to the actions taken by the Iowa continuum of sanctions. These graduated sanctions taken by the Wichita County Adult Probation Department are considered crucial in obtaining compliance from their supervised clients. The overall intent of such sanctions is to reduce their recidivism, not just technical violations, but also law violations. It is considered contempt of court when a probationer fails to observe one or more probation program conditions, and such a charge may be lodged against the offender. This means a new criminal charge may be added to the client's offense history. Probation authorities do not wish to contribute to an offender's criminal history; rather, they want to help offenders avoid such sanctions and punishments (Wichita County Adult Probation, 2006).

A third county-based program with graduated sanctions is the Williamson County Adult Probation Department in Texas (Williamson County Adult Probation, 2006). Their plan includes both pre-adjudication and post-adjudication continuums of sanctions. These include the following:

I. Pre-Adjudication

1. Pre-trial release

2. PSI reports

3. Deferred adjudication

II. Post-Adjudication

1. Diagnostic screening for alcohol and drugs; level of education; mental impairment

2. Sexual dysfunction

3. Supervision, including regular, specialized caseloads (sex offenders, special-needs offenders, substance abusers, ignition interlock, and absconders)

III. Residential/Custodial Facilities

1. Transition treatment centers

2. Halfway houses

3. Oxford Houses

4. 3/4 Homes

5. Intermediate sanctions facilities (ISF)

6. House arrest

7. Jail

8. Boot camp

9. State jail

10. Prison

IV. Adjunct Services/Sanctions

IVa. Cognitive Education Programs:

1. Substance abuse education

2. Cognitive education

IVb. Education Programs:

1. Education/vocational services

2. English speakers of other languages

3. Life skills training

4. Project Better Chance

V. Drug and Delinquency Prevention

VI. Electronic Monitoring

VII. Urinalysis

VIII. Community Service Restitution

IX. Y.I.E.L.D. Program

X. Alcohol and Drug Education

1. Repeat offender

2. Drug offender education

3. Basic drug education

4. Alcohol traffic safety/DWI education

5. MADD victim impact panel

6. Advanced alcohol and drug education

7. Outpatient treatment

8. Alcoholics Anonymous

9. Adult Children of Alcoholics

10. ALANON

XI. Assault Prevention Programs

1. Anger management

2. Assault prevention

3. Chronic anger management program

4. Family violence diversion network

5. Batterer's Intervention and Prevention Program (BIPP)

XII. Sex Offender Counseling

1. Individual

2. Group

XIII. Theft Prevention.

1. Bad Check Program

2. Crossroads Program

3. Multiple Offender Program

4. Shoplifting

XIV. Financial Counseling

1. Consumer credit counseling services

2. Crossroads Program

3. Money-sense class

4. Debtors Anonymous

The Williamson County Adult Probation Department says that the purpose of sanctions is to provide officers with a variety of sanctions that will aid in supervising offenders in the community as long as is possible or practical. The continuum of sanctions includes programs and services that are either operated by the department or contracted from within the community (Williamson County Adult Probation, 2006).

When probationers fail to abide by their program conditions, they face probation revocation. While judges are not disposed to locking up all persons who face revocation action, that option exists nevertheless. Much depends on the attitude of the offender, the nature and persistence of the offending as well as its seriousness, and the prospects for future good conduct from the offender if their probation program is continued. Under a worst-case scenario, probation revocation actions will occur.

THE PROBATION REVOCATION PROCESS

What if probationers violate one or more conditions of their probation? First, the program violation must be detected. Second, if it is detected, the detector, usually the PO, must decide whether to report it. Third, if it is reported, it may or may not be serious enough to warrant a hearing by a judge. Fourth, if it is serious enough to warrant a hearing by a judge, it may or may not result in the termination of the probationer's program. Fifth, if the probationer's probation program is terminated, it may or may not result in prison or jail confinement. This means that a judge could resentence the probationer to a different type of probation program involving more intensive supervised probation, perhaps a program involving home confinement and/or electronic monitoring. Therefore, the probation revocation process, whenever it is initiated, may lead anywhere (Barbee, Eosemberg, and Gunter, 2002). A North Carolina order on violation of probation is shown in Figure 6.5.

Technically, any probation program violation is regarded seriously whenever it is detected. If the PO determines that the probationer violated curfew by one or more minutes, this is a curfew violation and could be reported. If the probationer were to test positive for drugs or alcohol, this type of program violation is regarded as serious and could be reported. Much discretionary power rests with the PO and his or her relationship with the particular probationer/client. Usually an attempt is made to determine why the program violation occurred. Notes maintained by the PO indicate whether or not the offense has occurred before, and if so, how often. In reality, POs prioritize probation program requirements and treat their seriousness on a graduated scale known only to them. Reporting a probationer for a technical program violation involves a certain amount of paperwork and a subsequent court appearance. Thus, this is a time-consuming process and one that POs often seek to avoid. Therefore, only the most serious program violations are often considered for formal action, such as committing new crimes or being visibly impaired from chronic substance or alcohol abuse. Some POs use graduated sanctions as ways of encouraging their clients to become more law-abiding without formal court intervention (Howell and Gamble, 2006).

Interestingly, POs know much about their probationer/clients and whether they will complete their probation programs successfully. For instance, probationers with less education and a record of numerous prior arrests are more likely to fail in their probation programs. Less education would mean that certain offenders had not completed high school. Offenders with a history of substance abuse and who were under- or unemployed preceding their instant conviction offenses are also more likely to fail during the period of their probation. Those POs who take greater interest in their clients might likely refer them to certain community services where some or all of their needs can be addressed. But high PO caseloads in many jurisdictions often mean that POs can spend very little or no time face-to-face with their clients.

Whether formal probation revocation proceedings will occur involves a great deal of PO discretion. However, there are certain factors or events that are beyond a PO's direct control. For instance, a probationer may be arrested for and charged with a crime. The probationer may be carrying a concealed weapon and the weapon is discovered by police officers or detectives who are interviewing witnesses at a crime scene. The probationer may get in an automobile accident while driving a car he or she is not supposed to be driving. Official reports filed by different law enforcement agencies cannot be ignored. The fact that a person is

STATE OF NORTH CAROLINA

File No.
Co. Of Hearing

_____ County_____   Seat of Court

NOTE: *(This form is not to be used for structured sentencing offenses.)*

In The General Court Of Justice
☐ District ☐ Superior Court Division

STATE VERSUS

Name Of Defendant

Attorney For State

☐ Def. Found Not Indigent ☐ Def. Waived Attorney

Attorney For Defendant

☐ Appointed ☐ Retained

**ORDER ON VIOLATION
OF PROBATION
OR ON MOTION TO MODIFY**

☐ **AND COMMITMENT ON SPECIAL PROBATION**

G.S. 15A-1344, 15A-1345

The defendant was placed on probation pursuant to the following Judgment Suspending Sentence:

Date Of Judgment Suspending Sentence

☐ Superior Court
☐ District Court

Name Of County And File No. (County Of Original Conviction)

This matter is before the Court upon: *(check one option)*

☐ 1. review under G.S. 15A-1342(b) or (d). After reasonable notice to the defendant, the Court ☐ finds ☐ does not find that termination of probation is warranted by the defendant's conduct and the ends of justice.

☐ 2. a motion to modify the conditions of the defendant's probation for good cause without charge of violation. After notice and hearing, or upon the consent of the State and the defendant, the Court ☐ finds ☐ does not find that good cause has been shown to modify the original Judgment Suspending Sentence.

☐ 3. charge(s) of violation. After considering the record contained in the files numbered above, together with the evidence presented by the parties and the statements made on behalf of the State and the defendant, the Court finds that the defendant is charged with having violated specified conditions of the defendant's probation as alleged in the Violation Report or Notice

Upon due notice or waiver of notice, a hearing was held before the Court and:

☐ 1. the defendant admitted or the Court is reasonably satisfied in the exercise of its discretion that the defendant has violated each of the conditions of probation set forth in

☐ a. paragraphs _____ in the Violation Report or Notice of Hearing dated _____ .
☐ b. the attached sheet.

The defendant violated each condition willfully and without valid excuse; and each violation occurred at a time prior to the expiration or termination of the period of the defendant's probation.

☐ 2. by the evidence presented, the Court is not reasonably satisfied that the defendant has violated any of the conditions of the defendant's probation except those found above, if any.

ORDER

It is ORDERED that:

☐ 1. the original Judgment is modified as set forth below and, except as specifically so modified, shall remain in full force and effect.

☐ 2. the original Judgment is not modified, but remains in full force and effect.

☐ 3. the defendant's limited driving privilege is REVOKED; the defendant shall surrender all copies of that privilege to the Clerk of Superior Court for transmittal/notification to the Division of Motor Vehicles.

☐ 4. the defendant's probation is terminated.

☐ 5. all charges of probation violation in this case, which are not specifically found above, are dismissed.

☐ 6. the disposition of this matter is continued until _____ .

SPECIAL PROBATION/ACTIVE SENTENCE

☐ As a condition of special probation, the defendant shall ☐ serve an active term of _____ ☐ days ☐ months in the custody of the ☐ N.C. DOC. ☐ Sheriff of this County. ☐ submit to IMPACT imprisonment per attached AOC-CR-302, Page Two. ☐ pay jail ☐ work release recommended. **(NOTE:** *This term shall NOT be reduced by jail or treatment time, good time, gain time or parole.)*

The defendant shall report in a sober condition to begin serving this term on:

| Day | Date | Hour | ☐ AM ☐ PM | and shall remain in custody until: | Day | Date | Hour | ☐ AM ☐ PM |

☐ The defendant shall again report in a sober condition to continue serving this term on the same day of the week for the next _____ consecutive weeks, and shall remain in custody during the same hours each week.

MODIFIED MONETARY CONDITIONS

The "Monetary Conditions" in the Judgment Suspending Sentence are modified to read as follows: Pay to Clerk of Superior Court ☐ $_____ on or before _____ .

☐ the "Modified Amount Due" shown below, plus the monthly probation supervision fee set by law ☐ pursuant to a schedule determined by the probation officer ☐ at the rate of $_____ per _____ , beginning on _____ and continuing on the same day of each _____ thereafter until paid in full.

☐ Other:

| Balance On Original Obligation* | Arrearage On Probation Fee | Attorney Fee This Proceeding | Modified Amount Due |
| $ | $ | $ | $ |

*Equals "Total Amount Due" as shown on original Judgment, less all payments made to date, and adjusted to reflect any modifications on Side

AOC-CR-316, Rev. 9/02
© 2002 Administrative Office of the Courts

Material opposite unmarked squares is to be disregarded as surplusage.

FIGURE 6.5   North Carolina Order on Violation of Probation.

on probation is a matter of public record. When a probationer gets into any type of trouble with a law enforcement agency of any kind, there is bound to be a report made of that trouble to the court who has jurisdiction over that probationer.

Under present law in every U.S. jurisdiction, probationers are entitled to a hearing before the judge if their probation is in jeopardy. Thus, if a PO is charged with committing either a technical probation program violation (e.g., curfew violation, frequenting a place where alcoholic beverages are served) or a crime, then the matter of revoking one's probation is referred to the original sentencing court for further action.

OTHER MODIFICATIONS OF PROBATION

☐ 1. The defendant's term of probation is extended for a period of _____ , from _____ to _____ .

☐ 2. The defendant's assignment to the Intensive Probation Supervision Program is terminated and the defendant is continued on supervised probation.

☐ 3. The defendant is transferred to ☐ unsupervised ☐ supervised probation.

☐ 4. The defendant is allowed until _____ to comply with the following condition(s)

☐ 5. The special conditions of probation identified below, as numbered and set out in the Judgment Suspending Sentence, are modified as follows: *(state number of each condition to be modified and set out modification.)*

☐ 6. The defendant shall also comply with the following additional special conditions of probation which the Court finds are reasonably related to the defendant's rehabilitation:

    ☐ complete _____ hours of community service during the first _____ days of probation, as directed by the community service coordinator, and pay the fee prescribed by G.S. 143B-475.1(b).

    ☐ Other: *(set out conditions)*

☐ 7. Comply with the Additional Conditions of Probation which are set forth on AOC-CR-302, Page Two, attached.

CONTEMPT

NOTE: *This Contempt section applies to a defendant* <u>sentenced</u> *on or after May 1, 1994. [G.S. 5A-11(a)(9a) and 15A-1344.]*

Upon due notice or waiver of notice, a hearing was held before the Court and the defendant is found guilty of contempt beyond a reasonable doubt.
It is ORDERED that the defendant for willful contempt:

    ☐ a. be imprisoned for _____ days in the custody of the sheriff.

    ☐ b. pay a fine of _____ .

    ☐ c. Other: _____

AWARD OF FEE TO COUNSEL FOR DEFENDANT

☐ A hearing was held in open court in the presence of the defendant at which time a fee, including expenses, was awarded the defendant's appointed counsel or assigned public defender in this proceeding.

ORDER OF COMMITMENT/APPEAL ENTRIES

☐ 1. It is ORDERED that the Clerk deliver <u>two</u> certified copies of this Order and Commitment to the sheriff or other qualified officer and that the officer cause the defendant to be delivered with these copies to the custody of the agency named on the reverse to serve the sentence imposed or until the defendant shall have complied with the conditions of release pending appeal.

☐ 2. The defendant gives notice of appeal from the judgment of the District Court to the Superior Court. The current pretrial release order is modified as follows: _____

☐ 3. The defendant gives notice of appeal from the judgment of the Superior Court to the Appellate Division. Appeal entries and any conditions of post conviction release are set forth on form AOC-CR-350.

SIGNATURE OF JUDGE

Date	Name Of Presiding Judge (Type Or Print)	Signature Of Presiding Judge

CERTIFICATION

I certify that this Order and the attachment(s) marked below is a true and complete copy of the original which is on file in this case.
☐ 1. Appellate Entries (AOC-CR-350)
☐ 2. Additional Conditions Of Probation (AOC-CR-302, Page Two)
☐ 3. Judgment Suspending Sentence *(Check only if a term of imprisonment is imposed as a new condition of special probation.)*

Date Of Certification	Date Certified Copies Delivered To Sheriff	Signature And Seal
		☐ Deputy CSC ☐ Assistant CSC ☐ Clerk Of Superior Court

(NOTE: *Defendant signs the following statement in all cases of supervised probation except where probation is terminated or is not modified.)*
I have received a copy of this Order which contains modifications of my probation and I agree to them. I understand that no person who supervises me or for whom I work while performing community or reparation service is liable to me for any loss or damage which I may sustain unless my injury is caused by that person's gross negligence or intentional wrongdoing. I understand that my probation may be

Date Signed	Signature Of Defendant	Witnessed By

NOTE: *Send a Certified Copy to the Clerk of Superior Court of the County of Original Conviction, if Different.*

AOC-CR-316, Side Two, Rev. 9/02
©2002 Administrative Office of the Courts   Material opposite unmarked squares is to be disregarded as surplusage.

FIGURE 6.5   (Continued).

The court must conduct a two-stage proceeding. Allegations against the probationer must be heard by the judge. Supporting evidentiary information must be presented to show the probationer's guilt relating to the charges filed. The probationer is permitted to introduce exculpatory information on his or her own behalf and to offer supporting testimony. All of this evidence is heard in the first stage of a two-stage revocation process. Therefore, the first stage of a probation revocation hearing is to determine the guilt or innocence of the accused relating to the probation program violation, whatever it may be. If the judge determines that there is no basis for the allegations, then the matter is concluded. The probationer

STATE VERSUS	File No.
Name Of Defendant	

ADDITIONAL CONDITIONS OF PROBATION - G.S. 15A-1343(b1)

NOTE: *Use this page in conjunction with AOC-CR-302, "Judgment Suspending Sentence"; AOC-CR-310, "Impaired Driving Judgment Suspending Sentence"; or AOC-CR-316, "Order On Charge Of Violation Of Probation Or On Motion To Modify".*

In addition to complying with the regular and any special conditions of probation set forth in the "Judgment Suspending Sentence" entered in the above case(s), the defendant shall also comply with the following special conditions of probation and conditions of special probation, which the Court finds are reasonably related to the defendant's rehabilitation.

☐ Be assigned to the INTENSIVE PROBATION SUPERVISION PROGRAM for a period of not less than six months, obey all rules, regulations and directions of the program until discharged, and

1. Submit at reasonable times to warrantless searches by a probation officer of the defendant's person, and of the defendant's vehicle and premises while the defendant is present, for the following purposes which are reasonably related to the defendant's probation supervision:
☐ stolen goods ☐ controlled substances ☐ contraband ☐ _____

2. Not use, possess or control any illegal drug or controlled substance unless it has been prescribed for the defendant by a licensed physician and is in the original container with the prescription number affixed on it; not knowingly associate with any known or previously convicted users, possessors or sellers of any illegal drugs or controlled substances; and not knowingly be present at or frequent any place where illegal drugs or controlled substances are sold, kept or used.

3. Supply a breath, urine and/or blood specimen for analysis of the possible presence of a prohibited drug or alcohol, when instructed by the defendant's probation officer.

4. Complete not less than _____ hours or more than _____ hours of community or reparation service, as determined by the defendant's probation officer, and under the direction of the community service coordinator and pay the fee prescribed by G.S. 143B-475.1(b) ☐ within _____ days of this Judgment and before beginning service.

5. Participate in any evaluation, counseling, treatment or education program as directed by the defendant's probation officer, faithfully keep all scheduled appointments, and abide by all rules, regulations and directions of each program.

6. Not be away from the defendant's place of residence between the hours of _____ p.m. and _____ a.m. unless authorized in writing by the defendant's probation officer.

7. Not leave the defendant's county of residence without prior approval of the defendant's probation officer.

8. Other:

☐ Submit as directed by the defendant's probation officer to a medical evaluation by a physician approved by the officer and, if certified to be medically fit for participation in the Intensive Motivation Program of Alternative Correctional Treatment (IMPACT), further submit, as ordered by the officer, on the date and at the place specified, to imprisonment in a facility for youthful offenders for a period of 90 days from that date, and abide by all rules and regulations as provided in conjunction with the IMPACT program, provided:

a. at the end of this 90 day period, the defendant shall continue to submit to imprisonment for an additional period of 30 days if required to do so as provided in those rules and regulations, and

b. If, within _____ days from the date of this Judgment, the defendant is not certified to be medically fit for program participation or for any other reason is not ordered to submit to imprisonment as provided above then ☐ the defendant shall reappear before the Court as directed by the probation officer for a hearing to determine what modifications, if any, should be made to this Judgment.
☐ Other:

☐ *(Use this option when placing defendant under house arrest as a special condition of supervised probation in any case, or as a condition of supervised special probation upon conviction of DWI under G.S. 20-138.1 and imposition of Level One or Level Two imprisonment. In DWI cases, check the block at the end of this option, see G.S. 20-179(g) and (h), and designate days of imprisonment and house arrest accordingly.)* Be assigned to the Electronic House Arrest Program for a period of _____ days, submit to electronic monitoring and abide by all rules, regulations and directions of the program until discharged ☐ and before being assigned, serve a term of imprisonment of _____ days in the custody of the sheriff of this county.

☐ Other Conditions:

Date	Name Of Presiding Judge (Type Or Print)	Signature Of Presiding Judge

AOC-CR-302, Page Two, Rev. 7/2000
© 2000 Administrative Office of the Courts   Material opposite unmarked squares to be disregarded as surplusage.

FIGURE 6.5   (Continued).

remains on his or her probation program. However, if the judge determines that the probationer is guilty of the allegations, then a second stage is conducted. This second stage may be conducted in court after a recess. During this second stage of the two-stage process, the judge determines what the penalty should be for violating the particular program requirement(s).

Judges are encouraged to avoid incarcerating probationers if it is reasonable to do so under particular circumstances. Judges may determine that even though the probationer has violated one or more program conditions based on the evidence presented, that the probationer should be permitted to continue in his or her probation

BOX 6.3

INTERNATIONAL SNAPSHOT: PROBATION AND PAROLE IN CANADA

Canada is a federalist country and a member of the British Commonwealth, consisting of 10 provinces and two territories. A parliamentary democratic government consists of executive and legislative powers and is split between the central and provincial units. The criminal laws of Canada are based on the Canadian Criminal Code, which was enacted in 1892. Subsequently in 1955, there were substantial revisions and numerous amendments. The Criminal Code has been revised continuously up to the present, and it is based largely on the English system of criminal jurisprudence across the country. Parole in Canada was established in 1959 through the Parole Act and the National Parole Board was created. This act was amended in 1977 to enable individual provinces to establish their own parole boards for determining inmate early releases. Although parole boards exist now in most provinces, the National Parole Board continues to have jurisdiction in provinces that have not established their own parole boards.

A Narcotics Control Act was passed in 1970 because of increased drug trafficking and drug abuse. Shortly thereafter, the Bail Reform Act was passed in 1971. This act limits the warrantless arrest powers of police by requiring suspects to be released if police do not have reasonable or probable grounds to believe that the public interest or safety would be jeopardized if such persons were released. Today, the standard is that if someone is charged with a crime that has a five-years-or-less prison sentence associated with it, and if the police officer has no reasonable/probable grounds to believe that (1) continued detention is necessary in the public interest, (2) that the accused is unlikely to attend a subsequent trial if released, and (3) that the issue of releases is of such a serious nature that it should be dealt with by a justice of the peace, then bail will generally be granted to such persons. Furthermore, a Juvenile Offenders Act was passed in 1985. This act raised the age of minimum criminal responsibility to 12 years of age for all provinces

and territories. It also set the age of adult criminal responsibility at age 18 throughout all of Canada. It is possible for youthful offenders to be processed as adults at the recommendation of youth court judges. Juveniles may also avoid prosecution through diversion, which is practiced extensively. Diversion is an alternative measures program initiated at the request of the prosecutor. For juveniles especially, if they are subject to a formal prosecution, then there is a broad range of sentencing options usually imposed, consisting of community service, restitution, treatment, restorative justice, or possible secure custody to absolute discharge. Individual provinces are vested with powers to decide all juvenile cases involving persons age 12 or younger. Social service agencies are primarily responsible for regulating these youths.

Crimes are generally divided into three categories: (1) summary offenses, which are the least serious crimes (e.g., public disturbance, traffic violations); (2) indictable offenses, or the most serious crimes (e.g., murder, rape, robbery) and involve minimum confinement in a penitentiary for two or more years; and (3) hybrid offenses, which are dual offenses that can be prosecuted as either summary or indictable offenses, depending on prosecutorial discretion (e.g., breaking and entering, petty theft). Summary offenses are largely localized ordinances varying in complexity from one territory or province to the next. These are defined most often by municipal or provincial legislation. Summary offense punishments most often involve probation, fines with a maximum of $2,000, and/or a maximum of six months in a provincial prison. A special classification of crimes is known as supreme court exclusive offenses. Some of these offenses include treason and piracy. Definitions of indictable offenses are uniform throughout all Canadian jurisdictions.

The police forces of Canada are divided into provincial, municipal, and federal units. The federal police agency is the Royal Canadian Mounted Police. These officers have jurisdiction in all territories and provinces relating to crimes of a federal nature, much like the FBI in the United States. Municipal police have jurisdiction for various cities, including Toronto, Montreal, and other urban areas. Smaller city, village, county, and township police forces exist and are responsible for the enforcement of local laws. Suspects may be arrested with or without a warrant. Following arrests, suspects must be brought before justices of the peace within 24 hours for further processing. Pretrial detention is only infrequently used, except in the most serious cases. Determining bail can last up to eight days and is determined by the justice of the peace.

Persons accused of crimes are entitled to most rights associated with U.S. case processing. Suspects who are indigent will be provided court-appointed counsel to represent them. Most provinces have legal aid systems for this purpose. The police often serve as prosecutors. Private citizens may function as prosecutors under certain circumstances as well, in so-called private prosecutions. Trials are held for persons facing indictable offense charges, but defendants are given the choice of a trial by jury or a bench trial, where the judge decides the case exclusively. About 70–80 percent of all persons charged with indictable offenses will stand trial. Diversion exists as an alternative to trial for the least serious offenses as well as for more youthful first-offenders. Alternative dispute resolution and restorative justice programs operate in most Canadian jurisdictions. Only about 10 percent of all criminal cases each year are heard before a judge and jury.

The court system of Canada consists of the Supreme Court of Canada (like the U.S. Supreme Court), which hears appeals for both summary and indictable offense convictions. A Court of Appeal exists to hear summary and indictable offense conviction appeals in less serious cases. District and county courts and provincial courts/criminal division hear all summary offense cases. Each province has three levels of trial courts. The highest is the superior court of criminal jurisdiction. This court has jurisdiction over all indictable offense cases. The name of this court varies among provinces. The second type of court is the court of criminal jurisdiction. This court has jurisdiction over all indictable offenses except for the most serious offenses, which must be tried by the superior court of criminal jurisdiction. The third court is the summary conviction court. Provincial judges or magistrates preside over these courts and try only summary offenses. For juveniles there are youth courts. In cases involving native Canadian defendants, circle courts exist. These are located in more remote regions of Canada and are connected closely with close-knit community norms and laws. These involve restorative justice principles, and a panel of a defendant's peers, victims, family members, the prosecutor, the defense attorney, and other interested parties is convened to decide the case and potential punishment, which is almost always rehabilitative and oriented toward restitution and community service.

Once persons are convicted, the trial judge imposes the sentence. Judges are obliged to follow maximum, minimum, and fixed penalty guidelines that are provided by statute for all offense categories. There is no provision for a special sentencing hearing, although they do occur. Sentencing may occur at the time of conviction. All convictions may be appealed. Expert witnesses and others testify about accused persons and whether they are mentally fit. Judges consider the mental status of defendants when imposing sentences.

The range of penalties is from life imprisonment (Canada has no death penalty), to deprivation of liberty for a period of years or months, to control of freedom (through probation or some form of offender monitoring), verbal warnings and admonitions, community service orders, and restitution/compensation. Split sentences are possible where multiple offenses have been committed. Sentences may also be intermittent, involving serving time on weekends so that offenders may retain their present jobs and support their dependents.

Probation is used extensively. Probation conditions are similar to those in the United States. Probationers are required to abide by various conditions set by the court and enforced by the probation departments in the different provinces or territories. Most large urban areas

(*continued*)

BOX 6.3 (*Continued*)

have community residential centers, which probationers must attend on a regular basis and for fixed time periods. The aims of probation in Canada are rehabilitation, community reintegration, and self-improvement. These are accomplished by an interconnected network of social and vocational services, including counseling, vocational/educational training, and other treatments. There is a great deal of probation variation among provinces and territories. Thus the Canadian probation system is highly decentralized. Community service orders are frequently imposed, where probationers must work or donate their time to the community by the completion of so many community service hours. Imprisonment is considered as a last resort by Canadian authorities. It is unusual for first-offenders to be incarcerated unless a serious crime has been committed, such as murder, rape, robbery, or child sexual abuse. Offenders who serve probationary terms and are convicted of new offenses may be re-sentenced to probation. It may take five or six probation sentences before these persons will actually be imprisoned. Again, the thrust of the Canadian criminal justice system is on offender rehabilitation and reintegration.

The prison system of Canada is complex. There are federal penitentiaries where persons are housed who have committed federal crimes and are sentenced to two or more years. Other offenders serving shorter sentences are incarcerated in provincial prisons. Offenders entering all prisons are classified initially through a rigorous classification process. This classification enables prison officials to individualize offender needs and identify particular programming that will assist them most effectively. Vocational, educational, and counseling opportunities are provided in every prison for those inmates who desire to participate. Thus, there are prison industries that train inmates in various skills, such as laundry, shoe manufacture, clothing manufacture, farming, and machine operation. Inmates lacking education are encouraged to work toward their G E D or high school diplomas. They are also encouraged to enroll in college programs where offered. For certain inmates, participation is mandatory. Canada does not have any private prisons. Some privatization

has occurred through the establishment of halfway houses and other community services.

Parole may be granted once offenders have served one-sixth of their sentences. Both federal and provincial inmates may be released on full or day parole. Another type of parole is through the Mandatory Release Program. This is a federal program providing for the mandatory release of inmates who have served two-thirds of their prison time and who have exhibited good behavior. But they must remain in their communities under the supervision of parole officers until the duration of their original sentences expires. Parole officers assist parolees in finding employment, obtaining housing, and helping with personal problems.

Various Canadian provinces have Temporary Absence programs, which are similar to U.S. furloughs. Inmates may be released for short, unsupervised time periods of up to 15 days, but they must return to their prisons at specified times. There are harsh penalties for noncompliance with these directives. These Temporary Absence programs are pre-parole programs and are very effective at enabling inmates to locate work and housing and support their families and other dependents. Under mandatory release, parolees are not responsible to parole boards, but they are accountable to their parole officers, who exercise a great deal of discretion.

Probation services are operated through the Adult Corrections Services. In 2005 there were over 130,000 persons on probation. A total of 166,000 persons were under some form of correctional service supervision that same year. About 10 percent of these persons were women. One-third of all incarcerated females are Aboriginals, while 20 percent of all incarcerated male offenders are Aboriginals. There were approximately 1,200 parolees under supervision in the various provinces. One explanation for the relatively low number of parolees in Canada is that the prison population across all territories and provinces in 2005 was approximately 35,000. It has been estimated that probationers make up about 85 percent of all offenders under supervision during any given year, although these figures fluctuate. The amount of imprisonment in Canada has declined gradually between 1995 and 2005. Some reasons for this decrease include less reported crime in the provinces and territories during this period and greater use of community-based programming in lieu of imprisonment. For instance, in 2000 there were 1,900 parolees. The 2005 figure is substantially lower. Furthermore, more judges are crediting offenders with time served on remand or pretrial detention. Thus prison sentence lengths are shortened accordingly. Generally, govern-ment funding of correctional resources has declined over the years. This is due to decreased prison populations and growing community corrections, which cost far less to operate.

Sources: Adapted from Debra Cohen and Sandra Longtin, "Canada" *World Factbook of Criminal Justice Systems,* New York, 2004; "Adult Correctional Services, 2003/2004," *The Daily,* December 16, 2005; Saskatchewan Corrections and Public Safety, "Volunteers in Probation," November 2005.

program for its duration. Or judges may decide to impose additional conditions to one's program as sanctions or penalties. The offender may be required to make restitution to victims, pay a fine, or enter into mediation with one or more other parties. Or the offender may be placed in home confinement and/or electronic monitoring. Or the offender may be required to have more frequent face-to-face visits with the PO in an intensive supervision scenario. If the program violation is serious enough, the judge has the authority to terminate one's probation program and order the probationer incarcerated. These are the options available to judges. Below are some leading cases relating to probation revocation. The next section also contains several common scenarios involving probationers and how different state jurisdictions have concluded these revocation actions.

Special Circumstances: Mandatory Federal Probation Revocation

Federal district court judges have been exposed to numerous changes in sentencing laws during the 1980s and 1990s. The Sentencing Reform Act of 1984 led to the promulgation of **U.S. sentencing guidelines**, which went into effect in October 1987. Federal district court judges were obligated to follow these guidelines as closely as possible, although they have been allowed to engage in upward or downward departures from these guidelines in sentencing certain offenders, provided that they furnish a written rationale for doing so.

In 1994, Congress passed the Violent Crime and Law Enforcement Act (VCCA), which further affected federal judges and the sentences they imposed. Of particular interest were changes in sentencing regulations that pertained to revoking the probation programs of federal offenders. In the pre-VCCA period (pre–September 1994), federal district court judges could revoke a federal probationer's probation program, but the revocation sentence must fall within the guideline range available for the original sentence. However, in the post-VCCA period, a revocation sentence could be any sentence that the court could have imposed at the time of the original sentence. For example, if a probationer had originally been sentenced to 12 months of probation resulting from a recommendation from the federal prosecutor for a downward guideline departure, a subsequent revocation sentence from the court could be for a 24-month probationary sentence or even imprisonment, absent a renewal motion from the federal prosecutor. Under the post-VCCA sentencing scheme, a federal judge could impose any sentence that could have been imposed at the original sentencing date, regardless of prosecutorial recommendations.

Under a new post-VCCA provision, a revocation sentence resulting from drug possession must result in a term of imprisonment. This is a new mandatory sentence. Although it is mandatory, the court may determine that the revoked probationer may benefit from drug treatment as an alternative to incarceration. This is a very narrow option, which is contained in the new post-VCCA provisions. However, if the mandatory incarcerative term is imposed, it must be at least one-third of the maximum guideline provision for the original offense. Thus, if the original sentence had an upper guideline of 30 months, then the term of incarceration that the court must impose would be 10 months, absent any consideration given to one's amenability to drug treatment (Adair, 2000:67–68).

LANDMARK CASES AND SPECIAL ISSUES

In this section we examine several U.S. Supreme Court cases that have affected probationers and the conditions under which judges may revoke their probation programs. Several cases are highlighted that have had national significance and application. Other cases are described at the state level, where individual state supreme or appellate courts have ruled in particular probation revocation matters. The issues described in each of the following scenarios are generally applicable among the states, with very few and limited exceptions.

U.S. Supreme Court Cases

Mempa v. Rhay (1967).   Jerry Mempa was convicted of "joyriding" in a stolen vehicle on June 17, 1959. He was placed on probation for two years by a Spokane, Washington, judge. Several months later, Mempa was involved in a burglary on September 15, 1959. The county prosecutor in Spokane moved to have Mempa's probation revoked. Mempa admitted participating in the burglary. At his probation revocation hearing, the sole testimony about his involvement in the burglary came from his probation officer. Mempa was not represented by counsel, was not asked if he wanted counsel, and was not given an opportunity to offer statements in his own behalf. Furthermore, there was no cross-examination of the probation officer about his statements. The court revoked Mempa's probation and sentenced him to ten years in the Washington State Penitentiary.

Six years later in 1965, Mempa filed a writ of **habeas corpus**, alleging that he had been denied a right to counsel at the revocation hearing. The Washington Supreme Court denied his petition, but the U.S. Supreme Court elected to hear it on appeal. The U.S. Supreme Court overturned the Washington decision and ruled in Mempa's favor. Specifically, the U.S. Supreme Court said Mempa was entitled to an attorney but was denied one. While the Court did not question Washington authority to defer sentencing in the probation matter, it said that any indigent (including Mempa) is entitled at every stage of a criminal proceeding to be represented by court-appointed counsel, where "substantial rights of a criminal accused may be affected." Thus, the U.S. Supreme Court considered a probation revocation hearing to be a "critical stage" that falls within the due process provisions of the Fourteenth Amendment. In subsequent years, several courts also applied this decision to parole revocation hearings.

Gagnon v. Scarpelli (1973).   Gerald Scarpelli pled guilty to a charge of robbery in July 1965 in a Wisconsin court. He was sentenced to 15 years in prison. But the judge suspended this sentence on August 5, 1965, and placed Scarpelli on probation for a period of 7 years. The next day, August 6, Scarpelli was arrested and charged with burglary. His probation was revoked without a hearing and he was placed in the Wisconsin State Reformatory to serve his 15-year term. About three years later, Scarpelli was paroled. Shortly before his parole, he filed a *habeas corpus* petition, alleging that his probation revocation was invoked without a hearing and without benefit of counsel. Thus, this constituted a denial of due process. Following his parole, the U.S. Supreme Court acted on his original *habeas corpus* petition and ruled in his favor. Specifically, the U.S. Supreme Court said that Scarpelli was denied his right to due process because no revocation hearing was held and he was not represented by court-appointed counsel within the indigent claim. In effect, the Court, referring to *Morrissey v. Brewer* (1972), said that "a probation revocation, like parole revocation, is not a stage of a criminal prosecution, but does result in loss of liberty. . . . We hold that a probationer, like a parolee, is entitled to a preliminary hearing and a final revocation hearing in the conditions specified in *Morrissey v. Brewer.*"

The significance of this case is that it equated probation with parole as well as the respective revocation proceedings. While the Court did not say that all parolees and probationers have a right to representation by counsel in all probation and parole revocation proceedings, it did say that counsel should be provided in cases where the probationer or parolee makes a timely claim contesting the allegations. While no constitutional basis exists for providing counsel in all probation or parole revocation proceedings, subsequent probation and parole revocation hearings usually involve defense counsel if legitimately requested. The U.S. Supreme Court declaration has been liberally interpreted in subsequent cases.

Bearden v. Georgia (1983).   Bearden's probation was revoked by Georgia authorities because he failed to pay a fine and make restitution to his victim as required by the court. He claimed he was indigent, but the court rejected his claim as a valid explanation for his conduct. The U.S. Supreme Court disagreed. It ruled that probation may not be revoked in the case of indigent probationers who have failed to pay their fines or make restitution. They further suggested alternatives for restitution and punishments that were more compatible with the abilities and economic resources of indigent probationers, such as community service. In short, the probationer should not be penalized where a reasonable effort has been made to pay court-ordered fines and restitution. The states have ruled similarly in more recent cases (*People v. Bouyer,* 2002; *United States v. Jones,* 2002).

Offender indigence does not automatically entitle them to immunity from restitution orders. In a 1993 case, *United States v. Bachsian* (1993), Bachsian was convicted of theft. He was required to pay restitution for the merchandise still in his possession under the Victim Witness Protection Act. Bachsian claimed, however, that he was indigent and unable to make restitution. The Ninth Circuit Court of Appeals declared in Bachsian's case said that it was not improper to impose restitution orders on an offender at the time of sentencing, even if the offender was unable to pay restitution then. In this instance, records indicated that Bachsian was considered by the court as having a future ability to pay, based on a presentence investigation report. Eventually, Bachsian would become financially able and in a position to make restitution to his victim. His restitution orders were upheld. Also, bankruptcy does not discharge an offender's obligation to make restitution, although the amount and rate of restitution payments may be affected (*United States v. Leigh*, 2002).

Black v. Romano (1985).   A probationer had his probation revoked by the sentencing judge because of alleged program violations. The defendant had left the scene of an automobile accident, a felony in the jurisdiction where the alleged offense occurred. The judge gave reasons for the revocation decision, but did not indicate that he had considered any option other than incarceration. The U.S. Supreme Court ruled that judges are not generally obligated to consider alternatives to incarceration before they revoke an offender's probation and place him in jail or prison. Clearly, probationers and parolees have obtained substantial rights in recent years. U.S. Supreme Court decisions have provided them with several important constitutional rights that invalidate the arbitrary and capricious revocation of their probation or parole programs by judges or parole boards. The two-stage hearing is extremely important to probationers and parolees, in that it permits ample airing of the allegations against offender, cross-examinations by counsel, and testimony from individual offenders.

Selected State Cases

Separate punishment hearings are not required in probation revocation proceedings, where the probationer has an adequate opportunity to present mitigating evidence during the revocation proceeding. Euler was a Texas offender convicted of a crime and sentenced to four years' imprisonment, but the sentence was suspended and Euler was placed on probation instead (*Euler v. State*, 2005). During his probation program, he allegedly violated one or more terms of his probation program and a probation revocation action was undertaken. The trial court conducted a probation revocation hearing and determined that Euler had indeed violated the terms of his probation. The probation program was revoked and the judge ordered Euler to prison. Euler appealed, asking the court to conduct a separate punishment hearing where he could present mitigating evidence. The appellate court reviewed Euler's case and determined that since Euler had ample opportunity during the revocation proceeding to present any mitigating evidence in his behalf, he was not entitled to a separate punishment hearing. The significance of this case is that it is not necessary to conduct two separate hearings for probation revocation, provided that ample opportunity exists for probationers to present mitigating evidence during the revocation proceeding. Thus, a single proceeding involves both fact finding and a punishment phase without separating these phases into separate hearings.

   Statements made by a probation officer and committed to writing may not be relied upon exclusively to revoke one's probation without the direct testimony from the probation officer. Salter was an Alabama probationer who allegedly violated one or more conditions of his probation program. The probation officer summarized the nature of Salter's program violations in a report and submitted them to the court. The court relied upon these written statements in the officer's report but did not specifically require the officer to be present and state such violations for the record. Salter's probation program was revoked and an order for his imprisonment was issued. Salter appealed, alleging that he had a right to confront his accuser, the probation officer, and that reliance upon the report itself was insufficient to revoke his probation. An appellate court agreed and set aside his probation revocation order. Probation officers must be present to testify as to the contents of their written commentaries about alleged probation violations. Written reports alone are insufficient grounds to revoke one's probation (*Salter v. State,* 2004). Another Alabama probationer, Taylor, was involved in a similar case where the probation officer gave a report to the court in writing but did not personally testify. The outcome was the same and Taylor's probation revocation order was set aside (*Taylor v. State,* 2004).

Victims cannot dictate to courts whether convicted offenders should or should not have their probation programs revoked. Arnold was a North Carolina offender. At the time of his sentencing, Arnold was placed on probation. Subsequently, Arnold allegedly violated one or more terms of his probation program and a revocation hearing was held. Present at the hearing was the victim of Arnold's original conviction offense. The judge asked the victim what should be done in Arnold's case. The victim declared, "Arnold should go somewhere and grow up." The judge revoked Arnold's probation and ordered Arnold to prison. Arnold appealed, contending that victims should not determine whether one's probation program should be revoked. An appellate court agreed and set aside the probation revocation order. Victims cannot determine whether probation programs should be revoked in any specific instance of a probation revocation proceeding. This is a judicial responsibility and judges must decide, based on the evidence, whether probationers have violated the terms of their probation orders and what shall be the consequences (*State v. Arnold,* 2005).

Probation can be revoked while convicted offenders are serving a portion of their split sentences in jail. Bowen was a New York offender who was given a split sentence. One part of the sentence involved incarceration in a jail for a specified period, accompanied by a sentence of probation, to run concurrent with the jail time (*People v. Bowen,* 2005). While in jail, Bowen promoted prison contraband, thus violating a condition of his probation. The judge revoked Bowen's probation following the incident, allowing Bowen ample opportunity to present mitigating evidence in his own behalf. However, testimony from jail officials and eyewitnesses provided sufficient grounds to revoke Bowen's probation. Bowen objected, claiming that in order to revoke his probation program, he must actually be outside of jail on probation when a program violation is detected. An appellate court disagreed. Whenever split sentences involve concurrent probationary terms as well as jail time, offenses committed while in jail are sufficient to function as probation program violations, and judges are empowered to revoke one's probation program.

Judges must abide by restitution terms outlined in plea agreements when they accept such agreements for the purpose of imposing probation, and they cannot revoke probation for failure to pay amounts of restitution that are subsequently imposed in excess of the original amount of restitution ordered. Pursuant to a plea agreement, a federal offender, Fleischer, pleaded guilty to an offense and agreed to a restitution order of $12,500 as a part of his probation orders (*United States v. Fleischer,* 2005). However, subsequent to being placed on probation, the judge ordered to pay $237,000 in restitution. Fleischer objected and the judge moved to revoke his probation. Fleischer appealed and the Second Circuit Court of Appeals heard his case. The appellate court ordered the additional restitution set aside, reinstating Fleischer's probation program. The court declared that judges are bound to observed amounts of restitution as originally outlined in plea agreements when they are accepted. Additional amounts of restitution cannot be added by judges later as further punishment.

Judges may revoke one's probation program for willful failure to obey one or more conditions of the probation program. Harris was a Florida offender sentenced to probation, with the condition that he complete the Mentally Disordered Sexual Offender (MDSO) Treatment Program (*Harris v. State,* 2005). Subsequently it was determined by Harris's probation officer that Harris had not made any attempt to enroll in the MDSO program and that this action had been willful. Harris's probation program was revoked and Harris was ordered to prison. Harris appealed, alleging that his limited intellectual abilities prevented him from seeking MDSO assistance and participating in the program. An appellate court disagreed. At Harris's probation revocation hearing, testimony was presented by the program director and treating personnel, all of whom has examined Harris initially. There was sufficient evidence on the record that Harris's actions were willful, and that he deliberately disobeyed this important condition of his probation program.

Judges are prohibited from revoking one's probation program based on the mere fact that a probationer is arrested. Sharpston is a Florida probationer who was subsequently arrested for petty theft while on probation (*Sharpston v. State,* 2005). The arrest came to the attention of Sharpston's probation officer who reported the arrest to the court. Sharpston's probation program was revoked as a result of the arrest and Sharpston appealed. An appellate court set aside Sharpston's probation revocation, holding that a revocation of probation based solely on proof of an arrest is improper. Furthermore, the appellate court noted that not once during Sharpston's probation revocation proceeding was Sharpston actually asked if he had committed the petty theft offense of which he was accused.

Defendants may or may not refuse probation if the court imposes probation as a sentence, depending on the jurisdiction. In a case reported elsewhere in the text, Brown was a California defendant convicted of vandalizing his wife's car (*People v. Brown,* 2001). The judge imposed a sentence of probation, but Brown refused it, claiming that the probation conditions were too onerous. Brown settled for a six-month jail sentence instead. Brown's refusal of probation was upheld by a higher court.

However, in *Demarce v. Willrich* (2002), the Arizona defendant refused probation and opted for a jail sentence instead, under conditions similar to Brown's. In the *Demarce* case, an appellate court held that the defendant did not have the right to reject probation and elect incarceration for a lesser term after finding that the probation conditions were too onerous. Thus, it depends on the particular state jurisdiction whether defendants may reject probation if they don't like its conditions.

SUMMARY

Convicted offenders may or may not receive probation in lieu of incarceration. The most common form of probation is standard probation. Offenders are expected to comply with a list of behavioral requirements. Ordinarily, some form of reporting to probation agencies is specified so that probationers can have contact with their POs at regular intervals. Some offenders require closer supervision. Increasing the amount of contact between probationers and their supervising officers is intensive supervised probation. Intensive supervised probation refers to a wide range of nonincarcerative programs exerting variable control over probationers. Intensive supervision means different things depending on the jurisdiction. Most corrections professionals consider intensive supervision to mean frequent face-to-face contact with probationers. Thus, intensive supervision means to supervise probationers more closely than standard probationers. Often, intensive supervision is accompanied by home confinement and electronic monitoring, as well as other program conditions.

Unpopular with the general public, probation of any kind is designed to reintegrate offenders into their respective communities and assist jail and prison officials with their overcrowding problems. Intensive supervised probation programs in current use among the states are based on one or more correctional philosophies stressing contrasting orientations toward how offenders on probation ought to be controlled. The justice model is most punitive and emphasizes penalties for offenders that fit the crimes they committed. The limited risk control model is founded on the idea that an offender's degree of risk to the public can be measured and that the intensity of supervision imposed should vary with the severity of the offense. The treatment-oriented model is most closely aligned with the rehabilitative ideal of corrections and emphasizes community reintegration, community service, restitution, curfew, and home confinement alternatives.

Most intensive supervised probation programs are characterized with low probation officer caseloads and frequent face-to-face contact with probationers either at home or at work. Many of these programs include counseing or some form of vocational/educational training and/or restitution/public service. Three programs are the Georgia ISP program, the Idaho ISP program, and the South Carolina ISP program. These programs have similar elements and characteristics and are designed for low-risk nonviolent offenders. Georgia handpicks its probationers, and thus, only the most eligible offenders are included. This biases the program in such a way so as to maximize its success for clients. The Idaho ISP program uses teams of two POs and a supervisor who work in shifts to monitor offender conduct. South Carolina's ISP program utilizes specialized POs who have training specific to different offender needs. Offenders must also pay a regular, nominal program maintenance fee.

Another incarcerative alternative is shock probation. Shock probation, also known as split sentencing, involves a short period of incarceration followed by participation in a probation program. Mixed sentences, intermittent sentences, and jail are conditions of probation. The more popular terms are split sentencing and shock probation. Shock probation was pioneered in Ohio, although it is currently used in many other states as a sanction. The philosophy of shock probation is that offenders will be shocked into the realization that their crimes are serious and that incarceration is undesirable. Shock incarceration is sometimes known as a boot camp experience. Boot camp goals are multifaceted, emphasizing self-discipline, self-awareness, and various educational and vocational skills. Boot camps are aimed primarily at more youthful offenders, although older offenders are not excluded by most programs. Most states have either developed or are in the process of developing boot camp programs. Boot camp graduates tend to have low recidivism rates compared with standard probationers. Some boot camps are operated by county jails. These are known as jail boot camps. They have been instrumental in upgrading one's social and vocational skills as well as preparing participants for entering the workforce and supporting their families.

When one or more probation program requirements are violated, POs initiate action against probationers. Some program requirements are more important than others, and thus, in certain instances no action is taken. However, where new crimes are alleged or drug or alcohol dependencies are detected, some probationers are in jeopardy of having their probation programs revoked by their original sentencing judges. The probation revocation process is a formal, two-stage proceeding. The first stage determines one's guilt or innocence relating to the allegations of program violations. If judges find that probationers have indeed violated one or more probationary terms, then they must decide the punishment to impose. This occurs in the second phase of the proceeding. Punishment may be a simple return to one's probation program. In other instances, it may be a resentence to more intensive supervised probation. In yet other instances, some probationers may be placed in jails or prisons for a period of time. Several landmark cases have been decided by the U.S. Supreme Court to govern the probation revocation process.

QUESTIONS FOR REVIEW

1. Intensive supervised probation is characterized by what features?

2. How does standard probation differ from intensive supervised probation?

3. Differentiate between the Georgia and South Carolina intensive supervised probation models. How are participants selected for each program?

4. What are three correctional models that have influenced intensive supervised probation programs in recent years? How does each model modify or shape existing probation programs?

5. What are some general criticisms of the Idaho Intensive Supervised Probation Program?

6. What is meant by an intermittent sentence? Is intensive supervised probation an intermittent sentence? Why or why not?

7. What are some principal program components of the South Carolina and Idaho ISP programs?

8. What is a boot camp? What are its goals?

9. What is the philosophy of shock probation? Has shock probation achieved its general objectives? Why or why not?

10. What is meant by a jail boot camp? Describe a jail boot camp, including its goals or objectives. Are jail boot camps successful?

SUGGESTED READINGS

Chan, M. et al. (2005). "Evaluation of Probation Case Management (PCM) for Drug-Involved Women Offenders." *Crime and Delinquency* **51**:447–469.

Lutze, F.E. and C.A. Bell (2005). "Boot Camp Prisons as Masculine Organizations: Rethinking Recidivism and Program Design." *Journal of Offender Rehabilitation* **40**:133–152.

Mitchell, O., D.L. MacKenzie, and D.M. Perez (2005). "A Randomized Evaluation of the Maryland Correctional Boot Camp for Adults: Effects on Offender Antisocial Attitudes and Cognitions." *Journal of Offender Rehabilitation* **40**:71–86.

Seng, M. and A.J. Lurigio (2005). "Probation Officers' Views on Supervising Women Probationers." *Women and Criminal Justice* **16**:65–86.

Skeem, J.L., P. Emke-Francis, and J.E. Louden (2006). "Probation, Mental Health, and Mandated Treatment: A National Survey." *Criminal Justice and Behavior* **33**:158–184.

Wood, P.B., D.C. May, and H.G. Grasmick (2005). "Gender Differences in the Perceived Severity of Boot Camp." *Journal of Offender Rehabilitation* **40**:153–174.

INTERNET CONNECTIONS

Boot Camps
http://www.boot-camps-info.com/

Boot Camps for Struggling Teens
http://www.juvenile-boot-camps.com

Colorado Judicial Department Probation Program
http://www.courts.state.co.us/panda/statrep/ar2000/probnarr.pdf

Crawford County Intensive Supervised Probation
http://www.crawfordcocpcourt.org/ISProbation.htm

Department of Probation and Court Services
http://www.co.mchenry.il.us/CountyDpt/CourtServ/CSerAdult.asp

Michigan 36th District Court Probation Programs
http://www.36thdistrictcourt.org/probation-programs.html

Thunder Road Probation Program
http://www.thunder-road.org/programs_acp.html

U.S. Parole Commission
http://www.usdoj.gov/uspc/releasetxt.htm

CHAPTER 7

Jails and Prisons

Chapter Outline

Chapter Objectives

As the result of reading this chapter, the following objectives will be realized:

1. Describing jails and their major characteristics and primary functions.
2. Profiling jail inmates.
3. Describing prisons and their major characteristics and functions.
4. Understanding the relation between probation, parole, jails, and prisons.
5. Identifying several inmate classification systems.
6. Understanding the major differences between jails and prisons.
7. Understanding several important jail and prison issues, including overcrowding; violence and inmate discipline; jail and prison design and control; rehabilitative prison programs; and privatization.

• *Mark K. is a Illinois probationer. In October 2005, Mark K. was taken into custody after his apartment roommate was found in possession of an unlicensed dog. Furthermore, the dog had not been given rabies shots within the recent past. Citing these illegalities, Mark K.'s probation officer advised him that he was consorting with a person who was breaking the law, thus violating one of the terms of his probation orders. She took Mark K. into custody and had him confined in the county jail to await a judicial hearing. Mark K. was placed in a holding cell with six other inmates. Mark K. objected to being locked up and complained loudly to the jailers for relief. But his pleas were ignored. Instead, two inmates assaulted Mark K. and broke his nose, four ribs, and a facial bone during a lengthy beating. The next morning, a jail officer discovered Mark K. lying on the floor of the large cell and called for assistance to move Mark K. to the jail infirmary. An examination disclosed the extent of his injuries and he was subsequently transported to an area hospital for treatment. In the meantime, he failed to appear for a scheduled probation revocation hearing and the judge, unfamiliar with Mark K.'s beating, cited him for contempt and issued an order for his immediate arrest. Ultimately the contempt charges were dropped, and Mark K.'s probation was continued. The original grounds for jailing Mark K. were deemed "insufficient" to support a probation violation. Mark K. plans to sue the jail, the probation department, and the probation officer for permanent bodily injuries sustained as a result of the jail attack. He is also alleging false arrest and imprisonment. Should Mark K. be entitled to any damages from the jail, the probation department, or the probation officer? What sorts of protections exist for ensuring a probationer's safety while confined in jail? [Adapted from the Associated Press, "Roommate's Unlicensed Dog Results in Probationer Jail Beating, Lawsuit," June 1, 2006.].*

• *Luke R. is a California parolee who had been convicted of several weapons offenses. In March 2005 Luke R. was arrested by a California Highway Patrol officer for driving while intoxicated. Luke R. refused the breathalyzer test. This charge violated a parole provision and Luke R. was jailed pending a parole hearing. Shortly after being jailed, Luke R. submitted to a urinalysis to determine his blood alcohol level. Luke R. was placed in a cell with two other prisoners and confined for two weeks. Subsequently it was determined that Luke R.'s blood alcohol level was 0.0, and that he had not been drinking. Furthermore, no evidence of drugs, legal or otherwise, was detected in his urine. The charge that he had violated a parole condition was dismissed. Subsequently Luke R. developed a chest ailment and sought medical treatment. He was diagnosed as being in the preliminary stages of tuberculosis. It was revealed that another inmate celling with Luke R. had tuberculosis, although it had not been diagnosed by jail officials at the time of Luke R.'s confinement. Luke R. is presently undergoing treatment for tuberculosis and is expected to recover. What protections should jails establish to protect possible probation or parole violators who are celled with others for short periods? Is Luke R. entitled to any damages from the jail or its officers? [Adapted from the Associated Press, "Innocent Parolee Contracts Tuberculosis from Jail Inmate," July 7, 2006.].*

• *Magda G. is a 29-year-old Pennsylvania prostitute and a probationer. In January 2006 she was picked up by police officers for soliciting for prostitution in a county near Philadelphia. When it was discovered that she was a probationer, her probation officer was notified. He retrieved Magda G. from jail two days later and returned her to her residence. Magda G. claims that she was sexually assaulted repeatedly while confined in the county jail. She claims that two jail officers placed her in an isolated cell and took turns having sex with her for nearly two days, before the arrival of her probation officer. During that time, she said, her guards threatened her on more than one occasion that if she didn't want to go to prison, she should forget about what was happening to her. Furthermore, she added, the officers said she was a whore anyway, and who would believe her? She says she cooperated with them and did whatever they wanted to keep from going to prison. Her probation officer notified the county sheriff and chief jailer who both said they would look into the matter. What recourse should Magda D. have against the jail officers she says assaulted her? What are her chances of convincing anyone that she was ever assaulted? [Adapted from the Associated Press, "Female Jail Inmate Alleges Sexual Assault by Guards," August 15, 2006].*

• *Philip Z. is a New Mexico first-offender probationer who was convicted of vehicular theft. In February 2006 he was taken into custody by his probation officer for a routine curfew violation and jailed pending a revocation hearing by the local judge. While confined in a county jail near Albuquerque, Philip Z.'s two other cell mates used marijuana and other illegal drugs. Philip Z. was offered these substances but declined. Later, jail officers entered the cell and confiscated the illegal contraband and drugs. All three inmates, including Philip Z., were charged with marijuana and methampetamine possession. Philip Z. demanded a drug test, but a jail officer said the jail did not have the proper testing equipment. Neither of Philip Z.'s fellow inmates acknowledged that Philip Z. did not use these illegal substances. Philip Z.'s probation officer added the drug charges to the curfew violation charge and submitted the paperwork to the judge. In his own defense, Philip Z. admits to the curfew violation but claims that he missed the bus ordinarily taken to his residence because his construction work crew had to work overtime to complete a task. He attempted to reach his probation officer, but she was unavailable. Philip Z. says he left a message on her voice mail and she admits it was received. He also claims that he has never used drugs and did not use these drugs when celled with the other inmates in the county jail. How can Philip Z. persuade the judge that this was simply a case of guilt by association and that he didn't use drugs? Should Philip Z.'s probation program be revoked because of the actions of his jail cell mates? [Adapted from the Associated Press, "Probationer Claims Innocence on Drug Charges While Jailed," August 1, 2006.].*

INTRODUCTION

This chapter is abjout jails and prisons. Jails in the United States are one of the most maligned and forgotten components of the criminal justice system. In the first section, a brief history of jails in the United States is presented. Jail inmates are also profiled. Typically, jails are city- or county-funded and -operated facilities designed to confine offenders serving short sentences as well as those awaiting trial. Jails are an integral feature of U.S. corrections. In contrast, prisons are intended as long-term custodial facilities for more serious offenders. The second section of this chapter presents a brief history of prisons in the United States and discusses their characteristics and functions. In past years, we could distinguish clearly between prisons and jails in terms of whether convicted offenders had committed felonies or misdemeanors. Misdemeanants were usually sent to jails, while convicted felons were sent to prisons. This is no longer the case, since overcrowding of prisons has caused prison officials to negotiate with smaller jails to accommodate some of their inmate overflow. These inmates housed in local jails are **contract prisoners.** Both state and federal governments have contracted with many local jails as a means of housing a certain proportion of their offender populations. This contracting has directly aggravated existing jail overcrowding. Prison inmates are profiled and compared with jail inmates.

The last section of the chapter presents and discusses several important issues relevant for both jails and prisons. These issues include the overcrowding problem, the problem of inmate violence and discipline, the design and control of jails and prisons, vocational and educational programs for inmates, and privatization. It is important to understand some of the functions and culture of jails and prisons, since inmate conduct is one determinant of early-release decisions by parole boards. Also, inmate conduct is important for those offenders experiencing shock probation. This sentence prescribes one to four months of incarceration, whereupon judges remove offenders from jails and resentence them to probation. However, inmates who behave poorly while confined for these short terms may not be resentenced to probation. Judges exercise discretion and are influenced by inmate conduct. They must decide whether to continue incarcerating offenders or resentence them to probation after one or more months of confinement. Thus, jails and prisons play an important role in probation and parole programs.

JAILS AND JAIL CHARACTERISTICS

In 2006, there were 16 million admissions to and 14.9 million releases from U.S. jails, with an average daily jail population of 739,000. There are jail population increases and serious overcrowding problems in most city and county jails in most jurisdictions (U.S. Department of Justice, 2006). In turn, jail overcrowding has been directly or indirectly responsible for numerous inmate deaths and extensive violence, much offender litigation challenging among other things the constitutionality of the nature of their confinement and treatment, and administrative and/or supervisory problems of immense proportions. How did jails reach this stage and acquire these problems? A brief history of jails in the United States explains several contemporary jail problems.

The term **jail** is derived from the old English term **gaol** (also pronounced "jail"), which originated in 1166 A.D. through a declaration by Henry II of England. Henry II established gaols as a part of the Assize or Constitution of Clarendon. Gaols were locally administered and operated, and they housed many of society's misfits. Paupers or vagrants, drunkards, thieves, murderers, debtors, highwaymen, trespassers, orphan children, prostitutes, and others made up early gaol populations. Since the Church of England was powerful and influential, many religious dissidents were housed in these gaols as a punishment for their dissent. This practice continued for several centuries.

Local control over the administration and operation of jails by **shire-reeves** in England was a practice continued by the American colonists in later years. Most jails in the United States today are locally controlled and operated similar to their English predecessors. Thus, political influence upon jails and jail conditions is strong. In fact, changing jail conditions from one year to the next are often linked to local political shifts through elections and new administrative appointments. Also, the fact that local officials controlled jails and jail operations meant that no single administrative style typified these facilities. Each county (shire) was responsible for establishing jails and managing them according to their individual discretion. Current U.S. jail operations in most jurisdictions are characterized by this same individuality of style.

Originally, jails were designed as holding facilities for persons accused of crimes. Alleged law violators were held until court convened, when their guilt or innocence could be determined. Today, pre-trial detainees make up a significant proportion of the U.S. jail population. Shire reeves made their living through reimbursements from taxes collected in the form of fees for each inmate housed on a daily basis. For instance, the reeve would receive a fixed fee, perhaps 50 or 75 cents per day for each inmate held in the jail. Therefore, more prisoners meant more money for reeves and their assistants. Such a reimbursement scheme was easily susceptible to corruption, and much of the money intended for inmate food and shelter was pocketed by selfish reeves. Quite logically, the quality of inmate food and shelter was very substandard, and jails became notorious because of widespread malnutrition, disease, and death among prisoners.

Workhouses

Deplorable jail conditions continued into the sixteenth century, when workhouses were established largely in response to mercantile demands for cheap labor. A typical **workhouse** in the mid-sixteenth century was the **Bridewell Workhouse** established in 1557. This London facility housed many of the city's vagrants and general riffraff (Champion, 2007). Jail and workhouse sheriffs and administrators quickly capitalized on the cheap labor these facilities generated, and additional profits were envisioned. Thus, it became commonplace for sheriffs and other officials to "hire out" their inmates to perform skilled and semi-skilled tasks for various merchants. While the manifest functions of work houses and prisoner labor were supposed to improve the moral and social fiber of prisoners and train them to perform useful skills when they were eventually released, profits from inmate labor were often pocketed by corrupt jail and workhouse officials. Workhouses were also established in other countries such as Italy and the Netherlands during the same period. In the United States, workhouses were prevalent well into the 1800s and existed to house disreputable persons, such as prostitutes and drunkards.

Jails were commonplace throughout the colonies. Sheriffs were appointed to supervise jail inmates, and the fee system continued to be used to finance these facilities. All types of people were confined together in jails, regardless of their gender or age. Orphans, prostitutes, drunkards, thieves, and robbers were often contained in large, dormitory-style rooms with hay and blankets for beds. Jails were great melting pots of humanity, with little or no regard for inmate treatment, health, or rehabilitation. Even today, jails are characterized similarly.

The Walnut Street Jail

The Pennsylvania legislature authorized in 1790 the renovation of a facility originally constructed on Walnut Street in 1776, a two-acre structure initially designed to house the overflow resulting from overcrowding of the High Street Jail. The **Walnut Street Jail** was both a workhouse and a place of incarceration for all types of offenders. But the 1790 renovation was the first of several innovations in U.S. corrections. Specifically, the Walnut Street Jail was innovative because (1) it separated the most serious prisoners from others in 16 large solitary cells; (2) it separated other prisoners according to their offense seriousness; and (3) it separated prisoners according to gender. Besides these innovations, the Walnut Street Jail assigned inmates to different types of productive labor according to their gender and conviction offense. Women made clothing and performed washing and mending chores. Skilled inmates worked as carpenters, shoemakers, and other crafts. Unskilled prisoners beat hemp or jute for ship caulking. With the exception of women, prisoners received a daily wage for their labor, which was applied to defray the cost of their maintenance. The Quakers and other religious groups provided regular instruction for most offenders. The Walnut Street Jail concept was widely imitated by officials from other states during the next several decades. Many prisons were modeled after the Walnut Street Jail for housing and managing long-term prisoners (Champion, 2005).

The Quakers in Pennsylvania were a strong influence in jail reforms. In 1787 they established the **Philadelphia Society for Alleviating the Miseries of Public Prisons.** This society was made up of many prominent Philadelphia citizens, philanthropists, and religious reformers who believed prison and jail conditions ought to be changed and replaced with a more humane environment. Members of this Society visited each jail and prison daily, bringing food, clothing, and religious instruction to inmates. Some of these members were educators who sought to assist prisoners in acquiring basic skills such as reading and writing. Although their intrusion into prison and jail life was frequently resented and opposed by local authorities and sheriffs, their presence was significant and brought the deplorable conditions of confinement to the attention of politicians.

Subsequent Jail Developments

Information about the early growth of jails in the United States is sketchy. One reason is that there were many inmate facilities established during the 1800s and early 1900s serving many functions and operating under different labels. Sheriffs' homes were used as jails in some jurisdictions, while workhouses, farms, barns, small houses, and other types of facilities served similar purposes in others. Thus, depending on who did the counting, some facilities would be labeled as jails and some would not. Limiting jail definitions only to locally operated short-term facilities for inmates excluded also those state-operated jails in jurisdictions such as Alaska, Delaware, and Rhode Island. Another reason for inadequate jail statistics and information was that there was little interest in jail populations. Another problem was that it was difficult to transmit information from jails and jail inmates to any central location during that period of time. Often, local records were not maintained, and many sheriff's departments were not inclined to share information about their prisoners with others. Streamlined communications systems did not exist, and information was compiled very slowly, if at all. State governments expressed little or no interest in the affairs of jails within their borders, since these were largely local enterprises funded with local funds. Even if there had been a strong interest in jail information among corrections professionals and others, it would have been quite difficult to acquire.

The U.S. Census Bureau began to compile information about jails in 1880 (Champion, 2005). At ten-year intervals following 1880, general jail information was systematically obtained about race, nativity, gender, and age. Originally, the U.S. Census Bureau presented data separately for county jails, city prisons, workhouses, houses of correction, and leased county prisoners. But in 1923, these figures were combined to reflect more accurately what we now describe as jail statistics. A special report was prepared by the U.S. Census Bureau titled *Prisoners 1923.* And in that same year, Joseph Fishman, a federal prison inspector, published a book, *Crucible of Crime,* describing living conditions of many U.S. jails. Comparisons with 1880 base figures show the jail population of the United States to be 18,686 in 1880 and almost doubling to 33,093 by 1890.

Most reports about jail conditions in the United States have been largely unfavorable. The 1923 report by Fishman was based on his visits to and observations of 1,500 jails, describing the conditions he saw as horrible. More recent reports suggest these conditions have not changed dramatically since Fishman made his early observations. It was not until 1972 that national survey data about jails became available. Exceptions include the years 1910, 1923, and 1933, where jail inmate characteristics were listed according to several offense categories. A majority of jail inmates each of those years had committed petty offenses such as vagrancy, public drunkenness, and minor property crimes. Even since 1972, jail data have not been regularly and consistently compiled (Champion, 2005).

There are several reasons for many of the continuing jail problems in the United States. While some of these persistent problems will be examined in-depth later in this chapter, it is sufficient for the present to understand that (1) most of the U.S. jails today were built before 1970, and many were built five decades or more before that; (2) local control of jails often results in erratic policies that shift with each political election, thus forcing jail guards and other personnel to adapt to constantly changing conditions and jail operations; and (3) jail funding is a low-priority budget item in most jurisdictions, and with limited operating funds, the quality of services and personnel jails provide and attract is considerably lower compared with state and federal prison standards and personnel (Champion, 2005).

The Number of Jails in the United States

No one knows the exact number of jails in the United States at any given time. One reason is that observers disagree about how jails ought to be defined. Some people count only locally operated and funded, short-term incarceration facilities as jails, while other people include state-operated jails in their figures. In remote territories such as Alaska, World War II Quonset huts may be used to house offenders on a short-term basis. Work release centers, farms for low-risk inmates, and other facilities may be included or excluded from the jail definition. Sometimes, A **lock-up** (drunk tank, holding tank) might be counted as a jail, although such a facility exists primarily to hold those charged with public drunkenness or other minor offenses for up to 48 hours. These are not jails in the formal sense, but rather, they are simple holding tanks or facilities. The American Jail Association suggests that to qualify as a bonafide jail, the facility must hold inmates for 72 hours or longer, not 48 hours. One of the more accurate estimates of the number of jails in the United States is 3,328, reported by the U.S. **Department of Justice** jail census in 2004.

FUNCTIONS OF JAILS

Jails are more likely to receive, process, and confine mostly detached and disreputable persons rather than true criminals. Many noncriminals are arrested simply because they are offensive and not because they have committed crimes. Jails were originally conceived as short-term holding facilities for inmates serving short sentences as well as for those awaiting trial. The general and most basic function of jails is security. In the last 20 years, however, jails have changed considerably in response to public policy and practicality. Presently, jails perform a myriad of functions, some of which are unrelated to their original historical purpose. The following functions characterize a majority of jails in the United States:

Jails Hold Indigents, Vagrants, and the Mentally Ill.   Jails are generally ill-equipped to handle those with mental or physical disorders. Often, physicians are available only on an on-call basis from local clinics in communities, and no rehabilitative programs or activities exist. More than a few of these inmates have communicable diseases, such as HIV/AIDS or tuberculosis (Krebs, 2002; Valette, 2002).

Jails Hold Pretrial Detainees.   Offenders arrested for various crimes and cannot afford or are denied bail are housed in jails until their trial. For most defendants awaiting trial, their period of **pretrial detention** is fairly short. **Pretrial detainees** may be held in jail without bail if they pose an escape risk or are considered dangerous. Such action is sometimes known as **preventive detention.**

Jails House Witnesses in Protective Custody.   Material witnesses to crimes in key cases may be housed in jails until trials can be held, if it appears that their lives are in danger or their safety is threatened. Some witnesses may be reluctant to testify, and thus prosecutors may wish to guarantee their subsequent appearance by placing them in protective custody. Often, jails are designed so that special accommodations are provided these witnesses, and they do not ordinarily associate with offenders.

Jails House Convicted Offenders Awaiting Sentencing.   Convicted offenders awaiting sentencing are usually held in local jail facilities. These offenders may be federal, state, or local prisoners. When these offenders are housed in local jails, the jurisdiction is ordinarily reimbursed for offender expenses from state or federal funds.

Jails House Persons Serving Short-Term Sentences.   Jails were never designed to accommodate offenders for lengthy incarcerative periods beyond one year. Prisons were constructed and intended for that type of long-term inmate confinement. Many offenders still serve relatively short terms in jails, but increasing numbers of inmates are incarcerated for periods exceeding the one-year standard.

Jails House Some Juvenile Offenders.   Because of the **jail removal initiative,** most juveniles have been diverted from jails for processing. However, annually some juveniles are incarcerated in jails for short periods, until their identity can be verified. Many juveniles have fake IDs and lie to police about who they are and where they live. Some juveniles appear to be much older than they really are. Thus, jail authorities may not know that they are incarcerating juveniles if their fake IDs say otherwise and they appear to be adults. In those cases where juveniles are held in jails for brief periods, they are usually segregated from adult offenders, unless jail conditions do not permit such segregation. Despite the jail removal initiative and efforts from various vested interest groups to remove juveniles from adult jails, their numbers have increased over the years. For instance, there were 8,600 juveniles held in adult jails in 2006. Many of these juveniles were held for brief periods of less than six hours. One reason for this increase is that more jurisdictions are getting tough with youthful offenders and changing laws so that incarceration of younger youths in adult facilities is approved (U.S. Department of Justice, 2006).

Jails Hold Prisoners Wanted by Other States on Detainer Warrants.   Jails must often accommodate prisoners wanted by other jurisdictions in other states. **Detainer warrants** are notices of criminal charges or unserved sentences pending against prisoners. Even though these types of prisoners will eventually be moved to other jurisdictions when authorities from those jurisdictions take them into custody, detainees take up space and time when initially booked and processed.

Jails Hold Probation and Parole Violators.   If probationers or parolees violate one or more of their program conditions, they are subject to arrest and incarceration until authorities can determine what to do about their program violations. Often, sentencing judges will return probation program violators back out on the streets after finding that their program violations were not especially serious. Parole boards may release a certain proportion of parolees for similar reasons. Nevertheless, these persons take up valuable jail space while they are confined, even if the periods of confinement are brief.

Jails Hold Contract Prisoners from Other Jurisdictions.   More than a few jails in Texas, Virginia, Oregon, Washington, and other states work out agreements with state and federal prison systems to house a certain portion of their inmate population overflows. Many jurisdictions have serious inmate overcrowding problems. Thus, the existence of available jail space to accommodate some of this overflow is appealing to these state and federal jurisdictions. In effect, the state or federal government pays the county jail, wherever it is located, to house a certain number of prisoners for a specified period. These prisoners are known as contract prisoners. For instance, Hawaii has exported a large number of its state prisoners to Texas jails to be held for periods of one or more years. This transportation of inmates from Hawaii to the mainland has caused the families of many inmates to complain, since it is prohibitive to visit incarcerated relatives on a regular basis. However, prisoners have no right to determine where they are housed, as long as their accommodations are not cruel and unusual. Furthermore, family members of inmates have no legal rights in this decision making.

Jails Operate Community-Based Programs and Jail Boot Camps.   Increasingly, some of the larger jails are offering some inmates an opportunity to improve their employability by taking vocational and educational training at nearby schools. In more than a few jurisdictions, educational training is a mandatory part of one's incarceration experience (Glover, 2002). Some of these jails operate jail boot camps, which give inmates an opportunity to participate in counseling and self-help programs. Some of these programs are aimed at meeting their needs. If certain inmates are alcohol or substance abusers, they are permitted to join local Alcoholics Anonymous or Narcotics Anonymous groups for brief periods.

Jails Hold Mentally Ill Inmates Pending Their Removal to Mental Health Facilities. No one knows for sure how many mentally ill inmates pass through jails or prisons annually (Jacoby, 2002). The mentally ill pose supervisory and medical problems for jail staff, because often, their specific illnesses are undiagnosed and there is inadequate medical assistance available on the jail premises to treat them (Walters et al., 2002). Furthermore, some of the more serious mentally ill inmates may injure themselves or other inmates by committing acts of violence. No official estimates are available, although some observers have indicated that jails hold as many as 600,000 mentally ill persons annually (Cornelius, 1996). One major reason for larger numbers of mentally ill persons winding up in jails is massive deinstitutionalization of the mentally ill. In 1955, for example, there were 559,000 patients in state mental hospitals. In 2006 there were fewer than 40,000 patients in these same hospitals (U.S. Department of Justice, 2006). Theoretically, at least, patients who were discharged were supposed to receive out-patient follow-up care and services in their communities. But such care and services occurred in only a fraction of these cases. In recent years, this problem has received significant media attention as well as government recognition, and growing numbers of mentally ill offenders currently housed in jails and prisons are being discharged to appropriate medical and mental health centers for treatment rather than punishment.

A PROFILE OF JAIL INMATES

In 2006, approximately 90 percent of all jail inmates were male, while 43 percent were white and non-Hispanic (U.S. Department of Justice, 2006). The number of female arrestees has climbed slowly since 1990, from 9.2 percent to 14.1 percent in 2006. Figures for different ethnicities and races have remained fairly constant during the 1990s and into the 2000s. Some observers believe that selective law enforcement and racial profiling have contributed to the disproportionately large number of black jail inmates over the years, where they have accounted for about 46 percent of all jail inmates (U.S. Department of Justice, 2006). Over half of all jail inmates were not convicted of any crime. At midyear 2006, it was estimated that about 94 percent of all available jail space in the United States was occupied. Some of the types of occupants in U.S. jails are described below.

Drunks, Vagrants, and Juveniles. Many sorts of persons are processed through jails daily. In recent years, virtually every large U.S. city has experienced an escalation in the number of homeless persons, or those without any means of support and nowhere to stay except on city streets, in doorways, or in public parks. Police officers may bring loiterers and vagrants to jail and hold them temporarily until they can establish their identity and account for their conduct. These arrests and detentions most often result in releases several hours later. Drunk drivers are taken to jails by police officers every evening, and they are released in the morning, after they have sobered up. Some juveniles whose identities are unknown may be held in separate areas of jails for brief periods until they can be reunited with their families or guardians.

Pretrial Detainees and Petty Offenders.   Many jail inmates are held for the purpose of awaiting trial on assorted criminal charges. Other inmates are held for periods of less than a year for petty offense convictions.

Shock Probationers and Prison Inmate Overflow.   Scarce jail space must be found for a certain number of jail inmates who are known as shock probationers. These are persons who have been sentenced by judges to long prison terms. However, the judge's intention is to hold these persons in jails for periods ranging from 30 to 120 days. Then, these persons will be brought back before the judge and resentenced to probation. The judge merely wishes to scare these persons by

 **BOX 7.1**

 **CAREER SNAPSHOT**

Michael Pederson
Chief Juvenile Probation Officer, Elko County Juvenile Probation, Elko, Nevada

Statistics:

B.S. (criminal justice); M.S. (organizational management), Weber State University

Background:

I attended and graduated from Weber State University in Ogden, Utah, and graduated in 1992 with a B.S. degree, majoring in criminal justice and minoring in psychology. My initial plan when starting college was to enter the nursing field and become an officer in the military. After being looked over four years in a row, I switched my interest toward the law enforcement field and completed my degree over the next two years. In 1997 I went back and obtained a graduate degree in organizational management and started focusing on administrative duties.

Work Experience:

I was hired by a private security agency the day of graduation and worked for them until a slot was available in the local police academy. Upon graduation, I was hired by a small county agency in southern Utah. After a short time there, I was hired by a larger county law enforcement agency located in Utah. While an employee with this agency, I held the positions of deputy sheriff (working with pre- and post-convicted county inmates); classification deputy (assigned to the housing and safety of county inmates); and transportation deputy (assigned to the court and other secure transport of county inmates) within the jail division. After working two years at this job, I was promoted to the patrol division where I held assignments as patrol deputy and a member of the Fugitive Apprehension Team. After doing these two assignments for 16 months, I was promoted to sergeant and reassigned back to the Jail Division. While there, I supervised deputies in the jail booking area and inmate classification and discipline area for the next two years. In April 2001 my family relocated to Nevada and I

(Continued)

BOX 7.2 (*Continued*)

took a position as Deputy Chief in this department. My responsibilities included probation officer supervision, grant writing, and other administrative functions. In August 2005, I was promoted to Chief and assigned the responsibilities of developing programs, the continuation of writing departmental grants to fund these new programs, and working with the public to gain community support.

Insights:

Working with families with kids that struggle with the law can be challenging. Not only do you supervise the wayward child, but you also have to deal with stressed-out parents. I believe there is a vicious cycle that is created whenever a child grows up with a good home life and few boundaries. That child becomes a parent and provides the same experiences for his or her kids, not out of the desire to be a bad parent, but just because he or she doesn't know any better. If this chain is not reversed and new skills are not acquired by either the child or the entire family, I don't see any end in sight to delinquent behavior. Families are the most important unit in society. Society needs to start protecting them and providing them with the resources needed to help them stay strong. This is the main reason I have decided to leave the adult criminal justice system and try to make a difference in the juvenile arena. You can make all the money in the world and still be unproductive. Working with juveniles who struggle with the law and with families that are crying out for help is truly honorable and should be pursued.

Advice to Students:

Find the type of work you love to do. Don't worry if it takes months or even years to find the right job. Find the kind of job that motivates you to get out of bed and makes you want to work late. Choosing your occupation is one of the most important decisions you will ever make. If you love your work, it will be noticed by those who consider hiring you, those you end up working for and with, and the people you serve. In this line of work, families know if you care about helping them or not. They need dedicated probation officers that are concerned with the struggles they are facing. Some parents are honestly shocked whenever their child gets into trouble.

I recall a certain family that came to our department. The child had stolen money from her employer in the amount of thousands of dollars. This child was only 16 years old and was heavily influenced by peer pressure. The parents were totally blown away when the police department called and reported what their "angel" had done. I received the report and was assigned the responsibility of supervision. This child could have easily been sent off to the state juvenile corrections facility because of the seriousness of her delinquent actions. However, we worked through her issues, helped her complete her court-ordered sanctions, and helped her make restitution for the money she had stolen. After she was released from probation, I received flowers and a heartfelt letter from the child and family expressing their appreciation for helping their daughter. I still see this family around town and the experience has changed their lives for the better. This experience alone has made all of the schooling and training I have had worthwhile. These types of experiences happen frequently and they make working here worth getting up in the morning.

Struggling families are looking for allies to assist them to get their children back on course. You can be that person if you are committed to the cause. There is no better reward, no amount of money you can be paid, that will equal the satisfaction you receive from helping children turn their lives around and abandon the criminal behaviors they were attempting to pursue. If you have the integrity within you and the desire to serve others, then this line of work is for you.

incarcerating them for brief periods. The belief is that the shock value of short-term incarceration will act as a deterrent to further offending. Despite this noble crime prevention objective, shock probationers take up valuable jail space and are not considered particularly serious. However, another contingent of jail inmates consists of more serious offenders from various state and federal jurisdictions. State and federal prisons with overcrowding problems will contract with jail authorities to house a certain number of prisoners, thus reducing a certain amount of prison overcrowding. These contract prisoners are usually held for periods of one year or longer in designated jails with sufficient space to accommodate them. They take up scarce jail space on a long-term basis.

Contract prisoners are usually held in special cell blocks or on designated floors of jails. Furthermore, they are supervised more closely than other jail inmates, because they constitute a general inmate class that is considered more dangerous. Contract prisoners cost jails more to supervise, therefore, although this cost is offset by state and federal government funds that are allocated to particular counties where jail space is used. In 2006 there were 74,200 contract prisoners being housed in U.S. jails (U.S. Department of Justice, 2006).

Work Releasees and the Mentally Ill. Jail services also include managing a certain portion of offenders on work release programs in those jurisdictions that have them. Jail inmates sentenced to work release programs are low-risk and nonviolent offenders. Some observers question whether they should be incarcerated at all compared with persons who have been sentenced to standard probation.

Psychologically disturbed inmates may prove bothersome or disruptive to other inmates. These people pose additional problems to jail staff, because in especially small jail facilities, there are no separate facilities for segregating these from serious offenders. Often, local jail facilities are ill-equipped to meet the special needs of mentally ill offenders or those who may be retarded. In 2006 about a fourth of all U.S. jails had no psychological or health staff (U.S. Department of Justice, 2006).

Probationers and Parolees. A small proportion of jail inmates consists of probationers and parolees who have violated one or more conditions of their programs and are awaiting hearings to determine their dispositions and whether their programs should be revoked. About 8,000 jail inmates were probation or parole violators in 2005 (U.S. Department of Justice, 2006). About a fourth of these offenders (1,250) were being held in jails for allegedly committing new crimes.

PRISONS, PRISON HISTORY, AND PRISON CHARACTERISTICS

Prisons Defined

Prisons are state or federally funded and operated institutions to house convicted offenders under continuous custody on a long-term basis. Compared with jails, prisons are completely self-contained and self-sufficient. In 2005, there were over 2.4 million inmates in both federal and state penitentiaries (U.S. Department of Justice, 2006). Prisons were operating at 108 percent of their operating capacity. The Federal Bureau of Prisons was operating at 132 percent of its operating capacity, while New Jersey and Wisconsin were respectively operating at 147 percent and 142 percent of their operating capacities. Erving Goffman

(1961) has described a prison as a **total institution,** because it is an environmental reality of absolute dominance over prisoners' lives. These self-contained facilities have recreational yards, workout rooms, auditoriums for viewing feature films, and small stores for purchases of toiletries and other goods.

The Development and Growth of U.S. Prisons

Early English and Scottish penal methods were very influential on the subsequent growth and development of U.S. prisons. Most English and Scottish prisons that existed to house criminals and others often had operational policies that were influenced by economic or mercantile interests as well as those of the Church. **John Howard** (1726–1790), an influential English prison reformer, criticized the manner and circumstances under which prisoners were administered and housed. Howard had been a county squire and later, in 1773, he was the sheriff of Bedfordshire. He conducted regular inspections of gaol facilities and found that prisoners were routinely exploited by gaolers, since gaolers had no regular income other than that extracted from prisoners through their labor. Howard visited other countries to inspect their prison systems. He was impressed with the Maison de Force (House of Enforcement) of Ghent, where prisoners were treated humanely. They were clothed, lodged separately from others during evening hours, and wellfed. He thought that these ideas could be used as models for British prisons and gaols. He succeeded in convincing British authorities that certain reforms should be undertaken. In 1779, the Penitentiary Act was passed.

The Penitentiary Act provided that new facilities should be created, where prisoners could work productively at hard labor rather than suffer the usual punishment of **banishment.** Prisoners were to be well-fed, clothed, and housed in isolated, sanitary cells. They were to be given opportunities to learn useful skills and trades. Fees for their maintenance were abolished, rigorous inspections were conducted regularly, and balanced diets and improved hygiene were to be strictly observed. Howard believed that prisoners should be given a hearty work regimen. Through hard work, prisoners would realize the seriousness and consequences of their crimes. Thus, work was a type of penance. The new word *penitentiary* was originated and was synonymous with reform and punishment. Presently, penitentiaries in the United States are regarded as punishment-centered rather than reform-oriented, as significant philosophical shifts have occurred in American corrections (Champion, 2007).

State Prisons

The first state prison was established in Simsbury, Connecticut, in 1773. This prison was actually an underground copper mine that was converted into a confinement facility for convicted felons. It was eventually made into a permanent prison in 1790. Prisoners were shackled about the ankles, worked long hours, and received particularly harsh sentences for minor offenses. Burglary and counterfeiting were punishable in Simsbury by imprisonment not exceeding 10 years, while a second offense meant life imprisonment.

Actually, the Walnut Street Jail was the first true American prison that attempted to correct offenders. Compared with the Simsbury underground prison, a strictly punishment-centered facility, the Walnut Street Jail operated according to the rehabilitation model. A signer of the Declaration of Independence, Dr. Benjamin Rush (1745–1813), was both a physician and a humanitarian. He believed that punishment should reform offenders and prevent them from committing future crimes. He also believed that they should be removed temporarily from society until they became remorseful. Rush believed that prisoners should exercise regularly and eat wholesome foods. Thus, he encouraged prisoners to grow gardens where they could produce their own goods. Prisoner-produced goods were so successful at one point that produce and other materials manufactured or grown by inmates were marketed to the general public. Therefore, he pioneered the first prison industry, where prisoners could market goods for profit and use some of this income to defray prison operating expenses. Some of Rush's ideas were incorporated into the operation of the Walnut Street Jail, and eventually, the pattern of discipline and offender treatment practiced there became known popularly as the **Pennsylvania System.** The Walnut Street Jail Pennsylvania System became a model used by many other jurisdictions (Champion, 2005).

Auburn State Penitentiary

New York correctional authorities developed a new type of prison in 1816, the **Auburn State Penitentiary,** designed according to **tiers,** where inmates were housed on several different levels. The tier system became a common feature of subsequent U.S. prison construction, and today, most prisons are architecturally structured according to tiers. The term **penitentiary** is used to designate an institution that not only segregates offenders from society but also from each other. The original connotation of penitentiary was a place where prisoners could think, reflect, and repent of their misdeeds and possibly undergo reformation. Presently, the words *prison* and *penitentiary* are used interchangeably, since virtually every prison has facilities for isolating prisoners from one another according to various levels of custody and control. Thus, each state has devised different names for facilities designed to house its most dangerous offenders. Examples include Kentucky State Penitentiary, California State Prison at San Quentin, New Jersey State Prison, North Dakota Penitentiary, and Maine State Prison.

FIGURE 7.1 Men's Correctional Unit, North Dakota State Penitentiary.

At the Auburn State Penitentiary, prisoners were housed in solitary cells during evening hours. This was the beginning of what is presently known as **solitary confinement.** Another innovation at Auburn was that inmates were allowed to work together and eat their meals with one another during daylight hours. This was known as the **congregate system** (Champion, 2005). Auburn Penitentiary also provided for divisions among prisoners according to the nature of their offenses. The different tiers conveniently housed inmates in different offense categories, with more serious offenders housed on one tier and less serious offenders housed on another. Certain tiers were reserved for the most unruly offenders who could not conform their conduct to prison policies. The most dangerous inmates were kept in solitary confinement for long periods as punishment. These periods ranged from a few days to a few months, depending on the prison rule violated. Therefore, Auburn Penitentiary is significant historically because it provided for the minimum-, medium-, and maximum-security designations by which modern penitentiaries are known.

Prisoners were provided with different uniforms as well, to set them apart from one another. The stereotypical striped uniform of prison inmates was a novelty at Auburn that was widely copied as well. Over half of all state prisons patterned their structures after the Auburn system during the next half century, including the style of prison dress and manner of separating offenders according to their crime seriousness. Striped prison uniforms for prisoners continued until the 1950s when they became outmoded.

Other Prison Developments

Between 1816 and 1900, many other state prisons were established. One of the first successful prisons was constructed in Cherry Hill, Pennsylvania, in the early 1830s. This prison was considered successful because it was the first to offer a continuing internal program of treatment and other forms of assistance to inmates. The first state penitentiary in Ohio was opened in Columbus in 1834. The largest state prison of that time period was established in Jackson, Michigan, in 1839. By 1999, this State Prison of Southern Michigan had been torn down and rebuilt. It houses 615 male inmates. Another large state prison was built in Parchman, Mississippi, in 1900. In 1999, it housed 4,836 inmates. Louisiana claims one of the largest and oldest state prisons, however, being built in 1866 with a capacity of 4,747 inmates. In 2006, the Louisiana State Penitentiary in Angola housed 5,108 males (U.S. Department of Justice, 2006).

The American Correctional Association and Elmira Reformatory

In 1870 the **American Correctional Association (ACA)** was established and Rutherford B. Hayes, a future U.S. president, was selected to head that organization. The goals of the ACA were to formulate a national correctional philosophy, to develop sound correctional policies and standards, to offer expertise to all interested jurisdictions in the design and operation of correctional facilities, and to assist in the training of correctional officers. The ACA was originally called the National Prison Association, then the American Prison Association, and finally and more generally, the American Correctional Association.

The United States was entering a new era of correctional reform with the establishment of the ACA. Six years later, the Elmira State Reformatory in

Elmira, New York, was constructed. **Elmira Reformatory** experimented with certain new rehabilitative philosophies espoused by various penologists including its first superintendent, Zebulon Brockway (1827–1920). Brockway was critical of the harsh methods employed by the establishments he headed, and he envisioned better and more effective treatments for prisoners. He had his chance in 1876 when he was selected to head Elmira Reformatory. Elmira was considered the new penology and used the latest scientific information in its correctional methods. Penologists from Scotland and Ireland, **Captain Alexander Maconochie** and **Sir Walter Crofton,** were instrumental in bringing about changes in European correctional methods during the period when Elmira was established in the early 1870s. These men influenced American corrections by introducing the **mark system,** where prisoners could accumulate **tickets-of-leave,** which would enable them to be released early from their lengthy incarcerative sentences. Through hard work and industry, prisoners could shorten their original sentences, which earlier had to be served in their entirety (Champion, 2005).

Elmira was truly a reformatory and used a military model comparable to contemporary boot camps. Prisoners performed useful labor and participated in educational or vocational activities, where their productivity and good conduct could earn them shorter sentences. Elmira inmates were trained in close-order drill, wore military uniforms, and paraded about with wooden rifles. Authorities regarded this as a way of instilling discipline in inmates and reforming them. Historians credit Elmira Reformatory with individualizing prisoner treatment and the use of indeterminate sentencing directly suited for parole actions. Elmira Reformatory was widely imitated by other state prison systems subsequently.

THE FUNCTIONS OF PRISONS

The functions served by prisons are closely connected with the overall goals of corrections. Broadly stated, correctional goals include deterrence, rehabilitation, societal protection, offender reintegration, just-deserts, justice and due process, and retribution or punishment. The goals of prisons are listed and described below.

Prisons Provide Societal Protection.   Locking up dangerous offenders or those who are persistent nonviolent offenders means that society will be protected from them for variable time periods. It is not possible at present to lock up all offenders who deserve to be incarcerated. Space limitations are such that we would require at least four or five times the number of existing prisons to incarcerate all convicted felons and misdemeanants. Thus, the criminal justice system attempts to incarcerate those most in need of incarceration.

Prisons Punish Offenders.   Restricting one's freedoms, confining inmates in cells, and obligating them to follow rigid behavioral codes while confined is regarded as punishment for criminal conduct. The fact of incarceration is a punishment compared with the greater freedoms enjoyed by probationers and parolees.

Prisons Rehabilitate Offenders.   Few criminal justice scholars accept the idea that prisons rehabilitate inmates. Little support exists for the view that imprisonment does much of a rehabilitative nature for anyone confined.

 **BOX 7.2**

Japan has a largely centralized federal system of government. The government is divided into the executive, legislative, and judicial branches. A new constitution was established in 1947 called the Peaceful Constitution, and was directed at banning wars and establishing post-war harmony. A penal code was also established. Subsequently there have been numerous political reforms in Japan leading to their present governmental system. Presently the Japanese criminal justice system is accusatorial, where prosecutors and defense counsels argue cases before judges who decide them. The jury system in Japan was used for many decades but was suspended in 1943. In 2004 new jury laws were passed that were scheduled to be implemented in 2009.

The judicial system consists of summary courts, family courts, district courts, and high courts, where decisions can be appealed from district courts. Criminal appeals may be made to the Supreme Court, although most of these appeals involve constitutional issues. Summary courts are located in towns and cities and involve offenses punishable only by fines. There are over 60 district courts, which are the equivalent of basic criminal trial courts in the United States. High courts exist in all major cities with similar jurisdiction over more serious cases. The criminal code has set minimum and maximum sentences for offenses to individualize punishments for different types of offenders. Judges conduct trials and are authorized to examine witnesses, call for evidence, and decide one's guilt. Judges may also suspend the sentences of those convicted and place them on probation or order them to perform various types of services. Judges may also sentence offenders to prison.

Three general categories of crime in Japan are crimes against the state, crimes against society, and criminals against individuals. Crimes against individuals include homicide, assault, bodily injury, forcible rape, kidnapping, theft, fraud, robbery, and extortion. Theft has a very broad meaning and includes burglary, shoplifting, and stealing goods from cars. Crimes against society include arson, gambling, and indecent behavior in public. Special laws are in place to regulate possession and use of firearms and public morals. Compared with other industrialized countries, Japan's crime rate is among the lowest. Also, because of the upsurge in drug use on a worldwide basis, Japan has enacted stiff drug laws to punish those trafficking or using illegal drugs. Methamphetamine is the most frequently abused drug in Japan. The Ministry of Justice compiles crime statistics and other crime information and distributes such information regularly. In 2005 there were very low numbers of rapes and murders, less than 5,000. Larceny is the largest crime category, accounting for over 70 percent of all crimes committed.

The age of criminal responsibility is 20. Anyone under the age of 20 is considered a juvenile and subject to the jurisdiction of juvenile courts according to the Juvenile Law. Juveniles are most often subjected to treatment measures, which stress rehabilitation and reintegration, positive self-esteem development, counseling, and other highly individualized interventions. Protective measures for juveniles do not rule out placement in special training schools where juveniles may receive vocational and/or educational training and socialization to become more law-abiding citizens. Placements in such facilities are usually indeterminate, and often, probation officers who work with adult offenders also work with certain juveniles they are assigned.

Two general police agencies are prevalent. One is the National Police Safety Commission (NPSC) and the other is the National Police Agency (NPA). The NPSC is a policy-making body, while the NPA administers police business. Regional police bureaus have been established in all major cities. Each local city has Prefectural Police, or PP. These PP enforce all local laws, including traffic violations and other minor offenses. They also investigate more serious types of crime. Police officers rely heavily on local residents of communities to assist them in their law enforcement efforts. Therefore, community policing is commonplace in Japanese cities and towns. A high degree of citizen involvement occurs, and this extends to other dimensions of the criminal justice system as well. Several police academies are responsible for training law enforcement officers at all law enforcement levels.

Whenever police officers arrest offenders, prosecutors bring charges against them. The Japanese constitution sets forth various rights of accused persons, patterned after various Western models, such as the United States. If indigent defendants are charged, they are provided with legal counsel appointed by the government. Speedy and public trials are provided. Plea bargaining in Japan is not an option. Even where guilt is admitted through a confession, prosecutors must present evidence that establishes one's guilt in court. Suspects may be detained without bail pending a later trial, although bail is permitted in less serious cases. Prosecutions of cases have extremely high conviction rates. Over 90 percent of all prosecutions result in convictions. The types of penalties range from death, to imprisonment with labor, imprisonment without labor, fines, short-term detention (less than 30 days), and a variety of other penalties, such as asset forfeiture. Judges may also impose community punishments such as probation in various forms with a variety of conditions.

The Correction Bureau is responsible for administering Japan's prison system. There are three major types of prisons. These include prisons for convicted inmates who are sentenced to imprisonment with or without labor; juvenile prisons for convicted offenders under age 26, and with or without labor; and detention houses for unconvicted offenders such as those awaiting trial. New prison admissions largely consist of larceny and drug offenders. The treatment of prisoners in Japanese prisons is oriented toward rehabilitation and reintegration or resocialization. Prison treatment programs are specifically tailored for each inmate following a thorough classification process where one's needs are determined or assessed. Prison labor, vocational training, educational coursework, living guidance, counseling, learning social coping skills, and receiving various types of medical and mental health care are provided. In 2005 there were approximately 83,000 persons in Japanese prisons. About half were repeat offenders or recidivists. Less than 10 percent of all inmates were females. Most female offenders were convicted of property crimes, sex offenses, or drug violations.

The government assumes responsibilities for offenders far beyond simply warehousing them in the prison system. Noninstitutional treatment in the form of community corrections exists for a large portion of offenders convicted in criminal court proceedings. A large number of those receiving suspended sentences are assigned to professional probation officers for a fixed term of supervision and assistance. A Rehabilitation Bureau oversees community corrections and the operation of probation and parole. Although estimates are somewhat unreliable, it is believed that there were over 250,000 probationers and parolees in Japan in 2005. The responsibility for aftercare of these offenders is within the jurisdiction of the Rehabilitation Bureau, which supports approximately 1,400 probation officers and over 60,000 volunteer probation officers.

The volunteer probation system has been used in Japan since the 1980s. Community volunteers are persons selected from their communities to assist in probationer/parolee reintegration and rehabilitation. The ideal plan for the voluntee probation system is for each volunteer to supervise and work with up to five offenders, although most work only with two offenders at any given time. They are given the responsibility of ensuring that these offenders do not reoffend, largely by offering them assistance and guidance, as well as close supervision.

Critics of the volunteer probation officer system have said that often these volunteers are too old (more than 70 percent are over age 55 and retired) and thus cannot understand the complexity of problems faced by offenders. However, the selection of volunteers requires that such individuals be respected and financially secure. Almost all volunteers are men, and most are over age

(continued)

BOX 7.2 (Continued)

50. They come from diverse backgrounds, including fisherman or farmers, religious leaders, housewives, and retired persons. Nevertheless, the recidivism rate among offenders working with volunteer probation officers is less than 5 percent. This is remarkable, considering that these persons are essentially untrained compared with the country's professional probation officers who work with more serious offenders. Professional probation officers are trained persons who are under the jurisdiction of the Ministry of Justice and are assigned to regional parole boards or probation offices. They usually have a knowledge of psychology and/or sociology, and they have experience working with offenders who need social assistance and rehabilitation. They also work cooperatively with volunteer probation officers and give them additional assistance and information when needed. Crime and delinquency prevention are also important functions assumed by both professional and volunteer probation officers.

Prison inmates may become eligible for parole after serving a portion of their sentences. Regional parole boards have been established throughout Japan in different cities, and these parole boards hear and decide cases and whether to release certain offenders short of serving their maximum sentences. These parole boards may also revoke one's parole program if one or more parole program conditions are violated. About 15 percent of all supervised offenders under the jurisdiction of the Rehabilitation Bureau are parolees.

There is a very low recidivism rate among both probationers and parolees. One of the major reasons for this low recidivism is that in order to qualify for probation or parole, offenders must show a great deal of remorse and meet rigorous selective criteria before probation or parole is granted. Thus some creaming exists in the probation and parole system. Nevertheless, probation and parole in Japan seems highly successful, especially with the high degree of involvement of community volunteers. Social acceptance is crucial to offenders in Japanese society. Dishonor is taken

seriously, and families exert a powerful influence over offender conduct. Thus, volunteer probation officers work with offenders to get them jobs in their communities so that they may become law-abiding and productive. This individualization of treatment also contributes to low offender recidivism. When volunteer probation officers spend a great deal of time with offenders and give them intensive personalized attention, it makes a difference to offenders, who see their supervisors as mentors or friends rather than authority figures.

Both probation and parole programming in Japan have conditions similar to those attached to U.S. probation and parole programs. Probationers and parolees are subject to periodic checks of their employment and homes, and they are obligated to observe various behavioral requirements. Violating one or more of their program conditions can cause either judges or the parole board to revoke their programs. Each of Japan's major cities and most larger communities have community residential centers, similar to halfway houses in the United States. These residential centers offer offenders a variety of services, including educational/vocational training and job-seeking advice.

When probationers are initially sentenced to probation, they must report to the probation office where a professional probation officer interviews them and reviews their criminal history and problems. A special treatment plan is eventually established. Probation officers assign different probationers to volunteer probation officers for supervision. Parole works similarly. Each community residential center can accommodate up to 100 offenders, with some variation among different localities. Volunteer probation officers ensure that offenders keep in touch with their families on a regular basis, at least twice a month if not more often. Progress reports are prepared by these volunteers and submitted monthly to the probation office. More noncompliant probationers and parolees will be supervised by professional probation officers, who use more rigorous supervision methods. Japan's probation and parole systems utilize electronic monitoring and home confinement in different communities, and they have used such individualized tracking and placement methods since the early 1990s.

_____

Sources: Adapted from "Correctional Statistics," Japan Rehabilitation Bureau, Ministry of Justice, January 2006; "Volunteer Probation Officer Program," Unpublished paper, Onishi Yamagata, December 2005; "Parole and Probation Work in Japan," National Center for Policy Analysis, Washington, DC, December 2001; Noboru Hashimoto, "Parole in Japan," Tokyo Probation Office, November 2004; "Japan," World Factbook of Criminal Justice Systems, 2004.

Nevertheless, many prisons have vocational and educational programs, psychological counselors, drug dependency programming and counseling, and an array of services available to inmates in order that they might improve their skills, education, and self-concept (King et al., 2002). Prisons also have libraries for inmate self-improvement. More often than not, prisons also socialize inmates in adverse ways, so that they might emerge from prisons later as better criminals who have learned ways of avoiding detection when committing future crimes. One growing problem in prisons that often interferes with rehabilitative efforts of institutional programming is the greater cultural diversity of inmates and the lack of suitable interventions to fit different inmate needs.

Prisons Reintegrate Offenders. It might be argued that moving offenders from higher security levels, where they are more closely supervised, to lower security levels, where they are less closely supervised, helps them understand that conformity with institutional rules is rewarded. As prisoners near their release dates, they may be permitted unescorted leaves, known as furloughs or work/study release, where they may participate in work or educational programs and visit with their families during the week or on weekends. These experiences are considered reintegrative. Most prisons have such programs, but they are presumably aimed at certain offenders who are believed to no longer pose a threat to society. Prisons also provide parenting services and courses to younger inmates with children. While a lot of work has been done to foster more effective parenting for inmate mothers, inmate fathers are increasingly receiving this same type of parenting training (Muhammad, 2006).

Occasionally, officials wrongly estimate the nondangerousness of certain furloughees and work releasees. In any case, the intent of reintegrative prison programs is to provide those wanting such programs the opportunity of having them. At least some inmates derive value from such programs, although some observers believe the costs of operating them are far outweighed by the lack of rehabilitation and reintegration that actually occurs. High recidivism rates among those released from prisons and jails call the rehabilitative nature of prisons and jails into question (Spohn and Holleran, 2002).

INMATE CLASSIFICATION SYSTEMS

Religious movements are credited with establishing early prisoner classification systems in the eighteenth century. The Walnut Street Jail in 1790 in Philadelphia attempted to segregate prisoners according to age, gender, and offense seriousness.

Subsequent efforts were made by penal authorities to classify and separate inmates according to various criteria in many state and federal prison facilities. Adequate classification schemes for prisoners have yet to be devised. Classification schemes are based largely on psychological, behavioral, and sociodemographic criteria. The use of psychological characteristics as predictors of risk or dangerousness and subsequent custody assignments for prisoners was stimulated by research during the period 1910–1920 (Champion, 2005).

No single scheme for classifying offenders is foolproof, although several instruments have been used more frequently than others for inmate classification and placement. The Megargee Inmate Typology presumes to measure inmate adjustment to prison life (Megargee and Carbonell, 1985). Several items were selected from the Minnesota Multiphasic Personality Inventory (MMPI), a psychological assessment device, to define 10 prisoner types and to predict an inmate's inclination to violate prison rules or act aggressively against others. Basically a psychological tool, the Megargee Inmate Typology has been adopted by various state prison systems for purposes of classifying prisoners into different custody levels. The predictive utility of this instrument is questionable, however. One problem Megargee himself detected was that prisoner classification types based on his index scores change drastically during a one-year period. For some observers, this finding has caused serious questions about the reliability of Megargee's scale. For other observers, however, inmate score changes on Megargee's scale indicate behavioral change, possibly improvement. Thus, reclassifications are conducted of most prison inmates at regular intervals to chart their behavioral progress.

Besides Megargee, other professionals who have devised useful inmate classification criteria have not been particularly fruitful. For example, inmate misconduct is often correlated with being affiliated with street gangs. Other criteria have been used in different research throughout each of the state and federal systems with varying results (Dowdy, Lacy, and Unnithan, 2002). One's prior record of offending, age, unemployment history, and race have functioned as both legal and extralegal criteria and have been associated with program failures or successes under different research conditions. The present generation of objective prison classification systems must be capable of more than simple risk assessment. Systems must be able to identify the needs of an increasingly diverse population with changing characteristics to provide appropriate programs, services, and treatment opportunities, and prepare offenders for re-entry into their communities. Presently the focus of risk assessment development is on identifying high-risk, disruptive offenders in order to foster more effective correctional planning and monitoring, as well as promoting safer environments for staff and inmates.

One thing is certain about risk instruments and inmate classifications resulting from applications of these instruments. Exactly how prison inmates are initially classified and housed will directly influence their parole chances (Sullivan, 2006). Inmates classified as maximum security may not deserve this classification, since it means that the inmate is considered dangerous. Inmate opportunities for personal development and rehabilitation are limited in these classifications. However, inmates who are classified as minimum security have a wide variety of prison benefits and programs (Waters and Megathlin, 2002). They are neither supervised as closely nor considered dangerous. When minimum-security inmates face parole boards, their custody levels are assets. When maximum-security inmates face parole boards, their classification is a liability. An example of a prison risk assessment instrument to determine an inmate's placement or security level is the one used by the Alaska Department of Corrections and is illustrated in Figure 7.2.

STATE OF ALASKA DEPARTMENT OF CORRECTIONS

Security Designation Form for Long-Term Sentenced Prisoners

(1) _____   (3) _____
    Institution   Designation Staff Member

(2) _____   (4) _____
    Date   Supt. Signature (exception case only)

SECTION A   IDENTIFYING DATA

(1) _____
Prisoner's Name   Last   First   Middle Initial

(2) _____
    Date of Birth

(3) Type of Case: Regular _____   Exception _____   (4) OBSCIS _____

(5) Separatees: _____
_____

SECTION B   SECURITY SCORING

1. Type of Detainer:

   0 = None   3 = Class C Felony   7 = Unclassified or
   1 = Misdemeanor   5 = Class B Felony   Class A Felony   [ ] 1

2. Severity of Current Offense:

   1 = Misdemeanor   3 = Class C Felony   7 = Unclassified
                         5 = Class B Felony   or Class A Felony   [ ] 2

3. Time to Firm Release Date:

   0 = 0–12 months   3 = 60–83 months
   1 = 13–59 months   5 = 84 + months   _____   [ ] 3
                                                 Firm Release Date

4. Type of Prior Convictions:

   0 = None   1 = Misdemeanor   3 = Felony   [ ] 4

5. History of Escapes or Attempted Escapes:

	None	+15 Years	10–15 Years	5–10 Years	−5 Years	
Minor	0	1	1	2	3	
Serious	0	4	5	6	7	[ ] 5

6. History of Violent Behavior:

	None	+15 Years	10–15 Years	5–10 Years	−5 Years	
Minor	0	1	1	2	3	
Serious	0	4	5	6	7	[ ] 6

FIGURE 7.2 Alaska Security Designation for Long-Term Sentenced Prisoners.
Courtesy of the Alaska Department of Corrections, 2003.

---

7. SECURITY TOTAL   [ ] 7

8. Security Level:
    Minimum = 0–6 points   Medium = 7–13 points   Maximum = 14–36 points

9. Designated Custody Level:
    Community/Minimum   Medium   Close   Maximum
            0 – 6   7 – 13   14 – 25   26 – 36

10. Designation Staff Comments:

    _____

    _____

    _____

SECTION C   MANAGEMENT CONSIDERATION

---

1. Release Plans   5. Special Treatment   9. Residence
2. Medical   6. Ethnic/Cultural   10. Restitution Center
3. Psychiatric   Consideration   11. Contract Misdemeanant
4. Education   7. Overcrowding   Housing
                          8. Judicial Recommendation

FIGURE 7.2   (Continued).

All prisons in the United States have classifications that differentiate between prisoners and cause them to be placed under various levels of custody or security (Sullivan, 2006). One of the main purposes for the initial inmate classification is to identify those likely to engage in assaultive or aggressive disciplinary infractions. Prisoners are eventually channeled into one of several fixed custody levels known as (1) **minimum security,** (2) **medium security, and** (3) **maximum security.**

Minimum-Security Classification

Minimum-security prisons are facilities designed to house low-risk, nonviolent first-offenders. These institutions are also established to accommodate those serving short-term sentences. Sometimes, minimum-security institutions function as intermediate housing for those prisoners leaving more heavily monitored facilities on their way toward parole or eventual freedom. Minimum-security housing is often of a dormitory-like quality, with grounds and physical plant features resembling a university campus rather than a prison. Those assigned to minimum-security facilities are trusted to comply with whatever rules are in force.

Administrators place greater trust in inmates in minimum-security institutions, and these sites are believed to be most likely to promote greater self-confidence and self-esteem among prisoners. The rehabilitative value of minimum-security inmates is high. Also, family visits are less restricted. The emphasis of minimum-security classification is definitely on prisoner reintegration into society.

Medium-Security and Maximum-Security Classification

Sixty percent of all state and federal prisons in the United States are medium- and minimum-security institutions. A majority of state and federal prison facilities are designed to accommodate medium- and minimum-security inmates. As of 2006, of all U.S. penitentiaries, all but the one in Atlanta, Georgia, were classified as maximum security (U.S. Department of Justice, 2006). Medium-security facilities at both state and federal levels offer inmates opportunities for work release, furloughs, and other types of programs.

Forty percent of all U.S. prisons are maximum-security institutions. Ordinarily, those sentenced to serve time in maximum-security facilities are considered among the most dangerous, high-risk offenders. Maximum-security prisons are characterized by many stringent rules and restrictions, and inmates are isolated from one another for long periods in single-cell accommodations. Closed-circuit television monitors often permit correctional officers to observe prisoners in their cells or in work areas, which are limited. Visitation privileges are minimal. Most often, no efforts are made by officials to rehabilitate inmates.

An example of one of the most memorable maximum-security penitentiaries ever constructed was the federal prison at Alcatraz in San Francisco Bay. Alcatraz was constructed in 1934 but closed in 1963 because of poor sanitation and the great expense of prisoner maintenance. During the period Alcatraz was operated, Alcatraz held over 1,500 prisoners, including Al Capone and Robert "Birdman" Stroud. In maximum-security prisons, inmate isolation and control are stressed, and close monitoring by guards either directly or through closed-circuit television reduces prisoner misconduct significantly.

Maxi-Maxi, Admin Max, and Super Max Prisons

Prisons such as the federal penitentiary at Marion, Illinois, are considered maxi-maxi prisons. The Marion facility accommodated only 568 inmates in 2006, and those incarcerated at Marion are considered the very worst prisoners. Marion inmates are the most violence-prone, inclined to escape whenever the opportunity arises, and extremely dangerous. Two correctional officers were killed by prisoners in the Control Unit. When the riot was contained, Marion officials ordered a **lockdown,** where all prisoners were placed in solitary confinement and severe restrictions were imposed. For Marion inmates, lockdown meant confinement in isolation for $23^1/_2$ hours per day, with 30 minutes for exercise. Privileges were extremely limited. Prisons with the highest levels of security and inmate supervision are designated as **maxi-maxi.** In Colorado, the U.S. Bureau of Prisons operates the United States Penitentiary at Florence. This facility is designated as an **admin max** and houses only inmates with extensive criminal histories. Sometimes these prisons are known as **super max** facilities. It is believed that maxi-maxi, admin max, and super max all refer to essentially the same types of facilities with equivalent levels of the highest supervision and custody for the most dangerous offenders.

An example of a super max facility is Illinois's new Closed Maximum Security Correctional Center in Tamms. This facility is designed to house 520 of Illinois's most violent offenders. The closed maximum-security unit (CMAX) is the most secure. It is podular, with each pod containing 60 cells, 10 in each of six cellblocks. The cellblocks are arranged around a control station strategically positioned with visual access to all cells. Correctional officers assigned to each pod carry weapons and have access to tear gas. The facility supports the use of deadly force against inmates if it should become necessary. Cell furniture includes a concrete sleeping platform with a pad, a wall-mounted writing surface and shelf, a stainless steel "combi unit" (water closet, lavatory, and drinking fountain), and a small, stainless steel mirror. Strategically placed security vestibules provide additional circulation control and allow portions of the facility to be sealed off at will. Each bank of pods has an exterior evacuation area surrounded by a chain link fence and capped with razor wire.

It is apparent that there are many types of prisons, ranging from minimum-security, honor farm–type facilities to maxi-maxi penitentiaries. A low degree of violence is associated with minimum-security facilities. This is because inmates tend to be less dangerous and pose the least risk to the safety of correctional officers and others. Each prison setting with its peculiar inmate profile means that wardens or superintendents will be presented with different kinds of problems to resolve.

The Importance of Classification for Prisoners

Whether prisoners realize it or not, their classification when they enter prison has substantial influence on their early-release eligibility. Other factors, such as institutional conduct, not getting into fights with other inmates, avoiding disruptive behavior, controlling anger, participating in self-help programs, enrolling in counseling and other available prison services, all combine to influence parole board decision making when it comes time to decide whether any particular inmate should be released (Lahm, 2006).

Paroling authorities consider it significant, for instance, if an inmate enters prison and is placed in maximum-security or medium-security custody, and if that same inmate eventually works his or her way down to minimum-security custody. What this means is that the inmate has earned a level-of-custody reduction through good behavior. Parole boards are not going to grant parole easily to an inmate who has been placed in maximum-security custody and has remained there for several years. Furthermore, if an inmate advances to a higher custody level, such as moving from minimum-security to medium-security, this is evidence of poor conduct. The inmate may have a bad attitude, reject authority or any type of helpful intervention, or engage in disruptive behavior. Thus, it is definitely to an inmate's advantage to do the right types of things that will earn him or her level-of-custody reductions.

In Nevada, for instance, a parole-eligible inmate faced the parole board. He was a young man in his mid-20s. His record indicated that he lacked a high school education. He had been unemployed and on drugs at the time of his arrest for a property offense. He had served two years of a six-year term. The parole board asked him, "Well, why should we release you now? Have you worked on your GED? Have you done anything to correct your drug problem?" The inmate answered, condemning himself to further confinement. He said, "No, I haven't done any of that. I don't like education. I hate teachers. I don't think I've got a drug problem. I've been in this place for a few years and I don't do drugs. But I'm just not interested in those different things they say we can get involved in. I just hate authority." The Nevada Parole Board rejected his parole application. In this case, his own attitude about self-improvement was sufficient to cause the parole board to turn him down on his early-release request. Perhaps if he had obtained a GED or participated in drug therapy and counseling, the parole board may have granted him early release on that occasion.

In another case, the North Dakota Parole Board heard the early-release request from a young black inmate who was serving a four-year sentence for aggravated assault. He had assaulted his girlfriend. He had served two years and faced the parole board. One parole board member observed, "Lionel, it looks like you got into some trouble over the last few months. You've been in some fights. Got into some trouble. What about that?" Lionel looked at the parole board and said, "Listen, when some dude calls me a nigger, I'm not going to let it go. I'll fight him. That's what he wants, and that's what he's going to get from me." "Well," the parole board member further queried, "Why should we let you out now? You've served less than two years of a four-year sentence. Have you taken any anger management classes? You know that you are going to face that sort of thing no matter where you go. Are you always going to fight? What do you have to say about that?" Lionel told the parole board, "No, I haven't taken any anger management. I can control myself. It's just that these dudes are going to do anything they can to f__ me. They don't like me and they are going to try to get me into trouble by starting fights. The guards come along, they see two dudes fightin', and what do they do? They write both of us up. It ain't fair. No, I don't think I can walk away from that. But I think I can control my anger. About my parole, I think I deserve a 'cut' in my sentence. I know other guys who have got out early, and they're worse than me. I just think I deserve a 'cut.' " The parole board turned down Lionel for early release. When they advised him of their negative decision, he threw a pencil at one of the parole board members and cussed them out. He said he'd "max out" his time or serve his sentence in its entirety if it meant that he wouldn't have to put up with being called a nigger by some whitey in the 'block.

There are many self-help options available to most prisoners in most prisons in both the state and federal systems. They have to assist in their own defense, however. This means that they can't simply sit and wait for a parole board to grant them early release. They can do things to speed up the early-release process. One of these things is to earn a lower level of custody by following institutional rules and not causing trouble. Some inmates are incapable of understanding this, however.

A PROFILE OF PRISONERS IN U.S. PRISONS

Considerable diversity exists among prisoners in state and federal institutions. These differences include the nature and seriousness of their conviction offenses, age, and psychological or medical problems. In order to cope more effectively with meeting the needs of such diverse offenders, prisons have established different confinement facilities and levels of custody, depending on how each prisoner is classified. Overall, state and federal prisoner populations increased by nearly 184 percent between 1990 and 2005. Generally, the average increase in the federal and state prison inmate population was about 5 percent per year. This information is shown in Table 7.1.

In midyear 2005 7 percent of all state and federal prisoners were female (Harrison and Beck, 2005). Females have been incarcerated at increasing rates since the early 1990s. For instance, between 1990 and 2005, the average annual percentage of female inmates increased 4.7 percent, outpacing male incarcerations, which rose an average of 3.0 percent for the same period. Between 1995 and 2005, the female inmate population increased by 45 percent, while the male inmate population increased by 32 percent for the same period. The more rapid rise in female incarceration is mostly attributable to more property-related convictions among women than among men (Harrison and Beck, 2006). All prisoners under either state or federal jurisdiction for midyear 2005 are shown in Table 7.2.

TABLE 7.1

Change in the State and Federal Prison Populations, 1990–2005

Year	No. of Inmates	Annual Percent Change	Total Percent Change Since 1990
1990	773,124	—	—
1991	824,133	6.6	6.6
1992	883,593	7.2	14.2
1993	932,074	5.5	20.6
1994	1,016,691	9.1	31.5
1995	1,585,586	5.6	105.1
1996	1,646,020	3.8	112.9
1997	1,743,643	5.6	125.5
1998	1,816,931	4.2	135.1
1999	1,890,837	4.1	144.6
2000	1,937,482	2.5	150.6
2001	1,961,247	1.2	153.7
2002	2,033,331	3.7	163.0
2003	2,082,728	2.4	169.4
2004	2,131,180	2.3	175.7
2005	2,186,230*	2.6	182.8

Source: Paige M. Harrison and Allen J. Beck, *Prison and Jail Inmates at Midyear 2005.*
Washington, DC: U.S. Department of Justice, May 2006.
*midyear figures; does not include entire 2005 population.

TABLE 7.2

Prisoners Under the Jurisdiction of State or Federal Correctional Authorities, June 30, 2004, to June 30, 2005

Region and jurisdiction	Total 6/30/05	Total 12/31/04	Total 06/30/04	Percent change from— 6/30/04 to 06/30/05	Percent change from— 12/31/04 to 6/30/05	Prison incarceration rate, 6/30/05[a]
U.S. total	1,512,823	1,495,373	1,491,834	1.4%	1.2%	488
Federal	184,484	180,328	179,210	2.9	2.3	55
State	1,328,339	1,315,045	1,312,624	1.2	1.0	433
Northeast	173,125	170,980	173,967	−0.5%	1.3%	298
Connecticut	19,744	19,497	20,018	−1.4	1.3	375
Maine	2,084	2,024	2,014	3.5	3.0	153
Massachusetts	10,495	10,144	10,365	1.3	3.5	236
New Hampshire	2,561	2,448	2,441	4.9	4.6	196
New Jersey	28,124	26,757	28,107	0.1	5.1	323
New York	62,963	63,749	64,596	−2.5	−1.2	327
Pennsylvania	41,540	40,963	40,692	2.1	1.4	334
Rhode Island	3,639	3,430	3,701	−1.7	6.1	179
Vermont	1,975	1,968	2,033	−2.9	0.4	239
Midwest	252,406	250,702	249,732	1.1%	0.7%	380
Illinois	44,669	44,054	44,379	0.7	1.4	350

Region and jurisdiction	Total			Percent change from—		Prison incarceration rate, 6/30/05[a]
	6/30/05	12/31/04	06/30/04	6/30/04 to 06/30/05	12/31/04 to 6/30/05	
Indiana	24,244	24,008	23,760	2.0	1.0	386
Iowa	8,578	8,525	8,611	−0.4	0.6	289
Kansas	9,042	8,966	9,152	−1.2	0.8	329
Michigan	49,014	48,883	48,591	0.9	0.3	484
Minnesota	9,187	8,758	8,613	6.7	4.9	179
Missouri	31,066	31,188	30,542	1.7	−0.4	535
Nebraska	4,284	4,130	4,042	6.0	3.7	237
North Dakota	1,338	1,327	1,266	5.7	0.8	199
Ohio	44,976	44,798	44,770	0.5	0.4	392
South Dakota	3,344	3,095	3,101	7.8	8.0	430
Wisconsin	22,664	22,970	22,905	−1.1	−1.3	383
South	606,361	598,773	596,763	1.6%	1.3%	542
Alabama	27,740	25,873	26,521	4.6	7.2	587
Arkansas	13,469	13,655	13,477	−0.1	−1.4	480
Delaware	7,180	6,927	6,973	3.0	3.7	478
Florida	87,545	85,533	84,733	3.3	2.4	492
Georgia	47,682	50,979	48,625	−1.9	−6.5	526
Kentucky	18,897	17,790	17,763	6.4	6.2	432
Louisiana	37,254	36,939	36,745	1.4	0.9	824
Maryland	23,276	23,285	23,727	−1.9	0.0	405
Mississippi	20,856	20,983	20,429	2.1	−0.6	682
North Carolina	36,399	35,442	34,917	4.2	2.7	361
Oklahoma	23,702	23,319	23,284	1.8	1.6	655
South Carolina	23,896	23,428	24,173	−1.1	2.0	538
Tennessee	26,208	25,884	25,834	1.4	1.3	440
Texas	171,338	168,105	169,110	1.3	1.9	703
Virginia	35,667	35,564	35,472	0.5	0.3	471
West Virginia	5,252	5,067	4,980	5.5	3.7	287
West	296,447	294,590	292,162	1.5%	0.6%	421
Alaska	4,630	4,554	4,515	2.5	1.7	374
Arizona	32,664	32,515	31,631	3.3	0.5	502
California	166,532	166,221	166,053	0.3	0.2	456
Colorado	20,841	20,293	19,756	5.5	2.7	447
Hawaii	6,071	5,960	5,946	2.1	1.9	334
Idaho	6,136	6,375	6,312	−2.8	−3.7	429
Montana	3,369	3,164	3,123	7.9	6.5	360
Nevada	11,565	11,365	10,971	5.4	1.8	478
New Mexico	6,595	6,379	6,352	3.8	3.4	327
Oregon	13,317	13,180	13,219	0.7	1.0	365
Utah	6,013	5,990	5,802	3.6	0.4	240
Washington	16,688	16,614	16,559	0.8	0.4	283
Wyoming	2,026	1,960	1,923	5.4	2.3	398

Source: Paige M. Harrison and Allen J. Beck (2006). *Prison and Jail Inmates at Midyear 2005.* Washington, DC: Bureau of Justice Statistics. (Table 2, p. 3) public domain

The jail population in the United States for midyear 2005 was 819,434 (Harrison and Beck, 2006:7). Table 7.3 shows persons under jail supervision, by confinement status and type of program, for midyear 1995, 2000, and 2004–2005. There were 747,529 inmates held in jail, while 71,905 inmates were supervised outside of a jail facility, including weekender programs, electronic monitoring, day reporting, and home detention.

TABLE 7.3

Persons under jail supervision, by confinement status and type of program, midyear 1995, 2000, and 2004–05

Confinement status and type of program	Number of persons under jail supervision			
	1995	2000	2004	2005
Total	541,913	687,033	784,538	819,434
Held in jail	507,044	621,149	713,990	747,529
Supervised outside of a jail facility	34,869	65,884	70,548	71,905
Weekender programs	1,909	14,523	11,589	14,110
Electronic monitoring	6,788	10,782	11,689	11,403
Home detention	1,376	332	1,173	1,497
Day reporting	1,283	3,969	6,627	4,747
Community service	10,253	13,592	13,171	15,536
Other pretrial supervision	3,229	6,279	14,370	15,458
Other work programs	9,144	8,011	7,208	5,796
Treatment programs	. . .	5,714	2,208	1,973
Other	887	2,682	2,513	1,385

Source: Paige M. Harrison and Allen J. Beck (2006). *Prison and Jail Inmates at Midyear 2005.* Washington, DC: Bureau of Justice Statistics. (Table 8, p. 7) public domain

The gender, racial/ethnic, and conviction statuses of jail inmates for the years 1995, 2000, 2003, and 2004–2005 have been compared. These are shown in Table 7.4.

These figures show a greater proportion of females incarcerated in jails across the years surveyed compared with comparable prison population proportionate distributions. The proportion of female jail inmates grew from 1995 to 2005, from 10.2 percent to 12.7 percent. White inmates grew proportionately from 1995 to 2005, from 40.1 percent to 44.3 percent, while the black proportionate jail inmate population declined from 43.5 percent in 1995 to 38.9 percent in 2005. However, the Hispanic proportionate distribution of jail inmates grew slightly during the same period from 14.7 percent in 1995 to 15.0 percent in 2005. Also, fewer convicted offenders made up the jail population between 1995 and 2005, declining from 44.0 percent to 38 percent. At the same time, unconvicted offenders increased proportionately for the same period, from 56 percent to 62 percent (Harrison and Beck, 2006:8).

SOME JAIL AND PRISON CONTRASTS

Prisons are constructed to house long-term offenders who are convicted of serious offenses compared with those housed in jails. Below are some of the contrasts between prisons and jails. Compared with prisons:

1. The physical plant of jails is poorer, with many jails under court order to improve their physical facilities to comply with minimum health and safety standards.

2. Jails usually do not have programs or facilities associated with long-term incarceration such as vocational, technical, or educational courses to be

TABLE 7.4

Gender, race, Hispanic origin, and conviction status of local jail inmates, midyear 1995, 2000, and 2004–05

Characteristic	1995	2000	2004	2005
Total	100%	100%	100%	100%
Gender				
Male	89.8%	88.6%	87.7%	87.3%
Female	10.2	11.4	12.3	12.7
Race/Hispanic origin				
White	40.1%	41.9%	44.4%	44.3%
Black	43.5	41.3	38.6	38.9
Hispanic	14.7	15.1	15.2	15.0
Other	1.7	1.6	1.8	1.7
Two or more races				0.1
Conviction status				
Convicted	44.0%	44.0%	39.7%	38.0%
Male	39.7	39.0	34.8	33.2
Female	4.3	5.0	4.9	4.8
Unconvicted	56.0	56.0	60.3	62.0
Male	50.0	50.0	53.0	54.2
Female	6.0	6.0	7.3	7.7

Source: Paige M. Harrison and Allen J. Beck (2006). *Prison and Jail Inmates at Midyear 2005*. Washington, DC: Bureau of Justice Statistics. (Table 10, p. 8) public domain

taken by inmates, jail industries, recreation yards, or psychological or social counseling or therapy.

3. Jails have a greater diversity of inmates, including witnesses for trials, suspects or detainees, defendants awaiting trial unable to post bail or whose bail was denied, juveniles awaiting transfer to juvenile facilities or detention, those serving short-term sentences for public drunkenness, driving while intoxicated, or city ordinance violations, mentally ill or disturbed persons awaiting hospitalization, and overflow from state and federal prison populations.

4. Jail inmate culture is less pronounced and persistent. There is a high inmate turnover in jails, with the exception of the state and federal convict population.

5. The quality of jail personnel is lower, with many jail personnel untrained, undertrained, or otherwise less qualified to guard prisoners compared with their counterparts, prison correctional officers.

6. Jails are not usually partitioned into minimum-, medium-, or maximum-security areas. Control towers do not exist, where armed correctional officers patrol regularly. Jails are not surrounded by several perimeters, with barbed wire areas, sound-detection equipment, and other exotic electronic devices.

SELECTED JAIL AND PRISON ISSUES

This section examines briefly six major issues representing problems for both jails and prisons. These issues include: (1) jail and prison overcrowding; (2) violence and inmate discipline; (3) jail and prison design and control; (4) vocational/technical and educational programs in jails and prisons; (5) jail and prison privatization; and (6) gang formation and perpetuation.

Jail and Prison Overcrowding

Jails are expected to accomodate almost everyone brought to them for booking or proceesing. Murder suspects as well as public intoxication cases may be housed temporarily in the same tank or detention area to await further processing. The millions of admissions to and releases from jails annually only aggravate persistent jail overcrowding problems, despite the fact that most of those admitted to jails are not confined for lengthy periods. The volume of admissions and releases is severe enough and persistent enough to cause continuing jail overcrowding problems. Law enforcement arrest policies in many jurisdictions seriously aggravate jail overcrowding as well, as millions of arrestees occupy valuable jail space during booking and other perfunctory jail processing. The fact that numerous state and federal prisons contract with local jail authorities to house some of the prison inmate overflow suggests serious prison overcrowding as well.

Violent deaths, suicides, psychiatric commitments, and disciplinary infractions have been linked to jail and prison overcrowding. Some observers have argued that these results are very predictable. For instance, Wilkinson and Unwin (1999:98) have indicated, "Take a prison with inmates of many cultures, ethnic backgrounds and a basic tendency toward xenophobia: add a pinch of politically driven tightening of privileges; fold in a large dollop of life long lessons in mistrust and hatred; cook at 170 percent of design capacity and top off with hot and humid summer months. . .even the most bucolic of communities would be hard-pressed to exist, much less thrive, in such an environment. Yet we ask this of prison inmates every day." These researchers also note that many inmates come from backgrounds that allow little exposure to people of different races, religions, behaviors, and attitudes, that this ignorance becomes the root of many street and prison gangs. However, the overcrowding problem and the many conditions it generates that are adverse for inmates has often been dealt with in a piecemeal fashion. For instance, Ohio conducts a Corrections Training Academy, where cultural diversity is taught to prospective correctional officer recruits. Thus, staff are sensitized to overcrowding and the multicultural blend of inmates, but the inmates themselves are not offered similar experiences.

An endless string of solutions have been suggested to ease jail and prison overcrowding. Some of these solutions are labeled as front-door solutions, because they pertain to policies and practices by criminal justice officials who deal with offenders before and during sentencing. Other solutions are back-door solutions, where strategies are suggested to reduce existing prison populations through early release or parole, furlough, administrative release, and several other options.

Typically, front-door solutions to prison overcrowding are frequently directed at prosecutors and judges, and the way they handle offenders. Some observers suggest greater use of diversion and/or assignment to community service agencies, where offenders bypass the criminal justice system altogether and remain free within their communities. Greater use of probation by judges and recommendations of leniency from prosecutors have also been suggested, with an emphasis on some form of restitution, community service, victim compensation, and/or fine as the primary punishment. Other solutions include greater plea bargaining where probation is included; selective incapacitation, where those offenders deemed most dangerous are considered for incarceration; assigning judges a fixed number of prison spaces so that they might rearrange their sentencing priorities and incarcerate only the most serious offenders; and decriminalization of offenses to narrow the range of crimes for which offenders can be incarcerated (Auerbahn, 2002).

Some of the back-door proposals by observers include easing the eligibility criteria for early release or parole; the administrative reduction of prison terms, where the governor or others shorten originally imposed sentences for certain offenders; modifying parole revocation criteria so as to encourage fewer parole violations; and expanding the number of community programs such as mediation and including the use of intensive supervised parole for more serious offender groups (Adair, 2000).

Probably the most serious effect of prison overcrowding for inmates is upon their early-release chances. Parole-eligible inmates often find that because of prison overcrowding and the violence it generates, their parole chances are lessened. This is because there are far more inmates than self-help programs and prison labor can accommodate. Prisoners benefit if they can become involved in prison labor programs. However, only about 20 percent of all prisoners in the United States are included in such programs. Many services, such as group or individual counseling, vocational/technical, and educational programs, are chronically understaffed and cannot be offered to all inmates who need or desire them. Even where inmates want to become involved in these programs, the mere fact that so many inmates must be accommodated means that some inmates will be excluded from them. As a result, some inmates will not receive the needed services or programs. If they do receive some of these services, the quality of services or programming will be adversely affected because of larger numbers of inmates who must be accommodated. Many parole-eligible inmates, therefore, will not have adequate opportunities to show parole boards what they have accomplished. This is one of the adverse consequences of warehousing offenders under conditions of limited services and self-help programs.

Violence and Inmate Discipline

Prisons and jails are breeding grounds for inmate violence. Contributing to this potential for violence is the great mixture of races, ethnicities, and ages of inmates, together with chronic overcrowding. The increasingly visible presence of gangs has increased prison and jail violence as well, as inmates become affiliated with one gang or another, often for the purpose of self-protection (Straka, 2003). Every prison has screening mechanisms for new inmates according to standard criteria, but misclassifications frequently occur. Dangerous offenders and the mentally retarded or ill often commit aggressive acts against other inmates. But it is difficult to detect and distinguish between all offenders in terms of which ones pose the greatest risk to themselves or others. Placing inmates in solitary confinement for their own protection is most often not an option for the average prison. There is simply insufficient maximum-security space to accommodate all of those inmates who seek escape from other inmates who might wish to injure or exploit them. Also, there are limited policy provisions for insuring inmate safety from other violent inmates, although these provisions are not applied because of the exigencies of the situation. Drug abuse is also a contributing factor to inmate violence.

Much prison violence goes undetected. Inmate-on-inmate assault is the most frequent type of violence, where one or more inmates physically or sexually assault another inmate. The assaulted inmate does not report the incident for fear of retaliation, which is highly foreseeable. Not all assaults are sexually oriented or initiated. Many assaults by inmates upon other inmates are started over something as trivial as disagreements over telephone use. Many prisoners suffer physical injuries, and these incidents are frequently unreported or unrecorded. Even when correctional officers suspect or observe rule-breaking and certain forms of inmate violence, this behavior is frequently ignored. Some researchers indicate that correctional officers often ignore this misconduct in order to obtain inmate cooperation and compliance with prison rules. This fact gives prisoners some degree of psychological control or power over those correctional officers who look the other way when they observe rule infractions.

Increasingly common are sexual assaults and psychological harassment in jails and prisons (Tartaro, 2002). These incidents of violence are often attributable to growing numbers of inmates with antisocial personality disorders in both prison and jail settings (Wogan and MacKenzie, 2002). Both male and female inmates are aggressors in such assaults (Struckman-Johnson and Struckman-Johnson, 2002). Inmates with substance abuse problems has also contributed significantly to inmate violence. Prison violence has been mitigated successfully in at least some state prisons. In the Washington State Penitentiary at Walla Walla, for example, administrators have trained staff to cope with inmate violence through an approach known as prevention and reaction. With appropriate staff training, Washington correctional officers are learning to prevent new prisoners from joining prison gangs through various intervention activities.

Probably the most visible forms of prison violence are riots. Rioting is on the rise in U.S. prisons as well as other countries, such as Germany (Kury and Smartt, 2002). Rioting among jail and prison inmates is not unique to the United States. Rioting occurs in virtually every prison in every country at one time or another. Even women's prisons have had higher levels of violence in recent years (Suter et al., 2002). Whenever prisoners riot, they cause considerable damage to prison property and inflict physical injuries on inmates and prison and/or jail staff. Between 1990 and 2002, for instance, there were over 2,000 incidents of inmate rioting in U.S. prisons and jails (Suter et al., 2002). Causes of these riots have been attributable to racial tension, changes in rules and regulations, mass escape attempts, gang conflicts, rumors, disputes among inmates and between inmates and staff members, drug and alcohol use, complaints about food, security procedures, and inmate overcrowding (Rolison et al., 2002; Tartaro, 2002).

It is difficult for jail and prison administrators to prepare effectively for riots. Sometimes informants from among the prisoners will give correctional officers some advance warning that a riot is about to occur. But most often, riots are spontaneous and unplanned, at least from an administrator's perspective. Therefore, administrators have devised various strategies for coping with, containing, and eliminating riot behavior when it erupts. Some of these strategies include control of the news media, which often plays into the hands of inmates who are seeking external recognition of their grievance or plight. Force, negotiations, and administrative concessions are other strategies that help to end rioting when it occurs. Whenever rioting ends, command and control structures are reexamined. Some reorganization occurs, where prison and jail administrators attempt to implement new policies and procedures that will minimize or even eliminate further rioting. One typical response by prison administrators is to impose greater restrictions and rule enforcement on inmates following rioting. However, this action often causes more disciplinary problems than it resolves. It has been recommended that an official nonviolent attitude should be adopted by prison administrators in high-custody facilities while using whatever force is necessary to confine and control high-risk inmates. Such a nonviolent stance from administrators helps to ease inmate tensions and reduce the level of prison violence.

Some observers note that we know far more about the causes of aggression and violence among inmates than we do about their treatment (Stohr et al., 2002). Aggressive behavior is typically the result of an interaction between personal characteristics and situational factors. Our technology is such that we have the capability of reasonably identifying the perceptual and cognitive patterns, coping skills, contingencies, and values of those most deserving of special attention from prison programs. However, those most likely to engage in violence and aggressive behavior or are at the greatest risk levels are often the same persons who are least amenable to treatment. Thus, some intervention programs offered in prisons fail because they target inmates who cannot benefit from the program. Or our intervention programs work for some offenders but not for others. Or the program was a true failure because it did not provide a specific service that targeted a factor unrelated to violent conduct (Lemieux, 2002).

One administrative change that has had somewhat positive results is the establishment of inmate councils. These councils, sometimes called inmate disciplinary councils, exist apart from administrative sanctioning mechanisms. These councils are bodies that can hear and decide many low-level, nonserious inmate complaints against other inmates and even correctional officers or administrative policies. Usually, these councils can reach problem resolutions that satisfy most parties. All prisons at the state and federal levels currently have formal grievance procedures. These councils consist of inmates and a few prison correctional officers. Prisoners regard the addition of corrections officers as a way of providing these councils with some objectivity when hearing and deciding inmate grievances.

Hans Toch (1995:35) says that prisons gain from prison democracy when prisoners become committed to the improvement of prisons and from participating in decisions that affect their lives. From the perspective of prisoners, there are several positive benefits from greater participation in prison governance and self-regulation. Prisoners say, for instance, that they (1) have a chance to get rid of the them-and-us attitude; (2) have a more relaxed community atmosphere; (3) have more integration with staff; (4) have less boredom; (5) have less paranoia about release; (6) have more emphasis on the rehabilitation factor; and (7) have less bitterness against the system when released (Toch, 1995:36). For prospective parolees, these are very positive benefits that can ultimately drive down the amount of recidivism that typifies their conduct upon release.

Jail and Prison Design and Control

Some observers see a direct connection between new jail and prison design and a reduction in inmate violence (Sturges, 2002). Several proposals for resolving jail and prison problems are (1) to create new jails and prisons constructed in ways that will conserve scarce space and require fewer correctional officers; and (2) to reconstruct existing facilities to minimize prison violence and house more inmates. Prison construction in recent years has included increasingly popular modular designs. New modular designs also permit layouts and arrangements of cell blocks to enhance officer monitoring of inmates. But new prison construction is expensive, and many jurisdictions are either unwilling or unable to undertake new prison construction projects.

New jail and prison construction, the renovation or expansion of existing facilities, or the conversion of existing buildings previously used for other purposes take into account the matter of security and safety for both staff and inmates. Stairwells and areas otherwise hidden from the view of correctional officers encourage inmate sexual or otherwise physical assaults. These areas can either be reduced or eliminated entirely with new architectural designs. It is generally conceded that reducing blind spots or areas not directly visible to officers and other corrections officials help to reduce the incidence of inmate assaults (Reisig, 2002). The construction of safer jail and prison facilities can do much to minimize the incidence of inmate violence. Furthermore, institutional programming is enhanced, since there is better organization and planning through being able to anticipate the characteristics of future jail and prison clientele. If jail and prison officials have a better idea about the characteristics of those entering their facilities in future years, they can develop more effective programming to meet their needs. In the long run, inmates benefit from such planning (Prendergast et al., 2002).

Vocational/Technical and Educational Programs in Jails and Prisons

Most jails are not equipped to provide inmates with any vocational/technical and educational programs. Several reasons include the fact that most jails are not equipped with the space to offer such educational programming. Jail inmates do not have parole and good-time credit incentives compared with prison inmates. And jail inmates are usually serving short-term sentences that would interrupt any meaningful educational programming that might be contemplated. Even in those instances where jail educational programs have been devised and offered on a short-term basis to inmates, recidivism rates of graduates have not differed significantly from those who have not participated in educational programs offered at the jails.

Many prisons lack a broad variety of programs geared to enhance inmate skills and education. This state of affairs seems consistent with the view that the rehabilitation orientation in American prisons is on the decline. However, there have been several successes among state and federal prison systems. For instance, drug offenders in the U.S. Bureau of Prison's Choice program, a drug treatment and intervention program, have for the most part been successfully treated. Inmates with drug dependencies are subjected to a 10-month program, including intake/evaluation/follow-up, drug education, skills development, lifestyle modification, wellness, responsibility, and individualized counseling/case supervision. The emphasis in the Choice program is on education and the development of cognitive skills rather than on treatment and insight-oriented therapy.

In Washington, McNeil Island houses a portion of the state's serious offenders. In 1996 the prison facility, which houses 1,300 medium-security inmates, implemented an educational program known as the Work Ethic Camp (WEC) (Washington Work Ethic Camp, 2006). The camp recruits volunteers from among interested inmates who want to improve themselves. Designated correctional officers behave in ways that model demanding employers, although they develop a personally supportive relationship between themselves and participating inmates. Inmates, known as WECies, are expected to put in eight-hour workdays at different tasks. There is demanding work at the Island power station, motor pool, recycling plant, water-filtration plant, meat-packaging plant, and other facilities. Inmates learn boat repair and maintenance, road repair, building construction, facility maintenance, clerical work, farm work, and forest maintenance. WEC inmates are also taught basic work habits, including cleanliness, following instructions, planning tasks, teamwork, interpersonal skills, tool care, and supervisor–employee relationships. They also take courses in reading, writing, and math; adult basic education preparation; anger/stress management; victim awareness; community responsibility; dependable strengths articulation process; family dynamics; unlocking your potential; chemical dependency; health and wellness; job readiness; and transition planning. The WEC's objective is to produce productive, employable inmates who will leave McNeil Island ready to go to work for an employer on the outside. Evaluation of the program thus far has been favorable. Inmates are developing better self-images and self-respect. They are acquiring the skills necessary to make it more effectively on the outside when released. But much depends on whether inmates are motivated to become involved in programs such as the WEC. Taking advantage of institutional health services is considered essential for many inmates with mental illnesses and behavioral problems (Garrity et al., 2002).

Some vocational/technical and educational programs are tailored to meet the needs of female inmates, including an emphasis on life skills (Schram and Morash, 2002). However, some evidence suggests that significant numbers of females have psychopathy, and that they may respond in different and sometimes unpredictable ways to vocational/technical programs or interventions (Jackson et al., 2002). In an Oregon prison, for example, a program was established in 1992 called the Women in Community Service program (WICS). This program was assessed during the period 1992–1995 and was determined to be effective for female offenders in different ways. The WICS was established to improve one's life skills, self-esteem, and motivation to change behavior. Vocational

FIGURE 7.3   A female chain gang
Courtesy of J.Peter Mortimer, Getty Images, Inc.

skills were emphasized, as well as drug- and alcohol-awareness courses and programs. The program's success has been determined by low recidivism rates among WICS participants in follow-up investigations (Champion, 2005).

By the early 1990s, participation in jail or prison educational programs was mandatory in at least 13 states. Of those states making education mandatory, the primary inmate targets were those with obvious educational deficiencies who did not meet minimum educational criteria. Reduced sentence lengths were offered as incentives to participate in educational programs. The measure of success of these programs was whether inmates continue their education in jail or prison beyond the mandatory minimum. One of the more innovative inmate literacy programs is operated by the Virginia Department of Corrections. Commencing in 1986, the "no read, no release" program has emphasized literacy achievement at no lower than the sixth-grade level and has made such an achievement part of the parole decision-making process. Results have been favorably viewed by various states. However, compulsory educational programs in jails and prisons have been subjected to several constitutional challenges.

In recent years, more than a few prison systems have gravitated toward offering life skills programs as a part of their educational services. The Delaware Department of Correction, for instance, established a life skills program in 1997. This program was offered in each of its four state prisons, where 5,000 inmates were housed. Participation in the program was voluntary, but each year approximately 300 inmates have enrolled. Nearly 85 percent have graduated from the program. The Delaware Life Skills Program, as it is called, runs three hours a day for four months. Each of five teachers conducts a morning and an afternoon course with 12 to 15 inmates in each course. The curriculum stresses three areas: academics; violence reduction; and applied life skills. Academics includes reading comprehension, mathematics, and language expression. The violence reduction component includes moral recognition therapy, anger management, and conflict resolution training. The applied life skills component includes credit and banking; job search; motor vehicle regulations; legal responsibilities and restitution; family responsibilities and child support; health issues; social services; educational services; cultural differences; and government and law. An evaluation of the life skills program offered by Delaware shows that the recidivism rate among program graduates was only 19 percent. This compares quite favorably with a control group where the recidivism rate was 27 percent. Thus, the objective of reducing recidivism among life skills participants was realized at all four Delaware institutions.

Parolees often benefit from the array of services extended to them in prison settings. Participating in educational programs, Alcoholics Anonymous, or some other educational or counseling is viewed as a desire to better oneself and indicative that rehabilitation may have occurred. Rehabilitation may or may not occur for particular inmates, depending on whether they manipulate the system or use it for true self-improvement. In any case, parole boards seem impressed with whatever progress inmates manifest, regardless of an inmate's motives. Indeed, some research indicates that at least some parolees benefit in their post-release after participating in correctional higher education programs.

Jail and Prison Privatization

A proposal that has received mixed reactions in recent years is the privatization of jail and prison management by private interests. Legally, there is nothing to prevent private enterprises from operating prisons and jails as extensions of state and local governments and law enforcement agencies. Privatization has been most noticeable in the juvenile justice system. In fact, in 2002 over 30 percent of all incarcerated juveniles were being held in facilities owned and operated by private interests (Camp et al., 2002). Private interests argue that they can manage and operate jails and prisons more effectively and economically than many government agencies. Presently, this issue remains unresolved. However, there is no debating the fact that private sector proposals for the management of jails and other facilities have been increasing in recent years and result in considerable savings for the contracting local and state governments.

A significant hurdle is the political control issue. Who has control over offenders housed in and managed by persons in the private sector? Another issue is an administrative one. Should private enterprises be allowed to sanction convicted offenders? Will the current level of quality of inmate care be maintained when operated by private interests? Many government facilities are currently under court order to improve their living conditions for inmates. It is unlikely that the private sector would do a poorer managerial task relating to inmate management. But the accountability issue persists.

Privatization has spread to probation and parole program operations. Private corporations can prepare pre-sentence investigation reports. They can also assist probation and parole departments in supervising probationer- or parolee-clients. In fact, guidelines are presently available to local and state governments about how private interests can interface with their own program operations and organization. In fact, the privatization phenomenon in corrections is not unique to the United States.

A positive view of privatization in corrections is to view this phenomenon as an extension and a complement to existing public correctional programs. Private interests have been instrumental in devising many correctional innovations, including electronic monitoring and new technology for surveillance, control, and drug testing (Tarnai, 2006). Private innovators in corrections have made it possible for many convicted offenders to become enrolled in intermediate punishment programs and endure many sanctions imposed in lieu of traditional incarceration in a jail or prison.

Gang Formation and Perpetuation

One of the most serious problems in jails and prisons today is the prevalence and influence of gangs (Straka, 2003). A 2002 survey of all major U.S. prisons disclosed that although two-thirds had specific policies that prohibited gang recruitment, there was a gang presence in almost all facilities surveyed. About one-sixth of all institutions reported that gang members had assaulted correctional staff. Two-thirds of all institutions were providing some form of gang training for their correctional officers. Such training included recognition signs such as tattoos, clothing colors and trinkets, and hand gestures.

No one knows precisely how many gang members there are in U.S. prisons and jails today. And gangs are not exclusively a United States phenomenon. Gangs are found in virtually all prisons throughout the world (Straka, 2003). Estimates of 100,000 or more prison inmates involved in formal gang activity have been made, although that figure is probably much higher (Lowry, Eichhorn, and Argueta, 2006). Since many prison gang members were former street gang members, some

FIGURE 7.4   Isolating inmates defeats prison gang formation
Courtesy of John Chiasson, Getty Images, Inc.

idea of the prevalence of gangs in prisons can be gleaned by examining the prevalence and numbers of street gangs and their memberships. In 2002, for example, there were over 28,000 gangs and 780,000 gang members in the United States (Straka, 2003). Self-reports from a sample of gang members who were surveyed by researchers indicated that most of these gang members were involved in one or more illegal activities and were committing crimes. A sizeable portion of these gang members had served time in juvenile secure facilities, jails, or prisons.

Generally for prisons but also for jails, gang members are believed responsible for 50 percent or more of all institutional disturbances and problems. For this reason, several correctional systems have aggressively established programs designed to defeat gang influence and discourage gang recruitment and membership practices in a variety of ways. One effort is the Gang-Free Environment Program, established in Illinois in 1996. The Taylorville Correctional Center (TCC) was created as a gang-free institution. Inmates were selected on the basis of their non-gang status. Programs were created to emphasize self-improvement, education, and employability, and to deemphasize any need for gang affiliation. This meant that the institution had to create a safe environment for all inmates. Correctional officers received various types of training calculated to help them relate more effectively with inmates and to recognize any attempt at gang formation among the prisoners. One goal of the TCC is to encourage inmates to make general changes in their lifestyles. A Lifestyle Redirection Program has been initiated where various courses are offered to all inmates. Inmates are virtually free from any pressure to join gangs. The inmate selection process has been mostly successful (Alarid and Cromwell, 2002). Unfortunately, not all prisons are capable of offering such a luxury to their inmates. Prison gangs are not only pervasive but they are also powerful.

Prison gang development has been described. For instance, prospective recruits for existing prison gangs enter prison with feelings of fear of the new setting. They sense danger, feel isolated, and are lonely. There are virtually no rules for acceptance, no commitment to any group, no rules of conduct that are immediately apparent, and no formal leadership. Subsequently, many inmates gravitate toward one gang or another, often along racial or ethnic lines. The prison gang itself is characterized as having the following: (1) formal rules and constitution; (2) well-defined goals and philosophy; (3) hierarchy of formal leadership with clearly defined authority and responsibility; (4) membership for life; (5) members wear gang tattoos; (6) wholesale involvement in gang activities both inside and outside of the penal institution; and (7) ongoing criminal enterprise.

In many instances, gangs have controlled prison culture and what transpires behind prison walls. They have intimidated prison staff. Furthermore, there is evidence that the same gangs have affiliate gangs in prisons in other states besides the ones where they originate (Straka, 2003). Beyond the disruptive effects of gangs on prison order and their influence over others within institutions, there are far-reaching effects that extend to those released from prison. Once someone has joined a prison gang, he or she is a part of that gang for life. Usually the only way to leave a gang is by dying. The thought of betraying another gang member either within or without prison walls is reprehensible for most gang members. Therefore, when a gang member leaves prison either by serving his or her time or through parole, there is a continuing allegiance to the gang that is expected. If the gang member outside of prison can do one or more favors or perform services for other gang members inside prison, then he or she will perform these favors or services. In most instances, these favors involve criminal activity of one type or another.

POs have a strong interest in determining whether their clients are affiliated with gangs. They learn gang recognition signals and familiarize themselves with gang territories in areas where their clients live. Gangs are considered community threat groups. Different states and the U.S. Probation Office have established specialized threat group programs where they attempt to coordinate their resources to combat those gang members on probation or parole who pose a serious threat to their communities (Sheehy and Rosario, 2003). Certain POs have special gang expertise and work with offenders who are gang members. It is their responsibility to identify tell-tale signs of gang activity and whether their clients are continuing their gang affiliations and traditions despite probation or parole program requirements to the contrary.

For probationers and parolees, gangs have a pervasive influence on whether these persons can remain law-abiding and conform with their different programs. There is ample evidence that prison and street gangs are closely intertwined. If gang membership requires probationers or parolees to commit new offenses, such as requisitioning drugs or money for currently incarcerated inmate-gang members, then this is a serious situation that POs must confront and resolve.

Several methods are presently being employed to minimize the influence of gangs in both prisons and on the streets. Sophisticated tracking programs are being devised so that computer tracking of gang members can occur. Understanding the communication patterns of gang members both inside and outside of prison is crucial to effective PO work, especially for those POs who work closely with known gang members.

THE ROLE OF JAILS AND PRISONS IN PROBATION AND PAROLE DECISION MAKING

Whether inmates are in jails or prisons, they are obligated to comply with specific behavioral guidelines that will permit jail and prison officials to maintain order and discipline. Besides these requirements, many prisons and some jails have programs designed to assist inmates in different ways. Educational or vocational training are more readily available in prison settings, although some of the larger jails offer similar programs for long-term offenders. Remember that many jails have contracts with state and federal prison systems to house some of their inmate overflow. Thus, not every jail inmate is incarcerated for shorter intervals of a year or less. Counseling and other forms of assistance are available to inmates if these want such services (Eisenberg and Trusty, 2002).

Jail and prison officers and administrators are in positions of submitting written reports about inmate conduct while confined. These reports may contain favorable or unfavorable information. Ultimately, this information is made available to paroling authorities so that a more informed parole decision can be made. If inmates cannot conduct themselves in a setting with explicit rules and regulations, then it is presumed that they cannot function well in their communities if released short of serving their full prison terms.

The federal government and various states have experimented with various predictive classification systems used for pretrial detainees. Therefore, even in instances where one's guilt or innocence has not yet been established through trial, some preliminary screening mechanisms have already been implemented that may impact either favorably or unfavorably on a judge's sentencing decision later. In the Federal Bureau of Prisons, for instance, pretrial detainees have been screened by various instruments and according to different predictive criteria to determine which alleged offenders would be good candidates for pretrial release. The results of such experimentation have been thus far inconclusive. Similar attempts to classify offenders have been made in other countries, such as Canada (Loza and Loza, 2002).

Attempts have also been made to forecast the successfulness of probationers based, in part, on their incarcerative experiences. Some probationers have been held in jails in pretrial detention until their trials. Others have been released on their own recognizance (ROR). Interestingly, many offenders who are or have been incarcerated for periods exceeding two days seem to have a much higher rate of offending than those who are released on their own recognizance. Factors relating to one's successful probation completion include being older, employed, married, and having some previous military service. We might speculate here that offenders who are held in pretrial detention may be more serious offenders compared with those freed on their own recognizance pending a trial.

Some jails and most prisons attempt to screen incoming inmates according to their risk or dangerousness as well as their special needs (Lemieux, Dyeson, and Castiglione, 2002). Screening is also conducted to evaluate offenders and determine the most suitable level of custody for them. Since it becomes increasingly expensive to monitor offenders as the level of custody increases (e.g., from minimum security to medium security, from medium security to maximum security), it is in an institution's best interests economically to maintain prisoners at the least intense custody level while they are confined. This is why most prisons have reassessments of inmates periodically (e.g., every six months or a year) to determine whether their present level of custody should be increased or decreased.

For inmates in various state and federal prison systems, inmate classifications are very important in several respects. Imposing more stringent monitoring and closer custody on those prisoners who are considered most aggressive and violent will serve to protect less serious and nonviolent inmates. Beyond this, the lower one's classification level, the more the trust accorded that inmate. Parole boards consider one's present level of custody and whether one has behaved well while at that particular custody level. Again, it is in a prisoner's best interests to be confined at the lowest security level possible. Therefore, periodic reclassifications of offenders that tend to downgrade their present levels of custody are positive moves that influence one's parole chances accordingly. The prison system itself plays a crucial role in determining whether parole will be granted. Other relevant factors are the seriousness of the conviction offense, length of the original sentence, and the amount of time served in relation to that sentence length.

In sum, jails and prisons are playing increasingly important roles in probation and parole decision making. Jails are devising more sophisticated classification procedures commensurate with those used in most prison systems. These classification systems are helpful in separating offenders according to several criteria that optimize their safety and needs. As jails become more like prisons by establishing a broader array of inmate programs of an educational and vocational nature, inmates themselves will be able to do more to influence their chances of more favorable treatment (Levenson and Farrant, 2002). They can take affirmative steps to ensure their involvement in community correctional programs where fewer restrictions exist.

SUMMARY

Jails were originally conceived as short-term facilities to house offenders charged with minor offenses, pretrial detainees, and those serving relatively short sentences. The American Jail Association considers a facility a jail if it houses inmates for periods of 72 hours or longer. Those facilities holding persons overnight are either lockups or holding tanks. In 2001, there were between 3,300 and 3,400 jails in the United States. In recent decades, jails have inadvertently assumed additional functions and responsibilities, including housing juvenile offenders for short periods, holding federal and state prisoner overflows on a contractual basis with various government agencies, housing witnesses, and providing a temporary haven for those suffering from psychological or mental problems. Jails also house probation and parole violators. Jails have little or no control over the types of inmates housed. About half of all jail inmates are unconvicted offenders, including drunks and vagrants. Shock probationers are also accommodated for short periods as a part of their split sentences. Most jails in the United States are old, many having been constructed prior to 1950.

Prisons are long-term facilities designed to hold more serious offenders. Early U.S. prisons were constructed in the late 1700s in Connecticut and Pennsylvania. Auburn (New York) State Penitentiary introduced several important innovations in American corrections in the early 1800s, including the tier system, solitary confinement, and the congregate system. Striped uniforms also were pioneered by Auburn Penitentiary. Prisons are designed to provide societal protection, punish offenders, rehabilitate offenders, and assist in their eventual reintegration into society. Inmate classification is an important feature of prison systems. Prisons classify inmates into different security levels, such as minimum, medium, and maximum security. Inmate housing costs rise as their custody level increases.

Jails are acquiring many of the characteristics of prisons, as officials acknowledge a growing jail population consisting of federal and state prisoners in need of rehabilitative services and other amenities. Jails and prisons share several problems, including chronic overcrowding, inmate violence, and various types of inmate programs. Prison and jail overcrowding is chronic and is a problem for most institutional administrators. Many other problems faced by prison and jail staffs are directly or indirectly influenced by overcrowding. Efforts to alleviate overcrowding have included innovations in building design and architectural re-arrangements that permit more effective utilization of space and promote greater officer efficiency. Podular direct supervision jails and prisons are rapidly becoming popular as the most effective inmate management strategy. The private sector is gradually moving into jail and prison management and operations, effectively reducing inmate maintenance costs. Much privatization has thus far been restricted to juvenile facilities and aftercare, although more privately operated adult facilities are being established in different localities.

Prisons and jails also influence probationers and parolees by providing the courts and parole boards with feedback about inmate conduct while confined. Especially in prisons, an inmate's level of custody can be changed, either upwardly or downwardly, depending on their bad or good conduct. Favorable behavioral reports encourage judges and parole boards to grant probationers and parolees greater benefits and freedoms.

Several issues affecting jails and prisons have been highlighted. Jails and prisons are chronically overcrowded. Overcrowding occurs because there is insufficient space to accommodate all persons who should be incarcerated and there are inadequate resources for new jail and prison construction. Jail and prison overcrowding contribute to and cause various problems for administrators and other inmates. One problem is increasing prison violence and inmate rioting for various reasons. Efforts have been made to reduce the amount of inmate violence (Jiang and Fisher-Giorlando, 2002). Changes in the architectural design and structuring of jails and prisons have lessened the incidence of violence in certain jurisdictions. Furthermore, the addition of helpful programs and services for inmate use have assisted many inmates to improve their personal skills and self-images. Thus, both jails and prisons today have made a concerted effort to furnish inmates with ample opportunities for self-improvement through vocational/technical and educational classes, group or individual counseling programs, and courses relating to anger management and improvement in social skills and interpersonal relations. Increasingly, the privatization of jails and prisons is occurring, although only a small fraction of the U.S. jail and prison inmate population today is under the control of private interests. Finally, gang presence in jails and prisons has increased over the past several decades. The formation and perpetuation of gangs in prison settings was examined, as well as the continuing effects of gang membership on parolees when they reenter their communities.

QUESTIONS FOR REVIEW

1. What are some important events in the evolution of jails in the United States?
2. What are some general functions of jails? How do these contrast with the functions of prisons?
3. What were some of the innovations introduced by the Auburn State Penitentiary? Are any of these innovations still in evidence in modern-day prisons?

4. How do jails differ from lockups and drunk tanks?

5. What innovations did the Walnut Street Jail introduce? What was the influence of religion in correctional reforms during the 1700s and 1800s in the United States?

6. What is a detainer warrant? Who is likely to be served with a detainer warrant?

7. How do prisons and jails influence probation and parole violators?

8. What are some general factors considered important when classifying offenders for placement in prisons? What are risk elements?

9. Identify three major issues of relevance to both prisons and jails. Indicate in a brief paragraph how these issues are important to prison and jail operations and management.

10. What is a direct supervision jail? What are some of its characteristics for offender management?

SUGGESTED READINGS

Birzer, Michael and Delores Craig-Morehead (2006). "Why Do Jails Charge Housing Fees?" *American Jails* **20:**63–68.

Etter, Sr., Gregg W. and Robet L. Hinshaw (2006). "Managing High-Profile Inmates in a Jail Setting." *Corrections Today* **68:**28–31.

McCampbell, Susan W. (2006). "Gender-Responsive Strategies for Women Offenders: The Gender-Response Strategies Project: Jail Applications." *American Jails* **20:**15–22.

Nelson, Signe and Lynn Olcott (2006). "Jail Time Is Learning Time." *Corrections Today* **68:**26–31, 41.

Wener, Richard (2006). "Direct Supervision: Evolution and Revolution." *American Jails* **20:**21–24.

INTERNET CONNECTIONS

American Correctional Chaplains Association
http://www.correctionalchaplains.com/

American Correctional Health Services Association
http://www.corrections.com/achsa/indexl.html

American Civil Liberties Union
http://www.aclu.org

American Jail Association
http://www.corrections.com/aja

American Service Group, Inc.
http://www.asgr.com/

Amnesty International
http://www.amnesty.org

Caged Kittens
http://www.cagedkittens.com

Citizens for Effective Justice
http://www.okplus.com/fedup/

Citizens for Legal Responsibility
http://www.clr.org/

Connections: A Correctional Education Program Serving Offenders with Special Learning Needs
http://www.theconnectionsprogram.com/MainPageText.htm

Cook County Boot Camp
http://www.cookcountysheriff.org/bootcamp/

Correctional Medical Services
http://www.cmsstl.com

Corrections resources
http://www.officer.com/correct

CounterPunch
http://www.counterpunch.org

CSS Special Supervision Services
http://www.csosa.gov/css_specialsupervision.htm

Death Row Speaks
http://www.deathrowspeaks.net/

Federal Bureau of Prisons
http://www.bop.gov/

Federal Bureau of Prisons Library
http://www.bop.library.net/

Federal Prison Consultants
http://www.federalprisonconsultants.com/

Female Inmate Pen Pals
http://www.thepamperedprisoner.com

Female Special Needs Offenders
*http://www.stars.csg.org/slc/special/
2000/female_offenders.htm*

Gamblers Anonymous
http://www.gamblersanonymous.org/

George A. Keene, Inc.
http://www.keenejailequip.com/

International Association of Correctional
Training Personnel
http://www.iactp.org/

International Institute on Special Needs
Offenders
http://www.iisno.org.uk

Jail Management
*http://www.mmmicro.com/
jail_management.htm*

Koch Crime Institute
*http://www.kci.org/publications/bootcamp
/docs/nij/Correctional_Boot+Camps/
chpt17.htm*

NaphCare, Inc.
http://www.naphcare.com/

Narcotics Anonymous
http://www.na.org

Narcotics Complete Recovery Center
http://www.drugrehab.net

National Institute of Corrections
http://www.nicic.org/

National Institute of Corrections Jail
Administration Training Program
*http://www.nicic.org/services/training/
programs/jails/jail-admin.htm*

Objective Jail Classification
http://www.corrections.com/aja/training

Online Friends to Death Row Inmates
http://www.freeworldfriends.com

PRC Jail Record Management System
http://www.northrupgrummanit.com

PS.NET
http://www.ps.net/cms

Recovery Resources Online
http://www.soberrecovery.com

The Program for Female Offenders, Inc.
*http://www.fcnetworks.org/Dir98/
dir98front.html*

Unauthorized Federal Prison Manual
http://www.bureauofprisons.com/

Very Special Women
http://www.vswomen.com

Women Behind Bars
http://www.womenbehindbars.com/

Women in Criminal Justice
http://www.wicj.com

Women's Prison Association
*http://www.wpaonline.org/WEBSITE/
home.htm*

Chapter Outline

Chapter Objectives

As the result of reading this chapter, the following objectives will be realized:

1. Describing the history and evolution of parole in the United States.
2. Identifying key figures who created or devised new early release systems.
3. Understanding the philosophy of parole as well as highlighting some of the functions parole serves.
4. Describing some of the major functions of parole programs.
5. Profiling parolees, including successful and unsuccessful ones.
6. Examining reentry of parolees back into their communities and the many problems they face as they attempt to become reintegrated.
7. Highlighting some of the more important trends observed in contemporary parole in the United States.

• *Furnari was a federal prisoner convicted of offenses related to organized crime. After serving a portion of his sentence and thus becoming eligible for supervised release on parole, Furnari applied for parole but the U.S. Parole Commission denied his early release. Grounds cited for denying his early release from prison included evidence of his alleged participation in four murders and attempted murder, crimes that were uncharged and for which he was not convicted. Furnari objected to the fact that the U.S. Parole Commission relied in part on evidence of uncharged offenses in denying him early release and appealed. The Third Circuit Court of Appeals heard the case and upheld the U.S. Parole Commission's denial of Furnari's parole. The appellate court declared that the Parole Commission has broad discretionary authority in materials it considers for parole decisions, including dismissed counts of an indictment, hearsay evidence, and allegations of criminal activity for which the prisoner was not even charged.* [Furnari v. U.S. Parole Commission, *125 Fed.App. 435 (U.S.3rdCir.March) (2005)].*

• *Adams was a federal prisoner seeking parole. He filed a Section 1983 petition, alleging that his civil rights were violated by parole commission members who allegedly relied on erroneous information when they denied him early release. The Eighth Circuit Court of Appeals heard his case and upheld the U.S. Parole Commission's decision to deny him parole. The court said that Adams was seemingly attempting to correct allegedly erroneous information in his parole record rather than challenging the legality of his sentence or the factual bases for his conviction. Furthermore, Adams could not prove facts that would support his claims of discrimination or violations of his due process rights as alleged in his petition. The court also stated that inmates do not have a constitutionally protected liberty interest in the possibility of parole.* [Adams v. Agniel, *405 F.3d 643 (U.S.8thCir.May) (2005)].*

• *Johnson was a New York inmate convicted of a violent crime. When Johnson became eligible for parole, he sought early release from the New York State Board of Parole. The parole board convened and denied Johnson's request for early release, placing particular emphasis on Johnson's violent offense conviction to justify the parole denial. Johnson filed an appeal, alleging that the parole board is obligated to consider all factors equally, including his social history and background, institutional conduct, and efforts toward rehabilitation. Furthermore, Johnson claimed that the parole board decision was politically motivated and that it had a vested interest in denying violent offenders early release. An appeals court heard Johnson's case and upheld the parole board decision, stating that parole decisions are discretionary and that parole boards are not required to give equal weight to or specifically discuss every factor considered in making its decision. The allegations that the parole board decision in Johnson's case was politically motivated and that it automatically denied parole to all violent offenders were unsubstantiated and unpersuasive.* [Johnson v. New York State Board of Parole, *790 N.Y.S.2d 733 (N.Y.Sup.App.Div.March) (2005)*].

- *Seegars was an Oklahoma inmate who was seeking parole. During the time Seegars was confined in an Oklahoma prison, the Oklahoma legislature enacted a change in the law pertaining to the parole eligibility date for all inmates. The law change extended from one year to three years the time that must elapse before inmates may become parole-eligible. Seegars had served more than one year but less than three years when he sought parole, and the parole board applied the new law in denying Seegars early release. Seegars appealed, claiming that this parole denial violated* ex post facto *laws and thus violated his due process rights. A federal appeals court heard Seegars's case and upheld his parole denial. The court declared that although Oklahoma had changed the calculation of parole eligibility dates during Seegars's term of confinement, it did not alter the definition of criminal conduct or increase his punishment for his conviction offense. Thus, changing parole eligibility time guidelines does not violate inmate rights to due process because it doesn't change their punishment. Entitlement to parole is not a constitutionally protected right.* [Seegars v. Ward, *124 Fed.App. 637 (U.S.10th Cir.March) (2005)*].

INTRODUCTION

These scenarios suggest that parole is a complex decision that often involves a variety of criteria that are not clear-cut. In Furnari's case, he was denied parole partially on the basis of crimes he had not been convicted of committing. The parole board relied to some extent on hearsay rather than hard evidence of his guilt in these unproven crimes. Adams attempted to challenge his parole denial through a civil rights action that was deemed inappropriate and unsubstantiated on the record. Johnson, the New York inmate, found that the parole board did not have to give equal weight to all factors that might influence his early release and that parole is not a constitutionally protected right. Seegars argued ineffectively that legislative changes in parole policy and time guidelines for early release may be made without violating his due process rights, and that *ex post facto* law changes and their application, where one's punishment is not increased and one's criminal conduct is not redefined, are not unconstitutional.

This chapter looks at parole or early release from prison. A brief history of parole in the United States is provided. Included is a discussion of the philosophy of parole as well as several of its important functions. Parole has been criticized in recent years for various reasons. In some instances, dangerous persons have been paroled and they have committed serious crimes while under parole supervision. Some states have abolished parole outright. Thus, some consideration is given to the positive and negative aspects of parole decision making. Alternatives to parole are also examined. One consideration when contemplating parole for any particular offender is that offender's prior record. Thus, an examination of the types of persons who are paroled is provided.

A growing issue is the reentry of parolees back into their communities. This issue is examined in some detail. Covered are several programs designed to facilitate inmate reentry into their communities. Various obstacles are discussed that impede offender reentry. Methods for overcoming these obstacles are discussed.

Because many parolees have joined gangs while imprisoned, some attention is given to the growing presence in communities and how parolees are affected by such gangs. Gangs have a pervasive and continuing impact on ex-offenders, since there are considerable peer pressures both inside and outside of prison to remain affiliated with gangs and perform various services for them. Gang power over inmates and parolees is described.

PAROLE DEFINED

Parole is the conditional release of a prisoner from incarceration (either from prison or jail) under supervision after a portion of the sentence has been served. The major distinguishing feature between probation and parole is that parolees have served some time incarcerated in either jail or prison, while probationers have avoided incarceration. Some common characteristics shared by both parolees and probationers are that: (1) they have committed crimes, (2) they have been convicted of crimes, (3) they are under the supervision or control of probation or parole officers, and (4) they are subject to one or more similar conditions accompanying their probation or parole programs. Some general differences are that generally, parolees have committed more serious offenses compared with probationers. Also, parolees have been incarcerated for a portion of their sentences while probationers are not generally incarcerated following their convictions for crimes. Furthermore, parolees may have more stringent conditions (e.g., curfew, participation in drug or alcohol rehabilitation, counseling, halfway house participation, more face-to-face contacts with their POs) accompanying their parole programs compared with probationers.

THE HISTORICAL CONTEXT OF PAROLE

Parole existed in eighteenth-century Spain, France, England, and Wales. British convicts under sentence of death or convicted of other serious offenses created for England a problem currently confronting the United States: prison overcrowding. In the eighteenth century, Britain had no penitentiaries. But one option available was to export excess prisoners to the American colonies. After the Revolutionary War, this option no longer existed.

Seeking new locations for isolating its criminals from the rest of society, England selected Australia, one of several remote English colonies that had accommodated small numbers of offenders during the American colonial period when prisoner exportation was popular. The first large-scale **transportation** of convictsfrom England came to Australia in 1788. While many of these transportees were convicted of minor theft, it was intended by the English government that they should become builders and farmers. However, these were trades at which they were highly unsuccessful. It became apparent that officials needed to establish prisons to house some of their prisoner-transportees. One such outpost 1,000 miles off the coast of Australia was **Norfolk Island**, where a penal colony was established. Another was **Van Dieman's Land** (Champion, 2005).

The private secretary to the lieutenant governor of Van Diemen's land in 1836 was a former Royal Navy officer and social reformer, Alexander Maconochie (1787–1860). In 1840, Maconochie was appointed superintendent of the penal colony at Norfolk Island. When he arrived to assume his new duties, he was appalled by what he found. Prisoners were lashed repeatedly and tortured frequently by other means. Maconochie had personal views and a penchant for humanitarianism, and his lenient administrative style toward prisoners was unpopular with his superiors as well as other penal officials. For instance, Maconochie believed that confinement ought to be rehabilitative, not punitive. Also, he felt that prisoners ought to be granted early release from custody if they behaved well and did good work while confined. Thus, Maconochie established the **mark system** whereby he gave prisoners **marks of commendation** and authorized the early release of certain inmates who demonstrated a willingness and ability to behave well in society on the outside. This action was the early manifestation of indeterminate sentencing that was subsequently established in the United States. Maconochie's termination as superintendent at Norfolk Island occurred largely because he filed a report that condemned the English penal system and the disciplinary measures used by the island penal colony. He was sent back to England in 1844.

Maconochie's prison reform work did not end with this dismissal. During the next five years, Maconochie was transferred from one desk job to another, although he continued to press for penal reforms. Eventually he was reassigned, probably as a probationary move by his superiors, to the governorship of the new Birmingham Borough Prison. His position there lasted less than two years. His superiors dismissed him for being too lenient with prisoners. In 1853, he successfully lobbied for the passage of the English Penal Servitude Act that established several rehabilitation programs for inmates and abolished transporting prisoners to Australia. Because of these significant improvements in British penal policy and the institutionalization of early-release provisions throughout England's prison system, Maconochie is credited as being the father of parole.

Sir Walter Crofton, a prison reformer and director of Ireland's prison system during the 1850s, was impressed by Maconochie's work and copied his three-stage intermediate system whereby Irish prisoners could earn their early conditional release. Crofton, also known as another father of parole in various European countries, modified Maconochie's plan whereby prisoners would be subject to: (1) strict imprisonment for a time; (2) transferred to an intermediate prison for a short period where they could participate in educational programs and perform useful and responsible tasks to earn **good marks;** and (3) given tickets-of-leave where they would be released from prison on license under the limited supervision of local police. Under this third ticket-of-leave stage, released prisoners were required to submit monthly reports of their progress to police who assisted them in finding work. A study of 557 prisoners during that period showed only 17 had their tickets-of-leave revoked for various infractions. Thus, Walter Crofton pioneered what later came to be known as several major functions of parole officers: employment assistance to released prisoners, regular visits by officers to parolees, and the general supervision of their activities (Champion, 2005).

The United States connection with the European use of parole allegedly occurred in 1863 when Gaylord Hubbell, the warden at Sing Sing Prison, New York, visited Ireland and conferred with Crofton about his penal innovations and parole system. Subsequently, the National Prison Association convened in Cincinnati, Ohio, in 1870 and considered the Irish parole system as a primary portion of its agenda. Attending that meeting were Crofton, Hubbell, and other reformers and penologists. The meeting resulted in the establishment of a Declaration of Principles, which promoted an indeterminate sentence and a classification system based largely on Crofton's work. Crofton's mark system, which was intended to reward prisoners for behaving well while confined, was probably the forerunner of what is now known today as good-time credit. Inmates can accumulate good-time credit and apply it against their maximum sentences, which can be used for early release from prison.

Zebulon Brockway became the new superintendent of the New York State Reformatory at Elmira in 1876 and was instrumental in the passage of the first indeterminate sentencing law in the United States. He is also credited with introducing the first **good-time system** where an inmate's sentence to be served is reduced by the number of good marks earned. **Good time** was given, which was credit applied to one's maximum sentence. If an inmate accumulated sufficient good-time credit, then he or she could be released short of serving the full sentence originally imposed by the judge. Once this system was in operation and shown to be moderately effective, several other states patterned their own early-release standards after it in later years. Elmira Reformatory was important, in part, because it used the good-time release system for prisoners in 1876. Actually, the practice of using early release for inmates occurred in the United States much earlier. Parole was officially established in Boston by Samuel G. Howe in 1847. From 1790 to 1817, convicts were obligated to serve their entire sentences in prison (Champion, 2005).

In 1817, New York adopted a form of commutation or lessening of sentence that became known as good time. Through the accumulation of sufficient good time, an inmate could be granted early release through his good behavior. This good-time early release was essentially a **pardon,** an executive device designed to absolve offenders of their crimes committed and release them, thus alleviating the prison overcrowding situation. The unofficial practice of parole, therefore, preceded the unofficial practice of probation by several decades. Officially, however, true parole resulted from the ticket-of-leave practice and was first adopted by Massachusetts in 1884, also the state first implementing officially the practice of probation in 1878 (Champion, 2005).

PAROLE AND ALTERNATIVE SENTENCING SYSTEMS

A general relation exists between indeterminate sentencing and parole. However, when jurisdictions adopt indeterminate sentencing schemes, this does not mean that either parole or parole boards are automatically established. Indeterminate sentencing indicates a minimum and a maximum term of years or months inmates may serve. Ordinarily, inmates must serve the minimum amount of time specified, but they may be released in different ways short of serving their full terms. Ordinarily, parole boards determine early-release dates for inmates under this type of sentencing system. But there are other early-release options besides parole board actions. For example, by 1911, nine states were using indeterminate sentencing. However, 11 years earlier in 1900, 20 states had established parole plans to effect the early release of prison inmates. Some of these jurisdictions had mandatory sentencing provisions, while others had determinate sentencing schemes. Early release short of serving one's full term could be administratively granted, from prison officials or the governor, or through the accumulation of good-time credits applied against the maximum time to be served. In short, it is not the case that indeterminate sentencing and parole boards must coexist in any jurisdiction simultaneously.

Usually, a parole system in any state prison consisted of the warden and other local authorities including the prison physician, the superintendent of prisons, and certain community officials. The federal prison system had no formal parole board until 1910, and it was similarly comprised of officials making up state parole boards. Prior to the establishment of these boards and within the context of indeterminate sentencing, the discretion to release a prisoner short of serving his full term rested with the prison warden, superintendent, or state governor.

By 1944, all states had parole systems. The United States Congress formally established a United States Board of Parole in 1930. And by the 1960s, all states had some form of indeterminate sentencing. Apart from the obvious benefits of alleviating prison overcrowding, parole and indeterminate sentencing was perceived for nearly a century as a panacea for reforming criminals. The rehabilitative ideal dominated the structure and process of all phases of corrections as well as most corrections programs.

Not all states used parole for rehabilitative purposes, however. In 1893, California adopted parole as a way of minimizing the use of clemency by governors and to correct and/or modify excessive prison sentences in relation to certain crimes committed. In fact, officials who favored parole in California were skeptical about its rehabilitative value. Parole was seen primarily as a period during which the end of a determinate sentence would occur that was originally imposed by the court. But a majority of the states stressed the rehabilitative value of indeterminate sentencing and parole generally. While the principle of deterrence dominated corrections philosophy for most of the period 1820–1900, from 1900–1960, the principle of rehabilitation was of primary importance. Indeterminate sentencing was largely in the hands of corrections "observers" such as social workers, wardens, and probation and parole officers.

One early criticism of parole was contained in a series of reports issued in 1931 by the **Wickersham Commission,** a National Commission on Law Observance and Enforcement (National Commission on Law Observance and Enforcement, 1931). The Wickersham Commission derived its name from its chairman, George W. Wickersham, a former United States Attorney General. Prepared shortly after the Prohibition Era and the Depression, the Wickersham reports were very critical of most criminal justice agencies and how they dealt with crime and criminals. Parole was not the sole target of criticism by the Wickersham Commission. However, it did receive many criticisms. Among the criticisms was that parole released many dangerous criminals into society, and these offenders were not rehabilitated and were unsupervised. Also, the Wickersham Commission did not believe that a suitable system existed for determining which prisoners should be eligible for parole. While these reports caused considerable debate among corrections professionals for several years, nothing was done to alter the existing operations of state or federal parole systems. The rehabilitation or medical model became increasingly popular, together with social work and psychiatry, as members of these helping professions attempted to treat prisoner adjustment problems through therapy, medicine, and counseling.

Indeterminate Sentencing and Parole

Indeterminate sentencing is the only sentencing scheme that involves the intervention of parole boards. Because parole boards are vested with virtually absolute discretion concerning who does and doesn't get paroled, they are considered powerful entities. But because they have been responsible for the release of more than a few inmates who have subsequently committed violent crimes, they have attracted considerable adverse criticism. The major positive and negative aspects of indeterminate sentencing have been described. Some of the positive features of indeterminate sentencing include:

1. Allows for full implementation of rehabilitative ideal.
2. Offers best means of motivating involuntarily committed inmates to work for rehabilitation.
3. Offers maximum protection to society from hardcore recidivists and mentally defective offenders.
4. Helps maintain an orderly environment within the institution.
5. Prevents unnecessary incarceration of an offender and thus helps to prevent the correctional system from becoming a factory from which offenders emerge as hardened criminals.
6. Offers a feasible alternative to capital punishment.
7. Removes judgment as to length of incarceration from the trial court and puts it in the hands of a qualified panel of behavioral observers who make their final decision based on considerably more evidence than is available at the post-conviction stage of the trial.
8. Decision as to length of incarceration reflects the needs of the offender and not the gravity of the crime, in the best interests of both society and offender.
9. Prevents correctional authorities from being forced to release from custody an offender who is clearly not ready to rejoin society.
10. Prevents problem offender from retreating into a "sick" role during rehabilitation.
11. Acts as a deterrent to crime.

Some of the negative features of indeterminate sentences are:

1. Treatment is a myth, and vocational training is a fraud; inmates are neither treated, trained, nor rehabilitated.
2. Even if treatment were honestly attempted by staffs, psychotherapy with involuntarily committed patients is generally considered difficult; indeterminate sentencing supplies only negative motivation, which will be insufficient for long-range results.
3. Even if effective therapy were plausible for some offenders, it is neither justified nor proper for all offenders, and there should be a right not to receive unwanted therapy.
4. Treatment is tokenism and rehabilitation is almost nonexistent; therefore, the indeterminate sentence is a device to hide society's dehumanizing treatment of criminals, particularly those who are poor or members of minority groups.
5. While taking criminals off the street, indeterminate sentencing makes it easy for society to ignore the underlying causes of crime.
6. The indeterminate sentence is most often used as an instrument of inmate control.
7. Psychiatrists become more jailers than healers; they know they will have to testify later in court about the patient and recommend or not recommend a prisoner's release.

8. Designations of some offenders as mentally ill is extremely arbitrary; therefore, single treatment approaches are impossible to devise.

9. There is great danger that indeterminate sentencing will be used to punish persons for unpopular political beliefs and views; religious and political nonconformists are ones most likely to rebel against the therapeutic system.

10. Indeterminate sentencing encourages the smart or cunning offender and is more favorable to him than to the less intelligent offender.

11. Despite the fact that courts are supposed to retain some measure of control, there is no adequate protection from life imprisonment under the guise of indeterminate sentencing.

Because of rising crime rates, unacceptable levels of recidivism among parolees, and general dissension among the ranks of corrections professionals about the most effective ways of dealing with offenders, the 1970s reflected a gradual decline in the significance and influence of the rehabilitation model. However, selected jurisdictions have reported success with parole programs where effective community supervision and offender management have been provided, or where POs have performed their supervisory roles properly. Whether parole rehabilitates is arguable. In any case, the rehabilitation model has been largely replaced by the justice model. The mission of the justice model or perspective is fairness, where prison is regarded as the instrument whereby sentences are implemented and is not to be held accountable for rehabilitating offenders. The justice model has assisted greatly in prompting most states as well as the federal government to undertake extensive revisions of their sentencing guidelines. The general thrust of these revisions is toward a get-tough-on-crime crusade that is replacing reform with retribution.

Another goal of the justice model is to minimize if not eliminate entirely any sentencing disparities often associated with indeterminate sentencing schemes and the arbitrariness of parole board decisions. It is questionable, however, whether any sentencing scheme will achieve such desirable results. Some authorities suggest that there is every reason to believe that judges will continue to impose sentences according to previous discriminatory patterns where extralegal factors are influential. These extralegal factors include race, ethnicity, gender, age, and socioeconomic status.

The Shift to Determinate Sentencing

Nearly half of all states had shifted from indeterminate to determinate sentencing by 2005. These sentencing shifts have resulted in the abolition of paroling authority in a few states for making early prisoner release decisions. An additional consequence has been to limit the discretionary sentencing power of judges. The remaining states and the District of Columbia have also instituted numerous sentencing reforms calculated to deal more harshly with offenders, to reduce or eliminate sentencing disparities attributable to race, ethnicity, or socioeconomic status, to increase prisoner release predictability as well as the certainty of incarceration, and/or to deter or control crime. In many of these states, the authority of parole boards to grant early release as well as the calculation of good-time credits have been restricted to varying degrees.

On November 1, 1987, the United States Sentencing Commission revamped existing sentencing guidelines entirely for federal district judges

(Champion, 2005). The long-range implications of these changes are unknown. However, some preliminary estimates have been projected. For instance, the average time served prior to November 1, 1987, for kidnapping was from 7.2 to 9 years. Under the new guidelines, they provide an incarcerative term for offenders of from 4.2 to 5.2 years. However, for first-degree murder convictions, the new guidelines prescribe 30 years to life for all offenders compared with 10 to 12.5 years time served, on the average, under old sentencing practices by federal judges. Therefore, more convicted felons will go to prison, but many of these offenses will carry shorter incarceration terms.

While these sentencing guidelines are only applicable to United States district courts and federal judges and magistrates, some states have similar guidelines-based or presumptive sentencing schemes. Other states such as California, Minnesota, Pennsylvania, and Washington already have existing penalties for certain offenses that are similar in severity to those prescribed for the same offenses by the United States sentencing guidelines. By 2005, 32 states had established sentencing guidelines for their prison inmates (U.S. Department of Justice, 2006).

In Pennsylvania, for instance, sentencing guidelines were introduced in the early 1980s. Compared with an indeterminate sentencing scheme used prior to these guidelines, actual sentences imposed have become more severe for violent offenders. But sentencing severity has also increased for many nonviolent property offenders as well. It is unclear whether this outcome was contemplated by the Pennsylvania State Legislature when the guidelines were determined. At least one objective of Pennsylvania's guidelines was to remedy sentencing disparities. Some evidence suggests that this outcome has been realized in part. But the Pennsylvania state prison growth was 171 percent during the 1980s, so that by 1990, the prison system housing accommodated more than 24,000 inmates in space actually designed for 16,000 inmates. In 2005, Pennsylvania authorities were constructing new prison space to house 30,000 additional offenders at a cost of $2.4 billion.

Critics contend that while determinate sentencing may provide prisoners with release certainty and possibly result in more fairness in the sentencing process, there are several discretionary decisions at various stages in the adjudication and post-adjudication period uncontrolled by this sentencing form. Six decision-making stages and/or factors have been identified as critical to sentencing equity and predictability: (1) the decision to incarcerate; (2) the characteristics of the penalty scaling system, including the numbers of penalty ranges and offense categories; (3) presence or absence of aggravating or mitigating circumstances; (4) the parole review process; (5) the use of good time in calculating early release; and (6) the revocation from supervised release (Champion, 2005).

Additionally, prosecutorial discretion concerning which cases should be prosecuted, reports of arresting officers and circumstances surrounding arrests, evidentiary factors, and judicial idiosyncrasies figure prominently in many sentencing decisions at state and federal levels. Thus, regardless of the nature and scope of existing sentencing provisions, the prospects for the effective control over all of the relevant discretionary decisions that influence sentencing are not overwhelmingly favorable. Although parole boards in 36 states have continued to exercise discretion over the early release of prisoners, parole continues to draw criticism from both the public and corrections professionals.

The American Correctional Association established a Task Force on Parole to examine how states have established and implemented their present parole policies and guidelines (American Correctional Association, 2006). This task force has found that parole is undergoing alteration in various jurisdictions because of both political and public pressures. States such as Pennsylvania have established guidelines for their parole boards to follow for making their early-release decisions about offenders. These guidelines are similar to the ones created in these same states for judicial sentencing decisions.

Good-Time Credits and Early Release

Good-time credits may be called gain time, earned time, statutory time, meritorious time, commutation time, provisional credits, good conduct credits, or disciplinary credits. Whatever the term, good time is a reward for good behavior and a prevalent management tool in most U.S. prisons. For instance, Arkansas allows good-time credits for every 30 days served. Thus, when offenders are sentenced to 10 years in Arkansas, offenders know that for every month they serve, 30 days will be deducted from their 10-year maximum term. In Iowa, the standard of 15 days of good time for every 30 days served is used. Therefore, serving six years in an Iowa prison means that three years is deducted from one's original 10-year sentence. Accumulating good time and being released is not the same thing as being paroled. In the case of an Arkansas inmate who has served one-half of his or her original sentence, he or she is free from prison without conditions. This is not absolute in all jurisdictions, however. In some states, inmates released as the result of good-time credit accumulation must serve some or all of their remaining time on supervised **mandatory release**. Table 8.1 shows various states with different good-time provisions.

A majority of states permit the accumulation of good-time credit at the rate of 15 days or more per month served. The Federal Bureau of Prisons permits 54 days per year as good-time credit to be earned by federal prisoners. Some states permit

TABLE 8.1

Good-Time Credits for Different State Jurisdictions

More than 30 days per month:
Alabama, Oklahoma, South Carolina, Texas

30 days per month:
Arkansas, Florida, Illinois, Indiana, Kansas, Louisiana, Nevada, New Mexico, Virginia, West Virginia

20 days per month:
Maryland, Massachusetts

15 days per month:
Arizona, California, Connecticut, Kentucky, Maine, Nebraska, New Jersey, Rhode Island, South Dakota, Vermont, Washington, Wyoming

Less than 15 days per month:
Alaska, Colorado, Delaware, District of Columbia, Federal Bureau of Prisons, Iowa, Michigan, Mississippi, Missouri, New Hampshire, New York, North Carolina, North Dakota, Oregon, Tennessee

No good time given:
Georgia, Hawaii, Idaho, Minnesota, Ohio, Pennsylvania, Utah, Wisconsin

Source: Compiled by author.

additional good-time credits to be accumulated for participation in vocational or educational programs. States such as New Hampshire have an interesting variation on this theme. Instead of rewarding prisoners with good-time credits, New Hampshire authorities add 150 days to the minimum sentences imposed. These 150 days can be reduced at the rate of 12.5 days per month of good behavior or exemplary conduct, according to the New Hampshire prison system.

There are various motives behind different state provisions for good time. Prison overcrowding is perhaps the most frequently cited reason. However, good-time credit allowances can also encourage inmates to participate in useful vocational and educational programs. More than a few inmates abuse the good-time system by enrolling in these programs in a token fashion. But many inmates derive good benefits from them as well. Also, good-time credits influence one's security placement while institutionalized. Those inmates who behave well may be moved from maximum- to medium-, or from medium- to minimum-security custody levels over time. And we know that one's immediate classification level preceding a parole board hearing is taken into account as a factor influencing one's parole chances. Another reason for good-time allowances or credits is to maintain and improve inmate management by prison administrative staff. Well-behaved inmates make it easier for officials to administer prison affairs. Those who do not obey prison rules are subject to 30 days of good-time credit deductions and are "written up" by correctional officers for their misconduct. If inmates accumulate enough of these paper infractions, they may lose good-time credits or, as in New Hampshire, they may fail to reduce the extra time imposed above their minimum sentences.

THE PHILOSOPHY OF PAROLE

Like probation, parole has been established for the purpose of **rehabilitating** offenders and **reintegrating** them into society. Parole is a continuation of a parolee's punishment, under varying degrees of supervision by parole officers, ending when the originally imposed sentence has been served. Officials have noted that parole is **earned** rather than automatically granted after serving a fixed amount of one's sentence. The punitive nature of parole is inherent in the conditions and restrictions accompanying it, which other community residents are not obligated to follow.

Parole's eighteenth-century origins suggest no philosophical foundation. In the 1700s, **penological pragmatism** permitted correctional officials to use parole to alleviate prison overcrowding. Roughly between 1850 and 1970, the influence of social reformers, religious leaders, and humanitarians upon parole as a rehabilitative medium was quite apparent. But as has been seen, the pendulum has shifted away from rehabilitation (not entirely) and toward societal retribution. The early California experience with parole was anything but rehabilitative. Rather, it was a bureaucratic tool to assist gubernatorial decision making in clemency cases involving excessively long sentences.

THE FUNCTIONS OF PAROLE

The functions of parole are probably best understood when couched in terms of **manifest** and **latent functions. Manifest functions** are intended or recognized, apparent to all. Latent functions are also important, but they are hidden and less transparent. Two important manifest functions of parole are (1) to reintegrate parolees into society, and (2) to control and/or deter crime. Three latent functions of parole are (1) to ease prison and jail overcrowding, (2) to remedy sentencing disparities, and (3) to protect the public.

Offender Reintegration

Incarcerated offenders, especially those who have been incarcerated for long periods, often find it difficult to readjust to life in the community. Inmate idleness and a unique prison subculture, regimentation and strict conformity to numerous rules, and continuous exposure to a population of criminals who have committed every offense imaginable simply fail to prepare prisoners adequately for noncustodial living. Parole provides a means whereby an offender may make a smooth transition from prison life to living in a community with some degree of freedom under supervision. Parole functions as a reintegrative mechanism for both juveniles and adults.

Crime Deterrence and Control

It is believed by some correctional authorities that rewarding an inmate for good behavior while in prison through an early conditional release under supervision will promote respect for the law. Some persons believe that keeping an offender imprisoned for prolonged periods will increase the offender's bitterness toward society and result in the commission of new and more serious offenses. But there is some evidence to the contrary. For instance, a study of parole board decision making in Nebraska showed that parole-eligible inmates who were denied parole were more likely to comply with institutional rules and behave well following their parole denials. Institutional misconduct also decreased for offenders who were not granted parole hearings. This information suggests that once these inmates have been rejected for early release or denied a parole hearing, they may seek to conform with institutional rules to a greater degree than before they were granted hearings or were denied parole following hearings. Therefore, the prospect of parole provides a strong incentive for inmates to comply with institutional rules. While this doesn't mean that they will obey societal rules if released into their communities later, it is a good indication that they have the capacity to follow rules when they choose to do so, and if it is in their best interests. Parole boards are persuaded to grant early release to those offenders with good conduct records while incarcerated. They are deemed better risks than those who engage in institutional misconduct.

Early release from prison, under appropriate supervision, implies an agreement of trust between the state and offender. In many instances, this trust instills a degree of self-confidence in the offender, which yields the desired law-abiding results. Then again, there are those who claim parole is a failure, although they cannot say for certain whether the problem rests with parole itself or with the abuse of discretion on the part of parole-granting bodies. Deterrence and crime control actually extend beyond parole board decision making. PO supervisory practices within the community play an important part in controlling offender behaviors. Furthermore, POs can be of assistance in linking their clients with necessary community services, such as psychological counseling and programming, vocational/technical and educational programs, and other services.

 **BOX 8.1**

Lyndi N. Farnum
Juvenile Probation Officer
Case Manager, Juvenile Sex Offender Unit

Statistics:

B.S. (criminal justice administration), Bellevue University;
State of Nevada Peace Officer's Standards and Training Academy

Background:

It was while I was employed at the U.S. Attorney's Office–District of Montana and attending college that I truly became interested in the field of law enforcement and criminal justice. It was a very valuable experience that allowed me to see both sides of the spectrum and helped to cement in my mind that this was the way I wanted to spend my professional life. In August 2003, shortly after finishing my associate degree, I was hired by the Elko County Juvenile Probation Department as a probation officer and am currently working there today. I attended the State of Nevada Peace Officer's Standards and Training Academy and graduated as a Category II Peace Officer in May 2005. It was during this time that my interests in the criminal justice field broadened and I was allowed to come back for an additional seven weeks of training to become a Category I Peace Officer, enabling me to have more career options. I started to realize my need for higher education and I began to pursue my bachelor's degree and subsequently graduated in 2005 with a B.S. in criminal justice administration.

Work Experiences:

There is more than an abundance of work to be done in the juvenile justice field regardless of the geographical location. It is rarely uneventful and it seems as if the challenges come daily. Shortly after I came to work for the department, I expressed an interest in working with and learning about juvenile sex offenders. Subsequently, I was assigned to work in this area and have found the challenge to be what I enjoy the most. Although it can be difficult to separate yourself from the victim, one should keep in mind that the offender needs to be offered the services available to facilitate a healthy rehabilitation.

As a probation officer, you spend a lot of time solving problems. Just when you think that you should be nominated for "Probation Officer of the Year," you suddenly become grounded when yet another different situation presents itself. Just like other law enforcement fields, in juvenile probation, nine times out of 10, the families we deal with are in crisis mode and they feel as though their current situation needs more attention than anything else you might be dealing with. Constantly dealing with these circumstances is why some people get burned out with their jobs and try to find another, less stressful occupation.

Advice to Students:

The most important piece of advice I would give to students pursuing a field in juvenile probation or in law enforcement in general is to learn a second language, preferably one that is prevalent in the community where you work and live. This is extremely important because more and more we are dealing with families where the parents do not speak English and it's difficult to make them feel like you are trying to work with them if you can't communicate with them.

Another piece of advice I would give would be to get involved in any way you can with a law enforcement agency. Don't feel like anything is beneath you if it's in the field where you want to work. Most probation officers are recruited from within the juvenile detention centers, and so any way you can get your foot in the door would be beneficial in the long run.

Decreasing Prison and Jail Overcrowding

Another function of parole is to alleviate jail and prison overcrowding. Parole is a back-end solution, in as much as parole boards exercise considerable discretion about which offenders will be released short of serving their full terms, although more than a few parole board members in various jurisdictions do not perceive their decision making to be affected by prison overcrowding conditions. Every state has a paroling authority, although several states have eliminated parole as an early-release option. The fact that some states and the federal government have abolished parole and substituted other means whereby inmates may be freed short of serving their full sentences doesn't mean that those previously sentenced under an indeterminate sentencing scheme are no longer within the jurisdiction of parole boards (U.S. Sentencing Commission, 2006). For instance, Maine was the first state to abolish parole in 1976. However, its parole board continues to meet from time to time to hear early-release petitions from inmates who were convicted prior to 1976. The old rules for early release still apply to these offenders. But their numbers are diminishing. In 1999, for instance, Maine had only 31 parolees, with two released from parole supervision. The Maine Parole Board will continue to exist as long as there are parolees in the state. If one or more parolees violate their parole conditions, the Maine Parole Board must determine whether such violations are sufficient to revoke their parole programs. If so, some Maine parolees may be returned to prison.

Most states have significant numbers of parolees and are quite different from Maine. In fact, in 2006 there were approximately 742,000 persons on parole in the United States. Parole is definitely making a difference to jail and prison populations, since parolee numbers are about a third of the number of all incarcerated offenders. Also, there is a fairly brisk turnover among parolees annually, with slightly more parolees entering parole programs than are released from them (U.S. Department of Justice, 2006).

Interestingly, the influence of parole boards on prison population sizes may be overstated. Some jurisdictions, such as Florida, report that following their abolition of parole in 1983 and a transformation from indeterminate to determinate sentencing, average prison sentences of convicted offenders were reduced to a greater degree through statutorily mandated earned good-time credits. Thus, larger numbers of offenders were being released from Florida prisons earlier under determinate sentencing than under indeterminate sentencing where parole board discretion was exercised (Florida Department of Corrections, 2006).

Compensating for Sentencing Disparities

One of the criticisms of sentencing practices in both the states and federal system is that judges impose disparate sentences on the basis of race/ethnicity, age, gender,

BOX 8.2

INTERNATIONAL SNAPSHOT: PROBATION AND PAROLE IN SWEDEN

In 2005 Sweden had a population of over 11 million. The government of Sweden is a constitutional monarchy with a parliamentary form of government. The Parliament of Sweden makes all laws, including the criminal code. The maximum punishment in Sweden is life imprisonment, since Sweden has abolished the death penalty. The Swedish criminal justice system is accusatorial, consisting of a prosecutor who represents the state and defense counsel who represents accused persons. Presently all criminal laws are embodied within the Swedish Penal Code. The present penal code is based on a major revision of it that occurred in 1965. It has been revised extensively in subsequent years.

The age of criminal responsibility in Sweden is 15. However, for those between ages 15 and 21, special rules apply. Special grounds must exist in order for youths under age 18 to be imprisoned. Thus, for all practical purposes, incarcerative sentences are not normally imposed on persons under the age of 21 with exceptional circumstances. Sweden does not distinguish between crimes and infractions. Crime is categorized and statistics are compiled and published based on the types of crimes committed. These follow closely the definitions of crimes as outlined by the penal code. Swedish statistical reporting of crimes includes all crimes reported, whether they are solved or unsolved or founded. Special drug laws were passed in the early 1990s because of the escalating drug problem, both trafficking and illegal use, throughout the world. Types of crimes that would be considered violent crimes or crimes against the person in the United States (e.g., murder, forcible rape, robbery, aggravated assault) are relatively rare in Sweden. Most crime is property crime, principally theft. Burglary is the most frequent type of theft, followed by vehicular theft. Most crime occurs in Sweden's larger cities, while more rural areas report little or no criminal activity.

A major study of crime victims known as the Study of Living Conditions (ULF) was conducted in the 1970s. Essentially a self-report survey, the ULF determined that of all those surveyed, 29 percent had been crime victims during the past year. Most of these victimizations were thefts, many of which were unreported to police. Subsequently evidence has shown a gradual increase in the amount of violent crime, although compared with other countries, Swedish violent crime is relatively low. Those most likely to be victimized were young men subject to a high incidence of street crime; single mothers of young children subject to violence in the home; and certain police officers, restaurant staff, or medical staff subject to violence in the workplace.

The police of Sweden are under the jurisdiction of the National Police Board. A National Criminal Investigation Department exists to carry out criminal investigations. A National Police College exists to train and develop officers for law enforcement services in different communities and cities. Local police organizations include over 130 different police areas. There are also marine police who patrol Sweden's waters. The National Police Board assists local police jurisdictions with more serious types of criminal investigations, and under certain conditions, the National Police Board may take over and run these investigations independent of local police authority. The National Police College in Stockholm trains both uniformed officers and criminal investigators. Qualifications for police work include good health, good body, a driver's license, the ability to swim, and being at least 20 years of age. About a fourth of all police officers in Sweden in 2005 were women. Basic training for police recruits includes 10 months of basic training plus an additional 18 months as a trainee in one of the police districts located in various communities. This is the equivalent of in-service training police officers or correctional officers may receive through their own training programs in U.S. jurisdictions.

Criminal suspects in Sweden are subject to rights similar to those of suspects in U.S. jurisdictions. If probable cause exists, persons may be stopped and searched. They may be detained for further investigation if justification exists. Thus much discretionary power is given to police relating to citizen activities. It is unusual for police officers to detain suspects where the maximum punishment is a mere fine. However, persons who do not identify themselves may be held indefinitely until their identities are known, regardless of the crime(s) they are suspected of committing. Complaints against the police by the public are infrequent. Police disciplinary boards review all complaints and determine whether disciplinary action should be taken.

All suspects are entitled to a trial where guilt must be proven by prosecutors beyond a reasonable doubt. There are no jury trials. Trials consist of three to five judges sitting as a panel. All suspects are entitled to have counsel appointed for them by the state if they are indigent and cannot afford counsel. Private counsel do not need specialized legal training in Sweden. However, all defense counsel must be a trained lawyer and a member of the Swedish Bar Association. There is no plea bargaining in Sweden. Suspects cannot plead guilty to a lesser charge in exchange for leniency. All persons who are prosecuted for a crime where a prison sentence might be imposed must stand trial. Only the most serious offenses come to trial. Prosecutors have wide discretionary powers in determining whether charges should be brought against particular suspects. Even if confessions are voluntarily given or obtained, prosecutors must make a presentation to the court to show defendant guilt beyond a reasonable doubt. For juvenile offenders, most often prosecutors will waive prosecution or divert the case to the equivalent of social services.

Suspects may be held for up to 12 hours before criminal charges are filed against them. A statutory maximum time for arrest is 48 hours, and a request for a pretrial detention order is filed the same day one is arrested. A 72-hour period exists for applications for prolonged detention prior to a trial. Usually persons will be held without bail if they are considered dangerous or are regarded as flight risks.

The court system of Sweden is a three-tiered court structure. The highest court is the Supreme Court. The next highest court is the Court of Appeal. These courts are considered as the highest of three tiers. The other two tiers are district courts, which are courts of general jurisdiction and hear both serious and nonserious cases, and general courts, which are similar to municipal courts. These courts hear cases involving public order offenses, traffic violations, and other offenses. Other specialized courts exist to hear matters of administration, market matters, and rent/leasehold agreements. The majority of cases involved in both general and district courts are resolved by summary sentences and fines.

A finding of guilt results in a sentence that is always imposed by the judge. In the most serious cases, special hearings may be conducted similar to sentencing hearings. During these discussions, evidence may be presented to show aggravating and/or mitigating circumstances. These occasions may involve expert witnesses who testify as to the mental soundness of convicted offenders. All of this information is taken into account, including recommended treatment programs.

The Criminal Code provides for a broad range of penalties if defendants are convicted. Judges may impose probation or imprisonment. Probation is always a zonditional sentence that involves rehabilitative programming. Judges may also suspend sentences in lieu of alternative dispositions, which may include counseling, community service, restitution orders, fines, and other sanctions. If the judge decides on imprisonment, the minimum time to be served is 14 days. Life imprisonment may be imposed, although realistically it ranges from 14–16 years. It is significant to note that judges are admonished to use incarceration infrequently or as a last resort, if alternative punishments are warranted or justified by the individual circumstances of a case. Any punishments imposed are determined according to crime seriousness, the age and mental state of the offender, and family circumstances. It is not possible with any degree of consistency to say that a normal punishment for a particular offense is imprisonment of an exact number of years or months. Sentences are individualized and vary according to the different sentenced

(*Continued*)

BOX 8.2 (*Continued*)

offenders. Punishments are proportional to the crime committed, however. The more serious crimes will be punished more severely.

Sentences of probation are made at the recommendation of the prosecutor. Probation sentences must always be associated with crimes where the punishment is more severe than a fine. Probation programs consist of various behavioral conditions, and many of these programs include electronic monitoring, home confinement, counseling, attending vocational/educational programs, mental health outpatient treatment, drug abuse counseling, and other requirements. The rule is for probation with conditions to last up to three years. Such a punishment may include a fine. Home confinement with electronic surveillance is becoming increasingly popular. Home detention and electronic surveillance may be chosen by certain offenders, but they can only choose this option once. If they violate one or more of their probationary terms, they may never again be placed under such supervision. The Probation and Parole Service determines whether certain persons should receive home confinement with electronic surveillance, and for what period of time such supervision should occur. Usually these types of supervision are granted to parolees who are serving short prison sentences of less than three months. The purpose of such supervision is crime prevention. Community work orders may also be imposed. These are similar to community service orders in the United States and involve unpaid labor in the service of the community.

Those under age 21 are typically placed with a social service agency for supervision and aftercare. These sentences usually involve a one-year period of supervision followed by two years of provisional freedom, where no supervision occurs. If the offender commits a new offense while on the probationary term, then either a new supervision period commences or the offender is incarcerated.

Drug abusers may be sentenced to drug treatment under the Care of Alcoholics and Drug Abusers Act. These sentences are imposed only if the offender would have served a sentence of imprisonment for less than one year. Sweden uses day fines, which are calculated on the basis of the seriousness of the offense and one's financial situation. For virtually any offense alleged, prosecutors have discretion not to prosecute certain persons if they decide the evidence is insufficient to support a conviction. The overall goal is that of a drug-free society. Programs are created to reduce the harmful effects of drug use. Treatment is abstinence-based and coerced. Drug laws are strictly enforced, and urine and blood tests are mandatory for persons suspected of illicit drug use. Sweden has not typically had a significant drug problem, although during the 1980s and early 1990s, the amount of illicit drug use among Swedish persons, particularly youths, increased. Various treatment and prevention measures were implemented, including law changes to better address the escalating drug problem. Drug offenders may be sentenced to probation with community treatment orders. Such orders involve counseling and medical treatments designed to prevent the recurrence of drug problems.

There are approximately 80 Swedish prisons, divided into national and local prisons. National prisons usually house offenders who are serving sentences of more than one year and who require additional security for their confinement. Local prisons are similar to county jails and involve persons who are serving sentences of less than one year. Prison work programs exist in the national prisons, and prisoners are encouraged to learn various vocational skills or improve their educational attainment. All work in national prisons is designed to enhance or improve rehabilitation.

Contemporary Swedish developments pertaining to probation and parole have led to the establishment of Probation and Parole Services. The Probation and Parole Service is under the jurisdiction of the Swedish Prison and Probation Service (Krinalardsstyrelsen), which is directly answerable to the Ministry of Justice. The Probation and Parole Service has three major functions:

1. To provide supervision and support for offenders sentenced to probation, for offenders released from prison on early-release programs, and for offenders sentenced to community service orders, treatment orders, or home detention. In the event some offenders fail to fulfill the demands of their programs or court orders (e.g., treatment, contact with the probation and parole office), the matter is referred to a special board, the Probation and Parole Board, for consideration.
2. To assist the courts in determining appropriate sentences through an assessment of the accused's current and past social situations, the accused's need of and motivation for different forms of psychosocial treatment, the accused's suitability for placement in community-based programs, and an assessment of treatments likely to affect one's recidivism.
3. To coordinate the provision of treatment and/or support programs organized and administered by the local government bodies and/or voluntary organizations and when no appropriate programs are available in local communities, organize and implement programs that specifically target criminal behavior (e.g., programs for violent offenders or alcohol-/drug-related traffic offenses).

Preceding any sentencing of a convicted person, a social inquiry report is prepared, which is a detailed assessment of the person's needs and motivation for treatment or other forms of noncustodial care (e.g., community work orders, probation). This assessment is usually requested by the trial court and is used to determine the most appropriate sentence.

Parole is an option for incarcerated offenders once they have served at least two-thirds of their prison sentences. This is a harsher provision that existed prior to 1993 when offenders were parole-eligible after serving only one-half of their sentences. The Probation and Parole Board acts as a judiciary body in matters of discipline of persons sentenced to prison, probation, or others released from prison on parole. This board rules in all matters relating to early-release requests, sanctions for misbehavior or failure to follow program rules, and/or rehabilitative requirements to be met by persons sentenced to probation, parole, community work orders, community treatment orders, or home detention. The period of parole is usually determined for a one-year period following the date of one's release from prison. During this period, the parolee is expected to have continuous contact with his or her parole officer. Parolees must keep theirsupervising officers informed as to thei whereabouts, residence, employment, and means of financial support. Any misconduct occurring during this period may be grounds for revoking one's parole program. After the period of parole has been served, the remainder of one's prison sentence, whatever it may have been originally, is suspended or remitted.

The board may also rule in matters of extending the period of one's supervision if warranted by the facts and revoking one's program for the remaining period of one's incarceration. Sometimes parole is only partially revoked, for periods such as one month. If parole is to be revoked in its entirety, then the matter is referred to district courts for further action. The board also rules in matters of treatment outside of the prison system for inmates currently serving prison sentences, and the board hears offenders' appeals of decisions made by the Probation and Parole Service. The rate of recidivism for both probationers and parolees is quite low, less than 50 percent.

Sources: Adapted from Per-Olof H. Wikstrom and Lars Dolmen, "Sweden," *World Factbook of Criminal Justice Systems,* 2004; Probation and Parole Service, *Probation and Parole Service Nacka-Haninge: A Division of the Prison and Parole Service in Sweden,* Nacka-Haninge: SWE; Drug Policy Alliance, "Sweden," *Drug Policy Around the World,* Washington, DC: Drug Policy Alliance, December 2005; *Probation and Parole Statistics for Sweden,* Probation and Parole Service, January 2006.

and/or socioeconomic status. In an effort to remedy sentencing disparities, parole boards can exercise their discretion and adjust the sentences of those who appear to be unfairly penalized because of extralegal factors. Among the states to implement whole sale changes in their sentencing practices is Minnesota. Minnesota established sentencing guidelines in 1980, and officials noted substantial decreases in prior sentencing disparities attributable to race, ethnicity, age, gender, and socioeconomic status. Sentences were more uniform as to who goes to prison and how long they serve.

An informed parole board is capable of making decisions about early releases of inmates that are fairer than otherwise calculated through determinate sentencing provisions. In Ohio, parole boards permit victims of crimes, the sentencing judge, prosecutor, and the media to be notified of and attend parole hearings, and they actively solicit essential documentation to support their subsequent parole decision (Ohio Parole Board, 2006). Inmates have an opportunity to present evidence of their progress while in prison as well as their constructive parole plans. If granted early release, they must sign an agreement to abide by the conditions required for successful parole supervision, and they are ultimately responsible for their own conduct while completing the term of their parole.

Public Safety and Protection

One of the primary areas of concern for citizens relating to parole is offender **risk.** There are no foolproof ways of forecasting an offender's future dangerousness. Yet, dangerous offenders are freed by parole boards daily throughout the United States. Many of these offenders have demonstrated by their work in prison that they are potentially capable of leading law-abiding lives. Parole boards use different methods for determining which offenders should be released. Such forecasts of offender risk have been used since the 1920s. Predicting offender success on parole is a major policy issue in most jurisdictions. This issue has led to numerous reforms relating to sentencing and parole board decision making and the criteria used for risk forecasting. Presently there is no universal policy in effect throughout all U.S. jurisdictions. Each state and the federal government have independent criteria that are used for early-release decision making.

One critical issue is determining whose interests are more important—the public or the inmate. Parole offers inmates a chance to live reasonably normal lives in society. However, some risk is assumed by parole boards when parole is granted. No one knows for sure how each parolee will respond to his or her parole program. There are a certain proportion of parolee failures that cause people to view the whole idea of parole with skepticism. However, there are many other parolees who have successful experiences while on parole. They are able to readjust to community living and refrain from committing new offenses. For all practical purposes, they have become rehabilitated. In 2006 there were 442,200 parolees who were discharged from their parole programs, meaning that they endured their parole programs without incident and refrained from violating the law or their parole program conditions (U.S. Department of Justice, 2006). Proportionately, about a third of all parolees remain violation-free within their jurisdictions. This doesn't mean that the other two-thirds commit new crimes, but they may violate one or more of their parole program conditions, such as a curfew, or failing an alcohol or drug test.

Parole departments throughout the United States supervise their clients more or less intensively. Most departments have specialized units of parole officers to deal with parolees with particular problems, such as alcohol or substance abuse

FIGURE 8.1   Parole officer discusses parole plan with parolee. Courtesy of James Shaffer, Photoedit

issues. Different types of community services are available to parolees with various problems to enable them to improve themselves in different ways. However, evidence suggests that some parole departments and POs have negative views toward their clients and are predisposed to view them unfavorably. Thus, the assistance parolees receive from their POs may not be entirely supportive.

The fact is that society must cope with eventual offender releases, since many offenders serve their time and are released unconditionally anyway. The early release of a portion of these offenders is based on prior department practices and parole board dispositions. No offender who is seriously believed to pose a public risk is deliberately released short of serving his or her full term of confinement. Paroling authorities believe that they can predict with a reasonable degree of certainty that most of those who receive early release will be properly supervised and will live law-abiding lives. From the perspective of inmates, they deserve a chance within their communities to prove themselves capable of earning societal trust through their good works.

A PROFILE OF PAROLEES IN THE UNITED STATES

Numbers of Parolees Under Supervision

In 2004, 6.99 million persons were under some form of correctional supervision in the United States. Of these, 765,355, or about 11 percent, were on parole. About 10 percent of these were federal parolees, while the remainder were from state prisons. The parole population grew in the United States by 12.6 percent between 1995 and 2004. Table 8.2 shows the number of state and federal offenders on parole, according to both state and U.S. region, for 2004. Supervised releasees in the federal system accounted for 11.7 percent of all parolees.

TABLE 8.2

Adults on Parole, 2004

Region and Jurisdiction	Parole Population 1/1/04	2004 Entries	2004 Exits	Parole Population 12/31/04	Percent Change 2004	Number on Parole per 100,000 Adult Residents, 12/31/04
U.S. total	745,125	503,200	483,000	765,355	2.7%	347
Federal	86,567	37,712	34,149	89,821	3.8%	41
State (reported)	685,745	450,632	434,642	675,534	—	—
State (estimated)	658,558	465,500	448,800	675,534	2.6%	307
Northeast	152,488	69,100	66,800	154,819	1.5%	371
Connecticut	2,343	2,857	2,648	2,552	8.9	96
Maine	32	0	0	32	0.0	3
Massachusetts	3,597	4,862	4,605	3,854	7.1	78
New Hampshire	1,199	766	753	1,212	1.1	122
New Jersey	13,248	11,030	10,098	14,180	7.0	217
New York	55,853	23,715	25,044	54,524	−2.4	372
Pennsylvania	102,244	10,083	8,665	77,175	—	806
Rhode Island	363	403	398	368	1.4	44
Vermont	796	546	420	922	15.8	190
Midwest	122,678	101,898	96,736	127,840	4.2%	258
Illinois	35,008	35,260	35,991	34,277	−2.1	362
Indiana	7,019	7,028	6,548	7,499	6.8	162
Iowa	2,974	2,839	2,496	3,317	11.5	146
Kansas	4,145	4,542	4,162	4,525	9.2	221
Michigan	20,233	11,330	10,639	20,924	3.4	276
Minnesota	3,596	4,770	4,494	3,872	7.7	100
Missouri	15,830	13,299	11,729	17,400	9.9	398
Nebraska	648	1,112	955	805	24.2	61
North Dakota	225	650	636	239	6.2	48
Ohio	18,427	11,724	11,269	18,882	2.5	218
South Dakota	1,944	1,865	1,592	2,217	14.0	382
Wisconsin	12,629	7,479	6,225	13,883	9.9	330
South	224,995	106,059	98,779	231,994	3.1%	305
Alabama	6,950	3,999	3,204	7,745	11.4	225
Arkansas	13,180	7,182	5,518	14,844	12.6	715
Delaware	529	269	259	539	1.9	85
District of Columbia	4,861	2,203	1,746	5,318	9.4	1,198
Florida	5,098	5,540	5,750	4,888	−4.1	36
Georgia	21,161	13,178	10,995	23,344	10.3	359
Kentucky	7,744	4,083	3,821	8,006	3.4	253
Louisiana	23,743	13,517	12,873	24,387	2.7	728
Maryland	13,742	8,145	7,536	14,351	4.4	345
Mississippi	1,816	1,056	893	1,979	9.0	92
North Carolina	2,677	3,411	3,206	2,882	7.7	45
Oklahoma	4,047	1,926	1,644	4,329	7.0	163
South Carolina	3,242	1,313	1,263	3,292	1.5	104
Tennessee	7,957	3,394	2,660	8,410	5.7	186
Texas	102,271	33,463	33,662	102,072	−0.2	629
Virginia	4,834	2,601	3,043	4,392	9.1	78
West Virginia	1,143	779	706	1,216	6.4	85

TABLE 8.2 *(Continued)*

Region and Jurisdiction	Parole Population 1/1/04	2004 Entries	2004 Exits	Parole Population 12/31/04	Percent Change 2004	Number on Parole per 100,000 Adult Residents, 12/31/04
West	158,397	188,413	186,496	160,881	1.6%	324
Alaska	927	630	606	951	2.6	204
Arizona	5,367	8,211	7,907	5,671	5.7	135
California	110,338	154,402	155,046	110,261	−0.1	419
Colorado	6,559	6,094	5,270	7,383	12.6	216
Hawaii	2,240	831	775	2,296	2.5	238
Idaho	2,329	1,578	1,537	2,370	1.8	232
Montana	815	648	653	810	−0.6	113
Nevada	4,126	2,422	2,938	3,610	−12.5	209
New Mexico	2,328	2,062	1,714	2,676	14.9	190
Oregon	19,456	8,919	7,517	20,858	7.2	761
Utah	3,229	2,289	2,206	3,312	2.6	201
Washington	105	48	33	120	14.3	3
Wyoming	578	279	294	563	−2.6	145

Source: Lauren E. Glaze and Seri Palla (2005). *Probation and Parole in the United States, 2004.* Washington, DC: U.S. Department of Justice. (Table 4, p. 7) (public domain)

Profiling Parolees

Table 8.3 shows some of the primary characteristics of parolees in the United States for 2004. These characteristics are compared with the parolee population from 1995. One of the most significant changes from 1995 to 2004 is that female parolees have increased from 10 to 12 percent of the parolee population. Racially, white parolees increased proportionately from 34 to 40 percent, while black parolees declined from 45 to 41 percent. The proportion of Hispanic parolees declined from 21 to 18 percent during the 1995–2004 period (Glaze and Palla, 2005).

Further characterizing these parolees, 85 percent were on active parole status in 2004, compared with 78 percent active in 1995. The greatest proportion of parolees under parole supervision in 2004 were drug offenders (38 percent), followed by property offenders (26 percent) and violent offenders (24 percent). About 52 percent of all parolees were mandatory parolees, whereas 31 percent were discretionary parolees. Approximately 46 percent of parolees in 2004 successfully completed their parole programs and were released from the system. About 39 percent of all parolees had been returned to incarceration, with 12 percent jailed or imprisoned for a new conviction. Parolees awaiting a parole revocation hearing totaled 26 percent, while 10 percent of all parolees leaving parole were absconders (Glaze and Palla, 2005:9).

METHODS OF RELEASE FROM PRISON

Releases of large numbers of inmates on parole are the result of many factors (Clear, Majeed, and Bownoth, 2006). Some of these factors are prison overcrowding and good behavior of prisoners while confined. Also, prisons are attempting to

TABLE 8.3

Characteristics of Adults on Parole, 1995, 2000, and 2004

Characteristic	1995	2000	2004
Total	100%	100%	100%
Gender			
Male	90%	88%	88%
Female	10	12	12
Race/Hispanic origin			
White	34%	38%	40%
Black	45	40	41
Hispanic	21	21	18
American Indian/Alaska Native	1	1	1
Asian/Native Hawaiian/other Pacific Islander	–	–	1
Status of supervision			
Active	78%	83%	85%
Inactive	11	4	3
Absconder	6	7	7
Supervised out of State	4	5	4
Other	–	1	1
Sentence length			
Less than 1 year	6%	3%	5%
1 year or more	94	97	95
Type of offense			
Violent	–	–	24%
Property	–	–	26
Drug	–	–	38
Other	–	–	12
Adults entering parole			
Discretionary parole	50%	37%	31%
Mandatory parole	45	54	52
Reinstatement	4	6	8
Other	2	2	9
Adults leaving parole			
Successful completion	45%	43%	46%
Returned to incarceration	41	42	39
With new sentence	12	11	12
With revocation pending	18	30	26
Other	11	1	1
Absconder	**	9	10
Other unsuccessful	**	2	2
Transferred	2	1	1
Death	1	1	1
Other	10	2	1

Source: Lauren E. Glaze and Seri Palla (2005). *Probation and Parole in the United States, 2004.* Washington, DC: U.S. Department of Justice. (Table 6, p. 9) (public domain)

manage their scarce space in order to accommodate the most dangerous offenders. Another major contributing factor is court-ordered prison population reductions because of health and safety regulations and cruel and unusual punishment conditions associated with some prison facilities that have been unable to comply with federally mandated guidelines under which inmates may be confined. Some of the older prisons in the United States are rat-infested, roach-ridden structures without proper heat or ventilation in winter or summer months. Coupled with chronic overcrowding, some of these institutions are simply inhumane. This is where courts draw the line and require minimal conditions under which human beings can be held in confinement.

Amy Solomon (2006:28) has identified three major forms of release relevant for prison inmates. These forms of release include (1) discretionary release, (2) mandatory release, and (3) unconditional release.

Discretionary Release

Discretionary release involves a parole board decision to release prisoners before they have served their full sentences, serving the remainder of their sentences under community supervision. Parole boards essentially screen prisoners and use their discretion to determine who is the most ready to return to their communities. Parole boards may consider criminal histories, the incarceration offense, institutional conduct, prisoner attitude and motivation, participation in prison programming, and positive connections to the community such as employment, housing arrangements, and family ties. Prisoners released by parole boards are called **discretionary parolees.**

Mandatory Release

Mandatory release occurs whenever prisoners have served their original sentences, less any accumulated good-time credit, serving the balance of their sentences under supervision in the community. Mandatory releasees have not received a determination or evaluation of their fitness to return to the community from a parole board or any other authority. These persons are called **mandatory releasees.** Mandatory releasees account for the largest numbers of releasees from prisons.

Unconditional Release

Unconditional releasees leave prison after serving their full terms behind bars. These individuals were not granted early release via a parole board in states retaining discretionary parole, nor did they receive good-time credits enabling them to achieve mandatory release. Therefore, unconditional releasees exit prison without any conditions of release, community supervision, or reporting requirements. Some of these offenders may never have received any treatment or counseling for particular problems they may have (e.g., drug dependencies, learning disabilities, mental illnesses, or other problems) (Solomon, 2006).

PAROLEE REENTRY AND REENTRY ISSUES

Perhaps the major problem confronting paroling agencies today is parolee reentry. Reentry refers to releases of prison and jail inmates back into their communities after serving some or all of their sentences. Approximately 95 percent of all inmates confined in prisons and jails will eventually be released back into their communities (Taxman, 2006), although some estimates have been as high as 99 percent

(Cummings, 2003:9). But consistently and unfortunately, 65 percent or more of these parolees or releasees will eventually reoffend (Petersilia, 2003; Rhine, 2006).

The Urban Institute in Washington, DC, conducted an extensive study of 38,624 prisoners as a sample from 272,111 prisoners originally involved in a 1994 cohort study reported by the Bureau of Justice Statistics (Solomon, Kachnowski, and Bhati, 2005). One of the primary findings of this research was that no matter the type of parole supervision offenders received, their recidivism rates remained about the same as offenders who were released without supervision. Furthermore, investigators compared the recidivism rates of offenders released by different parole methods and discovered little, if any, significant differences in their recidivism rates. The conclusions from this research were that neither parole supervision nor the methods whereby offenders are released from prison had any significant impact on recidivism rates among these offenders.

Policymakers were shocked by these findings. Criminologists were equally surprised, in that it might be logical to expect at least some significant differences in recidivism rates among these parolees that would vary according to the nature of their supervision, if any, and the methods whereby they were released back into their communities. Edward Rhine, the Deputy Director of the Office of Policy and Offender Reentry at the Ohio Department of Rehabilitation and Reintegration, has noted that these discouraging findings have fueled renewed interest in the subject of inmate reentry, largely because legislators, correctional leaders, and other key stakeholders believe that public safety has been and is continuing to be sorely compromised when hundreds of thousands of prisoners released from prison are singularly ill-equipped and poorly supported in their attempts to succeed in their communities (Rhine, 2006:22). He adds pessimistically that if past and current recidivism trends offer an accurate barometer relative to the risks these offenders present to public safety in years to come, the forecast is sobering.

In this section, we examine the reentry issue in great detail. The following topics are featured: (1) prison-based initiatives to assist pre-parolees and their merits; (2) characteristics of parolees who reenter their communities; (3) obstacles to effective parolee reentry; (4) structured failure issues; (5) isolated parole agency–community initiatives to assist parolees; (6) the emergence of reentry courts; and (7) continuing reentry issues.

Prison-Based Initiatives to Assist Pre-Parolees and Their Merits

What Can Inmates Expect When They Enter Prison?   When inmates enter either federal or state prisons, what can they expect to receive as a part of prison services to assist them? Do prisoners have a right to be rehabilitated while in prisons or jails? Unless otherwise specified by particular state jurisdictions, prisoners do not have an absolute right to be rehabilitated (Palmer, 1997). The extent and nature of prison services for inmates varies greatly among prisons. Among these services are included varying opportunities for vocational and educational assistance. Reginald Wilkinson, for instance, has said that it is well established that providing opportunities to improve educational and work-related skills can reduce the risks of future offending. Employability is related to criminal involvement, since many offenders enter prison initially with poor work histories. Without the development of job skills while incarcerated, many eventual releasees will find their ability to obtain and sustain employment challenging. Attaining sustainable employment and acceptance into the workforce can serve as a building block to connecting with the community. Gainfully employed ex-offenders are more capable of taking care of themselves and their families, and they have a much better chance of being contributing members of their communities. Although many employers are reluctant to hire ex-offenders, corrections and the business community must work together to help overcome these barriers (Wilkinson, 2005:88).

However, generalizations about all prisons categorically cannot be made with any reliability. Some prisons provide more services than others. The federal prison system seems to offer the greatest variety of programming and services to its inmates compared with most state systems. But even in the federal system, such programming and services are limited.

Preliminary Classification and Segregation.   One of the first things that happen to prison inmates upon their entry into prison is that they are classified according to a variety of criteria. Homer Cummings describes some of the ways federal offenders are classified and processed. He acknowledges that classification is a very important task. Attempts are made to separate older from younger offenders. Those with various types of communicable illnesses and diseases are separated or segregated from more healthy inmates. Those considered less violent are separated and segregated from those considered more violent.

Cummings indicates that younger offenders who demonstrate an eagerness to learn new and useful skills are often placed in federal reformatories, such as the one at Chillicothe, Ohio, where they are educated and taught various trades. Those who lack ambition and responsibility are placed in federal mountain camps, such as the one in Kooskia, Idaho, or the one in the Catalina Mountains of Arizona. Physically handicapped and mentally ill federal offenders are sent to a federal hospital facility in Springfield, Missouri. Those addicted to narcotics and those with other types of dependencies are sent to specially equipped federal institutions where they can receive various treatments. Only 5 percent of the federal inmate population consists of women. These female offenders are usually accommodated at institutions such as Alderson, West Virginia. Television cooking hostess Martha Stewart, who was convicted of lying about her insider trading, served her time at Alderson, for instance. Habitual offenders and escape-prone inmates are confined in some of the older penitentiaries such as Atlanta or Leavenworth or Florence, Colorado. The facility at Florence is considered a supermax, maxi-maxi, or admin-max type of facility, which is almost totally escape-proof and reserved for only the most hardened offenders.

Cummings obviously recognizes the need for federal prisons, and all prisons for that matter, to make substantial commitments to programs that will prepare inmates for their eventual release back into society. He notes, for instance, that under a federal initiative, federal treatments for drug addictions increased from 385,000 to 900,000 from 1998 to 2003. This increase in drug treatment is one component of the overall improvement of inmate health (Cummings, 2003:10).

Presidential Promises for Corrections.   During the period 2002–2004, President George W. Bush allocated over $100 million into prison reentry and transitional services (Weedon, 2004:6). Through a program known as **Going Home,** the federal government recognized the importance of federal inmates participating in rehabilitative programming while confined as well as transitional assistance when about to return to their communities. The Going Home program, created through the Serious and Violent Offenders Reentry Initiative, was further bolstered by President Bush's 2004 State of the Union address, where he announced a new federal initiative to provide $300 million over the following four years to address three major elements of reentry: (1) mentoring, (2) transitional housing, and (3) job training and placement (Weedon, 2004:6). But an economic downturn, beginning in 2003, made it increasingly difficult if not impossible for correctional departments across the nation to implement all forms of programming that would enable their prisons to fulfill these goals. In fact, during the 2003–2004 period, there was a substantial decline in spending at the state level combined with rising expenditures for operating prison systems. These rising expenditures were largely due to the necessity to meet the health care needs of those at high risk for chronic and infectious diseases, and corrections officials have been forced to choose between institutional security, health care, and programming.

Faced with these three choices, officials generally opted to reduce programming. Thus, there has been a sharp reduction in programs in federal, state, and local correctional systems that provide offenders with the educational, vocational, and life skills necessary to prepare them for their eventual reintegration into society (Weedon, 2004:6). One major result of this reduced funding to correctional systems is the elimination of the federal Residential Substance Abuse Treatment (RSAT) program, which provided for intensive drug and alcohol treatment programs within many U.S. prisons. This program was the sole direct federal resource for prison drug treatment, and the loss of these federal programming dollars will have a long-range impact on states' abilities to provide offenders with drug/alcohol treatment programming. This cutback, in turn, will undermine general reentry efforts. Joey Weedon (2004:6) says that corrections is presently at a crossroad. The profession is being asked to invest in reentry while those programs upon which the success of reentry is built are being scaled back or eliminated in their entirety as the result of shifting priorities and budget cuts. Programs that have proved immensely successful, including RSAT, are not being funded adequately, and there is little new funding to replace them. The president's goal of reducing inmate recidivism coupled with the elimination of federal funding for correctional programs cannot coexist. If inmate recidivism is to be decreased, then greater funding for programming must be provided. We can't achieve one goal without realizing the other first. It simply can't be done.

The lack of funding for correctional institutional programming in recent years is underscored by Joan Petersilia. Petersilia (2003) says that during the 1990s, funding for prison vocational and educational programming for inmates was cut drastically, and that during the 1990s, vocational job training for inmates decreased from 32 to 27 percent. Participation in educational programs decreased during the same period from 42 to 34 percent. In addition, drug treatment programs were cut to the point that for those offenders who were drug- or alcohol dependent and need treatment, only 13 percent received such treatment during the 1990s. Over 85 percent of those leaving prison today need drug or alcohol treatment but did not receive it while confined.

First There Were Pell Grants for Inmates, Then There Weren't. In 1953, the University of Southern Illinois (USI) offered educational programming to inmates in several correctional institutions. Subsequently the first inmate/student graduates received bachelor's degrees from USI. USI's initiative was copied by several universities in other states, so that by 1965, there were 12 post-secondary educational programs in U.S. prisons. Also in 1965, the U.S. Congress passed Title IV of the Higher Education Act, granting prison inmates the right to apply for federal financial aid in the form of federal Pell grants. Federal Pell grants were noncompetitive, need-based grants available to all low-income students.

The Pell Grant program is a post-secondary education (PSCE) subsidy run by the federal government and named after Senator Claiborne Pell, although it is technically known as the Basic Educational Opportunity Grant program. These grants are awarded on the basis of financial need through a formula. The formula is the cost of attendance less the expected family contribution. This equals the financial need. Students under age 24 must report their parents' income on their Pell Grant applications whether they are living with them or not. Federal Pell Grants are not loans; they do not have to be repaid. Undergraduate students who have not earned a bachelor's degree or other professional degree are eligible.

By 1973, there were 182 higher education programs operating in different prison systems. By 1982, 350 higher education programs were being offered in U.S. prisons, and about 10 percent of all prisoners were taking advantage of the Pell Grant program to seek further education. However, not everyone was in favor of funding inmate education with federal tax dollars. Senator Jesse Helms of North Carolina introduced an amendment to the Higher Education Act of 1965 in 1991, which would cut off federal funds for education for inmates. He claimed that the money was spent to the disadvantage of "free" students. Republican Thomas Coleman of Missouri and Democrat Bart Gordon of Tennessee drafted a similar amendment that would prohibit inmates from receiving Pell Grants, but it was defeated. But in 1992, Congress passed the Higher Education Reauthorization Act, which proclaimed that prisoners can only use Pell Grant money for tuition and fees. Furthermore, inmates on death row or serving life-without-parole sentences became ineligible to receive Pell Grants (Great Books Foundation, 2006).

In 1994, when 25,169 inmates were receiving an average Pell Grant of $1,600 to defray a small portion of their educational expenses, the Violent Crime Control and Law Enforcement Act was passed by Congress, ending prisoner eligibility for federal Pell Grants after September 13, 1994. By 1997, higher education for inmates was virtually nonexistent behind bars. That year, only eight educational programs were being offered to U.S. inmates in selected prisons, and 25 states had eliminated or cut back their vocational training programs for inmates. Interestingly, these cuts in educational and vocational programming funding to inmates came at a time when numerous studies showed that inmate-participants exhibited dramatic decreases in recidivism when released from prison. A Bureau of Prisons report issued in 1987 found that the more education prisoners receive, the lower their recidivism. And holders of college degrees were the least likely to reenter prison. Inmates with some high school exhibited a 55 percent decrease in their recidivism when released compared with inmates not receiving this education (Great Books Foundation, 2006).

With the elimination of Pell Grants to inmates, much inmate discontent occurred. It wasn't so much the fact that numerous inmates were affected by the elimination of Pell Grants as it was that inmates no longer had the option of applying for them. Prisons breed bitterness. The curse of idleness is profound and long-lasting (Cummings, 2003:10). Eliminating Pell Grants launched numerous lawsuits, mostly dismissed by appellate courts. Prisoners initiating these lawsuits alleged that they were being deprived of a basic entitlement. But as has been seen, prisoners do not have either an absolute or constitutional right to be rehabilitated.

Isolated and Small-Scale Institutional Programs That Help Some Pre-Parolees.

Many prisons and some jails have limited or smaller-scale initiatives to assist certain inmates in becoming rehabilitated by offering particular vocational programming such as deep-sea diving, horse training, and even cooking. For instance, Susan Clayton (2005:79) reports on the introduction of a three-month-long program offered at the Montgomery County Correctional Facility in Clarksburg, Maryland, that is designed to teach inmates how to keep a job in the baking/food service industry upon release. Called the Sweet Release Program, the 40-hour-per-week course focuses on hands-on baking and sanitation skills as well as the process of making positive changes in the community. Five program goals are stressed: (1) reducing inmate recidivism; (2) assisting inmates in obtaining jobs in the foods sector; (3) teaching inmates how to get and keep a job; (4) teaching both basic and advanced elements of baking production so that permanent, full-time employment is possible; and (5) providing the education necessary so that each graduate can take and pass a national sanitation exam and obtain a food service manager license. Program eligibility is based on the following: (1) sentencing has occurred and at least three months remain on one's sentence; (2) prescreening and selection by counseling and correctional staff has been done; (3) participating inmates have expressed a strong interest in full-time employment; (4) inmates have expressed an interest in the baking/food services industry as a career opportunity; (5) inmates must have a good record during incarceration (no violent behavior); and (6) inmates must have the ability to read at at least the eighth-grade level. Applications are received from approximately 40 inmates every three months for six available spots. When inmates complete the program, they receive a certified food manager license from the Montgomery County Department of Health and Human Services. Graduates must still take and pass the national exam. Through jail administration contacts in the community, placing ex-offenders in employment in food services is a relatively easy task. By 2005, 26 out of 27 inmates at the facility had taken the national exam and passed (Clayton, 2005:130). Joanne Zacharias, a food service manager who works with these inmates, says that typically, "inmates are often released from jail with no money, no job, no home, no hope. However, when they get released from this program and reentry, whether they go through the prerelease center or not, hopefully we are going to have a job set up for them, a place to live, and a plan. That's what it's all about—successful reentry" (Clayton, 2005:130).

Yes, that's what it's all about. But the baking school operated by this jail only scratches the surface. It is not a program that all inmates everywhere can join and experience employment success. Positions in the food industry are limited. But at least a few inmates are being helped, and to that extent, at least, such limited programs are helpful.

Other limited institutional programs for inmates operated by some prisons and some jails include the Wild Horse and Burro Program in Oklahoma, the Comstock Wild Horse Training Program in Nevada, the NEADS Dogs for Deaf and Disabled Americans in Boston, the Prisoners and Pups Program in Oregon, and the Chino, California, Prison Deep-Sea Diving Program. The Wild Horse and Burro Program in Oklahoma is operated by the James Crabtree Correctional Center in Helena. Several hundred prisoners have helped train horses for over 10 years

(Crabtree Correctional Center, 2006). Steve Moore, a vocational/technical instructor at Crabtree, says that "a lot of guys who work with the mustangs will become interested in horses and taking the vo-tech courses allows them to gather some book knowledge about horses. Many of the guys leave the center and begin training horses as a profession." He adds that the program gives them something to look forward to and be responsible for (Crabtree Correctional Center, 2006:1). The average training time is three months, at an average training cost of $200 a month. Most released prisoners have not recidivated.

At Warm Springs Correctional Center in Carson City, Nevada, inmates help to tame wild horses also, similar to the program in Oklahoma. In the Warm Springs case, one inmate who had worked with wild horses for nine years remarked how therapeutic it was. The state prison director, Jackie Crawford, said, "It's therapeutic for the inmates and it is a management tool for the prison system because the inmates are productively busy. Not only are they easier to manage, but by training them with horses, when they go out, they may be a more productive citizen." Over 200 horses a year are tamed by this program. Once trained, they are turned over to new owners. Inmates selected for participation in the horse training program have evidenced past good behavior while imprisoned. It speaks well of them when appearing before parole boards. Recidivism rates among parolees who have participated in this horse training program have been remarkably low, less than 5 percent (Harper, 2000:1).

In Princeton, Massachusetts, local prison inmates are selected on the basis of their good institutional conduct to participate in dog training, especially seeing-eye training for deaf, blind, and otherwise disabled Americans, in a program operated by the National Education for Assistance Dog Services (NEADS) (NEADS, 2006). It takes up to a year to work with dogs where they are then able to benefit blind and disabled Americans who need them. Offenders develop patience and skill in training them to lead the blind. The work becomes very altruistic, and whatever antisocial attitudes prisoners may have had before entering this program are quickly dispelled. The success rate of parolees who have participated in the NEADS program with seeing-eye dogs is incredibly low, less than 5 percent.

Similar programs where inmates work with and train seeing-eye dogs are Puppies Behind Bars in New York City and Project Pooch in Woodburn, Oregon. In both programs, inmates apply for entry into these training programs and are carefully screened, primarily on the basis of their excellent institutional conduct and discipline. Not only are some dogs trained for seeing-eye work with blind persons, but some dogs are also trained for explosive detection or drug detection work with police and other law enforcement agencies. There are other similar programs in New York City called Guiding Eyes for the Blind, Guide Dog Foundation, Guide Dogs of America, and the Seeing Eye. Inmates in all of these programs are encouraged to take correspondence courses in veterinary assistance. The Prison Pup Program is located in Princeton, Massachusetts. It is operated by NEADS. Puppies are placed with inmates who train them to assist people who are deaf, hearing impaired, or physically disabled. At least five correctional facilities in the Massachusetts, Maine, and Connecticut areas are involved in the NEADS programming. One program, Prison Pet Partnership, is operated in Gig Harbor, Washington, at the Washington Correctional Center for Women. It was one of the first prison pup programs to be established (Operation Safety Net, 2006).

The Pennsylvania Approach to Reentry.   In recent years, the Pennsylvania Department of Corrections (PDOC) has realized the greater importance that should be given to inmate rehabilitation and institutional programming. Pennsylvania officials have observed numerous parolees leaving their prison system with few or no employment skills or prospects for meaningful work, low levels of education, and serious drug and alcohol problems. They have recognized that these persons need a place to live and some will need to be reunified with their families from which they may have become estranged before or during their incarceration (Beard and Gnall, 2003:68). Therefore, the PDOC created a new mission statement to protect the public by confining persons committed to our custody in safe, secure facilities and to provide opportunities for inmates to acquire the skills and values necessary to become productive, law-abiding citizens while respecting the rights of crime victims.

This new mission statement has meant a renewed commitment by the PDOC to prepare currently incarcerated men and women for more successful reentry into communities. A three-pronged approach has been devised. This approach consists of the following measures:

1. The PDOC conducts a thorough risk and needs assessment in each inmate. The risk component assesses the likelihood that offenders will commit new crimes if released on parole. Also assessed is the extent to which present inmates engage in disruptive actions while confined. The needs assessment detects issues that originally contributed to each offender's incarceration, such as low educational levels and few job skills.

2. The PDOC offers alcohol and other drug treatment and education programs, such as GED and vocational training, aimed at addressing offender needs.

3. The PDOC provides inmates with the opportunity to participate in the Community Orientation and Reintegration (COR) program, which teaches inmates skills on how to find and keep a job, and how to overcome the obstacles to successful reintegration. COR also acts as a booster, reminding inmates of the important lessons they have learned in prison programming that will help them in their attempt to become law-abiding community members (Beard and Gnall, 2003:68).

All new Pennsylvania male inmates are processed through the Diagnostic Center at the State Corrections Institution (SCI) at Camp Hill, while female inmates are diagnosed and evaluated at the Muncy SCI. One aspect of institutional life not overlooked by the PDOC is the criminogenic atmosphere of prisons. Criminogenic influences include acquiring or bolstering antisocial attitudes and associates, as well as criminal thinking, all of which are highly associated with greater recidivism. Hostility and anger of inmates were also measured, using appropriate personality assessment tools. The PDOC decided to utilize the Level of Service Inventory—Revised (LSI-R), a reliable risk-needs tool for its evaluations of parole-eligible inmates. The Pennsylvania Board of Probation and Parole was already using the LSI-R, and therefore, its costs and usefulness were easily adapted to the institutional population. As a result of these assessments, PDOC inmates were divided according to their risk and need levels. Those with the highest risks and needs according to these assessments were selected to receive the most intensive services, and over a longer time interval. At the same time, those designated as low risk/low needs were not directed to any type of treatment, since they were considered least likely to reoffend or being influenced by antisocial forces within their prisons. Assessment scores were not used exclusively. Clinicians also evaluated inmates and made independent judgments.

On the basis of these assessments, those inmates with the highest risk-needs levels were placed into particular inmate programs emphasizing work/education; citizenship; family/relationship/self; offense-related; and reentry. The overall goals of inmate programs are to enable inmates to (1) understand the effects and consequences of their criminal behavior on victims and their own families; (2) demonstrate an appropriate respect for authority, peers, and self by having a better understanding of community living; (3) understand their high-risk factors for reoffending; and (4) describe resources and intervention strategies for support to establish and maintain successful community adjustment.

The work/education programs offer adult basic education, GED and secondary diplomas, English as a second language, and special education programs. The citizenship program focuses on inmates as becoming law-abiding and productive community members. Through role-playing and prosocial activities, inmates would learn more about their own interpersonal relationships with other community members. The family/relationship/self program focuses on developing parenting skills, as well as understanding the special needs of older and female offenders. One purpose is to strengthen family ties, and another is to learn to accept responsibility and be accountable as parents. The offense-related category includes alcohol and other drug treatment, sex offender therapy, anger management and violence prevention, batterer treatment, and the impact of crime on victims.

The PDOC COR program is the department's transitional program designed to bridge the gap between prison and the community. COR addresses the needs to secure proper identification and finding employment and suitable housing. Effective community linkages are promoted. The COR program occurs about a month before an inmate's parole. The second phase occurs approximately 30–45 days following one's release and transition to parole supervision. Relapse prevention is stressed to promote greater offender stability while in their community. So far, the PDOC is optimistic about its initiative to assist inmates while still institutionalized. The program seems to be working. Recidivism among inmates who are eventually released are less than 10 percent.

And since the 1980s, a program for training deep-sea divers has been operated at the Chino, California, Prison. It trains selected inmates for deep-sea salvage work. It trains approximately 10 inmates at a time, and most of these inmates are placed with deep-sea salvage firms once they are released on parole. The success rate for reentering inmates into society is quite high, over 90 percent, which translates into a recidivism rate of less than 10 percent (Champion, 2005).

One problem with almost all of these small-scale programs is that they offer a very limited range of job opportunities for participating inmates. For inmates who are lucky enough to qualify for these programs, the rehabilitative effect couldn't be more favorable. But we must understand that over 2 million inmates were behind bars in prisons and jails in 2006. Less than 25 percent of all of these inmates had access to scarce prison jobs or educational/vocational programming. Fewer still had access to drug and alcohol counseling services, since monies for these programs have been seriously curtailed in recent years and most prisons do not have the luxury of providing such programming for those inmates in need of such assistance.

The Louisiana Department of Public Safety Initiative.   In 2005, Louisiana was releasing at least 15,000 inmates on parole. Based on prior information, the

Louisiana Department of Public Safety and Corrections (LDPSC) determined that about half of all of these releasees will return to prison within a five-year period. Richard Stalder, secretary of the LDPSC, observed that "we have to prepare people who leave our system, who go back to the community, to lead pro-social, law-abiding lives" (St. Gerard, 2005:17). Louisiana spends $567 million per year on incarcerating offenders, but only $5.5 million is allocated to rehabilitation programs. Stalder said also that 80 percent of all Louisiana inmates have substance abuse problems, and that a large portion have average reading skills at the fifth-grade level. Beginning with the 2005 year, Stalder said that the LDPSC is implementing new regulations requiring inmate evaluations and screenings to determine their educational and other needs. Two programs are in the process of being implemented on a pilot basis. They are faith-based programs utilizing volunteer services and bringing education into the prison. These programs will place inmates together in a separate dormitory setting and offer them studies and life-skills programs. These programs have demonstrably lower recidivism rates when used in other jurisdictions, according to recent LDPSC research (St. Gerard, 2005:17).

The Second Chance Act of 2005.   The U.S. Congress has become increasingly involved in American corrections. While several programs, such as Pell Grants for prisoners, have been curtailed or eliminated by Congress, at the same time, high rates of recidivism among parolees have caused politicians to rethink the problem of inmate reentry and consider new solutions for the high recidivism problem. The Act's name has been taken from a statement made by President George W. Bush to the effect that America is the land of second chance. The Second Chance Act of 2005 recognizes that the problems of prisoner reentry are complex. The Act impacts offender recidivism in diverse ways, from providing tools to address substance abuse, mental health, and other problems of inmates confined in state and federal prisons to strengthening families and communities across the country (Wilkinson and Rhine, 2005:55). The legislation proposes a seamless type of reentry program couched in a holistic framework, and it targets strengthening families and improving the quality of life in communities. It focuses also on reducing the barriers that confront offenders as they seek to reenter their communities following confinement.

The Act extends well beyond prison walls. It emphasizes the necessary integration of a variety of services, including programming, support, and offender accountability that extends from the time one is sentenced through any period of supervision in one's community when released. Collaborations between community groups, faith-based organizations, service providers, citizens, victims, and formerly incarcerated persons are crucial. Ensuring that offenders have appropriate treatment while they are confined is just as important as ensuring that their treatment is continued while being supervised by probation or parole officers in their communities. Under the Act, therefore, a variety of risk and needs assessment tools is contemplated in order to ensure that programming and service delivery can be prioritized according to those offenders most in need of treatment and services. One initiative is the establishment of both a juvenile and adult offender reentry resource center. The existence of such a center would provide a clearinghouse and national database whereby all levels of government, local jurisdictions and communities, and stakeholders who have an interest may go to learn more about what works and what is effective relative to offender reentry. They may also solicit technical assistance and training to adopt evidence-based practices germane to reentry (Wilkinson and Rhine, 2005:57). Actually, the Second Chance Act provides a very sensible balance that recognizes that reentry is about public safety as well as returning offenders home as tax-paying and productive citizens. This means drawing on reentry best practices, seeking active collaboration and sustainable community and **faith-based partnerships,** engaging families across the full spectrum of reentry, and reducing those barriers that undermine offenders' successful transitions from prison to home.

Faith-based partnerships involve services for inmates within their communities, including welfare support, job training, emergency shelter, food/clothing provisions and supplies, and other forms of relief through local religious organizations. The Center for Faith-Based and Community Initiatives (CFBCI) at the U.S. Department of Labor has sought to empower faith-based and community organizations in general as these organizations help their neighbors (parolees, ex-offenders) enter, succeed, and thrive in the workforce. Organizations are targeted for federal funding that provide valuable services for offenders. Many of these organizations may not presently be partnered with government programs. Therefore, to accomplish this mission, the CFBCI works to remove administrative and regulatory barriers and develop innovative programs to foster partnerships between federally funded programs and faith-based organizations. Organizations are educated about local opportunities for collaboration with and about opportunities to participate in national grant programs. The objective is to integrate the work of faith-based organizations into the strategic planning and service delivery processes of local workforce investment boards (U.S. Department of Labor, 2006:1). Some groups oppose the governmental integration of faith-based organizations with other public efforts to help parolees and other ex-offenders, primarily because of the separation of church and state doctrine, although it is generally believed that regardless of the conflict, any collaboration that benefits parolees is a good one (Americans United for Separation of Church and State, 2006; Welsh, 2004).

Seamless Parole and Parole Programs

Increasing numbers of states are adopting a variation of seamless probation as a means of assisting offenders in transition from prison to their communities. Known as **seamless parole,** the idea is to provide continuity of care for inmates while they are confined, and to continue this care and treatment into their community life once they leave the prison environment. This is not to be confused with seamless services that regulate interstate compact agreements, where parolees in one state are transferred and supervised by POs in other states (Oklahoma Department of Corrections, 2006). Program goals in such interstate compact agreements are intended to provide new sets of rules to establish a seamless method of supervision and ease the transition of offenders from one jurisdiction to another. Seamless parole is unrelated to the seamless dimension of interstate compact agreements, however.

For instance, the Texas Department of Criminal Justice instituted an innovative education, intervention, and treatment program, which commenced in 2005. Known as the Therapeutic Community Substance Abuse Aftercare Treatment Program, it administers a broad range of therapeutic, outpatient, and resource treatments. The program oversees and coordinates all interrelated state and private programs involved in substance abuse treatment for offenders, both inside and outside of prison. Case management and drug and alcohol testing are used, and the program ranges over 6–9 months inside prison, depending on offender needs and responses to provided services and treatments (Texas Department of Criminal Justice, 2006). Once the offender is transitioned into the community, an additional 12–15 months of aftercare are provided intensively to ensure a seamless continuum of treatment and services. Again, program length is determined according to an offender's progress and specific needs.

In New York, a competency-based training program has been established by the New York Division of Parole for the purpose of providing seamless parole to inmates in need of special services and treatments (New York State Division of Parole, 2006). Three Special Needs Units, located in prisons in different areas of New York, offer two-day modules that provide competency-based training in the following subjects: (1) person-centered practices, (2) a framework for planning, and (3) community corrections. The objective is that facility and parole agency personnel will acquire skills to improve their assistance to inmates reentering society. The overall objective of these units and the training they impart is to make it possible for returning offenders to put ex-offenders into various community positions where they can play more significant community membership roles. Thus, the overall seamless parole model being used is very much person-centered.

As we have seen, mental illnesses among prison inmates are fairly prevalent. In Georgia, for example, inmates who have been diagnosed with mental illnesses receive appropriate medical and psychiatric care while incarcerated. However, when they return to their communities, they suddenly acquire the burden of self-maintenance. Many of these mentally ill offenders cannot reliably take on these responsibilities, which may be onerous for them. The simple routine of keeping medical appointments, taking daily medications, and related responsibilities requires organization and sustained efforts, qualities that are often compromised by their mental condition (Georgia Department of Corrections, 2006). Georgia authorities indicate that the six-month period following one's release from prison is probably the most relapse-prone phase for all offenders, and for mentally ill offenders, the likelihood of relapse is intensified.

Thus, in 2005 the Georgia Parole Board intensified its efforts to improve mental health support for offenders under its supervision. Specialists were hired to coordinate mental health services for parolees and upgrade agency staff training and procedures related to mental health issues. A new program, Treatment and Aftercare for Probationers and Parolees (TAPP), promises to boost post-prison support for all of Georgia's mentally ill and retarded offenders. Not only is TAPP made available to current parolees, but also it is made available to those who have maxed out their sentences and are no longer under any type of supervision. Georgia's prison inmates will receive long-term medical and residential care, regular meals, and structured recreation under the supervision of mental health professionals. For unsupervised offenders who have maxed out their sentences but still have mental health issues, Georgia is making it possible for officials to negotiate with mental health counselors and assist these individuals who can be located. Much of the time, these offenders are living on their own. They are unemployed and living on the streets. One official noted that all offenders need structure when they return from prison to the community. It makes sense to build interagency alliances to strengthen services, and to develop new procedures that will promote the seamless transition of prison-to-community treatment monitoring (Georgia Department of Corrections, 2006:2).

Characteristics of Parolees Who Reenter Their Communities

Offenders are reentering their communities in greater numbers each year. Joan Petersilia indicated that in 2000, 600,000 or more offenders were being returned to their communities from prison. Subsequently these numbers have escalated dramatically (Lowenkamp and Latessa, 2005).

The profile of offenders who are reentering their communities is not especially positive. Among nonviolent offenders who reenter their communities from prison, for instance, about 40 percent have less than a high school education. Nearly 70 percent had been using drugs prior to being incarcerated for their conviction offense and admit to continuing dependencies on drugs. Approximately 25 percent were dependent on alcohol prior to entering prison. It is likely that their alcohol dependence will continue. Over 50 percent were unemployed when imprisoned initially.

Only about 20 percent of those leaving state and federal prisons on parole have received some form of drug treatment within six months of being discharged. Few offenders receive transitional services, especially those placed in halfway houses for brief periods following their prison releases (Pellisier and Cadigan, 2004:10).

Obstacles to Effective Parolee Reentry

Community Resistance: The NIMBY Syndrome Revisited.   One of the persistent problems facing those reentering communities is that citizens have a general aversion to ex-offenders. The common belief seems to be that these offenders are categorically dangerous and pose serious threats to community safety. These citizen fears are at times justified, since some offenders do commit serious offenses once they return to their communities. But aggressive parole programming can do much to foster a better working relationship and collaborative effort between the agency, business leaders, law enforcement, social services, and other interested stakeholders. The NIMBY syndrome means "not in my backyard." It implies a rejection of those attempting to readjust to society and become productive citizens. Therefore, some community cooperation and acceptance are necessary for more successful inmate reentry to occur. Thus, citizens need to be educated about how these offenders will be supervised or monitored. They will need to understand how these offenders require some form of employment and housing assistance, as well as other services, including counseling and various treatments for any problems they may have. Such educational initiatives will do much to decrease community resistance to inmate reentry.

The Costs and Benefits of Correctional Treatment Programs.   Brandon Welsh (2004) has addressed the costs and benefits of reentry programs that are currently being used for offender reintegration and rehabilitation. Communities need to realize that the investments they make in offender rehabilitation services are crucial in minimizing recidivism rates and producing more law-abiding citizens. Treatment resources must be expanded if offenders' chances for successful reintegration and reentry are to be improved significantly.

The nature of resource improvements pertains to greater educational opportunities, easier access to employment opportunities, a greater variety of health and social service use, and drug dependency services. Substantial economic returns are projected that stem from greater expenditures of funds in these important areas. Some of the long-term benefits addressed by Welsh include more transitional aid and assistance, greater financial and job placement assistance, increased employment, and ultimately reduced reliance on social services, such as welfare. These improvements can translate favorably into substantial monetary benefits for society (Welsh, 2004:12).

Parolee Restrictions and Collateral Sanctions. Jeremy Travis (2005) has indicated that most parolees face invisible punishments of different kinds when reentering their communities following their prison terms. These invisible punishments have been referred to as collateral sanctions, and they represent laws, regulations, and administrative rules that often operate largely outside of public view (Mauer and Chesney-Lind, 2002). They may carry serious, adverse, and unfair consequences for the individuals who are affected (Travis and Visher, 2005).

Precisely what is meant and included among these invisible punishments and collateral sanctions? Joan Petersilia (2005) has given us some specificity here. Clearly there is substantial bias and stigma associated with having a prison record. Persons with criminal records have a much more difficult time finding employment compared with those without criminal records. Public access to the Internet is such, and the information provided on the Internet is so extensive and detailed, that almost anyone can check out anyone else to see if he or she has a criminal past. In at least 25 states in 2005, one's criminal past was a matter of public record and could be easily accessed by any interested party, such as a prospective employer. If those with prior records lie about being convicted for a crime and the conviction is subsequently discovered by the employer, then this fact is sufficient grounds for terminating the employee. Petersilia has found that 65 percent of all employers would not knowingly hire an ex-offender, even if the ex-offender were qualified for the job anyway. Thus, the number of jobs for ex-offenders is declining rapidly.

Parolees with Serious Mental Illnesses. Many prison and jail inmates have mental disorders. A portion of these are diagnosed and limited treatment is available for the most obvious inmates with these problems. However, these diagnosed cases are only a small portion of the true numbers of inmates with mental issues of different kinds that remain untreated. Furthermore, many offenders with mental disorders also suffer from drug dependencies. Such offenders are called offenders with co-occurring disorders (CODs). They are doubly problematic because many inmates with drug dependencies are not easily recognizable either. Thus, many inmates with CODs in jails and prisons go undiagnosed and untreated. Subsequently they are released that way (Sacks and Pearson, 2003). Parole agencies receive these persons with no knowledge of their existing conditions. They become problems for supervising POs at one time or another, for various reasons, and many have their programs revoked because they more easily violate one or more of their parole program conditions. Thus, such persons are a part of the revolving door of corrections.

Some jurisdictions have established **mental health courts** to enable judges and supporting staff both within institutions and in the community to manage the needs and treatments of such inmates more effectively. Mental health courts operate very much like drug courts in that individualized treatment plans are established for affected inmates. Subsequently when these inmates are released into their communities, a pattern of seamless aftercare continues, with community support services to meet many of their special needs. But one major problem is that only those diagnosed with mental illnesses are targeted for mental health courts, and only a small portion of the true number of offenders with mental illnesses are ever diagnosed. And so only a minority of cases receive such individualized care and treatment services while institutionalized and later following their community reentry (Sachs and Pearson, 2003).

It is a fact that a majority of inmates with undiagnosed mental illnesses will eventually reenter their communities and fail in their parole programs. They do not respond in normal ways to instructions; they have trouble complying with parole program requirements; they have difficulties with finding suitable employment and retaining their jobs; and they do not behave predictably as POs might expect. Many of these offenders ought to be hospitalized, but mental hospitals are overburdened as it is. In fact, it is precisely because of overcrowding that mental hospitals turned out thousands of mentally ill persons several decades ago who now make up a substantial portion of the homeless and destitute on our city streets. A portion of these persons become jail and prison inmates, because their peculiar behaviors more easily attract police attention and action. Mental illness among reintegrated parolees is a definite obstacle to reentry (Petersilia, 2005; Seiter, 2004).

Structured Failure Issues

Parole Program Requirements: The Impossible Dream?   Often, the parole program requirements imposed on parolees are cumbersome and difficult to follow. For instance, most parole programs provide that parolees cannot associate with other offenders. This restriction pertains even to families who may have one or more family members who are criminally involved (Petersilia, 2005:69).

Parolees are expected to find housing as a part of their parole conditions, but often, parolees lack sufficient resources to afford down payments on homes or first and last months' rents for apartments or homes. In many areas, landlords require proof of current and past employment, and one's criminal record is quickly detected. These parolees are passed over by prospective landlords because of this ex-offender stigma. There are also public housing laws that allow public housing agencies to deny housing to certain types of felons, such as drug abusers and sex offenders. Even if such persons qualify for public housing, the waiting lists are often as long as two to three years. Thus, ex-inmates show up at overcrowded shelters with long waiting lists and limits on the number of days they may stay in residence (Petersilia, 2005:69).

One onerous concomitant of having a criminal record and reuniting with one's immediate family is that if the family is presently living in a Public Housing Authority–controlled area, the U.S. Department of Housing and Urban Development's (HUD) policy is "one strike and you're out." This means that if an ex-offender moves into a HUD-controlled dwelling with the family, his or her family can be evicted without notice or warning. Parolees are seldom allowed to live in public housing anyway (Petersilia, 2005:69). This vicious cycle is such that the housing policy contributes to substandard housing or no housing, which breeds homelessness, which in turn increases the likelihood of recidivism. Large numbers of transients, panhandlers, and vagrants heighten citizen fear, and that fear ultimately contributes to increased crime and violence.

Curfews for offenders may be unrealistic. Many parolees are prohibited from purchasing or leasing automobiles. Thus, they must rely on public transportation to carry them to and from their workplace, if they are employed. These schedules mean that if a bus is missed because an ex-offender is expected to do extra work and put in longer hours in one's workplace, then a bus may be missed and the offender may be late in returning to his or her residence. Parole officers may detect these curfew "violations" and move to have one's parole revoked, even if a satisfactory explanation is provided for the curfew violation.

Are All Parole Violations Created Equally?   The nature of parole supervision has received little or no attention in the research literature (Burke, 2004). Peggy Burke says that a key hurdle for parolees to overcome is completing their period of parole successfully without being returned to prison for committing new crimes or violating technical program rules (2004:25). However, Burke notes that in recent years, parolees have been returned to prison increasingly, not for committing new crimes but for committing a variety of technical program violations. Among the reasons these parolees "fail" is that they often are poorly equipped to return to their communities with prosocial skills or vocational/educational competencies to make their transition from prison to the community a successful one.

How significant are parole program violations in influencing one's return to prison? In 1980, for instance, less than 20 percent of all parole revocations and returns to prison were for technical program violations (e.g., violating curfew, testing positive for drugs/alcohol, possessing illegal contraband, associating with known offenders, obtaining credit cards or opening bank accounts with PO permission, failing to report a police officer contact such as a brief interrogation, falling behind on restitution orders, or failing to maintain a residence and/or employment). In 1999 35 percent of all parolee returns to prison were the result of technical program violations (Burke, 2004:25). Are all of these technical program violations of equal seriousness? No. Should they all have the same consequences and punishments? No.

Burke has reviewed at least four states and their prison admissions for 2001. Georgia, Kansas, New Jersey, and Rhode Island were selected for her analysis. While these states vary greatly in the numbers of inmates in their prisons, there was no consistent pattern of percentages of admissions to prison based on technical parole violations. It made no difference whether the particular state had large numbers of inmates or small numbers of inmates. State inmate population size was irrelevant. For instance, Georgia had the largest adult daily prison population of 21,305 inmates, although the proportion of inmates admitted for technical parole violations was only 5.7 percent. In contrast, New Jersey had an average daily inmate population of 13,499 for 2001, but with 30 percent of these inmates in prison for technical parole violations. Rhode Island had the fewest numbers of inmates, 3,462, and it also had the lowest proportionate number of inmates, 3 percent, in prison for technical program violations. Kansas, another state with a low average daily inmate population of 5,923, had 45 percent of its inmates incarcerated for technical parole program violations. Is there any rhyme or reason to such drastic fluctuations from state to state concerning the proportions of prisoners in prison for technical program violations?

Burke says that one of the major reasons for such disparate differences among states in the numbers of parole revocations because of technical program violations is that almost every paroling agency has different technical program violation policies. In most cases, paroling agencies, when asked, cannot answer the simple question, "What proportion of technical violators are revoked to prison?" They don't know. Parole management systems in most states do not keep track of this information. It is telling, however, if we examine how many states word their policy manuals. In one state, for instance, the manual may state, "A formal revocation action may be initiated when there has been a violation in a significant respect or when violations have been serious and persistent." With thousands of parole officers supervising offenders among the states, one PO's "violation in a significant respect" definition of a parolee's misconduct may be quite different from another PO's definition. Is parole officer discretion in which violations get reported and which ones don't get reported the crucial factor here? Is it an individual thing? It would seem so. It is clear that agencies have not been explicit about what they expect of a line PO. Given increasing caseloads, concerns about community safety, a surveillance mindset, and concerns about liability, these are significant pressures on POs to rely on revocation as the safe response to technical violations (Burke, 2004:30).

Few states had policies in place to mandate automatic filings of parole program violations if POs detected program infractions. Thus, a distinction is often made between formal and informal dispositions. If a formal disposition is made, this means that the parole officer files a formal violation report and action is taken by the parole board. Informal action means that the PO doesn't report the violation but handles the violation matter informally. Informal adjustments include more frequent or intense monitoring of offenders, referrals to various community programs, changing treatment strategies, or intensifying reporting requirements. Even in those states where formal actions were taken and revocation proceedings were initiated, there was great variation in hearing outcomes. One state that revoked inmate parole programs always returned those inmates to prison, whereas another state only returned to prison about half of the revoked clients (Burke, 2004:30).

One recommended action that few states follow in revocation proceedings is to determine the risk and/or dangerousness posed by offenders who are found guilty of violation technical program requirements. Do parole boards return to prison those offenders who present the greatest risk to their communities? In Burke's (2004:30) analysis, no state had information to answer this question. Although offender risk should be an important consideration in any parole revocation action, severity of the violation and repetitiveness of violations should also be factored into the revocation decision. One tentative conclusion reached by Burke is that many offenders are returned to prison who shouldn't be. And they take up valuable prison space that could otherwise be allocated to more dangerous offenders. What Burke suggests is that a collaborative policy team should exist in all states to improve violation practices and that will clarify the broader purposes of supervision and how an agency's mission and vision can best be achieved.

Unemployment, Unemployment, and More Unemployment. Perhaps the greatest difficulty facing those being released from prison is finding a job and holding on to it (Wilkinson, 2005). We know, or we think we know, that improving one's educational and work-related skills will reduce one's risk of reoffending. Poor work histories are frequently equated with high recidivism rates (McBride, Visher, and LaVigne, 2005). Some of the information generated by the Urban Institute, an organization that has studied inmate reentry aggressively for several years, discloses that the nature of parolee supervision seems unrelated or remotely related to one's propensity to recidivate. This doesn't mean that no parole supervision is best. Rather, it means that the emphasis placed on the value of parole supervision may be overstated. Perhaps parole officers could redirect their efforts in ways that would enable their clients to find work and keep it (Rhine, 2006).

One correlate of low or no employment is prior history of drug use. Employers are not inclined to hire those with prior histories of drug or alcohol dependencies. They believe, rightly in many instances, that reversion to drugs and/or alcohol is likely, and that once an offender has become addicted to an illegal substance, it is difficult to overcome dependency on it (Cadigan, 2004). In this regard, a survey of parole officers has disclosed that maintaining steady employment, staying drug-free, receiving support from family and friends, and developing stable patterns of behavior are the most critical aspects of success for successful prisoner reentry (Seiter, 2002:53). Helping parolees maintain employment was reported by interviewed POs as one of the most important aspects of their jobs. More paroling agencies are turning toward greater use of information technology as a means of keeping track of client progress on several fronts, including their employment success (Pattavina, 2004).

It would seem that assisting offenders in obtaining employment and keeping their jobs would have both short- and long-range benefits for the community. Faye Taxman's (2004:33) description of offenders as active participants in their own post-prison futures seems to coincide well with the view that ex-offenders benefit greatly by demonstrating their own financial independence.

Varieties of Reentry Programs and Their Successfulness in Assisting Parolees

Several transition models have been proposed for those reentering their communities following imprisonment. These include (1) the Transition from Prison to Community Initiative, (2) the Violent Offender Reentry Initiative, and (3) the Reentry Partnership Initiative.

The Transition from Prison to Community Initiative (TPCI). The Transition from Prison to Community Initiative (TPCI) is a prisoner reentry program whose goal is to improve public safety by reducing the risk that released offenders pose by using risk assessment instruments and identifying risk factors that can be reduced by linking offenders to evidence-based treatments while they are still in prison as well as while they are under post-prison supervision (Parent and Barnett, 2004:25–26). The TPCI should prepare offenders for their successful transition from prison to society through effective programming and services. Several agencies, including corrections, human services, law enforcement, and community-based groups, must also be involved in a collaborative way to improve offenders in making this important transition. Thus, there are three phases: the institutional phase, the reentry phase, and the community phase (Parent and Barnett, 2004:26). The TPCI model is shown in Figure 8.2.

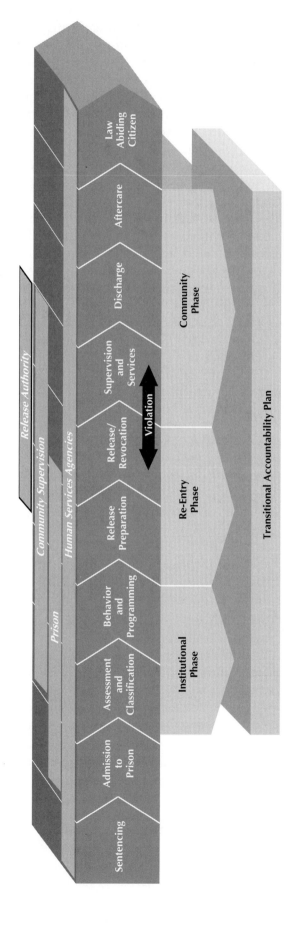

FIGURE 8.2 The TPCI Model. (from Parent and Barnett, 2004:26, *Federal Probation*, "Improving Offender Success and Public Safety Through System Reform: The Transition from Prison to Community Initiative." 68:25–31, p. 26.

During the institutional phase, which follows sentencing and admission to prison, offenders are classified and assessed according to their risks and needs. Their behavioral characteristics are examined and programming is designed to meet their needs, whatever they might be. These needs may be drug dependencies, alcohol treatment, mental health counseling, or other types of problems. At some point prior to an inmate's reentry into society, release preparation engages offenders in several of the adjustment problems and circumstances of community living. Following their discharge from prison, offenders have continued supervision and treatment, as needed. This aftercare is designed to assist them in becoming law-abiding and leading productive lives. During the period 2002–2003, several states, including Missouri and Oregon, began experiments with offenders and the implementation of TPCI. Primary challenges to all subsequent states who have joined these reentry efforts have been largely collaborative. Both institutional and community collaboration and coordination are critical to successful reentry. The primary obstacles to the successful implementation and operation of the TPCI are targeting the right offenders for interventions and reallocating scarce state resources so that proper treatments can be individualized according to offender needs.

The Serious Violent Offender Reentry Initiative (SVORI). The Serious Violent Offender Reentry Initiative (SVORI) program concerns serious and high-risk youthful offenders, although both adult and juvenile offenders are targeted for intervention. The SVORI initiative is a comprehensive effort to fund, develop, implement, enhance, and evaluate reentry strategies that will ensure the safety of the community and reduce serious and violent crime. This is accomplished by preparing targeted offenders to successfully return to their communities after having served a significant amount of time in secure confinement at a state training school, juvenile or adult correctional facility, or other secure institution. Communities that are selected for the SVORI have the opportunity to develop state-of-the-art reentry strategies and to acquire knowledge that will contribute to the establishment of national models of best practices (Office of Justice Programs, 2005).

Three phases of reentry are envisioned:

1. *Protect and Prepare: Institution-Based Programs.* These programs are designed to prepare offenders to reenter society. Services provided in this phase will include education, mental health and substance abuse treatment, job training, mentoring, and full diagnostic and risk assessment.

2. *Control and Restore: Community-Based Transition Programs.* These programs will work with offenders prior to and immediately following their release from correctional institutions. Services provided in this phase will include, as appropriate, education, monitoring, mentoring, life skills training, assessment, job skills development, and mental health and substance abuse treatment.

3. *Sustain and Support: Community-Based Long-Term Support Programs.* These programs will connect with individuals who have left the supervision of the justice system with a network of social service agencies and community-based organizations to provide ongoing services and mentoring relationships.

Examples of potential program elements include institution-based readiness programs, institutional and community assessment centers, reentry courts, supervised or electronically monitored boarding houses, mentoring programs, and community corrections centers (Office of Justice Programs, 2005:2).

The Reentry Partnership Initiative (RPI).   The Reentry Partnership Initiative (RPI) is designed to facilitate the smooth reentry of offenders into the community by providing the means of support through collaborative supervision as well as giving support to victims' rights without compromising public trust or safety. Inmates are targeted for treatment, education, and programs geared toward release preparedness during their incarceration. Inmates wishing to receive assistance must apply and sign an agreement to the conditions of this program. A close partnership between the community, businesses, and the system partners community at large is crucial in enhancing an offender's transition. The South Carolina Department of Probation, Parole, and Pardon Services is one site where the RPI has been implemented (South Carolina Department of Probation, Parole, and Pardon Services, 2006).

The eligibility criteria for participating South Carolina offenders, for example, include (1) inmates who have a residence plan in the South Carolina area; (2) offenders who live in South Carolina; (3) male and female offenders who are at least 18 years old; (4) offenders released to supervision; (5) offenders who have maxed out their sentences; and (6) offenders who are unemployed or underemployed. Participating offenders need an agreement date, special conditions specified, a needs assessment, and an action plan and referrals. Support services for the South Carolina RPI include vocational training; continued adult education; mental health counseling; local law enforcement; social services; faith-based community organizations; and a community workforce program.

The RPI expects to (1) enhance public safety by reducing reoffending among the released offender population; (2) build stronger police, corrections, and community partnerships and collaborations; (3) maximize offenders' accountability and positive contributions to the community; (4) strengthen support services for victims whose offenders are in the community; (5) increase the justice system's ability to identify offender needs and to match those needs with appropriate community resources; and (6) minimize prison returns due to technical violations of supervised release.

These and similar initiatives are interesting in that they have a number of common features despite being independently established. All stress public safety; institution–community integration; the need for prerelease preparation of offenders; vocational/educational training; and strong collaboration between different community agencies. Much of the success of each of these and similar programs is dependent upon such collaborative efforts. But often, one of the most difficult problems to overcome is community fear of offenders reentering their communities. There are two basic and competing needs operating here. One is the need for offenders to become rehabilitated in an accepting community milieu (Taxman et al., 2006). The other is the need for protection and security expressed by the community at large. It is imperative that a degree of trust should exist among community leaders that correctional authorities have targeted only the most eligible offenders for community participation. This places a great deal of importance on risk and needs assessment instrumentation, which has not been particularly good or effective in past years (Champion, 1994). It is quite difficult to identify those offenders who will do well and be responsive to institutional as well as community interventions designed to help them. Some offenders may become involved in institutional programming for its cosmetic value. It helps them look good to paroling authorities. Other inmates, however, get involved and are very sincere about this involvement. Distinguishing between those who are sincere about changing their behaviors and those who merely go through the motions to do whatever they have to do to earn early release is a very difficult task for stakeholders in such intervention programs (Petersilia, 2004, 2005; Taxman, 2004).

Isolated Parole Agency–Community Initiatives to Assist Parolees

The Civic Engagement Model of Reentry.   We have observed that there are numerous stumbling blocks for those reentering their communities following imprisonment. There has been a general decline in community involvement and civil commitment among parolees. Their prospects for obtaining and sustaining a safe, productive, and economically viable civic life in their communities have been greatly diminished. One primary reason for this is the structural obstacles to productive citizenship faced by persons currently or formerly under correctional supervision (Bazemore and Stinchcomb, 2004:14). Inmates in many states are automatically disenfranchised of their voting rights, and when these persons leave prison, they are unable to participate meaningfully in the political and social life of their communities because of such a limitation.

In order to improve one's reentry chances and general reintegration successfulness, a civil engagement intervention model has been proposed. Civic engagement practice and policy based on such a model would be expected to (1) weaken barriers to the development of prosocial identities for persons who have been under correctional supervision; (2) alter the community's image of such persons; and (3) mobilize community capacity to provide informal support and assistance (Bazemore and Stinchcomb, 2004:14). Such practices should promote desistance and successful reentry as well as enhance the democratic qualities, social justice, and safety of communities. Policy based on civil engagement theory features three primary dimensions: (1) decision making based on restorative justice principles; (2) civil community service; and (3) voting enfranchisement and democratic participation.

The disenfranchisement of voting rights is only one part of the picture, however. Bazemore and Stinchcomb (2004:22) note that the most formidable challenges to effective reentry are the many restrictions on employment, parental rights, voting rights, and other forms of exclusion and social stigma faced by returning offenders. Given their lack of crime control value, such restrictions can be justified only by the view that they represent additional punishments that are somehow deserved. Restorative justice principles seem highly compatible with both civic service and the removal of voting and other restrictions on those who have served their time. Restorative practices enable lawbreakers to make good by doing good as a means of earning their redemption in a way that helps others and builds community.

Faye S. Taxman (2004) is also supportive of civic engagement initiatives that restore offender rights as a part of a total picture of successful offender reintegration. Taxman says that a transition (reentry) process is needed that addresses both survival needs (e.g., food, housing, employment) and skill-based services (e.g., treatment, literacy, job training) to thwart the recycling of offenders from prison to the community and back to prison (2004:31). Taxman states that most intervention models that are currently utilized for reentry services for offenders are based on a model that the offender is the recipient of services that others, such as correctional and/or judicial agencies, deem necessary. This model is premised on the idea that the services to be provided are essential to an offender's successful reintegration and crime-free lifestyle. But this model fails to take into account the facts that (1) many offenders, even under court-ordered treatment services, do not attend these treatment services; and (2) in an era of intermediate sanctions, approximately one-third of these offenders have chosen jail or prison instead of community-based services, such as boot camps, day reporting programs, drug courts, or even intensive supervised probation/parole. In our present punitive-oriented correctional system today, offenders are released back into their communities with little more than they entered prison with, and they usually simply complete a form stating where they expect to live and what they expect to be doing (for an occupation).

Taxman suggests that an **active participant model** be used that involves five important steps and that integrates both institutional and post-institutional treatments and services. These steps include:

1. *Message to the offender.* The key messages to the offender must be that the offender controls his or her destiny; that the offender have options so that he or she can learn to make decisions in his or her own interest; and that these decisions be made during incarceration and pertain to the types of survival and skills-based services that offenders desire to ease their transition back into society.

2. *Institutional treatment.* Since many offenders lack basic employment skills, they should be provided with necessary educational, vocational, and clinical intervention services. The offender needs to identify his or her reintegration goals and become motivated to achieve them through aggressive involvement in institutional programming.

3. *Institutional/pre-release* (from 90 days before release to release day). Offenders should address their housing and employment plans as basic survival needs. Obtaining necessary identification cards, driver's licenses, Social Security cards, Medicare coverage, and other necessities will ease their integration back into the community. Attention to these details may involve local police departments and state agencies where these inmates will reside. Coordination among agencies is critical for this model's success.

4. *Post-release* (from release day to 30 days). Close monitoring of offenders during the initial 30-day release period is critical. The offender's perception of community adjustment should be assessed and even reassessed. Offenders should also be counseled about their vulnerability to involvement in criminal behavior. Offender stabilization is of paramount importance here.

5. *Integration* (from 30 days after release up to 2 years). This phase focuses on the gradual involvement in the community and offender stability over time. More offender-initiated decision making should be evident as crisis management becomes easier. Offenders should be involved in adjusting their plans based on their own experiences in the community (Taxman, 2004:34).

Improving Offender Success and Public Safety.   Can the successfulness of reentering ex-offenders and public safety coexist? Most intervention programs and reentry initiatives a rebased on this premise. Cooperation between correctional institutions, community corrections agencies, law enforcement, social services, and community businesses is vital to effective offender reintegration (Petersilia, 2005). But Brandon C. Welsh suggests that several forces are at work to interfere with effective offender reentry. First, fewer treatment resources are being provided while offenders are in prison. Second, changes in sentencing laws have reduced the motivation for prisoners to participate in self-help programs and take advantage of institutional services, even if they are provided. A third factor is diminishing transitional aid to offenders reentering society, including less employment and housing (Welsh, 2004:9). Using a strict cost–benefit analysis, Welsh has established a strong argument for revitalizing prison treatment programs and services. He stresses the great importance of institutional services and support, activities that occur before inmates reenter society, that may have the greatest impact on offender reentry. On the basis of his cost–benefit analysis, a case can be made for increasing the treatment resources for offenders while institutionalized, and this in turn may improve offenders' chances for a more successful return to society.

Public safety is always going to be a key concern of law-abiding citizens of every community. But the fact is that over 90 percent of all inmates will eventually come home. This is an undebatable fact of life (Cummings, 2003). Therefore, the issue of public safety is largely dependent upon how well adjusted these returning offenders happen to be and how well they are supervised if paroled. Many are released after maxing out their sentences, and thus they have no further requirement for supervision by anyone. Presently there are numerous reentry programs considering all possible factors that can impact on the successfulness of one's reentry (Seiter, 2004).

The Emergence of Reentry Courts

What Are Reentry Courts?   Former Attorney General Janet Reno announced an initiative in October 1999 intended to promote community safety and reduce recidivism among newly released prison inmates. The initiative, originally designed by Jeremy Travis who was the former Director of the National Institute of Justice, was the concept of the **reentry court.** Patterned after drug courts, where judges, not parole boards, continually oversee the progress of those with drug dependencies through a community network of counseling, treatment, and other services, reentry courts draw primarily on the authority of judges to promote positive behaviors among inmates who are returning to their communities. Various tools, such as the use of graduated sanctions and incentives, are a part of this process. The reentry court initiative relies on the involvement of other crucial partners including institutional and community corrections, law enforcement, faith-based organizations, social services, victim support groups, and neighborhood organizations, essential to build the necessary monitoring, coordinating services, and community linkages to support an offender's successful reentry and enhance public safety (Spelman, 2002, 2003). Reentry courts are designed to use the power of judicial authority to aggressively monitor offenders released into the community while at the same time providing them with a multitude of services facilitating their transition back into the community.

In 2000, the Office of Justice Programs articulated several important components or core elements of reentry courts. These include:

1. Offender assessment and planning, which will bring together reentry court personnel, such as a judge or parole or probation officer, to explain the reentry process to offenders and identify their needs upon release.

2. Active offender oversight, which would include routine judicial visits with all offenders.

3. Accountability to the community, to include the development of initiatives to ensure that offenders are held accountable both to victims and the community.

4. Graduated and parsimonious sanctions, or a predetermined range of sanctions for violations of the conditions of release that can be swiftly, predictably, and universally applied.

5. Access to an array of support services, which will include substance abuse treatment, job training programs, private employers, faith-based institutions, housing services, and community service providers.

6. Positive judicial reinforcement, or rewarding successful offender behavior and compliance with the condition of release (Spelman, 2002:23, 2003).

Subsequently several jurisdictions implemented reentry courts to serve offenders' needs and supervise their behavior over a period of time before and after their prison releases. Nine states were selected as sites for establishing reentry courts. One of these states was Ohio (Wilkinson, 2005:88).

Ohio's Reentry Courts. The Richland County, Ohio, Common Pleas Court established a reentry court shortly after the 2000 initiative announced by Janet Reno. The following agencies and/or individuals conducted numerous meetings to discuss and plan how Ohio's first reentry court would operate: the Ohio Department of Rehabilitation and Corrections; county and state offender supervision staff; the Ohio Adult Parole Authority; the Ohio Prison staff; community and prison caseworkers, and treatment providers; the Richland County Prosecutor; victim's services; community policing representatives; community corrections board members; and evaluation team members.

Originally it was agreed that the majority of offenders sentenced to a term of incarceration in the Richland County Court of Common Pleas would be expected to become participants in the reentry court project. Some categories of offenders would be automatically excluded. For instance, sex offenders and those with serious mental health disorders would be screened from program participation. The target population included both offenders who have been granted judicial release and/or given split sentences on the front end and those with parole and post-release control offenders on the back end. During the first 12 months of the project, it was expected that the program would accommodate 100 offenders released from prison under the direction of the court by either judicial release or split sentencing. Another 50–90 parole and post-release offenders would also become eligible to participate. Program goals include:

1. The authority to select cases for the reentry court, setting conditions of release, and deciding what sanctions and revocations will rest with the sentencing judge. The same authority will rest with the state parole board for parole and post-release cases.

2. Cases not eligible for community control (probation) that are ordinarily set for imprisonment will undergo further examination and assessment by the reentry court coordinator for the development of an institutional treatment plan. This plan will be the primary basis for judicial considering of their placement back into the community, either on judicial release or split sentencing, and it will be used in planning for parole or post-release control.

3. Prior to release from an institution, a transitional plan will be developed for each offender to ensure a smooth transition back into the community. A seamless continuum of treatment, employment, residential placement, and supervision issues will be addressed.

4. Offenders placed in the reentry court program shall be subject to active oversight through regular court appearances and the steady monitoring of their progress by the court and/or parole board.

5. The supervision of offenders subject to reentry court oversight requires and shall involve cooperation, information, information sharing, and collaboration among supervision officers, treatment providers, and community policing to ensure compliance with case management expectations. Examples of sanctions include community work service, electronic monitoring, financial fines; attendance at additional counseling programs; and 2- to 3-day punitive jail incarceration.

6. There shall be flexible and proportional responses to offender violations drawing on a continuum of graduated sanctions designed to encourage and support prosocial behavior.

7. Offender compliance with the conditions of supervision shall be rewarded with diminishing restrictions, positive reinforcement, and formal acknowledgment of the offender's efforts leading to the successful completion of the reentry court program (Spelman, 2002:24).

As of September 2001, 76 clients had participated in the reentry court project, with another 72 being monitored in prison for reentry consideration. Of the 76 reentry clients, 59 were under the authority of two common pleas judges, with 43 placed in the intensive supervision program, 10 placed in the substance abuse treatment court, and one client placed in the DUI program. The clients average approximately 4.5 months in the reentry court program, while the longest stay has been 10 months. One client had the shortest stay of one month. By September 2001, four revocation hearings were held where all four clients were dismissed from the program. By January 2002, 115 clients participated in the project, 30 of these being parolees and post-release control clients and 85 common pleas split-sentence clients. The failure rates of parole and post-release supervised clients thus far was 23 percent, while 12 percent failed from the common pleas court. The overall current failure rate is 16.5 percent, which is considered successful in view of the 30 percent informal recidivism standard used for general probation and program successes.

Continuing Reentry Issues

Increasing Need for Multicultural Competencies for Parolee Reentry. The social profile of prisoners has become more diverse during the past few decades. During the 1970s and 1980s, most prisoners in state and federal prisons and jails were largely white and black, with few Hispanics and others. While whites continue to account for a large proportion of inmates, black and Hispanic inmates have increased proportionately. Also, Asians and Pacific Islanders have added to the cultural diversity of our prison systems.

Greater cultural diversity in prisons and jails translates directly into greater cultural diversity in probation and parole. POs in all jurisdictions are having to supervise more culturally diverse offenders, many of whom have a limited understanding of English. For a growing number of offenders, Spanish is the primary language, or one of several Asian languages. The influx of Russians into the United States during the 1990s has also contributed to this cultural diversity (Glaze and Palla, 2005).

The proportionate numbers of culturally diverse offenders on probation or parole doesn't match the proportionate distributions of them in prisons and jails. For instance, 37 percent of all prison inmates were white in 2004, while 48 percent were black, and 20 percent were Hispanic. That same year, parolees consisted of 40 percent white, 41 percent black, and 18 percent Hispanic. A preliminary interpretation of these figures suggests that proportionately more whites than blacks or Hispanics are getting paroled, while there are decreases in the proportionate numbers of black and Hispanic parolees. These figures reflect back-end parole numbers. If we include probationers from the front end, there are also glaring discrepancies among races/ethnicities. For instance, in 2004 56 percent of all probationers were white, 30 percent were black, and 12 percent were Hispanic. Regardless of the reasons for these disproportionate figures, the fact remains that the parolee and probationer populations are sufficiently diverse to merit professional attention to multicultural differences.

It has been found that one of the major impediments to building an effective PO–client relationship is cross-cultural barriers. If counseling is going to be effective, for instance, it must reflect the differences in cultural values of the clientele supervised. This includes the totality of ideals, beliefs, skills, tools, customs, and institutions into which each member of society is born (Shearer and King, 2004:4). For instance, it has been found that some ethnic minorities do not take advantage of counseling services, and that whenever they do, they usually terminate their counseling prematurely. More culturally skilled staff are helpful in this regard. POs who receive cross-cultural training have more successful clients who are less likely to terminate their programs early.

Culturally aware POs are also more aware of their own preconceived notions and biases, and prejudicial attitudes, feelings, and beliefs, and they tend to avoid stereotyping and labeling. A culturally competent PO should exhibit sincerity, high service energy, knowledge of the client's culture, a nonjudgmental attitude, and resourcefulness. Ethnocultural competency is the ability of the PO to function effectively in the context of cultural differences. In fact, to improve general parole agency performance, it has been suggested that all officers should increase their multicultural knowledge and develop multicultural skills. Such improved competencies can achieve the following:

1. Knowledge of how a person's culture and heritage affect them personally and professionally.
2. Knowledge of how oppression and racism, discrimination, and stereotyping affect them personally.
3. How their negative and positive reactions toward other racial and ethnic groups may prove detrimental to the counseling relationship.
4. How poverty, racism, and stereotyping may affect the self-esteem and self-concept of racial and minority clients.
5. Knowledge of how institutional barriers prevent minorities from using mental health services.
6. Knowledge of the bias in assessment procedures.
7. Acting proactively to eliminate biases, prejudices, and discriminatory contents in conducting evaluations and providing interventions (Shearer, 2004:5).

There are several unknowns here. We don't know, for instance, whether multicultural training can impact significantly on the quality of parole services provided by supervising POs. We suspect that it can. Should POs be matched with clients based on culture, race, or ethnicity? This may be too much of a luxury for most parole departments. What sorts of multicultural competencies should be stressed? What should a multicultural curriculum look like? We don't know for sure. What is the current level of multicultural competency among the existing contingent of U.S. POs? We don't know. These are certainly issues worth exploring in future years. And resolving these and related issues can do much to improve PO effectiveness, especially in multicultural relationships with their clients.

Interagency Priorities at the Crossroads.   Interagency priorities have to do with different agencies in the community and funded by different sources that are designed to assist reentry offenders in different ways. Each agency has priorities that are seemingly closely intertwined with other agencies and their particular priorities. But information-sharing among agencies about ex-offender/clients is more easily said than done. For instance, Bernadette Pellissier and Timothy Cadigan studied drug treatment services received by inmates in the Federal Bureau of Prisons (BOP), the BOP's residential drug treatment program (RDAP), and transitional services (TS) (Pellissier and Cadigan, 2004:11). The RDAP is an institutional drug treatment program offered to inmates with drug dependencies within 36 months of their release from prison. TS focuses on outpatient treatments available to ex-offenders who are placed in halfway houses for varying periods following their release.

One of the first hurdles to be overcome by these researchers was gathering information from both RDAP and TS concerning the same offender/clients. The BOP operates an operational database, known as Sentry, where substance abuse treatment records are stored. Gaining access to this database was eventually achieved. It was important for these investigators to know which inmates had participated in both programs and which clients had failed in one or both of these drug treatment services. Their primary concern was the continuity of care these clients received both in and out of prison. What these researchers found was that continuity of care was spotty for both RDAP and TS. No consistent policies could be identified to link the two programs. These investigators concluded that for future years, it is imperative for both RDAP and TS to recognize their mutual need for a seamless system of care for all participating inmates or clients. The combined impact of these agencies and services would greatly benefit the offender population being served. Improved tracking and supervision were strongly recommended, as well as greater coordination between the different services, each striving to meet the needs of a common offender aggregate (Pelissier and Cadigan, 2004:13).

Lessons Learned from the "What Works" Approach.   Larry Sherman et al. (1998) have developed the Maryland Scale of Scientific Methods (MSSM) to identify crime prevention programs that work, especially with new parolees. The MSSM applies across all settings and includes core criteria that identify five levels of the scale. The higher the level, the more rigorous the research design and the lower the threat to internal validity. The MSSM ranks studies from 1 (weakest) to 5 (strongest) on overall internal validity. The scale uses the following levels to categorize evaluative studies by their rigor or scientific method:

1. Level 1: Correlation between a type or level of reentry program intervention (e.g., substance abuse treatment, violent or sex offender treatment, vocational training, work release, life skills) and an outcome measure at a single point in time (e.g., recidivism, return to custody, employment rate, drug use, academic achievement).

2. Level 2: Temporal sequence between the program (intervention) and outcome measure clearly observed or the presence of a comparison group without demonstrated comparability to the treatment group.

3. Level 3: A comparison between two or more comparable units of analysis, one with and one without the program.

4. Level 4: Comparison between multiple units with and without the program, controlling for other factors, or using comparison units that evidence only minor differences.

5. Level 5: Random assignment and analysis of comparable units to program and comparison groups (Sherman et al., 1998).

Sherman et al.'s (1998) examination of existing programs to assist those going through reentry yielded several positive findings. These investigators examined a variety of vocational and work programs, drug rehabilitation programs, education programs, sex and violent offender programs, halfway house programs, and prison pre-release programs. Their findings include (1) vocational training and/or work release programs are effective in reducing recidivism and improving job readiness skills for ex-offenders; (2) drug rehabilitation programs are effective in reducing arrests, drug-related offenses, continued drug use, and parole violations; (3) halfway house programs reduce the frequency and severity of future crimes; (4) there are promising results for several types of sex offender and violent offender programs; (5) educational programs increase educational achievement scores but do not decrease recidivism; and (6) pre-release programs improve the chances of successful inmate reentry. These findings are extremely useful for correctional policymakers. It can be concluded that to improve reentry success and reduce recidivism, those categories of reentry programs that work should be funded and expanded, and those with promising findings should undergo further evaluation (Seiter, 2004:33). One shortcoming associated with most programs was insufficient resources allocated to the programs. This translates into insufficient money to operate these programs adequately. If the money is not there or is allocated inappropriately, then less promising results for those going through the reentry process can be expected. It's not so much that money can buy rehabilitation, but the lack of adequate funding can certainly increase recidivism and create greater community harm.

They All Come Out.   It is a virtual certainty that most currently imprisoned offenders will eventually be released back into their communities (Cummings, 2003:9). They all come out, or at least most of them do eventually. Both Joan Petersilia (2004) and Homer Cummings (2003) place great emphasis, therefore, on offender classification, both at the front and back ends of one's confinement in prison. The presence of an effective offender classification system to assess one's risk and needs goes a long way to providing both institutional treatments and services as well as post-release aftercare and services. Petersilia (2004:5) believes that successful classifications of offenders and subsequent interventions useful for their reentry tend to emphasize behavioral and cognitive techniques, such as modeling, role playing, reinforcement, and cognitive restructuring. Treatment interventions should target those offenders deemed to pose the highest risk. The most effective strategy for discerning an offender's risk level is not clinical judgments but rather actuarial-based assessments, such as the Level of Service Inventory.

Petersilia says that correctional practitioners for the most part have traditionally relied on nonacademic solutions for formulating rehabilitation programming. At the same time, academics are attempting through meta-analyses and other methods to identify the most promising intervention research as a guide to best-practices policies. But when she compares correctional practitioners and academics, there is little or no evidence that research is driving policy or that policy is driving research. In order to improve this situation and develop the best solutions for offender programming and more successful reentry, both correctional practitioners and academics will have to collaborate to a greater degree and be more accepting of their respective solutions for common problems on the reentry issue. Presently, in Petersilia's opinion, we have not reached that stage where such positive collaboration has been achieved. However, Petersilia is optimistic and believes that a health collaboration between these two camps will eventually evolve (Petersilia, 2004:8).

Homer Cummings (2004) stresses a well-regulated parole system that would permit deserving prisoners the opportunity of leaving their cells and prisons for short periods of time, such as work or study release, to provide them with the opportunity to seek out potential job opportunities and eventually obtain permanent work outside of their institutions. This is where classification can be used most successfully. Those most eligible inmates can be assessed and identified. Allowing them a reasonable stake in their futures with such parole policies would have several advantages for the communities they will enter. They will be more easily employed, rely less on welfare and other social support services, and acquire more law-abiding attitudes on their way to becoming more productive citizens. Cummings also is against long prison terms, since he believes that prisons breed idleness and bitterness among inmates over time. In this respect, the Federal Bureau of Prisons operates prison industries that are able to provide at least 80 percent of all inmates with some form of work to prevent them from being idle. The average federal offender spends approximately 20 months behind bars. This is sufficient time for them to receive adequate treatments and counseling, as well as educational and vocational training. If they need mental health treatment or other health services, such services can be identified shortly after they enter federal prisons through proper classification mechanisms.

THE GROWING GANG PRESENCE

Increasing numbers of parolees are affiliated with gangs (Lowry et al., 2006). If convicted offenders are non-gang members when they enter prison, the likelihood is that when they leave prison on parole, they will be affiliated with a gang (Straka, 2003). Gang membership increases one's propensity to reoffend, since most gangs are involved in illicit criminal activities and induce their membership to engage in such criminal enterprises as drug trafficking.

Also, increasing numbers of offenders who enter jails and prisons are already affiliated with gangs. Most of these new inmates joined gangs as juveniles. It is generally acknowledged that gangs exist in all states, that they are involved with drug sales and distribution, and that they are highly structured. The variety and nature of gangs is explained by personal factors such as class, culture, race, and ethnicity, along with community factors such as poverty, social instability, and social isolation. Intergang violence is fairly common. Gang members are becoming older and remaining in gangs longer. Many of those entering prisons perpetuate their gang affiliations by joining existing gangs or forming their own groups for self-protection and other interests.

Parole officers have reported that one of their major problems in dealing with parolees is gang affiliation, which is not always apparent. Many parolees attempt to disguise their gang affiliation by removing recognizable gang tattoos or denying that they are gang members when visited by their POs. It is often difficult for POs to prescribe treatments or needed community services for those affiliated with gangs, since there is strong resistance from parolee-clients who are gang-affiliated to becoming meaningfully involved in helpful interventions.

Overcoming gang influence is difficult. POs may attempt to initiate contacts between parolees and their victims, where personal injuries or property losses were sustained as the result of crimes committed. Sometimes restorative justice methods are effective in increasing the likelihood that parolees will remain law-abiding while on parole (Schaefer et al., 2006). But despite the best intentions of POs and their agencies, there will always be a hardcore contingent of parolees who will prove to be unstable and not abide by their parole program conditions. Some may even abscond from their jurisdictions (Gunnison and Helfgott, 2006). Greater police presence in gang-dominated neighborhoods assists POs in their attempts to keep parolees from engaging in further criminal activities as the result of gang influence.

But the pervasiveness of gangs in areas where parolees are likely to reside, together with ready access to addictive substances and alcohol, mean that POs are fighting an uphill battle in their efforts to reform, rehabilitate, and reintegrate their parolee-clients (Powers and Wilson, 2006). In many jurisdictions, parolee failures are drug-related. Parolee failures attributable to substance abuse can sometimes be converted into positive experiences, however (Ryan, 2006). In Kentucky, for example, a program known as the Halfway Back Program provides an alternative to incarceration for parolees with nonviolent technical violations that might otherwise trigger revocation proceedings. In the Halfway Back Program, parolees caught violating technical program conditions sign an agreement to complete their programs and refrain from committing future technical violations. These agreements between parolees and their POs seem to offer strong incentives to remain law-abiding, despite the adverse influence gangs in the area may have. Other strategies, such as home confinement and electronic monitoring, may be necessary, however.

THE IDEA OF PAROLE IN RETROSPECT

It is evident that parole in the United States is increasing annually. This does not mean that the successfulness of parole is increasing to an equivalent degree. On the contrary. It would seem that much depends on the nature of particular parole programs and the intensity of supervised release relating to how parolees are managed. The federal government has replaced parole with supervised release. Parole has already been abolished in Maine, and several other states have given serious consideration to proposals for its elimination. At one extreme, the "just-deserts" philosophy is that offenders should be punished for their crimes in accordance with whatever the law prescribes. However, the laws are not formulated with the right degree of precision. For example, most offenses prescribe a term of incarceration up to X years or months and/or a fine of not more than X dollars. Thus, important decisions must be made by prosecutors, judges, and other officials that attempt to match the severity of the punishment imposed with the seriousness of the crime committed. This is far from an exact science, although social scientists and others for centuries have wrestled with the problems of defining appropriate punishments that fit each crime. Scientific investigations have attempted to evolve ideal models or schemes that might fit neatly into a sentencing scheme that states or the federal government might adopt. In fact, there is little or nothing scientific about state and federal statutes and their accompanying sentencing patterns in any jurisdiction.

At the other extreme are those labeled as rehabilitation-oriented and/or who promote or endorse nonincarcerative, reintegrative programs or the early release of offenders so as to minimize the criminogenic effects of prisons and jails. It is unlikely that parole will be abolished on a national scale, at least for the next several decades. Methods for controlling or monitoring offenders while on probation or parole are constantly being improved, and new and better devices are being developed to ensure greater supervisory effectiveness. Thus, better control of persons currently under PO supervision appears to be the most logical solution to present problems.

Prison overcrowding enters the picture as an extremely important intervening variable. Many state prison systems have contracts with local city or county jails to house some of their inmate overflow. Several state prison systems are currently under zero population growth court orders, where maximum prison capacities cannot be exceeded. A general shift in sentencing from indeterminate to determinate has eroded or eliminated parole board authority to grant prisoners early release. However, under determinate sentencing, considerable latitude in sentencing decisions and charging decisions exists for judges and prosecutors. One result of these sentencing reforms has been to increase the likelihood of being incarcerated for various offenses, although the length of incarceration has been significantly shortened.

The just-deserts and rehabilitative philosophies present corrections officials with an unresolvable dilemma. Standing on the sidelines of the great debate are observers who claim that nothing works. Many victims of offenders oppose their parole, believing that these offenders, if released, will reoffend and harm them (Wolf and Rodgers, 2006). While it is true that no offender rehabilitation program is 100 percent recidivism-free, this does not mean that the program ought to be scrapped. When particular parole programs have recidivism rates of 30 percent or less, they also have success rates of 70 percent or higher. Some offenders appear to be benefiting from program participation. One costly solution is to construct and staff more prisons to house more prisoners. But can the states and the federal government afford to do this? Consider California's dilemma. Presently, California places approximately 70 percent of its convicted felons on probation (U.S. Department of Justice, 2006). What if these felons had been sentenced to incarceration, even for short terms? Where would California prison officials put them? Furthermore, it is difficult and costly to attract and hire educated and competent persons to work in correctional officer and PO positions to supervise and manage offenders in or out of prison.

However, communities are playing an increasingly important role in offender management. In fact, many organizations are being established in the private sector to assume roles and offender management functions originally performed by understaffed and underpaid government bureaucracies. Parolees are becoming involved in new and innovative community programs featuring useful activities, such as employment assistance, individual and group counseling, educational training, literacy services, and valuable networking with other community agencies and businesses. More dangerous offenders who are released on parole are often placed in electronic monitoring programs and/or subject to house arrest or home confinement.

Additionally, inmates who are within a few months of their prospective parole dates are being released, with or without supervision, for short periods through work or study release programs. Other inmates are permitted short leaves from prison through furloughs. Yet other inmates are housed temporarily in halfway houses in communities, where they can ease back into community life gradually. Halfway houses are facilities with some rules and regulations, including curfew and drug and alcohol checks. Some inmates have a particularly difficult time coping with the relatively new freedoms of community life after the strict discipline and regimentation they experienced while incarcerated. These halfway houses and community residential centers provide diverse functions for many recently paroled offenders.

Almost all of the programs available to probationers are also made available to parolees. While differences between probationers and parolees were more pronounced in past decades, it is becoming increasingly the case that they bear more similarities to one another than differences. One reason is that there is so little room available in prisons and jails that many felons cannot be accommodated. Some states, such as California, place as many as 70 percent of their convicted felons on probation annually, simply because there is no room for them in existing prison and jail facilities. Even the vast construction programs in California and other states are falling behind in attempting to keep pace with increasing numbers of offenders falling within some form of probation or parole supervision annually.

One prediction is that government will rely more heavily in future years on private interests for offender management responsibilities. Numerous experiments are underway to see which programs have the best results and minimize parolee failures. Failures most often occur because of the fact that many parolees are either unsupervised or undersupervised during their parole activity. Many of them lack the ability to fill out application forms for jobs. Also, many have drug- or alcohol-related problems that got them into trouble initially. Rapidly expanding community services are doing more to fill important parolee needs. Volunteers and paraprofessionals are becoming more valuable components in these growing community programs as well.

SUMMARY

Parole is early release from prison short of serving one's full sentence originally imposed by the court. Parole originated in the eighteenth century in Spain, France, and England, and became popular in the United States in the mid-1800s as a means of alleviating prison overcrowding. The father of parole, Alexander Maconochie, was an early prison reformer who sought to assist prisoners to earn early release through marks of commendation or good marks. These types of rewards have been continued in United States prisons as good-time credits against time served.

United States sentencing reforms have resulted in the abolishment of parole boards in several states, although a majority of states continue to use indeterminate sentencing and parole boards as decision-making bodies to grant or refuse to grant prisoners early release. Parole boards have been criticized for their failure to recognize recidivists and/or dangerous prisoners who should be confined. However, no foolproof prediction tools presently exist to permit accurate predictions of dangerousness of prisoners or the risk to the public if offenders are released short of serving their full terms.

The philosophy of parole is prisoner rehabilitation through reintegrating offenders into society. The manifest and latent functions of parole include reintegrating offenders into society, controlling or deterring crime, alleviating prison overcrowding, remedying sentencing disparities attributable to race, ethnicity, or socioeconomic status, and public protection. No current profile of parolees exists other than selected characteristics of persons presently incarcerated in prisons. Few prisoners serve their full terms, and most are released either through parole board discretion or mandatorily after serving approximately one-third of their sentences.

Shifts in the nature of sentencing have done much to influence how parole is treated. Many states continue to use parole boards with discretionary powers to release inmates short of serving their full terms. Other states utilize mandatory supervised release as a way of rewarding those who have accumulated sufficient good-time credits and show promise for successful adaptations to community life if released. Many states are currently reevaluating their sentencing provisions and standards. Presently, there is considerable controversy concerning the contrasting philosophies of rehabilitation and just-deserts, where some corrections professionals seriously question the rehabilitative value of parole programs. The United States Sentencing Commission implemented new guidelines for federal judges to follow in November 1987, and the United States Parole Commission was scheduled for abolishment in 1992.

QUESTIONS FOR REVIEW

1. What is parole? What are some manifest and latent functions of parole?
2. What are some of the goals of parole? Do corrections professionals agree on these goals and the extent to which they are being achieved?
3. What contributions have the following persons made to the use of parole in the United States?
    a. Alexander Maconochie
    b. Walter Crofton
    c. Gaylord Hubbell
4. What is the relation between indeterminate sentencing and parole?
5. How does determinate sentencing modify parole?
6. What was the Wickersham Commission and what were some of its functions?
7. What are some of the pro's and con's of indeterminate sentencing in relation to parole?
8. How do the rehabilitative and justice models of parole differ?
9. What are some of the characteristics of parolees in the United States?
10. What are some of the major issues associated with prisoner reentry into their communities? How are correctional institutions, community agencies, and social services addressing these issues?

SUGGESTED READINGS

Allender, David M. (2004). "Offender Reentry: A Returning or Reformed Criminal?" *FBI Law Enforcement Bulletin* **73**:1–10.

Draine, M., T.L. Sia, and D.F. Dansereau (2006). "Improving Early Engagement and Treatment Readiness of Probationers: Gender Differences." *The Prison Journal* **86**:1552–1572.

Lowencamp, Christopher T. and Edward J. Latessa (2005). "Developing Successful Reentry Programs: Lessons Learned from the 'What Works' Research." *Corrections Today* **67**:72–76.

McBride, Elizabeth C., Christy Visher, and Nancy LaVigne (2005). "Informing Policy and Practice: Prisoner Reentry Research at the Urban Institute." *Corrections Today* **67**:90–93.

Seiter, Richard P. (2004). "Inmate Reentry: What Works and What to Do About It." *Corrections Compendium* **29**:2–5, 33–34.

Solomon, Amy L. (2006). "Does Parole Supervision Work?: Research Findings and Policy Opportunities." *APPA Perspectives* **30**:26–37.

Wilkinson, Reginald A. (2005). "Engaging Communities: An Essential Ingredient to Offender Reentry." *Corrections Today* **67**:86–89.

INTERNET CONNECTIONS

American Probation and Parole Association
http://www.appa-net.org/

Board of Prison Terms High Control Parolees
http://www.bpt.ca.gov/hcparolees.html

Crime Prevention Coalition of America
http://www.crimepreventioncoalition.org/

Federal Prison Consulants
http://www.federalprisonconsultants.com

Georgia Parolee Database
http://www.pap.state.ga.us/parolee_database.htm

International Corrections and Prisons Association
http://www.icpa.ca/related/parole

New Jersey State Parole Board
http://www.state.nj.us/parole

New York State Parole Department
http://www.parole.state.ny.us/specialrelease.html

Parole boards
http://crimelynx.com/stateparole

Parole links
http://www.tbcnet.com/~salsberry/Parole%20Sites

Parole Violators
http://www.bottomlinestudios.com/ParoleViolators.html

Parole Watch
http://www.parolewatch.org

Probation and parole sites
http://angelfire.com/md/ribit/states

Street Time
http://www.post-gazette.com/tv/20020623tvweek2p2.asp

U.S. Parole Commission
http://www.usdoj.gov/uspc/

CHAPTER 9

Early Release, Parole Programs, and Parole Revocation

Chapter Outline

Chapter Objectives

As the result of reading this chapter, the following objectives will be realized:

1. Describing the composition and orientations of parole boards and their functions.
2. Understanding the general orientations of parole boards' decision making.
3. Describing various alternative programs in lieu of/in addition to parole.
4. Investigating circumstances and procedures whereby parole is revoked, including case law relative to the revocation process.
5. Describing landmark cases in parolee rights relative to parole actions, including revocations of parole.
6. Reviewing the rights of parolees in probation and parole revocation proceedings.
7. Describing pre-release and work/study release programs in the United States, their historical development, and functions.
8. Describing the types of offenders most eligible for work/study release programs.
9. Describing the nature and functions of day reporting centers.
10. Describing furlough programs, their historical bases, functions, weaknesses, and strengths.
11. Understanding the origin and development of halfway houses and residential treatment centers in the United States.
12. Identifying community residential centers and day treatment programs.
13. Understanding the advantages and disadvantages of day treatment programs for clients and the community generally.
14. Describing other forms of sanctions, including fines, day fine programs, community service orders, and victim restitution/compensation.

• *Schwartz was a Wisconsin inmate who was convicted of armed robbery and subsequently paroled. While on parole, Schwartz violated one or more parole conditions and the state revoked his parole. In 2001 Wisconsin enacted a mandatory release law and Schwartz was paroled again. While Schwartz was out on parole a second time, Wisconsin officials determined through DNA evidence that Schwartz had been involved in another crime, which was committed during the period of his first parole term. His parole was therefore revoked again, and Schwartz appealed. Initially a circuit court declared that the Wisconsin Parole Board lacked jurisdiction to revoke his second parole program based on alleged parole violations committed by Schwartz during his first parole term. Eventually the Wisconsin Supreme Court resolved the matter and said that the parole board retained continuous jurisdiction over Schwartz throughout both of his parole terms, and that they could hold Schwartz accountable for all violations committed during his entire sentence. Based on the DNA evidence showing a parole violation, Schwartz's parole was revoked and he was returned to prison.* [State Department of Corrections v. Schwartz, 693 N.W.2d 703 (Wis.Sup.March) (2005)].

• *Ash was a federal offender convicted on charges of possession with intent to distribute cocaine. He was released on parole in 2001. A year later, he was charged with attempted murder, assault in the first and second degrees, and carrying a dangerous and concealed weapon. All of the criminal charges were subsequently dismissed. However, the Parole Commission revoked Ash's parole. At Ash's parole revocation hearing, two officers testified about what they knew about the allegations against Ash. Their testimony was basically hearsay, since they testified about what they had been told about Ash by others. Ash was not permitted to cross-examine the witnesses. Ash challenged the parole revocation on the basis that his due process rights were violated when he was denied the right to*

368 Chapter 9 Early Release, Parole Programs, and Parole Revocation

cross-examine the witnesses. Despite the fact that the Parole Commission regarded the testimony of the two witnesses as "reliable hearsay," denying Ash the opportunity to confront and cross-examine these witnesses violated his minimum due-process rights. Ash's parole revocation was set aside and a new hearing was scheduled where he could cross-examine these witnesses. [Ash v. Reilly, 354 F.Supp.2d 1 (U.S. D. D.C.Dec.) (2004)].

• *Booth was a Pennsylvania inmate who was paroled. As a part of Booth's parole program, he was ordered to a term of house arrest and electronic monitoring. During his parole term, it was alleged that he had violated one or more parole conditions and the parole board revoked his parole. He was returned to prison and ordered to serve his entire prison sentence. Booth appealed, contending that he should receive credit for time served on house arrest and electronic monitoring against his maximum sentence. The parole board denied his request and an appeals court heard his case. The appeals court declared that the conditions of Booth's home confinement and electronic monitoring were sufficiently limiting so as to constitute custody, and they granted him the time he served on home confinement and electronic monitoring against his maximum prison sentence.* [Booth v. Pennsylvania Board of Probation and Parole, 866 A.2d 1189 (Pa.Comm.Jan.) (2005)].

• *Stewart was an inmate convicted of a violent offense. The Kentucky State Parole Board granted Stewart early release and admitted him to a parole program with various conditions. Subsequently, Kentucky enacted a Sexual Offender Treatment Program and Stewart was brought back before the parole board and ordered to complete the new program. Stewart objected, contending that this provision was an ex post facto law and thus violated his rights as a parolee. The Kentucky court of appeals disagreed, holding that the parole board may rescind one or more parole provisions at any time and amend them to include new provisions, such as required participation in sex offender treatment. The retroactive application of the requirement that the parolee should complete a sex offender treatment program did not violate ex post facto prohibitions. Kentucky did not extend the length of Stewart's punishment, and it did not change the definition of his original crime.* [Stewart v. Commonwealth, 153 S.W.3d 789 (Ky.Sup.Jan.) (2005)].

• *Riesch was a Wisconsin prisoner who was placed on parole planning in anticipation of his mandatory release date. Prior to his actual release, Riesch learned that he would have to participate in a particular treatment program. Riesch became extremely uncooperative and unmanageable. Ultimately the parole board ordered Riesch transferred to a local jail and parole officials revoked his parole status. Riesch appealed, claiming that he had not yet been placed on parole, and thus the parole board had no basis for revoking his parole and was therefore improper. An appeals court disagreed, noting that it is not necessary for prisoners to be physically released from custody and placed on actual parole in order for their parole status to be revoked. Riesch's improper institutional conduct upon learning of his mandatory participation in a treatment program constituted a violation of one or more of his parole program conditions, and thus the parole board was within its authority to revoke his parole even though he had not been conditionally freed from custody.* [State ex rel. Riesch v. Schwarz, 692 N.W.2d 219 (Wis.Sup.Feb.) (2005)].

INTRODUCTION

This chapter is about parole board early-release decision making. It examines the options and alternatives available to parolees when parole is granted. With the exception of life imprisonment and death penalty cases, most offenders sentenced to incarceration are eventually released back into their communities, either through the natural conclusion of their original sentences or through some alternative early-release scheme such as parole. Parole is most frequently conditional, and parole programs involve filing reports with parole agencies, observing curfew, making restitution, performing community service, participating in individual or group counseling, or participating in educational or vocational/technical programs. There is considerable diversity among programs for parolees. Some of these programs are described. Furthermore, some parolees may need to be supervised intensively, while other clients may simply be required to report in a manner similar to standard probation. Many parolees may only be required to make contact by letter or telephone with their POs, while others must make themselves accessible to random face-to-face visits at home or in the workplace.

Compared with programs designed for probationers such as pretrial diversion, shock probation, split sentencing, and various forms of intensive probation supervision, programs for parolees are rather unique in that they are, for the most part, transitional programs. Transitional programs are designed to assist recently imprisoned offenders in making any necessary psychological and social adjustments to become reintegrated into their communities. Parolees with special problems (e.g., mental illness, mental retardation, alcohol or drug dependencies, and sex offenders) may be required to participate in community activities and programs that deal directly with these problems. Sometimes parolees will be expected to make restitution to their victims or perform a limited amount of community service for the duration of their original sentences. These are additional conditions that parole boards may see fit to make a part of an offender's parole program.

The first section of this chapter describes several pre-release programs. These involve releases of inmates for limited purposes, such as short-term work assignments and for the purpose of taking academic courses at nearby schools. Some inmates take courses to complete their GEDs. Other clients take courses or participate in group or individual therapy not ordinarily offered in prison settings. Work and study release are defined and their advantages and disadvantages for participating offenders are described. Furlough programs are also examined. Furloughs are short leaves from prison and are usually limited to weekends and involve visits with family members. Some furloughs may serve other purposes, such as performing work or community service or making restitution to victims. The functions, goals, and advantages and disadvantages of furlough programs are discussed. Most parole program options are community-driven. This means that community-based corrections often manages or supervises parolees.

The parole-granting process is described. This includes a discussion of parole board conduct as it relates to early-release decision making for eligible jail or prison inmates. Parole board composition and diversity is also discussed. Parole boards exist in most states. However, numerous modifications in sentencing strategies among the states and federal government have greatly modified parole-granting practices in more than a few jurisdictions. In some instances, parole has been eliminated entirely as an early-release option for inmates. Parole boards orient themselves in various ways toward inmates. Some of these parole board orientations are described. Parole boards also attempt to employ objective criteria when making parole decisions. Some of these criteria are presented and critically examined.

Risk assessment instruments are also used and provide parole boards with important data about the future conduct of inmates. Parole boards are fallible entities, and their decision making is imperfect. But this fact does not deter them from attempting to make accurate forecasts of future parolee conduct. The final part of this chapter describes several landmark cases pertaining to parole revocation. Parolees are entitled to two-stage hearings before their parole boards and have minimum due-process rights. The chapter catalogues several important legal rights of parolees and presents various scenarios involving legal challenges to the different conditions of their parole programs.

PRE-RELEASE PROGRAMS

Most programs available to parolees are similar to those for probationers. In some states and the federal system, parolees and probationers report to the same persons or agencies. One distinction previously made between probationers and parolees is that parolees have served time in prison. For this reason alone, parolees are considered more dangerous as an offender class compared with probationers. Parolees are granted early release from incarceration by parole boards or some other paroling authority. This does not mean that they will be removed entirely from supervision, however. Several different kinds of programs exist for particular types of parolees and require varying levels of parolee supervision and monitoring. This section examines seven of these programs. These include (1) pre-release, (2) work release and study release, (3) furloughs, (4) standard parole with conditions, (5) intensive supervised parole, (6) shock parole, and (7) halfway houses.

Pre-Release

Pre-release is any action that results in a jail or prison inmate being granted a temporary leave from his or her institution for various purposes. Usually these purposes include meeting with prospective employers and working at jobs on a part-time basis until one's parole or early release is granted; studying or taking courses at nearby schools for the purpose of completing degrees; and visiting with families for the purpose of reuniting with them and establishing harmonious familial relations. A **pre-release program** is any activity that enables inmates to leave their institutions on a temporary basis for purposes of employment, work, study, or familial contact. Pre-release programs are available to both male and female inmates. For example, the Program for Female Offenders, Inc., is operated by the Pennsylvania Department of Corrections to assist female inmates in learning word processing, data entry, and telecommunications skill training. Sometimes pre-release programs are calculated to assist particular inmates with various addictions or dependencies. For instance, pre-release might enable some inmates with drug, alcohol, or gambling problems to receive needed assistance from community services through their temporary releases from custody.

Pre-release programs are transitional programs in that they enable inmates to make a smoother transition into their communities through gradual reentry and temporary leaves from jail or prison. Sometimes these programs are called **pre-parole programs.** Oklahoma operates a Pre-Parole Conditional Supervision Program, or PPCSP. PPCSP is a traditional exit from the prison system for many inmates. In Oklahoma, many prisoners who are about to be paroled are released under close supervision for limited periods. The Oklahoma PPCSP requires inmates to submit a weekly parole plan to their POs, submit to drug and/or alcohol checks, observe a curfew, maintain employment, and pay court costs. They must return to their prisons on weekends. If any inmate does not have a job, he or she must obtain one within 30 days following their pre-parole release. Over 80 percent of all PPCSP releasees have some sort of job lined up before being released. In order to qualify for inclusion in this program, inmates must have served at least 15 percent of their time and are within one year of their scheduled parole eligibility date. Any institutional infraction will delay an inmate's acceptance into the pre-parole program. PPCSP clients must pay a $20 monthly supervision fee, restitution, court costs, and child support. Program recidivism averages 26 percent.

Work Release

Work release, also called **work furlough, day parole, day pass,** and **community work,** refers to any program that provides for the labor of jail or prison inmates in the community under limited supervision. Work release is designed to ease inmates gradually back into their communities by permitting them short leaves from prison to perform jobs and assist in supporting their dependents. Work release was unofficially commenced in the United States in 1906 when Vermont sheriffs assigned inmates to limited community work (Champion, 2005). Acting on their own authority, Vermont sheriffs assigned inmates to work outside jails in the community. At that time, sheriffs issued passes to certain low-risk inmates to work in the community during daytime hours, but they had to return to jail by a given curfew time. Work release was implemented in Wisconsin when the **Huber Law** was passed in 1913. Senator Huber of Wisconsin successfully secured the passage of a bill that permitted Wisconsin correctional institutions to grant temporary releases to low-risk misdemeanants. Most states have work release programs today, with over 65,000 inmates involved in such programs in 2006 (U.S. Department of Justice, 2006).

The Goals and Functions of Work Release Programs.   The goals of work release programs are to:

1. Reintegrate the offender into the community.
2. Give the offender an opportunity to learn and/or practice new skills.
3. Provide offenders with the means to make restitution to victims of crimes.
4. Give offenders a chance to assist in supporting themselves and their families.
5. Help authorities to more effectively predict the likelihood of offender success if paroled.
6. Foster improvements in self-images or self-concepts through working in a nonincarcerative environment and assuming full responsibility for one's conduct.

Specific benefits accruing to offenders and the community are that at least some inmates are not idle and exposed to continuous moral decay associated with incarceration; prisoners pay confinement costs and can support their families; and prisoners can receive rehabilitative treatment and possibly make restitution to their victims. The primary functions of work release for parolees are (1) community reintegration, (2) promotion of inmate self-respect, (3) repayment of debts to victims and society, and (4) provision of support for self and dependents.

Community Reintegration.   Work release enables the parolee to become reintegrated into the community. Even though parolees must return to their prisons or other places of confinement during nonworking hours, they enjoy temporary freedoms while performing useful work. Thus, when it comes time for them to be officially released through either a parole board decision, administrative action, or from the normal completion of their sentences, the adjustment to community life will not be abrupt and potentially upsetting psychologically or socially.

Work release has worked particularly well for female inmates who have become involved in a Delaware-sponsored program known as CREST (Farrell, 2000). In the CREST program, female inmates with drug dependencies and other problems have been able to seek and receive treatment from community agencies. Furthermore, these women have been able to work at jobs and form networks of social support among themselves

Promotion of Inmate Self-Respect.   Plans for inmate labor in some jurisdictions are designed with rehabilitation in mind. Most work study programs attempt to instill self-esteem within those inmates originally untrained and incapable of performing even menial labor in the private sector. These work experiences are designed to equip inmates with skills useful to employers on the outside. Furthermore, inmates can earn sufficient income to offset some of their own housing expenses while in prison and provide supplementary amounts to their families.

Repayment of Debts to Victims and Society.   On October 12, 1984, President Ronald Reagan signed Public Law 98-473, which established the Comprehensive Crime Control Act. This was the **Victims of Crime Act of 1984.** Currently, all states and the federal government have victim compensation programs. As a part of offender work release requirements, a certain amount of their earned wages may be allocated to restitution and to a general victim compensation fund. Thus, fines, restitution, and some form of community service have become common features of federal sentencing (18 U.S.C. Sec. 3563(a)(2), 2001). Almost every state has adopted some form of victim restitution program for offenders.

Provision of Support for Self and Dependents.   Those prisoners with wives and/or children ordinarily do not earn enough on work release to support their dependents totally. However, their income from work performed is helpful in providing for a portion of their dependents' necessities. Work release programs can function as incentives for prison inmates to comply with prison rules. Inmates who obey prison rules are slated for work release, while other inmates are denied it. Some of the money earned by inmates is used for supporting their families.

Determining Inmate Eligibility for Work Release Programs.   Not all inmates in prisons and jails are eligible for work release programs. Before an inmate may become eligible for such programs in some jurisdictions, they must serve a minimum portion of their originally prescribed sentences. Long-term inmates who have committed serious crimes are often automatically excluded from participation in work release because of their projected public risk if loosed in their communities. Statutory provisions in several states specify the minimum amount of time that must be served before inmates may make application to participate in work release. One advantage of participating in work release is that if looks good on an inmate's record when being considered for eventual parole. Those inmates who have completed work release programs stand a much better chance of being paroled than those who have not been selected for participation.

Study Release Programs

Study release programs are essentially the same as work release programs, but for the express purpose of securing educational goals. Several types of **study release** have been identified: adult basic education, high school or high school equivalency (GED), technical or vocational education, and college. In 2005, there were 2,400 inmates in study release programs (U.S. Department of Justice, 2006). One reason for such low numbers of study releasees is that many educational programs are offered online by computer or are available through correspondence. Also, most prison systems have educational programs that enable inmates to receive degrees at various educational levels.

Determining Inmate Eligibility for Study Release. An inmate's eligibility for study release involves several factors. First, inmates must be within a short time of being released anyway. For prospective parolees, study release may be granted to those within a year or less of being paroled. A second criterion is whether inmates have behaved well while institutionalized. Good behavior inside prison doesn't mean that inmates will behave well when placed on study release. However, compliance with institutional rules is generally a good predictor of compliance with program rules for study release. Few offenders will jeopardize their parole chances by violating program rules while on study release.

Eligible inmates must file a plan indicating the reasons for acquiring additional education and how their additional education will benefit them when released into the community. Educational training enhances an inmate's eligibility for particular kinds of work when parole is granted or whenever the offender is released from the system. More educated inmates are more employable. If restitution is a part of one's parole program, then acquiring greater amounts of education can assist in making restitution payments later.

Advantages and Disadvantages of Study Release Programs. Study release programs concern more than a few community residents who view such programs as threats to community safety. However, the failure rate of study releasees is so low that program advantages far outweigh community safety concerns. Study release helps to prepare inmates for different types of occupations or professions. The Tennessee Department of Corrections, for instance, has a study release program where selected inmates can learn data entry, building construction, welding, food services, industrial maintenance, surveying, and drafting. They become certificated upon completing their study release programs. Many of their educational credits are transferrable to colleges and universities where they can undertake advanced graduate study, if interested. However, some jurisdictions have reported inmate discontent with the types of jobs their education has qualified them to perform.

Some inmates do not actually utilize these study release programs for anything other than their cosmetic value for parole board appearances. For instance, a study of work and study release programs in two states, Oregon and California, have shown that many prisoners believe that they are "under pressure" to participate in these types of prison programs. Many prisoners believe that such participation would look good to their parole boards (U.S. Department of Justice, 2006). However, Tennessee and other jurisdictions report that inmates have demonstrated remarkable progress related to greater knowledge about the harmful effects of drug abuse, greater discipline, and improved development in self-awareness and self-concept.

Furlough Programs

A **furlough** is an authorized, unescorted leave from confinement granted for specific purposes and for designated time periods, usually from 24 to 72 hours, although it may be as long as several weeks or as short as a few hours (U.S. Department of Justice, 2006). The overall aim of furlough programs as a form of temporary release is to assist the offender in becoming reintegrated into society. Mississippi was the first state to use furloughs in 1918 on a limited basis for low-risk, minimum-security prison inmates who had served at least two or more years of their sentences and were regarded as good security risks. These furloughs usually involved conjugal visits with families or Christmas holiday activities for brief, 10-day periods and were believed valuable for preparing offenders for permanent reentry into their respective communities once parole had been granted (Montgomery, 2006). In 2005 there were approximately 20,000 inmates who participated in over 200,000 furloughs (U.S. Department of Justice, 2006). Thirty states and the federal government used furloughs for eligible offenders. Florida granted the largest number of furloughs (68,000), followed by Rhode Island (5,000), Vermont (3,900), the federal system (3,400), and Nebraska (2,900). The fewest number of furloughs granted occurred in Arkansas, Tennessee, and Wisconsin, with two each. During 2002 there were only about 100 inmates who absconded from their furlough programs in these states. Mississippi has permitted conjugal visits as a part of its furlough program. Such visits by spouses are believed to minimize prison violence (Hensley, Koscheski, and Tewksbury, 2002).

The prime beneficiaries of furlough programs are the prisoners themselves. The trust placed in them by the prison system is psychologically beneficial. However, some offenders on furlough may commit new crimes. It is impossible to know which inmates will or will not commit new offenses. But the screening process for inmate eligibility weeds out most of those likely to reoffend. Typically, inmates have served a significant portion of their originally prescribed sentences and are eligible for parole consideration. Successful completion of furlough programs increases one's parole chances.

The Goals of Furlough Programs.   The purposes of furloughs are several. Offenders are given a high degree of trust by prison officials and are permitted leaves to visit their homes and families. Interestingly, such furloughs are beneficial to both prisoners and to their families, because they permit family members to get used to the presence of the offender after a long incarcerative absence. Sometimes, prisoners may participate in educational programs (like study release) outside of prison as a type of study release. They can arrange for employment once paroled, or they can participate in vocational training for short periods. In Canada, for instance, furloughs may be granted to eligible inmates for the following reasons: to make contacts for employment; to visit close relatives; to obtain medical or psychiatric services; to visit seriously ill relatives or attend the funerals of close relatives; to appear before study groups; to make contacts for discharge; and to secure a residence upon release on parole or discharge. Such programs in Canada are called Temporary Absence Programs.

Furloughs also provide officials with an opportunity to evaluate offenders and determine how they adapt to living with others in their community. Thus, the furlough is a type of test to determine, with some predictability, the likelihood that inmates will conform to society's rules if they are eventually released through parole. Furloughs also function as incentives to conform to prison rules and regulations. Prisoners selected for participation in furlough programs are nearing the end of their sentences and will eventually be paroled or released anyway. They are good risks because the likelihood they will abscond while on a furlough is quite remote.

The Functions of Furlough Programs.   Furloughs are intended to accomplish the following functions: (1) offender rehabilitation and reintegration, (2) the development of self-esteem and self-worth, (3) opportunities to pursue vocational/educational programs, and (4) aiding parole boards in determining when inmates are ready to be released.

Offender Rehabilitation and Reintegration. The manifest intent of furloughs is to provide offenders with outside experiences to enable them to become accustomed to living with others in the community apart from the highly regulated life in prison or jail settings. Indications are that furloughs fulfill this objective in most instances. Furloughs assist inmates in making successful transitions from prison life to community living.

The Development of Self-Esteem and Self-Worth. Furloughs instill within inmates feelings of self-esteem and self-worth. Again, the element of trust plays an important role in enabling those granted furloughs to acquire trust for those who place trust in them. The development of self-esteem and self-worth are unmeasurable. Yet, many of those granted furloughs report that they believe they have benefited from their temporary release experiences.

Opportunities to Pursue Vocational/Educational Programs. Another benefit of furlough programs for those in jurisdictions where furloughs are permitted and granted is that opportunities are available for inmates to participate in programs not available to them in prisons or jails. Thus, if inmates wish to take courses in typing, art, automobile repair, or philosophically oriented offerings in social science or related areas, furloughs permit them the time to pursue such courses. Sometimes, these furloughs are labeled as study release, because they involve a program of study designed for the offender's specific needs.

Aiding Parole Boards in Determining When Inmates Ought to Be Released. A key function of furloughs as tests of inmate behavior are to alert parole boards which inmates are most eligible to be released and who will likely be successful while on parole. Indiana, for instance, has an 80 percent success rate with its furlough program as used for parole board decision making. In that jurisdiction, inmates are granted furloughs if they are within 60 days of being paroled. They are limited to three-day furloughs, where they can make home visits, obtain required medical treatment or psychological counseling, participate in special training courses, and perform work or other duties.

Determining Inmate Eligibility for Furloughs.   Furloughs are granted only to inmates who meet special eligibility requirements. Program participation is restricted to the following types of inmates: inmates must be at minimum-custody status; they must have served a fixed amount of their sentences and are within a short time of release; approval must be obtained from a committee that reviews all furlough applications; a clean institutional record is required; they must have a stable home environment; and they must not have prior records of violent offending (e.g., murder, aggravated assault, armed robbery, rape).

STANDARD PAROLE WITH CONDITIONS

In 2006, every state had parolees. Many of these offenders were granted early release by a parole board. There are some exceptions, however. In California, for example, most prison inmates receive a determinate sentence and are released on parole once they have served their prison terms, less good-time credit that they have accumulated. Following their release from prison, they have a three-year parole period. This involves supervision by POs wherever these offenders choose to locate within the state. They must abide by the same types of conditions required of probationers. Once they have successfully completed their three-year parole terms, they are officially released from the criminal justice system. For more serious California offenders who have been convicted of first- or second-degree murder, they have usually been sentenced to life terms with the possibility of parole. The California Board of Prison Terms meets and considers whether any of these offenders should be paroled. If they are eventually paroled, the length of their parole is for the rest of their lives. That is, they will be under PO supervision until they die. Both life and non-life parolees are periodically reviewed during their parole periods to determine their suitability for discharge from parole prior to their maximum discharge dates (Stephens, 2001:1).

Who Is Parole Eligible?

Since most states have revised or are revising their sentencing provisions, it is sometimes difficult to determine who is eligible for parole. Should parole be limited to nonviolent offenders, or should all types of offenders, even murderers and rapists, be paroled? Presently, all types of offenders may be considered for parole in those jurisdictions who use parole. As we observed earlier, most states have modified or drastically altered their sentencing provisions so that today, it is not unusual for some states to have vestiges of several types of sentencing schemes that affect particular cohorts of prisoners differently. Mississippi is a case in point. Mississippi has identified several different classes of offenders divided according to when they were convicted of crimes and sentenced. Mississippi uses the following scheme:

Parole Eligible/Earned Release Offenders

1. Crimes committed on or before June 30, 1995
2. Offenders required to serve 25 percent of their sentence
3. Eligible for parole after 25 percent of time served
4. Offender can "flat time" after serving only 50 percent of their sentence (offender is eligible for release)
5. Sex offenders, habitual offenders, or offenders with life sentences are not eligible

Truth-In-Sentencing Offenders

1. Crimes committed from July 1, 1995–December 31, 1999
2. Every offender must serve 85 percent of their sentence in incarceration
3. Remaining 15 percent of sentence served in community services under ERS supervision

First-Time Nonviolent Offenders Eligibility (Mississippi Senate Bill 3028)

1. Crimes committed from January 1, 2000, to present
2. Passed by Legislature on March 12, 2001
3. Nonviolent first-time offenders must serve 25 percent of their sentence in incarceration, then they are eligible for parole consideration (Mississippi Parole Board, 2006:1–2).

It seems that from this Mississippi example that the truth-in-sentencing provisions Mississippi introduced in 1995 caused their prison population to soar. In order to ease prison overcrowding, incarceration was reevaluated for first-time offenders so that their parole eligibility was restored to 1995 standards. Mississippi has indicated that depending on an inmate's sentence, some inmates are eligible to serve part of their sentence on parole. Although an inmate may be eligible for parole, it is not guaranteed that the inmate will be granted parole. A list of all inmates eligible for parole is generated by the Mississippi Department of Corrections and sent to the Mississippi Parole Board. The cases of the inmates on the list are reviewed by the parole board and a decision is made to grant or deny a parole hearing. At a parole hearing, the inmate's file is reviewed, including any rule violations during incarceration (Mississippi Parole Board, 2006:1).

In a state such as Maine, for instance, parole was abolished in 1976 as an early-release mechanism. However, there were still several Maine inmates who were considered parole eligible in 2004. These were convicts who committed their crimes prior to the abolition of parole in 1976. Thus, Maine maintains a part-time parole board that meets on occasion to decide parole for those few inmates who continue to be governed by the pre-1976 early-release standards under which they were sentenced. Regardless of how many sentencing changes have been implemented by any given state, for all parole-eligible inmates in all jurisdictions, there are several parole conditions that they must comply with if paroled.

Parole Conditions

All parole programs in all jurisdictions are conditional, in that they indicate what parolees must and must not do during their parole periods. For offenders with particular needs, such as alcohol or drug dependencies or gambling addictions, the conditions of their parole programs may include special provisions for community treatment on a regular basis. They may be required to attend Alcoholics Anonymous, Narcotics Anonymous, or Gamblers Anonymous meetings. Parole boards usually determine whatever additional conditions should be included when paroling particular offenders.

Most parole agreements include standard conditions and a space for special conditions of parole, at the parole board's discretion. For instance, Ohio has the following types of provisions for its parolees. In order to be admitted to the Ohio parole program, parole-eligible inmates must sign the following document containing these provisions:

In consideration of having been granted supervision on December 1, 2001, I agree to report to my probation/parole officer within 48 hours or according to the written instructions I have received and to the following conditions:

BOX 9.1

**CAREER
SNAPSHOT**

Mike Ebright
Captain, Nevada Department of Public Safety, Division of Parole and
Probation, Carson City, Nevada

Statistics:

B.A. (social services and corrections), University of Nevada–Reno;
Nevada State Police Officers Academy

Background:

During my first two years of college, I had an
undeclared major because I had no idea
what I wanted to be when I grew up. Then a
friend explained to me the work she did at a
juvenile detention center and spoke of a desire to become a juvenile probation officer.
This intrigued me, and I declared a major in
the same college as hers—social services and
corrections. I began volunteer work with juveniles in a Big Brother–type program
through the local YMCA and quickly found
that working with juveniles was too frustrating—these were good kids who had difficult
home situations, and I wanted to get to the
root of the problem. In the spring of my junior year, a fellow student came to speak to
my criminology class about a volunteer program at the adult parole and probation office. I inquired about becoming a Volunteer
in Probation (VIP) and I never looked back.

I did two semesters of internship at Parole and Probation and continued my volunteer work between semesters. In the spring
of 1980 I tested for an Officer (PO) position
and the experience as a VIP definitely
helped me breeze through the oral boards.
Even in 1980 there was a need for bilingual
officers, and so I obtained a minor in Spanish through a summer program in Mexico. It
was a great way to increase my value as a PO
candidate and give myself a nice college
graduation gift at the same time. I graduated
in August 1980, interviewed for a job later
that month and, after a mandatory background investigation, was hired on November 4, 1980. Although it is rare these days, I
have spent my entire 26-year career at the
same agency.

Work Experiences:

Initially I was assigned a court officer position
conducting and writing pre-sentence investigation (PSI) reports in our Reno, Nevada, office. This was a great introduction to the job
because it is where the process begins. It was
very intimidating the first time I appeared in
court to represent the agency and support the
investigations I performed. However, after
getting my feet wet, I found attending court
and playing the game with the attorneys to be
challenging and enjoyable. One really gets a
sense of doing something worthwhile for their
community when a judge follows their recommendation to either order appropriate as programming special conditions of probation or
to send a dangerous criminal to prison for a
maximum term. Likewise, this initial assignment introduced me to the real world of dealing with heroin addicts and career convicts.
This was also the time I completed the
Nevada Peace Officer's Standards and Training Basic Academy and the Division's preser-
vice training.

After my first year, I was transferred to a
general supervision caseload made up of approximately 80 probationers and parolees, including those who had transferred to Nevada
via Interstate Compact. This job is complex
and one does not truly begin to feel comfortable knowing the job for a couple of years. Of
course, back then technology was not what it
is today. Case notes were done by hand in
paper files and reports were typed by clerical
staff on typewriters. Copy machines were expensive to use, and so carbon paper was
hoarded by officers. (Oh, how the times have
changed—everything is automated now and
basic computer skills are second nature.)

Learning the 100-plus forms, how they were to be completed, and the paperwork flow was a job in itself. Then one had to learn everything they could about all of their offenders, from what special conditions of supervision they needed to complete, to family names, to how their homes were laid out, and to the cars they drove. All good POs get to know their offenders better than the offenders know themselves. The small details, such as an offender missing one counseling session, give POs the hint that the offender may be regressing. Some can be helped to become successful, productive citizens and others have too many negative influences in their lives so that no one can stop them from repeating their criminal behavior. I served six years "on the streets" in Reno.

My first promotion to a Senior Officer in a small rural office in Carson City turned out to be the best three years of my career. In this position I had a great variety of duties that kept the job very interesting. I handled a caseload of 150 offenders who had transferred to other states pending Interstate Compact acceptance; another 100 offenders who were fugitives; and about another 50 offenders who were on a minimum bank because they did not need close supervision, but who couldn't be released from supervision for a variety of reasons. Additionally, I was the District's Evidence Officer, Firearms Instructor, and Prisoner Transport Coordinator. If that wasn't enough, I acted as a backup for officers when they were on leave and helped to train a few new officers. One needs to thrive on stress and chaos to really enjoy this field.

My next promotion was to a first-line supervisory position (now known as a sergeant). In any job, when one moves into a supervisory/management position, their job/life changes forever. It is similar to how one's life changes when they become a parent. I have always referred to moving into management as "going over to the dark side." Even though I think I was as successful as I could have been at maintaining a balance of being supportive of my officers and being their boss, I still became their "enemy." One cannot assign and proofread work, audit work, and discipline staff, and still be their "friend." I have never met a first-line supervisor who wasn't initially astounded at how much time is spent on personnel issues. However, most of all, I missed working in the field with the offenders.

One year later, my position was upgraded to lieutenant due to the size and rural nature of our office. The job did not change that much, but I was more involved in the decision making regarding hiring, resource usage, procedures, and the like. I spent seven years as a lieutenant and then seven years as a captain. Captains are involved in hiring, testifying before the legislature, developing the budget, formulating policies and procedures for the Division, and performing other administrative duties.

One Quick "War Story":

A few years ago some of my officers had information that one of our fugitives, who had a serious criminal record, was hiding in a house with a methamphetamine-abusing female who was acting as a caretaker for an elderly woman. The house was surrounded by an extremely foul odor. The female told the officers that the fugitive was not there, but she would not let them into the house initially. The female then ran from the house, but the officers caught her and placed her in handcuffs. Being suspicious, the officers called a local sheriff's deputy and me to the house. The female continued to deny that our fugitive was in the house and that there was nothing illegal in the house. After calming down the female and telling her that we were only interested in getting our fugitive, she agreed to let us enter the house. However, she did not want us to go into her charge's bedroom. Guess where we thought the fugitive was hiding?

We surrounded the house and made entry. The odor was sickening, but we could not determine its origin. The house seemed to be clean. The female explained that the odor was coming from *Depends* diapers. We searched the house, except for the charge's room, without results. When we told the female we were concerned about the elderly woman's safety, the female started to freak out.

(continued)

BOX 9.1 (*Continued*)

We had to prone her out and, due to what we felt were exigent circumstances, we entered the charge's bedroom. We found the woman alone, but she had been dead for a long time—estimation by a pathologist was three months.

Advice to Students:

- Obtain on-the-job experience through an internship or other volunteer work and/or do "ride-alongs" with officers from the agency where you think you may want to work. This gives you the knowledge, skills, and abilities to become a more valuable candidate, smooths the testing process, and affords you the opportunity to see if this is really what you want to do for a living.

- Question officers about their jobs and learn about the pros and cons of this work. There are too many to mention here, but keep in mind that you have to be willing to exchange money for excitement. There is nothing boring about this job.

- Be patient during the hiring process. These are government agencies and not corporations. If you really want to work in this field, you have to understand that bureaucracies move slowly, and most probation/parole agencies require time-consuming background investigations.

- Do not become complacent, but maintain a sense of humor and a good support system. This can be a dangerous job and it will eat you up if you allow it. You have to work hard, but you have to play hard too.

1. I will obey federal, state, and local laws and ordinances, and all rules and regulations of the Fifth Common Pleas Court or the Department of Rehabilitation and Correction.

2. I will always keep my probation/parole officer informed of my residence and place of employment. I will obtain permission from my probation/parole officer before changing my residence or my employment.

3. I will not leave the state without written permission of the Adult Parole Authority.

4. I will not enter upon the grounds of any correctional facility nor attempt to visit any prisoner without the written permission of my probation/parole officer nor will I communicate with any prisoner without first informing my probation/parole officer of the reason for such communication.

5. I will comply with all orders given to me by my probation/parole officer or other authorized representative of the court, the Department of Rehabilitation and Correction, or the Adult Parole Authority, including any written instructions issued at any time during the period of supervision.

6. I will not purchase, possess, own, use, or have under my control any firearms, deadly weapons, ammunition, or dangerous ordnance.

7. I will not possess, use, purchase, or have under my control any narcotic drug or other controlled substance, including any instrument, device, or other object used to administer drugs or to prepare them for administration, unless it is lawfully prescribed for me by a licensed physician. I agree to inform my probation/parole officer promptly of any such prescription and I agree to submit to drug testing if required by the Adult Parole Authority.

8. I will report any arrest, citation of a violation of the law, conviction, or any other contact with a law enforcement officer to my probation/parole officer no later than the next business day, and I will not enter into any agreement or other arrangement with any law enforcement agency that might place me in the position of violating any law or condition of my supervision unless I have obtained permission in writing from the Adult Parole Authority, or from the court if I am a probationer.

9. I agree to a search without warrant of my person, my motor vehicle, or my place of residence by a probation/parole officer at any time.

10. I agree to sign a release of confidential information from any public or private agency if requested to do so by a probation/parole officer.

11. I agree and understand that if I am arrested in any other state or territory of the United States or in any foreign country, my signature as witnessed at the end of the page will be deemed to be a waiver of extradition and that no other formalities will be required for authorized agents of the State of Ohio to bring about my return to this state for revocation proceedings.

12. I also agree to the following Special Conditions as imposed by the court or the Adult Parole Authority:

    I have read or had read to me the foregoing conditions of my parole. I fully understand these conditions, I agree to comply with them, and I understand that violation of any of these conditions may result in the revocation of my parole. In addition, I understand that I will be subject to the foregoing conditions until I have received a certificate from the Adult Parole Authority or a Journal Entry from the Court if I am a probationer, stating that I have been discharged from supervision.

The parolee signs this form and a witness also signs.

This agreement contains several important stipulations that are contained in virtually every parole agreement. First, the prospective parolee must agree to stay in continuous contact with his or her parole officer during the parole period, however long it may be. The offender may not possess firearms or dangerous weapons. The offender must remain in the state unless permission to leave it is obtained from the PO in advance. Drugs and alcohol are to be avoided, and drug and alcohol checks are to be permitted whenever the PO sees fit to administer them. In this particular form, the offender agrees to be extradited from external jurisdictions, even foreign countries, in the event that he or she absconds. And the prospective parolee agrees to warrantless searches at any time by his or her PO. If there are special conditions of parole, these must be complied with to the letter. If counseling or sex offender treatment is required, then the parolee must satisfy that condition. If attending Alcoholics Anonymous or some other group is required, this condition is mandatory. All conditions are mandatory.

The prospective parolee must agree to all of these conditions. Failure to agree to these conditions and sign the document will mean that parole will not be granted. While it may seem unusual for a prospective parolee not to sign this document and obtain early release, some inmates believe that the parole conditions are too stringent. They may exercise their right to remain in prison and serve out their sentences, particularly if they are within a few months or years of mandatory release anyway. And if the offender accepts these conditions and violates any one or more of them, he or she is liable of having his or her parole program revoked. A majority of parolees in the United States are currently under standard parole with conditions (U.S. Department of Justice, 2006).

Discretionary and Mandatory Parole

Two types of parole are **discretionary parole** and **mandatory parole.** Discretionary parole is the most common form of parole used by parole boards. The parole board's task is to determine whether an inmate is suitable to be paroled and that his or her release is in the best interest of the public. Some of the many reasons that influence a parole board to grant or deny parole include:

1. The serious nature of the offense
2. The number of offenses committed
3. The offender's psychological and/or psychiatric history
4. Community opposition
5. Insufficient time served
6. Prior misdemeanor or felony convictions
7. Police and/or juvenile record
8. History of drug and/or alcohol abuse
9. History of violent conduct
10. Escape or escape attempts
11. Crimes committed while incarcerated
12. Participation or lack of participation in complete rehabilitative prison programming
13. Arrangements or lack of arrangements for employment and/or residence

Figure 9.1 is an example of a federal parole acknowledgment letter, and it shows where the inmate may either accept or reject parole release. A list of conditions is supplied with this form, although they may not be shown here. In some jurisdictions, parole may be mandatory and cannot be rejected for any reason.

Mandatory parole is the automatic release of an offender from prison, usually six months prior to the completion of his or her sentence. In contrast with discretionary parole, parole boards normally do not vote on mandatory parole, since it is established by law. Mandatory parole may also include special conditions. Also, mandatory parolees are not necessarily permitted to leave prison grounds for a period of time, in order to allow them to gradually adjust to noninstitutional life. Many prisons have conventional housing on prison grounds where mandatory parolees can live for a short period. Thus, not all mandatory parolees are automatically freed directly into the community. Furthermore, the parole board may impose additional post-incarcerative supervision for mandatory parolees if it feels such supervision is necessary for the successful reintegration of the offender (Virginia Department of Corrections, 2003).

Figure 9.2 is an example of the Alaska Board of Parole Order of Mandatory Parole. It specifies most parole conditions, in that other special conditions of parole may be included as ordered by the Alaska Board of Parole. These conditions may include special individual or group counseling, participation in vocational/educational programming, or other community services. If the parolee has problems with drugs or alcohol, then the parole board may direct the parolee to participate in appropriate treatment or programs suitable for these different forms of substance abuse. The parolee is given a six-page statement of supplemental conditions, which may or may not be imposed by the parole board. The parolee does not have to sign the form, since parole

PAROLE ACKNOWLEDGEMENT LETTER		REPORT DATE *(YYYYMMDD)*
1. INMATE NAME *(Last, First, Middle)*	**2. SSN**	**3. ID NUMBER**

4. CORRECTIONS FACILITY

5. ACKNOWLEDGEMENT

I have read and understand the attached notice of approval/disapproval of my parole.

6. PAROLE APPROVAL

☐ I accept parole release. I understand my release is conditional upon continued good behavior and acceptance for supervision by a US Probation/Parole Officer.

☐ I do not accept parole release.

7. PAROLE DENIAL

INSTRUCTIONS

You have the right to appeal the determination of the Service Clemency and Parole Board denying your release on parole. You may submit your appeal through the commanding officer of your confinement facility within 30 days of receipt of the attached denial letter. The appeal application may include any new or additional information which was not previously considered by the Service Clemency and Parole Board.

APPEAL SELECTION

☐ I desire to appeal the denial of my parole by the Service Secretary Clemency and Parole Board. I understand the decision on my appeal by the designee of the Service Secretary is final.

☐ I do not desire to appeal the denial of my parole by the Service Secretary Clemency and Parole Board.

PRIVACY ACT STATEMENT

AUTHORITY: 10 U.S.C. §951, P.L. 90-377, and E.O. 9397.

PRINCIPAL PURPOSE(S): To notify an offender of approval for parole release and record the individual's acceptance or rejection of parole. This form is also used to notify an offender of a negative determination by the Service Clemency and Parole Board and to record an offender's decision to appeal or not appeal the decision denying parole.

ROUTINE USE(S): To the Department of Justice, in instances where the prisoner is incarcerated in a Federal Bureau of Prisons facility for incarceration.

DISCLOSURE: Voluntary; however, failure to provide the requested information may result in denial of parole or forfeiture of opportunity to elect appeal rights as to parole denial.

8. INMATE SIGNATURE	**9. DATE** *(YYYYMMDD)*
10. WITNESS NAME. GRADE AND TITLE *(Last, First, Middle)*	**11. SIGNATURE**	**12. DATE** *(YYYYMMDD)*

DD FORM 2716, NOV 1999

FIGURE 9.1   Federal Parole Acknowledgment Letter.

granting in Alaska is mandatory. Parolees must accept these parole conditions, as well as any other special supplemental conditions the Alaska Board of Parole deems fit to impose. Failure to comply with one or more of these conditions at any time may subject the parolee to parole revocation and subsequent return to prison.

ALASKA BOARD OF PAROLE

ORDER OF MANDATORY PAROLE

Parolee _____ DOB_____ Released_____ Supv. Expires _____

The following terms and conditions are effective on the release date shown on the CERTIFICATE OF GOOD TIME AWARD (AS 33.20.030) for all prisoners released pursuant to AS 33.16.010(c) or AS 33.20.040. I understand I am required by law to abide by the conditions imposed, whether or not I sign these conditions. The Parole Board may have me returned to custody at any time when it determines a condition of parole has been violated.

CONDITIONS OF MANDATORY PAROLE

1. REPORT UPON RELEASE: I will report in person no later than the next working day after my release to the P.O. located at _____, and receive further reporting instructions. I will reside at: _____.

2. MAINTAIN EMPLOYMENT/TRAINING/TREATMENT: I will make a diligent effort to maintain steady employment and support my legal dependents. I will not voluntarily change or terminate employment without receiving permission from my Parole Officer (P.O.) to do so. If discharged or if employment is terminated (temporarily or permanently) for any reason, I will notify my P.O. the next working day. If I am involved in an education, training or treatment program, I will continue active participation in the program unless I receive permission from my P.O. to quit. If I am released, removed or terminated from the program for any reason, I will notify my P.O. the next working day.

3. REPORT MONTHLY: I will report to my P.O. at least monthly in the manner prescribed by my P.O. I will follow any other reporting instructions established by my P.O.

4. OBEY LAWS/ORDERS: I will obey all state, federal and local laws, ordinances, orders, and court orders.

5. PERMISSION BEFORE CHANGING RESIDENCE: I will obtain permission from my P.O. before changing my residence. Remaining away from my approved residence for 24 hours or more constitutes a change in residence for the purpose of this condition.

6. TRAVEL PERMIT BEFORE TRAVEL OUTSIDE ALASKA: I will obtain the prior written permission of my P.O. in the form of an interstate travel agreement before leaving the State of Alaska. Failure to abide by the conditions of the travel agreement is a violation of my order of parole.

7. NO FIREARMS/WEAPONS: I will not own, possess, have in my custody, handle, purchase or transport any firearm, ammunition or explosives. I may not carry any deadly weapon on my person except a pocket knife with a 3" or shorter blade. Carrying any other weapon on my person such as a hunting knife, axe, club, etc. is a violation of my order of parole. I will contact the Alaska Board of Parole if I have any questions about the use of firearms, ammunition or weapons.

8. NO DRUGS: I will not use, possess, handle, purchase, give or administer any narcotic, hallucinogenic (including marijuana/THC), stimulant, depressant, amphetamine, barbiturate or prescription drug not specifically prescribed by a licensed medical professional.

9. REPORT POLICE CONTACT: I will report to my P.O., not later than the next working day, any contact with a law enforcement officer.

10. DO NOT WORK AS AN INFORMANT: I will not enter into any agreement or other arrangement with any law enforcement agency which will place me in the position of violating any law or any condition of my parole. I understand that Department of Corrections and Parole Board policy prohibit me from working as an informant.

11. NO CONTACT WITH PRISONERS OR FELONS: I may not telephone, correspond with or visit any person confined in a prison, penitentiary, correctional institution or camp, jail, halfway house, work release center, community residential center, juvenile correctional center, etc. Contact with a felon during the course of employment or during Corrections-related treatment is not prohibited if approved by my P.O. Any other knowing contact with a felon is prohibited unless approved by my P.O. I will notify my P.O. the next working day if I have contact with a prisoner or felon.

12. CANNOT LEAVE AREA: I will receive permission from my P.O. before leaving the area of the state to which my case is assigned. My P.O. will advise me in writing of limits to the area to which I have been assigned.

13. OBEY ALL ORDERS / SPECIAL CONDITIONS: I will obey any special instructions, rules or orders given to me by the Board of Parole or by my P.O. and I will follow any special conditions imposed by the Board of Parole or my P.O.

14. WAIVE EXTRADITION: I will waive extradition to the State of Alaska from any state or territory of the United States, and I will not contest efforts to return me to Alaska by the Board of Parole or my P.O.

15. PROVIDE DNA SAMPLE: I will provide a blood and/or oral sample when requested by a health care professional acting on behalf of the State, if I am being released after a conviction of an offense requiring the State to collect the sample(s) for the DNA identification system under AS 44.41.035.

I have received a copy of these conditions of parole. I have had the opportunity to read these conditions or to have them read to me if I cannot read. My mandatory parole can be revoked and I can be required to serve the remainder of my sentence if I violate any parole conditions. I understand it is my responsibility to contact my P.O. if I have a question about the meaning or intent of any parole condition. I realize I can be arrested by a P.O. at any time with or without a warrant if my conduct so dictates.

_____   _____   _____   _____
Parolee signature   Date   Witness Signature   Title

DISTRIBUTION: WHITE - Board of Parole   YELLOW - Institution   PINK - Parolee   GOLD - Parole Officer

Alaska Board of Parole, P.O. Box 112000, Juneau, AK 99811-2000
Rev. 3/99; Alaska Board of Parole [g:\parole\forms\Standard MR Cond.doc]

FIGURE 9.2   Alaska Board of Parole Order of Mandatory Parole.

INTENSIVE SUPERVISED PAROLE

Parolees are often subject to precisely the same kinds of behavioral requirements as probationers who are involved in intensive supervision programs. The **New Jersey Intensive Probation Supervision Program** is made up of inmates who have served at least three or four months of their prison terms. In fact, the term **shock parole** has been applied to this and similar programs, because an inmate is shocked with what it is like to be incarcerated. The use of house arrest, electronic monitoring, and several other programs may be a part of one's conditional early release from prison. The level of monitoring will vary according to the risk posed by the offender. But it is quite difficult to predict accurately one's risk to the public or general dangerousness.

Most parolees are **standard parolees,** in the sense that they are obligated to adhere to certain standard early-release agreements formulated by paroling authorities. In 1987, the United States Sentencing Commission implemented new guidelines that included the following policy statement of recommended conditions of probation and **supervised release:**

1. The defendant shall not leave the judicial district or other specified geographical area without the permission of the court or PO.

2. The defendant shall report to the PO as directed by the court or PO and shall submit a truthful and complete written report within the first five days of each month.

3. The defendant shall answer truthfully all inquiries by the PO and follow the instructions of the PO.

4. The defendant shall support his dependents and meet other family responsibilities.

5. The defendant shall work regularly at a lawful occupation unless excused by the PO for schooling, training, or other acceptable reasons.

6. The defendant shall notify the PO within 72 hours of any change in residence or employment.

7. The defendant shall refrain from excessive use of alcohol and shall not purchase, possess, use, distribute, or administer any narcotic or other controlled substance, or any paraphernalia related to such substances, except as prescribed by a physician.

8. The defendant shall not frequent places where controlled substances are illegally sold, used, distributed, or administered, or other places specified by the court.

9. The defendant shall not associate with any persons engaged in criminal activity, and shall not associate with any person convicted of a felony, unless granted permission to do so by the PO.

10. The defendant shall permit a PO to visit him at any time at home or elsewhere and shall permit confiscation of any contraband observed in plain view by the PO.

11. The defendant shall notify the PO within 72 hours of being arrested or questioned by a law enforcement officer.

12. The defendant shall not enter into any agreement to act as an informer or a special agent of a law enforcement agency without the permission of the court.

13. As directed by the PO, the defendant shall notify third parties of risks that may be occasioned by the defendant's criminal record or personal history or characteristics, and shall permit the probation officer to make such notifications and to confirm the defendant's compliance with such notification requirement (U.S. Sentencing Commission, 1987).

Additional special provisions pertain to possession of weapons, restitution, fines, debt obligations, access to financial information, community confinement, home detention, community service, occupational restrictions, substance abuse program participation, and mental health program participation (U.S. Sentencing Commission, 2003:5.7–5.10).

The New Jersey Intensive Supervision Parole Program

One of the better **intensive supervised parole (ISP)** programs in the United States has been devised by New Jersey. The New Jersey Intensive Supervision Program (NJISP) was established in June 1983. Originally, the program was influenced by the traditional, treatment-oriented rehabilitation model and has been designed to target the least serious incarcerated offenders. Since 1983 the NJISP has become a model program that other states have emulated. Its program components are discussed at length in this section because of its successfulness.

Program Goals. The goals of the NJISP are (1) to reduce the number of offenders serving state prison sentences by permitting them to be resentenced to an intermediate form of punishment; (2) to improve the utilization of correctional resources by making additional bed space available for violent criminals; and (3) to test whether supervising selected offenders in the community is less costly and more effective than incarceration.

Program Eligibility. Who qualifies for the NJISP? First, anyone incarcerated in a New Jersey prison may apply for admission to the NJISP. In fact, once an offender has been convicted of a crime and incarcerated in a New Jersey prison or county jail, he or she may apply for admission into the NJISP. However, there are mandatory exclusions consisting of the following:

1. Persons who have been convicted of homicide, a sex offense, a crime of the first degree, and robbery.
2. Persons who are serving sentences of life without the possibility of parole.
3. Persons who have convictions for organized crime activity.

For all other offenders, applications will be received and reviewed by an ISP Screening Panel. The ISP Screening Panel is comprised of three members drawn from 25 judges and citizen members. The Screening Panel screens applications received from eligible inmates. The screening standards are rigorous. Between 1983 and 1999, for instance, 38,000 applications from inmates were received. Only 19 percent (7,220) of these applications were approved and inmates were admitted into the NJISP.

The application process is more than merely rubber-stamping someone's application for inclusion. Applicants who are deemed eligible for the NJISP are interviewed by program staff. They must develop detailed case plans that set forth their goals and objectives for achieving program success. Participant goals include remaining free from illegal substances, strengthening relationships, maintaining steady employment, resolving legal problems, and paying required financial obligations. Applicants must also state that they will attend self-help sessions of Alcoholics Anonymous, take adult education courses, or receive family counseling, depending on individual offender circumstances. Applicants must indicate their willingness to abide by the NJISP conditions by signing their case plans.

Applicants must also obtain a sponsor within the community and they are encouraged to develop network teams. Community sponsors assist participants in complying with the NJISP conditions. They may provide participants with transportation to and from required meetings or to obtain employment. Community sponsors also sign an applicant's case plan and can offer suggestions about how to strengthen it. During the applicant investigation process, recommendations are solicited from the original sentencing judge, the prosecutor, previous probation and parole officers, victims, and the local police. This information is referred to as an assessment report and is forwarded to the ISP Screening Board for review. The Board deliberates in groups of three and decides whether to accept or reject particular applicants.

The Provisional Process. An ISP Resentencing Panel receives recommendations from the ISP Screening Board and admits or denies program admission for each applicant. Accepted applicants are immediately released from prison or jail and placed into the NJISP. Those denied admission are returned to the New Jersey Department of Corrections.

The process is provisional, since all applicants must endure a 90-day trial period. The progress of each participant is tracked and reviewed by the Panel in 90-day intervals. Participants reappear before the Panel for formal resentencing into the program after they have been under supervision for 180 days. Prior to resentencing, participants are considered to be on conditional release from their prisons or jails.

The NJISP stresses that it does not overturn the original sentencing judge's decision; rather, the ISP Resentencing Panel merely changes the place of confinement. Furthermore, the ISP Resentencing Panel does not declare that the original sentence was inappropriate. The Resentencing Panel stands by the original sentence imposed and deems it proper and justified. The NJISP is not a slap on the wrist. It is a demanding program requiring the participant to adhere to many stringent program requirements. Some applicants have been known to withdraw their applications once they learn that they will be under ISP supervision for 16–22 months. Finally, the NJISP is not a widening of the net of social control over offenders. Only those sentenced to serve incarcerative terms are considered eligible for program admission. Judges are prohibited from sentencing offenders directly into the NJISP.

Participants are advised that if they are admitted into the program, they can expect to be on the program for at least 16 months, and for a longer period if their original sentence was five or more years. If any program condition is violated while they are on the NJISP, then they may be expected to remain in the program for longer periods.

Program Requirements. The NJISP requirements are among the most rigorous found in any state or federal ISP program. These are listed below.

Conditions of the Intensive Supervision Program (ISP)

You have been placed on the Intensive Supervision Program (ISP) by the ISP Resentencing Panel for a trial period of 90 days subject to your compliance with your case plan and the conditions listed below. If you are arrested for a new offense, the ISP Resentencing Panel may issue a warrant to detain you in custody, without bail, to await disposition on the new charges.

1. I will obey the laws of the United States, and the laws and ordinances of any jurisdiction in which I may be residing.

2. I am required to promptly notify my ISP Officer if I am arrested, questioned, or contacted by any law enforcement official whether summoned, indicted, or charged with any offense or violation.

3. I will report as directed to the Court or to my ISP Officer.

4. I will permit the ISP Officer to visit my home.

5. I will answer promptly, truthfully, and completely all inquiries made by my ISP Officer and must obtain approval prior to any residence change. If the change of address or residence is outside the region in which I am under supervision, I will request approval at least 30 days in advance.

6. I will participate in any medical and/or psychological examinations, tests, and/or counseling as directed.

7. I will support my dependents, meet my family responsibilities, and continue full time (35 hours or more per week), gainful employment. I will notify my ISP Officer prior to any change in my employment or if I become unemployed.

8. I will not leave the State of New Jersey without permission of my ISP Officer.

9. If I abscond from supervision (keep my whereabouts unknown to my ISP Officer), I may be charged with a new crime of Escape under 2C: 29-5, which may subject me to an additional sentence of up to five years consecutive to any ISP violation time.

10. I will not have in my possession any firearm or other dangerous weapon.

11. I will perform community service of at least 16 hours per month, unless modified by the ISP Resentencing Panel.

12. I will participate in ISP group activities as directed.

13. I will maintain a daily diary of my activities and a weekly budget while under supervision.

14. I will not borrow any money, loan any money, or make credit purchases without permission of my ISP Officer. I may be required to surrender any credit cards in my possession to my officer.

15. I will maintain weekly contact with my community sponsor and network team.

16. I will comply with the required curfew of 6:00 P.M. to 6:00 A.M. unless modified by my ISP Officer. If unemployed, I will abide by a 6:00 P.M. curfew unless modified by my ISP Officer.

17. I will submit at any time to a search of my person, places, or things under my immediate control by my ISP Officer.

18. I will abstain from all illegal drug use and consumption of alcohol (including nonalcoholic beer) and submit to drug and/or alcohol testing as directed. I also will not ingest any product containing poppy seeds. I will not use any medications, including over-the-counter medications, which contain alcohol.

19. I will notify my employer of my participation in ISP within 30 days after commencing employment.

20. I will not ingest any medication prescribed to someone else and will inform my ISP Officer of any medication prescribed to me by a physician or dentist.

21. I will file my Federal and State tax returns by the lawfully prescribed date and provide copies of the returns to my ISP Officer.

22. In accordance with State law, I cannot vote in any public election while under ISP supervision.

23. I will maintain telephone service at my approved residence. If the telephone service is discontinued, I will notify my ISP Officer immediately. I am not permitted to have a caller ID or call forwarding services on my telephone.

24. I cannot collect unemployment benefits, disability assistance, or welfare benefits without permission.

25. I cannot possess a pager (beeper) and/or cellular telephone unless approved by my ISP Officer.

26. I cannot visit inmates in county or state correctional facilities until I have completed six months of satisfactory ISP supervision and with the permission of the ISP Regional Supervisor.

27. I may not serve in the capacity of an informant for a law enforcement agency. If requested to do so, I must decline and inform my ISP Officer of the request.

28. I will not engage in any gambling including the purchase of lottery tickets. I will not enter a gambling establishment (casino) unless employed at such an establishment or given permission to visit such establishment by my ISP Officer.

29. I will turn in to my ISP Officer my driver's license (if driving privileges have been revoked), firearms ID card, and hunting license if any of them are in my possession.

30. I will comply with any and all directives from the ISP Resentencing Panel or my officer.

These are very rigorous conditions. All participants must agree to them in writing. A violation of any one or more of these conditions means that the Resentencing Panel will hear the charges and decide on the punishment. Program violations are cause for terminating one's involvement in the program and returning the offender to prison. The Resentencing Panel usually sits in parties of three and conducts hearings at least 4 times per month. Hearings are held in various locations throughout New Jersey's 21 counties in an effort to acquaint judges and other judicial employees with the functions of the Resentencing Panel.

PO Responsibilities.   ISP officers spend about 80 percent of their time in direct field supervision. In 1998, for instance, officers conducted 556,202 participant contacts. Since 1984, POs have conducted almost 4 million contacts. Caseloads of POs are a maximum of 20 clients. Participants do not visit regional officers. Rather, POs visit participants at their workplaces, homes, and other places as deemed appropriate by the PO. Participants can reach their POs 24 hours a day. All POs are equipped with a message paging device that can be accessed through a toll-free 800 number. If any participant absconds from the program, the ISP arranges for and assists in the execution of arrest warrants. Violators will be tracked down by any and all means available to the State of New Jersey.

POs are unarmed. This is a concern for many POs involved in the NJISP. Strategies for working in unsafe areas have been devised. These include arranging meetings with community sponsors as escorts and the use of prearranged sites. All ISP officers and community development specialists are equipped with portable cellular telephones to assist in their monitoring and surveillance duties. ISP officers may search a participant's home, person, or vehicle without a warrant. Searches are conducted at random to determine whether participants are in possession of firearms or illegal contraband, or if they have any other prohibited items such as credit cards or cellular telephones or pagers.

Client Responsibilities.   All ISP participants must maintain employment. They must be economically self-sufficient. During 1998, for instance, ISP participants had an average full-time income of $15,000. Participants are obligated to observe a curfew ranging from 6:00 P.M. to 6:00 A.M. These curfews may be changed with PO approval. Curfews are monitored through random visits, telephone calls, electronic surveillance, and by community sponsors and network team and family members. Participants can modify their curfews as they progress successfully through their programs. Participants must pay all court-ordered financial obligations, which may include restitution, child support, court-mandated fines, drug penalties, Victim Crime Compensation Board fees, and other payments. Participants must perform at least 16 hours of community service each month. Projects may include maintenance work at hospitals, nursing homes, and geriatric institutes; cleaning municipal vehicles; picking up litter at parks and roadways; stuffing envelopes for nonprofit agencies; painting; carpentry; plumbing; tutoring; and clerical work for charitable organizations.

Clients must submit to urine monitoring to detect drug use. Alcohol ingestion is detected by using a Breathalyzer. The majority of participants have substance abuse problems. Participants are screened as often as three times a week. Positive tests are often confirmed by gas chromatography. Participants with positive tests are immediately confronted. Admission of drug use is considered to be a crucial element in the recovery process. Most participants admit to using drugs when confronted. ISP uses more than 100 outpatient and inpatient substance abuse, alcohol abuse, and psychological treatment providers. Educational seminars are held regularly for participants, and their attendance at these seminars is mandatory. Sanctions are imposed for any program violation. The seriousness of the sanction depends on the seriousness of the violation. The most commonly applied sanctions are increased curfew restrictions, additional community service hours, increased treatment requirements, home detention, and short-term incarceration.

The Successfulness of the NJISP.   How does the NJISP measure the successfulness of its program? Client recidivism is used. By March 1999, there were 7,154 participants, with about 44 percent of these (3,164) graduating. There were 2,774 (39 percent) participants returned to custody for violating program conditions. Of the program graduates, the recidivism figures have been most impressive. Using a 60-month follow-up of the NJISP graduates, only 7.5 percent had recidivated. This is a success rate of 92.5 percent.

The cost of the NJISP is low compared with incarceration. In New Jersey, it cost $31,000 to house one offender in prison or jail for a year. The NJISP program costs for each participant per year were only $7,158.

A Profile of NJISP Clientele.   In 1999 the active caseload of all NJISP clients was 1,133. Of these, 86 percent were male. The average sentence length for

BOX 9.2

The government of England and Wales consists of the monarchy, Parliament, the House of Lords, and the House of Commons, and the laws are derived largely from common law. Statutory instruments or delegated legislation is the basis of British laws and may be promulgated by government ministers or departments. Acts of Parliament override common law provisions, and later acts take precedence over earlier ones. The court system in England and Wales is adversarial. The rights of accused persons are similar to those enjoyed by defendants in U.S. courts. Any indigent defendant has the right to a court-appointed attorney or solicitor. Legal advice is provided to all defendants charged with a criminal offense, however. Duty solicitors are available in court at all times to provide legal representation for any person accused of a crime. Plea bargaining is an accepted practice, and about 50 percent of all criminal cases are concluded through guilty pleas. Prosecutors are obligated to disclose case information to any accused person and his or her attorney, although discovery is not reciprocal. Defense counsels are not obligated to make similar disclosures of evidence to the prosecution.

Crimes in England and Wales are classified according to their seriousness. They also may be classified according to how they are brought to trial. The age of criminal responsibility is 10, and children between ages 10 and 17 are brought before a youth court if charged with a criminal offense. Punishments imposed on juvenile offenders are largely nominal and include fines or restitution, which often become the responsibility of the parents. In the most serious juvenile cases, compulsory attendance may be required at attendance centers where youths may receive counseling and instruction. The aim of such centers is rehabilitation and reintegration, to instill within youths a law-abiding demeanor. Persons age 18 or older are subject to adult court jurisdiction and accompanying punishments upon conviction.

The least serious offenses are summary offenses. These include such behaviors as public intoxication, mischief, public disorder, and other nuisance offenses. More serious offenses are known as indictable offenses, and these include rape, murder, robbery, assault, and other serious crimes. Sometimes a third class of offense exists known as a hybrid offense, the seriousness of which is based on prosecutorial discretion. The most prevalent types of offenses are property offenses, accounting for over 90 percent of all crime. These offenses include burglary, theft, fraud, and criminal damages. Drug offending is increasing, however, as world drug markets are expanding. Despite the increased use of illegal drugs, drug abuse accounts for a very small proportion of crimes committed. England and Wales have some of the lowest violent crime statistics of all industrialized countries. There are several reasons for these low figures, although strict firearms regulation and prohibition figure prominently in these low violent crime rates. Crime figures are summarized regularly in the *British Crime Survey,* which is essentially a victimization survey. In 2004 there were over 11.7 million crimes reported. In England and Wales, crime peaked in 1995 and has declined perceptibly since then.

Summary offenses are usually tried in magistrate's courts, while more serious offenses are tried in Crown Courts. There are approximately 100 Crown Courts in England and Wales located in different jurisdictions. Juries may hear more serious cases, although bench trials where judges decide are also prevalent. Juries consist of 12 persons, and guilt must be established beyond a reasonable doubt. Majority votes in determining one's guilt are permissible, such as a jury vote of 10–2. Any conviction in a magistrate's court, or court of first instance, is appealable to a Crown Court. Appeals of convictions in Crown Courts are made in the Court of Appeal Criminal Division. The House of Lords hears cases involving matters of national law,

(continued)

BOX 9.2 (*Continued*)

similar to appeals directed to the U.S. Supreme Court.

Magistrate's courts are usually comprised of three-judge panels. Legally experienced clerks advise them on matters of law. Sometimes judges sit alone to hear the least serious offenses. When persons are convicted in magistrate's courts, the magistrate or panel of magistrates will determine the appropriate sentence. In Crown Courts, verdicts of guilty are followed by sentences imposed by judges.

The court system is such that following guilty verdicts either by judges or juries, a sentencing hearing may be conducted. This hearing is preceded by an order for a pre-sentence report similar to a pre-sentence investigation report that probation officers in U.S. jurisdictions might prepare. The Probation Service is charged with the preparation of such reports, which are given to judges to advise them as to the proper sentence to impose. These sentencing recommendations are customarily made. Similar to U.S. judges, however, British judges may impose sentences different from those recommended in pre-sentence reports by probation officers. Defense counsels may attempt to mitigate the harshness of the sentences imposed on their clients by including facts of mitigation into the record during the sentencing hearing. The ultimate sentencing responsibility, however, rests with judges. Prosecutors and victims have no input in the sentencing process.

The range of punishments in England and Wales extends from verbal warnings and fines to incarceration for specified periods, depending on offense seriousness. Over 80 percent of all convictions result in fines. Besides fines, periods of incarceration may be imposed. Furthermore, community service orders or community work, and probation supervision, may be authorized. Community service or work can be imposed up to 240 hours. Victim compensation or restitution orders may be imposed as well. Usually about 20 percent of all persons found guilty of indictable offenses are incarcerated. Sentences of imprisonment may be suspended or begun immediately, again depending on offense seriousness. There is no death penalty, although the most serious offenders may receive terms of life imprisonment.

Criminal proceedings against various suspects begin with arrests and charges filed. Prosecutors typically dismiss between 25–30 percent of these cases because of a lack of evidence or other factors. The Crown Prosecution Service conducts prosecutions against criminal suspects in Crown Courts. Prosecutors may defer prosecution against certain suspects for up to six months, and they may discharge defendants at their discretion based on conduct. These actions are similar to deferred prosecutions and pretrial diversion in U.S. jurisdictions. Furthermore, some offenses may be diverted to a mediation process similar to alternative dispute resolution, particularly where property damage has occurred. The aim of such mediation is restitution or restoration. Criminal trials are averted as a result of this process.

Pretrial detention of suspects occurs, especially for most serious indictable offenses. However, a type of speedy trial provision exists wherein a criminal defendant must come to trial within 70 days of being charged with an offense. Bail is extended to those entitled to bail, similar to the bail process in the United States. New bail provisions were established under the Criminal Justice and Public Order Act of 1994. Bail may be denied for those deemed a risk to society or those who may flee the jurisdiction.

Following a trial, the range of penalties may involve unconditional discharges, where persons are simply fined and freed. For more serious crimes, incarceration of varying durations may be imposed. Imprisoned offenders may serve only a portion of their sentences. If they are granted early release, they are placed on probation. England and Wales has a Parole Board, although persons granted parole are placed on probation, not parole. All conditional prison releasees are called probationers. In 2005 sentences in Crown Courts and magistrate's courts resulted in 8 percent discharged, 71 percent receiving fines, 13 percent receiving community sentences(probation), and 7 percent being incarcerated in prison.

In 2005 there were 139 prisons in England and Wales. The prison population was approximately 76,000. Most prisons were publicly operated, although several were privately operated. Prisons are designed to allow for different levels of offenders, usually according to the type of crime they have committed. Category A prisoners are those who are most likely to escape. These are held under the most secure conditions. Category B prisoners don't require maximum security, but they need close monitoring. Category C prisoners can't be trusted in open conditions but are not likely to attempt escape. The least serious inmate is Category D. These prisoners are trusted enough to wander about the prison freely but must report for daily roll calls. Less than 10 percent of all prisoners are women. While confined, prisoners may enjoy various amenities, including television and radio. They receive regular health care, educational opportunities, vocational training, religious worship, and visitation privileges from family or friends. Youthful offenders under age 21 are usually accommodated in Secure Training Centers, Local Authority Secure Children's Homes, and Youth Offending Institutes.

Probation can be imposed in the following ways. When an offender leaves prison, or receives a community sentence, he or she will be put on probation, which means they will be supervised by a probation officer. Thus, offenders are placed on probation when:

1. Judges sentence them to a community sentence, as an alternative to prison.
2. The Parole Board decides the offender can be released short of serving the full term of imprisonment.
3. The offender is automatically released from prison after serving three-fourths of the original sentence imposed.

Being on probation in England and Wales involves conditions, similar to those imposed on U.S. probationers and parolees. If one or more rules of probation are violated, violators face revocation of their probation

and possible return or placement in prison. Offenders are obligated to report regularly to their probation officers and attend supervision sessions on a regular basis. If they miss a session, they will receive one warning. If they miss a second session, they will be sent to court and possibly be imprisoned for a short time period. Other probation requirements include:

1. Completing community sentences successfully.
2. Completing alcohol and/or drug treatment.
3. Staying in a probation hostel.
4. Staying away from the area where the crime was committed.

Community sentences may include compulsory work, such as cleaning up local areas and removing graffiti, which may allow offenders to acquire new skills while repaying societal debts; community rehabilitation, which may involve regular meetings with probation officers to facilitate behavioral changes; and/or curfews, where offenders must stay indoors at certain times under a form of house arrest or home confinement. The aims of sentencing include protecting the public, punishing offenders, reducing crime, rehabilitating offenders, and repairing harm to society through restorative justice. Sentences by judges are influenced by the seriousness of the offense, one's remorsefulness, and the defendant's prior record.

In 2005 probation officers supervised approximately 250,000 offenders. About 70 percent of these probationers were serving community sentences and were not formerly imprisoned. The remaining 30 percent consisted of those who had served various terms before being released on probation. The role of probation officers is multifaceted, and it includes rehabilitating offenders; enforcing the conditions of offenders' court orders and release licenses; conducting offender risk assessments to protect the public; and resolving problems that may have led offenders to commit the crime in the first place. Greater emphasis has been given in recent years to

(continued)

BOX 9.2 (Continued)

community safety and security. Consistent with this emphasis is the use of better offender management methods, including the use of home confinement and electronic monitoring. More demanding community sentences have been imposed, together with greater accountability measures. More severe sanctions have been created for chronic or persistent offenders. The probation service is under the jurisdiction of Her Majesty's Inspectorate of Probation, which is an independent organization that reports on probation officer performance and provides Home Office ministers with reports and advice for improving probation services.

In 2006 the Sentencing Guidelines Council, which was created in 2004, articulated a set of guidelines for sentencing procedures in all courts. These guidelines are referred to as the National Allocation Guidelines and are proposed to assist courts in dealing with criminal cases throughout England and Wales. These guidelines provide a level of uniformity among courts that previously did not exist. Similar to the federal sentencing guidelines currently in effect in the United States, the purpose of these guidelines is to

provide guidance to those making sentencing decisions, namely the judiciary. The guidelines themselves do not set forth specific minimum and maximum penalties for specific offenses. Rather, they detail procedural matters relative to all aspects of the sentencing process, such as the conditions that must prevail in order for plea bargains to be offered and completed. Guilty pleas and sentence reductions are addressed. Procedures for summary trials are detailed, including the information courts should deliver to criminal suspects as a part of their processing. At this writing, these guidelines were considered draft guidelines, and thus they were not yet officially approved. But their creation suggests strong governmental interest in formalizing and systematizing the sentencing process.

Sources: Adapted from Corretta Phillips, Gemma Cox, and Ken Pease, "England and Wales," *The World Factbook of Criminal Justice Systems*, 2004; *National Allocation Guidelines 2006*, London: Sentencing Guidelines Council, 2006; British Home Office, *National Community Safety Plan 2006–2009*, London, 2006; "Crime Reduction in the UK," British Home Office, London, November, 2005.

males was 51 months compared with 49 months for female offenders participating in the program. A majority of offenders were convicted for drug use and sales (63.7 percent for men and 73.1 percent for women). A majority of participants were never married. About 12 percent of all participants, both male and female, were married. The median educational level of all participants was 11 years. About 60 percent of all participants were high school graduates. A majority were employed (62 percent for men and 53 percent for women). About 38 percent of all male participants were first-offenders, while 49 percent of all female participants were first-offenders.

In New Jersey, at least, the public likes the NJISP. The media have given the NJISP very favorable coverage. There have been relatively few incidents involving victimizations through violent offending. One reason for this is that applicants are so rigorously screened before they are accepted into the program. ISP has had a very positive effect on most participants, by presenting educational seminars, offering courses in parenting skills, GED preparation, job searches and job application form assistance, and literacy courses.

The New Jersey Intensive Supervision Program is by no means the only program of its type in the United States. It has been widely copied in other jurisdictions. One common thread running through almost all of these ISP programs is the continuous monitoring and random checking of offenders (Marciniak, 2000).

ISP means closer offender monitoring. This means that fewer clients will have a chance to use drugs or alcohol and avoid being detected through random checks. This constant monitoring seems to work in most ISP programs. Face-to-face contacts improve client compliance with program conditions. There is some variation among programs relating to client recidivism. Not all offenders are monitored as closely as they are in the New Jersey ISP. However, the two most important factors relating to program failure were drug/alcohol abuse and unemployment.

The Nevada Intensive Supervision Program

Nevada has established an intensive supervision program for both its probationers and parolees. The Nevada ISP program is one component of case management and a tool in assisting the Nevada Division of Parole and Probation in achieving its overall mission. It is also the ultimate level of supervision that the Nevada agency can provide for community safety and offender rehabilitation. The common elements of Nevada's ISP are as follows:

1. Frequent contacts with offenders
2. Smaller caseloads
3. A system of phases or levels
4. Curfews or electronic monitoring
5. Drug and alcohol testing
6. Graduated internal sanctions
7. Treatment and other interventions
8. Required employment
9. Employment-seeking activities or schooling

All specialized caseloads are fielded to District IV (Las Vegas), which is the largest ISP unit within Nevada. These caseloads encompass residential confinement, mandatory parole release, offenders in need of true ISP monitoring, and the sex offender unit. These caseloads in 2001 totaled 1,044 offenders. The Nevada legislature authorized a 30:1 ratio for residential confinement and ISP offenders, and a 40:1 ratio for all others. The Division of Parole and Probation screens offenders for inclusion in its ISP program according to: (1) crimes of violence; (2) crimes involving drug trafficking or sales of controlled substances; (3) criminal activity of a sophisticated nature; (4) active gang affiliation; (5) sustained or chronic substance abuse history; (6) history of mental illness; and (7) court/board ordered. One or all of these criteria might function to deny admission to the ISP program for any particular offender.

The ISP encompasses two phases, whose duration is determined by a specific period of time. The first phase consists of a 90-day period; during this time, the offender is placed either on court/board house arrest or curfew. The house arrest monitoring is provided by a contracted private company, who sets the fee for such service, and the offender is required to meet that financial obligation. Curfew can either be monitored by the appropriate officer or the offender may be referred to the private company offering that service (the offender is responsible for fee assessments when referred to the private company). During this initial 90-day period, the offender will be aggressively encouraged to enroll in and complete short-term goals such as outpatient substance abuse or alcohol counseling, employment counseling, and anger management.

The second phase of this program consists of either a 30- or 60-day period, during which time the offender is made ready to enter the general supervision population. During this time frame, the offender is taken off residential confinement or curfew and supervision requirements are greatly relaxed. If the offender relapses during this phase of supervision, then he or she is allowed one more opportunity to reenter Phase I and again attempt to change his behavior to a positive vein, indicating that he or she can be managed in a general supervision population. Thus, the ISP was restructured with the intent of providing an ultimate level of ISP and rehabilitation to promote long-term behavioral change that would eventually lead to enhanced public safety. If those efforts fail and result in a violation process, this Division could positively assure that there would be no other supervision strategies available to the offender.

The following are contract requirements for each phase or level of supervision:

Phase/Level I:

1 home contact

1 monthly report

2 field contacts or 2 surveillance contacts or 1 each

1 employment program/program verification

Special conditions as applicable

Phase/Level II:

1 home contact

1 monthly report

1 field contact or 1 surveillance

1 employment/program verification

Special conditions as applicable

Offenders on Residential Confinement:

2 home contacts

1 monthly report

1 residence verification

1 face-to-face contact

2 employment/program verifications

Special conditions as applicable

Surveillance of an offender may be considered to be a field contact with supervisory approval. All surveillance time shall be recorded in a surveillance log. The surveillance log is turned into and maintained by the officer's immediate supervisor at the end of each month. At the beginning of 2001, the ISP unit worked a seven-day schedule, with a day and a swing shift. Caseloads were assigned according to geographic location. The team concept is utilized within this unit and generally the officers work with assigned partners when working the field. Most caseloads are integrated with both the residential confinement and ISP offenders and this was decided on because of two factors. First, the geographic location, and second, every officer cross-trains in all phases, therefore making it easier to have the same level of expertise throughout the seven-day period. The sex offender subunit presently has 10 officers, and at this time, their contact requirements are constantly changing. They generally work alone with the exception of a planned search/arrest. The program was implemented during the Spring/Summer of 2000. Ten percent of all offenders were returned to either the court or parole board, which resulted in a 3 percent revocation rate (Konopka, 2001:1–4).

SHOCK PAROLE

Shock parole, sometimes called shock probation, refers to a planned sentence where judges order offenders imprisoned for periods ranging from 30, 60, 90, or even 120 days. The terms of imprisonment are actually longer, such as one or more years. However, offenders are removed from their jails or prisons after these short periods and resentenced to probation or parole, provided that they behaved well while incarcerated. The shock factor relates to the shock of being imprisoned. Theoretically, this trauma will be so dramatic that offenders will not want to reoffend and return to prison. Therefore, there is a strong deterrent factor associated with these shock parole sentences. Ohio introduced the first shock probation law in 1965. Several other states have adopted similar laws in recent years (Champion, 2005). It is important to note that offenders who are sentenced to shock parole do not know that this sentence is actually being imposed. In their own minds, they are being sentenced to terms of one or more years in prison. Thus, when they are suddenly removed from prison and resentenced to parole, this shock of resentencing sends them an important message to refrain from lawless conduct and remain law-abiding.

The success of shock parole is measured by the recidivism rates of shock parolees. New York State Department of Corrections estimates savings per inmate of up to $10,000 per year, while other jurisdictions using shock incarceration report similar savings (New York State Department of Correctional Services, 2006). Recidivism figures for shock probationers in Ohio and other jurisdictions have been unusually low compared with the recidivism rates of offenders involved in other types of programs such as intensive supervised probation, furloughs, or work release. It is perhaps too early to tell whether shock incarceration will make an important difference in the long run as a crime control strategy, although preliminary reports are favorable.

HALFWAY HOUSES AND COMMUNITY RESIDENTIAL CENTERS

Halfway Houses Defined

One of the most important components of transitional corrections is the **halfway house.** Halfway houses are either publicly or privately operated facilities staffed by professionals, paraprofessionals, and volunteers. They are designed to assist parolees in making the transition from prison to the community. They provide food, clothing, temporary living quarters, employment assistance, and limited counseling. Again, if the parolee has been confined for a long period, the transition can be difficult, possibly even traumatic. Sometimes these facilities are known as **community residential centers.**

In 2005, 43 states and the federal government operated halfway houses for parolees. There were 39,222 halfway house clients (U.S. Department of Justice, 2006). While the precise origin of halfway houses is unknown, some observers say evidence of halfway houses existed during the Middle Ages as a part of Christian charity. The Salvation Army is associated with halfway house operations in the United States in the early 1900s, although there were shelters such as the Philadelphia House of Industry in existence to serve the various needs of parolees as early as 1889. Much earlier in 1817, some reformist groups lobbied for halfway houses as a means of solving prison overcrowding problems. At that time, these proposals were rejected because of the belief that prisoners would contaminate one another if they lived together in common quarters. Temporary facilities for released prisoners were established also in New York City as early as 1845. The Quakers operated the Isaac T. Hopper Home for those released from prison. In 1864, the Temporary Asylum for Disadvantaged Female Prisoners was established in New York City as well.

In many jurisdictions, halfway houses offer services to offenders on a voluntary basis. They assist greatly in helping former inmates make the transition from rigid prison life to community living. There was resistance to halfway houses when they were first proposed, because the public feared **criminal contamination.** This was the belief that if ex-offenders lived together, they would spread their criminality like a disease. Subsequently, the public warmed to the idea of halfway houses once it was learned that they exerted a high degree of supervision and control over halfway house clientele.

Sponsorship of halfway houses for the next 150 years stemmed primarily from private and/or religious sources. In 1845, the Quakers opened the **Isaac T. Hopper Home** in New York City, followed by the Temporary Asylum for Disadvantaged Female Prisoners, established in Boston in 1864 by a reformist group. In 1889, the House of Industry was opened in Philadelphia, and in 1896, Hope House was established in New York City by Maud and Ballington Booth. Receiving considerable financial support from a missionary religious society called the Volunteers of America, the Boothes were able to open what became known as **Hope Houses** in future years in Chicago, San Francisco, and New Orleans.

State and federal governments during the 1800s and early 1900s continued to work toward the creation of halfway houses apart from those established in the private sector, however. In 1917, the Massachusetts Prison Commission recommended the establishment of houses to accommodate recently released offenders who were indigent. But this plan was rejected. Eventually in the 1960s, Attorney General Robert F. Kennedy recommended government sponsorship and funding for halfway house programs. In 1965, the Prisoner Rehabilitation Act was passed, which authorized the establishment of community-based residential centers for both juvenile and adult pre-release offenders.

One of the most significant events to spark the growth of state-operated halfway houses was the creation of the **International Halfway House Association (IHHA)** in Chicago in 1964. Although many of the halfway house programs continued to be privately operated after the formation of the IHHA, the growth in the numbers of halfway houses was phenomenal during the next decade. For instance, from 1966 to 1982, the number of halfway houses operating in the United States and Canada rose from 40 to 1,800 (Wilson, 1985:154). These figures are probably lower than the actual number of halfway houses in existence during those time periods, since these numbers were based on affiliation with the IHHA and the American Correctional Association through a directory that was devised.

Halfway House Variations

Because there are so many different government-sponsored and private agencies claiming to be halfway houses, it is impossible to devise a consistent definition of one that fits all jurisdictions. There is extensive variation in the level of custody for clients ranging from providing simple shelter on a voluntary basis to mandatory confinement with curfew. There are also many different services provided by halfway houses. These might include alcohol- or drug-related rehabilitation facilities with some hospitalization on premises, minimal or extensive counseling services, and/or employment assistance. Also, halfway house programs are designed for offenders ranging from probationers and pre-releasees to parolees and others assigned to community service with special conditions.

Halfway-In and Halfway-Out Houses

The concept of a halfway house is closely connected with the reintegrative aim of corrections. In recent years, at least two hyphenated versions of the term have emerged. First, **halfway-out** houses are facilities designed to serve the immediate needs of parolees from those established to accommodate probationers in the community. Second, **halfway-in** houses provide services catering to probationers in need of limited or somewhat restricted confinement apart from complete freedom of movement in the community.

Halfway-in houses are deliberately intended to create uncomfortable atmospheres for them. Halfway-in houses structure the lives of probationers in various ways, mostly by making them comply with various program requirements (e.g., curfew, random drug and alcohol checks, and other technical details). In contrast, halfway-out houses, for parolees, are designed to provide homelike and supportive environments aimed at aiding the offender's readjustment to society. Like halfway-in houses, these homes also continue punishment through the high degree of supervision or offender control exerted by halfway-out house staff. But because their clientele are parolees and have served substantial time behind bars, their functions are more therapeutic, rehabilitative, and reintegrative rather than punishment-centered.

The Philosophy and Functions of Halfway Houses

Halfway houses typify the transition prisoners must make from prisons and jails to their communities. Halfway houses furnish living accommodations and food, job placement services for parolees, group and/or individual counseling, medical assistance, placement assistance in vocational/technical training programs, and numerous other forms of assistance to clients.

The major functions of halfway houses overlap some of those associated with other programs for parolees. These include (1) parolee rehabilitation and reintegration into the community; (2) provisions for food and shelter; (3) job placement, vocational guidance, and employment assistance; (4) client-specific treatments; (5) alleviating jail and prison overcrowding; (6) supplementing supervisory functions of probation and parole agencies; and (7) monitoring probationers, work/study releasees, and others with special program conditions.

Parole Rehabilitation and Reintegration into the Community

The major function of halfway houses is to facilitate offender reintegration into the community. This is accomplished, in part, by providing necessities and making various services accessible to offenders. The administrative personnel of halfway houses as well as the professional and paraprofessional staff members assist in helping offenders with specific problems they might have such as alcohol or drug dependencies. Often, parolees have worked out a plan for themselves in advance of their parole date. This plan is subjected to scrutiny by parole board members, and the parolee often has the assistance of a PO in its preparation.

Provisions for Food and Shelter

Some parolees have acquired savings from their work in prison industries, while other parolees have no operating capital. Thus, halfway houses furnish offenders with a place to stay and regular meals while they hunt for new occupations and participate in self-help programs. Furthermore, halfway house personnel help offenders locate apartments or more permanent private housing for themselves and their families.

Job Placement, Vocational Guidance, and Employment Assistance

Almost every halfway house assists offenders by furnishing them job leads and negotiating contacts between them and prospective employers. Some halfway houses provide offenders with financial subsidization, which must be repaid when the offender has successfully acquired employment and is relatively stable.

Client-Specific Treatments. Offenders with special needs or problems, such as sex offenders, drug addicts or alcoholics, or mentally retarded clients, benefit from halfway houses by being permitted the freedom to take advantage of special treatment programs. They may receive counseling, medical treatment, or other services custom-designed for their particular needs. If these offenders were to be placed on the street on parole directly from a prison or jail, the transition for some would be too traumatic, and it is likely that they would revert to old habits or dependencies.

Alleviating Jail and Prison Overcrowding. Any program that provides a safety valve for prison or jail populations contributes to alleviating overcrowding problems. Probably the major function of halfway houses is to assist offenders in becoming reintegrated into society after long periods in secure confinement. But the functions of such houses have become diversified over the years. In any case, the existence of halfway houses has contributed to some reduction in jail and prison overcrowding as both a front-end and back-end solution.

Supplementing Supervisory Functions of Probation and Parole Agencies. A latent function of halfway houses is to exercise some degree of supervision and control over both probationers and parolees. These supervisory functions are ordinarily performed by probation or parole officers. However, when some inmates are released to halfway houses, halfway house staff assume considerable responsibility for client conduct.

Monitoring Parolees, Work/Study Releasees, and Others with Special Program Conditions.   Many parolees have conditional parole programs that require their attendance at meetings and regular counseling. Thus, halfway houses can not only provide the basic necessities such as food, clothing, and shelter, but they can also offer assistance in transporting clients to and from their required meetings and counseling sessions.

Strengths and Weaknesses of Halfway Houses

Blanket generalizations about halfway house effectiveness are difficult because there is so much diversity among halfway house programs. Furthermore, these programs have been established on widely different philosophical bases or rehabilitative models. But several attempts to measure halfway house effectiveness have been observed. Effectiveness of halfway houses has been measured primarily in one of three ways. First, are halfway houses more cost-effective compared with incarceration? Second, do halfway houses actually assist in reintegrating offenders into society? And third, do halfway houses reduce recidivism to a greater degree among parolees compared with other programs such as standard parole? The cost-effectiveness of halfway houses is undisputed when contrasted with the cost of maintaining inmates in prisons or jails. For instance, it costs about $43 per day to maintain a client in a halfway house (U.S. Department of Justice, 2006). This is less than half of the cost of incarcerating offenders in most prisons.

Some of the major strengths and weaknesses of halfway house programs are as follows:

1. Halfway houses are effective in preventing criminal behavior in the community as alternatives that involve community release.
2. The placement of halfway houses in communities neither increases nor decreases property values.
3. Halfway houses assist their clients in locating employment but not necessarily maintaining it.
4. Halfway houses are able to provide for the basic needs of their clients as well as other forms of release.
5. At full capacity, halfway houses cost no more, and probably less, than incarceration, although they cost more than straight parole or outright release from correctional systems (Champion, 2005).

OTHER PAROLE CONDITIONS

Parolees are subject to several different kinds of conditions while serving their parole terms. These conditions may be to attend Alcoholics Anonymous, Narcotics Anonymous, and Gamblers Anonymous meetings, participate in individual or group counseling, take vocational/educational training, and seek and obtain continuous employment to support their dependents. Other conditions include (1) day reporting centers, (2) fines, (3) day fines, (4) community service orders, and (5) restitution.

Day Reporting Centers

For parolees, day treatment centers are operated primarily during daytime hours for the purpose of providing diverse services to offenders and their families. Day reporting centers are highly structured, nonresidential programs utilizing supervision, sanctions, and services coordinated from a central focus. Offenders live at home and report to these centers regularly, and daily. As a part of community residential treatment centers, day treatment programs provide services according to offender needs. These services might include employment assistance, family counseling, and educational/vocational training. Day treatment centers can also be used for supervisory and/or monitoring purposes. Client behavior modification is a key goal of such centers. Limited supervisory functions can be performed by day treatment centers as well, such as employment verification and evidence of law-abiding conduct for probationers and parolees. These centers are also operated for the purpose of providing family counseling in **juvenile delinquency** cases through parent education and support groups.

Fines

Fines and Criminal Statutes. An integral part of sentencing in an increasing number of cases is the use of fines. The use of fines as sanctions can be traced to preindustrialized and non-Western societies. Estimates suggest that over 14 million persons are arrested each year in the United States, and that a significant portion of these receive fines upon conviction. Ordinarily, state and federal criminal statutes provide for various incarcerative lengths upon conviction. Additionally, various fines are imposed as and/or conditions exercised at the discretion of sentencing judges. For instance, if law enforcement officers were to violate one's civil rights by the unlawful use of physical force or excessive force in making an arrest, they might be subject to penalties, including confinement in a state penitentiary up to five years and a fine of "not more than" $10,000. This means that if these law enforcement officers are convicted of violating one's civil rights, the judge can sentence them to prison for up to five years and impose a fine of $10,000. This would be within the judge's discretionary powers.

Types of Fines and Fine Collection Problems. Different types of scenarios involving fines have been described. These include: (1) fines plus jail or prison terms; (2) fines plus probation; (3) fines plus suspended jail or prison terms; (4) fines or jail alternatives ($30 or 30 days); (5) fines alone, partially suspended; and (6) fines alone. The arguments for and against the use of fines as sanctions have also been clearly delineated. It has been argued that (1) fines are logically suited for punishment because they are unambiguously punitive; (2) many offenders are poor and cannot afford fines; (3) because the poor cannot afford fines as easily as the rich, there is obvious discrimination in fine imposition; (4) someone else may pay the fine other than the offender; (5) often, fine payments are enforceable because of offender absconding; (6) courts lack sufficient enforcement capability; and (7) fines may actually increase crime so that the poor can get enough money to pay previously imposed fines. The problems of fine collection are such that less than half of the fines imposed are ever collected in most U.S. courts. Billions of dollars are involved in fine nonpayment. In more than a few jurisdictions, fine payment rates at the time of conviction have only been 14 percent.

Suspending Fines.   In many criminal cases, however, fines are either not imposed or suspended. This is because often, indigent or poor offenders cannot pay these fines or would have great difficulty paying them and supporting their families or fulfilling any of their other financial obligations. From our examination of probation and parole revocation, we know that one's probation or parole program cannot be revoked simply because of one's inability to pay program fees or fines. Thus, many judges do not impose fines because they will be uncollectible. Also, fines are not imposed in many cases because of certain jurisdictional precedents. In other instances, fines may be imposed but those obligated to pay fines will abscond. Even if those assessed fines do not abscond, the collection procedures in different jurisdictions are lax or unenforced.

Day Fines

Day fines are an early European invention. Day fines are a two-step process whereby courts (1) use a unit scale or benchmark to sentence offenders to certain numbers of day-fine units (e.g., 15, 30, 120) according to offense severity and without regard to income; and (2) determine the value of each unit according to a percentage of the offender's daily income; total fine amounts are determined by multiplying this unit value by the number of units accompanying the offense. For instance, if Offender X were convicted of simple assault, this might have a unit value of 30. The offender may have a net daily income of $50. Suppose the percentage of one's net daily income to be assessed as a fine is 10 percent. This means that one's total fine would be $50 10% $\times$ 30 units (for simple assault), or $5 $\times$ 30 = $150. This $150 fine would be assessed an offender at the time of sentencing, and the method of fine payment would be determined as well. Fine payments may be in installments, usually over no longer than a three-month period.

The Staten Island Day Fine Experiment.   In August 1988, judges in the New York City borough of Staten Island established a day-fine system similar to that developed earlier in Europe. This experiment was conducted because this jurisdiction and others like it in New York had considerable trouble collecting fines imposed when offenders were convicted of crimes. It was believed by Staten Island officials that day fines would actually increase the rate of fine payments, since day fines were determined in accordance with one's ability to pay. The project's planners had several goals in mind. These included:

1. A system of sentencing benchmarks proposing a specific number of day-fine units for each criminal offense.
2. A system for collecting necessary information about offenders concerning their ability to pay.
3. Policy guidelines and easy-to-use methods for establishing the value of each day-fine unit imposed for each offender.

4. Strategic improvements in the court's collection and enforcement mechanisms.

5. A microcomputer-based information system that automates and records collection and enforcement activities.

Establishing the amount of a day-fine unit involved determining one's net daily income expected as well as the number of one's dependents. Day-fine unit amounts would be scaled down according to increased numbers of dependents, for instance. Thus, every effort was made to distribute day fines equitably, according to one's ability to pay. This is in stark contrast with the idea of a fixed-fine system imposed on offenders, regardless of their earnings or numbers of dependents. The Staten Island experiment wanted to determine several things. First, were day fines higher or lower than fines previously assessed for similar offenses? Second, would the burden of calculating one's day fine amount deter fine collection? And third, would the new collection techniques used with day fines have any favorable impact on collection outcomes? The results were favorable. For instance, between April 1987 and March 1988, the total fine amounts imposed by the courts increased by 14 percent, while fines for average penal law offenses increased by 25 percent. Most important, collection rates under the new day-fine system rose to 85 percent. Capped collection amounts were those governed by statute. Thus, day-fine payments could not exceed statutory maximum fines for specific offenses, despite the fact that a day-fine amount may be generated in excess of this statutory maximum. An average of $440.83 was collected using uncapped day fines compared with $205.66 collected under pre-day-fine traditional fine methods.

The new collection techniques established by the Staten Island project has had the following advantages over traditional or more routine court procedures related to fine assessments and payment: (1) more extended terms for payment of the larger day fines; (2) fewer costly court appearances; and (3) fewer warrants for nonappearance at post-sentence hearings.

Considered significant in the Staten Island experiments was the individualized nature of fine assessments and collection. Clearly, determining one's fine according to their ability to pay and arranging for installment payments of these fines is a more profitable way of court operation as well as a means of enhancing offender accountability. Similar experiments have been conducted in Milwaukee with consonant results.

Community Service Orders

Increasingly, conditions are imposed on parolees that provide for fines and some amount of community service. Community service sentencing is one of the best examples of the use of parole as a means of achieving offender accountability. Under the **Victim and Witness Protection Act of 1982** (18 U.S.C. Sec. 3579-3580, 2007), community service orders were incorporated as an option in addition to incarceration at the federal level. One flaw of the Act was that it left unspecified when community service orders were to be imposed. Thus, judges could impose community service orders at the time of sentencing, or parole boards could make community service a provisional requirement for an inmate's early release. Victim advocates strongly urge that community service orders be an integral feature of the sentencing process. For instance, California has adopted community service orders as an integral part of their parole process (Stephens, 2001).

Community service means that parolees perform services for the state or community. The nature of community service to be performed is discretionary with the sentencing judge or paroling authority. In some jurisdictions, prisoners must perform a specified number of hours of community service such as lawn maintenance, plumbing and other similar repairs, or services that fit their particular skills. The philosophy underlying community service is more aligned with retribution than rehabilitation.

Forms of Community Service.   Community service is considered a punishment and is court-imposed. Many types of projects are undertaken by offenders as community service. Usually, these projects are supervised by POs or other officials, although reports are sometimes solicited from private individuals such as company managers or supervisors. A portion of offender earnings is allocated to victims as well as to the state or local public or private agencies overseeing the community services provided. In New Jersey, for example, community service orders include the following: assisting Community Food Banks throughout New Jersey with food drives; Adopt-a-Highway; the March of Dimes Walk-A-Thon; and assisting various Goodwill sites with sorting and cleaning donated items. Other community service projects include scraping, sanding, and digging; building renovations; maintenance of recreational areas; and assistance in the operation of governmental facilities and nonprofit charitable events.

The Effectiveness of Community Service.   Serious questions are raised by authorities about the effectiveness of community service and restitution as sentencing options or parole program requirements. The fact that offenders are released into their communities for the purpose of performing community service raises a **public risk** issue for some people, although those offenders ordinarily selected for community service are low risk and nonviolent. Other questions relate to the personal philosophies of judicial and correctional authorities, the offender eligibility and selection criteria used among jurisdictions, organizational arrangements, the nature of supervision over offenders performing community services, and how such services are evaluated. Community service is a just and fitting accompaniment to whatever sentence is imposed by judges or whatever conditions are established by paroling authorities when considering inmates for early release. The element of retribution is strong, and it is believed by some observers that offenders are better able to understand the significance of the harm they inflicted on others by their criminal acts.

Restitution

An increasingly important feature of probation programs is restitution. Restitution is the practice of requiring offenders to compensate crime victims for damages offenders may have inflicted. Several models of restitution have been described. These include:

The Financial/Community Service Model.   The Financial/Community Service model stresses the offender's financial accountability and community service to pay for damages inflicted upon victims and to defray a portion of the expenses of court prosecutions. It is becoming more commonplace for probationers and divertees to be ordered to pay some restitution to victims and to perform some type of community service. Community service may involve clean-up activities in municipal parks, painting projects involving graffiti removal, cutting courthouse lawns, or any other constructive project that can benefit the community. These community service sentences are imposed by judges. Probation officers are largely responsible for overseeing the efforts of convicted offenders in fulfilling their community service obligations. These sentencing provisions are commonly called **community-service orders**.

Community-service orders are symbolic restitution, involving redress for victims, less severe sanctions for offenders, offender rehabilitation, reduction of demands on the criminal justice system, and a reduction of the need for vengeance in a society, or a combination of these factors. Community-service orders are found in many different countries and benefit the community directly. Furthermore, where convicted offenders are indigent or unemployed, community service is a way of paying their fines and court costs. Some of the chief benefits of community service are: (1) the community benefits because some form of restitution is paid; (2) offenders benefit because they are given an opportunity to rejoin their communities in law-abiding, responsible roles; and (3) the courts benefit because sentencing alternatives are provided. Usually, between 50 and 200 hours of community service might be required for any particular convicted offender.

The Victim–Offender Mediation Model.   The **Victim–Offender Mediation model** focuses on victim–offender reconciliation. Alternative dispute resolution is used as a mediating ground for resolving differences or disputes between victims and perpetrators. Usually, third-party arbiters, such as judges, lawyers, or public appointees, can meet with offenders and their victims and work out mutually satisfactory arrangements whereby victims can be compensated for their losses or injuries.

The Victim/Reparations Model.   The **Victim/Reparations model** stresses that offenders should compensate their victims directly for their offenses. Many states have provisions that provide **reparations** or financial payments to victims under a Crime Victims Reparations Act. The Act establishes a state-financed program of reparations to persons who suffer personal injury and to dependents of persons killed as the result of certain criminal conduct. In many jurisdictions, a specially constituted board determines, independent of court adjudication, the existence of a crime, the damages caused, and other elements necessary for reparation. Reparations cover such economic losses as medical expenses, rehabilitative and occupational retraining expenses, loss of earnings, and the cost of actual substitute services. Restitution can heighten accountability and result in a reduction in recidivism among offenders. However, if restitution is not properly implemented by the court or carefully supervised, it serves little deterrent purpose.

PAROLE BOARDS AND EARLY-RELEASE DECISION MAKING

Parole Boards, Sentencing Alternatives, and the Get-Tough Movement

By 2006, most states had changed their sentencing provisions (Champion, 2007). In many instances, these changes in sentencing provisions significantly limited the discretionary authority of parole boards to grant prisoners early release. By 2005 12 states and the federal government had abolished parole in favor of determinate sentencing (Champion, 2005). Nevertheless, all states continue to use parole boards for those offenders sentenced under indeterminate sentencing and prior to parole's abolishment in specified jurisdictions.

Maine was the first state to abolish parole in 1976. Other states abolished parole in later years: Minnesota (1982), Florida (1983), Washington and the Federal Bureau of Prisons (1984), Oregon (1989), Delaware (1990), Kansas (1993), Arizona and North Carolina (1994), Virginia (1995), Ohio (1996), and Wisconsin (1999) (Champion, 2005). The primary reason given for abolishing parole in these jurisdictions was to remove early-release authority from parole boards, which tended to exhibit discrimination and often used extralegal factors in the parole-granting process. Furthermore, critics of parole believed that many offenders were being released too early. Thus, whenever parole boards released inmates short of serving their full sentences, these decisions were opposed by many citizens. Interestingly, since parole has been abolished in various states, the amount of time actually served by inmates in these states has decreased through the accumulation of good-time credits under determinate and guidelines-based sentencing. The question of abolishing parole boards in any jurisdiction is a hotly contested issue and one not likely resolvable in the near future.

Parole Board Composition and Diversity

Much diversity exists in the composition of parole boards in the United States. Most parole board members, whether full or part time, are governor-appointed. There are no special qualifications for parole board membership in most jurisdictions (Paparozzi, 2006). Some parole board members might be former correctional officers or prison superintendents, while others might be retired judges, school teachers, or university professors.

Massachusetts probably has the most stringent criteria for parole board membership compared with other jurisdictions. Members of the Massachusetts Parole Board must possess a bachelor's degree and five or more years of experience in corrections, law enforcement, social work, or other related field. One parole board member must be an attorney, while another must be a physician. States such as Texas, Oregon, and North Dakota do not require their parole board members to possess special qualifications. Since governors make parole board appointments in most jurisdictions, membership on these boards is largely political.

Parole boards are known by different names, depending on the jurisdiction. The diversity of names given to parole boards is shown in Table 9.1.

Functions of Parole Boards

The primary functions of parole boards are to:

1. Evaluate prison inmates who are eligible for parole and act on their application to approve or deny parole.
2. Convene to determine whether a parolee's parole should be revoked on the basis of alleged parole violations.
3. Evaluate juveniles to determine their eligibility for release from detention.
4. Grant pardons or a **commutation** of sentences to prisoners, where mitigating circumstances or new information is presented that was not considered at trial.

TABLE 9.1

Parole Boards for Federal and State Jurisdictions, 2006

State	2006 Parole Board Name
Alabama	Board of Pardons and Paroles (3 full-time members; governor-appointed)
Alaska	Board of Parole (5 part-time members; governor-appointed)
Arizona	Board of Executive Clemency (5 full-time members; governor-appointed)
Arkansas	Post-Prison Transfer Board (7 members, 3 full time, 4 part time; independent)
California	Board of Prison Terms (7 full-time members; governor-appointed)
Colorado	Board of Parole (7 full-time members; governor-appointed)
Connecticut	Board of Parole (12 part-time members, chairman full time; governor-appointed)
Delaware	Board of Parole (1 full-time, 4 part-time members; governor appointed)
District of Columbia	U.S. Parole Commission (7 full-time members; appointed by U.S. Attorney General)
Florida	Parole Commission (3 full-time members; governor-appointed)
Georgia	Board of Pardons and Paroles (5 full-time members; autonomous)
Hawaii	Paroling Authority (3 full-time, 2 part-time members, 1 full-time chairman; governor-appointed)
Idaho	Commission of Pardons and Parole (5 part-time members; appointed by Board of Corrections)
Illinois	Prisoner Review Board (12 full-time members; governor-appointed)
Indiana	Parole Board (5 full-time members; governor-appointed)
Iowa	Board of Parole (5 full-time members; governor-appointed)
Kansas	Parole Board (4 full-time members; governor-appointed)
Kentucky	Parole Board (8 full-time members; governor-appointed)
Louisiana	Board of Parole (7 full-time members; governor-appointed)
Maine	Parole Board (5 part-time members; governor-appointed; hears only cases pre–April 1976)
Maryland	Parole Commission (8 full-time members; appointed by Secretary of Public Safety and Correctional Services)
Massachusetts	Parole Board (6 full-time members; governor-appointed)
Michigan	Parole Board (10 full-time unclassified employees; appointed by Director of the Department of Corrections)
Minnesota	Board of Pardons (3 full-time members: governor, chief justice, attorney general) Hearings and Release Unit (8 full-time officers set terms of supervised release for adults and parole for juveniles)
Mississippi	Parole Board (5 full-time members; governor-appointed)
Missouri	Board of Probation and Parole (6 full-time members; governor-appointed)
Montana	Board of Pardons (3 part-time and 2 auxiliary members; governor-appointed)
Nebraska	Board of Parole (5 full-time members; governor-appointed)
Nevada	Board of Parole Commissioners (7 full-time members; governor-appointed)
New Hampshire	Board of Parole (7 part-time members; governor-appointed)
New Jersey	Parole Board (9 full-time members; governor-appointed)
New Mexico	Adult Parole Board (4 full-time members; governor-appointed)
New York	Board of Parole (19 full-time members; governor-appointed)
North Carolina	Post-Release Supervision and Parole Commission (5 full-time commissioners; governor-appointed)
North Dakota	Parole Board (3 part-time members; governor-appointed)
Ohio	Adult Parole Authority (12 full-time members; 3 chief hearing officers; 19 hearing officers; 24 parole board parole officers; appointed by Director of Department)
Oklahoma	Pardon and Parole Board (5 part-time members, 3 appointed by governor, 1 by Court of Criminal Appeals, and 1 by Supreme Court)

State	2006 Parole Board Name
Oregon	Board of Parole and Post-Prison Supervision (3 full-time members; governor-appointed)
Pennsylvania	Board of Probation and Parole (5 full-time members; governor-appointed)
Rhode Island	Parole Board (6 part-time members; governor-appointed)
South Carolina	Board of Paroles and Pardons (7 part-time members; governor-appointed)
South Dakota	Board of Pardons and Paroles (7 part-time members; independent and responsible to Department of Corrections)
Tennessee	Board of Paroles (7 full-time members; governor-appointed)
Texas	Board of Pardons and Paroles (18 full-time members; convene in 3-member panels; independent)
Utah	Board of Pardons and Parole (5 full-time members; governor-appointed)
Vermont	Board of Parole (5 part-time members; governor-appointed)
Virginia	Parole Board (5 full-time members; governor-appointed)
Washington	Indeterminate Sentence Review Board (3 part-time members, governor-appointed; determines parole for offenders sentenced prior to July 1984)
West Virginia	Parole Board (5 full-time members; governor-appointed)
Wisconsin	Parole Commission (5 full-time members; governor-appointed)
Wyoming	Board of Parole (7 full-time members; governor-appointed)
Federal	U.S. Parole Commission (7 full-time members; appointed by U.S. Attorney General)

Sources: Compiled by author from the American Correctional Association, *Probation and Parole Directory 2006.* Lanham, MD: American Correctional Association, 2006.

5. Make provisions for the supervision of adult offenders placed on parole; to establish supervisory agencies and select parole officers to monitor offender behavior.

6. Provide investigative and supervisory services to smaller jurisdictions within the state.

7. Grant reprieves in death sentence cases and to commute death penalties.

8. Restore full civil and political rights to parolees and others on **conditional release** including probationers.

9. Review disparate sentences and make recommendations to the governor for clemency.

10. Review the pardons and executive clemency decisions made by the governor (American Correctional Association, 2006).

Most parole boards make parole decisions exclusively. In some jurisdictions, several additional functions, such as sentence commutations and reprieves from death sentences, are performed, either according to statute or at the pleasure of the governor. In other jurisdictions, the paroling authority is vested in agencies independent of the governor.

Parole Board Standards

Parole boards evolve certain standards by which to function, subject to legislative approval. For instance, the Connecticut Parole Board has articulated the following standards:

1. The nature and circumstances of inmate offenses and their current attitudes toward them.

2. The inmate's prior record and parole adjustment if paroled previously.

3. Inmate's attitude toward family members, the victim, and authority in general.

4. The institutional adjustment of inmates, including their participation in vocational/educational programs while incarcerated.

5. Inmate's employment history and work skills.

6. Inmate's physical, mental, and emotional condition as determined from interviews and other diagnostic information available.

7. Inmate's insight into the causes of his or her own criminal behavior in the past.

8. Inmate's personal efforts to find solutions to personal problems such as alcoholism, drug dependency, and need for educational training or developing special skills.

9. The adequacy of the inmate's parole plan, including planned place of residence, social acquaintances, and employment program (Connecticut Board of Parole, 2006).

Parole Board Decision Making and Inmate Control

Parole board decision making is influenced by many factors. One of these factors is prison overcrowding. Dramatic increases in parole supervision have been observed, as the number of parole releases and revocation hearings have grown substantially over the years (Ryan, 2006). The aims of parole boards are similar to those of sentencing: treatment, incapacitation, deterrence, and deserts. A significant question for parole boards is determining when it is appropriate to release inmates. Some states have attempted to objectify parole guidelines. However, many parole boards oppose adopting objective parole guidelines. One reason is the fear of losing a certain amount of control or discretionary authority over inmate releases. Also, parole boards do not know which variables are most crucial in making the best early-release decisions for specific parole-eligible inmates. Using risk-screening instruments for determining which offenders should be paroled have exhibited unimpressive results, for instance (Champion, 1994).

Cases that Parole Boards Must Review

Many parole board decisions involve property offenders, although persons convicted of murder, robbery, assault, rape, and other violent crimes face parole boards as well. Notorious inmates, such as Sirhan Sirhan, convicted killer of Robert Kennedy; Charles Manson, Patricia Krenwinkle, Leslie Van Houten, convicted murderers of heiress Abigail Folger and actress Sharon Tate and others; convicted murderer James Richardson, who murdered his seven children by using a poison insecticide in Arcadia, Florida, on October 25, 1967; and confessed serial killer Joel Rifkin, who murdered at least 13 prostitutes on Long Island and in upstate New York between 1990 and 1993, are among those inmates considered parole-eligible.

Cases That Parole Boards Do Not Have to Review

Ordinarily parole boards do not have to review cases where offenders have been sentenced to life-without-parole terms or death. However, under certain circumstances and in particular jurisdictions, parole boards may be asked by inmates to have their sentences commuted from life-without-parole to life, which is of considerable significance to the inmate. If the parole board is authorized to make such a change, then a "life sentence" makes the offender parole-eligible and then the parole board must eventually hear the case and decide whether to grant early release. Only exceptional circumstances must exist when parole boards make these types of decisions. Not all parole boards have this type of authority. There is considerable variation among state parole boards in this matter.

Are All Offenders Eligible for Parole Granted Parole?

Additionally when offenders do become eligible for parole, this does not mean parole will automatically be granted by the parole board. Parole boards have considerable discretionary power, and in many jurisdictions, they have absolute discretion over an inmate's early-release potential. In fact, when federal courts have been petitioned to intervene and challenge parole board actions, the decisions of parole boards have prevailed (*Tarlton and Clark,* 1971). It is helpful to review briefly some of the more important factors influencing parole board decision making. In deciding whether to grant parole or not grant parole for given inmates, the following factors are considered:

1. The commission of serious disciplinary infractions while confined
2. The nature and pattern of previous convictions
3. The adjustment to previous probation, parole, and/or incarceration
4. The facts and circumstances of the offense
5. The aggravating and mitigating factors surrounding the offense
6. Participation in institutional programs that might have led to the improvement of problems diagnosed at admission or during incarceration
7. Documented changes in attitude toward self or others
8. Documentation of personal goals and strengths or motivation for law-abiding behavior
9. Parole plans
10. Inmate statements suggesting the likelihood that the inmate will not commit future offenses
11. Court statements about the reasons for the sentence.

When parole boards grant inmates parole, the parole program is always conditional and subject to various rules and regulations. If the parole board denies parole to inmates, the reasons for these denials must be specified in writing and given to the inmate. Supposedly, this written justification for parole denial gives the inmate an opportunity to improve in those areas cited by the board as unsatisfactory or unfavorable. Rehearings in every jurisdiction with parole boards are conducted at regular intervals, such as every one or two years.

Parole Board Orientations

Decisions made by parole boards are classified into six categories. These categories reflect a particular value system. These are the (1) jurist value system,

(2) sanctioner value system, (3) treater value system, (4) controller value system, (5) citizen value system, and (6) regulator value system. The **jurist value system** regards parole decisions as a natural part of criminal justice where fairness and equity predominate. Emphasized are an inmate's rights, and parole board members strive to be sensitive to due process. The **sanctioner value system** equates the seriousness of the offense with the amount of time served. In some respects, this is closely connected with the just-deserts philosophy. The **treater value system** is rehabilitative in orientation, and decisions are made in the context of what might most benefit the offender if parole is granted. Thus, participation in various educational or vocational programs, therapy or encounter groups, restitution, and other types of conditions might accompany one's early release. The **controller value system** emphasizes the functions of parole supervision and monitoring. The conditions are established that increase the degree of control over the offender. The controller value system views offender incapacitation or severe restrictions of freedom as desirable, because this system is most concerned with the risk posed to the public by the offender's early release.

The **citizen value system** is concerned with appealing to public interests and seeing that community expectations are met by making appropriate early-release decisions. How will the public react to releasing certain offenders short of serving their full terms? Will public good be served by such decisions? The **regulator value system** is directed toward inmate reactions to parole board decisions. How will current inmates react to those decisions in view of their own circumstances? Will the parole supervision system be undermined or enhanced as the result of parole board decision making?

Developing and Implementing Objective Parole Criteria

Is it possible to establish objective parole criteria to govern all parole board decision making? Objective parole criteria would insulate parole board members from criticisms of racism when releasing disproportionately large numbers of offenders of particular races or ethnic backgrounds. Parole board member liability would be limited in those instances where offenders are granted early release who are especially dangerous and pose the greatest risk to their communities. **Objective parole criteria** have been compared with determinate sentencing policies, while traditional parole criteria have been equated with indeterminate sentencing systems. Among the advantages of objective parole criteria are:

1. Inmates know their presumptive release dates within several months of their incarceration.
2. The paroling authority is bound or obligated to meet the presumptive release date.
3. The paroling authority uses scores consisting of an inmate's criminal history and offense severity to determine time ranges for parole release.
4. The paroling authority uses a composite group score representing criminal histories of similar offenders to predict parole success.

However, objective parole criteria are used to restrict parole board discretionary power and flexibility. Therefore, while fairness to offenders and parole board accountability are increased by making the parole release decision-making process more explicit and consistent, there are some undesirable, unanticipated consequences. For example, the Florida Parole Commission implemented new objective parole criteria in 1980. Prior to 1980, adult inmates of Florida's prisons had filed an average of 400 civil lawsuits annually. After the objective criteria went into effect, the number of lawsuits increased to more than 1,800 per year. The Florida Parole Commission's legal department had to increase its staff of attorneys from two to seven. Florida inmate lawsuits involved primarily four issues directly related to the new objective parole criteria. First, inmates alleged that objective scoring system errors led to unfavorable classifications and unjustifiably longer incarceration terms. Second, inmates claimed they originally had been placed in the wrong level of offense severity, often stemming from an erroneous interpretation of their plea agreements. Third, the inmates claimed parole board members inconsistently extended or shortened their incarceration length by either considering or failing to consider certain aggravating circumstances such as using a weapon during the commission of the crime or causing serious injury to victims. The fourth issue alleged parole board failure to consider mitigating circumstances that would lessen the length of incarceration. All of these issues seemingly could be remedied by close monitoring of all parole board decision making and a demand for fairness and consistency in the application of objective parole criteria (Champion, 2005).

Interest in devising consistent and objective early release criteria is probably as old as parole itself. Most of the popular and more scientific methods for devising predictive criteria have been developed since the late 1960s, however. In 1972, the United States Parole Commission started to use an actuarial device in predicting parole success of federal prisons. By the early 1980s, every state had either devised a system or was using one originated by another jurisdiction whereby parole decision making could be objectified (Schlager and Robbins, 2006).

Theoretically at least, the technology exists that can classify offenders accurately on the basis of their potential risk to public safety, social service, educational and vocational needs, and individual behavioral profiles. However, many paroling bodies have not used this technology. One reason is the low predictive power and insufficient validation of prediction instruments that have been devised. Another reason is that despite using objective criteria, recidivism rates among parolees continue to be 65 percent or higher. Some states have attempted to adopt objective parole criteria, however. The Ohio Parole Board uses the following criteria for its early-release decision making:

1. Current offense and details of the crime
2. Prior record: felonies–misdemeanors–juvenile
3. Supervision experiences: parole–furlough–probation
4. Institution adjustment: job assignment–work evaluation–rule infractions
5. Substance abuse program participation
6. Vocational or academic training
7. Personality evaluation: I.Q.–highest grade completed
8. Psychological reports
9. Psychiatric reports
10. Personal history factors: marital status–employment history–work skills–special problems
11. Parole plan: living arrangements–employment plans

12. Community attitude: prosecutor's recommendation–judge's recommendation–police or sheriff's recommendation–victim's statement

13. Detainers

14. Type and number of prior hearings

15. Results of prehearing conference with Case Manager or Unit Manager (Ohio Department of Correction and Rehabilitation, 2006).

These criteria are only guidelines, as noted by the Ohio Adult Parole Authority. Therefore, there may be departures that are based on the degree of aggravation or mitigation accompanying any eligible inmate's early-release request. It is Ohio's experience that using these criteria in conjunction with several other measures will increase their Adult Parole Authority effectiveness to about 75 percent. In short, Ohio authorities believe that 75 percent of their early-release decision making with these guidelines will result in successful decision making. Viewed another way, Ohio authorities expect no more than a 25 percent degree of recidivism among those paroled. Ohio bases their guidelines system on five major components. These components include:

1. *Risk Instrument.* The risk instrument is critical to the guidelines system. It looks at several factors dealing with an inmate's prior criminal history including the number of probations, paroles, and revocations. Age at first felony conviction and substance abuse history are also related to risk assessed points. The risk level totals equal 1, 2, or 3. The higher the number, the higher the risk.

2. *Offense Score.* Included in the guideline system are several offenses designated as "Endangering Offenses." If an inmate has ever been convicted of an Endangering Offense, either a juvenile or adult, one point is assessed toward the total score.

3. *Institutional Score.* The Parole Board will make a determination of the inmate's institutional adjustment at the time of the hearing. If the inmate is now serving or has recently served time in Disciplinary Control, Local Control, or Administrative Control, one (1) point will be assessed toward the total score.

4. *Aggregate Score.* The sum total of the Risk Score, the Offense Score, and the Institution Score equals the Aggregate Score.

5. *Matrix.* The Matrix is a grid containing twenty-four (24) cell divisions. Each cell contains the guidelines procedure into which an inmate is placed and a continuance range if the decision is not to release. The horizontal axis of the grid is the "Aggregate Score" 1–5. The vertical axis is the felony level reflecting the inmate's sentence. Sentences range from fourth degree to life (Ohio Department of Correction and Rehabilitation, 2006).

Each state has devised independent criteria governing early-release decision making for its parole board. All of these criteria are related to a degree, although there are significant variations. For example, Massachusetts has devised a parole risk instrument. For instance, the Massachusetts Parole Board uses a Release Risk Classification Instrument consisting of (1) number of returns to higher custody since Controlling Effective Date of Commitment; (2) custody standing prior to the Controlling Effective Date of Commitment; (3) total number of parole revocations; (4) number of adult convictions for property offenses; (5) number of charges for a person offense as a juvenile; (6) age at release hearing; and (7) evidence of heroin, opiate, or crack cocaine use. Both the number of returns to higher custody and age have maximum scores of "6" for four or more returns to higher custody and being 23 years of age or younger. One's custody standing and evidence of drug use each contribute 2 points, while the other factors are weighted by 1 point each. A high score of 19 points is possible. Such a person might be a 22-year-old cocaine addict who has prior offenses of burglary as an adult and robbery as a juvenile, who has been returned to a higher custody level on four previous occasions, has one previous parole revocation, and was incarcerated prior to the Controlling Effective Date. A three-part scale is used: 0–4 = low risk, 5–10 = moderate risk, and 11+ = high risk.

Utah uses the following factors to determine one's parole eligibility: (1) age at first arrest; (2) prior juvenile record; (3) prior adult arrests; (4) correctional supervision history; (5) supervision risk; (6) percentage of time employed in last 12 months, prior to incarceration; (7) alcohol usage problems; (8) drug usage problems; (9) attitude (motivation to change, willing to accept responsibility); (10) address changes during last 12 months (prior to incarceration); (11) family support; and (12) conviction or juvenile adjudication for assaultive offense in last five years.

Age, prior record, and drug/alcohol dependencies are obviously considered significant risk factors, at least for these instruments developed in these particular jurisdictions. In fact, these are critical components of most scales examined. Many jurisdictions believe that one's employment history and attitude (measured different ways) are also crucial to good parole decision making. The rationale for including these different components is grounded in considerable empirical research. We have already seen that many studies have focused on recidivism and the characteristics of recidivists. Most of these studies have provided us with the bases for making actuarial predictions for various offender aggregates. Thus, younger offenders have higher recidivism rates than older offenders. The age at which the onset of criminal behavior occurs is an important predictor. The earlier the onset of criminal conduct, the more likely recidivism will occur.

Similar to initial classifications conducted by prison officials and subsequent reassessments of inmates, parole boards also utilize reassessments of client risk after parolees have functioned for several months in their respective parole programs. Some jurisdictions have established rather specific prediction schemes based on some or all of these criteria. For example, Michigan has created five risk groupings based primarily on one's age, marital status, and previous institutional conduct. These are shown below.

Risk Group

Very High Risk: Instant offense of rape, robbery, or homicide and serious misconduct or security segregation and first arrest before 15th birthday.

High Risk: Instant offense of rape, robbery, or homicide and serious misconduct and age of first arrest was 15 or over.

Middle Risk: Instant offense either rape, robbery, or homicide and no serious misconduct; or instant offense not rape, robbery, or homicide (may be other assaultive crime) and no reported felony while juvenile and never been married at time of instant offense.

Very Low Risk: Instant offense not rape, robbery, or homicide and no reported felony while juvenile and not serving on other assaultive crime and has been married (Michigan Department of Corrections, 2006).

Risk assessment devices are being used by most states, including California, South Carolina, Oregon, Alaska, Illinois, Louisiana, and Tennessee (Ratansi et al., 2006). The Council's survey of existing or currently used instruments indicates the following factors that most often appear as risk predictors:

1. Number of prior convictions
2. Number of prior incarcerations
3. Age at first commitment, conviction, or arrest
4. Drug abuse history
5. Convictions for burglary, forgery, theft
6. Alcohol abuse history
7. Employment history
8. School adjustment
9. Probation/parole history
10. Peer involvement

Regardless of the predictive utility of these items, the Council has exhibited a failure rate for various sample predictions of about 30 percent. According to the Council, their primary problem is that accurate data concerning prospective parolees is often difficult to obtain. Therefore, predictions of success for different offender aggregates are always tainted by the unknown influence of extraneous variables.

SALIENT FACTOR SCORES AND PREDICTING PAROLEE SUCCESS ON PAROLE

Although a weighting system for parole prognosis was developed by **Ernest W. Burgess** of the University of Chicago in 1928, the development of currently applicable objective parole decision-making guidelines can be traced to the pioneering work of Don Gottfredson and Leslie Wilkins, leaders of the Parole Decision-Making Project in the early 1970s. At that time, the National Council on Crime and Delinquency and the United States Parole Commission (originally the United States Board of Parole) were interested in parole decision making and solicited the assistance of social scientists to examine various criteria involved in early-release decisions. The Parole Decision-Making Project led to the adoption of a preliminary set of guidelines that provided parole board members with specific criteria to assess the successfulness of granting parole to various offenders. Categories of offenders were established by these guidelines and based, in part, on a ranking of **offense severity** as well as a salient factor score. A salient factor score is a numerical classification that supposedly predicts the probability of a parolee's success if parole is granted.

Ideally, the **salient factor score (SFS)** was designed to assist parole board members to make fair, objective, and just parole decisions. Unusual departures from these guidelines by parole boards were to be accompanied by written rationales outlining the reasons for such departures. In 1973, the United States Parole Commission formally adopted these parole decision guidelines and SFSs were used in all federal parole hearings. This was largely the result of a federal court order for the United States Board of Parole to articulate specifically its policies for granting parole (*Childs v. United States Board of Parole*, 1973). Subsequently, the Federal Bureau of Prisons devised several prediction devices to determine early release for parole-eligible federal inmates. One of these devices is the Salient Factor Score, or SFS, 81. An earlier version was the SFS 76.

The Federal Bureau of Prisons devised the **Salient Factor Score 81 (SFS 81)** for determining parole eligibility or, more recently, supervised release, for its eligible inmates. The Salient Factor Score Index consists of six criteria, including (1) prior convictions/delinquency adjudications; (2) prior commitments of more than 30 days (either as an adult or as a juvenile); (3) age at current offense/prior commitments; (4) recent commitment-free period (three years); (5) Probation/Parole/Confinement/Escape status violator this time; and (6) heroin/opiate dependence. Eligible federal inmates receive up to 3 points for no prior convictions or delinquency adjudications, up to 2 points for no prior commitments of more than 30 days (as either an adult or a juvenile), up to 2 points for being age 26 or older at the time of the current offense, and 1 point each for no prior commitment (in last three years), no probation/parole/confinement/escape status at time of current offense, and no history of opiate addiction. Thus, federal inmates can score a possible 10 points and minimize their parole risk status. Scores of zero (0) or close to zero mean higher or highest parole risk.

At the federal level, the salient factor score was made up of seven criteria and was refined in 1976. This was referred to as **SFS 76**. In August 1981, the salient factor scoring instrument underwent further revision and a new, six-factor predictive device, **SFS 81,** was constructed. A comparison of the revised SFS 81 with its previous counterpart (SFS 76) was made according to validity, stability, simplicity, scoring reliability, and certain ethical concerns. Both instruments appeared to have similar predictive characteristics, although the revised device possesses greater scoring reliability. Of even greater significance is that SFS 81 places considerable weight on the extent and recency of an offender's criminal history. Up to seven points can be earned by having no prior convictions or adjudications (adult or juvenile), no prior commitments of more than 30 days, and being 26 years of age or older at the time of the current offense (with certain exceptions). Figure 9.3 shows the six-item federal Salient Factor Score instrument, **SFS 81**. Classification systems, such as the SFS 81 instrument, are simply models. These models are assigned names such as the National Institute of Corrections Prison Classification Model or the Iowa Risk Assessment Model.

Several dimensions of the SFS 81 are worth noting. First, great emphasis is placed on one's prior juvenile record. Items 1, 2, and 4 refer to prior behaviors of parolees that may have involved their juvenile pasts. A total of six points on this 10-point scale may be accumulated, depending on whether one has a juvenile record. Furthermore, age is considered significant. The younger one enters a life of crime, the more seriously it is regarded. There are sound sociological and psychological reasons for this assumption. Thus, one's juvenile record plays a heavy role in determining one's subsequent risk to society. Finally, the SFS 81 contains information about drug use, specifically heroin or opiate dependence. Therefore, one's youthfulness when committing offenses, prior juvenile adjudications, and involvement with heroin or opiates serve to undermine one's parole chances.

SALIENT FACTOR SCORE INDEX

1. Prior convictions/adjudications (adult or juvenile):
   None (3 points)
   One (2 points)
   Two or three (1 point)
   Four or more (0 points)   _____

2. Prior commitments of more than 30 days (adult or juvenile):
   None (2 points)
   One or two (1 point)
   Three or more (0 points)   _____

3. Age at current offense/prior commitments:
   25 years of age or older (2 points)
   20–25 years of age (1 point)
   19 years of age or younger (0 points)   _____

4. Recent commitment-free period (three years):
   No prior commitment of more than 30 days (adult or
   juvenile) or released to the community from last such
   commitment at least three years prior to the commencement
   of the current offense (1 point)
   Otherwise (0 points)   _____

5. Probation/parole/confinement/escape status violator this time:
   Neither on probation, parole, confinement, or escape
   status at the time of the current offense, nor committed as a
   probation, parole, confinement, or escape status violator this
   time (1 point)
   Otherwise (0 points)   _____

6. Heroin/opiate dependence:
   No history of heroin/opiate dependence (1 point)
   Otherwise (0 points)   _____
   Total score =   _____

FIGURE 9.3   Salient Factor Score Index, SFS 81

Source: U.S. Parole Commission, *Rules and Procedures Manual*. Washington, DC: U.S. Parole Commission, 1985. Updated by author 2006.

The SFS 81 is scored in the following manner:

Raw Score	Parole Prognosis
0–3	Poor
4–5	Fair
6–7	Good
8–10	Very Good

Thus, the larger the score, the better the prognosis for parole. Federal paroling authorities are not bound by the results of this instrument. Other factors, such as the offenders's PSI report, together with information from victims or victims' relatives, are considered as well. Judicial recommendations and commentary are also available. One's SFS score alone does not determine one's parole eligibility.

GRANTING OR DENYING PAROLE

Parole boards of all states using parole as an early-release mechanism always consider one's prior institutional behavior, the seriousness of the conviction offense, one's parole plan, the demeanor of the parole-eligible offender, and a host of other factors in making their decisions. Each case is different and requires differential consideration of various factors that may or may not influence one's successfulness on parole if that is the parole board's decision. Figures 9.4 and 9.5 are two examples taken from actual closed parole files from the Texas Department of Criminal Justice, illustrating respectively a successful and an unsuccessful parole request. The names of the inmates and other parties have been changed, as well as the dates and other specific identifying information for purposes of confidentiality.

These cases show that a great deal of information is compiled and factor into early-release decision making. The impressions and recommendations from parole officers who are assigned to make individual assessments of prospective parole-eligible offenders carry great weight with the parole board. In cases where inmates

---

Successful Parole Request
TEXAS DEPARTMENT OF CRIMINAL JUSTICE

INSTITUTIONAL DIVISION PAROLE CASE SUMMARY

UNIT: Ferguson   **PMA ( )**   **PPT ( )**   **PIA ( )**   **"3g"(N)**

NAME: OWENBY, Richard Allen   **TDC:** 68491936   **DATE:** 12-3-06   **CODE:** 12/00

MINIMUM EXPIRATION DATE: 1-13-08   **MAXIMUM EXPIRATION DATE:** 7-12-11

CALENDAR TIME SERVED: 10 Yrs 8 Mos   **ON:** 20 Years   **DOCKET:** 5-04

PROPOSED RELEASE PLAN: **DISTRIBUTION:**   Central Office

(1) Grandmother and Sister: Region I
Matilda Cummings & Tanisha Jones,   Dallas District

4159 1st Avenue,
Huntsville IPO
Dallas, Dallas County, Texas 75210.
Telephone number: (214) 555-3111,
Sister: (214) 555-8645.
(2) None.

HALFWAY HOUSES: Dallas, Forth Worth, or Waco, Texas.

JOB/SKILLS: Will seek employment as a cook. Claims prior experience.

OTHER/COMMENTS: None.

RESTITUTION: None.

REPORTING INSTRUCTIONS: **IN PERSON:**   **TELEPHONE:**   **LETTER:**

FIGURE 9.4 Successful Parole Request

DPO: **DISTRICT:**   **COUNTY:**   **APPROVED:**

COMMITMENT DATA INFORMATION

COUNTY	CAUSE #	OFFENSE:	SENTENCE:	DATE:
Dallas	F93-415-IU	AGG ROBBERY W/ DEADLY WPN (5-10-92)	20 YEARS	8-28-96

TOTAL SENTENCE: 20 YEARS   **SENTENCE BEGIN DATE:** 7-15-96

AGE: 31 (12-13-75)   **RACE:** Black   **SEX:** M   **HEIGHT:** 6'2″   **WEIGHT:** 210

EDUCATION: GED

DETAINERS: None.

PAROLE SUBJECT TO APPROVED RELEASE PLAN

This parole approval is not effective or final until a formal parole agreement is entered into and signed by the inmate and the State of Texas acting through the Board of Pardons and Paroles. The approval may be withdrawn by the Board or the Governor at any time prior to the acceptance and execution of the formal parole agreement.

PAROLE PANEL ACTION:

_____   _____

BOARD MEMBER'S INITIALS   **DATE**

PAROLE IS HEREBY ADOPTED AND APPROVED UPON ISSUANCE OF PAROLE CERTIFICATE AND EXECUTION OF PAROLE AGREEMENT.

CRIMINAL HISTORY: TP: 0;   **OP:** 0;   **TR:** 0;   **OR:** 0.

JUVENILE: None.

ADULT PROBATIONS: None.

ADULT INCARCERATIONS: None.

OTHER ARRESTS:
Attempt to Commit Capital Murder on a Police Officer (1), dismissed (1).

INSTANT OFFENSE SUMMARY:

Aggravated Robbery With a Deadly Weapon: On 5-10-95, in the daytime in Dallas, Texas, the subject and Michael Wilson (Life sentence, TDC-ID, Coffield Unit) were allegedly walking down a bike trail in a city park. A statement from the victim states that Wilson pulled a knife and allegedly threatened the victim. The victim states that they became involved in a fight and Wilson cut the victim on the wrist and on the chin. The victim allegedly also pulled a knife but claims that he did not use the weapon. However, the subject states that he and codefendant were accused of allegedly hiding in bushes and then jumping out at the victim who was riding the bicycle and demanded his bicycle. According to the victim, he refused to give up is bicycle and Wilson became infuriated and tried to stab the victim. Wilson allegedly cut the victim's throat. When witnesses came on the scene, the subject and codefendant fled on foot. They then apparently threw the knives used in the offense in some bushes and officers recovered both knives, one of which had fresh blood on it. The

FIGURE 9.4   (*Continued*)

subject states that he and the codefendant were arrested later that day hiding in some business near the scene. According to the subject, the victim was not injured that severely, however, he did require treatment at an emergency room. The subject states that he was released on bond for approximately three weeks and claims he was never arrested during this time. Rationale of Present Offense: "I didn't know it was happening."

Substance Abuse History:

Drugs: From the age of 15 until this incarceration, the subject admits to smoking approximately two marijuana cigarettes every other day. He denies the use of any other narcotics. He denies the sale of narcotics. He reports no drug treatment. He claims he was not under the influence of any drugs at the time of the Present Offense.

Alcohol: The subject denies the use of alcohol.

Physical/Mental: None.

Social History:

The subject claims he completed the 10th grade in public school. His longest employment was for two years as a barbeque cook for his uncle's restaurant on weekends. He attended public school during the week. During the last two years in society, he was employed in this capacity and was employed in this capacity at the time of the Present Offense. He reports no military history.

Institutional Adjustment:

The subject is an SAT III status assigned as a Dryer Operator in the laundry. He presently does not participate in any self-improvement programs. The subject completed his GED certificate from Adams School District on 4-90 (verified). He has had the following disciplinary cases: Failure to Complete Work (1); Refusing to Obey an Order (1); Possession of Contraband (2); Trafficking and Trading (1); and Refusing to Work (2), all of which were minor cases and he has lost no good time. He has had no furlough.

Impression Section:

Mr. Owenby is a 31-year-old first offender incarcerated for Aggravated Robbery with a Deadly Weapon sentenced to 20 years. Mr. Owenby initially was sentenced to 45 years; however, his case was overturned and the sentence was reduced from 45 years to 20. He reports no juvenile criminal history. He does report one other arrest for Capital Murder on a Police Officer; however, he claims this case was dismissed. Mr. Owenby admits to being involved in the Present Offense; however, he claims he was basically a bystander observing a fight. He claims that he was not involved in any robbery and there were no intentions of robbing the victim. He claims that the codefendant and the victim just got into a fight. Mr. Owenby had a good attitude and cooperated in this interview. Positive factors affecting Mr. Owenby's release would be his limited criminal history, he completed his GED certificate, and he plans to reside with his grandmother and sister while returning to employment as a cook for his uncle's restaurant. Negative factors affecting Mr. Owenby's release would be the nature and seriousness of the present offense. In addition, he does not report any serious substance abuse history. Mr. Owenby has been incarcerated since 1996. It appears likely that he may encounter adjustment problems upon release due to his rather long incarceration. It would appear that a pre-parole transfer to a halfway house would benefit Mr. Owenby's adjustment upon release. However, his present aggravated offense excludes him from this program. Perhaps he could still be considered for PPT due to the fact that he has no history of other type of assaultive convictions and the fact that he was limitedly involved in the Present Offense. In addition, Mr. Owenby's sentence was reduced from 45 years to 20 years. Mr. Owenby was counseled regarding the services offered by the Project RIO Office, that can assist him in job placement upon his release from prison.

SUBMITTED BY: Fred Drennon
Transitional case manager
DATE: 11-9-06

Result: Mr. Owenby was paroled subject to parole conditions.

FIGURE 9.4   (Continued)

Unsuccessful Parole Request

TEXAS DEPARTMENT OF CRIMINAL JUSTICE
BOARD OF PARDONS AND PAROLES CASE SUMMARY

UNIT: Coffield

NAME: JACOBS, Norman Kingsley   **TDC NO:** 43218   **DATE:** 10-14-06

MINIMUM EXPIRATION DATE: 10-6-05   **MAXIMUM EXPIRATION DATE:** 1-4-08

CALENDAR TIME SERVED: 3 Years   **ON:** 5 Years   **DOCKET:** 9-06   **EMS DATE:** 10-06

PROPOSED RELEASE PLAN: **DISTRIBUTION:**   Central Office
(1)   Mother, Mabel Jacobs   Region I
       2222 2nd Avenue   Dallas District
       Dallas, Dallas County, Texas 75211   Huntsville IPO
                                                                              Palestine IPO

HALFWAY HOUSES: Refused any choices as placement under any circumstances.

JOB/SKILLS: He will seek employment as a roofer.

OTHER/COMMENTS: None.

RESTITUTION: None.

REPORTING INSTRUCTIONS: **IN PERSON**   **TELEPHONE:**   **LETTER:**

                                DISTRICT: **COUNTY:**   **APPROVED**

COMMITMENT DATA INFORMATION

COUNTY:	CAUSE#:	OFFENSE:	SENTENCE:	DATE:	TYPE:
Dallas	F02-33315	AGG ROBBERY/W DEADLY WPN (9-19-02)	5 Years	12-1-05	

TOTAL SENTENCE: 5 Years   **SENTENCE BEGIN DATE:** 6-14-03
AGE: 26 (7-14-80)   **RACE:** White   **SEX:** M   **HEIGHT:** 5'11"   **WEIGHT:** 160
EDUCATION: 9th grade

DETAINERS: None.

PAROLE PANEL ACTION: _____   _____
                            BOARD MEMBER'S INITIALS   DATE

                            PAROLE DENIED

CRIMINAL HISTORY: TF-0; **OP**-0; **TE**-0; **OR**-0

JUVENILE: Detailed 13-15, Riot, released to parents; Theft (2), released to parents.

ADULT INCARCERATIONS: None.

FIGURE 9.5   Unsuccessful Parole Request

OTHER ARRESTS:

Mr. Jacobs admits to other arrests for: Unlawful Carrying Weapon and Violation of Controlled Substance Act, dismissed as part of plea bargain.

INSTANT OFFENSE SUMMARY:

AGGRAVATED ROBBERY WITH A DEADLY WEAPON: On 9-19-02, Mr. Jacobs is alleged to have taken the keys to the victim's vehicle by threatening him with a .38 caliber pistol. He fled the scene and was arrested approximately 6 hours later. Identification was made by the victim to the police and arrest was made by the license plate number. He was not released on bond. His rationale, "He loaned it to me."

SUBSTANCE ABUSE HISTORY:

DRUGS: Mr. Jacobs admits use of marijuana beginning at age 13 up to the time of incarceration on an occasional basis of approximately once or twice monthly. He also states he began using cocaine by injection and smoking at age 21 for approximately 2 years up to the time of incarceration. This was on a once or twice monthly basis. He denies sale of drugs or treatment for substance abuse.

ALCOHOL: Mr. Jacobs admits consumption of beer beginning at age 13 up to the time of incarceration. At the time of the Instant Offense, he states he had consumed approximately one-fifth of whiskey by drinking it with water over the last eight hours. He states he is not an alcoholic and also "I'm not going to stop drinking."

PHYSICAL/MENTAL:

PHYSICAL: TDC medical records and the inmate indicate he is diagnosed as having the following problems: high blood pressure, for which is prescribed Verapamil, 80mg, once daily; a sinus condition, for which is prescribed Pseudoephedrin (Actifed), one tablet twice daily; asthma condition, for which is prescribed Alupent Inhaler to be used as needed and Theador, 300mg, twice daily; a heart condition, for which he is prescribed Capoten, 25mg, twice daily; and an ulcer condition, for which is prescribed Tagamet, 400mg, twice daily. It is apparent that employment possibilities will be severely restricted due to these conditions.

MENTAL: TDC medical records contain a Psychological Examination dated 1-16-04. At that time, he was diagnosed as Schizophrenia, Paranoid Chronic with accompanying Depression and Alcohol Dependency. In the past, he has been prescribed Valium, and while in county jail, he was prescribed Mellaril. This was due to feeling depressed off and on for several years. File material contains reports of two suicide attempts by overdosing on various types of pills. This was apparently done to gain attention but the inmate states "I didn't care about living no more." Collateral contact with unit psychological staff shows that he is currently undergoing therapy consisting of listening to relaxation tapes. The length of time necessary for maximum benefit was not determined. Evaluation at the time of release may be necessary to determine if MHMR services are necessary upon his return to society.

SOCIAL HISTORY:

Mr. Jacobs completed the ninth grade in regular education. He has received no vocational training. His longest prior employment was for two years as a roofer. At the time of the Instant Offense, he reports being unemployed for the previous one year and was a roofer prior to that. He has no military history.

INSTITUTIONAL ADJUSTMENT:

Mr. Jacobs is a Line Class II inmate assigned as a Clerk to the Records Conversion Area. He is not participating in any educational, vocational, or character development programs. He has received no furloughs. He has received three minor rule infraction violations in addition to the following ones: On 2-2-05, he was placed in solitary confinement for Refusing to Obey Orders; On 3-30-05, he was placed in solitary confinement and reduced to SAT IV for use of Indecent or Vulgar Language. On 5-7-05, he was again cited for Refusing to Obey Orders and Threatening an Officer, at which time he was reduced to Line Class II and forfeited 40 days of good conduct time. He states that he did not threaten the officer and that the officer lied concerning the circumstances of the case.

FIGURE 9.5   *(Continued)*

IMPRESSION SECTION:

Mr. Jacobs is a 26-year-old offender at TDC for his first incarceration. He has attempted supervised release on two occasions, one resulting in success. His current incarceration is due to a probation revocation due to Failure to Report and Failure to Pay Fees. His rationale for this felony conviction seems to be that he denies the seriousness of the circumstances and events that led to his conviction. It appears his assaultiveness should be of concern to decision makers when considering him for return to society. His conduct during this incarceration has not been satisfactory, which is reflected by his disciplinary record and being in a reduced time earning category with forfeited good conduct time. Additionally, he has been placed in solitary confinement on two occasions. He is not likely to complete a release without benefit of supervision and other programs.

While incarcerated, Mr. Jacobs has not participated in unit programs. Major areas of concern are his deficiencies in educational achievements, vocational skills, control of drug and alcohol use, and his apparent mental condition. Monitored abstinence from drug and alcohol use by urinalysis may be beneficial in determining relapse into past criminal behavioral activity. Supervision concerning completion of basic education and attaining vocational skills should be required during incarceration and after release until completion. Also compliance with treatment plans for psychiatric problems may be necessary. Attention to these areas after release could enhance his possibilities for remaining in society as a productive member.

Upon release Mr. Jacobs plans to reside with his family and seek employment as a roofer. Assistance from TEC or TRC could provide initial possibilities for gainful employment. Also inmate MHMR services may be necessary to assist his reintegration process. When asked concerning his thoughts about being paroled, he said, "I'm not going to stop drinking, regardless of the programs they send me to." This statement was reflective of his negative attitude concerning the criminal justice system, possible benefits from MHMR services, and substance abuse counseling. His poor physical and mental health conditions are negative factors toward an overall picture of his apparently poor chance for successful release.

Result: Mr. Jacobs was denied parole.

FIGURE 9.5   *(Continued)*

are subsequently paroled, their institutional conduct is generally satisfactory, with few write-ups or incident reports. Furthermore, they have participated in self-help groups and other programming offered by their prison. They acknowledge their problems and seek ways to remedy them. Less successful parole-eligible inmates deny they have problems, refuse to participate in prison programming, and may have poor attitudes concerning any assistance that may be offered. If they have alcohol or drug problems, they may deny the existence of such problems. If asked why they committed their conviction offenses, they are inclined to blame others for what happened, or they minimize their role in the crime (Clear et al. 2006).

THE PROCESS OF PAROLE REVOCATION

Parole revocation is a two-stage proceeding. Parolees who are in jeopardy of having their parole programs revoked through **revocation actions** are entitled to **minimum due process** rights. The governing case in all parole revocation proceedings is *Morrissey v. Brewer* (1972), discussed in the following section. The primary reason for extending minimum due process rights to parolees is that they are in jeopardy of losing their liberty. They can be reincarcerated if the parole board determines that the nature of their parole program violation is sufficiently serious.

However, a majority of parolees are not returned to prison. Rather, they are placed under more intensive and restrictive supervision from their POs. Some parolees are electronically monitored and placed in home confinement with strictly enforced curfews. Those who failed in their programs because of alcohol or substance abuse may be required to participate in counseling or group therapy. Self-help groups, such as Alcoholics Anonymous or Narcotics Anonymous, may be recomended as a part of their continuing parole program.

 **BOX 9.3**

EXCUSES FOR VIOLATING PAROLE CONDITIONS

**Montie Guthrie, Dallas, Texas,
Parole Officer.**

During the 1990s, Montie Guthrie was employed with the Texas Department of Criminal Justice Parole Division. Guthrie supervised hundreds of parolees and prepared thousands of reports. He visited his parolee-clients in dangerous Dallas neighborhoods that were gang-infested and full of violence. On more than one occasion, his life was threatened by neighborhood toughs. Luckily for Guthrie, his parolee-clients always bailed him out. On one occasion, for example, Guthrie was visiting a dangerous parolee who had been convicted of aggravated assault and murder. The parolee was gigantic, with massive arms and chest. He was known to pummel his victims into submission or death. When Guthrie visited, another man, a gang member, was at the parolee's residence. The visitor didn't like Guthrie's inquiries of his parolee-client and the fact that Guthrie was looking around the apartment for possible illegal contraband. The visitor insulted Guthrie and invited him outside to fight. Instead, the parolee rose from his chair and advised his visiting friend that he, the parolee, would be stepping outside with his friend, not the parole officer. He advised his friend to "keep quiet" or suffer the consequences. He pointed his finger at his parole officer and said, "That's the man keeping me out of prison. Nobody lays a finger on him. Now sit down and keep quiet." Sometimes it pays to have friends in low places.

As Guthrie reflects on his years with the Texas Department of Criminal Justice as a parole officer, he is amused at some of the incidents that involved some of his parolee-clients. In one particularly hilarious incident, Guthrie described a parolee who went hunting and shot an award-winning 18-point buck with a high-powered rifle. The shooting merited a visit from photographers and a reporter from a Dallas newspaper. Subsequently, the parolee's picture was printed in the paper, with the parolee holding the buck for everyone to see. The caption read, "Mr. _____ shot his trophy 18-point buck in northeast Coleman County just before Christmas. Mr. _____ said the buck would field dress about 150 pounds. The rack measured 18 inches. Mr. _____ was headed for the taxidermist and will probably soon have a fine trophy on the wall of his home." Ironically, Mr. _____ was a parolee. One of his parole program conditions was that he not possess or use firearms. This hunting antic came to Guthrie's attention when he read the morning newspaper. Mr. _____ had his parole revoked for the firearms violation and he was returned to prison.

Early in his career as a parole officer, Guthrie visited numerous clients. Some of them tested positive for drugs or alcohol. Others weren't home when they were supposed to be there. Some clients didn't report to his office when scheduled to do so at regular intervals. Still others absconded from the jurisdiction, only to be apprehended later. Each parolee had one or more excuses for violating his or her parole conditions. Guthrie catalogued these excuses:

- I didn't report because I was shot.
- I forgot.
- I don't know.
- My Corry [family member] died.
- I thought you said I didn't have to.
- I thought I was an annual [meaning once-a-year visit].
- I thought I would be arrested.
- I went to jail.
- I was sick.
- I came up here but you weren't here.
- My car broke down.
- I couldn't report because of my sister's drinking problem and I had to stay and watch her kids.
- I got married.
- My family said he [the parole officer] had homosexual tendencies and I was afraid he would come on to me.
- The reason I was positive [for cocaine] was my girlfriend put it on my _____ and then sucked it.

(continued)

BOX 9.3 (*Continued*)

- You see, I'm always positive [for cocaine] because I go out to these clubs and these girls, man, they always want to get with me, right? So, when I'm not looking, they put coke in my drink to get me high so I'll get with them.
- Well, I didn't do no crack, man, I was just cookin' the stuff.
- I was just around a bunch of people smokin'.
- I didn't do no drugs! My girl, man, she smoked the stuff and it must have got on me when I went down on her.
- My neighbors sneaked into my house and put cocaine in my sugar.
- It was on the counter and when I brushed it off, it must have got in me.
- They do coke at this bar a lot on the table, and when I put the pretzels on the bar, some must a got on them and me when I ate them.
- I smoke weed because I'm trying to gain weight and I know I'll get the munchies if I don't.
- I was having sex with a guy who was high and he ejaculated in me.
- I was at a club and my friend saw a guy put something in my drink and didn't tell me.
- It's just weed!

- I'm taking vitamins and antibiotics.
- I smoke because I want to get with women.
- My girl was going back to school and I wanted to be sure to give it to her good before she went back so she'll think about me.
- I cut so much cocaine it must have absorbed into my skin.
- They're not as bad as they seem.
- My friends stole the car, and then they picked me up at the house in it.
- It wasn't crack—it was just a ball of soap.
- I don't remember.
- It was self-defense. He started calling my grandmother bad names, and so I stabbed him.
- I left because they were selling drugs where I lived. I didn't have time to tell you where I moved to.
- I didn't go to GED classes because someone is trying to kill me. They'll kill me if I go to that class.

As Guthrie says, once you think you've heard it all, you hear something new. There's never a dull moment in parole work!

Courtesy of Montie Guthrie. Compiled by author, February 2001.

The parole revocation process involves two stages. The first stage involves an offender's appearance before the parole board to answer the allegations relating to the parole program violation(s). If the parole board determines that the offender is guilty of one or more program rule infractions, then it must decide the punishment. Meeting to determine the punishment is the second stage. If a parolee's program is revoked, the parole board must furnish the parolee with its reasons for the revocation action in writing. Furthermore, the parole board recommends what the parolee must do in order to earn another chance at parole. Below are several cases involving parole revocation.

LANDMARK CASES AND SELECTED ISSUES

Morrissey v. Brewer (1972). The first landmark case involving the constitutional rights of parolees was *Morrissey v. Brewer* (1972). In 1967, John Morrissey was convicted by an Iowa court for "falsely drawing checks" and sentenced to not more than seven years in the Iowa State Prison. He was eventually paroled from prison in June 1968. However, seven months later, his parole officer learned that while on parole, Morrissey had bought a car under an assumed name and operated it without permission, obtained credit cards under a false name, and gave false information to an insurance company when he was involved in a minor automobile accident. Also, Morrissey had given his parole officer a false address for his residence.

The parole officer interviewed Morrissey and filed a report recommending that parole be revoked. The reasons given by the officer were that Morrissey admitted buying the car and obtaining false ID, obtaining credit under false pretenses, and he also admitted being involved in the auto accident. Morrissey claimed he "was sick," and that this condition prevented him from maintaining continuous contact with his parole officer. The parole officer claimed that Morrissey's parole should be revoked because Morrissey had a habit of "continually violating the rules." The parole board revoked Morrissey's parole and he was returned to the Iowa State Prison to serve the remainder of his sentence. Morrissey was not represented by counsel at the revocation proceeding. Furthermore, he was not given the opportunity to cross-examine witnesses against him, he was not advised in writing of the charges against him, no disclosure of the evidence against him was provided, and reasons for the revocation were not given. Morrissey also was not permitted to offer evidence in his own behalf or give personal testimony.

Morrissey's appeal to the Iowa Supreme Court was rejected, but the U.S. Supreme Court heard his appeal. While the Court did not address directly the question of whether Morrissey should have had court-appointed counsel, it did make a landmark decision in his case. It overturned the Iowa Parole Board action and established a two-stage proceeding for determining whether parole ought to be revoked. The first or preliminary hearing is held at the time of arrest and detention, where it is determined whether probable cause exists that the parolee actually committed the alleged parole violation. The second hearing is more involved and establishes the guilt of the parolee relating to the violations. This proceeding must extend to the parolee certain minimum due process rights. These rights are:

1. The right to have written notice of the alleged violations of parole conditions.
2. The right to have disclosed to the parolee any evidence of the alleged violation.
3. The right of the parolee to be heard in person and to present **exculpatory evidence** as well as witnesses in his behalf.
4. The right to confront and cross-examine adverse witnesses, unless cause exists why they should not be cross-examined.
5. The right to a judgment by a neutral and detached body, such as the parole board itself.
6. The right to a written statement of the reasons for the parole revocation.

Thus, the significance of the Morrissey case is that it set forth minimum due process rights for all parolees, creating a two-stage proceeding whereby the alleged infractions of parole conditions could be examined and a full hearing conducted to determine the most appropriate disposition of the offender.

For several decades, interest in the rights of probationers and parolees has increased considerably. Not only has more attention been devoted to this subject in the professional literature, but various courts in different jurisdictions, including the U.S. Supreme Court, have set forth landmark decisions that influence either positively or negatively the lives of those in probation or parole programs.

Revoking Parole: Selected Issues

Samson v. California (2006).   Donald Samson was a California parolee who had previously been convicted of illegal possession of a firearm, a felony. In September 2002 in San Bruno, California, a police officer saw Samson walking with a woman and child and believed that Samson was wanted on a warrant. He approached Samson and asked him whether he was facing an arrest warrant, which Samson denied. The officer confirmed this fact by contacting his police station. Nevertheless, because of Samson's status as a parolee, the police officer decided to search Samson. The officer retrieved a cigarette box containing a plastic baggie containing methamphetamine and arrested Samson. Samson was returned to prison, not only for the parole violation, but also for the new felony conviction of illegal possession of drugs. Samson appealed, alleging that his Fourth Amendment right against unreasonable searches and seizures had been violated by the officer, since the officer had no reasonable suspicion or probable cause to search Samson's person. Samson's conviction and parole revocation were affirmed by appellate courts and eventually the U.S. Supreme Court heard Samson's case. The U.S. Supreme Court upheld the search of Samson's person as reasonable, since one condition of a parolee's release permits law enforcement officers and parole officers the right to search a parolee's person and premises without cause. There is no reasonable expectation of privacy afforded parolees while on their parole programs.

Pennsylvania Board of Probation and Parole v. Scott (1998).   Scott, a parolee, was suspected of possessing firearms in violation of his parole conditions. Parole officers conducted a warrantless search of his premises and discovered firearms. Scott's parole was revoked on the basis of the discovered evidence and he was recommitted to prison. Scott appealed, alleging that his Fourth Amendment right against unreasonable searches and seizures had been violated and that evidence thus seized was not admissible in a **parole revocation hearing.** The U.S. Supreme Court held that a parolee's Fourth Amendment rights do not apply in parole revocation hearings, and that incriminating evidence discovered and seized in violation of a parolees' Fourth Amendment rights may be introduced at parole revocation proceedings.

Pennsylvania Department of Corrections v. Yeskey (1998).   Yeskey was a Pennsylvania prison inmate who was sentenced to 18–36 months in a correctional facility, but was recommended for placement in a Motivational Boot Camp that, if successfully completed, would have led to his parole in just six months. Yeskey was rejected by the boot camp officials because of a medical history of hypertension. Yeskey sued the Pennsylvania Department of Corrections, alleging that the exclusion violated the Americans with Disabilities Act (ADA), and the federal court rejected his claim, contending that the ADA was inapplicable to state prison inmates. The Third Circuit Court of Appeals reversed and remanded, and the government appealed to the U.S. Supreme Court who heard the case. The U.S. Supreme Court affirmed the appellate court, declaring that the ADA provision prohibiting a public entity from discriminating against qualified individuals with disabilities on account of that person's disability applied to inmates in state prisons.

Pardons

When the U.S. President or a state governor pardons someone who may or may not be on probation or parole, the effect of these pardons is different, depending on the jurisdiction. Generally, a pardon is tantamount to absolution for a crime previously committed. Someone has been convicted of the crime, and the intent of a pardon is to terminate whatever punishment has been imposed. In *United States v. Noonan* (1990), for instance, Gregory Noonan was convicted and sentenced in 1969 for "failing to submit to induction into the armed forces." President Jimmy Carter granted a pardon to Noonan on January 21, 1977, wherein Carter declared a "full, complete and unconditional pardon" to persons convicted during the Vietnam War for refusing induction. Noonan sought to have his record of the original conviction expunged. An **expungement order** has the effect of wiping one's slate clean, as though the crime and the conviction had never occurred. Noonan believed that his conviction, which remained on his record, adversely affected his employment chances. Thus, he sought to expunge his record because of the pardon he had received from Carter. However, the Third Circuit Court of Appeals, a federal appellate court, refused to grant him this request. The Court declared that "a pardon does not blot out guilt nor does it restore the offender to a state of innocence in the eye of the law." In short, at least in Noonan's case, the presidential pardon was effective in removing the punishment but not the criminal record.

Not all courts agree with the Third Circuit Court of Appeals. In some state appellate courts, a different position has been taken regarding the influence of a pardon on one's criminal record. Following the lead of a Pennsylvania court of appeals, the Indiana Court of Appeals declared in the case of *State v. Bergman* (1990) that a pardon does expunge one's criminal record. The Governor of Indiana had pardoned a convict, Bergman, for a crime he had previously committed. Bergman sought to have his record expunged, in much the same way as Noonan. The Indiana Court of Appeals declared that pardons "block out the very existence of the offender's guilt, so that, in the eye(s) of the law, he is thereafter as innocent as if he had never committed the offense." Subsequent state court decisions have concurred with both Pennsylvania and Indiana.

Despite the fact that some offenders have been pardoned, this does not always exempt them from having their pardoned offense used against them in subsequent court proceedings involving new crimes. For instance, Moore was pardoned for a crime he committed in Louisiana (*Moore v. State,* 2002). Moore eventually moved to Mississippi where he was arrested and charged with felony driving under the influence. He was convicted and his prior Louisiana criminal record was used against him in a Mississippi court to enhance his sentence. Moore appealed, alleging that his pardoned offense was in effect expunged and that it could no longer be considered of relevance in any future sentencing. The Mississippi appellate court disagreed, citing Louisiana law in defense of the enhanced Mississippi criminal court sentence. Under Louisiana law, automatic pardon provisions do not restore defendants to the status of innocence. Thus, the court held that Mississippi could utilize the "pardoned offense" to enhance Moore's sentence for a crime he committed in Mississippi.

Parolee Program Conditions

When probationers or parolees are subject to having their programs revoked by respective authorities, what is the nature of evidence that can be used against them to support their program revocation? What are their rights concerning PO searches of their premises? What about the program conditions they have been obligated to follow? What about parole board recognition of and obligation to follow minimum-sentence provisions from sentencing judges? These issues and several others are discussed briefly below.

Parole Board Actions and Parolee Rights

Parole boards have considerable discretionary powers. They may deny parole or grant it. They may revoke one's parole and return the offender to prison, or they may continue the offender's parole program, with additional supervision and other conditions. Below are listed a variety of cases dealing with numerous issues. Some of these issues may appear trivial, although their significance to affected probationers or parolees is profound.

Inmates who become eligible for parole are not automatically entitled to parole. More than a few inmates think that when they have served a certain portion of their sentences, they should automatically be granted parole. This is not true. Parole boards have considerable discretion whether to grant or deny parole to any inmate. Short of serving their full sentences or completing a portion of their term less any applicable good-time credit, inmates are not automatically entitled to be paroled. In a Pennsylvania case, a parole statute was amended during the time an offender was incarcerated. When his parole date occurred, he appeared before the parole board, expecting to be paroled. But the parole board used the amended parole statute to deny him parole. He claimed that this was an *ex post facto* application of an existing statute and should have no bearing on his own parole. However, an appellate court determined that the use of amended statute by the parole board to deny him parole did not violate his constitutional rights. Furthermore, under the new provisions of the statute, the same considerations for early release were weighted by the parole board to justify his parole denial (*Bonsall v. Gillis,* 2005).

Sometimes extensive media coverage and the sensationalism surrounding one's original conviction offense will influence parole boards to deny parole to otherwise parole-eligible inmates, regardless of their suitability for parole. In California, for example, Leslie Van Houten, age 56, a former follower of Charles Manson, was convicted of murder in 1970 and sentenced to death. Subsequently, her sentence was commuted to life imprisonment, which made her parole-eligible. As of 2006 she had made 16 visits to the California Board of Prison Terms for consideration for early release. On each of these occasions, her parole requests were denied. Prior to her 2002 parole hearing, Van Houten filed a suit requesting the court to order her release from prison. The court rejected her request. It is doubtful that Van Houten will ever be paroled. This is due primarily to the politically charged nature of her conviction offense and the unfavorable publicity for parole officials and the California governor that her parole would likely generate. In the meantime, the California Board of Prison Terms has paroled numerous murders who have committed far more heinous acts than Van Houten ("Van Houten fails," 2006). Political pressures exerted on parole board members are found beyond California. In 2003 New Jersey Parole Board members admitted off the record that their parole decision making was strongly influenced by the New Jersey governor's office, and that if they failed to make decisions consistent with their governor's sentiments, their jobs would be in jeopardy (Baldwin and McClure, 2003).

In the case of Lee, a Pennsylvania inmate, a judge earlier had sentenced Lee to an indeterminate prison term, identifying a minimum sentence as well as a maximum one (*Commonwealth v. Lee,* 2005). The minimum sentence imposed on Lee was the factual point at which Lee would become eligible for parole. However, the Pennsylvania Parole Board has the exclusive right to grant or deny parole. The fact that a sentencing judge imposed a minimum sentence to be served by Lee did not mean that the parole board was obligated to parole Lee when that minimum sentence had been served. An appellate court upheld the right of the parole board to deny Lee his early release from prison.

Parole boards do not have to recognize explicit parole guidelines when determining an inmate's parole eligibility. Weintraub was a federal inmate serving a lengthy term (*United States v. Weintraub,* 2005). During his confinement, he complied dutifully with all terms of his confinement, participating in self-help counseling, educational and vocational programs, and other activities designed to enhance his subsequent rehabilitation and reintegration. He even was able to pay a fine and make restitution to his victim while confined. However, when he appeared before the U.S. Parole Commission to be placed on supervised release, the Commission denied him early release. The Commission cited factors such as his leadership role in the crime's commission and placing numerous persons at serious risk to their health (he had illegally removed and disposed of a large quantity of asbestos from his real estate holdings). Weintraub argued that the Commission was obligated to free him, but an appellate court held otherwise, noting that the Commission's reasons for deciding not to release Weintraub do not have to comply fully with paroling guidelines.

Inmates who serve time in a state parole program may not apply this time against a federal sentence for a new crime. Buchanan was a state prisoner who was paroled for a crime (*Buchanan v. U.S. Bureau of Prisons,* 2005). Between his state prison time and parole, he had spent 46 months under state supervision. During this period, however, Buchanan was arrested and convicted of a federal crime for which a lengthy sentence was imposed. Buchanan demanded that he be credited with 46 months against his new federal sentence as an entitlement to being in state custody. An appellate court ruled against Buchanan, holding that because his parole revocation was based on conviction of a new offense punishable by imprisonment, the Commission was required to order forfeiture of all prior time spent on parole, including the time he spent in state prison.

Parolees who are placed on home confinement as a condition of their parole program cannot count the time served under house arrest against their maximum sentences if they subsequently violate one or more conditions of their parole and it is revoked. A Nevada offender was placed on parole with the condition that he remain under house arrest for a period of time, with numerous conditions and restrictions (*State v. Second Judicial District Court,* 2005). Despite the stringent conditions, the offender was permitted to travel to and from grocery shopping, her employment, medical appointments, counseling, and court appearances. She was even permitted to travel to Las Vegas to get married. However, she violated one or more of her parole conditions apart from those related to her house arrest and her parole was revoked. She was returned to prison to serve the remainder of her sentence. She filed a motion to have the time spent on house arrest count against her maximum prison sentence. However, the Nevada Parole Board denied her request and she appealed. The appellate court upheld the decision of the parole board denying her credit for the time she served while under house arrest. Indeed, the appellate court said that her house arrest was merely a reasonable condition that did not count as time spent in confinement, which would have entitled her to credit against her sentence.

Inmates who have been paroled and who subsequently commit a new violent act while on parole may have their parole programs revoked and be returned to prison to serve the remainder of their sentences in their entirety. Lychanko was a federal releasee who had served a portion of his lengthy sentence in a federal prison (*Lychanko v. Davis,* 2005). While on release, Lychanko committed a new and violent offense. He was subsequently convicted and returned to prison where he was obligated to serve the remaining portion of his original sentence. He appealed but an appellate court upheld the U.S. Parole Commission in its decision, ordering him to serve the remaining portion of his sentence before serving his new prison term for the new criminal conviction.

Convicted offenders may be declared violent offenders and parole ineligible if they are convicted of vehicular homicide. Boehrns was a South Dakota offender convicted of vehicular homicide. He was therefore classified under South Dakota law as a violent offender and designated not eligible for parole (*Boehrns v. S.D. Board of Pardons and Paroles,* 2005). The South Dakota Code (Section 22-16-41, 2007) reads that a crime of violence includes any felony in the commission of which the perpetrator uses force, or was armed with a dangerous weapon. Boehrns claimed that his automobile was not a firearm or other dangerous weapon under the South Dakota Code and appealed his parole ineligibility on this ground. After debating the issue of whether his automobile was a dangerous weapon under the meaning of the statute, the appellate court upheld the decision to make Boehrns ineligible for parole. In convoluted wording, the appellate court said that it could not say that the designation of Boehrns's offense as a violent offense for the purpose of parole eligibility was improper.

Offenders convicted of two or more crimes may be paroled for one sentence but be required to continue to serve the other sentence. Deutsch was a federal inmate convicted of two separate federal offenses *United States v. Deutsch,* 2005). He was sentenced to two separate terms of imprisonment to run concurrently with one another. At one point during his prison term, he became eligible for parole. The parole board granted him early release on one of his sentences but denied him early release on the other sentence. Deutsch had to serve more prison time, despite the early-release decision on one of his conviction offenses. He appealed. The appellate court upheld the right of the board to not grant him early release on the other sentence. Deutsch must serve more time and cannot be released from prison because of the two convictions.

Offenders who are serving time on parole in one state for a crime they committed in another state may be returned to the original state for a determination of whether their parole should be revoked. Fisher was serving time on parole in Delaware for a New Jersey conviction under an interstate compact agreement (*Fisher v. Carroll,* 2005). Delaware authorities tried and convicted Fisher for his Delaware crimes, and then Delaware returned Fisher to New Jersey to face parole revocation proceedings. In New Jersey, the parole board revoked

Fisher's parole for his Delaware offenses and obligated him to serve the remainder of his prison sentence in a New Jersey prison. Fisher believed that his action violated his constitutional right against double jeopardy and appealed. The appellate court disagreed with Fisher and upheld the ruling of the New Jersey Parole Board. When new violations of one's parole occur, a parole revocation action is permissible, including a return to prison, even if the new parole violations are conviction offenses in other states.

SUMMARY

Several pre-release programs are available to parole-eligible inmates who are within a short time of being released. Some of these programs include work release, where inmates may be granted temporary leaves from their prisons to work at jobs in their communities. Other temporary leaves may be used for earning academic degrees. These programs are known as study release. Variations from standard parole include halfway houses and furloughs. These are community-based programs and provide offenders with opportunities for reintegration into the community. Halfway houses or community residential centers may be either publicly or privately operated. They exist to provide offenders with housing, food, counseling, and other services while on parole. These programs are considered transitional because they permit offenders to gradually reenter society and make an adjustment from highly structured and regulated prison life. Furloughs are temporary leaves designed to permit offenders to become reunited with families or to engage in employment. Most of the time, these programs are granted to low-risk minimum-security offenders.

Other programs include standard parole with conditions. All parole programs are conditional, in that there are certain expectations made of all parolees. These conditions prohibit the use of alcohol or illegal drugs, ownership of firearms, and cellular telephones and beepers. Furthermore, parolees must permit their supervising POs to visit their premises and conduct searches without warrant at any time. Some parole programs involve intensive parolee supervision. One of these programs is the New Jersey Intensive Supervision Program. This program selects participants from numerous applicants annually. Any interested New Jersey jail or prison inmate may apply for entry into the New Jersey ISP. However, New Jersey authorities only accept about 19 percent of all applicants. Several types of inmates are automatically excluded, including those with violent criminal records, sex offenders, and those affiliated with organized crime. The New Jersey program boasts a recidivism rate of less than 10 percent and has successfully operated since 1983.

Other conditions may be imposed by a paroling authority, including community service and victim restitution. Together with fines and day fines, community service partially defrays the costs associated with the offender's crime, such as medical bills and property damage. There are many forms of community service and restitution. Not everyone agrees how or when these types of sanctions ought to be applied, however. Also, it is difficult to evaluate the effectiveness of these sanctions as deterrents to further criminal activity.

By 1988, all states had modified their existing sentencing provisions. Maine abolished parole in 1976, and the federal government technically abolished parole in 1992, although supervised early-release procedures have been continued. Many states are moving toward some form of determinate sentencing or presumptive or guidelines-based sentencing schemes. A majority of states continue to use parole boards for granting early release to prisoners. Parole board composition varies among jurisdictions, and the criteria for granting parole vary considerably as well. In many jurisdictions, prisoners may acquire good-time credits, which serve to reduce their sentences a certain number of days for each month served.

Parole boards attempt to predict which inmates should receive early release. They also determine dates for first parole consideration, fix the minimum time to be served, and award good-time credits to inmates who have earned them. Studies of parole board decision making reveal that predictions of dangerousness are complex and far from error-free. Parole board members further complicate the early-release decision-making process by reflecting different correctional orientations including jurist, treater, sanctioner, controller, citizen, and regulator philosophies. The primary criticisms of parole boards focus on a lack of consistent parole criteria. Many parole boards use salient factor scores made up of an inmate's prior record, age, and prospects for adjusting to community life.

Parole revocation is the process of returning an inmate to prison for one or more technical violations or for committing new crimes. The revocation process has been examined by the United States Supreme Court, and several landmark cases have presented parolees with specific rights. Parole revocation now consists of two hearings, one to determine if probable cause exists that a violation occurred, and the other to determine whether parole ought to be revoked.

Parolees and probationers have been vested with several important constitutional rights in the last few decades, as the U.S. Supreme Court has extended due process and equal protection to encompass them as well as other citizens. Before parolees have their parole revoked, a two-stage hearing is mandatory, where probable cause is first determined, and then an appropriate disposition of each case is made by an impartial body. It is likely that other significant rights will be obtained for parolees in future years as the U.S. Supreme Court faces new and different appeals from parolees and probationers.

QUESTIONS FOR REVIEW

1.   What is meant by pre-release? What are several types of pre-release programs? Describe each.

2.   What is work release? What are some potential benefits for inmates who participate in work release?

3.   What are furloughs? Are furloughs the same as work release? What are some advantages of furloughs for prisoners?

4.   What are some important functions performed by parole boards? What criteria do they usually employ when reaching decisions about individual inmates?

5.   What is the Salient Factor Score Index? Is there any apparent bias associated with this index?

6.   What rights do offenders have before officials can revoke their parole? What are some cases that are important in the matter of parole revocation? What were the issues involved in these cases?

7.   Who makes up a parole board? Are these persons corrections officers? Why or why not?

8.   What are four different orientations of parole board members besides the sanctioner orientation? Define each.

9.   What are some objective parole criteria? Why are they considered objective?

10.   What is a salient factor score? How is it used by parole boards to determine one's early-release eligibility?

SUGGESTED READINGS

Belenko, S. (2006). "Assessing Released Inmates for Substance-Abuse-Related Service Needs." *Crime and Delinquency* **52**:94–113.

Burke, Peggy B. (2004). "Parole Violations: An Important Window on Offender Reentry." *APPA Perspectives* **28**:24–31.

Hanrahan, K., J.J. Gibbs, and S.E. Zimmerman (2005). "Parole and Revocation: Perspectives of Young Adult Offenders." *The Prison Journal* **85**:251–269.

Klag, S., F. O'Callaghan, and P. Creed (2005). "The Use of Legal Coercion Treatment of Sustance Abusers: An Overview and Critical Analysis of Thirty Years of Research." *Substance Use and Misuse* **40**:1777–1795.

Morgan, K.D. and B. Smith (2005). "Parole Decisions Revisited: An Analysis of Parole Release Decisions for Violent Inmates in a Southeastern State." *Journal of Criminal Justice* **33**:277–287.

Paparozzi, M.A. and P. Gendreau (2005). "An Intensive Supervision Program that Worked: Service Delivery, Professional Orientation, and Organizational Supportiveness." *The Prison Journal* **85**:445–466.

INTERNET CONNECTIONS

Administrative Office of the U.S. Courts
http://www.uncle-sam.com/uscourts.html,
http://www.uscourts.gov/

American Psychological Association
http://www.apa.org

Correctional Industries Association
http://www.corrections.com/industries/

Corrections Corporation of America
http://www.correctionscorp.com/

Faith to Faith Friends
http://www.f2ff.com

Furlough programs
http://www.xpay.net/SevFurloughProgram
.htm

Gender Programming Training and Technical Assistance Initiative
http://www.girlspecificprogram.org

Glaser Institute on Reality Therapy
http://www.wglasserinst.com/whatisrt

Gurley House Women's Recovery Center
http://www.thegurleyhouse.org

ISCOS Halfway Houses
iscos.org.sq/halfway.shtml

National Association of Social Workers
http://www.naswdc.org

National Corrections Corporation
http://www.nationalcorrections.com

National State History of Halfway Houses
http://www.ni-cor.com/halfwayhouses.html

North Carolina Study Release Program
http://www.doc.state.nc.us/DOP/Program/
studyrel.htm

PACER Service Center
http://www.pacer.psc.uscourts.gov/

Probation and Parole Compact Administrators Association
http://www.ppcaa.net/

Reynolds Work Release Second Chance Program
http://www.wa.gov/doc/REYN02DSWR
description.htm

Social work agencies
http://www.sc.edu/swan/national

Work furlough programs
http://www.dcn.davis.ca.us/YoloLINK/
services/S0026.html

Work release frequently asked questions
http://www.dc.state.fl.us/oth/inmates/wr
.htm

Probation/Parole Organization and Operations: Recruitment, Training, and Officer–Client Relations

Chapter Outline

Chapter Objectives

As the result of reading this chapter, the following objectives will be realied:

1. Distinguishing between correctional officers, probation officers, and parole officers, and examining how different jurisdictions view these work roles.
2. Profiling probation and parole officers and describing their primary characteristics and training.
3. Describing the recruitment and selection requirements for those performing probation and parole officer functions.
4. Describing the education and training received by probation and parole officers.
5. Describing various caseload models used by probation/parole agencies.
6. Understanding the structure and function of probation and parole departments.
7. Describing the qualifications and selection criteria of probation and parole officers.
8. Understanding how caseloads for POs are assigned.
9. Understanding the nature of officer/client interactions.
10. Describing the ethics of performing PO work.

THE GOOD

- *Eugene Wardford, a parole officer at the Outer District Parole Office in Michigan, received the Michigan Department of Corrections Award for Meritorious Service. Wardford has been with the department for 14 years. In a case involving a parolee, Wardford suspected that an 11-month-old infant was in danger because of a drug relapse of his female parolee. The woman took her infant and absconded from the jurisdiction. Fearing for the infant's safety, Wardford contacted family and child protective services and conducted an independent investigation, using his informants and other sources to discover the woman's whereabouts. A search of the woman's possible hideouts led to her discovery by Wardford, who took her and her infant into custody without incident. The infant was turned over to child protective services in good health and the parolee was lodged in jail. Nancy Spigliano, the Parole/Probation Manager, said of Wardford, "He is a good investigator with good hunches and good intuition. He never hesitates to share his knowledge with less experienced agents". [Source: Adapted from the Michigan Department of Corrections, "Parole Officer Eugene Wardford Receives Director's Award for Meritorious Service," March 20, 2003].*

- *A Dover, Delaware, probation officer was honored by the Delaware Department of Corrections for saving the life of one of its officers. Probation Officer Doug Watts received the Commendation of Valor for his action taken on March 24, 2001. Watts and another officer, David Spicer, were on Operation Safe Streets duty in Dover when they stopped two individuals who were acting suspiciously. The persons fled and Watts and Spicer pursued them. They fired at the officers, wounding Spicer badly. Watts returned fire, wounding one of the suspects. Officer Watts was able to get Officer Spicer to the hospital where he received life-saving treatment. The suspects were apprehended and turned out to have lengthy criminal records. The activity prompting Watts and Spicer out on Dover streets late at night was an initiative created by the Governor's Task Force on Violent Crime. Operation Safe Streets partners with police to comb "hot spots" for violent crime and actively track high-risk probationers at night. Teams also conduct spot checks of homes and hangouts of high-risk probationers, ensuring that they adhere to the strict terms of their probation. [Source: Adapted from the State of Delaware Department of Corrections, "Probation Officer to be Honored by Dover Police Department," October 9, 2001].*

• *Craig B. Milledge, a Probation Officer II with the Albany, Georgia, Probation Office, received a Public Safety Award from the Georgia Department of Corrections for his life-rescuing efforts resulting from a car crash. Officer Milledge was the first to arrive at a two-car accident and provided assistance to both parties while calling for emergency help. Officer Milledge then provided assistance to one of the drivers, an elderly man who had obtained a deep cut and was bleeding badly. He applied pressure to stop the bleeding until local emergency authorities could respond, and then he assisted police officers with traffic control afterward. Michael Nail, the Director of the Probation Division, said, "It is a pleasure to have someone of the caliber of Officer Milledge on our staff. We are proud that his efforts were recognized in such a prestigious manner." [Source: Adapted from the Georgia Department of Corrections, "6th Annual Governor's Public Safety Awards: Albany Resident Craig B. Milledge Nominated," October 16, 2003].*

THE BAD

• *Former Probation Officer John Santy, Franklin County, New York, was convicted of stealing $52,512 from various probationers under different pretexts. He received monies directly from probationers who were paying court-ordered fines and for monies paid for community services they performed. He would then alter public records in the probation office and court offices to show that the fines and community service payments had been made and the probationer work had been performed. On one occasion, he fixed the case of a probationer charged with drunk driving by extorting money from him and altering records to show that his fines had been paid. His pattern of fraud was eventually exposed. He was sentenced to five concurrent two- to six-year terms in prison on several counts of third-degree larceny, second-degree forgery, and first-degree tampering with public records. [Source: Adapted from Denise A. Raymo and the* Press Republican, *"Former Probation Officer Gets Prison Time for Stealing from Clients," September 14, 2005].*

• *In July 1994, Andrew Elem, Jr., age 47, was convicted in Milwaukee, Wisconsin, and placed on probation for delivery of cocaine. In July 1997, three days before the end of his probation term, his probation officer, Emily C. Lewandowski, forged his name on a document that extended his probationary term for two additional years. Subsequently, Elem was arrested and convicted of fourth-degree sexual assault while on probation. He was imprisoned for a lengthy period, aggravated in large part because his criminal conduct was also a violation of his probation. Later, Elem was assigned a court-appointed attorney who discovered the forgery on Elem's probation document. A suit was filed against Lewandowski and the probation department alleging severe mental and emotional damages as well as economic loss. In the meantime, Lewandowski, age 32, pleaded no contest to a charge of misconduct in public office in 2000 in connection with forging Elem's name on the document extending his probationary term. She was sentenced to 3 years of probation and is no longer a probation officer. [Source: Adapted from Gina Barton and the* Milwaukee Journal Sentinel, *"Man Sues Ex-Probation Officer," June 10, 2003].*

• *In Arlington Heights, Illinois, Brian Leden, a former Lake County probation officer, was convicted of official misconduct because of a $25,000 bribe he accepted from a parolee he was assigned to supervise. The convict was paroled and assigned to Leden. In exchange for the $25,000, Leden would allow the parolee to roam freely within his community without supervision of any kind. Also, Leden would intervene and fix court documents in the event the parolee got into trouble. Leden, age 33, entered a guilty plea and was sentenced to serve 30 months on probation, with 9 months on jail work release. [Source: Adapted from Tony Gordon and the* Daily Herald, *"Probation Officer Pleads Guilty to Taking Money," May 7, 2005].*

• *In Bexar County, Texas, several probation officers are under investigation for various offenses. Allegations include a female probation officer who is accused of having sex with one of her probationers. Two other officers are accused of stealing money orders from probationers who were paying fines. The officers would cash the money orders and alter court records to show that their payments were made. Another officer is accused of using a county automobile for personal use. Another officer was arrested for misconduct at a local bar and resisting arrest. Bill Fitzgerald, in charge of the Bexar County Probation Office, says, "They cannot cross the line on ethical or moral issues. In each case, if the officer is guilty, he or she will lose their badge. Internal affairs is handling all of these incidents." [Source: Adapted from the* San Antonio News, *"5 Probation Officers Accused of Crimes," February 11, 2004].*

THE UGLY

• *In Eaton, Ohio, a Preble County grand jury indicted Douglas E. Moore, age 32, a probation officer with the Preble County Juvenile Court, on two counts of sexual battery after he was accused of having sexual relations with a 17-year-old under his supervision. Police reports disclose that at the time of the alleged violation, the victim, a male teen, was placed under Moore's supervision while on probation. Moore's residence was searched and a computer containing pornographic materials was seized. Moore resigned his position on August 3, 2004.[Source: Adapted from* WHIOTV.com, *August 30, 2004].*

• *Nicole Waite, age 36, a probation officer, was arrested for turning a male juvenile delinquent under her probation supervision into her personal boy-toy in exchange for a favorable pre-sentencing report. During the sexual encounters alleged, the teen and Waite smoked pot, drank alcohol, and had sex. After receiving the favorable pre-sentencing report, which helped the teen get community service, the teen turned in the probation officer because she "kept bugging me for sex," he said. Commissioner Rose Gill Hearn said, "The conduct of this probation officer was egregious and goes against everything expected from representatives of law enforcement. If convicted, Waite faces up to seven years in prison.[Source: Adapted from Barbara Ross and Bill Hutchinson,* Daily News, *October 2, 2003].*

• *In Havre, Montana, Edward L. Schmidt, a 13-year veteran with the Department of Corrections, faces an official misconduct charge for allegedly engaging in sexual acts with a woman he supervised. He is accused of requiring the 40-year-old woman to call him and explicitly tell him about sexual matters as well as engaging in various sexual acts. Investigators found seminal fluid on the woman's couch and carpet that matched genetic material from Schmidt.*

• *In Kansas City, Missouri, Randall Nester, age 37, a former probation officer, pleaded guilty to four counts of sexual misconduct and acceding to corruption by a public servant. Nester threatened his probationers with jail time if they didn't do what he wanted. Several of his female probationers claimed that he groped them inappropriately and/or had sexual relations with them. Nester worked with the Johnson County Department of Corrections from 1997 to 2002. He was ordered to serve 30 months in prison and one year in jail for the sexual misconduct charges.*

• *Frank Keith Cochran, age 41, of New Port Richey, Florida, was a former probation officer who was accused of having sexual relations with a woman he supervised. Cochran pleaded no contest to charges that he engaged in official misconduct as well as sexual misconduct. The victim was one of his probationers, an exotic dancer, Melinda Starnes. On his first probation visit to her home, Cochran found a bottle of wine in her refrigerator and asked her if she wanted to go to jail. When she said "No," he said "Well then, you're going to cooperate." They had sex that night and Starnes moved in with Cochran shortly thereafter. They smoked pot together and got drunk frequently. Cochran altered official records to prevent the woman from violating the terms of her probation. Cochran oversaw hundreds of probationers and house arrests, ensuring that they passed drug tests and showed up for their work, even when they didn't. Cochran could have been sentenced to five years, but instead, he received two years of house arrest and three years of probation.*

• *A Charlevoix, Michigan, probation officer, Charles Abraham, age 45, pleaded guilty to sexual misconduct when he assaulted with intent to commit sexual penetration a probationer under his supervision. Waiving his right to a preliminary examination, Abraham, an 18-year veteran with the probation department, admitted to kissing and embracing the woman and touching her breast while at her home. The woman said that Abraham showed up at her home after she failed to keep an appointment with him at his office earlier that day. The charges against Abraham were subsequently reduced through a plea agreement to fourth-degree sexual assault, a serious misdemeanor. He could have served up to 10 years in prison on the original charges. The Michigan Department of Corrections said, "We want to make sure the message is clear and unambiguous to anyone who would engage in this kind of behavior. We think it's deserving of a felony." [Source: Adapted from the Associated Press and the* Billings Gazette, *"Probation Officer Faces Charges," January 11, 2004; adapted from Patrick Winderl and the* Havre Daily News, *"Former Probation Officer is Convicted of Misconduct," June 23, 2004; adapted from the* Jefferson City News Tribune, *"Former Kansas Probation Officer Sentenced for Sexual Misconduct," April 8, 2005; adapted from Richard Raeke and the* St. Petersburg Times, *"Ex-Probation Officer Sentenced in Misconduct Case," March 23, 2004; adapted from the* Record Eagle, *"Probation Officer Pleads Guilty: Charles Abraham Admits Fondling Woman on Probation Under His Supervision," May 5, 1999].*

INTRODUCTION

Probation and parole officers are honored annually for acts of heroism, accomplishments, and assistance to others above and beyond the call of duty. They play important roles in assisting those they supervise to remain law-abiding and becoming rehabilitated. They are trained to act in professional ways, and they are equipped with the necessary skills to do so. They have substantial powers over their clients, and their recommendations carry great weight with courts. But with such powers, some officers may stray and take advantage of particular clients, whether it is for money, sex, or some other illicit objective. Most probation and parole officers in the United States are those who conform with the rules of their offices. Like any organization, however, there are a few who violate the trust given them by their office. Disciplinary actions such as those described in the scenarios above are taken whenever abuses of one's position are reported and confirmed.

This chapter is about the recruitment, selection, and training of probation and parole officers. When a mandate was issued by the President's Commission of 1967, significant developments occurred in corrections and probation/parole that led to improvements in programs, personnel, and policies in almost every local, state, and federal jurisdiction. We examine the contemporary condition of probation and parole services as well as the state of these services in previous years. While considerable improvements have been made in efforts to recruit and retain quality personnel and upgrade the quality of services provided offenders, much more needs to be done. This chapter assesses the progress made as well as highlights those areas in need of improvement.

Correctional officers are prison or jail staff and their supervisors who manage inmates, while probation and parole officers supervise and manage probationers and parolees in a variety of offender aftercare programs (American Correctional Association, 2006). Since the departments of correction in many states select POs as well as prison staff and conduct training programs for all of their correctional personnel, similar criteria are often used for selecting correctional officers as well as for POs. Thus, useful information will be gleaned from the general correctional literature, which is applicable to POs as well as prison and jail personnel. This does not mean that prison and jail correctional officers necessarily share the same characteristics with POs. One major difference is that correctional officers manage and interact with incarcerated offenders, while POs manage and interact with nonincarcerated criminals. There are also differing pay scales, work requirements, and other important characteristics that serve to distinguish between these two officer populations that deal with offenders at different points in time.

There has been a substantial and continuing increase in the number of personnel working in the area of adult and juvenile corrections. In early 2006 there were over 800,000 personnel in corrections for both adults and juveniles (American Correctional Association, 2006). There were 310,000 correctional officers in U.S. jails and prisons at the beginning of 2006. Also, there were 460,000 personnel working in adult and juvenile probation and parole services for the same period (American Correctional Association, 2006). Thus, probation and parole personnel made up about 65 percent of all persons working with convicted offenders.

Probation officers are hired to manage probationers exclusively in many jurisdictions, while parole officers deal only with parolees. Some observers believe that probation officers deal with lower-risk and less dangerous offenders compared with parole officers. Parole officers are assigned ex-convicts who have already served a portion of their sentences in prisons or jails, usually because of felony convictions. Confinement implies a greater level of dangerousness compared with those who are selected to participate in probation programs. However, evidence suggests that probation officers are receiving more dangerous offenders into their charge annually through felony probation, as prison and jail overcrowding make it impossible to incarcerate all criminals who should be incarcerated.

In many jurisdictions, probation and parole officers supervise both types of offenders interchangeably (American Correctional Association, 2006). In many states, probation and parole officers are combined in official reports of statistical information to organizations such as the American Correctional Association. Within the adult category, states such as Alabama, Florida, Virginia, Washington, and Wyoming report total numbers of probation and parole aftercare personnel rather than distinguish them.

THE ORGANIZATION AND OPERATION OF PROBATION AND PAROLE AGENCIES

Different departments and agencies in each state administer probation and parole departments. Most states have departments of corrections that supervise both incarcerated and nonincarcerated offenders; these tasks are sometimes overseen in other jurisdictions by departments of human services, departments of youth services, or some other umbrella agency.

Functions and Goals of Probation and Parole Services

The functions and goals of probation and parole services are to:

- supervise offenders;
- ensure offender-client compliance with program conditions by conducting random searches of offender premises, maintaining contact with offender-client employers, and otherwise maintaining occasional face-to-face spot checks;
- conduct routine and random drug/alcohol checks;

- provide networking services for employment assistance;
- direct offender-clients to proper treatment, counseling, and other forms of requested assistance;
- protect the community and its residents by detecting program infractions and reporting infractions to judges and parole boards;
- assist offenders in becoming reintegrated into their communities; and
- engage in any rehabilitative action that will improve offender-client skills and law-abiding behavior.

Organization and Administration of Probation and Parole Departments

Each state and large city has its own organization for administering and supervising probationers and parolees. The volume of offenders makes a significant difference in how departments are managed and the sizes of caseloads POs have. In some areas of the country, such as New York, PO caseloads for supervising probationers are as high as 400. In other parts of the country, caseloads for POs may be as low as 10. Obviously in those areas where PO caseloads are sizeable, the nature of supervision exercised over these offenders is different from the supervision received by clients when client caseloads are under 25 (American Correctional Association, 2006).

Some jurisdictions have drive-in windows established in shopping centers where clients may drive up to a window like they are going to withdraw cash from an automated teller machine. However, instead of withdrawing cash, they place their hands on a surface that reads their palm prints and verifies their whereabouts. In other locations, such as Long Beach, California, large numbers of probationers and some parolees report monthly to a central office to verify that they are employed and are remaining law-abiding. These check-ins mean that numerous offenders can be supervised. However, the nature of the supervision is questionable. Without frequent, random, and direct face-to-face contact with offender-clients, POs have no way of knowing whether these clients are law-abiding or engaging in some illicit behavior. Only those brought to the attention of police come to the attention of POs. Also, POs may detect probation or parole program violations during random visits to offender-clients' premises at odd hours.

Most states and the federal government attempt to divide clients according to the seriousness of their prior offending. Some offenders are deemed at greater risk of reoffending than others. Therefore, they are targeted for more intensive supervision. Lower-risk offenders are less likely to reoffend, and therefore their supervision does not need to be that intense. One example of a probation and parole agency is the Field Services Division Central Office in North Dakota. Figure 10.1 shows a diagram of this office. There is a director, a program manager, business officer, release program manager, three community offender services program managers, and an institutional offender services manager.

One good feature of Figure 10.1 is that it is relatively simple. There simply aren't that many persons on probation or parole in North Dakota. For example, in 2005, there were 4,286 probationers and 467 parolees in North Dakota to be supervised (U.S. Department of Justice, 2006). Despite these low numbers, even the North Dakota Probation and Parole Field Services division can be fairly complex. Figure 10.2 shows a diagram of the division of labor for Parole and Probation Field Services.

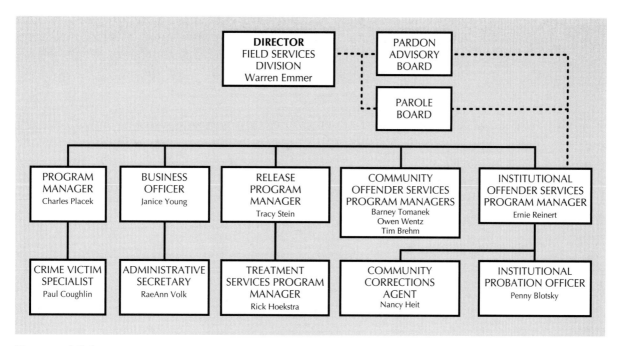

FIGURE 10.1   North Dakota Field Division Central Office.
(Courtesy of Elaine Little, Director, North Dakota Department of Corrections and Rehabilitation)

In Figure 10.2, there is a general manager over four major regions of North Dakota, together with a manager who supervises an intensive program for offenders who need to be more closely monitored. North Dakota is a large state geographically, and thus it is imperative to divide it according to quadrants, with a West Region Supervisor, a Central Region Supervisor, a South Region Supervisor,

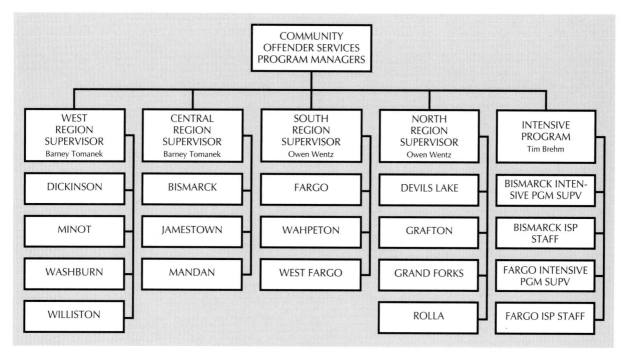

FIGURE 10.2   North Dakota Parole and Probation Field Services.
(Courtesy of Elaine Little, Director, North Dakota Department of Corrections and Rehabilitation)

and a North Region Supervisor. Notice in Figure 10.2 that there are 14 major cities and surrounding areas served by these four regions. Under the Intensive Program, there are four major intensive supervision supervisors and support staff to supervise offenders. These programs operate primarily out of Bismarck or Fargo.

The general mission of the Field Services Division overseeing probationers, parolees, and other community-based clients is to protect society by ensuring that the community-placed offenders are provided responsible supervision that requires them to be an active participant in their rehabilitation. Supervising offenders requires proactive intervention and case management strategies. The Field Services Division continuously reviews and modifies programs it provides to address community safety issues, prison overcrowding, and offender needs. The Intensive Supervision Program and comprehensive Day Reporting Program typify programming designed to facilitate the supervision of those offenders posing the greatest risks and needs. Halfway houses, home confinement programs, and curfews are some of the intermediate sanctions used to verify compliance with supervision sanctions. Electronic monitoring and on-site drug testing are also tools used regularly by POs to supervise offenders (Tarnai, 2006).

Probation and parole departments in various states are administered by different agencies and organizations. Although most states have departments of corrections that supervise both incarcerated and nonincarcerated offenders, these tasks are sometimes overseen in other jurisdictions by departments of human services, departments of youth services, or some other umbrella agency that may or may not have the expertise to service these clients adequately. Many jurisdictions have **interstate compact agreements,** whereby offenders who are from states other than where they are convicted may be returned to their home states for probation or parole supervision (Swan, 2006). These interstate compact agreements are useful in that offenders often have an easier time finding work if they are familiar with where they live. There are other advantages as well (Blackburn, 2006).

During the 1990s, a growing concern has been the **professionalization** of all correctional personnel. When the President's Commission on Law Enforcement and Administration of Justice made its recommendations in 1967, few standards were in place in most jurisdictions to guide administrators in their selection of new recruits. Thus, it was not unusual for critics of corrections to frequently make unfavorable remarks about and unflattering characterizations of those who manage criminals and oversee their behaviors. Because of the complexity of contemporary correctional roles, new pools from which to recruit, and greater social science training, different types of officers may be required in future years with a broader range of skills.

Selected Criticisms of Probation and Parole Programs

Probation and parole programs have been viewed unfavorably over the years, both in the United States and in other countries such as England. There have been claims that probation and parole don't work as rehabilitative strategies, and that POs are not doing their jobs properly because of the actions of their probationers and parolees. Consequently, both state and federal policymakers have targeted probation, parole, and the field of corrections generally for massive institutional changes and reforms. In the early years of correctional reforms, officials believed that the treatment or medical model was sound, and that rehabilitation on a large scale was possible for both incarcerated and nonincarcerated offenders. Of course, rehabilitation was projected as the direct result of proper therapeutic programs

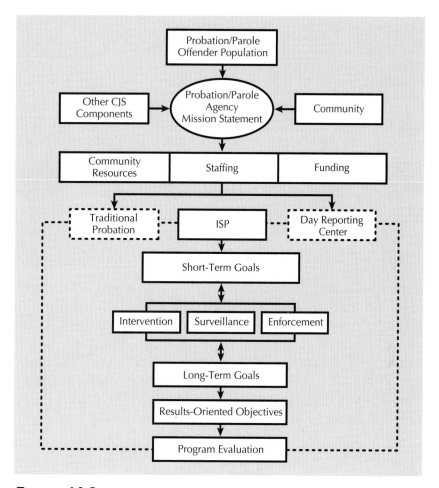

FIGURE 10.3   Program Development Process.
Source: From Fulton, Gendreau, and Paparozzi, 1995:26; reprinted with the permission of the American Probation and Parole Association.

and treatments. Educational and vocational-technical programs were coupled with group and individual counseling in prisons and jails. Offenders sentenced to probation were slotted for involvement in various training courses and assigned to programs designed to improve their self-concept, skills, and marketability as job-holders and breadwinners.

The rehabilitative aim of corrections was not entirely abandoned, but over the years, an increasingly skeptical public became disenchanted with what corrections officials espoused and how they sought to rehabilitate offenders. Too many ex-convicts were committing new crimes and subject to rearrests. Former clients of probation or parole programs were also apprehended for new law violations. Furthermore, rearrests of offenders frequently occurred while they were on probation or parole.

Efforts have been made to link the failure of rehabilitation in probation and parole with specific programs and personnel. The most common criticisms of rehabilitation programs are that they are disorganized as well as inadequately funded and staffed. Few programs dependent upon public funds for their operation and continuation will acknowledge adequate staffing and funding. Thus, most programs are perpetually in a state of need, where requests are made annually for larger portions of public resources and budgets are stretched to justify greater allocations for agency funding.

What evidence suggests that enlarging correctional staffs and spending more money on correctional programs will necessarily result in lower recidivism rates? Interestingly, the enlargement of correctional staffs, especially in probation and parole, has made it possible in some jurisdictions for officers to supervise their clients more closely through lower offender caseloads. However, greater supervision of offenders has resulted occasionally in an increase in the number of reported technical violations of an offender's probation or parole program (Baumer et al., 2002). Technical violations do not mean that crime among probationers and parolees has increased, only that they are now more frequently observed and recorded. These offenders stand a good chance of having their probation or parole revoked because of such violations, thus giving the public the impression that their criminal activity is increasing.

Criticisms of POs generally have centered on the inadequacy of their training, lack of experience, and poor educational background. For example, studies of POs have shown that they are typically white, come from rural areas, are politically conservative, have mixed job histories, have entered corrections work at a turning point or after failure in another career, or are merely holding their present job while anticipating a career move to a more promising alternative.

To the extent that probation and parole officers are similar in their backgrounds and training compared with corrections officers who perform inmate management chores, these characteristics have implications for the quality of services delivered by probation and parole agencies. If it is true that a majority of probation and parole officers enter this work with little or no training, that they lack the enthusiasm and energy to perform their jobs efficiently and effectively, and that they lack basic educational skills for dealing with offender clients, then it may be that these factors significantly influence the quality of services delivered to offenders. If probation and parole officers cannot cope effectively with the demands of their jobs because of their own limited resources and experiences, then suggested reforms involving their professionalization would be justified (Morton and Stone, 2006).

Professionalization is often equated with acquiring more formal education rather than practical skills involving one-to-one human relationships with different types of offender-clients. Educational programs for officers often overemphasize the laws and rules of institutions and the mechanics of enforcement. Often underemphasized are people skills and the ability to cope with human problems (e.g., physically or mentally impaired clients), those abilities required if the quality of officers is to be raised (Griffin, 2002). Although the following list is not exhaustive, it contains some of the more prevalent reasons for criticisms of probation and parole programs and personnel:

1. Probation and parole programs have historically been fragmented and independent of other criminal justice organizations and agencies. Without any centralized planning and coordinating, probation and parole programs have developed haphazardly in response to varying jurisdictional needs.

2. The general field of corrections has lacked professionalization associated with established fields with specialized bodies of knowledge. Often, corrections officers have secured their training through affiliation with an academic program in sociology, criminal justice, or political science. While these programs offer much relating to the correctional field, they are not designed to give corrections career–oriented students the practical exposure to real problems faced by officers on duty and dealing with real offenders.

3. Most jurisdictions have lacked licensing mechanisms whereby officers can become certified through proper in-service training and education. However, this situation has greatly improved during the last few decades. In 2006, probation and parole officers averaged 252 hours of training, including 44 hours of in-service training. Also in 2006, there were formal training programs in all U.S. jurisdictions (U.S. Department of Justice, 2006).

4. Until the early 1980s, only one state required a college education of probation or parole officer applicants, and some states had as their only prerequisite the ability to read and write, presumably for the purpose of completing PSI reports. Despite the fact that the relation between a college education and probation or parole officer effectiveness has not been demonstrated conclusively, some evidence suggests that college training is particularly helpful in the preparation of pre-sentence investigations and understanding criminal law and potential legal issues and liabilities that might arise in the officer–client relationship.

5. Past selection procedures for probation and parole officers have focused on physical attributes and security consideration. An emphasis in recruitment upon physical attributes has historically operated to exclude women from probation and parole work, although there is evidence showing a greater infusion of women into correctional roles in recent years. For example, in 1986 only 12 percent of all POs in the United States were women. But by 2006, the proportion of female POs had risen to about 50 percent (U.S. Department of Justice, 2006). In recent years, screening mechanisms have changed to include psychological interviews and personality assessment inventories for the purpose of identifying those most able to handle the **stress** and psychological challenges of probation and parole work, with less emphasis on physical abilities. Several studies have found that PO work generally is more enriching and complicated in the sense that one's personal problem-solving skills are becoming more important compared with past years, where learned standard solutions were applied consistently to situations with general similarities. Thus, PO work is becoming more of an art rather than the application of a limited range of standard strategies for diverse client problems, regardless of whether those strategies are applicable or inappropriate.

6. Probation and parole officer training has often been based on the military model used for police training. In those states with centralized corrections officer training and in-service programs for those preparing for careers in probation and parole work, a fundamental program flaw has been overreliance upon police training models whose relevance is frequently questioned by new recruits. Highly structured training programs frequently fail to provide prospective probation and parole officers with the sorts of practical experiences they will encounter face-to-face with offender-clients.

PROBATION AND PAROLE OFFICERS: A PROFILE

Interacting with ex-offenders, visiting their homes or workplaces, and generally overseeing their behavior while on probation or parole is a stressful experience. The dangerousness associated with PO work is well documented, and each day exposes most POs to risks similar to those encountered by police officers. Of course, offenders are obliged to comply with probation or parole program requirements, whatever they might be, and to be responsive and accessible whenever POs wish to contact them.

The primary control mechanism that POs exercise over offenders is the probation or parole revocation power possessed by POs. While their recommendations for a parole or probation revocation are not binding on any parole board convened to hear allegations of violations against an offender, reports filed by POs commence revocation proceedings. An unfavorable report about an offender may involve a technical violation or a serious criminal allegation. POs often overlook minor supervision violations, in part because they judge such violations not to be serious and also because they do not wish to prepare the extensive paperwork that is a preliminary requirement for a formal probation/parole revocation hearing. Despite the leverage POs have over their offender-clients, the possibility of violent confrontation with injury or death, and hostility from the public-at-large make PO work increasingly stressful and demanding.

Characteristics of Probation and Parole Officers

Who are probation and parole officers? What are their characteristics? Although little comprehensive information about POs exists, surveys have been conducted in recent years that depict the characteristics of those performing various correctional roles. These surveys indicate a gradual move toward greater corrections officer professionalization. Historically, evidence of professionalizing probation work has been found in various cities, such as Chicago, during the period 1900–1935. One indication of greater professionalization of the corrections profession has been the movement toward accreditation and the establishment of accreditation programs through the American Correctional Association (ACA) and the American Probation and Parole Association (APPA) (American Correctional Association, 2006).

 **BOX 10.1**　　　　　　　　　　　　 **CAREER SNAPSHOT**

Chris Callahan
Chief Probation Officer, Claremont District Office, New Hampshire Department of Corrections

Statistics:

B.S. (sociology-crime and delinquency sequence), Suffolk University, Boston; M.S. (juvenile justice), Eastern Kentucky University.

Background:

My interest in criminal justice began during my years at Suffolk University (1973–1977). I entered college with a tentative career objective of becoming a lawyer. My initial major was government. I found this major to be populated by students with an interest and knowledge in politics. I had neither.

Fortunately, I had a chance encounter with a sociology major who introduced me to the study of crime and delinquency. For whatever reason, I never had even thought about social science devoted to the study of crime and the society's response to it. I took a few crime and delinquency courses and was hooked.

During my senior year, I completed a field study placement at a district court probation office in Concord, Massachusetts. The probation officers (POs) appeared to me to be problem solvers. The court sentenced adults and juveniles to probation supervision and the POs had to devise some sort of strategy to deal with the underlying issues with the ultimate goal of preventing further criminality. After assessing the probationer's situation, the POs would bring to bear whatever social, educational, and mental health resources were available. It was social work with criminals and delinquents. My direct contact was with a few juvenile delinquents in a supportive or mentoring-type role. Most of the time, I simply observed the probation officers and tagged along. I left there after the semester was over. Looking back now, it seems like just a snapshot, but it left an impression on me.

Work Experience:

My actual work experience in criminal/juvenile justice began in 1980 in the juvenile detention center of the Fayette County Jail in Lexington, Kentucky. Juvenile Detention was operated by the Division of Children's Services. I was hired as a juvenile detention counselor. I was responsible for the security and care of juveniles, generally ages 12–17, held there for status or delinquency offenses. This largely entailed sitting with them in the day room area or "pod" and supervising their activities. Detention was temporarily housed in the adult detention center while a separate juvenile detention center was being built. After a few years, we moved to our own secure facility. I spent a lot of time listening to and observing these youthful offenders. It was an extremely valuable experience. I learned a lot about the behavior and thinking of these youthful offenders and about correctional security practices.

While working in the juvenile detention center, I attended Eastern Kentucky University's College of Law Enforcement and earned my master's degree in juvenile justice. Dick Jones, Director of Juvenile Detention, was supportive of my educational effort. Working in the field of juvenile justice reinforced what I was learning in graduate school and vice versa. After completing the master's degree, I was promoted to Detention Social Worker. This was a grant-funded position working with serious and violent juvenile offenders. I oversaw some of the family visitation and did some pre-release training and follow-up.

My adult correctional career began with accepting a position as a probation/parole officer (PPO) in Alexandria, Virginia. I worked there for approximately one year, and then I accepted a PPO position in Brattleboro, Vermont. My motivation for the change was to be closer to family in New England (I was born and raised in Massachusetts). As a PPO in Vermont, I found the Department of Corrections to be very active in developing rehabilitative programs, such as for batterers, sexual offenders, and youthful offenders, a definite plus. However, I also found there to be a lack of court-imposed punitive sanctions for those who chose not to participate in such programs or who continued their criminal and high-risk behaviors. As a criminal justice practitioner, you will find philosophical and operational differences from state to state, even within states. I became acquainted with PPOs from New Hampshire. The criminal justice system in New Hampshire had a philosophy that was more in line with my personal correctional philosophy. In 1988 I became a PPO in New Hampshire.

The criminal justice system in New Hampshire is more enforcement-oriented than the previous two states where I had worked. A probationer or parolee who deliberately fails to comply with their release conditions is likely to face incarceration as a consequence. Such incarceration may be short- or long-term depending on the level of noncompliance and their prior record. Conditions of probation or parole are very similar in New Hampshire. They are tailored to enhance public safety and to mandate rehabilitative programming for offenders. The reality of incarceration for noncompliance and the perception by offenders of that reality enhances the effectiveness of alternative sentences such as probation and parole. At the same time, this mechanism for returning an offender to incarceration enhances public safety.

(continued)

BOX 10.1 *(Continued)*

As PPOs, we are constantly assessing risk. We do this by gathering information about the offenders, such as offense information, prior criminal records, and their current life situations. We evaluate their behavior in the community by office and field visits and collateral contacts. We refer them for appropriate rehabilitative programming and maintain contact with program providers to assess their participation and progress. We are not merely enforcers of rules. Analytical skills and independence of thought are also important. In my opinion, a PPO can do no finer work than when he or she prevents new victimizations by successfully employing rehabilitative resources or by removing an offender from the community who is a menace to people and property. That is crime prevention.

New Hampshire PPOs are authorized to make arrests of noncompliant probationers and parolees. We carry firearms, OC spray (pepper gas), and handcuffs. We have ballistic vests. We have law enforcement radios, handheld and in the cars. Since some of our training is law enforcement–related, we are certified through the New Hampshire Standards and Training Council. The minimum requirements to become a PPO I are a bachelor's degree (with related coursework) and 3 years of related experience.

Since 2002 I have been Chief Probation/Parole Officer for Sullivan County in New Hampshire. My office is located in Claremont. Claremont is a small city on the western side of New Hampshire. I supervise an office of three other PPOs, a case technician, and a secretary. I am part manager and part PPO. I am enjoying the challenges management offers, but I also continue to enjoy the work and variety of situations that we encounter on a daily basis in probation and parole. I still need to get away from the desk and out into the field.

Advice to Students:

If you are tentatively thinking about a career in criminal justice, an introduction to criminal justice course is a good starting point. If you "know" what you want to be in the criminal justice field, still give a good look at all of the possible career paths in criminal justice. I would hazard to say that there are more choices than you realize. Regardless of your particular career goal in criminal justice, learn about all of the components and players in the system. When you find a particular job or area of interest, learn as much about it as you can. As you can see from my background, it sometimes takes a while to get into a particular field. While being a PPO has been my favorite job, I truly value the time I spent as a Juvenile Detention Counselor.

A majority of PO staff are female (58 percent), white (78 percent), possess bachelor's degrees (76 percent), and have 9–12 years experience. Entry-level salaries for POs ranged in 1999 from a low of $18,200 in Kentucky to a high of $45,600 in California, with the average entry-level salary being about $26,000 (U.S. Department of Justice, 2006). Maximum salaries among jurisdictions for POs ranged from a low of $30,000 in West Virginia to a high of $88,000 in Alaska (Camp and Camp, 2003), with the average highest salary at $56,000. The federal probation system had an entry-level salary of $28,000, with a high salary of $97,500, averaging $49,900. Most state systems presently require bachelor's degrees as the minimum education for entry-level parole officer positions. In a few states, the general entry-level requirements for PO positions are less stringent. In 1990, for instance, a few jurisdictions required a bachelor's degree or equivalent experience. By 2006, a majority of jurisdictions required bachelor's degrees for entry-level positions (U.S. Department of Justice, 2006).

Considering the relatively low salaries of POs compared with those in other correctional positions and in the private sector, their higher median ages, and their comparatively lower educational levels, it is understandable that probation and parole have drawn criticism in the last few decades concerning the lack of professionalism POs seem to exhibit. This problem is explained, in part, by the lack of professional identity characterizing PO work, the fact that there is no recognized professional school to prepare leaders for probation, and no nationally recognized scholars or administrators who can be called eminent leaders in probation or parole.

What Do POs Do?

Studies of correctional personnel have focused on prison and jail correctional officers, their behaviors and backgrounds, and work orientations. It has been reported that POs have negative self-images and impressions. Although there have been gains in the selection, recruitment, and professionalization of POs, attitude changes about their work roles and relationships with offender-clients have been slowly changing. The highest labor turnover among POs usually occurs during the early years of their employment.

At least 23 different PO functions have been identified, reflecting considerable diversity associated with PO roles. These include supervision, surveillance, investigation of cases, assisting in rehabilitation, develop and discuss probation conditions, counsel, visit homes and work with clients, make arrests, make referrals, write PSI reports, keep records, perform court duties, collect fines, supervise restitution, serve warrants, maintain contracts with courts, recommend sentences, develop community service programs, assist law enforcement officers and agencies, assist courts in transferring cases, enforce criminal laws, locate employment for clients, and initiate program revocations.

A direct relation exists between professionalism and the nature and quality of work performed in the organization. Where POs lack self-esteem and are often scorned by others because of their apparent leniency with the offenders they manage, they have sometimes acquired counterproductive definitions of their work roles and functions. An element of cynicism exists among POs and their work attitudes. Some of the major orientations manifested by POs are summarized as follows:

1. Probation officers are mere instruments to be utilized for larger organizational ends. Their body of professional skills cannot be autonomously employed but must be exercised within the framework of precise organizational limits and objectives.

2. Probation officers' lack of genuine professional status in the court is a constant source of personal anxiety, work alienation, and general dissatisfaction.

3. The pre-sentence investigation document is often cynically employed to validate judicial behavior or is otherwise used to reinforce administrative action already taken. The circumstances under which probation reports are prepared cast serious doubts as to their objectivity, validity, and integrity.

4. Frustrated as professionals, stripped of real decision-making power, lacking a genuine career motif, and assigned relatively low status by the

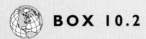 **BOX 10.2**

INTERNATIONAL SNAPSHOT: PROBATION AND PAROLE IN COSTA RICA

Costa Rica is a Central American country with approximately 4 million inhabitants. The Spanish colonial system has had a pervasive influence on Costa Rica's criminal justice system. The government is best described as a constitutional democracy with a unicameral Legislative Assembly elected freely every four years. The economy of Costa Rica is predominantly light industry, tourism, and agriculture. The penal code of Costa Rica has been revised numerous times, the most recent revision occurring in 2004. A separate penal code exists for juveniles under the 1996 Penal Juvenile Justice Law.

Crimes in Costa Rica are categorized into two major classifications. The most serious crimes are the equivalent of U.S. felonies, and they are known as *delitos*. These include crimes against life or family, sex crimes, property damage, human rights crimes, drug trafficking, robbery, burglary, and aggravated assault. These carry penalties of fines and/or imprisonment in Costa Rican prisons for periods of one year or longer. The second crime class includes misdemeanors or contravention offenses. Such offenses might include crimes against public safety, minor property offending, and minor physical injury. The punishment for such offending is less than one year in a jail or prison. Judges may suspend incarcerative penalties at their discretion.

The age of criminal responsibility in Costa Rica is 18, with the exception of persons who are close to the legal age (e.g., 16–17 years of age) who have committed heinous crimes. Costa Rica subscribes to the United Nations definition of rights for juveniles. A further distinction is made for children age 12 or over, and under 18. Those over 12 and under 18 and who have committed one or more crimes are sent to rehabilitative facilities. The focus of these facilities is entirely on rehabilitation of a vocational and/or educational nature. For those under age 12, no punitive action is taken. Social agencies accept responsibility for the welfare of such children and their proper placement with families who will assume responsibility for their conduct.

The most frequent crimes committed are robbery and larceny. There are relatively few murders and rapes annually, given a population in excess of 4 million. Drug offenses have increased in frequency in recent years, primarily in costal communities with sea access. Victim's assistance agencies have been established to look after the needs of crime victims and their close relatives affected by crime. Crime victims are given the opportunity to have input in one's sentencing if convicted of a crime. This input is similar to victim impact statements victims may prepare for pre-sentence investigation reports or sentencing hearings in the United States.

The police forces of Costa Rica are divided into six classes. The judicial police are under the executive branch of government and are the equivalent of the FBI in the United States. Another division consists of the Metro police who enforce laws in the greater San Jose metropolitan area. The Guardia de Asistencia Rural (GAR) has jurisdiction for all rural areas of Costa Rica. There are also local law enforcement departments in smaller communities. Officers act much like police officers in the United States, in that they may make arrests of persons who are seen committing crimes. They may also make arrests of persons based on reports by private citizens who observed crimes occur. In this respect, police must have probable cause to stop, detain, and/or apprehend a person for suspicion of committing an offense. Under circumstances where police officers do not actually observe a crime occur, they may transport suspects to local judicial officials for further investigation. No charges are filed until concrete evidence exists that a crime was committed and the suspect in custody committed it. Suspects may be held for 24 hours before charges must be filed. Officers do not make custody decisions. These are determined by the judge or presiding official who decides to detain or release the suspect from custody. Costa Rica does not have a formal military force. Formal investigations of suspects are conducted by the Department of Justice, not by the police department. Searches of one's premises require a search warrant issued by a presiding judge in the jurisdiction.

Persons who are arrested have the right to an attorney. If they cannot afford an attorney, one will be appointed for them by the court. The Justice Department conducts all interrogations, and confessions are admissible against suspects after they are warned of the serious implications of confessing to a crime. Persons accused of a crime in Costa Rica have various rights. They have rights similar to criminal suspects in the United States. These rights include notice of charges against them; the right against self-incrimination; the right to an attorney or to have one appointed for them if they cannot afford one; the right to bail; and the right to a speedy trial.

When a person is first arrested, he or she is brought before a fact-finding authority where an initial questioning period is conducted. If the case has merit, it proceeds to the next level, where the Ministerio Publico or prosecutor conducts an official prosecution. Evidence is gathered and witnesses are obtained. There is no plea bargaining in Costa Rica. Accused persons may not accept lighter sentences in exchange for testimony against others or for confessions. However, judges may impose lighter sentences at their discretion if they believe the information provided by the accused is noteworthy and leads to a successful prosecution. Pretrial detention exists in Costa Rica. Whether a suspect is allowed to post bail depends on the offenses alleged, the person's prior criminal record, the reliability of the offender, and the impact on the community. Factors such as the mother's family background, the accused level of education, number of children, job performance, marital status, and leisure time activities are all considered in the bail decision. About 85 percent of all persons charged with crimes are released on bail annually. Those held in pretrial detention are held in holding facilities until they have their day in court.

Not all cases result in formal court action. There is pretrial diversion, which is an option used by prosecutors with judicial approval. Of the 103,000 cases processed in 1999, for instance, about 26 percent were dismissed without trial. Pretrial diversion was recommended in about 5 percent of these cases, while the majority of other cases processed resulted in relatively minor penalties, including home confinement and fines.

The court system in Costa Rica is multileveled. The highest court is the supreme court, or the Salas Corte Suprema de Justicia. There are several courts of appeal, and several types of lower courts. The lowest court consists of Alcaldias who handle misdemeanor offenses or minor crimes, with punishments of less than three years. The next higher court is the Juzgados or courts of First Instance. These deal with crimes whose penalties are more than three years. The Tribunal Superior and the Supreme Tribunal are courts of appeal for lower courts as well as trial courts for felonies. There are seven provinces in Costa Rica, with three lower courts to serve them. In 2000 there were 103 Alcaldia courts, 84 Juzgados courts, 10 Tribunal Superior courts, and one Supreme Court. Judicial appointments are made by the Judicial Counsel. These individuals must be certified attorneys with a high level of education. Those who anticipate being judges are encouraged to take their legal training in Spain, England, or the United States. Most cases are resolved through a trial process, even where persons plead guilty to crimes.

When a person is found guilty of a crime, the judge or panel of judges imposes a sentence. Sentences are determined by the penal code, although judges have some flexibility in how the law is interpreted and applied. Sentencing hearings are conducted in many serious cases, where input is given by social workers, clergy, psychologists, and other professionals. The range of penalties include fines, imprisonment, and house arrest. While most crimes carry 1- to 25-year sentences, longer sentences may be imposed under special circumstances. There is no death penalty in Costa Rica.

(continued)

BOX 10.2 (Continued)

Fines are assessed on the basis of the number of days a convicted offender is sentenced to pay a prescribed percentage of his income. Offenders have 15 days to pay their fines or they are imprisoned. This time period may be extended at the discretion of the judge.

Four major prisons existed in Costa Rica in 2005. There was at least one jail in each of Costa Rica's seven provinces. One maximum-security institution existed for men and one existed for women. A separate juvenile facility existed for males only, and one juvenile facility existed that was co-correctional. There are no precise figures on how many persons are incarcerated in Costa Rica at any given time. Estimates range from 2,500 to 4,000 persons in prisons and local jails. No information is available about the nature of persons incarcerated, such as the number of murderers, robbers, rapists, and others. The ratio of prison guards to inmates is about 1 to 20.

Inmates may earn time off for good behavior up to 50 percent of their maximum sentence being served. Thus, there is parole in Costa Rica. Determining who should receive early release is an interesting process. A judge refers each case to the Criminology Institute, where a criminological diagnosis of the inmate is made. A report is submitted by the institute attesting to whether the offender has complied with all penal conditions and whether basic treatments should be ordered. For first-offenders, it is possible to earn early release after serving only six months. Again, much depends on the good conduct of the applicant for early release. When parole is granted, judges have the right to impose any conditions they consider advisable to impose, given the nature of the conviction offense. The report from the Criminology Institute is an important document and it functions much like a pre-sentence investigation report for judges in U.S. jurisdictions. The numbers of persons on probation and parole are unknown, since formal records of these proceedings are not made available to the general public.

While in prison, although inmates are not made to work, they are encouraged to take advantage of various rehabilitative programs of a vocational and/or educational nature. Such training can prepare them for easing back into their communities, finding jobs, and supporting their dependents. Costa Rican prisoners have many amenities enjoyed by U.S. prisoners. They have group therapy sessions, anger management training, counseling, educational/vocational training, television sets, radios, and the right to possess a certain amount of their personal property. Conjugal and family visits are permitted on a regular basis. Medical care and religious services are provided.

There is no formal probation protocol in Costa Rica. The closest thing to probation is a suspension of proceedings against a criminal suspect. This is similar to pretrial diversion in the United States. Thus, divertees are placed on suspension for a period of time with conditions. Depending on whether they comply with their conditions, their cases may be dismissed at the end of their suspension period. The conditions under which suspension is granted are similar to probation conditions. Accused persons are not permitted to frequent establishments where liquor is served; they are not permitted to associate with known criminals; they must take special treatment programs designated for them depending on their offenses and particular needs; they must accept being under surveillance; and they are not allowed to possess weapons.

Sources: Adapted from Bureau of Democracy, Human Rights, and Labor, "Costa Rica: Country Reports on Human Rights Practices, 2001," Washington, DC, March 4, 2002; United Nations, Committee Against Torture, "Convention Against Torture and Other Cruel, Inhuman or Degrading Treatment or Punishment," New York, November 13, 2000; Henry Q. Giralt, "Costa Rica," *World Factbook of Criminal Justice Systems,* Fairbanks, AK, March 2004; Caroline C. Williams, "Costa Rica," *World Factbook of Criminal Justice Systems,* Directorate of Citizen Security, 2003; *2004 Penal Procedural Code,* "Statistics and Trends," National Assembly, December 2005.

community, it is not surprising that probation workers often develop a high degree of cynicism.

5. Probation officers come to view their administrators as frightened, insecure, petty officials who will respond to any organization need at the expense of workers and clients. There is a constant undercurrent of antagonism between probation workers and their supervisors.

While POs themselves may be at fault directly or indirectly by being ill-prepared or undereducated for the roles they perform, probation and parole agencies must absorb some of the blame. It has been suggested by more than one critic that probation and parole organizations and agencies often fail to clarify their own goals and objectives for the staff to achieve. If the goals of the organization itself are diffuse, it is difficult for agency members to adhere to particular policies or move in constructive directions when helping their offender-clients.

Some fragmentation of effort exists among many POs who have their own ideas about how their jobs ought to be performed and what correctional philosophies should guide their own thinking about themselves and what they do. Increasing PO accountability through more effective leadership from administrators is one possible solution. Agency management must be willing to establish reasonable standards of performance for both staff and clients. They must then follow through by monitoring and assessing performance objectively.

Frequently, organizational constraints inhibit the development of professional orientations toward probation and parole work, while more educated POs are sought by probation/parole agencies. When they begin their PO duties, these duties remain perfunctory or routine and custodial. Thus, more educated POs are not permitted the latitude to adapt their skills and education to their supervisory tasks and dealings with offender-clients. Many PO training programs, where they exist, simply fail to train new POs to deal effectively with the practical problems they will encounter on the job. It also seems the case that they are neither allowed nor encouraged to utilize the skills they have developed.

Tenured POs feel threatened by what they perceive as greater emphasis on education, which operates to the exclusion of prior experience. These feelings foster interpersonal strains between senior/experienced and newer POs with vastly different educational backgrounds and experiences. The importance of dealing effectively with the offender-client is shifted to a lower priority, as POs spend more time dealing with conflicting role and training expectations and less time helping offenders. Accordingly, more highly educated POs reflect greater disappointment with their work, where they were promised more challenging tasks but must often perform routine and menial ones.

Observers have concluded that POs experience much frustration in the performance of their work roles and associations with colleagues and clients, and that much of this frustration is organizationally induced. Greater professionalization is called for, and it has been suggested that such professionalization can be engendered through greater participation in decision making by the POs themselves.

POs spend much of their time preparing reports or PSIs for convicted offenders at the request of judges. They must maintain contact with all offenders assigned to their supervision. They must be aware of community agencies and employment opportunities so that their function as resource staff may be maximized. They must perform informal psychological counseling. They must enforce the laws and ensure offender compliance with the requirements of the particular probation or parole program. When faced with dangerous or life-threatening situations in their contacts with offenders, they must be able to make decisions about how best to handle these situations. They must be familiar with their legal rights, the rights of offenders, and their own legal liabilities in relation to clients. POs must be flexible enough to supervise a wide variety of offender-clients. Increasing numbers of PO clients are from different ethnicities and cultures. Thus, greater cultural awareness is required of today's POs.

A summary of the primary duties of probation and parole officers in North Dakota seems to typify this general work:

1. Supervise offenders to ensure compliance with parole, probation, or community placement agreements.

2. Perform scheduled and unscheduled home visits.

3. Conduct searches, with or without a warrant, of homes, vehicles, and possessions of criminal offenders to determine if they have dangerous, illegal, or stolen goods, or for any other evidence that might indicate criminal behavior.

4. Manage cases by means of direct contact with offenders, indirect contact through individuals who are acquainted with or have an impact on the offender's life, and the maintenance of records required by the Department of Corrections and Rehabilitation.

5. Conduct investigations, prepare reports, and make recommendations for the offender's placement and level of risk to the community.

6. Notify court-mandated sex offenders of their responsibility to register with local law enforcement and monitor their adherence to this statute.

7. Assist law enforcement in criminal investigations.

8. Collect, handle, and maintain evidence in accordance with evidentiary law.

9. Maintain necessary certifications and licensures (North Dakota Department of Corrections and Rehabilitation, 2004:1–4).

Recruitment of POs

When POs are recruited, what type of training should they receive? How much education should be required, and what educational subjects have the greatest relevance for correctional careers? No immediate answers are available for these questions. While most of us would agree that PhD degrees are not essential for the effective performance of PO work, some educational training is desirable. Currently, observers disagree about how much education should be officially required as a part of the recruitment process.

The selection requirements and recruitment procedures included in this section are not exhaustive. But they serve as a set of standards against which PO recruitment, selection, and training programs may be evaluated. Traditional PO selection procedures have tended to focus on weeding out those unfit for PO work rather than on selecting those possessing the skills needed for successful job performance. PO training in most states includes several weeks of class time (e.g., social sciences, humanities, and/or police sciences) and two or more weeks of in-service training (American Correctional Association, 2004; Camp and Camp, 2003). However, some states had no in-service or course requirements in place for

BOX 10.3

JOB ANNOUNCEMENTS FOR PROBATION/PAROLE OFFICER POSITIONS

• **Probation Officer/Probation Officer Trainee**

DATE OF EXAMINATION: February 4, 2006

LAST FILING DATE: December 28, 2005

LOCATION OF EMPLOYMENT: Livingston County (New York) Probation Department

SALARY: Trainee: $15.50–$21.05 (2005)
Officer: $16.55–$22.50

EXAMINATION NUMBER: 61-002
CANDIDATES MUST HAVE BEEN LEGAL RESIDENTS OF LIVINGSTON COUNTY FOR AT LEAST FOUR MONTHS IMMEDIATELY PRECEDING THE DATE OF THE WRITTEN TEST AND MUST CONTINUOUSLY MAINTAIN THEIR RESIDENCY THROUGH THE DATE OF APPOINTMENT.

An official application form must be filed for *each* examination. You are responsible for completing *all* sections of the application. Exam number and title must be recorded on the application.

List Certification: A single eligible list will be established as a result of this examination. Candidates who are successful in this examination and possess the minimum qualifications for Probation Officer will be certified for appointment as a Probation Officer. Those eligible for Probation Officer Trainee will be certified at the trainee level. Persons appointed at the trainee level will be advanced to Probation Officer without further examination upon satisfactory completion of the one-year traineeship. Probation Officer eligibles will have their names certified for appointment before those eligible for Probation Officer Trainee. If candidates originally placed on the eligible list as a Probation Officer Trainee acquire the training or experience necessary to meet the minimum qualifications for Probation Officer during the life of the list, they may submit a new application and may then be certified as a Probation Officer.

MINIMUM QUALIFICATIONS:
Probation Officer
Master's degree or Doctorate in social work, education, administration, law, sociology, psychology, criminology, or related field *OR* Bachelor's degree and two years' experience in counseling or casework in a recognized agency adhering to acceptable standards in probation, parole, social services, psychiatric or medical social work, or related work; *OR* appropriate combination of above training and experience.

Special Requirements:

1. Applicants must possess a valid New York State driver's license at the time of appointment, or have other suitable means of transportation.

2. A probation office position is a peace officer under State Law. All candidates will be required to participate in and satisfactorily complete all requirements of a training program. Training will include classroom instructions in such areas as basic law, social work practice and case management, use of deadly physical force, firearms and other weapons training, and arrest procedures. Successful completion of the program is mandatory for continued employment.

3. An applicant who is offered employment must be willing to submit to criminal history checks by both the Division of Criminal Justice Services and the Federal Bureau of Investigation. Those checks will be subject to a fee determined by each respective agency, and that fee must be paid by the applicant at the time the fingerprints are taken.

DUTIES: This is the beginning position at the professional level of probation work. The duties require the application of modern

(continued)

BOX 10.3 (*Continued*)

social work techniques in making evaluations of adults or juveniles and in supervising persons on probation. A Probation Officer is called upon to exercise sound professional judgment in analyzing data and in making recommendations concerning court dispositions. He/she assists persons on probation and other persons whom the probation agency services. A Probation Officer works under the supervision of a higher ranking professional employee and may help to supervise the work of Probation Assistants, Probation Officer Trainees, or volunteers.

Probation Officer Trainees are automatically appointed to this title if they have satisfactorily completed one year of service.

• **TITLE: Probation and Parole Unit Supervisor (5120)**

LOCATION: Statewide—Applications are being accepted for the purpose of maintaining registers of eligibles who would be available for employment as vacancies occur with the Board of Probation and Parole of the Department of Corrections. Currently the Board of Probation and Parole utilizes this classification in various locations throughout the State. When vacancies occur, the names of eligibles available for employment in the county where the vacancy is located will be certified in grade order for employment consideration.

ANNUAL SALARY: $35,076–$51,372

BENEFITS: Missouri State Employee Retirement System (MOSERS) provides retirement, life insurance, survivor and disability benefits; Missouri Consolidated Healthcare Plan (MCHCP) provides medical, vision, dental, and Employee Assistance Program benefits (some of these benefits may not be available in all areas of the state); Missouri Deferred Compensation Plan (PEBSCO); Missouri Cafeteria Plan; Missouri Voluntary Life Insurance; 15 days paid annual leave per year for new full-time employees (accrual rates increase with years of service); 15 days paid sick leave per year.

DEFINITION: This is professional supervisory adult probation and parole work in the Board of Probation and Parole. An employee in this class may serve as the assistant to the District Administrator, supervise a unit in a moderate to large district office, or have programmatic supervision for a specialized program such as community sentencing, intensive supervision, electronic monitoring, or residential treatment. Work involves providing supervision and training to staff with emphasis on professional performance of duties and conformance with the policies and procedures set forth in the rules, regulations, and manuals of the Board of Probation and Parole. General supervision is received from a designated administrative superior through conferences and reviews of records and reports; however, the employee exercises considerable discretion and independent judgment in the performance of the assigned responsibilities within established policies and procedures.

EXPERIENCE AND EDUCATION QUALIFICATIONS: Three years of professional experience in adult probation and parole or corrections casework; and graduation from an accredited four-year college or university with specialization in criminal justice, social work, sociology, or psychology. (Graduate work from an accredited college or university in the specified education areas may be substituted on a year-for-year basis for a maximum of one year of the stated experience. Additional qualifying experience, substance abuse counseling or closely related work may be substituted on a year-for-year basis for deficiencies in the stated education. Two years of less related social casework, employment interviewing, or counseling may be substituted for each year of deficiency in the stated education.)

EXAMINATION COMPONENT: Rating of Education and Experience, 100%.

HOW TO APPLY: To secure an Official Application Form, visit the Division of Personnel website *www.oa.mo.gov/pers/howtoapply.htm*, or contact the Division via telephone. Note: The Division of Personnel only accepts electronic applications for some classes, *http://www.ease.mo.gov/*.

- **Chief Probation Officer**

Mohave County Probation, Kingman (AZ)

Full-time benefits eligible position $2,661.60–$4,128.80 biweekly (Hire in Salary is Negotiable Depending on Qualifications)

At-will position appointed by and serving at the pleasure of the presiding superior court judge. Position is responsible for planning, developing, organizing, and directing the activities and staff of the adult and juvenile probation department, currently comprised of 122 staff in four branch offices and a juvenile detention facility. Requires a Master's degree in business, management, the social sciences, or a related field degree from an accredited college or university, 10 years' experience in the fields of correction or probation, or working with offenders or delinquents in some equivalent capacity, with at least five years of progressively increasing responsibility in an administrative and supervisory capacity. The successful candidate will be at least 21 years of age, a citizen of the United States or have legal resident status, and will be required to undergo a polygraph, psychological, and criminal background check.

To apply, submit letter of interest and resume, completed court application for employment, probation supplemental packet, and questionnaire to the address listed. Position is open until filled; however, the selection committee has initiated review of applications.

- **Deputy Probation Officer I/II**

AGENCY: Santa Cruz County, CA

COMPENSATION: Deputy Probation Officer I: $2,770–$3,505/Month; Deputy Probation Officer II: $3,061–$3,872/Month (Check with County for most recent pay scales)

CLOSING DATE: All applications on file in the Personnel Department as of 5:00 P.M. on the Friday before the 1st and 3rd Thursday of each month will be reviewed and scheduled for testing the following week. The exams are scheduled to take place the 1st and 3rd Thursday of each month at 5:30 P.M. **SUPPLEMENTAL APPLICATION REQUIRED.**

TO APPLY: Contact Santa Cruz County Personnel Department, 701 Ocean Street, Room 310, Santa Cruz, CA 95060. (831) 454-2600. TDD# (831) 454-2123. *www.co.santa-cruz.ca.us* EOE.

DESCRIPTION: Deputy Probation Officers perform referral, supervision, counseling, and rehabilitation services for a caseload of adult and juvenile offenders on probation and their families. Deputy Probation Officer I is the trainee level in the probation officer series. Deputy Probation Officer II is the journey level in the professional Probation Officer series.

THE REQUIREMENTS: Deputy Probation Officer I: Equivalent to a Bachelor's degree from an accredited four-year college or university, in psychology, sociology, social services, humanities, criminal justice, or a related field; OR, two years of experience performing duties comparable to those of Probation Aide with the County of Santa Cruz.

Deputy Probation Officer II: One year of experience performing duties comparable to a Deputy Probation Officer I in Santa Cruz County and successful completion of the core training course for Probation Officers as mandated by the Standards and Training for Corrections Program.

- **Probation Officer Entry: Adult Probation Countywide (Yavapai County, AZ Government, Employment Opportunity)**

Status: Full-time

Salary: $16.92 per hour

Classification: Classified, Non-Exempt

Open Date: 02/08/06

Close Date: Open until filled

Position Summary: Under close supervision performs professional duties of moderate difficulty in providing correctional casework services to assigned probationers at the direction of the Superior Court; performs other work as required or assigned. Supervises a caseload of assigned probationers requiring minimum to maximum supervision; conducts pre-sentence investigations and writes pre-sentence reports; compiles and maintains social histories and case histories; interviews probationers, families, authorities, employers, and victims; reviews and evaluates criminal records, police

(*continued*)

BOX 10.3 (Continued)

reports, and psychiatric and psychological reports; evaluates criminal personalities, behaviors, and rehabilitation potential; testifies in Court; provides for counseling for probationers; performs searches; and makes arrests.

Minimum Qualifications: A Bachelor's degree with a preference in the behavioral sciences or a related field from an accredited college or university; a minimum 21 years of age; a U.S. citizen or have legal resident status; maintain a valid Arizona driver's license, must successfully pass a pre-employment character and fitness background records check and psychological evaluation; submit to and pass an alcohol and illegal drug use screening; meet and be able to perform the required training and job duties with or without reasonable accommodation; may be required to submit to a polygraph. All results of pre-employment screening results will be kept confidential.

Preferences: Preferences may be given to candidates who are computer literate and bilingual in Spanish.

• **CAREER OPPORTUNITY, Klamath County, Oregon**

Probation Officer III, Community Corrections Department

Overview of the Position: Performs duties of Parole and Probation Officer as defined in ORS 181.610(13), 137.620, and 1367.630. Perform probation and parole counseling with adult offenders; conduct needs assessments and develop case plans; monitor probation and parole compliance and maintain caseload records.

Responsibilities/Duties:

Interview adult offenders on Probation, Parole, or Post-Prison Supervision to assess client needs; assess social, emotional, and economic status; determine treatment goals and refer clients to community agencies, if needed; counsel clients on probation/parole/PPS procedures, issues, and personal problems; counsels clients in establishing personal goals and plans; and confer with clients' family, support group, and community.

Maintain regular contact with clients and monitor activities; offer continuing assessment and counseling according to clients' needs and progress; monitor progress of meeting probation/parole/PPS conditions such as fines, restitution, participation in drug/alcohol treatment, employment or cognitive programs; contract service agencies, employers, clients' family, support group, and community.

Write reports for and confer with courts, or supervisory authority, on client probation/parole/PPS compliance; report problems and progress.

Prepare pre-sentence reports for courts; investigate offender's legal case and personal background; make recommendations on sentencing requirements.

Attend court hearings; document, testify, and make recommendations at probation/parole/PPS compliance hearings; testify at pre-sentence hearings.

Maintain records of client casework, including interviews, assessments, services provided, and probation/parole/PPS progress.

Participate in service resource development for client treatment and in-service evaluation.

May carry firearm for self-defense while performing duties as described in ORS and according to department policy.

Conduct arrest and search procedures in the office and field.

Attend staff meetings, professional conferences, and training programs; network professionally with criminal justice agencies and treatment providers.

Perform other related duties as assigned.

OCCUPATIONAL CERTIFICATES/LICENSES: Maintain valid Oregon driver's license.

Acquire within 1 year, and maintain, Parole and Probation Basic Certification from DPSST.

Acquire, and maintain, LEDS Certification.

EDUCATIONAL/VOCATIONAL PREPARATION: Possession of a Bachelor's degree from an accredited college or university with major study in criminal justice; behavioral science, social work, or related field; or an Associate's degree with at least four years responsible experience in probation/parole/PPS counseling, corrections, or social service counseling; or any satisfactory equivalent combination of experience and training.

EXCELLENT BENEFITS AND COMPENSATION: The hourly range for this position is $18.48 per hour up to $20.79 per hour with future increases extended up to a current maximum of $23.38 per hour. Starting compensation is determined by Klamath County based on skill. This position is represented by the Federation of Parole and Probation Officers. The normal work schedule is eight hours a day, five days a week. This position is classified as Non-Exempt under the Fair Labor Standards Act (FSLA) and therefore is eligible for overtime pay.

Klamath County offers a competitive benefits and compensation package. Employee benefits include the following:

Excellent Medical, Dental, Vision, and Prescription Insurance options

Life Insurance and Short-Term Disability programs

No-cost Flexible Spending Account (Section 125) Tax-Savings Plan

Paid holidays, vacation, and sick leave benefits

Excellent Klamath County Pension/Retirement Plan

Employee Wellness Program

On-going professional training and development programs

No-cost Employee Assistance Plan (EAP)

Deferred Compensation (Section 457) Plan options

AFLAC supplemental insurance options

Credit Union membership
Free parking

APPLICATION AND SELECTION PROCESS: To apply, return a completed Klamath County Employment Application. When applying, please reference job number **06-023-3821.** This position closes March 31, 2006, by 5:00 P.M. ***Applicant must complete attached questions.** Application materials are available from the Klamath County Human Resources Department located in the Government Center, Room 216, 305 Main Street, Klamath Falls, Oregon 97601-6332. Our telephone number is (541) 883-4296 or toll-free (888) 339-KCHR. Our facsimile number is (541) 883-4270. You may submit your application in person, fax, or online via our website, *www.co.klamath.or.us.* The selection process will consist of a review and evaluation of the knowledge and skills on the applications and resumes submitted. The best-qualified applicants, as determined by Klamath County, will be considered for employment.

For additional information, visit us online, or call our 24-hour job information hotline at 541-883-4188. *Klamath County enforces a drug-free workplace. Successful applicants will be required to submit to a pre-employment drug screening.*

• **Probation Officer I (Grand Junction, Colorado) $3,012–$4,038/Month**

To Establish an Eligibility List
Definition of Work: Monitors lower risk offenders or an administrative caseload and may provide supervision and/or investigatory work of probationers.

Minimum Qualifications: Bachelor's degree (BA) from four-year college or university with major coursework preferably in criminal justice, sociology, psychology, social work, or related field. Upon hire and as a condition of continued employment, the employee must: (1) complete the Basic Safety course as per state policy; and (2) complete Mandatory New Employee Training required by the Colorado Judicial Branch.

Applications To: Susan Gilbert, Chief Probation Officer, 125 N. Spruce, P.O. Box 20000, Grand Junction, Colorado 80502-5042. *Applications must be postmarked by January 6, 2006.* Position #TBD.

• **Probation Officer II** (Grand Junction, Colorado) $3,165–$4,243/Month

(*continued*)

BOX 10.3 (Continued)

Promotional Opportunity for Colorado Judicial Branch Employees Only

To Establish Eligibility List

Definition of Work: Provides supervision and/or investigatory work of probationers for a probation department.

Minimum Qualifications: Bachelor's degree (B A) from four-year college or university with major preferably in criminal justice, sociology, psychology, social work, or related field. Must have worked a minimum of one continuous year as a Probation Officer or Alcohol and Drug Evaluation Specialist and completed the following training courses: the Training and Advanced Training tracks of the Colorado Judicial Branch Probation Officer Career Track Program; the Mandatory New Employee Training required by the Colorado Judicial Branch; and the Basic Safety Course as per state policy. If field visits are being conducted, must complete the Defensive Skills course per state policy as a condition of continued employment, **OR** Bachelor's degree (BA) from a four-year college or university with major coursework preferably in criminal justice, sociology, psychology, social work, or related field and three years of experience working directly with probationers, parolees, or like work. Upon hire, and as a condition of continued employment, the employee must: (1) complete the Basic Safety course as per state policy; (2) if field visits are being conducted, must complete the Defensive Skills course per state policy; (3) complete the Training Track of the Colorado Judicial Branch Probation Officer Career Track Program within the first year of employment; (4) complete Mandatory New Employee Training required by the Colorado Judicial Branch as per state policy.

Applications To: Susan Gilbert, Chief Probation Officer, 125 N. Spruce, P.O. Box 20000, Grand Junction, Colorado, 80502-5042. **Applications must be postmarked by January 6, 2006.** Position #TBD.

• **Probation Officer III** *(Grand Junction, Colorado)* $3,325–$4,457/Month

Promotional Opportunity for Colorado Judicial Branch Employees Only

To Establish an Eligibility List

Definition of Work: Provides supervision and/or investigation of probationers for a probation department.

Minimum Qualifications: Bachelor's degree (B A) from four-year college or university with major coursework preferably in criminal justice, sociology, psychology, social work, or related field. Must have worked a minimum of two continuous years as a Probation Officer or Alcohol and Drug Evaluation Specialist and completed the following training: three tracks of the Colorado Judicial Branch Probation Officer Career Track Program, which must have included completion of the Apprenticeship Track; the Mandatory New Employee Training required by the Colorado Judicial Branch; and the Basic Safety course as per state policy. If field visits are being conducted, the employee must complete the Defensive Skills course as per state policy; **OR** Bachelor's degree (BA) from a four-year college or university with major coursework preferably in criminal justice, sociology, psychology, social work, or related field and five years of experience working directly with probationers, parolees, or like field. Upon hire and as a condition of continued employment, the employee must: (1) complete Basic Safety course as per state policy and if field visits are being conducted, must be able to complete the Defensive Skills course as per state policy; (2) complete the Training Track of the Colorado Judicial Branch Probation Officer Career Track Program within the first year of employment; and (3) complete Mandatory New Employee Training required by the Colorado Judicial Branch.

Applications To: Susan Gilbert, Chief Probation Officer, 125 N. Spruce, P.O. Box 20000, Grand Junction, Colorado 80502-5042. **Applications must be postmarked by January 6, 2006. Position #TBD.**

those aspiring to PO roles. By 2002, most states had minimum numbers of introductory hours that ranged from 40 to 1,480, while in-service hours ranged from 20 to 160 (Camp and Camp, 2003).

Minimum Educational Requirements for POs.   In 2003, minimum educational requirements of those entering the correctional field were a high school diploma or the GED for an entry-level PO position; community college (two years) diploma; or some college work. Because of the recent emphasis on professionalization, increasing numbers of jurisdictions are requiring a bachelor's degree for entry-level PO jobs (American Correctional Association, 2004).

The Use of Written Examinations for Screening Applicants.   While over 80 percent of the programs required a written examination, only about 20 percent subjected recruits to psychological screening. The Minnesota Multiphasic Personality Inventory and Inwald Personality Inventory appear to be those most popularly applied, when any are used. Very few programs included physical examinations, medical checks, or FBI inquiries. Several programs had no formal testing or examination procedures as a means of screening PO candidates (American Correctional Association, 2003). By 2003, most jurisdictions had considerably more rigorous physical and psychological qualifications for starting positions (American Correctional Association, 2004).

In 1981 the National Institute of Corrections (NIC) responded to the need for greater **professionalization** and training among POs by sponsoring a series of training programs in various jurisdictions. The American Correctional Association (ACA) was selected to administer some of these programs and eventually developed the Development of Correctional Staff Trainers program, which provided comprehensive, experience-based training for more than 1,000 trainers and other professionals between 1981 and 1985. In 1985 over 6,000 individuals had enrolled in ACA correspondence courses and participated in related programs, seminars, and workshops on a variety of correctional topics. These training programs are being continued, and enrollments have escalated considerably well beyond 2002 (American Correctional Association, 2003).

Stressed in these programs and workshops have been legal liabilities of POs and other types of corrections officers, as well as the cultivation of skills in the management and supervision of offender-clients. Additionally, programs and coursework are offered for managing stress, crisis intervention and hostage negotiations, proposal and report writing, legal issues training, managing community corrections facilities, dealing with the mentally ill offender, and suicide prevention (Fitzgerald et al., 2006).

One way of gauging the nature and quantity of education that should logically be expected of potential POs is to examine the situations they would ordinarily encounter. The fact that POs interact with violent and nonviolent offenders requires more than one approach or solution to any situation. Certain types of offenders on probation or parole are dangerous, and incarceration has not necessarily made them less dangerous than they were when they originally committed serious crimes. For example, female POs risk sexual assault if they are assigned especially violent sex offenders with one or more previous rape convictions. Both male and female POs risk injury through assault if they make decisions that affect offender freedoms such as recommendations for parole or probation revocations because of program violations they detect (Smith, 2006).

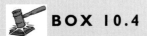

BOX 10.4

CAREER SNAPSHOT ON THE IMPORTANCE OF INTERNSHIPS

Monika D. Kinsman
Former FBI Intern, Law Enforcement Communication Unit, FBI National Academy, Quantico, VA

Statistics:

B.A. (law and justice) *magna cum laude,* Central Washington University; M.S. in Organizational Development, Central Washington University; M.A. (criminal justice management and administration), University of Alaska–Fairbanks.

Background:

Since the time I was first able to understand the concept of crime, I have sought to understand why people engage in antisocial criminal behavior. As I grew older, I decided that I wanted to make a career for myself in the field of law enforcement, where I can make a difference in stopping criminals, or otherwise work to reduce the impact of crime on society. Some time ago, I concluded that the ideal employer for me would be the Federal Bureau of Investigation (FBI). Based on the reading I had done, it was obvious to me that the FBI is one of the world's best law enforcement organizations. Although I knew that my own motivation and skill-set are key determinants of whatever I accomplish, I knew that the environment in which I work is also a key factor. Therefore, if I wanted to be the best, it was important for me to work with the best.

When the Internet first became popular, I began watching for job opportunities on the FBI's website. Although I had not even graduated from high school at that point, I was determined to do whatever it took to get on board with the FBI in some capacity. Because many of the FBI's jobs require a four-year baccalaureate degree, I knew that the first step was to go to college and obtain a bachelor's degree. As a part of that process, I decided that I would apply for one of the FBI's many internship opportunities, even though they were extremely competitive.

The Application Process:

Some time during my junior year (November 2003), I submitted my internship application.

Because the FBI has numerous opportunities available and students are permitted to apply for multiple opportunities simultaneously, I sent in three separate applications—one to the FBI Honor's Internship Program, one to the FBI's National Center for the Analysis of Violent Crime (NCAVC), and one to the FBI Academy's Behavioral Science Unit (BSU). In addition, I applied for a full-time paid job opportunity in the local Seattle field office as an Investigative Assistant.

To my surprise I was selected to interview for every position where I had applied. I flew to Washington, DC, and had a joint interview with the NCAVC and BSU, then I interviewed at the local FBI Seattle field office for the Honor's Internship Program, and also for the paid job opportunity. The interviews went well, and I was invited back shortly thereafter for a second interview for the Honor's Internship Program, where I was informed that I was one of the top five candidates for Washington State (the FBI only selects one student from each state for this internship position).

Much to my dismay, I received rejection letters for each of the positions I had applied for—you can imagine how disappointed I was! Thankfully, I was not discouraged and decided to reapply four months later. To be on the safe side, I sent in five applications this time around. Although I could not reapply for the Honor's Internship Program (applications are only accepted once per year for this program), I reapplied to the BSU and NCAVC, as well as to three additional units at the FBI National Academy. About a month later, I got a telephone call from Supervisory Special Agent Andre Simons of the Law Enforcement Communication Unit (LECU) who wanted to interview me, and a few days later he offered me the position.

The FBI Employment Process:

Although I was ready to leave for the Academy as soon as possible, amazingly it took a full year from the time Agent Simons offered me the position to the time the FBI completed the background process and I had clearance to go. Believe it or not, I had actually completed my undergraduate degree by that point, and had begun graduate education in Central Washington University's MS in Organizational Development program.

No one was kidding when they said that the FBI background process is thorough. It involves providing a full account of your entire personal history—every place you have lived in your life; every place you have been employed since age 16; information about educational achievements and a review of your transcripts; a list of three references and social acquaintants; a full list of any foreign travel; your full court record; your financial status; information about all of your immediate relatives; your drug history; and every individual with whom you have resided in the last five years for a period of 30 days or more. In addition, you must provide your fingerprints, participate in a personal security interview, participate in a polygraph examination, and submit to a drug test.

Once that entire process was nearing completion, I began seeking out housing and travel arrangements. Unfortunately, the FBI does not provide any assistance to interns in locating housing, and by sheer luck, I met an instructor at the Academy who was looking for an intern to rent a room. As soon as my housing was in place, I booked a flight to Virginia immediately and quickly entered into what would become one of the most valuable experiences of my life.

The Internship Process:

The Law Enforcement Communication Unit (LECU) is responsible for training newly hired FBI agents as well as law enforcement officers from all over the world who come to the FBI for specialized training in topics pertaining to communication. This includes interviewing and interrogation, effective writing, media relations, organizational communication, statement analysis, and more. The LECU is also tasked with publishing the *FBI Law Enforcement Bulletin* each month, which is read by over 200,000 members of the law enforcement community.

My responsibilities at the LECU included assisting in the analysis and reporting of data collected for various research projects; developing and collating information from various sources for writing and editing assignments; conducting literature searches and preparing annotated bibliographies and article summaries on topics such as interviewing, interrogation, deception, and statement analysis; and assisting LECU instructional staff in lesson plans and student practical exercises for New FBI Agent and National Academy classes.

In addition to my work, I was able to take advantage of working on the site of the world's most elite educational institution for law enforcement officers. I had the opportunity to attend several New Agent and National Academy classes each week—not just in my unit, but at the entire FBI Academy. Some of the classes I attended included statement analysis, counterintelligence, asset development, psychopathy, computer crimes for police supervisors, counterterrorism, domestic terrorism, international terrorism, defensive driving tactics, explosives and explosive devices, school violence, espionage, case management, interviewing and interrogation, cognitive interviewing, and more. I spent about 30 percent of my time at the Academy attending classes.

Work Experience:

Although I am still in graduate school, I have already had relevant work experience in the fields of investigation and law enforcement. I have worked full time as a Communications Officer for the Washington State Patrol, and on a part-time basis I have

(*continued*)

BOX 10.4 (*Continued*)

performed support work for a private investigator. Two years prior to my FBI Internship, I had the opportunity to do an investigative internship with the Washington State Bar Association in the Office of Disciplinary Counsel. And lastly, when I was in high school, I volunteered as a Police Cadet for the Bellevue Police Department in Bellevue, Washington.

Advice to Students:

If you, too, think you'd like to support the mission of the FBI or other organization charged with the enforcement of laws and supervising offenders, you can visit the FBI Jobs website at www.fbijobs.com and become familiar with all of the internship opportunities that exist (and what the deadlines are for applying). Regardless of your field of study, you're likely to find something that relates to you and will be invaluable to enhancing your future career possibilities. Here's a few additional tips that should not be overlooked:

- Know the deadline for each internship you would like to apply for and prepare your application packet early; do not wait until the last minute.

- Set high standards for yourself and keep your grades up; most of the internship programs require at least a 3.0 grade point average, and if you want to be competitive, aim much higher.

- Be professional! Practice your interviewing skills, finetune your resume with a career counselor, and be prepared.

- Be honest and do not make false statements during the hiring process. The study of law and justice is the study of a particular branch of ethics. The hallmark of any serious academic study of ethics is a commitment to the truth. Students choosing law and justice-related

careers are expected to meet rigorous standards of honesty.

- Remember that your background encompasses far more than your employment experience and education. Your background includes your character, reputation, training, abilities, involvement in civic and community activities, military service, financial matters, criminal history, drug history, and many other aspects of your life. The FBI is looking for bright individuals who possess "Fidelity, Bravery, and Integrity," which is the FBI motto and motivating force behind the men and women of the FBI. The most important thing you can do prior to applying for employment with the FBI is to carry out your personal affairs and professional business in a responsible manner.

- Remember to be persistent. If you get turned down the first time, try and try again. It worked for me.

- Buy a book by Thomas C. Ackerman called *FBI Careers: The Ultimate Guide to Landing a Job as One of America's Finest.* It is a small investment for the benefits it could help you gain.

I want to do something important with my life, and while I've always known that I didn't want to become a sworn law enforcement officer, I can think of no better career than one that supports the mission of the law enforcement community—to protect the safety of the public. The internship I participated in at the FBI provided me with a unique perspective of FBI operations and gave me an insider's perspective of what it is like working for one of the most elite law enforcement organizations in the world. While I anticipate my specific career goals will shift as I encounter new ideas and information, I am committed to doing what I can do to support those in the law enforcement community who give so selflessly of themselves to help others in need.

Furthermore, drug- or alcohol-dependent offenders are less predictable and may become violent even if they were convicted of nonviolent offenses.

Offenders on probation or parole as well as those incarcerated are frequently adept at manipulating those supervising them. Thus, in some jurisdictions, POs receive training for resisting group pressure, acquiring self-control, and making less risky decisions (American Correctional Association, 2003). In addition, they receive offensive and defensive training for self-protection as well as their own manipulative skills for eliciting and altering offenders' values and beliefs about themselves in both formal and informal counseling.

Increasing the amount of training considered relevant by prospective POs through simulated situations of officer–offender interactions is one means of increasing the professionalism of officers generally. Many POs believe they need more practical training as a part of their training programs, rather than mere attendance in awareness or other related educational courses. One reason for a more practical training emphasis is that the kinds of persons traditionally attracted to corrections positions have not been particularly excited about or motivated to participate in academic programs. Thus, topics such as when to use deadly force and spotting those situations likely to create legal liability are directly relevant to the future tasks performed by POs. Those officers most likely to leave the correctional field often lack the motivation, education, and commitment, but a more relevant curriculum could function to reduce labor turnover significantly in various training programs.

PO TRAINING AND SPECIALIZATION

Assessment Centers and Staff Effectiveness

The focus on behaviorally based methods for selecting and evaluating POs not only results in the hiring of better line personnel, but it also functions to identify those most able to perform managerial tasks. It is clear that a key element in the success of any probation program is the quality of line staff. A key element in maintaining line staff quality is managerial adequacy.

Assessment centers are useful for identifying potential chief probation officers and administrators for probation/parole programs. These assessment centers are often patterned after those used in the selection of law enforcement officers. Personality tests are often used to identify those prospective officers who would have the right temperament for PO work.

If the right kinds of managers can be selected and promoted, line staff can be molded into productive work units to better serve offender-clients. Managers can assist their probation/parole organizations to devise more clearly defined mission statements of goals and objectives and to establish greater uniformity of quality of performance among staff members. While assessment centers are not foolproof and should not be considered as cookbook methods for selecting "good managers," they are helpful by providing for specific tests and assessments of those desirable qualities of leadership and managerial effectiveness that should be seriously considered by administrators. Criminal justice generally has had a continuing need for better managers, and thus criminal justice professionals including corrections personnel should explore every management evaluation tool available, including assessment centers.

FIGURE 10.4   Increasing Numbers of Jail Officers are Better Trained and Educated.

The Florida Assessment Center

The Dade County, Florida, Department of Corrections and Rehabilitation was one of the first state corrections agencies to establish an **assessment center** for the selection of entry-level officers (Page, 1995). While using assessment centers to screen personnel for organizational positions is not a new concept, especially in private industry, the use of such centers in corrections recruitment and training is innovative. Currently, a large number of law enforcement agencies employ assessment centers or other pivotal screening facilities to separate the fit from the unfit among applicants for law enforcement positions.

The **Florida Assessment Center** moves beyond traditional selection mechanisms such as the use of paper-and-pencil measures, standard personality, interests, and aptitude/IQ tests or inventories by examining a candidate's potential on the basis of the full scope of the job. This is accomplished by a previously established job task analysis made of the different correctional chores to be performed by prospective applicants. The Dade County Assessment Center has identified the following skills associated with corrections work of any kind: (1) the ability to understand and implement policies and procedures; (2) the ability to be aware of all elements in a given situation, and to use sensitivity to others and good judgment in dealing with the situation; and (3) the ability to communicate effectively (Page, 1995).

On the basis of various measures designed to tap into each of these personal and social skills, the most qualified candidates are targeted for further testing and interviews. These tests include preparations of written reports, role-playing and acting out problem situations, and videotaped situational exercises. The Center strives to provide candidates with as much realism as possible concerning the kinds of situations they will encounter in dealing with criminals either inside or outside of prison. Also emphasized is an awareness of race, gender, and ethnicity in the social dimension of relating with offenders. Three-person teams of evaluators screen applicants on the basis of their objectivity and manner in responding to various job-related simulated challenges. A key objective is to assist prospective corrections personnel to avoid legal challenges and suits by clients and/or prisoners. Thus, when subsequent decisions are made by corrections officers and others and challenged in court, the basis for the challenges will be unlikely attributable to faults associated with the selection process.

The evaluators in the Florida Assessment Center are themselves trained by other assessors or correctional officers so that they may more readily determine those most appropriate candidates for correctional posts. Observing, categorizing, and evaluating candidate skills are procedures requiring extensive training, and the Assessment Center continually subjects its own selection process to both internal and external scrutiny and evaluation. Assessment center officials in both Florida and other jurisdictions where such centers are used believe that the training their officers receive also helps to reduce their potential for lawsuits from clients (Dear et al., 2002).

The Use of Firearms in Probation and Parole Work

Because the idea of POs carrying firearms is fairly new, little information exists about it. Also, it is too early to evaluate the long-range implications of PO firearms use in the field. In 2000, there were 24 states that authorized the use of firearms for parole officers. Twenty-six states authorized firearms use for their probation officers (American Correctional Association, 2003). More probation and parole officer training programs are featuring topics related to PO safety, especially in view of the shift from the medical model toward more proactive, client-control officer orientations (Holcomb, 2006). Few professionals in criminology and criminal justice question that each generation of probationers and parolees includes more dangerous offenders. Largely because it is impossible at present to incarcerate everyone convicted of crimes, the use of probation and parole as front-end and back-end solutions to jail and prison overcrowding is increasing. Also increasing are reports of victimization from POs working with probationers and parolees in dangerous neighborhoods. It is not necessarily the case that probationer-clients or parolee-clients are becoming more aggressive or violent toward their PO supervisors, although there have been reports of escalating client violence against their supervising POs. The fact is that POs are obligated to conduct face-to-face visits with their clients, and that in many instances, these face-to-face visits involve potentially dangerous situations and/or scenarios. However, some evidence suggests a decline in the future of home visits as a standard PO function (Holcomb, 2006).

Life-Threatening Situations and Assaults Against POs by Their Clients. Anonymous interviews with POs supervising both adults and juveniles give us some insight as to the potential hazards of PO work. One PO supervising juvenile offenders in Cincinnati, Ohio, for instance, reported that she was assaulted and physically beaten by youth gang members associated with one of her juvenile clients. The juvenile client himself was apologetic and promised to advise his gang members to leave her alone the next time she appeared in his neighborhood. However, her broken arm, jaw, and lost teeth will be reminders of her neighborhood visit. In another situation, a male PO visited a parolee in a run-down section of Los Angeles. The parolee had been drinking excessively. When the PO entered the client's apartment, the parolee held a rifle to his own chin, threatening suicide. At one point, as the parolee continued to drink, he pointed the rifle at the PO and said, "You're the reason its come to this . . . I might as well blow your fuckin' head off too." After three hours of talking, the parolee was coaxed into surrendering his weapon with a promise from the PO "not to do anything." The PO left and never said a word about the incident. Within a month, the PO had resigned and became a postal worker. Increasingly, PO training involves understanding about how to deal with drug- or alcohol-dependent clients in productive ways (Champion, 2005).

The hazards of PO work are clearly portrayed in the results of a nationwide survey conducted by the Federal Probation and Pretrial Officers Association in 1993 (Bigger, 1993:14–15). This study disclosed the following assaults or attempted assaults against officers nationwide since 1980:

Murders or attempted murders	16
Rapes or attempted rapes	7
Other sexual assaults or attempted sexual assaults	100
Shot and wounded or attempted shot and wounded	32
Uses or attempted use of blunt instrument or projectile	60
Slashed or stabbed or attempted slashed or stabbed	28
Car used as weapon or attempted use of car as weapon	12
Punched, kicked, choked, or other use of body/attempted	1,396
Use or attempted use of caustic substance	3
Use or attempted use of incendiary device	9
Abducted or attempted abduction and held hostage	3
Attempted or actual unspecified assaults	944
TOTAL	2,610

A more recent survey of 1,120 state and county probation and parole officers in Minnesota raises several concerns about officer safety. Of the sample surveyed, 19 percent reported one or more physical assaults during their career, while 74 percent reported being verbally or physically threatened one or more times. About 4 percent actually were physically assaulted one or more times in the past year, while 37 percent reported being physically or verbally threatened one or more times during the past year (Arola and Lawrence, 1999:32).

Self-Protection or Provocation?   Whether POs should arm themselves during their visits to clients is often a moot question, since they arm themselves anyway, regardless of probation/parole office policy. When POs are put to a vote, however, the results are often divided 50–50. For instance, a study of 159 POs attending an in-service training session in 1990 at a state probation training academy investigated these POs' opinions about their right to carry firearms while on the job. A carefully worded question, "Should POs be given the legal option to carry a firearm while working?," was asked of these 159 POs. Responses indicated that 59 percent of the officers believed that they should have the legal option to carry a firearm. This doesn't mean that 59 percent of these officers would carry firearms on the job; rather, they supported the idea of one's choice to carry a firearm while working if such a choice were made available. In the same study, POs were asked whether they would endorse a requirement to carry a firearm as a part of one's PO work. Over 80 percent of the female POs interviewed opposed such a requirement, while about 69 percent of the male POs responded similarly. However, 80 percent of all officers interviewed said that they would carry a firearm if required to do so.

Opposition to POs carrying firearms is largely that this moves POs into a law enforcement function. Furthermore, if it becomes generally known that POs carry firearms, this may escalate a situation between a PO and an armed client to the point where injuries or deaths could occur. In contrast, other professionals argue that changing offender populations have transformed into successive generations of more dangerous, violent clientele (Gahl et al., 2006). A fundamental issue at the center of this controversy is the amount and type of training POs receive who will carry these firearms. States such as Florida have authorized their POs to use firearms as of July 1992. However, their POs have received extensive firearms training as well as psychological training so that the necessity of using a firearm will be for self-protection and a last resort (Gahl et al., 2006).

Establishing Negligence in Training, Job Performance, and Retention

Not only is PO work increasingly hazardous, but POs are becoming increasingly liable for their actions taken in relation to the clients they supervise. Lawsuits against POs are becoming more commonplace. Many of these lawsuits are frivolous, but they consume much time and cause many job prospects to turn away from PO work. There are three basic forms of immunity: (1) absolute immunity, meaning that those acting on behalf of the state can suffer no liability from their actions taken while performing their state tasks (e.g., judges, prosecutors, and legislators); (2) qualified immunity, such as that enjoyed by probation officers if they are performing their tasks in good faith; and (3) quasi-judicial immunity, which generally refers to PO preparation of PSI reports at judicial request. In the general case, POs enjoy only qualified immunity, meaning that they are immune only when their actions were taken in good faith. However, there is some evidence that the rules are changing related to the types of defenses available to POs, although the limits of immunity continue to be vague and undefined. At least two different conditions that seem to favor POs in the performance of their tasks and the immunity they derive from such conditions have been identified:

1. Probation officers are considered officers of the court and perform a valuable court function, namely the preparation of PSI reports.
2. Probation officers perform work intimately associated with court process, such as sentencing offenders.

Despite these conditions, it is unlikely that POs will ever be extended absolute immunity to all of their work functions. Judicial immunity and qualified immunity are two types of immunity that are generally available to public officials including POs. Judicial liability is like absolute immunity, described earlier. Judges must perform their functions and make decisions that may be favorable or unfavorable to defendants. Lawsuits filed against judges are almost always routinely dismissed without trial on the merits. Parole boards also possess such judicial immunity in most cases. In contrast, qualified immunity ensues only if officials, including POs, did not violate some client's constitutional rights according to what a reasonable person would have known.

One of the ambiguities of PO work is the fact that often, the letter of the law is replaced by the spirit of the law. POs simply create their own informal rules for dealing with their clients. Annual regional and national conferences of probation and parole officers, such as those sponsored by the American Correctional Association, the American Jail Association, and the American Probation and Parole Association, optimize conditions where officers from different jurisdictions can exchange information with one another about how their work is performed. Much of this informal dialogue is casual conversation, but in many instances, POs glean from their counterparts in other jurisdictions certain ideas about rule-bending. Not all of this dialogue is nefarious, however. Often, a PO in South Carolina will tell another PO from California that South Carolina POs have a right to do one or more different things that affect client programs. The California PO may be surprised, because in California, PO interference with or modification of client programs may be prohibited.

For example, in South Carolina, POs may place clients in halfway houses for up to 75 days; they may place offenders in residential or nonresidential treatment; they may restructure the supervision of a client's plan of action; they may increase the numbers of supervisory contacts; and they may order up to 40 hours of community service. But in Florida, some or all of these actions by POs are strictly prohibited. For instance, in *Reynard v. State* (1993), a PO had ordered a client to perform so many hours of community service. However, a Florida Appellate Court struck down the community service orders because the sentencing judge had not included such community service orders as one of the probation conditions.

Liability Issues Associated with PO Work

A summary of some of the key liability issues related to PO work is provided below.

1. Some information about a PO's clients is subject to public disclosure whereas some information isn't subject to public disclosure. POs must constantly reassess their working materials about specific clients and decide which information is relevant under certain circumstances. It would be advisable, for instance, to inform prospective employers of certain probationers or parolees if the work involves custodial services in a large apartment complex and the particular probationers/parolees are convicted voyeurs, rapists, exhibitionists, or burglars. POs might also inform banks that particular probationers/parolees have been convicted of embezzlement if these clients are seeking work in a bank setting or any other business where they will be working around and handling money. But it may not be appropriate to advise an employer that the probationer/parolee is a convicted drug dealer if the client is seeking to become a car salesperson or factory worker. Also, in most states, if POs know that their clients have AIDS, it is improper for POs to report this fact to a client's employer. This is because there are statutory prohibitions against such disclosures except under certain circumstances. These circumstances vary considerably among state jurisdictions. Some states have no policy on this issue. Thus, it is up to individual agencies to adopt their own policies. A general rule within most PO agencies is that if a probationer or parolee obtains a job on his or her own, there is no officer or agency liability because reliance is absent. However, an agency's rules may require disclosure by the officer when he or she learns of the probationer or parolee's job, even if the job was obtained by the offender.

2. POs have a duty to protect the public. Their work in this regard may subject them to lawsuits. This issue relates closely to the first. If particular probationers or parolees have made threats to seek revenge against particular persons or organizations, it would be advisable for POs to report that these clients are in the community and may pose a risk to one or more former victims. There are some notable distinctions in degrees of liability, however. If a probationer says he is going to kill his wife and the PO does nothing about it, liability may attach and the PO may be liable for not warning the wife or notifying authorities. But if a parolee tells his PO that he feels like going out to commit armed robbery and actually carries it out, the liability of the PO is questionable, since it is unreasonable for us to assume that the PO knew where and when the client would commit the robbery. Furthermore, saying one may go out and commit armed robbery and actually committing the robbery are two different matters. The PO may conclude that his or her client is simply blowing off steam, getting emotions out in the open where they can be dealt with productively, or some other such similar interpretation.

3. PO use of firearms may create hazards for both POs and their clients. POs are increasingly carrying firearms for their personal protection when entering dangerous neighborhoods or housing projects where their clients reside. If they use their firearms, there is some likelihood that someone, possibly the probationer/parolee, the PO, or an innocent bystander or relative, may be seriously or fatally injured. Liability of this sort is always possible. One way of minimizing such liability is to provide POs with proper firearms training prior to authorizing them to carry dangerous weapons. While this doesn't guarantee that they will avoid lawsuits and liability, it does minimize the risk of such legal actions by others. Often, POs are sued by their clients or others (U.S. Code, Title 42 Section 1983, which is the **Civil Rights Act**), civil rights actions are involved. These are usually tort actions and settled in civil courts rather than criminal courts.

4. POs may supervise their clients in a negligent manner. In an Arizona case, POs were sued because of victim injuries sustained as the result of a failure to properly supervise a dangerous client. In the Arizona case (*Acevedo v. Pima County Adult Probation Department,* 1984), a convicted felon, a child sexual abuser, was placed on probation and subsequently sexually molested several children of the plaintiff. The POs supervising this offender knew of his sexual deviance and propensities. However, they allowed him to rent a room on premises where the plaintiff and her five children resided. The Arizona Supreme Court observed that while POs do many diverse tasks and have demanding responsibilities, they must not knowingly place clients in situations where their former conduct might create a hazard to the public. In this case, the lawsuit against the POs was successfully pursued. It may also be argued that these POs failed to warn the plaintiff of their client's sexual propensities. This, too, could have warranted a lawsuit against these POs.

5. PO PSI report preparation may result in liability. One of the more important PO functions is the preparation of PSI reports at the request of judges prior to offender sentencing. Much information is contained in these PSI reports, some of which may not be directly relevant to sentencing. Thus, it may not be necessary to disclose the entire contents of PSIs at any particular time. At the federal level, at least, federal judges may disclose the contents of PSI reports except where (1) disclosure

might disrupt rehabilitation of the defendant; (2) the information was obtained on a promise of confidentiality; and (3) harm may result to the defendant or to any other person. Subsequently, when inmates are about to be paroled, the PSI report may again be consulted. Obviously, the long-term impact of a PSI report is substantial. Errors of fact, unintentional or otherwise, may cause grievous harm to inmates and jeopardize seriously their chances for early release. If the information barring them from early release is contained in the PSI document, and if the parole board relies heavily upon this information in their denial of parole to particular offenders, and if the information contained therein is inaccurate or false, a cause of action or lawsuit may be lodged against the original PO who prepared the PSI report.

6. Liabilities against POs and/or their agencies may ensue for negligent training, negligent retention, and deliberate indifference to client needs. POs may not have particular counseling skills when dealing with certain offenders who have psychological problems. They may give poor advice. Such advice may cause offenders to behave in ways that harm others. Also, POs may not be adequately prepared or trained to carry firearms. They may discharge their firearms under certain circumstances than can cause serious injury or death. These are examples of negligent training. Negligent retention might be a situation where certain POs are maintained by a probation agency after they have exhibited certain conduct or training deficiencies that they have failed to remedy. Failing to rid an organization of incompetent employees is negligent retention. Finally, when POs meet with their probationer/parolee clients, they may believe particular offenders need certain community services or assistance. However, these POs may deliberately refrain from providing such assistance or making it possible for their clients to receive such aid. If certain clients are drug-dependent and obviously in need of medical services, deliberate indifference on the part of the PO would be exhibited if the PO did nothing to assist the client in receiving the needed medical treatment. This would be an example of deliberate indifference. Deliberate indifference may be a vengeful act on the part of the PO, an omission, or simple failure to act promptly.

While the above list of PO legal liabilities is not exhaustive, it represents the major types of situations where POs incur potential problems from lawsuits. Several types of defenses are used by POs when performing their work. These defenses are not perfect, but they do make it difficult for plaintiffs to prevail under a variety of scenarios. These defenses include the following:

1. POs were acting in good faith while performing the PO role.
2. POs have official immunity, since they are working for and on behalf of the state, which enjoys sovereign immunity.
3. POs may not have a special relationship with their clients, thus absolving them of possible liability if their clients commit future offenses that result in injuries or deaths to themselves or others.

Probation and Parole Officer Labor Turnover

In 2002, there was a turnover among probation and parole officers of 16 percent. Among probation/parole officer recruits in training, the turnover rate was higher at 23 percent (Camp and Camp, 2003). In view of a number of continuing problems confronting those entering probation and parole service as a career, it is understandable why there is a high degree of **labor turnover** among POs. There are several explanations for this turnover. First, the rapid increase in the offender population managed by POs has created significant logistical problems. Some observers have indicated that POs must continue to maintain their current level of activity in an environment where the public demands greater punishment, incarceration, and a decrease in public expenditures (Camp and Camp, 2003). Furthermore, there is a lack of consensus among POs about their goals and professional objectives, as well as how these goals ought to be realized. Some POs see themselves as a **broker** who provides referral services to their offender-clients or arrange offender contacts with community agencies that provide special services, including counseling and training. Other POs see themselves as a **caseworker** who attempts to change offender behavior through educating, enabling, or mediating whenever offender problems occur. Many POs have asked whether the public has come to expect too much from them, particularly in view of financial cutbacks and greatly increased offender caseloads.

PROBATION AND PAROLE OFFICER CASELOADS

The **caseload** of a probation or parole officer is considered by many authorities to be significant in affecting the quality of supervision POs can provide their clients. Caseloads refer to the number of offender-clients supervised by POs. Caseloads vary among jurisdictions (American Correctional Association, 2003). Theoretically, the larger the caseload, the poorer the quality of supervision and other services. Intensive probation supervision (IPS) is based on the premise that low offender caseloads maximize the attention POs can give their clients, including counseling and employment, social, and psychological assistance (Coleman, Sharp, and Green, 2006). The success of such IPS programs suggests that lower caseloads contribute to lower recidivism rates among parolees and probationers. It is also conceded that other program components such as fines, curfews, and community service may have some influence on the overall reduction of these rates.

Ideal Caseloads

The earliest work outlining optimum caseloads for professionals was Chute (1922). Chute advocated caseloads for POs no larger than 50. Similar endorsements of a 50-caseload limit were made by Edwin Sutherland in 1934, the American Prison Association in 1946, the Manual of Correctional Standards in 1954, and the National Council of Crime and Delinquency in 1962 (Champion, 2005). The 1967 President's Commission on Law Enforcement and Administration of Justice lowered the optimum caseload figure to 35.

In 2006, actual caseloads of POs varied greatly, ranging from a low of 50 clients in Nebraska to a high of 104 clients in California (U.S. Department of Justice, 2006). IPS had caseloads ranging from nine per officer in Wyoming to a high of 51 in Rhode Island. Considerable jurisdictional variation exists regarding both regular and intensive supervision caseloads for POs.

Presently there is no agreement among professionals as to what is an ideal PO caseload. On the basis of evaluating caseloads of POs in a variety of jurisdictions, there is evidence that (1) no optimal caseload size has been demonstrated, and (2) no

FIGURE 10.5   Office Visits with POs Increase Caseload Sizes.

clear evidence of reduced recidivism, simply by reduced caseload size, has been found (Champion, 2005). This declaration applies mainly to standard probation/ parole supervision, and it is not intended to reflect on the quality of recent ISP programs established in many jurisdictions. Because the composition of parolees and probationers varies considerably among jurisdictions, it is difficult to develop clear-cut conclusions about the influence of supervision on recidivism and the delivery of other program services (Lemke, Lowenkamp, and Smith, 2006). An arbitrary caseload figure based on current caseload sizes among state jurisdictions would be about 30 clients per PO. This is perhaps the closest number to an ideal caseload size. The average caseload for POs in 1999 was 124, while the average intensive supervision caseload was 25. This small difference suggests that different jurisdictions have variable ideas about what is or isn't standard or intensive supervision.

Changing Caseloads and Officer Effectiveness

Do smaller PO caseloads mean greater effectiveness and quality of services provided clients by their supervising POs? It is assumed that POs have fewer clients to supervise, then they will be able to supervise their clients more effectively. There is great variation among jurisdictions about how optimum caseloads, large or small, should be defined. If POs are asked, they will almost always say that the lower their caseload, the more effective they are at helping their probationers and parolees. If probationers and parolees are asked the same question, they will tell a similar story. Close supervision of their behaviors while on probation or parole is more often viewed as assistance rather than punishment. This is especially true for those clients with drug or alcohol dependencies.

As we have moved into the twenty-first century, the nature of PO client supervision is changing. We are increasingly relying upon technology in our relations with probationers and parolees. Electronic monitoring and home confinement, drive-by check-ins at probation department offices, and distance contacts between offenders and their supervisors by mail or other means suggests less face-to-face encounters. It is clear that officer safety is becoming increasingly crucial and is presently a dominant issue in discussions of how best to supervise offenders.

PO jobs are becoming increasingly complex, and POs are learning to be more effective as service brokers. This means that they are networking their clients with more community services annually to provide improved treatments and other offender needs (Arthur, 2000). At the same time, some jurisdictions are experimenting with group reporting. In Anoka County, Minnesota, group reporting involves offender/clients reporting to their probation departments at particular times and meeting as a group with their assigned POs. Thus, this gives POs a chance to meet face-to-face with a large number of clients at any given time, rather than to hazard visits to dangerous neighborhoods for face-to-face visits on a one-on-one basis.

Technology is being incorporated into the PO–client relation in other ways as well. More probationers are having to undergo polygraph or lie detector testing as a condition of their probation or parole programs. If there is a criminal investigation, some clients on probation or parole may become suspects. Therefore, their submission to a polygraph test will either include or exclude them as suspects. Also, these clients can be asked about program infractions, which are not easily detected, such as drug use or associating with known criminals. If the answers to these questions are incriminating, they may be the preliminary grounds to seek a revocation of one's program.

Caseload Assignment and Management Models

The court sentences offenders to probation, while parole boards release many prisoners short of serving their full terms. POs must reckon with fluctuating numbers of offenders monthly, as new assignments are given them and some offenders complete their programs successfully. No particular caseload assignment method has been universally adopted by all jurisdictions. Rather, depending on the numbers of offenders assigned to probation and parole agencies, PO caseload assignment practices vary. Variations in caseload assignment schemes have been observed. There are four popular varieties of assignment methods: (1) the conventional model, (2) the numbers game model, (3) the conventional model with geographic considerations, and (4) specialized caseloads (Champion, 2005).

The Conventional Model. The conventional model involves the random assignment of probationers or parolees to POs. Thus, any PO must be prepared to cope with extremely dangerous offenders released early from prison on parole, those with drug or alcohol dependencies or in need of special treatment programs, and those requiring little, if any, supervision. However, those convicted of violent offenses may no longer be violent. Spouses may kill in the heat of passion, but it is highly unlikely that they will kill again. By the same token, it is possible that low-risk, less dangerous property offenders may become violent through offense escalation.

The conventional model is probably used most frequently in probation and parole agencies throughout the United States. There are no specific logistical problems that need to be dealt with, and POs can be assigned offender-clients on an as-needed basis. The major drawback is that POs must be extremely flexible in their management options, because of the diversity of clientele they must supervise.

The Numbers Game Model. The **numbers game model** is similar to the conventional model. In order to apply this model, the total number of clients is divided by the number of POs, and POs are given the designated number randomly. For instance, if there are 500 offenders and 10 POs, 500/10 = 50 offenders per PO. Another version of the numbers game model is to define an optimum caseload such as 40, and determine how many POs are required to supervise 40 offenders each. Thus, PO hiring is influenced directly by the numbers of offenders assigned to the jurisdiction and whatever is considered the optimum caseload.

The Conventional Model with Geographic Considerations. The **conventional model with geographic considerations** is applied on the basis of the travel time required for POs to meet with their offender-clients regularly. Those POs who supervise offenders in predominantly rural regions are given lighter caseloads so that they may have the time to make reasonable numbers of contacts with offenders on a monthly or weekly basis. Those POs who supervise largely urban offenders are given heavier caseloads because less travel time between clients is required.

The Specialized Caseloads Model. Sometimes caseload assignments are made on the basis of PO specialties. The **specialized caseloads model** pertains to PO assignments to clients who share particular problems, such as drug or alcohol dependencies. The POs assigned to these clients have special skills relating to these dependencies. Often, these POs have developed liaisons with Alcoholics Anonymous or other organizations so that their service to clients can be enhanced. Perhaps certain POs have had extensive training and education in particular problem areas to better serve certain offender-clients who may be retarded or mentally ill (Carr, Collins, and Leary, 2006). Some POs by virtue of their training may be assigned more dangerous offenders. Those POs with greater work experience and legal training can manage dangerous offenders more effectively compared with fresh, new PO recruits. In some respects, this is close to client-specific planning, where individualization of cases is stressed (Fitzgerald et al., 2006).

It is believed that caseloads ought to be refocused to heighten offender accountability through cognitive restructuring and restorative case management. Traditional caseloads are oriented largely toward offender monitoring and control. Offenders need to experience some actual change in their behavior while on probation or parole. They need to learn about the adverse impact they had on possible victims of their crimes. Their accountability should be heightened and their self-awareness in this regard sharpened. Basically, the intent of restorative case management is to provide an ethical foundation and specific direction for the function of offender case management. Attention of supervising POs is shifted toward the offender's level of cognitive distortion and skill defects, the level of antisocial behaviors, and the ability of offenders to provide restoration to communities and victims. The emphasis of restorative case management is on the victims of offenders, although offenders themselves should acquire a greater degree of empathy with their victims. This program is similar to the balanced approach. The **balanced approach,** devised originally for juvenile offenders, stresses heightening offender accountability, individualizing sanctions or punishments, and promoting community safety as critical program components (Morton and Stone, 2006). Restorative case management synthesizes these elements and blends them with heightened offender awareness through cognitive restructuring.

OFFICER–CLIENT INTERACTIONS

Although recruitment for POs is designed to identify and select those most capable of performing increasingly demanding PO tasks, little uniformity exists among jurisdictions regarding the types of POs ultimately recruited. Each PO brings to the job a philosophy of supervision based, in part, on agency expectations. Furthermore, each PO has individual differences and attitudes toward work that influence their supervisory style. Some POs are more punitive than others, while some see themselves as rehabilitators or therapists.

In the course of interacting with different kinds of offenders, it is not unusual for POs to acquire a certain amount of cynicism about their jobs and those they supervise. If an offender recidivates by committing a new offense, some POs may take this new offense personally and consider it an indication of their failure at helping certain offender-clients. The nature of PO work is multifaceted and is constantly changing. Sometimes, these work roles come into conflict with one another. Administrators often make abrupt changes in one's duties, and therefore, POs need to have a degree of flexibility in adapting to their particular tasks as well as the different clients they may be assigned (Meierhoefer et al., 2006).

These work roles include, but are not limited to, the following: (1) the **detector,** where the PO attempts to identify troublesome clients or those who have one or more problems that could present the community with some risk; (2) the broker, where the PO functions as a referral service and supplies the offender-client with contacts with agencies who provide needed services; (3) the **educator, enabler,** and **mediator,** where the PO seeks to instruct and assist offenders to deal with problems as they arise in the community; and (4) the **enforcer,** where POs perceive themselves as enforcement officers charged with regulating client behaviors.

Since POs are obligated to check up on their clients, they are viewed with suspicion and apprehension by probationers and parolees. One important concern for parolees is the confidentiality of the relationship between themselves and their supervisors (Meierhoefer et al., 2006). According to the rules and terms of one's probation or parole, infractions of any kind are to be reported to agency authorities and dealt with accordingly. However, if every single infraction observed by POs was reported and acted upon officially, there would be an endless series of hearings about whether probation or parole should be revoked in each reported case. The required attendance and participation of POs at such hearings would consume virtually every minute of their time, and little or no time would be left to supervise and help other offenders. Therefore, the PO–offender/client relationship often becomes one of negotiation, where the PO conveniently overlooks certain rule infractions, particularly minor ones, and where the offender-client conscientiously attempts to adhere to the more important probation or parole provisions. This means that often, an unwritten relationship is established whereby the PO and offender can help each other in complementary ways.

Role conflict is inherent in the PO–offender relationship. It cannot be eliminated. The PO desires a successful outcome for the client, where the terms of the probation or parole are fulfilled and where the client emerges from the program to lead a productive life. But often, the circumstances leading to an offender's original arrest and conviction continue to exist and influence offender behaviors. Old acquaintances, family circumstances, and the added pressures of maintaining a job and complying with stringent probation or parole program conditions cause problems for more than a few offenders. Many revert to their old ways by committing new crimes and/or violating one or more program requirements.

If a PO reports a parolee or probationer for violating a program rule, there is a possibility that the offender will eventually retaliate by either threatening the PO or carrying out aggressive acts. At the same time, the PO has considerable power and can influence significantly the life chances of those supervised. An unfavorable report may mean prison for probationers or a longer term in prison for parolees. Objectivity is required of all POs, although achieving objectivity and detachment in performing the PO role is difficult. Many POs take it personally whenever one of their offenders fails or is returned to prison. They regard offender failure as their own failure. After all, some of these POs entered their profession originally to help others. When their strategies for helping others are apparently ineffective, this failure reflects adversely on their own job performance. Seasoned POs recommend to those entering the field initially that they should not get too friendly with their offender-clients. They must constantly divorce their emotions from their work roles. There is some evidence, however, that POs find this difficult to do. POs attempt to perform helping functions, while at the same time they must be enforcers of legal conditions (Meierhoefer et al., 2006).

Women on probation or parole are considered troublesome by many POs, especially those with chemical dependencies or mental illnesses (Freiburger, 2006). Some POs feel women take up too much of their time with a variety of what agents consider minor problems. Additionally, female clients evidence problems of adjustment related to family, children, and employment. For these and related reasons, women are less likely than men to be reported for anything but the most serious kinds of rule infractions. Researchers suggest that POs treat female probationers and parolees differently because of their paternalistic beliefs that womens' family-based obligations are more important than mens' (Hennessey, 2006).

Many POs are frustrated because they lack the time and resources to do the kind of job they believe is maximally helpful to their clients. Because of their increasing caseload responsibilities, POs cannot possibly devote the proper amount of time to any given offender without interfering with their time allocations to other clients. The immense paperwork associated with the PO role has caused more than a few POs to opt for alternative professions. The progress of offenders must be reported regularly to the courts, parole boards, and various agencies. These reports are tedious to complete. Increased caseloads and work pressures are not only stressful, they also lead to a reduction in the quality of general services and supervision extended to offender-clients.

One important implication for POs of the reduction of the quality of client supervision is the increased potential for lawsuits arising from their negligent supervision of clients (Harris, 2006). While POs cannot guarantee public safety completely by their supervision of offenders, it is generally believed that the more intense the supervision, the less likely offenders will commit dangerous offenses. Where supervision by POs is less intense, the risk to the public posed by the offender theoretically increases. In a 1986 Alaska case, the Alaska Supreme Court ruled that state agencies and their officers may be held liable for **negligence** when probationers and parolees under their supervision commit violent offenses (*Division of Corrections v. Neakok,* 1986). Thus, POs are increasingly at risk through tort actions filed by victims harmed by the crimes committed by their offender-clients. The American Correctional Association currently conducts seminars and other types of training to make POs more knowledgeable about their personal liabilities, especially if one or more of their clients harm victims while under PO supervision.

A CODE OF ETHICS FOR POs

POs abide by a general code of ethics. Ethical codes have been developed for most professional organizations. A **code of ethics** refers to regulations formulated by major professional societies that outline the specific problems and issues frequently encountered by persons who practice the profession. POs are in continuous contact with criminals who are either on probation or parole. Often, POs must make ethical choices that involve moral dilemmas. POs exercise considerable discretion over their clients, and they are expected to exercise their discretion wisely. Thus, POs have a responsibility to act properly in controlling individual clients. But at the same time, they must balance societal interests against the interests of their clients.

For example, POs are expected to monitor their clients closely and report any infractions of probation or parole programs. However, POs have been known to give second and third chances to their clients in order to help them avoid imprisonment. Furthermore, when probation officers prepare presentence investigation reports for judges, they can sway the judge one way or another toward the offender, depending on how they choose to prepare their report. POs choose what should be entered into PSI reports, and on occasion, they may omit a fact that could seriously affect a convicted offender's freedom. If the offender used a firearm during the commission of a felony, for instance, the PO could omit this fact from the PSI report. The use of a firearm would lead to a mandatory period of incarceration. But there may be mitigating circumstances that change how the PO views the use of the firearm by the particular offender. POs also work closely with prosecutors and are intimately familiar with the nuances of plea bargaining. Often, prosecutors will reduce charges against criminal suspects in exchange for a guilty plea to a less serious offense. More often than not, the prosecutor will encourage the PO to prepare a PSI report that omits certain factual information that the judge might otherwise consider. With the information included, the judge may not accept the plea agreement and the case might have to be tried before a jury. This is not always a desirable outcome for prosecutors. Thus, there is an element of collusion between prosecutors and POs. For some POs, this is an ethical dilemma.

For POs who are considered educators and enablers, they may wish to maintain clients under their supervision in the belief that they can make a difference in their lives. If their clients violate minor program rules, such as curfew, POs may overlook the curfew violation in order to continue the offender's treatment in counseling or participation in an educational or vocational program.

POs are not supposed to have malicious motives when referring their clients to judges or parole boards for revocation actions. If a PO reports a program violation in order to teach the client the importance of obeying program rules, that is one thing. If the PO reports a program violation to the parole board because the offender is black or Hispanic, then this action is discriminatory and clearly wrong. In another situation, if a PO does not violate a probationer or parolee for failing a drug test, the PO may be facilitating their program success by encouraging them to be law-abiding and refrain from further drug use. However, the PO may also be enabling the offender's addictive behavior.

The American Probation and Parole Association has evolved a code of ethics for its membership, which follows:

1. I will render professional service to the justice system and the community at large in effecting the social adjustment of the offender.

2. I will uphold the law with dignity, displaying an awareness of my responsibility to offenders while recognizing the right of the public to be safeguarded from criminal activity.

3. I will strive to be objective in the performance of my duties, recognizing the inalienable right of all persons, appreciating the inherent worth of the individual, and respecting those confidences that can be reposed with me.

4. I will conduct my personal life with decorum, neither accepting nor granting favors in connection with my office.

5. I will cooperate with my coworkers and related agencies and will continually strive to improve my professional competence through the seeking and sharing of knowledge and understanding.

6. I will distinguish clearly, in public, between my statements and actions as an individual and as a representative of my profession.

7. I will encourage policy, procedures, and personnel practices that will enable others to conduct themselves in accordance with the values, goals, and objectives of the American Probation and Parole Association.

8. I recognize my office as a symbol of public faith and I accept it as a public trust to be held as long as I am true to the ethics of the American Probation and Parole Association.

9. I will constantly strive to achieve these objectives and ideals, dedicating myself to my chosen profession (American Probation and Parole Association, 2006).

Federal probation officers have also established an ethical code to abide by when supervising offenders. This code is as follows:

1. As a Federal Probation Officer, I am dedicated to rendering professional service to the courts, the parole authorities, and the community at large in effecting the social adjustment of the offender.

2. I will conduct my personal life with decorum, will neither accept nor grant favors in connection with my office, and will put loyalty to moral principles above personal consideration.

3. I will uphold the law with dignity and with complete awareness of the prestige and stature of the judicial system of which I am a part. I will be ever cognizant of my responsibility to the community that I serve.

4. I will strive to be objective in the performance of my duties; respect the inalienable rights of all persons; appreciate the inherent worth of the individual; and hold inviolate those confidences that can be reposed with me.

5. I will cooperate with my fellow workers and related agencies and will continually attempt to improve my professional standards through seeking of knowledge and understanding.

6. I recognize my office as a symbol of public faith and I accept it as a public trust to be held as long as I am true to the ethics of the Federal Probation Service. I will constantly strive to achieve these objectives and ideals, dedicating myself to my chosen profession (Administrative Office of U.S. Courts, 2001).

Several different kinds of probation/parole officers have been identified: (1) punitive officers, (2) welfare officers, (3) passive officers, and (4) synthetic officers.

Punitive Officers.   Punitive officers are very dogmatic and orient themselves toward their clients as law enforcement officers. They put societal interests above the interests of their clients. They file petitions to violate their clients' programs with great frequency. The punitive officer seeks to control offender behavior through threats and intimidation.

Welfare Officers.   Welfare officers are like social workers in that they focus on treatment and rehabilitation. Such officers focus their attention on advocating, brokering, education, enabling, and mediating. They assist their clients in finding employment and even help them fill out job applications. They consider their roles as largely therapeutic.

Passive Officers.   Passive officers care little about the needs of society or their clients. They merely go through the day in a perfunctory way, performing their jobs in minimal ways. Their primary interest is getting through the day, the week, the month, and the year, and eventually retiring with full pension and benefits. They seek to advance their own positions within their agencies. They simply follow the rules set forth for them to follow—nothing more, nothing less.

Synthetic Officers.   Synthetic officers are actually a blend of enforcers and social workers. They want very much to supervise their offenders so that they will remain law-abiding. They work closely with police departments. But at the same time, they understand the complexities of probationers' and parolees' problems and the limitations of working through those problems. These officers are both humanitarian and justice oriented.

It is unknown how many officers of particular types there are throughout the different state and federal agencies and organizations. All officers share a common bond, however, in that they should be guided by the ethic of care, the central goal of which is to reintegrate offenders into their communities. Thus, they must continually reevaluate their positions and how they relate with their clients. The PO–client relation is a dynamic one and is ever-changing.

PO UNIONIZATION AND COLLECTIVE BARGAINING

Historically, American probation and parole officers have been among the last professional aggregates to organize for the purpose of forming unions and engaging in collective bargaining. A survey of the professional literature found in the source files of *Criminal Justice Abstracts* during the period 1968–2005 reveals that 92 percent of all references to unions and collective bargaining relate primarily to police organizations (Champion, 2005). Most of the remaining articles and books on the subject of unions and collective bargaining pertain to correctional officers who are affiliated with prisons and jails. Several reasons for these early developments and the emphasis on unionization for police officers and correctional staff are that criminal suspects and inmates have been the most volatile aggregates to file lawsuits against specific officers. Often these lawsuits have proved groundless. However, individual officers have had to hire their own defense counsels for the purpose of self-protection against frivolous suits. Through unionization, police officer and correctional officer unions now provide ample funds for defense work where individual officers are sued by citizens or inmates. Another objective of these unions is to secure additional benefits pertaining to working conditions, officer safety, and retirement (Crawley, 2002).

But during the 1990s, POs have organized at local, state, and federal levels to establish collective bargaining mechanisms and unions for common purposes. Virtually every major city and all states have probation and parole officer unions today that represent PO interests. One of the oldest unions is the L.A. County Probation Officers Union. This was an outgrowth of the American Federal, State, County, and Municipal Employees (AFSCME), one of the country's largest public employees' unions. AFSCME is affiliated with the AFL-CIO and began as a series of smaller unions during the 1930s. In 1955, the membership of AFSCME numbered 100,000 employees. Shortly after World War II in 1945, a group of World War II veterans who became employed as probation officers in Los Angeles County in California founded AFSCME Local 685. In 1969, Local 685, under the strong leadership of Henry Fiering, began to aggressively fight for the rights of its employees with the L.A. County Probation Department in all matters concerning wages, hours, benefits, and working conditions, including caseload assignments.

The L.A. County Probation Officers Union is only one of hundreds of local unions across the country today who lobby for the rights and entitlements of POs. In New York, for example, the New York State Probation Officers Association (NYSPOA) was formed during the late 1960s to represent the interests of line officers working in the field of probation. The preamble to the constitution of the NYSPOA says that the association, recognizing the need to preserve human dignity through acceptance, empathy, and understanding, advocates the use of those corrective facilities, professions, skills, and rehabilitative procedures that will best protect society through the reduction of crime and delinquency. Over the years, the NYSPOA has strived to write, influence, and/or support legislative endeavors that would permit probation officers to perform their functions effectively, efficiently, and safely. The NYSPOA works with other professional organizations, such as the American Probation and Parole Association, to further its interests and objectives. The NYSPOA is continually striving to upgrade the quality of professional services rendered by its affiliate officers. In 1991, for instance, an annual conference was proposed that would provide low-cost training for interested POs and address their diverse needs.

Probation and parole officer unions also arbitrate and settle grievances, whether they are generated by probationers or parolees or by POs themselves. In some instances, grievances pertain to the pay POs should receive for overtime they engage in while supervising their clients. For instance, a New Jersey county settled a grievance originating from New Jersey PO supervisors who had been given additional supervisory responsibilities to supervise other POs. The pay differential was only 94 cents per hour, and the county balked at paying the additional hourly wage. But the union representing the POs arbitrated a settlement, with the county paying over $5,800 in monies owed to PO supervisors.

Salary increases at fixed rates are also negotiated by unions through collective bargaining. In one county, for example, a cost-of-living pay raise was negotiated at 4 percent for January 1998, 3 percent for January 1999, 3 percent for January 2000, and 2 percent for January 2001. If POs in this particular county should be promoted, demoted, or transferred, there are contract provisions calling for salary adjustments to levels consistent with the salary range held prior to the promotion, transfer, or demotion.

At the city level, probation and parole unions are having a more significant voice and power over the lives of affiliate POs. In Portland, Oregon, for instance, the city council has recognized the Parole and Probation Employee's Association (PPEA) to represent its membership as a collective bargaining unit. Some of the issues negotiated include caseloads, working hours, compensation for overtime, confidentiality issues, PSI report preparation time, fringe benefits relating to vacations, and retirement. Regarding caseloads, the Department of Corrections has alleged that POs have caseloads of 8 under ISP and 50 cases per PO under standard supervision. However, the PPEA has alleged that standard caseloads are closer to 100 clients per PO. A PPEA representative said that because of the sheer volume of cases, "we've become a bunch of desk-bound pencil pushers" (Probation and Parole Employee's Association, 2001:2).

Probation and parole officer unions are not unique to the United States. For instance, there are probation and parole officer unions in Canada and other countries. In Ontario, Canada, for instance, there is a Probation Officers Association of Ontario, Inc. (POAO). The POAO is committed to the following objectives:

1. Speak with credibility on issues in criminal justice.
2. Facilitate increased understanding of the specialized role of the Probation Officer.
3. Provide representative perspectives on legislative issues to policymakers.
4. Provide a forum for an exchange of professional experience and opinion.
5. Promote good fellowship and esprit de corps among members.
6. Foster goodwill, understanding, and cooperation with others working in the criminal justice system.
7. Educate and involve the community in corrections.

The POAO expects its membership to subscribe to the following values:

1. That Probation Officers achieve professional status and continue to receive on ongoing education.
2. That its members are fully committed to a Code of Ethics.
3. That community corrections programs retain their validity as an effective means of rehabilitation for offenders.
4. That autonomy be maintained, while at the same time the responsibilities of the Ministries, OPSEU, and other components of the criminal justice system be acknowledged.
5. That involvement in the decision-making process be democratic and participatory at all levels.

Over 600 probation and parole officers belong to the POAO and they supervise more than 60,000 offenders in the community. POs supervise probation orders, parole, conditional sentences, and conditional supervision orders. They monitor and enforce compliance with these court orders and others such as restitution to victims and community service orders. These professionals prepare detailed and comprehensive pre-sentence investigation reports and pre-dispositional reports for juveniles. Pre-parole reports are also prepared for the Ontario Board of Parole.

SUMMARY

Both adult and juvenile corrections have escalated during the last few decades. POs have assumed increased responsibilities and supervisory tasks in dealing with an increasingly diverse and dangerous clientele. In 2001 there were over 630,000 personnel working in corrections, with about 60 percent of these working in probation and parole services. The functions of probation and parole services are to supervise offenders; ensure offender compliance with program goals and provisions; conduct routine alcohol/drug checks; provide networking services for employment assistance; direct offender-clients to proper treatment, counseling, and other forms of assistance; protect the community by detecting a client's program infractions and reporting them to judges or parole boards; assisting offenders in becoming integrated into their communities; and engaging in any useful rehabilitative enterprise that will improve offender-client skills.

The organization and administration of probation and parole services is most often within the scope of the Department of Corrections in most states. Services vary among the states, although there are common elements to all probation and parole services and programs. The complexity of organizational structure is highly dependent upon the nature of clientele supervised and their special needs. The rehabilitative aim of corrections has not been particularly successful. For this and other reasons, probation and parole departments have drawn extensive criticism from an increasingly discontent public. Criticisms have focused on the lack of skills and training of POs and the ineffectiveness of their performance. Professionalization through organizations such as the American Correctional Association and the American Probation and Parole Association have attempted to raise standards relating to the selection, recruitment, and training of POs throughout the nation.

In 2001, POs averaged $23,000 as an entry-level salary, while top PO positions reached $93,400. Few jurisdictions required bachelor's degrees for PO work, however, a majority of POs had some college education or had completed college. Increased education is the primary means for improving one's professionalization. Observers suggest that there is a high correlation between higher education achieved and work effectiveness among POs. Because of an increasingly ethnically and racially diverse clientele, POs have received additional training in cultural diversity. Some POs are recruited for dealing with special offender populations where English is a second language. Assessment centers are used for PO training. One assessment center is the Florida Assessment Center, which focuses on selecting and evaluating the best POs for supervising offenders in a **Florida community control program (FCCP).**

One important issue that is being raised in greater numbers of jurisdictions is whether POs should carry firearms. About half the states authorized the use of firearms for POs in 2006. There is a controversy over whether POs should go armed. Some persons feel that armed POs tend to provoke their clients, while others see carrying a weapon as a reasonable means of self-protection, particularly if POs must enter dangerous, gang-controlled neighborhoods to visit their clients. One of the hazards of PO work is the lawsuit syndrome, where clients sue POs for various reasons. Thus, a part of PO training is designed to acquaint them with the conditions and situations that are most likely to result in lawsuits. Thus, the potential for lawsuits can be avoided or minimized. POs are continually subjected to periodic evaluations to determine their competence in job performance. Labor turnover among POs averages about 15 percent per year.

Most POs who leave the profession tend to seek better jobs in the private sector or graduate to federal employment where the pay and benefits are substantially greater than state compensation.

Another important issue is the matter of caseloads. Caseloads refer to the number of clients managed by POs in any state or federal agency. POs supervise offenders either intensively or generally, depending on the programs imposed by judges and parole boards. No precise figures have been agreed upon as to what constitutes an optimum caseload size for POs. There are different caseload assignment models. These include the conventional model, the numbers-game model, the conventional model with geographic considerations, and the specialized caseloads model. Officer–client interactions are affected by different factors, including the orientations of POs toward offenders. Some of these orientations are detectors, enablers, educators, mediators, and enforcers. Depending on a PO's orientation, interactions with clients are positively or negatively influenced. Some amount of role conflict therefore exists, as POs attempt to perform their jobs under different sets of circumstances established by each jurisdiction. Most POs belong to one or more organizations where codes of ethics have been promulgated. These codes of ethics obligate POs to adhere to stringent behavioral guidelines in the performance of their jobs. It is expected that PO adherence to these codes of ethics will eventually improve their effectiveness and job performance, and that, ultimately, client recidivism will decline.

Probation and parole officers have formed unions and engage in collective bargaining in all states. Many of these unions are at local, county, and state levels, and all unionization is designed to achieve better conditions for POs. Issues involve pay, retirement benefits, caseloads and assignments, promotional opportunities, and various types of grievances about the job and its benefits. Each union has articulated objectives. Union representatives are authorized to negotiate contracts with city, county, state, and federal governments to determine pay scales, working hours and conditions, and other matters of relevance to their memberships. Unions also attempt to improve the quality of professionalism among their memberships by sponsoring annual conferences where workshops are conducted to learn various skills. All union members are encouraged to improve their skills on a regular basis to promote their own interests within their respective probation or parole agencies.

QUESTIONS FOR REVIEW

1. What are some functions and goals of probation and parole services?
2. Are all probation and parole agencies organized in the same way? What are some reasons for different organizational arrangements?
3. What are several criticisms of probation and parole programs?
4. What is the essence of the argument advanced by Robert Martinson that "nothing works" when applied to probation and parole?
5. What sort of profile do probation and parole officers have? What are some of their primary characteristics?
6. What are some of the major duties and responsibilities of POs?
7. What seems to account for comparatively high levels of labor turnover in corrections work in relation to other occupations or professions? How do many POs perceive correctional work and what reasons do they cite for leaving it?

8. Is there an ideal caseload for a PO? How are caseloads determined?

9. Identify and describe four types of caseload assignment methods.

10. How does the size of caseload relate to a PO's effectiveness?

SUGGESTED READINGS

Czuchry, M., T.L. Sia, and D.F. Dansereau (2006). "Improving Early Engagement and Treatment Readiness of Probationers: Gender Differences." *The Prison Journal* **86**:56–74.

DeAmicis, Albert P. (2006). "An Ethical Dilemma in Corrections." *American Jails* **20**:77–82.

Hatcher, Loran D. (2006). "Security Threat Groups: It Is More than Managing Gangs in a Local Facility." *Corrections Today* **68**:54–58.

Paparozzi, Mario A. (2005). "Caseload Size in Probation and Parole." *APPA Perspectives* **29**:23–25.

White, William L. et al. (2005). "The Other Side of Burnout." *APPA Perspectives* **29**:26–31.

INTERNET CONNECTIONS

American Correctional Association
http://www.corrections.com/aca/index

Burnout in Billings
http://www.cannabisnews.com/news/16/thread16603.shtml

Citizens for Legal Responsibility
http://www.clr.org

Corrections Industries Association
http://www.correctionalindustries.org

Corrections industries links
http://www.corrections.com/industries

Corrections news
http://www.newstopics.corrections.com

Intermediate Skills
http://www.ojdda.org/intlesplan.html

International Corrections and Prisons Association
http://www.icpa.ca/home.html

Naber Technical Enterprises: Correctional Training, Correctional Consulting, Jail Research for Criminal Justice and Public Safety
http://www.nteusa.orgflyers/08.html

National Institute of Corrections
http://www.nicic.org

Probation officer recruitment
http://www.wvmccd.cc.ca.us/wvmccd/police/officer_hire.html

Ventura County Probation Agency
http://www.ventura.org/vcap/recruitm.htm

Chapter Outline

Chapter Objectives

As the result of reading this chapter, the following objectives will be realized:

1. Examining the PO–client relation and the changing nature of PO work.
2. Describing problems of parole officers including stress, burnout, and turnover.
3. Describing the role of volunteers in probation, parole, and community corrections work.
4. Discussing some of the criticisms leveled at volunteers in probation/parole and community corrections roles.
5. Discussing the legal liabilities of volunteers.
6. Describing the roles and responsibilities of paraprofessionals.
7. Examining the legal liabilities of paraprofessionals in probation/parole and community corrections.
8. Discussing the future involvement of volunteers and paraprofessionals in assisting probationers and parolees.

• *Jerry M. liked his probation work in New York. He entered the field to help others. He had completed a university degree and had taken additional study to prepare him for dealing with clients with special needs. In his early months of in-service training, Jerry M. spent a lot of time observing and learning by watching how other probation officers did their jobs. Jerry M. was assigned a lot of paperwork and assisted his associates in the completion of pre-sentence investigation reports. This tedious but necessary work gave him valuable insights into why certain offenders got into trouble. After several months, Jerry M. was assigned a caseload of 45 low-risk probationers. After two years, his case load had risen to 178 probationers. Even in his early months of dealing with lower numbers of clients, he found that he could not spend a great deal of time with each of them. His visits to client homes and places of work were limited by time. There's only so much you can do during the day. Jerry M. began extending his own working hours, without additional pay. He wanted to make a difference in his clients' lives. But with nearly 200 probationers to supervise, it didn't take long for Jerry M. to become disenchanted with his work. Most of his clients would come to his office and report on a regular basis. He would file their routine reports, spend five minutes asking them questions about their employment, how they were doing, and if they needed any special assistance. Not that he could have provided any special assistance if it were requested, since the resources of his probation department were severely limited. Finally, during the third year of employment with his department, Jerry M. abruptly quit. When asked why he would give up his job to go to work in his brother's car dealership as a car salesman, Jerry M. said simply, "There's not enough of me to go around. I found that I couldn't do what I wanted to do. My job as an officer became meaningless. My clients were still committing crimes and I couldn't do a thing about it. I quit." Jerry M. is not alone. New York is one of many states reporting high rates of labor turnover among its probation officers annually. Such turnover is costly, and the reasons cited for leaving usually have to do with job stress and burnout. [Source: Adapted from the Associated Press, "Stresses of Probation Work Lead to High Officer Turnover in New York Probation Office," March 7, 2006].*

• *Marcia L. is a 52-year-old volunteer. She works with parolees at a halfway house in Connecticut. Marcia L. receives no money for her work. She helps parolees learn how to read. She helps some of them fill out job applications. She reads to them and offers short classes on different subjects. She spends 8 or 9 hours a day working with her clients, who have come to trust her and confide in her. Marcia L. loves her work. She says that working with parolees is not as dangerous as her friends have advised. "Some of my best friends think*

I'm crazy, hanging out with dangerous felons. But while they have committed terrible crimes in the past, the ones I deal with are very respectful and protective of me. One of my 'boys' got me out of trouble with some teenage gang members in the tough neighborhood where our house is located. They wanted money and one of my boys came along and set them straight. I won't say what he did exactly, but those particular gangsters avoid me like I've got some contagious disease nowadays. I really love what I do." [Adapted from Fred West and the Associated Press, "Volunteer at Halfway House Improves Client Literacy," May 3, 2006].

• Jose R., age 61, is a volunteer assigned to work at a day reporting center in a Chicago suburb. Jose R. works with low-risk probationers who must stop in regularly at the center to be checked for drug or alcohol use. While at the center, clients may meet with probation officers, paraprofessionals, and volunteers for different purposes. A limited number of courses are offered for those lacking vocational and educational skills. Most clients reporting to the center have not graduated from high school and some are illiterate. Jose R. is divorced and he is on disability, retired from his high school teaching job. One of his clients is Manuel M., a 24-year-old parolee with a wife and two children to support. On more than one occasion, Manuel M. has confided in Jose R. about his rocky marital relationship. Manuel M. has had difficulty finding work and keeping it. He is barely making ends meet at home, and his wife is critical of him. During one of his sessions with Manuel M., Jose R. made some casual observations about Manuel M.'s wife and her unrealistic expectations. Jose R. suggested that Manuel M. should tell his wife to be more supportive of him and his efforts to find work and keep it. He even suggested some dialogue, things to say. About a week later, Manuel M. reported to the center, complaining that his wife was seeking a divorce and alleging that Jose R. had interfered in their marriage. Manuel M. has been forced out of his apartment and is now hard-pressed to find an apartment he can afford. He is suing the probation department largely because of the actions and advice received from Jose R., whose services with the center have been terminated. [Adapted from the Associated Press, "Lawsuit Filed for Bad Advice," June 1, 2006].

INTRODUCTION

This chapter examines the changing PO role. There are serious concerns throughout the correctional community about whether POs are peace officers or police officers. PO responsibilities include supervising dangerous clients and ensuring that they are in compliance with their probation or parole program requirements. One of the first things POs attempt to do is ascertain the degree of risk posed by the offenders they supervise. The first part of this chapter examines the assessment of offender risk. Several risk measures are presented. Since POs are expected to assist their clients as well as monitor their behaviors, some of these instruments attempt to determine offender needs as well as their risk levels. Needs instruments are described. It is very important to define an offender's needs in order for POs to network and coordinate the most appropriate community services as interventions in a client's behalf.

PO work is increasingly specialized. More offenders who are freed on probation or parole abscond or leave their jurisdictions without PO permission. They cannot be immediately located. Thus, many probation and parole agencies have established apprehension units to track down absconders and return them to their jurisdictions. If absconders are located and returned, they face possible probation or parole program revocation. Therefore, it is dangerous business to be a part of apprehension units and to hunt fugitives who want to avoid capture.

Gangs are a pervasive part of our society. Thousands of gangs exist throughout the United States. Gangs are commonplace in prisons and jails as well as on city streets. Therefore, it is essential that POs familiarize themselves with gang recognition signs and symbols. When POs enter particular neighborhoods where their clients reside, often these neighborhoods are gang-dominated. Thus, there is an element of danger that exists merely during the act of checking up on a PO's clients. The gang phenomenon is examined to the extent that it influences PO work and how POs do their jobs, especially where a portion of one's probationer- or parolee-clients are gang members. Probation and parole agencies also have research units whose task it is to study client profiles and devise new and improved supervision procedures. Some of the activities of these research units are described.

PO work is stressful. There are numerous demands on POs, including their work for criminal courts, their supervision of dangerous clientele, and other general occupational hazards. The stresses of PO work are examined, including a discussion of possible sources of stress. Stress often leads to burnout, which in turn causes POs to become less effective in the performance of their work. Burnout is examined, including a discussion of how it is assessed. Several solutions are proposed to alleviate stress and burnout associated with the PO role.

The final part of this chapter examines the roles of volunteers and paraprofessionals who often assist with offender management in a variety of ways. Volunteers are unsalaried workers. Often they are found working with offenders in halfway houses. They assist them with filling out job applications and perform teaching functions. Usually, volunteers have no legal training or qualifications that authorize them to direct probationers or parolees in their required programming by the court or parole board. Nevertheless, they do perform several valuable services for probation and parole departments and officers. Paraprofessionals have some amount of formal training working with offenders. Many paraprofessionals have college degrees in disciplines that complement probation and parole work, such as criminal justice, sociology, political science, psychology, or social work. Their roles are also described. Finally, because volunteers and paraprofessionals are not as well trained as regular POs, they are unusually vulnerable to legal liabilities of different kinds. They may give offenders the wrong type of advice. Or they may give illegal assistance to offenders without the knowledge that what they are doing is wrong or should not be done. Thus, the legal liabilities of these volunteers and paraprofessionals are examined and discussed.

PROBATION AND PAROLE: RISK/NEEDS ASSESSMENTS

Assessing Offender Risk: A Brief History

Many **risk assessment** measures have been devised and are used largely for the purpose of determining probabilities that offender/clients will engage in dangerous or maladjusted behaviors. These probabilities are subsequently used for placement, program, and security decision making. Needs measures and instruments enable corrections personnel and administrative staffs to highlight client weaknesses or problems that may have led to their convictions or difficulties initially (Ratansi et al., 2006). Once problem areas have been targeted, specific services or treatments might be scheduled and provided. Various Christian Reform movements have been credited with establishing an early prisoner **classification system** in the eighteenth century. Behavioral scientists, especially psychiatrists and psychologists, conducted research during the period 1910–1920, and found that custody-level placements of inmates as well as other program assignments could be made by using certain psychological characteristics as predictors.

Criminologists and criminal justice scholars have become increasingly involved in devising risk assessment inventories and needs indices, using combinations of psychological, social, socioeconomic, and demographic factors and related criteria to make dangerousness forecasts and behavioral predictions. One of the reasons for developing such instrumentation is the frequency of rapes among inmates. In fact, the incidence of such sexual assaults among inmates has drawn the attention of the federal government and the enactment of the Prison Rape Elimination Act of 2003 (Harrison, Johnson, and Beck, 2006). One dimension of this act is to identify those more aggressive inmates likely to engage in rape and isolate them from other offenders while incarcerated. They may also receive special counseling and therapy in addition to their isolation. Risk assessment inventories enhance the ability of prison authorities to identify such persons, isolate them, and treat them.

Formal, paper-and-pencil risk and needs instruments began to proliferate during the 1960s (Champion, 1994). Some of this instrumentation was used with juvenile offenders. Later, numerous behavioral and psychological instruments were devised and used for the purpose of assessing client risk or inmate dangerousness. The Minnesota Multiphasic Personality Inventory (MMPI), consisting of 550 true–false items, was originally used in departments of corrections for personality assessments. While this instrument is still applied in many correctional settings, some researchers, such as Edwin Megargee, have extracted certain items from the MMPI for use as predictors of inmate violence and adjustment. The use of **classification** devices such as Megargee's are often designated as MMPI-based assessments or classifications. Applications of scales such as Megargee's have received mixed results and evaluations. In at least some studies, such scales have demonstrably low reliability (Tjaden and Layton, 2006).

Herbert Quay's work preceded the work of Megargee (Quay and Parsons, 1971). Quay devised a relatively simple typology of delinquent behavior, classifying delinquents into four categories: Undersocialized Aggression, Socialized Aggression, Attention Deficit, and Anxiety–Withdrawal–Dysphoria. Juveniles would complete a self-administered questionnaire and their personality scores would be quickly tabulated. Depending on how particular juveniles were depicted and classified, different treatments would be administered to help them. Later, Quay devised a scale, which he called AIMS, or the Adult Internal Management System (Quay, 1984). Again, Quay used a self-administered inventory, the Correctional Adjustment Checklist and the Correctional Adjustment Life History. His adult typology consisted of five types of inmates: Aggressive Psychopathic, Manipulative, Situational, Inadequate–Dependent, and Neurotic–Anxious. Another system is the I-Level Classification, referring to the Interpersonal Maturity Level Classification System. It is based on a mixture of developmental and psychoanalytic theories and is administered by psychologists or psychiatrists in lengthy clinical interviews. Clients are classified as being at particular "I-Levels," such as I-1, I-2, and so on, up to I-7. Each I-level is a developmental stage reflecting one's ability to cope with complex personal and interpersonal problems. The higher the I-level, the better adjusted the client.

It was not until the 1980s, however, that state corrections departments began to create and apply risk assessment schemes with some regularity and in correctional areas beyond the institutional setting. For example, Arizona created its first Offender Classification System manual in 1986 (Arizona Department of Corrections, 2006). Instrumentation for risk assessment was established in Illinois in the mid-1980s. Tennessee sought requests for proposals in 1987 to devise risk measures for its inmate population. Missouri introduced a variation of AIMS for use in its Department of Corrections in 1988. Many jurisdictions are currently revising or have recently revised their risk and needs instruments (Tjaden and Layton, 2006). Iowa's Risk/Needs Classification System was implemented in December 1983 and revised extensively in 2005 (Iowa Department of Correctional Services, 2006). The Iowa Department of Corrections Reassessment of Client Risk is shown in Figure 11.1.

1. Classification systems enable authorities to make decisions about appropriate offender program placements.

2. Classification systems help to identify one's needs and the provision of effective services in specialized treatment programs.

3. Classification assists in determining one's custody level if confined in either prisons or jails.

4. Classification helps to adjust one's custody level during confinement, considering behavioral improvement and evidence of rehabilitation.

5. While confined, inmates may be targeted for particular services and/or programs to meet their needs.

6. Classification may be used for offender management and deterrence relative to program or prison rules and requirements.

7. Classification schemes are useful for policy decision making and administrative planning relevant for jail and prison construction, the nature and number of facilities required, and the types of services to be made available within such facilities.

8. Classification systems enable parole boards to make better early-release decisions about eligible offenders.

9. Community corrections agencies can utilize classification schemes to determine those parolees who qualify for participation and those who don't qualify.

10. Classification systems enable assessments of risk and dangerousness to be made generally in anticipation of the type of supervision best suited for particular offenders.

11. Classification schemes assist in decision making relevant for community crime control, the nature of penalties to be imposed, and the determination of punishment.

12. Classification may enable authorities to determine whether selective incapacitation is desirable for particular offenders or offender groupings.

Dangerousness and risk are often used interchangeably. Dangerousness and risk both convey propensities to cause harm to others or oneself. What is the likelihood that any particular offender will be violent toward others? Does an offender pose any risk to public safety? What is the likelihood that any particular offender will commit suicide or attempt it? Risk (or dangerousness) instruments are screening devices intended to distinguish between different types of offenders for purposes of determining initial institutional classification, security placement and inmate management, early release eligibility, and the level of supervision required under conditions of probation or parole. Most state jurisdictions and the federal government refer to these measures as risk instruments rather than dangerousness instruments. There is considerable variance among states regarding the format and content of

IOWA DEPARTMENT OF CORRECTIONS REASSESSMENT OF CLIENT RISK

Client Name_____ ICBC# _____
      Last   First   Middle

Date of Reassessment _____ Officer's Name _____

Offense _____

INSTRUCTIONS: Score Items and add total score.   **SCORE**

1. Age at first Adult Conviction/Juvenile Adjudication (include deferreds)	24 or older	= –2	[ ]
	20 to 23	= 0	[ ]
	19 or younger	= 1	[ ]
2. Prior Juvenile Commitments	None	= 0	[ ]
	One or more	= 2	[ ]
3. Prior Probations/Parole Supervisions (Adult/Juvenile Adjudications)	One or more	= 2	[ ]
	None	= 0	[ ]
4. Number of Prior Probation/Parole Revocations (Adult/Juvenile Adjudications)	One or more	= 2	[ ]
	None	= 0	[ ]
	One or more	= 2	[ ]
5. Felony/Misdemeanor Convictions (include present offense, deferreds, Juvenile Adjudications); Circle applicable and add for score. Do not exceed a total of 3.	Burglary or Robbery	= 1	[ ]
	Theft, Forgery, FUFI, Fraudulent Practices	= 1	
	Assault, Weapons Public Order		
6. Misdemeanor Conviction History (Simple & Serious Misdemeanors Only) Include present offense, deferreds & Juvenile Adjudications.	Offenses	= 1	
	None	= 0	[ ]
	None or one	= 0	
	Two or more	= 1	[ ]
7. Sex	Female	= 0	
	Male	= 1	[ ]
8. Alcohol Usage Problems	No interference	= 0	
	Occasional abuse	= 1	
9. Drug Usage Problems	Frequent abuse	= 2	[ ]
	No interference	= 0	
	Occasional abuse	= 1	
	Frequent abuse	= 2	[ ]

*10. **Employment** Satisfactory one year or longer	=	–2	
Secure or not applicable	=	0	
Unsatisfactory or Unemployed, unemployable	=	2	[ ]

(continued)

FIGURE 11.1   Iowa Department of Corrections Reassessment of Client Risk.

Source: Iowa Department of Correctional Services, 2003.

*11.	**Companions** No adverse relationships	=	0		
	Associations occasionally negative	=	1		
	Associations almost completely negative	=	2	[	]
*12.	**Problems with Current Living Situation** Relatively stable relationships and/or address	=	0		
	Moderate disorganization or stress	=	1		
	Major disorganization/ stress	=	2	[	]
*13.	**Response to Supervision Conditions** No problems of consequence	=	0		
	Moderate compliance problem	=	1		
	Frequently unwilling to comply	=	3	[	]
*14.	**New Arrests** None	=	0		
	One or more arrests	=	3	[	]
*15.	**Use of Community Resources**				
	Not needed	=	0		
	Productively utilized	=	0		
	Needed, but not available	=	1		
	Utilized, but not beneficial	=	2		
	Client rejected referral	=	3	[	]

TOTAL SCORE   [   ]

Clients are assigned to the highest level of supervision indicated on the following scale:

Risk

31 to 15	Intensive
14 to 8	Normal
7 to 2	Minimum
1 to −5	Administrative

Levels of Supervision

1	Intensive
2	Normal
3	Minimum
4	Administrative

FIGURE 11.1   *(Continued)*

such measures. An example of one of the less elaborate versions of a risk assessment instrument is one used by the Massachusetts Parole Board, illustrated in Figure 11.2.

Additionally, needs assessment devices are instruments that measure an offender's personal/social skills, health, well-being and emotional stability, educational level and vocational strengths and weaknesses, alcohol/drug dependencies, mental ability, and other relevant life factors, and that highlight those areas for which services are available and could or should be provided. Needs assessment devices,

Reason for Override

0   Assaultive offense
1   Severity of offense
2   Special conditions set by parole board, court, or district
3   Client not available for active supervision
4   Force field indicates high needs

5   Other_____

_____

_____

_____

_____

_____

_____

Comments_____

_____

_____

_____

_____

Level   [   ]

Revised Level   [   ]

Override reason code   [   ]

_____
Override approval/date

FIGURE 11.1   (Continued)

measures, scales, or inventories identify the types of services offenders might require if incarcerated. If some offenders are illiterate, they may be placed, either voluntarily or involuntarily, into an educational program at some level, depending on the amount of remedial work deemed necessary. Psychologically disturbed or mentally ill offenders may require some type of counseling or therapy (Fitzgerald et al., 2006). Some offenders may require particular medications for illnesses or other maladies. Sometimes instruments are designed in such a way so as to assess both needs and risk. In Figure 11.3, the Kansas Department of Corrections has devised a risk and needs assessment coding form for assessing the future conduct and needs of parolees.

Risk and need assessments may also be referred to jointly and contained in a longer inventory or measure, labeled a risk–need assessment. An inspection of these devices and the individual items included within them will indicate which factors seem to have the greatest priority and predictive utility. The Alaska offender need assessment scale shown in Figure 11.4 also assigns greater or lesser weights to different items, which focus on various dimensions of one's life. Those areas having the largest number of points potentially assigned include employment, emotional stability, and alcohol usage. These items have possible large scores of "5," "6," and "5," respectively. All other items, including academic/vocational skills, financial status, other substance abuse, mental ability, health, living arrangements, sexual

MASSACHUSETTS PAROLE BOARD
Release Risk Classification Instrument

Name:_____   MCI-Number_____

SID:_____   Actual Release Date:_____

Hearing Location:_____   Hearing Date:_____

Completed By:_____   Completion Date:_____

Controlling Effective Date of Commitment:_____

1. Number of returns to higher custody since the Controlling Effective Date of Commitment: (Count all revocations, returns from escape and probation surrenders):	0 = 0 points 1 = 2 points 2, 3 = 4 points 4 or more = 6 points	[ ]
2. Custody standing prior to the Controlling Effective Date of Commitment:	Not under custody = 0 points On street supervision = 1 point Incarceration = 2 points	[ ]
3. Total number of parole revocations on prior state sentences:	None = 0 points 1 or more = 1 point	[ ]
4. Number of adult convictions for property offenses prior to the Controlling Effective Date of Commitment:	None = 0 points 1 or more = 1 point	[ ]
5. Number of charges for a person offense as a juvenile:	None = 0 points 1 or more = 1 point	[ ]
6. Age at release hearing:	34 or older = 0 points 28–33 = 2 points 24–27 = 4 points 23 or younger = 6 points	[ ]
7. Evidence of heroin, cocaine, or crack cocaine use: Notes (verbal admission):_____	No = 0 points Yes = 2 points	[ ]
8. SCORE: Add the numerical scores of questions 1 through 7 and enter the total score in this box.		[ ]

SCORING: A score between 0–4 = Low Risk; 5–10 = Moderate Risk, 11 or more = High Risk

FIGURE 11.2   Massachusetts Parole Board Release Risk Classification Instrument.

Source: Massachusetts Parole Board, 2003.

behavior, and the officer's impression of a client's needs have a largest weight of "4" or less. Again, on the basis of one's cumulative score or raw point total, interpretive tables are consulted to determine one's level of needs and types of needs that should be addressed with one or more services. These services might include alcohol or drug abuse treatment programs, vocational/educational training, employment counseling, or individual/group therapy. Those areas most indicative of one's greatest weaknesses or needs are typically those with the largest score weights.

There are also specific needs-assessment instruments. Figure 11.4 is an example of the Alaska Department of Corrections Offender Need Assessment Scale.

Kansas Department of Corrections

Parolee Risk and Needs Assessment Coding Form

Name _____

Number _____

Assessment Date _____

MO _____ DA _____ YR _____

Type of Assessment _____

Action Code: [ ]

District [ ]

PO NO. _____

Risk Assessment

Pts	Item		Code
[ ]	1.	Severity Level I Offense	
[ ]	2.	# Prior Periods Prob/Par Sup	
[ ]	3.	Attitude	
[ ]	4.	Age 1st Felony Conviction	
[ ]	5.	# Prior Felony Convictions	
[ ]	6.	Convictions Certain Offenses	
[ ]	7.	# Prior Prob/Par Revocations	
[ ]	8.	Alcohol Usage Problems	
[ ]	9.	Other Drug Usage	
[ ]	10.	# Address Changes	
[ ]	11.	% Time Employed	
[ ]	12.	Social Identification	
[ ]	13.	Problem Interpersonal Rel.	
[ ]	14.	Use of Community Resources	
[ ]	15.	Response to Supervision	
[ ]	16.	Risk Total	

Needs Assessment

Item		Pts	Code
17.	Academic/Vocational	[ ]	
18.	Employment	[ ]	
19.	Financial Management	[ ]	
20.	Marital Family	[ ]	
21.	Companions	[ ]	
22.	Emotional Stability	[ ]	
23.	Alcohol Usage	[ ]	
24.	Other Drug Usage	[ ]	
25.	Mental Ability	[ ]	
26.	Health	[ ]	
27.	Sexual Behavior	[ ]	
28.	Officer Impression	[ ]	
29.	Needs Total	[ ]	

Decision

		Code
30.	Supervision Determination	
31.	Over-ride	
32.	Supervision Level Assigned	
33.	Next Assessment Date	

MO _____ YR _____

ASSESSMENT COMPLETED BY: Signature _____

Distribution
Original—Data Entry
Copy—PO File
Copy—Deputy Secretary If Override Required

May 20. 1988 (Amended)

FIGURE 11.3 Kansas Department of Corrections Parolee Risk and Needs Assessment.

Source: Kansas Department of Corrections, 2003.

OFFENDER NEED ASSESSMENT

Client's Name_____   Officer's_____

Select the appropriate answer and enter the associated weight in the score column.   Total all
scores to arrive at the need assessment score.

                                                                                    SCORE
1. ACADEMIC/VOCATIONAL SKILLS:
    a. High school or above skill level..0   [   ]
    b. Has vocational training; additional not needed............................1   [   ]
    c. Has some skills; additional needed..2   [   ]
    d. No skills; training needed..3   [   ]
2. EMPLOYMENT:
    a. Satisfactory employment for 1 year or longer..............................0
    b. Employed; no difficulties reported; or homemaker, student, retired or
        disabled and unable to work..2   [   ]
    c. Part-time, seasonal, unstable employment or needs additional employment;
        unemployed, but has a skill..3   [   ]
    d. Unemployed & virtually unemployable; needs training.......................5   [   ]
3. FINANCIAL STATUS:
    a. Longstanding pattern of self-sufficiency.................................0   [   ]
    b. No current difficulties..1   [   ]
    c. Situational or minor difficulties..2   [   ]
    d. Severe difficulties..4   [   ]
4. LIVING ARRANGEMENTS (Within last six months):
    a. Stable and supportive relationships with family or others in living group.0
    b. Client lives alone or independently within another household.............1
    c. Client experiencing occasional, moderate interpersonal problems
        within living group..2
    d. Client experiencing frequent and serious interpersonal problems within
        living group...4   [   ]
5. EMOTIONAL STABILITY:
    a. No symptoms of instability...0
    b. Symptoms limit, but do not prohibit adequate functioning.................3
    c. Symptoms prohibit adequate functioning...................................5   [   ]
6. ALCOHOL USAGE (Current):
    a. No interference with functioning...0
    b. Occasional abuse; some disruption of functioning.........................3
    c. Frequent abuse; serious disruption; needs treatment......................6   [   ]
7. OTHER SUBSTANCE USAGE (Current):
    a. No interference with functioning...0   [   ]
    b. Occasional substance abuse; some disruption of functioning; may need
        treatment..3
    c. Frequent substance abuse; serious disruption; needs treatment............5   [   ]
8. MENTAL ABILITY:
    a. Able to function independently...0
    b. Some need for assistance; potential for adequate adjustment;
        mild retardation...2
    c. Deficiencies suggest limited ability to function independently;
        moderate retardation...3   [   ]
9. HEALTH:
    a. Sound physical health; seldom ill..0
    b. Handicap or illness interferes with functioning on a recurring basis.....1
    c. Serious handicap or chronic illness; needs frequent medical care.........3   [   ]
10. SEXUAL BEHAVIOR:
    a. No apparent dysfunction..0
    b. Real or perceived situational or minor problems..........................2
    c. Real or perceived chronic or severe problems.............................3   [   ]
11. OFFICER'S IMPRESSION OF CLIENT NEEDS:
    a. None...0
    b. Low..1
    c. Moderate...2
    d. High...4   [   ]

                                                TOTAL SCORES 1 THROUGH 11   [   ]

FIGURE 11.4   Alaska Department of Corrections Offender Need Assessment Scale.
Source: Alaska Department of Corrections, 2003.

It measures 11 different factors, including one's academic/vocational skills, employment history, financial status, living arrangements, emotional stability, alcohol and/or substance abuse, mental ability, general health and well-being, and sexual behavior, with the evaluating officer's impression of the clients' needs.

Types of Risk Assessment Instruments

Three basic categories of risk classifications have been identified (Morris and Miller, 1985:13–14):

1. **Anamnestic prediction.** This is a prediction of offender behavior according to past circumstances. The circumstances are similar now, therefore, it

is likely they will behave the same way now. For example, a pre-sentence investigation report may show that an offender was alcohol- and drug-dependent, unemployed, inclined toward violence because of previous assault incidents, and poorly educated. Recidivists convicted of new crimes may exhibit present circumstances similar to those that prevailed when they were convicted of their earlier offense. Thus, judges and others might rely heavily upon the situational similarity of past and present circumstances to measure offender risk. However, if some offenders have made a significant effort between convictions to obtain additional education or training for better job performance, or if they are no longer alcohol- or drug-dependent, other types of behavioral forecasts will have to be made. This is because different circumstances exist now compared with previous circumstances.

2. **Actuarial prediction.** This type of prediction is based on the characteristics of a class of offenders similar to offenders being considered for probation, parole, or inmate classification. Considering others like them, situated as they are, this is how they behaved in the past. Therefore, it is likely that those persons who exhibit similar characteristics to the general class of offenders considered for these different sanctioning and classification options will behave in ways similar to that particular class. In effect, this is an aggregate predictive tool. For instance, assume we have targeted a large sample of persons placed on probation and track them over a two-year period. We determine that 65 percent of these probationers did not complete their probationary periods satisfactorily. We describe these failures as follows: they are predominantly young, black, unemployed or underemployed, lack a high school education, were victims of child abuse, and are drug-dependent. Now, whenever young, black, unemployed, less-educated, drug-dependent, former child-abuse victims are considered for probation, parole, inmate classification, or some intermediate sanctioning option, their chances of being placed in one program or another, or of being classified one way or another, may be influenced greatly by the general characteristics of previous program failures. Interestingly, it seems that program failures are more often described and used to structure risk instruments than are program successes (Fields and McNamara, 2003).

3. **Clinical prediction.** This type of prediction is based on the predictor's professional training and experience working directly with the offender. Based on extensive diagnostic examinations, the belief is that the offender will behave in a certain way. The subjectivity inherent in clinical prediction is apparent. The skills of the assessor are prominent. However, such prediction is more expensive, since each clinical prediction is individualized. Both anamnestic and actuarial prediction respectively utilize situational factors and general characteristics of offenders in forecasting their future risk. Interestingly, the highest degrees of validity are associated with actuarial and anamnestic predictions (for instance, those currently used by parole boards), and they are considered very reliable. Predictors in clinical predictions are usually psychiatrists or psychologists with extensive clinical training and experience with deviant conduct and criminal behavior. Actuarial prediction seems superior in its predictive utility compared with clinical prediction.

Any prediction tools that are used, and any claims about their validity and reliability, and/or the recommendations concerning their applicability to specific offender situations, are subject to certain limitations. For instance, Morris and Miller (1985:35–37) have suggested three guiding principles for parole boards to consider when making early release decisions. These include:

1. Punishment should not be imposed, nor the term of punishment extended, by virtue of a prediction of dangerousness, beyond that which would be justified as a deserved punishment independently of that prediction.

2. Provided this limitation is respected, predictions of dangerousness may properly influence sentencing decisions and other decisions under criminal law.

3. The base expectancy rate of violence for the criminal predicted as dangerous must be shown by reliable evidence to be substantially higher than the base expectancy rate of another criminal with a closely similar criminal record and convicted of a closely similar crime but not predicted as unusually dangerous, before the greater dangerousness of the former may be relied on to intensify or extend his or her punishment.

Judges and especially probation officers are also interested in behavioral prediction. The PSI report prepared for any offender sometimes contains a recommendation for some form of probation or incarceration (American Correctional Association, 1994). This recommendation is based on the probation officer's belief that the offender will either be a good risk or a poor risk for probation. This is behavioral prediction. **Prediction** means an assessment of some expected future behavior of a person including criminal acts, arrests, or convictions. Predictions of future criminal behavior date back to Biblical times, although our concern here is with contemporary developments and the current state-of-the-art prediction and assessment devices. Assessments of offender risk have been devised by most departments of corrections throughout the United States. Iowa, Kansas, and Massachusetts are only a few of the states that have devised such instruments. Several important and desirable characteristics of these instruments have been outlined. These include:

1. The model should be predictively valid.
2. The model should reflect reality.
3. The model should be designed for a dynamic system and not remain fixed over time.
4. The model should serve practical purposes.
5. The model should not be a substitute for good thinking and responsible judgment.
6. The model should be both qualitative and quantitative (Rans, 1984:50).

The paroling authority next consults a table of offense characteristics consisting of categories varying in offense severity. Adult ranges in numbers of months served are provided for each category and are cross-tabulated with the four-category parole prognosis above. Thus, a parole board can theoretically apply a consistent set of standards to prisoners committing similar offenses. When the board departs from these standards, especially when parole is possible for an offender but denied, a written rationale is provided for both the prisoner and appellate authorities. And an inmate has the right to appeal the decision of the parole board to a higher authority such as the National Appeals Board (18 U.S.C. Sec. 4215, 2001). Consistency is highly desirable in the application of any parole criteria. Many inmate lawsuits involve allegations of inconsistent application of parole eligibility guidelines.

The Effectiveness of Risk Assessment Devices

Present efforts to develop classification schemes to predict offender future behavior remain at best an unstable business. This criticism applies to both adult and juvenile risk assessment measures that are currently applied. Risk assessment devices developed and used in one state are often not applicable to offenders in other states. In some states such as Massachusetts, risk assessment instruments are used by probation officers to decide which probationers should be supervised with varying frequency. Results were favorable (i.e., lower recidivism rates were observed) where certain high-risk offenders received greater supervision by probation officers compared with high-risk offenders not receiving greater supervision.

Two important questions in designing any instrument to predict future criminal conduct are (1) which factors are most relevant in such predictions? and (2) what weight should be given each of these factors? We don't know for sure. One recurring criticism of prediction studies and the development of risk assessment instruments is that much work is needed on the definition and measurement of criteria. This does not mean that all of the instruments presently developed are worthless as predictors of success on probation or parole. But it does suggest these measures are imperfect. Therefore, it may be premature to rely exclusively on instrument scores to decide who goes to prison and who receives probation. But in many jurisdictions, risk assessment scores are used precisely for this purpose (Robinson, 2002).

The LSI-R and Addiction Severity Index.   Two important indices developed for psychological screenings of subjects, including inmates and probationers/parolees, are the **Level of Service Inventory—Revised (LSI-R)** and the **Addiction Severity Index.** The LSI-R is a quantitative survey of attributes of offenders and their situations. In order for the device to be administered correctly, clients must be at least age 16 or older. The LSI-R purportedly assesses one's successfulness on parole, participation in halfway houses, institutional misconduct, and recidivism. The LSI-R is legally based. This means that it is based on legal requirements that could be used in official hearings involving clients or inmates and possibly in court proceedings. The LSI-R samples four major risk factors: (1) criminal history, (2) criminal attitudes, (3) criminal associates, and (4) antisocial personality patterns. There is considerable evidence of both the reliability and validity of the LSI-R in clinical studies of inmates and probationer/parolee client populations.

The LSI-R utilizes a manual with complete instructions for administering the instrument. It can easily be used by probation and parole officers, correctional workers at jails or prisons, detention facilities, and correctional halfway houses. It can be used to record any and all relevant factors to be used in case classification and to assist in distributing resources most effectively on a case-by-case basis. LSI-R results enable users to make decisions regarding placement into halfway houses and to make appropriate security level classifications. The importance of the LSI-R is that it is a structured means of determining one's risk and needs, as well as the level of care and services required for clients and/or inmates. Don Andrews and James Bonta

(2006) have indicated that LSI-R results should never be used in isolation. Other defining criteria relating to offender needs should be used as well, such as therapist recommendations or counseling results.

A continuum of care is designated by LSI-R results. Ten content areas that can provide useful information for planning one's rehabilitative program include (1) criminal history; (2) education/employment; (3) financial stability; (4) family/marital situation; (5) accommodations/housing; (6) leisure/recreational activities; (7) companions and support group, if any; (8) emotional/personal; (9) attitudes/orientation; and (10) alcohol/drug dependencies. An individual evaluation is made and a client is referred to particular services, depending on the LSI-R results. For instance, the measure may suggest that evaluation and treatment for substance abuse is needed, or that a mental health assessment should be conducted. If the client is not financially independent, community resources can be utilized to enable the client to become employed or work at a trade for which he or she is qualified. The scale, according to Andrews and Bonta, is cost-effective, comprehensive, easy to understand, and highly useful in a clinical sense as well as in several practical ways.

The Addiction Severity Index (ASI) is another assessment tool that is widely used in the evaluation of substance abusers, particularly those who are alcohol- or drug-dependent. The ASI is a comprehensive interview that assesses the history, frequency, and consequences of alcohol use, as well as five additional domains that are commonly associated with drug use: medical, legal, employment, social/family, and psychological functioning. The higher the score on the ASI, the greater the need for treatment. ASI scores help POs, corrections personnel, and various social service agencies to focus on any given patient's problem areas and the best plan for effective treatment of them.

It is beyond the scope of this book to replicate the ASI here. However, it may be found on the Internet at http://cnx.rice.edu/content/m12681/latest/. It consists of a detailed, five-page instrument that collects much information, including one's name; address; birth date; race; religion; prior record and incarcerations, if any; gender; medical status (detailed medical profile); employment status (e.g., education completed, professional skills, trades); driver's license; automobile for personal use; usual occupation/profession; full-time or part-time work; drug/alcohol use (e.g., types of drugs, amount of use, frequency of use, days of treatment for drug or alcohol abuse as outpatient or inpatient); legal status (e.g., arrests, probationary or parole status, different types of crimes committed, length of incarcerations, numbers of incarcerations); family history (e.g., whether different family members have had drug or alcohol dependencies in the past); family/social relationships; and psychiatric status (self-expressed feelings, attitudes, emotions). This index is easily administered. A manual exists for interpreting the results, although there is a high degree of subjectivity inherent in the instrument (Gustafson, 2006).

Both the LSI-R and the ASI contain individual components that exist on the various state and federal scales of risk and needs that have been examined in this chapter. Risk and needs indices of all types contain similar information, because so many of these common variables are correlated strongly with problem behaviors. There are strong psychological elements or components on both the LSI-R and the ASI. These features do not detract from their utility as risk and needs predictors. However, as Andrews and Bonta (2006) have suggested, scores from these instruments should not be used exclusively in the analysis of any particular client or the therapy plan devised for him or her. A more complete analysis is recommended.

Some Applications of Risk/Needs Measures

We have already discussed several of the many potential applications of **risk/needs instruments** and measures. One convenient way of highlighting the most common applications of these instruments by the different states is to examine their own utilization criteria and objectives. The following state utilization criteria are not intended to represent *all* other states or to typify them. Rather, they have been highlighted because of their diversity of objectives. For example, Iowa's Classification Risk Assessment Scale is used for the following purposes: (1) program planning; (2) budgeting and deployment of resources; (3) evaluating services, programs, procedures, and performances; (4) measuring the potential impact of legislative and policy changes; (5) enhancing accountability through standardization; (6) equitably distributing the workload; and (7) improving service delivery to clients (Iowa Department of Correctional Services, 2006).

The above goals for Iowa are couched in the context of initial placement decisions and closely related to management objectives, including allocating scarce resources most profitably in view of system constraints. Theoretically, if the system's processual features are optimized, offender management is also. Presumably, the quality of services available to offender-clients would also be improved. But as we have seen, risk assessments serve purposes. For instance, the Ohio Parole Board uses a guideline system for determining early releases of certain offenders through parole or furlough. This guideline system incorporates a risk assessment instrument and has the following objectives:

1. To provide for public protection by not releasing those inmates who represent a high risk of repeating violent or other serious crimes
2. To provide an appropriate continuum of sanctions for crime
3. To cooperate with correctional management in providing safe, secure, and humane conditions in state correctional institutions
4. To recognize the achievement of those inmates with special identifiable problems relating to their criminal behavior who have participated in institutional programs designed to alleviate their problems
5. To make the decision-making process of the Adult Parole Authority more open, equitable, and understandable both to the public and to the inmate (Ohio Parole Board, 2006).

In Ohio, the parole board guideline system objectives differ substantially from those of Iowa. The Ohio risk assessment objectives are more offender-oriented, with emphases on the appropriateness of sanctions and identifying offender-client needs that may be met by particular services. There are also greater concerns for public safety and greater community comprehension of the parole decision-making process. Most states distinguish between offender evaluations for the purpose of determining their *institutional risk* and their public risk. Again, the device contents are often identical or very similar. An examination of the utilization criteria for other state risk assessment devices yields similar diversity of instrument goals. It is possible to group these diverse objectives according to several general applications. Thus, we may conclude that for most states, the following general applications are made of risk assessment instruments at different client-processing stages:

1. To promote better program planning through optimum budgeting and deployment of resources.

2. To target high-risk and high-need offenders for particular custody levels, programs, and services without endangering the safety of others.

3. To apply the fair and appropriate sanctions to particular classes of offenders and raise their level of accountability.

4. To provide mechanisms for evaluating services and programs as well as service and program improvements over time.

5. To maximize public safety as well as public understanding of the diverse functions of corrections by making decision making more open and comprehensible to both citizens and offender-clients (Champion, 1994).

Selective Incapacitation

Selective incapacitation is incarcerating certain offenders deemed high risks to public safety and not incarcerating other offenders determined to be low risks, given similar offenses. Selective incapacitation applies to certain high-risk offenders and is designed to reduce the crime rate by incapacitating only those most likely to recidivate (Jefferies et al., 2006). Obviously, selective incapacitation is discriminatory in its application, and the ethics and fairness of predictive sentencing are frequently called into question. Professionals who deal with violent persons on a regular basis—mental health professionals and psychiatrists—also question the accuracy of dangerousness indices, especially when such devices are used for justifying preventive detention. There are too many variables that can interfere with proper prediction of individual behaviors. If we factor in one's drug abuse, substance abuse, or some other chemical dependency, our prediction attempts become increasingly unreliable (Barrett, Jacobs, and Clawson, 2006).

In Washington, for instance, specific types of offenders have been targeted for special punishment following their conventional sentences. Washington State's legislature passed the Sexual Predatory Act in 1990, which allows for the civil commitment of sex offenders in a mental health facility if they are deemed to pose a future danger to others. Identifying a specific offender aggregate for more extensive punishment when they have served their full terms raises questions about the fairness of their extended terms, even though these extended terms are mental hospitals and not prisons. Some critics label Washington's Sexual Predator Act as premature and unscientific, since we currently lack scientific skills to make precise predictions about one's future conduct (Martin and Sundberg, 2006). Similarities have been drawn between the treatment of habitual sex offenders and habitual drunk drivers, for example (Smith, 2006). One conclusion is that we have created a special category of offenders from which there is no escape. The only real predictor to be inferred based on current knowledge is that patients with a history of sexually violent behavior are in a high-risk group for committing future acts of this nature. Therefore, anyone treated for sexual deviance is at high risk for repeating such acts (Martin and Sundberg, 2006). In many of these situations, the law selects poor candidates for more extensive treatment in mental hospitals. The use of preventive detention for such purposes raises both moral and legal questions for analysis.

THE CHANGING PROBATION/PAROLE OFFICER ROLE

The quality of PO personnel is increasing compared with past years (Champion, 2005). The American Correctional Association and several other agencies are expanding their training options and arrangements to permit larger numbers of prospective corrections recruits to acquire skills and training. Raising the minimum standards and qualifications associated with corrections positions generally and PO work specifically will eventually spawn new generations of better-trained officers to manage growing offender populations. New generations of POs are also having to familiarize themselves with computers and computer software programs designed for offender control and surveillance.

One belief is that more educated POs may be able to better manage the stress associated with PO work. But at the same time, there are indications that more educated POs and other corrections officers have higher levels of dissatisfaction with their work compared with less educated officers. Personality factors appear crucial for making successful adaptations to PO work. Also, there is high labor turnover among corrections personnel. This means that comparatively few officers remain in PO work long enough to acquire useful skills and abilities to assist their clients effectively. While the composition of the PO workforce is changing gradually each year, technological developments and changes in the laws governing PO–offender/client interactions and the rights of offenders are also occurring. For instance, the use of electronic monitoring of offenders is making it possible to increase officer caseloads dramatically without affecting seriously the amount of time officers spend monitoring offender whereabouts. This is especially applicable in the case of low-risk offenders sentenced to probation or paroled property offenders.

But electronic monitoring, together with home incarceration, is inadvertently changing the qualifications of those who supervise offenders with these electronic devices. Private enterprises are entering the correctional field in increasing numbers, and their involvement in probation or parole programs where electronic monitoring and house arrest are used as sanctions is apparent. What kinds of POs will be needed in future years to read computer printouts, drive by offender homes with electronic receiving devices, and conduct telephonic checks of offenders? Not all clients on probation or parole are nonviolent, low-risk offenders. Increasing numbers are dangerous felons who have committed violent crimes. Therefore, POs are required who possess more than minimal qualifications in order to adequately supervise those uncharacteristic of the average probationer or parolee. While in-service training is desirable, not all states include in-service training in their recruitment process. Unless there are drastic changes in both the image and rewards associated with PO work in the near future, more offenders will receive increasingly inadequate services from probation and parole professionals as caseloads are enlarged. This circumstance will only serve to increase recidivism rates associated with various probation and parole programs (Camp and Camp, 1999).

Global Positioning Satellite Systems: Tracking Offenders from Outer Space

Technological advancements in offender monitoring also modify PO roles and how they do their jobs. One of the more recent developments is the global positioning satellite (GPS) system, which is a method of locating an offender's whereabouts by using satellites in outer space (Arnold, 2006). Using space-age technology, the Florida Department of Corrections began a pilot project in 1997 to track the location and movements of offenders in real time, 24 hours a day, and notifying probation officers of any violations as they occurred. The pilot program was conducted at probation offices in Tampa and Clearwater. GPS is a network of satellites, used by the U.S. Department of Defense, that pinpoints targets and guides bombs. It has been used for everything from helping hikers find their way through the woods to guiding law enforcement to locate stolen vehicles. With GPS, POs can track an offender on a computer screen and can tell POs what street the offender is on, anywhere in the state (Arnold, 2006).

The GPS can actually customize equipment for particular offenders and create zones of inclusion or exclusion. Thus, POs can be warned if offenders approach their former victims in any way, or enter their neighborhoods. Some areas can simply be declared off limits, and these rules can be enforced easily through GPS. GPS offenders strap pager-size units to their ankles and carry lunchbox-size personal tracking devices (PTDs). POs can send instant messages to their clients through these PTDs and can warn offenders to leave particular locations immediately. One immediate benefit of such a system is to protect victims from various clients (iSECUREtrac, 2006).

A survey of Florida POs who have used GPS and PTD reveals mixed feelings. Some Florida POs say that the primary usefulness of GPS is to enforce curfews and whether offenders are present or absent in their homes or other places. The GPS system is not designed to show where offenders are during approved absence periods. Furthermore, the GPS system doesn't show what an offender is doing at any particular location. Most POs agreed that those offenders who could use GPS and PTDs the most were violent sex offenders and predators with prior criminal histories. According to some Florida POs, the technology is so new that some Florida judges don't know what they are dealing with. They sometimes assign traffic violators, bad check writers, and drug addicts to GPS and PTDs. These systems are not designed to deter traffic misconduct, bad check writing, or illegal use of drugs. Another problem is the technical failure of GPS or PTD devices, such as battery failure or system malfunctions. One skeptical judge, Judge John Kuder of Pensacola, decided to test the GPS system before sentencing convicted offenders to it. He wore the GPS and PTD devices for five days, doing everything he could to try and outsmart the system. Kuder went to a movie theater that had been designated as "off limits" for the test and left a note at the box office saying, "The mouse was here." Four minutes later, a Florida Department of Corrections PO signed the same note at the box office, saying, "So was the smart cat. Busted!" Judge Kuder said, "This is one challenge I'm very glad I lost" (Mercer, Brooks, and Bryant, 2000:80).

Is technology going to replace PO surveillance functions? Probably not. At least it will probably operate similar to electronic monitoring and home confinement programs that are a part of Florida's community control program. GPS and PTDs are simply alternative systems for tracking offenders' whereabouts. POs are still needed to conduct face-to-face visits with their clients, administer substance abuse kits and determine program violations related to illegal substances or alcohol, and determine other types of program violations. But the system does seem to suggest that surveillance techniques in the future will become increasingly sophisticated and that perhaps POs can use the extra time saved to do other, more important things to assist their clients in becoming reintegrated and rehabilitated (Arnold, 2006).

APPREHENSION UNITS

One fact of life faced by all probation and parole agencies is that some proportion of their clients will abscond or flee the jurisdiction. After all, probationers and parolees have the freedom and mobility to move about within their communities. If they choose to do so, they can flee the jurisdiction and attempt to elude their supervisors by living in other jurisdictions. Absconders also include a portion of jail and prison inmates who have been placed on work release, study release, or furloughs. However, these inmates are almost always within a few months of being released anyway. Thus, prisons and jails do not regard them as serious escape risks if they are entrusted not to abscond if given temporary leaves for various purposes. Fortunately, the proportion of absconders in probation and parole is quite low, less than 5 percent (Camp and Camp, 2003). The same is true for inmates of prisons and jails who abscond while on work and study release or are in furlough programs. The rate of apprehension of these fugitives is over 90 percent. Thus, most of these offenders are eventually apprehended.

All departments of correction throughout the United States have **apprehension units** to track **absconders.** Absconders are persons who are on work release, study release, furlough programs, probation, or parole and who flee their jurisdictions without permission. Apprehension units are dedicated departments consisting of specialists who engage in offender tracking and apprehension. Their business is to find absconders and bring them back to their jurisdictions for punishment. Absconders are subject to penalties such as five years' imprisonment for escape. This is an additional sentence in relation to the sentences they are serving for other crimes. For instance, when offenders sign intensive supervised probation documents, they often agree not to oppose extradition from another jurisdiction if they flee and are eventually apprehended. Probation and parole departments attempt to cover all contingencies relating to the retrieval of escapees from their various programs. Responses to absconders have included greater line officer responsibility; new information sources to locate absconders; expanded agency fugitive units; and tying sanctions for absconding to offender risk.

New York State has an apprehension unit, for example, that is dedicated to tracking down offenders who escape from work release and other temporary leave programs (Champion, 2005). The Maricopa County, Arizona, Adult Probation Department also has an apprehension unit for locating absconders. The goal of the apprehension unit in Maricopa County is to locate absconders before they have an opportunity to commit new offenses. They rely primarily on case files and telephone contact for potential leads about absconders. In the early 1990s, for instance, absconders were often detected when they committed crimes in other jurisdictions. Cursory records checks by other jurisdictions revealed detainer warrants that had been issued by the originating jurisdictions. These jurisdictions were therefore notified of the offender's whereabouts and POs could travel to these other jurisdictions and bring back the absconders. About 50 percent of all absconders were tracked according to their new offense records. But utilizing case files and telephone contacts resulted in a drastic improvement in apprehension rates. Nearly 65 percent of all absconders were located shortly after their escapes from supervision. In these instances, family members and friends were called and notified authorities where these persons could be located. Thus, many absconders were caught before they could commit new crimes.

Locating absconders using case files for tracking purposes is not new. The U.S. Probation Office and U.S. Marshals Service have tracked offenders in this fashion for decades. Whenever offenders are processed during booking, they are fingerprinted, photographed, and interviewed by authorities. They are required to provide all relevant contact information, including names, addresses, and telephone numbers of family members and where they have lived during the most recent 10-year period. This information is cross-checked to determine its validity and reliability. If some of these offenders escape later, this case file information is consulted and greatly assists U.S. Marshals in tracking down federal fugitives.

There have been numerous attempts to forecast potential absconders in advance. Using actuarial methods, potential Texas absconders seem to exhibit the following characteristics. They are often older, minorities, have fewer skills, outstanding debts, credit problems or bad credit, prior extensive unemployment, greater drug or alcohol abuse, had more unsavory friends with prior criminal records, and were serving longer sentences. Interestingly, many of these characteristics typified absconders from New York. Even absconders from halfway houses shared many of these same traits. More recent evidence about absconders from parole programs has shown that they tend to be less dangerous and pose less societal risk, although they do have extensive prior criminal records, are emotionally unstable, and have more parole supervisions and revocations. Mental illness seems associated with absconding in selected jurisdictions.

One major issue that has arisen to confront probation and parole agencies is how to punish absconders. Before extensive prison and jail overcrowding, the simple solution and punishment was simply to reconfine these offenders for prolonged periods. However, with chronic prison and jail overcrowding, this option is rapidly diminishing. Also, more than a few probation and parole departments have oversized caseloads and cannot allocate sufficient resources to locate absconders. The reduced availability of prison sanctions whenever absconders are located underscores the need to highlight and target high-risk offenders as potential absconders and streamlining the procedures for apprehending them and returning them to custody. Those considered to be high risk are clients who are serving longer prison terms and have previously been in prison or jail. However, no present methods are foolproof for identifying those most likely to abscond.

GANG UNITS

In 2002 there were over 29,000 known gangs in the United States (Thornberry et al., 2003). About 22,000 of these gangs were in large and small cities compared with suburban or rural counties. There was a total membership of over 800,000 gang members. Since gangs are a pervasive phenomenon in American society, they have become a major problem for POs who have found that increasing numbers of their clients are current or former gang members. One response has been the formation of **gang units.** Gang units were created originally to identify gang presence

 **BOX 11.1**

Josie A. Hermann
Parole/Probation Officer II
Baker City, Oregon

Statistics:

B.S. (sociology/anthropology), Eastern Oregon University; Cognitive Restructuring Facilitator, Blue Mountain Community College/Powder River Correctional Facility, Department of Public Safety Standards Training, Monmouth, Oregon.

Background:

I attended Eastern Oregon University majoring in sociology/psychology with the intent that I would get into the field of juvenile counseling. Prior to graduation, I got married, and while completing my degree, I worked full time for the State of Oregon as a Court Operations Specialist II. I worked both in District Court (small claims, traffic, misdemeanor, trial) and then moved to Circuit Court (felony criminal, divorce, civil cases, juvenile cases). At that time, I did not know that this background in the criminal justice system would be very helpful when I finally started in the parole/probation field. I finally graduated after taking classes at night and on my lunch hour.

I moved around with my husband and had my children, finding jobs in the court system, when we were finally moved to Baker City, Oregon, where I grew up as a child. My kids were small and I looked for a part-time job. There was an opening in the probation/parole office as an aide. I did not know what I would be doing, but it looked interesting. As the aide for the officers, I set up the work crews, wrote pre-sentence investigation reports for the court, and just about anything that I was asked to do. I was included in many of the trainings that were given to the officers and learned about what direction the prisons/community corrections fields were taking. There were many changes in the field during that time and I was laid off. But as I say, when one door closes, look for another to open, and it did. I applied for a job with Blue Mountain Community College to facilitate a cognitive restructuring class for inmates at Powder River Correctional Facility. This job just enhanced my learning in the field and I was soon asked back to my old job as an aide. I worked both jobs for a while, but when I was asked to go to the academy to get certified as a parole/probation officer, I chose the full-time job and have never looked back. I have been a certified parole/probation officer (P/PO) for over five years and was just promoted to parole/probation officer II, supervisor under the director.

Work Experiences:

I work with very diversified people. During the day you may work with other P/POs, police officers, corrections officers, mental health therapists, alcohol and drug counselors, child welfare workers, clergy, and of course, offenders. Each and every one of these people have a different point of view about what you are working on, and so you have to be very flexible and be able to stand your ground also. This field changes to meet the needs of victims, the offenders, and the taxpayers. For years you will focus on the rehabilitation of the offender, and then the focus will change to be on paying back to the victims. You just learn the risk assessments for offenders and then they change them. Sometimes this is very frustrating, but it is always challenging.

Visits to the offenders' homes usually turn up interesting and sometimes dangerous situations. Our office does its home visits in

(continued)

BOX 11.1 (Continued)

pairs. One day my partner and I walked in on an active methamphetamine lab. We each had an offender there and two juveniles. A backpack was found near the lab with a pistol in it. We called in the drug task force and they brought in the clean-up crew. Due to the offenders being contaminated from the lab, we had to wait until the offenders were cleaned off by the fire department before we could take them to the jail.

When you do home visits you never know what you will have to decide to do. Again my partner and I were doing a home visit on an offender who lived in a cabin 35 miles from town. When we got there, we saw two freshly killed elk. We knew that we needed to call in the State Police Game Officer and so we turned around and went out to where we could get cell phone reception. When the trooper got there, we went back to the cabin. The offender was high on methamphetamines, his girlfriend's mother was drunk, and the girlfriend was 9 months' pregnant with twins. After doing an investigation with the trooper regarding who killed the elk, we decided to take the offender to jail for a probation violation and new charges. My partner and the trooper were ready to go, but I insisted that we take the pregnant girlfriend out to a friend's home in town. That night the girlfriend went into labor and had the twins. If we had not decided to take the girlfriend into town, she may have died in labor.

Being a P/PO is not all fun and games. There is the time spent on the computer. As you know, most everything is done on the computer now and you have to be computer literate. Reports to the court and chronological entries are done on the computer, and the faster you are in keyboarding them, the more time you will have to complete other things that need to be done.

Working in a small office in eastern Oregon has helped me learn all the aspects of the job. We are not just assigned to do one piece of the job, but we must do all of the pieces from intake to completing their parole/probation, either successfully or not. You get to know the offender very well, maybe too well. They tell you about their sex lives, their family lives, their addictions, and things that you may not want to know. You are there to help them through their parole/probation, but you find that you help them learn about other parts of their lives. Many offenders do not know how to budget or do their taxes, how to get on lists for housing, get a divorce, or get a restraining order. I don't mean that we give legal advice, but we need to be able to help them go to where they can get the help they need. This is where my working with the court system has worked for me.

Advice to Students:

1. You will be working with many types of people and you will need to be open-minded, flexible, interested in their beliefs, and how they got those beliefs. They may have very different life experiences that can open your eyes to their needs. Those needs may need to be addressed to help them successfully get off parole/probation. Be a good listener but do not be manipulated, because offenders are very good at manipulation.

2. Learn about other sources in your community, who runs them, and who to talk to about them. These sources may be able to help the offender access money for schooling or housing, clothing for work, the counseling they may need, and help with physical/mental health problems.

3. Continue your own education. Take some college courses if they are available. Go to as many trainings as you can and continue to learn. Trainings not only teach you about the new things being used with offenders, but it also is networking for you with other P/POs and treatment providers. Trainings also relieve stress, since they are usually out of the workplace and are fun places to be.

4. Become an active member of your community. This can be done by going to church or working with children at your local YMCA, going to school activities, or helping with community activities for

special occasions. By doing activities with the community, you are seen as a good role model for the offenders, and the community members will become the eyes and ears for you if your offenders violate their probation or parole conditions. Community members can also help with finding housing for offenders who are having trouble in the community or getting the offender working when they have no experience.

5. Try not to become tainted with your thoughts. Not everyone walking down the street is an offender. Try not to judge people before you get to know them.

6. Always remember that you are important and you will do what you need to go home to your family at night. Be aware of who you are with, where you are going, and who you may meet there. This is a dangerous job and you need to keep up with your training in self-defense and the weapons you may carry. Always remember that the best weapon you have is your mind.

in neighborhoods as well as gang influence. Gang membership was also indicative of likely criminality, since most gangs are involved in illicit activities, particularly drugs and drug trafficking. However, gangs have been increasingly linked with violent crimes including homicides. Gang units were originally formed by police departments to combat gang-related crime in larger cities where gangs were most visible (Lowry et al., 2006).

During the last few decades, both juvenile and adult probation and parole departments have established specialized gang units to learn more about their gang-affiliated clientele. One result has been that POs have learned a lot more in recent years about gang activities in neighborhoods where clients are supervised; gang member personal alcohol and drug use; and antisocial peer networks distinguishing between gang and non-gang members. What is even more compelling about the work of probation and parole agency gang units is that they are discovering a closer connection between prison and street gangs and their relation with organized crime on several levels. Examples of the interplay between prison and street gangs are Chicago's Gangster Disciples and Latin Kings. These are gangs who have moved from disorganized collectivities to smooth-running organized crime groups with corporate divisions of labor and contemporary conceptual frameworks for conducting illegal businesses (Lowry et al., 2006).

But not all gang activity occurs in major cities in states with large populations. In Virginia, for instance, there are approximately 320 gangs. According to probation department personnel, many of these gang members are probationers or have previously been on probation. Assault, vandalism, and intimidation are most often linked with gang activities, although about half appear to be involved in drug trafficking and gun distribution. Gangs are not strictly a U.S. phenomena, but rather, they are found in other parts of the world. Often, gangs in other countries are loosely linked with their U.S. counterparts.

Of particular concern to POs is the link between street gangs and prison gangs. Many inmates of prisons and jails are gang members. When they are eventually released on parole, they link up with their gang counterparts in cities where they become involved in their parole programs. PO concerns stem from the fact that when ex-convicts return to the streets and reinvolve themselves in gang activities, ex-convicts have a proclivity toward greater violence, which spills over into street gang activities. Thus, the involvement of ex-convicts in youth gangs increases the life of the gangs and their level of violent crime. Nearly half of all gangs report such increased violence as the result of ex-convicts returning to their gangs.

POs strive to enhance their knowledge of both street and prison gangs in order to more effectively supervise them. This means learning gang jargon and prison argot or the use of special phrases and hand gestures that are relevant only to gang members. Such argot, jargon, and hand signals are ways of communicating among gang members, even with prison staff or POs present, and without their awareness or knowledge. However, as POs become more aware of this new language, they can interdict at appropriate times and take the necessary steps to control their clients. Thus, an important training component for both POs and correctional officers in institutions is gang interpersonal communications skills to help prepare them to interact with offender populations whose speech is intended to manipulate or misdirect. Sometimes, POs work with tactical police officers, community youth workers, and neighborhood representatives to work toward reducing violent criminal activity. One project was known as the Little Village Gang Violence Reduction Project in Chicago. POs were able to learn much about gang phenomena generally and become better at performing their supervisory responsibilities, particularly where gang members were involved. One outcome of such experiments has been more effective social intervention by POs of specific gang members as clients, greater crime prevention, and general gang suppression (Lowry et al., 2006).

The U.S. Probation Office has special teams to handle community threat groups in designated areas of the country. There are street and youth gangs, former inmate gang members, organized crime groups, and prison gangs in most cities. The presence of these gangs shows no signs of abating. A specialized community threat group program has been established with the primary activities of assigning probation office personnel to specialized work with community threat group offenders and developing an intensive training curriculum for the general staff. The ultimate objective would be a massive interdiction effort to reduce or eliminate gang activity, especially pertaining to federal offenders.

RESEARCH UNITS

An essential component of any probation or parole department is a research unit. Research units compile extensive information about probationer and parolee characteristics as well as information about inmate populations of jails and prisons. It is important for POs to have an accurate profile of the clients they are supervising or will eventually supervise. Research units are essential to effective probation and parole program planning. Networking with established community services can be achieved more effectively if offender needs can be anticipated.

Research units are also in the business of devising risk–needs instrumentation for use by judges and paroling authorities. Again, it is imperative for these persons and agencies to have indicators at their disposal concerning offender needs and the risks they might pose if granted probation or parole. Research units are also involved in departmental and organizational programming, both within their own agencies and throughout the community. They devise new and improved strategies for offender supervision and management, as well as better ways of administering agency resources. For example, Kentucky has a Criminal Justice Statistical Analysis Center for the purpose of compiling much valuable information about offenders and their risks and needs (Champion, 2005).

Research units are also important in effective court management, which can eventually ease the problems of POs in their supervisory duties (Morton and Stone, 2006). Research units for the courts, probation and parole departments, and police agencies have existed for several decades, and they have proved instrumental at providing essential information for task coordination and crime reduction.

STRESS AND BURNOUT IN PROBATION/PAROLE OFFICER ROLE PERFORMANCE

The selection and recruitment of the right kinds of personnel to perform PO work roles is designed to identify those most able to handle the stresses and strains accompanying the job. The concern about occupational stress has been rising steadily in recent years. Virtually all occupations and professions have varying degrees of stress associated with them. Probation and parole work is not immune from stress and **burnout.** Many probation and parole officers tend to offer more negative than positive comments about their work when interviewed. Often, studies of POs show stress levels comparable to police officers as well as significant job burnout, stress levels, and **job dissatisfaction.**

Possible Gender and Age Differences in Stress and Burnout Associated with PO Work. Do female POs have more or less stress and burnout compared with their male PO counterparts? Not according to a review of research on the subject. Apparently, the problems of women officers are the problems of male officers, so that neither gender requires special attention. Both males and females who pursue PO careers may have similar personality backgrounds. The premise of personality as a determinant has not been systematically studied thus far. This applies similarly to studies of male and female police officer stress levels.

Age as a factor in burnout also seems to be a contributing factor. We might simplify such thinking by stating that as POs get older, the more burnout they experience. This postulation has little consistent empirical support. In short, some studies show this happens, whereas other studies show it doesn't happen. For instance, older POs (age 51 or older) may experience more emotional exhaustion and low feelings of personal accomplishment. In turn, this sensed lack of accomplishment may lead to decreased client contact, which, in turn, has decreased PO work effectiveness. Younger POs may exhibit greater role conflict and emotional exhaustion, accompanied by greater client contact. Younger officers may be driven toward greater client contact to resolve role conflict situations and reduce emotional exhaustion, while older officers are driven away from clients because of feelings of depersonalization and a lack of accomplishment.

Stress

Stress is a nonspecific response to a perceived threat to an individual's well-being or self-esteem (Cheeseman, 2006). It is important that we recognize that these stress responses are not specific, and that each person reacts differently to the same situation triggering stress. Some people react to stress with somatic complaints of aches and pains, while others may exhibit irritability, loss of attention span, or fatigue. Furthermore, what is stressful for one person may not be stressful to another. Therefore, several factors including one's previous experiences with the event, constitutional factors, and personality may function to mediate the stress and one's reaction to the event (Hogan, Lambert, and Barton, 2006). In-service training is regarded by many departments of correction as important, since the training exposes new recruits to different officer–offender relationships that generate stress. Becoming familiar with a variety of officer–offender interactions and recognizing potentially problematic interpersonal situations is one means of effectively combating stress, or at least minimizing it. Although it is not known precisely how education relates to stress reduction, more educated POs probably are more aware of several behavioral or interactional options whenever problems arise between themselves and probationers or parolees. While this finding is not consistent among all jurisdictions, greater stress has been reported in those agencies where high caseload assignments are received.

Some stress is good. A moderate amount of stress enhances the learning and creative processes, while too little stress may induce boredom or apathy. However, we don't know for sure how much stress is too much. We do know that correctional officers have twice the national average divorce rate. Also, they have the highest heart attack rates among all types of state employees, including police officers. These statistics appear to result directly from the stressful aspects of corrections work.

Burnout

Burnout is one result of stress (Hogan et al., 2006). Burnout emerged as a popular term in the mid-1970s to describe work alienation, apathy, depersonalization, depression, and a host of other job-related complaints (Bingham, 2006). Not everyone agrees about how burnout ought to be defined. Maslach (1982a:30–31) has identified at least 15 different connotations of the term. These are:

1. A syndrome of emotional exhaustion, depersonalization, and reduced personal accomplishment that can occur among individuals who do people work of some kind.

2. A progressive loss of idealism, energy, and purpose experienced by people in the helping professions as a result of the conditions of their work.

3. A state of physical, emotional, and mental exhaustion marked by physical depletion and chronic fatigue, feelings of helplessness and hopelessness, and the development of a negative self-concept and negative attitudes toward work, life, and other people.

4. A syndrome of inappropriate attitudes toward clients and self, often associated with uncomfortable physical and emotional symptoms.

5. A state of exhaustion, irritability, and fatigue that markedly decreases the worker's effectiveness and capability.

6. To deplete oneself. To exhaust one's physical and mental resources. To wear oneself out by excessively striving to reach some unrealistic expectations imposed by oneself or by the values of society.

7. To wear oneself out doing what one has to do. An inability to cope adequately with the stresses of work or personal life.

8. A malaise of the spirit. A loss of will. An inability to mobilize interests and capabilities.

9. To become debilitated or weakened because of extreme demands on one's physical and/or mental energy.

10. An accumulation of intense negative feelings that is so debilitating that a person withdraws from the situation in which those feelings are generated.

11. A pervasive mood of anxiety giving way to depression and despair.

12. A process in which a professional's attitudes and behavior change in negative ways in response to job strain.

13. An inadequate coping mechanism used consistently by an individual to reduce stress.

14. A condition produced by working too hard for too long in a high-pressure environment.

15. A debilitating psychological condition resulting from work-related frustrations, which results in lower employee productivity and morale.

The common elements of these definitions seem to be emotional, mental, and physical exhaustion, which debilitates and weakens one's ability to cope with situations. Definitions 2, 3, and 4 above are particularly crucial for PO work, since POs must maintain effective relations with their clients on a continuous basis and regularly evaluate their progress. When stress rises to the level where burnout is generated, offender-clients experience corresponding decreases in the quality of delivery services from probation/parole personnel. The importance of burnout is that it signifies a reduction in the quality or effectiveness of an officer's job performance. Such debilitating reductions in effectiveness are often accompanied by higher recidivism rates among probationers and parolees, more legal problems and case filings from officer–client interactions, and greater labor turnover among POs (Bingham, 2006).

Sources of Stress

Stress among POs and other professionals emanates from several sources. Stress researchers have targeted the following as the chief sources of stress among POs: (1) job dissatisfaction, (2) role conflict, (3) role ambiguity, (4) officer–client interactions, (5) excessive paperwork and performance pressures, (6) low self-esteem and public image, and (7) job risks and liabilities.

Job Dissatisfaction.   Job dissatisfaction is somewhat unwieldy, as it occurs as the result of a variety of factors. Some of these overlap those cited above, which generate work-related stress. Low pay, burgeoning caseloads, and unchallenging work figure prominently in an officer's decision to leave PO work for better employment opportunities elsewhere (Cheeseman, 2006).

Role Conflict.   Role conflict occurs as the result of having to adhere to conflicting expectations. When POs collect supervision fees from their indigent clients, this often creates a type of conflict about their roles as rehabilitators and enforcers. The expectations of the probation officer role are unusual and sometimes conflicting. These expectations may be those of supervisors, and they sometimes are in conflict with a PO's concept of how the job ought to be performed. Sometimes role conflict occurs when the probation supervisor and administrator each expects the PO to complete different tasks at the same time. The logistical complications are apparent, and role conflict ensues.

Role Ambiguity.   Closely related to role conflict is **role ambiguity.** Role ambiguity occurs whenever POs have inadequate or even conflicting information about their work roles, the scope and responsibilities of the job, and the ethics of certain unwritten practices that are commonplace among many POs. Observers have long been critical of probation and parole agencies and organizations for failing to make explicit program goals and mission statements. The fact that often probation and parole program goals are diffuse or unspecified makes it difficult for POs working with those programs to focus their energies in productive directions consistent with program objectives.

Officer–Client Interactions.   Work overload, inadequate agency resources, and problems related to client contact often contribute to job stress. In some instances, officers felt that their efforts in relating to offender-clients were frequently misunderstood and they were perceived as antagonistic toward those they were supposed to help. Mismatching of officers and their clients also accounts for a certain proportion of interpersonal problems that arise in various agencies. Workload deployment systems based on a successful match between officer skills and clients to be supervised can make a significant difference in the day-to-day operation of probation/parole agencies.

Excessive Paperwork and Performance Measures.   The larger a PO's caseload, the more paperwork associated with the clients supervised. A growing problem is increased caseloads in many jurisdictions without an accompanying increase in the numbers of POs to perform the greater amount of work. Officers working under increased work pressure must produce more work in the same amount of time. The preparation of PSIs takes time. During any given period, the amount of time devoted to report preparation accounts for almost three-fourths of the PO's 40-hour work week. Closely related to excessive paperwork and performance pressures is the fact of bureaucratization. Bureaucratization stresses adherence to abstract rules, a hierarchy of authority, task specialization, explicit spheres of competence, emotional neutrality, and promotion on the basis of merit and expertise (Champion, 2003). Probation departments have been depicted by various investigators as more or less bureaucratic. As a result of these variable bureaucratic features either present or absent in probation/parole agencies, POs acquire different orientations toward their work (Garland and McCarty, 2006).

Low Self-Esteem and Public Image.   The low self-esteem and public image of POs is well known, and it invariably influences the quality of work they perform. There is little POs can do in the short range to modify significantly their low public image. However, as recruitment efforts are more successful in attracting better-qualified applicants for PO positions, it is likely that the quality of services delivered will improve. One result of improved delivery of services may be a better public image associated with PO work.

High Risks and Liabilities.   Those working with criminals incur several risks. Some risk may be associated with the type of offender clientele served. Parolees who have been formerly convicted of aggravated assault, murder, rape, or some other type of violent crime may pose a degree of risk to the personal safety of POs. There is also an element of risk incurred from a client's associates who may be violent criminals. These are unknown and incalculable hazards. In addition to these personal risks, however, are legal liabilities incurred by POs who must interact with their offender-clients. In the course of furnishing them with counseling, job assistance, and other services, POs risk giving them poor advice, violating their privacy, maligning them to others, and preventing them from participating in various programs. POs must be aware of their legal responsibilities. At the same time, they must be aware of those actions that may lead to lawsuits against them from dissatisfied offender clientele. Many POs indicate that their training may not be sufficient to equip them with the legal and practical expertise needed to do good jobs.

Mitigating Factors to Alleviate Stress and Burnout

It is believed by many authorities that probation and parole organizations and agencies are at fault in creating dangerously high stress and burnout levels among POs and other correctional officers. Organizational factors may directly contribute to employee stress. When a calling becomes a job, one no longer lives to work but works to live. Thus, POs may lose enthusiasm, excitement, and a sense of mission about the work. While some observers say that it is virtually impossible to prevent burnout among POs, regardless of their coping strategies and mechanisms, it is possible for the organization to implement changes to minimize it. If organizational heads will recognize what causes stress and burnout, they have a better than even chance of dealing with it effectively (Wargent, 2002). One way of alleviating stress and burnout is to incorporate features into PO training programs to make them more streetwise so as to be safer when conducting face-to-face visits with their clients. This might encompass hand-to-hand combat training and other self-defense skills.

Participative Management.   Participative management is the philosophy of organizational administration where substantial input is solicited from the work staff and used for decision-making purposes where one's work might be affected. Thus, subordinates' opinions become as crucial to organizational decision making, as lower-level participants are given a greater voice in how the organization is operated or administered. Organizational solutions stress greater employee involvement in the decision-making process relating to offender treatment and supervision. Generally, a lack of participation in decision making is a key source of stress and burnout. Employee commitment to do better work can be enhanced through bringing a PO's goals into harmony with those of the organization. Management by Objectives, or MBO, has been suggested as one means of accomplishing participatory goal setting between organizational heads and agency personnel, although MBO has lost momentum as a goal-setting and motivating strategy in recent years.

VOLUNTEERS IN PROBATION/PAROLE WORK

Who Are Volunteers? **A corrections volunteer** is any unpaid person who performs auxiliary, supplemental, augmentative, or any other work or services for any law enforcement, court, or corrections agency. Corrections volunteers vary greatly in their characteristics and abilities, in their ages, and in their functions.

What Do Corrections Volunteers Do? Some volunteers are retired school teachers who work with jail and prison inmates to assist them in various kinds of literacy programs. The Gray Panthers, an organization of elderly volunteers, provide various services and programs targeting older inmates specifically. Some volunteers, such as septuagenarian Brigitte Cooke in Huntington, Pennsylvania, work with death row inmates or those serving life sentences. Her services include spiritual guidance, support, and compassion. Some volunteers are crime victims who confront criminals who have committed crimes suffered by victims. Yet other volunteers provide religious training and conduct services for inmates and others. Other types of volunteers work as day care service personnel to care for young children of female parolees and probationers who perform full-time work in connection with their probation or parole programs.

Some Examples of Correctional Volunteer Work

One volunteer program designed for working with female offenders both in prison and in community-based programs is called the Program for Female Offenders. This program provides for volunteers who visit the Allegheny County, Pennsylvania, Jail three times a week and the State Correctional Institution at Muncy on a less frequent but regular basis (Arnold, 1993:120). Incarcerated women are assisted by volunteers who help them adjust to prison life. Certain family and legal problems may be dealt with, using the volunteers as intermediaries. For those women who have been recently released, the agency operates a training center, two residential facilities, and a day treatment program. All of these facilities are located in Pittsburgh (Arnold, 1993:120). One facility, the Program Center, is a work release facility that serves 34 female prisoners. Volunteers provide these women with job assistance, GED preparation, and life skills. Parenting programs and day care services are also provided largely through the use of volunteer services. Arnold (1993:120–122) says that volunteers deserve special recognition for the unpaid services. This Pennsylvania program has outlined some valuable types of functions performed by these volunteers. These functions include:

1. serving as tutors at the skill training center and handling most GED preparation;
2. providing transportation to parenting sessions at their residential centers;
3. teaching women hobby skills such as knitting, sewing, and dressmaking;
4. teaching computer and job search skills at the skill training center; and
5. providing gifts for women and their children every Christmas.

Arnold says that often, these tasks lead to friendships between volunteers and inmate/clients. Arnold also advises that it is important to place volunteers in positions where they will feel safe and comfortable. She suggests the following guidelines:

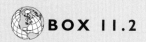 **BOX 11.2**

**INTERNATIONAL SNAPSHOT:
PROBATION AND PAROLE
IN NORWAY**

Norway is a unified state consisting of three branches: the legislative, judiciary, and executive. The executive branch is made up of the King and members of the Cabinet. The national parliament, known as the *Stortinget,* is comprised of 157 members who are democratically elected. These persons pass all laws, both criminal and civil. All bills submitted for passage must be approved by the King. Norway is divided into 19 counties *(fylker),* and about 475 municipalities, or *kommuners.* The Ministry of Justice and the Police is responsible for financing and operating the Norwegian criminal justice system through a highly centralized government apparatus, although each large city and smaller community has local police officers to enforce all laws.

The court system of Norway is quite autonomous. The courts do not use *stare decisis* as is the case with other countries who rely heavily on common law. Instead, the courts act independently and make individualized decisions about defendants on a case-by-case basis. Norwegian courts also allow virtually all evidence to be submitted, regardless of how it was obtained or its authenticity or veracity. All information about crimes is considered relevant and given appropriate weight by the judiciary. Courts are less formal in Norway compared with other countries. Judicial officials do not have to undergo any particular judicial training, and most judges are lay judges who may have no legal qualifications. Thus the courts use lay juries and lay judges to decide both criminal and civil matters. Some judges are professionally trained, however, and they sit with lay judges to decide important criminal cases.

All criminal laws have been codified under successive revisions of the Penal Code and Criminal Procedure Act. In fact, the Act on Rules of Judicial Procedure in Criminal Cases was first implemented and formalized in 1986. A distinction is made between the civil administration of criminal laws and the Military Penal Code, which is exclusively applicable to military personnel. In the early 1990s the Criminal Law Commission was appointed to revise the criminal code. Subsequently this code was extensively revised.

Presently the age of criminal responsibility in Norway is 15. Persons under 15 years of age are under the jurisdiction of social welfare agencies that exist throughout Norway. The efforts of these agencies are to rehabilitate youths rather than punish them. Youths are provided with vocational and educational opportunities, counseling, and other forms of assistance based on their individual needs. The Norwegian government assumes a prominent role in administering the affairs of juveniles in ways similar to the doctrine of *parens patriae* in the United States. For persons age 15 or over, these individuals are held criminally responsible for any crime they may commit.

The penal code of Norway distinguishes between felonies and misdemeanors, with felonies incurring sentences of three months or longer in prison or local jail facilities. Misdemeanors are subject to a wide range of lesser punishments. Incarceration is used minimally in Norway, since it is believed to be counterproductive to one's rehabilitation and societal reintegration. Felonies include offenses such as rape, arson, perjury, murder, larceny, embezzlement, fraud and breach of trust, robbery, and assault. Misdemeanors have a maximum incarcerative penalty of three months or less, together with fines. Drug offenses are considered especially serious and can draw sentences as punishments of up to 10 years in prison. In 2005, there were approximately 450,000 crimes reported to the police. About a third of these offenses were misdemeanors, while the remainder were felonies. Rape and murder occur infrequently. Tracking crime statistics in Norway reveals that crime tended to peak during the period 1994–1996, and subsequently crime has become somewhat stable over time. This is consistent with crime trends reported in other

(continued)

BOX 11.2 (Continued)

countries such as the United States, England, and Australia.

In 2005 there were 7 police regions and 62 police districts. Districts are overseen by police commissioners, *politimestre,* and assistant commissioners and superintendents, *politiinspektorer* and *politifullmektiger,* respectively. All police forces are administered by the Ministry of Justice and Police, and the Public Prosecution Authority has the principal lead in criminal investigations and prosecutions. Overseeing the prosecutions of all offenses is the Director General of Public Prosecutions, or *Riksadvokaten.* The Director General is appointed by the King. There are approximately 55 public prosecutors assigned to various geographical jurisdictions. All public prosecutors are appointed by the King and must have sufficient legal training. Rural area law enforcement is conducted by sheriffs or *lensmenn.* Sheriffs are answerable to the local police commissioners. There are approximately 400 districts in Norway with police commissioners. The police in all areas of Norway are separate from the military, and their law enforcement duties are based on customary law rather than statutory law. However, legal statutes are binding on all law enforcement agencies, regardless of the region. Police have a great deal of autonomy and discretion in deciding when to make arrests. In 2005 there were over 9,000 sworn police officers in Norway, with about 20 percent of all officers being women. Police officers are authorized to carry weapons, including firearms and batons. Their use of force is authorized according to the seriousness demanded by each situation they confront. Citizens may make citizen arrests, although similar to the United States, such arrests by citizens are not advisable. Nevertheless, such arrests may be made if crimes are observed. Normally, however, police officers are contacted to perform these dangerous tasks. Suspects are arrested on the basis of just cause. Searches and seizures of persons and their property may be conducted with judicial approval. Judicial approval is not required where persons are observed in the act of committing crimes.

Whenever someone is accused of a crime, they have rights similar to those enjoyed by U.S. citizens. All persons who are indigent are entitled to a court-appointed attorney to defend them. Suspects may not be compelled to give confessions, although their conversations and interviews with police may be recorded. Persons who plead guilty may have their cases disposed of in courts of summary jurisdiction without a formal trial. Courts may or may not involve juries. Usually the matter of whether a jury sits and decides one's guilt is at the discretion of the judiciary in charge of the case. There is no defendant right to a jury trial. Also, defendants are not entitled to be present at all proceedings where testimony is given by various witnesses. Under certain circumstances, usually to protect particular witnesses, defendants may be escorted from the courtroom while these witnesses are examined and cross-examined. All court judgments of guilt or innocence must be supported in writing with a detailed rationale and supporting evidence. All convicted offenders have the right to appeal their convictions and sentences to higher courts. Where appeals are lodged by convicted offenders, such appeals of verdicts that carry sentences of six or more years must involve a jury to determine the issue of guilt in the High Court where such appeals are directed.

Depending on the seriousness of charges against accused persons, there are alternatives to trials. These alternatives often involve fines, which are assessed according to one's ability to pay and the seriousness of the charges. These fines, or *foreleggs,* are often assessed for traffic violations and other minor offenses. Prosecuting attorneys have considerable discretion and may decline to prosecute certain cases, depending on the availability and quality of evidence. In many cases involving youths under age 18, even though criminal responsibility attaches at age 15, discretion to decide what is best for these persons shifts to municipal child welfare boards instead of the courts. Other alternatives to prosecution include deferred prosecution, which is similar to diversion. Some accused persons may be placed in such simulated diversionary circumstances and be required to perform certain services such as community service or receive recommended counseling or other treatments. Or such persons may simply be freed with the condition that they refrain from further criminal offending. Obviously if they commit new offenses later, they will be severely punished, which is the result of contempt of court and refusal to obey the requirements set forth by prosecutors. About half of all cases charged will eventually proceed to trial. Norway also has restorative justice, where many criminal cases can be diverted to arbitration and Conflict Boards. Pretrial detention occurs in about 20 percent of all cases. In the remaining 80 percent of all cases scheduled for trial, persons are generally released on their own recognizance.

When persons are convicted of various criminal offenses, the courts determine the sentence. Courts of the first instance are comprised of two lay judges and one professional judge. Together they decide what sentence should be imposed. In jury trial cases, sentences are determined by professional judges, the jury foreman, and three jury members. Victim input is important in all sentencing matters. Victim opinions about punishments are given appropriate weight. The types of penalties courts may impose include fines, social service, and imprisonment. Maximum prison sentences are 21 years. Such sentences are imposed for murder, rape, and serious drug offending. Suspended sentences are given to younger or first-time offenders where minor crimes are involved. Such sentences, *betinget dom,* account for about a third of all sentences imposed annually. Fines usually accompany most sentences of imprisonment or sentence suspensions.

Community service involves unpaid labor to the community performed by offenders for up to 360 hours. Such community service is imposed for crimes punishable by up to one year in prison. Community service punishment may also involve fines. Another punishment is detention or *forvaring,* which is rarely used. Most persons sentenced to preventive detention are recidivists with a strong likelihood of reoffending.

Persons who are sentenced to prison are exposed to various forms of rehabilitative measures, including vocational and educational training. These programs are run by the Ministry of Education. All levels of education are offered to prisoners. Prisoners have visitation privileges with their families as well as the right to be outdoors at least an hour a day. Prisoners who have served two-thirds of their sentences are entitled to apply for parole, which is often granted. Persons who have served 50 percent of their sentences may also apply for early release, although this is seldom granted.

Generally Norwegian corrections is under the Prison and Probation Department. This department is the superior authority for the Prison Service and the Probation Service. The department is divided into the administrative section, which oversees personnel and personnel matters, and the client section, which oversees individuals serving sentences of probation or incarceration. The Prison Service is responsible for implementing custodial sentences and preventive detention, and in ways that the adverse effects of incarceration are minimized. This is the strong rehabilitation emphasis given to incarcerated offenders. The Probation Service enforces community sanctions and measures, such as community service orders, drunk-driving prevention programs, and early release and suspended sentence supervision, which is the equivalent to U.S. probationary action. Some offenders may serve time under house arrest or home confinement, and the Probation Service oversees such persons. The Norwegian Correctional Service is responsible for monitoring offenders in all programs, and it also prepares the equivalent of pre-sentence investigation reports for judges to consider when offenders are prosecuted. The Correctional Service was established in 2001 and is administered by the Ministry of Justice. The main goals of this organization are to enforce reactions set by the prosecuting authority and by the courts, as soon as they are legally binding, and to enable offenders through their own initiative to change their own criminal behavior for purposes of reintegration and rehabilitation. The central administration of

(*continued*)

BOX 11.2 (Continued)

the Correctional Service consists of KITT, which is the information technology center and KRUS, which is the Prison and Probation Staff Education Center. In 2005 there were 4 halfway houses, 21 probation offices, and 42 prisons under the Correctional Service authority. No precise figures are presently available to indicate how many persons are under suspended sentences, under house arrest, or on probation or parole. Estimates suggest that overall, there are approximately 35,000 persons presently under the supervision of the Correctional Service. Available information for 2005 indicates that 12,130 persons were serving prison sentences that year. Approximately 2,100 persons were awaiting sentences that same year. About 5,500 persons were serving community sanctions in 2005.

Several offense-specific treatment programs are worth mentioning. Various programs of an educational or rehabilitative nature are strongly supported by the Norwegian government. These include cognitive skills programs; offender substance abuse assistance and treatment; choices, which assists persons in proper law-abiding decision making; a Brotts-brytet (Stop Crime) program, which is aimed at crime prevention methods; a WIN program, which is a change program for women offenders; a one-to-one program, a cognitive activity for use in both prisons and communities relying heavily on counseling; ATV, which involves discussion groups for violent sex offenders; an anger management program; and a sexual offenders program. These programs are operated for both individuals or groups. The recidivism rate in Norway is less than 30 percent. Compared with other countries, such a low recidivism rate is remarkable and likely attributable to the strong rehabilitative emphasis throughout the Norwegian correctional system.

Sources: Adapted from Lee Bygrave, "Norway," *World Factbook of Criminal Justice Systems,* Washington, DC, 1997; *The Norwegian Correctional Service,* Central Administration of the Correctional Service, Oslo, Norway 2006; "The Prison and Probation Department," *Execution of Sentence: Care and Confinement of Convicts in Norway,* Oslo, Norway, 2005; *Norwegian Statistics on Prison and Probation, 2005,* Prison and Probation Department, Oslo, Norway, 2006.

1. Don't take offenders home or lend them money.
2. Don't share your troubles with offenders.
3. Learn to listen effectively.
4. Don't try to solve offenders' problems.
5. Don't make judgments.
6. Report irregular behavior to the agency staff. This is not being disloyal.
7. Don't provide drugs or alcohol to offenders.
8. Don't always expect to be appreciated.
9. Do have empathy and patience.
10. Do care. (Arnold, 1993:122).

Criticisms of Volunteers in Correctional Work

There is Pervasive Volunteer Naivete.   Not everyone is enthusiastic about volunteer involvement in law enforcement, the courts, or corrections. There arise unusual situations from time to time where inmates and other types of offenders might harm volunteers or be harmed by the very volunteers trying to help them. One problem that is cited frequently by critics of correctional volunteerism is volunteer naivete.

Volunteers Do Not Make Long-Term Commitments with Clients.   Because of the voluntary, unpaid nature of volunteer work, many volunteers may be in correctional settings for brief periods, tire of their activities, and leave. While POs generally held positive attitudes about the influence of volunteers in assisting them in their regular duties, the most frequent criticism was that a significant proportion of volunteers do not stay with their clients for adequate time periods. Often, clients are shuffled back and forth between volunteers and regular POs. As a result, clients feel manipulated or "let down" by the particular volunteer absence.

Volunteers Often Do Not Want to Work Independently.   Some volunteers do not wish to work independently from POs in assisting their clients. This situation has necessitated a considerable and unnecessary expenditure of valuable time on the part of the supervising PO, who is often overworked with heavy caseloads and numerous other required duties.

Volunteers Often Lack Expertise and Experience.   Often a chief concern of POs is that volunteers lacked general knowledge about the specific rules and policies of their probation/parole offices (Florida Department of Corrections, 1993). Thus, if some offenders violate program rules, volunteers may experience difficulty reporting them for these infractions. Volunteers seem to be more easily manipulated compared with regular POs.

Law Enforcement Agencies and the Courts are Reluctant to Share Information about Offenders with Volunteers Serving PO Functions.   It is probably natural for law enforcement organizations and the courts to take a dim view of disclosing confidential information about offender-clients to volunteers who are operating in unofficial capacities. Thus, the confidential issue continues to be pervasive among probation departments (American Correctional Association, 1993).

Volunteers Threaten Job Security.   It seems to follow that if a department or agency utilizes the services of volunteers to supplement the work performed by full-time staff, then some of those full-time staff may not be needed in future months or years. Some employees of corrections agencies have expressed this particular fear, regardless of its foundation in truth.

Since Volunteers Are Unpaid, They Don't Respond to Orders Like Regular Staff.   Unpaid personnel who work with corrections agencies on a voluntary basis are under no special obligation to adhere to specific working hours or schedules. Most volunteers wish to comply with the requirements of the tasks they are assigned. But volunteers may have a totally different type of commitment to work compared with paid staff members. If volunteers don't like certain tasks they are assigned, they don't have to reappear at work in the future.

Some Volunteers May be Aiders and Abetters.   In some instances, volunteers have developed relationships with offenders that interfere with the objectivity of their work. They may smuggle contraband into prisons or settings where such contraband is prohibited. They may even make it possible for certain offenders to escape. These instances and others involving volunteers have sometimes been reported.

Because of the nonprofessional nature of volunteer work generally, questions often arise concerning the quality of work volunteers can perform. If volunteers are assigned case-sensitive work, such as working with probationers and/or parolees, they must necessarily become exposed to confidential materials or information about their clients. In fact, some volunteers in certain probation/parole agencies often act on instructions from these agencies to obtain such information from law enforcement sources or the courts. Should these volunteers be granted access to this information? Agencies interested in using volunteers should do the following:

1. Evaluate the need.
2. Develop goals and job descriptions.
3. Involve staff.
4. Actively recruit volunteers.
5. Educate volunteers about inmates.
6. Explain security needs to volunteers.
7. Give volunteers the big picture.
8. Evaluate program effectiveness.
9. Recognize your volunteers' contributions.

Furthermore, it is recommended that volunteers be. (1) ethical, (2) good listeners, (3) empathetic, but not gullible, (4) respectful, (5) genuine, (6) patient, (7) trustworthy, (8) confrontive, (8) objective—don't take sides, (9) nonhostile, and (10) nonexpectant of thanks (Champion, 2005).

PARAPROFESSIONALS IN PROBATION/PAROLE WORK

Paraprofessionals in virtually every field are salaried assistants who work with professionals. A corrections paraprofessional is someone who possesses some formal training in a given correctional area, is salaried, works specified hours, has formal duties and responsibilities, is accountable to higher-level supervisors for work quality, and has limited immunity under the theory of agency. Agency is the special relation between an employer and an employee whereby the employee acts as an agent of the employer, able to make decisions and take actions on the employer's behalf (Black, 1990:62).

The Roles of Paraprofessionals

The quality of paraprofessional work reflects the amount of training these personnel receive. For instance, in various prisons, paraprofessionals are used to assist mental health professionals and psychiatrists. Some correctional staff may have demonstrable abilities as mental health caregivers. Other volunteers are especially good working with children. In some jurisdictions, corrections personnel are given specialized mental health training and experience with mental health counseling. While the primary professional goals of clinical and correctional staff may conflict from time to time, it is apparent that the two professions

 **BOX 11.3**

ON THE ETHICS OF USING VOLUNTEERS

Prospective volunteers with some suggestions and rules:

1. Use appropriate language. Don't pick up inmate slang or vulgarity. Using language that isn't a part of your style can label you a phoney.

2. Do not volunteer if you are a relative or visitor of an inmate in that institution.

3. Do not engage in political activities during the time voluntary services are being performed.

4. Do not bring contraband into prison. If you are not sure what is contraband, ask the staff. People who bring in contraband are subject to permanent expulsion and/or arrest.

5. Do not bring anything into or out of a facility for an inmate at any time, no matter how innocent or trivial it may seem, unless with the written permission of the superintendent. Volunteers should adopt a policy of saying no to any request by an inmate to bring in cigarettes, money, magazines, or letters. If in doubt, ask a staff member.

6. Keep everything in the open. Do not say or do anything with an inmate you would be embarrassed to share with your peers or supervisors.

7. Do not give up if you failed at your first try. Try again.

8. Don't overidentify. Be a friend, but let inmates carry their own problems. Be supportive without becoming like the inmates in viewpoint or attitude.

9. Do not take anything, including letters, in or out of a correctional facility without permission. Respect the confidentiality of records and other privileged information.

10. Do not bring unauthorized visitors or guests with you to the institution. They will be refused admission.

11. Do not give out your address or telephone number. If asked, you might say, "I'm sorry, but I was told that it was against the rules to do that."

12. Do not correspond with inmates in the facility in which you volunteer or accept collect telephone calls from them at your place of residence.

13. Be aware that the use of, or being under the influence of, alcohol or drugs while on institution grounds is prohibited.

14. Don't impose your values and beliefs on inmates. Do not let others impose a lower set of values on you.

15. Don't discuss the criminal justice system, the courts, inconsistency in sentencing, or related topics. Although everyone is entitled to his or her own opinion, what volunteers say can have serious repercussions in the dorms or with staff.

16. Ask for help. If you are uncertain about what to do or say, be honest. It is always best to tell the inmate that you will have to seek assistance from your supervisor. Inmates don't expect you to have all the answers.

17. Know your personal and professional goals. Be firm, fair, and consistent.

18. If you have done something inappropriate, tell your coordinator regardless of what happened. It is far better to be reprimanded than to become a criminal.

Source: Adapted from D.J. Bayse (1993). *Helping Hands: A Handbook for Volunteers in Prisons and Jails.* Laurel, MD: American Correctional Association. Pps. 48–50.

share common functions. Actually, properly trained correctional staff as mental health paraprofessionals can supply quality mental health care compared with the work quality of many professionals who work with inmates.

Virginia's Department of Corrections has invested considerable time and effort to establish literacy programs for its prison inmates and community corrections clients. Paraprofessionals have been used extensively in several Virginia DOC projects. The Wechsler Adult Intelligence Scale was used by Virginia officials to define offenders with IQ levels ranging from 72 to 90. Also, males age 16–19 were chosen who had reading levels that were from 50 to 83 percent below normal grade level. Paraprofessionals were hired to read in unison with these offenders. Reading material would be chosen and read several times to establish a fluent, normal reading pattern. Through the use of paraprofessionals in these educational endeavors, Virginia officials estimate that they were able to raise the reading level of most offenders by more than four years (Virginia Department of Corrections, 2006).

Paraprofessionals working with family therapists in this fashion learn about family and juvenile laws and how youths should be counseled and treated. In Seattle, Washington, for instance, paraprofessionals are used to counsel repeat runaway offenders through the Community Services Section of the Seattle Police Department (Seattle Police Department, 2006). Paraprofessionals have also been used in mediation projects, such as alternative dispute resolution. As we have seen, alternative dispute resolution is a civil alternative to a criminal prosecution. Impartial arbiters reconcile differences between offenders and their victims and attempt to mediate these conflicts in an equitable manner.

Legal Liabilities of Volunteers and Paraprofessionals

The Case of Hyland v. Wonder (1992).   One of the few higher-profile legal cases involving volunteers was the case of *Hyland v. Wonder* (1992). This case involved a volunteer who had worked at a juvenile probation department for several years. After serving as a volunteer and working with juveniles during this period, the volunteer became critical of how the probation office was being managed. He wrote a letter to those overseeing the probation department where he was volunteering, outlining various complaints and asserting how certain improvements would benefit the office. His services as a volunteer were subsequently terminated. He sued, claiming that his criticisms of the probation department were protected by the free speech provision of the First Amendment. Furthermore, he contended that he had a protected liberty interest in his continued status as a volunteer, and that this liberty interest was protected by the "due process" clause of the Fourteenth Amendment. The federal Ninth Circuit Court of Appeals heard his appeal after his complaint was dismissed by a U.S. District Court earlier. The Appellate Court determined that the agency could not deprive the defendant of a valuable government benefit as punishment for speaking out on a matter of public concern. The nature of his public concern was government inefficiency, incompetence, and waste. But the Court declared that he was not vested with a property/liberty interest in his volunteer position, however. Thus, he was not in the position of being able to state or create a claim of entitlement for the purposes of the due process clause of the Fourteenth Amendment.

In the *Hyland* case, a volunteer had spent so much time in his volunteer work with the probation department that he came to regard his position and opinions as equivalent with regular full-time employees, or so it would appear. His lawsuit is evidence of his enthusiasm for the work and the seriousness he attached to it. However, the Court was unsympathetic to the extent that his volunteer time accrued did not vest him with any real standing regarding office policies. This is a good example of how some volunteers can lose their perspective of who they are and why they are there. It is also a good example of one pitfall of volunteer work.

As employees of various helping agencies associated with law enforcement, the courts, and corrections, paraprofessionals enjoy immunity from prosecution similar to that of regular law enforcement officers, corrections officers, and POs. This immunity is not absolute, but rather, it is limited to acts within the scope of one's duties and responsibilities. Thus, paraprofessionals act on behalf of the agencies employing them. Under certain conditions, organizations that employ staff who injure or cause harm to others may be liable under the theory of ***respondeat superior.*** This doctrine is based on the principle of master and servant. If the servant does something to harm others while performing work for the master, then the master might be liable. An example might be if a Los Angeles County Probation Officer shot and wounded a probationer during a confrontation, the Los Angeles County Probation Department might be liable under certain conditions. However, public agencies, such as the Los Angeles County Probation Department, enjoy some qualified immunity from lawsuits, many of which are often frivolous.

The liability coverage of paraprofessionals is very similar to that of volunteers. Organizations using both volunteers and paraprofessionals are subject to lawsuits in the event an action by a paraprofessional or volunteer results in damages to inmates or offender-clients. This is especially true if paraprofessionals are used in counseling and other programs involving sex offenders, where their potentially insufficient training may generate various liability issues (Martin and Sundberg, 2006). These damages may be monetary, physical, or intangible, such as psychological harm. Title 42, Section 1983 of the **U.S. Code Annotated** (2007) outlines various types of civil rights violations that might be used as bases for lawsuits. Among the bases for different lawsuits by offender-clients are allegations of negligence. Negligence may include:

1. Negligent hiring (e.g., organization failed to "weed out" unqualified employees who inflicted harm subsequently on an inmate or probationer/parolee).

2. Negligent assignment (e.g., employee without firearms training is assigned to guard prisoners with a firearm; firearm discharges, wounding or killing an inmate).

3. Negligent retention (e.g., an employee with a known history of poor work and inefficiency is retained; subsequently, work of poor quality performed by that employee causes harm to an inmate or offender-client).

4. Negligent entrustment (e.g., employee may be given confidential records and may inadvertently furnish information to others that may be harmful to inmates or offender-clients).

5. Negligent direction (e.g., directions may be given to employees that are not consistent with their job description or work assignment; this may result in harm to inmates or offender-clients).

6. Negligent supervision (e.g., employee may supervise prisoners such that inmate problems are overlooked, causing serious harm and further injury or death to inmate or offender-client).

One way of minimizing lawsuits against paraprofessionals and other employees of correctional agencies is to train them so that they can perform their jobs appropriately. Several criteria are important to establish as a part of a training program for paraprofessionals and others in the event subsequent lawsuits are filed. These include:

1. The training was necessary as validated by a task analysis.
2. The persons conducting the training were, in fact, qualified to conduct such training.
3. The training did, in fact, take place and was properly conducted and documented.
4. The training was "state-of-the-art" and up-to-date.
5. Adequate measures of mastery of the subject matter can be documented.
6. Those who did not satisfactorily "learn" in the training session have received additional training and now have mastery of the subject matter.
7. Close supervision exists to monitor and continually evaluate the trainee's progress.

These criteria alone are insufficient to insulate fully one's organization against lawsuits from offender-clients. Nevertheless, they provide some suitable criteria that can be cited in the event an organization or its employees are ever sued. One recommendation is to document that such training is provided and has occurred (*Whitley v. Warden,* 1971). The theory is that if an event is not documented, it did not happen, as in training.

SUMMARY

POs are supervising an increasingly dangerous clientele. Annually, the numbers of probationers and parolees is escalating. Many of these new entries into probation and parole programs are gang members with prior histories of violence. Therefore, it is imperative for POs to have some detailed information about the clientele they will be supervising. One method of determining the risk posed by such clients is to apply risk assessment measures. Probationers as well as parolees are administered risk assessment instruments, either by probation departments or by parole boards. The intent is to determine which offenders are most likely to reoffend and pose safety risks to the public and their supervising POs.

Assessing offender risk has been done for many decades. All states and the federal government have devised risk inventories with differing degrees of sophistication to anticipate one's future dangerousness. Classification is an attempt to place offenders in those programs that will enable them to maximize the program benefits. Some offenders have needs, such as low levels of education and a lack of work skills. Such offenders will need more assistance than others when it comes to networking with community agencies. Thus, one function of classification is to identify not only the level of risk posed by offenders, but also to provide some indication of the types of needs that must be addressed. PO supervisory responsibilities can be enhanced to the extent that they can anticipate offender needs and match them with appropriate community agencies for counseling or treatment.

Risk assessments can be classified according to whether they are actuarial, anamnestic, or clinical. Actuarial devices, which are the most popular, attempt to identify the characteristics of program failures. Thus the focus is on which characteristics tend to be associated with probationers and parolees who do not succeed in their programs. Thus, probation-eligible or parole-eligible offenders may either be granted or denied probation or parole on the basis of the extent to which they match the characteristics of program failures. Actuarial prediction is popular largely because anyone can administer a paper-and-pencil questionnaire delving into superficial details of one's background and prior criminal record. Anamnestic prediction is using one's past experiences and comparing them with one's anticipated future experiences. Parole boards are especially adept at ascertaining whether one's parole plan is sufficiently unique to show them that the conditions under which a parolee will be living will be substantially different from the conditions that originally led to trouble with the law. Thus, anamnestic prediction compares past circumstances with future circumstances and predictions are made about how these changed circumstances will modify the future behaviors of prospective parolees. Clinical prediction is the least used of the three types of prediction. The main reason is that it is too costly to administer on a large-scale basis. Clinicians, psychologists, and psychiatrists must become involved with probationers or parolees, and this involvement is time-consuming and expensive. Few jurisdictions have the resources to apply clinical prediction. Ultimately, no single prediction method is foolproof, and virtually every method is flawed where future behaviors are predicted. Thus, one method is about as good as the others for predicting one's future risk or dangerousness, despite how much one prediction form is marketed or promoted over the others as the best method.

Risk assessment instruments are used for diverse purposes. Not only are they useful for making offender forecasts of future conduct while on probation or parole, but they are also used for classifying offenders for institutional custody levels, such as minimum-, medium-, or maximum-security confinement. Some parole-eligible inmates may not be granted parole because they are deemed to pose too great a risk to society and their recidivism potential is high. Therefore, selective incapacitation is used to confine those least likely to complete their parole programs successfully.

The roles of POs are gradually changing. One reason for such change is technological advancements relating to client supervision. Global satellite tracking systems are currently being used in growing numbers of jurisdictions to determine offender whereabouts. Furthermore, like electronic monitoring, while such tracking systems cannot control behavior, they can offer probation agencies and POs an early warning of whether their clients are entering restricted areas where former victims of their crimes reside. Thus, there is a safety element introduced through such tracking systems, although there is presently some controversy among POs about the usefulness and applications of such technology.

In every probation and parole department, there are apprehension units, or special departments whose personnel have the responsibility of tracking down program absconders. Every year, there is a proportion of absconders who leave their jurisdictions without permission and attempt to elude capture. In 1999 about 4 percent of all clients under different forms of supervision in the community were absconders. These included some inmates who were granted temporarily releases, such as work release, study release, or furloughs. Even some halfway house residents have absconded from their parole programs. Several factors were identified with absconders.

Most probation and parole departments in the larger cities have gang units, or special task forces who study gang formation and operations. More POs are interacting with gang members who not only are affiliated with street gangs but associated with other gang members while incarcerated in prisons and jails. Finally, most larger probation and parole departments have research units who compile valuable statistical information about those supervised and their characteristics.

PO work is stressful. Stress is a nonspecific response to a perceived threat to an individual's well-being or self-esteem. Stress may lead to burnout, which directly interferes with a PO's work performance. Some of the sources of stress include job dissatisfaction, role conflict, role ambiguity, excessive paperwork obligations, high caseloads, and high risks and liabilities that accompany supervising dangerous offenders. Assisting POs in their supervisory work are volunteers and paraprofessionals. Volunteers are unpaid, yet they perform valuable services such as teaching parolees and probationers how to read and fill out job applications. They perform other tasks as well, depending on the particular jurisdiction and PO needs. Paraprofessionals have had some training related to the work they perform, although they do not have the requisite skills to be full-fledged POs. Their work is more advanced compared with volunteers, and they are paid for what services they render. Both volunteers and paraprofessionals are at risk regarding their legal liabilities. No one working with probationers or parolees is immune from lawsuits that might be filed. Usually, the least-experienced workers are most vulnerable to lawsuits from clients, since they may offer adverse advice unintentionally. The legal liabilities of volunteers and paraprofessionals were described and discussed.

QUESTIONS FOR REVIEW

1. What is risk assessment? What are risk assessment instruments?
2. What is meant by classification? What are some of its functions?
3. Identify three types of prediction. Which type of prediction is best? Discuss.
4. What is meant by selective incapacitation? Is it constitutional? Why or why not?
5. How is technology changing the PO role?
6. What is a global satellite tracking system? How is it used to monitor an offender's whereabouts?
7. What is the doctrine of *respondeat superior?* Do organizations have absolute immunity against lawsuits filed against them because of poor work done by their employees?
8. Is it ethical to use volunteers where these volunteers have access to confidential records of inmates, probationers, or parolees? Why or why not?
9. What is a corrections paraprofessional?
10. What are some of the roles of paraprofessionals in corrections generally? What about paraprofessional involvement with juvenile offenders?

SUGGESTED READINGS

Butler, Richard and Vanessa Garcia (2006). "The Parole Supervision of Security Threat Groups: A Collaborative Response." *Corrections Today* **68**:60–63.

Clark, Michael D. (2006). "Entering the Business of Behavior Change: Motivational Interviewing for Probation Staff." *APPA Perspectives* **30**:38–45.

Gottfredson, S.D. and L.J. Moriarty (2006). "Statistical Risk Assessment: Old Problems and New Applications." *Crime and Delinquency* **52**:178–200.

Philipse, M.W. et al. (2005). "Reliability and Discriminant Validity of Dynamic Reoffending Risk Indicators in Forensic Clinical Practice." *Criminal Justice and Behavior* **32**:643–664.

Surrett, R. (2006). "CCTV and Citizen Guardianship Suppression: A Questionable Proposition." *Police Quarterly* **9**:100–125.

Thompson, C. and A.B. Lopez (2005). "Adjustment Patterns in Incarcerated Women: An Analysis of Differences Based on Sentencing Length."*Criminal Justice and Behavior* **32**:714–732.

INTERNET CONNECTIONS

Fugitive Apprehension Unit
http://www.doc.missouri.gov/Horizon/fugitive05_k03.htm

Gang unit resources
http://www.officer.com/special_ops/gang.htm

Paraprofessionals
http://www.ptcwct.ptc.edu:8800/public/CRJ244OSM/

Parole officer stress
http://www.enlightenedsentencing.org/what-probation-officers-say.htm

Probation in the New Century
http://www.dcor.state.ga.us/pdf/proFY01.pdf

Support staff probation
http://www.bvsd.k12.co.us/sb/policies/GDM.htm

Violent Fugitive Apprehension Section
http://www.state.ma.us/msp/unitpage/violent.htm

Volunteers and paraprofessionals in probation and parole
http://www.copbiz.com/Products/Books/corrections.htm

Volunteers In Prevention, Probation, and Prisons, Inc.
http://www.comnet.org/vip/

Volunteers of America
http://www.voa.org/

Worcester County Gang Unit
http://www.worcester.da.com/daunits/gangst.html

CHAPTER 12 | *Offender Supervision: Types of Offenders and Special Supervisory Considerations*

Chapter Outline

Chapter Objectives

As the result of reading this chapter, the following objectives will be realized:

1. Understanding the general nature and composition of the special-needs offender population.
2. Understanding the problems of mentally ill offenders on probation and parole.
3. Describing HIV/AIDS and drug/alcohol dependent offenders and the supervisory problems they pose for POs.
4. Describing gang members and how POs supervise them.
5. Understanding sex offenders and other special-needs offenders and the various programs used to treat them.
6. Describing drug courts and the drug court movement.
7. Describing various interventions, including the idea of the therapeutic community.
8. Understanding the functions of Alcoholics Anonymous, Narcotics Anonymous, and Gamblers Anonymous.
9. Describing gang members, their characteristics, and tattoo removal programs.

• *Near Dallas, Texas, a parole officer was conducting a routine visit in the neighborhood of one of his new parolees. According to a report of the parolee's prior institutional conduct, the parolee, Nathan M., had a history of violence. The violence included sporadic fights with both staff and other inmates. Nathan M. had been placed in solitary confinement for several months during the four years he was confined. When the parole officer knocked on Nathan M.'s apartment, someone yelled out, "Come in." The parole officer opened the apartment door and found himself staring down the barrel of a 12-gauge shotgun in the hands of Nathan M. The situation was potentially lethal. The probation officer was armed with a 9mm semiautomatic pistol. He closed the apartment door and attempted to determine why Nathan M. had a weapon and why the officer was being threatened with it. Nathan M. began to rant and rave about "voices in my head" telling him to do things. The parole officer was a suspected alien from another planet. After nearly four hours at shotgun point, Nathan M. suddenly put down the shotgun and went into another room to urinate. The officer moved quickly and unloaded the weapon. He drew his own weapon and when Nathan M. reentered the room, he was quickly subdued. Later at the jail, the parole officer related what Nathan M. had said and believed to detectives who decided to bring in a consulting psychiatrist. Nathan M. was thoroughly examined and determined to have paranoid schizophrenia. Subsequent searching revealed that at no time during Nathan M.'s conviction offense, trial, or at any other stage did attorneys for either side seek a psychiatric evaluation of Nathan M. Nathan M. had gone almost five years without any kind of diagnosis of his mental condition. He is now receiving treatment and is housed in a state mental facility where he receives medication for his illness. He is a compliant patient. [Source: Adapted from the Associated Press, "Parolee Determined to be Psychotic and is Hospitalized," August 1, 2006].*

• *Donna Marley, age 38, and Chris Williams, age 19, both of Plattsburgh, New York, were at low points in their lives. They were both drug dependent and addicted to crack cocaine. Williams had dropped out of high school and was dependent upon alcohol and marijuana as well as crack cocaine. He had already been arrested multiple times for various offenses and had spent a lot of time in the Clinton County Jail. Marley was struggling with a three-year crack-cocaine addiction. Like Williams, Marley had seen a jail cell on more than one occasion. Both felt their lives were quickly slipping away and that they had lost control over their destinies. Then something happened to change their lives permanently. Plattsburgh and Clinton County established a drug court in 2003. Marley and Williams were the first new drug court cases. City Court Judge Penelope Clute and a Drug Court team, comprised of several treatment providers and representatives from the Probation Department and the District Attorney's Office, worked closely with Marley and Williams to find them work and provide them with the treatment necessary to keep them drug-free. At first it was difficult for Marley to find employment, but the Drug Court team intervened and found her full-time work that she enjoyed. She reverted once and used drugs, but was brought back to jail briefly and reassigned to the Drug Court program. In February 2005, Marley and Williams became the first graduates of the Drug Court program. Between the time of their initial involvement in Drug Court and graduation, both Marley and Williams were closely monitored and submitted to biweekly checks. Probation officers worked closely with both clients and monitored them closely, conducting frequent drug tests on them. Any relapses were instantly reported and court response was swift. Judge Kevin Ryan, who presides over the county's Drug Court program, said that this is the most rewarding thing he's ever done as a judge. He said that people with long-standing addictions were constantly in trouble with the law, and typically, through traditional court processing, they never received the proper treatment for these addictions. Now the Drug Court program is in place and gives the participants a chance to reconnect with their families and become financially stable. While drug treatment and programs such as those in place in New York don't always work for everyone, the court, through a variety of means, offers encouragement to those in need of treatment, and the process works much quicker. [Source: Adapted from Anna Jolly and the* Press Republican, *"Drug Courts Turning Out Drug-Free Citizens," February 11, 2005].*

• *When a city doesn't have adequate space for rehabilitating sex offenders, where should they be placed? They should be placed somewhere, shouldn't they? Chicago is one of many cities struggling with the problem of what to do with its growing population of sex offenders in need of treatment, counseling, and rehabilitation. One questionable solution is to dump excess numbers of sex offenders in poorer neighborhoods, where they will be less visible to the public. In fact, according to Alderman Carrie Austin of the 34th Ward, this is an increasingly common practice. "They dump every damn thing here. It's a disrespect to our community. If they're ours, then we have to accept ours. But [state corrections officials] don't care—just so they have them off their books at my community's expense," says Austin. The state requires paroled sex offenders to spend time in a transitional facility before moving to more permanent homes. But the number of homes for sex offenders is not keeping pace with the growing numbers of these offenders, and state officials are having to send these offenders into a broader range of communities, despite protests from citizens. Sometimes the results are tragic. A 32-year-old homeless man and convicted sex offender, Vincent Hudson, was charged with three counts of first-degree murder and aggravated criminal sexual assault. The bodies of two of his alleged victims were found dumped in a lot near some railroad tracks. Another was found in a vacant lot. Blunt force trauma and strangulation were causes of death, and all three victims were sexually mutilated. Hudson's DNA was found on all three victims, thus linking him directly with their deaths. Hudson's victims were prostitutes plying their trade in high-risk areas of Chicago. Hudson had a lengthy arrest record and numerous phony addresses. He was arrested at a homeless shelter in a poor South Chicago area. Hudson had never undergone a psychiatric evaluation, despite evidence that he might be psychologically disturbed and have mental problems. Who should bear the blame for the deaths of Hudson's victims? Hudson himself? The state? [Adapted from skcentral.com, "Man Charged with Three Rapes, Murders on South Side," February 6, 2006].*

INTRODUCTION

This chapter deals with special-needs offenders. They may be drug-dependent, sexual predators, have mental diseases or defects, have HIV/AIDS, or one of several other types of problems. They pose substantial risks to POs in their supervisory roles. As POs supervise an increasingly diverse clientele, their jobs become more dangerous, and their stress levels and anxieties are elevated.

In the 1950s and 1960s, POs enjoyed far greater predictability in their work than today. Conventional distinctions were made between property offenders (e.g., burglars, thieves, those convicted of vehicular theft) and violent offenders, or those who committed crimes against the person (e.g., homicide, aggravated assault, forcible rape, and robbery). Although there always have been offenders with problems, substance abuse, mental illness, and communicable diseases have become pervasive in American society, especially since the 1970s (Hammett, Harmon, and Rhodes, 2002). Contemporary probationers and parolees as clients have special problems and are in need of unconventional services and resources.

In 2005, for instance, an estimated 600,000 mentally ill offenders were incarcerated in U.S. prisons and jails. Among probationers and parolees that same year, 700,000 were identified as mentally ill, while over 500,000 reported a mental or emotional condition, and 281,200 had been admitted overnight to a mental hospital for treatment (U.S. Department of Justice, 2006). Over half of all mentally ill clients have prior histories in jails and prisons of institutional violence. It is not unexpected, therefore, that such violence will carry over into their probation and parole programs as a part of a continuing pattern. Relatively little has been done to intervene and assist mentally ill inmates and subsequent PO clients. They continue to pose supervisory hazards for their POs, largely because of their unpredictability. Thus, the first part of this chapter examines mentally ill offenders who are under PO supervision.

A second type of offender POs supervise is the sex offender. Some of these sex offenders are child sexual abusers. They may be required to avoid frequenting areas where small children are located, such as schools and parks. While sex offenders are not especially abundant, there are sufficient numbers such that POs assigned to supervise them must pay particular attention to their whereabouts and activities. Many sex offenders are obligated to attend individual and group counseling and participate in sex offender programs as a part of their special parole and probation program conditions. These activities require continuous monitoring by attentive POs. Also, these offenders cannot be monitored on a 24/7 basis, and thus their freedom to roam about in their communities means that they may be able to reoffend without their POs' knowledge at different times. Problems of monitoring sex offenders are also examined.

A third type of offender is described. Increased numbers of HIV/AIDS cases have occurred, largely because of indiscriminate drug use, needle-sharing, and unprotected sex. Prisons and jails are optimum breeding grounds for the transmission of HIV/AIDS, since they place offenders in close proximity with one another where stronger offenders can sexually exploit the weaker ones. Some same-sex relations are consensual. Furthermore, HIV/AIDS is not restricted to the male inmate population. Female inmates are exhibiting increased rates of HIV/AIDS in recent years. Therefore, POs are supervising increased numbers of clients with such communicable diseases as HIV/AIDS. However, tuberculosis among offenders has increased in the United States in recent years. This is a highly contagious disease and presents greater dangers for POs since it can be transmitted more easily than HIV/AIDS. For POs, supervising POs with tuberculosis places them at far greater risk. HIV/AIDS offender-clients are described, as well as the special supervisory provisions for POs who must monitor them.

By far the largest category of offenders in need of close supervision are substance abusers. Substance abuse is considered the single most important problem among probation and parole offenders. It has been estimated that between 55 and 80 percent of all probationers and parolees have been involved with drugs or alcohol, and that illicit substances were involved in their original offenses. The incidence of relapse is especially high for substance-abusing offenders, and POs must devise innovative strategies for their supervision. Because substance-abusing offenders are so prevalent within the probationer and parolee community, and because of the unique problems they pose for their supervising POs, improved screening mechanisms have been devised to detect illegal drug use of offenders under supervision. POs have had to work harder to link these offenders with necessary community services so that they can receive appropriate therapy and treatment. Furthermore, they are inclined to relapse at high rates. This means that POs must be more vigilant at detecting relapses and rapidly moving to control such behavior when it occurs.

One response to greater drug use among offenders has been the development of specialized courts to deal only with drug abusers. These are drug courts, and they provide therapies and recommended programs to involve those most in need of treatment and community services. They also make provisions for follow-up monitoring by POs as well as appropriate sanctions if their relapses are chronic or repetitive over time. These drug courts are described, including their operations and services. POs increasingly rely on therapeutic communities or treatment models that emphasize integrated community services at several different levels to meet the complex needs of substance-abusing offenders and others. Therapeutic communities and their functions are described. A part of the therapeutic community are interventions such as Alcoholics Anonymous for those with alcohol addictions, Narcotics Anonymous for those with drug dependencies, and Gambler's Anonymous for those addicted to gambling. Therapeutic communities also exist for developmentally disabled, handicapped, and/or mentally retarded offenders. These programs are described.

The chapter concludes with a discussion of gang members on probation and parole. A growing segment of the offender population both within and without the prison setting are gang members. Gang members present supervision problems for POs for a variety of reasons. One of these reasons is that gangs tend to form subcultures with strong group norms. In turn, these norms create a substantial resistance to change. Thus, when POs attempt to intervene in the lives of gang members and help them become more law-abiding, they often encounter subcultural barriers that are gang-generated. Thus, the process of coping with gang-affiliated clients is discussed. Some of the strategies for overcoming resistance to change are highlighted, including recently developed tattoo removal programs.

TYPES OF OFFENDERS: AN OVERVIEW

In this section, an overview of **special-needs offenders** is presented. This overview is intended to describe the various types of offender populations that POs supervise. When certain probationers and parolees have serious needs and dependencies, this requires special services from POs and an extraordinary amount of care and supervision. In some probation and parole agencies, special assignments are made to certain POs with skills relevant for those clients with particular disabilities or problems. These are referred to as specialized case-loads. Many probation and parole departments do not have the resources or personpower to allocate POs for specialized services. Thus, POs must supervise all offenders, regardless of whether or not they have special problems requiring unconventional community intervention, assistance, or programming.

What must POs do to manage or supervise offenders with serious dependencies and other problems? What are the pressures on POs to monitor these offenders closely? What should POs do when they detect program violations among those most likely to relapse and commit program violations? There are no easy answers to these questions. In a later section of this chapter, several of these different types of special-needs offenders are examined in closer detail. In the last section, several interventions and community programs are described that are used in conjunction with special-needs offender supervision.

Coping with Special-Needs Offenders

Any correctional program, whether it is institutional corrections or community-based corrections, will inevitably have to deal with and make provisions for special-needs offenders. Special-needs offenders include physically, mentally, psychologically, or socially impaired or handicapped offenders who require extraordinary care and supervision. Sometimes, elderly offenders are classified as special-needs offenders to the extent that they might require special diets, medicines, or environments. Mental retardation, illiteracy, and physical disabilities are some of the many kinds of problems associated with special-needs offenders. Some definitions of special-needs offenders include women, although female offenders and their problems and programs are treated elsewhere. Operators of community-based correctional facilities face continual dilemmas over the need to accommodate these offenders in special facilities and the need to move offender-clients generally into mainstream society and assist them to live independently.

Regarding the provisions for special-needs offenders in many community corrections programs, major problems have been identified, including lack of access to adequate mental health services, inadequate information and training among court and corrections personnel, and insufficient interagency coordination and cooperation (Bowen et al., 2002). In more than a few instances, some of these inmates have attempted suicide or have assaulted other inmates. Some suicide attempts have been successful, and some inmate assaults have been fatal.

Some community corrections facilities are linked closely with other close-custody prisons, such as the Massachusetts Correctional Institution (MCI) for women at Framingham. The Framingham institution, which houses 575 female convicts, offers assistance in the following areas: (1) mental health counseling;

(2) substance abuse treatment; (3) parenting and family services; (4) employment planning, education, and vocational counseling; and (5) health screenings, treatment, and referrals. These services seem offender-relevant, since a lack of education and drug abuse are two of the major obstacles to finding employment (Dennehy, 2006).

In Texas, for example, a Special Needs Parole Program has been established to provide for an early parole review for offenders with special health needs who require 24-hour skilled nursing care. Between 2000 and 2005, for instance, the number of cases screened for the program declined markedly by 40 percent, as did those referred to the parole board for early release. Those released on Special Needs Parole declined by 45 percent. These declines were attributable to ineffective and inadequate screening procedures as well as tougher parole criteria. It was found that over 50 percent of all referred cases in 2005 were simply ineligible for parole because of Texas statutes. However, 40 percent were referred for parole anyway, and of these, 34 percent were granted early release (Breston, 2006).

Almost contemporaneously with the Texas Special Needs Program, an independent survey was undertaken of U.S. state prisons during the period 1991–1997. It was found that the number of inmates age 50 and over increased by 115 percent during this period, while the overall prison population grew by almost 84 percent. It was also found that increasing numbers of prisons were housing special-needs offenders, older offenders with health problems, and disabled inmates in special prison areas or including them in programs specifically designed for their conditions. This means that Texas and perhaps other jurisdictions are retaining more special-needs offenders for longer prison terms, although corrections officials are having to make special (and more expensive) arrangements for their care and treatment. Eventually, a portion of these offenders will be released on parole, and the problems of the institution will be passed along to paroling authorities.

Community corrections may not provide the degree of protection that might need to be extended to persons with one or more disabilities or handicaps. Those who are mentally ill may not be able to function normally in their communities. Some offenders who are mentally impaired may require constant monitoring and supervision, primarily for their own protection (Fitzgerald et al., 2006). Some observers believe that it will be necessary for entire Departments of Correction in each state to address the problems of special-needs offenders from a total systems approach. A comprehensive corrections plan can be effective at maximizing the cost efficiency of correctional construction. The growing number of special-needs populations will require new thinking by architects and administrators to meet inmates' and clients' special health, program, and management needs.

Sex offenders often pose special problems for community corrections staff. Sex offenders may have committed rape, incest, voyeurism, or any of several other sexual behaviors and/or perversions. Treatments of sex offenders sometimes involve the hormonal drug Depo-Provera, and some patients may be monitored by a penile plethysmograph, a device that measures the significance of various sexual stimuli relating to one's arousal (Smith, 2006).

Many offenders involved in community-based corrections programs have learning disabilities. Special education courses and services are needed to meet their needs more effectively. Several components of successful correctional special educational programs have been identified. These include functional assessments of the skills and learning needs of handicapped offenders, a curriculum that teaches functional academic and living skills, vocational special education, and transitional programs that facilitate moving from correctional systems to community living. In more than a few instances, inmate mothers about to be released may have previously been addicted to crack cocaine or other drugs. It is imperative that they should be put in contact with appropriate agencies or community centers upon their release so that they can continue to receive information and education about the dangers of drug use and how such use might imperil their children.

Correctional agencies must manage a wide range of offenders including those with special problems. These offenders or clients present unusual challenges for probation and parole officers as well as program administrators who must adjust their supervisory methods and program components accordingly. Special types of offenders may have deep-seated psychological problems that are not immediately diagnosed. They may react in unpredictable ways to various types of treatments or therapy. Because their behaviors may be unexpected or unanticipated, they may become violent and harm themselves or others. Persons who are abnormal in some respects behave in abnormal ways. Probation and parole personnel are not always prepared for each and every contingency that may arise. It is a good idea to know about these special types of offenders and their needs, behavior patterns, and what, if anything, of an unusual nature might be expected from them.

Unfortunately, there is often inadequate communication between institutional staff and community services or institutional care officials who can intercede and recommend appropriate treatment for inmates who misbehave or exhibit unconventional behaviors. For example, front-line correctional staff of prisons may not deem it necessary to report to mental health officials that certain inmates are cutting themselves, masturbating publicly, or smearing feces on their cell walls. One reason for not reporting such incidents is that some correctional staff have acquired cynical attitudes about inmates and their attempts to seek recognition from others. Attracting officer and medical attention by engaging in unconventional behaviors are sometimes used to manipulate staff. Thus, correctional officers may dismiss such behaviors as unimportant when they may, indeed, be indicative of deep-seated personality disturbances in need of attention or treatment.

This overview encompasses the following offender aggregates: (1) mentally ill offenders; (2) sex offenders and child sexual abusers; (3) drug-/alcohol-dependent offenders; (3) HIV/AIDS offenders; (4) gang members; and (5) developmentally disabled offenders.

Mentally Ill Offenders

No one knows how many mentally ill inmates there are in prisons and jails throughout the United States (Fitzgerald et al., 2006). Estimates suggest that as many as 600,000 mentally ill offenders are currently incarcerated (U.S. Department of Justice, 2006). Mentally ill or retarded inmates present correctional officials with problems similar to those who have drug/alcohol dependencies. Also, because of their mental conditions, some of their behavior is disruptive. This disruptive behavior occurs not only during confinement but later, when these inmates are discharged. In many jurisdictions, treatment services for mentally retarded offenders receive a low budgetary and program priority (Paradis et al., 2000).

 **BOX 12.1**

Patti Boberschmidt
Client Manager/Parole Officer, Division of Youth Services, State of Colorado

Statistics:

B.S. (rehabilitation and psychology), University of Northern Colorado.

Background Information and Experience:

When I first began college at the University of Northern Colorado in 1974, like many college students I had no idea what I was going to do with my life. In fact in 1978 when I was scheduled to graduate, I still did not have a solid career plan. I knew that I wanted to work in the human services area, but that is a broad area. When it came time to set up my internship, I decided to visit a secure treatment facility for adolescent males that was located in Golden, Colorado. The great thing about this was that it was a short, 10-minute drive from my home. I was aware of this placement all through my junior high school and high school years. It was the place that "those" kids that got into trouble were sent. Never to be heard from again. Coming from a home that was the model for a "perfect" family, it was always a mystery to me, and a bit daring. I spoke with the director who was eager to assist me. After the required semester it was obvious, and I was hooked. I was hired within a couple of months after graduation, and I have never looked back. That was 28 years ago.

The first 12 years I remained in locked facilities working with youth who were incarcerated for everything from trespassing and truancy to sexual offenses and manslaughter. A normal day consisted of waking up the residents, serving breakfast, chores and hygiene, school on facility grounds, and then back to the unit to begin treatment groups. After a break for dinner, there was usually scheduled programming. If not, additional treatment groups were conducted and then planned leisure activities. I used to joke that I was

"locked up" as well. Definitely not a 9-to-5 job. My family got used to me working holidays, nights, and weekends. Just because some people had jobs where things closed down, that was never the case with this business. I have fond memories of spending Christmas with all of these kids. Most of them had no family involved. Since the units that we worked in had kitchens, we would arrange with the main dining hall to give us our turkey and everything else that went with it so that we could cook with the residents. Even though it was a locked facility, we would manage to make Christmas an event for these kids. Sometimes even more of an event than they had ever had at home. This was not always a happy time for some kids; in fact, this was true of most holidays. Most of them had come from some pretty dysfunctional families, and this was a time when other families were celebrating in a traditional manner. They were dealing with situations where the family might not have had money to buy gifts, or spent the holidays intoxicated; some had parents who were incarcerated in prison or jail. Many of these kids remember spending them in a foster placement or on the street. Not good memories of happy family gatherings. Believe it or not, these were some of my most rewarding memories. I could never stress enough the importance of the relationships that were developed during the duration of a youth's stay.

Eventually it was time for me to broaden my horizons. I was somewhat "paroled" to work in the community as an independent living counselor. This included teaching skills such as interviewing, finding and keeping a job, interpreting a lease, locating resources such as accessing health care, and budgeting and money management. I found it amazing that so many kids are expected to emancipate when they turn 18 years of age. We were asking them to do something that so many people much older have difficulty doing.

In 1994 I decided to make another change within the field. I became a part of a team that piloted and implemented the Division of Youth Corrections, Pre-Service Academy. This worked well with my skills as a trainer, and I was able to incorporate areas for training and curriculum development from my knowledge of at-risk youth.

In 1998 I decided that it was time that I got back to what I loved the most: direct services. I was hired as a client manager/parole officer for the Division of Youth Corrections. It was extremely fortunate that I happened to work in a state that recognizes the importance of continuity of care. I am assigned a youth's case immediately upon commitment by the courts. From that moment on, I make all decisions regarding that youth's stay. I write the treatment plan and contract services, serve as a liaison with the courts, schools, families, and treatment providers. Once a youth has completed all treatment requirements for transition into the community, I present the case to a community review board. After a successful community transition, I would then present the case to the Juvenile Parole Board. Once paroled, the work would begin all over again. In fact, this is where the rubber meets the road.

My motto is "Expect the unexpected, because it will happen." This is where I earn my whole paycheck. The best-case scenario is for the youth to return home. When a youth returns home, he or she has earned it through hard work, addressing his or her treatment issues, learning his or her cycles, and obtaining skills to aid him or her in his or her success. This is all good, but unfortunately most of the time, home life has not changed. This is where you find out if all of the treatment and groups that helped empower this youth with new skills to deal with all of the challenges that they would be exposed to really worked. If the family counseling sessions helped the family communicate, problems would be solved more effectively.

One of the most important things that needs to be recognized, whether a youth is incarcerated or free in the community, is that you need to meet them where they are. In other words, expectations should not exceed what that youth is able to do. Where youths are in their adolescent development stage is crucial to the abilities they are able to display and the level of success they can achieve. That is not to say that it can't be done eventually, but it is a long process. There are so many things that interfere with normal adolescent development. I think that this is something that is easy to overlook. When a youth begins using drugs or alcohol at age 13 and has continued using until some entity, such as the court, intervenes, then basically you might in reality have a 17-year-old, but emotionally the youth is stuck at age 13 in terms of the way he or she thinks and copes with the world. The same goes for youths who have lived in an unsafe environment where they have been neglected or abused (e.g., sexually, emotionally, or physically). Youth with mental health issues and pregnancy also apply to this. It is our job to move them through the stages of adolescent development, teaching them skills that they will need to have successful, productive lives.

It was amazing working with so many youth over the years that I can look back and remember names and faces and histories of these kids as if no time has passed. It is not uncommon for me to get a call from a client that I had 2, 5, or even 10 years ago. Or a youth checking in with me even though he or she is on escape status just to let me know that everything is okay. I love this. I genuinely feel the loss when I close a case. I always let them know that I am available for advice or resources if they ever have the need for either.

Advice to Students:

1. Give praise and develop realistic expectations.
2. Establish healthy boundaries, not only in your personal relationship with your clients but also with your personal life. This job will have a way of following you home.

(*continued*)

BOX 12.1 (*Continued*)

3. Remember that the judge punished them by committing them; our job is to help them address whatever it is they need in order for them to be successful when they return to the community. Don't judge or criticize.

4. Families are the key. Include them and make them feel a part of the success.

5. Don't take it personally. Frequently a youth that you have an excellent relationship with will let you down. This is when you use it as a learning experience.

6. Seek opportunities for growth; this is what keeps you energized as well as current with best practice.

7. Kids know when you like them, if this is a JOB, it might not be the correct profession for you.

8. Ask questions. Don't assume.

9. Walk your talk. You can't expect a behavior that you are not willing to model.

Sex Offenders and Child Sexual Abusers

Another category of offenders receiving special emphasis from corrections are sex offenders, including child sexual abusers. Sometimes these offenders are grouped with criminals who are mentally ill and deserve special services, while others feel they should receive no unique consideration. Since many sex offenses are committed against victims known by the offender as a friend or family member, a large number of these incidents are not reported to the police. Thus, no one really knows how many sex offenders there are in the United States at any given time (Smith, 2006).

Drug-/Alcohol-Dependent Offenders

Drug and alcohol abuse are highly correlated with criminal conduct. Large numbers of pretrial detainees are characterized as having drug and/or alcohol dependencies. Furthermore, there is evidence that many offenders suffer from polysubstance abuse. Offenders with drug or alcohol dependencies present several problems for correctional personnel. Often, jails are not equipped to handle their withdrawal symptoms, especially if they are confined for long periods. Also, the symptoms themselves are frequently dealt with rather than the social and psychological causes for these dependencies. Thus, when offenders go through alcohol detoxification programs or are treated for drug addiction, they leave these programs and are placed back into the same circumstances that caused the drug or alcohol dependencies originally.

HIV/AIDS Offenders

A growing problem in corrections is HIV/AIDS, or human immunodeficiency virus/acquired immune deficiency syndrome. Estimates are that by 2005, there were over 5 million HIV/AIDS cases in the United States, and that the number of AIDS cases was doubling about every 8 to 10 months (Office of Justice Programs, 2006). AIDS is particularly prevalent among jail and prison inmates. Prisoners living in close quarters are highly susceptible to the AIDS virus because of the likelihood of anal–genital or oral–genital contact.

Gang Members

In 2006 there were over 1.1 million active gang members in 30,000 youth gangs throughout the United States, both on the streets and in U.S. prisons and jails (U.S. Department of Justice, 2006). Virtually every city with a population of 250,000 or greater reported the presence of gangs. Furthermore, there were significant gang increases in suburban and rural areas of the United States, as the number of gang members in these areas increased by 70 percent from 1996 to 2006. These gangs pose threats to community stability and citizen safety. Many gang members have antisocial personalities and have difficulty relating or coping with others.

Developmentally Disabled Offenders

A growing but neglected population of offenders are those with physical handicaps. Some offenders are confined to wheelchairs, and therefore, special facilities must be constructed to accommodate their access to probation or parole offices or community-based sites. Other offenders have hearing or speech impairments that limit them in various ways. Physically challenged offenders often require greater attention from their POs. Acquiring and maintaining employment is sometimes difficult for persons with different types of physical handicaps. Many POs become brokers between their own agencies and community businesses who are encouraged to employ certain of these clients with special problems. Community volunteers are increasingly helpful in assisting probation and parole agencies with physically handicapped clients.

MENTALLY ILL OFFENDERS

Thousands of mentally ill individuals pass through local correctional facilities annually. One quarter of all inmates in prisons and jails in 2005 reported that they had been diagnosed or treated for one type of mental illness or another (U.S. Department of Justice, 2006). Nearly 100,000 of these inmates said that they were on some form of prescription medication for a mental illness, while another 65,000 reported that they had been admitted to a mental health program at one time or another during their commission of crimes. Offenders who are mentally ill are incarcerated disproportionately in relation to other offenders (Carr et al., 2006). Mentally ill inmates tend to mask their limitations and are highly susceptible to prison culture and inmate manipulation. Also, these offenders are often unresponsive to traditional rehabilitation programs available to other inmates. They present correctional officers with unusual discipline problems unlike other inmates. Corrections officers often are high-school educated with little, if any, training in dealing with mentally ill individuals. Obviously, proper classification systems should be devised to identify different types of disabled inmates. Similar classification systems are currently being devised in many jail settings and corrections generally is becoming more responsive to the needs of these types of offenders.

A deinstitutionalization movement commenced in 1968 in the United States, where mentally ill offenders were increasingly shifted from institutional to community care. This movement has not been uniform throughout all jurisdictions, however. One aim of deinstitutionalization has been to reduce jail and prison populations by diverting the mentally ill or retarded to nonincarcerative surroundings such as hospitals. However, deinstitutionalization has not been entirely successful in this respect. One unintended consequence of deinstitutionalization has been to discharge large numbers of mentally disturbed offenders back into the community prematurely after a short hospitalization. Police once again encounter these offenders because of their inability to cope with the rigors of the street. In fact, the police bring these same individuals back into jails and prisons through "mercy bookings," where they mistakenly believe correctional personnel can take care of them more effectively. Thus, the cycle is repeated, where the stresses of jail or prison exacerbate latent psychotic, convulsive, and behavioral factors (Carr et al., 2006).

Of course, deinstitutionalization of mentally ill offenders does not significantly alleviate the burden on probation and parole departments who must supervise these clients. POs and their agencies have had to make significant adjustments and programmatic changes to accommodate mentally ill offenders. One of the greatest areas of concern, from the standpoint of agency personnel, relates to supervising those who are learning disabled or mentally retarded. Often, because these offenders cannot express themselves or indicate their needs, it is difficult to identify the most appropriate services or legal assistance they might require. Many POs lack skills in dealing with these clients, although many agencies throughout the United States are improving their services delivery (Carr et al., 2006).

For institutional corrections, the problems of mentally ill persons are manifold. Many mentally ill offenders are violent, and they are recidivists (Zhang and Jung, 2006). A study of mentally ill patients was conducted in 1998, which was known as the MacArthur Violence Risk Assessment Study. The sample investigated consisted of 1,136 persons who had been hospitalized for mental disorders. Many of these persons had criminal records, and self-disclosures by these patients concluded that about a third had violent thoughts. Many patients were self-proclaimed substance abusers, and they predicted that they would leave their institutions and commit violent acts if given the opportunity. A correlation was demonstrated between their psychopathy, anger, and impulsiveness. The disturbing fact is that many of these patients, when released, will actually carry out their violent thoughts and act accordingly. Therefore, many new commitments to jails and prisons are former mental patients with histories of violence. A sample of New York inmates revealed that a high percentage of older detainees, age 62 or older, were charged with violent felonies and had previously been hospitalized in New York or elsewhere (Paradis et al., 2000). Many of those committed to jails reported that they previously had been diagnosed with mental problems and reportedly had paranoid delusions, which were known to psychiatric staff. However, little or no attempt was made to detain them beyond short-term observation periods in the facilities where they were confined.

Many mentally ill inmates of prisons and jails slip through the cracks and are not diagnosed as mentally ill. Rather, they are simply regarded as violent inmates by correctional officers. Thus, they avoid treatment for their mental problems altogether. Some prisoners develop psychoses of one type or another as the result of confinement. For instance, prisoners placed in solitary confinement seem to have a higher incidence of onset of psychiatric disorders compared with those not placed in solitary confinement.

Most prisons in the United States and in other English-speaking countries such as England and Canada attempt to screen incoming inmates for mental disorders. For instance, in England at the Durham Prison, new inmates undergo health assessments designed to determine their mental conditions. Many of these inmates were improperly diagnosed, however, and almost all of them were placed in the general population with other inmates. Researchers who investigated this situation concluded that the reason for these misclassifications and misdiagnoses was attributable to inappropriate staff training and experience. Furthermore, when incoming prisoners were screened, they were discouraged by staff from carrying on conversations where their mental illnesses might become more apparent (Birmingham et al., 2000). Even when mentally ill offenders are processed or screened properly, they may not receive the appropriate therapy. In some instances, they may receive no therapy at all.

Court intervention has not always been helpful. During the 1980s and 1990s, the verdict of guilty-but-mentally-ill was increasingly used. This verdict enabled juries to convict mentally ill offenders of crimes, which resulted in their hospitalization rather than incarceration. Supposedly, these offenders would receive appropriate treatment and then be released into the general inmate population of the nearest prison. However, many of these offenders have escaped incarceration when civil authorities have authorized their release from hospital custody.

When these offenders are eventually transferred to parole services, their mental problems accompany them. In more than a few instances, POs do not know that these persons are mentally disturbed. But increasing numbers of states are devising risk/needs assessment devices that permit POs the opportunity of detecting some of the more mentally disordered clients. Despite these advancements in technology and test improvements, it is still difficult for many authorities to detect antisocial personalities and those most likely to become violent and reoffend. The most direct indicators of problem parolees is through contacts with prison officials who have supposedly had an opportunity to examine these parole-eligible inmates and determine their psychopathy. However, all too often, inmates with serious psychological problems are improperly diagnosed or not diagnosed at all. Therefore, it is unexpected whenever POs discover mentally unstable clients among their caseloads where no prior warning had been given from institutional officials. Again, the problem was often attributable to a lack of properly trained jail or prison staff who either didn't take the time to diagnose certain inmates properly or failed to recognize the signs of mental illness whenever they were prevalent.

One attempt to aggressively deal with the mentally ill population was implemented in Maryland in 1994 following a pilot study of assessing mental illness among inmates in jails and prisons and how communities and institutions were coping with it. In the early 1990s, it was estimated that approximately 700 inmates were being confined in local facilities in Maryland. However, Maryland, not unlike other jurisdictions, lacked sufficient and adequately trained staff to properly screen and treat the mentally ill that were processed by local jails. Often, mentally ill individuals were simply ignored, unless they proved disruptive or attempted suicide. After several pilot projects, Maryland officials created the Community Criminal Justice Treatment Program, or MCCJTP. This program was founded on two principles: (1) the target population requires a continuum of care provided by a variety of service professionals in jail and in the community that is coordinated at both the state and local levels; and (2) local communities are in the best position to plan and implement responses to meet the needs of the mentally ill offenders in their jurisdictions (Champion, 2005).

BOX 12.2

INTERNATIONAL SNAPSHOT: PROBATION AND PAROLE IN GHANA

The government of Ghana is a multiparty parliamentary government with a President who is elected and is the head of state and chief of the executive branch. A legislature exists to create all civil and criminal laws, and it consists of the President and the National Assembly. There are regional leaders who report to the central government on matters of public policy. The government oversees the court system and all police services as well as the prison system. All high officials, including the Chief Justice of the Supreme Court, the Director of Prisons, and the Inspector General of Police, are all appointed by the President. Ghana is a member of the Economic Community of West African States (ECOWAS) and the Organization for African Unity (OAU).

The historical roots of Ghana's political system are English and common law, which is based on *stare decisis* or judicial precedent and is a dominant theme. Statutory law dominates most areas of Ghana, although in remote rural regions of the country, tribal chiefs and elders are permitted to administer justice in accordance with tribal traditions. Ghana was once known as the Gold Coast, and in 1957 it ceased being dependent upon Great Britain. Despite achieving independence from England, Ghana continues to employ many of the British traditions in its legal system, including how laws are defined and how crimes are punished.

Crimes in Ghana are divided into serious and nonserious offenses, such as felonies and misdemeanors. The most serious offenses are murder, assault, rape, robbery, extortion, possession of dangerous drugs, counterfeiting, forgery, and abduction. Drug possession and trafficking is a growing problem. The three major drugs manufactured and distributed by Ghanan criminals are cocaine, heroin, and Indian hemp. These and other serious crimes are punishable by fines and imprisonment. Misdemeanors, such as traffic offenses, public drunkenness, and tax evasion, are punished usually by fines. The age of criminal responsibility is 18. Crime victims have little or no role in the sentencing process. If they are involved, they are involved as witnesses. They have no input regarding the sentences imposed if their victimizers are convicted. No systematic records are kept to determine the profiles of those most frequently victimized or the true nature of crime in Ghana. There are no victim assistance programs.

Five degrees of offenses in Ghana have been identified. Capital offenses where the death penalty may be administered include murder, treason, or piracy. First-degree felonies punishable by life imprisonment include manslaughter, rape, and mutiny. Second-degree felonies punishable by up to 10 years in prison include intentional harm to persons, perjury, and robbery. Misdemeanors include assault, theft, official corruption, and public nuisance activity. These are punishable by either fines or various short terms of imprisonment. Corporal punishment is not permitted. No juveniles may be imprisoned, and no one under the age of 18 may be executed, regardless of the heinous nature of the offense. Although there are no official laws prohibiting trafficking in persons, Ghana does have laws forbidding slavery and child exploitation. But it is well documented that human trafficking occurs with some frequency in Ghana, and persons are sold to criminals in other countries for prostitution and other illegal activities. Various governmental efforts are underway to prevent or minimize such human trafficking.

Ghana is divided into 11 different regions. Police officers are recruited from a centralized source and distributed or assigned to these regions as needed. All regional police agencies report directly to the Ghana Police Regional Headquarters. Ghana police are responsible for law enforcement, offender apprehension, crime detection and investigation, and protection of lives and property. They also have licensing duties relating to hunting and other activities where firearms are used.

The Ghana Police Training Center (PTC) is similar to POST in that it is a centralized training facility for all persons who perform police tasks. Recruits undergo a rigorous training program of six months before assuming the duties of police officers in the different regions. Deadly force may be used to combat resisting suspects where crimes have been committed and threats to officers are perceived as real. Although warrants are technically required before police conduct searches of one's premises, often these warrants are ignored and searches and seizures are conducted without them. Any statement by an arrested suspect may be admitted into evidence at a subsequent trial, with or without the presence of an attorney. Police officers have extensive discretionary powers, and they may arrest and charge virtually any person whom they believe has committed a crime. It is up to individual officers whether to bring persons before magistrates for a hearing and subsequent trial.

Defendants in criminal actions have rights similar to those of U.S. citizens. If defendants are indigent, then counsel will be appointed to represent them. Defendants may plead guilty to avoid a trial, but such confessions or admissions do not necessarily automatically mean leniency will be forthcoming from sentencing judges. The maximum penalty for the most serious offenses is death. Any person charged with a crime that may result in the death penalty is entitled to a trial before the High Court. For lesser offenses, such as misdemeanors, these cases may be tried by magistrates in a summary fashion and fines may be imposed. All other serious cases are tried in either a Circuit Court or the High Court and are preceded by an indictment. Ghana does not have jury trials. Defendants cannot plea bargain in Ghana. Police officers who make the arrests of suspects become prosecutors and pursue cases against specific suspects they arrested. Police officers may also give testimony relating to the cases they prosecute. There is no accurate information about the number of crimes committed in Ghana annually or the number of persons who are arrested and go to trial.

Bail is available, provided that a friend or relative of the defendant can post it. If the crime is alleged to have been committed by a property owner, then he or she may be released on their own recognizance until trial. However, it is possible to hold persons until their trials if they are believed to pose societal risks or are likely to flee Ghana to avoid prosecution. Usually about a third of all defendants are held until trial annually. All others are released on their own recognizance.

The court system of Ghana is somewhat complex. The highest court is the Supreme Court and is the equivalent of the U.S. Supreme Court or court of last resort. This court consists of a chief justice and six other justices. A Court of Appeal has appellate jurisdiction over High Courts and Circuit Courts. High Courts and Circuit Courts are comprised of from one to three judges who sit and decide cases. Each of the districts in Ghana has a District Court to hear local cases. The lowest courts are Customary Courts, and these are usually located in the most rural regions. A separate Juvenile Court exists to hear matters involving criminal acts committed by youths under the age of 18. They consist of four persons: a laywoman, a layman, and two magistrates. All juvenile cases are handled informally, and these judicial bodies are transient. There are probably fewer than 20 juvenile sessions conducted in Ghana during any given year. The punishments for juveniles are almost always exclusively rehabilitative, and vocational and educational training are emphasized and encouraged. There are at least seven industrial schools throughout Ghana to accommodate juveniles who are in need of special training, counseling, or services.

The sentencing process in Ghana is strictly up to the presiding judge or judges. Sentencing decisions must be unanimous if more than one judge hears a particular case. The only persons having input in sentencing matters are professionals such as psychiatrists

(continued)

BOX 12.2 (Continued)

and social workers. Medical experts may also be consulted, as well as probation officers.

The range of punishments includes fines, community service, restitution, probation, or prison. Prison terms are imposed from one year to life, although the death penalty may be administered for the most serious crimes. Most persons who are executed have been convicted of treason, murder, or attempting to overthrow the government.

It is unknown how many persons are under the supervision of probation officers. Persons who are imprisoned can be released short of serving their full terms, provided they exhibit good behavior. Thus, a form of parole exists. Early releases are usually based on good conduct. Inmates who participate in self-help programs, counseling, anger management, vocational or educational courses, and other rehabilitative services earn good-time credit against their maximum sentences. Interestingly, paroled persons or any convicted person is virtually unaffected by their convictions and sentences served when they seek employment, since it is forbidden for employers to inquire about prior criminal records of their prospective employees. The Director of Prisons oversees all administrative decision making in all Ghanan prisons. Prison officers in Ghana are well trained, with many of them trained in England and other countries besides Ghana's own prison officer training program.

Visitations by family and friends are permitted inmates in Ghana's prisons. These include both maximum- and medium-security prisons. Some prisons are considered "open," where prisoners are kept on their honor not to attempt escape. Conjugal visits are permitted offenders in these types of facilities. Ghana's prisons are notoriously overcrowded. In a system designed to house 7,500 inmates, there were over 15,000 inmates being housed in Ghana's prisons in 2005. At this writing, the Ghana government was examining various solutions to the problem of prison overcrowding, including granting earlier releases to the current inmate population. Thus it is anticipated that in future years, the number of parolees who are supervised by probation officers will rise appreciably.

Sources: Adapted from Robert Winslow, *Crime and Society: A Comparative Criminology Tour of the World,* San Diego, CA: San Diego State University, 2005; "Ghana: The Prison System," *Ghana Ministry of Justice,* 2006; *Trafficking in Persons Report,* Office to Monitor and Combat Trafficking in Persons, Washington, DC, June 14, 2004; Obi N.I. Ebbe, "Ghana," *World Factbook of Criminal Justice Systems,* 2005; Graphic Communications Limited, "A-G Wants Death Penalty Abolished,"*Graphic Ghana,* October 26, 2005; "The Constitution of Ghana," Ministry of Justice, 2006; "Penal Reform Planned for Prisons," Washington, DC: UN Integrated Regional Information Networks, 2005; "Country Reports on Human Rights Practices," Washington, DC: Bureau of Democracy, Human Rights, and Labor, February 23, 2001; "Ghana: Criminal Justice, the Courts, and the Judiciary," Ministry of Justice, Ghana, 2006.

The goals of the MCCJTP are to improve the identification and treatment of mentally ill offenders and increase their chances of successful independent living, thereby preventing their swift return to jail, mental hospitals, homelessness, or hospital emergency rooms. In some locations, MCCJTP also aims to reduce the period of incarceration, through post-booking diversion and even reduce the likelihood of incarceration altogether.

The MCCJTP works as follows:

1. Preliminary identification of candidates for program services is made following arrest, after self-referral by the defendant, or as the result of referrals by the arresting officer, the classification officer, jail medical staff, the substance abuse counselor, or other jail personnel.

2. The MCCJTP case manager meets with candidates to conduct an in-jail diagnostic interview and an individual needs assessment.

3. While in jail, the inmate meets with the case manager for counseling and the development of an aftercare plan. A typical plan will include substance abuse counseling, educational services, recreational services, employment training, and eventually, suitable housing.

4. MCCJTP case mangers help link clients to specified services, such as psychiatric day treatment, substance abuse treatment, vocational rehabilitation, and educational services.

5. Case managers were responsible for monitoring offenders for program compliance and to ensure their compliance with housing agreements and participation in daily activities and treatment plans.

6. The length of stay in the MCCJTP depends on client progress, which is monitored daily. Judicial approval is required. The case is left open for one year. At the end of the year, the judge either closes the case or reopens it.

The probation department actively assists the MCCJTP in a variety of ways, usually through networking with community agencies to provide clients with needed services and programs. Between 1994 and 1998, the program has been highly successful. While persons with mental illnesses have not been cured outright, most have been brought to a level where they can function fairly normally with assistance from caregivers provided through the MCCJTP.

State and federal probation and parole services have gradually increased their roles in assessing the prevalence of mental illness among their clientele. In 2005, 46 states indicated that mental health agencies, private practitioners, or the courts were the primary determinants of one's mental condition. Only 14 states had provisions for and kept records of the prevalence of mental illness among their probation and parole populations. While these figures have improved in recent years, there are still inadequate assessments of mentally ill clients among a majority of state probation and parole agencies (U.S. Department of Justice, 2006).

SEX OFFENDERS

It has been estimated that convicted rapists make up about 2 percent of the prison population in the United States in 2005 (Martin and Sundberg, 2006). About 268,000 sex offenders were under some form of correctional supervision during the same period (U.S. Department of Justice, 2006). Sex offenders are persons who commit a sexual act prohibited by law. Fairly common types of sex offenders include rapists and prostitutes, although sex offenses may include voyeurism ("Peeping Toms"), exhibitionism, child sexual molestation, incest, date rape, and marital rape. This list is not exhaustive. Child sexual abusers are adults who involve minors in virtually any kind of sexual activity ranging from intercourse with children to photographing them in lewd poses. Although the exact figure is unknown, it is believed that approximately 2 million children are sexually victimized annually. It is also estimated that 90 percent of all child sexual abuse cases are never prosecuted, although this situation appears to be changing.

Public interest in and awareness of sex offenders is based on the belief that most convicted sex offenders will commit new sex offenses when released.

Regardless of the diverse motives of sex offenders, there is general agreement among professionals that these offenders usually need some form of counseling or therapy. Many jurisdictions currently operate sex therapy programs designed to rehabilitate sex offenders, depending on the nature of their sex crime (Smith, 2006).

Sex offenders offer POs a unique challenge. First, sex offenders expect some amount of assistance from community programs designed to counsel and treat them. Thus, they believe they are in a therapeutic milieu whenever they are freed on probation or parole with conditions. In accordance with their program expectations, they obtain honest employment and attempt to lead law-abiding lives. Most sex offenders do not have lengthy criminal records, nor do they have moderate or severe substance-abuse problems or dependencies or unstable lifestyles. But the media and public have quite a different view of sex offenders. They are viewed as unstable predators who seek to repeat their victimizations whenever possible (Lindsey, 2006). Reports of escapes of violent sexual predators from treatment centers and mental hospitals do little to dispel public sentiment against sex offenders. In support of this belief, 48 states had passed community notification legislation by 1998 so that sex offenders would be required to register whenever they relocated to different communities to start new lives. Obviously the public regards sex offending as a most egregious activity and desires to punish it most severely. Thus, the dilemma arises about how POs can effectively supervise these offenders without posing a risk to public safety, and at the same time avoid undercutting the offender's ability to get back on to a crime-free path. There are no easy answers to this dilemma (Smith, 2006).

The **Missouri Sexual Offender Program (MOSOP)** targets the needs of incarcerated, nonpsychotic sexual offenders. The program can supervise effectively over 700 offenders who are required to complete the program before becoming eligible for parole. MOSOP approaches sex offenders on the assumption that their sex offenses resulted from learned patterns of behavior associated with anxious, angry, and impulsive individuals. The three-phase program obligates offenders to attend 10 weeks of courses in abnormal psychology and the psychology of sexual offending. In other phases, inmates meet in group therapy sessions to talk out their problems with counselors and other inmates. MOSOP officials believe that if the program can reduce sex offender recidivism by only 3 percent, it will pay for itself from the savings of court costs and inmate processing and confinement.

Sex offenders, especially child sexual abusers, pose significant problems for both jail and prison authorities as well as community-based corrections personnel. Child sexual abusers are often abused themselves by other inmates when their crimes become known to others. Other sex offenders become the prey of stronger inmates who use these offenders for their own sexual gratification. Many sex offenders request that they be segregated from other prisoners because of danger to themselves. But because of limited resources and space, jail and prison officials cannot often segregate these offenders effectively from other inmates. Within communities, many sex offenders and child sexual abusers are placed in community-based facilities for treatment and counseling (Martin and Sundberg, 2006). The most frequently used treatment method in sex offender treatment agencies is peer group counseling.

Various models of PO training and caseload assignments have been described that include sex offender specialization. Some officers are specialists in that they have received unique training in counseling sex offenders. Some POs have acquired M S W degrees and are certified counselors for those with sex or alcohol problems. One of these PO training models is the specialized caseloads model, where clients are assigned according to their particular offenses and/or psychological problems. Sex offenders and child sexual abusers are among those clients receiving particular supervision from PO specialists, just as chemically dependent persons might be supervised by special POs who have acquired additional chemical dependency training (Martin and Sundberg, 2006).

OFFENDERS WITH HIV/AIDS

Although there has been much improvement in creating greater AIDS awareness among inmates through educational programs, the fact is that AIDS education in incarcerative settings has not slowed the spread of this disease appreciably. By the beginning of 2006, for instance, there were 41,556 AIDS-infected inmates in state prisons and 3,222 AIDS-infected inmates in federal penitentiaries (Office of Justice Programs, 2006). Interestingly, female inmates in state and federal prisons had a higher AIDS infection rate compared with men. For male prisoners, about 2.2 percent were infected with AIDS compared with 3.5 percent of all female inmates.

It follows that if AIDS is prevalent and increasing among jail and prison inmates, then it is prevalent and increasing among probationers and parolees as well. Thus, AIDS has become a primary topic of concern among POs and their agencies. In view of the various circumstances under which AIDS has been transmitted in recent years, from saliva or blood residue from dentists and others working in different health professions, POs have perceived that their risk of being infected with the AIDS virus has increased greatly. Many probationers and parolees are former drug offenders. Drug-dependent clients represent a special danger, since AIDS is known to be easily transmitted when drug addicts share their needles used to inject heroin and other substances. It is widely known from media reports that some crimes have been perpetrated by some offenders wielding needles and other objects they say have been infected with AIDS. Thus, these actions pose additional risks for supervising POs who must be on their guard and protect themselves from becoming infected.

Indirectly related to the rise in HIV/AIDS in prisons, jails, and probation and parole programs is the rise in tuberculosis. Between 1976 and 1996, for instance, there was a 50 percent increase in the number of New York State prison inmates infected with tuberculosis. Much of this tuberculosis is untreatable and fatal. It is more easily transmitted than HIV/AIDS, although HIV/AIDS inmates and clients seem at greater risk of contracting tuberculosis than other inmates who are HIV/AIDS-free. Today, virtually every prison conducts a routine tuberculosis skin test to determine whether particular inmates are infected. If they are infected, then they are almost always isolated from the general inmate population in an effort to control the spread of this disease. Some of the nation's larger jails, such as the Los Angeles County Jail, conducts routine mini chest films, which are single-view, low-dose, screening radiographs to detect active pulmonary disease. Thus, early detection of this disease can be immediately isolated and treated.

Inmates, probationers, and parolees with HIV/AIDS are at risk of transmitting their disease to others. While institutionalized, inmates with HIV/AIDS are often isolated physically from the general inmate population to prevent the spread of their disease to other inmates. However, their isolation cannot be continued indefinitely. Institutionalization may be the last chance many of these persons will have to receive appropriate treatment under any type of meaningful supervision. Even while some prisoners with HIV/AIDS are confined, particularly in local jails, sometimes they are ill-treated or denied treatment by insensitive jail personnel as a punishment for their condition. At some point, most of these offenders will be paroled. When they come under the supervision of paroling authorities, they are often assigned to a PO that is trained in sexually transmitted diseases. These are specialized caseloads. POs with special knowledge can be more effective in the management and supervision of HIV/AIDS-infected clients.

It is often the case that HIV/AIDS-infected inmates are known to POs before their arrival. This way, POs can arrange appropriate community services and treatment so that when their clients arrive, their therapy can continue without interruption (Anno, 1998). Often, new clients with AIDS/HIV have other problems, such as drug dependencies. POs must also plan to address these types of problems as well. Increasing numbers of HIV/AIDS-infected clients are women. If some of these women are pregnant or have borne children prior to their earlier confinement, then POs must arrange to educate them concerning how to prevent the spread of HIV/AIDS. Some investigations have revealed that the knowledge among women with HIV/AIDS, how it was acquired, and how it can be transmitted is extremely low. Thus, it is critical that these persons receive special education courses or a general exposure to knowledge about HIV/AIDS and its transmission. Usually, a community agency can assist in this regard.

Some inmates with HIV/AIDS who are within a short time of early release may be granted work or study release from their confinement. There are obvious risk factors associated with permitting these persons to work for limited periods outside of prison walls. However, if these persons are properly supervised within a supportive community environment, then their transition back into their communities later may go more smoothly.

SUBSTANCE-ABUSING OFFENDERS

Offenders who are arrested and convicted for substance abuse are increasing compared with other offender groups. It is estimated that when alcohol abusers are combined with drug abusers within the offender population, between 80 and 90 percent of them have some type of addiction or problem. Between 1990 and 2006, for instance, the number of state and local arrests for drug offenses rose from 1,350,000 to 2,446,000 (U.S. Department of Justice, 2006). The population of chronic illicit drug users consists largely of poor, undereducated, unemployed, and uninsured persons. These persons commit crimes at disproportionately higher rates than other criminals and they pose substantial health risks to their associates. Furthermore, they comprise the population of probationers and parolees most likely to relapse while free within their communities under PO supervision. Thus, they present fairly serious monitoring problems for POs in all jurisdictions. And this problem is increasing rather than diminishing.

A fairly common offender category under PO supervision is the DWI or DUI offender. These are persons who have been convicted of drunk driving or driving under the influence of alcohol or drugs. It has been estimated that

814,600 persons convicted of drunk driving were under correctional supervision during 2005. For POs, it is important to note that during the early 2000s, the correctional supervision rate for drunk drivers rose from 151 for every 1,000 DWI arrests to 368 for every 1,000 DWI arrests (U.S. Department of Justice, 2006). DWI or DUI offenders must complete special conditions of probation relating to attending Alcoholics Anonymous meetings, Mothers Against Drunk Drivers meetings, and driving schools in various jurisdictions. All of this information must be documented and filed with the probation office. POs must keep track of all of these offenders in order to ensure program compliance.

Prisons and jails do not always insulate inmates from continued drug or alcohol abuses. Illegal substance abuse is prevalent among inmates in state and federal prisons. Corrections employees are often about as likely as prisoners to abuse drugs, since the employees themselves are frequently the major conduits for smuggling drugs into prison settings. Currently, many state, local, and federal agencies conduct routine urinalyses of their employees to detect and/or deter drug abuse among them as well as inmates (Dunlap and Ciccel, 2006).

Pretrial detainees have often been involved in additional criminality while awaiting trial. Even samples of pretrial detainees who were subjected to periodic drug tests as a specific deterrent were found to have high failure-to-appear rates and rearrests. Drug dependencies also account for greater numbers of dropouts and failures among those involved in both juvenile and adult intervention programs. For those on either probation or parole, drug and/or alcohol dependencies present various problems and account for program infractions, rearrests, and general adjustment and reintegration problems.

Those reentering the community on parole after years of incarceration are especially vulnerable to drug dependencies during the first six months following their release. Individual or group counseling and other forms of therapy are recommended for drug- or alcohol-dependent clients, although many clients are considered treatment-resistant. Since 1972, various community-based treatment programs have been implemented to treat and counsel drug-dependent clients. These community-based programs have been collectively labeled **Treatment Alternatives to Street Crime (TASC)** and currently are being operated in numerous jurisdictions throughout the United States to improve client abstinence from drugs, increase their employment potential, and improve their social/personal functioning.

For POs, an effective supervision strategy requires a reliable drug-testing program as well as a consistent and well-formulated policy that holds offenders accountable for their decision to use drugs or otherwise violate the special drug aftercare consideration. The range of consequences for drug aftercare violations must be clearly spelled out in the office policy manual and overseen by unit supervisors; the expectations of abstinence and possible sanctions must be carefully reviewed with the offender during the initial interview; and, most essential, the threatened sanctions must be imposed when and if violations occur if we are to be effective in controlling and treating drug offenders.

In the early 1990s, the typical response whenever drug or alcohol abusers were encountered in courts was to place them under intensive probation or parole supervision, with considerable monitoring and randomized drug and alcohol checks. While these types of checks are still conducted in most if not all state and federal jurisdictions, they do not appear to be working to decrease the extent of substance abuse. What does seem to work is combining prevention and education programs for non-drug users with treatment programs for users. This is acknowledged as the most effective strategy for reducing drug demand. Treatment for incarcerated and nonincarcerated offenders not only reduces drug use but also suppresses the criminal activity associated with it. Moreover, offenders who are forced into drug treatment by legal mandates are just as successful in recovery as those who voluntarily enter treatment programs, and they often remain in their programs for longer periods.

In other jurisdictions, more aggressive offender monitoring and supervision has been proposed. For instance, the traditional medical model, which considers drug and alcohol dependence as a disease that can be cured with some type of long-term therapy and treatment, may not be suitable for criminal offenders who have serious addictions. The medical model is closely associated with the social work approach and places POs in positions to be manipulated by their addicted clients. Few offenders are willing to oblige their supervising POs or anyone else to give up drugs or alcohol voluntarily. What usually happens is that there are frequent relapses where POs merely suggest starting over or trying again with a particular therapy. Also, many addicted clients are master manipulators and design various methods to beat the systems that are designed to test whether they are using specific drugs. It is not unusual for POs to give offenders chance after chance following drug tests that disclose the use of one or more drugs within the past 24 or 48 hours. For many POs, this is part of establishing rapport with their clients and earning their trust. Some clients, for instance, object to being ordered to refrain from using alcohol, if their addiction happens to be cocaine. Why should they be expected to refrain from alcohol use if they have another type of addiction? One answer is that alcohol consumption is associated with a higher rate of relapse involving their drug of choice, whether it is cocaine, heroin, or some other addictive substance. The most common positives for drugs include cocaine, amphetamines, morphine, and marijuana. Other drugs include anabolic steroids, barbiturates, phencyclidine (PCP), and prescription medications such as diazepam (Valium), codeine, and methadone (Curtis, 2003).

Many offenders attempt to beat the tests administered by POs or private contractors by doing different things to contaminate their urine or blood specimens. Some of the techniques offenders use include using a rubber penis filled with clean urine; attaching to the unobserved side of the penis a tube leading to a container under the armpit; inserting a small bottle of clean urine into the vagina; pouring clean urine into a specimen bottle; dipping the bottle into the urinal or toilet and filling it with water; or contaminating the urine sample with various foreign substances, such as Drano, chlorine, or bleach. Other clients flush their specimens. This is one of the more common ways of trying to beat the tests. Flushing means to consume large quantities of water, coffee, or other liquids to dilute the concentration of drugs in the body and accelerate the excretion. The greater the liquid intake, the lower the concentration of the drug and the quicker the excretion rate. Some offenders simply fail to show up for their counseling sessions or treatment. Skipping meetings means no test and no detection. For many POs, someone who fails to appear for a counseling session may be less serious than testing positive for drugs.

Sam Torres, a former federal probation officer, believes that a continuum of sanctions should be imposed instead of the usual course of treatment prescribed by the medical model. The sanctions are as follows:

1. Admonishment, which is a verbal warning that the test was positive, or that the offender failed to report for testing.

2. Verbal admonishment by a probation officer, which is a verbal warning issued to the offender that further drug use will have consequences, such as mandatory participation in a 12-step program or other activities.

3. Written admonishment by the probation officer, which is a formal letter to the offender advising him or her of the consequences for continuing to test positive for drug use.

4. Verbal admonishment by the probation officer and supervisor, which adds weight to the admonishment.

5. Written admonishment by the U.S. Parole Commission, if the client is a federal probationer or parolee.

6. Verbal admonishment by the court.

7. Lengthen the time in the current phase, or simply extending the time period of their current phase level.

8. Increase the client's phase level to closer supervision and testing.

9. Increase the level of supervision, including more frequent offender monitoring.

10. Community service as a punishment.

11. Alcoholics Anonymous or Narcotics Anonymous mandatory meetings; offenders must sign cards at these meetings to signify they attended.

12. Outpatient counseling.

13. Electronic monitoring.

14. Community correctional center participation.

15. Reside and participate in a sober-living program.

16. Arrest, short-term custody, and reinstatement to supervision.

17. Intermittent incarceration.

18. Therapeutic community (residential drug treatment).

19. Arrest, custody, and recommendation for program revocation (Torres, 1998:38–44).

The importance of these different stages of increasing sanctions is to make it clear to offenders that their relapses will have specific consequences. It is insufficient to merely threaten to do something. The PO actually has to follow through and do it. Torres recommends a zero-tolerance policy, and he believes that offenders should be held accountable for their decision to use drugs. They are engaging in a rational choice to violate program requirements. Clients are given numerous opportunities to overcome their addictions. Complete abstinence is the recommended therapy according to this model.

Unfortunately, it is a fact that if drug-abusing offenders are eventually incarcerated, they will easily acquire drugs in their institutions from other inmates. There is about as much drug use, if not more, in prisons and jails than there is on city streets. Inmates use a multitude of methods to smuggle drugs into their institutions. And there are many creative ways of paying for these drugs in order to continue their addictions.

Drug Screening and Methadone Treatment

Detecting drug abuse is most often accomplished through clinical screenings performed by addiction counselors or others. A clinical screening is an initial gathering and compiling of information to determine if an offender has a problem with alcohol or drug (AOD) abuse and if so, whether a comprehensive clinical assessment is warranted. Screening is accomplished through a structured interview or instruments designed to get offenders to self-report information. Screening also filters out individuals who have medical, legal, or psychological problems that must be addressed before they can participate fully in treatment.

Some agencies use the Psychopathic Personality Inventory (PPI), which is a 56-item, self-report inventory that provides a total score on psychopathy and factor scores on eight dimensions of psychopathy: Machiavellian egocentricity; social potency; cold-heartedness; carefree nonplanfulness; fearlessness; blame externalization; impulsive nonconformity; and stress nonimmunity. The major screening and assessment is a standardized set of procedures designed to: (1) establish baseline information about AOD dependence; (2) assess client readiness for counseling; and (3) serve as treatment planning tools for counseling by identifying (a) the client's high-risk situations for AOD use and (b) the client's coping strengths and weaknesses (Brody and Rosenfeld, 2002).

Clients are considered ready for treatment when they perceive and accept that they have a problem or "own" the problem. In many instances, however, clients do not appear ready for treatment. They tend to minimize, deny, or reject and resist any attempt to help them from counselors. Certainly a part of this resistance or denial is related to their present addictive state, since they are not rational enough to appreciate the logical curative consequences of withdrawal.

Perhaps the most serious problem associated with deterring substance abusers from persisting in their addictions is the physical reactions offenders experience during the withdrawal period. In instances of heroin addiction, for instance, complete and immediate abstinence from heroin causes intense pain throughout the body, complete with nausea, vomiting, and cramping. These symptoms continue for several days. Withdrawal from drugs is not a pleasant experience. Additionally, there is always the possibility that because of one's bodily condition and weakness, the physical stress of withdrawal can be debilitating, causing permanent nerve damage, even death. Therefore, in certain cases where serious addictions to drugs exist, the withdrawal treatment is gradual. Several drugs are used in the withdrawal process. These drugs, such as methadone, are also narcotics, but they cause fewer violent withdrawal symptoms. For instance, methadone is a synthetic narcotic used to treat morphine and heroin addiction. Actually, it is more powerful than morphine, but it has fewer debilitating side effects and the body can withstand adverse withdrawal reactions more easily. In short, drug withdrawal with the assistance of other drugs is more easily tolerated by the body. Many treatment programs that are conducted under controlled hospital conditions utilize methadone and other substances to treat serious addictions.

Some observers believe that the use of methadone in treating heroin and morphine addiction is merely substituting one narcotic for another, and that one can become addicted to methadone. However, this observation neglects the fact that there are other dimensions to one's overall treatment program, which include chemical dependency education, counseling, and other nondrug therapies. Furthermore, offenders receive continuous monitoring and are medically evaluated on a regular basis to determine how their body is responding to treatment. With the volume of drug-abusing offenders entering the criminal justice system, one increasingly used response is the drug court.

Drug Courts and the Drug Court Movement

Drug courts are special courts that are dedicated exclusively to the needs of drug-abusing offenders. They work with prosecutors, defense counsels, treatment professionals, probation officers, and other community agencies to achieve case outcomes for drug abusers that will maximize their successful treatment. Drug courts were established in 1989 in Dade County, Florida. Since 1989 and through 2006, drug courts have been implemented in over 1,000 jurisdictions. More than 350,000 drug-using offenders have participated in drug court programs. Of these, about 65 percent have successfully completed their programs or are actively participating in them (McGuire and Hendrickson, 2006).

One unique feature of drug courts is the specialization they exhibit toward drug-abusing offenders (Fulkerson and Smith, 2006). Most other courts are courts of general criminal jurisdiction, where drug offenders are combined with other types of criminals and punished similarly. However, drug courts recognize the atypicality of drug abusers and their need for special services provided only through an integrated community program involving several helping agencies. Although drug courts are currently enjoying a remarkable degree of success in the treatment of drug-abusing offenders, not everyone is enthusiastic about their emergence and persistence. One criticism is that for some drug abusers, being sent to a drug court for processing is more stigmatizing than therapeutic. Thus, the reintegrative intentions of drug courts may be defeated in part because of their specialization in dealing exclusively with drug offenders. Thus, diversion to drug court may be regarded as discriminatory by some drug abusers, who in turn will reject the reintegrative efforts of those seeking to assist them (Collins, 2006).

Despite this criticism, drug courts show no signs of abating in the near future. If anything, they are being expanded in more diverse areas of the country annually, and at a phenomenal growth rate (Fulkerson and Smith, 2006). Furthermore, drug courts are not exclusively focused on drugs. There are drug courts that address alcohol dependency as well as hard drugs. A unique DWI drug court has been established in Las Cruces, New Mexico, for example, where specially trained court personnel assess first- and second-time DWI offenders for symptoms of alcoholism. A subsequent treatment program is prescribed by the judge, which includes individual, group, and family counseling sessions.

One feature of drug courts is that they provide for more consistent and frequent monitoring of participating offenders who are ordered into particular therapies. Not only is the supervision more comprehensive, but there are increased rates of retention in treatment and reduced drug use and criminal behavior while participants are in these programs. Drug courts are designed to handle more serious offenders, many of whom have prior criminal histories with a myriad of physical and mental health needs. Recidivism rates almost always decline following one's participation in such programs (Collins, 2006).

The Drug Court Model.   A general model typically followed by drug courts has the following characteristics: (1) a single drug court judge and staff who provide leadership and focus; (2) expedited adjudication through early identification of appropriate program participants and referral to treatment as soon as possible after arrest; (3) intensive long-term treatment and aftercare for appropriate drug-using offenders; (4) comprehensive and well-coordinated supervision through regular status hearings before a single drug court judge to monitor treatment progress through program compliance; (5) increased defendant accountability through a series of graduated sanctions and rewards; and (6) mandatory and frequent drug testing (Champion, 2005).

A study of 24 drug courts by Columbia University's National Center on Addiction and Substance Abuse (CASA) has provided one of the first major academic reviews and analyses of drug court effectiveness. How has the model worked with offenders? Essentially, the study found that drug courts provide closer, more comprehensive supervision and much more frequent drug testing and monitoring than conventional forms of community supervision, such as probation or parole. More important, drug use and criminal behavior are substantially reduced while offenders are participating in drug court programs. The CASA study further summarizes findings from older and newer drug courts. The results are fairly consistent in that:

- Drug courts have been successful in engaging and retaining felony offenders in programmatic and treatment services who have substantial substance abuse and criminal histories but little prior treatment engagement.
- Drug courts provide more comprehensive and closer supervision of the drug-using offender than other forms of community supervision.
- Drug use and criminal behavior are substantially reduced while clients are participating in drug court.
- Criminal behavior is lower after program participation, especially for graduates, although few studies have tracked recidivism for more than one year post-program.
- Drug courts generate cost savings, at least in the short term, from reduced jail/prison use, reduced criminality, and lower criminal justice system costs.
- Drug courts have been successful in bridging the gap between the court and the treatment/public health systems and spurring greater cooperation among the various agencies and personnel within the criminal justice system, as well as between the criminal justice system and the community.

The cost effectiveness of drug courts has been assessed. In Multnomah County, Oregon, a program known as the STOP Drug Court Diversion Program was evaluated. A sample of 150 participants was compared with three other groups, including STOP noncompleters (persons who failed drug tests or did not appear at their status hearings). For every taxpayer dollar spent on programming costs of STOP, a $2.50 savings to taxpayers was realized. If victimization costs are factored in, then the cost savings rises to about $10 for every dollar spent on programming.

The Jefferson County (Kentucky) Drug Court Program. An example of one drug court in action is the Jefferson County Drug Court Program in Kentucky. Based on the Dade County, Florida, model, this model diverts first-time drug possession offenders into a 12-month community treatment program that includes acupuncture and the development of social and educational skills (Jefferson County Drug Court, 2006). It is monitored directly by the drug court judge, who helps to supervise the offender's treatment program. The model breaks down the traditional adversarial roles of prosecutors and defense attorneys. If the judge believes that offenders are trying to break the pattern of addiction, then the offenders remain in treatment even after they test positive for drugs several times. Therefore, the treatment program may be continued indefinitely until the offender successfully completes the program.

The drug court judge extends judicial oversight throughout all phases of the program. Clients are required to attend sessions of drug court on a schedule set by the judge. Before weekly sessions of drug court, the judge is provided with individualized progress reports for all participants. During these court sessions, the judge reviews the program progress of each client. Upon review, the judge may (1) continue client participation; (2) permanently remove the client from the program; or (3) remain the client to a term of jail incarceration for failure to meet program requirements.

Participation in drug court is voluntary. Referrals are made to the drug court from prosecutors or public or private attorneys. Clients must be 18 years of age and meet the following criteria established by the prosecutor:

1. Possession versus trafficking cases: preference is given to cocaine possession cases; trafficking cases are considered after a review of possession cases.
2. Prior drug arrests: defendants with multiple trafficking arrests in their history are not considered.
3. No history of violent offenses: offenders with a history of violent crimes are not eligible for inclusion in the program.
4. Eligibility: only Jefferson County cases are eligible for inclusion.
5. Police approval: the lead officer in the case is consulted in the decision to recommend a client for diversion into the drug court program.
6. Quantity of cocaine: any offender in possession of one or more ounces of cocaine is not eligible for drug court; any offender with five or more grams of cocaine is presumed to be trafficking in drugs and is placed on the trafficking list of offenders eligible for program review (Jefferson County Drug Court, 2006).

After all applicants are screened and meet the initial screening criteria, they must undergo a psychological assessment. The purpose of the assessment is to determine whether the client is amenable to treatment and does not pose a risk to the community. Drug court participants must abide by all program conditions. All drug court participants must be punctual, attend all required program sessions, be nonviolent, refrain from attending treatment sessions while under the influence of drugs, and behave lawfully. The aim is to create and maintain a receptive treatment environment, promote prosocial behavior, and establish a sense of individual accountability among clients. The various treatment programs offered through the drug court include acupuncture, meditation, individual counseling, group therapy, Alcoholics Anonymous (AA), Narcotics Anonymous (NA), and chemical dependency education.

There are three treatment phases, described below.

Phase I: Detoxification (10 days)

1. Four random drug tests
2. Attendance at a minimum of five weekly meetings of AA/NA

3. Participation in all individual and group counseling sessions as determined by program staff

4. Optional acupuncture and/or meditation sessions

In order to move to phase II, the client must receive a maximum of four negative drug screens, attend all assigned individual and group therapy sessions, and attend all weekly AA/NA meetings.

Phase II: Stabilization (108 days)

1. Acupuncture and/or meditation sessions as needed/requested

2. Two weekly drug tests (a minimum number of positive drug screenings during each of the first four weeks and no positive drug screens by the sixth week of this phase are necessary to move to phase III)

3. Attendance at a minimum of four AA/NA meetings as prescribed by the treatment plan; clients must obtain an AA/NA sponsor

4. Attendance at all individual and group counseling sessions as prescribed by the treatment plan

5. Significant progress toward meeting treatment plan goals as determined by treatment program staff and the drug court judge

Phase III: Aftercare (six months)

1. Acupuncture and/or meditation sessions as requested by the client

2. Random drug tests

3. Participation in educational, vocational, remedial, and other training programs as specified in the individual treatment plan

4. Individual and group counseling as needed

5. Attendance at a minimum of three AA/NA meetings per week

6. Maintenance of and regular contact with a full-time AA/NA sponsor

In order to graduate from the drug court program, clients must meet the following requirements: (1) remaining drug-free as shown by the results of their drug tests in the last two months of this phase; and (2) securing or maintaining employment or enrolling or maintaining enrollment in an educational program and/or engaging in full-time parenting responsibilities. Only those clients who have paid all accrued fees will be permitted to graduate from drug court (Jefferson County Drug Court, 2006).

Results from the Jefferson County Drug Court Program were based on an analysis of 237 clients who were screened and included in the program. They were compared with a sample of 76 persons who were screened but not included in the program. Reconviction was used as the recidivism measure and indicator of program failure. There were significant differences in failure rates of graduates compared with nonparticipants. Graduates of drug court had a reconviction rate of 13 percent, while the reconviction rate of the comparison group was 55 percent. This finding suggests that the Jefferson County Drug Court treatment program has been successful. However, the graduates were also compared according to whether they were subsequently charged with a drug-/alcohol-related offense. This time, about 43 percent of the graduates had been charged during the follow-up period; however, these figures are slightly lower than the nongraduates, of whom 46 percent were charged with new drug offenses. Thus, nearly half of all drug court graduates were unable to avoid relapses back to drugs. One recommendation was that drug court graduates should continue to receive regular drug testing and monitoring in order to maintain their resistance to drugs (Jefferson County Drug Court, 2006).

Drug court programs in other jurisdictions have had similar success rates. The Brooklyn, New York, Treatment Court was commenced in 1996. Over 1,000 drug abusers were placed in treatment programs by this drug court during the interval 1996–1999. Two-thirds were still actively involved in the program, and about one-third had completed 180 days of treatment. While there were relapses, relapse rates were similar to the Jefferson County, Kentucky, rates of about 50 percent. And in Riverside, California, a drug court operated a Recovery Opportunity Center (ROC), which was a drug treatment day program. There were 103 ROC clients who were followed up after 20 months from program admission. Of the graduates, 58 percent showed no signs of substance abuse. Recidivism rates for graduates were about 15 percent, again comparable with the Jefferson County program (Jefferson County Drug Court, 2006).

COMMUNITY PROGRAMS FOR SPECIAL-NEEDS OFFENDERS

Therapeutic Communities

A **therapeutic community** is a treatment model in which all activities, both formal and informal, are viewed as interrelated interventions that address the multidimensional disorder of the whole person. These activities include educational and therapeutic meetings and groups, as well as interpersonal and social activities of the community. Within this theoretical framework, social and psychological change evolves as a dynamic interaction between the individual and the peer community, its context of activities, and expectations for participation (Deitsch et al., 2001:26).

Therapeutic communities are often mandated by the courts or parole boards for persons with particular substance-abuse problems or chemical dependencies. For instance, 720 offenders were mandated by the court for drug treatment into three highly structured therapeutic communities in the northeastern United States during the period 1990–1993. They were subjected to a battery of tests, including the Circumstances, Motivation, Readiness, and Suitability attitudinal scale. In the cases of these court-placed offenders, the periods of their detention were unspecified. It remained at the discretion of program authorities to determine when they had successfully completed their programs by participating in community programming as outlined by their therapeutic community plan. Many therapeutic community models are commenced in prison or jail settings and subsequently continued in an offender's city or town. Therefore, therapeutic community clientele have the benefit of continuing their treatment and programming under limited supervision following their release from incarceration. Often, these therapeutic community programs are designed for offenders with chemical dependencies rather than for mentally ill patients (Stohr et al., 2002). Programs have been established in Texas, Washington, DC, and Delaware.

A Delaware-based therapeutic community has been created, known as CREST. CREST is prison-based and is applied to females who are encouraged to form networks of support for one another. During an experimental period in the mid-1990s, 41 female participants were involved in CREST, including a control group of 39 female work releasees. Both groups were compared while in prison, as well as in 6- and 18-month follow-ups after they were released from incarceration. Women participating in the CREST program were more successful in remaining law-abiding, with a 39 percent recidivism rate. However, those who were on standard work release had a recidivism rate of 50 percent. Thus, the likelihood of relapse was greater for those who were not a part of the CREST program (Farrell, 2000). A similar study of substance-abusing clients was conducted in Washington, DC.

For POs, therapeutic community involvement of parolees alleviates some of their pressure to locate and integrate offender programming. It is already in place for some of these offenders. Thus, a PO's job is made much easier by simply having to supervise offenders already networked within their therapeutic community environments. A PO's work might consist primarily of performing periodic and random drug or curfew checks. The concept of therapeutic community is being considered and applied in countries outside of the United States. It appears to be gaining in popularity as an intervention for persons with serious addiction problems (Thomas, Holzer, and Wall, 2002).

Alcoholics Anonymous, Narcotics Anonymous, and Gamblers Anonymous Programs.

As we have seen in therapeutic community and drug court interventions, Alcoholics Anonymous and Narcotics Anonymous programs have played major roles as community support mechanisms in order to provide social support for recovering alcohol and drug abusers. Alcoholics Anonymous and Narcotics Anonymous programs are designed to provide information and guidance for those with alcohol and drug dependencies. They are offered to inmates in prisons and jails as well as in their communities. They both involve a series of steps where participants admit that they are powerless to control their cravings for alcohol or drugs. These programs are frequently linked with probation and parole programs. Other programs deal with offenders who have been convicted of domestic violence–related offenses (Harrell et al., 2006). Judges and parole boards often require probationers and parolees to attend their meetings as one of their special conditions of probation or parole.

Similar to the 12-step program used by Alcoholics Anonymous, the 12-step program for Narcotics Anonymous is as follows:

1. We admitted that we were powerless over our addiction, that our lives had become unmanageable.
2. We came to believe that a Power greater than ourselves could restore us to sanity.
3. We made a decision to turn our will and our lives over to the care of God as we understood Him.
4. We made a searching and fearless moral inventory of ourselves.
5. We admitted to God, to ourselves, and to another human being the exact nature of our wrongs.
6. We were entirely ready to have God remove all these defects of character.
7. We humbly asked Him to remove our shortcomings.
8. We made a list of all persons we had harmed, and became willing to make amends to them all.

9. We made direct amends to such people whenever possible, except when to do so would injure them or others.

10. We continue to take personal inventory and when we were wrong promptly admitted it.

11. We sought through prayer and meditation to improve our conscious contact with God as we understood Him, praying only for knowledge of His will for us and the power to carry that out.

12. Having had a spiritual awakening as a result of these steps, we tried to carry this message to addicts, and practice these principles in all our affairs.

Meetings of these groups are usually announced in local newspapers daily throughout the nation. Persons are advised of their street locations and times. Some meetings are "closed," meaning that they are not open to the general public. These are occasions where permanent membership can band together and discuss intimate details of their alcohol and narcotics addictions with one another. Other meetings are open, and the public is invited. Only those with drug or alcohol dependencies are encouraged to attend these open meetings, although it is unlikely that someone wishing to see what goes on at these meetings would be barred from participating. During the meetings, which usually last one hour, each person is given an opportunity to stand, identify themselves by first name only, and indicate the nature of their addiction. Some attendees take this opportunity to apologize to the group for their addictions. They elicit acceptance and empathy from other attendees. At the end of the meeting, a prayer is uttered, with all of those willing to do so linking hands in a large circle.

The religious components in both Alcoholics Anonymous and Narcotics Anonymous have alienated certain drug abusers who are atheists and do not believe in God. Several options have been made available to them, including various secular organizations that are organized along lines similar to those of AA and NA.

The value of AA and NA as viable interventions has been criticized. Where convicted offenders are required to attend such meetings as a part of their probation programs, there is no way that they can be induced to participate actively in these meetings once there. They sign a card signifying their attendance. There is no pressure on them to become actively involved in discussions. No one can compel them to say anything about themselves. Nevertheless, POs continue to encourage those with alcohol and drug dependencies to attend these meetings, and attend them with great frequency.

Increasingly recognized as a serious addiction is gambling. Where it is permitted, gambling is not illegal. Nevertheless, it is addictive in much the same sense that alcohol and drugs are addictive. In many areas of the country, organizations have been established to treat gambling addiction, especially where it has been related to criminal activity. Persons who gamble may lose a lot of money. They may resort to crime to obtain additional money to pursue their gambling addiction. Usually, Gamblers Anonymous organizations have included 12-step programs similar to AA and NA, although they also include educational programming emphasizing personal financial counseling. Individual and group therapy also accompany Gamblers Anonymous programming, depending on the jurisdiction. Gamblers Anonymous organizations have been in existence for several decades.

GANG MEMBERS

It is difficult to understand why youth gangs form and perpetuate themselves over long periods of time. Gangs emerge, grow, dissolve, and disappear for reasons that are poorly understood. Gangs are defined as self-formed associations of peers, united by mutual interests, with identifiable leadership and internal organization, who act collectively or as individuals to achieve specific purposes, including the conduct of illegal activity and control of a particular territory, facility, or enterprise. They may include either adults or juveniles.

Several problems confront POs who must supervise gang members. When gang members have been incarcerated for a period of time, they emerge from prisons or jails and seem to increase the level of violence among their street gang affiliate memberships. POs must interact with these gang members, often on their own turfs, where gang members utilize hand signs and special language to deceive POs and mislead them. There are also dangers whenever POs enter known gang-controlled neighborhoods for the purpose of visiting other gang-member clients. It has been reported that over 50 percent of all gang members in the United States have used firearms at one time or another during the commission of a violent crime. This is one of the reasons many POs have sought to carry firearms when they make house visits to their clients. About half of all states have approved firearms use for their POs, in part because these are potential dangers to PO lives and security.

Gangs are prevalent in schools throughout the United States. Many of these students bring firearms to their schools at different times. Illicit drug use among gang members on school property is reported. Gangs also create a pattern of resistance to change. Thus, when POs attempt to intervene and intercede with any particular offender, there is an overpowering sense of betrayal on the part of the gang member-client if he or she accepts the PO's suggested intervention. This does not always occur. But POs encounter resistance from more than a few gang member-clients nevertheless.

Many gangs are involved in illicit activities, such as dealing drugs or transporting firearms. When POs supervise gang members, there is always the possibility that they are continuing their involvement in these illicit activities. However, actual drug use by probationers or parolees can easily be checked with various devices at random times. Thus, many gang members are smart enough not to get caught doing drugs while serving time in probation or parole programs. Despite these checks, POs often regard their interventions with gang members as unproductive, since it is difficult to overcome the influence of gang membership. Self-definitions of gang membership and involvement in delinquent activities are strong (Bjerregaard, 2002).

The National Youth Gang Survey is disturbing in a number of respects. First, it demonstrates the pervasiveness of gangs in American society. Second, it shows the strength gangs have in virtually every locality where they exist. Third, it demonstrates the interaction between prison/jail inmates and street gangs. And fourth, it illustrates the diverse forms of criminal activities associated with gang membership. As we have seen, in 2006 there were at least 1 million known gang members in over 3,000 gangs in the United States.

What is even more disturbing is that during the last half-century since the 1950s, there have been numerous changes in the structure, organization, and activities of gangs. Gangs are increasingly lethal in their choice of weaponry, which often includes automatic weapons used in conventional warfare between nations. Other changes include the fact that no longer are gangs confined to large urban centers. They have branched out into smaller communities and towns. Furthermore, more gang members are remaining in their gangs well into their adult years. More gangs are graduating into large-scale drug trafficking and gun sales both nationally and internationally. Gangs are big business, and many gangs are increasingly organized according to corporate structural models, complete with executive boards and chairmen.

The public is more frequently aware of gang presence by the incidence of drive-by shootings that occur in larger cities, such as Los Angeles, New York, and Chicago. Often, these drive-by shootings involve deaths of innocent bystanders who are standing in close proximity to rival gang members who are the intended targets. Relatively little is known by the public about gang involvement in large-scale drug trafficking and other criminal enterprises.

Considerable investigation has been conducted concerning why persons become affiliated with gangs initially. Psychological and social maladjustments are often cited, such as low self-esteem and being an isolate in schools and other social settings (Sutherland and Shepherd, 2002). Both male and female gang members appear to have joined gangs for essentially the same reasons. Yet other persons join gangs for mutual protection. They feel safe where there is strength in numbers.

POs have an uneasy relation with clients who are affiliated with gangs. We have already examined some of these reasons earlier in this chapter. Gangs exert considerable social and psychological influence over their memberships, and this influence often undermines PO attempts to change the attitudes of gang member-clients. Furthermore, there is the possibility and likelihood that gang member-clients will continue to engage in illicit activities of their gangs without PO knowledge.

Community and PO response to gangs and gang interventions are usually broken down into the following categories: (1) community organization or neighborhood mobilization; (2) social intervention, which involves youth outreach and street work counseling; (3) opportunities provision, which involves jobs, job training, and education; (4) suppression, which involves arrest, incarceration, and supervision; and (5) organizational development, which involves adapting organizations to facilitate dealing with gangs, such as the development of gang units in police departments.

Increasingly, gang intervention programs are emphasizing partnerships with different agencies, including schools. The GREAT (Gang Resistance Education and Training) program involves school resource officers and works in conjunction with gang units from police departments to educate non-gang members in schools to avoid gangs. Other programs are geared toward younger youths.

In order for early childhood or adolescent programs to maximize their effectiveness, they must target those persons most susceptible to gang membership. These are known as at-risk children. One way of identifying at-risk factors is to study the characteristics and background of known gang members and work backward to non-gang adolescents with those same characteristics. For example, gang members exhibit the following characteristics: they are largely male, socially inept, maladjusted, sexually promiscuous, suffering from low self-esteem, ethnic minorities, exhibit sociopathic personalities, and are closely associated with antisocial peers (Frankfort-Howard and Romm, 2002). Geographically, areas characterized with high unemployment, poverty, the absence of meaningful jobs, and economically distressed neighborhoods seemed to be breeding grounds for prospective gang members. Clearly, the identification of at-risk youths is at best diffuse. Given this diffuseness, a comprehensive gang model has been recommended, which is a multifaceted approach targeting individual youths, peer groups, families, and the community (Brownfield and Thompson, 2002).

What can POs do to intervene where gang members form a portion of their clientele? One program that was initiated in Boston is Operation Night Light. Commenced in 1992, Operation Night Light is a specialized unit with two goals: (1) curbing gang violence and (2) enforcing court-ordered conditions of probation. The program involves teams of police officers and probation officers who visit the homes of probationers who are known gang members. The objective of these visits is to ensure program compliance with curfews and to conduct visual inspections of one's premises for illegal contraband, cellular telephones, illegal beepers, and other items that might be used for illicit purposes. Operation Night Light, which eventually became Operation Tracker, has been successful enough to eliminate the blind spots of communication between the police and POs.

What seems to have emerged from Operation Tracker and similar programs is that in order to maximize their effectiveness, POs need to be in greater contact with police organizations and communicate with them. Probation officers need to equip themselves with the knowledge and techniques to recognize the presence of gang activity. One method of obtaining such knowledge is increased communication with various criminal justice agencies, primarily police departments. It is the case that whenever police officers stop a person on the street for investigation, they may not know that the person is a parolee or probationer. With more frequent communication between POs and police officers, these communication gaps can be narrowed such that offender accountability can be improved.

Tattoo Removal Programs

Whenever gang members wish to leave gangs, they often find it hard to do so. If they relocate to other regions of the country, chances are there will be affiliate gangs in those new territories who will recognize those who recently moved there. One of the telltale signs of gang membership is a gang **tattoo.** Gang members place tattoos on their hands, arms, feet, faces, and other places on their bodies as symbols of their gang affiliation. If these tattoos are in conspicuous places, then it attracts the attention of affiliate gang members. One of the most frequent locations where tattoos are given to new gang members is in prisons and jails. Other inmates use crude instruments to install permanent tattoos on their new members. The tattoo is seemingly a symbol of ownership, implying that the gang owns the gang member forever. Once a gang member, always a gang member, or so some gang members would like their membership to believe. Some gangs are so deeply entrenched in one's social and personal world that they will not let anyone leave their gang under penalty of death. Gang membership is often taken that seriously. More than a few deaths have been the result of persons attempting to leave their gangs.

Increasingly, POs and police agencies are offering to remove these symbols of gang membership for those desiring to detach themselves from gangs. The Ventura County, California, Sheriff's Department has a **tattoo removal program,** where gang members can have their tattoos removed at no charge through laser surgery. According to this program, whenever a gang member gets smart and wants to get out of the gang and find employment, it is almost impossible to do so. This is because employers fear gang members and can easily recognize them through the tattoos they wear. Tattoos are essentially a stigma that follows them through life. They cannot get a job, nor can they have a lasting relationship with anyone. Thus, they cannot become productive members of society.

The tattoo removal program operated by the Ventura County Sheriff's Department consists of the following process. First, gang members must attend a tattoo removal screening. They are interviewed about why they want their tattoos removed. They are asked about where they plan to relocate to escape contact with their former gang associates. They must perform a certain number of community service hours in order to pay for the removal of their tattoos. Once they have been interviewed and performed the necessary hours of community service, which may include graffiti removal of their own gangs' symbols, they will have their tattoos removed free of charge. Thus, they can detach themselves from gang membership by having the most visible signs of gangs removed from their bodies. Once these tattoos are removed, these persons can leave their communities and establish new lives elsewhere where others do not know about their prior affiliation with gangs (Ventura County Sheriff's Department, 2001). Tattoo removal programs similar to the one operated by the Ventura County Sheriff's Department are operated in other parts of the country with positive results.

SUMMARY

Special-needs offenders present diverse problems for probation agencies and paroling authorities throughout the United States. Special-needs offenders include those who are drug- or alcohol-dependent, the mentally ill, sex offenders and child sexual abusers, developmentally disabled offenders, and offenders with HIV/AIDS or other communicable diseases such as tuberculosis. POs have increasing responsibilities for networking among various community-based agencies that offer diverse services for offender-clients. Many communities do not have adequate services that coincide with some of the problems manifested by offenders. Attempts are being made to individualize offender treatments, to provide family counseling and parenting education as a means of preventing family violence, and to provide offenders with parenting skills so that better childhood interventions can be employed (McMahon and Pence, 2003). Supervising offenders is hazardous work. POs need to acquire greater training to anticipate the types of offenders they will supervise and how different psychological and social offender problems should be resolved whenever they arise.

Mentally ill offenders are abundant in our prisons and jails. Many of these persons become clients of POs, and POs must learn different ways of supervising these clients whose behaviors are often violent and unpredictable. Another class of special needs offender is the sex offender. While sex offenders make up only a small proportion of jail and prison inmates as well as clients of POs, they are regarded as a most heinous aggregate by citizens generally. Thus, POs have increased responsibilities to monitor sex offenders of different types very closely as a way of protecting the community from them. Most, however, have no prior criminal histories, are nonviolent, and pose little or no danger to others.

Drug- and/or alcohol-dependent offenders are associated with over 80 percent of all criminal activity and arrests. The likelihood of relapse is greatest among this offender aggregate. Therefore, POs must monitor their progress closely, often by administering urinalyses and other types of tests to determine the presence of illegal substances. Another class of offender is the client with HIV/AIDS and/or tuberculosis. Tuberculosis cases have been rising in the United States at an alarming rate. While POs have a low likelihood of contracting HIV/AIDS from their clients, they are at far greater risk when interacting with tuberculosis-infected clients.

Gang members comprise another offender category that requires special treatment and supervision. POs must be cognizant of gang signs and symbols as well as the dangers of entering gang territories for the purpose of visiting their gang-member clientele. Developmentally disabled offenders must be accommodated as well. While there aren't many of these offenders in the population, their numbers are growing. POs must increasingly network with various community agencies to see that these persons have their needs met appropriately.

Various types of interventions have been recommended for each of these offender groupings. For sex offenders, community treatment programs and sex therapy classes are often required as a part of their probation or parole programs. Offenders with HIV/AIDS or tuberculosis must be linked with appropriate agencies so that they can learn how to avoid transmitting their diseases to others. Thus, educational courses of various kinds are recommended or required as a part of their therapeutic treatment.

The largest aggregate of offenders under PO supervision have drug or alcohol dependencies. In recent years, drug courts have been established in most jurisdictions. These drug courts are specialized courts that hear only DWI or drug cases. Appropriate treatments are recommended or required. Drug courts work closely with a network of persons and agencies to ensure that drug-dependent offenders receive appropriate instruction and treatment as needed. Often, counseling on an individual or group basis is recommended. Several drug court programs in different parts of the United States were described.

Increasingly, therapeutic communities are being established in different communities as treatment models for persons with different types of addictions or dependencies. A therapeutic community refers to multiple interventions and agencies networked in such a way so as to achieve a positive result for participating clients (Hiller et al., 2002). Therapeutic communities are often commenced in prisons and jails, although they continue once offenders leave incarceration on probation or parole. Assisting offenders in their rehabilitation are private self-help organizations, such as Alcoholics Anonymous, Narcotics Anonymous, and Gamblers Anonymous. Often, attendance at these meetings is compulsory for probationers or parolees with drug or alcohol or gambling addictions.

Gang members are pervasive in American society. Their numbers, organizational structure, and operational sophistication are such that many POs find it difficult to relate with them. Learning programs are established to inform and advise POs about the latest advancements in gang psychology and methodology. Police agencies and parole/probation departments are working closer together in those areas where gang presence is especially strong. Greater communication between these agencies assists POs in heightening offender accountability. If gang members want to leave their gangs, there are tattoo removal programs to assist them free of charge in ridding themselves of telltale tattoos that often are used to control and manipulate them. Without identifying tattoos, such persons can move to other parts of the country and start new lives without the fear of being recognized by other gang members and enlisted involuntarily into illicit gang activities.

QUESTIONS FOR REVIEW

1. Who are special-needs offenders? What problems do they pose for supervising POs?

2. How do probationers and parolees with HIV/AIDS or tuberculosis pose special supervisory problems for POs?

3. Who are developmentally disabled offenders? What special provisions for these offenders must be made by supervising POs?

4. How many mentally ill offenders are under the supervision of POs throughout the United States? In what ways do mentally ill offenders pose a danger to POs during their supervision?

5. Why are sex offenders, who are relatively few in number compared with other offender groups, given so much attention by the media and public? How does this attention affect how POs supervise them?

6. Identify some of the special programs that have been created for sex offenders and are a mandatory part of their probation or parole programs.

7. Drug- and alcohol-dependent offenders are associated with 80 percent of all crimes committed. Why is this offender aggregate troublesome for their supervising POs? What is the rate of relapse among drug- and alcohol-dependent offenders?

8. Sam Torres recommends a continuum of sanctions against drug/alcohol abusers. Identify some of these sanctions.

9. What are Alcoholics Anonymous, Narcotics Anonymous, and Gamblers Anonymous? What is their relation to religion, if any? How do they operate in relation to various offender treatment programs?

10. What is a tattoo removal program and what are its objectives?

SUGGESTED READINGS

Addy, Jim and Travis Parker (2006). "The Lancaster County, Nebraska Mental Health Jail Diversion Project." *American Jails* **20**:27–35.

Bowker, Art and Michael Gray (2004). "An Introduction to the Supervision of the Cybersex Offender." *Federal Probation* **68**:3–8.

Cramer, Martha L. and Shirley C. Scott (2006). "Seventy Percenters: An Innovative Domestic Violence Program at the Pima County Jail." *Corrections Today* **68**:32–33.

Cumming, Georgia and Robert McGrath (2005). *Supervision of the Sex Offender: Community Management, Risk Assessment, and Treatment.* Lexington, KY: American Probation and Parole Association.

Kielar, Marie (2006). "Collaboration for Success: Denver County's Justice Center Program." *Corrections Today* **68**:38–41.

Macher, Abe M. (2006). "Clenbuterol Adulterated Heroin." *American Jails* **20**:17–20.

Riley, William (2006). "Interpreting Gang Tattoos." *Corrections Today* **68**:46–53.

INTERNET CONNECTIONS

Adcare Correctional Drug and Alcohol Treatment Programs
http://www.adcare.com/correc/

Addictions page
http://www.well.com/user/woa

Alcoholics Anonymous
http://www.alcoholics-anomymous.org

International Institute on Special Needs Offenders
http://www.iisno.org.uk/

MAN Domestic Violence Offender Treatment Program
http://www.themangroup.org/downloads/Offender_Treat_Recs4-17.pdf

Shadow Track Technologies
http://www.shadowtrack.com/?sources=Overture

Smart Recovery
http://www.smartrecovery.org

Special Offenders and Special-Needs Offenders
http://www.shsu.edu/~icc_rjh/364f00.htm

Texas Council on Offenders with Mental Impairments
http://www.tdcj.state.tx.us/tcomi-contcare.htm

2003 International Conference on Special Needs Offenders
http://www.specialneedsoffenders.org/aboutus.html

CHAPTER 13 | *Juvenile Probation and Parole*

Chapter Outline

Chapter Objectives

As the result of reading this chapter, the following objectives will be realized:

1. Defining and describing juveniles and juvenile delinquency, including its various forms.
2. Identifying status offenses and the process of deinstitutionalization of status offenses.
3. Examining the juvenile justice system, including its various components and dispositional alternatives.
4. Highlighting landmark juvenile cases involving U.S. Supreme Court decisions extending various rights to juveniles.
5. Describing the nature of juvenile offenses and offense seriousness.
6. Describing various probation programs for juveniles, including diversion and probation.
7. Identifying various detention and parole programs available for juveniles.
8. Highlighting several important trends in juvenile parole

• *DePugh was a New York juvenile accused of a violent crime and convicted in criminal court. At the time of his sentencing, DePugh asked the court to grant him youthful offender status. The judge rejected the request and sentenced DePugh as an adult. DePugh appealed and a New York appeals court heard the case. It was noted by the appeals court that the judge relied on information contained in a pre-sentence investigation report, which included both mitigating and aggravating factors, and adequately explained the court's reasons for denying youthful offender status. The appeals court upheld the judge's order to sentence DePugh as an adult offender and noted that the sentence imposed on DePugh was not unusually harsh or severe. [People v. DePugh, 791 N.Y.S.2d 234 (N.Y.Sup.App.Div.March) (2005)].*

• *Christopher M. was a California juvenile adjudicated delinquent on a robbery charge that was also interpreted as a hate crime. Christopher M. was placed on probation, with one of the conditions being that all records relating to his medical and psychological treatment be made available to the court and probation personnel. Christopher M. objected, claiming that such disclosure of his personal information was a violation of his right to privacy and thus unconstitutional. Furthermore, Christopher M. claimed that the information between himself and his psychotherapist was protected by the psychotherapist–patient privilege. The appeals court upheld the judge's order to disclose Christopher M.'s information. It cited Christopher M.'s lack of empathy toward others; his gang-banging activities; his participation in criminal conduct that involved violence against innocent victims; his unwillingness to take responsibility for his antisocial behavior; his substance abuse problems; and his refusal to participate in counseling and substance abuse programs. Granting the probation department and personnel access to Christopher M.'s personal records will help to further the department's interest in his rehabilitation and reformation, treatment in succeeding in helping him to overcome his psychological, behavioral, and substance abuse problems. Disclosure of confidential information to relevant parties in the probation department also enables the department to deal more effectively with Christopher M.'s antisocial behavior, which was the very purpose of the psychotherapy Christopher M. received. Given the limited scope of the disclosure to probation department authorities, it could not be said that the probation condition violated the psychotherapist–patient privilege. [In re Christopher M.,* 26 *Cal.Rptr.3d 61 (Cal.App.March) (2005)].*

- *M.J.A. was a Texas juvenile who was placed in a foster home as a condition of his probation. M.J.A. objected to the out-of-home placement and the matter was appealed. The appellate court agreed with the judge and permitted the out-of-home placement, arguing that the juvenile had been adjudicated on a charge of burglary. The court heard testimony from M.J.A.'s neighbors, all of whom indicated the risk he posed if left at home. Even M.J.A.'s mother testified that she would be unable to control M.J.A. if he were left at home. Under these circumstances, there was ample support for the out-of-home placement where M.J.A. would be able to receive the quality of care and level of support and supervision needed to meet the conditions of his probation. [Matter of M.J.A.,* 155 *S.W.3d 575 (Tex.App.Dec.) (2004)].*

- *J.F. was a Florida juvenile placed on probation for a property offense. Subsequently, J.F.'s probation officer was notified by an informant that she had seen J.F. driving in a car with various stolen items. The probation officer reported this hearsay information to the court where the judge ordered J.F. arrested. Subsequently, J.F.'s probation program was revoked as the result of the testimony from the probation officer. J.F.'s attorney objected, arguing that hearsay evidence and an arrest without any supporting evidence do not constitute proper grounds for a revocation of the youth's probation program. An appellate court heard J.F.'s case and reinstated his probation program. The appellate court declared that the probation officer who gave evidence at J.F.'s probation revocation hearing did not personally see J.F. in a car with stolen items. Rather, this officer was relaying information received from another person. Probation revocation cannot be based on hearsay evidence. Probation may be revoked upon a combination of hearsay and nonhearsay evidence, and furthermore, probation may not be revoked merely on the basis of the fact that a probationer has been arrested. Because there was insufficient evidence of the juvenile's commission of a new crime of grand theft, the order revoking his probation had to be reversed. [J.F. v. State,* 889 *So.2d 130 (Fla.Dist.App.Dec.) (2004)].*

- *B.S. was a Florida juvenile on parole. At one point, information came to the attention of B.S.'s parole officer that B.S. had violated one or more conditions of his parole program. An order for his commitment was filed, but B.S.'s defense attorney objected, raising several arguments that prompted a stay of his commitment. Shortly thereafter, however, and without any oral argument, the stay of B.S.'s commitment order was lifted and B.S. was confined in a Florida industrial school. B.S.'s attorney filed an appeal, which was subsequently heard by an appellate court. The court set aside the order that had lifted B.S.'s stay of commitment, declaring that B.S. was entitled to the basic rudiments of due process, which had been ignored. The state had failed to provide B.S. with written notice of his parole violations. Furthermore, it had denied his attorney's discovery request as well as a demand from B.S. for a statement of the alleged violations committed. Also, B.S.'s counsel was permitted no time to prepare a defense for B.S. even though he has requested a continuance, which was denied. In short, B.S. had been denied his due process rights and his order of parole revocation had to be set aside. [B.S. v. State,* 886 *So. 2d 1062 (Fla.Dist.App.Nov.) (2004)].*

INTRODUCTION

This chapter is about juvenile probation and parole. There is little consistency among jurisdictions throughout the United States about how juvenile probation and parole are handled. No national policies exist that apply to every jurisdiction. Thus, it is impossible to make blanket generalizations about the juvenile probation and parole process, except in the broadest of terms. The first section describes juveniles and juvenile delinquency. How are juvenile delinquents defined? Another class of juvenile is the status offender. Status offenders differ in several significant ways from juvenile delinquents. These differences are described. The deinstitutionalization of status offenders is a movement that commenced in the 1970s to remove status offenders from incarcerative settings normally used for more serious juveniles. While many states have implemented the deinstitutionalization of status offenders, other states are either undecided on the issue or are moving slowly toward such a policy. This policy is described and its significance and relevance for affected juveniles is explained.

The second section presents an overview of the juvenile justice system, describing briefly the origins and functions of juvenile courts. The doctrine of parens patriae, inherited from England, has had a profound influence on juvenile courts in the United States. The juvenile justice system or process is presented from the point of juvenile arrests, intake, petitions and adjudicatory proceedings, and judicial dispositions. Various dispositional options available to juvenile court judges are listed and described. These include nominal, conditional, and custodial dispositional options. The next section of the chapter examines various juvenile probation and parole programs. It is not intended to be comprehensive, since juvenile justice textbooks cover this information in far greater detail. Nevertheless, several key programs are described that provide the reader with a broad perspective of available juvenile probation and parole programs.

The final section describes the juvenile probation and parole revocation process. Almost no U.S. Supreme Court action has been taken regarding revocations of juvenile probation and parole. Often, state and local jurisdictions have followed the guidelines of probation and parole revocations set forth by various precedent-setting landmark cases for adult criminals. They included *Mempa v. Rhay* (1967), *Gagnon v. Scarpelli* (1973), and *Morrissey v. Brewer* (1972), described in earlier chapters. Juvenile courts and revocation proceedings are not bound by these adult cases, however. But the cases do serve as guidelines for juvenile courts to follow at their option. Several state cases involving juvenile probation and parole revocation are presented, however, in order to illustrate how different jurisdictions deal with juvenile probation or parole program violations.

JUVENILES AND JUVENILE DELINQUENCY

Juvenile Offenders.   **Juvenile offenders** or **juvenile delinquents** are classified and defined according to several different criteria. For instance, the 1899 Illinois **Juvenile Court Act** that created juvenile courts determined that the jurisdiction of juvenile courts extended to all juveniles under the age of 16 who were found to be in violation of any state or local laws. About a fifth of all states, including Illinois, currently place the upper age limit for juveniles at either 15 or 16. In the remaining states, the upper limit for juveniles is age 17 (except for Wyoming, where it is age 18). Ordinarily, the jurisdiction of juvenile courts includes all young persons who have not yet attained the age at which they should be treated as adults for purposes of criminal law (Black, 1990:867). At the federal level, juveniles are considered to be persons who have not yet attained their 18th birthday (18 U.S.C., Sec. 5031, 2001).

Upper and Lower Jurisdictional Age Limits. While fairly uniform upper age limits for juveniles have been established in all U.S. jurisdictions (either under 16, under 17, or under 18 years of age), there is no uniformity concerning applicable lower age limits. English common law placed juveniles under age 7 beyond the reach of criminal courts, since it was believed that those under age 7 were incapable of formulating criminal intent or *mens rea*. However, many juvenile courts throughout the United States have no specified lower age limits for those juveniles within their purview. Few, if any, juvenile courts will process three-year-olds who kill others through the juvenile court, although these courts technically can do so in some jurisdictions.

Delinquency and Juvenile Delinquents

The majority of youthful offenders who appear before juvenile courts are those who have violated state or local laws or ordinances. The federal government has no juvenile court. Rather, federal cases involving juveniles infrequently are heard in federal district courts, but adjudicated juveniles are housed in state or local facilities if the sentences involve commitment to secure youth facilities. The majority of U.S. jurisdictions restrict their definitions of juvenile delinquency to any act committed by a juvenile, which, if committed by an adult, would be considered a crime (Tracy, 2002).

Status Offenders

Status offenses are any acts committed by juveniles that would (1) bring the juveniles to the attention of juvenile courts and (2) not be crimes if committed by adults. Common juvenile status offenses include running away from home, truancy, and curfew violations. Many of the youths who engage in this conduct are incorrigible, habitually disobedient, and beyond parental control. Truants and liquor law violators may be more inclined to become chronic offenders and to engage in more serious, possibly criminal, behaviors. An influential factor contributing to juvenile offender chronicity and persistence is contact with juvenile courts. Contact with juvenile courts, especially frequent contact, is believed by some researchers to stigmatize youths and cause them either to be labeled or acquire self-concepts as delinquents or deviants (Rhyne and Scott, 2006). Therefore, diversion of certain types of juvenile offenders from the juvenile justice system has been advocated and recommended to minimize these potentially adverse consequences of systemic contact.

AN OVERVIEW OF THE JUVENILE JUSTICE SYSTEM

The Origins and Purposes of Juvenile Courts

The **juvenile justice system** consists of a more or less integrated network of agencies, institutions, organizations, and personnel that process juvenile offenders. This network is made up of law enforcement agencies; prosecutors and courts; corrections, probation, and parole services; and public and private community-based treatment programs that provide youths with diverse services. Juvenile courts are a relatively recent American creation. Figure 13.1 shows a diagram of the juvenile justice system.

Modern American juvenile courts have various, less formal European antecedents. While the origin of this cutting point is unknown, the age of 7 was used in Roman times to separate **infants** from those older children who were accountable to the law for their actions. England used the age of 7 as the age of accountability for youths, and this practice has continued to the present day in the United States. Children presently under the age of 7 in most jurisdictions are not presumed capable of formulating criminal intent.

The Case of Ex parte Crouse.   Until the late 1830s, little consistency was apparent related to the division of labor between parental, religious, and state authority over juveniles. In 1838, a decision in a state case invested juvenile authorities with considerable parental power. The case of *Ex parte Crouse* (1838) involved a father who sought custody of his daughter from the Philadelphia House of Refuge. The girl had been committed to that facility by the court because

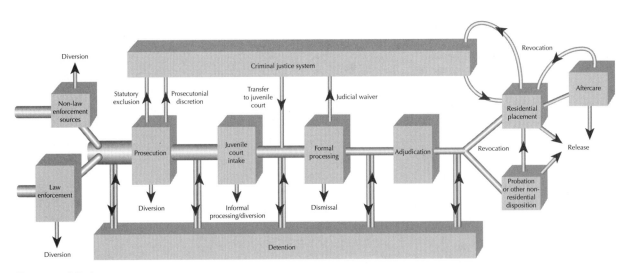

FIGURE 13.1   The Juvenile Justice System.
Source: Office of Juvenile Justice and Delinquency Prevention (2003).

she was declared unmanageable. She was not given a jury trial. Rather, the judge arbitrarily committed her. A higher court rejected the father's claim that parental control of children is exclusive, natural, and proper. It upheld the power of the state to exercise necessary reforms and restraints to protect children from themselves and their environments. While this decision was only applicable to Pennsylvania citizens and their children, other states took note of it and sought to invoke similar controls over errant children in their jurisdictions. In effect, children (at least in Pennsylvania) were temporarily deprived of any legal standing to challenge decisions made by the state in their behalf. This was the general state of juvenile affairs until the post–Civil War period known as Reconstruction.

Reform Schools.   In a period prior to the Civil War, **reform schools** were established and proliferated. One of the first state-operated reform schools was established in Westboro, Massachusetts, in 1848. By the end of the century, all states had reform schools. All of these institutions were characterized by strict discipline, absolute control over juvenile behavior, and compulsory work at various trades. Another common feature was that they were controversial.

Dependent and Neglected Children.   Few legal challenges of state authority over juveniles were lodged by parents during the 1800s. But in 1870, an Illinois case made it possible for special courts to be established to dispose of juvenile matters and represented an early recognition of certain minimal rights they might have. Daniel O'Connell, a youth who was declared vagrant and in need of supervision, was committed to the Chicago Reform School for an unspecified period (*People ex rel. O'Connell v. Turner,* 55 Ill. 280, 1870). O'Connell's parents challenged this court action, claiming that his confinement for vagrancy was unjust and untenable. Existing Illinois law vested state authorities with the power to commit any juvenile to a state reform school as long as a reasonable justification could be provided. In this instance, vagrancy was a reasonable justification. The Illinois Supreme Court distinguished between misfortune (vagrancy) and criminal acts in arriving at its decision to reverse Daniel O'Connell's commitment. In effect, the court nullified the law by declaring that reform school commitments of youths could not be made by the state if the "offense" was simple misfortune. They reasoned that states' interests would be better served if commitments of juveniles to reform schools were limited to those committing more serious criminal offenses rather than those who were victims of misfortune. Those who were considered victims of misfortune were called **dependent and neglected children.**

The First Juvenile Court.   Three decades later, the Illinois legislature established the first juvenile court on July 1, 1899, by passing the Act to Regulate the Treatment and Control of Dependent, Neglected, and Delinquent Children, or the Juvenile Court Act. This act provided for limited courts of record, where notes might be taken by judges or their assistants, to reflect judicial actions against juveniles. The jurisdiction of these courts, subsequently designated as "juvenile courts," would include all juveniles under the age of 16 who were found in violation of any state or local law or ordinance. Also, provision was made for the care of dependent and/or neglected children who had been abandoned or who otherwise lacked proper parental care, support, or guardianship. No minimum age was specified that would limit the jurisdiction of juvenile court judges. However, the act provided that judges could impose secure confinement on juveniles 10 years of age or over by placing them in state-regulated juvenile facilities such as the state reformatory or the State Home for Juvenile Female Offenders. Judges were expressly prohibited from confining any juvenile under 12 years of age in a jail or police station. Extremely young juveniles would be assigned POs who would look after their needs and placement on a temporary basis. Between 1900 and 1920, 20 states passed similar acts to establish juvenile courts. By the end of World War II, all states had created juvenile court systems. However, considerable variation existed among these court systems, depending on the jurisdiction.

MAJOR DIFFERENCES BETWEEN CRIMINAL AND JUVENILE COURTS

1. Juvenile courts are civil proceedings exclusively designed for juveniles, whereas criminal courts are proceedings designed for alleged violators of criminal laws. In criminal courts, alleged criminal law violators are primarily adults, although selected juveniles may be tried as adults in these same courts.

2. Juvenile proceedings are informal, whereas criminal proceedings are formal. Attempts are made in many juvenile courts to avoid the formal trappings that characterize criminal proceedings.

3. In most states, juveniles are not entitled to a trial by jury, unless the juvenile judge approves.

4. Both juvenile and criminal proceedings are adversarial. Juveniles may or may not wish to retain or be represented by counsel. Today, most states make provisions in their juvenile codes for public defenders for juveniles if they are indigent and cannot afford to hire private counsel.

5. Criminal courts are courts of record, whereas juvenile proceedings may or may not maintain a running transcript of proceedings.

6. The standard of proof used for determining one's guilt in criminal proceedings is beyond a reasonable doubt. In juvenile courts, judges use the same standard for juvenile delinquents who face possible commitment to secure juvenile facilities. In other court matters leading to non-commitment alternatives, the court uses the civil standard of preponderance of the evidence.

7. The range of penalties juvenile judges may impose is more limited than criminal courts. Both juvenile and criminal courts can impose fines, restitution, community service, probation, and other forms of conditional discharge. Juvenile courts can also impose residential secure or nonsecure placement, group homes, and camp/ranch experiences. Long terms of commitment to secure facilities are also within the purview of juvenile court judges. In most criminal courts, however, the range of penalties may include life imprisonment or the death penalty in those jurisdictions where the death penalty is used.

This comparison indicates that criminal court actions are more serious and have more significant long-term consequences for offenders compared with actions taken by juvenile courts. For instance, the Miranda Warning is given to juveniles when they are arrested or taken into custody. Most jurisdictions have forms for this purpose. Figure 13.2 shows a Miranda Warning form used by an Arkansas county. Accompanying this form may be a Waiver of Right

MIRANDA WARNING

1. You have the right to remain silent. *(You do not need to say anything).*

    _____

2. Anything you say can and will be used against you in a court of law. *(Anyone you say anything to, i.e.:
    neighbor, friend, police officer, teacher or anyone else, can come to court and repeat what you told them).*

    _____

3. You have the right to talk to a lawyer, one will be appointed, free of charge, to represent you before any
    questioning, if you wish.

    _____

4. If you cannot afford to hire a lawyer, one will be appointed, free of charge, to represent you before any
    questioning, if you wish. *(This is a decision you have to make. It does not depend upon whether you or your
    parents have the money to hire an attorney).*

    _____

5. You can decide at anytime to exercise these rights and not answer any questions or make any statements, or
    have a lawyer present. *(If you decide to answer questions, you may, or you can stop the questioning anytime
    you want. It is your decision if you want to have an attorney present at this time).*

    _____

6. Do you understand each of these rights I have explained to you?

    _____

7. Having these rights in mind, do you wish to talk to us now? *(Remember, you have the right to talk with an
    attorney before you make any statements. If you wish to do so, we will provide you with the name and
    telephone number of the Public Defender. The Public Defender is an attorney provided by Baxter County to
    speak on your behalf to the court or any authorities you want him to).*

    _____

Public Defender: KENFORD CARTER, P.O. BOX 1438, FLIPPIN, AR 72634 - 870/453-1462

Juvenile	Date	Parent/Guardian	Date
Attorney	Date	Juvenile Officer	Date

FIGURE 13.2   Miranda Warning Form. (From Baxter County, AR).

to Counsel form, which arrested juveniles and their parents may be asked to
sign. An example of this form is shown in Figure 13.3.

While many critics see juvenile courts moving toward a just-deserts philosophy in the treatment and **adjudication** of juveniles, many youths are still subject to
treatment-oriented, nonsecure alternatives rather than custodial options. Thus, it is
in the best interests of the state to provide alternatives to incarceration for both
adult and juvenile offenders. This "best interests" philosophy of juvenile courts is
based on an early doctrine known as *parens patriae* (Sharp and White, 2006).

Parens Patriae

Juvenile courts have always had considerable latitude in regulating the affairs
of juveniles. This freedom to act in a child's behalf was rooted in the largely

WAIVER OF RIGHT OF COUNSEL

Case No:_____

IN THE MATTER OF _____, A JUVENILE

NOW COMES _____, the juvenile

respondent, in the above titled and numbered case, in person and together with his/her

parent(s) in writing and in the presence of _____

and after having been informed of his/her right to an attorney, and that the court would

appoint counsel to represent him/her at no cost, nevertheless knowledgeable and willfully

waives his right to be represented by legal counsel during the following stages of the

proceedings in this case:

_____   Intake Interview

_____   Plea and Arraignment

_____   Adjudication and Disposition

No promises or threats have been made to me; and no pressure or coercion of any kind has
been used against me.

_____   _____
Juvenile Officer   Juvenile Respondent

_____   _____
Date   Date

_____   _____
Parent   Parent

_____   _____
Date   Date

FIGURE 13.3   Waiver of Right to Counsel Form. (From Baxter County, AR).

unchallenged doctrine of ***parens patriae***. The *parens patriae* doctrine received formal recognition in U.S. courts in the case of *Ex parte Crouse* (1838).
This case involved the commitment of an unruly and incorrigible female child
to a state agency. When the parents of the child attempted to regain custody
over her later, their request was denied. She remained a ward of the state by
virtue of the power of the state agency charged with her supervision. This case
set a precedent in that the state established almost absolute control over juvenile custody matters. The primary elements of *parens patriae* that have contributed to its persistence as a dominant philosophical perspective in the
juvenile justice system are summarized as follows:

1. *Parens patriae* encourages informal handling of juvenile matters as
   opposed to more formal and criminalizing procedures.
2. *Parens patriae* vests juvenile courts with absolute authority to provide what
   is best for youthful offenders (e.g., support services and other forms of care).

3. *Parens patriae* strongly encourages benevolent and rehabilitative treatments to assist youths in overcoming their personal and social problems.

4. *Parens patriae* avoids the adverse labeling effects that formal court proceedings might create.

5. *Parens patriae* means state control over juvenile life chances.

Arrests and Other Options

Law enforcement officers require little justification to apprehend juveniles or take them into custody. An arrest is the legal detainment of a person to answer for criminal charges or (infrequently at present) civil demands. Arrests of juveniles are more serious than being taken into custody. Suspected runaways, truants, or curfew violators are taken into custody for their own welfare or protection. Suspected juvenile delinquents are often arrested. Following being taken into custody or an arrest, the first screening of juveniles is intake.

Intake Screenings

Intake or an **intake screening** is the second major step in the juvenile justice process. It is a more or less informally conducted screening procedure whereby intake POs or other juvenile court officers, including the prosecutor, decide whether detained juveniles should be (1) unconditionally released from the juvenile justice system; (2) released to parents or guardians subject to a subsequent juvenile court appearance; (3) released or referred to one or more community-based services or resources; (4) placed in secure detention subject to a **detention hearing;** (5) referred to teen court, youth court, or peer court for resolution; or (6) waived or transferred to the jurisdiction of criminal courts.

Petitions and Adjudicatory Proceedings

Jurisdictional Variations in Juvenile Processing.   There is considerable variation in different jurisdictions about how juvenile courts are conducted. Increasingly, juvenile courts are emulating criminal courts in many respects (Brown and D'Angelo, 2006). Most of the physical trappings are present, including the judge's bench, tables for the prosecution and defense, and a witness stand. Either prosecutors file **petitions** or act on the petitions filed by others. Petitions are official documents filed in juvenile courts on the juvenile's behalf, specifying reasons for the youth's court appearance. These documents assert that juveniles fall within the categories of dependent or neglected, status offender, or delinquent, and the reasons for such assertions are usually provided. Filing a petition formally places the juvenile before the juvenile judge in many jurisdictions. But juveniles may come before juvenile judges in less formal ways. Those able to file petitions against juveniles include their parents, school officials, neighbors, or any other interested party. The legitimacy and factual accuracy of petitions are evaluated by juvenile court judges. An example of a delinquency petition is shown in Figure 13.4.

In most jurisdictions, juvenile judges have almost absolute discretion in how their courts are conducted. Juvenile defendants alleged to have committed various crimes may or may not be granted a trial by jury, if one is requested. Few states permit jury trials for juveniles in juvenile courts, according to legislative mandates. After hearing the evidence presented by both sides in any juvenile proceeding, the judge decides or adjudicates the matter. An **adjudication** is a judgment or action on the petition filed with the court by others. If the petition alleges delinquency on the part of certain juveniles, the judge determines whether the juveniles are delinquent or not delinquent. If the petition alleges that the juveniles involved are dependent, neglected, or otherwise in need of care by agencies or others, the judge decides the matter. A disproportionately large number of female delinquents receive greater attention from juvenile court judges compared with male juveniles. This is in part because of the paternal nature of juvenile court judges and their views about how female juvenile delinquents ought to be treated (King, Bierdeman, and Jordan, 2006). Some persons

---

PETITION
(DELINQUENT/UNRULY)

IN THE JUVENILE COURT OF GLYNN COUNTY, GEORGIA

In the interest of: Case _____

_____   Sex _____

    A Child   DOB:_____

TO THE JUVENILE COURT OF GLYNN COUNTY, GEORGIA:

    1. Your petitioner alleges the child named above to be of the sex and age and to have the name there set forth; that the father of said child is_____, who resides at _____ the mother is _____ who resides at _____ said child resides at _____ _____in said county and state, and is in the custody and control of _____who resides at said place; that the said child is subject to the jurisdiction of this Court.

    2. That the within petition is filed in the best interest of the public and the within named child.

    3. That said child has violated the section of the code cited below and is a delinquent/unruly child by reason of the facts set forth below:

    A.

    4. That said child is in need of supervision, treatment or rehabilitation. That said child is/is not currently in detention in the _____ Center, having been placed there at _____ on _____, 2004.

    Petitioner prays that process issue, directed to the parties hereto, requiring them to show cause why said child should not be dealt with according to law.

_____
(Petitioner)

Subscribed and sworn to before me, on information and belief, this the_____day of _____, 2004. _____
(Attesting Officer)

The above petition is approved to be filed in the best interest of the public and the named child.
This_____day of_____, 2004.

_____
(Court Designee)

FIGURE 13.4 Delinquency Petition. (From Glynn County, Georgia).

believe this differentiation on the basis of gender is discriminatory and should be discontinued (McCoy and Moak, 2006).

If the result of an adjudicatory hearing is a finding that the juvenile is delinquent, the judge has several options available. The most likely option of choice to most juvenile court judges is to place the juvenile on probation for a specified time period. The term of probation varies, depending on the seriousness of the adjudication offense. Figure 13.5 shows a probation order.

In more than a few instances, delinquent youths will have one or more problems that got them into trouble initially. Some of these problems can be addressed through special conditions of probation. These special conditions may include various treatments for drug dependencies, counseling, vocational education, compulsory school attendance, restitution, or any other reasonable condition judges wish to impose. A form showing the conditions of probation and special conditions of probation is shown in Figure 13.6.

IN THE JUVENILE COURT OF GLYNN COUNTY
STATE OF GEORGIA

IN THE INTEREST OF:

| CASE NUMBER: _____

| SEX: _____

| D.O.B.: _____

|
_____ |
       A CHILD | AGE: _____

ORDER OF PROBATION

Petition(s) having been filed in this Court and after hearing evidence in this Court, this court has determined that the above-named child is subject to the jurisdiction and protection of this Court as provided by law: and

After hearing evidence the Court finds the child committed the following act(s), to wit:

Upon dispositional hearing and after hearing evidence the Court finds that said child is hereby found to be unruly/delinquent and in need of treatment, rehabilitation, or supervision.

It is ordered that said child be and hereby is placed on Probation (pursuant to O.C.G.A. 15-11-66 (a) (2)) to this Court for a period of time not to exceed six months unless extended pursuant to O.C.G.A. 15-11-70 said probation to be supervised by an Officer of this Court under the conditions and stipulations attached hereto and made hereof by reference.

CONSIDERED, ORDERED AND ADJUDGED on this the _____ day of _____, 2004.

_____
George M. Rountree, Judge

FIGURE 13.5 Probation Order. (From Glynn County, Georgia).

IN THE JUVENILE COURT OF GLYNN COUNTY, GEORGIA

*

*

*

IN THE INTEREST OF   *   **CASE NO.** _____

CONDITIONS OF PROBATION

In accordance with the laws of Georgia, you have been placed on probation for a period of 6 months. **IT IS THE ORDER OF THIS COURT** that you comply with the following conditions of probation.

1. Do not violate any State, Federal or Local Laws.
2. Discuss with your parents any planned outside activities including places, associations and hours, and have approval before leaving home.
3. You shall have a curfew of on weekdays and on Friday and Saturday.
4. You shall attend school each school day and abide by all school rules.
5. Do not change your place of residence without first notifying your court officer.
6. You shall report to your court officer every other week beginning and obey such specific orders and directions as may be issued by the Judge or your court officer.

SPECIAL CONDITIONS

7. You shall perform _____ sessions of community service located at _____ on the following dates _____.
8. You shall submit to random drug testing as ordered.
9. You shall pay restitution in the amount of _____.
10. You shall surrender your driver's license until _____
11. You shall attend and complete the Gateway MRT or Gate program and abide by all rules of the program.
12. You shall attend the S.T.A.R Program as deemed appropriate by your Court Officer.

AGREEMENT AND AFFIDAVIT

By my signature, I certify that I have read and understand the conditions of probation as set forth and will abide by them.

Child: _____

GUARDIAN'S RECEIPT AND AGREEMENT

I acknowledge receipt of a copy hereof and understand these conditions placed upon my child. I promise to make every effort to uphold the conditions outlined above.

Guardian: _____

Court Officer: _____   Date: _____

FIGURE 13.6   Conditions and Special Conditions of Probation. (From Glynn County, Georgia).

Once the term of probation has been concluded successfully, a judgment may be entered by the court to terminate one's probation program. This order is filed only if all conditions of the program have been met and a favorable report has been filed by the juvenile's supervising PO. Such an order is shown in Figure 13.7.

**IN THE JUVENILE COURT OF GLYNN COUNTY
STATE OF GEORGIA**

IN THE INTEREST OF:

DOB:

<u>TERMINATION OF PROBATION ORDER</u>

It appearing to the court that the above-named child, having been placed on probation under the supervision of this court, has made satisfactory adjustment while on probation.

It is further Ordered and decreed that the above named child is hereby released from probation and the jurisdiction of this Court terminated.

SO ORDERED THIS THE 20TH DAY OF DECEMBER, 2004.

_____
George M. Rountree, Judge

FIGURE 13.7   Termination of Probation Order. (From Glynn County, Georgia).

If the adjudicatory proceeding fails to support the facts alleged in the petition filed with the court, the case is dismissed and the youth is freed. If the adjudicatory proceeding supports the allegations, then the judge must adjudicate the youth as either a delinquent, a status offender, or a youth in need of special treatment or supervision. Then, the juvenile court judge must dispose of the case according to several options.

TEEN COURTS

Teen Court Variations

One alternative for formal juvenile court appearances and adjudications are teen courts. Increasing numbers of jurisdictions are using **teen courts** as an alternative to formal juvenile court proceedings for determining one's punishment (Butts and Buck, 2002). Teen courts are informal jury proceedings, where jurors consist of teenagers who hear and decide minor cases. First-offender cases, where status offenses or misdemeanors have been committed, are given priority in a different type of court setting involving one's peers as judges. Judges may divert minor youth cases to these teen courts. Adults function only as presiding judges, and these persons are often retired judges, lawyers, or others with substantial courtroom experience who perform such services voluntarily and in their spare time. The focus of teen courts is on therapeutic jurisprudence, with a strong emphasis on restitution, community service, and rehabilitation. One objective of such courts is to teach empathy to offenders. Victims are encouraged to take an active role in these courts. Youths become actively involved as advisory juries (Peterson, 2005).

Teen courts are also known as **youth courts, peer courts,** and **student courts** (Preston and Roots, 2004). Their growing appeal as an alternative to formal juvenile court processing is evident. In 1997 there were 78 active teen courts. By 2005 there were 1,019 youth court programs operating in juvenile justice systems, schools, and community-based organizations throughout the United States, with an anticipated 2,000 youth courts or more being established over the next few years (Peterson, 2005). The American Probation and Parole Association has recognized the significance and contributions of teen courts by establishing September as National Youth Court Month to highlight the activities of youth courts and their contributions to the youth justice system (American Probation and Parole Association, 2006). Several variations of teen courts have been described (Butts and Buck, 2002). Four courtroom models of teen courts include (1) adult judge, (2) youth judge, (3) peer jury, and (4) tribunal.

Adult Judge Teen Court Model.   Adult judge teen courts use adult judges to preside over all actions. The judge is responsible for managing all courtroom dynamics. Generally, a youth volunteer acting as the prosecutor presents each case against a juvenile to a jury comprised of one's peers. This is similar to a prosecutor in the adult system presenting a case against a defendant in a grand jury action. A juvenile defense counsel offers mitigating evidence, if any, which the jury may consider. The jury is permitted to ask the youthful defendant any question in an effort to determine why the offense was committed and any circumstances surrounding its occurrence. Subsequently, the jury deliberates and determines the most fitting punishment. This is a recommendation only. The suitability of the recommended punishment, which is most often some form of community service and/or victim compensation or restitution, is decided by the judge. About half of all teen courts in the United States use the adult judge model.

Youth Judge Model.   The youth judge variation of teen courts uses a juvenile judge instead of an adult judge. Youths are used as prosecutors and defense counsel as well. This teen court variation functions much like the adult judge teen court model. Again, a sentence is recommended by a jury, and the appropriateness of the sentence is determined by the juvenile judge. About a third of all teen courts use this model.

Peer Jury Model.   In the peer jury model, an adult judge presides, while a jury hears the case against the defendant. There are no youth prosecutors or defense counsels present. After hearing the case, which is usually determined through jury questioning of the defendant directly, the jury deliberates and decides the sentence, which the judge must approve.

Tribunal Model.   Under the tribunal model, one or more youths act as judges, while other youths are designated as prosecutors and defense counsels. The prosecution and defense present their side of the case against the youthful defendant to the judges, who subsequently deliberate and return with a sentence. All sentences may be appealed. Again, the sentences usually involve restitution or some form of victim compensation, community service, or a combination of punishments depending on the circumstances. This tribunal model is very popular and is used in many jurisdictions.

Each of these models is summarized below:

	Judge	Youth Attorneys	Jury/Role of Jury
Adult Judge Model	Adult	Yes	Recommend sentence
Youth Judge Model	Youth	Yes	Recommend sentence

Peer Jury Model	Adult	No	Questions defendant, recommends sentence
Tribunal Model	Youths (1–3)	Yes	No jury present

Some Teen Court Examples

Two examples of teen courts are described here. These are the Abilene Teen Court and the Restorative Justice Teen Court.

The Abilene Teen Court.   Based on the Peer Jury Model, selected juveniles are referred to the Abilene Teen Court by juvenile court judges. Qualifying for Teen Court are youths ages 10 to 18 who have received a Class C misdemeanor violation and who are currently enrolled in school or seeking a high school diploma. Youth who have not participated in a Teen Court program within the past two years may request Teen Court. All participating youths must plead "guilty" or "no contest." They must pay $20 as an administrative court fee.

The Abilene Teen Court's goals are to (1) provide a program offering youth valuable education and hands-on experience in the legal and judicial system; (2) provide meaningful and constructive alternatives to the formal court process of juvenile offenders; (3) reduce the number of youths in juvenile court by intervening early and interrupting developing patterns of criminal behavior; (4) give an opportunity to make restitution through community service, written letters of apology, and Teen Court participation; (5) allow youth to participate in the role of a juror to experience the other side of the justice system by determining consequences for peers; (6) create awareness in youthful offenders of the harmful consequences their actions may have on others; and (6) build positive habits and skills, such as reporting to work on time, cooperating with coworkers, accepting constructive criticism, and successfully completing tasks.

The dress code for Teen Court is very conservative. The dress code is strictly enforced. The following things are *not allowed. Do not wear* shorts, tank tops, bare midriffs, headgear (e.g., caps, scarves, rags, or bandannas), visible facial piercing, chains, spiked jewelry, clothing with inappropriate pictures or slogans, extreme makeup or hair colors, flip flops, or house shoes. Dress nicely, as if you were attending a graduation or church. For males, they must wear dress slacks, nice pants, or at least nice jeans without tears or holes. They must wear nice pressed shirts, or at least a shirt without holes or tears. They must wear dress shoes, boots, or athletic shoes. For females, they must wear dress pants, or at least jeans without holes or tears. They must wear nice pressed shirts, or at least a shirt without holes or tears. They may also wear a dress or skirt. The skirt must be no shorter than 2 inches above the knee. Wear dress shoes, boots, or athletic shoes.

Teens appear in Teen Court for his or her trial. They must arrive on time. Check-in time is usually 5:00 P.M. Cell phones are to be turned off or silenced. No recording devices are permitted. Food, drink, gum, and tobacco products are prohibited. No displays of anger are permitted. Courteousness and respectfulness are expected of all participants, including volunteers. They must be alert, attentive, and businesslike. They must speak only at appropriate times and in a loud, clear voice, using acceptable language. They must refrain from any unnecessary talking, laughing, or noise of any kind. They must show respect for the court at all times. They must maintain good posture, and not put their feet on the furnishings. They must address the judge properly, by "Your Honor." They must follow *all* rules and dress codes for the community service agencies where they are assigned later.

Subsequently the teen is questioned by defense and prosecuting attorneys, who are volunteers, and then sentenced by a jury of their peers, who are teens that have been sentenced to serve on the Teen Court jury. The jury assesses punishment based on a grid system, called the Discipline Grid. The youth will be sentenced to community service and jury duty.

The youth is assigned to jury duty the week following their trial. Once all requirements have been met, Teen Court will submit the citation to the referring court for dismissal. If the youth fails to complete the Teen Court experience successfully, the citation is referred back to the referring court for further action. If this occurs, then the citation will be entered onto the youth's record as a disposition, the original fine will be assessed, and in some cases, the youth's driver's license will be suspended or denied.

The benefits of the Abilene Teen Court for the community, youth, and parents are apparent. For the community, fewer juvenile repeat offenders free up law enforcement officers and agencies to focus their attention on more serious criminals. By interrupting errant juvenile patterns of behavior, the expense of future imprisonment will be minimized. Community service work performed at nonprofit organizations improves operating conditions and reduces workload.

For youth benefits, Teen Court challenges youth to perform at their highest levels of ability and places high priority on educating the youth for life responsibilities as individuals, citizens, and family members. Peer group interpersonal relations are strengthened, together with a greater awareness of and compliance with the law. Teens become acquainted with the judicial system and experience the satisfaction of contributing to the community, while gaining valuable work experience. Completion of requirements within the specified time results in dismissals, which keep offenses off of the youth's record.

Parents benefit because it provides a framework of positive peer pressure and discipline. It also provides an opportunity for children to make amends to the community through community service work. It gives their children a reason not to repeat their mistakes.

The official statutes governing the Abilene Teen Court indicate that:

A justice or municipal court may defer proceedings against a defendant who is under the age of 18 or enrolled full time in an accredited secondary school in a program leading to a high school diploma for not more than 180 days if the defendant is (1) charged with an offense that the court has jurisdiction over; (2) pleads *nolo contendere* or guilty to the offense in open court with the defendant's parent, guardian, or managing conservator present; (3) presents to the court an oral or written request to attend a teen court program; and (4) has not successfully completed a teen court program in the two years preceding the date that the alleged offense occurred.

The teen court program must be approved by the court. A defendant for whom the proceedings are deferred shall complete the teen court program not later than the 90th day after the date of the teen court hearing to determine punishment is held or the last day of the deferral period, whichever date is earlier. The justice or municipal court shall dismiss the charge at the time the defendant has successfully completed the teen court program. A charge dismissed under these conditions may not be part of the defendant's criminal record or driving record or used for any purpose. However, if the charge was for a traffic offense, the court shall report to the Department of Public Safety that the defendant successfully completed the teen court program and the date of completion for inclusion in the defendant's driving record. The justice or municipal court may require a person who requests a teen court program to pay a fee not to exceed $10 that is set by the court to cover the costs of administering this article. Fees collected by a municipal court shall be deposited in the municipal treasury. Fees collected by a justice court shall be deposited in the county treasury of the county in which the court is located. A person who requests a teen court program and fails to complete it is not entitled to a refund of the fee. A court may transfer a case in which proceedings have been deferred to a court in another county if the court to which the case is transferred consents. A case may not be transferred unless it is within the jurisdiction of the court to which it is transferred.

The successfulness of the Abilene Teen Court has been exceptional. Most offenders who are processed through this Teen Court seldom recidivate. Most go on to complete their high school diplomas, and many pursue higher degrees at colleges or universities. Thus, they have escaped the unfavorable label of delinquent by avoiding a juvenile court appearance. All of this is done in lieu of a formal juvenile court adjudication.

The Barron County Restorative Teen Court.   In Barron County, Wisconsin, a Restorative Justice Teen Court (RJTC) has been established. The mission of the RJTC is the help juvenile offenders restore their relationships with the community through alternative methods of adjudicating minor juvenile offenses, including programs that teach responsibility and positive decision making and restore a sense of safety in the community. The Barron County RJTC is based on the philosophy that a youthful law violator does not continue to be an offender when a peer jury decides punishment. It will provide a way for first-offenders to keep their records clean. The program focuses on youth accountability and development. RJTC is designed to interrupt patterns of criminal behavior by promoting positive feelings of self-esteem, motivating self-improvement, and developing a healthy attitude toward authority.

Respondent participation in this program is voluntary and requires an advance guilty plea. The program is available to juvenile offenders ages 12 to 18, and still in school. Respondents must have parental or guardian consent and participation. In the RJTC, the judge introduces the respondent to teenage peer jurors who are informed of the charge against the respondent. After hearing the evidence presented by a teenage prosecutor and defense attorney, the jury considers the appropriate sanctions for the offense. The decision is reviewed by the judge and read to the respondent. Eligible offenses for the RJTC include minor traffic violations; misdemeanors such as public intoxication, theft, retail theft, property damage, vandalism, disorderly conduct; possession of alcohol, or small amounts of marijuana; trespassing; curfew violation; and other minor offenses. The RJTC sanctions are designed to fit the offense and involve restitution, community service, and prevention education. Referrals in Barron County are received from courts, probation and parole, schools, human services, or law enforcement. Referral forms are available from the Barron County Court. A referral form is shown in Figure 13.8.

Once a case has been referred to the RJTC, an Agreement to Participate and Waiver of Liability form must be signed. This form is shown in Figure 13.9. Furthermore, instructions are given to each defendant/youth. These instructions pertain to time of appearance, dress, protocol to be followed while in court, turning off cell telephones and pagers, observance of court decorum, and a general procedural statement to clarify each stage of the proceedings. Figure 13.10 provides Instructions for Procedures for Respondents in subsequent RJTC actions.

All participants, including parents, respondent, teen jurors, prosecutor, judge, defense counsel, and other interested parties, including the victim, if any, are assembled. The procedure is outlined in Figure 13.11.

The protocol followed in Figure 13.11 is quite explicit, including the sanctions available to judges at the end of the proceedings, as outlined in procedure #16. The RJTC is responsible for enforcing the terms of the jury verdict and punishment. Failure to comply with any of its terms will nullify the agreement and the juvenile will be referred to juvenile court for further proceedings. However, successful completion of the RJTC's terms and conditions will mean an expungement of one's juvenile record related to that offense.

B A R R O N   C O U N T Y

Restorative Justice Programs, Inc.

2850 COLLEGE DRIVE, RICE LAKE, WI 54868

715-736-0940

REFERRAL FORM

Check appropriate box: Office use:

☐ **VICTIM OFFENDER CONFERENCE**

TEEN COURT case #
_____
Date rec'd:

☐ **RESTORATIVE TEEN COURT**

Date closed:

_____

| **VOC** case # _____ |
| Date rec'd: _____ |
| Date closed: _____ |

Referred By _____

Phone # _____

Please include any of the applicable: victim statement, statement of loss, teacher statement, police report, any other pertinent information.

Offender Information (use separate form for each offender)

Name _____

Address _____

Male _____ Female _____ Age or DOB _____ Home Phone

Number _____

Grade in school _____ Name of teacher (If in elementary) _____

If under 18, parents/guardians names and addresses _____

_____

Names of offender/s: _____

Do victim and offender know each other? Yes _____ No _____

If related, how _____

Has anyone spoken to victim about Victim-Offender Conferencing or Teen Court at this point? _____

If so, who: _____

Additional information:

_____

Names of other offenders in the
case _____

Were others referred to Victim-Offender Conferencing? Yes _____ No _____

Were others referred to Teen Court?   Yes _____ No _____

Employer _____

School _____

Offense/s

_____

Date of Offense/s _____

Was a citation Issued? _____

Summary of offense and nature of damages

Victim Information
(additional forms for multiple victims)

Name _____

Address _____ Home Phone

_____

Male _____ Female _____ Age or DOB _____

Grade in school _____ Name of teacher (if in elementary) _____

If under 18, parents/guardians names and

addresses _____

_____

Other victims: Yes _____ No _____ Were others referred to VOC or Teen Court: Yes _____
No _____

use attached multiple victims form

Names of
Offender/s:_____

Do Victim and offender know each other? Yes _____ No_____
    If related, how _____

Has anyone spoken to victim about Victim-Offender Conferencig or Teen Court at this
point?_____
If so, who:_____

Additional Information:

FIGURE 13.8   Referral Form (Barron County, Wisconsin, Restorative Teen Court Program).

BARRON COUNTY

Restorative Justice Programs, Inc.

2850 COLLEGE DRIVE, RICE LAKE, WI 54868

715-736-0940

RESTORATIVE JUSTICE TEEN COURT

AGREEMENT TO PARTICIPATE and WAIVER OF LIABILITY

Restorative Teen Court is a diversion program specifically designed for misdemeanor youthful offenders who have no prior court record. Participation by all parties is completely voluntary. All participants are required to tell the truth and each takes an Oath of Confidentiality. In Restorative Teen Court, specially trained teenagers fulfill the roles of prosecuting and defense attorneys, clerks, bailiffs, and jurors.

The puerpose of Restorative Teen Court is to direct cases away from the circuit and municipal court and provide a forum for respondents (who admit guilt) to explain their involvement in the offense. Their peers sanction the respondents in Restorative Teen Court. Specially trained teen panelist question the respondent about his/her involvement in the case as a jury of specially trained volunteers and previously sanctioned respondents listen. It is then the duty of the jury to talk over the important points raised during court and unanimously agree to appropriate sanctions. The judge approves the sanctions and the respondent and their parent/guardian sign a contract to carry out the sanctions imposed.

As a RESPONDENT, you need to know and understand that only when these sanctions and conditions have been successfully completed will the referring agency be notified to close your case, with no further action taken. In addition, you will have no public court record at that time.

As a RESPONDENT, you need to know and understand that if you fail to complete each and every sanction, and/or condition, as set forth in the time frame given, and if you are arrested before you have completed the sanctions, or if you fail to attend your Restorative Teen Court trial, you will automatically be expelled from the Restorative Teen Court program, and referred back to the referring agent. There is no constitutional right to an attorney for Restorative Teen Court, however, if your case is returned to the referring agent, you may want to contact an attorney.

IT IS FURTHER AGREED AND UNDERSTOOD THAT AS A WAIVER OF LIABILITY and as a condition of participation in the Restorative Teen Court Program, you and your parent/guardian promise to hold harmless the Restorative Teen Court Board of Directors, its Coordinators, employees and volunteers, any school district in Barron County and its employees, duly authorized law enforcement officers in any municipality in Barron County, Barron County Restorative Justice Programs, Inc., and its volunteers and any community service agency or individuals, from any and all the Restorative Teen Court Program, including any coming and going.

A **sixty-five dollar fee** for participation in the Restorative Teen Court program is due at the time of trial. Only cash or money order can be accepted.

I authorize the Restorative Teen Court Coordinator to release information to participants in the Restorative Teen Court Program.

With my signature, I acknowledge that I have read, or that someone has read and explained to me, the contents of the above mentioned AGREEMENT TO PARTICIPATE IN TEEN COURT. I understand my obligations to the program and will abide by its requirements.

_____   _____
Respondent   Parent/Guardian

_____   _____
Restorative Teen Court Coordinator   Parent/Guardian

_____
Date

FIGURE 13.9 Agreement to Participate and Waiver of Liability (Barron County, Wisconsin, Restorative Teen Court Program).

BARRON COUNTY

Restorative Justice Programs, Inc.

2850 COLLEGE DRIVE, RICE LAKE, WI 54868

715-736-0940

Restorative Justice Programs, Inc.

2850 COLLEGE DRIVE, RICE LAKE, WI 54868

715-736-0940

RESTORATIVE JUSTICE TEEN COURT

INSTRUCTIONS AND PROCEDURES FOR RESPONDENTS

You are to appear for your Teen Court hearing, accompanied by a parent/guardian, on the date and time on your **Notice to Appear in Teen Court.**

Please dress appropriately—neat and clean clothes are required; no shorts, hats, or torn clothing; shoes and shirts are required; no gum chewing, smoking, food, or soda allowed.

Check in with the Restorative Teen Court Representative when you arrive at the Courthouse.

You will meet with your defense attorney to prepare your case. You will then wait in the lobby area for your hearing to be called.

A Restorative Teen Court representative will escort you to the courtroom for your hearing.

Your parents/guardians may sit in the front row of the courtroom.

The Clerk will introduce the case, and swear in the jurors.

You will be sworn in by the Clerk, and then questioned by the defense and prosecution attorneys, or a peer panel. Your parents may be questioned as well.

The jury will receive instructions from the Judge, and be escorted by the Bailiff to the deliberation room.

The Judge will decide if the sanctions are fair, and the Foreperson will read the sanctions.

The court will be dismissed.

You and your parent/guardian will be escorted by Restorative Teen Court Staff to sign the constructive sanction agreement, and go over the completion guidelines.

FIGURE 13.10   Instructions for Procedures for Respondents in Subsequent RJTC Actions. (Barron County, Wisconsin, Restorative Teen Court Program.

In the RJTC example above, several possible sanctions could be imposed, including restitution, community service, or victim compensation. Court and other maintenance fees could also be assessed. In certain jurisdictions, such as Holland, Michigan, teen courts include letters of apology to victims and others, as well as restitution contracts. A letter of apology is illustrated in Figure 13.12. A contract ordering a specific amount of restitution is shown in Figure 13.13 from the same Holland, Michigan, jurisdiction. Each jurisdiction has the discretionary power to devise different means for offenders to apologize to their victims, make restitution, or perform other duties such as community service.

The successfulness of the Barron County Restorative Justice Teen Court is based on a restorative justice model, which is becoming increasingly popular for both adult and juvenile offenders. It seeks to involve more community members and enlists their support in order to enable offenders to reflect on the harm they have inflicted on their victims and have their accountability heightened. Restorative justice is not revenge-centered. It is often victim-centered, although some models have been offender-centered where benefits are obvious for defendants who may face criminal or delinquent proceedings if they do not comply with teen court conditions and requirements. The success rate of such programs is remarkable. Very few juveniles return to law-breaking behaviors. Having the opportunity to participate and judge others enables them to see both sides of the law in retrospect. Their appreciation for the juvenile justice system is enhanced.

BARRON COUNTY
Restorative Justice Programs, Inc.
2850 COLLEGE DRIVE, RICE LAKE, WI 54868
715-736-0940

Restorative Justice Programs, Inc.
2850 COLLEGE DRIVE RICE LAKE, WI 54868
715-736-0940

PROCEDURE FOR RESTORATIVE TEEN COURT

1.   Bailiff calls the court to order and announces the judge. **"Please rise. This court in and for Barron County is now in session. Honorable _____ presiding".**

2.   The Judge may make any opening statements, such as:

   "I would like to welcome everyone to Teen Court. The respondent has voluntarily agreed to come to Restorative Teen Court and has already admitted guilt. The respondent will receive constructive sanctions after hearing testimony."

3.   The judge explains confidentiality before the oath is given. The Judge stresses the importance of confidentiality and the meaning of confidentiality.

   "Confidentiality is a serious expectation in Restorative Teen Court. You have the responsibility as a member of the court not to share personal information about the case with anyone. That means do not tell the name or any identifying characteristics of the respondent to your family, your best friend, your teacher, or anyone else. You have a serious responsibility and obligation to keep these proceedings confidential. Anyone who breaks confidentiality may, and probably will, be charged with contempt of court."

   Ask everyone in the courtroom to stand and raise their right hand.

   "Do you solemnly swear or affirm that you will not divulge, either by words or signs, any information which comes to your knowledge in the course of a Restorative Teen Court session, and that you will keep secret all said proceedings, which will be held in your presence."

   "You may be seated."

4.   The Judge asks the respondent to please rise and face the jury.

   "Does anyone on the jury know this respondent?"
   "How do you know the respondent?"
   "Will it affect your ability to determine fair constructive sanctions?"
   "Does anyone on the jury know the lawyers?"
   "Will it affect your ability to determine fair constructive sanctions?"
   "Is there any jury member who feels that they cannot be fair for any reason?"

   "Do the prosecution and defense accept the jury?"

5.   Ask the Clerk to call the case.

   "Case number _____ in the interest of _____."

6. The jury stands and raises their right hand. The Clerk swears in the jury.

   "Do you solemnly swear or affirm that you will objectively weigh the issues in this case and render fair constructive sanctions according to the testimony, and guidelines of Restorative Teen Court?"

7. The judge asks the prosecuting attorney to make the appearances. After the appearances, the Judge asks:

   "Are the prosecution and defense ready to proceed?"

8. The prosecution and defense make their opening statements.

9. The Judge asks the defense attorney to call their first witness. The respondent is sworn in by the Clerk, **"Do you solemnly swear or affirm to tell the truth, the whole truth, and nothing but the truth?"** The Judge then asks the respondent to take the witness stand.

10. The defense and the prosecution attorneys examine the respondent. Redirect/Re-cross are offered to the attorneys. The jury is allowed to ask questions. The Judge may ask questions.

11. The Judge asks the defense attorneys to call their next witness. The parent(s) or guardian(s) are sworn in and questioned by the defense and prosecution attorneys. Redirect/Re-Cross are offered. The jury may ask questions. The Judge may ask any questions.

12. If the victim wishes to speak, they may do so at this time; or if there is a victim impact statement it is read at this time by the prosecuting attorney.

13. Closing arguments by the prosecution, first, then the defense. Rebuttal is offered to the prosecution.

14. The Judge gives instructions to the jury, of constructive sanctioning options and jury duties.

    YOUR FIRST DUTY WHEN YOU RETIRE IS TO SELECT A FOREPERSON. THE DECISION YOU MAKE MUST BE UNANIMOUS. DURING YOUR DELIBERATION ALL PERTINENT MATTERS (SUCH AS WHETHER THE RESPONDENT IS REMORSEFUL; WHETHER PUNISHMENT HAS BEEN RECEIVED FROM PARENTS OR OTHERS FOR THE OFFENSE; AND THE SPECIFICS OF THE EVENT SHOULD BE CONSIDERED. REMEMBER THAT IT IS EACH JUROR'S DUTY TO THE RESPONDENT AND THE COMMUNITY TO SPEAK THEIR MIND. IF A JUROR SIMPLY GOES ALONG WITH THE CROWD, THEY ARE NOT DOING THEIR JOB. USE THE CONSTRUCTIVE SANCTIONING FORM TO GUIDE YOU. THE MINMUM CONSTRUCTIVE SANCTIONS THAT YOU CAN GIVE ARE THE TEEN/PARENT WORKSHOP AND AT LEAST ONE NIGHT OF JURY DUTY. PLEASE THINK ABOUT YOUR DECISION CAREFULLY BECAUSE I MAY MODIFY THE SANCTIONS IF I FEEL IT NECESSARY. BAILIFF, PLEASE ESCORT THE JURY TO THE JURY ROOM."

14. After the Panel returns, the Bailiff brings the sanctioning forms to the Judge who reads over and signs the forms. If the constructive sanctions are acceptable to the Judge, the Judge states that there is no need to modify the decisions. If the Judge modifies the decisions, the court is informed.

15. The Bailiff returns the form to the Foreperson. The Judge asks the respondent and his/her parents(s)/guardian(s) to rise individually when their constructive sanctions are read. The Foreperson reads the sanctions. After the reading, the Judge asks each of the respondent(s) and the parent(s)/guardian(s) if they understand the sanctions; the sanctions; and if they accept the sanctions. The Bailiff then takes the constructive form to the Clerk.

16. The Judge says:

    "Please remember your oath of confidentiality. The names and events of Restorartive Teen Court Trials are not to be discussed with anyone. Thank you for your participation."

    The Judge then makes the following final comments to the respondents:

    a. There is only one opportunity to attend Restorative Teen Court.
    b. All Sanctions must be completed within 60 days.
    c. That only when the sanctions are completed will the Restorative Teen Court Coordinator ask for a dismissal of the charges.

d. After they finish the Restorative Teen Court Program, the respondents will not have a public recor.

e. If sanctions are not completed within 60 days, they will be referred back to the referrimg agent for further action.

f. If during the 60 days the respondent becomes involved in addtional charges, they will immediately be dismissed from the Restorative Teen Court Program, and not be eligible for its benefits

   "A Restorative Teen Court Staff member will meet with each of you and explain the constructive sanctions and answer any questions you may have"

17. The Bailiff then adjourns court: "ALL RISE, THIS COURT IS NOW ADJOURNED." The Bailiff leads the Panel out of the courtroom.

19. The respondent(s), along with their parent(s)/guardian(s), goes with the Restorative Teen Court Staff for processing as the next case prepares. The courtroom remains quiet.

FIGURE 13.11   Procedure for Restorative Justice Teen Court.

TEEN COURT

LETTER OF APOLOGY

Dear Teen Court Defendant,

An apology is a part of the recommended sentence of City of Holland Teen Court. Nearly every minor who comes before Teen Court is required to apologize either orally, in writing, or both. The sentencing report that was given to you after the Teen Court hearing will indicate your apology sentence. Completed letters should be sealed, addressed, stamped and given to the Teen Court Coordinator to be mailed.
IMPORTANT: If it is unclear to whom the letter should be sent, please send it to your parent(s) or guardian.

If you choose, you can use the following worksheet to help you organize the information to express your thoughts and feelings. Please call Teen Court Coordinator _____ with any questions at _____

_____
A letter of apology should include the following:

Date _____
Name of person or organization _____
Street Address _____
City, State, Zip Code _____

Dear _____,

I was responsible for (doing what)
_____
_____(when)_____
_____
_____
I am sorry because (why)_____

_____
Since the offense I have taken responsibility by (doing what)

_____
_____

The experience of my arrest, court hearing, and consequences has taught me that

_____

I realize now that my offense hurt (who) _____

_____

and I regret (what)_____

_____

Sincerely,

_____

FIGURE 13.12 Letter of Apology (Holland, Michigan, Teen Court). (public domain)
Source: Holland Teen Court, Holland, Michigan

TEEN COURT RESTITUTION CONTRACT

Date of Referral _____   Case No _____

Juvenile Name _____

Address _____   Phone _____

Victim _____

Address _____   Phone _____

Offense & Date of Offense

_____

_____

_____

_____

Type of Restitution (Include Specific Amount & Time)

_____

_____

_____

_____

I agree that the above information is acceptable to me and will comply to the best of my ability

_____   Teen Court Coordinator
Juvenile

_____   _____
Juvenile's Parent or Guardian   Juvenile's Parent or Guardian

FIGURE 13.13 Teen Court Restitution Contract. (Holland, Michigan, Teen Court). (public domain)
Source: Holland Teen Court, Holland, Michigan.

The Successfulness of Teen Courts

Teen courts are increasingly popular as alternatives to formal juvenile court actions attests to their successfulness in sanctioning first-time low-risk youthful offenders (Patrick et al., 2004). Being judged by one's peers seems to be an effective method of imposing sanctions. Youths who function as judges, prosecutors, and defense counsels usually receive a certain number of hours of training to perform these important roles (Carrington and Schulenberg, 2004). In New York, for instance, an average of 16–20 hours of training is required of youth court juvenile officials (Butts and Buck, 2002). In some instances, written tests are administered following one's training. These are the equivalent of bar exams for youths, to ensure that they understand some basic or fundamental legal principles.

Several national youth court guidelines have been articulated. These guidelines have been developed for (1) program planning and community mobilization; (2) program staffing and funding; (3) legal issues; (4) identified respondent population and referral process; (5) volunteer recruitment and sentencing options; (6) volunteer training; (7) youth court operations and case management; and (8) program evaluation.

Recidivism rates of teen courts have not been studied consistently throughout all jurisdictions. However, available information suggests that the recidivism rates among youthful defendants who have gone through the teen court process are very low, less than 20 percent. One positive consequence that is reported in many jurisdictions is that processed youth emerge with a greater appreciation for the law, a greater understanding of it, and a greater respect for authority figures. They appear to be more law-abiding compared with youths adjudicated in more traditional ways through juvenile courts (Butts and Buck, 2002). A majority of states have adopted teen court models of one type or another, and many are in the process of considering legislation to establish them (Chapman, 2005).

States vary in terms of the eligibility age limits and types of offenses that youth courts may consider. Mostly first-offense, low-level misdemeanors or status offenses are included. More serious offenses are usually passed along to the juvenile court beyond the intake stage. The accountability of participating youths is heightened considerably inasmuch as youths must admit guilt before participating in teen courts (Butts and Buck, 2002). Furthermore, they must waive their confidentiality rights in most jurisdictions.

JUVENILE RIGHTS

During the mid-1960s and for the next 20 years, significant achievements were made in the area of juvenile rights. The U.S. Supreme Court has vested youths with certain constitutional rights. These rights do not encompass all of the rights extended to adults who are charged with crimes.

1. ***Kent v. United States (1966).*** *Kent v. United States* (1966) established the universal precedents of (1) requiring waiver hearings before juveniles can be transferred to the jurisdiction of a criminal court (excepting legislative or automatic waivers, although reverse waiver hearings must be conducted at the juvenile's request), and (2) juveniles are entitled to consult with counsel prior to and during such hearings.

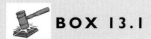

George Epp
Director, Colorado Division of Emergency Management
Former Chairman, Colorado Juvenile Parole Board

Statistics:

B.A. (sociology), University of Colorado; Colorado Peace Officer Certification.

Background:

First, my prior work experience includes being Executive Director, Sheriffs of Colorado; Sheriff, Boulder County; Sheriff's Division Commander, Watch Commander, Detective Sergeant, Detective, Patrol Officer, and Jail Officer. I've chaired the Colorado Juvenile Parole Board and been involved in numerous other chair positions for the governor of Colorado and other officials.

I've been interested in criminal and social justice as long as I can remember. While still in high school, I was part of a group that traveled from Colorado to Alabama to participate in the civil rights march from Selma to Montgomery. I went to college in the late 1960s, which were troubled times. Challenges to authority, the Vietnam War, and questioning of our basic institutions, together with growing claims to basic rights by minorities, were the order of the day. I was an ardent admirer of President John F. Kennedy, his brother, Bobby, and Martin Luther King, Jr. Assassins gunned all of them down.

I spent my first three years in college as a geology major. But I was attracted to courses in social science, and eventually I changed my major. The University of Colorado had no major in criminal justice in 1972, but I graduated with a degree in sociology, with an emphasis on juvenile delinquency. As a part of my coursework, I served as a volunteer juvenile probation officer.

My first real job was a deputy sheriff, working the midnight shift in the county jail. At that time, certification for peace officers was just beginning, and no formal training or certification were required to work in

jails. A new sheriff had been elected; he was young, idealistic, and determined to professionalize his department. Change was the only constant during the first years I worked for the sheriff's department. When I started, there were 50 employees and a county population of 120,000. Thirty years later, the sheriff's office employed 325 persons and served a county of 300,000. With no prior experience myself, I went from jail officer to patrol officer to detective during my first year on the job. There were few policies and procedures, and the ones we had changed often. Escapes from our jail were embarrassingly frequent; most were the result of poor facility design combined with a lack of staff training and supervisory problems.

In spite of and perhaps because of the chaos of those early years, our organization matured and improved. We built a new jail, developed personnel policies, created training programs, and sought help to improve our organizational structure. I had wonderful opportunities over the next 18 years to serve in patrol, detectives, and in the jail, both at the line level and as a supervisor and administrator. In 1990, Brad Leach, the sheriff who had led us for 20 years, announced he was stepping down. I decided to run for this office. I won both the primary and general election and served as the sheriff for several terms. In 1994, voters statewide passed a constitutional amendment placing term limits on all local and state office holders, which meant that I could not run again in 2002. I was fortunate to be hired as the director of our state's sheriff's association. After three years working for this organization, I

(continued)

BOX 13.1 (*Continued*)

was asked by Governor Bill Owens to become Director of the Division of Emergency Management. Beginning in 2000, I was appointed by the governor to serve on the Colorado Juvenile Parole Board. Prior to that, most of my professional experience had dealt with adult offenders.

Most everyone wonders, guesses, and assumes why some people break the law and some do not. It has been a question I have often pondered and discussed with others. During my time on the Juvenile Parole Board, I reviewed files and conducted interviews with about 1,500 kids who had been in trouble with the law. When I began, I expected to find that many kids had come from troubled families. But I was shocked to see that well over 90 percent of the kids in serious trouble had been abandoned, abused, or neglected by their parents. I did my first two full days of hearings before I came to the first youth who still lived with both parents, and in that case, the father had just been released from prison for sexually assaulting the youth's older sister. What inner strength allows some kids in these horrible situations to avoid trouble and become successful? And what can we do, both as citizens and as criminal justice professionals, to protect children from their parents?

2. **In re Gault (1967).** The *Gault* case is the most significant of all landmark juvenile rights cases. Certainly it is considered the most ambitious. In a 7–2 vote, the U.S. Supreme Court articulated the following rights for all juveniles: (1) the right to a notice of charges; (2) the right to counsel; (3) the right to confront and cross-examine witnesses; and (4) the right to invoke the privilege against self-incrimination.

3. **In re Winship (1970).** *Winship* established an important precedent in juvenile courts relating to the standard of proof used in established defendant guilt. The U.S. Supreme Court held that "beyond a reasonable doubt," a standard ordinarily used in adult criminal courts, was henceforth to be used by juvenile court judges and others in establishing a youth's delinquency. Formerly, the standard used was the civil application of "preponderance of the evidence."

4. **McKeiver v. Pennsylvania (1971).** The *McKeiver* case was important because the U.S. Supreme Court held that juveniles are not entitled to a jury trial as a matter of right.

5. **Breed v. Jones (1975).** This case raised the significant constitutional issue of "double jeopardy." The U.S. Supreme Court concluded that after a juvenile has been adjudicated as delinquent on specific charges, those same charges may not be alleged against those juveniles subsequently in criminal courts through transfers or waivers.

6. **Schall v. Martin (1984).** In this case, the U.S. Supreme Court issued juveniles a minor setback regarding the state's right to hold them in preventive detention pending a subsequent adjudication. The Court said that the preventive detention of juveniles by states is constitutional, if judges perceive these youths to pose a danger to the community or an otherwise serious risk if released short of an adjudicatory hearing.

OFFENSE SERIOUSNESS AND DISPOSITIONS: AGGRAVATING AND MITIGATING CIRCUMSTANCES

Aggravating and Mitigating Circumstances

Aggravating Circumstances.   Aggravating circumstances are those that enhance penalties imposed by juvenile court and criminal court judges. Key aggravating factors include the following:

1. Death or serious bodily injury to one or more victims.
2. An offense committed while an offender is awaiting resolution of other delinquency charges.
3. An offense committed while the offender is on probation, parole, or work release.
4. Previous offenses for which the offender has been punished.
5. Leadership in the commission of a delinquent act involving two or more offenders.
6. A violent offense involving more than one victim.
7. Extreme cruelty during the commission of the offense.
8. The use of a dangerous weapon in the commission of the offense, with high risk to human life.

Mitigating Circumstances.   Mitigating factors are those that lessen penalties imposed by these respective courts. Key mitigating factors include the following:

1. No serious bodily injury resulting from the offense.
2. No attempt to inflict serious bodily injury on anyone.
3. Duress or extreme provocation.
4. Circumstances that justify the conduct.
5. Mental incapacitation or physical condition that significantly reduced the offender's culpability in the offense.
6. Cooperation with authorities in apprehending other participants, or making restitution to the victims for losses they suffered.
7. No previous record of delinquent activity.

JUDICIAL DISPOSITIONAL OPTIONS

Below is a summary of judicial options. One or more of the following 11 options may be exercised in any delinquency adjudication:

Nominal Sanctions
1. A stern reprimand may be given.
2. A verbal warning may be issued

Conditional Sanctions

3. An order may be given to make restitution to victims.

4. An order may given to pay a fine.

5. An order may be given to perform some public service.

6. An order may be given to submit to the supervisory control of some community-based corrections agency on a probationary basis.

7. A sentence may be imposed, but the sentence may be suspended for a fixed term of probation.

Custodial Sanctions (Nonsecure and Secure)

8. An order may be issued for the placement of the juvenile in a foster home.

9. An order may be issued for the placement of the juvenile n a residential center or group home.

10. An order may be given to participate under supervision at a camp ranch or special school (either nonsecure or secure detention).

11. An order may be given to be confined in a secure facility for a specified period.

Nominal and Conditional Sanctions

Nominal dispositions are verbal and/or written warnings or reprimands issued to low-risk juvenile offenders, often first-offenders, for the purpose of alerting them to the seriousness of their acts and their potential for receiving severe conditional punishments if they ever should reoffend. These sanctions are the least punitive alternatives.

Conditional sanctions most often include probation. Most juvenile court judges choose probation as the sanction to apply for juveniles most frequently. It places juveniles under the supervision of juvenile POs and they can report directly to the judge if juveniles misbehave or do not follow their probation orders. Probation for juveniles is pretty much like it is for adults. Juveniles also have intensive probation supervision, sometimes called **juvenile intensive supervised probation (JISP)**.

Custodial Sanctions

The custodial options available to juvenile court judges are of two general types: nonsecure facilities and secure facilities. Nonsecure custodial facilities are those that permit youths freedom of movement within the community. Youths are generally free to leave the premises of their facilities, although they are compelled to observe various rules, such as curfew, avoidance of alcoholic beverages and drugs, and participation in specific programs that are tailored to their particular needs (Schaps and Solomon, 2003). These types of nonsecure facilities include foster homes, group homes and halfway houses, camps, ranches, experience programs, and wilderness projects.

Nonsecure Facilities.   If the juvenile's natural parents are considered unfit, or if the juvenile is abandoned or orphaned, **foster homes** are often used for temporary placement. Those youths placed in foster homes are not necessarily law violators. They may be **children in need of supervision (CHINS)** or **persons in**

need of supervision (PINS) (*Matter of Zachary "I"*, 1993). Foster home placement provides youths with a substitute family. A stable family environment is believed by the courts to be beneficial in many cases where youths have no consistent adult supervision or are unmanageable or unruly in their own households.

Another nonsecure option for juvenile judges is the assignment of juveniles to **group homes.** Placing youths in group homes is considered an intermediate option available to juvenile court judges. Group homes are community-based operations that may be either publicly or privately administered. Usually, group homes will have counselors or residents to act as parental figures for youths in groups of 10 to 20. Certain group homes, referred to as family group homes, are actually family-operated, and thus, they are in a sense an extension of foster homes for larger numbers of youths. Several other options include wilderness experiences, camps, placement on ranches or other similar facilities, or even boot camps for temporary periods. The boot camps for juveniles are very similar to those for adults.

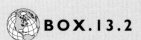

BOX.13.2

INTERNATIONAL SNAPSHOT: PROBATION AND PAROLE IN AUSTRALIA

Australia is a commonwealth nation comprised of a national government and six state governments. The six states includes Queensland, Western Australia, Tasmania, New South Wales, Victoria, and South Australia. Each state establishes its own criminal codes similiar to U.S. states in relation to the federal government. Within each state are shires, which are the equivalent of U.S. counties. The commonwealth of Australia is a federalist government and has laws enforceble in all states. The most frequently prosecuted federal crimes include drug importation and violation of social security laws. Within each state, local communities may pass their own laws and ordinance, such as traffic enforcement and public order laws. Because of the strong influences of Great Britian on Auatralia, there is a pervasive influence of common law distinguished from codified law. There is a great deal of common law in Australia, and it varies considerably in its usage among the different states. Australia also has a large population of Aborigines, tribes of person who have evolved their own customs and laws. Quite often, crimes committed among Aboriginal tribes are settled by custom rather than by external law enforcement bodies.

Crimes in Australia are defined as any conduct that is prohibited by law that may result in punishment. Crimes are either felonies, misdemeanors, or minor offences, but most often these are reffered to as indictable or non-indictable offences. Indictable offences, the equivalent of U.S. felonies, are tried in superior courts in each of the states or in federal courts, and they may require juries. But the vast majority of Australia offending involves nonindictable offences, which are heard and decided in magistrate's local courts. Generally, however, crimes are divided according to crimes against the person, crimes against property, and "other."

The minimum age of criminal responsibility follows common law precedent, which indicates anyone below the age of 7 is not accountable. Only persons age 16 or older can be tried in an adult court, however. There is considerable variation among the states regarding juvenile court jurisdiction, with some states having a 10–17 age range, while others have an 8–17 or a 7–16 age range. Some generalities include that any youth over the age of 7 and who is charged with homicide may be tried in adult court. In some rare instances, youths over

(*continued*)

BOX 13.2 (*Continued*)

the age of 7 but under the age of 18 can be tried in adult court for rape or treason.

The police forces of Australia are similar to those of the United States. A federal police force exists, much like the FBI. It is known as the Australian Federal Police, or AFP. There is a separate police force for each of the six states and for the Northern Territory. In all there are eight separate police forces in Australia. Each community or town has its own police contingent as well. In 2005 there were over 35,000 police officers in Australia in all states, towns, and communities. All police officers may carry firearms and batons, and deadly force may be used if one's life is endangered by a criminal suspect. Most arrests of suspects occur without warrant, although warrants are required to search one's automobile and home. Police officers also have considerable discretionary authority to caution suspects. Thus, there is widespread use of police cautioning, where possible criminal suspects are merely warned rather than arrested and charged. All of this is at the discretion of the police officer in any police–citizen contact. All interviews with suspects and any confessions given are videotaped for all serious cases.

The rights of accused persons are similar to those rights enjoyed by U.S. citizens. All persons have the right to defend themselves, or to have an attorney appointed for them if they are indigent. Under a national system, all indigent accused persons may be represented by attorneys who provide free legal services. A Legal Aid Commission oversees assignments of public defenders to indigents. Aboriginals have their own legal services. Both prosecutors and defense counsels have the right to cross-examine persons during trials. In all serious cases, persons who are arrested are also booked, fingerprinted, and photographed. If charges are not brought against suspects, they are released subsequently. Police officers permit arrested persons to telephone others for assistance. Police officers also investigate crimes and furnish prosecutors with evidence in all criminal matters. Guilty pleas are acceptable and judges may decide to dispense with trials and impose sentences at the time guilty pleas are entered. This process

speeds up case processing considerably, and there is rarely a backlog of court cases in any Australian court. The most serious cases are heard in court, where an accused person is entitled to a 12-member jury trial. While plea bargaining is not officially condoned in Australia, a form of it exists through charge bargaining, where some charges against suspects are dropped in exchange for a plea of guilty to other more serious charges.

Persons who are charged with crimes may or may not be entitled to bail. Bail is provided in less serious cases, if the suspect is not likely to flee the jurisdiction, and if the crime(s) alleged do not pose a serious risk to others or the general public. There is a strong presumption in granting bail in virtually every jurisdiction. Those charged with murder, robbery, or rape may be held without bail and are said to be remanded to custody until their trial dates. About 15 percent of all persons charged with serious crimes are subject to remand annually.

The court system of Australia is hierarchical, headed by the High Court of Australia. This is final court of appeal for all lower state courts and appellate bodies. Each state and territory has a supreme court, much like each U.S. state. Depending on the particular state and population, there are intermediate appellate courts. In heavily populated areas, there are district courts and criminal courts. In more rural areas there are county courts. Each town or community has a magistrate's court. Approximately 90 percent of all criminal cases are heard and decided in magistrate's courts. Special juvenile courts exist that are closed to the press and public for a youth's privacy and confidentiality. When cases are decided in criminal matters, pre-sentence investigation reports are prepared by probation officers much like they are in the United States. Victim impact statements may be appended to these reports, and during sentencing hearings, which occur in the most serious cases, victims may give their opinions about judicial sentencing options. Thus, there is significant victim involvement in sentencing. Probation officers have a great deal of influence in offender sentencing, since they prepare pre-sentence investigation reports and make sentencing recommendations. Probation is used frequently as an optional punishment.

All prisons in Australia are the responsibility and are under the control of the states or territories. There are no federal penitentiaries. The most recent figures reported in 2006 were for the 2004 year. A census of Australian prisons is conducted every June 30, and in 2004 there were 24,171 persons in prison. This is a 2.6 percent increase over the number of Australian inmates incarcerated in 2003. Men make up about 93 percent of all inmates, similar to U.S. prison figures. In an unofficial report, there were approximately 55,000 persons under noncustodial supervision (probation or parole) in 2005. This is an increase of 7 percent from 2004. And the 55,000 figure is over triple the incarcerated inmate population from 1993, which was 14,335.

The range of penalties available to criminal court judges includes fines, probation, and incarceration of varying durations, depending on the crime seriousness and other factors. Judges may also impose home confinement, community service orders, restitution, and almost every other type of intermediate punishment available to convicted offenders in the United States. The probation orders received by probationers in Australia look very much like U.S. state and federal probation orders. Australia does not have the death penalty, as it was abolished in 1967. The most prevalent offenses profiling inmates in Australian prisons include 42 percent violent offenders, about 15 percent drug offenders (as drug offenses have climbed systematically over the last 10-year period), and approximately 40 percent property offending. All prisoners have vocational and educational opportunities while they are imprisoned. Additionally, counseling programs for different types of offenders exist, including drug treatment programs for drug-dependent persons. The prisons of Australia all have different security levels, and each inmate can earn more privileges and less secure confinement through good conduct. Furloughs are permitted after prisoners have served a portion of their sentences with good conduct reports. These furloughs are almost always weekend leaves to rejoin their families and look for work in their post-prison period following parole-granting. The primary goals of the Australian criminal justice system are retribution, incapacitation, rehabilitation, and crime prevention or deterrence. Restorative justice is used frequently, particularly among Aborigines and their tribes. This procedure avoids the adverse labeling effects of criminal prosecutions, as families and offenders and victims are able to come together and resolve their differences in civil ways.

Parole is used in Australia. Persons become parole-eligible after serving two-thirds of their maximum sentences. In 2005, there were approximately 220,000 persons under probation or parole supervision. Probation and parole officers who supervise offenders employ varying strategies in dealing with their criminal clients. These supervisors must often be teachers, social workers, and counselors as well as enforcers of probation or parole program conditions. Probation and parole officers must function in different ways as negotiators; brokers for individualized community services for their clients; help to bridge the needs of their clients and make available community resources when needed; be intermediaries between offenders and different agencies; and be social resource managers.

The Prisons Department and the Probation and Parole Service attempt to deal with a variety of client problems, and they provide different treatment programs, including individual counseling, group work, and engage in family work and liaison with other agencies in the substance abuse field. An aggressive attempt is made to recruit only the best persons to serve as probation and parole officers, and they are carefully trained in in-service programming for many months before performing their jobs on their own with individual clients. Coordination is emphasized, together with accurate record keeping, documentation, and individual evaluation and progress reports.

Actually, the list of tasks performed by Australian probation and parole officers is extensive. It includes (1) managing and supervising offenders who have received

(continued)

BOX 13.2 (*Continued*)

community-based supervision orders, including home detention, probation, bail, or parole, and they must make sure that persons comply with their program conditions; (2) monitoring home detainees by means of home visits and electronic monitoring technology, which is increasing, and they must report any violations detected; (3) developing and implementing community-based work programs; (4) assessing placement and management of offenders placed on community service work orders, bonds, fine options, and penalties; (5) interviewing offenders and their families, employers, or teachers to obtain information; (6) submitting reports and recommendations on whether parole should be granted or continued; (7) providing advice to assist the courts in determining the suitability of offenders to be placed on community-based orders; (8) arranging the employment of offenders as directed by the courts; (9) identifying the social development needs of offenders and referring them to appropriate programs; (10) advising parolees and those on community-based orders on matters such as education, employment, finance, housing, and other community services that may help in their rehabilitation; (11) conducting regular interviews with parolees and report on their progress; (12) maintaining contact with families to help solve problems of readjustment and rehabilitation; (13) assisting in preparing briefs for prosecuting offenders who fail to comply with community-based orders or who breach parole conditions; (14) maintaining and developing client records and administrative

procedures; (15) taking part in staff development and training programs, and providing training for new staff; and (16) participating on various committees to assist in policy, practice, and community development.

Like probation officers in the United States, Australian probation and parole officers may work in offices or in noninstitutionalized community corrections centers. A portion of their time is spent in court and visiting prisons to interview and assess various offenders and prisoners. Personal requirements as qualifications for PO work include having maturity, patience, tolerance, and discretion; having the ability to assist people and assess situations; having a genuine interest in people and their welfare; and having good communication skills.

Sources: Adapted from David Biles, "Australia," *World Factbook of Criminal Justice Systems,* Washington, DC, 2005; Australian Institute of Criminology, *Probation and Parole 2000,* Canberra: Australian Institute of Criminology, 2000; "Community Based Corrections," Australian Institute of Criminology, December 30, 2005; "ACT Corrective Services," Australian Institute of Criminology, December 30, 2005; *Australian Crime: Facts and Figures 2005,* Canberra: Australian Institute of Criminology, 2006; *The Weekend Australian,* "Prison Population Up," March 25, 2006; Department of Corrective Services, *Annual Report 2004/2005,* Sydney, AUS: Department of Corrective Services, 2005; New South Wales Department of Corrective Services, "Government Departments and Agencies," Sydney, AUS: Department of Corrective Services, 2006; Commonwealth of Australia, "Probation Officer/Parole Officer," March 2006; Australian Institute of Criminology, "Offender Development Teams and Substance Abuse," Canberra: Australian Institute of Criminology, January 2006.

Secure Confinement.   **Secure confinement** for juveniles in the United States emulate adult prisons or penitentiaries in several of their characteristics. There is considerable peer violence in many juvenile institutions, similar to violence in adult settings (Peterson-Badali and Koegl, 2002). They are also either short term or long term. These terms are ambiguous as they pertain to juvenile secure custody facilities. Short-term confinement facilities, sometimes referred to as **detention,** are designed to accommodate juveniles on a temporary basis. These juveniles are either awaiting a later juvenile court adjudication, subsequent foster home or group home placement, or a transfer to criminal court. Sometimes youths will be placed in short-term confinement because their identity is unknown and it is desirable that they should not be confined in adult lock-ups or jails (Neustatter, 2002). The average duration of juvenile incarceration nationally is about six months. The average short-term detention is 30 days. Most juvenile court judges use incarceration as a last resort. By far the most frequently used sanction against juveniles is probation (Feld, 2003).

JUVENILE POs AND PRE-DISPOSITIONAL REPORTS

Juvenile Probation Officers

Many probation officers who work with juveniles report that their work is satisfying. Many of them see themselves as playing an important part in shaping a youth's future by the nature of the relationship they can establish between themselves and the juveniles with whom they work. There is a keen sense of professionalism among most probation and parole officers. The American Correctional Association and the American Probation and Parole Association are two of the most important professional organizations today that disseminate information about corrections and probation and parole programs and provide workshops and various forms of professional training. Many probation and parole officers attend the meetings of these and other professional organizations to learn about the latest innovations and probation programs. Sweet (1985) views probation work with juveniles as a timely opportunity to intervene and make a difference in their lives. Thus, he sees probation as a type of therapy. He divides the therapy function that probation officers can perform into five simple steps:

1. Case review—probation counselors need skills to read the behaviors of the youths they supervise and their probable antecedents.
2. Self-awareness—probation counselors need to inspect their own reactions to youths; are they too impatient or overly sensitive? Traditional transference and countertransference issues must be addressed.
3. Development of a relationship—great patience is required; children are often rejected, and probation officers must learn to accept them and demonstrate a faith in their ability to achieve personal goals.
4. The critical incident—the testing phase of the relationship, where juveniles may deliberately act up to test honesty and sincerity of POs.
5. Following through—successive tests will be made by juveniles as they continue to verify the PO's honesty and sincerity; POs do much of the parenting that their clients' parents failed to do. Sweet considers these stages integral features of action therapy that can often be more effective than insight-oriented therapy (Sweet, 1985:90).

Because of their diverse training, POs often orient themselves toward juvenile clients in particular ways that may be more or less effective. Because many juvenile offenders are considered manipulators who might take advantage of a PO's sympathies, some POs have devised interpersonal barriers between themselves and their youthful clients. Other POs have adopted more productive interpersonal strategies. In most juvenile cases, POs seek to instruct and assist offenders to deal with their personal and social problems in order to fit better into their community environments. If POs continuously check up on their youthful clients or regard them with suspicion, they inhibit the growth of productive interpersonal relations that might be helpful in facilitating a youth's reentry into society. Enforcement-oriented officers and those who attempt to detect rule infractions almost always create a hostile working relationship with their clients, and communication barriers are often erected that inhibit a PO's effectiveness.

Juvenile Probation Officer Functions

The functions of juvenile POs are diverse, and they include such tasks as report preparation, home and school visits, and a variety of other client contacts. They often arrange contacts between their clients and various community-based corrections agencies who provide services and specific types of psychological and social treatments. POs themselves perform counseling tasks with their clients. They also must enforce laws associated with probation or parole program conditions. Thus, if offenders have been ordered to comply with a specific curfew and/or reimburse victims for their financial losses, POs must monitor them to ensure that these program conditions have been fulfilled. Some of the most important juvenile PO functions are:

1. Problem solving (problem analysis—the ability to grasp the source, nature, and key elements of problems; judgment—recognition of the significant factors to arrive at sound and practical decisions)

2. Communication (dialogue skills—effectiveness of one-on-one contacts with youthful clients, small group interactions; writing skills—expression of ideas clearly and concisely)

3. Emotional and motivational (reactions to reassure—functioning in a controlled, effective manner under conditions of stress; keeping one's head; drive—the amount of directed and sustained energy to accomplish one's objectives)

4. Interpersonal (insight into others—the ability to proceed, giving due consideration to the needs and feelings of others; leadership—the direction of behavior of others toward the achievement of goals)

5. Administrative (planning—forward thinking, anticipating situations and problems, and preparation in advance to cope with these problems; commitment to excellence—determination that the task will be done-well).

In 2006 it was estimated that there were 35,000 juvenile probation officers in the United States. These officers provided intake services for over 2 million juveniles, pre-dispositional studies of over 800,000 cases, and received over 800,000 cases for supervision (U.S. Department of Justice, 2006). These cases are not distributed evenly throughout the various juvenile probation departments in the United States. Thus, caseloads for some POs are considerably larger than they are for others. A high caseload is arbitrarily defined as 50 or more juvenile clients, although caseloads as high as 300 or more have been reported in some jurisdictions. When caseloads are particularly high, this places an even greater burden on the shoulders of juvenile POs who must often prepare pre-dispositional reports for youths at the juvenile court judge's direction.

Pre-dispositional Reports

Juvenile court judges in many jurisdictions order the preparation of **pre-dispositional reports,** which are the functional equivalent of pre-sentence investigation reports for adults. Pre-disposition reports are intended to furnish judges with background information about juveniles to make a more informed sentencing decision. They also function to assist probation officers and others to target high-need areas for youths and specific services or agencies for individualized referrals. This information is often channeled to information agencies such as the National Center for Juvenile Justice in Pittsburgh, Pennsylvania, so that researchers may benefit in the juvenile justice investigations. They may analyze the information compiled from various jurisdictions for their own research investigations.

Pre-dispositional reports are completed for more serious juveniles and function like pre-sentence investigation reports prepared by POs for adults. Juvenile court judges order these prepared in most cases, unless there are statutory provisions in certain jurisdictions that govern their automatic preparation. These pre-dispositional reports contain much of the same information as PSI reports. Sometimes, juveniles whose families can afford them have private pre-dispositional reports prepared to influence judges to exert leniency on the juvenile offender.

Four important reasons for why pre-dispositional reports should be prepared are that (1) these reports provide juvenile court judges with a more complete picture of juvenile offenders and their offenses, including the existence of any aggravating or mitigating circumstances; (2) these reports can assist the court in tailoring the disposition of the case to an offender's needs; (3) these reports may lead to the identification of positive factors that would indicate the likelihood of rehabilitation; and (4) these reports provide judges with the offender's treatment history, which might indicate the effectiveness or ineffectiveness of previous dispositions and suggest the need for alternative dispositions (Champion, 2007).

It is important to recognize that pre-dispositional reports are not required by judges in all jurisdictions. By the same token, legislative mandates obligate officials in other jurisdictions to prepare them for all juveniles to be adjudicated. Also, there are no specific formats universally acceptable in these report preparations. Figure 13.14 provides two examples of pre-dispositional reports from two different jurisdictions. These are real pre-dispositional reports from actual cases, although the names of critical participants have been changed for purposes of confidentiality and anonymity.

As can be readily seen from the two different pre-dispositional reports shown in Figure 13.14, they can vary considerably in completeness and detail. All of this is dependent upon the nature of the case, the jurisdiction, the protocol followed by particular courts, and other factors. In some jurisdictions, there are orderly forms to fill out, with spaces clearly marked. Again, it varies according to the formality of the jurisdiction. For instance, in the Indiana example shown in Figure 13.15, a standardized form may be used as an alternative to the free-flowing type of report depicted here. A sample report is shown in Figure 13.6.

Rogers (1990:44) indicates that pre-disposition reports contain insightful information about youths that can be helpful to juvenile court judges prior to sentencing. Six social aspects of a person's life are crucial for investigations, analysis, and treatment. These include: (1) personal health, physical and emotional; (2) family and home situation; (3) recreational activities and use of

I. New Mexico Predispositional Report

CHILDREN, YOUTH AND FAMILIES DEPARTMENT
JUVENILE JUSTICE DIVISION

IDENTIFYING INFORMATION*

***Fictitious names because of**

New Mexico confidentiality provisions

NAME: Mary Verdugo

DOB: October 15, 1992

SSN: n/a

ADDRESS: 301 1st St.

Las Cruces, NM

PHONE NUMBER: (444)(555-1212)

P/G/C: Parents

RELIGIOUS PREF: unknown

PRIMARY LANGUAGE SPOKEN: English

COURT INFORMATION

COMPLETED BY: Ann Ames

DATE COMPLETED: October 10, 2006

CASE NUMBER: 123456

CAUSE NUMBER: 7890

JUDGE: Hon. Mark Jones

COUNTY: McNabb

DEFENSE ATTY: Charles Barkin

CCA: unknown

FINAL DISPOSITION: No contest plea

FINAL DISPOSITION DATE: Pending

AKA: n/a

I. Referral Information

Current Offense: On 1-02-2006 at 3:40 AM, Mary Verdugo was taken (by her parents) to the hospital after she was bleeding profusely. Doctors there notified Mary Verdugo's parents that it was apparent that she had just given birth to a baby. The location of the baby was unknown at the time and doctors suspected that Mary Verdugo had possibly killed the baby. Police were notified and searched her room where they found a full-term baby (deceased) in a trash can. Mary Verdugo allegedly told police that she did not know she was pregnant, but gave birth to the baby, by herself, on 12-30-05. An autopsy report indicates that the baby girl, who was found with the umbilical cord still attached, and wrapped around her neck, was alive at birth and died of asphyxiation. Mary Verdugo was arrested on 1-11-06 and booked into McNabb County Jail, Juvenile Unit, at approximately 6:00 PM.

On 1-13-06, a petition was filed charging Mary Verdugo with Count 1: Child Abuse (intentionally caused) (death), or in the alternative: Child Abuse (negligently caused)(death), or in the alternative; Child Abuse (negligently permitted)(death) and Count 2: Tampering with Evidence. Mary Verdugo's parents were able to post the 10 percent cash deposit of $10,000 bond and Mary Verdugo was released home on January 14, 2006. A forensic evaluation was ordered at this time.

On September 22, 2006, Mary Verdugo entered into a plea agreement with the Children's Court Attorney. Mary Verdugo pleaded No Contest to Alternative Count 1: Child Abuse (negligently permitted)(death). In exchange for the plea, the remaining counts in the petition were dismissed and the state agreed to handle the case in a juvenile setting. There was no agreement as to the disposition in the matter and a Pre-dispositional Report was ordered.

Number of Co-Offenders: 0

Victim Impact Mailed: ☐ Yes   ☐ No   ☐ N/A   Response: ☐ Yes   ☐ No

Victim Requests Restoration:

Victim Impact Summary: A victim impact statement is not applicable in this case. It should be noted, however, that Mary Verdugo has given two names for the father of her child. Initially, Mary Verdugo told investigators that she had sexual intercourse with Walter Brooks and that the condom broke. She said she had taken a pregnancy test at Planned Parenthood with negative results. During this officer's conversation with

Mary Verdugo, however, she indicated that the father is John Johnson. She said that Johnson denied that he is the father and that they do not have any contact with each other.

Chronological report attached: ☐ Yes   ☐ No

Currently on Probation/Parole: ☐ Yes   ☐ No   Location:

Prior Supervision:

Cause No.	Begin Date	Type	Length	Expiration	Release Date	Release Type
N/A	10-13-04	Informal supervision	3 months	1-12-05	1-12-05 under	Now supervising conditional release.

Comments: Mary Verdugo was placed on Informal Supervision after her first referral to the probation department in October 2004. Mary Verdugo was referred to Juvenile Probation for a citation she had received for Criminal Trespass. Mary Verdugo and her two sisters were cited as a group of teens caught loitering at Grady's, a restaurant and popular hangout for youth. Mary Verdugo came to see this officer at least one time every week, without fail. Mary Verdugo turned in weekly grade checks from school and attendance was verified.

Prior Commitment to Correctional Facility:

Cause No.	Commit Date	Type	Length	Expiration	Dis.Date	Dis.Type
N/A	N/A	N/A	N/A	N/A	N/A	N/A

Comments: Mary Verdugo has had no prior commitments to correctional facilities.

Prior Youthful Offender: ☐ Yes   ☐ No

Outstanding Restitution: ☐ Yes   ☐ No   Amount: $0.00

Outstanding Community Service: ☐ Yes   ☐ No   Hours: 0

II. SOCIAL, EDUCATIONAL, AND SUBSTANCE ABUSE HISTORY

(Please include information on siblings, dependents, employment, parents' marital status, primary language spoken in home, current school status, special expectations, truancy, behavior problems, gang activity, weapons, extracurricular activities, alcohol, marijuana, and other drug use.)

A. Social

Mary Verdugo is the youngest of three daughters born to Martin and Jane Verdugo. Jean Verdugo is 19 years old, married, and living with her husband, William Smith, 21, and their infant son, Frederick. Olivia Verdugo (18), lives in the family home along with Mary Verdugo. The family lives in a rented house in the northeast heights of Las Cruces, and have for the past four years. The home is a three-bedroom home that appears cluttered but clean. The front and back yards seem moderately maintained and the inside is well furnished. The ashes of Mary Verdugo's (deceased baby) sit on the fireplace mantel in an urn the shape of an angel. Baby Verdugo was cremated on 1-28-06, after the Office of Medical Investigators released the body. For weeks after the incident, the mailbox outside the house and the cars belonging to the family and friends were decorated with tiny pink ribbons in remembrance of the baby. Mary Verdugo has moved out of the bedroom that she resided in at the time of the incident. Mary Verdugo's parents have moved into that room and report that Mary Verdugo is unable (emotionally) to go in there. Mary Verdugo is currently working at Best Industries, as of May 1, 2006. Mary Verdugo previously worked at McDonald's but lost her job shortly after the events of this case came to light. Mary Verdugo had to take four months off of work after the incident. She was an emotional wreck, making her "dysfunctional" and therefore unable to complete her job as expected. Taking this time off paid its toll on the family as well, and Martin Verdugo was forced to work even more at his job of 11 years. Martin Verdugo said that he had to "keep the family going" in a time when it seemed everything was falling apart. Mary Verdugo is currently working with her father at Best Industries where she is working in the mailroom. Mary Verdugo is currently considered a part-time employee, although she works 7.5 hours/day. Mary Verdugo has been there for three months and currently makes $6.50/hour. The remainder of her day is spent on her home schooling. Mary Verdugo spends much of her weekends babysitting her 5-month-old nephew, Frederick.

Mary Verdugo attended Las Cruces Elementary School where her mother was the President of the PTA. Both Mrs. Verdugo and her father report that Mary Verdugo was a good student and did fine in elementary school. Once in middle school, Mary Verdugo attended Craig Middle School. She and her family lived in the south valley and Mary Verdugo said she was one of the very few blonde-haired, blue-eyed girls there. Mary Verdugo reported that she did fine in school, but had problems with peers because of her race. The family eventually moved and Mary Verdugo began attending Burgess Middle School. Mary Verdugo reported no problems at Burgess. Once in high school, Mary Verdugo began attending informal student parties and that she was very much into marijuana her ninth grade year. Mary Verdugo became involved with a boyfriend who proved to be a bad influence on her. After her ditching classes became a habit, Mary Verdugo was referred to a truancy officer and ordered to complete community service. Mary Verdugo reportedly got back on track after her parents placed her on more structure and restriction. By the time this incident took place, Mary Verdugo was seemingly doing much better. Mary Verdugo was in the midterm of her sophomore year when this incident occurred and did not return following her arrest in January 2006. Mary Verdugo plans to continue with her home schooling until graduation. Incidentally, Mary Verdugo has done very well in this program and is now classified as a junior, ahead of her schedule in a mainstream educational setting. Mary Verdugo's sister, Olivia, left her school after the incident as well when the publicity brought adverse reactions from her peers. Olivia, however, has since returned to the school and is reportedly not having any problems there. Jean Verdugo graduated from school before any of these circumstances arose.

As mentioned earlier, Mary Verdugo was referred to the probation department on one other occasion. In July 2004, police officers working a tac-plan in Northeast Heights cited Mary Verdugo and her sisters for trespassing at a local restaurant. Officers were working in an effort to reduce the number of young people loitering in the various parking lots. Mary Verdugo and her sisters were at Grady's when the three of them were cited. Mary Verdugo came in to see this officer for her Preliminary Inquiry on 10-13-04 and was placed on informal supervision. Mary Verdugo made weekly visits with this officer, called in regularly, and turned in school reports as requested. There does not appear to be any other legal history with the family, however, it has been reported that things have been tense at home.

There does not appear to be any physical evidence in the home, however, it has been reported that there is tension and that marital conflict is present. According to the Forensic Evaluation, dated 1-20-05, there were frequent fights about issues relating to the three daughters, money, and dad's drinking. Martin Verdugo has been said to have a "long-standing alcohol abuse Hell." Counseling was offered initially to help cope with the surrounding offense and any issues exacerbated by it, however, Martin Verdugo advised that he does not need any more counseling. Martin Verdugo reports that he will support Mary Verdugo throughout her counseling, but that he has no intention of continuing himself. Martin Verdugo reported that he does not believe the incident should be "dwelled on" and that "you have to go on, or it will tear you up." It was unclear if Martin Verdugo would participate in further counseling or not.

Initially, Martin Verdugo sought counseling services for his family through the Employee Assistance Program that his employer provides. This program only allowed for five visits and the family quickly exhausted that service. Dr. Martha Ames, a private psychologist, was recommended and Mary Verdugo has been seeing her for some time now. Mary Verdugo sees Dr. Ames every two weeks, but no other family member attends. Mary Verdugo's sessions are on average one hour at a time. Mary Verdugo reports that she likes Dr. Ames and feels comfortable in working with her.

Mary Verdugo has admitted to using substances in the past such as marijuana and acid. It is this officer's understanding that Mary Verdugo used acid on an experimental basis only and that marijuana was her drug of choice while in the ninth grade. It is also this officer's understanding that Mary Verdugo has not used any marijuana since June 2005. It is a concern, however, that Mary Verdugo admits to using alcohol on New Year's Eve 2004. This apparently took place at the house with her parents present along with other friends drinking as well. It is disconcerting that Mary Verdugo's parents would allow minors to drink in their home. This was not typical, however, according to Mary Verdugo, but rather something of a celebration of the upcoming new year. Mary Verdugo advised her parents allow drinking on special occasions only.

B. Education/Employment

Diploma:

☐ HS Diploma   ☐ GED Certificate

Graduation date: Pending   GED Date: N/A

Special Education:

☐ Eligible for Sp.Ed.   ☐ Ineligible for Sp.Ed.   ☐ May require Sp.Ed.

Qualifications for Sp.Ed: N/A

Level: N/A   Effective Date: N/A

C. School History

School Name	Type	Program	Prog. Type	Grade/Sp.Ed.	Start Date Stat.
Hardcourt Learning Direct	Home School	Mail/correspondence school	Regular Education	10 school	03/01/06

Comments: As mentioned earlier, Mary Verdugo is doing well in school and is now classified as a junior in high school. Mary Verdugo mails in her schoolwork and completes the assignments that she is provided through the Hardcourt Learning Direct Program. Mary Verdugo has goals of completing her high school education and eventually obtaining a degree in Auto Mechanics.

D. Mental Health/Substance Use History
  Treatment:

Prior Treatment Outpatient   Prior Treatment Outpatient   Date of Last Psych. Eval: 4-17-05

Substance Use:

☐ Alcohol   Frequency: Special Occasions
☐ Marijuana   Frequency: Daily in the past
☐ Drugs   Frequency: Experimental
☐ Solvents   Frequency:

Date Updated: 11-7-05

Comments: Please refer to Section II above for details.

III. JPPO OVERVIEW RECOMMENDATION

(Include core services, P/G/C and client's view of needs, issues and strengths, treatment/residential placement, JPPO areas of concern and community-based service required if removal of client from home is recommended.)

Mary Verdugo appeared to be very nervous about the outcome of this case. Mary Verdugo acknowledged that she would like to continue working and complete her education. Mary Verdugo described herself as a very caring person who is "good minded" and prides herself in her good grades and employment history. Mary Verdugo's father was equally complimentary in his description of Mary Verdugo. Martin Verdugo described Mary Verdugo as a hard worker, energetic, focused, and good with chores at home, never having to be reminded to do them. The only negative issue hat Mary Verdugo and her father could pinpoint was her need to stay on track with school. Nothing was mentioned in regards to counseling or the deep issues associated with the death of her child.

It is difficult to ascertain what Mary Verdugo's thoughts are about the incident itself. It is unfortunate that she was able to plead No Contest in that she now can keep her side of the story to herself. It has been very difficult to assess the situation given that much of the very important information will never have to be given by Mary Verdugo. It impedes treatment as well by not having to talk about the incident or specific actions in the matter as long as that is the case. Mary Verdugo's own state of mind is at risk. As Dr. Ames described it, Mary Verdugo has been greatly limited in her ability to work with other students, as she has not been permitted to talk about the offense. Dr. Ames has been hampered in her ability to investigate with Mary Verdugo and her family the causes of the offense and to directly address them. When weighing the distinction between Retribution, safety of the public, and the best interest of the child, it is difficult to suggest that incarceration is the most appropriate outcome. Mary Verdugo has been afforded the opportunity to show that she can comply with the structure and rules that the probation department can provide and she has done that. Incarcerating her at this point would serve no purpose other than punishment and this could impede the treatment process even further. Dr. Ames feels that Mary Verdugo does not lack the capacity for empathy and the concern for others. Furthermore, it is this officer's understanding that Mary Verdugo does not pose a threat to anyone. The amount of denial in this case is insurmountable and the plea agreement encourages it. It is imperative that Mary Verdugo be allowed to engage in therapy to the point that she can talk about the incident and work, with her parents, to move past this and begin the lengthy process of intensive therapy. It is equally important that Mary Verdugo's family engage in therapy. According to the Forensic Evaluation, a likely factor in Mary Verdugo's situation is the stress in the family characterized by parental alcohol abuse, depression, and chronic marital conflict. The results of these family problems affected the whole family. Mary Verdugo, it has been reported, is deficient in coping skills, judgment, problem solving, and decision making. Mary Verdugo, according to the Forensic, appears to be "overwhelmed by especially stressful circumstances, and to ill-judged behavior at such times." Mary Verdugo, it reports, "does not seem to be a girl with antisocial or prominent aggressive tendencies, or characteristic tendencies toward remorseless use of others." Given these findings, it would seem appropriate to think that with support and supervision, and with intense therapy to recognize these contributing factors, Mary Verdugo would seem to be a low risk for repeat offenses and danger to others.

It is this officer's recommendation that Mary Verdugo be given a term of probation, for an extended period of time, to be determined by the court, but that addresses these crucial elements. It is highly recommended that Mary Verdugo be monitored closely to determine her progress and participation. It is also recommended that Mary Verdugo's parents be made party to the petition and monitored for their compliance in therapy as well. A referral to the JIPS program could also be made to address what could be a rocky transition from intense publicity of this case back to more routine circumstances. It is also recommended that Mary Verdugo continue with intense psychotherapy and address specifics of the incident. The probation department would ideally work with the therapist in maintaining compliance and progress. Incarceration at this point would serve no other purpose than to address punishment and retribution. These issues could be served in the context of probation supervision just as well, while allowing Mary Verdugo to obtain the therapy that she desperately needs. Periodic Judicial Reviews could be used to further monitor compliance and progress. Community service is advised and possible options with meaningful results could be explored through the context of therapy.

IV. CLINICAL SOCIAL WORKER COMMENTS

(Must be completed for mandatory referrals and court order.)

Please refer to Forensic Evaluation dated 1-20-06.

_____
Clinical Social Worker

Respectfully Submitted,   Approved;

_____   _____
Emilio Ramirez, JPPO   Chief JPPO/Supervisor
Count 1: Robbery

2. Indiana Predispositional Report

PREDISPOSITIONAL REPORT

James Allenbeck

8522C114 005362 0110

COUNT I: RUNAWAY

OCTOBER 16, 2006

LEGAL HISTORY:

PAST OFFENSES:

November 19, 2000	An Information Petition is received from the Terre Hauste Police Department,aleging Criminal Mischief
December 8,.2000	A Preliminary Inquiry is conducted. This matter is taken under advisement, pending request for restitution.
March 1, 2001	No requests for restitution are received and this matter is filed as inactive.

PRESENT OFFENSE

April 22, 2006	The minor child is arrested for Runaway.
April 23, 2006	A Preliminary Inquiry is conducted and this matter is filed with the prosecutor.
June 9, 2006	The State of Indiana files Count I: Runaway.
September 11, 2006	Matter comes on for Arraignment. The minor child appears in person with his mother and stepfather. The Constitutional Rights are read and explained. The petition is read and `allegation contained therein admitted to. A PredispositionalReport is ordered and Disposition is set.

SOURCES OF INFORMATION

James Allenbeck, Offender
Tom and Rachel Jamison, offender's mother and stepfather
Records, Terre Haute Police Department
Records, Vigo County School Corporation
Records, Vigo County Juvenile Justice Center

SOCIAL HISTORY

NATURAL MOTHER

Rachel Allenbeck Jamison, age 43, was born on December 19, 1962, in Terre Haute, Indiana. She has an 11th-grade education from Madison High School and is employed by Indiana State University as a supervisor for Special Education.

NATURAL FATHER

James Allenbeck's father died in December 1999. His name was Michael Arthur Allenbeck. He was born on August 25, 1957, in Franklin, Kentucky. He graduated from Franklin High School and attended one year at Western Kentucky University. He was employed as a truck driver with Moody Trucking.

Michael and Rachel Allenbeck were married in January 1985. James is the only child from this union. This was Michael Allenbeck's only marriage. Rachel Allenbeck had been married previously to Peter Kruittschnitt. The couple married in September 1979 and divorced in 1981, with no children being born in the union. Rachel bore James on December 29, 1993. She is presently married to Tom Jamison. The couple married in October 2005 and have no children together.

HOME ENVIRONMENT

James resides with his mother and stepfather at 1111 23rd Drive, Terre Haute, Indiana. The family is buying their two-bedroom, one-and-a-half bath home. According to Rachel, James does what he is asked to do without any backtalk. She further states he is a sneak and will break things on purpose, has stolen from family members, and continues to smoke cigarettes after being told to stop. Rachel states that she and James have a good relationship together, but he seems to go out of his way to "piss off" his stepfather. A copy of a list of concerns and complaints from Rachel is attached to this report. Rachel feels that James acts appropriate, but seems to be another person when your back is turned.

EDUCATION

James is a ninth-grade student at Terre Haute North Vigo High School. According to mother and stepfather, James is doing well in school. A copy of his grades are attached to this report. He did have six Saturday Schools last year for not doing homework and one Saturday School for throwing pizza in another student's face. James does not intend to graduate from high school.

PHYSICAL AND MENTAL HEALTH

James enjoys good health at this time. No serious injuries or illnesses were reported to this officer by the mother. James has no history of contact with a mental health facility for counseling. He does smoke cigarettes and has been caught stealing cigarettes from his stepfather. He has admitted to stealing over $400 in liquor and trading it for cigarettes. James has also stolen oxycodine from his stepfather.

HOBBIES AND RECREATION

James enjoys television, talking on the telephone, reading *Harry Potter* books.

RECOMMENDATION

It is respectfully recommended that James Allenbeck be placed on 6 months' strict Formal Probation, Court Ordered to attend school, Court Ordered to participate in Family Preservation Program at Hamilton Center, and to pay $127 in Court Costs, a $100 Administration Fee, and a $10 monthly User Fee.

FIGURE 13.14 Two sample Pre-Dispositional Reports

leisure time; (4) peer group relationships (types of companions); (5) education; and (6) work experience. According to the National Advisory Commission on Criminal Justice Standards and Goals as outlined in 1973, pre-dispositional reports have been recommended in all cases where the offenders are minors. In actual practice, however, pre-dispositional reports are only prepared at the request of juvenile court judges. No systematic pattern typifies such report preparation in most U.S. jurisdictions.

Rogers (1990:46) says that the following characteristics were included in 100 percent of all of the cases: (1) gender, (2) ethnic status, (3) age at first

PROBATION OFFICERS REPORT OF PRELIMINARY INQUIRY AND / OR PREDISPOSITIONAL REPORT

STATE OF INDIANA
COUNTY OF VIGO

In the Matter of: _____
A Child Alleged to be a Delinquent Child

Date Completed: _____

Assigned P.O.: _____   Report Prepared By: _____

JUVENILE INFORMATION

Case No.(s): _____

Legal Name: _____

Alias(es)/Nickname(s): _____

Custodial Person(s) or Agency: _____

Street Address: _____

City: _____

Telephone: _____   Social Security No.: _____

DOB: _____   POB: _____

Age: _____ Race: _____ Gender: _____ Ht: _____ Wt: _____ Eyes: _____ Hair: _____

ID Marks: _____

Driver's Lic. No.: _____ State of Issue: _____ Status: _____

JUVENILE LEGAL INVOLVEMENT

_____Chg(s) pending_____Detainer(s)____Inf.Adj._____Probation_____Res.Plemnts._____IDOC

_____DFCS Ward _____Violations _____Parole_____Waived ____Adult Status ____Other Contacts

DELINQUENT ACT(S) INFORMATION

Alleged Offense: _____ Date Committed: _____

I.C. _____ Class (if committed by an adult): _____ Felony/Misdemeanor

Alleged Offense: _____ Date Committed: _____

I.C. _____ Class (if committed by an adult): _____ Felony/Misdemeanor

Alleged Offense: _____ Date Committed: _____

I.C. _____   Class (if committed by an adult): _____ Felony/Misdemeanor

Referring Agency: _____

Custody Status: _____

_____

Co-Offender(s) Status: _____

Case No.(s): _____

PRIOR LEGAL HISTORY

Date of Referral	Charges	County/ P.O	Disposition (Date / Type)
_____	_____	_____	_____
_____	_____	_____	_____
_____	_____	_____	_____

EDUCATION, HEALTH, EMP0LOYMENT

School: _____   Grade: _____   Credits: _____

Special Education Classification: _____ Yes _____ No   Suspension/Expulsions: _____

Special Educational Placement: _____ Yes _____ No   Special Ed. Classification: _____

Mental Health Referrals: _____ Yes _____ No   Therapist: _____
                                                            Doctor: _____
Reasons for Referral: Diagnosis: _____
_____   Medication: _____
_____   Dates: _____
_____

Physical Problems: _____ Yes _____ No   Diagnosis: _____

                                                          Doctor Name: _____

                                                          Last Visit: _____

Description: _____

_____

_____

Alcohol/Drug Use: _____ Yes _____ No   Substance of Choice: _____
                                                         Frequency: _____
                                                         Last Usage: _____
                                                         Addicted ?: _____
                                                         Source: _____
                                                         Parent Awareness: _____

Employer: _____

Position: _____   Hours: _____ $ _____ /hr.

ADDITIONAL INFORMATION

_____

_____

_____

FAMILY INFORMATION

Father's Name: _____ SSN _____ (if available)
Address: _____   D.O.B. _____
Employment: _____   Hours: _____
Home Telephone: _____   Work Telephone: _____

Mother's Name: _____ SSN _____ (if available)
Address: _____   D.O.B. _____
Employment: _____   Hours: _____
Home Telephone: _____   Work Telephone: _____

Guardian: _____ SSN _____ (if available)
Address: _____   D.O.B. _____
Employment: _____   Hours: _____
Home Telephone: _____   Work Telephone: _____

Significant Other(s): _____ Relationship: _____
Address: _____
Employment: _____   Hours: _____
Home Telephone: _____   Work Telephone: _____
Siblings:

NAME	REL.	AGE	ADDRESS	LEGAL HISTORY
_____	_____	_____	_____	_____
_____	_____	_____	_____	_____
_____	_____	_____	_____	_____
_____	_____	_____	_____	_____

Who Resides in the Home?   How does the Child behave in the Home?
_____   _____
_____   _____
_____   _____

What type of Relationship does he/she have with their parent/sibling?
_____
_____
_____

EVALUATION/SUMMARY

_____

_____

_____

_____

_____

_____

_____

RECOMMENDATIONS

Preliminary Inquiry:

_____ Dismissal   _____ Referral to other agency
_____ Informal Adjustment   _____ Warning and Release
_____ File Petition   _____ Other _____

Reason for recommendation: _____

_____

_____

Custody Recommendation:

_____ Release to Parent   _____ Release to Guardian   _____ Informal Home Detention
_____ Formal Home Detention   _____ Electronic Surveillance   _____ Shelter Care
_____ Juvenile Center   _____ Not in Custody   _____ Other _____

Comments:

_____

_____

Predispositional Report:

If juvenile admits to charge, recommendations for disposition (Complete if applicable): _____

_____

_____

_____

_____

_____

FIGURE 13.15   Standardized Pre-dispositional Report from Indiana, County of Vigo.

juvenile court appearance, (4) source of first referral to juvenile court, (5) reason(s) for referral; (6) formal court disposition; (7) youth's initial placement by court; (8) miscellaneous court orders and conditions, (9) type of counsel retained, (10) initial plea, (11) number of prior offenses, (12) age and time of initial offense, (13) number of offenses after first hearing, (14) youth's total offense number, (15) number of companions, first offense, (16) number of detentions, and (17) number of out-of-home placements. These pre-disposition reports may or may not contain victim impact statements. Pre-sentence investigation reports, or PSIs, prepared for adults convicted of crimes are the equivalent of pre-dispositional reports. It is more common to see such victim impact statements in adult PSI reports, although some pre-dispositional reports contain them in certain jurisdictions. These statements are often prepared by victims themselves and appended to the report before the judge sees it. They are intended to provide judges with a sense of the physical harm and monetary damage victims have sustained, and thus, they are often aggravating factors that weigh heavily against the juvenile to be sentenced (DeAngelo and Blackburn, 2006).

JUVENILE PROBATION AND PAROLE PROGRAMS

Over 2 million juvenile cases are processed annually by juvenile courts. About 900,000 of these are assigned to POs for predispositional study, while 700,000 cases are assigned for supervision (U.S. Department of Justice, 2006). The most common form of probation is standard probation. Standard juvenile probation is more or less elaborate, depending on the jurisdiction. Of all sentencing options available to juvenile court judges, standard probation is the most commonly used. The first probation law was enacted in Massachusetts in 1878, although probation was used much earlier. John Augustus is credited with inventing probation in Boston in 1841. **Standard probation programs** are either a conditional or unconditional nonincarcerative sentence of a specified period following an adjudication of delinquency.

Unconditional and Conditional Probation

Probation programs for juveniles are either unconditional or conditional and exhibit many similarities with adult probation programs. Unconditional standard probation basically involves complete freedom of movement within the juvenile's community, perhaps accompanied by periodic reports by telephone or mail with a PO or the probation department. Because a PO's caseload is often high, with several hundred juvenile clients that must be managed, individualized attention cannot be given to most juveniles on standard probation. Sometimes police officers are called upon to assist POs in their supervisory tasks. The period of unsupervised probation varies among jurisdictions depending on offense seriousness and other circumstances. Juveniles placed on probation for a period of time must sign a form acknowledging their probation orders and special conditions, if any. An example of the types of instructions to juveniles placed on probation is shown in Figure 13.16.

Conditional probation programs may include optional conditions and program requirements, such as performing a certain number of hours of public or community service, providing restitution to victims, payment of fines, employment, and/or participation in specific vocational, educational, or therapeutic programs. It is crucial to any probation program that an effective classification system is in place so that juvenile judges can sentence offenders accordingly. One variation of the National Institute of Corrections' (NIC) Model Classification Project scheme is used for juvenile classifications, where both risk and

---

Instructions to Juvenile Offenders

1. Cooperate with the juvenile probation or parole officer and answer all questions honestly.

2. Provide or authorize release of any records requested by the juvenile probation or parole officer. These may include legal, medical, psychological, substance abuse treatment, educational, military, employment, financial, juvenile court, or other records.

3. As a condition of supervision, the offender is subject to random urine testing for alcohol and drug usage at such times as he or she is ordered to submit to these by a juvenile probation or parole officer.

4. Be advised that failure or refusal to submit to such testing or tampering with a urine specimen should be considered the same as a "positive" test.

5. Any positive result can lead to revocation and incarceration or such lesser penalty as may be appropriate.

6. Inform the juvenile probation or parole officer of all arrests and convictions. Inform the juvenile probation or parole officer of any new arrests that occur prior to sentencing in this case.

ACKNOWLEDGMENT

I the undersigned, have read or had read to me the above information and understand these instructions. I understand that the court will be informed if I fail to cooperate or provide false, incomplete, or misleading information.

_____
Probation or Parole Officer

_____
Signature of Juvenile

_____
Date

FIGURE 13.16 Instructions to Juvenile Offenders.

needs are assessed. Generally, the terms of standard probation include the following:

1. To obey one's parents or guardians.
2. To obey all laws of the community, including curfew and school laws.
3. To follow the school or work program approved by the PO.
4. To follow instructions of the PO.
5. To report in person to the PO or court at such times designated by the PO.
6. To comply with any special conditions of probation.
7. To consult with the PO when in need of further advice.

Juveniles sentenced to standard probation experience little change in their social routines. Whenever special conditions of probation are included, these special conditions usually mean more work for POs. Some of these conditions might include medical treatments for drug or alcohol dependencies, individual or group therapy or counseling, or participation in a driver's safety course. In some instances involving theft, burglary, or vandalism, restitution provisions may be included, where youths must repay victims for their financial losses. Most standard probation programs in the United States require little, if any, direct contact with the probation office. Logistically, this works out well for POs, who are frequently overworked and have enormous client caseloads of 300 or more youths. However, greater caseloads means less individualized attention devoted to youths by POs, and some of these youths require more supervision than others while on standard probation. In growing numbers of jurisdictions, juvenile and adult probation services are merging in an effort to hold down operating costs and offender supervision expenses (Ball and Bingham, 2006).

Standard probation exhibits relatively high rates of recidivism, ranging from 40 to 75 percent. Even certain youth camps operated in various California counties have reported recidivism rates as high as 76 percent. Therefore, it is often difficult to forecast which juveniles will have the greatest likelihood of reoffending, regardless of the program we are examining.

The following are elements that appear to be predictive of future criminal activity and reoffending by juveniles: (1) one's age at first adjudication; (2) a prior criminal record (a combined measure of the number and severity of priors); (3) the number of prior commitments to juvenile facilities; (4) drug/chemical abuse; (5) alcohol abuse; (6) family relationships (parental control); (7) school problems; and (8) peer relationships. An additional factor not cited by Baird but may have significant predictive value is whether youths who are currently on probation violate one or more conditions of their probation programs (Champion, 2005). Needs assessments should be individualized, based on the juvenile's past record and other pertinent characteristics, including the present adjudication offense. The level of supervision should vary according to the degree of risk posed to the public by the juvenile. While a weighting procedure for the different risk factors is not provided, a description of a supervisory scheme that acts as a guide for juvenile probation and aftercare is given. This scheme would be applied based on the perceived risk of each juvenile offender. The scheme would include:

Regular or Differential Supervision
1. Four face-to-face contacts per month with youth.
2. Two face-to-face contacts per month with parents.
3. One face-to-face contact per month with placement staff.
4. One contact with school officials.

Intensive Supervision
1. Six face-to-face contacts per month with youth.
2. Three face-to-face contacts per month with parents.
3. One face-to-face contact per month with placement staff.
4. Two contacts with school officials.

Alternative Care Cases
1. One face-to-face contact per month with youth.
2. Four contacts with agency staff (one must be face-to-face).
3. One contact every two months with parents.

An assignment to any one of these supervision levels, including **alternative care cases,** should be based on both risk and needs assessments. Baird says that often, agencies make categorical assignments of juveniles to one level of supervision or another, primarily by referring to the highest level of supervision suggested by two or more scales used (Champion, 2005). Each juvenile probation agency prefers specific predictive devices, and some agencies use a combination of them. Again, no scale is foolproof, and the matter of false positives and false negatives arises, as some juveniles receive more supervision than they really require, while others receive less than they need.

Not all probation orders involving juveniles are lenient. In the *Matter of Jessie GG* (1993), for instance, a New York high school student was placed on a two-year probationary term and ordered to pay $1,500 restitution for damages to a victim's property. The two-year probationary period coincided with his ability to pay. Furthermore, it was the harshest disposition the juvenile court judge could impose.

Juvenile probationers do not have the same rights as adult probationers (Ball and Bingham, 2006). For instance, a California juvenile probationer, Michael T., was placed on probation with the provision that supervising POs and police could conduct warrantless searches of his premises at any time (*In re Michael T.,* 1993). A similar provision for warrantless searches and seizures on a juvenile probationer's premises has been made in the case of *In re Bounmy V.* (1993), where the offender was a known cocaine dealer and was suspected of secreting cocaine on his premises at different times.

Intensive Supervised Probation (ISP) Programs

Intensive supervised probation (ISP) programs, alternatively known as intensive probation supervision (IPS) programs, have become increasingly popular for managing nonincarcerated offender populations. Since the mid-1960s, these programs have been aimed primarily at supervising adult offenders closely, and in recent years, ISP programs have been designed for juvenile offenders as well. Intensive supervised probation is a highly structured and conditional supervision program for either adult or juvenile offenders that serves as an alternative to incarceration and provides for an acceptable level of public safety. Some researchers argue that the effectiveness of ISP is how well certain risk control factors are managed by supervising POs rather than the sheer intensity of their supervision over clients.

Characteristics of ISP Programs.   ISP programs for juveniles have been developed and are currently operating in about one-third to one-half of all U.S. jurisdictions. Similar to their adult ISP program counterparts, **juvenile intensive supervision programs (JISPs)** are ideally designed for secure detention-bound youths and are considered as acceptable alternatives to incarceration. This is what JISPs were always meant to be. JISPs are differentiated from other forms of standard probation by citing obvious differences in the amount of officer/client contact during the course of the probationary period. For example, standard probation is considered no more than two face-to-face officer/client contacts per month. JISPs might differ from standard probation according to the following face-to-face criteria: (1) two or three times per week versus once per month; (2) once per week versus twice per month; or (3) four times per week versus once per week (the latter figure being unusually high for standard probation contact).

Different types of PO dispositions toward their work are evident in descriptions of the various services provided by different JISPs. For example, 55 programs examined revealed the following range of services, skills, and resources were mentioned as being brokered by POs in different jurisdictions:

1. Mental health counseling
2. Drug and alcohol counseling
3. Academic achievement and aptitude testing
4. Vocational and employment training
5. Individual, group, and family counseling
6. Job search and placement programs
7. Alternative education programs
8. Foster grandparents programs
9. Big Brother/Big Sister programs

Not all JISPs are alike, however. Nevertheless, many JISPs share similarities, including the following:

1. Recognition of the shortcomings of traditional responses to serious and/or chronic offenders (e.g., incarceration or out-of-home placement)
2. Severe resource constraints within jurisdictions that compel many probation departments to adopt agency-wide classification and workload deployment systems for targeting a disproportionate share of resources for the most problematic juvenile offenders
3. Program hopes to reduce the incidence of incarceration in juvenile secure detention facilities and reduce overcrowding
4. Programs tend to include aggressive supervision and control elements as a part of the "get tough" movement, and
5. All programs have a vested interest in rehabilitation of youthful offenders.

From these analyses of JISP content generally, we can glean the following as basic characteristics of JISPs:

1. Low officer/client caseloads (i.e., 30 or fewer probationers)
2. High levels of offender accountability (e.g., victim restitution, community service, payment of fines, partial defrayment of program expenses)
3. High levels of offender responsibility
4. High levels of offender control (home confinement, electronic monitoring, frequent face-to-face visits by POs)
5. Frequent checks for arrests, drug and/or alcohol use, and employment/school attendance (drug/alcohol screening, coordination with police departments and juvenile halls, teachers, family).

The Ohio Experience

The value of JISP can be appreciated by what Weibush has described as the **Ohio Experience.** Weibush has compared three different Ohio counties that have used different ISPs for their juvenile offenders, as well as the Ohio Department of Youth Services (ODYS). The counties include Delaware County (predominantly rural), Lucas County (Toledo), and Cuyahoga County (Cleveland). The ODYS is state-operated and manages the most serious offenders, since these are exclusively felony offenders on parole from secure detention. In each of the county jurisdictions, most of the offenders are detention-bound, with the exception of the Lucas County juveniles who are sentenced to ISP after having their original sentences of detention reversed by juvenile court judges.

Targeted by the Delaware JISP are those juveniles with a high propensity to recidivate as well as more serious felony offenders who are detention-bound. Youths begin the program with a five-day detention, followed by two weeks of house arrest. Later, they must observe curfews, attend school and complete schoolwork satisfactorily, report daily to the probation office, and submit to periodic urinalysis. Each youth's progress is monitored by intensive counselors and surveillance staff 16 hours a day, seven days a week. Weibush says that although the Delaware program has a rather strict approach, it embodies rehabilitation as a primary program objective. The Delaware program has about a 40 percent recidivism rate, which is high, although it is better than the 75 percent rate of recidivism among the general juvenile court population of high-risk offenders elsewhere in Ohio jurisdictions.

Lucas County program officials select clients from those already serving sentences of detention and who are considered "high-risk" offenders. Lucas County officials wished to use this particular selection method, since they wanted to avoid any appearance of "net widening" that their JISP might reflect. Drawing from those already incarcerated seemed the best strategy in this case. The Lucas program is similar to the Delaware program in its treatment and control approaches. However, the Lucas program obligates offenders to perform up to 100 hours of community service as a program condition. House arrest, curfew, and other Delaware program requirements are also found in the Lucas program. The successfulness of the Lucas program has not been evaluated fully, although it does appear to have reduced institutional commitments by about 10 percent between 1986 and 1987.

The Cuyahoga County program (Cleveland) was one of the first of several ISP programs in Ohio's metropolitan jurisdictions. It is perhaps the largest county program, with 1,500 clients at any given time, as well as six juvenile court judges and 72 supervisory personnel. One innovation of the Cuyahoga program was the development of a team approach to client surveillance and management. This program, like the other county programs, performs certain broker functions by referring its clients to an assortment of community-based services and treatments during the program duration. Currently, there are six teams of surveillance officers who each serve about 60 youths. These teams are comprised of a team leader, two counselors, and three surveillance staff. Recidivism rates averaged about 31 percent in a longitudinal follow-up.

The ODYS program operates the state's nine training schools in addition to supervising the 3,000 youths each year who are released on parole. The ODYS has 93 youth counselors to staff seven regional offices. The ODYS commenced JISP in February 1988 and supervised those high-risk offenders with a predicted future recidivism rate of 75 percent or higher. Since these clients were all prior felony offenders with lengthy adjudication records, they were considered the most serious group to be supervised compared with the other programs. Accordingly, the ODYS supervision and surveillance structure exhibited the greatest degree of offender monitoring. The team approach has been used by the ODYS, with teams consisting of three youth counselors and two surveillance staff. Since its creation, the JISP operated by the ODYS has exhibited a drop in its recidivism rate. On the basis of a comparison of the first year of its operation with recidivism figures for its clients from the previous year, the ODYS program had a 34 percent reduction in its rate of recidivism. Furthermore, a 39 percent reduction in parole revocations occurred. This is significant, considering the high-risk nature of the offender population being managed.

All of these programs have required enormous investments of time and energy by high-quality staff, according to Weibush. Furthermore, each program has illustrated how best to utilize existing community resources to further its objectives and best serve juvenile clients in need. However, Weibush says that what is good for Ohio probationers and parolees may not necessarily be suitable for those offenders of other jurisdictions. Nevertheless, these programs function as potential models after which programs in other jurisdictions may be patterned.

Other Juvenile Probation and Parole Programs

Electronic Monitoring for Juvenile Offenders.   An electronic monitoring program has been used for juvenile offenders in Allen County, Indiana. Known as the Allen County, Indiana, Juvenile Electronic Monitoring Program Pilot Project, or EMP, this program was commenced as an experimental study in October 1987 and was conducted for nine months through May 1988. At the time the study started, the probation department had 25 POs who were appointed by the court and certified by the Indiana Judicial Conference. During 1987, 2,404 juveniles were referred to the probation department by the court. About 34 percent of these were female offenders. During that same year, 167 youths were incarcerated in secure facilities for delinquents at a total cost of $1.5 million. Because of fiscal constraints, Allen County agreed to place only six juveniles in the electronic monitoring program. However, two of these youths recidivated and were dropped from it shortly after it started. The remaining four youths remained in the program. The juvenile judge in these cases sentenced each youth to a six-month probationary period with electronic monitoring. Each youth wore a conspicuous wristlet, which eventually became a symbol of court sanctions. Like the proverbial string tied around one's finger, the wristlet was a constant reminder that these juveniles were "on probation." Furthermore, others who became aware of these electronic devices became of assistance in helping these youths to avoid activities that might be considered in violation of probation program conditions.

Despite the small number of participants in this study, the findings are of interest and suggest similar successful applications on larger offender aggregates. Each juvenile was interviewed at the conclusion of the program. They reported that their wristlets were continuous reminders of their involvement in the probation program. However, they didn't feel as though program officials were spying on them. In fact, one of the youths compared his experience with electronic monitoring with his previous experience of being supervised by a PO. He remarked that whenever he was under the supervision of the PO, he could do whatever he wished, and there was little likelihood that his PO would ever find out about it. However, he was always under the threat of being discovered by the computer or by the surveillance officer.

Another interesting phenomenon was the fact that the wristlet enabled certain offenders to avoid peer pressure and "hanging out" with their friends. Since they had wristlets, they had good excuses to return home and not violate their curfews. Also, the families of these juveniles took a greater interest in them and their program. In short, at least for these four youths, the program was viewed very favorably and considered successful. Parents who were also interviewed at the conclusion of the program agreed that the program and monitoring system had been quite beneficial for their sons. While electronic monitoring for juveniles is still in its early stages of experimentation in various jurisdictions, it is a cost-effective alternative to incarceration.

Home Confinement and Juveniles.   In many jurisdictions, home confinement is supplemented with electronic monitoring. Relatively little is known about the extent to which home confinement is used as a sentencing alternative for juvenile offenders. Since probation is so widely used as the sanction of choice except for the most chronic recidivists, home confinement is most often applied as an accompanying condition of electronic monitoring. However, this type of sentencing may be redundant, since curfew for juvenile offenders means home confinement anyway, especially during evening hours. As a day sentence, home confinement for juveniles would probably be counterproductive, since juveniles are often obligated to finish their schooling as a probation program condition. Again, since school hours are during the daytime, it would not make sense to deprive juveniles of school opportunities through some type of home detention.

Shock Probation and Boot Camps.   Shock probation has sometimes been compared erroneously with **Scared Straight,** a New Jersey program implemented in the late 1970s. Scared Straight sought to frighten samples of hardcore delinquent youths by having them confront inmates in a Rahway, New Jersey, prison. Inmates would yell at and belittle them, calling them names, cursing, and yelling. Inmates would tell them about sexual assaults and other prison unpleasantries in an attempt to get them to refrain from reoffending. However, the program was unsuccessful. Despite early favorable reports of recidivism rates of less than 20 percent, the actual rate of recidivism among these participating youths was considerably higher. Furthermore, another control group not exposed to Scared Straight had a lower recidivism rate. The Scared Straight program is perhaps closer in principle to the **SHAPE-UP Program** implemented in Colorado and discussed as a diversionary measure earlier. However, SHAPE-UP Program authorities deny any program similarities other than prisoner-client interaction for brief periods.

The juvenile version of shock probation or shock incarceration is perhaps best exemplified by juvenile boot camps. Also known as the Army Model, boot camp programs are patterned after basic training for new military recruits. Juvenile offenders are given a taste of hard military life, and such regimented activities and structure for up to 180 days are often sufficient to "shock" them into giving up their lives of delinquency or crime and staying out of jail. Boot camp programs in various states have been established, including the Regimented Inmate Discipline program in Mississippi, the About Face program in Louisiana, and the shock incarceration program in Georgia.

Two good examples of boot camp programs are the U.S. Army Correctional Activity (USACA) in Fort Riley, Kansas, established in 1968, and the Butler (New York) Shock Incarceration Correctional Facility. In both programs, inmates wear army uniforms, learn basic army drills, salute, and participate in a rigorous correctional treatment program. Ordinarily, youthful first-offender felons are targeted for involvement in these programs. The Butler Shock program, for instance, involves young offenders ranging in age from 16 to 29. They must stay in the camp for six months and comply with all program rules. About 88 percent of all boot camp trainees are successful and win a parole later. The Butler facility has inmates who have been heavily involved in drug-dealing. About 90 percent of all participants have been convicted of drug offenses. They have rigorous work details, must complete schoolwork, and adhere to a highly disciplined regimen. They are given eight minutes for meals, and they must carry their leftovers in their pockets.

Their days begin at 5:30 A.M., with reveille blaring over the intercom. Immediately, drill instructors start screaming at them. Besides military drilling, all inmates must experience drug counseling and study. At the Fort Riley facility, inmates may learn vocational skills and crafts. They also receive counseling and other therapy and treatment. At both camps, physicians and other support staff are ready to furnish any needed medical treatment. When they eventually leave the facility, most have changed their outlook on life and have acquired new lifestyles not associated with crime. Again, recidivism rates among these inmates are under 30 percent, which is considered an indication of program success. Similar successes have been observed in other jurisdictions, such as Michigan (Nicol and McCree, 2006).

GRADUATED SANCTIONS FOR JUVENILE OFFENDERS

Similar to adult probationers and parolees, juveniles in most jurisdictions are subject to a continuum of sanctions that ranges from verbal warnings or reprimands to incarceration in a secure facility. Most jurisdictions regard locking up juveniles as the last resort. In Tennessee, for instance, electronic monitoring and house arrest are considered "last resorts" by most counties with electronic monitoring programs. If juveniles fail in these programs, then juvenile court judges have no other option than to lock up these persistent offenders for a short period of time to send them a message not to reoffend.

The Office of Juvenile Justice and Delinquency Prevention (OJJDP) has devised a suggested list of graduated sanctions for youths. The graduated sanction plan is a part of the OJJDP's Comprehensive Strategy for Serious, Violent, and Chronic Juvenile Offenders. Of course, the reduction of risk factors and enhancement of protective factors in youths' lives is the first line of defense against juvenile delinquency. As a complement to a delinquency prevention approach, however, an effective juvenile justice system program model for the treatment and rehabilitation of delinquent offenders is one that combines accountability and sanctions with increasingly intensive treatment and rehabilitation services. These graduated sanctions must be wide-ranging to fit the offense and include both intervention and secure corrections components. The graduated sanctions continuum deals with individuals who may have shown initial signs of delinquency, such as vandalism or truancy, or they may be repeat nonviolent offenders. A small number may even be dangerously homicidal and in need of secure incarceration or intensive treatment (Pacific Hills Treatment, 2006).

Because there is such a wide array of juvenile misbehavior, juvenile justice must be dealt with appropriately through relevant services and programs. A model graduated sanctions continuum combines treatment and rehabilitation with reasonable, fair, humane, and appropriate sanctions while offering a continuum of care consisting of diverse programs. At each level there should be a number of sublevels or gradations that serve to curb delinquency by inducing law-abiding behavior as early as possible. The Rhode Island Department of Corrections has created a graduated sanctions continuum. The continuum includes the following levels:

1. *Prevention.* Programs and resources that decrease risk factors and enhance protective factors in order to minimize the risk of future delinquent behavior.

2. *Intervention.* Involves swift, well-defined, and consistent sanctions by the community. Usually used for first-time, nonviolent offenders. Intervention often includes diversion, counseling, restitution, and community service.

3. *Immediate sanctions.* Used for first-time delinquent offenders (misdemeanors and nonviolent felonies) and nonserious repeat offenders (generally misdemeanants). Nonresidential community-based programs are often appropriate and involve community police officers to assist in monitoring progress and ensure deterrence from future delinquent activities.

4. *Intermediate sanctions.* Used for offenders whose offenses do not warrant immediate sanctions (usually first-time serious or violent offenders). Also used for those who fail to respond successfully to immediate sanctions as evidenced by repeated offenses (e.g., property offenders or drug-involved juveniles). These sanctions may be residential or nonresidential including intensive supervision programs, day treatment programs, and/or tracking programs as an alternative to secure incarceration and staff-secure residential programs.

5. *Secure sanctions.* Incarceration that is reserved for the most serious and violent repeat-offenders. The Rhode Island Training School for Youth is the only secure facility for juvenile offenders in Rhode Island. Exceptions of course include those juveniles who are waived to the Adult Correctional Institution due to the serious and/or violent nature of their offenses.

6. *Aftercare.* Upon release from secure sanctions, a juvenile receives an individualized program of assistance beyond traditional parole. These programs often include high levels of treatment and social control while integrating case management, community restitution, education, job training, substance abuse rehabilitation, and other components as needed.

At every phase of the continuum, offenders should be subject to increasingly severe sanctions if they continue delinquent activities. Objective risk assessments should be employed to determine the most appropriate sanction for each individual, with assessments based on the risk the offender poses to society, the nature of the offense, the number and nature of prior offenses, and the presence of other relevant risk factors.

Additionally, programs must be small enough to ensure that youth receive individualized attention. Treatment plans need to be appropriate for each youth, and should involve families whenever possible. Residential programs must have a strong aftercare component to involve the family and community in reintegrating the youth into the community. The graduated sanctions continuum must also have as a distinct goal the implementation of a restorative justice system rather than one based merely on retribution. This distinction is essential if we are to make communities devastated by crime and violence whole again. Juvenile crime victimizes real people and real communities. In the past, the adversarial justice system has focused on punishment, deterrence, and containment of crime, with little if any concern for repairing the harm done to the victims and the community. Restorative justice requires the involvement of not only the city and state, but also the victims, offenders, and communities in the justice process. Offenders must be held accountable by accepting responsibility for the damage and suffering they have caused by being required to make amends. Components may include victim–offender mediation, community conferencing, alternative dispute resolution, work experience, and meaningful restitution and community service projects (Rhode Island Department of Corrections, 2006).

With graduated sanctions in place in many jurisdictions, youths have considerable notice before they face full-fledged formal probation or parole revocation proceedings. Thus, whenever youths appear before their parole boards or face juvenile court judges in such proceedings, it is assumed that most of these youths have already had first, second, third, fourth, and fifth chances to succeed in their probation or parole programs. Probation or parole revocation is a last resort, and most judges and parole boards hate to see these youths reappear before them for violating their program conditions. Such youths suggest program and intervention failures. Therefore, incarceration in a secure facility is often the undesirable sanction of choice when rendering judgments.

REVOKING JUVENILE PROBATION AND PAROLE

Parole for juveniles is similar to parole for adult offenders. Those juveniles who have been detained in various institutions for long periods may be released prior to serving their full sentences.

Purposes of Juvenile Parole

The general purposes of parole for juveniles are:

1. to reward good behavior while youths have been detained;
2. to alleviate overcrowding,
3. to permit youths to become reintegrated back into their communities and enhance their rehabilitation potential; and
4. to deter youths from future offending by ensuring their continued supervision under juvenile parole officers.

Numbers of Juveniles on Parole

Estimates vary about how many juvenile offenders are on parole at any given time. The present lack of coordination among jurisdictions relating to juvenile offender record-keeping makes it difficult to determine actual numbers of juvenile parolees or probationers at any given time. Furthermore, some jurisdictions continue to prevent public scrutiny of juvenile court adjudicatory proceedings or their results. Since one's juvenile record is expunged or sealed upon reaching adulthood, even historical research on this subject is limited by various systemic constraints. About 30,000 youths were involved in some form of juvenile parole program in 2006 (American Correctional Association, 2006).

Juvenile parolees share many of the same programs used to supervise youthful probationers. Intensive supervised probation programs are used for both probationers and parolees in many jurisdictions. Furthermore, juvenile POs often perform dual roles as juvenile parole officers as they supervise both types of offenders. Studies of juvenile parolees tend to show that the greater the intensity of parole, the lower the recidivism. Influencing the successfulness of juvenile parole is whether juveniles are successfully employed or actively involved in development or counseling programs. For most juveniles who spend time behind bars or reform school walls, this experience is traumatic. About 65 percent of the juveniles on parole refrain from committing new offenses (Champion, 2007).

Juvenile Parole Decision Making

The decision to parole particular juveniles is left to different agencies and bodies, depending on the jurisdiction. Studies of imposing secure confinement upon juvenile delinquents indicate that in 45 state jurisdictions, the lengths of secure confinement are indeterminate. In 32 states, early-release decisions are left up to the particular juvenile correction agency, whereas six states use parole boards exclusively, and five other states depend on the original juvenile court judge's decision. Only a few states had determinate schemes for youthful offenders, and therefore, their early release from secure custody would be established by statute in much the same way as it is for adult offenders (American Correctional Association, 2006).

A seven-member parole board in New Jersey is appointed by the governor and grants early release to both adult and juvenile inmates. Utah uses a Youth Parole Authority, a part-time board consisting of three citizens and four staff members from the Utah Division of Youth Corrections. This board employs objective decision-making criteria to determine which juveniles should be paroled. However, sometimes discrepancies exist between what the Authority actually does and what it is supposed to do. Some criticisms have been that the primary parole criteria are related to one's former institutional behavior rather than to other factors, such as one's prospects for successful adaptation to community life, employment, and participation in educational or vocational programs.

Similar criticisms have been made about youth parole boards in other states. Many of these juvenile parole boards consist of persons who make subjective judgments about youths on the basis of extralegal and subjective criteria. Predispositional reports prepared by juvenile POs, records of institutional behavior, a youth's appearance and demeanor during the parole hearing, and the presence of witnesses or victims have unknown effects on individual parole board members. Parole decision making is not an exact science. Subjectivity is endemic to this process. When subjective criteria impact this decision-making process, a juvenile's parole chances are significantly subverted. Thus, parole board decision-making profiles in various jurisdictions may show evidence of early-release disparities attributable to racial, ethnic, gender, or socioeconomic factors.

Juvenile Parole Policy

Various state juvenile parole programs and provisions have been investigated. At least eight different kinds of juvenile parole have been used more or less frequently among the states. These are:

1. Determinate parole (length of parole is linked closely with the period of commitment specified by the court; paroling authorities cannot extend

confinement period of juvenile beyond original commitment length prescribed by judge; juvenile can be released short of serving the full sentence).

2. Determinate parole set by administrative agency (parole release date is set immediately following youth's arrival at secure facility).

3. Presumptive minimum with limits on the extension of the supervision period for a fixed or determinate length of time (minimum confinement period is specified, and youth must be paroled after that date unless there is a showing of bad conduct).

4. Presumptive minimum with limits on the extension of supervision for an indeterminate period (parole should terminate after fixed period of time; parole period is indeterminate, where PO has discretion to extend parole period with justification; parole length can extend until youth reaches age of majority and leaves juvenile court jurisdiction).

5. Presumptive minimum with discretionary extension of supervision for an indeterminate period (same as #4 except PO has discretion to extend parole length of juvenile with no explicit upper age limit; lacks explicit standards limiting the extension of parole).

6. Indeterminate parole with a specified maximum and a discretionary minimum length of supervision.

7. Indeterminate parole with legal minimum and maximum periods of supervision.

8. Indeterminate or purely discretionary parole.

Recidivism and Probation/Parole Revocation

Juvenile Probation and Parole Revocation. probationand parole revocations are the termination of one's probation or parole program (PPP), usually for one or more program violations. Figure 13.17 shows a probation revocation form that is used in Arkansas for initiating probation revocation hearings and other actions. A review hearing is conducted, and if revocation is recommended, the reasons must be set forth in writing. Figure 13.17 shows disposition information available to juvenile court judges when conducting such hearings. A statement of a juvenile's rights is given to the juvenile and juvenile's parents prior to the hearing. An example of a statement of rights for juvenile parole revocations is shown in Figure 13.18.

When one's PPP is terminated, regardless of who does the terminating, there are several possible outcomes. One is that the offender will be returned to secure detention. This is the most severe result. A less harsh alternative is that offenders will be shifted to a different kind of PPP. For instance, if a juvenile is assigned to a halfway house as a part of a parole program, the rules of the halfway house must be observed. If one or more rules are violated, such as failing to observe curfew, failing drug or alcohol urinalyses, or committing new offenses, a report is filed with the court or the juvenile corrections authority for possible revocation action. If it is decided later that one's PPP should be terminated, the result may be to place the offender under house arrest or home confinement, coupled with electronic monitoring. Thus, the juvenile would be required to wear an electronic wristlet or anklet and remain on the premises for specified periods. Other program conditions would be applied as well. The fact is that one is not automatically returned to detention following a parole revocation.

COVER SHEET
STATE OF ARKANSAS
CHANCERY COURT: JUVENILE (CONTINUED PROCEEDINGS:
REVIEW, PROBATION REVOCATION & PARENTAL RIGHTS TERMINATION)

The juvenile division reporting form and the information contained here in shall not be admissible as evidence in any court proceeding or replace or supplement the filing and service of pleadings, orders, or other papers as required by law or Supreme Court Rule. This form is required pursuant to Administrative Order Number 8. Instructions are located on the back of the form.

===

FILING INFORMATION:

County: _____ District: _____ Case Number: _____

Judge: _____ Division: _____ petition Filing Date: _____

Name of Juvenile: _____ Date of Birth: _____
　　　　　　　　　　Last, First, Middle

Social Security No. _____

Original Petition Field:　　　• FINS　　　• Dependency/Neglect　　　• Delinquency

===

DISPOSITION INFORMATION:

Probation Revocation Hearing:　　　Hearing Date: _____　　Child's Attorney Present: • Yes • No

　　　　　　　　　　　　　　　　　　Type:　• Bench　• Plea

　　　　　　　　　　　　Order Date: _____

• Extend Probation　　　　　　　• Impose Additional Conditions of Probation

• Commit to DYS

• Place In:　　　• Juvenile Detention Facility　　• Home Detention with Electronic Monitoring

• Transfer Custody:　　• DHS　　• Licensed Agency　　• Relative　　• Otherr

• Grant Permanent Custody to an individual

• Order Juvenile/Family Member to Submit to Evaluations:　　• Physical　　• Psychiatric　　• Psychological

• Order Parent/Guardian to Attend Parental Responsibility Training Program

• Order Parent/Guardian to Pay Juvenile Cost of:　　• Commitment　　• Detention　　• Foster Care

• Order:　　　• Probation　　• Restitution $_____　　　• Public Service
　　　　　　• Fine $_____　　• Court Costs $_____　　　• Other

• Suspended Driver's License　　　　　• Order Restricted Driving Permit

---

Review Hearing:　　Hearing Date: _____　　Child's Guardian Ad Litern Present: • Yes • No

　　　　　　　　Type: • 6 Month • 18 Month　Other　Child's Attorney Present:　　　　• Yes • No

　　　　　　　　Order Date: _____　　　　Parent's Attorney Present: • Yes • No

Disposition　　• Return Juvenile to Parent, Guardian or Custodian
(6 Month)　　　• Continue Out-of-Home Placement
Disposition:　　• Return Juvenile to Parent, Guardian or Custodian
(18 Month)　　• Authorize Plan for Termination of Parent/Child Relationship, Guardianship or Custody
　　　　　　　• Place Juvenile in Foster Care
　　　　　　　• Continue Out-of-Home Placement
　　　　　　　• Other _____

Parental Rights
Termination Hearing: Hearing Date: _____ Child's Guardian Ad Litern Present: • Yes • No

Child's Attorney Present: • Yes • No

Order Date: _____ Parent's Attorney Present: • Yes • No

Termination: • Granted • Denied

_____

Clerk Signature

Form AOC 9/96

_____

Date

Send 1 Copy to AOC upon filing.
Send 1 Copy to AOC upon disposition.
Keep original in Court file.

FIGURE 13.17 Review, Probation Revocation, and Parental Rights Termination (Arkansas Form).

STATEMENT OF RIGHTS
JUVENILE PROBATION REVOCATION

A probation revocation is a hearing before a judge to decide if a juvenile violated a term or condition of probation, and if so, whether the judge should change the disposition.

You will be asked to admit or deny the allegations of the probation violation. You have the following rights:

1.   You have the right to have an attorney represent you. You may have the right to an attorney appointed at public expense.

2.   If you deny the allegations of the probation violation, you have a right to a hearing before a judge. The hearing must be held within seven days if you are removed from your home. If you are allowed to remain in your home pending the probation revocation hearing, the hearing must be held within a reasonable time. If you admit the probation violation, you give up your right to a probation revocation hearing.

3.   Before the hearing, you are entitled to receive all the evidence of the probation violation that will be used against you, including probation revocation reports and all records relating to the proceedings.

4.   At the probation revocation hearing, both you and the prosecuting attorney have the right to offer evidence, make arguments, subpoena witnesses, and call and cross-examine witnesses. You may testify in your own defense or remain silent throughout the hearing. You may present mitigating circumstances or other reasons why the probation violation, if proved, should not result in a change in the disposition order.

5.   The probation violation must be proved by clear and convincing evidence. You have the right to appeal the decision of the court after a revocation hearing.

DATE: _____   _____
            (Signature of Child)

DATE: _____   _____

(Signature of Parent, Legal Guardian, or Legal Custodian)

FIGURE 13.18 Statement of Rights, Juvenile Probation Revocation.

Usually, if a return to incarceration or detention is not indicated, the options available to judges, parole boards, or others are limited only by the array of supervisory resources in the given jurisdiction. These options ordinarily involve more intensive supervision or monitoring of offender behaviors. Severe overcrowding in many juvenile detention facilities discourages revocation action that would return large numbers of offenders to industrial schools or youth centers. Intermediate punishments, therefore, function well to accommodate larger numbers of serious offenders, including those who have their parole revoked.

The process of PPP revocation for juveniles is not as clear-cut as it is for adult offenders. The U.S. Supreme Court has not ruled decisively thus far about how juvenile PPP revocation actions should handled. Prior to several significant U.S. Supreme Court decisions, either PPP revocation could be accomplished for adult offenders on the basis of reports filed by POs that offenders were in violation of one or more conditions of their PPPs. Criminal court judges, those ordinarily in charge of determining whether to terminate one's probationary status, could decide this issue on the basis of available evidence against offenders. For adult parolees, former decision making relative to terminating their parole could be made by parole boards without much fanfare from offenders. In short, parole officers and others might simply present evidence that one or more infractions or violations of PPP conditions had been committed. These infractions, then, could form the basis for revoking PPPs as well as a justification for these decisions.

Juvenile Case Law on Probation Revocations

When youths are placed on probation, the most frequently used dispositional option by juvenile court judges, they are subject to having their program revoked for one or more violations of program conditions. Several cases are presented below to show how different juvenile courts handle probation revocations.

Can juvenile courts revoke a youth's probation and re-dispose a juvenile to a longer probationary term? Yes. Stephanie N. was an Arizona youth who violated one or more of her probationary terms. The juvenile court revoked Stephanie N.'s probation and reimposed a new probationary term of one year. Stephanie N. appealed, claiming that the juvenile court lacked jurisdiction to revoke her probation program and extend the probationary term beyond the one-year period originally imposed. The Arizona appellate court heard the case and upheld the judge's decision to extend Stephanie N.'s probation for a one-year period beyond the point where her probation program violations were detected and reported by her juvenile probation officer. In this case, the court held that the age of majority in Arizona for youth is 18. Once a juvenile reaches age 18, one's probationary term ends and the juvenile court has no further jurisdiction over youths originally disposed to probation in their courts. In Stephanie N.'s case, she was under age 18, had her probation revoked and a new one-year term of probation imposed, and this new one-year term of probation did not overlap her 18th birthday (*In re Stephanie N.,* 2005).

Can juvenile courts revoke a youth's probation program on hearsay evidence? Are youths entitled to Fifth Amendment protection in probation revocation hearings? Must probationers give incriminating testimony about their alleged probation violations in probation revocation proceedings? Yes, no, and yes. E.P. was a Florida youth who had his probation program revoked and was committed to a residential program for a designated period of time. During his probation revocation proceeding, his mother gave information to the court that E.P. had failed to respond to two prior enrollment appointments with programs he was ordered to attend. E.P. was also called as a witness and admitted, over his defense counsel's objection, that he never went back to the designated program once he had enrolled in it. E.P. appealed, claiming that his probation program should not have been revoked because the juvenile court relied on hearsay evidence from his mother and he was compelled to give self-incriminating testimony in violation of his Fifth Amendment right against self-incrimination. The Florida court of appeals rejected both arguments, holding that sufficient evidence existed in the record of E.P.'s willful and substantial program violations. Furthermore, the juvenile court properly accepted E.P.'s admissions over the defense counsel's objection. The appellate court further stated that while Fifth Amendment protection exists for persons who may be compelled to give incriminating evidence against themselves in a trial court, juvenile probationers may not refuse to answer questions during probation revocation proceedings, merely because such questions might disclose a probation violation. When a juvenile's probation orders are issued initially by a juvenile court judge, the juvenile signs a waiver agreeing to accept the probation program terms, including a waiver of the right against self-incrimination. Fifth Amendment protection does not cover admissions from probationers about possible violations of their probation conditions. Furthermore, E.P.'s mother's testimony is considered evidence for purposes of considering probation revocation. Hearsay evidence is therefore admissible during these proceedings (*E.P. v. State,* 2005).

Can juvenile courts require youths placed on probation to submit to periodic polygraph (lie detector) tests to determine whether they are complying with their probation orders? Yes. D.S. is an Ohio youth who was placed on probation based on charges of rape and gross sexual imposition. As a part of his dispositional orders, D.S. was required to submit to a full disclosure polygraph and such further maintenance polygraphs as may be directed by his probation officers/therapists. D.S. appealed, claiming that this required polygraph condition was unreasonable and violated his constitutional rights for various reasons. One reason given was that polygraph test results are not admissible in trial proceedings; therefore, they should not be permitted while a youth is under probation supervision. The Ohio court of appeals reviewed his case and upheld the juvenile court judge's original decision in the matter. The Ohio court noted that polygraph results are admissible in trial proceedings where both sides stipulate to their use for witness impeachment or corroboration purposes. But such an application is separate and distinct from a probation condition. Several courts have authorized the use of polygraphs because of their rehabilitative potential and offender treatment. The court noted that juvenile courts have broad authority to impose reasonable conditions of probation on juveniles. The conditions of probation must be related to the interests of doing justice, rehabilitating the offender, and ensuring the offender's good behavior. The juvenile court should consider whether the condition (1) is reasonably related to rehabilitating the offender; (2) has some relationship to the crime committed; and (3) is related to conduct that is criminal or is reasonably related to future criminality and serves the statutory ends of probation. Other courts have found that polygraph conditions are reasonably related to one's rehabilitation, related to one's crime, and serve the statutory ends of probation. The polygraph has been generally accepted as a useful tool in the treatment and rehabilitation of sex offenders. The overriding factor administering polygraph tests is truthfulness. Probationers are required to tell the truth. D.S. also made a Fifth Amendment claim to the effect that polygraph tests required him to make self-incriminating statements and thus were unconstitutional. The court rejected this claim as well, since D.S. agreed to all probation conditions including the waiver of his Fifth Amendment right against self-incrimination during probation revocation proceedings (*In re D.S.,* 2005).

Can juveniles be required to pay restitution as a part of their probation program where restitution amounts are determined by victim estimates of costs? Yes. James C. is a Rhode Island youth who was adjudicated delinquent and disposed to probation for larceny. As a part of his probation program, James C. was ordered to pay restitution to the victim in an amount estimated by various body shops for repairs to a vehicle he vandalized. James C. appealed, claiming that reliance on such estimates by the victim was in violation of his right to due process and should be disregarded. A Rhode Island appellate court heard the case and disagreed. The court held that the victim's testimony about the estimates of costs related to car repairs based on body shop estimates was reliable, credible, and proper. While a juvenile is entitled to a hearing to determine the amount of restitution, the proceeding need not be formal and may be conducted in a summary manner (*In re James C.,* 2005).

Can juvenile courts revoke a youth's probation and order them to a secure facility for 12 months without considering less restrictive alternatives to incarceration? Yes. Generally, juvenile courts are encouraged, but not obligated, to consider the least restrictive alternatives when disposing youths to probation, including placement in a secure facility. This is consistent with the Juvenile Justice and Delinquency Prevention Act of 1974 and its subsequent modifications and provisions. In this instance, Stacy S. was a New York youth who violated one or more terms of her probation program and was ordered to serve 12 months in a secure institution. She appealed the decision and argued that the juvenile court was obligated to consider less restrictive alternatives to secure confinement. The New York appellate court disagreed. The court held that juvenile courts must consider the needs and best interests of youths adjudicated and disposed. The record in this instance established that the least restrictive alternative in this case was placement in a secure institution. Placement in the secure facility for one year would provide Stacy S. with counseling, as well as educational and psychological assistance. Stacy S. had a history of violent and unlawful behavior. Thus, placement in a secure facility would facilitate community protection. The juvenile court is not required to experiment with the lowest form of intervention, have it fail, and then try each succeeding level of intervention before ordering placement to a secure facility (*Matter of Stacy S.,* 2005).

Can juveniles be ordered to serve time in a secure facility if, during their original adjudicatory hearing, they did not knowingly and intelligently waive their right to counsel? No. J.R.I. is a Florida youth who was adjudicated delinquent in juvenile court and placed on probation. During his probationary term, J.R.I. violated one or more probation conditions and the court re-disposed him to serve a period of months in a secure facility. J.R.I. appealed, contending that during the original adjudicatory proceedings, he did not knowingly and intelligently waive his right to counsel, and thus the trial court could not commit him to any period of confinement, despite the probation violation. The Florida appellate court reversed the decision of the juvenile court to commit J.R.I. to a secure facility. It held that since J.R.I. did not knowingly and intelligently waive his right to counsel in the original adjudicatory hearing, a fact admitted by the prosecution, the juvenile court could not impose incarceration of any kind on J.R.I. The court said that absent a knowing and intelligent waiver, no person may be imprisoned for any offense, unless he was represented by counsel at his trial. Therefore, he cannot be sentenced to a term of imprisonment upon the revocation of his probation. Upon revoking one's probation program, however, the juvenile court judge may impose any sanction (such as community service, restitution, house arrest, electronic monitoring) that otherwise could have been imposed on J.R.I. at the original dispositional hearing other than any type of incarceration. (*J.R.I. v. State,* 2005).

Can juvenile courts extend a youth's term of probation beyond the age of majority? Do state juvenile courts disagree on this issue? Yes and yes. Carliesha C. is a New York juvenile probationer who violated a condition of her probation program by failing to make restitution to a victim. Carliesha C. was originally disposed to a probationary term of one year, which would exceed her 18th birthday. During her probationary term and following her 18th birthday, Carliesha C. was found in violation of her probation orders by failing to pay restitution, and the juvenile court judge ordered her to serve one additional year on probation. Carliesha C. appealed, contending that the juvenile court no longer had jurisdiction over her following her 18th birthday. The New York appellate court heard the case and upheld the judge's decision. While 18 is the age of majority in New York State, juvenile court orders of probation may extend beyond one's 18th birthday. Furthermore, if probation program orders are violated at any time during the probationary period, juvenile court judges may impose additional probationary terms of one year, even though such orders are issued after a youth becomes an adult. In this case, the probationary term remained in effect beyond Carliesha C.'s 18th birthday, and thus the juvenile court judge retained jurisdiction to impose an additional year of probation. Not all state courts are consistent in this regard. See *In re Stephanie N.,* above, for a comparison of how different state courts interpret juvenile court jurisdiction and when it terminates (*In re Carliesha C.,* 2005).

Can juvenile courts order juvenile sex offenders to register as state sex offenders? Yes. D.L. is a Texas juvenile adjudicated for a sex offense. According to Texas law, all sex offenders must register with the state as sex offenders. D.L. took issue with this mandatory sex offender registration requirement and appealed, contending that being required to register as a sex offender amounted to cruel and unusual punishment in violation of his Eighth Amendment rights. A Texas appellate court upheld the juvenile court order requiring D.L. to register with the state as a sex offender. According to the Juvenile Code, juvenile sex offender registration is mandatory and does not violate one's Eighth Amendment right against cruel and unusual punishment (*Matter of D.L.,* 2005).

Must probation orders for juveniles be orally pronounced by juvenile court judges during adjudicatory and dispositional hearings in order to be enforceable? No. D.G. is a Florida juvenile who was adjudicated delinquent during an adjudicatory proceeding. In D.G.'s case, the juvenile court judge merely filed a dispositional order for probation with the court clerk. D.G. appealed, contending that his right to due process was violated since the judge did not verbally spell out the probation conditions. Thus, the probation program and its accompanying orders were unenforceable. The Florida appellate court heard the case and disagreed. The court declared that oral pronouncements of one's delinquency and orders of probation are not a requirement of the punishment process. Rather, these orders may be in writing and are fully enforceable (*D.G. v. State*, 2005).

Juvenile Case Law on Parole Revocations

There is very little current information about juvenile parole revocation. A few of the cases involving parole eligibility and/or revocation involving juveniles are reported below.

Can juveniles have their parole programs revoked for failure to observe curfew? Yes. Gunter was a Florida juvenile who was placed on parole after serving 16 months of a 24-month disposition to a secure facility. Gunter was 17 years of age, and he was working in a fast-food restaurant. One evening he came home late, well beyond his curfew hour of 7:00 P.M. His parole officer was waiting for him, and Gunter was asked why he was late. He replied that he had to work late at the restaurant and missed his bus. He had to take a later bus. The parole officer checked with the restaurant and they indicated that Gunter left at 5:30 P.M. according to his time card and that he did not have to work late on that particular evening. The parole officer reported this apparent curfew violation to the parole board who summoned Gunter before them. Gunter was evasive and claimed that his parole officer was fabricating a story about his curfew violation. But Gunter's father testified before the parole board about Gunter's late appearance at the home. The parole board revoked. On the basis of the information provided by Gunter's parole officer and Gunter's father, Gunter was remanded to the secure facility where he would have to serve the remainder of his disposition. Gunter appealed, claiming that the action of the parole board was arbitrary and discriminatory. A Florida appellate court heard his case and upheld the action of the parole board, noting that sufficient evidence of Gunter's program violation existed. The court also noted that Gunter's attitude and reaction were adverse to the good conduct expected of him, and that his lack of truthfulness more than justified the parole board decision (*In re Gunter,* 2006).

Can juvenile parole be revoked merely by associating with former gang members? Yes. Terrence M. is a Mississippi juvenile and former gang member who was serving a 12-month placement in a secure facility for drug possession and use as well as assaultive behavior resulting from a gang-affiliated activity. The juvenile parole board decided to parole Terrence M. three months short of serving his full term. Two weeks into his parole term, Terrence M. was spotted at a local game center associating with three known members of his former gang. One of his parole conditions was that he should not have any contact with his former gang members. An informant advised Terrence M.'s parole officer who went to the game center and saw Terrence M. talking with the gang members. Terrence M. was taken into custody and subsequently appeared before the juvenile parole board. The parole board decided to revoke Terrence M.'s parole program and he was returned to the secure facility. He appealed the decision, but a Mississippi appellate court upheld the decision of the parole board in his case. An eyewitness, together with the testimony of Terrence M.'s parole officer, were sufficient documentation that he had violated an important parole program condition. His appeal was rejected (*Terrence M. v. State*, 2006).

Can juveniles have their parole programs revoked on hearsay evidence of drug use? No. Felicia L. is a 17-year-old Texas female who was paroled from a secure facility after serving four months for possession of illegal prescription medication and forgery. While on parole, Felicia L. was placed in foster care. According to her foster parents, she was continuously absent from the home without a valid excuse, was verbally abusive, and acted in an erratic manner. The family notified the parole officer and declared that they believed Felicia L. was using methamphetamine and other illegal drugs. The parole officer brought Felicia L. before the parole board, and on the basis of a written statement from the foster father, the parole board voted to revoke her parole. She appealed, declaring that her due process rights were violated and that she did not have an opportunity to confront her accuser. Her attorney was given no opportunity to challenge the veracity of the written statements of the foster father. Furthermore, no drug tests were performed to determine whether Felicia L. had indeed consumed illegal substances. A Texas appellate court reversed the parole board decision and reinstated Felicia L.'s parole program, holding that she had been deprived of a fundamental right to confront and cross-examine the persons giving testimony, oral or written, against her. The written declarations by Felicia L.'s foster father were labeled as hearsay, and a valid reconfinement to a secure facility could not be based on hearsay alone (*Felicia L. v. State,* 2006).

Prospective juvenile parolees are entitled to certain minimum due process rights in various states similar to those articulated in the adult cases. Similar procedures are followed in several other states. Despite these procedural safeguards, parole revocation hearings for juveniles are often scripted in advance.

Because the literature on juvenile parole violators is scant, it is difficult to profile them. Early research has shown, however, that those parolees who have had the longest institutional commitment lengths are also the more likely to have their parole revoked (Haapanen and Britton, 2002). However, this may be a somewhat self-fulfilling observation, since the most serious offenders are given the longest sentences anyway, and they are more likely to recidivate.

TRANSFERS, WAIVERS, OR CERTIFICATIONS

As a last resort, and usually for only the most serious offenders, juvenile court judges may waive their jurisdiction over certain juveniles to the jurisdiction of criminal courts for adults. These waivers of jurisdiction are not undertaken routinely. In fact, fewer than 1 percent of all juveniles charged with delinquent offenses are transferred each year.

Transfers refer to changing the jurisdiction over certain juvenile offenders to another jurisdiction, usually from juvenile court jurisdiction to criminal court jurisdiction (Flowers, 2002). Transfers are also known as waivers, referring to a **waiver** or change of jurisdiction from the authority of juvenile court judges to criminal court judges. Prosecutors or juvenile court judges decide that in some cases, juveniles should be waived or transferred to the jurisdiction of criminal courts. Presumably, those cases that are waived or transferred are the most serious cases, involving violent or serious offenses, such as homicide, aggravated assault, forcible rape, robbery, or drug-dealing activities. Some jurisdictions such as Utah certify juveniles as adults. **Certification** is a formal procedure whereby the state declares the juvenile to be an adult for the purpose of a criminal prosecution. The results of certifications are the same as for waivers or transfers. Several reasons for the use of transfers, waivers, or certifications include the following:

1. To make it possible for harsher punishments to be imposed.
2. To provide just-deserts and proportionately severe punishments on those juveniles who deserve such punishments by their more violent actions.
3. To foster fairness in administering punishments according to one's serious offending.
4. To hold serious or violent offenders more accountable for what they have done.
5. To show other juveniles who contemplate committing serious offenses that the system works and that harsh punishments can be expected if serious offenses are committed.
6. To provide a deterrent to decrease juvenile violence.
7. To overcome the traditional leniency of juvenile courts and provide more realistic sanctions.
8. To make youths realize the seriousness of their offending and induce remorse and acceptance of responsibility.

In 2005, out of 2.2 million youths brought to the attention of juvenile courts, only 11,300 youths were transferred to criminal court. Most juveniles transferred were male, with only 800 females being waived (U.S. Department of Justice, 2006). About 5,700 of all transferred juveniles were black or another minority, despite the fact that white juveniles comprised about 65 percent of all cases referred to juvenile court. Furthermore, those charged with person offenses and waived to criminal court made up only 40 percent of those transferred. About 42 percent of those charged with property or public order offenses were waived to criminal courts, while about 12 percent of those waived were charged with drug offenses (U.S. Department of Justice, 2006). In 2005, nine states and all federal districts indicated no specified age for transferring juveniles to criminal courts for processing. Two states, Vermont and Wisconsin, specified age 10 as the minimum age at which a juvenile could be waived. Colorado, Missouri, Montana, and Oregon established age 12 as the earliest age for a juvenile waiver. Eighteen states used age 14 as the youngest transfer age, while the District of Columbia set the minimum transfer age at 15, and one state, Hawaii, used the minimum transfer age of 16. There are four types of waiver actions. These are: (1) judicial waivers, (2) direct file, (3) statutory exclusion, and (4) demand waivers.

Judicial Waivers

The largest numbers of waivers from juvenile to criminal court annually come about as the result of direct judicial action. **Judicial waivers** give the juvenile court judge the authority to decide whether to waive jurisdiction and transfer the case to criminal court.

There are three kinds of judicial waivers. The first type, **discretionary waivers,** empower the judge to waive jurisdiction over the juvenile and transfer the case to criminal court. An example of a discretionary waiver form used to waive jurisdiction over juveniles to criminal court is shown in Figure 13.19.

Because of this type of waiver, judicial waivers are sometimes known as discretionary waivers. The second type of judicial waiver is the **mandatory**

COURT OF COMMON PLEAS, JUVENILE COURT DIVISION
CUYAHOGA COUNTY, OHIO

IN THE MATTER OF:

CASE NO:

JUDGE

<u>JOURNAL ENTRY</u>

DISCRETIONARY TRANSFER

This matter came on for hearing this_____day of_____, 2002, before the Honorable

The Court finds that notice requirements have been met and all necessary parties were present in court.
☐ *The complaint was read in open court.* ☐ *Reading of the complaint was waived.* ☐ *The Court explained legal rights, procedures, and consequences of the hearing pursuant to Ohio Juvenile Rule 29 and Ohio Revised Code Section 2152.12.*
The Court further finds that the child is represented by counsel. Upon the conclusion of all evidence presented relating to the matter herein and the arguments of counsel, the Court finds that the child was _____ years of age at the time of the conduct charged and that there is probable cause to believe that the child committed an act that would be the crime of _____, in violation of Section _____ of the Ohio Revised Code and classified as ☐ *Aggravated Murder*
☐ *a felony of the first degree if committed by an adult.*
☐ *It is ordered that this matter is continued to a later date for a full investigation, including a mental examination, pursuant to Ohio Juvenile Rule 30. Child is remanded to secure detention pending further hearing. ? The Court finds that the child, through counsel, waives a mental examination.*
☐ *The Court finds after a full investigation, including a mental and physical examination of said child made by a duly qualified person(s), and after full consideration of the child's prior juvenile record, family environment, school record, efforts previously made to treat and rehabilitate the child, including prior commitments to the Ohio Department of Youth Services, the nature and severity of the offense herein, the age, physical, and mental condition of the victim as effected by the matter herein, and other matters of evidence, there are reasonable grounds to believe that the child herein is not amenable to care or rehabilitation within the juvenile system. The Court further finds that the safety of the community may require that the child be subject to adult sanctions.*

The Court considered the relevant factors in favor of transfer pursuant to R. C. 2152.12(D) and makes the following findings:
☐ *The victim suffered physical or psychological harm, or serious economic harm.*
☐ *The physical or psychological harm suffered by the victim was exacerbated because of the physical or psychological vulnerability or the age of the victim.*
☐ *The child's relationship with the victim facilitated the act charged.*
☐ *The child allegedly committed the act charged for hire or as a part of a gang or other organized criminal activity.*
☐ *The child had a firearm on or about the child's person or under the child's control at the time of the act charged, the act charged is not a violation of section 2923.12 of the Revised Code, and the child, during the commission of the act charged, allegedly used or displayed the firearm, brandished the firearm, or indicated that the child possessed a firearm.*
☐ *At the time of the act charged, the child was awaiting adjudication or disposition as a delinquent child, was under a community control sanction, or was on parole for a prior delinquent child adjudication or conviction.*

JOURNAL ENTRY   **CASE NUMBER**   **PAGE 2**

☐ *The results of any previous juvenile sanctions and programs indicate that rehabilitation of the child will not occur in the juvenile system.*
☐ *The child is emotionally, physically, or psychologically mature enough for the transfer.*
☐ *There is not sufficient time to rehabilitate the child within the juvenile system.*
☐ *Other:*

The Court considered the relevant factors against transfer pursuant to R. C. 2152.12(E) and makes the following findings:

☐ *The victim induced or facilitated the act charged.*

☐ *The child acted under provocation in allegedly committing the act charged.*

☐ *The child was not the principal actor in the act charged, or, at the time of the act charged, the child was under the negative influence or coercion of another person.*

☐ *The child did not cause physical harm to any person or property, or have reasonable cause to believe that harm of that nature would occur, in allegedly committing the act charged.*

☐ *The child previously has not been adjudicated a delinquent child.*

☐ *The child is not emotionally, physically, or phychologically mature enough for the transfer.*

☐ *The child has a mental illness or is a mentally retarded person.*

☐ *There is sufficient time to rehabilitate the child within the juvenile system and the level of security available in the juvenile system provides a reasonable assurance of public safety.*

☐ *Other:*

☐ *It is therefore ordered pursuant to O.R.C. 2152.12(B), that the matter herein is transferred to the General Trial Division of the Cuyahoga County Common Pleas Court for further proceedings pursuant to law. It is further ordered that the child herein is remanded to the county jail for detention pending further proceedings. It is further ordered that the child herein may be released pending trial upon entering into a recognizance with good and sufficient surety in the sum of $_____ to assure his/her appearance before the said General Trial Division, at such time as may be fixed by that Court, it is further ordered that should such recognizance be filed, it is to be transferred to the said General Trial Division.*

_____

JUDGE   DATE

FILED WITH THE CLERK AND JOURNALIZED
ON _____
BY _____ DEPUTY CLERK

FIGURE 13.19   Discretionary Transfer. (From Cuyahoga County, Ohio).

waiver. In the case of a mandatory waiver, the juvenile court judge *must* waive jurisdiction over the juvenile if probable cause exists that the juvenile committed the alleged offense. The third type of judicial waiver is called a **presumptive waiver.** Under the presumptive waiver scenario, the burden of proof concerning a transfer decision is shifted from the state to the juvenile. It requires that certain juveniles be waived to criminal court unless they can prove that they are suited to juvenile rehabilitation.

Direct File

Under **direct file,** the prosecutor has the sole authority to decide whether any given juvenile case will be heard in criminal court or juvenile court. Essentially, the prosecutor decides which court should have jurisdiction over the juvenile. Prosecutors with direct file power are said to have **concurrent jurisdiction.** This is another name for direct file. In Florida, for example, prosecutors have concurrent jurisdiction. They may file extremely serious charges (e.g., murder, rape, aggravated assault, robbery) against youths in criminal courts and present cases to grand juries for indictment action. Or prosecutors may decide to file the same cases in the juvenile court.

Statutory Exclusion

Statutory exclusion means that certain juvenile offenders are automatically excluded from the juvenile court's original jurisdiction. Legislatures of various states declare a particular list of offenses to be excluded from the jurisdiction of juvenile courts. Added to this list of excluded offenses is a particular age range. Sometimes this action is referred to as a **legislative waiver** or an **automatic waiver**.

Demand Waivers

Under certain conditions and in selected jurisdictions, juveniles may submit motions for **demand waivers**. Demand waiver actions are requests or motions filed by juveniles and their attorneys to have their cases transferred from juvenile courts to criminal courts. Why would juveniles want to have their cases transferred to criminal courts? One reason is that most U.S. jurisdictions do not provide jury trials for juveniles in juvenile courts as a matter of right (*McKeiver v. Pennsylvania,* 1971). However, about a fifth of the states have established provisions for jury trials for juveniles at their request and depending on the nature of the charges against them.

Other Types of Waivers

Reverse Waivers.   **Reverse waivers** are actions by the criminal court to transfer direct file or statutory exclusion cases from criminal court back to juvenile court, usually at the recommendation of the prosecutor. Typically, juveniles who would be involved in these reverse waiver hearings would be those who were automatically sent to criminal court because of statutory exclusion. Thus, criminal court judges can send at least some of these juveniles back to the jurisdiction of the juvenile court. Reverse waiver actions may also be instigated by defense counsels on behalf of their clients. **Reverse waiver hearings** are held in these matters.

Once An Adult/Always An Adult.   **The once an adult/always an adult provision** is perhaps the most serious and long-lasting for affected juvenile offenders. This provision means that once juveniles have been convicted in criminal court, they are forever after considered adults for the purpose of criminal prosecutions.

Waiver Hearings

All juveniles who are waived to criminal court for processing are entitled to a hearing on the waiver if they request one (Champion, 2007). Thus, a **waiver hearing** is a formal proceeding designed to determine whether the waiver action taken by the judge or prosecutor is the correct action, and that the juvenile should be transferred to criminal court. Waiver hearings are initiated through a **waiver motion**, where the prosecutor usually requests the judge to send the case to criminal court. In those jurisdictions with direct file or statutory exclusion provisions, juveniles and their attorneys may contest these waiver actions through **reverse waiver hearings**. Reverse waiver hearings are conducted before criminal court judges to determine whether to send the juvenile's case back to juvenile court.

BLENDED SENTENCING STATUTES

A vast improvement over transfers, waivers, or certifications is what is called **blended sentencing. Blended sentencing statutes** refer to the imposition of juvenile and/or adult correctional sanctions on serious and violent juvenile offenders who have been adjudicated in juvenile court or convicted in criminal court. Blended sentencing options are usually based on age or on a combination of age and offense. There are five blended sentencing models. These include (1) juvenile–exclusive blend; (2) juvenile–inclusive blend; (3) juvenile–contiguous blend; (4) criminal–exclusive blend; and (5) criminal–inclusive blend.

1. **The juvenile–exclusive blend** involves a disposition by the juvenile court judge that is either a disposition to the juvenile correctional system or to the adult correctional system, but not both. Thus, a judge might order a juvenile adjudicated delinquent for aggravated assault to serve three years in a juvenile industrial school, or the judge may order the adjudicated delinquent to serve three years in a prison for adults. The judge cannot impose *both* types of punishment under this model, however. In 2004, only one state, New Mexico, provided such a sentencing option for its juvenile court judges.

2. **The juvenile–inclusive blend** involves a disposition by the juvenile court judge that is both a juvenile correctional sanction and an adult correctional sanction. In cases such as this, suppose the judge had adjudicated a 15-year-old juvenile delinquent on a charge of vehicular theft. The judge might impose a disposition of two years in a juvenile industrial school or reform school. Furthermore, the judge might impose a sentence of three additional years in an adult penitentiary. However, the second sentence to the adult prison would typically be suspended, unless the juvenile violated one or more conditions of his or her original disposition and any conditions accompanying the disposition. Usually, this suspension period would run until the youth reaches age 18 or 21. If the offender were to commit a new offense or violate one or more program conditions, he or she would immediately be placed in the adult prison to serve the second sentence originally imposed.

3. **The juvenile–contiguous blend** involves a disposition by a juvenile court judge that may extend beyond the jurisdictional age limit of the offender. When the age limit of the juvenile court jurisdiction is reached, various procedures may be invoked to transfer the case to the jurisdiction of adult corrections. This particular sentencing blend seems most effective at punishing serious and violent offenders while providing them with a final chance to access certain provided Texas rehabilitative programs.

4. **The criminal–exclusive blend** involves a decision by a criminal court judge to impose either a juvenile court sanction or a criminal court sanction, but not both. For example, a criminal court judge may hear the case of a 15-year-old youth who has been transferred to criminal court on a rape charge. The youth is convicted in a jury trial in criminal court. At this point, the judge has two options: the judge can sentence the offender to a prison term in an adult correctional facility, or the judge can impose an incarcerative sentence for the youth to serve in a juvenile facility. The judge may believe that the 15-year-old would be better off in a juvenile industrial school rather than in an adult

prison. The judge may impose a sentence of adult incarceration, but he or she may be inclined to place the youth in a facility where there are other youths in the offender's age range.

5. **The criminal–inclusive blend** involves a decision by the criminal court judge to impose both a juvenile penalty and a criminal sentence simultaneously. Again, as in the juvenile court–inclusive blend model, the latter criminal sentence may be suspended depending on the good conduct of the juvenile during the juvenile punishment phase. There is a special strength of this blend. If the juvenile violates one or more conditions of his or her confinement in the juvenile facility, the judge has the power to revoke that sentence and invoke the sentence of incarceration in an adult facility. Thus, a powerful incentive is provided for the youth to show evidence that rehabilitation has occurred. It is to the youth's advantage to behave well while confined, since a more ominous sentence of confinement with adult offenders may be imposed at any time.

Blended sentencing statutes are intended to provide both juvenile and criminal court judges with a greater range of dispositional and/or sentencing options. In the 1980s and earlier, juvenile courts were notoriously lenient on juvenile offenders. Dispositions of juvenile court judges were mostly nominal or conditional, which usually meant verbal warnings and/or probation. While probation continues to be the sanction of choice in a majority of juvenile courts following delinquency adjudications, many states have armed their juvenile and criminal court judges with greater sanctioning powers. Thus, it is now possible in states, such as Colorado, Arkansas, or Missouri, for either juvenile court judges to impose sanctions that extend well beyond their original jurisdictional authority. Juvenile court judges in New Mexico, for instance, can place certain juveniles in either adult or juvenile correctional facilities. Criminal court judges in Florida, Idaho, Michigan, or Missouri can place those convicted of crimes in either juvenile or adult correctional facilities, depending on the jurisdiction. These are broader and more powerful dispositional and sentencing options to hold youthful offenders more accountable for the serious offenses they commit.

SUMMARY

Juvenile delinquents commit acts that would be crimes if committed by adults. Status offenders commit acts that would not be crimes if committed by adults. Considerable variation exists among juvenile court jurisdictions. Most juvenile court jurisdictions throughout the United States deal with juveniles charged with delinquent offenses. In a minority of jurisdictions, status offenders are co-processed with delinquent offenders. The juvenile court is a civil court. Thus, when juveniles' cases are presented and decided, this results in an adjudication or judgment. This adjudication is not the same as a criminal conviction. Juveniles do not acquire criminal records from juvenile court adjudications of any kind. Sometimes, if the offense warrants, juveniles may be waived, certified, or transferred to criminal courts and tried as if they were adults. A greater range of severe penalties may be imposed on those convicted of crimes in criminal courts. Most cases commenced in the juvenile justice system remain within it, where juvenile court judges have various options if offenders are adjudicated delinquent. These options include nominal, conditional, and custodial dispositions. The most frequently used option by juvenile court judges is probation. Frequently, juveniles who have been adjudicated delinquent and have recidivated at a later date will be placed on probation again. In fact, secure confinement of juveniles is considered as a last resort in most juvenile court jurisdictions.

Many of the probation and parole programs for adults are emulated in the juvenile justice system. Juveniles may be placed on unconditional or conditional diversion, unconditional or conditional probation, intensive supervised probation, and with or without conditions, including victim compensation or restitution, fines, community service, electronic monitoring, home confinement, and/or suggested psychological treatments or counseling. No U.S. Supreme Court case law exists governing probation and parole revocation proceedings for juveniles. Many jurisdictions are influenced by some of the major cases decided for adult probationers and parolees facing revocation of their programs. In some instances, juvenile court judges require juvenile POs to prepare predispositional reports to assist judges in the dispositions they impose for adjudicated juveniles.

The most successful probation and parole programs for juveniles involve activities that improve their coping skills, self-images, and self-respect. Accountability is an important component of these programs as well. The Ohio Experience emphasizes community protection, offender accountability, and individualizing sanctions for specific youths. This particular program underscores the continuing importance of the *parens patriae* doctrine. Boot camps and shock probation or incarceration seem useful as well for instilling youths with greater individual responsibility and accountability.

QUESTIONS FOR REVIEW

1. How do delinquents differ from status offenders? What are the major criteria used in these different definitions?

2. What is the extent of juvenile court jurisdiction over children who are dependent and neglected?

3. What is the doctrine of *parens patriae* and how has it influenced today's juvenile courts?

4. What was the significance of the following cases: (a) *Schall v. Martin;* (b) *Ex parte Crouse;* (c) *In re Gault;* and (d) *In re Winship?*

5. What are some of the major differences between criminal and juvenile courts?

6. What are graduated sanctions continuums? How do they work for juveniles? What are some of their intended aims?

7. What are waivers? What are four different types of waivers? Do these proceedings require a hearing? Why or why not?

8. What are blended sentencing statutes? How do they differ from waivers?

9. What is the process of revoking a youth's probation or parole program?

10. What are some of the causes for revoking a juvenile's probation or parole?

SUGGESTED READINGS

Blomberg, Thomas G. et al. (2006). "Juvenile Justice Education, No Child Left Behind, and the National Collaboration Project." *Corrections Today* **68**:143–145.

Marcell, Frank (2006). "Security Threat Groups' Effect on Corrections During the Past Decade." *Corrections Today* **68**:56–59.

Meyers, D.L. (ed.) (2005). *Boys Among Men: Trying and Sentencing Juveniles as Adults.* Westport, CT: Praeger.

Sridharan, Sanjeev, Lynette Greenfield, and Baron Blakley (2004). "A Study of Prosecutorial Certification Practice in Virginia." *Criminology and Public Policy* **4:**605–632.

Steiner, Benjamin, Craig Hemmens and Valerie Bell (2006). "Legislative Waiver Reconsidered: General Deterrent Effects of Statutory Exclusion Laws Enacted Post-1979." *Justice Quarterly* **23:**34–58.

Vandiver, D.M. and R. Teske (2006). "Juvenile Female and Male Sex Offenders: A Comparison of Offender, Victim, and Judicial Processing Characteristics." *International Journal of Offender Therapy and Comparative Criminology* **50:**148–165.

INTERNET CONNECTIONS

ABA Juvenile Justice Center
http://www.abanet.org/crimjust/juvjus/home.html

Building Blocks for Youth
http://www.buildingblocksforyouth.org/issues/girls/resources.html

Center for Court Innovation
http://www.courtinnovation.org/

Communication Works
http://www.communicationworks.org

Council of Juvenile Correctional Administrators
http://www.corrections.com/cjca

Juvenile Boot Camp Directory
http://www.kci.org/publication/bootcam/prerelease.htm

Juvenile Intensive Probation Supervision
http://www.nal.usda.gov/pavnet/yf/yfjuvpro.htm

Juvenile Justice Reform Initiatives
http://www.ojjdp.ncjrs.org/pubs/reform/ch2_k.html

National Council of Juvenile and Family Court Judges
http://www.ncjfcj.unr.edu/

National Girls' Caucus
http://www.pacecenter.org

National Youth Court Center
http://www.youthcourt.net

North Carolina IMPACT Boot Camps
http://www.doc.state.nc.us/impact/

Office of Juvenile Justice and Delinquency Prevention
http://www.ojjdp.ncjrs.org

PACE Center for Girls, Inc.
http://www.pacecenter.org

Rights for All
http://www.amnesty-usa.org/rightsforall/juvenile/dp/section2.html

Riker's Island High Impact Incarceration Program
http://www.correctionhistory.org/html/chronicl/nycdoc/html/hiip.html

Teen Boot Camp
http://www.teenbootcamps.com

Teen Court
http://www.teen-court.org

Texas Juvenile Probation Commission
http://www.tjpc.state.tx.us/

Wilderness Programs, Inc.
http://www.wildernessprogramsetc.com

Youth Alternatives, Inc.
http://www.volunteersolutions.org/volunteer/agency/one_177937.html

Youthful Offenders Parole Board
http://www.yopb.ca.gov/

CHAPTER 14 | *Evaluating Programs: Balancing Service Delivery and Recidivism Considerations*

Chapter Outline

Chapter Objectives

As the result of reading this chapter, the following objectives will be realized:

1. Defining recidivism and examining several popular meanings of the term as pertaining to probation and parole.
2. Examining recidivism and parole and probation revocation.
3. Describing characteristics of recidivists, including their offenses and other pertinent traits.
4. Comparing and contrasting recidivism between parolees and probationers.
5. Examining the views of probationers and parolees and the reports they make about those factors most influential in curbing their own recidivism.

- *John Evander Couey was a chronic recidivist. He had been arrested over 30 times and had a lengthy criminal record with many convictions for both violent and property offenses. In 2003 he was arrested and convicted of a serious DUI charge, but he was given probation. Subsequently, he violated one or more terms of his probation in 2004 and was promptly put on probation again. Another probation violation got him 59 days in jail. When he was released from jail, he wandered about, eventually encountering 9-year-old Jessica Lunsford in Citrus County, Florida, in March 2005. He kidnapped her, raped her repeatedly, and then murdered her. What should be done with John Couey? What should be his punishment? Should a prior judge have locked him up in prison for many years for his numerous crimes? Who is to blame for John Couey's crimes? [Adapted from Robert James Bidinotto and the Associated Press, "What Is Justice? What is Crime? And What Should the Criminal Justice System Be Doing?", March 30, 2005].*

- *Royce Timmons was paroled in California and shortly thereafter began a six-day crime spree that started with an argument with his girlfriend, who he stabbed repeatedly in the neck, face, and chest. She nearly died. Later that same day, Timmons hijacked a woman sitting in her car at a fast-food restaurant and drove her to three different places, raping her at each stop. She managed to escape on their fourth stop. Over the next few days, Timmons robbed two women at a small business, carjacked another vehicle, and robbed and kidnapped the clerk at a convenience store and raped her. On the day he was eventually apprehended by police, he began by carjacking a Ford Explorer from an auto dealership, scored some crack cocaine, and drove around town getting high. Coincidentally, a police cruiser spotted the stolen Ford Explorer and followed Timmons. Timmons became aware that he was being followed and a high-speed chase ensued. The chase ended when Timmons rolled the Explorer on its side. When police approached the overturned vehicle, Timmons was laying on his side, smoking a crack cocaine pipe. The prosecutor, Victor Stull, said, "Even though he's been in this chase, and the car's tipped over, the most important thing in his mind is to take one more hit on his crack pipe." In his jail photo taken about an hour later, Timmons, 46, appeared to be in a daze, his bloodshot eyes glassed over, and his face splotched with several days of uneven growth of salt-and-pepper facial hair. Timmons was last seen sitting in a San Bernardino County Jail, facing 18 criminal counts, including attempted murder, carjacking, robbery, kidnapping to commit robbery/rape, rape by force, sodomy with force, and sexual penetration with a foreign object. It is likely that Timmons will become the poster person for Governor Arnold Schwarzenegger's tough-on-crime prison-reform agenda. [Source: Adapted from Stephen James and the* Sacramento News and Review, *"Meet Arnold's Willie Horton," May 19, 2005].*

- *In 1997, Collier, Florida, sheriff's officials proclaimed a 30 percent recidivism rate for graduates of DRILL, a boot camp for juvenile delinquents. In 1999 a recidivism figure of 19 percent was cited. And on September 6, 2005, the sheriff disclosed that of the first 165 boys to graduate from DRILL, 97 percent were eventually rearrested. How can that be? First, when the 1997 figures were cited, the 30 percent recidivism rate was for persons who failed to complete the program. In 1999, the figures disclosed recidivism of graduates within the first year of their program graduation. Subsequently a five-year study was commissioned. This time, it showed that 97 percent of all graduates had been rearrested or reconvicted of new offenses. As a result, the DRILL program has been terminated. Other states may face budget cuts with their boot camp programs if similar results are disclosed with longer follow-up periods for tracking recidivists. For instance, Missouri claims a 9 percent recidivism rate, but it only counts juveniles who are sent to jail within a year of their release as recidivists. Also not counted are those who turn 18 years old and become part of the adult offender system when they recidivate. The Florida sheriff's study suggests that the rehabilitation of chronic delinquents through boot camp programs may be just wishful thinking. [Source: Adapted from Brent Batten and the* Naples Daily News, *"Success Rates of Juvenile Boot Camps Can Be Quite Deceptive," September 8, 2005].*

• *Operation Triggerlock is a Weed and Seed intervention program established and implemented in Harrisburg, Pennsylvania. It is designed to remove violent felons, illegal firearms, and narcotics from crime-ridden communities. Operation Triggerlock involves intensive surveillance operations, undercover investigations, and arrests of criminal suspects. Saturation patrols are conducted throughout various neighborhoods. The patrols serve a dual purpose: they reassure law-abiding citizens and discourage criminal elements. Operation Triggerlock is an integral part of Weed and Seed, a federal community-building initiative that assists Pennsylvania and other states in fighting back against drugs, crime, and poverty to restore neighborhood quality of life. The "Weed" component involves intensive efforts to improve public safety, followed by a "Seed" component involving citizen-driven revitalization strategies. During 2002, for instance, an evaluation study of Operation Triggerlock operations disclosed 4,659 arrests and 834 warnings. Additionally, police seized 75 firearms, 67 vehicles, and illegal cash totalling more than $163,000. [Source: Adapted from the PR Newswire, "PA Commission on Crime and Delinquency Presents Funding to Pennsylvania State Police for 'Operation Triggerlock,' " September 29, 2003].*

INTRODUCTION

How do we know if community-based correctional programs for probationers and parolees work? Because there are so many programs out there, which ones are most effective? Do these programs achieve their objectives, and to what degree? This chapter is about program evaluation and recidivism. Every intervention program applied to both juveniles and adults is subject to evaluation at one time or another. Investigators want to know whether a particular program is cost-effective and whether it accomplishes its stated goals. Programs are either successful or unsuccessful. Offender-clients either "fail" or "succeed." How is the successfulness or unsuccessfulness of programs and offender-clients measured? The first part of this chapter examines the criteria conventionally used to evaluate program effectiveness. Both objective and subjective criteria are considered in this discussion.

Because there are so many different kinds of offenders of various ages, there are numerous intervention, rehabilitation, and reintegration programs designed to assist them in meeting their diverse needs. We will find that program success is subject to widely different interpretations, and many professionals use diffuse and even inconsistent criteria to evaluate whether a program's goals are attained. Because the successfulness of programs often depends on the nature of the program clientele, some attention is given to how clients are selected for inclusion in particular programs. Some programs engage in creaming, where only the most low-risk and eligible offenders are included. Thus, some bias exists at the outset favoring program successfulness. If only the most desirable clients are included, more favorable results will be expected, compared with those programs that include more dangerous and higher-risk clientele.

Recidivism is an important measure of program success or failure. Therefore, considerable attention is devoted to describing recidivism and its many varieties. Recidivism is examined in the context of both juvenile and adult probationers and parolees. Probationer recidivism is compared with parolee recidivism to determine any significant differences, if any (Hepburn, 2005). What kinds of offenders are more likely to recidivate, and under what types of conditions? What factors are useful in decreasing recidivism? Recidivism seems to fluctuate among probationers and parolees according to various program conditions. Which program conditions seem most likely to reduce recidivism? The chapter concludes with an examination of attitudes expressed by probationers and parolees themselves about their reasons for recidivating.

PROGRAM EVALUATION: HOW DO WE KNOW PROGRAMS ARE EFFECTIVE?

Program evaluation is the process of assessing any intervention or program for the purpose of determining its effectiveness in achieving manifest goals. Program evaluation investigates the nature of organizational intervention strategies, counseling, interpersonal interactions, staff quality, expertise, and education, and the success or failure experiences of clients served by any program. Several examples below illustrate what is meant by program evaluation.

Example 1. Connie Ireland and JoAnn Prause (2005) studied recidivism differences between parolees released according to a mandatory release policy and those leaving prison early through discretionary parole release. In the present research, the "intervention" or "program" consisted of the two different early-release methods: discretionary release and mandatory release. Discretionary parole release is the practice of parole review and determination of prison release for offenders sentenced under indeterminate sentencing schemes. These discretionary releases are largely subjective, relying heavily on personal judgments of an offender's future potential for success on parole according to various criteria. In contrast, mandatory release is the automatic discharge from prison of inmates after they have served a specified time in prison. Mandatory release has become increasingly popular, since it objectifies early-release criteria and removes subjective and potentially adverse release disparities from paroling authorities according to extralegal factors such as race/ethnicity, age, gender, and socioeconomic status. These investigators gathered parolee release information from national figures reported for 1995. Ireland and Prause wanted to know which release method was more successful in reducing recidivism rates among parolees. The evaluation or measure of parole success consisted of comparing recidivism rates of parolees released under different release methods.

What did Ireland and Prause find? Parolees under mandatory release were far more likely to fail in their parole programs and parole supervision compared with those parolees under discretionary release. These researchers adjusted for numerous factors, including type of offense, time served, age, ethnicity, and gender when conducting their comparisons of parolee successfulness. While their study is not definitive, Ireland and Prause have suggested strongly that discretionary parole, despite its controversial dimensions, is more effective in promoting parolee success compared with mandatory release. Maybe having parole boards involved in early-release decision making isn't so bad after all.

Example 2. Alexander Cowell, Nahama Broner, and Randolph Dupont (2004) were interested in the cost effectiveness of a jail diversion program for incarcerated persons diagnosed with mental disorders and histories of substance abuse. The "intervention" or "program" was jail diversion. Jail diversion is a post-booking program where booked offenders who have been jailed are removed from custody prior to prosecution and conviction and placed in a community treatment system where they can receive various services, counseling, and other types of assistance. Targeted for jail diversion were persons with co-occurring mental disorders (e.g., schizophrenia, depression, and bipolar disorder) and substance abuse or dependence disorders. At the time these researchers conducted their research, nine cities were experimenting with jail diversion with co-occurring mental illness and substance abuse disorders. Four sites were selected for study, and participants were tracked over a 12-month period. The evaluation was multifaceted. It consisted of the cost effectiveness of jail diversion compared with the actual costs of incarceration; whether participants had higher levels of mental functioning after a one-year follow-up; and whether there was any evidence of substance abuse within a year following program completion.

What did these researchers find? Although the four sites differed from one another according to various success criteria, an overall assessment was that jail diversion was less costly than incarceration. Furthermore, a slight increase in mental functioning occurred, attributed to the community treatment and programming received by study participants. Relapse rates for those arrested for substance abuse problems were also lower. The general implication is that jail diversion works, at least among the sites studied in this research, for improving mental health and reducing substance abuse among arrestees.

Example 3. Ralph Fretz (2005) investigated reentry problems and issues arising from a large sample of state and federal offenders released from prisons. He observed that many parolees had problems adjusting to community living and that many had high relapse rates because of drug and alcohol dependencies and a failure to get and keep a job. In recent years, community education centers (CECs) have been established based on a continuum-of-care model that incorporates step-down or transitional programming from institutional to community correctional settings. Fretz noted that only 7 percent of all parolees were involved in CEC programming, and that about two-thirds of all released offenders will be rearrested within three years following their release. Fretz wanted to evaluate the effectiveness of CECs, the "program" or "intervention," on a sample of parolees and whether the continuum-of-care model worked to lower their recidivism rates (the measure of program success). Fretz used a case approach, where he tracked a sample of offenders who participated in CEC programming. The CEC program involved assessing offenders and their needs while they were institutionalized. Subsequently they would be assisted on parole through halfway house living with structured reentry and reintegration. They would be provided with various treatments, including cognitive-behavioral therapy and various prosocial behavioral experiences.

What did Fretz find? Offenders who participated in CEC programming reintegrated more successfully into their communities. They networked more closely with their families and received continuing assistance and treatment for their former substance abuse problems. The intervention of CEC was regarded as successful.

Example 4. Jill Levenson and Leo Cotter (2005) investigated the impact of Megan's Law on a sample of sex offenders. Megan's Law was enacted in 1996 and named after Megan Kanka who was a New Jersey child murdered by a child sexual abuser. The U.S. Congress passed the law requiring all sex offenders to register with local law enforcement agencies so that their current whereabouts would be known to others. Megan's Law required states to initiate notification procedures to inform the public about sex offenders who live in close proximity to them. According to Levenson and Cotter, the purpose of their research was to better understand the positive and negative, intended or unintended, consequences of community notification laws on sex offender rehabilitation and reintegration. In this study, the "intervention" was Megan's Law. Florida was selected for study and a sample of 183 sex offenders were recruited and studied from various outpatient and sex offender counseling centers. One reason Florida was targeted for this investigation was that it required lifetime registration of sex offenders; all sex offenders in the state are subject to public disclosure; few guidelines are provided for notification procedures; and each local law enforcement agency is allowed to notify its community residents in any manner deemed appropriate. Levenson and Cotter wanted to know whether community notification might increase an offender's awareness of their risk, thus facilitating engagement in more treatment and risk management. The "outcome" would be sex offender impressions and evaluations of notification procedures and how they viewed their own rehabilitation and community reintegration.

What did Levenson and Cotter find? First, door-to-door warnings appeared to be the most widely used instrument of community notification that sex offenders were living nearby. Half of all participating sex offenders had no idea how residents were being advised of their presence. About a third of all sex offenders reported losses of jobs and homes, threats of harassment, and/or property damage. Most offenders believed that community notification laws were unfair. However, they said it was fair for law enforcement agencies to take their fingerprints, photographs, and descriptions of their offenses. Fewer than 10 percent believed that it was fair for the public to know their telephone numbers, addresses, work locations, and vehicle information. Of those surveyed, only 18 percent of the sex offenders said that they were at risk of reoffending. Most said they would never reoffend. Interestingly, most sex offenders reported that their lack of social support from community residents would function as a dynamic risk factor for sex offense recidivism. About half of the respondents said that posted Internet information about them was factually incorrect or inaccurate. Few sex offenders believed that communities are safer because of Megan's Law. One implication of this research was the suggestion to implement a tier system of notification similar to that adopted by California. This system would identify the most high-risk offenders and permit lower-risk offenders a better chance to become rehabilitated. Finally, Levenson and Cotter discovered that studying the ability of community notification to reduce sex offense recidivism is methodologically challenging.

SOME RECOMMENDED OUTCOME MEASURES

The American Probation and Parole Association (APPA) conducted a longitudinal investigation and survey to determine various alternative outcome measures for assessing intermediate punishment program effectiveness. Various organizational heads were surveyed throughout the United States and Canada. The APPA asked the following question:

"Assume that your department is going to be evaluated by an outside evaluator. The results of the evaluation will determine the level of funding for the next fiscal year. What outcome measure(s) would you want the evaluator to use in 'measuring' the success of your program(s)? What outcome measure(s) would you *not* want the evaluator to use in the evaluation?"

The results were as follows in order *or* most cited to least cited: (1) amount of restitution collected; (2) number of offenders employed; (3) technical violations; (4) alcohol/drug test results; (5) new arrests; (6) fines/fees collected; (7) number completed supervision; (8) hours of community service; (9) number of sessions of treatment; (10) number/ratio revocations; (11) percent financial obligations collected; (12) employment stability/days employed; (13) new arrests: crime type/seriousness; (14) meeting needs of offenders; (15) family stability; (16) education attainment; (17) costs/benefits/services/savings; (18) days alcohol-/drug-free; (19) number of treatment referrals; (20) time between technical violations; (21) marital stability; (22) wages/taxes paid; and (23) compliance with court orders.

Community-based programs are increasingly incorporating elements that heighten offender accountability. Making restitution to victims or to the community is an increasingly common program element. Employment is also a key agency goal of many community-based agencies. Thus, many officials selected the number of offenders employed as another preferred indicator of agency effectiveness. Other criteria in the top five included technical violations, alcohol/drug test results, and new arrests. Possibly because agencies have more effective monitoring mechanisms in place and improved supervision styles, it is less likely for program clients to engage in technical program violations, fail in drug/alcohol test results, and be rearrested for new offenses.

Probably every community-based corrections program has eligibility criteria used for selecting prospective clientele from among the offender population. Many programs regarded as successful in fulfilling their objectives and aims are guilty of selecting only the most success-prone clients. These include low-risk offenders and first-offenders. Particular types of offenders are deliberately excluded. For instance, some programs may declare that if offenders have a history of violent conduct, are mentally ill or psychologically disturbed, or are sex offenders, then they will be ineligible for inclusion in those programs. If only the most problem-free offenders are selected from the jail- or prison-bound offender population for probation or placement in a community-based correctional program, then the program effectiveness will be enhanced simply because a higher quality of clientele is being included. Those who are unlikely to succeed in these programs are systematically excluded. This is called creaming. The term no doubt derives from dairying, where the cream is skimmed from fresh milk. In a sense, the best of all eligible offenders is included in various intervention programs and influence in a positive way the successfulness of those programs.

The New Jersey IPS program for parolees is an example of creaming. By way of brief review, the New Jersey IPS program had a strict client selection process.

For instance, it consists of several screening stages. Final decisions on which applicants would be accepted were made by a resentencing panel of Superior Court judges. Reasons for rejecting applicants included first- and second-degree felonies, too many prior felony convictions, prior crimes of violence, and applicant reluctance to comply with IPS provisions. Thus, the New Jersey program was targeted for low-risk offenders with the least likelihood of recidivating. Not unexpectedly, the New Jersey ISP program reported recidivism rates of less than 20 percent. Thus, a type of self-fulfilling prophecy is created, where the program will succeed because we have done everything in our power to enhance the success of the program, including a careful screening of program applicants. The true test of any intervention program is whether it can make a difference for the hardcore offender aggregate. Short of permanently incarcerating all of our hardcore offenders, one important goal of community-based intervention programs should be to reintegrate unreintegratable offenders into their communities with some measure of success. Not many community-based corrections organizations are willing to implement programs that cater to the least successful clientele pool.

BALANCING PROGRAM OBJECTIVES AND OFFENDER NEEDS

The major objectives of community-based probation and parole programs for juveniles and adults are summarized as follows:

1. Facilitating offender reintegration
2. Continuing offender punishment
3. Heightening offender accountability
4. Ensuring community protection or safety
5. Promoting offender rehabilitation
6. Improving offender skills and coping mechanisms
7. Resolving offender social and psychological problems
8. Alleviating jail and prison overcrowding
9. Monitoring offender behaviors
10. Reducing offender chemical dependencies
11. Collecting fines, restitution payments, and other fees
12. Enforcing the law, including community service orders
13. Employing support personnel, corrections workers, and professionals/paraprofessionals
14. Producing low rates of recidivism among agency clientele
15. Coordinating and networking agency tasks and functions with other community agencies.
16. Justifying agency budget

This list is not exhaustive. Many functions or objectives above overlap with one another. The fact is that agencies are multifaceted, striving to achieve diverse goals or aims. Many of these organizational aims are mentioned by Petersilia and Turner (1993). She notes the following agency goals with accompanying performance indicators:

1. Assessing offenders' suitability for placement (performance indicators = accuracy and completeness of PSIs; timeliness of revocation and termination hearings; validity of classification/prediction instrument; percent of offenders receiving recommended sentence or violation action; and percent of offenders recommended for community who violate)

2. Enforcing court-ordered sanctions (performance indicators = number of arrests and technical violations during supervision; percent of ordered payments collected; number of hours/days performed community service; number of favorable discharges; numbers of days employed, in vocational education or school; and drug-free and/or alcohol-free days during supervision)

3. Protecting the community (performance indicators = number and type of supervision contacts; number and type of arrests during supervision; number and type of technical violations during supervision; number of absconders during supervision)

4. Assisting offenders to change (performance indicators = number of times attending treatment/work programming; employment during supervision; number of arrests and/or technical violations during supervision; number drug-free and/or alcohol-free days during supervision; and attitude change)

5. Restoring crime victims (performance indicators = payment of restitution; extent of victim satisfaction with service and department).

Thus, these programs exist for a variety of reasons. Some of these reasons are totally unrelated to offender needs, such as employment of agency personnel and justifying the agency budget. It is important to coincide agency processes with offender needs as a way of demonstrating program effectiveness. Petersilia and Turner (1993) has reduced almost all of these agency functions to things that can be counted. We can count the amount of collected fine payments and restitution. We can count numbers of days alcohol-free or drug-free. We can count numbers of rearrests, numbers of favorable discharges, numbers of days employed. There are many intangibles, however, that cannot be counted. We do not know, for instance, whether offender familial relations are actually improving. We might count the number of "911 calls," however, for reports of spousal abuse or other forms of familial conflict for various offender-clients. This might be a negative gauge of positive family functioning. Also, we do not know whether true psychological changes are occurring within any particular offender-client (White et al., 2002). We only know that these offender-clients have been provided with the means for change. We don't know for sure whether changes actually occur in designated or targeted program areas.

When PSI reports are prepared for any offender, POs make a point of identifying problem areas that could or should be addressed by subsequent programming. These are identified as offender needs. We have an array of risk–needs instruments that assess both an offender's dangerousness and the special needs they might exhibit. When inmates are classified upon entry into jails or prisons, they are usually assessed with either self-administered or other types of paper-and-pencil tests or devices that seek to determine their most appropriate placement, whether it is a particular custody level or rehabilitation/educational/vocational/counseling program. In Virginia, for instance, inmates with low reading levels are tracked to special educational classes designed to improve their literacy levels. It is logical to assume that if the literacy levels of inmates can be improved, then their chances for employment are also improved. Completing job application forms requires a minimum amount of literacy, for example.

Offenders with psychological or social adjustment problems may benefit from individual or group therapy or various forms of sensitivity training.

What about alcohol or drug usage? In prisons, there is a low likelihood that alcoholism or drug dependency will continue to be problematic for offenders. We know that inmates have access to drugs in most prisons or jails. But what can we do now that will help offenders cope with their community environment when they are subsequently released from prison? If alcohol or drug dependencies contributed to their crimes, then what coping mechanisms can be provided these offenders while they are institutionalized? Drug and alcohol dependency classes are provided inmates with these kinds of problems (identifiable need areas). But do these classes prevent subsequent recurrences of alcohol and drug dependency?

Parole boards in most jurisdictions face offenders every day, both adults and juveniles, who are chronic recidivists with drug and alcohol dependencies (Parker, 2001). They ask prospective parolees, "Did you participate in Alcoholics Anonymous while in prison?" Prospective parolee: "Yes." Parole board: "But you have been convicted of a new crime, and when you were caught, you were drunk. What happened?" Prospective parolee: "I got in with the wrong crowd," or "I had a setback," or "I had some personal problems," or "I just couldn't pass up a drink," or "I went along with the crowd for old time's sake." Some offenders never escape the problems that contributed to their criminal activity, no matter how much training, coursework, therapy, or counseling they receive.

Any community-based corrections program attempts to provide useful interventions that will assist offender-clients in various ways. Some of these interventions include the use of injectable methadone administered to drug addicts on an outpatient basis (Beaumont, 2001). Assisting former gang members in avoiding subsequent renewed contact with their gang associates is also important (Curry, Decker, and Egley, 2002). Volunteers and paraprofessionals assist offender-clients in filling out job application forms, in reading programs, or in other reintegrative or rehabilitative activities. Meeting diverse offender needs is viewed as a primary way of reducing or eliminating recidivism. And recidivism is probably the most direct way of measuring program effectiveness, despite other program components, aims, or alternative outcome measures.

RECIDIVISM DEFINED

A conceptual Tower of Babel exists regarding recidivism. Numerous investigations of this phenomenon have been conducted, although no consensus exists about the meaning of the term. Criminologists and other observers can recite lengthy lists of characteristics that describe recidivists. But describing recidivists and using those characteristics as effective predictors of recidivism are two different matters. For example, if a parole board uses a salient factor score to predict an offender's degree of success on parole, some inmates will be refused parole because their scores suggest they are poor risks. At the same time, other inmate scores may indicate good risks. The poor risks are denied parole, while the good risks are granted it. However, among the poor risks are inmates who will never recidivate, while among the good risks (who eventually become parolees) are serious recidivists. Parole boards are interested in minimizing the frequency of both false positives and false negatives. When a false positive is denied parole, certain moral, ethical, and legal issues are raised about continuing to confine otherwise harmless persons. When a false negative is granted parole and commits a new, serious offense, the public is outraged, the parole board is embarrassed, and the integrity of test developers and the validity of prediction instruments are called into question. Judges who impose probation instead of incarceration or incarceration instead of probation are subject to similar attacks on similar grounds. Numerical scales are often used as more objective criteria for probation or parole decision making. It is not necessarily the case that these scales are superior to personal judgments by judges or parole boards. But references to numbers seem to objectify early-release or probation-granting decisions compared with visual appraisals of offenders and subjective interpretations of their backgrounds contained in PSIs. Several problems have been identified relating to recidivism and its measurement. A brief listing of some of the more common problems is provided below:

1. The time interval between commencing a probation or parole program and recidivating is different from one study to the next. Some studies use six months, while others use a year, two years, or five years.

2. There are at least 14 different meanings of recidivism. Comparing one definition of recidivism with another is like comparing apples with oranges.

3. Recidivism is often dichotomized rather than graduated. Thus, people either recidivate or they don't recidivate. No variation exists to allow for degrees of seriousness of reoffending of any type.

4. Recidivism rates are influenced by multiple factors, such as the intensity of supervised probation or parole, the numbers of face-to-face visits between POs and their clients, and even the rate of prison construction.

5. Recidivism rates may be indicative of program failures rather than client failures.

6. Recidivism only accounts for official rule or law violations; self-reported information indicates that higher rates of recidivism may actually exist compared with those that are subsequently reported and recorded.

7. Considerable client variation exists, as well as numerous programmatic variations. Depending on the client population under investigation, recidivism is more or less significant.

8. Policy shifts in local and state governments may change how recidivism is used or defined as well as the amount of recidivism observed in given jurisdictions.

We know, or at least we think we know, that recidivists tend to be male, black, younger, less educated, and have lengthy prior records. In fact, having a lengthy prior record appears to be most consistently related to recidivism. Therefore, should we make it official judicial or parole board policy not to grant probation or parole to younger, less educated, black males with lengthy prior records? No. These are aggregate characteristics and do not easily lend themselves to individualized probation or parole decision making.

One continuing problem is that while these and other characteristics describe the general category of recidivists (whomever they may be), these characteristics are also found among many nonrecidivists. Thus, based on relevant information about offenders, prediction measures must be devised and tested to improve their validity. A related problem is determining whether recidivism has occurred. This means some degree of agreement needs to be established concerning what does and does not mean recidivism.

Existing measures of recidivism complicate rather than simplify its definition. It is important to pay attention to how recidivism is conceptualized in the research literature, since probation or parole program failures or successes are measured by recidivism rates. And a general standard has emerged among professionals that a failure rate above 30 percent means that a probation or parole program is ineffective. Ineffective in what sense? Reducing crime? Rehabilitating offenders? Both?

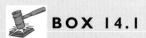 **BOX 14.1**　　　　　　　　　　　　

CAREER SNAPSHOT

Mario A. Paparozzi
Chair, Department of Sociology and Criminal Justice, University of North Carolina at Pembroke
Former Chairman, New Jersey State Parole Board (ret.)

Statistics:

Ph.D. (sociology), Rutgers University

Background:

Upon graduation from college, most of us had one major objective in mind: to get a job that makes use of our hard-earned degree! I was no different at the time of my graduation in 1972. I also recall that back in 1972 the prospects of getting a job for college graduates were said to be from poor to nonexistent. Sound familiar? I majored in sociology, and I was determined to beat the odds.

I applied for just about every job imaginable at the county, state, and federal government levels that required a bachelor's degree. I even applied for some jobs in the private sector (e.g., Wall Street, insurance companies, personnel). It took six months, but I finally succeeded. On February 6, 1973, I started my first day on the job as a New Jersey Parole Officer Trainee in Newark.

Little did I know that this day was going to be the first day of what is now a 33-plus year career in criminal justice, or that I would end up with opportunities to work within the system as an assistant commissioner of corrections and state parole board chairman. This wonderful career also gave me opportunities to serve as president of the American Probation and Parole Association and the International Association of Reentry, and in a myriad of professional capacities in over 20 state, national, and international professional associations. It is also of note that because of my career in corrections and parole, I had opportunities to be on numerous television and radio programs in the United States and Canada (e.g., *Geraldo Rivera, Dateline, A&E American Justice*) and to speak at conferences in 44 states as well as Canada, France (at the Council of Europe), and England (where I was introduced as the keynote speaker by Princess Anne). These kinds of opportunities await you too if you choose a profession within probation, parole, or community corrections—remember, I was no different from any of you when it all began.

I hope that my brief introduction has intrigued you enough to read on. You see, I also know that too many students skip over these highlight boxes when doing their assigned readings. Yet it is within these highlights that a student can gain a real insight into how his or her studies might actually shape his or her future. Now let us turn to some of my personal realities as I moved along my corrections and parole career path.

The Dual Responsibilities of Casework and Law Enforcement.

In 1973 parole officers in New Jersey were unarmed and not considered law enforcement

(continued)

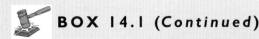 **BOX 14.1** (*Continued*)

officers. By the time I left, and I am pleased to have been a part of the change, parole officers were armed and had full police powers. Whether armed or not, parole and probation officers always have the threefold responsibilities of doing offender treatment, offender surveillance, and law enforcement—and in that order. When parole and probation officers become armed and have police powers, as I did, we do so to become better parole and probation officers but not to become surrogate police officers.

I felt strongly that arming parole officers was necessary because my caseload of 100 parolees lived in the high-rise public housing projects of Newark's Central Ward. At the time, my assigned territory was said to have one of the highest crime rates in the nation, the highest rate of infant mortality, the highest high school dropout rate, and the highest tuberculosis rate. As well, unemployment rates at the time were often equated with the rates experienced in the Great Depression of the 1930s. I am sure that you can imagine the difficult environment within which I was expected to carry out my parole officer responsibilities. Crime was rampant, and there simply were not enough services to ameliorate the serious social and personal problems facing the parolees on my caseload or their families.

In order to do my job as a parole officer, it was necessary for me to visit parolees at their homes frequently. I quickly realized how dangerous home visits would be when, early on, I was confronted by a group of young men blocking my entrance to a building (remember, I was unarmed). One of the men was displaying a large switchblade, another three a bullet at me and said, "Next time I ain't gonna throw it." On another occasion, I was on the 11th floor of one of the housing projects, and I was confronted by a group of teens who walked toward me and blocked my exit to the staircase. The backed-up incinerator smoke on the 11th floor was so thick that we could barely see each other. I took advantage of the poor visibility to fake reaching under my jacket for a gun, then in the most threatening voice I could muster, I said, "Freeze, you're under arrest." I am sure

that I added a few appropriate expletives too! In any case, my prospective attackers scattered and I walked away unharmed. These are but two examples underscoring the need for parole and probation officers to carry firearms, two-way radios, and other accoutrements of law enforcement. But they must never forget that these are merely tools to be better parole and probation officers and not surrogate police officers.

In the absence of being properly equipped and trained, many parole and probation departments, including my own department in the early years of my career, supported and continue to support policies that do not require home visits. These kinds of policies, often known as the redlining of dangerous geographical areas, are for the benefit of officer safety. However, public safety is jeopardized to the extent that parole and probation officers do not conduct home visits of convicted offenders under conditional release in the community. In fact, this is a good example of the type of practice that has caused many politicians, victims' groups, and the general public to be critical of parole and probation. In this regard, parole and probation are too often thought of as a slap on the wrist, a joke, or worse. In short, when parole and probation officers cannot proactively supervise offenders in the community, their criminal justice system value and contributions to public safety and justice are greatly diminished.

One of the best examples I can give you to highlight the need for home visits and the dangerous potential of redlining policies involves the well-known case of Jeffrey Dahmer. Dahmer was on probation when he engaged in murder and cannibalism of young men over a period of time. Dahmer sometimes cooked his victims' body parts in his apartment and also stored them in his refrigerator and elsewhere in his small apartment. The story that I am about to recount played significantly into my quest for parity between the law enforcement functions and casework functions of parole and probation officers so that parole and probation officers can do the job expected of them.

I once was invited to give a major address to a correctional association in Wisconsin. As I had done so many times in my career, I gave my talk and then joined the conference attendees for their luncheon. I walked over to an empty seat at one of the tables and joined a group of probation and parole officers. As we talked, I learned the probation/parole officer sitting next to me had been Jeffrey Dahmer's officer. Innocently, I asked how the officer did not notice anything unusual (visually, or through foul smells in Dahmer's apartment) when conducting home visits. Dahmer's assigned officer told me that no visits to Dahmer's home were ever conducted. The officer then went on to explain that the requirement to conduct home visits was waived because Dahmer lived in a dangerous area—a clear case of redlining policy. I could not help but think then, as I have done so many times since, about the possibility that one or more of Dahmer's victims might have been spared their horrific fate if a probation/parole officer had conducted home visits!

On a personal note, I recall an instance when a parolee was prohibited from residing with his wife and her five school-age daughters. The parolee met and married his wife while he was serving 20 years in prison for murder (she was introduced to the parolee through a friend on a prison visit). I decided to conduct an unannounced home visit at the home of the parolee's wife just to be sure that there were no problems and that the parolee was not living with her. I found the parolee hiding in the closet—he was arrested, placed in jail, and a parole violation hearing was scheduled. At the parole violation hearing, the parolee's wife begged for the parolee's continuance on parole. She even agreed to place her school-age daughters in foster homes so that she could live with her husband. The parolee was released on parole, and he did live alone with his wife for a few months until he murdered her by slitting her throat. One can only wonder what the fate of the school-age children might have been if they had been living with the couple also.

Parole, Probation, and Community Corrections Are Public Safety:

These two stories illustrate how important it is to take parole and probation seriously. Parole and probation officers do enhance prospects for public safety, but only if the policies and practices that they work under permit them to do so. Most individuals on parole and probation are not murderers. They are individuals who are in need of assistance to turn their lives around. To be sure, they are individuals who have a known track record for breaking the law. Offenders under conditional community release should be assisted in their rehabilitation, they should always be watched, and when necessary, they should be placed in secure custody to protect the public. In other words, parole and probation = treatment + surveillance + enforcement—in that order.

Recidivism means program failure. Or does it? There is a wide variety of probation and parole programs available to the courts and corrections officials for many different kinds of offenders. One common problem faced by all programs is that observers have trouble matching the right programs with the right clientele. We have much descriptive information about recidivists. Numerous evaluation studies are conducted annually of various offender programs and virtually all strategies for dealing with offenders are examined and reexamined. No matter the cure proposed, the illness remains. Treatments are rarely pure, however, and therefore, their evaluations are necessarily complicated. Probationers or parolees who violate one or more terms of their probation or parole, regardless of the type of program examined, are considered recidivists. This chapter is about recidivism among probationers and parolees. Recidivism in the general case is examined, and recidivists are described. Also examined here are some of the factors contributing to recidivism and strategies officials use to combat recidivism.

If rehabilitation is the probation or parole program goal, then recidivism rates seem appropriate measures of program success or failure. However, if control and community protection are program goals, then a success might be viewed as the identification and quick revocation of persons who are committing crimes. After all, the police are in the business of surveillance and control, and they judge an arrest a success, whereas we deem it a failure. If community safety is the primary goal, then perhaps an arrest and revocation should be seen as a success and not a failure. Recidivism seems relevant when we are interested in the rehabilitative value of programs, but many programs involving intensive supervision of parolees and probationers seem focused primarily on crime control. Some of the different ways of operationalizing recidivism are:

1. Rearrest
2. Parole or probation revocation or unsatisfactory termination
3. Technical parole or probation rule violations
4. Conviction for a new offense while on parole or probation
5. Return to prison
6. Having a prior record and being rearrested for a new offense
7. Having a prior record and being convicted for a new offense
8. Any new commitment to a jail or prison for 60 days or more
9. Presence of a new sentence exceeding one year for any offense committed during a five-year parole follow-up
10. Return of released offenders to custody of state correctional authorities
11. Return to jail
12. Reincarceration
13. The use of drugs or alcohol by former drug or alcohol abusers
14. Failure to complete educational or vocational/technical course or courses in or out of prison/jail custody

The most commonly used conceptualizations include rearrests, reconvictions, revocations of parole or probation, reincarcerations, and technical program violations.

Rearrests

As a measure of recidivism, **rearrest** is frequently used in evaluation studies of parole/probation program effectiveness, although rearrests are highly misleading. The most obvious flaw is that it is uncertain whether offenders have actually committed new offenses. Sometimes, if a crime has been committed in the neighborhood where particular clients are residing in a halfway house, *and* if the crime is similar in nature to the crime(s) for which the ex-offenders were previously convicted, detectives and police may look up the offenders and interview them. Since offender associations with police authorities are inherently strained anyway, it is likely that police would interpret an offender's nervousness as a sign of guilt. Thus, the offender might be subject to rearrest based on the suspicions of officers. The crucial element is whether the officers have probable cause to justify the client's arrest. The totality of circumstances may be such that officers may in good faith believe they have reasonable suspicion that the client has committed a crime or has guilty knowledge. They have wide discretion to question ex-offenders in an effort to learn more about the crime and the potential culpability of those they interview. In New York, for instance, whenever an inmate is granted parole, the supervising PO brings the parolee's fingerprints and criminal record to the local police precinct where the offender resides. Thus, police are notified of the parolee's return to their community. Constitutional safeguards exist, of course, to protect all citizens from unreasonable arrests by police. However, law enforcement officers find it relatively easy to justify their actions to the court when dealing with former offenders and parolees, even where the Constitutional rights of ex-offenders have been infringed.

Another problem associated with using rearrests to measure recidivism is that ex-offenders may be released after police determine that they are not likely suspects. However, a rearrest is interpreted as recidivism by some researchers, and this means program failure. Rearrested offenders are not necessarily taken to jail or returned to prison; they may continue in their present probation or parole programs. Of course, it is also possible that the ex-offender did, indeed, commit a new crime. But this must be proved, beyond a reasonable doubt, in a court of law. Some jurisdictions use the preponderance of evidence standard for probation/parole revocations. This standard is less stringent than the beyond-a-reasonable-doubt standard.

In New York, for instance, many probationers/parolees adjourn their revocation hearings pending the outcome of their court cases. If they are acquitted of criminal charges, this obviously impacts their probation/parole revocation process favorably. If the result of a trial is a conviction for the probationer/parolee, then a revocation hearing on the violation will not be conducted. A certificate of disposition would suffice as evidence of a conviction and sentence. However, not all parolees or probationers who are rearrested for new crimes are prosecuted for those crimes. They may instead be sent to prison. Due to the *Morrissey v. Brewer* (1972) decision, however, two hearings (i.e., one to determine probable cause and the other an actual revocation proceeding) are required before the paroling authority can summarily revoke parole.

Reconvictions

Reconviction for a new offense is probably the most reliable indicator of recidivism as well as the most valid definition of it. This represents that at least one new crime has been committed by an offender while on probation or parole, and the court has determined offender guilt beyond a reasonable doubt. Some observers may counter by saying that any failure to observe probation or parole conditions or placing oneself in a position of increasing the likelihood of arrest (e.g., violating curfew or associating with other offenders) is evidence that offender rehabilitation has not occurred. However, if crime control is of primary importance to those involved with probationers and parolees, then this argument fails to hold.

Revocations of Probation or Parole

A **revocation** of probation or parole means that parolees or probationers have violated one or more of the conditions associated with their supervision status. These conditions may be as harmless as missing a 10:00 P.M. curfew by five minutes or as serious as committing and being convicted of a new felony. Parole and probation officers have some discretionary authority where technical program violations are involved. They may overlook these incidents or report them. If the incident is a re-arrest, the discretion passes to others such as arresting officers and prosecutors or is at least "shared." If interpersonal relations between clients and POs have become strained, the PO may exaggerate the violation, regardless of how minor it may be.

BOX 14.2

INTERNATIONAL SNAPSHOT: PROBATION AND PAROLE IN THE NETHERLANDS

The Netherlands consists of the Netherlands, Aruba, and the Netherlands Antilles. It is a kingdom divided into 12 provinces and 689 municipalities. The government of the Netherlands has a constitution, although the Netherlands also has a hereditary monarchy, where the first-born child is the Crown. The Crown makes all important appointments, including the 28-member Council of State. The Crown is the titular president of the Council, although routine operations are carried out by an appointed vice president. The government consists of the Crown and a Parliament, comprised of two chambers. The first or upper chamber consists of elected persons from each of the provincial states, while the second or lower chamber is elected by a national vote by all adult Netherlands citizens.

At the head of the Netherlands criminal justice system is the Ministry of Justice. A unitary governmental structure exists that is governed by laws embodied within the constitution and the Criminal or Penal Code, and the Code of Criminal Procedure and Special Acts. The criminal justice system is modified by a continuing series of acts, including the Police Act, which was rewritten during the late 1990s. A probation service exists and was established in 1986. The activities and powers of the police and prosecution service are regulated by similar acts and undergo periodic change and improvement.

The legal system of the Netherlands is set in motion with the commission of a crime. If a perpetrator is suspected, an accusation is made. Measures, such as telephone wiretaps and other information-acquiring procedures, are conducted by police as they investigate to see whether a case merits further investigation. The trial itself is an accusatorial process. The purpose of criminal trials is to determine the truth about the crime, how it occurred, and who committed it. Interestingly, only judges are permitted to ask questions of witnesses and suspects during trials. Prosecutors and defense counsels are permitted to ask a limited range of questions, although such questions are primarily supplementary ones. Cross-examination of witnesses does not occur in Netherlands courts. Once a case has been decided, the principle of *stare decisis* does not exist, meaning that higher court opinions are not binding on lower courts. Traditionally, however, most lower courts follow higher court precedents.

The power of prosecutors is extensive. Prosecutors can elect to keep cases from courts. They can engage in conditional waivers or transaction. Conditional waivers involve informal dispositions of cases, which may include minimal restrictive conditions. Transaction can be used in much the same way as a deferred prosecution to keep accused persons out of the formal court system. Actually, transaction is a measure vesting prosecutors with the authority to impose fines on accused persons where their potential maximum sentences are six years. If the offender agrees to pay a stipulated fine, then this out-of-court monetary settlement concludes the case. All payments are made to the Netherlands Treasury. Plea bargaining is forbidden. Guilty pleas are acceptable, although no expectation of leniency from persons pleading guilty exists. Prosecutors may hold suspects for several months before bringing formal charges against them. Their ability to interview and interrogate suspects is virtually unlimited, and defense counsel are restricted in the nature of contacts they have with the accused.

The court system is somewhat complex. In 2005, the judiciary consisted of 62 cantonal courts, 19 district courts, 5 courts of appeal, and a supreme court with 24 justices. Cantonal courts hear both civil and criminal cases. These are like circuit courts in various states such as Tennessee. A single judge presides in such courts. District courts hear both civil and criminal matters, but in these types of courts, there are panels of three judges who hear each case. Courts of appeal hear both civil and criminal cases decided in the lower district courts. All judges serving in all of these courts are appointed by the Crown for life but retire at age 70. All lower-court cases are subject to appeals, and once the Supreme Court has heard an appealed case, the case is concluded. If the case is overturned, then this does not mean that similar cases are affected. Each case is heard on its own merits, and no particular case is binding for all similar cases in lower courts, although informally, lower court judges are influenced by what actions the Supreme Court has chosen to take.

The range of criminal penalties for judges in all lower criminal courts includes fines (from the Financial Penalties Act of 1983); suspended sentences, which were commenced in 1986 contiguous with the introduction of probation; automatic release from prison after serving two-thirds of one's maximum sentence; and community service, which was introduced as an alternative punishment in 1989. All prohibited acts are divided into crimes or felonies (*misdrijven*) and infractions or transgressions (*overtredingen*). All acts are differentiated as either crimes or infractions by the legislature. Felonies are similar to those in the United States and include offenses such as murder, rape, robbery, theft combined with violence, and assault. Less serious offenses are the equivalent of misdemeanors and are considered transgressions, and these might include traffic offenses or public order offenses. All transgressions are tried in the cantonal courts, while all crimes are tried in the district courts.

The age of criminal responsibility in the Netherlands is 12. However, juveniles between ages 12 and 18 are subject to juvenile criminal laws. Juveniles are dealt with far less severely than adult offenders. However, youths who are between ages 16 and 18 may be tried in adult criminal courts. This is similar to the transfer or waiver process. Such consideration as adults would be under extraordinary circumstances, such as committing serious offenses such as murder, robbery, or rape. In rare instances, juvenile law may continue to be applicable to persons between the ages of 18 and 21. All persons age 21 or older are subject to adult criminal penalties, regardless of all other circumstances.

In 2005 the population of the Netherlands was 17 million. The capital is Amsterdam, with major cities being The Hague, Rotterdam, and Utrecht. The predominant ethnic group is Dutch, although there are large minority communities consisting of Moroccans, Turks, and Surinamese. The amount of violence in the Netherlands generally is quite low. For instance, in 2005 there were only two murders per 100,000 persons. Attempted murder and manslaughter rates were only 16 per 100,000 that same year. The most serious offenses are punishable by long terms of imprisonment. The Netherlands does not have the death penalty. In fact, the maximum punishment for the most serious offense is 20 years and/or a fine. Property crime is another matter. Much of the crime in the Netherlands is property offending, with approximately 4,000 thefts per 100,000 persons. One growing problem in the Netherlands is drug offending. Drug trafficking has become widespread and is considered sufficiently serious that several drug acts have been passed to deter drug offenders. The drug of choice for drug offending is Ecstasy (MDMA), a synthetic narcotic. The Netherlands is considered somewhat of an illegal drug–producing mecca for many countries. In 2003, for instance, approximately 13 million MDMA tablets were seized by foreign governments including the United States, which had been exported from the Netherlands. It is presently unknown what quantity of illegal drugs actually enters these countries originally manufactured in the Netherlands. Aggressive prevention efforts on the part of the government have seriously

(continued)

BOX 14.2 (Continued)

curtailed drug production and distribution in recent years, however. For instance, the Dutch Opium Act punishes the possession, commercial distribution, production, import, and export of all illicit drugs. Drug use itself, however, is not an offense. Interestingly, the Netherlands has a rather liberal policy about drug use, and it is fairly easy to purchase small quantities of drugs, even Ecstasy, in local coffee shops. Distinguished also are hard and soft drugs, with heroin being considered a hard drug with serious dependency issues. Nevertheless, such drugs, hard or soft, may be purchased openly on Netherlands city streets every day and used publicly. With this policy of openness, it is easy to understand how easy it is to export larger quantities of these drugs without a great deal of detection by Dutch authorities.

Dutch authorities treat criminals in unique ways. For instance, if offenders are convicted in court of crimes such as murder or rape, they may be imprisoned for a time and then sent to a mental institution for continuous examination. Sexual offending especially draws time in a mental institution as a form of TBS (*ter beschikking stelling*). Theoretically, a sex offender can spend an indeterminate amount of time in a mental hospital, even the remainder of his or her life, if a committee believes he or she poses serious risks to society.

There are victim's assistance groups in the Netherlands. The Ministry of Justice, under the National Victim Support Organization, supports and subsidizes victim support programs in various cities and towns. Paid professionals assist victims in coping with crimes perpetrated against them. However, victims are prohibited from expressing their opinions in criminal trials. Victims do not have a right to be heard during a trial, but they are entitled to seek compensation from their victimizers through the Criminal Injuries Compensation Fund Act, which was established in 1975.

Little information exists about police arrests and their frequency. Police may make arrests with reasonable suspicion. They require arrest warrants only if suspects are located in their homes. Most arrests are made without a warrant. The rights of accused persons are quite different from those of U.S. citizens. For instance, a fast-track version of U.S. speedy trials exists wherein the accused can petition the court to dismiss a case if it's not brought to trial within an especially short time interval. Thus, police officers are hard-pressed to collect incriminating evidence sufficient to sustain a conviction. However, all suspects are entitled to an attorney, regardless of whether they are affluent or indigent. Defendants may or may not elect to be present at their own trials. Defendants have the right to remain silent and refrain from giving testimony in a case. Defense counsels may not question witnesses directly; rather, defense counsels ask judges to ask witnesses particular questions; it is up to individual judges whether to ask questions requested by counsel. There is no right to cross-examination. Legal Assistance Bureaus exist to provide legal services for indigents.

The sole responsibility for conducting a prosecution is the public prosecutor. Prosecutors decide whether sufficient evidence exists to proceed with particular cases. Judges have no authority over decisions by prosecutors not to proceed against particular suspects, despite evidence to the contrary. The pretrial alternative of expediency or opportunity exists in all Dutch courts. This principle permits prosecutors to dismiss cases as a matter of public interest. Public prosecutors have a wide range of options, including dismissing charges. Sometimes prosecutors may decline to prosecute certain suspects, but they may order treatment for them. Such would be the case in alcohol-dependent or drug-dependent cases. Restitution may also be ordered by prosecutors. As we have seen, prosecutors may also impose fees or fines on convicted offenders so that they may not have to serve time in prison.

In the Netherlands, only about one-third of all cases eventually go to trial. About two-thirds of all cases are disposed of by prosecutors through transaction or dismissal. Of those that reach the court, there are relatively high conviction rates of 85 percent or more. Detention rates are fairly low, since prosecutors make decisions about who to detain and who to free while awaiting a trial or further legal action. There is no legal entitlement to bail. Relatively few defendants are incarcerated under pretrial conditions. Less than 10 percent of all persons charged with crimes are kept in detention for any length of time.

There are exceptions. In July 2005, Mohammed Bouyeri was sentenced to life in prison without the possibility of early release for the murder of Dutch filmmaker Theo van Gogh, a distant relative of artist/painter Vincent van Gogh. Bouyeri shot and stabbed the filmmaker in Amsterdam on a city street in broad daylight. In the case of Bouyeri, the life sentence was imposed as a true life sentence. He will never be paroled, with the exception of a rare royal pardon, which is rarely granted to anyone.

The range of punishments available to sentencing judges is vast. Primary penalties include fines, imprisonment, detention for brief periods, community service, and court-ordered treatments, depending on one's needs. Assisting judges in sentencing decision making are reports similar to pre-sentence investigation reports prepared by U.S. probation officers. These are known as social enquiry reports. These reports may also be prepared by private agencies and persons, much like they may be prepared in the United States. The minimum incarcerative sentence is one day. Maximum sentences are 15 years, or 20 years for murder, unless aggravating circumstances exist. Life sentences may be imposed in these cases, as we have seen. Failure to pay a fine may result in imprisonment for varying periods. This is known as fine default detention. Judges set the term of confinement for nonpayment of fines, and the length of time served is proportional to the amount of the imposed fine. One day of detention is the equivalent of 50–100 guilders. Other punishments may include property seizures and dispossession of certain rights, such as the right to hold particular jobs. Prison sentences of three or fewer years may be suspended. However, judges may not suspend prison sentences longer than three years. Suspended sentences may involve conditions similar to probation orders and accompanying restrictions.

Until the 1980s crime in the Netherlands was relatively low. However, Netherlands prisons grew in population from approximately 3,000 spaces to over 15,000 spaces by 2005. This change in prison growth is not necessarily the result of a new Dutch crime wave; rather, sentencing policy changes have occurred during the early 2000s to create longer prison sentences to be served by offenders. As has been observed, prisoners are entitled to release, under ordinary circumstances, after serving two-thirds of their prison sentences. These releases are almost always unconditional. Thus, no supervision of releasees is necessary. In recent years, however, there have been initiatives designed to introduce supervised release for convicted offenders who have served two-thirds of their sentences. Supervision is believed fundamental to successful reintegration back into society. Netherlands prisons have work programs and educational facilities designed to assist inmates in their societal reintegration efforts. Approximately 20,000 offenders have obtained early release from prison during the period 2000–2005, and about half of these offenders are under some form of supervision. The Netherlands utilizes electronic monitoring and home confinement, together with community service and other conditions, as a part of their continuing supervision and assistance programming.

The prison system of the Netherlands consists of institutions differentiated according to the types of prisoners held. There are closed or high-security prisons; semi-open prisons or normal-security institutions; open institutions with minimal security; and extra-high-risk security units to house inmates who are high escape risks or who pose a risk to other inmates because of their exhibited violent conduct. Placement in an extra-high-risk security unit may be for periods up to six months or more, depending on one's conduct. The Principles of Prison Administration Act has vested prisoners with rights entitling them to rehabilitative measures, including spiritual and social care, discipline, recreating, and work. Work is a requirement, and prisoners

(continued)

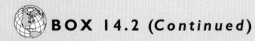

BOX 14.2 (Continued)

who perform work are paid. Prisoners who refuse to work are punished by confinement in solitary cells for five-day periods. Vocational and educational opportunities are made available to all prisoners, to enable them to transition more easily back into society when they are eventually released.

The probation service oversees numerous offenders who are convicted but freed without serving time in either jail or prison. Probation supervision is minimally intrusive. Dutch probation officers are primarily brokers and educators, whose primary role relates to offender rehabilitation. They provide networking services between their offender-clients and the business community in order to provide work for convicted offenders. Dutch probation officers do not consider themselves enforcers, and thus their efforts are concentrated on helping offenders

rather than punishing them. It is unknown exactly how many offenders are under probation supervision at any given time, but a good estimate is approximately 60,000 persons in 2005.

[Sources: Adapted from U.S. Department of State, *The Netherlands,* Washington, DC: U.S. Department of State, Bureau of Consular Affairs, March 24, 2006; Alexis A. Aronowitz, "The Netherlands," *The World Factbook of Criminal Justice Systems,* Washington, DC, 2005; Public and Cultural Affairs Press, "Drug Policy and Crime Statistics," Washington, DC, December 24, 2005; Bureau of European and Eurasian Affairs, *Background Note: The Netherlands,* Washington, DC: U.S. Department of State, Bureau of European and Eurasian Affairs, May 2005; Associated Foreign Press, "Radical Gets Life Term for Killing Van Gogh," July 27, 2005; Bart van der Linden, "The Return of Early Conditional Release in the Netherlands," *The Peninsula,* November 2000; *The Netherlands: Criminal Justice System and Statistics,* The Hague, NETH: Ministry of Internal Affairs, March 2006].

Many factors influence a parole or probation revocation decision. Prison or jail overcrowding is one of them. The seriousness of the violation is also considered. A third factor is the recommendation of the PO. The main problem with a technical violation of parole or probation, however, is that often it is not related to crime of any kind. Therefore, a revocation based solely on technical criteria is irrelevant as a crime control strategy, unless it can be demonstrated empirically that failure to revoke would have resulted in a new crime being committed. And most, if not all, observers are not prepared to make such assertions at present. A revocation of probation or parole does not necessarily mean a return to prison or jail, however. Depending on the grounds for the revocation and other factors, an offender may be placed on a probation or parole program with a higher control level. This is one reason why revocations of probation and parole cannot be equated directly with reincarceration.

Reincarcerations

The use of **reincarceration** as a measure of recidivism is as misleading as counting the numbers of rearrests and revocations among probationers and parolees. Reincarceration does not specify the type of incarceration. After probation is revoked, a probationer may be placed in a state or federal prison. After a federal parolee's status has been revoked, the parolee may be placed in a city or county jail for a short period rather than returned to the original federal prison. The most frequent usages of recidivism include rearrests, reconvictions, and reincarcerations, although many other meanings have been given it. Arguably, it seems that the most relevant connotation applied to recidivism is a new conviction for a criminal offense as opposed to a simple rearrest or parole revocation for a technical program violation, both of which might be grounds for reincarceration. Reincarceration as a measure of recidivism is unreliable as well because it fails to distinguish between the true law breaker and the technical rule violator.

Technical Program Violations

Technical program violations might include curfew violations, failing a drug or alcohol urinalysis, failing to report employment or unemployment, failing to check in with the PO, failing to file a monthly status report in a timely way, or missing a group therapy meeting. Technical program violations are not crimes. However, they are legitimate conditions of probation or parole that are enforceable. Failure to comply with any one or more of these program requirements (e.g., making restitution to victims, performing so many hours of community service) may be the basis for a possible probation or parole revocation action.

While technical program violations have been used as recidivism measures, they are not particularly the best indicators. Prioritizing the most frequently used measures of recidivism, we might list reconvictions, reincarcerations, rearrests, and probation/parole revocations, in that order. Several suggestions have been made about how to use recidivism in program evaluation and research. These include: (1) standardizing the definition of recidivism; (2) discouraging the use of recidivism as the only outcome measure for community corrections programs; (3) defining alternative outcome measures for the evaluation of community corrections programs; (4) educating interested stakeholders, including the general public, on the alternative measures; and (5) encouraging researchers, evaluators, and agency personnel to use appropriate outcome measures to evaluate program success/failure (Champion, 2005).

It is unrealistic to expect that these suggestions will ever be implemented. There is simply too much variety among community corrections programs presently. Too many different vested interests have a stake in seeing recidivism conceptualized in different ways to fit neatly into particular funding priorities by showing program "successes." The public as well as stakeholders definitely need to be educated concerning various ways of measuring agency success or effectiveness. True, recidivism is not the only way successfulness or effectiveness should be measured. The last three of Boone's suggestions suggest both short- and long-range planning to allow for testing alternative outcome measures of program accomplishments.

RECIDIVIST OFFENDERS AND THEIR CHARACTERISTICS

Avertable and Nonavertable Recidivists

Recidivists with prior records of incarceration have been classified into avertable recidivists and nonavertable recidivists. **Avertable recidivists** are those offenders who would have still been in prison serving their original sentences in full at the time they were confined for committing new offenses. **Nonavertable recidivists** are those offenders whose prior sentences would not have affected the commission of new crimes. Examples of avertable and nonavertable recidivists using more recent sentencing periods are as follows. Suppose John Doe is a new 2007 prison admission. Doe was previously incarcerated in 1990 for armed robbery and given a 2- to 20-year sentence in a state prison. The parole board released

Doe in 2003 whereupon Doe began committing new burglaries. Eventually he was apprehended by police and convicted of burglary in 2007. Had he still been in prison serving his maximum 20-year sentence, those burglaries he committed from 2003–2007 never would have occurred. Doe is called an avertable recidivist, because his crimes occurred within the maximum range of his original sentence.

John Doe's sister, Jane, was convicted in 1995 of vehicular theft. Jane was sentenced to five years in prison. Jane served all of her time and was eventually released. Jane obeyed the law for several years, but in 2007 she was arrested for and convicted of stealing another automobile. Since she had already served the maximum sentence of five years for vehicular theft from 1995–2000, the maximum range of her original sentence no longer applied. Jane is classified as a nonavertable recidivist. Both she and her brother, John, are recidivists, because they are criminal offenders who have been convicted of previous crimes. But John's new crimes may have been averted had John been forced to serve his maximum sentence. This doesn't rule out the possibility that when John finally served the maximum 20-year sentence for armed robbery, he could commit new crimes and therefore be classified as a nonavertable recidivist like his sister.

Nonavertable recidivists tend to account for substantially higher percentages of crimes compared with avertable recidivists in virtually every crime category. Second, nonavertable recidivists compared with first-timers account for substantially smaller percentages of violent crimes and drug offenses but somewhat higher percentages of property crimes, with few exceptions. The percent of offenses under the avertable recidivists category theoretically represents the proportion of crimes that would not have been committed by these offenders had they been obligated to serve out their entire sentences.

Public Policy and Recidivism

State legislators and policymakers have seized results such as these as foundations for arguments that mandatory and/or determinate sentencing and more rigorous parole criteria ought to be employed. In view of the sentencing reforms enacted by various states and current trends, these figures have apparently been persuasive or at least influential in changing sentencing policies and parole criteria.

The study conducted by the Bureau of Justice Statistics (BJS) is one of the larger surveys of recidivists and their characteristics. But each year, new waves of offenders enter jails and prisons. The profile changes, probably daily. But there are some general patterns that emerge, not only from this analysis but from other research as well. According to the BJS survey, using reconviction as an indicator of an adult recidivist, recidivists appear to share the following characteristics:

1. Recidivists tend to be male.
2. Recidivists tend to be younger (under age 30), and recidivism declines with advancing age.
3. Recidivists tend to have an educational level equivalent to high school or less.
4. Recidivists tend to have lengthy records of arrests and/or convictions.
5. Recidivists tend to be under no correctional supervision when committing new offenses.
6. Recidivists tend to have a record of juvenile offenses.
7. Recidivists tend to commit crimes similar to those for which they were convicted previously.

8. Recidivists tend to have alcohol or drug dependency problems associated with the commission of new offenses.

9. Recidivists tend not to commit progressively serious offenses compared with their prior records.

10. Recidivists tend to be unmarried, widowed, or divorced.

11. Recidivists tend to be employed, either full time or part time, when committing new offenses (U.S. Department of Justice, 2006).

Again, these characteristics considered singly or in any combination make predictions of dangerousness or public risk difficult at best. Parole boards might use such information as supplemental when interviewing prospective parolees. Judges might consider such information when deciding the appropriate sentence for a convicted offender. The odds favor future offender behaviors consistent with previous offender behaviors. The odds increase as the number of characteristics associated with recidivists increases. But the certainty of recidivism for any specific offender can never be predicted in any absolute sense. Prediction schemes seem more effective when large numbers of offenders sharing similar characteristics are aggregated, but parole boards and judges make decisions about individual offenders, not groups of them.

PROBATIONERS, PAROLEES, AND RECIDIVISM

The immense interest of states in sentencing reforms directed away from rehabilitation and toward justice with greater certainty of punishment stems, in part, from public dissatisfaction with how the courts and corrections have dealt with offenders in recent decades. Recidivism spells failure to many citizens, and judicial leniency in sentencing, real or imagined, has contributed to a backlash of sorts. This backlash is similar to the public reaction to John Hinckley's acquittal on charges that he attempted to assassinate President Ronald Reagan, on the grounds that he was insane at the time the offense was committed. The insanity defense was quickly abolished in several states and vastly overhauled in others. This occurred despite the fact that the insanity defense is used in fewer than 1 percent of all criminal prosecutions and is successfully used in only a small fraction of those cases.

Alarming statistics stimulate public concern about parole and probation programs. The United States Department of Justice says that 65 percent of released prisoners will return to prison within two years, and most of these will occur within one year from one's release. Parole may hold down prison populations, but there may be a trade-off through increased street crime (U.S. Department of Justice, 2006). Greater certainty of incarceration coupled with longer terms of confinement for law violators are advanced by reformers as solutions for reducing and controlling crime. However, research has never demonstrated conclusively that longer prison sentences make ex-offenders less likely to commit new crimes. In view of public sentiment favoring longer prison sentences for offenders, we may conclude that the primary goal achieved by longer incarcerative sentences is incapacitation and control rather than deterrence. "Getting tough" on crime is best illustrated to the public by imposing harsher and longer sentences on convicted offenders. Again, the deterrent value of lengthy incarceration is questionable.

Curbing Recidivism

Strategies for decreasing recidivism rates include incarceration, intensive supervised probation/parole, and a wide range of intermediate punishments already discussed including electronic monitoring, house arrest, and community-based treatment programs (Bloom et al., 2002). The more intensive monitoring an offender receives, the less the recidivism, although some intensively supervised offenders recidivate. The treatment or rehabilitation orientation is not a bad one, although many observers feel that many established treatment programs do not fulfill their stated goals. The fact that 50 percent or more of all offenders, incarcerated or on probation, will recidivate in the future at some unspecified time is evidence of the rehabilitative failure of any program, including incarceration. However, one influential but conservative voice favoring incapacitation is James Q. Wilson who argues that while imprisonment may not rehabilitate offenders, it does keep them off the streets away from the general public. And this may be the most effective means of crime control. Another controversial solution recommended by some observers is selective incapacitation (Auerbahn, 2002).

SUMMARY

Program evaluation is the process of assessing any corrections intervention or program for the purpose of determining its effectiveness in achieving manifest goals. Program evaluation almost always involves recidivism as an indicator of program goal attainment. However, other alternative outcome measures are used, including costs, benefits, and savings to communities, wages and taxes paid, and compliance with court orders. Recidivism refers to repeat offending, although it has no universally applicable definition. It applies to criminals who commit or are suspected of committing new offenses, and connotations of term are associated with rearrests, reconvictions, reincarcerations, parole/probation revocations, and technical program violations.

Parole boards and judges are interested in minimizing recidivism in their parole-granting and sentencing capacities. Often, salient factor scores are useful in forecasting one's potential successfulness as a parolee, and judges rely on presentence investigations of offenders when deciding the correct sentence to impose. No technique or measure accurately forecasts recidivism, however. False positives and false negatives attest to the low predictive power of instruments purportedly designed to measure dangerousness or public risk. Recidivists tend to be younger males with lengthy prior records of convictions. They usually, though not always, have less education, are from lower socioeconomic statuses, and tend to commit new offenses similar to their prior offense convictions. Recidivism declines with advancing age.

Factors influencing recidivism appear to be probation or parole status, length of prison term, and type of offense. Property offenders tend to recidivate more than violent offenders. Parolees tend to recidivate more than probationers. The greater the level of probation/parole supervision, the less the recidivism while on probation/parole. The length of incarceration appears to have little influence on recidivism. This finding undermines arguments advanced by observers that longer prison terms will reduce crime and recidivism.

Probation and parole programs and their administration can be improved. Many programs are either new or in early experimental stages so that definite conclusions about their effectiveness cannot be drawn. Probationers themselves believe increased contact with probation officers and program incentives and rewards for compliance ought to be incorporated as a means of increasing program effectiveness and reducing recidivism. Differential supervision may actually be an incentive for many probationers/parolees. The longer one remains violation-free while under supervision, the less intense will be the supervision. Some states have automatic probation/parole program discharges, where probationers/parolees will automatically be released from the criminal justice system after successfully completing a three-year term of supervision with incurring revocations or program violations.

QUESTIONS FOR REVIEW

1. What is meant by creaming? How does creaming influence program effectiveness?
2. What is a "needs instrument"? What types of items are included on "needs" instruments?
3. Differentiate between avertable recidivists and nonavertable recidivists. Give some examples.
4. Identify at least six different connotations of recidivism. Which recidivism measures are most popular?
5. Which recidivism measure seems most realistic and why?
6. What are some characteristics of recidivists? Are observers in agreement about these characteristics? Why or why not?
7. How well can recidivist characteristics be used to predict offender risk or dangerousness?
8. What kinds of changes do probationers feel ought to be made in probation programs?
9. Does the length of incarceration exert any impact on the likelihood of recidivism?
10. Some researchers believe that recidivists tend to commit more serious offenses. Is this true? Why or why not?
11. Which offenders tend to have higher recidivism rates: property or violent offenders? What differences in recidivism rates would you expect when comparing probationers with parolees? Cite a study where such a comparison was made.
12. Why are parole boards and judges concerned about false positives and false negatives?

SUGGESTED READINGS

Bureau of Justice Statistics (2006). *State Justice Statistics Program.* Washington, DC: Office of Justice Programs, Bureau of Justice Statistics.

Commission on Virginia Alcohol Safety Action Program (2006). *Habitual Offenders Relapse Prevention.* Fairfax, VA: Commission on Virginia Alcohol Safety Action Program.

Connecticut Department of Corrections (2006). *Recidivism.* Wethersfield, CT: Connecticut Department of Corrections.

Florida Department of Corrections (2006). *Evidence-Based Practices: Programs That Work in the Florida Department of Corrections.* Tallahassee: Florida Department of Corrections.

National Institute of Justice (2006). *Drug Courts: The Second Decade.* Washington, DC: National Institute of Justice.

Urban Institute (2006). *Prisoner Reentry and Community Policing: Strategies for Enhancing Public Safety.* Washington, DC: The Urban Institute.

INTERNET CONNECTIONS

Abstract on recidivism
http://www.hare.org/abstracts/loza1.html

Basic Guide to Program Evaluation
http://www.eval.org/EvaluationDocuments/progeval.html

Bureau of Data and Research Program Accountability Measures
http://www.djj.state.fl.us/RnD/r_digest/issue37/issue37.pdf

Expert Program Evaluation Services
http://www.statistics-talk.com

Guidelines for State Parole Program Evaluation
http://www.csulb.edu/~ddowell/guidelines.htm

The NIJ Research Review
http://www.ncjrs.org/rr/vol1_1/17.html

Oregon Department of Corrections Recidivism of New Parolees
http://www.doc.state.or.us/research/Recid.pdf

Recidivism of Adult Felons
http://www.auditor.leg.state.mn.us/ped/pedrep/9701-sum.pdf

Recidivism of Adult Probationers
http://www.co.hennepin.mn.us/commcorr/reports/RecidivismofAdultProbationers.htm

Glossary

Abnormal physical structure Explanation of criminal conduct using physical indicators such as the shape of earlobes, head shapes and contours, and body deformities that are viewed as contributory to deviance or crime.

Absconders Persons who flee their jurisdictions while on probation, parole, work release, study release, or furloughs without permission.

Acceptance of responsibility Acknowledgment by convicted offenders that they are responsible for their actions and have rendered themselves totally and absolutely accountable for the injuries or damages they may have caused; used by judges to mitigate sentences during sentencing hearings; an integral factor in U.S. sentencing guidelines offense severity calculations, influencing numbers of months of confinement offenders may receive.

Actuarial prediction Forecast of future inmate behavior based on a class of offenders similar to those considered for parole.

Actus reus Criminal act. One component of a crime.

Adjudication Decision by juvenile court judge deciding whether juvenile is delinquent, status offender, or dependent/neglected; finding may be "not delinquent."

Adjudicatory hearing Formal proceeding involving a prosecutor and defense attorney where evidence is presented and the juvenile's guilt or innocence is determined by the juvenile court judge.

Admin max Level of security designation to denote a penitentiary that holds only prisoners with extensive criminal histories and are escape-prone or especially violent. The highest security level exists at such facilities.

Aftercare General term to describe a wide variety of programs and services available to both adult and juvenile probationers and parolees; includes halfway houses, psychological counseling services, community-based correctional agencies, employment assistance, and medical treatment for offenders or ex-offenders.

Agency The special relation between an employer and an employee whereby the employee acts as an agent of the employer, able to make decisions and take actions on the employer's behalf.

Aggravating circumstances Factors that enhance one's sentence; these include whether serious bodily injury or death occurred to a victim during crime commission and whether offender was on parole at time of crime.

Allegheny Academy In 1982, this Pennsylvania facility was opened and operated by the Community Specialists Corporation, a private, nonprofit corporation headquartered in Pittsburgh and specializing in the community-based treatment of young offenders; general aim is to change the negative behavior of offenders; targeted are juvenile offenders who have failed in other, traditional probation programs.

Alternative care cases Borderline cases where judges may sentence offenders to either incarceration or probation subject to compliance with various conditions.

Alternative dispute resolution (ADR) Procedure whereby a criminal case is redefined as a civil one and the case is decided by an impartial arbiter, where both parties agree to amicable settlement; criminal court is not used for resolving such matters; usually reserved for minor offenses.

Alternative sentencing Also creative sentencing where judge imposes sentence other than incarceration; often involves good works such as community service, restitution to victims, and other public service activity.

American Correctional Association (ACA) Esta-blished in 1870 to disseminate information about correctional programs and correctional training; designed to foster professionalism throughout correctional community.

Anamnestic prediction Forecast of inmate behavior according to past circumstances.

Anomie Condition of normlessness as set forth in Robert K. Merton's theory of anomie.

Anomie theory Robert Merton's theory, alleging persons acquire desires for culturally approved goals to strive to achieve, but they adopt innovative, sometimes deviant, means to achieve these goals; anomie implies normlessness; innovators accept societal goals but reject institutionalized means to achieve them.

Apprehension units Specific departments within correctional services who pursue those who leave their jurisdictions without permission or abscond; probation and parole departments have apprehension units dedicated to hunting down absconders.

Arraignment Proceeding following an indictment by a grand jury or a finding of probable cause from a preliminary hearing; determines (1) plea, (2) specification of final charges against defendant(s), and (3) trial date.

Arrest Taking persons into custody and restraining them until they can be brought before court to answer the charges against them.

Assessment center Agency designed for selecting entry-level officers for correctional work; assessment centers hire correctional officers and probation or parole officers.

Auburn State Penitentiary Prison constructed in New York in 1816; known for its creation of tiers, or different levels of custody for different types of offenders; known for use of "striped" clothing for prisoners to distinguish them from the general population if prisoners escape confinement; known for congregate system, where offenders could dine in large eating areas; also used solitary confinement; custody levels are medium and maximum.

Augustus, John Private citizen acknowledged as formulator of probation in the United States in Boston in 1841.

Automatic waivers (also **legislative waivers**) Actions initiated by state legislatures whereby certain juvenile offenders are sent to criminal courts for processing rather than to juvenile courts; usually requires a certain age range (16–17) and prescribed list of offenses (e.g., rape, homicide, armed robbery, arson); a type of certification or waiver or transfer.

Avertable recidivists Offenders who would still have been in prison serving a sentence at a time when a new offense was committed.

Bail A surety to procure the release of those under arrest and to ensure that they will appear later to face criminal charges in court; also known as a bail bond.

Balanced approach View of offender rehabilitation that stresses heightening offender accountability, individualizing sanctions or punishments, and promoting community safety.

Banishment Punishment form used for many centuries as a sanction for violations of the law or religious beliefs; those found guilty of crimes or other infractions were ordered to leave their communities and never return; in many instances, this was the equivalent of the death penalty, since communities were often isolated and no food or water were available within distances of hundreds of miles from these communities. *See also* **Transport.**

Behavioral reform John Augustus's attempt to change behaviors of persons charged with crimes in the early 1840s; Augustus believed that changes in one's behaviors could be influenced by periods of probation, contrition, and abstinence (e.g., alcohol).

Beyond a reasonable doubt Standard used in criminal courts to establish guilt or innocence of criminal defendant.

Biological theories Explanations of criminal conduct that emphasize the genetic transmission of traits that figure prominently in deviant behavior; any explanation that focuses on biology and heredity as sources of criminal behavior.

Bonding theory A key concept in a number of theoretical formulations. Emile Durkheim's notion that deviant behavior is controlled to the degree that group members feel morally bound to one another, are committed to common goals and share a collective conscience. In social control theory, the elements of attachment, commitment, involvement, and belief; explanation of criminal behavior implying that criminality is the result of a loosening of bonds or attachments with society; builds on differential association theory. Primarily designed to account for juvenile delinquency.

Booking An administrative procedure designed to furnish personal background information to a bonding company and law enforcement officials. Booking includes compiling a file for defendants, including their name, address, telephone number, age, place of work, relatives, and other personal data.

Boot camps Highly regimented, military-like, short-term correctional programs (90–180 days) where offenders are provided with strict discipline, physical training, and hard labor resembling some aspects of military basic training; when successfully completed, boot camps provide for transfers of participants to community-based facilities for nonsecure supervision.

Boston House of Corrections Jail where convicted offenders were confined for various offenses, including drunkenness and disorderly behavior; operated during the 1830s and 1840s.

Boston Offender Project (BOP) Experimental juvenile treatment program commenced in 1981 through the Massachusetts Department of Youth Services; aimed at reducing recidivism, reintegrating youths, and increasing offender accountability.

Bridewell Workhouse Established in 1557 in London, England; designed to house vagrants and general riffraff; noted for exploitation of inmate labor by private mercantile interests.

Brockway, Zebulon First superintendent of New York State Reformatory at Elmira in 1876; arguably credited with introducing first "good time" system whereby inmates could have their sentences reduced or shortened by the number of good marks earned through good behavior.

Broker Probation/parole officer work role orientation where PO functions as a referral service and supplies offender-client with contacts with agencies who provide needed services.

Bureau of Justice Statistics Organization created in 1979 to distribute statistical information concerning crime, criminals, and crime trends.

Burgess, Ernest W. Collaborated with Robert Park to devise concentric zone hypothesis to explain crime in different Chicago city sectors.

Burnout Psychological equivalent of physical stress, characterized by a loss of motivation and commitment related to task performance.

Camps Nonsecure youth programs, usually located in rural settings, designed to instill self-confidence and interpersonal skills for juvenile offenders; also known as wilderness programs.

Career criminals Those offenders who earn their living through crime; they go about their criminal activity in much the same way workers or professional individuals engage in their daily work activities; career criminals often consider their work as a "craft," since they acquire considerable technical skills and competence in the performance of crimes.

Caseload Number of clients or offenders probation or parole officers must supervise during any given time period, such as one week or one month.

Caseworker Any probation or parole officer who works with probationers or parolees as clients; term originates from social work where caseworkers attempt to educate, train, or rehabilitate those without coping skills.

Cellular telephone devices Electronic monitoring equipment worn by offenders that emits radio signals received by local area monitor.

Certification *See* **Transfers.**

Charge reduction bargaining Type of plea bargaining where the inducement from the prosecutor is a reduction in the seriousness of charge or number of charges against a defendant in exchange for a guilty plea.

Children in need of supervision (CHINS) Any youth who has no responsible parent or guardian and needs one.

Children's tribunals Early form of court dealing with juvenile offending in the 1850s through the 1890s; informal judicial mechanisms for evaluating seriousness of juvenile offenders and prescribing punishments for them.

Child-saver movement Largely religious in origin, loosely organized attempt to deal with unsupervised youth following the Civil War; child-savers were interested in the welfare of youths who roamed city streets unsupervised.

Child-savers Philanthropists who believed that children ought to be protected; originated following the Civil War.

Child Sexual Abuse Treatment Program Individual counseling for all family members of offender-clients, including mother–daughter counseling, marital counseling, father–daughter counseling, and group counseling, where such counseling is based on the principles of humanistic psychotherapy; self-help groups are also provided; volunteer men's collectives, social services agencies, and women's shelters are often effective in changing behaviors of offender-abusers.

Child sexual abusers Adults who involve minors in virtually any kind of sexual activity ranging from intercourse with children to photographing them in lewd poses.

Chronic offenders Repeat offenders who continually reoffend; repeat offenses and new convictions may be for misdemeanors or felonies, but there is a continuation of offending over a period of years; persistent offenders.

Citizen value system Parole board decision-making model appealing to public interests in seeing that community expectations are met by making appropriate early-release decisions.

Civil Rights Act Title 42, Section 1983 of the U.S. Code permitting inmates of prisons and jails as well as probationers and parolees the right to sue their administrators and/or supervisors under the "due process" and "equal protection" clauses of the Fourteenth Amendment.

Clark, Benjamin C. Philanthropist and "volunteer" probation officer who assisted courts with limited probation work during the 1860s; carried on John Augustus's work commenced in the early 1840s.

Classification Attempts to categorize offenders according to type of offense, dangerousness, public risk, special needs, and other relevant criteria; used in institutional settings (prisons) for purposes of placing inm-ates in more or less close custody and supervision.

Classification system Means used by prisons and probation/parole agencies to separate offenders according to offense seriousness, type of offense, and other criteria; no classification system has been demonstrably successful at effective prisoner or client placements; any means of determining the dangerousness or risk of offenders in order to place them in either specific community programs or appropriate custody levels while confined.

Clinical prediction Forecast of inmate behavior based on professionals' expert training and working directly with offenders.

Code of ethics Regulations formulated by major professional societies that outline the specific problems and issues that are frequently encountered in the types of research carried out within a particular profession. Serves as a guide to ethical research practices.

Cognitive development Stages in the learning process where one acquires abilities to think and express him- or herself; thoughts about the feelings of others are acquired.

Cognitive development theory Also called dev-elopmental theory, stresses stages of learning process whereby persons acquire abilities to think and express themselves, respect the property and rights of others, and cultivate a set of moral values.

Combination sentence *See* **Split sentencing.**

Common law Authority based on court decrees and judgments that recognize, affirm, and enforce certain usages and customs of the people. Laws determined by judges in accordance with their rulings.

Community-based corrections Several types of programs that manage offenders within the community instead of prison or jail; includes electronic monitoring, day fine programs, home confinement, intensive supervised probation/parole.

Community-based supervision Reintegrative programs operated publicly or privately to assist offenders by providing therapeutic, support, and supervision programs for criminals; may include furloughs, probation, parole, community service, and restitution.

Community control A Florida community-based correctional program involving home confinement and electronic monitoring for offender supervision.

Community control house arrest Florida program where offenders are confined to their own homes, instead of prison, where they are allowed to serve their sentences.

Community corrections Any one of several different types of programs designed to supervise probationers and parolees; includes but not limited to home confinement, electronic monitoring, day reporting centers, probation, parole, intensive supervised probation, intensive supervised parole, furloughs, halfway houses, work release, and study release.

Community corrections act Statewide mechanism included in legislation whereby funds are granted to local units of government and community agencies to develop and deliver "front-end" alternative sanctions in lieu of state incarceration.

Community model Relatively new concept based on the correctional goal of offender reintegration into the community; stresses offender adaptation to the community by participating in one or more programs that are a part of community-based corrections.

Community reintegration Process whereby an offender who has been incarcerated is able to live in community under some supervision and gradually adjust to life outside of prison or jail; theory is that transition to community life from regimentation of prison life can be eased through community-based correctional program and limited community supervision.

Community residential centers Transitional agencies located in neighborhoods where offenders may obtain employment counseling, food and shelter, and limited supervision pertaining to one or more conditions of probation or parole; example might be day reporting/treatment program.

Community service Sentence imposed by jud- ges in lieu of incarceration where offenders are obligated to perform various tasks that assist the community and help to offset the losses suffered by victims or the community-at-large.

Community-service orders Symbolic restitution, involving redress for victims, less severe sanctions for offenders, offender rehabilitation, reduction of demands on the criminal justice system, and a reduction of the need for vengeance in a society, or a combination of these factors.

Community Services System A coordinated system of community-based social services integrating at least 70 agencies with varying funding sources, governing bodies, and philosophies.

Community work *See* **Work release.**

Commutation Administratively authorized early release from custody (e.g., prisoners serving life terms may have their sentences commuted to 10 years).

Concurrent jurisdiction *See* **Direct file.**

Conditional dispositions Punishments imposed by juvenile courts that most often involve probation.

Conditional diversion program Supervisory method where divertee is involved in some degree of local monitoring by probation officers or personnel affiliated with local probation departments.

Conditional release Any release of inmates from custody with various conditions or program requirements; parole is a conditional release; any release to a community-based corrections program is a conditional release.

Conflict criminology *See* **Radical Criminology.**

Conflict/Marxist theory *See* **Radical Criminology.**

Conflict theory *See* **Radical Criminology.**

Congregate system Inmates are allowed to work together and eat their meals with one another during daylight hours.

Containment theory Explanation elaborated by Walter Reckless and others that positive self-image enables persons otherwise disposed toward criminal behavior to avoid criminal conduct and conform to societal values. Every person is a part of an external structure and has a protective internal structure providing defense, protection, and/or insulation against one's peers, such as delinquents.

Continuous signaling devices Electronic monitoring devices that broadcast an encoded signal that is received by a receiver-dialer in the offender's home. *See* **Electronic monitoring.**

Continuous signaling transmitters Appara-tuses worn about the ankle or wrist that emit continuous electronic signals, which may be received by POs who drive by an offender's dwelling with a reception device.

Continuum of sanctions, graduated sanctions A system of punishments ranging from verbal reprimands and self-imposed behavioral restrictions to imprisonment. Such systems of sanctions are graduated or graduated such that each violation of a probation's program results in a possible transfer to a more serious level of supervision and punishment. The aim of such continuums is to encourage offender compliance with program rules and reduce the chance of probation revocation.

Contract prisoners Inmates from state or federal prison systems who are accommodated in local jails for designated periods such as one or more years at reduced rates in order to reduce prison overcrowding.

Controller value system Parole board decision-making system emphasizing the functions of parole supervision and management.

Conventional model Caseload assignment model where probation or parole officers are assigned clients randomly.

Conventional model with geographic considerations Similar to conventional model; caseload assignment model is based on the travel time required for POs to meet with offender-clients regularly.

Cook, Rufus R. Philanthropist who continued John Augustus's work, particularly assisting juvenile offenders through the Boston Children's Aid Society in 1860.

Corrections The aggregate of programs, services, facilities, and organizations responsible for the management of people who have been accused or convicted of criminal offenses.

Corrections officers Personnel who work in any correctional institution, such as a jail, prison, or penitentiary; formerly known as "guards"; preferred term currently as per American Correctional Association and American Jail Association resolutions.

Corrections volunteer Any unpaid person who performs auxiliary, supplemental, or any other work or services for any law enforcement, court, or corrections agency.

Courts Public judiciary bodies that apply the law to controversies and oversee the administration of justice.

Creaming Term to denote taking only the most qualified offenders for succeeding in a rehabilitative program; these offenders are low risk, unlikely to reoffend.

Creative sentencing Name applied to a broad class of punishments that offer alternatives to incarceration and that are designed to fit a particular crime.

Crime classification index Selected list of offenses that are used to portray crime trends; index offenses are usually divided into Type I or more serious offenses and Type II offenses or less serious offenses; compiled by Federal Bureau of Investigation and Department of Justice.

Crime control A model of criminal justice that emphasizes containment of dangerous offenders and societal protection.

Crimes Violations of the law by persons held accountable under the law; must involve *mens rea* and *actus reus* as two primary components.

Crimes against the person Less frequently used term to describe a criminal act involving direct contact with another person and/or injury to that person, usually where a dangerous weapon is used; person crimes include aggravated assault, rape, homicide, and robbery; more recently designated as violent crime; presently such crimes are considered violent crimes or crimes of violence.

Crimes against property Any criminal act not directly involving a victim (e.g., burglary, vehicular theft [not carjacking], larceny, arson [of an unoccupied dwelling]); more recently designated as property crime.

Crimes of violence Any crime involving potential or actual injury to a victim, and where a weapon is used to facilitate the offense; usually includes homicide, rape, or aggravated assault.

Criminal contamination Belief that if ex-offenders live together or associate closely with one another, they would spread their criminality like a disease; fear originally aroused from construction of halfway houses for parolees.

Criminal justice system Integrated network of law enforcement, prosecution and courts, and corrections designed to process criminal offenders from detection to trial and punishment; interrelated set of agencies and organizations designed to control criminal behavior, detect crime, and apprehend, process, prosecute, rehabilitate, and/or punish criminals.

Criminal trial An adversarial proceeding within a particular jurisdiction, where a judicial determination of issues can be made, and where a defendant's guilt or innocence can be decided impartially.

Criminogenic environment Typically, prisons are viewed as "colleges of crime" where inmates are not rehabilitated but rather learn more effective criminal techniques; any interpersonal situation where the likelihood of acquiring criminal behaviors is enhanced.

Critical criminology A school of criminology that holds that criminal law and the criminal justice system have been created to control the poor and have-nots of society. Crimes are defined depending on how much power is wielded in society by those defining crime.

Crofton, Sir Walter Director of Ireland's prison system during the 1850s; considered "father of parole" in various European countries; established system of early release for prisoners; issued "tickets of leave" as an early version of parole.

Cultural transmission theory Explanation emphasizing transmission of criminal behavior through socialization. Views delinquency as socially learned behavior transmitted from one generation to the next in disorganized urban areas.

Custodial dispositions Punishments imposed by juvenile courts that may involve either secure or nonsecure confinement in a detention facility or group home.

Dangerousness Defined differently in several jurisdictions; prior record of violent offenses; potential to commit future violent crimes if released; propensity to inflict injury.

Day fines A two-step process whereby courts (1) use a unit scale or benchmark to sentence offenders to certain numbers of day-fine units (e.g., 15, 30, 120) according to offense severity and without regard to income; and (2) determine the value of each unit according to a percentage of the offender's daily income; total fine amounts are determined by multiplying this unit value by the number of units accompanying the offense.

Day parole *See* **Work release.**

Day pass *See* **Work release.**

Day reporting centers Operated primarily during daytime hours for the purpose of providing diverse services to offenders and their families; defined as a highly structured nonresidential program utilizing supervision, sanctions, and services coordinated from a central focus; offenders live at home and report to these centers regularly; provides services according to offender needs, which may include employment assistance, family counseling, and educational/vocational training; may be used for supervisory and/or monitoring purposes; client behavior modification is a key goal of such centers.

Defendants Persons who have been charged with one or more crimes.

Defendant's sentencing memorandum Version of events leading to conviction offense in the words of the convicted offender; version may be submitted together with victim impact statement.

Defense counsel Any lawyer who represents and defends someone accused of a crime in court.

Delinquency Any act committed by an infant of not more than a specified age who has violated criminal laws or engages in disobedient, indecent, or immoral conduct, and is in need of treatment, rehabilitation, or supervision; status acquired through an adjudicatory proceeding by juvenile court.

Delinquent subcultures Close associations formed between youths who have committed crimes; bonds formed and patterns of behavior closely resemble societal rules such that these groupings are referred to as subcultures; characteristics include ways of gaining status and recognition or promotion.

Delinquents Juveniles who commit an offense that would be a crime if committed by an adult.

Demand waivers Actions filed by juveniles and their attorneys to have a case in juvenile court transferred to the jurisdiction of criminal courts.

Department of Justice Organization headed by attorney general of United States; responsible for prosecuting federal law violators; oversees Federal Bureau of Investigation and the Drug Enforcement Administration.

Dependent and neglected children Official category used by juvenile court judges to determine whether juveniles should be placed in foster homes and taken away from parents or guardians who may be deemed unfit; children who have no or little familial support or supervision.

Deserts model Way of viewing punishment in proportion to offense seriousness; the punishment should fit the crime.

Detainer warrants Notices of criminal charges or unserved sentences pending against prisoners in the same or other jurisdictions.

Detector PO work role orientation where PO attempts to identify troublesome clients or those who are most likely to pose high community risk.

Detention Any holding of a juvenile for a specified period to await an adjudicatory proceeding.

Detention hearing Judicial or quasi-judicial proceeding held to determine whether or not it is appropriate to continue to hold or detain a juvenile in a shelter facility.

Determinate sentencing Sentence involving confinement for a fixed period of time and that must be served in full and without parole board intervention, less any "good time" earned in prison.

Deterrence Actions that are designed to prevent crime before it occurs by threatening severe criminal penalties or sanctions; may include safety measures to discourage potential lawbreakers such as elaborate security systems, electronic monitoring, and greater police officer visibility.

Differential association theory Edwin Sutherland's theory of deviance and criminality through associations with others who are deviant or criminal. Theory includes dimensions of frequency, duration, priority, and intensity; persons become criminal or delinquent because of a preponderance of learned definitions that are favorable to violating the law over learned definitions unfavorable to it.

Differential reinforcement theory In social learning theory, strengthening or increasing the likelihood of the future occurrence of some voluntary act. Positive reinforcement is produced by rewarding behavior, negative reinforcement by an unpleasant or punishing stimulus. Differential reinforcement is produced when a person comes to prefer one behavior over another as the result of more rewards and less punishment. Self-reinforcement refers to self-imposed positive or negative sanctions.

Direct file Condition where prosecutor has sole authority to determine whether juvenile will be prosecuted in juvenile or criminal court.

Direct supervision jails Constructed so as to provide officers with 180-degree lines of sight to monitor inmates; employ a podular design; modern facilities also combine closed-circuit cameras to continuously observe inmates while celled.

Discretionary waivers *See* **Judicial waivers.**

Diversion The official halting or suspension of legal proceedings against criminal defendants after a recorded justice system entry, and possible referral of those persons to treatment or care programs administered by a nonjustice or private agency. *See also* **Pretrial release.**

Diversion programs Several types of programs preceding formal court adjudication of charges against defendants; defendants participate in therapeutic, educational, or other helping programs; may result in exp-ungement of criminal charges originally filed against defendant; may include participation in Alcoholics Anonymous or driver's training programs. *See also* **Diversion.**

Divertees Persons who participate in a diversion program or who is otherwise granted diversion.

Double jeopardy Fifth Amendment guarantee that protects against a second prosecution for the same offense following acquittal or conviction for the offense and against multiple punishments for the same offense.

Drug courts Special courts that handle only drug cases and are designed to work with prosecutors, defense counsels, treatment professionals, and probation officers to achieve a case outcome that is in the best interests of drug-involved offenders; established in 1989.

Due process model Emphasizes one's constitutional right to a fair trial and consistent treatment under the law; the "equal protection" clause of the Fourteenth Amendment is also stressed; sentencing disparities attributable to race, ethnicity, gender, or socioeconomic status should not be tolerated. *See also* **Justice model.**

Early Release *See* **Parole.**

Earned good time Credit earned and applied against one's maximum sentence through participation in GED programs, vocational/ technical programs, counseling, and self-help groups while in prison.

Ectomorph Body type described by Sheldon; person is thin, sensitive, delicate.

Educator *See* **Enabler.**

Ego Sigmund Freud's term describing the embodiment of society's standards, values, and conventional rules.

Electronic monitoring Use of telemetry devices to verify that an offender is at a specified location at specified times.

Elmira Reformatory Institution constructed in Elmira, New York, in 1876; experimented with certain new rehabilitative philosophies espoused by various penologists including its first superintendent, Zebulon Brockway (1827–1920); considered the new penology and used the latest scientific information in its correctional methods; used a military model comparable to contemporary boot camps; prisoners performed useful labor and participated in educational or vocational activities, where their productivity and good conduct could earn them shorter sentences; inmates were trained in close-order drill, wore military uniforms, and paraded about with wooden rifles; authorities regarded this as a way of instilling discipline in inmates and reforming them; credited with individualizing prisoner treatment and the use of indeterminate sentencing directly suited for parole actions; widely imitated by other state prison systems subsequently.

Enabler PO work role orientation where PO seeks to instruct and assist offenders in dealing with problems as they arise.

Endomorph Body type described by Sheldon; person is fat, soft, plump, jolly.

Enforcer PO work role orientation where POs see themselves as enforcement officers charged with regulating client behaviors.

Exculpatory evidence Any evidence or material that shows or supports a defendant's innocence.

Experience programs *See* **Wilderness programs.**

Expungement The act of removing one or more records of an arrest or conviction from an offender's court files and other legal documents; usually ordered by the court following a successful diversion program.

Expungement order Act of removing a juvenile's record from public view; issued by juvenile court judges, order instructs police and juvenile agencies to destroy any file material related to juvenile's conduct. *See also* **Sealing of Record.**

False negatives Offenders predicted not to be dangerous but who turn out to be dangerous.

False positives Offenders predicted to be dangerous but who turn out not to be dangerous.

Federal Bureau of Investigation (FBI) Invest- igative agency that is the enforcement arm of the Department of Justice; investigates over 200 different kinds of federal law violations; maintains extensive files on criminals; assists other law agencies.

Felony Crime punishable by imprisonment for a term of one or more years; a major crime; an index crime.

Felony probation Procedure of granting convicted felons probation in lieu of incarceration, usually justified because of prison overcrowding; involves conditional sentence in lieu of incarceration.

Fines Financial penalties imposed at time of sentencing convicted offenders; most criminal statutes contain provisions for the imposition of monetary penalties as sentencing options.

First-offenders Criminals who have no prior record of criminal activity.

First-time offenders Criminals who have no previous criminal records; these persons may have committed crimes, but they have only been caught for the instant offense.

Flat time Actual amount of incarceration inmates must serve before becoming eligible for parole or early release.

Florida Assessment Center One of the first state corrections agencies to establish center for selection of entry-level correctional officers; uses intensive screening procedures for selecting applicants for officer positions.

Florida Community Control Program (FCCP) Florida program seeking to provide a milieu of accountability for offender-clients; established in 1983, the FCCP has served more than 40,000 clients; supervision of Florida offenders placed in this program is intense; offenders must have a minimum of 28 supervisory contacts per month; supervising officers have caseloads of between 20 and 25 offenders; caseloads are very low compared with standard probation or parole supervision; utilizes home confinement; offenders are regularly screened for drug and alcohol use, and offenders are monitored to ensure their payment of victim compensation, restitution, and/or community service; offenders also pay supervision fees to offset some of the program costs; recidivism is less than 20 percent for FCCP clients.

Foster homes Temporary placements in a home where family setting is regarded as vital; children in need of supervision targeted for out-of-own-home placement.

Freedom of Information Act (FOIA) Act that makes it possible for private citizens to examine certain public documents containing information about them, including IRS information or information compiled by any other government agency, criminal or otherwise.

Front-end solution Any solution for jail and prison overcrowding prior to placement of convicted offenders in jail or prison settings; programs include diversion, probation, and any community-based correctional program.

Furlough Authorized, unescorted leave from confinement granted for specific purposes and for designated time periods.

Furlough programs Authorized, unescorted leaves for inmates; designed to permit incarcerated offenders opportunity of leaving prison temporarily to visit their homes with promise to return to facility at expiration of furlough.

Gang Self-formed associations of peers, united by mutual interests, with identifiable leadership and organization, who act collectively or as individuals to achieve specific purposes, including the conduct of illegal activity, or the control of a particular territory, facility, or enterprise.

Gang units Special departments in police, probation, or parole agencies dedicated to identifying and supervising the activities of gang members.

Gaol Early English term for a contemporary jail (pronounced "jail").

Georgia Intensive Supervision Probation Program (GISPP) Program commenced in 1982 that established three phases of punitive probation conditions for probationers; phases moved probationers through extensive monitoring and control to less extensive monitoring, ranging from 6 to 12 months; program has demonstrated low rates of recidivism among participants.

Get-tough movement General trend among sentencing reformers and others to toughen current sentencing laws and punishments to require offenders to serve more time; philosophy of punishment advocating less use of probation and more use of incarceration.

Global Positioning Satellite system Network of satellites, used by the U.S. Department of Defense, that pinpoints targets and guides bombs. Currently used by some jurisdictions for the purpose of tracking probationers and parolees and their whereabouts.

Good marks Credits obtained by prisoners in nineteenth-century England where prisoners were given credit for participating in educational programs and other self-improvement activities.

Good time Credit applied to a convicted offender's sentence based on the amount of time served; states vary in allowable "good time"; average is 15 days off of maximum sentence for every 30 days served in prison or jail; incentive for good behavior, thus called "good time"; the amount of time deducted from the period of incarceration of a convicted offender; calculated as so many days per month on the basis of good behavior while incarcerated.

Good-time system Method introduced by Elmira Reformatory in 1876 where an inmate's sentence to be served is reduced by the number of good marks earned; once this system was in operation and shown to be moderately effective, several other states patterned their own early-release standards after it in later years.

Graduated sanctions, continuum of sanctions *See* **Continuum of Sanctions.**

Grand jury Special jury convened in about one-half of all states; comprised of various citizens; numbers vary among states; purposes are to investigate criminal activity or determine probable cause that a crime has been committed and a designated suspect probably committed it; yields "true bill" or indictment or presentment, or "no true bill," finding insufficient probable cause to merit indictment.

Group homes Also known as group centers or foster homes, these are facilities for juveniles that provide limited supervision and support; juveniles live in home-like environment with other juveniles and participate in therapeutic programs and counseling; considered nonsecure custodial.

Guidelines-based sentencing Also known as presumptive sentencing, this form of sentencing specifies ranges of months or years for different degrees of offense seriousness or severity and one's record of prior offending; the greater the severity of conduct and the more prior offending, the more incarceration time is imposed; originally used to create objectivity in sentencing and reduce sentencing disparities attributable to gender, race, ethnicity, or socioeconomic status.

Habeas corpus Writ meaning "produce the body"; used by prisoners to challenge the nature and length of their confinement.

Habitual offenders Criminals who engage in continuous criminal activity during their lives; recidivists who continually commit and are convicted of new crimes.

Halfway house Any nonconfining residential facility intended to provide alternative to incarceration as a period of readjustment of offenders to the community after confinement.

Halfway-in houses Places that provide services catering to those probationers in need of limited or somewhat restricted confinement apart from complete freedom of movement in the community.

Halfway-out houses Facilities designed to serve the immediate needs of parolees from those established to accommodate probationers in the community.

Heredity Theory that behaviors are result of characteristics genetically transmitted; criminal behaviors would be explained according to inherited genes from parents or ancestors who are criminal or who have criminal propensities.

Home confinement Called house arrest or home incarceration, intended to house offenders in their own homes with or without electronic devices; reduces prison overcrowding and prisoner costs; intermediate punishment involving the use of offender residences for mandatory incarceration during evening hours after a curfew and on weekends.

Home incarceration *See* **Home confinement**.

Homeward Bound Established in Massachusetts in 1970; program designed to provide juveniles with mature responsibilities through the acquisition of survival skills and wilderness experiences; six-week training program subjected 32 youths to endurance training, physical fitness, and performing community service.

Hope Center Wilderness Camp Organized network of four interdependent, small living groups of 12 teenagers each; goals are to provide quality care and treatment in a nonpunitive environment, with specific emphases on health, safety, education, and therapy; emotionally disturbed youths whose offenses range from truancy to murder are selected for program participation; informal techniques used, including "aftertalk" (informal discussion during meals), "huddle up" (a group discussion technique), and "pow wow" (a nightly fire gathering); special nondenominational religious services are conducted; participants involved in various special events and learn to cook meals outdoors, camp, and other survival skills.

Hope Houses In 1896, Hope House was established in New York City by Maud and Ballington Booth; receiving considerable financial support from a missionary religious society called the Volunteers of America, the Boothes were able to open additional Hope houses in future years in Chicago, San Francisco, and New Orleans.

House arrest *See* **Home confinement**.

Howard, John (1726–1790) English prison reformer who influenced upgrading prison conditions throughout England and the United States.

Huber law Legislation passed in Wisconsin in 1913 authorizing the establishment of work release programs.

Id The "I want" part of a person, formed in one's early years; Sigmund Freud's term to depict that part of personality concerned with individual gratification.

Idaho Intensive Supervised Probation Program Launched as a pilot project in 1982; a team consisting of one PO and two surveillance officers closely supervised a small group of low-risk offenders who normally would have been sent to prison; the program was quite successful; in October 1984, Idaho established a statewide ISP program with legislative approval; this step was seen as a major element in the "get tough on crime" posture taken by the state.

Implicit plea bargaining Entry of guilty plea by defendant with the expectation of receiving a more lenient sentence from authorities.

Incidents A specific criminal act involving one or more victims.

Indeterminate sentencing Sentences of imprisonment by the court for either specified or unspecified durations, with the final release date determined by a parole board.

Index offenses Includes eight serious types of crime used by the FBI to measure crime trends; information is also compiled about 21 less serious offenses ranging from forgery and counterfeiting to curfew violations and runaways; index offense information is presented in the UCR for each state, city, county, and township that has submitted crime information during the most recent year.

Indictment A charge against a criminal defendant issued by a grand jury at the request of the prosecutor; the establishment of probable cause by a grand jury that a crime has been committed and a specific named individual committed it.

Infants Legal term applicable to juveniles who have not attained the age of majority; in most states, age of majority is 18.

Information Prosecutor-initiated charge against criminal defendant; a charge against a criminal defendant issued by a prosecutor and based on a finding of probable cause.

Initial appearance First formal appearance of criminal suspect before a judicial magistrate, usually for the purpose of determining the nature of criminal charges and whether bail should be set.

Inmate classification Typology schemes based largely on psychological, behavioral, and sociodemographic criteria; the use of psychological characteristics as predictors of risk or dangerousness and subsequent custody assignments for prisoners was stimulated by research during the period 1910–1920.

Intake Process of screening juvenile offenders for further processing within the juvenile justice system.

Intake screening Critical phase where determination is made by probation officer to release juvenile, to detain juvenile, or to release juvenile to parents pending subsequent court appearance.

Intensive probation supervision (IPS) programs Any program designed to supervise probationers closely, with increased numbers of face-to-face visits by POs and more frequent drug and alcohol checks.

Intensive supervised parole (ISP) Intensified monitoring by POs where more face-to-face visits and drug/alcohol testing are conducted; seems to have a lower amount of recidivism compared with more standardized parole programs.

Intensive supervised probation (ISP) programs Supervised probation under probation officer; involves close monitoring of offender activities by various means (also known as intensive probation supervision, or IPS).

Intermediate punishments Sanctions involving punishments existing somewhere between incarceration and probation on a continuum of criminal penalties; may include home incarceration and electronic monitoring.

Intermittent confinement Sentence where offender must serve a portion of sentence in jail, perhaps on weekends or specific evenings; considered similar to probation with limited incarceration. *See also* **Split sentence**.

Intermittent sentence This type of sentence occurs when offenders are sentenced to a term requiring partial confinement; perhaps the offender must serve weekends in jail; a curfew may also be imposed; in all other respects, the nature of intermittent sentencing is much like probation.

International Halfway House Association (IHHA) State-operated halfway houses was the creation of the IHHA in Chicago in 1964; although many of the halfway house programs continued to be privately operated after the formation of the IHHA, the growth in the numbers of halfway houses was phenomenal during the next decade; for instance, from 1966 to 1982, the number of halfway houses operating in the United States and Canada rose from 40 to 1,800.

Interstate compact agreements Contracts between two or more states where offenders are supervised by POs or housed in jails or prisons in their home states different from the states where they were convicted.

Isaac T. Hopper Home Opened by the Quakers in 1845 in New York City; followed by the Temporary Asylum for Disadvantaged Female Prisoners established in Boston in 1864 by a reformist group.

Jail A facility built to house short-term offenders serving sentences of less than one year.

Jail as a condition of probation Sentence where judge imposes limited jail time to be served before commencement of probation. *See also* **Split sentence**.

Jail boot camps Short-term programs for offenders in a wide age range; those in New York and New Orleans have age limits of 39 years and 45 years, respectively; many of the existing jail boot camps target probation or parole violators who may face revocation and imprisonment.

Jail overcrowding Condition that exists whenever the number of inmates in a jail exceeds the number designated as the operating capacity for the jail.

Jail removal initiative Movement to remove juveniles from adult jails.

Jails Facilities designed to house short-term offenders for terms less than one year; also a place for persons awaiting trial or on trial; funded and operated by city/county funds; American Jail Association defines jails as facilities that hold offenders for periods of 72 hours or longer.

Job dissatisfaction Lack of interest in work performed by correctional officers; apathy or discontentment with tasks or assignments.

Judicial plea bargaining Type of plea bargaining where judge offers a specific sentence.

Judicial reprieves Temporary relief or postponement of the imposition of a sentence; commenced during Middle Ages at the discretion of judges to permit defendants more time to gather evidence of their innocence or to allow them to demonstrate that they had reformed their behavior.

Judicial waivers Transfer of jurisdiction over juvenile offenders to criminal court, where judges initiate such action; also called discretionary waivers.

Jurisdiction Power of a court to hear and determine a particular case.

Jurist value system Category of decision making by parole boards where parole decisions are regarded as a natural part of the criminal justice process where fairness and equity predominate.

Jury trial An entitlement of being charged with a crime carrying a penalty of incarceration of six months or more; an adversarial proceeding involving either a civil or criminal matter that is resolved by a vote of a designated number of one's peers, usually 12 members; as opposed to a "bench trial," where a judge hears a case and decides guilt or innocence of defendants or whether plaintiffs have prevailed against defendants in civil cases.

Just-deserts model *See also* **Deserts model**.

Justice model Punishment orientation emphasizing fixed sentences, abolition of parole, and an abandonment of the rehabilitative ideal; philosophy that emphasizes punishment as a primary objective of sentencing; fixed sentences, an abolition of parole, and an abandonment of the rehabilitative ideal.

Juvenile Also known as an infant legally; a person who has not attained his or her 18th birthday.

Juvenile Court Act Provided for limited courts of record in 1899 in Illinois, where notes might be taken by judges or their assistants to reflect judicial actions against juveniles; the jurisdiction of these courts, subsequently designated as "juvenile courts," would include all juveniles under the age of 16 who were found in violation of any state or local law or ordinance; also, provision was made for the care of dependent and/or neglected children who had been abandoned or who otherwise lacked proper parental care, support, or guardianship.

Juvenile delinquency Violation of the law by a person prior to his or her 18th birthday; any illegal behavior committed by someone within a given age range punishable by juvenile court jurisdiction.

Juvenile delinquents Any minor who commits an act that would be a crime if committed by an adult.

Juvenile Diversion/Non-Custody Intake Program California juvenile program implemented in 1982 targeted for more serious juvenile offenders; characterized by intensive supervised probation, required school attendance, employment, and counseling.

Juvenile Diversion Program (JDP) Any program for juvenile offenders that temporarily suspends their processing by the juvenile justice system; similar to adult diversion programs; program established in 1981 in New Orleans, Louisiana, by District Attorney's Office where youths could receive treatment before being petitioned and adjudicated delinquent. *See also* **Diversion**.

Juvenile Intensive Supervision Programs (JISPs) Intensive supervision programs for youthful offenders; they possess many of the same features as programs for adults, including more frequent face-to-face visits, curfews, drug and alcohol checks, electronic monitoring, and home confinement.

Juvenile justice system The process through which juveniles are processed, sentenced, and corrected after arrests for juvenile delinquency.

Juvenile offenders *See* **Juvenile delinquents**.

Labeling theory Explanation of crime attributed to Edwin Lemert whereby persons acquire self-definitions that are deviant or criminal; persons perceive themselves as deviant or criminal through labels applied to them by others; the more people are involved in the criminal justice system, the more they acquire self-definitions consistent with the criminal label.

Labor turnover The degree to which new POs and correctional officers replace those who quit, die, or retire.

Latent functions Unrecognized, unintended functions; associated with probation or parole, latent functions might be to alleviate prison or jail overcrowding.

Law enforcement The activities of various public and private agencies at local, state, and federal levels that are designed to ensure compliance with formal rules of society that regulate social conduct.

Law Enforcement Assistance Administration (LEAA) Program commenced in 1968 and terminated in 1984, designed to provide financial and technical assistance to local and state police agencies to combat crime in various ways.

Legislative waiver *See* **Statutory exclusion**.

Level of custody Degree of supervision and confinement for inmates, depending on the type of crime committed, whether they pose a danger to themselves or other prisoners, and their past institutional history; varies from minimum-, medium-, to maximum-security conditions.

Libido Sigmund Freud's term describing the sex drive believed innate in everyone.

Limited risk control model Method of supervising offenders based on anticipated future criminal conduct; uses risk assessment devices to place offenders in an effective control range.

Lockdown Security measure implemented in prisons that have undergone rioting; usually involves solitary confinement of prisoners for undetermined period; removal of amenities, such as televisions, store privileges.

Lock-up Short-term facilities to hold minor offenders; includes drunk tanks, holding tanks; while these facilities are counted as jails, they exist primarily to hold those charged with public drunkenness or other minor offenses for up to 48 hours; the American Jail Association suggests that to qualify as a true jail, the facility must hold inmates for 72 hours or longer, not 48 hours.

Maconochie, Captain Alexander (1797–1860) Prison reformer and former superintendent of the British penal colony at Norfolk Island and governor of Birmingham Borough Prison; known for humanitarian treatment of prisoners and issuance of "marks of commendation" to prisoners that led to their early release; considered the forerunner of indeterminate sentencing in the United States.

Mandatory release Type of release from jail or prison where inmates have served their full terms or when they have fulfilled sentences specified according to a particular sentencing scheme, such as guidelines-based sentencing or determinate sentencing; mandatory releasees would be subject to automatic release upon serving some portion of their incarcerative terms less good-time credits applied for so many months or days served.

Mandatory sentencing Court is required to impose an incarcerative sentence of a specified length, without the option for probation, suspended sentence, or immediate parole eligibility.

Mandatory waivers Transfers initiated by judges who are required to waive jurisdiction over a juvenile to criminal court.

Manifest functions Intended or recognized functions; associated with probation and parole, manifest functions are to permit offender reintegration into society.

Mark system *See* **Tickets of leave**.

Marks of commendation Points accrued by convicts for good behavior under Alexander Maconochie's (1840s) term of leadership at Norfolk Island; authorized early release of some inmates who demonstrated a willingness and ability to behave well in society on the outside; this action was forerunner of indeterminate sentencing subsequently practiced in the United States.

Marxist criminology *See* **Radical criminology**.

Maxi-maxi Level of custody that accommodates the most violence-prone inmates who are inclined to escape whenever the opportunity arises, and who are considered extremely dangerous; in many cases, maxi-maxi prison inmates are placed in solitary confinement and severe restrictions are imposed; confinement in isolation for $23^1/_2$ hours per day, with 30 minutes for exercise is not uncommon; privileges are extremely limited. *See also* **Maximum security**.

Maximum-security Level of custody where prisoners are closely supervised and given little freedom; subject to constant surveillance, often solitary confinement; limited privileges.

Mediation The process of working out mutually satisfactory agreements between victims and offenders; an integral part of alternative dispute resolution.

Mediator *See* **Enabler**.

Medical model Also known as "treatment model," this model considers criminal behavior as an illness to be treated.

Medium-security Level of custody in a prison where inmates are given more freedoms compared with maximum-security facilities; their movements are monitored; often, these facilities are dormitory-like, and prisoners are eligible for privileges.

Mens rea Criminal mind or guilty mind. One component of a crime.

Meritorious good time Credit earned and applied against one's maximum sentence to be served in prison for engaging in acts of heroism or other feats that should be recognized for their merit; used in conjunction with determinate sentencing schemes.

Mesomorph Body type described by Sheldon; person is strong, muscular, aggressive, tough.

Minimum due process Rights accorded parolees resulting from *Morrissey v. Brewer* (1972) landmark case; two hearings are required: (1) a preliminary hearing to determine whether probable cause exists that a parolee has violated any specific parole condition, and (2) a general revocation proceeding; written notice must be given to the parolee prior to the general revocation proceeding; disclosure must be made to the parolee concerning the nature of parole violation(s) and evidence obtained; parolees must be given the right to confront and cross-examine their accusers unless adequate cause can be given for prohibiting such a cross-examination; a written statement must be provided containing the reasons for revoking the parole and the evidence used in making that decision; the parolee is entitled to have the facts judged by a detached and neutral hearing committee. *See also* **Due process**.

Minimum-security Level of custody in a prison that is designated for nonviolent, low-risk offenders; housed in efficiency apartments; inmates permitted family visits, considerable inmate privileges.

Minnesota sentencing grid Sentencing guidelines established by Minnesota legislature in 1980 and used by judges to sentence offenders; grid contains criminal history score, offense seriousness, and presumptive sentences to be imposed; judges may depart from guidelines upward or downward depending on aggravating or mitigating circumstances.

Misdemeanant One who commits a misdem-eanor.

Misdemeanor Crime punishable by confinement in city or county jail for a period of less than one year; a lesser offense.

Missouri Sexual Offender Program (MOSOP) Program targeted to serve the needs of incarcerated, nonpsychotic sexual offenders; the program can supervise effectively over 700 offenders who are required to complete the program before becoming eligible for parole; approach is that sex offenders' behaviors resulted from learned patterns of behavior associated with anxious, angry, and impulsive individuals; the three-phase program obligates offenders to attend 10 weeks of courses in abnormal psychology and the psychology of sexual offending. In other phases, inmates meet in group therapy sessions to talk out their problems with counselors and other inmates.

Mitigating circumstances Factors that lessen the severity of the crime and/or sentence; such factors include old age, cooperation with police in apprehending other offenders, and lack of intent to inflict injury.

Mixed sentence Two or more separate sentences imposed where offenders have been convicted of two or more crimes in the same adjudication proceeding. *See also* **Split sentence**.

Modes of adaptation Robert Merton's typology of how persons orient themselves to societal goals and the means used to achieve those goals.

Narrative Portion of pre-sentence investigation report prepared by probation officer or private agency where description of offense and offender are provided; culminates in and justifies a recommendation for a specific sentence to be imposed on the offender by judges.

National Crime Victimization Survey (NCVS) A random survey of approximately 60,000 dwellings, about 127,000 persons age 12 and over, and approximately 50,000 businesses; smaller samples of persons from these original figures form the database from which crime figures are compiled; carefully worded questions lead people to report incidents that can be classified as crimes. This material is statistically manipulated in such a way so as to make it comparable with *Uniform Crime Report* statistics; this material is usually referred to as victimization data.

National Incident-Based Reporting System (NIBRS) A compendium of incident-level data for a broad range of offenses; all incidents involving crimes are counted, even if they arise out of an ongoing sequence of criminal events (e.g., a suspect robs a liquor store, shoots the clerk, assaults customers, steals a car, and commits vehicular homicide before being arrested by police).

Needs assessment instrument Any questionnaire device that is designed to forecast an offender's problems and required community services (e.g., physical and/or mental health, education, counseling).

Negligence Liability accruing to prison or correctional program administrators and POs as the result of a failure to perform a duty owed clients or inmates or the improper or inadequate performance of that duty; may include negligent entrustment, negligent training, negligent assignment, negligent retention, or negligent supervision (e.g., providing POs with revolvers and not providing them with firearms training).

Net-widening Pulling juveniles into juvenile justice system who would not otherwise be involved in delinquent activity; applies to many status offenders; also known as "widening the net."

Neutralization theory Explanation holds that delinquents experience guilt when involved in delinquent activities and that they respect leaders of the legitimate social order. Their delinquency is episodic rather than chronic, and they adhere to conventional values while drifting into periods of illegal behavior. In order to drift, the delinquent must first neutralize legal and moral values.

New Jersey Intensive Supervision Program Supervisory method commenced in 1983 to serve low-risk incarcerated offenders and draws clients from inmate volunteers; program selectivity limits participants through a seven-stage selection process; participants must serve at least four months in prison or jail before being admitted to program, which monitors their progress extensively; similar to Georgia Intensive Probation Supervision Program in successfulness and low recidivism scores among participants.

New York House of Refuge Established in New York City in 1825 by the Society for the Prevention of Pauperism; an institution largely devoted to managing status offenders, such as runaways or incorrigible children; compulsory education and other forms of training and assistance were provided to these children; the strict, prison-like regimen of this organization was not entirely therapeutic for its clientele; any of the youthful offenders who were sent to such institutions, including the House of Reformation in Boston, were offspring of immigrants.

NIMBY syndrome Meaning "not in my backyard"; refers to attitudes of property owners who live near where community-based correctional facilities are planned for construction; property owners believe they will suffer declined property values and will be at risk because of felons roaming freely near their homes; opposition opinion toward construction of community-based correctional facilities.

No bill, no true bill Finding of a grand jury that insufficient evidence exists to find probable cause against a criminal defendant that a crime was committed and that the suspect committed it.

Nominal dispositions Juvenile punishments resulting in lenient penalties such as warnings and/or probation.

Nonavertable recidivists Offenders whose prior sentence would not have affected the commission of new crimes.

Norfolk Island Penal colony established on this island in 1840s supervised by Alexander Maconochie; noted for establishment of mark system and marks of commendation leading to contemporary use of good-time credits in U.S. prisons and jails.

Numbers game model Caseload assignment model for probation or parole officers where total number of offender/clients is divided by number of officers.

Objective parole criteria General qualifying conditions that permit parole boards to make nonsubjective parole decisions without regard to an inmate's race, religion, gender, age, or socioeconomic status.

Offender control Philosophy that says if we can't rehabilitate offenders, we can control their behavior while on probation; priority shift in probationer management toward greater use of intermediate punishments designed for better offender monitoring.

Offender rehabilitation Condition achieved when criminals are reintegrated into their communities and refrain from further criminal activity. *See* **Rehabilitation**.

Offenders Persons convicted of a crime.

Offense seriousness score Number based on criminal offense severity; often used in guidelines-based sentencing schemes such as are used in Minnesota; U.S. sentencing guidelines uses offense seriousness scores to calculate numbers of months of incarceration for convicted offenders, together with one's criminal history score.

Offense severity Seriousness of offense, according to monetary amount involved in theft, embezzlement; degree of injuries infli-cted on one or more victims; amount of drugs involved in drug transactions; other alternative measures of crime seriousness.

Ohio Experience Several different types of programs established in Ohio during late 1980s for juvenile offenders; uses home confinement, electronic monitoring, intensive supervised probation; has three goals of heightening offender accountability, individualizing punishments, and promoting community safety.

Once an adult/always an adult provision When juveniles are transferred to criminal court for processing in particular jurisdictions, they will forever after be treated as adults if they commit new offenses, regardless of whether they are still juveniles.

180 Degrees, Inc. Similar to a halfway house for parolees, but it is designed for those who have received no previous treatment for their sex offenses; participation is limited only to those offenders willing to admit they have committed one or more sex offenses and who can function as group members; offenders form men's sexuality groups that meet for 90-minute meetings over a 13-week period; all participants contract with officials to write an autobiography of their offense, a description of the victim, a listing of sexual abuse cues, the development of a control plan, and personal affirmations.

Overcharging Action by prosecutors of charging a defendant with more crimes than are reasonable under the circumstances; raising the charge to a more serious level, expecting a conviction of lesser crime.

Overcrowding Condition that exists when numbers of prisoners exceed the space allocations for which the jail or prison is designed; often associated with double-bunking or putting two prisoners per cell.

Paraprofessional Someone who possesses some formal training in a given correctional area, is salaried, works specified hours, has formal duties and responsibilities, is accountable to higher-level supervisors for work quality, and has limited immunity under the theory of agency.

Pardon An executive device designed to absolve offenders of their crimes committed and release them, thus alleviating the prison overcrowding situation.

Parens patriae Literally "parent of the country" and refers to doctrine where state oversees the welfare of youth; originally established by King of England and administered through chancellors.

Parole Status of offenders conditionally released from a confinement facility prior to expiration of their sentences, placed under supervision of a parole agency.

Parole board Body of governor-appointed or elected persons who decide whether eligible inmates may be granted early release from incarceration.

Parole officers (POs) Corrections officers who supervise and counsel parolees and perform numerous other duties associated with parolee management.

Parole revocation Two-stage proceeding that may result of a parolee's reincarceration in jail or prison; first stage is a preliminary hearing to determine whether parolee violated any specific parole condition; second stage is to determine whether parole should be cancelled and the offender reincarcerated.

Parole revocation hearing A formal meeting of a parolee with a parole board, where the parole board determines whether a parolee is guilty or innocent of a parole program infraction or rule violation; if guilt is established, then parole board must determine punishment to be imposed, which may include intensification of supervision in present parole program or return to prison; two-stage proceeding to determine (1) whether parolee has committed offense or offenses requiring revocation of parole; and (2) what punishment should be imposed; a critical stage.

Parolees Offenders who have served some time in jail or prison, but have been released prior to serving their entire sentences imposed upon conviction.

Penitentiary Facility generally designed to be self-contained and to house large numbers of serious offenders for periods of one year or longer; characterized by manned perimeters, walls, electronic security devices, and high custody levels.

Pennsylvania System Devised and used in Walnut Street Jail in 1790 to place prisoners in solitary confinement. Predecessor to modern prisons. Used solitude to increase penitence and prevent cross-infection of prisoners. Encouraged behavioral improvements.

Persistent felony offenders Persons who continually commit new felonies and are convicted of them; repeat offenders.

Persistent offenders Persons who are convicted multiple times for crimes during their lives.

Persons in need of supervision (PINS) Youths who need the supervision and management of an adult guardian or parent.

Petitions Official documents filed in juvenile courts on the juvenile's behalf specifying reasons for court appearance.

Philadelphia Society for Alleviating the Miseries of Public Prisons Established in 1787, Quaker society devoted to improving jail conditions in Philadelphia; consisted of philanthropists and religionists.

Plea bargaining A preconviction agreement between the defendant and the state whereby the defendant pleads guilty with the expectation of either a reduction in the charges, a promise of sentencing leniency, or some other government concession short of the maximum penalties that could be imposed under the law.

Prediction An assessment of some expected future behavior of a person including criminal acts, arrests, or convictions.

Predispositional reports Document prepared by juvenile intake officer for juvenile judge; purpose of report is to furnish the judge with background about juveniles to make a more informed sentencing decision; similar to PSI report.

Preliminary hearing, preliminary examination Hearing by magistrate or other judicial officer to determine if person charged with a crime should be held for trial; proceeding to establish probable cause; does not determine guilt or innocence.

Pre-parole programs Any transitional programs, including work release, study release, furloughs, or other temporary leaves, for various purposes; inmates are usually within several months of being granted early release; the intent of such programs is to reintegrate these offenders into their communities gradually and avoid the shock of shifting from highly structured and regulated prison life into community living without prison restrictions and regulations.

Preponderance of evidence Standard used in civil courts to determine defendant or plaintiff liability.

Pre-release Any transitional program that assists inmates in prisons or jails in adapting or adjusting to life in their communities by offering them temporary leaves from their institutions.

Pre-release program Prior to granting parole, inmates may be placed on furloughs or work or study release to reintegrate them gradually back into their communities.

Pre-sentence investigation (PSI) Report prepared either by a probation officer or private organization to assist judges in sentencing convicted offenders; includes description of offense, work background and social history of offender, victim impact statement, educational attainment, work record, and other important details.

Pre-sentence investigation report (PSI) Docu- ment prepared by a probation officer, usually at the request of a judge, wherein a background profile of a convicted offender is compiled; includes PO's version of crime committed, convicted offender's statement, victim impact statement, and other relevant data compiled from court records and interviews with persons who know offender and victim.

Presentment A charge issued by a grand jury upon its own authority against a specific criminal defendant; a finding of probable cause against a criminal suspect that a crime has been committed and the named suspect committed it.

President's Commission on Law Enforcement and the Administration of Justice 1967 panel empowered to investigate the state of training and standards used for police officer selection; made recommendations to President of United States to authorize funds to improve officer selection and training methods for general improvement of law enforcement effectiveness.

Presumptive sentencing Punishment prescribed by statute for each offense or class of offense; the sentence must be imposed in all unexceptional circumstances, but where there are mitigating or aggravating circumstances, the judge is permitted some latitude in shortening or lengthening the sentence within specific boundaries, usually with written justification.

Presumptive waiver Burden of proof in transfer decision making shifts from the state to the juvenile; juvenile must be waived to criminal court for processing unless he or she can prove suitable for rehabilitation.

Pretrial detainees Persons charged with crimes and who are placed in custody, usually a jail, prior to their trial.

Pretrial detention Order by court for defendant (juvenile or adult) to be confined prior to adjudicatory proceeding; usually reserved for defendants considered dangerous or likely to flee the jurisdiction if released temporarily.

Pretrial diversion Act of deferring prosecution of a criminal case by permitting defendant to complete a specified period of months or years, usually with conditions; usually persons who comply with behavioral requirements of diversion may have their original charges dismissed, reduced, or expunged.

Pretrial release Freedom from incarceration prior to trial granted to defendants. *See* **ROR**.

Pretrial services Various duties performed by probation officers for either state or federal courts; may include investigations of persons charged with crimes and bail recommendations.

Preventive confinement Placement of alleged offenders in custody, usually a city or county jail, prior to trial; also known as preventive detention.

Preventive detention Constitutional right of police to detain suspects prior to trial without bail, where suspects are likely to flee from the jurisdiction or pose serious risks to others.

Primary deviation Minor violations of the law that are frequently overlooked by police (including "streaking" or swimming in a public pool after hours).

Prison overcrowding Condition resulting whenever inmate population exceeds rated or design capacity.

Prisons Facilities designed to house long-term serious offenders; operated by state or federal government; houses inmates for terms longer than one year.

Privatization General movement in corrections and law enforcement to supplement existing law enforcement agencies and correctional facilities with privately owned and operated institutions, organizations, and personnel; theory is that private management of such organizations can be more cost-effective and reduce capital outlays (taxation) associated with public expenditures for similar functions.

Probable cause Reasonable belief that a crime has been committed and that a specified person accused of the crime committed it.

Probatio A period of proving or trial or forgiveness.

Probation Sentence not involving confinement that imposes conditions and retains authority in sentencing court to modify conditions of sentence or resentence offender for probation violations.

Probation officer caseloads The number of probationer/clients supervised by probation officers; caseloads are determined in different ways, depending on particular probation agency policies.

Probation officers (POs) Corrections official who functions to monitor convict's progress outside of prison.

Probation revocation The process whereby a judge conducts a two-stage proceeding to determine whether a probationer's probation program should be revoked or terminated; such terminations are based on one or more program infractions, which may include curfew violations, use of illegal drugs, possession of illegal contraband, or commission of a new offense.

Probation Subsidy Program California program implemented in 1965 and providing for local communities with supplemental resources to manage larger numbers of probationers more closely; a part of this subsidization provided for community residential centers where probationers could "check in" and receive counseling, employment assistance, and other forms of guidance or supervision.

Probationers Persons who do not go to jail or prison, but rather serve a term outside of prison subject to certain behavioral conditions.

Professionalization Equated with acquiring more formal education rather than practical skills involving one-to-one human relationships with different types of offender-clients; more recently associated with improvements in officer selection, training, and education; accreditation measures are implemented to standardize curricula and acquisition of skills that improve one's work proficiency.

Professionals Persons who are members of a learned profession or have achieved a high level of proficiency, competency, and training.

Program evaluation The process of assessing any corrections intervention or program for the purpose of determining its effectiveness in achieving manifest goals; investigates the nature of organizational intervention strategies, counseling, interpersonal interactions, staff quality, expertise, and education, and the success or failure experiences of clients served by any program.

Program for Female Offenders, Inc. (PFO) Pennsylvania program commenced in 1974, guided by two goals: reforming female offenders and creating economically dependent women; started with a job placement service; training centers were eventually created and operated by different counties on a nonprofit basis; center offerings have included remedial math instruction, English instruction, and clerical classes such as word processing, data entry, and telecommunications skill training; counseling has also been provided for those women with social and psychological problems; currently serves 300 women per year, and the community facilities have a low recidivism rate of only 3.5 percent.

Programmed contact devices Electronic monitoring devices; similar to continuous signal units, except that a central computer calls at random hours being monitored to verify that offenders are where they are supposed to be; offenders answer the telephone and their voices are verified by computer.

Progressive Era 1960s and 1970s time period where liberals stressed rehabilitation for convicted offenders rather than lengthy prison sentences.

Project New Pride Program established in Denver, Colorado, in 1973 and blends education, counseling, employment, and cultural education for children ages 14 through 17; eligible juveniles include those with two prior adjudi- cations for serious misdemeanors and/or felonies; goals are to reintegrate juveniles into their communities through school participation and employment and reduce recidivism rates of juveniles.

Property crimes Illegal acts that do not involve direct contact with specific victims; examples include theft, burglary of unoccupied dwellings, vehicular theft (not car-jacking), embezzlement, fraud.

Prosecutions Carrying forth of criminal proceedings against a person culminating in a trial or other final disposition such as a plea of guilty in lieu of trial.

Prosecutors Court officials who commence criminal proceedings against defendants; represents state interests or government interest; prosecutes defendants on behalf of state or government.

Psychoanalytic theory Sigmund Freud's theory of personality formation through the id, ego, and superego at various stages of childhood. Maintains that early life experiences influence adult behavior.

Public defender Court-appointed attorney for indigent defendants who cannot afford private counsel.

Public risk A subjective gauge of an offender's perceived dangerousness to the community if released, either on probation or parole; sometimes assessed through risk assessment instruments.

Radical criminology Stresses control of the poor by the wealthy and powerful. Crime is defined by those in political and economic power in such a way so as to control lower socioeconomic classes (e.g., vagrancy statutes are manifestations of control by wealthy over the poor).

Ranches Nonsecure facilities for juvenile delinquents designed to promote self-confidence and self-reliance; located in rural settings; involves camping out and other survival activities for confidence-building. *See also* **Wilderness programs.**

Rand Corporation Private institution that conducts investigations and surveys of criminals and examines a wide variety of social issues; located in Santa Monica, California; distributes literature to many criminal justice agencies; contracts with and conducts research for other institutions.

Reality therapy Behavior modification method focusing on the collaborative relation between a PO and a client; client is accepted for what he or she is, but where behavior is unacceptable; rationalization for behavior is rejected; an outgrowth of developmental theory.

Rearrest One indicator of recidivism; consists of taking parolee or probationer into custody for investigation in relation to crimes committed; not necessarily indicative of new crimes committed by probationers or parolees; may be the result of police officer suspicion.

Recidivism New crime committed by an offender who has served time or was placed on probation for previous offense; tendency to repeat crimes.

Recidivism rates Proportion of offenders who, when released from probation or parole, commit further crimes; measured several different ways, including probation revocation, parole revocation, violating curfew, testing positive for drugs or alcohol, or failing to appear for weekly or monthly meetings with POs.

Recidivists Offenders who have committed previous offenses and are convicted of new crimes.

Reconviction Measure of recidivism where former convicted offenders are found guilty of new crimes by a judge or jury.

Reentry Reintegration of an offender into society after being released from prison by either mandatory release, discretionary release, or unconditional release.

Reform schools Early establishments providing secure confinement for more serious types of juvenile offenders; juvenile equivalent to prisons; taught youths various crafts and trade skills; intended to reform youth's behavior; unsuccessful at behavior modification.

Regulator value system Parole board orientation directed toward inmate reactions to parole board decisions; deals with issues such as how current inmates will react to those decisions in view of their own circumstances or how the parole supervision system can be undermined or enhanced as the result of parole board decision making.

Rehabilitation Correcting criminal behavior through educational and other means, usually associated with prisons.

Rehabilitation model Orientation toward offenders which stresses reintegration into society through counseling, education and learning new ways of relating to others.

Rehabilitative ideal *See* **Rehabilitation**.

Reincarceration Return to prison or jail for one or more reasons including parole or probation violations and revocations, rearrests, and reconvictions.

Released on own recognizance Act of releasing defendants charged with crimes into the community prior to trial, without bail or other restrictions; usually ROR defendants have strong community ties and have committed minor or nonviolent offenses. *See* **ROR**.

Reparations Damages paid an offender to victims for injuries and property loss because of a crime.

Repeat-offenders Habitual offenders who continually reoffend and are convicted of new offenses during a span of years.

Respondeat superior Doctrine that holds master (supervisor, administrator) liable for actions of slave (employees).

Restitution Stipulation by court that offenders must compensate victims for their financial losses resulting from crime; compensation for psychological, physical, or financial loss by victim; may be imposed as part of an incarcerative sentence.

Restorative justice Every action that is primarily oriented toward doing justice by repairing the harm that has been caused by a crime.

Reverse waiver hearings Formal meetings with juvenile court judge and criminal court to determine whether youths who have been transferred to criminal court for processing as the result of an automatic waiver or legislative waiver can have this waiver set aside so that the case may be heard in juvenile court.

Reverse waivers Actions filed by juveniles to have their transferred cases waived from criminal court back to juvenile court.

Revocation Action taken by parole board or judge to revoke or rescind the parolee's or probationer's program because of one or more program violations.

Revocation actions Any decision by a judge or parole board to consider revoking a probationer's or parolee's program based on one or more reasons related to program violations.

Reynolds, James Bronson Early prison reformer, established the University Settlement in 1893 in New York; settlement project ultimately abandoned after Reynolds and others could not demonstrate its effectiveness at reform to politicians and the public generally.

Risk Danger or potential harm posed by an offender, convicted or otherwise; likelihood of being successful if placed in a probation or parole program intended to reintegrate or rehabilitate through community involvement.

Risk assessment Any attempt to characterize the future behaviors of persons charged with or convicted of crimes; involves behavioral forecasts of one's propensity to pose harm or a danger to themselves or to others; usually paper-and-pencil devices that yield scores of one's potential dangerousness; used for probation and parole decision making.

Risk assessment instruments Predictive device intended to forecast offender propensity to commit new offenses or recidivate.

Risk–needs instruments The same type of device as a risk-assessment instrument, with the exception that items are included that attempt to determine or define necessary services, counseling, education, or any other helpful strategy that will deter offenders from future offending.

Role ambiguity Lack of clarity about work expectations; unfamiliarity with correctional tasks.

Role conflict Clash between personal feelings and beliefs and job duties as probation, parole, or correctional officer.

Rules of Criminal Procedure Formal rules followed by state and federal governments in processing defendants from arrest through trial; these vary from state to state.

Runaways Juveniles who leave their home for long-term periods without parental consent or supervision; unruly youths who cannot be controlled or managed by parents or guardians.

Salient Factor Score (SFS), SFS 76, SFS 81 Score that is used by parole boards and agencies to forecast an offender's risk to the public and future dangerousness; numerical classification that predicts the probability of a parolee's success if parole is granted; different numerical designations indicate years when scoring devices were created.

Sanctioner value system Model used by parole boards in early-release decision making where amount of time served is equated with seriousness of conviction offense.

Scared Straight New Jersey program devised in the 1980s where juveniles visit inmates in prisons; inmates talk to youths and scare them with stories of their prison experiences; int-ended as a delinquency deterrent.

Screening cases Procedure used by prosecutor to define which cases have prosecutive merit and which ones do not; some screening bur-eaus are made up of police and lawyers with trial experience.

Seamless parole to provide continuity of care for inmates while they are confined, and to continue this care and treatment into their community life once they leave the prison environment. Such parole programs are often used with drug-dependent offenders. The program oversees and coordinates all interrelated state and private programs involved in substance abuse treatment for offenders, both inside and outside of prison. Case management and drug and alcohol testing are used, and the program ranges over 6–9 months inside prison, depending on offender needs and responses to provided services and treatments.

Seamless probation An integrated model of care where the treatment (social services) and supervision staff (POs) jointly conduct screenings and assessments for treatment and offer cognitive-behavioral therapeutic group sessions. Offenders are transitioned into different levels of care as they progress through their treatment programs by either increasing or decreasing the level of care.

Secondary deviation Law violations that have become incorporated into a person's lifestyle or behavior pattern.

Secure confinement Incarceration of juvenile offender in facility that restricts movement in community; similar to adult penal facility involving total incarceration.

See Our Side Program (SOS) Prince George's County, Maryland, program established in 1983; SOS is referred to by its directors as a "juvenile aversion" program, and dissociates itself from "scare" programs such as Scared Straight; seeks to educate juveniles about the realities of life in prison through discussions and hands-on experience and attempts to show them the types of behaviors that can lead to incarceration; clients coming to SOS are referrals from various sources, including juvenile court, public and private schools, churches, professional counseling agencies, and police and fire departments; youths served by SOS range in age from 12 to 18, and they do not have to be adjudicated as delinquent in order to be eligible for participation. SOS consists of four, three-hour phases.

Selective incapacitation Selectively incarcerating individuals who show a high likelihood of repeating their previous offenses; based on forecasts of potential for recidivism; includes but is not limited to dangerousness.

Self-reported information Any data about one's personal criminal offending disclosed by the offender other than by official recordings of arrests; any disclosures of crimes committed by offenders that are otherwise unknown to police.

Sentence recommendation plea bargaining Agreement between defense counsel and prosecutor where prosecutor recommends a specific sentence to the judge in exchange for a defendant's guilty plea.

Sentencing Phase of criminal justice process where judge imposes a penalty for a criminal conviction; penalty may include a fine and/or incarceration in a jail or prison for a period of months or years; may also include numerous nonincarcerative punishments, such as community-based corrections.

Sentencing hearing A formal procedure following one's criminal conviction where judge hears evidence from convicted offender and others concerning crime seriousness and impact; PSI report introduced as evidence to influence judicial decision making; additional testimony heard to either mitigate or aggravate sentence imposed.

Sentencing memorandum, defendant's Core element of presentence investigation report where offenders provide their version of the offense and the nature of their involvement in that offense; may include mitigating factors that might lessen sentencing severity.

Sentencing Reform Act of 1984 Act that provided federal judges and others with considerable discretionary powers to provide alternative sentencing and other provisions in their sentencing of various offenders.

Services to Unruly Youth Program Established in Franklin County, Ohio, in January 1975; designed to provide crisis intervention and counseling as well as other services to unruly youth (status offenders) and their families; has served over 19,000 youths and their families since its inception.

Sex offenders Persons who commit a sexual act prohibited by law; common types of sex offenders include rapists and prostitutes, although sex offenses may include voyeurism ("Peeping Toms"), exhibitionism, child sexual molestation, incest, date rape, and marital rape.

Shire-reeves The early English term used to refer to the chief law enforcement officer of counties (shires) who was known as a reeve. Contemporary usage of the term has been abbreviated to "sheriff," who is the chief law enforcement officer of U.S. counties.

Shock incarceration *See* **Shock probation.**

Shock parole *See* **Shock probation.**

Shock probation Placing an offender in prison for a brief period, primarily to give him or her a taste of prison life (for "shock value") and then releasing the person into the custody of a probation/parole officer. *See also* **Shock probation program.**

Shock probation program Derives from the fact that judges initially sentence offenders to terms of incarceration, usually in a jail; after offenders have been in jail for a brief period (e.g., 30, 60, 90, or 120 days), they are brought back to reappear before their original sentencing judges; these judges reconsider the original sentences they imposed on these offenders; provided that these offenders behaved well while incarcerated, judges resentence them to probation for specified terms; first used in Ohio in 1964.

Shock probationers Any convicted offenders sentenced to a shock probation program.

Situational offenders First-offenders who commit only the offense for which they were apprehended and prosecuted and are unlikely to commit future crimes.

Social casework An approach to modifying the behavior of criminals by developing a close relation between the PO and client, within a problem-solving context, and coordinated with the appropriate use of community resources.

Social control theory Explanation of criminal behavior that focuses on control mechanisms, techniques, and strategies for regulating human behavior, leading to conformity or obedience to society's rules, and that posits that deviance results when social controls are weakened or break down, so that individuals are not motivated to conform to them.

Social learning theory Applied to criminal beh-avior, theory stressing importance of learning through modeling others who are criminal; criminal behavior is a function of copying or learning criminal conduct from others.

Social process theories Explanations of criminal conduct that arise from one's social environment and close associations with others.

Socialization Learning through contact with others.

Sociobiology Scientific study of causal relation between genetic structure and social behavior.

Solitary confinement Technically originated with Walnut Street Jail; used subsequently and origin attributed to the Auburn (New York) State Penitentiary in 1820s, where prisoners were housed individually in separate cells during evening hours.

See Our Side Program (SOS) Juvenile aversion program in Prince George's County, Maryland, designed to prevent delinquency.

South Carolina Intensive Supervised Probation Program Supervision method implemented in 1984; primary aims of the ISP program were to heighten surveillance of participants, increase PO–client contact, and increase off-ender accountability; started ISP program as a pilot or experimental project.

Specialized caseloads model PO caseload model based on POs' unique skills and knowledge relative to offender drug or alcohol problems; some POs are assigned particular clients with unique problems that require more than average PO expertise.

Specialized Offender Accountability Program (SOAP) Program operated by the Lexington Correctional Center in Oklahoma for juveniles under 22 years of age; based on military disciplinary model, individualized treatment is provided, although a strict military regimen is observed.

Special-needs offenders Inmates, probationers, and parolees with unique problems, such as drug or alcohol dependencies, communicable diseases such as tuberculosis or HIV/AIDS, mental illness, or developmental disabilities and mental retardation; may include gang members who require unconventional interventions.

Split sentencing Procedure whereby judge imp-oses a sentence of incarceration for a fixed period, followed by a probationary period of a fixed duration; similar to shock probation.

Standard parolees Anyone on parole who must comply with the basic parole program conditions; as opposed to someone who is intensively supervised by POs with frequent face-to-face visits and random drug and alcohol checks.

Standard probation programs Probationers conform to all terms of their probation program, but their contact with probation officers is minimal; often, their contact is by telephone or letter once or twice a month.

Status offenders Any juveniles who commit offenses that would not be crimes if committed by adults (e.g., runaway behavior, truancy, curfew violation).

Status offenses Violations of statutes or ordinances by minors, which, if committed by adult, would not be considered either felonies or misdemeanors.

Statutory exclusion Certain juveniles, largely because of their age and offense committed, are automatically excluded from juvenile court jurisdiction.

Statutory good time Credit prescribed by the U.S. Congress and state legislatures that prisoners may apply toward their maximum sentences; a method of obtaining early release under determinate sentencing schemes.

Stigmatization Social process whereby offenders acquire undesirable characteristics as the result of imprisonment or court appearances; undesirable criminal or delinquent labels are assigned to those who are processed through the criminal and juvenile justice systems.

Strain theory A criminological theory positing that a gap between culturally approved goals and legitimate means of achieving them causes frustration, which leads to criminal behavior.

Stress Negative anxiety that is accompanied by an alarm reaction, resistance, and exhaustion; such anxiety contributes to heart disease, headaches, high blood pressure, and ulcers.

Study release Essentially the same as work release programs, but study release is for the express purpose of securing educational goals; several types of study release have been identified: adult basic education, high school or high school equivalency (GED), technical or vocational education, and college.

Study release programs *See* **Study release.**

Subculture of violence Subculture with values that demand the overt use of violence in certain social situations. Marvin Wolfgang and Franco Ferracuti devised this concept to depict a set of norms apart from mainstream conventional society, in which the theme of violence is pervasive and dominant. Learned through socialization with others as an alternative lifestyle.

Subcultures Social cliques and behavior patterns of selected groups, such as gangs.

Summary offense Any petty crime punishable by a fine only.

Super max Level of security designed for the most dangerous inmates with extensive criminal histories.

Superego Sigmund Freud's term describing that part of personality concerned with moral values.

Supervised release Any type of offender management program where clients must be sup-ervised by probation/parole officers more or less intensively.

Suspended execution of a sentence A constitutional, statutorily authorized form of judicial clemency, similar to a pardon. Judges or juries find offenders guilty, enter a judgment of a conviction, but suspend imposing the sentence, such as a fine and/or prison term, pending the performance of various acts by the offender (e.g., community service, maintenance fee payments, remaining law-abiding for a period of time) over a given time interval. Once the time interval passes and the offender has satisfactorily complied with the judge's demands, the sentence is suspe-nded. However, the offender remains convicted of the offense.

Suspended imposition of a sentence A contitutional, statutorily authorized action by a judge stemming from a conviction by either a judge or jury, but where the judge doesn't enter the conviction on the record. The judge delays entering the conviction pending some action on the part of the offender (e.g., community service, maintaining employment, being law-abiding) over a given time interval, such as one year. After the successful compliance with the judge's behavioral expectations for the offender, the conviction is set aside or dismissed and the offender is freed. This is similar to an expungement order, where the record of the conviction is eliminated.

Tattoo Symbol of gang membership that is placed on the body in different locations to signify one's gang affiliation.

Tattoo removal program Any process whereby gang members can have their gang tattoos removed in order to escape gang control.

Technical program violations Any infractions by probationers or parolees of the terms of their probation or parole agreements; some violations may include failing drug or alcohol checks, violating curfew, associating with known felons, possessing firearms, cellular telephones, or pagers.

Temporary release programs Any type of program for jail or prison inmates designed to permit them absence from confinement, either escorted or unescorted, for short-term periods; work release, study release, and furloughs are most common types of temporary release.

Theory An integrated body of propositions, definitions, and assumptions that are related in such a way so as to explain and predict the relation between two or more variables.

Theory of opportunity Explanation of deviant behavior and criminality which is class-based and suggests that persons in the lower socioeconomic classes have less opportunity to acquire scarce goods; therefore, they obtain these goods by illegal means.

Therapeutic community A treatment model in which all activities, both formal and informal, are viewed as interrelated interventions that address the multidimensional disorder ofthe whole person. These activities include educational and therapeutic meetings and groups, as well as interpersonal and social activities of the community; within this theoretical framework, social and psychological change evolves as a dynamic interaction between the individual and the peer community, its context of activities, and expectations for participation.

Therapeutic jurisprudence View of judges which attempts to combine a "rights" perspective—focusing on justice, rights, and equality issues—with an "ethic of care" perspective—focusing on care, interdependence, and response to need.

Tickets-of-leave Document given to a prisoner as the result of accumulating good time marks and which would obligate the prisoner to remain under limited jurisdiction and supervision of local police.

Tier system Auburn (New York) State Penitentiary innovation in 1820s designed to established multiple levels of inmate housing, probably according to type of conviction offense and institutional conduct.

Tiers Different floors of a prison or penal institution designed to hold prisoners who have committed various types of offenses.

Tort Civil wrong, omission where plaintiff seeks monetary damages; as distinguished from crimes, where incarceration and fines may be imposed.

Total institution Erving Goffman's term describing self-contained nature of prisons; depicts all community functions inside prison walls, including social exchange, living.

Totality of circumstances Sometimes used as the standard whereby offender guilt is determined or where search and seizure warrants may be obtained; officers consider entire set of circumstances surrounding apparently illegal event and act accordingly.

Traditional treatment-oriented model Stresses traditional rehabilitative measures that seek to reintegrate the offender into the community through extensive assistance; may include elements of the justice and limited risk control models, its primary aim is "long-term change in offender behavior"; includes strategies, such as (a) developing individual offender plans for life in the community such as work, study, or community service; (b) full-time employment and/or vocational training; and/or (c) using community sponsors or other support personnel to provide assistance and direction for offenders.

Transfer hearing Also known as certification or waiver, this is a proceeding to determine whether juveniles should be certified as adults for purposes of being subjected to jurisdiction of adult criminal courts where more severe penalties may be imposed.

Transfers Proceedings where juveniles are remanded to the jurisdiction of criminal courts to be processed as though they were adults; also known as certification and waiver.

Transportation This form of punishment was banishment to remote territories or islands where law violators would work at hard labor in penal colonies isolated from society.

Treater value system Parole board decision-making system where emphasis is on rehabilitation, and where early-release decisions are made on the basis of what will best suit the offender.

Treatment Alternatives to Street Crime (TASC) Since 1972, various community-based treatment programs have been implemented to treat and counsel drug-dependent clients; currently being operated in numerous jurisdictions throughout the United States to improve client abstinence from drugs, increase their employment potential, and improve their social/personal functioning.

Treatment model *See* **Medical model.**

True bill Finding by grand jury that probable cause exists that a crime was committed and a specific person or persons committed it; an indictment; a presentment.

Truth-in-sentencing provisions Legislatively mandated proportionately longer incarcerative terms that must be served by inmates before they become parole-eligible; the federal government requires that its inmates must serve at least 85 percent of their imposed sentences before they are eligible for supervised release.

Unconditional diversion program No restrictions are placed on offender's behavior; no formal controls operate to control or monitor divertee's behavior.

Unconditional release Any authorized release from custody, either as a defendant or convicted offender, without restriction; usually applicable to inmates who have served their statutory time in jail or prison; diversion or probation may be unconditional.

Uniform Crime Reports (UCR) Published annually by the Federal Bureau of Investigation; includes statistics about the number and kinds of crimes reported in the United States annually by over 15,000 law enforcement agencies; the major sourcebook of crime statistics in the United States; compiled by gathering information on 29 types of crime from participating law enforcement agencies; crime information is requested from all rural and urban law enforcement agencies and reported to the FBI.

University Settlement Privately operated facility in New York commenced in 1893 by James Bronson Reynolds to provide assistance and job referral services to community residents; settlement involved in probation work in 1901; eventually abandoned after considerable public skepticism, and when political opponents withdrew their support.

U.S. Code Annotated Comprehensive compe-ndium of federal laws and statutes, including landmark cases and discussions of law applications.

U.S. sentencing guidelines Standards of punishment implemented by federal courts in November 1987 obligating federal judges to impose presumptive sentences on all convicted offenders; guidelines exist based on offense seriousness and offender characteristics; judges may depart from guidelines only by justifying their departures in writing.

User fees Monthly fees paid by divertees or probationers during the diversion or probationary period to help defray expenses incurred by the public or private agencies who monitor them.

Van Dieman's Land 1780s English island penal colony established off the coast of Australia; used to accommodate dangerous prisoners convicted of crimes in England.

Victim compensation Any financial restitution payable to victims by either the state or convicted offenders.

Victim impact statement (VIS) Statement filed voluntarily by victim of crime, appended to the pre-sentence investigation report as a supplement for judicial consideration in sentencing offender; describes injuries to victims resulting from convicted offender's actions.

Victim and Witness Protection Act of 1982 Federal Act designed to require criminals to provide restitution to victims; provides a sentencing option that judges may impose.

Victim–offender reconciliation Any mediated or arbitrated civil proceeding or meeting between offender and victim where a mutually satisfactory solution is agreed upon and criminal proceedings are avoided.

Victim–Offender Reconciliation Project (VORP) A specific form of conflict resolution between the victim and the offender; face-to-face encounter is the essence of this process; Elkhart

County, Indiana, has been the site of VORP since 1987; primary aims of VORP are to (1) make offenders accountable for their wrongs against victims, (2) reduce recidivism among participating offenders, and (3) heighten responsibility of offenders through victim compensation and repayment for damages inflicted.

Victimization data Carefully worded questions lead people to report incidents that can be classified as crimes; this material is statistically manipulated in such a way so as to make it comparable with UCR statistics; this material is usually referred to as victimization data.

Victimizations The basic measure of the occurrence of a crime and is a specific criminal act that affects a single victim.

Victims of Crime Act of 1984 Under Public Law 98-473 the Comprehensive Crime Control Act was established; Chapter 14 of this act is known as the **Victims of Crime Act of 1984**; as a part of all state and federal government victim compensation programs, work release requirements, a certain amount of earned wages of work releasees may be allocated to restitution and to a general victim compensation fund.

Violence Behaviors and individuals that intentionally threaten, attempt, or inflict physical harm on others.

Violent crimes Any criminal act involving direct confrontation of one or more victims; may or may not involve injury or death; examples are aggravated assault, robbery, forcible rape, homicide.

VisionQuest A type of wilderness program; a private, for-profit enterprise operated from Tucson, Arizona; program operates in about 15 states, serves about 500 juveniles annually, and is about half of the cost of secure institutionalization.

Volunteers Hardworking, unpaid, dedicated individuals who fill in the gaps for correctional agencies and provide much-needed services that victims, inmates, parolees, probationers, and their families might otherwise not receive because of limited funding for programs.

Waiver hearing Motion by prosecutor to transfer juvenile charged with various offenses to a criminal or adult court for prosecution; waiver motions make it possible to sustain adult criminal penalties.

Waiver motion Move by defense or prosecution to transfer juvenile to jurisdiction of criminal court.

Waivers *See* **Transfers.**

Walnut Street Jail Pennsylvania legislature authorized in 1790 the renovation of a facility, originally constructed on Walnut Street in 1776, to house the overflow resulting from overcrowding of the High Street Jail; used as both a workhouse and a place of incarceration for all types of offenders; 1790 renovation was the first of several innovations in U.S. corrections, including (1) separating the most serious prisoners from others in 16 large solitary cells; (2) separating other prisoners according to their offense seriousness; and (3) separating prisoners according to gender.

White-collar crime Offenses committed by someone in the course of performing their jobs or occupations; embezzlement and fraud are examples of white-collar crime.

Wickersham Commission A National Commission on Law Observance and Enforcement established in 1931 and chaired by George W. Wickersham; evaluated and critiqued parole as well as the practices of various criminal justice agencies in managing the criminal population.

Wilderness program Any nonsecure outdoors program that enables juvenile delinquents to learn survival skills, self-confidence, self-reliance, and self-esteem; used for secure-confinement bound offenders.

Women's Activities and Learning Center (WALC) Program The Kansas Department of Corrections established a program for women with children that has been patterned after PATCH (Parents and Their Children) commenced by the Missouri Department of Corrections and MATCH (Mothers and Their Children) operated by the California Department of Corrections; Topeka facility has the primary goal of developing and coordinating a broad range of programs, services, and classes and workshops that will increase women offender's chances for a positive reintegration with their families and society upon release.

Work furlough *See* **Work release.**

Workhouse Incarcerative facilities in England in 1700s where sheriffs and other officials "hired out" their inmates to perform skilled and semi-skilled tasks for various merchants; the manifest functions of workhouses and prisoner labor were supposed to improve the moral and social fiber of prisoners and train them to perform useful skills when they were eventually released; however, profits from inmate labor were often pocketed by corrupt jail and workhouse officials.

Work release Any program where inmates in jails or prisons are permitted to work in their communities with minimal restrictions and supervision, are compensated at the prevailing minimum wage, and must serve their nonworking hours housed in a secure facility.

Youth at-risk program Any juvenile program targeting youths considered "at risk" because of low socioeconomic status, poor family relationships, members of families with known criminal parents or siblings; any program designed to improve a youth's skills in various educational and social areas, where such immediate limitations make conditions favorable for acquiring delinquent characteristics and behaviors.

Youth Service Bureaus (YSBs) Established in numerous jurisdictions in order to accomplish diversions several objectives; places within communities where "delinquent-prone" youths could be referred by parents, schools, and law enforcement agencies; forerunners of contemporary community-based correctional programs, since they were intended to solicit volunteers from among community residents and to mobilize a variety of resources that could assist in a youth's treatment; the nature of treatments for youths, within the YSB concept, originally included referrals to a variety of community services, educational experiences, and individual or group counseling; original YSBs attempted to compile lists of existing community services, agencies, organizations, and sponsors who could cooperatively coordinate these resources in the most productive ways to benefit affected juveniles.

References

ABILENE TEEN COURT (2006). *Abilene Teen Court*. Abilene, TX: Author.

ADAIR, JR., DAVID N. (2000). "Revocation Sentences: A Practical Guide." *Federal Probation* **64**:67–73.

ADDY, JIM and TRAVIS PARKER (2006). "The Lancaster County, Nebraska, Mental Health Jail Diversion Project." *American Jails* **20**:27–35.

ADMINISTRATIVE OFFICE OF U.S. COURTS (2001). *Federal Probation Officer Code of Ethics*. Washington, DC: Author.

ADMINISTRATIVE OFFICE OF U.S. COURTS (2006). *PSI Reports: Preparation and Examples*. Washington, DC: Author.

AGNEW, ROBERT ET AL. (2002). "Strain, Personality Traits, and Delinquency: Extending General Strain Theory." *Criminology: An Interdisciplinary Journal* **40**:43–72.

ALARID, LEANNE FIFTAL and PAUL F. CROMWELL (2002). *Correctional Perspectives: Views from Academics, Practitioners, and Prisoners*. Los Angeles: Roxbury Publishing Company.

ALBRECHT, HANS JOERG (2002). "Electronic Monitoring." *MonatSchrift fuer Kriminologie und Strafrechtsreform* **85**:84–104.

ALBRECHT, HANS JEORG and ANTON VAN KALMTHOUT (2002). *Community Sanctions and Measures in Europe and North America*. Frieburg, Germany: Max Planck Institut fur Auslandisches und Internationls Strafrecht.

ALEMI, F. ET AL. (2004). "Activity Based Costing of Probation With and Without Substance Abuse Treatment: A Case Study." *Journal of Mental Health Policy and Economics* **7**:51–57.

AMERICAN CORRECTIONAL ASSOCIATION (1993). *Juvenile and Adult Correctional Departments, Institutions, Agencies and Paroling Authorities: United States and Canada*. College Park, MD: American Correctional Association.

AMERICAN CORRECTIONAL ASSOCIATION (1994). *Field Officer and Resource Guide*. Laurel, MD.

AMERICAN CORRECTIONAL ASSOCIATION (2003). *Probation and Parole Directory 2003–2005*. Lanham, MD: Author.

AMERICAN CORRECTIONAL ASSOCIATION (2004). *2003 Directory, Adult and Juvenile*. Lanham, MD: American Correctional Association.

AMERICAN CORRECTIONAL ASSOCIATION (2006). *2006 Directory, Adult and Juvenile*. Lanham, MD: Author.

AMERICAN PROBATION AND PAROLE ASSOCIATION (2006). *The American Probation and Parole Association Code of Ethics*. Lexington, KY: Author.

AMERICANS UNITED FOR SEPARATION OF CHURCH AND STATE (2006). *Faith-Based Initiatives: Taxpayer Funded Religious Discrimination*. Washington, DC: Author.

AMES, LYNDA J. and KATHERINE T. DUNHAM (2002). "Asymptotic Justice: Probation as a Criminal Justice Response to Intimate Partner Violence." *Violence Against Women* **8**:6–34.

ANDREWS, DON, and JAMES L. BONTA (2006). *Level of Service-Revised*. Ottawa, CAN: Jopie van Rooyen & Partners.

ANTONOPOULOS, GEORGIOS A. (2002). "Evaluating the Juvenile Delinquency Prevention Policies in the United States, Japan, and Australia: What Lessons for Best Practice Emerge?" *Die Kriminalpraevention* **6**:111–115.

ANNO, B. JAYE (ED.) (1998). "HIV Infection among Incarcerated Women." *Journal of Correctional Health Care* **5**:123–254.

AOS, STEVE, JOHN ROMAN, and MARLENE BECKMAN (2006, July). "Understanding Cost Effectiveness of Probation and Parole: A Toolbox for Community Corrections Practitioners." Unpublished paper presented at the annual meeting of the American Probation and Parole Association, Chicago.

ARIZONA DEPARTMENT OF CORRECTIONS (2006). *Offender Classification System (OCS): Classification Operating Manual Revised*. Phoenix, AZ: Author.

ARNOLD, ERIC C. (2006, July). "Eye in the Sky: Enhanced Supervision and Case Management with Integrated Mobile Data Technology." Unpublished paper presented at the annual meeting of the American Probation and Parole Association, Chicago.

AROLA, TERRYL and RICHARD LAWRENCE (1999). "Assessing Probation Officer Assaults and Responding to Officer Safety Concerns." *APPA Perspectives* **22**:32–35.

ARTHUR, LINDSAY G. (2000). "Punishment Doesn't Work!" *Juvenile and Family Court Journal* **51**:37–42.

AUERBAHN, KATHLEEN (2002). "Selective Incapacitation, Three Strikes, and the Problem of Aging Prison Populations: Using Simulation Modeling to See the Future." *Criminology and Public Policy* **1**:353–388.

AUGUSTUS, JOHN (1852). *A Report of the Labors of John Augustus for the Last Ten Years: In Aid of the Unfortunate*. New York: Wright and Hasty.

AUSTIN, JAMES (2006). "What Should We Expect from Parole?" *APPA Perspectives* **30**:46–53.

BALDWIN, TOM and SANDY McCLURE (2003). "Parole Board Officials Cite Pressures." Trenton, NJ: Gannett State Bureau.

BALL, CHRISTINA and ROBERT L. BINGHAM (2006, July). "Probation Consolidation: A Current Urban Experience." Unpublished paper presented at the annual meeting of the American Probation and Parole Association, Chicago.

BANDURA, ALBERT (1977). *Social Learning Theory*. Englewood Cliffs, NJ: Prentice-Hall.

BARBEE, ANDY, MIKE EOSEMBERG, and ANGIE GUNTER (2002). *Trends, Profiles, and Policy Issues Related to Felony Probation Revocations in Texas*. Austin, TX: Texas Criminal Justice Policy Council.

BARRETT, CHERYL, LISA JACOBS, and ELYSE CLAWSON (2006, July). "Implementing Evidence-Based Practices Through Judicial Education." Unpublished paper presented at the annual meeting of the American Probation and Parole Association, Chicago.

BARRON COUNTY RESTORATIVE JUSTICE TEEN COURT (2006). *Barron County Restorative Justice Teen Court*. Barron County, WI: Author.

BASILE, VINCENT D. (2002). "A Model for Developing a Reentry Program." *Federal Probation* 66:55–58.

BATCHELDER, JOHN STUART and J. MARVIN PIPPERT (2002). "Hard Time or Idle Time: Factors Affecting Inmate Choices Between Participation in Prison Work and Education Programs." *Prison Journal* 82:269–280.

BAUMER, ERIC P. ET AL. (2002). "Crime, Shame, and Recidivism." *British Journal of Criminology* 42:40–59.

BAZEMORE, GORDON and JEANNE STINCHCOMB (2004). "A Civic Engagement Model of Reentry: Involving Community Through Service and Restorative Justice." *Federal Probation* 58:14–24.

BEARD, JEFFREY A. and KATHLEEN GNALL (2003). "The Pennsylvania Approach to Reentry." *Corrections Today* 65:68–73.

BEAUMONT, BETTY (2001). "Survey of Injectable Methadone Prescribing in General Practice in England and Wales." *International Journal of Drug Policy* 12:91–101.

BECKER, HOWARD S. (1963). *Outsiders: Studies in the Sociology of Deviance*. New York: Free Press.

BENDA, BRENT B., NANCY J. TOOMBS, and MARK PEACOCK (2002). "Ecological Factors in Recidivism: A Survival Analysis of Boot Camp Graduates After Three Years." *Journal of Offender Rehabilitation* 35:63–85.

BERGERON, LINDSEY and JEFF BOUFFARD (2006, March). "The Implementation and Effectiveness of a Reentry Program for Serious and Violent Offenders in a Small Urban Area." Unpublished paper presented at the annual meeting of the Academy of Criminal Justice Sciences, Baltimore.

BERNBURG, JON GUNNAR and MARVIN D. KROHN (2003). "Labeling: Life Chances and Adult Crime: The Direct and Indirect Effects of Official Intervention in Adolescence on Crime in Early Adulthood." *Criminology* 41:1287–1318.

BEYMER, JUDITH K. and ROGER L. HUTCHINSON (2002). "Profile of Problem Children from a Rural County in Indiana." *Adolescence* 37:183–208.

BIGGER, PHILLIP J. (1993). "Officers in Danger: Results of the Federal Probation and Pretrial Officers Association's National Study on Serious Assaults." *APPA Perspectives* 17:14–20.

BINGHAM, ROBERT L. (2006, July). "Morale—Slaying the Hydra or at Least Wounding It." Unpublished paper presented at the annual meeting of the American Probation and Parole Association, Chicago.

BIRMINGHAM, LUKE ET AL. (2000). "Mental Illness At Reception Into Prison." *Criminal Behaviour and Mental Health* 10:77–87.

BJERREGAARD, BETH (2002). "Self-Definitions of Gang Membership and Involvement in Delinquent Activities." *Youth and Society* 34:31–54.

BLACK, HENRY CAMPBELL (1990). *Black's Law Dictionary (6th Ed.)*. St. Paul, MN: West Publishing Company.

BLACKBURN, DON (2006, July). "Interstate Compact for Adult Offender Supervision." Unpublished paper presented at the annual meeting of the American Probation and Parole Association. Chicago.

BLOOM, BARBARA ET AL. (2002). "Moving Toward Justice for Female Juvenile Offenders in the New Millenium: Modeling Gender-Specific Policies and Programs." *Journal of Contemporary Criminal Justice* 18:37–56.

BOEHNKE, KLAUS and DAGMAR WINKELS (2002). "Juvenile Delinquency Under Conditions of Rapid Social Change." *Sociological Forum* 17:57–79.

BOHN, MARTIN J., JOYCE L. CARBONELL and EDWIN I. MEGARGEE (1995). "The Applicability and Utility of the MMPI-Based Offender Classification System in a Mental Health Unit." *Criminal Behaviour and Mental Health* 5:14–33.

BOND-MAUPIN, LISA J. and JAMES R. MAUPIN (2002). "The (Mis)uses of Detention and the Impact of Bed Space in One Jurisdiction." *Juvenile and Family Court Journal* 53:21–31.

BOSWELL, GWYNETH ET AL. (2002). "Working with Young Adults Sentenced to Life." *British Journal of Community Justice* 1:77–89.

BOSWELL, GWYNETH and PETER WEDGE (2002). *Imprisoned Fathers and Their Children*. Belmont, CA: Wadsworth Publishing Company.

BOWEN, ERICA ET AL. (2002). "Evaluating Probation Based Offender Programs for Domestic Violence Perpetrators: A Pro-Feminist Approach." *Howard Journal of Criminal Justice* 41:221–236.

BOWERS, DAVID, JENNIFER LANGHINRICHSEN-ROHLING, and CATALINA ARATA (2006, March). "Examining the Role of Gender in Gottfredson and Hirschi's General Theory: A Test with an Adolescent Sample." Unpublished paper presented at the annual meeting of the Academy of Criminal Justice Sciences, Baltimore.

BRALLEY, JAMES and JOHN PROVOST (2001). "Reinventing Supervision: Georgia Parole's Results-Driven Supervision." *Corrections Today* 63:120–123.

BRESTON, DAVID A. (2006). *Parole: Frequently Asked Questions*. Houston, TX: David A. Breston State and Federal Criminal Investigation.

BRODY, YOSEF and BARRY ROSENFELD (2002). "Object Relations in Criminal Psychopaths." *International Journal of Offender Therapy and Comparative Criminology* 46:400–411.

BROWN, MICHAEL P. and JILL D'ANGELO (2006, March). "Juvenile Justice Decision-Making: An Examination of Gender Equity." Unpublished paper presented at the annual meeting of the Academy of Criminal Justice Sciences, Baltimore.

BROWN, SAMMIE (2000). "Into the Millennium with Comprehensive Objective Prison Classification Systems." *Corrections Today* 62:138–139.

BROWNFIELD, DAVID and KEVIN THOMPSON (2002). "Distinguishing the Effects of Peer Delinquency and Gang Membership on Self-Reported Delinquency." *Journal of Gang Research* 9:1–10.

BRUCE, A.A. ET AL. (1928). *Parole and the Indeterminate Sentence*. Springfield: Illinois Parole Board.

BURKE, PEGGY B. (2004). "Parole Violations: An Important Window on Offender Reentry." *APPA Perspectives* 28:24–31.

BURRUSS, GEORGE W. and KIMBERLY KEMPF-LEONARD (2002). "The Questionable Advantage of Defense Counsel in Juvenile Court." *Justice Quarterly* **19**:37–67.

BUTTS, JEFFREY A. and JANEEN BUCK (2002). *The Sudden Popularity of Teen Courts.* Washington, DC: Urban Institute.

CADIGAN, TIMOTHY P. (2004). "Instituting a 'Reentry' Focus in the Federal Probation System." *Federal Probation* **68**:36–40.

CAMP, CAMILLE GRAHAM and GEORGE M. CAMP (2003). *Corrections Yearbook 2002.*

CAMP, SCOTT D. ET AL. (2002). "Using Inmate Survey Data in Assessing Prison Performance: A Case Study Comparing Private and Public Prisons." *Criminal Justice Review* **27**:26–51.

CARR, BRENT A., LINDA COLLINS, and PAM LEARY (2006, July). "Mental Health Diversion Program: Diverting Persons with Mental Impairments Out of the Traditional Criminal Court Process." Unpublished paper presented at the annual meeting of the American Probation and Parole Association, Chicago.

CARRINGTON, PETER J. and JENNIFER L. SCHULENBERG (EDS) (2004). "The Youth Criminal Justice Act." *Canadian Journal of Criminology and Criminal Justice* **46**:219–389.

CEPEDA, ALICE and VALDEZ AVELARDO (2003). "Risk Behaviors Among Young Mexican-American Gang-Associated Females: Sexual Relations, Partying, Substance Abuse, and Crime." *Journal of Adolescent Research* **18**:90–106.

CHAMPION, DEAN J. (ED.) (1989). *The U.S. Sentencing Guidelines: Implications for Criminal Justice.* New York: Praeger.

CHAMPION, DEAN J. (1994). *Measuring Offender Risk: A Criminal Justice Sourcebook.* Westport, CT: Greenwood Press.

CHAMPION, DEAN JOHN (2003). *Administration of Criminal Justice: Structure, Function, and Process.* Upper Saddle River, NJ: Prentice Hall/Pearson Education.

CHAMPION, DEAN J. (2004). *Review of Literature Relating to Collective Bargaining and Probation and Parole Officers.* Laredo: Texas A & M International University.

CHAMPION, DEAN JOHN (2005). *Corrections in the United States: A Contemporary Perspective, 4e.* Upper Saddle River, NJ: Prentice Hall/Pearson Education.

CHAMPION, DEAN JOHN (2007). *The Juvenile Justice System: Delinquency, Processing, and Law.* Upper Saddle River, NJ: Prentice Hall/Pearson Education.

CHAPMAN, JACK (1998). "Bigger, Better, Safer, Faster, and Less Expensive." *American Jails* **12**:9–17.

CHAPMAN, YVONNE K. (2005). "Teen Courts and Restorative Justice." Unpublished paper presented at the annual meeting of the Academy of Criminal Justice Sciences, Chicago (March).

CHEESEMAN, KELLY (2006, March). "'I Can't Get No Satisfaction': Assessing Causes of Stress and Job Dissatisfaction among Correctional Officers." Unpublished paper presented at the annual meeting of the Academy of Criminal Justice Sciences, Baltimore.

CHUTE, C.L. (1922). "Probation and Suspended Sentence." *Journal of the American Institute of Criminal Law and Criminology* **12**:558.

CLARK, PATRICIA M. (1995). "The Evolution of Michigan's Community Corrections Act." *Corrections Today* **57**:38–39, 68.

CLAYTON, SUSAN L. (2005). "Jail Inmates Bake Their Way to Successful Reentry." *Corrections Today* **67**:78–80, 130.

CLEAR, TODD R. and HARRY R. DAMMER (2000). *The Offender in the Community.* Belmont, CA: Wadsworth.

CLEAR, TODD R., NATALIE MAJEED, and FELICIA BOWNOTH (2006, March). "Long-Term Prisoners: A Review of the Literature." Unpublished paper presented at the annual meeting of the Academy of Criminal Justice Sciences, Baltimore.

COHEN, ALBERT K. (1955). *Delinquent Boys.* Glencoe, IL: Free Press.

COHN, ALVIN W. ET AL. (2002). "What Works in Corrections?" *Federal Probation* **66**:4–83.

COLEMAN, RICH, BETH SHARP, and CATHIE GREEN (2006, July). "Partnering for Successful Reentry (Help, There's an Offender in My Office)." Unpublished paper presented at the annual meeting of the American Probation and Parole Association, Chicago.

COLLINS, PETER A. (2006, March). "Substance Abuse Treatment in Idaho: Measuring the Cost Through the Use of Administrative Data Bases." Unpublished paper presented at the annual meeting of the Academy of Criminal Justice Sciences, Baltimore.

CONNECTICUT BOARD OF PAROLE (2006). *Mission and Procedures.* Hartford, CT: Author.

CORNELIUS, GARY F. (1996). *Jails in America: An Overview of Issues (2/e).* Laurel, MD: American Correctional Association.

CORRECTIONAL ASSOCIATION OF NEW YORK (2000). *Health Care in New York State Prisons: A Report of Findings and Recommendations By the Visiting Committee on Correctional Association of New York.* New York: Correctional Association of New York Prison Visiting Committee.

COURTRIGHT, KEVIN E., BRUCE L. BERG, and ROBERT J. MUTCHNICK (1997). "The Cost Effectiveness of Using House Arrest with Electronic Monitoring for Drunk Drivers." *Federal Probation* **61**:19–22.

COWELL, ALEXANDER J., NAHAMA BRONER, and RANDOLPH DUPONT (2004). "The Cost-Effectiveness of Criminal Justice Diversion Programs for People with Serious Mental Illness Co-Occurring with Substance Abuse." *Journal of Contemporary Criminal Justice* **20**:292–315.

COWLES, ERNEST L., THOMAS C. CASTELLANO and LAURA A. GRANSKY (1995). *Boot Camp Drug Treatment and Aftercare Intervention: An Evaluation Review.* Washington, DC: U.S. Government Printing Office.

CRABTREE CORRECTIONAL CENTER (2006). *Work Experience Program Benefits Wild Horses and Inmates.* Helena, OK: Author.

CRAWLEY, ELAINE (2002). "Bringing It All Back Home? The Impact of Prison Officers' Work on Their Families." *Probation Journal* **49**:277–286.

CUMMINGS, HOMER (2003). "They All Come Out." *Federal Probation* **67**:9–11.

CURRIE, DAN (2001). *A Short History of Vera's Work on the Judicial Process.* Albany, NY: Vera Institute of Justice.

CURRY, G. DAVID, SCOTT H. DECKER, and ARLEN EGLEY JR. (2002). "Gang Involvement and Delinquency in a Middle School Population." *Justice Quarterly* **19**:275–292.

CURTIS, RIC (2003). "Crack, Cocaine, and Heroin: Drug Eras in Williamsburg, Brooklyn, 1960–2000." *Addiction Research and Theory* **11**:47–63.

DALLEY, LANETTE P. (2002). "Policy Implications Relating to Inmate Mothers and Their Children: Will the Past Be Prologue?" *Prison Journal* **82**:234–268.

DEANGELO, ANDREW and SUSAN BLACKBURN (2006, July). "Competency Development Through Community/Victim Services." Unpublished paper presented at the annual meeting of the American Probation and Parole Association, Chicago.

DEAR, GREG E. ET AL. (2002). "Prisoners' Willingness to Approach Prison Officers for Support: The Officer's Views." *Journal of Offender Rehabilitation* **34**:33–46.

DEITCH, DAVID A. ET AL. (2001). "Does In-Custody Therapeutic Community Substance Abuse Treatment Impact Custody Personnel?" *Corrections Compendium* **26**:1–24.

DENNEHY, KATHLEEN M. (2006). *Massachusetts Correctional Institution (MCI)*. Milford, MA: DOC Central Headquarters.

DOELLING, DIETER, ARTHUR HARTMANN, and MONIKA TRAULSEN (2002). "Legalbewachrung Nach Tacter-Opfer-Ausgleich im Jugendstrafrecht." *Monatsschrift fuer Krimmologie und Strafrechtsreform* **85**:185–193.

DOWDY, ERIC R., MICHAEL G. LACY, and N. PRABHA UNNITHAN (2002). "Correctional Prediction and the Level of Supervision Inventory." *Journal of Criminal Justice* **30**:29–39.

DUNLAP, KAREN L. and J. DE CARLO CICCEL (2006, July). "Providing Effective Community Supervision of Impaired Driving Offenders." Unpublished paper presented at the annual meeting of the American Probation and Parole Association, Chicago.

DUROSE, M.R. and C.J. MUMOLA (2004). *Profile of Nonviolent Offenders Exiting State Prisons*. Washington, DC: U.S. Department of Justice, Office of Justice Programs.

DZUR, ALBERT W. and ALAN WERTHEIMER (2002). "Forgiveness and Public Deliberation: The Practice of Restorative Justice." *Criminal Justice Ethics* **21**:3–20.

EDLESON, JEFFREY L. ET AL. (2003). "How Children are Involved in Adult Domestic Violence: Results from a Four-City Telephone Survey."*Journal of Interpersonal Violence* **18**:18–32.

EISENBERG, MICHAEL and BRITTANI TRUSTY (2002). *Overview of the InnerChange Freedom Initiative: The Faith-Based Prison Program within the Texas Department of Criminal Justice*. Austin, TX: Texas Criminal Justice Policy Council.

EMPEY, LAMAR T. and JEROME RABOW (1961). "The Provo Experiment in Delinquency Rehabilitation." *American Sociological Review* **26**:679–695.

EVANS, DONALD G. (2005). "Community Engagement: A Challenge for Probation/Parole." *APPA Perspectives* **67**:117–119.

FABELO, TONY (2002). "The Impact of Prison Education on Community Reintegration of Inmates: The Texas Case." *Journal of Correctional Education* **53**:106–110.

FALS, STEWART WILLIAM (2003). "The Occurrence of Partner Physical Aggression on Days of Alcohol Consumption: A Longitudinal Diary Study." *Journal of Counseling and Clinical Psychology* **71**:41–52.

FARRALL, STEPHEN ET AL. (2002). "Long-Term Absences from Probation: Officers' and Probationers' Accounts." *Howard Journal of Criminal Justice* **41**:263–278.

FARRELL, AMY (2000). "Women, Crime, and Drugs: Testing the Effect of Therapeutic Communities." *Women and Criminal Justice* **11**:21–48.

FARRELL, JILL, DOUGLAS YOUNG, and KARL MOLINE (2006, March). "The Creation and Implementation of an Intake Risk-Needs Assessment Instrument for Juveniles." Unpublished paper presented at the annual meeting of the Academy of Criminal Justice Sciences, Baltimore.

FAULKNER, DAVID (2002). "Prisoners as Citizens." *British Journal of Community Justice* **1**:11–19.

FELD, BARRY C. (2003). "The Constitutional Tension Between *Apprendi* and *McKeiver*: Sentence Enhancements Based on Delinquency Convictions and the Quality of Justice in Juvenile Courts." *Wake Forest Law Review* **38**:1111–1224.

FERRARO, KATHLEEN J. (2003). "The Words Change, But the Melody Lingers: The Persistence of Battered Woman Syndrome in Criminal Cases Involving Battered Women." *Violence Against Women* **9**:110–129.

FESTERVAN, EARLENE (2003). *Women Probationers: Supervision and Success*. Lanham, MD: American Correctional Association.

FIELDS, SCOTT A. and JOHN R. MCNAMARA (EDS.) (2003). "The Prevention of Child and Adolescent Violence: A Review." *Aggression and Violent Behavior* **8**:61–91.

FINN, MARY A. and SUZANNE MUIRHEAD-STEVES (2002). "The Effectiveness of Electronic Monitoring with Violent Male Parolees." *Justice Quarterly* **19**:293–312.

FITZGERALD, BILL ET AL. (2006, July). "Working Together: Providing Residential Treatment to the Mentally Impaired Offender." Unpublished paper presented at the annual meeting of the American Probation and Parole Association, Chicago.

FLORIDA ADVISORY COUNCIL (2006). *Local Government and the State-Level Partnership*. Tallahassee, FL: Florida Advisory Council on Intergovernmental Relations.

FLORIDA DEPARTMENT OF CORRECTIONS (1993). *Status Report on Elderly Inmates*. Tallahassee, FL: Florida Department of Corrections Youth and Special Needs Program Office.

FLORIDA DEPARTMENT OF CORRECTIONS (2006). *Florida's Community Supervision Population Monthly Status Report*. Tallahassee, FL: Florida Department of Corrections, Bureau of Research and Data Analysis, Community Supervision Section.

FLOWERS, R. BARRI (2002). *Kids Who Commit Adult Crimes: Serious Criminality by Juvenile Offenders*. Binghamton, NY: Haworth Press.

FRANCIS, TERESA (2006, March). "Cruel and Unusual Punishment: Privatization of Health Care in the Jail and Prisons." Unpublished paper presented at the annual meeting of the Academy of Criminal Justice Sciences, Baltimore.

FRANKFORT-HOWARD, ROBYNE and STEPHAN ROMM (2002). "Outcomes of a Residential Treatment of Antisocial Youth: Development of or Cessation from Adult Antisocial Behavior." *Residential Treatment for Children and Youth* **19**:53–70.

FREIBURGER, TINA L. (2006, March). "Re-Entry of Mentally Ill Female Offenders." Unpublished paper presented at the annual meeting of the Academy of Criminal Justice Sciences, Baltimore.

FRETZ, RALPH (2005). "'Step Down' Programs: The Missing Link in Successful Inmate Reentry." *Corrections Today* **67**:102–107.

FROST, GREGORY A. (2002). "Florida's Innovative Use of GPS for Community Corrections." *Journal of Offender Monitoring* **15**:6.

FULKERSON, ANDREW and TONI SMITH (2006, March). "Family Group Conferences in the Drug Treatment Court." Unpublished paper presented at the annual meeting of the Academy of Criminal Justice Sciences, Baltimore.

GAHL, NANCY ET AL. (2006, July). "Killed in the Line of Duty: 20 Years Later, What Have We Learned?" Unpublished paper presented at the annual meeting of the American Probation and Parole Association, Chicago.

GARBARINO, JAMES ET AL. (2002). "Trauma and Juvenile Delinquency: Theory, Research, and Interventions." *Journal of Aggression, Maltreatment, and Trauma* **6**:1–264.

GARLAND, BRETT and BILL McCARTY (2006, March). "Explaining Perceptions of Administrative Support among Prison Treatment Staff." Unpublished paper presented at the annual meeting of the Academy of Criminal Justice Sciences, Baltimore.

GARRITY, THOMAS F. ET AL. (2002). "Factors Predicting Illness and Health Services Use Among Male Kentucky Prisoners with a History of Drug Abuse." *Prison Journal* **82**:295–313.

GEORGIA DEPARTMENT OF CORRECTIONS (2006). *Mentally Ill Parolees: Providing a Chain of Care to Break the Cycle of Crime.* Atlanta, GA: Author.

GIBLIN, MATTHEW J. (2002). "Using Police Officers to Enhance the Supervision of Juvenile Probationers: An Evaluation of the Anchorage CAN Program." *Crime and Delinquency* **48**:116–137.

GLASSER, WILLIAM (1976). *The Identity Society.* New York: Harper and Row.

GLAZE, LAUREN E. (2003). *Probation and Parole in the United States, 2002.* Washington, DC: Bureau of Justice Statistics.

GLAZE, LAUREN E. and SERI PALLA (2005). *Probation and Parole in the United States, 2004.* Washington, DC: Bureau of Justice Statistics.

GLOVER, WILLIAM V. (2002). "Successfully Implementing a Full Mandatory Attendance Policy in the Arkansas Department of Correction School District." *Journal of Correctional Education* **53**:101–105.

GOFF, MARIE and DONALD B. GOFF (2006, July). "Family Group Conferencing in a Rural Setting and Collaboration: Make It Happen!" Unpublished paper presented at the annual meeting of the American Probation and Parole Association, Chicago.

GOFFMAN, ERVING (1961). *Asylums.* Garden City, NY: Anchor Press.

GRABAREK, JOANNA K., MICHAEL L. BOURKE, and VINCENT VAN HASSELT (2002). "Empirically Derived MCMI-III Personality Profiles of Incarcerated Female Substance Abusers." *Journal of Offender Rehabilitation* **35**:19–29.

GREAT BOOKS FOUNDATION (2006). *Education and Incarceration: A History.* Washington, DC: Author.

GREENE, JUDITH and VINCENT SCHIRALDI (2002). *Cutting Correctly: New Prison Policies for Times of Fiscal Crisis.* Washington, DC: Justice Policy Institute.

GRIETENS, HANS, JACOBUS RINK, and WALTER HELLINCKX (2003). "Nonbehavioral Correlates of Juvenile Delinquency: Communications of Detained and Nondetained Young People About Social Limits." *Journal of Adolescent Research* **18**:68–89.

GRIFFIN, MARIE L. (2002). "The Influence of Professional Orientation on Detention Officers' Attitudes Toward the Use of Force." *Criminal Justice and Behavior* **29**:250–277.

GUNNISON, ELAINE and JACQUELINE HELFGOTT (2006, March). "Community Corrections Officer Perceptions of Ex-Offender Reentry Needs." Unpublished paper presented at the annual meeting of the Academy of Criminal Justice Sciences, Baltimore.

GURA, PHILLIP F. (2002). *Buried from the World: Inside Massachusetts Prisons.* Boston: Massachusetts Historical Society.

GUSTAFSON, DAVID (2006). *Addiction Severity Index.* Washington, DC: Creative Commons.

HAAPANEN, RUDY and LEE BRITTON (2002). "Drug Testing for Youthful Offenders on Parole: An Experimental Evaluation." *Criminology and Public Policy* **1**:217–244.

HAGHIGHI, BAHRAM and ALMA LOPEZ (1993). "Success/Failure of Group Home Treatment Programs for Juveniles." *Federal Probation* **57**:53–58.

HAMMETT, THEODORE M., MARY PATRICIA HARMON, and WILLIAM RHODES (2002). "The Burden of Infectious Disease among Inmates of and Releasees from United States Correctional Facilities." *American Journal of Public Health* **92**:1789–1794.

HARNISH, AARON A. (2006, March). "A Multifaceted Leadership Program for At-Risk Youth." Unpublished paper presented at the annual meeting of the Academy of Criminal Justice Sciences, Baltimore.

HARPER, RAY (2000). "Inmate Help Tame Wild Horses." *Reno Gazette-Journal,* December 8, 2000:B1.

HARRELL, ADELE V. ET AL. (2006, July). "Supervising Domestic Violence Offenders on Probation: Improving Compliance and Protecting Victims." Unpublished paper presented at the annual meeting of the American Probation and Parole Association, Chicago.

HARRIS, DAVID (2006, July). "Judicial Immunity and Probation: What Does That Mean?" Unpublished paper presented at the annual meeting of the American Probation and Parole Association, Chicago.

HARRIS, ROBERT J. and T. WING LO (2002). "Community Service: Its Use in Criminal Justice." *International Journal of Offender Therapy and Comparative Criminology* **46**:427–444.

HARRISON, PAIGE M. and ALLEN J. BECK (2005). *Prisoners and Jail Inmates at Midyear 2004.* Washington, DC: Bureau of Justice Statistics.

HARRISON, PAIGE M., CANDICE M. JOHNSON, and ALLEN J. BECK (2006, July). "Implementing the Prison Rape Elimination Act: Sexual Violence Reported By Former Inmates." Unpublished paper presented at the annual meeting of the American Probation and Parole Association, Chicago.

HARRISON, PAIGE M. and ALLEN J. BECK (2006). *Prison and Jail Inmates at Midyear 2005.* Washington, DC: Bureau of Justice Statistics.

HENNESSEY, MAYA (2006, July). "Gender Competence with Female Offenders." Unpublished paper presented at the annual meeting of the American Probation and Parole Association, Chicago.

HENSLEY, CHRISTOPHER, MARY KOSCHESKI, and RICHARD TEWKSBURY (2002). "Does Participation in Conjugal Visitations Reduce Prison Violence in Mississippi? An Exploratory Study." *Criminal Justice Review* **27**:52–65.

HEPBURN, JOHN R. (2005). "Recidivism among Drug Offenders Following Exposure to Treatment." *Criminal Justice Policy Review* **16**:237–259.

HERBST, DOMINIC P. (2006, July). "Resolving Rage, Restoring Relationships and Reducing Recidivism." Unpublished paper presented at the annual meeting of the American Probation and Parole Association, Chicago.

HILLER, MATTHEW L. ET AL. (2002). "Motivation as a Predictor of Therapeutic Engagement in Mandated Residential Substance Abuse Treatment." *Criminal Justice and Behavior* **29**:56–75.

HIRSCHI, TRAVIS (1969). *Causes of Delinquency.* Berkeley: University of California Press.

HOBBS, JILL, PATRICK JABLONSKI, and GARNETT AHERN (2006, July). "If You Can Measure It, You Can Manage It: The Use of Data in Community Corrections." Unpublished paper presented at the annual meeting of the American Probation and Parole Association, Chicago.

HOGAN, NANCY, ERIC LAMBERT, and SHANNON BARTON (2006, March). "The Impact of Stressors on the Work-Family

Conflict of Staff at a Private Midwestern Prison." Unpublished paper presented at the annual meeting of the Academy of Criminal Justice Sciences, Baltimore.

HOLCOMB, DEBI and MOLLY GLENN (2006, July). "Increasing Offender Success: Victim Services Liaisons in Parole." Unpublished paper presented at the annual meeting of the American Probation and Parole Association, Chicago.

HOLCOMB, JEFFERSON (2006, July). "Probation Officer Risk and the Carrying of Firearms." Unpublished paper presented at the annual meeting of the Academy of Criminal Justice Sciences, Baltimore.

HOLT, VICTORIA L. ET AL. (2003). "Do Protection Orders Affect the Likelihood of Future Partner Violence and Injury?" *American Journal of Preventive Medicine* **24:** 16–21.

HOOTON, ERNEST (1939). *Crime and the Man.* Westport, CT: Greenwood Press.

HOSSAIN, MOKERROM and JOY COMBS-MARSHALL (2006, March). "Taking Care of Teenage Mothers and Their Children: A Way to Reduce Juvenile Delinquency." Unpublished paper presented at the annual meeting of the Academy of Criminal Justice Sciences, Baltimore.

HOWELL, JAMES C. and DAVID GAMBLE (2006, July). "A Practical Approach to Linking Graduated Sanctions with a Continuum of Effective Programs." Unpublished paper presented at the annual meeting of the American Probation and Parole Association, Chicago.

INDIANA DEPARTMENT OF CORRECTIONS (2001). *An Assessment of Furlough Programs: Preliminary Report.* Indianapolis, IN: Author.

IOWA DEPARTMENT OF CORRECTIONAL SERVICES (2005). *Corrections Continuum: Intermediate Criminal Sanctions Program.* Davenport, IA: Author.

IOWA DEPARTMENT OF CORRECTIONAL SERVICES (2006). *Iowa Classification System: Assessment & Reassessment of Client Risk Instructions & Scoring Guide.* Davenport, IA: Author.

IRELAND, CONNIE STIVERS and JOANN PRAUSE (2005). "Discretionary Parole Release: Length of Imprisonment, Percent of Sentence Served, and Recidivism." *Journal of Crime and Justice* **28:**27–49.

iSECUREtrac (2006, July). "Effective GPS Programs: How to Launch, Manage, and Grow." Unpublished paper presented at the annual meeting of the American Probation and Parole Association, Chicago.

ISRAEL, MARK and JOHN DAWES (2002). "Something from Nothing': Shifting Credibility in Community Correctional Programs in Australia." *Criminal Justice: The International Journal of Policy and Practice* **2:**5–25.

JACKSON, REBECCA L. ET AL. (2002). "Psychopathy in Female Offenders: An Investigation of Its Underlying Dimensions." *Criminal Justice and Behavior* **29:**692–704.

JACOBY, JOSEPH E. (2002). "The Endurance of Failing Correctional Institutions: A Worst Case Study." *Prison Journal* **82:**168–188.

JAMES, TOM, GEOBOO SONG, and SEBASTIAN DAVIS (2006, March). "Identification of High-Risk Areas for Targeting Policies and Programs to Deal with Juvenile Crime and Gang Activities." Unpublished paper presented at the annual meeting of the Academy of Criminal Justice Sciences, Baltimore.

JEFFERIES, ROGER ET AL. (2006, July). "Managing High Risk/Need Offenders—Where the Rubber Meets the Road." Unpublished paper presented at the annual meeting of the American Probation and Parole Association, Chicago.

JEFFERSON COUNTY DRUG COURT (2006). *The Use of Drug Courts: Some Successful Experiences.* Jefferson County, KY: Author.

JESNESS, CARL F. (1987). "Early Identification of Delinquent-Prone Children: An Overview." In *The Prevention of Delinquent Behavior,* John D. Burchard and Sara N. Burchard (eds.). Newbury Park, CA: Sage.

JIANG, SHANHE and FISHER-GIORLANDO (2002). "Inmate Misconduct: A Test of the Deprivation, Importation, and Situational Models." *Prison Journal* **82:**335–358.

JOHANSSON-LOVE, JILL and JAMES H. GEER (2003). "Investigation of Attitude Change in a Rape Prevention Program." *Journal of Interpersonal Violence* **18:**84–89.

JOHNSTON, C. WAYNE (2006, March). "Principles of Prosecutorial Diversion Policies: Do No Harm." Unpublished paper presented at the annual meeting of the Academy of Criminal Justice Sciences, Baltimore.

KARP, DAVID R. and NICK ADORNETTO (2005). "Research on Reentry." *APPA Perspectives* **29:**20–21.

KING, RYAN S. ET AL. (2002). *Distorted Priorities: Drug Offenders in State Prisons.* Washington, DC: The Sentencing Project.

KING, TAMMY A., JEN BIERDEMAN, and TOM C. JORDAN (2006, March). "Female Juvenile Delinquency." Unpublished paper presented at the annual meeting of the Academy of Criminal Justice Sciences, Baltimore.

KITSUSE, J.I. (1962). "Societal Reaction to Deviant Behavior: Problems of Theory and Method." *Social Problems* **9:** 247–256.

KLEIN, SHIRLEY R., GEANNINA S. BARTHOLOMEW, and JEFF HIBBERT (2002). "Inmate Family Functioning." *International Journal of Offender Therapy and Comparative Criminology* **46:**95–111.

KOHLBERG, L. (1963). "The Development of Children's Orientations Toward a Moral Order: Sequence in the Development of Human Thought." *Vita Humana* **6:**11–33.

KONOPKA, AL (2001). *Nevada ISP Program.* Las Vegas, NV: Division of Parole and Probation. (personal communication, March 8, 2001)

KREBS, CHRISTOPHER P. (2002). "High-Risk HIV Transmission Behavior in Prison and the Prison Subculture." *Prison Journal* **82:**19–49.

KURY, HELMUT and URSULA SMARTT (2002). "Prisoner-on-Prisoner Violence: Victimization of Young Offenders in Prison." *Criminal Justice: The International Journal of Policy and Practice* **2:**411–437.

LAHM, KAREN (2006, March). "Importation Theory Revisited: Measuring Inmate's Pre-Prison Attitudes." Unpublished paper presented at the annual meeting of the Academy of Criminal Justice Sciences, Baltimore.

LAMBERT, ERIC G. ET AL. (2005). "The Good Life: The Impact of Job Satisfaction and Occupational Stressors on Correctional Staff Life Satisfaction: An Exploratory Study." *Journal of Crime and Justice* **28:**1–27.

LATESSA, EDWARD J., LAWRENCE F. TRAVIS, and ALEXANDER HOLSINGER (1997). *Evaluation of Ohio's Community Corrections Act Programs and Community-Based Correctional Facilities.* Cincinnati, OH: Division of Criminal Justice, University of Cincinnati.

LE, THAO (2002). "Delinquency among Asian/Pacific Islanders: Review of Literature and Research." *Justice Professional* **15:**57–70.

LEIBER, MICHAEL, JOSEPH JOHNSON, and KRISTAN FOX (2006, March). "An Evaluation of an Aftercare Program for Delinquent Youth." Unpublished paper presented at the annual meeting of the Academy of Criminal Justice Sciences, Baltimore.

LEMERT, EDWIN M. (1951). *Social Pathology.* New York: McGraw-Hill.

LEMIEUX, CATHERINE M. (2002). "Social Support among Offenders with Substance Abuse Problems: Overlooked and Underused?" *Journal of Addictions and Offender Counseling* **23**:41–57.

LEMIEUX, CATHERINE M., TIMOTHY B. DYESON, and BRANDI CASTIGLIONE (2002). "Revisiting the Literature on Prisoners Who Are Older: Are We Wiser?" *Prison Journal* **82**:440–458.

LEMKE, RICHARD, CHRISTOPHER LOWENKAMP, and PAULA SMITH (2006, March). "The Effect of Incarceration on Recidivism: A Re-Examination of Spohn and Holleran." Unpublished paper presented at the annual meeting of the Academy of Criminal Justice Sciences, Baltimore.

LEMLEY, ELLEN C. (2006, March). "Restorative Justice and Social Altruism: An Exploration." Unpublished paper presented at the annual meeting of the Academy of Criminal Justice Sciences, Baltimore.

LEVENSON, JILL S. and LEO P. COTTER (2005). "The Effect of Megan's Law on Sex Offender Reintegration." *Journal of Contemporary Criminal Justice* **21**:49–66.

LEVENSON, JOE and FINOLA FARRANT (2002). "Unlocking Potential: Active Citizenship and Volunteering by Prisoners." *Probation Journal* **49**:195–204.

LINDSEY, MARIAN (2006, July). "Victim Services: Beyond Notification." Unpublished paper presented at the annual meeting of the American Probation and Parole Association, Chicago.

LOMBROSO, CESARE (1918). *Crime: Its Causes and Remedies.* Boston: Little, Brown.

LOWENKAMP, CHRISTOPHER T. and EDWARD J. LATESSA (2005). "Developing Successful Reentry Programs: Lessons Learned from the 'What Works' Research." *Corrections Today* **67**:72–77.

LOWRY, KEVIN, ANDY EICHHORN, and SERGIO ARGUETA (2006, July). "Hug-A-Thug or Lock-'Em Up: The Nassau County Collaborative Approach to Gang Member Rehabilitation." Unpublished paper presented at the annual meeting of the American Probation and Parole Association, Chicago.

LOZA, WAGDY and AMEL FANOUS LOZA (2002). "The Effectiveness of the Self-Appraisal Questionnaire as an Offender's Classification Measure." *Journal of Interpersonal Violence* **17**:3–13.

LUCKEN, KAROL (1997a). "The Dynamics of Penal Reform." *Crime, Law, and Social Change* **26**:367–384.

LUCKEN, KAROL (1997b). "Privatizating Discretion: 'Rehabilitating' Treatment in Community Corrections." *Crime and Delinquency* **43**:243–259.

LURIGIO, ARTHUR J., ANGIE ROLLINS, and JOHN FALLON (2004). "The Effects of Serious Mental Illness on Offender Reentry." *Federal Probation* **68**:45–52.

MARCINIAK, LIZ MARIE (2000). "The Addition of Day Reporting to Intensive Supervision Probation: A Comparison of Recidivism Rates." *Federal Probation* **64**:34–39.

MARION, NANCY (2002). "Effectiveness of Community-Based Correctional Programs: A Case Study." *Prison Journal* **82**:478–497.

MARSHALL, FRANKLIN H. (1989). "Diversion and Probation." In *The U.S. Sentencing Guidelines: Implications for Criminal Justice,* Dean J. Champion (ed.). New York: Praeger.

MARTIN, GREG and JEFF SUNDBERG (2006, July). "Treating Sex Offenders in Rural America." Unpublished paper presented at the annual meeting of the American Probation and Parole Association, Chicago.

MARTINEZ, PABLO (2006, March). "Probation is Failing—A Need for a New Paradigm?" Unpublished paper presented at the annual meeting of the Academy of Criminal Justice Sciences, Baltimore.

MARTINSON, ROBERT (1974). "What Works? Questions and Answers about Prison Reform." *The Public Interest* **35**: 22–54.

MASLACH, CHRISTINA (1982a). *Burnout: The Cost of Caring.* Englewood Cliffs, NJ: Prentice-Hall.

MASLACH, CHRISTINA (1982b). "Understanding Burnout: Definitional Issues in Analyzing a Complex Phenomenon." In *Job Stress and Burnout,* W. S. Paine (ed.). Beverly Hills, CA: Sage.

MAUER, M. and MEDA CHESNEY-LIND (2002). *Invisible Punishment: The Collateral Consequences of Mass Imprisonment.* New York: The New Press.

MAXEY, WAYNE (2002). "The San Diego Stalking Strike Force: A Multi-Disciplinary Approach to Assessing and Managing Stalking and Threat Cases." *Journal of Threat Assessment* **2**:549–558.

McBRIDE, ELIZABETH C., CHRISTY VISHER, and NANCY LaVIGNE (2005). "Informing Policy and Practice: Prisoner Reentry Research at the Urban Institute." *Corrections Today* **67**: 90–93.

McCOY, TANA and STACY C. MOAK (2006, March). "Examining Gender Bias in Use in Detention Among Female Status Offenders." Unpublished paper presented at the annual meeting of the Academy of Criminal Justice Sciences, Baltimore.

McGRATH, ROBERT J., GEORGIA CUMMING, and JOHN HOLT (2002). "Collaboration among Sex Offender Treatment Providers and Probation and Parole Officers: The Beliefs and Behaviors of Treatment Providers." *Sexual Abuse: A Journal of Research and Treatment* **14**:49–65.

McGRATH, ROBERT J. ET AL. (2003). "Outcome of a Treatment Program for Adult Sex Offenders: From Prison to Community." *Journal of Interpersonal Violence* **18**:3–17.

McGUIRE, MIKE P. and MARK A. HENDRICKSON (2006, July). "Community Drug Court: Bridging Community Members and Offenders Together to Increase Accountability and Positive Outcomes." Unpublished paper presented at the annual meeting of the American Probation and Parole Association, Chicago.

McKEAN, LISE and JODY RAPHAEL (2002). *Drugs, Crime and Consequences: Arrests and Incarceration in North Lawndale.* Chicago: Center for Impact Research.

McMAHON, MARTHA and ELLEN PENCE (2003). "Making Social Change: Reflections on Individual and Institutional Advocacy with Women Arrested for Domestic Violence." *Violence Against Women* **9**:47–74.

MEARS, DANIEL P. ET AL. (2003). *Drug Treatment in the Criminal Justice System: The Current State of Knowledge.* Washington, DC: Urban Institute Series on Drug Treatment in the Criminal Justice System.

MEGARGEE, EDWIN I. and JOYCE CARBONELL (1985). "Predicting Prison Adjustment with MMPI Correctional Scales." *Journal of Consulting and Clinical Psychology* **53**: 874–883.

MEIERHOEFER, BARBARA ET AL. (2006, July). "Stop Counting Contacts and Make Supervision Count." Unpublished paper presented at the annual meeting of the American Probation and Parole Asociation, Chicago.

MEMORY, JOHN M. ET AL. (1999). "Comparing Disciplinary Infraction Rates of North Carolina Fair Sentencing and Structured Sentencing Inmates: A Natural Experiment. "*Prison Journal* **79**:45–71.

MERCER, AMY (2006, March). "Juvenile Parole and Aftercare in the United States: A Contemporary Critical Review." Unpublished paper presented at the annual meeting of the Academy of Criminal Justice Sciences, Baltimore.

MERCER, RON, MURRAY BROOKS, and PAULA TULLY BRYANT (2000). "Global Positioning Satellite System: Tracking Offenders in Real Time."*Corrections Today* **62**:76–80.

MERTON, ROBERT KING (1938). "Social Structure and Anomie."*American Sociological Review* **3**:672–682.

MERTON, ROBERT KING (1957). *Social Theory and Social Structure.* New York: Free Press.

MICHAUD, PETER A. (2003). "Adding Crime Victims to the Reentry Equation."*Corrections Today* **65**:84–85, 89.

MICHIGAN DEPARTMENT OF CORRECTIONS (2006). *Objective Parole Criteria: Working Paper.* Lansing, MI: Author.

MISSISSIPPI PAROLE BOARD (2006). *Parole.* Jackson, MS: Author.

MONTGOMERY, JESSE, Jr. (2006, July). "Operation Spotlight: An Initiative in Our Parole Division." Unpublished paper presented at the annual meeting of the American Probation and Parole Association, Chicago.

MORRIS, NORVAL and MARC MILLER (1985). "Predictions of Dangerousness." In *Crime and Justice: An Annual Review of Research, Vol. 6.* Michael Tonry and Norval Morris (eds). Chicago: University of Chicago Press.

MORTON, WANDA and REGINALD STONE (2006, July). "Making the Transition: Line Staff to Management." Unpublished paper presented at the annual meeting of the American Probation and Parole Association, Chicago.

MUHAMMAD, BAHIYYAH (2006, March). "Children of Incarcerated Parents: How Many?" Unpublished paper presented at the annual meeting of the Academy of Criminal Justice Sciences, Baltimore.

MULLER, NICHOLAS and KAREN DUNLAP (2005). "Effective Supervision and Gun Violence Reductions." *APPA Perspectives* **30**:34–37.

MULLINS, TRACY GODWIN and ROBERT SUDLOW (2006, July). "The Role of Probation in Youth Court Programs." Unpublished paper presented at the annual meeting of the American Probation and Parole Association, Chicago.

NATIONAL COMMISSION ON LAW OBSERVANCE AND ENFORCEMENT (1931). *Wickersham Commission Reports.* Washington, DC: U.S. Government Printing Office.

NATIONAL EDUCATION FOR ASSISTANCE DOG SERVICES (NEADS) (2006). *Dogs for Deaf and Disabled Americans.* Princeton, MA: Author.

NELLIS, MIKE (2002). "Community Justice, Time, and the New National Probation Service."*Howard Journal of Criminal Justice* **41**:59–86.

NEUSTATTER, ANGELA (2002). *Locked In-Locked Out: The Experience of Young Offenders Out of Society and in Prison.* Washington, DC: U.S. Government Printing Office.

NEW YORK STATE DEPARTMENT OF CORRECTIONAL SERVICES (2006). *Absconders and Parolees from Work Release: 1988–1992.* Albany, NY: Author.

NEW YORK STATE DIVISION OF PAROLE (2006). *Special Needs Units and Prisoner Reentry.* Ithaca, NY: Cornell University.

NICOL, MARK and DERRICK MCCREE (2006, March). "Evaluating Michigan's Juvenile Boot Camp Program." Unpublished paper presented at the annual meeting of the Academy of Criminal Justice Sciences, Baltimore.

NIJBOER, JAN ET AL. (2002). "Recidivism." *Justiele Verkenningen* **8**:9–107.

NORTH DAKOTA DEPARTMENT OF CORRECTION AND REHABILITATION (2004). *Probation/Parole Officer Duties and Responsibilities.* Bismarck: North Dakota Department of Correction and Rehabilitation.

NURSE, ANNE M. (2002). *Fatherhood Arrested: Parenting from Within the Juvenile Justice System.* Nashville, TN: Vanderbilt University Press.

OFFICE OF JUSTICE PROGRAMS (2005). *Learn About Reentry.* Washington, DC: Author.

OFFICE OF JUSTICE PROGRAMS (2006). *AIDS-HIV-Infected Inmates in State and Federal Prisons.* Washington, DC: U.S. Government Printing Office.

OHIO DEPARTMENT OF CORRECTION AND REHABILITATION (2006). *Revised Guidelines for Paroling Offenders.* Columbus, OH: Author.

OHIO PAROLE BOARD (2006). *Revised Parole Board Guidelines.* Columbus, OH: Author.

OKLAHOMA DEPARTMENT OF CORRECTIONS (2006). *Parole and Interstate Services.* Oklahoma City, OK: Interstate Commission for Adult Offender Supervision.

OLDFIELD, MARK and M. OLDFIELD (2002). "What Works and the Conjunctural Politics of Probation: Effectiveness, Managerialism, and Neo-Liberalism."*British Journal of Community Justice* **1**:79–97.

OLIVERO, J. MICHAEL and RODRIGO MURATAYA (2006, March). "At-Risk Youth and Psychopathology." Unpublished paper presented at the annual meeting of the Academy of Criminal Justice Sciences, Baltimore.

OPERATION SAFETY NET (2006). *Have a Heart for Companion Animals.* Boston: Operation Safety Net.

PACIFIC HILLS TREATMENT (2006). *Juvenile Risk Factors and the Continuum of Sanctions.* Los Angeles, CA: Pacific Hills Treatment.

PAGE, BRIAN (1995). *Assessment Center Handbook.* Longwood, FL: Gould Publications.

PALMER, CARLETON A. and MARK HAZELRIGG (2000). "The Guilty But Mentally Ill Verdict: A Review and Conceptual Analysis of Intent and Impact."*Journal of the American Academy of Psychiatry and the Law* **28**:47–54.

PALMER, JOHN W. (1997). *The Constitutional Rights of Prisoners 5/e.* Cincinnati, OH: Anderson.

PALOMBO, BERNADETTE (2006, March). "'Doing Time' At Riker's Island: 'War Stories' Regarding Female Corrections Officers' Work-Related Experiences." Unpublished paper presented at the annual meeting of the Academy of Criminal Justice Sciences, Baltimore.

PAPAROZZI, MARIO (2006, March). "National Profile of Educational, Work Experience, and Training Requirements for Parole Board Members." Unpublished paper presented at the annual meeting of the Academy of Criminal Justice Sciences, Baltimore.

PARADIS, CHERYL ET AL. (2000). "Mentally Ill Elderly Jail Detainees: Psychiatric, Psychosocial, and Legal Factors."*Journal of Offender Rehabilitation* **31**:77–86.

PARENT, DALE G. and LIZ BARNETT (2004). "Improving Offender Success and Public Safety Through System Reform: The Transition from Prison to Community Initiative." *Federal Probation* **68**:25–30.

PARKER, HOWARD (2001). "Drug Interventions in the Youth Justice System." *Probation Journal* **48**:110–118.

PATRICK, STEVEN ET AL. (2004). "Control Group Study of Juvenile Diversion Programs." *Social Science Journal* **41**:129–135.

PATTAVINA, APRIL (2004). "The Emerging Role of Information Technology in Prison Reentry Initiatives." *Federal Probation* **68**:40–44.

PAYNE, BRIAN K. and RANDY R. GAINEY (2002). "The Influence of Demographic Factors on the Experience of House Arrest." *Federal Probation* **66**:64–70.

PELISSIER, BERNADETTE and TIMOTHY CADIGAN (2004). "Interagency Priorities at the Crossroads: Aftercare among Drug Users." *Federal Probation* **68**:10–14.

PELISIER, BERNADETTE and TIMOTHY CADIGAN (2004). "Interagency Priorities at the Crossroads: Aftercare Among Drug Users." *Federal Probation* **68**:10–14.

PETERSILIA, JOAN (2001). "Prisoner Reentry: Public Safety and Reintegration Challenges." *The Prison Journal* **81**:360–375.

PETERSILIA, JOAN (2003). *When Prisoners Come Home: Parole and Prisoner Reentry.* New York: Oxford University Press.

PETERSILIA, JOAN (2004). "What Works in Prisoner Reentry? Reviewing and Questioning the Evidence." *Federal Probation* **68**:4–8.

PETERSILIA, JOAN (2005). "Hard Time: Ex-Offenders Returning Home After Prison." *Corrections Today* **67**:66–69, 77.

PETERSILIA, JOAN M. and SUSAN TURNER (1993). *Evaluating Intensive Supervision Probation/Parole: Results of a Nationwide Experiment.* Washington, DC: U.S. Department of Justice, Office of Justice Programs.

PETERSON, SCOTT (2005). *The Growth of Teen Courts in the United States.* Washington, DC: Office of Juvenile Justice and Delinquency Prevention.

PETERSON-BADALI, MICHELE and CHRISTOPHER J. KOEGL (2002). "Juveniles' Experiences of Incarceration: The Role of Correctional Staff in Peer Violence." *Journal of Criminal Justice* **30**:41–49.

PHILADELPHIA POLICE DEPARTMENT (1998). *Philadelphia Police Department Grievance Guide.* Philadelphia: Morrison Press.

PHILADELPHIA PRISON SYSTEM (1990). *Philadelphia Prisons Pre-Release Program—Policy and Operations Manual.* Philadelphia: Author.

PHILLIPS, AMY K. (1997). "Thou Shalt Not Kill Any Nice People: The Problem of Victim Impact Statements in Capital Sentencing." *American Criminal Law Review* **35**:93–118.

PIAGET, J. (1948). *The Moral Judgment of the Child.* New York: Free Press.

PIEHL, ANNE MORRISON (2006). "Debating the Effectiveness of Parole: Does Parole Work?" *APPA Perspectives* **30**:54–61.

POOLE, LINDSEY, STEPHEN WHITTLE, and PAULA STEPHENS (2002). "Working with Transgendered and Transsexual People as Offenders in the Probation Service." *Probation Journal* **49**:227–338.

POVNER, GAIL A. (2002). "An Exercise in Therapeutic Jurisprudenc: Its Inception and Some Preliminary Observations." *American Jails* **16**:62–68.

POWERS, EDWARD and JANET K. WILSON (2006, March). "Serious and Violent Offender Reentry: Barriers to Effective Practice." Unpublished paper presented at the annual meeting of the Academy of Criminal Justice Sciences, Baltimore.

PRENDERGAST, MICHAEL L. ET AL. (2002). "Involuntary Treatment within a Prison Setting: Impact on Psychosocial Change During Treatment." *Criminal Justice and Behavior* **29**:5–26.

PRESTON, FREDERICK W. and ROGER I. ROOTS (EDS.) (2004). "When Laws Backfire: Unintended Impacts of Public Policy." *American Behavioral Scientist* **47**:1371–1466.

PROBATION AND PAROLE EMPLOYEE'S ASSOCIATION (2001). *Minutes of January 2001.* Portland, OR: Author.

PROBATION ASSOCIATION (1939). *John Augustus: The First Probation Officer.* New York: Author.

PURKISS, MARCUS ET AL. (2003). "Probation Officer Functions: A Statutory Analysis." *Federal Probation* **67**:12–23.

QUAY, HERBERT C. (1984). *Managing Adult Inmates.* College Park, MD: American Correctional Association.

QUAY, HERBERT C. and L.B. PARSONS (1971). *The Differential Behavioral Classification of the Adult Male Offender.* Philadelphia: Temple University [Technical report prepared for the U.S. Department of Justice Bureau of Prisons, Contract J-1C-22, 253].

RASMUSSEN, ALAN C. (2003). "Successful Supervision System for the Substance Abuser." *APPA Perspectives* **27**:30–31.

RASMUSSEN, DAVID W. and BRUCE L. BENSON (1994). *Intermediate Sanctions: A Policy Analysis Based on Program Evaluations.* Report prepared for the Collins Center for Public Policy, Tallahassee, FL.

RATANSI, SHAMIR ET AL. (2006, March). "The Effectiveness of Risk Assessment Tools for Parolees." Unpublished paper presented at the annual meeting of the Academy of Criminal Justice Sciences, Baltimore.

RATH, QUENTIN C. (1991). "Minnesota Corrections: Perspectives from Probation and Parole Officers." *Corrections Today* **53**:228–230.

REBELLON, CESAR J. (2002). "Reconsidering the Broken Homes/Delinquency Relationship and Exploring Its Mediating Mechanisms." *Criminology: An Interdisciplinary Journal* **40**:103–136.

RECKLESS, WALTER C. (1961). *The Crime Problem.* New York: Appleton-Century-Crofts.

RECKLESS, WALTER C. (1967). *The Crime Problem 2/e.* New York: Appleton-Century-Crofts.

REISIG, MICHAEL D. (2002). "Administrative Control and Inmate Suicide." *Homicide Studies* **6**:84–103.

RHINE, EDWARD E. (2006). "Recasting Parole Supervision as We Know It." *APPA Perspectives* **30**:22–24.

RHOADES, PHILLIP W. and MARYLIN VENEGAS (2006, March). "Probationer Satisfaction Surveys: Program and Personal Evaluation Tools." Unpublished paper presented at the annual meeting of the Academy of Criminal Justice Sciences, Baltimore.

RHODE ISLAND DEPARTMENT OF CORRECTIONS (2006). *Graduated Sanctions Continuum for Youth.* Cranston, RI: Author.

RHYNE, CHARLENE and WAYNE SCOTT (2006, July). "The Changing Face of Juvenile Justice." Unpublished paper presented at the annual meeting of the American Probation and Parole Association, Chicago.

RICHMOND TIMES-DISPATCH (1990). "Virginia County Tries Home Incarceration Program." *Corrections Today* **52**:100.

ROBERTS, JULIAN V. (2002). "Alchemy in Sentencing: An Analysis of Sentencing Reform Proposals in England and Wales." *Punishment and Society* **4**:425–442.

ROGERS, JOSEPH W. (1990). "The Predisposition Report: Maintaining the Promise of Individualized Juvenile Justice." *Federal Probation* **54**:43–57.

ROBINSON, GWEN (2002). "Exploring Risk Management in Probation Practice: Contemporary Developments in England and Wales." *Punishment and Society* **4**:5–25.

ROLISON, GARRY L. ET AL. (2002). "Prisoners of War: Black Female Incarceration at the End of the 1980s." *Social Justice* **29**:131–143.

ROULET, SISTER ELAINE (1993). "New York's Prison Nursery/Children's Center." *Corrections Compendium* **18**:4–6.

RYAN, JAMES (2006, March). "Who Gets Revoked? An Update of Intensive Supervision Successes and Failures in Vermont." Unpublished paper presented at the annual meeting of the Academy of Criminal Justice Sciences, Baltimore.

SACKS, STANLEY and FRANK PEARSON (2003). "Co-Occurring Substance Use and Mental Disorders in Offenders: Approaches, Findings and Recommendations." *Federal Probation* **67**:32–39.

SCHAEFER, BILL ET AL. (2006, July). "Applying Restorative and Community Justice Principles to Domestic Violence Cases." Unpublished paper presented at the annual meeting of the American Probation and Parole Association, Chicago.

SCHAPS, ERIC and DANIEL SOLOMON (2003). "The Role of the School's Social Environment in Preventing Student Drug Use." *Journal of Primary Prevention* **23**:299–328.

SCHARR, TIMOTHY M. (2001). "Interactive Video Training for Firearms Safety." *Federal Probation* **65**:45–51.

SCHLAGER, MELINDA and KELLY ROBBINS (2006, March). "Does Parole Work—Revisited: Revisiting the Discussion on the Effect of Post-Prison Success and Outcome." Unpublished paper presented at the annual meeting of the Academy of Criminal Justice Sciences, Baltimore.

SCHMITZ, RICHARD J., PINKY S. WASSENBERG, and MARISA E. PATTERSON (2000). *Evaluations of the Christian County Extended Day Program, Peoria County Anti-Gang and Drug Abuse Unit, and Winnebago Day Reporting and Assessment Centers.* Chicago: Illinois Criminal Justice Information Authority.

SCHRAG, CLARENCE (1971). *Crime and Justice: American Style.* Washington, DC: U.S. Government Printing Office.

SCHRAM, PAMELA J. and MERRY MORASH (2002). "Evaluation of a Life Skills Program for Women Inmates in Michigan." *Journal of Offender Rehabilitation* **34**:47–70.

SEATTLE POLICE DEPARTMENT (2006). *Community Policing Programs.* Seattle, WA: Author.

SEITER, RICHARD P. (2002). "Prisoner Reentry and the Role of Parole Officers." *Federal Probation* **66**:50–54.

SEITER, RICHARD P. (2004). "Inmate Reentry: What Works and What To Do About It." *Corrections Compendium* **29**:1–5, 33–35.

SHARP, CHRISTY and DODD WHITE (2006, July). "Promoting a Coordinated and Integrated Child Welfare and Juvenile Justice System." Unpublished paper presented at the annual meeting of the American Probation and Parole Association, Chicago.

SHARP, SUSAN F. and ROSLYN MURASKIN (2003). *The Incarcerated Woman: Rehabilitative Programming in Women's Prisons.* Upper Saddle River, NJ: Prentice Hall.

SHAW, CLIFFORD R. and HENRY D. MCKAY (1929). *Juvenile Delinquency and Urban Areas.* Chicago: University of Chicago Press.

SHEARER, ROBERT A. (2004). "Multicultural Competencies in Probation: Issues and Challenges." *Federal Probation* **68**:3–9.

SHEEHY, ROBERT D. and EFRAIN A. ROSARIO (2003). "Connecting Drug Paraphernalia to Drug Gangs." *FBI Law Enforcement Bulletin* **72**:1–6.

SHELDON, WILLIAM H. (1949). *Varieties of Delinquent Youth.* New York: Harper and Row.

SHERMAN, LAWRENCE W. ET AL. (1998). *Preventing Crime: What Works, What Doesn't, What's Promising.* Washington, DC: U.S. Department of Justice, National Institute of Justice.

SHORT, JAMES F. (2002). "Criminology: The Chicago School and Sociological Theory." *Crime, Law, and Social Change* **37**:107–115.

SIGLER, ROBERT T. and DAVID LAMB (1995). "Community-Based Alternatives to Prison: How the Public and Court Personnel View Them." *Federal Probation* **59**:3–9.

SIGLER, ROBERT T. and DAVID LAMB (1996). "Community Based Alternative Sanctions: How the Public and Court Personnel View Them." *Journal of Offender Monitoring* **9**:1–8.

SMITH, CARA (2006, July). "Managing Sex Offenders Under a Microscope and in a Sea of Legislative Change." Unpublished paper presented at the annual meeting of the American Probation and Parole Association, Chicago.

SOLOMON, AMY L. (2006). "Does Parole Supervision Work? Research Findings and Policy Opportunities." *APPA Perspectives* **30**:26–37.

SOLOMON, AMY, V. KACHNOWSKI, and A. BHATI (2005). *Does Parole Work? Analyzing the Impact of Postprison Supervision on Rearrest Outcomes.* Washington, DC: The Urban Institute.

SONTHEIMER, HENRY and TRACI DUNCAN (1996). *Assessment of County Intermediate Punishment Programs.* Harrisburg: Pennsylvania Commission on Crime and Delinquency.

SOUTH CAROLINA DEPARTMENT OF PROBATION, PAROLE, AND PARDON SERVICES (2006). *Reentry Initiative: A Partnership for Change.* Columbia, SC: Author.

SPANGENBERG, ROBERT L. ET AL. (1987). *Assessment of the Massachusetts Probation System.* West Newton, MA: Spangenberg Group.

SPELMAN, JEFFREY B. (2002). "Ohio's First Reentry Court." *APPA Perspectives* **26**:22–24.

SPELMAN, JEFFREY B. (2003). "An Initial Comparison of Graduates and Terminated Clients in America's Largest Reentry Court." *Corrections Today* **65**:74–77, 83.

SPOHN, CASSIA and DAVID HOLLERAN (2002). "The Effect of Imprisonment on Recidivism Rates of Felony Offenders: A Focus on Drug Offenders." *Criminology* **40**:329–358.

ST. GERARD, VANNESSA (2005). "Louisiana Makes Plans to Tackle Recidivism." *Corrections Today* **67**:17.

STARR, RANDY (2002). "A Successful Reintegration into the Community: One NGRI Acquittee's Story." *Federal Probation* **66**:59–63.

STARZYK, KATHERINE B. and WILLIAM L. MARSHALL (2003). "Childhood Family and Personological Risk Factors for Sexual Offending." *Aggression and Violent Behavior* **8**:93–105.

STEINMAN, RICK M. (2006, March). "A Potentially New Role for Criminal Defense Counsels: Therapeutic Jurisprudence." Unpublished paper presented at the annual meeting of the Academy of Criminal Justice Sciences, Baltimore.

STEPHENS, REGINA (2001). Personal letter. Sacramento, CA: Department of Corrections; Regina Stephens, Deputy Director, Parole and Community Services Division.

STEURY, ELLEN HOCHSTEDLER (1989). "Prosecutorial and Judicial Discretion." In *The U.S. Sentencing Guidelines: Implications for Criminal Justice,* Dean J. Champion (ed.). New York: Praeger.

STOHR, MARY K. (2002). "Comparing Inmate Perceptions of Two Residential Substance Abuse Treatment Programs." *International Journal of Offender Therapy and Comparative Criminology* **46**:699–714.

STOHR, MARY K. ET AL. (2002). "Inmate Perceptions of Residential Substance Abuse Treatment Programming." *Journal of Offender Rehabilitation* **34**:1–32.

STOUTHAMER-LOEBER, MAGDA and ROLF LOEBER (2002). "Lost Opportunities for Intervention: Undetected Markers for the Development of Serious Juvenile Delinquency." *Criminal Behavior and Mental Health* **12**:69–82.

STRAKA, RICHARD (2003). "The Violence of Hmong Gangs and the Crime of Rape." *FBI Law Enforcement Bulletin* **72**:12–16.

STRUCKMAN-JOHNSON, CINDY and DAVID STRUCKMAN-JOHNSON (2002). "Sexual Coercion Reported by Women in Three Midwestern Prisons." *Journal of Sex Research* **39**:217–227.

STURGES, JUDITH E. (2002). "Visitation at County Jails: Potential Policy Implications." *Criminal Justice Policy Review* **13**:32–45.

SULLIVAN, CHRISTOPHER (2006, March). "Classification and Specialization: Assessing the Relevance of Conviction Offense as a Means of Defining Offending Patterns." Unpublished paper presented at the annual meeting of the Academy of Criminal Justice Sciences, Baltimore.

SUNDT, JODY ET AL. (1998). "What Will the Public Tolerate?" *APPA Perspectives* **22**:20–26.

SUTER, JENNIFER M. ET AL. (2002). "Anger in Prisoners: Women Are Different from Men." *Personality and Individual Differences* **32**:1087–1100.

SUTHERLAND, J. and J.P. SHEPHERD (2002). "A Personality-Based Model of Adolescent Violence." *The British Journal of Criminology* **42**:433–441.

SWAN, ROBERT (2006, March). "Ghosts in the Machine: Administrative Intent and the Interstate Corrections Compact." Unpublished paper presented at the annual meeting of the Academy of Criminal Justice Sciences, Baltimore.

SWEET, JOSEPH (1985). "Probation as Therapy." *Corrections Today* **47**:89–90.

SYKES, GRESHAM (1974). "The Rise of Critical Criminology." *Journal of Criminal Law and Criminology* **65**:39–45.

SYKES, GRESHAM M. and DAVID MATZA (1957). "Techniques of Neutralization: A Theory of Delinquency?" *American Sociological Review* **22**:664–670.

TARLOW, BARRY (2005). *Bail Pending Appeal: The Bail Reform Act.* Washington, DC: National Association of Criminal Defense Lawyers.

TARLTON V. CLARK, 441 F. 2d. 384 (1971)

TARNAI, LISA (2006, July). "Drug Testing: A Cat and Mouse Game." Unpublished paper presented at the annual meeting of the American Probation and Parole Association, Chicago.

TARTARO, CHRISTINE (2002). "The Impact of Density on Jail Violence." *Journal of Criminal Justice* **30**:499–510.

TAXMAN, FAYE (2004). "The Offender and Reentry: Supporting Active Participation in Reintegration." *Federal Probation* **68**:31–36.

TAXMAN, FAYE (2006). "What Should We Expect from Parole (and Probation) Under a Behavioral Management Approach?" *APPA Perspectives* **30**:38–45.

TAXMAN, FAYE, S. SIMPSON, and N. PIQUERO (2002). "Measuring and Calibrating Therapeutic Integration in Drug Treatment Programs." *Journal of Criminal Justice* **30**:159–257.

TAXMAN, FAYE ET AL. (2006). *From Prison Safety to Public Safety: Innovations in Offender Reentry.* Washington, DC: The Urban Institute.

TAYLOR, SCOTT ET AL. (2006, July). "APPA's Reentry Initiative." Unpublished paper presented at the annual meeting of the American Probation and Parole Association, Chicago.

TEXAS DEPARTMENT OF CRIMINAL JUSTICE (2006). *The Therapeutic Community Substance Abuse Aftercare Treatment Program.* Austin, TX: Author.

THOMAS, CHRISTOPHER R., CHARLES E. HOLZER, and JULIE WALL (2002). "The Island Youth Programs: Community Interventions for Reducing Youth Crime and Violence." *Adolescent Psychiatry* **26**:125–143.

THORNBERRY, TERENCE P. ET AL. (2003). *Gangs and Delinquency in Developmental Perspective.* Cambridge, UK: Cambridge University Press.

TIMASHEFF, NICHOLAS S. (1941). *One Hundred Years of Probation, 1841–1941.* New York: Fordham University Press.

TJADEN, CLAUS D. and LINDA LAYTON (2006, July). "Exploring the Relationship Between Assessment and Reoffending." Unpublished paper presented at the annual meeting of the American Probation and Parole Association, Chicago.

TOCH, HANS (1995). "Inmate Involvement in Prison Governance." *Federal Probation* **59**:34–39.

TOLMAN, RICHARD M. (1996). "Expanding Sanctions for Batterers: What Can We Do Besides Jailing and Counseling Them?" In *Future Interventions with Battered Women and Their Families,* Jeffrey L. Edleson and Zvi Eisikovits (eds.). Thousand Oaks, CA: Sage.

TOMKINS, ALAN J. ET AL. (2002). "International Perspectives on Restorative and Community Justice." *Behavioral Sciences and the Law* **20**:307–436.

TOOMBS, THOMAS G. (1995). "Monitoring and Controlling Criminal Offenders Using the Satellite Global Positioning System Coupled to Surgically Implanted Transponders." *Criminal Justice Policy Review* **7**:341–346.

TORRES, SAM (1998). "A Continuum of Sanctions for Substance-Abusing Offenders." *Federal Probation* **62**:36–45.

TRACY, PAUL E. (2002). *Decision Making and Juvenile Justice: An Analysis of Bias in Case Processing.* Belmont, CA: Wadsworth Publishing Company.

TRAVIS, JEREMY (2005). *But They All Come Back: Facing the Challenges of Prisoner Reentry.* Washington, DC: The Urban Institute.

TRAVIS, JEREMY and CHRISTY VISHER (2005). *Prisoner Reentry and Public Safety in America.* New York: Cambridge University Press.

TREGLIA, GAIL HOLOVAC (2006, March). "Opening the Door for Reentry Into Our Community." Unpublished paper presented at the annual meeting of the Academy of Criminal Justice Sciences, Baltimore.

TUMPERI, ERIC (2006, July). "Enhancing Graduated Sanctions with Everyday Technology." Unpublished paper presented at the annual meeting of the American Probation and Parole Association, Chicago.

UNDERWOOD, LEE A. and SALLY H. FALWELL (2002). "Screening and Assessing Co-Occurring Disorders." *Corrections Today* **64**:22–23.

UNITED STATES V. RAMIREZ-FRANCO, 122 Fed.Appx. 324 (U.S.9thCir.Jan) (2005)

U.S. CODE ANNOTATED (2007). *United States Code Annotated.* St. Paul, MN: West Publishing Company.

U.S. DEPARTMENT OF JUSTICE (2005). *State and Federal PSI Report Preparation: Criteria and Regulations.* Washington, DC: Author.

U.S. DEPARTMENT OF JUSTICE (2006). *State and Federal Corrections Statistics.* Washington, DC: Author.

U.S. DEPARTMENT OF LABOR (2006). *Center for Faith-Based and Community Initiatives: CFBCI Mission Statement.* Washington, DC: Author.

U.S. SENTENCING COMMISSION (1987). *United States Sentencing Commission Guidelines Manual.* Washington, DC: U.S. Sentencing Commission.

U.S. SENTENCING COMMISSION (2003). *United States Sentencing Commission Guidelines Manual Revised.* Washington, DC: U.S. Sentencing Commission.

U.S. SENTENCING COMMISSION (2006). *United States Sentencing Commission Guidelines Manual.* Washington, DC: Author.

VALETTE, DELPHINE (2002). "AIDS Behind Bars: Prisoners' Rights Guillotined." *Howard Journal of Criminal Justice* **41**:107–122.

VANDER SANDEN, BRUCE and RICK FAULKNER (2003). "Accountability Through Innovation and Collaboration." *Corrections Today* **65**:56–58, 65.

"VAN HOUTEN FAILS IN NEW PAROLE BID." *Los Angeles Times,* July 14, 2006:B1.

VENTURA COUNTY SHERIFF'S DEPARTMENT (2001). *Tattoo Removal Program.* Ventura, CA: Author.

VIRGINIA DEPARTMENT OF CORRECTIONS (2003). *Probation and Parole: Frequently Asked Questions.* Richmond, VA: Author.

VIRGINIA DEPARTMENT OF CORRECTIONS (2006). *The Use of Paraprofessionals in Working with Offenders.* Richmond, VA: Author.

WALKLATE, SANDRA (2002). "So Who Are the Victims Now?" *British Journal of Community Justice* **1**:47–63.

WALTERS, GLENN D. ET AL. (2002). "Assessing Change with the Psychological Inventory of Criminal Thinking Styles: A Controlled Analysis and Multisite Cross-Validation." *Criminal Justice and Behavior* **29**:308–331.

WARGENT, MARTIN (2002). "The New Government of Probation." *Howard Journal of Criminal Justice* **41**:182–200.

Washington Work Ethic Camp (2006). *Washington McNeil Island Work Ethic Camp Elements.* Seattle, WA: Author.

WASSERMAN, GAIL A. and DEBRA L. KAPLAN (2006, July). "Project Connect: Probation Officer Gatekeeper Training in Mental Health Screening." Unpublished paper presented at the annual meeting of the American Probation and Parole Association, Chicago.

WATERS, J. EUGENE and WILLIAM L. MEGATHLIN (2002). "Evaluating Change in Social Climate in a Close Security State Correctional Facility." *Journal of Offender Rehabilitation* **34**:71–84.

WEEDON, JOEY R. (2002). "Drug War Undergoes Reform." *Corrections Today* **64**:24.

WEEDON, JOEY R. (2004). "The Foundation of Reentry." *Corrections Today* **66**:6.

WELLS, JAMES B. ET AL. (2006, March). "Variables Predictive of Recidivism among Juveniles Released from Out-of-Home Placements." Unpublished paper presented at the annual meeting of the Academy of Criminal Justice Sciences, Baltimore.

WELSH, BRANDON C. (2004). "Monetary Costs and Benefits of Correctional Treatment Programs: Implications for Offender Reentry." *Federal Probation* **68**:9–13.

WHITE, ROBERT J. ET AL. (2002). "Extent and Characteristics of Woman Batterers among Federal Inmates." *International Journal of Offender Therapy and Comparative Criminology* **46**:412–426.

WICHITA COUNTY ADULT PROBATION (2006). *Sanctions.* Wichita County, TX: Author.

WILKINSON, REGINALD A. (2005). "Engaging Communities: An Essential Ingredient to Offender Reentry." *Corrections Today* **67**:86–89.

WILKINSON, REGINALD A., G.A. BUCKHOLTZ, and G.M. SEIGFRIED (2004). "Prison Reform Through Offender Reentry: A Partnership Between the Courts and Corrections." *Pace Law Review* **24**:609–629.

WILKINSON, REGINALD A. and EDWARD E. RHINE (2005). "Confronting Recidivism: Inmate Reentry and the Second Chance Act of 2005." *Corrections Today* **67**:54–57.

WILKINSON, REGINALD A. and TESSA UNWIN (1999). "In Prison: A Recipe for Disaster." *Corrections Today* **60**:98–102.

WILLIAMSON COUNTY ADULT PROBATION (2006). *Continuum of Sanctions.* Williamson County, TX: Author.

WILSON, GEORGE P. (1985). "Halfway House Programs for Offenders." In *Probation, Parole, and Community Corrections,* Lawrence Travis III (ed.). Prospect Heights, IL: Waveland Press.

WILSON, JAMES Q. and RICHARD J. HERNSTEIN (1985). *Crime and Human Nature.* New York: Simon and Schuster.

WITT, BETSY (2006, March). "Implementation of a Mental Health Court: Process and Evaluation." Unpublished paper presented at the annual meeting of the Academy of Criminal Justice Sciences, Baltimore.

WOGAN, MICHAEL and MARCI MACKENZIE (2002). "Antisocial Personality Disorder in a Sample of Imprisoned Non-Sex, Non-Arson Adult Male Offenders." *Journal of Offender Rehabilitation* **35**:31–49.

WOLF, ANNE W. and MARY B. RODGERS (2006, July). "Are You Here to Oppose Parole?" Unpublished paper presented at the annual meeting of the American Probation and Parole Association, Chicago.

WOLF, YVAL (2002). "Violations of Out-Group and In-Group Regulations in the Eyes of Ordinary and Protected Prisoners: An Instance of Judgmental Modularity." *International Journal of Offender Therapy and Comparative Criminology* **46**:206–219.

WOLFGANG, MARVIN E. and FRANCO FERRACUTI (1967). *The Subculture of Violence.* London: Tavistock.

WOLFGANG, MARVIN E., ROBERT M. FIGLIO, and THORSTEN SELLIN (1972). *Delinquency in a Birth Cohort.* Chicago: University of Chicago Press.

YOCHELSON, SAMUEL and STANTON E. SAMENOW (1976). *The Criminal Personality.* New York: Jason Aronson.

ZHANG, YAN and PILSOO JUNG (2006, March). "The Lifetime Distribution of Recidivists for Different Types of Offenses." Unpublished paper presented at the annual meeting of the Academy of Criminal Justice Sciences, Baltimore.

Cases Cited

Name Index

Subject Index